SIGMUND COLLEC

VOL. 1 – SIX BOOKS

1. A General Introduction To Psychoanalysis (1920)
2. Three Contributions To The Theory Of Sex (1905)
3. Totem And Taboo (1913)
4. Dream Psychology (1901)
5. Leonardo Da Vinci (1910)
6. Psychopathology Of Everyday Life (1904)

(TRANSLATOR: G. Stanley Hall)

CONTENTS

BOOK ONE
A GENERAL INTRODUCTION TO PSYCHOANALYSIS

PREFACE

Few, especially in this country, realize that while Freudian themes have rarely found a place on the programs of the American Psychological Association, they have attracted great and growing attention and found frequent elaboration by students of literature, history, biography, sociology, morals and aesthetics, anthropology, education, and religion. They have given the world a new conception of both infancy and adolescence, and shed much new light upon characterology; given us a new and clearer view of sleep, dreams, reveries, and revealed hitherto unknown mental mechanisms common to normal and pathological states and processes, showing that the law of causation extends to the most incoherent acts and even verbigerations in insanity; gone far to clear up the *terra incognita* of hysteria; taught us to recognize morbid symptoms, often neurotic and psychotic in their germ; revealed the operations of the primitive mind so overlaid and repressed that we had almost lost sight of them; fashioned and used the key of symbolism to unlock many mysticisms of the past; and in addition to all this, affected thousands of cures, established a new prophylaxis, and suggested new tests for character, disposition, and ability, in all combining the practical and theoretic to a degree salutary as it is rare.

These twenty-eight lectures to laymen are elementary and almost conversational. Freud sets forth with a frankness almost startling the difficulties and limitations of psychoanalysis, and also describes its main methods and results as only a master and originator of a new school of thought can do. These discourses are at the same time simple and almost confidential, and they trace and sum up the results of thirty years of devoted and painstaking research. While they are not at all controversial, we incidentally see in a clearer light the distinctions between the master and some of his distinguished pupils. A text like this is the most opportune and will naturally more or less supersede all other introductions to the general subject of psychoanalysis. It presents the author in a new light, as an effective and successful popularizer, and is certain to be welcomed not only by the large and growing number of students of psychoanalysis in this country but by the yet larger number of those who wish to begin its study here and elsewhere.

The impartial student of Sigmund Freud need not agree with all his conclusions, and indeed, like the present writer, may be unable to make sex so all-dominating a factor in the psychic life of the past and present as Freud deems it to be, to recognize the fact that he is the most original and creative mind in psychology of our generation. Despite the frightful handicap of the *odium sexicum*, far more formidable today than the *odium theologicum*, involving as it has done for him lack of academic recognition and even more or less social ostracism, his views have attracted and inspired a brilliant group of minds not only in psychiatry but in many other fields, who have altogether given the world of culture more new and pregnant *appercus* than those which have come from any other source within the wide domain of humanism.

A former student and disciple of Wundt, who recognizes to the full his inestimable services to our science, cannot avoid making certain comparisons. Wundt has had for decades the prestige of a most advantageous academic chair. He founded the first laboratory for experimental psychology, which attracted many of the most gifted and mature students from all lands. By his development of the doctrine of apperception he took psychology forever beyond the old associationism which had ceased to be fruitful. He also established the independence of psychology from physiology, and by his encyclopedic and always thronged lectures, to say nothing of his more or less esoteric seminary, he materially advanced every branch of mental science and extended its influence over the whole wide domain of folklore, mores, language, and primitive religion. His best texts will long constitute a thesaurus which every psychologist must know.

Again, like Freud, he inspired students who went beyond him (the Wurzburgers and introspectionists) whose method and results he could not follow. His limitations have grown more and more manifest. He has little use for the unconscious or the abnormal, and for the most part he has lived and wrought in a preevolutionary age and always and everywhere underestimated the genetic standpoint. He never transcends the conventional limits in dealing, as he so rarely does, with sex. Nor does he contribute much likely to be of permanent value in any part of the wide domain of affectivity. We cannot forbear to express the hope that Freud will not repeat Wundt's error in making too abrupt a break with his more advanced pupils like Adler or the Zurich group. It is rather precisely just the topics that Wundt neglects that Freud makes his chief corner-stones, viz., the unconscious, the abnormal, sex, and affectivity generally, with many genetic, especially ontogenetic, but also phylogenetic factors. The Wundtian influence has been great in the past, while Freud has a great present and a yet greater future.

In one thing Freud agrees with the introspectionists, viz., in deliberately neglecting the "physiological factor" and building on purely psychological foundations, although for Freud psychology is mainly unconscious, while for

2

the introspectionists it is pure consciousness. Neither he nor his disciples have yet recognized the aid proffered them by students of the autonomic system or by the distinctions between the epicritic and protopathic functions and organs of the cerebrum, although these will doubtless come to have their due place as we know more of the nature and processes of the unconscious mind.

If psychologists of the normal have hitherto been too little disposed to recognize the precious contributions to psychology made by the cruel experiments of Nature in mental diseases, we think that the psychoanalysts, who work predominantly in this field, have been somewhat too ready to apply their findings to the operations of the normal mind; but we are optomistic enough to believe that in the end both these errors will vanish and that in the great synthesis of the future that now seems to impend our science will be made vastly richer and deeper on the theoretical side and also far more practical than it has ever been before.

G. STANLEY HALL, Clark University, April, 1920.

PART I. THE PSYCHOLOGY OF ERRORS

FIRST LECTURE: INTRODUCTION

I DO not know how familiar some of you may be, either from your reading or from hearsay, with psychoanalysis. But, in keeping with the title of these lectures—*A General Introduction to Psychoanalysis*—I am obliged to proceed as though you knew nothing about this subject, and stood in need of preliminary instruction.

To be sure, this much I may presume that you do know, namely, that psychoanalysis is a method of treating nervous patients medically. And just at this point I can give you an example to illustrate how the procedure in this field is precisely the reverse of that which is the rule in medicine. Usually when we introduce a patient to a medical technique which is strange to him we minimize its difficulties and give him confident promises concerning the result of the treatment. When, however, we undertake psychoanalytic treatment with a neurotic patient we proceed differently. We hold before him the difficulties of the method, its length, the exertions and the sacrifices which it will cost him; and, as to the result, we tell him that we make no definite promises, that the result depends on his conduct, on his understanding, on his adaptability, on his perseverance. We have, of course, excellent motives for conduct which seems so perverse, and into which you will perhaps gain insight at a later point in these lectures.

Do not be offended, therefore, if, for the present, I treat you as I treat these neurotic patients. Frankly, I shall dissuade you from coming to hear me a second time. With this intention I shall show what imperfections are necessarily involved in the teaching of psychoanalysis and what difficulties stand in the way of gaining a personal judgment. I shall show you how the whole trend of your previous training and all your accustomed mental habits must unavoidably have made you opponents of psychoanalysis, and how much you must overcome in yourselves in order to master this instinctive opposition. Of course I cannot predict how much psychoanalytic understanding you will gain from my lectures, but I can promise this, that by listening to them you will not learn how to undertake a psychoanalytic treatment or how to carry one to completion. Furthermore, should I find anyone among you who does not feel satisfied with a cursory acquaintance with psychoanalysis, but who would like to enter into a more enduring relationship with it, I shall not only dissuade him, but I shall actually warn him against it. As things now stand, a person would, by such a choice of profession, ruin his every chance of success at a university, and if he goes out into the world as a practicing physician, he will find himself in a society which does not understand his aims, which regards him with suspicion and hostility, and which turns loose upon him all the malicious spirits which lurk within it.

However, there are always enough individuals who are interested in anything which may be added to the sum total of knowledge, despite such inconveniences. Should there be any of this type among you, and should they ignore my dissuasion and return to the next of these lectures, they will be welcome. But all of you have the right to know what these difficulties of psychoanalysis are to which I have alluded.

First of all, we encounter the difficulties inherent in the teaching and exposition of psychoanalysis. In your medical instruction you have been accustomed to visual demonstration. You see the anatomical specimen, the precipitate in the chemical reaction, the contraction of the muscle as the result of the stimulation of its nerves. Later the patient is presented to your senses; the symptoms of his malady, the products of the pathological processes, in many cases even the cause of the disease is shown in isolated state. In the surgical department you are made to witness the steps by which one brings relief to the patient, and are permitted to attempt to practice them. Even in psychiatry, the demonstration affords you, by the patient's changed facial play, his manner of speech and his behavior, a wealth of observations which leave far-reaching impressions. Thus the medical teacher preponderantly plays the role of a guide and instructor who accompanies you through a museum in which you contract an immediate relationship to the exhibits, and in which you believe yourself to have been convinced through your own observation of the existence of the new things you see.

Unfortunately, everything is different in psychoanalysis. In psychoanalysis nothing occurs but the interchange of words between the patient and the physician. The patient talks, tells of his past experiences and present impressions, complains, confesses his wishes and emotions. The physician listens, tries to direct the thought processes of the patient, reminds him of things, forces his attention into certain channels, gives him explanations and observes the reactions of understanding or denial which he calls forth in the patient. The uneducated relatives of our patients—persons who are impressed only by the visible and tangible, preferably by such procedure as one sees in the moving picture theatres—never miss an opportunity of voicing their scepticism as to how one can "do anything for the malady through mere talk." Such thinking, of course, is as shortsighted as it is inconsistent. For these are the very persons who know with such certainty that the patients "merely imagine" their symptoms. Words were originally magic, and the word retains much of its old magical power even to-day. With words one man can make another blessed, or drive him to despair; by words the teacher transfers his knowledge to the pupil; by words the speaker sweeps his audience with him and determines its judgments and decisions. Words call forth effects and are the universal means of influencing human beings. Therefore let us not underestimate the use of words in psychotherapy, and let us be satisfied if we may be auditors of the words which are exchanged between the analyst and his patient.

But even that is impossible. The conversation of which the psychoanalytic treatment consists brooks no auditor, it cannot be demonstrated. One can, of course, present a neurasthenic or hysteric to the students in a psychiatric lecture. He tells of his complaints and symptoms, but of nothing else. The communications which are necessary for the analysis are made only under the conditions of a special affective relationship to the physician; the patient would become dumb as soon as he became aware of a single impartial witness. For these communications concern the most intimate part of his psychic life, everything which as a socially independent person he must conceal from others; these communications deal with everything which, as a harmonious personality, he will not admit even to himself.

You cannot, therefore, "listen in" on a psychoanalytic treatment. You can only hear of it. You will get to know psychoanalysis, in the strictest sense of the word, only by hearsay. Such instruction even at second hand, will place you in quite an unusual position for forming a judgment. For it is obvious that everything depends on the faith you are able to put in the instructor.

Imagine that you are not attending a psychiatric, but an historical lecture, and that the lecturer is telling you about the life and martial deeds of

Alexander the Great. What would be your reasons for believing in the authenticity of his statements? At first sight, the condition of affairs seems even more unfavorable than in the case of psychoanalysis, for the history professor was as little a participant in Alexander's campaigns as you were; the psychoanalyst at least tells you of things in connection with which he himself has played some role. But then the question turns on this—what set of facts can the historian marshal in support of his position? He can refer you to the accounts of ancient authors, who were either contemporaries themselves, or who were at least closer to the events in question; that is, he will refer you to the books of Diodor, Plutarch, Arrian, etc. He can place before you pictures of the preserved coins and statues of the king and can pass down your rows a photograph of the Pompeiian mosaics of the battle of Issos. Yet, strictly speaking, all these documents prove only that previous generations already believed in Alexander's existence and in the reality of his deeds, and your criticism might begin anew at this point. You will then find that not everything recounted of Alexander is credible, or capable of proof in detail; yet even then I cannot believe that you will leave the lecture hall a disbeliever in the reality of Alexander the Great. Your decision will be determined chiefly by two considerations; firstly, that the lecturer has no conceivable motive for presenting as truth something which he does not himself believe to be true, and secondly, that all available histories present the events in approximately the same manner. If you then proceed to the verification of the older sources, you will consider the same data, the possible motives of the writers and the consistency of the various parts of the evidence. The result of the examination will surely be convincing in the case of Alexander. It will probably turn out differently when applied to individuals like Moses and Nimrod. But what doubts you might raise against the credibility of the psychoanalytic reporter you will see plainly enough upon a later occasion.

At this point you have a right to raise the question, "If there is no such thing as objective verification of psychoanalysis, and no possibility of demonstrating it, how can one possibly learn psychoanalysis and convince himself of the truth of its claims?" The fact is, the study is not easy and there are not many persons who have learned psychoanalysis thoroughly; but nevertheless, there is a feasible way. Psychoanalysis is learned, first of all, from a study of one's self, through the study of one's own personality. This is not quite what is ordinarily called self-observation, but, at a pinch, one can sum it up thus. There is a whole series of very common and universally known psychic phenomena, which, after some instruction in the technique of psychoanalysis, one can make the subject matter of analysis in one's self. By so doing one obtains the desired conviction of the reality of the occurrences which psychoanalysis describes and of the correctness of its fundamental conception. To be sure, there are definite limits imposed on progress by this method. One gets much further if one allows himself to be analyzed by a competent analyst, observes the effect of the analysis on his own ego, and at the same time makes use of the opportunity to become familiar with the finer details of the technique of procedure. This excellent method is, of course, only practicable for one person, never for an entire class.

There is a second difficulty in your relation to psychoanalysis for which I cannot hold the science itself responsible, but for which I must ask you to take the responsibility upon yourselves, ladies and gentlemen, at least in so far as you have hitherto pursued medical studies. Your previous training has given your mental activity a definite bent which leads you far away from psychoanalysis. You have been trained to reduce the functions of an organism and its disorders anatomically, to explain them in terms of chemistry and physics and to conceive them biologically, but no portion of your interest has been directed to the psychic life, in which, after all, the activity of this wonderfully complex organism culminates. For this reason psychological thinking has remained strange to you and you have accustomed yourselves to regard it with suspicion, to deny it the character of the scientific, to leave it to the laymen, poets, natural philosophers and mystics. Such a delimitation is surely harmful to your medical activity, for the patient will, as is usual in all human relationships, confront you first of all with his psychic facade; and I am afraid your penalty will be this, that you will be forced to relinquish a portion of the therapeutic influence to which you aspire, to those lay physicians, nature-cure fakers and mystics whom you despise.

I am not overlooking the excuse, whose existence one must admit, for this deficiency in your previous training. There is no philosophical science of therapy which could be made practicable for your medical purpose. Neither speculative philosophy nor descriptive psychology nor that so-called experimental psychology which allies itself with the physiology of the sense organs as it is taught in the schools, is in a position to teach you anything useful concerning the relation between the physical and the psychical or to put into your hand the key to the understanding of a possible disorder of the psychic functions. Within the field of medicine, psychiatry does, it is true, occupy itself with the description of the observed psychic disorders and with their grouping into clinical symptom-pictures; but in their better hours the psychiatrists themselves doubt whether their purely descriptive account deserves the name of a science. The symptoms which constitute these clinical pictures are known neither in their origin, in their mechanism, nor in their mutual relationship. There are either no discoverable corresponding changes of the anatomical organ of the soul, or else the changes are of such a nature as to yield no enlightenment. Such psychic disturbances are open to therapeutic influence only when they can be identified as secondary phenomena of an otherwise organic affection.

Here is the gap which psychoanalysis aims to fill. It prepares to give psychiatry the omitted psychological foundation, it hopes to reveal the common basis from which, as a starting point, constant correlation of bodily and psychic disturbances becomes comprehensible. To this end, it must divorce itself from every anatomical, chemical or physiological supposition which is alien to it. It must work throughout with purely psychological therapeutic concepts, and just for that reason I fear that it will at first seem strange to you.

I will not make you, your previous training, or your mental bias share the guilt of the next difficulty. With two of its assertions, psychoanalysis offends the whole world and draws aversion upon itself. One of these assertions offends an intellectual prejudice, the other an aesthetic-moral one. Let us not think too lightly of these prejudices; they are powerful things, remnants of useful, even necessary, developments of mankind. They are retained through powerful affects, and the battle against them is a hard one.

The first of these displeasing assertions of psychoanalysis is this, that the psychic processes are in themselves unconscious, and that those which are conscious are merely isolated acts and parts of the total psychic life. Recollect that we are, on the contrary, accustomed to identify the psychic with the conscious. Consciousness actually means for us the distinguishing characteristic of the psychic life, and psychology is the science of the content of consciousness. Indeed, so obvious does this identification seem to us that we consider its slightest contradiction obvious nonsense, and yet psychoanalysis cannot avoid raising this contradiction; it cannot accept the identity of the conscious with the psychic. Its definition of the psychic affirms that they are processes of the nature of feeling, thinking, willing; and it must assert that there is such a thing as unconscious thinking and unconscious willing. But with this assertion psychoanalysis has alienated, to start with, the sympathy of all friends of sober science, and has laid itself open to the suspicion of being a fantastic mystery study which would build in darkness and fish in murky waters. You, however, ladies and gentlemen, naturally cannot as yet understand what justification I have for stigmatizing as a prejudice so abstract a phrase as this one, that "the psychic is consciousness." You cannot know what evaluation can have led to the denial of the unconscious, if such a thing really exists, and what advantage may have resulted from this denial. It sounds like a mere argument over words whether one shall say that the psychic coincides with the conscious or whether one shall extend it beyond that, and yet I can assure you that by the acceptance of unconscious processes you have paved the way for a decisively new orientation in the world and in science.

Just as little can you guess how intimate a connection this initial boldness of psychoanalysis has with the one which follows. The next assertion which psychoanalysis proclaims as one of its discoveries, affirms that those instinctive impulses which one can only call sexual in the narrower as well as in the wider sense, play an uncommonly large role in the causation of nervous and mental diseases, and that those impulses are a causation which has never been adequately appreciated. Nay, indeed, psychoanalysis claims that these same sexual impulses have made contributions whose value cannot be overestimated to the highest cultural, artistic and social achievements of the human mind.

According to my experience, the aversion to this conclusion of psychoanalysis is the most significant source of the opposition which it encounters. Would you like to know how we explain this fact? We believe that civilization was forged by the driving force of vital necessity, at the cost of instinct-satisfaction, and that the process is to a large extent constantly repeated anew, since each individual who newly enters the human community repeats the sacrifices of his instinct-satisfaction for the sake of the common good. Among the instinctive forces thus utilized, the sexual impulses play a significant role. They are thereby sublimated, i.e., they are diverted from their sexual goals and directed to ends socially higher and no longer sexual. But this result is unstable. The sexual instincts are poorly tamed. Each individual who wishes to ally himself with the achievements of civilization is exposed to the danger of having his sexual instincts rebel against this sublimation. Society can conceive of no more serious menace to its civilization than would arise through the satisfying of the sexual instincts by their redirection toward their original goals. Society, therefore, does not relish being reminded of this ticklish spot in its origin; it has no interest in having the strength of the sexual instincts recognized and the meaning of the sexual life to the individual clearly delineated. On the contrary, society has taken the course of diverting attention from this whole field. This is the reason why society will not tolerate the above-mentioned results of psychoanalytic research, and would prefer to brand it as aesthetically offensive and morally objectionable or dangerous. Since, however, one cannot attack an ostensibly objective result of scientific inquiry with such objections, the criticism must be translated to an intellectual level if it is to be voiced. But it is a predisposition of human nature to consider an unpleasant idea untrue, and then it is easy to find arguments against it. Society thus brands what is unpleasant as untrue, denying the conclusions of psychoanalysis with logical and pertinent arguments. These arguments originate from affective sources, however, and society holds to these prejudices against all attempts at refutation.

However, we may claim, ladies and gentlemen, that we have followed no bias of any sort in making any of these contested statements. We merely wished to state facts which we believe to have been discovered by toilsome labor. And we now claim the right unconditionally to reject the interference in scientific research of any such practical considerations, even before we have investigated whether the apprehension which these considerations are meant to instil are justified or not.

These, therefore, are but a few of the difficulties which stand in the way of your occupation with psychoanalysis. They are perhaps more than enough for a beginning. If you can overcome their deterrent impression, we shall continue.

SECOND LECTURE. THE PSYCHOLOGY OF ERRORS

WE begin with an investigation, not with hypotheses. To this end we choose certain phenomena which are very frequent, very familiar and very little heeded, and which have nothing to do with the pathological, inasmuch as they can be observed in every normal person. I refer to the errors which an individual commits—as for example, errors of speech in which he wishes to say something and uses the wrong word; or those which happen to him in writing, and which he may or may not notice; or the case of misreading, in which one reads in the print or writing something different from what is actually there. A similar phenomenon occurs in those cases of mishearing what is said to one, where there is no question of an organic disturbance of the auditory function. Another series of such occurrences is based on forgetfulness—but on a forgetfulness which is not permanent, but temporary, as for instance when one cannot think of a name which one knows and always recognizes; or when one forgets to carry out a project at the proper time but which one remembers again later, and therefore has only forgotten for a certain interval. In a third class this characteristic of transience is lacking, as for example in mislaying things so that they cannot be found again, or in the analogous case of losing things. Here we are dealing with a kind of forgetfulness to which one reacts differently from the other cases, a forgetfulness at which one is surprised and annoyed, instead of considering it comprehensible. Allied with these phenomena is that of erroneous ideas— in which the element of transience is again prominent, inasmuch as for a while one believes something which, before and after that time, one knows to be untrue—and a number of similar phenomena of different designations.

These are all occurrences whose inner connection is expressed in the use of the same prefix of designation *("Fehl-leistungen.")*. They are almost all unimportant, generally temporary and without much significance in the life of the individual. It is only rarely that one of them, such as the phenomenon of losing things, attains to a certain practical importance. For that reason also they do not attract much attention, they arouse only weak affects.

It is, therefore, to these phenomena that I would now direct your attention. But you will object, with annoyance: "There are so many sublime riddles in the external world, just as there are in the narrower world of the psychic life, and so many wonders in the field of psychic disturbances which demand and deserve elucidation, that it really seems frivolous to waste labor and interest on such trifles. If you can explain to us how an individual with sound eyes and ears can, in broad daylight, see and hear things that do not exist, or why another individual suddenly believes himself persecuted by those whom up to that time he loved best, or defend, with the most ingenious arguments, delusions which must seem nonsense to any child, then we will be willing to consider psychoanalysis seriously. But if psychoanalysis can do nothing better than to occupy us with the question of why a speaker used the wrong word, or why a housekeeper mislaid her keys, or such trifles, then we know something better to do with our time and interest."

My reply is: "Patience, ladies and gentlemen. I think your criticism is not on the right track. It is true that psychoanalysis cannot boast that it has never occupied itself with trifles. On the contrary, the objects of its observations are generally those simple occurrences which the other sciences have thrown aside as much too insignificant, the waste products of the phenomenal world. But are you not confounding, in your criticism, the sublimity of the problems with the conspicuousness of their manifestations? Are there not very important things which under certain circumstances, and at certain times, can betray themselves only by very faint signs? I could easily cite a great many instances of this kind. From what vague signs, for instance, do the young gentlemen of this audience conclude that they have won the favor of a lady? Do you await an explicit declaration, an ardent embrace, or does not a glance, scarcely perceptible to others, a fleeting gesture, the prolonging of a hand-shake by one second, suffice? And if you are a criminal lawyer, and engaged in the investigation of a murder, do you actually expect the murderer to leave his photograph and address on the scene of the crime, or would you, of necessity, content yourself with fainter and less certain traces of that individual? Therefore, let us not undervalue small signs; perhaps by means of them we will succeed in getting on the track of greater things. I agree with you that the larger problems of the world and of science have the first claim on our interest. But it is generally of little avail to form the definite resolution to devote oneself to the investigation of this or that problem. Often one does not know in which direction to take the next step. In scientific research it is more fruitful to attempt what happens to be before one at the moment and for whose investigation there is a discoverable method. If one does that thoroughly without prejudice or predisposition, one may, with good fortune, and by virtue of the connection which links each thing to every other (hence also the small to the great) discover even from such modest research a point of approach to the study of the big problems."

Thus would I answer, in order to secure your attention for the consideration of these apparently insignificant errors made by normal people. At this point, we will question a stranger to psychoanalysis and ask him how he explains these occurrences.

His first answer is sure to be, "Oh, they are not worth an explanation; they are merely slight accidents." What does he mean by this? Does he mean to assert that there are any occurrences so insignificant that they fall out of the causal sequence of things, or that they might just as well be something different from what they are? If any one thus denies the determination of natural phenomena at one such point, he has vitiated the entire scientific viewpoint. One can then point out to him how much more consistent is the religious point of view, when it explicitly asserts that "No sparrow falls from the roof without God's special wish." I imagine our friend will not be willing to follow his first answer to its logical conclusion; he will interrupt and say that if he were to study these things he would probably find an explanation for them. He will say that this is a case of slight functional disturbance, of an inaccurate psychic act whose causal factors can be outlined. A man who otherwise speaks correctly may make a slip of the tongue—when he is slightly ill or fatigued; when he is excited; when his attention is concentrated on something else. It is easy to prove these statements. Slips of the tongue do really occur with special frequency when one is tired, when one has a headache or when one is indisposed. Forgetting proper names is a very frequent occurrence under these circumstances. Many persons even recognize the imminence of an indisposition by the inability to recall proper names. Often also one mixes up words or objects during excitement, one picks up the wrong things; and the forgetting of projects, as well as the doing of any number of other unintentional acts, becomes conspicuous when one is distracted; in other words, when one's attention is concentrated on other things. A familiar instance of such distraction is the professor in *Fliegende Blätter*, who takes the wrong hat because he is thinking of the problems which he wishes to treat in his next book. Each of us knows from experience some examples of how one can forget projects which one has planned and promises which one has made, because an experience has intervened which has preoccupied one deeply.

This seems both comprehensible and irrefutable. It is perhaps not very interesting, not as we expected it to be. But let us consider this explanation of errors. The conditions which have been cited as necessary for the occurrence of these phenomena are not all identical. Illness and disorders of circulation afford a physiological basis. Excitement, fatigue and distraction are conditions of a different sort, which one could designate as psycho-physiological. About these latter it is easy to theorize. Fatigue, as well as distraction, and perhaps also general excitement, cause a scattering of the attention which can result in the act in progress not receiving sufficient attention. This act can then be more easily interrupted than usual, and may be inexactly carried out. A slight illness, or a change in the distribution of blood in the central organ of the nervous system, can have the same effect, inasmuch as it influences the determining factor, the distribution of attention, in a similar way. In all cases, therefore, it is a question of the effects of a distraction of the attention, caused either by organic or psychic factors.

But this does not seem to yield much of interest for our psychoanalytic investigation. We might even feel tempted to give up the subject. To be sure, when we look more closely we find that not everything squares with this attention theory of psychological errors, or that at any rate not everything can be directly deduced from it. We find that such errors and such forgetting occur even when people are not fatigued, distracted or excited, but are in every way in their normal state; unless, in consequence of these errors, one were to attribute to them an excitement which they themselves do not acknowledge. Nor is the mechanism so simple that the success of an act is assured by an intensification of the attention bestowed upon it, and endangered by its diminution. There are many acts which one performs in a purely automatic way and with very little attention, but which are yet carried out quite successfully. The pedestrian who scarcely knows where he is going, nevertheless keeps to the right road and stops at his destination without having gone astray. At least, this is the rule. The practiced pianist touches the right keys without thinking of them. He may, of course, also make an occasional mistake, but if automatic playing increased the likelihood of errors, it would be just the virtuoso whose playing has, through practice, become most automatic, who would be the most exposed to this danger. Yet we see, on the contrary, that many acts are most successfully carried out when they are not the objects of particularly concentrated attention, and that the mistakes occur just at the point where one is most anxious to be accurate— where a distraction of the necessary attention is therefore surely least permissible. One could then say that this is the effect of the "excitement," but we do not understand why the excitement does not intensify the concentration of attention on the goal that is so much desired. If in an important speech or discussion anyone says the opposite of what he means, then that can hardly be explained according to the psycho-physiological or the attention theories.

There are also many other small phenomena accompanying these errors, which are not understood and which have not been rendered comprehensible to us by these explanations. For instance, when one has temporarily forgotten a name, one is annoyed, one is determined to recall it and is unable to give up the attempt. Why is it that despite his annoyance the individual cannot succeed, as he wishes, in directing his attention to the word which is "on the tip of his tongue," and which he instantly recognizes when it is pronounced to him? Or, to take another example, there are cases in which the errors multiply, link themselves together, substitute for each other. The first time one forgets an appointment; the next time, after having made a special resolution not to forget it, one discovers that one has made a mistake in the day or hour. Or one tries by devious means to remember a forgotten word, and in the course of so doing loses track of a second name which would have been of use in finding the first. If one then pursues this second name, a third gets lost, and so on. It is notorious that the same thing can happen in the case of misprints, which are of course to be considered as errors of the typesetter. A stubborn error of this sort is said to have crept into a Social-Democratic paper, where, in the account of a certain festivity was printed, "Among those present was His Highness, the Clown Prince." The next day a correction was attempted. The paper apologized and said, "The sentence should, of course, have read 'The Clown Prince.'" One likes to attribute these occurrences to the printer's devil, to the goblin of the typesetting machine, and the like—figurative expressions which at least go beyond a psycho-physiological theory of the misprint.

I do not know if you are acquainted with the fact that one can provoke slips of the tongue, can call them forth by suggestion, as it were. An anecdote will serve to illustrate this. Once when a novice on the stage was entrusted with the important role in *The Maid of Orleans* of announcing to the King, "Connétable sheathes his sword," the star played the joke of repeating to the frightened beginner during the rehearsal, instead of the text, the following, "Comfortable sends back his steed,"[1] and he attained his end. In the performance the unfortunate actor actually made his début with this distorted announcement; even after he had been amply warned against so doing, or perhaps just for that reason.

These little characteristics of errors are not exactly illuminated by the theory of diverted attention. But that does not necessarily prove the whole theory wrong. There is perhaps something missing, a complement by the addition of which the theory would be made completely satisfactory. But many of the errors themselves can be regarded from another aspect.

Let us select slips of the tongue, as best suited to our purposes. We might equally well choose slips of the pen or of reading. But at this point, we must make clear to ourselves the fact that so far we have inquired only as to when and under what conditions one's tongue slips, and have received an answer

---

[1] In the German, the correct announcement is, "Connetable schickt sein Schwert zurück." The novice, as a result of the suggestion, announced instead that "Komfortabel schickt sein Pferd zurück."

on this point only. One can, however, direct one's interest elsewhere and ask why one makes just this particular slip and no other; one can consider what the slip results in. You must realize that as long as one does not answer this question—does not explain the effect produced by the slip—the phenomenon in its psychological aspect remains an accident, even if its physiological explanation has been found. When it happens that I commit a slip of the tongue, I could obviously make any one of an infinite number of slips, and in place of the one right word say any one of a thousand others, make innumerable distortions of the right word. Now, is there anything which forces upon me in a specific instance just this one special slip out of all those which are possible, or does that remain accidental and arbitrary, and can nothing rational be found in answer to this question?

Two authors, Meringer and Mayer (a philologist and a psychiatrist) did indeed in 1895 make the attempt to approach the problem of slips of the tongue from this side. They collected examples and first treated them from a purely descriptive standpoint. That, of course, does not yet furnish any explanation, but may open the way to one. They differentiated the distortions which the intended phrase suffered through the slip, into: interchanges of positions of words, interchanges of parts of words, perseverations, compoundings and substitutions. I will give you examples of these authors' main categories. It is a case of interchange of the first sort if someone says "the Milo of Venus" instead of "the Venus of Milo." An example of the second type of interchange, "I had a blush of rood to the head" instead of "rush of blood"; a perseveration would be the familiar misplaced toast, "I ask you to join me in hiccoughing the health of our chief."[2] These three forms of slips are not very frequent. You will find those cases much more frequent in which the slip results from a drawing together or compounding of syllables; for example, a gentleman on the street addresses a lady with the words, "If you will allow me, madame, I should be very glad to *inscort* you."[3] In the compounded word there is obviously besides the word "escort," also the word "insult" (and parenthetically we may remark that the young man will not find much favor with the lady). As an example of the substitution, Meringer and Mayer cite the following: "A man says, 'I put the specimens in the letterbox,' instead of 'in the hot-bed,' and the like."[4]

The explanation which the two authors attempt to formulate on the basis of this collection of examples is peculiarly inadequate. They hold that the sounds and syllables of words have different values, and that the production and perception of more highly valued syllables can interfere with those of lower values. They obviously base this conclusion on the cases of fore-

---

[2] "Aufstossen" instead of "anstossen."
[3] "Begleit-digen" compounded of "begleiten" and "beleidigen."
[4] "Briefkasten" instead of "Brütkasten."

sounding and perseveration which are not at all frequent; in other cases of slips of the tongue the question of such sound priorities, if any exist, does not enter at all. The most frequent cases of slips of the tongue are those in which instead of a certain word one says another which resembles it; and one may consider this resemblance sufficient explanation. For example, a professor says in his initial lecture, "I am not *inclined* to evaluate the merits of my predecessor."("Geneigt" instead of "geeignet.") Or another professor says, "In the case of the female genital, despite many *temptations* ... I mean many attempts ... etc." ("Versuchungen" instead of "Versuche.")

The most common, and also the most conspicuous form of slips of the tongue, however, is that of saying the exact opposite of what one meant to say. In such cases, one goes far afield from the problem of sound relations and resemblance effects, and can cite, instead of these, the fact that opposites have an obviously close relationship to each other, and have particularly close relations in the psychology of association. There are historical examples of this sort. A president of our House of Representatives once opened the assembly with the words, "Gentlemen, I declare a quorum present, and herewith declare the assembly *closed*."

Similar, in its trickiness, to the relation of opposites is the effect of any other facile association which may under certain circumstances arise most inopportunely. Thus, for instance, there is the story which relates that on the occasion of a festivity in honor of the marriage of a child of H. Helmholtz with a child of the well-known discoverer and captain of industry, W. Siemon, the famous physiologist Dubois-Reymond was asked to speak. He concluded his undoubtedly sparkling toast with the words, "Success to the new firm—Siemens and—Halski!" That, of course, was the name of the well-known old firm. The association of the two names must have been about as easy for a native of Berlin as "Weber and Fields" to an American.

Thus we must add to the sound relations and word resemblances the influence of word associations. But that is not all. In a series of cases, an explanation of the observed slip is unsuccessful unless we take into account what phrase had been said or even thought previously. This again makes it a case of perseveration of the sort stressed by Meringer, but of a longer duration. I must admit, I am on the whole of the impression that we are further than ever from an explanation of slips of the tongue!

However, I hope I am not wrong when I say that during the above investigation of these examples of slips of the tongue, we have all obtained a new impression on which it will be of value to dwell. We sought the general conditions under which slips of the tongue occur, and then the influences which determine the kind of distortion resulting from the slip, but we have in no way yet considered the effect of the slip of the tongue in itself, without regard to its origin. And if we should decide to do so we must finally have the courage to assert, "In some of the examples cited, the product of the slip also makes sense." What do we mean by "it makes sense"? It means, I think, that the product of the slip has itself a right to be considered as a valid psychic act which also has its purpose, as a manifestation having content and meaning. Hitherto we have always spoken of errors, but now it seems as if sometimes the error itself were quite a normal act, except that it has thrust itself into the place of some other expected or intended act.

In isolated cases this valid meaning seems obvious and unmistakable. When the president with his opening words closes the session of the House of Representatives, instead of opening it, we are inclined to consider this error meaningful by reason of our knowledge of the circumstances under which the slip occurred. He expects no good of the assembly, and would be glad if he could terminate it immediately. The pointing out of this meaning, the interpretation of this error, gives us no difficulty. Or a lady, pretending to admire, says to another, "I am sure you must have messed up this charming hat yourself." ("Aufgepatzt" instead of "aufgeputzt.") No scientific quibbles in the world can keep us from discovering in this slip the idea "this hat is a mess." Or a lady who is known for her energetic disposition, relates, "My husband asked the doctor to what diet he should keep. But the doctor said he didn't need any diet, he should eat and drink whatever *I* want." This slip of tongue is quite an unmistakable expression of a consistent purpose.

Ladies and gentlemen, if it should turn out that not only a few cases of slips of the tongue and of errors in general, but the larger part of them, have a meaning, then this meaning of errors of which we have hitherto made no mention, will unavoidably become of the greatest interest to us and will, with justice, force all other points of view into the background. We could then ignore all physiological and psycho-physiological conditions and devote ourselves to the purely psychological investigations of the sense, that is, the meaning, the purpose of these errors. To this end therefore we will not fail, shortly, to study a more extensive compilation of material.

But before we undertake this task, I should like to invite you to follow another line of thought with me. It has repeatedly happened that a poet has made use of slips of the tongue or some other error as a means of poetic presentation. This fact in itself must prove to us that he considers the error, the slip of the tongue for instance, as meaningful; for he creates it on purpose, and it is not a case of the poet committing an accidental slip of the pen and then letting his pen-slip stand as a tongue-slip of his character. He wants to make something clear to us by this slip of the tongue, and we may examine what it is, whether he wishes to indicate by this that the person in question is distracted or fatigued. Of course, we do not wish to exaggerate the importance of the fact that the poet did make use of a slip to express his meaning. It could nevertheless really be a psychic accident, or meaningful only in very rare cases, and the poet would still retain the right to infuse it with meaning through his setting. As to their poetic use, however, it would not be surprising if we should glean more information concerning slips of the tongue from the poet than from the philologist or the psychiatrist.

Such an example of a slip of the tongue occurs in *Wallenstein* (*Piccolomini*, Act 1, Scene 5). In the previous scene, Max Piccolomini has most passionately sided with the Herzog, and dilated ardently on the blessings of peace which disclosed themselves to him during the trip on which he accompanied Wallenstein's daughter to the camp. He leaves his father and the courtier, Questenberg, plunged in deepest consternation. And then the fifth scene continues:

Q.   Alas! Alas! and stands it so?
     What friend! and do we let him go away
     In this delusion—let him go away?
     Not call him back immediately, not open
     His eyes upon the spot?

OCTAVIO.   (*Recovering himself out of a deep study*)
     He has now opened mine,
     And I see more than pleases me.

Q.   What is it?

OCTAVIO.   A curse on this journey!

Q.   But why so? What is it?

OCTAVIO.   Come, come along, friend! I must follow up
     The ominous track immediately. Mine eyes
     Are opened now, and I must use them. Come! (*Draws Q. on with him.*)

Q.   What now? Where go you then?

OCTAVIO.   (*Hastily.*) To *her* herself

Q.   To—

OCTAVIO.   (*Interrupting him and correcting himself.*) To the duke. Come, let us go—.

Octavio meant to say, "To him, to the lord," but his tongue slips and through his words "*to her*" he betrays to us, at least, the fact that he had quite clearly recognized the influence which makes the young war hero dream of peace.

A still more impressive example was found by O. Rank in Shakespeare's *Merchant of Venice*, in the famous scene in which the fortunate suitor makes his choice among the three caskets; and perhaps I can do no better than to read to you here Rank's short account of the incident:

"A slip of the tongue which occurs in Shakespeare's *Merchant of Venice*, Act III, Scene II, is exceedingly delicate in its poetic motivation and technically brilliant in its handling. Like the slip in *Wallenstein* quoted by Freud (*Psychopathology of Everyday Life*, 2d ed., p. 48), it shows that the poets well know the meaning of these errors and assume their comprehensibility to the audience. Portia, who by her father's wish has been bound to the choice of a husband by lot, has so far escaped all her unfavored suitors through the fortunes of chance. Since she has finally found in Bassanio the suitor to whom she is attached, she fears that he, too, will choose the wrong casket. She would like to tell him that even in that event he may rest assured of her love, but is prevented from so doing by her oath. In this inner conflict the poet makes her say to the welcome suitor:

PORTIA:

I pray you tarry; pause a day or two,

Before you hazard; for, in choosing wrong

I lose your company; therefore, forbear a while:

There's something tells me, (but it is not love)

I would not lose you: * * *   * * * I could teach you

How to choose right, but then I am forsworn,

So will I never be: so may you miss me;

But if you do, you'll make me wish a sin

That I had been forsworn. Beshrew your eyes.

They have o'erlook'd me, and divided me;

One half of me is yours, the other half *yours*,

Mine own, I would say: but if mine, then yours,

And so all yours.

Just that, therefore, which she meant merely to indicate faintly to him or really to conceal from him entirely, namely that even before the choice of the lot she was his and loved him, this the poet—with admirable psychological delicacy of feeling—makes apparent by her slip; and is able, by this artistic device, to quiet the unbearable uncertainty of the lover, as well as the equal suspense of the audience as to the issue of the choice."

Notice, at the end, how subtly Portia reconciles the two declarations which are contained in the slip, how she resolves the contradiction between them and finally still manages to keep her promise: "* * * but if mine, then yours, And so all yours."

Another thinker, alien to the field of medicine, accidentally disclosed the meaning of errors by an observation which has anticipated our attempts at explanation. You all know the clever satires of Lichtenberg (1742-1749), of which Goethe said, "Where he jokes, there lurks a problem concealed." Not infrequently the joke also brings to light the solution of the problem. Lichtenberg mentions in his jokes and satiric comments the remark that he always read "Agamemnon" for "angenommen," (verb meaning "to accept) so intently had he read Homer. Herein is really contained the whole theory of misreadings.

At the next session we will see whether we can agree with the poets in their conception of the meaning of psychological errors.

THIRD LECTURE. THE PSYCHOLOGY OF ERRORS—(Continued)

AT the last session we conceived the idea of considering the error, not in its relation to the intended act which it distorted, but by itself alone, and we received the impression that in isolated instances it seems to betray a meaning of its own. We declared that if this fact could be established on a larger scale, then the meaning of the error itself would soon come to interest us more than an investigation of the circumstances under which the error occurs.

Let us agree once more on what we understand by the "meaning" of a psychic process. A psychic process is nothing more than the purpose which it serves and the position which it holds in a psychic sequence. We can also substitute the word "purpose" or "intention" for "meaning" in most of our investigations. Was it then only a deceptive appearance or a poetic exaggeration of the importance of an error which made us believe that we recognized a purpose in it?

Let us adhere faithfully to the illustrative example of slips of the tongue and let us examine a larger number of such observations. We then find whole categories of cases in which the intention, the meaning of the slip itself, is clearly manifest. This is the case above all in those examples in which one says the opposite of what one intended. The president said, in his opening address, "I declare the meeting closed." His intention is certainly not ambiguous. The meaning and purpose of his slip is that he wants to terminate the meeting. One might point the conclusion with the remark "he said so himself." We have only taken him at his word. Do not interrupt me at this point by remarking that this is not possible, that we know he did not want to terminate the meeting but to open it, and that he himself, whom we have just recognized as the best judge of his intention, will affirm that he meant to open it. In so doing you forget that we have agreed to consider the error entirely by itself. Its relation to the intention which it distorts is to be discussed later. Otherwise you convict yourself of an error in logic by which you smoothly conjure away the problem under discussion; or "beg the question," as it is called in English.

In other cases in which the speaker has not said the exact opposite of what he intended, the slip may nevertheless express an antithetical meaning. "I am not *inclined* to appreciate the merits of my predecessor." "*Inclined*" is not the opposite of "*in a position to*," but it is an open betrayal of intent in sharpest contradiction to the attempt to cope gracefully with the situation which the speaker is supposed to meet.

In still other cases the slip simply adds a second meaning to the one intended. The sentence then sounds like a contradiction, an abbreviation, a condensation of several sentences. Thus the lady of energetic disposition, "He may eat and drink whatever *I* please." The real meaning of this abbreviation is as though the lady had said, "He may eat and drink whatever he pleases. But what does it matter what *he* pleases! It is *I* who do the pleasing." Slips of the tongue often give the impression of such an abbreviation. For example, the anatomy professor, after his lecture on the human nostril, asks whether the class has thoroughly understood, and after a unanimous answer in the affirmative, goes on to say: "I can hardly believe that is so, since the people who understand the human nostril can, even in a city of millions, be counted on *one finger*—I mean, on the fingers of one hand." The abbreviated sentence here also has its meaning: it expresses the idea that there is only one person who thoroughly understands the subject.

In contrast to these groups of cases are those in which the error does not itself express its meaning, in which the slip of the tongue does not in itself convey anything intelligible; cases, therefore, which are in sharpest opposition to our expectations. If anyone, through a slip of the tongue, distorts a proper name, or puts together an unusual combination of syllables, then this very common occurrence seems already to have decided in the negative the question of whether all errors contain a meaning. Yet closer inspection of these examples discloses the fact that an understanding of such a distortion is easily possible, indeed, that the difference between these unintelligible cases and the previous comprehensible ones is not so very great.

A man who was asked how his horse was, answered, "Oh, it may *stake*—it may take another month." When asked what he really meant to say, he explained that he had been thinking that it was a *sorry* business and the coming together of "*take*" and "*sorry*" gave rise to "*stake*." (Meringer and Mayer.)

Another man was telling of some incidents to which he had objected, and went on, "and then certain facts were *re-filed*." Upon being questioned, he explained that he meant to stigmatize these facts as "*filthy*." "*Revealed*" and "*filthy*" together produced the peculiar "*re-filled*." (Meringer and Mayer.)

You will recall the case of the young man who wished to "*inscort*" an unknown lady. We took the liberty of resolving this word construction into the two words "*escort*" and "*insult*," and felt convinced of this interpretation without demanding proof of it. You see from these examples that even slips can be explained through the concurrence, the interference, of two speeches of different intentions. The difference arises only from the fact that in the one type of slip the intended speech completely crowds out the other, as happens in those slips where the opposite is said, while in the other type the intended speech must rest content with so distorting or modifying the other as to result in mixtures which seem more or less intelligible in themselves.

We believe that we have now grasped the secret of a large number of slips of the tongue. If we keep this explanation in mind we will be able to understand still other hitherto mysterious groups. In the case of the distortion of names, for instance, we cannot assume that it is always an instance of competition between two similar, yet different names. Still, the second intention is not difficult to guess. The distorting of names occurs frequently enough not as a slip of the tongue, but as an attempt to give the name an ill-sounding or debasing character. It is a familiar device or trick of insult, which persons of culture early learned to do without, though they do not give it up readily. They often clothe it in the form of a joke, though, to be sure, the joke is of a very low order. Just to cite a gross and ugly example of such a distortion of a name, I mention the fact that the name of the President of the French Republic, *Poincaré*, has been at times, lately, transformed into "*Schweinskarré*." It is therefore easy to assume that there is also such an intention to insult in the case of other slips of the tongue which result in the distortion of a name. In consequence of our adherence to this conception, similar explanations force themselves upon us, in the case of slips of the tongue whose effect is comical or absurd. "I call upon you to *hiccough* the health of our chief."[5] Here the solemn atmosphere is unexpectedly disturbed by the introduction of a word that awakens an unpleasant image; and from the prototype of certain expressions of insult and offense we cannot but suppose that there is an intention striving for expression which is in sharp contrast to the ostensible respect, and which could be expressed about as follows, "You needn't believe this. I'm not really in earnest. I don't give a whoop for the fellow—etc." A similar trick which passes for a slip of the tongue is that which transforms a harmless word into one which is indecent and obscene. The two examples are untranslatable: "apopos" instead of "apropos," and "eischeiszwaibehen" for "eiweiszscheibehen)

We know that many persons have this tendency of intentionally making harmless words obscene for the sake of a certain lascivious pleasure it gives them. It passes as wit, and we always have to ask about a person of whom we

_____

[5] The young man here said "aufzustossen" instead of "anzustossen."

hear such a thing, whether he intended it as a joke or whether it occurred as a slip of the tongue.

Well, here we have solved the riddle of errors with relatively little trouble! They are not accidents, but valid psychic acts. They have their meaning; they arise through the collaboration—or better, the mutual interference—of two different intentions. I can well understand that at this point you want to swamp me with a deluge of questions and doubts to be answered and resolved before we can rejoice over this first result of our labors. I truly do not wish to push you to premature conclusions. Let us dispassionately weigh each thing in turn, one after the other.

What would you like to say? Whether I think this explanation is valid for all cases of slips of the tongue or only for a certain number? Whether one can extend this same conception to all the many other errors—to misreading, slips of the pen, forgetting, picking up the wrong object, mislaying things, etc? In the face of the psychic nature of errors, what meaning is left to the factors of fatigue, excitement, absent-mindedness and distraction of attention? Moreover, it is easy to see that of the two competing meanings in an error, one is always public, but the other not always. But what does one do in order to guess the latter? And when one believes one has guessed it, how does one go about proving that it is not merely a probable meaning, but that it is the only correct meaning? Is there anything else you wish to ask? If not, then I will continue. I would remind you of the fact that we really are not much concerned with the errors themselves, but we wanted only to learn something of value to psychoanalysis from their study. Therefore, I put the question: What are these purposes or tendencies which can thus interfere with others, and what relation is there between the interfering tendencies and those interfered with? Thus our labor really begins anew, after the explanation of the problem.

Now, is this the explanation of all tongue slips? I am very much inclined to think so and for this reason, that as often as one investigates a case of a slip of the tongue, it reduces itself to this type of explanation. But on the other hand, one cannot prove that a slip of the tongue cannot occur without this mechanism. It may be so; for our purposes it is a matter of theoretical indifference, since the conclusions which we wish to draw by way of an introduction to psychoanalysis remain untouched, even if only a minority of the cases of tongue slips come within our conception, which is surely not the case. I shall anticipate the next question, of whether or not we may extend to other types of errors what we have gleaned from slips of the tongue, and answer it in the affirmative. You will convince yourselves of that conclusion when we turn our attention to the investigation of examples of pen slips, picking up wrong objects, etc. I would advise you, however, for technical reasons, to postpone this task until we shall have investigated the tongue slip itself more thoroughly.

The question of what meaning those factors which have been placed in the foreground by some authors,—namely, the factors of circulatory disturbances, fatigue, excitement, absent-mindedness, the theory of the distraction of attention—the question of what meaning those factors can now have for us if we accept the above described psychic mechanism of tongue slips, deserves a more detailed answer. You will note that we do not deny these factors. In fact, it is not very often that psychoanalysis denies anything which is asserted on the other side. As a rule psychoanalysis merely adds something to such assertions and occasionally it does happen that what had hitherto been overlooked, and was newly added by psychoanalysis, is just the essential thing. The influence on the occurrence of tongue slips of such physiological predispositions as result from slight illness, circulatory disturbances and conditions of fatigue, should be acknowledged without more ado. Daily personal experience can convince you of that. But how little is explained by such an admission! Above all, they are not necessary conditions of the errors. Slips of the tongue are just as possible when one is in perfect health and normal condition. Bodily factors, therefore, have only the value of acting by way of facilitation and encouragement to the peculiar psychic mechanism of a slip of the tongue.

To illustrate this relationship, I once used a simile which I will now repeat because I know of no better one as substitute. Let us suppose that some dark night I go past a lonely spot and am there assaulted by a rascal who takes my watch and purse; and then, since I did not see the face of the robber clearly, I make my complaint at the nearest police station in the following words: "Loneliness and darkness have just robbed me of my valuables." The police commissioner could then say to me: "You seem to hold an unjustifiably extreme mechanistic conception. Let us rather state the case as follows: Under cover of darkness, and favored by the loneliness, an unknown robber seized your valuables. The essential task in your case seems to me to be to discover the robber. Perhaps we can then take his booty from him again."

Such psycho-physiological moments as excitement, absent-mindedness and distracted attention, are obviously of small assistance to us for the purpose of explanation. They are mere phrases, screens behind which we will not be deterred from looking. The question is rather what in such cases has caused the excitement, the particular diversion of attention. The influence of syllable sounds, word resemblances and the customary associations which words arouse should also be recognized as having significance. They facilitate the tongue slip by pointing the path which it can take. But if I have a path before me, does that fact as a matter of course determine that I will follow it? After all, I must have a stimulus to make me decide for it, and, in addition, a force which carries me forward on this path. These sound and word relationships therefore serve also only to facilitate the tongue slip, just as the bodily dispositions facilitate them; they cannot give the explanation for the word itself. Just consider, for example, the fact that in an enormously large number of cases, my lecturing is not disturbed by the fact that the words which I use recall others by their sound resemblance, that they are intimately associated with their opposites, or arouse common associations. We might add here the observation of the philosopher Wundt, that slips of the tongue occur when, in consequence of bodily fatigue, the tendency to association gains the upper hand over the intended speech. This would sound very plausible if it were not contradicted by experiences which proved that from one series of cases of tongue-slips bodily stimuli were absent, and from another, the association stimuli were absent.

However, your next question is one of particular interest to me, namely: in what way can one establish the existence of the two mutually antagonistic tendencies? You probably do not suspect how significant this question is. It is true, is it not, that one of the two tendencies, the tendency which suffers the interference, is always unmistakable? The person who commits the error is aware of it and acknowledges it. It is the other tendency, what we call the interfering tendency, which causes doubt and hesitation. Now we have already learned, and you have surely not forgotten, that these tendencies are, in a series of cases, equally plain. That is indicated by the effect of the slip, if only we have the courage to let this effect be valid in itself. The president who said the opposite of what he meant to say made it clear that he wanted to open the meeting, but equally clear that he would also have liked to terminate it. Here the meaning is so plain that there is nothing left to be interpreted. But the other cases in which the interfering tendency merely distorts the original, without bringing itself to full expression—how can one guess the interfering meaning from the distortion?

By a very sure and simple method, in the first series of cases, namely, by the same method by which one establishes the existence of the meaning interfered with. The latter is immediately supplied by the speaker, who instantly adds the originally intended expression. "It may *stake*—no, it may *take* another month." Now we likewise ask him to express the interfering meaning; we ask him: "Now, why did you first say *stake*?" He answers, "I meant to say—'This is a *sorry* business.'" And in the other case of the tongue slip—*re-filed*—the subject also affirms that he meant to say "It is a *filthy* business," but then moderated his expression and turned it into something else. Thus the discovery of the interfering meaning was here as successful as the discovery of the one interfered with. Nor did I unintentionally select as examples cases which were neither related nor explained by me or by a supporter of my theories. Yet a certain investigation was necessary in both cases in order to obtain the solution. One had to ask the speaker why he made this slip, what he had to say about it. Otherwise he might perhaps have passed it by without seeking to explain it. When questioned, however, he furnished the explanation by means of the first thing that came to his mind. And now you see, ladies and gentlemen, that this slight investigation and its consequence are already a psychoanalysis, and the prototype of every psychoanalytic investigation which we shall conduct more extensively at a later time.

Now, am I unduly suspicious if I suspect that at the same moment in which psychoanalysis emerges before you, your resistance to psychoanalysis also raises its head? Are you not anxious to raise the objection that the information given by the subject we questioned, and who committed the slip, is not proof sufficient? He naturally has the desire, you say, to meet the challenge, to explain the slip, and hence he says the first thing he can think of if it seems relevant. But that, you say, is no proof that this is really the way the slip happened. It might be so, but it might just as well be otherwise, you say. Something else might have occurred to him which might have fitted the case just as well and better.

It is remarkable how little respect, at bottom, you have for a psychic fact! Imagine that someone has decided to undertake the chemical analysis of a certain substance, and has secured a sample of the substance, of a certain weight—so and so many milligrams. From this weighed sample certain definite conclusions can be drawn. Do you think it would ever occur to a chemist to discredit these conclusions by the argument that the isolated substance might have had some other weight? Everyone yields to the fact that it was just this weight and no other, and confidently builds his further conclusions upon that fact. But when you are confronted by the psychic fact that the subject, when questioned, had a certain idea, you will not accept that as valid, but say some other idea might just as easily have occurred to him! The trouble is that you believe in the illusion of psychic freedom and will not give it up. I regret that on this point I find myself in complete opposition to your views.

Now you will relinquish this point only to take up your resistance at another place. You will continue, "We understand that it is the peculiar technique of psychoanalysis that the solution of its problems is discovered by the analyzed subject himself. Let us take another example, that in which the speaker calls upon the assembly 'to *hiccough* the health of their chief.' The interfering idea in this case, you say, is the insult. It is that which is the antagonist of the expression of conferring an honor. But that is mere interpretation on your part, based on observations extraneous to the slip. If in this case you question the originator of the slip, he will not affirm that he intended an insult, on the contrary, he will deny it energetically. Why do you not give up your unverifiable interpretation in the face of this plain objection?"

Yes, this time you struck a hard problem. I can imagine the unknown speaker. He is probably an assistant to the guest of honor, perhaps already a minor official, a young man with the brightest prospects. I will press him as to whether he did not after all feel conscious of something which may have worked in opposition to the demand that he do honor to the chief. What a fine success I'll have! He becomes impatient and suddenly bursts out on me, "Look here, you'd better stop this cross-examination, or I'll get unpleasant. Why, you'll spoil my whole career with your suspicions. I simply said '*auf*-gestossen' instead of '*an*-gestossen,' because I'd already said '*auf*' twice in the same sentence. It's the thing that Meringer calls a perservation, and there's no other meaning that you can twist out of it. Do you understand me? That's all." H'm, this is a surprising reaction, a really energetic denial. I see that there is nothing more to be obtained from the young man, but I also remark to myself that he betrays a strong personal interest in having his slip mean nothing. Perhaps you, too, agree that it is not right for him immediately to become so rude over a purely theoretical investigation, but, you will conclude, he really must know what he did and did not mean to say.

Really? Perhaps that's open to question nevertheless.

But now you think you have me. "So that is your technique," I hear you say. "When the person who has committed a slip gives an explanation which fits your theory, then you declare him the final authority on the subject. 'He says so himself!' But if what he says does not fit into your scheme, then you suddenly assert that what he says does not count, that one need not believe him."

Yet that is certainly true. I can give you a similar case in which the procedure is apparently just as monstrous. When a defendant confesses to a deed, the judge believes his confession. But if he denies it, the judge does not believe him. Were it otherwise, there would be no way to administer the law, and despite occasional miscarriages you must acknowledge the value of this system.

Well, are you then the judge, and is the person who committed the slip a defendant before you? Is a slip of the tongue a crime?

Perhaps we need not even decline this comparison. But just see to what far-reaching differences we have come by penetrating somewhat into the seemingly harmless problems of the psychology of errors, differences which at this stage we do not at all know how to reconcile. I offer you a preliminary compromise on the basis of the analogy of the judge and the defendant. You will grant me that the meaning of an error admits of no doubt when the subject under analysis acknowledges it himself. I in turn will admit that a direct proof for the suspected meaning cannot be obtained if the subject denies us the information; and, of course, that is also the case when the subject is not present to give us the information. We are, then, as in the case of the legal procedure, dependent on circumstances which make a decision at one time seem more, and at another time, less probable to us. At law, one has to declare a defendant guilty on circumstantial evidence for practical reasons. We see no such necessity; but neither are we forced to forego the use of these circumstances. It would be a mistake to believe that a science consists of nothing but conclusively proved theorems, and any such demand would be unjust. Only a person with a mania for authority, a person who must replace his religious catechism with some other, even though it be scientific, would make such a demand. Science has but few apodeictic precepts in its catechism; it consists chiefly of assertions which it has developed to certain degrees of probability. It is actually a symptom of scientific thinking if one is content with these approximations of certainty and is able to carry on constructive work despite the lack of the final confirmation.

But where do we get the facts for our interpretations, the circumstances for our proof, when the further remarks of the subject under analysis do not themselves elucidate the meaning of the error? From many sources. First of all, from the analogy with phenomena extraneous to the psychology of errors; as, for example, when we assert that the distortion of a name as a slip of the tongue has the same insulting significance as an intentional name distortion. We get them also from the psychic situation in which the error occurred, from our knowledge of the character of the person who committed the error, from the impressions which that person received before making the error, and to which he may possibly have reacted with this error. As a rule, what happens is that we find the meaning of the error according to general principles. It is then only a conjecture, a suggestion as to what the meaning may be, and we then obtain our proof from examination of the psychic situation. Sometimes, too, it happens that we have to wait for subsequent developments, which have announced themselves, as it were, through the error, in order to find our conjecture verified.

I cannot easily give you proof of this if I have to limit myself to the field of tongue slips, although even here there are a few good examples. The young man who wished to "*inscort*" the lady is certainly shy; the lady whose husband may eat and drink whatever *she* wants I know to be one of those energetic women who know how to rule in the home. Or take the following case: At a general meeting of the Concordia Club, a young member delivers a vehement speech in opposition, in the course of which he addresses the officers of the society as: "Fellow committee lenders." We will conjecture that some conflicting idea militated in him against his opposition, an idea which was in some way based on a connection with money lending. As a matter of fact, we learn from our informant that the speaker was in constant money difficulties, and had attempted to raise a loan. As a conflicting idea, therefore, we may safely interpolate the idea, "Be more moderate in your opposition, these are the same people who are to grant you the loan."

But I can give you a wide selection of such circumstantial proof if I delve into the wide field of other kinds of error.

If anyone forgets an otherwise familiar proper name, or has difficulty in retaining it in his memory despite all efforts, then the conclusion lies close at hand, that he has something against the bearer of this name and does not like to think of him. Consider in this connection the following revelation of the psychic situation in which this error occurs:

"A Mr. Y. fell in love, without reciprocation, with a lady who soon after married a Mr. X. In spite of the fact that Mr. Y. has known Mr. X. a long time, and even has business relations with him, he forgets his name over and over again, so that he found it necessary on several occasions to ask other people the man's name when he wanted to write to Mr. X." (From C. G. Jung)

Mr. Y. obviously does not want to have his fortunate rival in mind under any condition. "Let him never be thought of."

Another example: A lady makes inquiries at her doctor's concerning a mutual acquaintance, but speaks of her by her maiden name. She has forgotten her married name. She admits that she was much displeased by the marriage, and could not stand this friend's husband. (From A. A. Brill.)

Later we shall have much to say in other relations about the matter of forgetting names. At present we are predominantly interested in the psychic situation in which the lapse of memory occurs.

The forgetting of projects can quite commonly be traced to an antagonistic current which does not wish to carry out the project. We psychoanalysts are not alone in holding this view, but this is the general conception to which all persons subscribe the daily affairs, and which they first deny in theory. The patron who makes apologies to his protegé, saying that he has forgotten his requests, has not squared himself with his protegé. The protegé immediately thinks: "There's nothing to that; he did promise but he really doesn't want to do it." Hence, daily life also proscribes forgetting, in certain connections, and the difference between the popular and the psychoanalytic conception of these errors appears to be removed. Imagine a housekeeper who receives her guest with the words: "What, you come to-day? Why, I had totally forgotten that I had invited you for to-day"; or the young man who might tell his sweetheart that he had forgotten to keep the rendezvous which they planned. He is sure not to admit it, it were better for him to invent the most improbable excuses on the spur of the moment, hindrances which prevented him from coming at that time, and which made it impossible for him to communicate the situation to her. We all know that in military matters the excuse of having forgotten something is useless, that it protects one from no punishment; and we must consider this attitude justified. Here we suddenly find everyone agreed that a certain error is significant, and everyone agrees what its meaning is. Why are they not consistent enough to extend this insight to the other errors, and fully to acknowledge them? Of course, there is also an answer to this.

If the meaning of this forgetting of projects leaves room for so little doubt among laymen, you will be less surprised to find that poets make use of these errors in the same sense. Those of you who have seen or read Shaw's *Caesar and Cleopatra* will recall that Caesar, when departing in the last scene, is pursued by the idea that there was something more he intended to do, but that he had forgotten it. Finally he discovers what it is: to take leave of Cleopatra. This small device of the author is meant to ascribe to the great Caesar a superiority which he did not possess, and to which he did not at all aspire. You can learn from historical sources that Caesar had Cleopatra follow him to Rome, and that she was staying there with her little Caesarion when Caesar was murdered, whereupon she fled the city.

The cases of forgetting projects are as a rule so clear that they are of little use for our purpose, i.e., discovering in the psychic situation circumstantial evidence of the meaning of the error. Let us, therefore, turn to a particularly ambiguous and untransparent error, that of losing and mislaying objects. That we ourselves should have a purpose in losing an object, an accident frequently so painful, will certainly seem incredible to you. But there are many instances similar to the following: A young man loses the pencil which he had liked very much. The day before he had received a letter from his brother-in-law, which concluded with the words, "For the present I have neither the inclination nor the time to be a party to your frivolity and your idleness." (From B. Dattner) It so happened that the pencil had been a present from this brother-in-law. Without this coincidence we could not, of course, assert that the loss involved any intention to get rid of the gift. Similar cases are numerous. Persons lose objects when they have fallen out with the donors, and no longer wish to be reminded of them. Or again, objects may be lost if one no longer likes the things themselves, and wants to supply oneself with a pretext for substituting other and better things in their stead. Letting a thing fall and break naturally shows the same intention toward that object. Can one consider it accidental when a school child just before his birthday loses, ruins or breaks his belongings, for example his school bag or his watch?

He who has frequently experienced the annoyance of not being able to find something which he has himself put away, will also be unwilling to believe there was any intent behind the loss. And yet the examples are not at all rare in which the attendant circumstances of the mislaying point to a tendency temporarily or permanently to get rid of the object. Perhaps the most beautiful example of this sort is the following: A young man tells me: "A few years ago a misunderstanding arose in my married life. I felt my wife was too cool and even though I willingly acknowledged her excellent qualities, we lived without any tenderness between us. One day she brought me a book which she had thought might interest me. I thanked her for this attention, promised to read the book, put it in a handy place, and couldn't find it again. Several months passed thus, during which I occasionally remembered this mislaid book and tried in vain to find it. About half a year later my beloved mother, who lived at a distance from us, fell ill. My wife left the house in order to nurse her mother-in-law. The condition of the patient became serious, and gave my wife an opportunity of showing her best side. One evening I came home filled with enthusiasm and gratitude toward my wife. I approached my writing desk, opened a certain drawer with no definite intention but as if with somnambulistic certainty, and the first thing I found is the book so long mislaid."

With the cessation of the motive, the inability to find the mislaid object also came to an end.

Ladies and gentlemen, I could increase this collection of examples indefinitely. But I do not wish to do so here. In my *Psychopathology of Everyday Life* (first published in 1901), you will find only too many instances for the study of errors.[6]

All these examples demonstrate the same thing repeatedly: namely, they make it seem probable that errors have a meaning, and show how one may guess or establish that meaning from the attendant circumstances. I limit myself to-day because we have confined ourselves to the purpose of profiting in the preparation for psychoanalysis from the study of these phenomena. I must, however, still go into two additional groups of observations, into the accumulated and combined errors and into the confirmation of our interpretations by means of subsequent developments.

The accumulated and combined errors are surely the fine flower of their species. If we were interested only in proving that errors may have a meaning, we would limit ourselves to the accumulated and combined errors in the first place, for here the meaning is unmistakable, even to the dullest intelligence, and can force conviction upon the most critical judgment. The accumulation of manifestations betrays a stubbornness such as could never come about by accident, but which fits closely the idea of design. Finally, the interchange of certain kinds of error with each other shows us what is the important and essential element of the error, not its form or the means of which it avails itself, but the purpose which it serves and which is to be achieved by the most various paths. Thus I will give you a case of repeated forgetting. Jones recounts that he once allowed a letter to lie on his writing desk several days

---

[6] So also in the writings of A. Maeder (French), A. A. Brill (English) J. Stärke (Dutch) and others.

for reasons quite unknown. Finally he made up his mind to mail it; but it was returned from the dead letter office, for he had forgotten to address it. After he had addressed it he took it to the post office, but this time without a stamp. At this point he finally had to admit to himself his aversion against sending the letter at all.

In another case a mistake is combined with mislaying an object. A lady is traveling to Rome with her brother-in-law, a famous artist. The visitor is much fêted by the Germans living in Rome, and receives as a gift, among other things, a gold medal of ancient origin. The lady is vexed by the fact that her brother-in-law does not sufficiently appreciate the beautiful object. After she leaves her sister and reaches her home, she discovers when unpacking that she has brought with her—how, she does not know—the medal. She immediately informs her brother-in-law of this fact by letter, and gives him notice that she will send the medal back to Rome the next day. But on the following day, the medal has been so cleverly mislaid that it can neither be found nor sent, and at this point it begins to dawn upon the lady that her "absent-mindedness" means, namely, that she wants to keep the object for herself.[7]

I have already given you an example of a combination of forgetfulness and error in which someone first forgot a rendezvous and then, with the firm intention of not forgetting it a second time, appeared at the wrong hour. A quite analogous case was told me from his own experience, by a friend who pursues literary interests in addition to his scientific ones. He said: "A few years ago I accepted the election to the board of a certain literary society, because I hoped that the society could at some time be of use to me in helping obtain the production of my drama, and, despite my lack of interest, I took part in the meetings every Friday. A few months ago I received the assurance of a production in the theatre in F., and since that time it happens regularly that I forget the meetings of that society. When I read your article on these things, I was ashamed of my forgetfulness, reproached myself with the meanness of staying away now that I no longer need these people and determined to be sure not to forget next Friday. I kept reminding myself of this resolution until I carried it out and stood before the door of the meeting room. To my astonishment, it was closed, the meeting was already over; for I had mistaken the day. It was already Saturday."

It would be tempting enough to collect similar observations, but I will go no further; I will let you glance instead upon those cases in which our interpretation has to wait for its proof upon future developments.

The chief condition of these cases is conceivably that the existing psychic situation is unknown to us or inaccessible to our inquiries. At that time our

---

[7] From R. Reitler.

interpretation has only the value of a conjecture to which we ourselves do not wish to grant too much weight. Later, however, something happens which shows us how justified was our interpretation even at that time. I was once the guest of a young married couple and heard the young wife laughingly tell of a recent experience, of how on the day after her return from her honeymoon she had hunted up her unmarried sister again in order to go shopping with her, as in former times, while her husband went to his business. Suddenly she noticed a gentleman on the other side of the street, and she nudged her sister, saying, "Why look, there goes Mr. K." She had forgotten that this gentleman was her husband of some weeks' standing. I shuddered at this tale but did not dare to draw the inference. The little anecdote did not occur to me again until a year later, after this marriage had come to a most unhappy end.

A. Maeder tells of a lady who, the day before her wedding, forgot to try on her wedding dress and to the despair of the dressmaker only remembered it later in the evening. He adds in connection with this forgetfulness the fact that she divorced her husband soon after. I know a lady now divorced from her husband, who, in managing her fortune, frequently signed documents with her maiden name, and this many years before she really resumed it. I know of other women who lost their wedding rings on their honeymoon and also know that the course of the marriage gave a meaning to this accident. And now one more striking example with a better termination. It is said that the marriage of a famous German chemist did not take place because he forgot the hour of the wedding, and instead of going to the church went to the laboratory. He was wise enough to rest satisfied with this one attempt, and died unmarried at a ripe old age.

Perhaps the idea has also come to you that in these cases mistakes have taken the place of the *Omina* or omens of the ancients. Some of the *Omina* really were nothing more than mistakes; for example, when a person stumbled or fell down. Others, to be sure, bore the characteristics of objective occurrences rather than that of subjective acts. But you would not believe how difficult it sometimes is to decide in a specific instance whether the act belongs to the one or the other group. It so frequently knows how to masquerade as a passive experience.

Everyone of us who can look back over a longer or shorter life experience will probably say that he might have spared himself many disappointments and painful surprises if he had found the courage and decision to interpret as omens the little mistakes which he made in his intercourse with people, and to consider them as indications of the intentions which were still being kept secret. As a rule, one does not dare do this. One would feel as though he were again becoming superstitious via a detour through science. But not all omens come true, and you will understand from our theories that they need not all come true.

FOURTH LECTURE. THE PSYCHOLOGY OF ERRORS—(Conclusion)

WE may certainly put it down as the conclusion of our labors up to this point that errors have a meaning, and we may make this conclusion the basis of our further investigations. Let me stress the fact once more that we do not assert—and for our purposes need not assert—that every single mistake which occurs is meaningful, although I consider that probable. It will suffice us if we prove the presence of such a meaning with relative frequency in the various forms of errors. These various forms, by the way, behave differently in this respect. In the cases of tongue slips, pen slips, etc., the occurrences may take place on a purely physiological basis. In the group based on forgetfulness (forgetting names or projects, mislaying objects, etc.) I cannot believe in such a basis. There does very probably exist a type of case in which the loss of objects should be recognized as unintentional. Of the mistakes which occur in daily life, only a certain portion can in any way be brought within our conception. You must keep this limitation in mind when we start henceforth from the assumption that mistakes are psychic acts and arise through the mutual interference of two intentions.

Herein we have the first result of psychoanalysis. Psychology hitherto knew nothing of the occurrence of such interferences and the possibility that they might have such manifestations as a consequence. We have widened the province of the world of psychic phenomena quite considerably, and have brought into the province of psychology phenomena which formerly were not attributed to it.

Let us tarry a moment longer over the assertion that errors are psychic acts. Does such an assertion contain more than the former declaration that they have a meaning? I do not believe so. On the contrary, it is rather more indefinite and open to greater misunderstanding. Everything which can be observed about the psychic life will on occasion be designated as a psychic phenomenon. But it will depend on whether the specific psychic manifestations resulted directly from bodily, organic, material influences, in which case their investigation will not fall within the province of psychology, or whether it was more immediately the result of other psychic occurrences back of which, somewhere, the series of organic influences then begins. We have the latter condition of affairs before us when we designate a phenomenon as a psychic manifestation, and for that reason it is more expedient to put our assertion in this form: the phenomena are meaningful; they have a meaning. By "meaning" we understand significance, purpose, tendency and position in a sequence of psychic relations.

34

There are a number of other occurrences which are very closely related to errors, but which this particular name no longer fits. We call them *accidental and symptomatic* acts. They also have the appearance of being unmotivated, the appearance of insignificance and unimportance, but in addition, and more plainly, of superfluity. They are differentiated from errors by the absence of another intention with which they collide and by which they are disturbed. On the other side they pass over without a definite boundary line into the gestures and movements which we count among expressions of the emotions. Among these accidental acts belong all those apparently playful, apparently purposeless performances in connection with our clothing, parts of our body, objects within reach, as well as the omission of such performances, and the melodies which we hum to ourselves. I venture the assertion that all these phenomena are meaningful and capable of interpretation in the same way as are the errors, that they are small manifestations of other more important psychic processes, valid psychic acts. But I do not intend to linger over this new enlargement of the province of psychic phenomena, but rather to return to the topic of errors, in the consideration of which the important psychoanalytic inquiries can be worked out with far greater clarity.

The most interesting questions which we formulated while considering errors, and which we have not yet answered, are, I presume, the following: We said that the errors are the result of the mutual interference of two different intentions, of which the one can be called the intention interfered with, and the other the interfering intention. The intentions interfered with give rise to no further questions, but concerning the others we want to know, firstly, what kind of intentions are these which arise as disturbers of others, and secondly, in what proportions are the interfering related to the interfered?

Will you permit me again to take the slip of the tongue as representative of the whole species and allow me to answer the second question before the first?

The interfering intention in the tongue slip may stand in a significant relation to the intention interfered with, and then the former contains a contradiction of the latter, correcting or supplementing it. Or, to take a less intelligible and more interesting case, the interfering intention has nothing to do with the intention interfered with.

Proofs for the first of the two relations we can find without trouble in the examples which we already know and in others similar to those. In almost all cases of tongue slips where one says the contrary of what he intended, where the interfering intention expresses the antithesis of the intention interfered with, the error is the presentation of the conflict between two irreconcilable strivings. "I declare the meeting opened, but would rather have it closed," is the meaning of the president's slip. A political paper which has been accused of corruptibility, defends itself in an article meant to reach a climax in the words: "Our readers will testify that we have always interceded for the good of all in the most *disinterested* manner." But the editor who had been entrusted with the composition of the defence, wrote, "in the most *interested* manner." That is, he thinks "To be sure, I have to write this way, but I know better." A representative of the people who urges that the Kaiser should be told the truth "*rückhaltlos*," hears an inner voice which is frightened by his boldness, and which through a slip changes the "*rückhaltlos*" into "*rückgratlos*."[8]

In the examples familiar to you, which give the impression of contraction and abbreviation, it is a question of a correction, an addition or continuation by which the second tendency manifests itself together with the first. "Things were revealed, but better say it right out, they were *filthy*, therefore, things were *refiled*."[9]

"The people who understand this topic can be counted on the *fingers of one hand*, but no, there is really only *one* who understands it; therefore, counted *on one finger*." Or, "My husband may eat and drink whatever *he* wants. But you know very well that *I* don't permit him to want anything; therefore he may eat and drink whatever *I want*." In all these cases, therefore, the slip arises from the content of the intention itself, or is connected with it.

The other type of relationship between the two interfering intentions seems strange. If the interfering intention has nothing to do with the content of the one interfered with, where then does it come from and how does it happen to make itself manifest as interference just at that point? The observation which alone can furnish an answer here, recognizes the fact that the interference originates in a thought process which has just previously occupied the person in question and which then has that after-effect, irrespective of whether it has already found expression in speech or not. It is therefore really to be designated as perseveration, but not necessarily as the perseveration of spoken words. Here also there is no lack of an associative connection between the interfering and the interfered with, yet it is not given in the content, but artificially restored, often by means of forced connecting links.

Here is a simple example of this, which I myself observed. In our beautiful Dolomites, I meet two Viennese ladies who are gotten up as tourists. I accompany them a short distance and we discuss the pleasures, but also the

---

[8] In the German Reichstag, November, 1908. "Rückhaltlos" means "unreservedly." "Rückgratlos" means "without backbone."

[9] "Zum Vorschein bringen," means to bring to light. "Schweinereien" means filthiness or obscurity. The telescoping of the two ideas, resulting in the word "Vorschwein," plainly reveals the speaker's opinion of the affair.

difficulties of the tourist's mode of life. One lady admits this way of spending the day entails much discomfort. "It is true," she says, "that it is not at all pleasant, when one has tramped all day in the sun, and waist and shirt are soaked through." At this point in this sentence she suddenly has to overcome a slight hesitancy. Then she continues: "But then, when one gets *nach Hose*, and can change...."[10] We did not analyze this slip, but I am sure you can easily understand it. The lady wanted to make the enumeration more complete and to say, "Waist, shirt and drawers." From motives of propriety, the mention of the drawers (Hose) was suppressed, but in the next sentence of quite independent content the unuttered word came to light as a distortion of the similar word, house (Hause).

Now we can turn at last to the long delayed main question, namely, what kind of intentions are these which get themselves expressed in an unusual way as interferences of others, intentions within whose great variety we wish nevertheless to find what is common to them all! If we examine a series of them to this end, we will soon find that they divide themselves into three groups. In the first group belong the cases in which the interfering tendency is known to the speaker, and which, moreover, was felt by him before the slip. Thus, in the case of the slip "*refilled*," the speaker not only admits that he agreed with the judgment "*filthy*," on the incidents in question, but also that he had the intention (which he later abandoned) of giving it verbal expression. A second group is made up of those cases in which the interfering tendency is immediately recognized by the subject as his own, but in which he is ignorant of the fact that the interfering tendency was active in him just before the slip. He therefore accepts our interpretation, yet remains to a certain extent surprised by it. Examples of this situation can perhaps more easily be found among errors other than slips of the tongue. In a third group the interpretation of the interfering intention is energetically denied by the speaker. He not only denies that the interfering tendency was active in him before the slip, but he wants to assert that it was at all times completely alien to him. Will you recall the example of "hiccough," and the absolutely impolite disavowal which I received at the hands of this speaker by my disclosure of the interfering intention. You know that so far we have no unity in our conception of these cases. I pay no attention to the toastmaster's disavowal and hold fast to my interpretation; while you, I am sure, are yet under the influence of his repudiation and are considering whether one ought not to forego the interpretation of such slips, and let them pass as purely physiological acts, incapable of further analysis. I can imagine what it is that frightens you off. My interpretation draws the conclusion that intentions of which he himself knows nothing may manifest themselves in a speaker, and

---

[10] The lady meant to say "Nach Hause," "to reach home." The word "Hose" means "drawers." The preservating content of her hesitancy is hereby revealed.

that I can deduce them from the circumstances. You hesitate before so novel a conclusion and one so full of consequences. I understand that, and sympathize with you to that extent. But let us make one thing clear: if you want consistently to carry through the conception of errors which you have derived from so many examples, you must decide to accept the above conclusion, even though it be unpleasant. If you cannot do so, you must give up that understanding of errors which you have so recently won.

Let us tarry a while over the point which unites the three groups, which is common to the three mechanisms of tongue slips. Fortunately, that is unmistakable. In the first two groups the interfering tendency is recognized by the speaker; in the first there is the additional fact that it showed itself immediately before the slip. In both cases, however, *it was suppressed. The speaker had made up his mind not to convert the interfering tendency into speech and then the slip of the tongue occurred; that is to say, the suppressed tendency obtains expression against the speaker's will, in that it changes the expression of the intention which he permits, mixes itself with it or actually puts itself in its place.* This is, then, the mechanism of the tongue slip.

From my point of view, I can also best harmonize the processes of the third group with the mechanism here described. I need only assume that these three groups are differentiated by the different degrees of effectiveness attending the suppression of an intention. In the first group, the intention is present and makes itself perceptible before the utterance of the speaker; not until then does it suffer the suppression for which it indemnifies itself in the slip. In the second group the suppression extends farther. The intention is no longer perceptible before the subject speaks. It is remarkable that the interfering intention is in no way deterred by this from taking part in the causation of the slip. Through this fact, however, the explanation of the procedure in the third group is simplified for us. I shall be so bold as to assume that in the error a tendency can manifest itself which has been suppressed for even a longer time, perhaps a very long time, which does not become perceptible and which, therefore, cannot be directly denied by the speaker. But leave the problem of the third group; from the observation of the other cases, you most draw the conclusion that *the suppression of the existing intention to say something is the indispensable condition of the occurrence of a slip.*

We may now claim that we have made further progress in understanding errors. We know not only that they are psychic acts, in which we can recognize meaning and purpose, and that they arise through the mutual interference of two different intentions, but, in addition, we know that one of these intentions must have undergone a certain suppression in order to be able to manifest itself through interference with the other. The interfering intention must itself first be interfered with before it can become interfering. Naturally,

38

a complete explanation of the phenomena which we call errors is not attained to by this. We immediately see further questions arising, and suspect in general that there will be more occasions for new questions as we progress further. We might, for example, ask why the matter does not proceed much more simply. If there is an existing purpose to suppress a certain tendency instead of giving it expression, then this suppression should be so successful that nothing at all of the latter comes to light; or it could even fail, so that the suppressed tendency attains to full expression. But errors are compromise formations. They mean some success and some failure for each of the two purposes. The endangered intention is neither completely suppressed nor does it, without regard to individual cases, come through wholly intact. We can imagine that special conditions must be existent for the occurrence of such interference or compromise formations, but then we cannot even conjecture what sort they may be. Nor do I believe that we can uncover these unknown circumstances through further penetration into the study of errors. Rather will it be necessary thoroughly to examine other obscure fields of psychic life. Only the analogies which we there encounter can give us the courage to draw those assumptions which are requisite to a more fundamental elucidation of errors. And one thing more. Even working with small signs, as we have constantly been in the habit of doing in this province, brings its dangers with it. There is a mental disease, combined paranoia, in which the utilization of such small signs is practiced without restriction and I naturally would not wish to give it as my opinion that these conclusions, built up on this basis, are correct throughout. We can be protected from such dangers only by the broad basis of our observations, by the repetition of similar impressions from the most varied fields of psychic life.

We will therefore leave the analysis of errors here. But may I remind you of one thing more: keep in mind, as a prototype, the manner in which we have treated these phenomena. You can see from these examples what the purposes of our psychology are. We do not wish merely to describe the phenomena and to classify them, but to comprehend them as signs of a play of forces in the psychic, as expressions of tendencies striving to an end, tendencies which work together or against one another. We seek a dynamic conception of psychic phenomena. The perceived phenomena must, in our conception, give way to those strivings whose existence is only assumed.

Hence we will not go deeper into the problem of errors, but we can still undertake an expedition through the length of this field, in which we will reëncounter things familiar to us, and will come upon the tracks of some that are new. In so doing we will keep to the division which we made in the beginning of our study, of the three groups of tongue slips, with the related forms of pen slips, misreadings, mishearings, forgetfulness with its subdivisions according to the forgotten object (proper names, foreign words, projects, impressions), and the other faults of mistaking, mislaying and losing objects. Errors, in so far as they come into our consideration, are grouped in part with forgetfulness, in part with mistakes.

We have already spoken in such detail of tongue slips, and yet there are still several points to be added. Linked with tongue slips are smaller effective phenomena which are not entirely without interest. No one likes to make a slip of the tongue; often one fails to hear his own slip, though never that of another. Tongue slips are in a certain sense infectious; it is not at all easy to discuss tongue slips without falling into slips of the tongue oneself. The most trifling forms of tongue slips are just the ones which have no particular illumination to throw on the hidden psychic processes, but are nevertheless not difficult to penetrate in their motivation. If, for example, anyone pronounces a long vowel as a short, in consequence of an interference no matter how motivated, he will for that reason soon after lengthen a short vowel and commit a new slip in compensation for the earlier one. The same thing occurs when one has pronounced a double vowel unclearly and hastily; for example, an "eu" or an "oi" as "ei." The speaker tries to correct it by changing a subsequent "ei" or "eu" to "oi." In this conduct the determining factor seems to be a certain consideration for the hearer, who is not to think that it is immaterial to the speaker how he treats his mother tongue. The second, compensating distortion actually has the purpose of making the hearer conscious of the first, and of assuring him that it also did not escape the speaker. The most frequent and most trifling cases of slips consist in the contractions and foresoundings which show themselves in inconspicuous parts of speech. One's tongue slips in a longer speech to such an extent that the last word of the intended speech is said too soon. That gives the impression of a certain impatience to be finished with the sentence and gives proof in general of a certain resistance to communicating this sentence or speech as a whole. Thus we come to borderline cases in which the differences between the psychoanalytic and the common physiological conception of tongue slips are blended. We assume that in these cases there is a tendency which interferes with the intention of the speech. But it can only announce that it is present, and not what its own intention is. The interference which it occasions then follows some sound influences or associative relationship, and may be considered as a distraction of attention from the intended speech. But neither this disturbance of attention nor the associative tendency which has been activated, strikes the essence of the process. This hints, however, at the existence of an intention which interferes with the purposed speech, an intention whose nature cannot (as is possible in all the more pronounced cases of tongue slips) this time be guessed from its effects.

Slips of the pen, to which I now turn, are in agreement with those of the tongue to the extent that we need expect to gain no new points of view from them. Perhaps we will be content with a small gleaning. Those very common little slips of the pen—contractions, anticipations of later words, particularly of the last words—again point to a general distaste for writing, and to an impatience to be done; the pronounced effects of pen slips permit the nature and purpose of the interfering tendency to be recognized. One knows in general that if one finds a slip of the pen in a letter everything was not as usual with the writer. What was the matter one cannot always establish. The pen slip is frequently as little noticed by the person who makes it as the tongue slip. The following observation is striking: There are some persons who have the habit of always rereading a letter they have written before sending it. Others do not do so. But if the latter make an exception and reread the letter, they always have the opportunity of finding and correcting a conspicuous pen slip. How can that be explained? This looks as if these persons knew that they had made a slip of the pen while writing the letter. Shall we really believe that such is the case?

There is an interesting problem linked with the practical significance of the pen slip. You may recall the case of the murderer H., who made a practice of obtaining cultures of the most dangerous disease germs from scientific institutions, by pretending to be a bacteriologist, and who used these cultures to get his close relatives out of the way in this most modern fashion. This man once complained to the authorities of such an institution about the ineffectiveness of the culture which had been sent to him, but committed a pen slip and instead of the words, "in my attempts on mice and guinea pigs," was plainly written, "in my attempts on people."[20][11] This slip even attracted the attention of the doctors at the institution, but so far as I know, they drew no conclusion from it. Now what do you think? Might not the doctors better have accepted the slip as a confession and instituted an investigation through which the murderer's handiwork would have been blocked in time? In this case was not ignorance of our conception of errors to blame for an omission of practical importance? Well, I am inclined to think that such a slip would surely seem very suspicious to me, but a fact of great importance stands in the way of its utilization as a confession. The thing is not so simple. The pen slip is surely an indication, but by itself it would not have been sufficient to instigate an investigation. That the man is preoccupied with the thought of infecting human beings, the slip certainly does betray, but it does not make it possible to decide whether this thought has the value of a clear plan of injury or merely of a phantasy having no practical consequence. It is even possible that the person who made such a

---

[11] The German reads, "bei meinen Versuchen an Mausen," which, through the slip of the pen, resulted in "bei meinen Versuchen an Menschen."

slip will deny this phantasy with the best subjective justification and will reject it as something entirely alien to him. Later, when we give our attention to the difference between psychic and material reality, you will understand these possibilities even better. Yet this is again a case in which an error later attained unsuspected significance.

In misreading, we encounter a psychic situation which is clearly differentiated from that of the tongue slips or pen slips. The one of the two rival tendencies is here replaced by a sensory stimulus and perhaps for that reason is less resistant. What one is reading is not a production of one's own psychic activity, as is something which one intends to write. In a large majority of cases, therefore, the misreading consists in a complete substitution. One substitutes another word for the word to be read, and there need be no connection in meaning between the text and the product of the misreading. In general, the slip is based upon a word resemblance. Lichtenberg's example of reading "*Agamemnon*" for "*angenommen*" (a verb, meaning "to accept) is the best of this group. If one wishes to discover the interfering tendency which causes the misreading, one may completely ignore the misread text and can begin the analytic investigation with the two questions: What is the first idea that occurs in free association to the product of the misreading, and, in what situation did the misreading occur? Now and then a knowledge of the latter suffices by itself to explain the misreading. Take, for example, the individual who, distressed by certain needs, wanders about in a strange city and reads the word "*Closethaus*" on a large sign on the first floor of a house. He has just time to be surprised at the fact that the sign has been nailed so high up when he discovers that, accurately observed, the sign reads "*Corset-haus.*" In other cases the misreadings which are independent of the text require a penetrating analysis which cannot be accomplished without practice and confidence in the psychoanalytic technique. But generally it is not a matter of much difficulty to obtain the elucidation of a misreading. The substituted word, as in the example, "*Agamemnon,*" betrays without more ado the thought sequence from which the interference results. In war times, for instance, it is very common for one to read into everything which contains a similar word structure, the names of the cities, generals and military expressions which are constantly buzzing around us. In this way, whatever interests and preoccupies one puts itself in the place of that which is foreign or uninteresting. The after-effects of thoughts blur the new perceptions.

There are other types of misreadings, in which the text itself arouses the disturbing tendency, by means of which it is then most often changed into its opposite. One reads something which is undesired; analysis then convinces one that an intensive wish to reject what has been read should be made responsible for the alteration.

In the first mentioned and more frequent cases of misreading, two factors are neglected to which we gave an important role in the mechanism of errors: the conflict of two tendencies and the suppression of one which then indemnifies itself by producing the error. Not that anything like the opposite occurs in misreading, but the importunity of the idea content which leads to misreading is nevertheless much more conspicuous than the suppression to which the latter may previously have been subjected. Just these two factors are most tangibly apparent in the various situations of errors of forgetfulness.

Forgetting plans is actually uniform in meaning; its interpretation is, as we have heard, not denied even by the layman. The tendency interfering with the plan is always an antithetical intention, an unwillingness concerning which we need only discover why it does not come to expression in a different and less disguised manner. But the existence of this unwillingness is not to be doubted. Sometimes it is possible even to guess something of the motives which make it necessary for this unwillingness to disguise itself, and it always achieves its purpose by the error resulting from the concealment, while its rejection would be certain were it to present itself as open contradiction. If an important change in the psychic situation occurs between the formulation of the plan and its execution, in consequence of which the execution of the plan does not come into question, then the fact that the plan was forgotten is no longer in the class of errors. One is no longer surprised at it, and one understands that it would have been superfluous to have remembered the plan; it was then permanently or temporarily effaced. Forgetting a plan can be called an error only when we have no reason to believe there was such an interruption.

The cases of forgetting plans are in general so uniform and transparent that they do not interest us in our investigation. There are two points, however, from which we can learn something new. We have said that forgetting, that is, the non-execution of a plan, points to an antipathy toward it. This certainly holds, but, according to the results of our investigations, the antipathy may be of two sorts, direct and indirect. What is meant by the latter can best be explained by one or two examples. If a patron forgets to say a good word for his protegé to a third person, it may be because the patron is not really very much interested in the protegé, therefore, has no great inclination to commend him. It is, at any rate, in this sense that the protegé will construe his patron's forgetfulness. But the matter may be more complicated. The patron's antipathy to the execution of the plan may originate in another quarter and fasten upon quite a different point. It need not have anything to do with the protegé, but may be directed toward the third person to whom the good word was to have been said. Thus, you see what doubts here confront the practical application of our interpretation. The protegé, despite a correct interpretation of the forgetfulness, stands in danger of becoming too suspicious, and of doing his patron a grave injustice. Or, if an individual forgets a rendezvous which he has made, and which he had resolved to keep, the most frequent basis will certainly be the direct aversion to encountering this person. But analysis might here supply the information that the interfering intention was not directed against that person, but against the place in which they were to have met, and which was avoided because of a painful memory associated with it. Or, if one forgets to mail a letter, the counter-intention may be directed against the content of that letter, yet this does not in any way exclude the possibility that the letter is harmless in itself, and only subject to the counter-intention because something about it reminds the writer of another letter written previously, which, in fact, did afford a basis for the antipathy. One can say in such a case that the antipathy has here transferred itself from that former letter where it was justified to the present one in which it really has no meaning. Thus you see that one must always exercise restraint and caution in the application of interpretations, even though the interpretations are justified. That which is psychologically equivalent may nevertheless in practice be very ambiguous.

Phenomena such as these will seem very unusual to you. Perhaps you are inclined to assume that the "indirect" antipathy is enough to characterize the incident as pathological. Yet I can assure you that it also occurs in a normal and healthy setting. I am in no way willing to admit the unreliability of our analytic interpretation. After all, the above-discussed ambiguity of plan-forgetting exists only so long as we have not attempted an analysis of the case, and are interpreting it only on the basis of our general suppositions. When we analyze the person in question, we discover with sufficient certainty in each case whether or not it is a direct antipathy, or what its origin is otherwise.

A second point is the following: when we find in a large majority of cases that the forgetting of a plan goes back to an antipathy, we gain courage to extend this solution to another series of cases in which the analyzed person does not confirm, but denies, the antipathy which we inferred. Take as an example the exceedingly frequent incidents of forgetting to return books which one has borrowed, or forgetting to pay one's bills or debts. We will be so bold as to accuse the individual in question of intending to keep the books and not to pay the debts, while he will deny such an intention but will not be in a position to give us any other explanation of his conduct. Thereupon we insist that he has the intention, only he knows nothing about it; all we need for our inference is to have the intention betray itself through the effect of the forgetfulness. The subject may then repeat that he had merely forgotten it. You now recognize the situation as one in which we once before found ourselves. If we wish to be consistent in our interpretation, an interpretation which has been proved as manifold as it is justified, we will be unavoidably forced to the conclusion that there are tendencies in a human being which can become effective without his being conscious of them. By so doing, however, we place ourselves in opposition to all the views which prevail in daily life and in psychology.

Forgetting proper names and foreign names as well as foreign words can be traced in the same manner to a counter-intention which aims either directly or indirectly at the name in question. I have already given you an example of such direct antipathy. The indirect causation, however, is particularly frequent and generally necessitates careful analysis for its determination. Thus, for example, in war times which force us to sacrifice so many of our former inclinations, the ability to recall proper names also suffers severely in consequence of the most peculiar connections. A short time ago it happened that I could not reproduce the name of that harmless Moravian city of Bisenz, and analysis showed that no direct dislike was to blame, but rather the sound resemblance to the name of the Bisenzi palace in Orrieto, in which I used to wish I might live. As a motive for the antagonism to remembering the name, we here encounter for the first time a principle which will later disclose to us its whole tremendous significance in the causation of neurotic symptoms, viz., the aversion on the part of the memory to remembering anything which is connected with unpleasant experience and which would revive this unpleasantness by a reproduction. This intention of avoiding unpleasantness in recollections of other psychic acts, the psychic flight from unpleasantness, we may recognize as the ultimate effective motive not only for the forgetting of names, but also for many other errors, such as omissions of action, etc.

Forgetting names does, however, seem to be especially facilitated psycho-physiologically and therefore also occurs in cases in which the interference of an unpleasantness-motive cannot be established. If anyone once has a tendency to forget names, you can establish by analytical investigation that he not only loses names because he himself does not like them, or because they remind him of something he does not like, but also because the same name in his mind belongs to another chain of associations, with which he has more intimate relations. The name is anchored there, as it were, and denied to the other associations activated at the moment. If you will recall the tricks of mnemonic technique you will ascertain with some surprise that one forgets names in consequence of the same associations which one otherwise purposely forms in order to save them from being forgotten. The most conspicuous example of this is afforded by proper names of persons, which conceivably enough must have very different psychic values for different people. For example, take a first name, such as Theodore. To one of you it will mean nothing special, to another it means the name of his father, brother, friend, or his own name. Analytic experience will then show you that the first person is not in danger of forgetting that a certain stranger bears this name, while the latter will be constantly inclined to withhold from the stranger this name which seems reserved for intimate relationships. Let us now assume that this associative inhibition can come into contact with the operation of the unpleasantness-principle, and in addition with an indirect mechanism, and you will be in a position to form a correct picture of the complexity of causation of this temporary name-forgetting. An adequate analysis that does justice to the facts, however, will completely disclose these complications.

Forgetting impressions and experiences shows the working of the tendency to keep unpleasantness from recollection much more clearly and conclusively than does the forgetting of names. It does not, of course, belong in its entirety to the category of errors, but only in so far as it seems to us conspicuous and unjustified, measured by the measuring stick of our accustomed conception—thus, for example, where the forgetfulness strikes fresh or important impressions or impressions whose loss tears a hole in the otherwise well-remembered sequence. Why and how it is in general that we forget, particularly why and how we forget experiences which have surely left the deepest impressions, such as the incidents of our first years of childhood, is quite a different problem, in which the defense against unpleasant associations plays a certain role but is far from explaining everything. That unpleasant impressions are easily forgotten is an indubitable fact. Various psychologists have observed it, and the great Darwin was so struck by it that he made the "golden rule" for himself of writing down with particular care observations which seemed unfavorable to his theory, since he had convinced himself that they were just the ones which would not stick in his memory.

Those who hear for the first time of this principle of defense against unpleasant recollections by means of forgetting, seldom fail to raise the objection that they, on the contrary, have had the experience that just the painful is hard to forget, inasmuch as it always comes back to mind to torture the person against his will—as, for example, the recollection of an insult or humiliation. This fact is also correct, but the objection is not valid. It is important that one begin betimes to reckon with the fact that the psychic life is the arena of the struggles and exercises of antagonistic tendencies, or, to express it in non-dynamic terminology, that it consists of contradictions and paired antagonisms. Information concerning one specific tendency is of no avail for the exclusion of its opposite; there is room for both of them. It depends only on how the opposites react upon each other, what effects will proceed from the one and what from the other.

Losing and mislaying objects is of especial interest to us because of the ambiguity and the multiplicity of tendencies in whose services the errors may act. The common element in all cases is this, that one wished to lose something. The reasons and purposes thereof vary. One loses an object when it has become damaged, when one intends to replace it with a better one, when one has ceased to like it, when it came from a person whose relations to one have become strained, or when it was obtained under circumstances of which one no longer wishes to think. The same purpose may be served by letting the object fall, be damaged or broken. In the life of society it is said to have been found that unwelcome and illegitimate children are much more often frail than those born in wedlock. To reach this result we do not need the coarse technique of the so-called angel-maker. A certain remissness in the care of the child is said to suffice amply. In the preservation of objects, the case might easily be the same as with the children.

But things may be singled out for loss without their having forfeited any of their value, namely, when there exists the intention to sacrifice something to fate in order to ward off some other dreaded loss. Such exorcisings of fate are, according to the findings of analysis, still very frequent among us; therefore, the loss of things is often a voluntary sacrifice. In the same way losing may serve the purposes of obstinacy or self-punishment. In short, the more distant motivation of the tendency to get rid of a thing oneself by means of losing it is not overlooked.

Mistakes, like other errors, are often used to fulfill wishes which one ought to deny oneself. The purpose is thus masked as fortunate accident; for instance, one of our friends once took the train to make a call in the suburbs, despite the clearest antipathy to so doing, and then, in changing cars, made the mistake of getting into the train which took him back to the city. Or, if on a trip one absolutely wants to make a longer stay at a half-way station, one is apt to overlook or miss certain connections, so that he is forced to make the desired interruption to the trip. Or, as once happened to a patient of mine whom I had forbidden to call up his fiancée on the telephone, "by mistake" and "absent-mindedly" he asked for a wrong number when he wanted to telephone to me, so that he was suddenly connected with the lady. A pretty example and one of practical significance in making a direct mistake is the observation of an engineer at a preliminary hearing in a damage suit:

"Some time ago I worked with several colleagues in the laboratory of a high school on a series of complicated elasticity experiments, a piece of work which we had undertaken voluntarily but which began to take more time than we had expected. One day as I went into the laboratory with my colleague F., the latter remarked how unpleasant it was to him to lose so much time that day, since he had so much to do at home. I could not help agreeing with him, and remarked half jokingly, alluding to an incident of the previous week: 'Let's hope that the machine gives out again so that we can stop work and go home early.'

"In the division of labor it happened that F. was given the regulation of the valve of the press, that is to say, he was, by means of a cautious opening of the valve, to let the liquid pressure from the accumulator flow slowly into the cylinder of the hydraulic press. The man who was directing the job stood by the manometer (pressure gauge) and when the right pressure had been reached called out in a loud voice: 'Stop.' At this command F. seized the valve and turned with all his might—to the left! (All valves, without exception, close to the right.) Thereby the whole pressure of the accumulator suddenly became effective in the press, a strain for which the connecting pipes are not designed, so that a connecting pipe immediately burst—quite a harmless defect, but one which nevertheless forced us to drop work for the day and go home.

"It is characteristic, by the way, that some time afterward when we were discussing this occurrence, my friend F. had no recollection whatever of my remark, which I could recall with certainty."

From this point you may reach the conjecture that it is not harmless accident which makes the hands of your domestics such dangerous enemies to your household property. But you can also raise the question whether it is always an accident when one damages himself and exposes his own person to danger. There are interests the value of which you will presently be able to test by means of the analysis of observations.

Ladies and gentlemen, this is far from being all that might be said about errors. There is indeed much left to investigate and to discuss. But I am satisfied if, from our investigations to date, your previous views are somewhat shaken and if you have acquired a certain degree of liberality in the acceptance of new ones. For the rest, I must content myself with leaving you face to face with an unclear condition of affairs. We cannot prove all our axioms by the study of errors and, indeed, are by no means solely dependent on this material. The great value of errors for our purpose lies in the fact that they are very frequent phenomena that can easily be observed on oneself and the occurrence of which do not require a pathological condition. I should like to mention just one more of your unanswered questions before concluding: "If, as we have seen in many examples, people come so close to understanding errors and so often act as though they penetrated their meaning, how is it possible that they can so generally consider them accidental, senseless and meaningless, and can so energetically oppose their psychoanalytic elucidation?"

You are right; that is conspicuous and demands an explanation. I shall not give this explanation to you, however, but shall guide you slowly to the connecting links from which the explanation will force itself upon you without any aid from me.

PART II: THE DREAM

FIFTH LECTURE: THE DREAM

Difficulties and Preliminary Approach

ONE day the discovery was made that the disease symptoms of certain nervous patients have a meaning.[12] Thereupon the psychoanalytic method of therapy was founded. In this treatment it happened that the patients also presented dreams in place of their symptoms. Herewith originated the conjecture that these dreams also have a meaning.

We will not, however, pursue this historical path, but enter upon the opposite one. We wish to discover the meaning of dreams as preparation for the study of the neuroses. This inversion is justified, for the study of dreams is not only the best preparation for that of the neuroses, but the dream itself is also a neurotic symptom, and in fact one which possesses for us the incalculable advantage of occurring in all normals. Indeed, if all human beings were well and would dream, we could gain from their dreams almost all the insight to which the study of the neuroses has led.

Thus it is that the dream becomes the object of psychoanalytic research— again an ordinary, little-considered phenomenon, apparently of no practical value, like the errors with which, indeed, it shares the character of occurring in normals. But otherwise the conditions are rather less favorable for our work. Errors had been neglected only by science, which had paid little attention to them; but at least it was no disgrace to occupy one's self with them. People said there are indeed more important things, but perhaps something may come of it. Preoccupation with the dream, however, is not merely impractical and superfluous, but actually ignominious; it carries the odium of the unscientific, awakens the suspicion of a personal leaning towards mysticism. The idea of a physician busying himself with dreams when even in neuropathology and psychiatry there are matters so much more serious—tumors the size of apples which incapacitate the organ of the psyche, hemorrhages, and chronic inflammations in which one can demonstrate changes in the tissues under the microscope! No, the dream is much too trifling an object, and unworthy of Science.

And besides, it is a condition which in itself defies all the requirements of exact research—in dream investigation one is not even sure of one's object. A delusion, for example, presents itself in clear and definite outlines. "I am the Emperor of China," says the patient aloud. But the dream? It generally cannot be related at all. If anyone relates a dream, has he any guarantee that he has told it correctly, and not changed it during the telling, or invented an addition which was forced by the indefiniteness of his recollection? Most dreams cannot be remembered at all, are forgotten except for small fragments. And

---

[12] Josef Breuer, in the years 1880-1882. Cf. also my lectures on psychoanalysis, delivered in the United States in 1909.

upon the interpretation of such material shall a scientific psychology or method of treatment for patients be based?

A certain excess in judgment may make us suspicious. The objections to the dream as an object of research obviously go too far. The question of insignificance we have already had to deal with in discussing errors. We said to ourselves that important matters may manifest themselves through small signs. As concerns the indefiniteness of the dream, it is after all a characteristic like any other. One cannot prescribe the characteristics of an object. Moreover, there are clear and definite dreams. And there are other objects of psychiatric research which suffer from the same trait of indefiniteness, e.g., many compulsion ideas, with which even respectable and esteemed psychiatrists have occupied themselves. I might recall the last case which occurred in my practice. The patient introduced himself to me with the words, "I have a certain feeling as though I had harmed or had wished to harm some living thing—a child?—no, more probably a dog—perhaps pushed it off a bridge—or something else." We can overcome to some degree the difficulty of uncertain recollection in the dream if we determine that exactly what the dreamer tells us is to be taken as his dream, without regard to anything which he has forgotten or may have changed in recollection. And finally, one cannot make so general an assertion as that the dream is an unimportant thing. We know from our own experience that the mood in which one wakes up after a dream may continue throughout the whole day. Cases have been observed by physicians in which a psychosis begins with a dream and holds to a delusion which originated in it. It is related of historical personages that they drew their inspiration for important deeds from dreams. So we may ask whence comes the contempt of scientific circles for the dream?

I think it is the reaction to their over-estimation in former times. Reconstruction of the past is notoriously difficult, but this much we may assume with certainty—if you will permit me the jest—that our ancestors of 3000 years ago and more, dreamed much in the way we do. As far as we know, all ancient peoples attached great importance to dreams and considered them of practical value. They drew omens for the future from dreams, sought premonitions in them. In those days, to the Greeks and all Orientals, a campaign without dream interpreters must have been as impossible as a campaign without an aviation scout to-day. When Alexander the Great undertook his campaign of conquests, the most famous dream interpreters were in attendance. The city of Tyrus, which was then still situated on an island, put up so fierce a resistance that Alexander considered the idea of raising the siege. Then he dreamed one night of a satyr dancing as if in triumph; and when he laid his dream before his interpreters he received the information that the victory over the city had been announced to him. He ordered the attack and took Tyrus. Among the Etruscans and the Romans other methods of discovering the future were in use, but the interpretation of dreams was practical and esteemed during the entire Hellenic-Roman period. Of the literature dealing with the topic at least the chief work has been preserved to us, namely, the book of Artemidoros of Daldis, who is supposed to have lived during the lifetime of the Emperor Hadrian. How it happened subsequently that the art of dream interpretation was lost and the dream fell into discredit, I cannot tell you. Enlightenment cannot have had much part in it, for the Dark Ages faithfully preserved things far more absurd than the ancient dream interpretation. The fact is, the interest in dreams gradually deteriorated into superstition, and could assert itself only among the ignorant. The latest misuse of dream interpretation in our day still tries to discover in dreams the numbers which are going to be drawn in the small lottery. On the other hand, the exact science of to-day has repeatedly dealt with dreams, but always only with the purpose of applying its physiological theories to the dream. By physicians, of course, the dream was considered as a non-psychic act, as the manifestation of somatic irritations in the psychic life. Binz (1876) pronounced the dream "a bodily process, in all cases useless, in many actually pathological, above which the world-soul and immortality are raised as high as the blue ether over the weed-grown sands of the lowest plain." Maury compared it with the irregular twitchings of St. Vitus' Dance in contrast to the co-ordinated movements of the normal person. An old comparison makes the content of the dream analogous to the tones which the "ten fingers of a musically illiterate person would bring forth if they ran over the keys of the instrument."

Interpretation means finding a hidden meaning. There can be no question of interpretation in such an estimation of the dream process. Look up the description of the dream in Wundt, Jodl and other newer philosophers. You will find an enumeration of the deviations of dream life from waking thought, in a sense disparaging to the dream. The description points out the disintegration of association, the suspension of the critical faculty, the elimination of all knowledge, and other signs of diminished activity. The only valuable contribution to the knowledge of the dream which we owe to exact science pertains to the influence of bodily stimuli, operative during sleep, on the content of the dream. There are two thick volumes of experimental researches on dreams by the recently deceased Norwegian author, J. Mourly Vold, (translated into German in 1910 and 1912), which deal almost solely with the consequences of changes in the position of the limbs. They are recommended as the prototype of exact dream research. Now can you imagine what exact science would say if it discovered that we wish to attempt to find the meaning of dreams? It may be it has already said it, but we will not allow ourselves to be frightened off. If errors can have a meaning, the dream can, too, and errors in many cases have a meaning which has escaped exact science. Let us confess to sharing the prejudice of the ancients and the common people, and let us follow in the footsteps of the ancient dream interpreters.

First of all, we must orient ourselves in our task, and take a bird's eye view of our field. What is a dream? It is difficult to say in one sentence. But we do not want to attempt any definition where a reference to the material with which everyone is familiar suffices. Yet we ought to select the essential element of the dream. How can that be found? There are such monstrous differences within the boundary which encloses our province, differences in every direction. The essential thing will very probably be that which we can show to be common to all dreams.

Well, the first thing which is common to all dreams is that we are asleep during their occurrence. The dream is apparently the psychic life during sleep, which has certain resemblances to that of the waking condition, and on the other hand is distinguished from it by important differences. That was noted even in Aristotle's definition. Perhaps there are other connections obtaining between the dream and sleep. One can be awakened by a dream, one frequently has a dream when he wakes spontaneously or is forcibly awakened from sleep. The dream then seems to be an intermediate condition between sleeping and waking. Thus we are referred to the problem of sleep. What, then, is sleep?

That is a physiological or biological problem concerning which there is still much controversy. We can form no decision on the point, but I think we may attempt a psychological characterization of sleep. Sleep is a condition in which I wish to have nothing to do with the external world, and have withdrawn my interest from it. I put myself to sleep by withdrawing myself from the external world and by holding off its stimuli. I also go to sleep when I am fatigued by the external world. Thus, by going to sleep, I say to the external world, "Leave me in peace, for I wish to sleep." Conversely, the child says, "I won't go to bed yet, I am not tired, I want to have some more fun." The biological intention of sleep thus seems to be recuperation; its psychological character, the suspension of interest in the external world. Our relation to the world into which we came so unwillingly, seems to include the fact that we cannot endure it without interruption. For this reason we revert from time to time to the pre-natal existence, that is, to the intra-uterine existence. At least we create for ourselves conditions quite similar to those obtaining at that time—warmth, darkness and the absence of stimuli. Some of us even roll ourselves into tight packages and assume in sleep a posture very similar to the intra-uterine posture. It seems as if the world did not wholly possess us adults, it has only two-thirds of our life, we are still one-third unborn. Each awakening in the morning is then like a new birth. We also speak of the condition after sleep with the words, "I feel as though I had been born anew," by which we probably form a very erroneous idea of the general feeling of the newly born. It may be assumed that the latter, on the contrary, feel very uncomfortable. We also speak of birth as "seeing the light of day." If that be sleep, then the dream is not on its program at all, rather it seems an unwelcome addition. We think, too, that dreamless sleep is the best and only normal sleep. There should be no psychic activity in sleep; if the psyche stirs, then just to that extent have we failed to reduplicate the foetal condition; remainders of psychic activity could not be completely avoided. These remainders are the dream. Then it really does seem that the dream need have no meaning. It was different in the case of errors; they were activities of the waking state. But when I am asleep, have quite suspended psychic activity and have suppressed all but certain of its remainders, then it is by no means inevitable that these remainders have a meaning. In fact, I cannot make use of this meaning, in view of the fact that the rest of my psyche is asleep. This must, of course, be a question only of twitching, like spasmodic reactions, a question only of psychic phenomena such as follow directly upon somatic stimulation. The dream, therefore, appears to be the sleep-disturbing remnant of the psychic activity of waking life, and we may make the resolution promptly to abandon a theme which is so ill-adapted to psychoanalysis.

However, even if the dream is superfluous, it exists nevertheless and we may try to give an account of its existence. Why does not the psyche go to sleep? Probably because there is something which gives it no rest. Stimuli act upon the psyche, and it must react to them. The dream, therefore, is the way in which the psyche reacts to the stimuli acting upon it in the sleeping condition. We note here a point of approach to the understanding of the dream. We can now search through different dreams to discover what are the stimuli which seek to disturb the sleep and which are reacted to with dreams. Thus far we might be said to have discovered the first common element.

Are there other common elements? Yes, it is undeniable that there are, but they are much more difficult to grasp and describe. The psychic processes of sleep, for example, have a very different character from those of waking. One experiences many things in the dream, and believes in them, while one really has experienced nothing but perhaps the one disturbing stimulus. One experiences them predominantly in visual images; feelings may also be interspersed in the dream as well as thoughts; the other senses may also have experiences, but after all the dream experiences are predominantly pictures. A part of the difficulty of dream telling comes from the fact that we have to transpose these pictures into words. "I could draw it," the dreamer says frequently, "but I don't know how to say it." That is not really a case of diminished psychic activity, like that of the feeble-minded in comparison with the highly gifted; it is something qualitatively different, but it is difficult to say wherein the difference lies. G. T. Fechner once hazarded the conjecture that the scene in which dreams are played is a different one from that of the waking perceptual life. To be sure, we do not understand this, do not know what we are to think of it, but the impression of strangeness which most dreams make upon us does really bear this out. The comparison of the dream activity with the effects of a hand untrained in music also fails at this point. The piano, at least, will surely answer with the same tones, even if not with melodies, as soon as by accident one brushes its keys. Let us keep this second common element of all dreams carefully in mind, even though it be not understood.

Are there still further traits in common? I find none, and see only differences everywhere, differences indeed in the apparent length as well as the definiteness of the activities, participation of effects, durability, etc. All this really is not what we might expect of a compulsion-driven, irresistible, convulsive defense against a stimulus. As concerns the dimensions of dreams, there are very short ones which contain only one picture or a few, one thought—yes, even one word only—, others which are uncommonly rich in content, seem to dramatize whole novels and to last very long. There are dreams which are as plain as an experience itself, so plain that we do not recognize them as dreams for a long time after waking; others which are indescribably weak, shadowy and vague; indeed in one and the same dream, the overemphasized and the scarcely comprehensible, indefinite parts may alternate with each other. Dreams may be quite meaningful or at least coherent, yes, even witty, fantastically beautiful. Others, again, are confused, as if feeble-minded, absurd, often actually mad. There are dreams which leave us quite cold, others in which all the effects come to expression—pain deep enough for tears, fear strong enough to waken us, astonishment, delight, etc. Dreams are generally quickly forgotten upon waking, or they may hold over a day to such an extent as to be faintly and incompletely remembered in the evening. Others, for example, the dreams of childhood, are so well preserved that they stay in the memory thirty years later, like fresh experiences. Dreams, like individuals, may appear a single time, and never again, or they may repeat themselves unchanged in the same person, or with small variations. In short, this nightly psychic activity can avail itself of an enormous repertoire, can indeed compass everything which the psychic accomplishes by day, but yet the two are not the same.

One might try to give an account of this many-sidedness of the dream by assuming that it corresponds to different intermediate stages between sleeping and waking, different degrees of incomplete sleep. Yes, but in that case as the psyche nears the waking state, the conviction that it is a dream ought to increase along with the value, content and distinctiveness of the dream product, and it would not happen that immediately beside a distinct and sensible dream fragment a senseless and indistinct one would occur, to be followed again by a goodly piece of work. Surely the psyche could not change its degree of somnolence so quickly. This explanation thus avails us nothing; at any rate, it cannot be accepted offhand.

Let us, for the present, give up the idea of finding the meaning of the dream and try instead to clear a path to a better understanding of the dream by means of the elements common to all dreams. From the relation of dreams to the sleeping condition, we concluded that the dream is the reaction to a sleep-disturbing stimulus. As we have heard, this is the only point upon which exact experimental psychology can come to our assistance; it gives us the information that stimuli applied during sleep appear in the dream. There have been many such investigations carried out, including that of the above mentioned Mourly Vold. Indeed, each of us must at some time have been in a position to confirm this conclusion by means of occasional personal observations. I shall choose certain older experiments for presentation. Maury had such experiments made on his own person. He was allowed to smell cologne while dreaming. He dreamed that he was in Cairo in the shop of Johann Marina Farina, and therewith were linked further extravagant adventures. Or, he was slightly pinched in the nape of the neck; he dreamed of having a mustard plaster applied, and of a doctor who had treated him in childhood. Or, a drop of water was poured on his forehead. He was then in Italy, perspired profusely, and drank the white wine of Orvieto.

What strikes us about these experimentally induced dreams we may perhaps be able to comprehend still more clearly in another series of stimulated dreams. Three dreams have been recounted by a witty observer, Hildebrand, all of them reactions to the sound of the alarm clock:

"I go walking one spring morning and saunter through the green fields to a neighboring village. There I see the inhabitants in gala attire, their hymn books under their arms, going church-ward in great numbers. To be sure, this is Sunday, and the early morning service will soon begin. I decide to attend, but since I am somewhat overheated, decide to cool off in the cemetery surrounding the church. While I am there reading several inscriptions, I hear the bell ringer ascend the tower, and now see the little village church bell which is to give the signal for the beginning of the service. The bell hangs a good bit longer, then it begins to swing, and suddenly its strokes sound clear and penetrating, so clear and penetrating that they make an end of—my sleep. The bell-strokes, however, come from my alarm clock.

"A second combination. It is a clear winter day. The streets are piled high with snow. I agree to go on a sleighing party, but must wait a long time before the announcement comes that the sleigh is at the door. Then follow the preparations for getting in—the fur coat is put on, the footwarmer dragged forth—and finally I am seated in my place. But the departure is still delayed until the reins give the waiting horses the tangible signal. Now they pull; the vigorously shaken bells begin their familiar Janizary music so powerfully that instantly the spider web of the dream is torn. Again it is nothing but the shrill tone of the alarm clock.

"And still a third example. I see a kitchen maid walking along the corridor to the dining room with some dozens of plates piled high. The pillar of porcelain in her arms seems to me in danger of losing its balance. 'Take care!' I warn her. 'The whole load will fall to the ground.' Naturally, the inevitable retort follows: one is used to that, etc., and I still continue to follow the passing figure with apprehensive glances. Sure enough, at the threshold she stumbles—the brittle dishes fall and rattle and crash over the floor in a thousand pieces. But—the endless racket is not, as I soon notice, a real rattling, but really a ringing and with this ringing, as the awakened subject now realizes, the alarm has performed its duty."

These dreams are very pretty, quite meaningful, not at all incoherent, as dreams usually are. We will not object to them on that score. That which is common to them all is that the situation terminates each time in a noise, which one recognizes upon waking up as the sound of the alarm. Thus we see here how a dream originates, but also discover something else. The dream does not recognize the alarm—indeed the alarm does not appear in the dream—the dream replaces the alarm sound with another, it interprets the stimulus which interrupts the sleep, but interprets it each time in a different way. Why? There is no answer to this question, it seems to be something arbitrary. But to understand the dream means to be able to say why it has chosen just this sound and no other for the interpretation of the alarm-clock stimulus. In quite analogous fashion, we must raise the objection to the Maury experiment that we see well enough that the stimulus appears in the dream, but that we do not discover why it appears in just this form; and that the form taken by the dream does not seem to follow from the nature of the sleep-disturbing stimulus. Moreover, in the Maury experiments a mass of other dream material links itself to the direct stimulus product; as, for example, the extravagant adventures in the cologne dream, for which one can give no account.

Now I shall ask you to consider the fact that the waking dreams offer by far the best chances for determining the influence of external sleep-disturbing stimuli. In most of the other cases it will be more difficult. One does not wake up in all dreams, and in the morning, when one remembers the dream of the night, how can one discover the disturbing stimulus which was perhaps in operation at night? I did succeed once in subsequently establishing such a sound stimulus, though naturally only in consequence of special circumstances. I woke up one morning in a place in the Tyrolese Mountains, with the certainty that I had dreamt the Pope had died. I could not explain the dream, but then my wife asked me: "Did you hear the terrible bell ringing that broke out early this morning from all the churches and chapels?" No, I had heard nothing, my sleep is a sound one, but thanks to this information I understood my dream. How often may such stimuli incite the sleeper to dream without his knowing of them afterward? Perhaps often, perhaps infrequently; when the stimulus can no longer be traced, one cannot be convinced of its existence. Even without this fact we have given up evaluating the sleep disturbing stimuli, since we know that they can explain only a little bit of the dream, and not the whole dream reaction.

But we need not give up this whole theory for that reason. In fact, it can be extended. It is clearly immaterial through what cause the sleep was disturbed and the psyche incited to dream. If the sensory stimulus is not always externally induced, it may be instead a stimulus proceeding from the internal organs, a so-called somatic stimulus. This conjecture is obvious, and it corresponds to the most popular conception of the origin of dreams. Dreams come from the stomach, one often hears it said. Unfortunately it may be assumed here again that the cases are frequent in which the somatic stimulus which operated during the night can no longer be traced after waking, and has thus become unverifiable. But let us not overlook the fact that many recognized experiences testify to the derivation of dreams from the somatic stimulus. It is in general indubitable that the condition of the internal organs can influence the dream. The relation of many a dream content to a distention of the bladder or to an excited condition of the genital organs, is so clear that it cannot be mistaken. From these transparent cases one can proceed to others in which, from the content of the dream, at least a justifiable conjecture may be made that such somatic stimuli have been operative, inasmuch as there is something in this content which may be conceived as elaboration, representation, interpretation of the stimuli. The dream investigator Schirmer (1861) insisted with particular emphasis on the derivation of the dream from organic stimuli, and cited several splendid examples in proof. For example, in a dream he sees "two rows of beautiful boys with blonde hair and delicate complexions stand opposite each other in preparation for a fight, fall upon each other, seize each other, take up the old position again, and repeat the whole performance;" here the interpretation of these rows of boys as teeth is plausible in itself, and it seems to become convincing when after this scene the dreamer "pulls a long tooth out of his jaws." The interpretation of "long, narrow, winding corridors" as intestinal stimuli, seems sound and confirms Schirmer's assertion that the dream above all seeks to represent the stimulus-producing organ by means of objects resembling it.

Thus we must be prepared to admit that the internal stimuli may play the same role in the dream as the external. Unfortunately, their evaluation is subject to the same difficulties as those we have already encountered. In a large number of cases the interpretation of the stimuli as somatic remains uncertain and undemonstrable. Not all dreams, but only a certain portion of them, arouse the suspicion that an internal organic stimulus was concerned in their causation. And finally, the internal stimuli will be as little able as the external sensory stimuli to explain any more of the dream than pertains to the direct reaction to the stimuli. The origin, therefore, of the rest of the dream remains obscure.

Let us, however, notice a peculiarity of dream life which becomes apparent in the study of these effects of stimuli. The dream does not simply reproduce the stimulus, but it elaborates it, it plays upon it, places it in a sequence of relationships, replaces it with something else. That is a side of dream activity which must interest us because it may lead us closer to the nature of the dream. If one does something under stimulation, then this stimulation need not exhaust the act. Shakespeare's *Macbeth*, for example, is a drama created on the occasion of the coronation of the King who for the first time wore upon his head the crown symbolizing the union of three countries. But does this historical occasion cover the content of the drama, does it explain its greatness and its riddle? Perhaps the external and internal stimuli, acting upon the sleeper, are only the incitors of the dream, of whose nature nothing is betrayed to us from our knowledge of that fact.

The other element common to dreams, their psychic peculiarity, is on the one hand hard to comprehend, and on the other hand offers no point for further investigation. In dreams we perceive a thing for the most part in visual forms. Can the stimuli furnish a solution for this fact? Is it actually the stimulus which we experience? Why, then, is the experience visual when optic stimulation incited the dream only in the rarest cases? Or can it be proved, when we dream speeches, that during sleep a conversation or sounds resembling it reached our ear? This possibility I venture decisively to reject.

If, from the common elements of dreams, we get no further, then let us see what we can do with their differences. Dreams are often senseless, blurred, absurd; but there are some that are meaningful, sober, sensible. Let us see if the latter, the sensible dreams, can give some information concerning the senseless ones. I will give you the most recent sensible dream which was told me, the dream of a young man: "I was promenading in Kärtner Street, met Mr. X. there, whom I accompanied for a bit, and then I went to a restaurant. Two ladies and a gentleman seated themselves at my table. I was annoyed at this at first, and would not look at them. Then I did look, and found that they were quite pretty." The dreamer adds that the evening before the dream he had really been in Kärtner Street, which is his usual route, and that he had met Mr. X. there. The other portion of the dream is no direct reminiscence, but bears a certain resemblance to a previous experience. Or another meaningful dream, that of a lady. "Her husband asks, 'Doesn't the piano need tuning?' She: 'It is not worth while; it has to be newly lined.'" This dream reproduces without much alteration a conversation which took place the day before between herself and her husband. What can we learn from these two sober dreams? Nothing but that you find them to be reproductions of daily life or ideas connected therewith. This would at least be something if it could be stated of all dreams. There is no question, however, that this applies to only a minority of dreams. In most dreams there is no sign of any connection with the previous day, and no light is thereby cast on the senseless and absurd dream. We know only that we have struck a new problem. We wish to know not only what it is that the dream says, but when, as in our examples, the dream speaks plainly, we also wish to know why and wherefore this recent experience is repeated in it.

I believe you are as tired as I am of continuing attempts like these. We see, after all, that the greatest interest in a problem is inadequate if one does not know a path which will lead to a solution. Up to this point we have not found this path. Experimental psychology gave us nothing but a few very valuable pieces of information concerning the meaning of stimuli as dream incitors. We need expect nothing from philosophy except that lately it has taken haughtily to pointing out to us the intellectual inferiority of our object. Let us not apply to the occult sciences for help. History and popular tradition tell us that the dream is meaningful and significant; it sees into the future. Yet that is hard to accept and surely not demonstrable. Thus our first efforts end in entire helplessness. Unexpectedly we get a hint from a quarter toward which we have not yet looked. Colloquial usage—which after all is not an accidental thing but the remnant of ancient knowledge, though it should not be made use of without caution—our speech, that is to say, recognizes something which curiously enough it calls "day dreaming." Day dreams are phantasies. They are very common phenomena, again observable in the normal as well as in the sick, and access to their study is open to everyone in his own person. The most conspicuous feature about these phantastic productions is that they have received the name "day dreams," for they share neither of the two common elements of dreams. Their name contradicts the relation to the sleeping condition, and as regards the second common element, one does not experience or hallucinate anything, one only imagines it. One knows that it is a phantasy, that one is not seeing but thinking the thing. These day dreams appear in the period before puberty, often as early as the last years of childhood, continue into the years of maturity, are then either given up or retained through life. The content of these phantasies is dominated by very transparent motives. They are scenes and events in which the egoistic, ambitious and power-seeking desires of the individual find satisfaction. With young men the ambitionphantasies generally prevail; in women, the erotic, since they have banked their ambition on success in love.

But often enough the erotic desire appears in the background with men too; all the heroic deeds and incidents are after all meant only to win the admiration and favor of women. Otherwise these day dreams are very manifold and undergo changing fates. They are either, each in turn, abandoned after a short time and replaced by a new one, or they are retained, spun out into long stories, and adapted to changes in daily circumstances. They move with the time, so to speak, and receive from it a "time mark" which testifies to the influence of the new situation. They are the raw material of poetic production, for out of his day dreams the poet, with certain transformations, disguises and omissions, makes the situations which he puts into his novels, romances and dramas. The hero of the day dreams, however, is always the individual himself, either directly or by means of a transparent identification with another.

Perhaps day dreams bear this name because of the similarity of their relation to reality, in order to indicate that their content is as little to be taken for real as that of dreams. Perhaps, however, this identity of names does nevertheless rest on a characteristic of the dream which is still unknown to us, perhaps even one of those characteristics which we are seeking. It is possible, on the other hand, that we are wrong in trying to read a meaning into this similarity of designation. Yet that can only be cleared up later.

SIXTH LECTURE: THE DREAM

Hypothesis and Technique of Interpretation

WE must find a new path, a new method, in order to proceed with the investigation of the dream. I shall now make an obvious suggestion. Let us assume as a hypothesis for everything which follows, that *the dream is not a somatic but a psychic phenomenon.* You appreciate the significance of that statement, but what justification have we for making it? None; but that alone need not deter us from making it. The matter stands thus: If the dream is a somatic phenomenon, it does not concern us. It can be of interest to us only on the supposition that it is a *psychic* phenomenon. Let us therefore work upon that assumption in order to see what comes of it. The result of our labor will determine whether we are to hold to this assumption and whether we may, in fact, consider it in turn a result. What is it that we really wish to achieve, to what end are we working? It is what one usually seeks to attain in the sciences, an understanding of phenomena, the creation of relationships between them, and ultimately, if possible, the extension of our control over them.

Let us then proceed with the work on the assumption that the dream is a psychic phenomenon. This makes it an achievement and expression of the dreamer, but one that tells us nothing, one that we do not understand. What do you do when I make a statement you do not understand? You ask for an explanation, do you not? Why may we not do the same thing here, *ask the dreamer to give us the meaning of his dream?*

If you will remember, we were in this same situation once before. It was when we were investigating errors, a case of a slip of the tongue. Someone said: "*Da sind dinge zum vorschwein gekommen,*" whereupon we asked— no, luckily, not we, but others, persons in no way associated with psychoanalysis—these persons asked him what he meant by this unintelligible talk. He immediately answered that he had intended to say "*Das waren schweinereien,*" but that he had suppressed this intention, in favor of the other, more gentle "*Da sind dinge zum vorschein gekommen]* (The reader will recall the example: "things were re-filled) I explained at the time that this inquiry was typical of every psychoanalytical investigation, and now you understand that psychoanalysis follows the technique, as far as possible, of having the subjects themselves discover the solutions of their riddles. The dreamer himself, then, is to tell us the meaning of his dream.

It is common knowledge, however, that this is not such an easy matter with dreams. In the case of slips, our method worked in a number of cases, but we encountered some where the subject did not wish to say anything—in fact, indignantly rejected the answer that we suggested. Instances of the first method are entirely lacking in the case of dreams; the dreamer always says he knows nothing. He cannot deny our interpretation, for we have none. Shall we then give up the attempt? Since he knows nothing and we know nothing and a third person surely knows nothing, it looks as though there were no possibility of discovering anything. If you wish, discontinue the investigation. But if you are of another mind, you can accompany me on the way. For I assure you, it is very possible, in fact, probable, that the dreamer does know what his dream means, but does *not know that he knows, and therefore believes he does not know.*

You will point out to me that I am again making an assumption, the second in this short discourse, and that I am greatly reducing the credibility of my claim. On the assumption that the dream is a psychic phenomenon, on the further assumption that there are unconscious things in man which he knows without knowing that he knows, etc.—we need only realize clearly the intrinsic improbability of each of these two assumptions, and we shall calmly turn our attention from the conclusions to be derived from such premises.

Yet, ladies and gentlemen, I have not invited you here to delude you or to conceal anything from you. I did, indeed, announce a *General Introduction to Psychoanalysis,* but I did not intend the title to convey that I was an oracle, who would show you a finished product with all the difficulties carefully concealed, all the gaps filled in and all the doubts glossed over, so that you might peacefully believe you had learned something new. No, precisely because you are beginners, I wanted to show you our science as it is, with all its hills and pitfalls, demands and considerations. For I know that it is the same in all sciences, and must be so in their beginnings particularly. I know, too, that teaching as a rule endeavors to hide these difficulties and these incompletely developed phases from the student. But that will not do in psychoanalysis. I have, as a matter of fact, made two assumptions, one within the other, and he who finds the whole too troublesome and too uncertain or is accustomed to greater security or more elegant derivations, need go no further with us. What I mean is, he should leave psychological problems entirely alone, for it must be apprehended that he will not find the sure and safe way he is prepared to go, traversable. Then, too, it is superfluous for a science that has something to offer to plead for auditors and adherents. Its results must create its atmosphere, and it must then bide its time until these have attracted attention to themselves.

I would warn those of you, however, who care to continue, that my two assumptions are not of equal worth. The first, that the dream is a psychic phenomenon, is the assumption we wish to prove by the results of our work. The other has already been proved in another field, and I take the liberty only of transferring it from that field to our problem.

Where, in what field of observation shall we seek the proof that there is in man a knowledge of which he is not conscious, as we here wish to assume in the case of the dreamer? That would be a remarkable, a surprising fact, one which would change our understanding of the psychic life, and which would have no need to hide itself. To name it would be to destroy it, and yet it pretends to be something real, a contradiction in terms. Nor does it hide itself. It is no result of the fact itself that we are ignorant of its existence and have not troubled sufficiently about it. That is just as little our fault as the fact that all these psychological problems are condemned by persons who have kept away from all observations and experiments which are decisive in this respect.

The proof appeared in the field of hypnotic phenomena. When, in the year 1889, I was a witness to the extraordinarily enlightening demonstrations of Siebault and Bernheim in Nancy, I witnessed also the following experiment: If one placed a man in the somnambulistic state, allowed him to have all manner of hallucinatory experience, and then woke him up, it appeared in the first instance that he knew nothing about what had happened during his hypnotic sleep. Bernheim then directly invited him to relate what had happened to him during the hypnosis. He maintained he was unable to recall anything. But Bernheim insisted, he persisted, he assured him he did know, that he must recall, and, incredible though it may seem, the man wavered, began to rack his memory, recalled in a shadowy way first one of the suggested experiences, then another; the recollection became more and more complete and finally was brought forth without a gap. The fact that he had this knowledge finally, and that he had had no experiences from any other source in the meantime, permits the conclusion that he knew of these recollections in the beginning. They were merely inaccessible, he did not know that he knew them; he believed he did not know them. This is exactly what we suspect in the dreamer.

I trust you are taken by surprise by the establishment of this fact, and that you will ask me why I did not refer to this proof before in the case of the slips, where we credited the man who made a mistake in speech with intentions he knew nothing about and which he denied. "If a person believes he knows nothing concerning experiences, the memory of which, however, he retains," you might say, "it is no longer so improbable that there are also other psychic experiences within him of whose existence he is ignorant. This argument would have impressed us and advanced us in the understanding of errors." To be sure, I might then have referred to this but I reserved it for another place, where it was more necessary. Errors have in a measure explained themselves, have, in part, furnished us with the warning that we must assume the existence of psychic processes of which we know nothing, for the sake of the connection of the phenomena. In dreams we are compelled to look to other sources for explanations; and besides, I count on the fact that you will permit the inference I draw from hypnotism more readily in this instance. The condition in which we make mistakes most seem to you to be the normal one. It has no similarity to the hypnotic. On the other hand, there is a clear relationship between the hypnotic state and sleep, which is the essential condition of dreams. Hypnotism is known as artificial sleep; we say to the person whom we hypnotize, "Sleep," and the suggestions which we throw out are comparable to the dreams of natural sleep. The psychical conditions are in both cases really analogous. In natural sleep we withdraw our attention from the entire outside world; in the hypnotic, on the other hand, from the whole world with the exception of the one person who has hypnotized us, with whom we remain in touch. Furthermore, the so-called nurse's sleep in which the nurse remains in touch with the child, and can be waked only by him, is a normal counterpart of hypnotism. The transference of one of the conditions of hypnotism to natural sleep does not appear to be such a daring proceeding. The inferential assumption that there is also present in the case of the dreamer a knowledge of his dream, a knowledge which is so inaccessible that he does not believe it himself, does not seem to be made out of whole cloth. Let us note that at this point there appears a third approach to the study of the dream; from the sleep-disturbing stimuli, from the day-dreams, and now in addition, from the suggested dreams of the hypnotic state.

Now we return, perhaps with increased faith, to our problem. Apparently it is very probable that the dreamer knows of his dream; the question is, how to make it possible for him to discover this knowledge, and to impart it to us? We do not demand that he give us the meaning of his dream at once, but he will be able to discover its origin, the thought and sphere of interest from which it springs. In the case of the errors, you will remember, the man was asked how he happened to use the wrong word, "*vorschwein*," and his next idea gave us the explanation. Our dream technique is very simple, an imitation of this example. We again ask how the subject happened to have the dream, and his next statement is again to be taken as an explanation. We disregard the distinction whether the dreamer believes or does not believe he knows, and treat both cases in the same way.

This technique is very simple indeed, but I am afraid it will arouse your sharpest opposition. You will say, "a new assumption. The third! And the most improbable of all! If I ask the dreamer what he considers the explanation of his dream to be, his very next association is to be the desired explanation? But it may be he thinks of nothing at all, or his next thought may be anything at all. We cannot understand upon what we can base such anticipation. This, really, is putting too much faith in a situation where a slightly more critical attitude would be more suitable. Furthermore, a dream is not an isolated error, but consists of many elements. To which idea should we pin our faith?"

You are right in all the non-essentials. A dream must indeed be distinguished from a word slip, even in the number of its elements. The technique is compelled to consider this very carefully. Let me suggest that we separate the dream into its elements, and carry on the investigation of each element separately; then the analogy to the word-slip is again set up. You are also correct when you say that in answer to the separate dream elements no association may occur to the dreamer. There are cases in which we accept this answer, and later you will hear what those cases are. They are, oddly enough, cases in which we ourselves may have certain associations. But in general we shall contradict the dreamer when he maintains he has no associations. We shall insist that he must have some association and—we shall be justified. He will bring forth some association, any one, it makes no difference to us. He will be especially facile with certain information which might be designated as historical. He will say, "that is something that happened yesterday" (as in the two "prosaic" dreams with which we are acquainted); or, "that reminds me of something that happened recently," and in this manner we shall notice that the act of associating the dreams with recent impressions is much more frequent than we had at first supposed. Finally, the dreamer will remember occurrences more remote from the dream, and ultimately even events in the far past.

But in the essential matters you are mistaken. If you believe that we assume arbitrarily that the dreamer's next association will disclose just what we are seeking, or must lead to it, that on the contrary the association is just as likely to be entirely inconsequential, and without any connection with what we are seeking, and that it is an example of my unbounded optimism to expect anything else, then you are greatly mistaken. I have already taken the liberty of pointing out that in each one of you there is a deep-rooted belief in psychic freedom and volition, a belief which is absolutely unscientific, and which must capitulate before the claims of a determinism that controls even the psychic life. I beg of you to accept it as a fact that only this one association will occur to the person questioned. But I do not put one belief in opposition to another. It can be proved that the association, which the subject produces, is not voluntary, is not indeterminable, not unconnected with what we seek. Indeed, I discovered long ago—without, however, laying too much stress on the discovery—that even experimental psychology has brought forth this evidence.

I ask you to give your particular attention to the significance of this subject. If I invite a person to tell me what occurs to him in relation to some certain element of his dream I am asking him to abandon himself to free association, *controlled by a given premise*. This demands a special delimitation of the attention, quite different from cogitation, in fact, exclusive of cogitation. Many persons put themselves into such a state easily; others show an extraordinarily high degree of clumsiness. There is a higher level of free association again, where I omit this original premise and designate only the manner of the association, e.g., rule that the subject freely give a proper name or a number. Such an association would be more voluntary, more indeterminable, than the one called forth by our technique. But it can be shown that it is strongly determined each time by an important inner mental set which, at the moment at which it is active, is unknown to us, just as unknown as the disturbing tendencies in the case of errors and the provocative tendencies in the case of accidental occurrences.

I, and many others after me, have again and again instigated such investigations for names and numbers which occur to the subject without any restraint, and have published some results. The method is the following: Proceeding from the disclosed names, we awaken continuous associations which then are no longer entirely free, but rather are limited as are the associations to the dream elements, and this is true until the impulse is exhausted. By that time, however, the motivation and significance of the free name associations is explained. The investigations always yield the same results, the information often covers a wealth of material and necessitates lengthy elaboration. The associations to freely appearing numbers are perhaps the most significant. They follow one another so quickly and approach a hidden goal with such inconceivable certainty, that it is really startling. I want to give you an example of such a name analysis, one that, happily, involves very little material.

In the course of my treatment of a young man, I referred to this subject and mentioned the fact that despite the apparent volition it is impossible to have a name occur which does not appear to be limited by the immediate conditions, the peculiarities of the subject, and the momentary situation. He was doubtful, and I proposed that he make such an attempt immediately. I know he has especially numerous relations of every sort with women and girls, and so am of the opinion that he will have an unusually wide choice if he happens to think of a woman's name. He agrees. To my astonishment, and perhaps even more to his, no avalanche of women's names descends upon my head, but he is silent for a time, and then admits that a single name has occurred to him—and no other: *Albino*. How extraordinary, but what associations have you with this name? How many albinoes do you know? Strangely enough, he knew no albinoes, and there were no further associations with the name. One might conclude the analysis had proved a failure; but no—it was already complete; no further association was necessary. The man himself had unusually light coloring. In our talks during the cure I had frequently called him an albino in fun. We were at the time occupied in determining the feminine characteristics of his nature. He himself was the Albino, who at that moment was to him the most interesting feminine person.

In like manner, melodies, which come for no reason, show themselves conditioned by and associated with a train of thought which has a right to occupy one, yet of whose activity one is unconscious. It is easily demonstrable that the attraction to the melody is associated with the text, or its origin. But I must take the precaution not to include in this assertion really musical people, with whom, as it happens, I have had no experience. In their cases the musical meaning of the melody may have occasioned its occurrence. More often the first reason holds. I know of a young man who for a time was actually haunted by the really charming melody of the song of Paris, from *The Beautiful Helen*, until the analysis brought to his attention the fact that at that time his interest was divided between an Ida and a Helen. If then the entirely unrestrained associations are conditioned in such a manner and are arranged in a distinct order, we are justified in concluding that associations with a single condition, that of an original premise, or starting point, may be conditioned to no less degree. The investigation does in fact show that aside from the conditioning which we have established by the premise, a second farther dependence is recognizable upon powerful affective thoughts, upon cycles of interest and complexes of whose influence we are ignorant, therefore unconscious at the time.

Associations of this character have been the subject matter of very enlightening experimental investigations, which have played a noteworthy role in the history of psychoanalysis. The Wundt school proposed the so-called association-experiment, wherein the subject is given the task of answering in the quickest possible time, with any desired reaction, to a given stimulus-word. It is then possible to study the interval of time that elapses between the stimulus and the reaction, the nature of the answer given as reaction, the possible mistake in a subsequent repetition of the same attempt, and similar matters. The Zurich School under the leadership of Bleuler and Jung, gave the explanation of the reactions following the association-experiment, by asking the subject to explain a given reaction by means of further associations, in the cases where there was anything extraordinary in the reaction. It then became apparent that these extraordinary reactions were most sharply determined by the complexes of the subject. In this matter Bleuler and Jung built the first bridge from experimental psychology to psychoanalysis.

Thus instructed, you will be able to say, "We recognize now that free associations are predetermined, not voluntary, as we had believed. We admit this also as regards the associations connected with the elements of the dream, but that is not what we are concerned with. You maintain that the associations to the dream element are determined by the unknown psychic background of this very element. We do not think that this is a proven fact. We expect, to be sure, that the association to the dream element will clearly show itself through one of the complexes of the dreamer, but what good is that to us? That does not lead us to understand the dream, but rather, as in the case of the association-experiment, to a knowledge of the so-called complexes. What have these to do with the dream?"

You are right, but you overlook one point, in fact, the very point because of which I did not choose the association-experiment as the starting point for this exposition. In this experiment the one determinate of the reaction, viz., the stimulus word, is voluntarily chosen. The reaction is then an intermediary between this stimulus word and the recently aroused complex of the subject. In the dream the stimulus word is replaced by something that itself has its origin in the psychic life of the dreamer, in sources unknown to him, hence very likely itself a product of the complex. It is not an altogether fantastic hypothesis, then, that the more remote associations, even those that are connected with the dream element, are determined by no other complex than the one which determines the dream element itself, and will lead to the disclosure of the complex.

Let me show you by another case that the situation is really as we expect it to be. Forgetting proper names is really a splendid example for the case of dream analysis; only here there is present in one person what in the dream interpretation is divided between two persons. Though I have forgotten a name temporarily I still retain the certainty that I know the name; that certainty which we could acquire for the dreamer only by way of the Bernheim experiment. The forgotten name, however, is not accessible. Cogitation, no matter how strenuous, does not help. Experience soon tells me that. But I am able each time to find one or more substitute names for the forgotten name. If such a substitute name occurs to me spontaneously then the correspondence between this situation and that of the dream analysis first becomes evident. Nor is the dream element the real thing, but only a substitute for something else, for what particular thing I do not know, but am to discover by means of the dream analysis. The difference lies only in this, that in forgetting a name I recognize the substitute automatically as unsuitable, while in the dream element we must acquire this interpretation with great labor. When a name is forgotten, too, there is a way to go from the substitute to the unknown reality, to arrive at the forgotten name. If I centre my attention on the substitute name and allow further associations to accumulate, I arrive in a more or less roundabout way at the forgotten name, and discover that the spontaneous substitute names, together with those called up by me, have a certain connection with the forgotten name, were conditioned by it.

I want to show you an analysis of this type. One day I noticed that I could not recall the name of the little country in the Riviera of which Monte Carlo is the capital. It is very annoying, but it is true. I steep myself in all my knowledge about this country, think of Prince Albert, of the house of Lusignan, of his marriages, his preference for deep-sea study, and anything else I can think of, but to no avail. So I give up the thinking, and in place of the lost name allow substitute names to suggest themselves. They come quickly—Monte Carlo itself, then Piedmont, Albania, Montevideo, Colico. Albania is the first to attract my attention, it is replaced by Montenegro, probably because of the contrast between black and white. Then I see that four of these substitutes contain the same syllable *mon*. I suddenly have the forgotten word, and cry aloud, "*Monaco.*" The substitutes really originated in the forgotten word, the four first from the first syllable, the last brings back the sequence of syllables and the entire final syllable. In addition, I am also able easily to discover what it was that took the name from my memory for a time. Monaco is also the Italian name of Munich; this latter town exerted the inhibiting influence.

The example is pretty enough, but too simple. In other cases we must add to the first substitute names a long line of associations, and then the analogy to the dream interpretation becomes clearer. I have also had such experiences. Once when a stranger invited me to drink Italian wine with him, it so happened in the hostelry that he forgot the name of the wine he had intended to order just because he had retained a most pleasant memory of it. Out of a profusion of dissimilar substitute associations which came to him in the place of the forgotten name, I was able to conclude that the memory of some one named Hedwig had deprived him of the name of the wine, and he actually confirmed not only that he had first tasted this wine in the company of a Hedwig, but he also, as a result of this declaration, recollected the name again. He was at the time happily married, and this Hedwig belonged to former times, not now recalled with pleasure.

What is possible in forgetting names must work also in dream interpretation, viz., making the withheld actuality accessible by means of substitutions and through connecting associations. As exemplified by name-forgetting, we may conclude that in the case of the associations to the dream element they will be determined as well by the dream element as by its unknown essential. Accordingly, we have advanced a few steps in the formulation of our dream technique.

SEVENTH LECTURE: THE DREAM

Manifest Dream Content and Latent Dream Thought

WE have not studied the problem of errors in vain. Thanks to our efforts in this field, under the conditions known to you, we have evolved two different things, a conception of the elements of the dream and a technique for dream interpretation. The conception of the dream element goes to show something unreal, a substitute for something else, unknown to the dreamer, similar to the tendency of errors, a substitute for something the dreamer knows but cannot approach. We hope to transfer the same conception to the whole dream, which consists of just such elements. Our method consists of calling up, by means of free associations, other substitute formations in addition to these elements, from which we divine what is hidden.

Let me ask you to permit a slight change in our nomenclature which will greatly increase the flexibility of our vocabulary. Instead of hidden, unapproachable, unreal, let us give a truer description and say inaccessible or unknown to the consciousness of the dreamer. By this we mean only what the connection with the lost word or with the interfering intention of the error can suggest to you, namely, unconscious *for the time being*. Naturally in contrast to this we may term *conscious* the elements of the dream itself and the substitute formations just gained by association. As yet there is absolutely no theoretical construction implied in this nomenclature. The use of the word unconscious as a suitable and intelligible descriptive epithet is above criticism.

If we transfer our conception from a single element to the entire dream, we find that the dream as a whole is a distorted substitute for something else, something unconscious. To discover this unconscious thing is the task of dream interpretation. From this, three important rules, which we must observe in the work of dream interpretation, are straightway derived:

1. What the dream seems to say, whether it be sensible or absurd, clear or confused is not our concern, since it can under no condition be that unconscious content we are seeking. Later we shall have to observe an obvious limitation of this rule. 2. The awakening of substitute formations for each element shall be the sole object of our work. We shall not reflect on these, test their suitability or trouble how far they lead away from the element of the dream. 3. We shall wait until the hidden unconscious we are seeking appears of itself, as the missing word *Monaco* in the experiment which we have described.

Now we can understand, too, how unimportant it is how much, how little, above all, how accurately or how indifferently the dream is remembered. For the dream which is remembered is not the real one, but a distorted substitute, which is to help us approach the real dream by awakening other substitute formations and by making the unconscious in the dream conscious. Therefore if our recollection of the dream was faulty, it has simply brought about a further distortion of this substitute, a distortion which cannot, however, be unmotivated.

One can interpret one's own dreams as well as those of others. One learns even more from these, for the process yields more proof. If we try this, we observe that something impedes the work. Haphazard ideas arise, but we do not let them have their way. Tendencies to test and to choose make themselves felt. As an idea occurs, we say to ourselves "No, that does not fit, that does not belong here"; of a second "that is too senseless"; of a third, "this is entirely beside the point"; and one can easily observe how the ideas are stifled and suppressed by these objections, even before they have become entirely clear. On the one hand, therefore, too much importance is attached to the dream elements themselves; on the other, the result of free association is vitiated by the process of selection. If you are not interpreting the dream alone, if you allow someone else to interpret it for you, you will soon discover another motive which induces you to make this forbidden choice. At times you say to yourself, "No, this idea is too unpleasant, I either will not or cannot divulge this."

Clearly these objections are a menace to the success of our work. We must guard against them, in our own case by the firm resolve not to give way to them; and in the interpretation of the dreams of others by making the hard and fast rule for them, never to omit any idea from their account, even if one of the following four objections should arise: that is, if it should seem too unimportant, absurd, too irrelevant or too embarrassing to relate. The dreamer promises to obey this rule, but it is annoying to see how poorly he keeps his promise at times. At first we account for this by supposing that in spite of the authoritative assurance which has been given to the dreamer, he is not impressed with the importance of free association, and plan perhaps to win his theoretic approval by giving him papers to read or by sending him to lectures which are to make him a disciple of our views concerning free association. But we are deterred from such blunders by the observation that, in one's own case, where convictions may certainly be trusted, the same critical objections arise against certain ideas, and can only be suppressed subsequently, upon second thought, as it were.

Instead of becoming vexed at the disobedience of the dreamer, these experiences can be turned to account in teaching something new, something which is the more important the less we are prepared for it. We understand that the task of interpreting dreams is carried on against a certain *resistance* which manifests itself by these critical objections. This resistance is independent of the theoretical conviction of the dreamer. Even more is apparent. We discover that such a critical objection is never justified. On the contrary, those ideas which we are so anxious to suppress, prove *without exception* to be the most important, the most decisive, in the search for the unconscious. It is even a mark of distinction if an idea is accompanied by such an objection.

This resistance is something entirely new, a phenomenon which we have found as a result of our hypotheses although it was not originally included in them. We are not too pleasantly surprised by this new factor in our problem. We suspect that it will not make our work any easier. It might even tempt us to abandon our entire work in connection with the dream. Such an unimportant thing as the dream and in addition such difficulties instead of a smooth technique! But from another point of view, these same difficulties may prove fascinating, and suggest that the work is worth the trouble. Whenever we try to penetrate to the hidden unconscious, starting out from the substitute which the dream element represents, we meet with resistance. Hence, we are justified in supposing that something of weight must be hidden behind the substitute. What other reason could there be for the difficulties which are maintained for purposes of concealment? If a child does not want to open his clenched fist, he is certainly hiding something he ought not to have.

Just as soon as we bring the dynamic representation of resistance into our consideration of the case, we must realize that this factor is something quantitatively variable. There may be greater or lesser resistances and we are prepared to see these differences in the course of our work. We may perhaps connect this with another experience found in the work of dream interpretation. For sometimes only one or two ideas serve to carry us from the dream element to its unconscious aspect, while at other times long chains of associations and the suppression of many critical objections are necessary. We shall note that these variations are connected with the variable force of resistance. This observation is probably correct. If resistance is slight, then the substitute is not far removed from the unconscious, but strong resistance carries with it a great distortion of the unconscious and in addition a long journey back to it.

Perhaps the time has come to take a dream and try out our method to see if our faith in it shall be confirmed. But which dream shall we choose? You cannot imagine how hard it is for me to decide, and at this point I cannot explain the source of the difficulty. Of course, there must be dreams which, as a whole, have suffered slight distortion, and it would be best to start with one of these. But which dreams are the least distorted? Those which are sensible and not confused, of which I have already given you two examples? This would be a gross misunderstanding. Testing shows that these dreams have suffered by distortion to an exceptionally high degree. But if I take the first best dream, regardless of certain necessary conditions, you would probably be very much disappointed. Perhaps we should have to note such an abundance of ideas in connection with single elements of dream that it would be absolutely impossible to review the work in perspective. If we write the dream out and confront it with the written account of all the ideas which arise in connection with it, these may easily amount to a reiteration of the text of the dream. It would therefore seem most practical to choose for analysis several short dreams of which each one can at least reveal or confirm something. This is what we shall decide upon, provided experience should not point out where we shall really find slightly distorted dreams.

I know another way to simplify matters, which, moreover, lies in our path. Instead of attempting to interpret entire dreams, we shall limit ourselves to single dream elements and by observing a series of examples we shall see how these are explained by applying our method.

1. A lady relates that as a child she often dreamt "*that God had a pointed paper hat on his head.*" How do you expect to understand that without the help of the dreamer? Why, it sounds quite absurd. It is no longer absurd when the lady testifies that as a child she was frequently made to wear such a hat at the table, because she could not help stealing glances at the plates of her brothers and sisters to see if one of them had gotten more than she. The hat was therefore supposed to act as a sort of blinder. This explanation was moreover historic, and given without the least difficulty. The meaning of this fragment and of the whole brief dream, is clear with the help of a further idea of the dreamer. "Since I had heard that God was all-knowing and all-seeing," she said, "the dream can only mean that I know everything and see everything

just as God does, even when they try to prevent me." This example is perhaps too simple.

2. A sceptical patient has a longer dream, in which certain people happen to tell her about my book concerning laughter and praise it highly. Then something is mentioned about a certain "*'canal,' perhaps another book in which 'canal' occurs, or something else with the word 'canal' ... she doesn't know ... it is all confused.*"

Now you will be inclined to think that the element "canal" will evade interpretation because it is so vague. You are right as to the supposed difficulty, but it is not difficult because it is vague, but rather it is vague for a different reason, the same reason which also makes the interpretation difficult. The dreamer can think of nothing concerning the word canal, I naturally can think of nothing. A little while later, as a matter of fact on the next day, she tells me that something occurred to her that *may perhaps* be related to it, a joke that she has heard. On a ship between Dover and Calais a well-known author is conversing with an Englishman, who quoted the following proverb in a certain connection: "*Du sublime au ridicule, il n'y a qu'un pas.*" (From the sublime to the ridiculous is but a narrow passage.) The author answers, "*Oui, le pas de Calais,*" (Yes, the passage from Calais) with which he wishes to say that he finds France sublime and England ridiculous. But the "*Pas de Calais*" is really a canal, namely, the English Channel. Do I think that this idea has anything to do with the dream? Certainly, I believe that it really gives the solution to the puzzling dream fragments. Or can you doubt that this joke was already present in the dream, as the unconscious factor of the element, "canal." Can you take it for granted that it was subsequently added to it? The idea testifies to the scepticism which is concealed behind her obtrusive admiration, and the resistance is probably the common reason for both phenomena, for the fact that the idea came so hesitatingly and that the decisive element of the dream turned out to be so vague. Kindly observe at this point the relation of the dream element to its unconscious factor. It is like a small part of the unconscious, like an allusion to it; through its isolation it became quite unintelligible.

3. A patient dreams, in the course of a longer dream: "*Around a table of peculiar shape several members of his family are sitting, etc.*" In connection with this table, it occurs to him that he saw such a piece of furniture during a visit to a certain family. Then his thoughts continue: In this family a peculiar relation had existed between father and son, and soon he adds to this that as a matter of fact the same relation exists between himself and his father. The table is therefore taken up into the dream to designate this parallel.

This dreamer had for a long time been familiar with the claims of dream interpretation. Otherwise he might have taken exception to the fact that so trivial a detail as the shape of a table should be taken as the basis of the investigation. As a matter of fact we judge nothing in the dream as accidental or indifferent, and we expect to reach our conclusion by the explanation of just such trivial and unmotivated details. Perhaps you will be surprised that the dream work should arouse the thought "we are in exactly the same position as they are," just by the choice of the table. But even this becomes clear when you learn that the name of the family in question is *Tischler*. By permitting his own family to sit at such a table, he intends to express that they too are *Tischler*. Please note how, in relating such a dream interpretation, one must of necessity become indiscreet. Here you have arrived at one of the difficulties in the choice of examples that I indicated before. I could easily have substituted another example for this one, but would probably have avoided this indiscretion at the cost of committing another one in its place.

The time has come to introduce two new terms, which we could have used long ago. We shall call that which the dream relates, the manifest content of the dream; that which is hidden, which we can only reach by the analysis of ideas we shall call latent dream thoughts. We may now consider the connection between the manifest dream content and the latent dream thoughts as they are revealed in these examples. Many different connections can exist. In examples 1 and 2 the manifest content is also a constituent part of the latent thought, but only a very small part of it. A small piece of a great composite psychic structure in the unconscious dream thought has penetrated into the manifest dream, like a fragment of it, or in other cases, like an allusion to it, like a catchword or an abbreviation in the telegraphic code. The interpretation must mould this fragment, or indication, into a whole, as was done most successfully in example 2. One sort of distortion of which the dream mechanism consists is therefore substitution by means of a fragment or an allusion. In the third, moreover, we must recognize another relation which we shall see more clearly and distinctly expressed in the following examples:

4. The dreamer "*pulls a certain woman of his acquaintance from behind a bed.*" He finds the meaning of this dream element himself by his first association. It means: This woman "has a pull" with him. (*"Vorzug." "Vom Bett hervorziehen."*)

5. Another man dreams that "*his brother is in a closet.*" The first association substitutes *clothes-press* for closet, and the second gives the meaning: his brother is *close-pressed* for money. (*"Schränkt sich ein".*)

6. The dreamer "*climbs a mountain from the top of which he has an extraordinarily distant view.*" This sounds quite sensible; perhaps there is nothing about it that needs interpretation, and it is simply necessary to find out which reminiscence this dream touches upon and why it was recalled. But you are mistaken; it is evident that this dream requires interpretation as well

as any other which is confused. For no previous mountain climbing of his own occurs to the dreamer, but he remembers that an acquaintance of his is publishing a "*Rundschau*," which deals with our relation to the furthermost parts of the earth. The latent dream thought is therefore in this case an identification of the dreamer with the "*Rundschauer*."

Here you find a new type of connection between the manifest content and the latent dream element. The former is not so much a distortion of the latter as a representation of it, a plastic concrete perversion that is based on the sound of the word. However, it is for this very reason again a distortion, for we have long ago forgotten from which concrete picture the word has arisen, and therefore do not recognize it by the image which is substituted for it. If you consider that the manifest dream consists most often of visual images, and less frequently of thoughts and words, you can imagine that a very particular significance in dream formation is attached to this sort of relation. You can also see that in this manner it becomes possible to create substitute formations for a great number of abstract thoughts in the manifest dream, substitutions that serve the purpose of further concealment all the same. This is the technique of our picture puzzle. What the origin is of the semblance of wit which accompanies such representations is a particular question which we need not touch upon at this time.

A fourth type of relation between the manifest and the latent dream cannot be dealt with until its cue in the technique has been given. Even then I shall not have given you a complete enumeration, but it will be sufficient for our purpose.

Have you the courage to venture upon the interpretation of an entire dream? Let us see if we are well enough equipped for this undertaking. Of course, I shall not choose one of the most obscure, but one nevertheless that shows in clear outline the general characteristics of a dream.

A young woman who has been married for many years dreams: "*She is sitting in the theatre with her husband; one side of the orchestra is entirely unoccupied. Her husband tells her that Elise L. and her bridegroom had also wished to come, but had only been able to procure poor seats, three for 1 Fl., 50 Kr. and those of course they could not take. She thinks this is no misfortune for them.*"

The first thing that the dreamer has to testify is that the occasion for the dream is touched upon in its manifest content. Her husband had really told her that Elise L., an acquaintance of about her age, had become engaged. The dream is the reaction to this news. We already know that in the case of many dreams it is easy to trace such a cause to the preceding day, and that the dreamer often gives these deductions without any difficulty. The dreamer also places at our disposal further information for other parts of the manifest dream content. Whence the detail that one side of the orchestra is unoccupied? It is an allusion to an actual occurrence of the previous week. She had made up her mind to go to a certain performance and had procured tickets in advance, so much in advance that she had been forced to pay a preference tax (this is called "Vorverkaufsgebühr" In German). When she arrived at the theatre, she saw how needless had been her anxiety, for *one side of the orchestra was almost empty*. She could have bought the tickets on the day of the performance itself. Her husband would not stop teasing her about her excessive haste. Whence the 1 Fl. 50 Kr.? From a very different connection that has nothing to do with the former, but which also alludes to an occurrence of the previous day. Her sister-in-law had received 150 florins as a present from her husband, and knew no better, the poor goose, than to hasten to the jeweler and spend the money on a piece of jewelry. Whence the number 3? She can think of nothing in connection with this unless one stresses the association that the bride, Elise L., is only three months younger than she herself, who has been married for almost ten years. And the absurdity of buying three tickets for two people? She says nothing of this, and indeed denies all further associations or information.

But she has given us so much material in her few associations, that it becomes possible to derive the latent dream thought from it. It must strike us that in her remarks concerning the dream, time elements which constitute a common element in the various parts of this material appear at several points. She attended to the tickets *too soon*, took them *too hastily*, so that she had to pay more than usual for them; her sister-in-law likewise *hastened* to carry her money to the jeweler's to buy a piece of jewelry, just as if she might *miss* it. Let us add to the expressions "*too early*," "*precipitately*," which are emphasized so strongly, the occasion for the dream, namely, that her friend only three months younger than herself had even now gotten a good husband, and the criticism expressed in the condemnation of her sister-in-law, that it was *foolish* to hurry so. Then the following construction of the latent dream thought, for which the manifest dream is a badly distorted substitute, comes to us almost spontaneously:

"How *foolish* it was of me to hurry so in marrying! Elise's example shows me that I could have gotten a husband later too." (The precipitateness is represented by her own behavior in buying the tickets, and that of her sister-in-law in purchasing jewelry. Going to the theatre was substituted for getting married. This appears to have been the main thought; and perhaps we may continue, though with less certainty, because the analysis in these parts is not supported by statements of the dreamer.) "And I would have gotten 100 times as much for my money." (150 Fl. is 100 times as much as 1 Fl. 50 Kr.). If we might substitute the dowry for the money, then it would mean that one buys a husband with a dowry; the jewelry as well as the poor seats would represent the husband. It would be even more desirable if the fragment "3 seats" had something to do with a husband. But our understanding does not penetrate so far. We have only guessed that the dream expresses her *disparagement* of her own husband, and her regret at having *married so early*.

It is my opinion that we are more surprised and confused than satisfied by the result of this first dream interpretation. We are swamped by more impressions than we can master. We see that the teachings of dream interpretation are not easily exhausted. Let us hasten to select those points that we recognize as giving us new, sound insight.

In the first place, it is remarkable that in the latent thought the main emphasis falls on the element of haste; in the manifest dream there is absolutely no mention of this to be found. Without the analysis we should not have had any idea that this element was of any importance at all. So it seems possible that just the main thing, the central point of the unconscious thoughts, may be absent in the manifest dream. Because of this, the original impression in the dream must of necessity be entirely changed. Secondly: In the dream there is a senseless combination, 3 for 1 Fl. 50 Kr.; in the dream thought we divine the sentence, "It was senseless (to marry so early)." Can one deny that this thought, "It was senseless," was represented in the manifest dream by the introduction of an absurd element? Thirdly: Comparison will show that the relation between the manifest and latent elements is not simple, certainly not of such a sort that a manifest element is always substituted for the latent. There must rather be a quantitative relationship between the two groups, according to which a manifest element may represent several latent ones, or a latent element represented by several manifest elements.

Much that is surprising might also be said of the sense of the dream and the dreamer's reaction to it. She acknowledges the interpretation but wonders at it. She did not know that she disparaged her husband so, and she did not know why she should disparage him to such a degree. There is still much that is incomprehensible. I really believe that we are not yet fully equipped for dream interpretation, and that we must first receive further instruction and preparation.

EIGHTH LECTURE: THE DREAM

Dreams of Childhood

WE think we have advanced too rapidly. Let us go back a little. Before our last attempt to overcome the difficulties of dream distortion through our technique, we had decided that it would be best to avoid them by limiting ourselves only to those dreams in which distortion is either entirely absent or of trifling importance, if there are such. But here again we digress from the history of the evolution of our knowledge, for as a matter of fact we become aware of dreams entirely free of distortion only after the consistent application of our method of interpretation and after complete analysis of the distorted dream.

The dreams we are looking for are found in children. They are short, clear, coherent, easy to understand, unambiguous, and yet unquestionable dreams. But do not think that all children's dreams are like this. Dream distortion makes its appearance very early in childhood, and dreams of children from five to eight years of age have been recorded that showed all the characteristics of later dreams. But if you will limit yourselves to the age beginning with conscious psychic activity, up to the fourth or fifth year, you will discover a series of dreams that are of a so-called infantile character. In a later period of childhood you will be able to find some dreams of this nature occasionally. Even among adults, dreams that closely resemble the typically infantile ones occur under certain conditions.

From these children's dreams we gain information concerning the nature of dreams with great ease and certainty, and we hope it will prove decisive and of universal application.

1. For the understanding of these dreams we need no analysis, no technical methods. We need not question the child that is giving an account of his dream. But one must add to this a story taken from the life of the child. An experience of the previous day will always explain the dream to us. The dream is a sleep-reaction of psychic life upon these experiences of the day.

We shall now consider a few examples so that we may base our further deductions upon them.

a). A boy of 22 months is to present a basket of cherries as a birthday gift. He plainly does so very unwillingly, although they promise him that he will get some of them himself. The next morning he relates as his dream, "*Hermann eat all cherries.*"

b). A little girl of three and a quarter years makes her first trip across a lake. At the landing she does not want to leave the boat and cries bitterly. The time of the trip seems to her to have passed entirely too rapidly. The next morning she says, "*Last night I rode on the lake.*" We may add the supplementary fact that this trip lasted longer.

c). A boy of five and a quarter years is taken on an excursion into the Escherntal near Hallstatt. He had heard that Hallstatt lay at the foot of the Dachstein, and had shown great interest in this mountain. From his home in Aussee there was a beautiful view of the Dachstein, and with a telescope one could discern the Simonyhütte upon it. The child had tried again and again to see it through the telescope, with what result no one knew. He started on the excursion in a joyously expectant mood. Whenever a new mountain came in sight the boy asked, "Is that the Dachstein?" The oftener this question was answered in the negative, the more moody he became; later he became entirely silent and would not take part in a small climb to a waterfall. They thought he was overtired, but the next morning, he said quite happily, "*Last night I dreamed that we were in the Simonyhütte*." It was with this expectation, therefore, that he had taken part in the excursion. The only detail he gave was one he had heard before, "you had to climb steps for six hours."

These three dreams will suffice for all the information we desire.

2. We see that children's dreams are not meaningless; they are *intelligible, significant, psychic acts*. You will recall what I represented to you as the medical opinion concerning the dream, the simile of untrained fingers wandering aimlessly over the keys of the piano. You cannot fail to see how decidedly these dreams of childhood are opposed to this conception. But it would be strange indeed if the child brought forth complete psychic products in sleep, while the adult in the same condition contents himself with spasmodic reactions. Indeed, we have every reason to attribute the more normal and deeper sleep to the child.

3. Dream distortion is lacking in these dreams, therefore they need no interpretation. The manifest and latent dreams are merged. *Dream distortion is therefore not inherent in the dream.* I may assume that this relieves you of a great burden. But upon closer consideration we shall have to admit of a tiny bit of distortion, a certain differentiation between manifest dream content and latent dream thought, even in these dreams.

4. The child's dream is a reaction to an experience of the day, which has left behind it a regret, a longing or an unfulfilled desire. *The dream brings about the direct unconcealed fulfillment of this wish.* Now recall our discussions concerning the importance of the role of external or internal bodily stimuli as disturbers of sleep, or as dream producers. We learned definite facts about this, but could only explain a very small number of dreams in this way. In these children's dreams nothing points to the influence of such somatic stimuli; we cannot be mistaken, for the dreams are entirely intelligible and easy to survey. But we need not give up the theory of physical causation entirely on this account. We can only ask why at the outset we forgot that besides the physical stimuli there are also psychic sleep-disturbing stimuli. For we know that it is these stimuli that commonly cause the disturbed sleep of adults by preventing them from producing the ideal condition of sleep, the withdrawal of interest from the world. The dreamer does not wish to interrupt his life, but would rather continue his work with the things that occupy him, and for this reason he does not sleep. The unfulfilled wish, to which he reacts by means of the dream, is the psychic sleep-disturbing stimulus for the child.

5. From this point we easily arrive at an explanation of the function of the dream. The dream, as a reaction to the psychic stimulus, must have the value of a release of this stimulus which results in its elimination and in the

continuation of sleep. We do not know how this release is made possible by the dream, but we note that *the dream is not a disturber of sleep*, as calumny says, *but a guardian of sleep, whose duty it is to quell disturbances.* It is true, we think we would have slept better if we had not dreamt, but here we are wrong; as a matter of fact, we would not have slept at all without the help of the dream. That we have slept so soundly is due to the dream alone. It could not help disturbing us slightly, just as the night watchman often cannot avoid making a little noise while he drives away the rioters who would awaken us with their noise.

6. One main characteristic of the dream is that a wish is its source, and that the content of the dream is the gratification of this wish. Another equally constant feature is that the dream does not merely express a thought, but also represents the fulfillment of this wish in the form of a hallucinatory experience. "*I should like to travel on the lake*," says the wish that excites the dream; the dream itself has as its content "*I travel on the lake*." One distinction between the latent and manifest dream, a distortion of the latent dream thought, therefore remains even in the case of these simple children's dreams, namely, *the translation of the thought into experience.* In the interpretation of the dream it is of utmost importance that this change be traced back. If this should prove to be an extremely common characteristic of the dream, then the above mentioned dream fragment, "*I see my brother in a closet*" could not be translated, "*My brother is close-pressed*," but rather, "I wish that my brother were close-pressed, *my brother should be close-pressed.*" Of the two universal characteristics of the dream we have cited, the second plainly has greater prospects of unconditional acknowledgment than the first. Only extensive investigation can ascertain that the cause of the dream must always be a wish, and cannot also be an anxiety, a plan or a reproach; but this does not alter the other characteristic, that the dream does not simply reproduce the stimulus but by experiencing it anew, as it were, removes, expels and settles it.

7. In connection with these characteristics of the dream we can again resume the comparison between the dream and the error. In the case of the latter we distinguish an interfering tendency and one interfered with, and the error is the compromise between the two. The dream fits into the same scheme. The tendency interfered with, in this case, can be no other than that of sleep. For the interfering tendency we substitute the psychic stimulus, the wish which strives for its fulfillment, let us say, for thus far we are not familiar with any other sleep-disturbing psychic stimulus. In this instance also the dream is the result of compromise. We sleep, and yet we experience the removal of a wish; we gratify the wish, but at the same time continue to sleep. Both are partly carried out and partly given up.

8. You will remember that we once hoped to gain access to the understanding of the dream problem by the fact that certain very transparent phantasy formations are called *day dreams*. Now these day dreams are actual wish fulfillments, fulfillments of ambitious or erotic wishes with which we are familiar; but they are conscious, and though vividly imagined, they are never hallucinatory experiences. In this instance, therefore, the less firmly established of the two main characteristics of the dream holds, while the other proves itself entirely dependent upon the condition of sleep and impossible to the waking state. In colloquial usage, therefore, there is a presentment of the fact that the fulfillment of a wish is a main characteristic of the dream. Furthermore, if the experience in the dream is a transformed representation only made possible by the condition of sleep—in other words, a sort of nocturnal day dream—then we can readily understand that the occurrence of phantasy formations can release the nocturnal stimulus and bring satisfaction. For day dreaming is an activity closely bound up in gratification and is, indeed, pursued only for this reason.

Not only this but other colloquial usages also express the same feeling. Well-known proverbs say, "The pig dreams of acorns, the goose of maize," or ask, "Of what does the hen dream? Of millet." So the proverb descends even lower than we do, from the child to the animal, and maintains that the content of a dream is the satisfaction of a need. Many turns of speech seem to point to the same thing—"dreamlike beauty," "I should never have dreamed of that," "in my wildest dreams I hadn't imagined that." This is open partisanship on the part of colloquial usage. For there are also dreams of fear and dreams of embarrassing or indifferent content, but they have not been drawn into common usage. It is true that common usage recognizes "bad" dreams, but still the dream plainly connotates to it only the beautiful wish fulfillment. There is indeed no proverb that tells us that the pig or the goose dreams of being slaughtered.

Of course it is unbelievable that the wish-fulfillment characteristic has not been noted by writers on the dream. Indeed, this was very often the case, but none of them thought of acknowledging this characteristic as universal and of making it the basis of an explanation of the dream. We can easily imagine what may have deterred them and shall discuss it subsequently.

See what an abundance of information we have gained, with almost no effort, from the consideration of children's dreams—the function of the dream as a guardian of sleep; its origin from two rival tendencies, of which the one, the longing for sleep, remains constant, while the other tries to satisfy a psychic stimulus; the proof that the dream is a significant psychic act; its two main characteristics: wish fulfillment and hallucinatory experience. And we were almost able to forget that we are engaged in psychoanalysis. Aside from its connection with errors our work has no specific connotation. Any psychologist, who is entirely ignorant of the claims of psychoanalysis, could have given this explanation of children's dreams. Why has no one done so?

If there were only infantile dreams, our problem would be solved, our task accomplished, and that without questioning the dreamer, or approaching the unconscious, and without taking free association into consideration. The continuation of our task plainly lies in this direction. We have already repeatedly had the experience that characteristics that at first seemed universally true, have subsequently held good only for a certain kind and a certain number of dreams. It is therefore for us to decide whether the common characteristics which we have gathered from children's dreams can be applied universally, whether they also hold for those dreams that are not transparent, whose manifest content shows no connection with wishes left over from the previous day. We think that these dreams have undergone considerable distortion and for this reason are not to be judged superficially. We also suspect that for the explanation of this distortion we shall need the psychoanalytic method which we could dispense with in the understanding of children's dreams.

There is at any rate a class of dreams that are undistorted, and, just like children's dreams, are easily recognizable as wish fulfillments. It is those that are called up throughout life by the imperative needs of the body—hunger, thirst, sexual desire—hence wish fulfillments in reaction to internal physical stimuli. For this reason, I have noted the dream of a young girl, that consisted of a menu following her name (Anna F......, strawberry, huckleberry, egg-dish, pap), as a reaction to an enforced day of fasting on account of a spoiled stomach, which was directly traceable to the eating of the fruits twice mentioned in the dream. At the same time, the grandmother, whose age added to that of her grandchild would make a full seventy, had to go without food for a day on account of kidney-trouble, and dreamed the same night that she had been invited out and that the finest tid-bits had been set before her. Observations with prisoners who are allowed to go hungry, or with people who suffer privations on travels or expeditions, show that under these conditions the dreams regularly deal with the satisfaction of these needs. Otto Nordenskjold, in his book *Antarctic* (1904), testifies to the same thing concerning his crew, who were ice-bound with him during the winter (Vol. 1, page 336). "Very significant in determining the trend of our inmost thoughts were our dreams, which were never more vivid and numerous than just at this time. Even those of our comrades who ordinarily dreamed but seldom, now had long stories to tell, when in the morning we exchanged our latest experiences in that realm of phantasy. All of them dealt with that outside world that now was so far away from us, but often they fitted into our present condition. Food and drink were most often the pivots about which our dreams revolved. One of us, who excelled in going to great dinners in his sleep, was most happy whenever he could tell us in the morning that he attended a dinner of three courses; another one dreamed of tobacco, whole mountains of tobacco; still another dreamed of a ship that came along on the open sea, under full sail. One other dream deserves mention: The postman comes with the mail and gives a long explanation of why it is so late; he had delivered it to the wrong address and only after great trouble on his part had succeeded in getting it back. Of course one occupies himself with even more impossible things in sleep, but in nearly all the dreams that I myself dreamed or heard tell of, the lack of phantasy was quite striking. It would surely be of great psychological interest if all these dreams were recorded. It is easy to understand how we longed for sleep, since it could offer us everything for which each one of us felt the most burning desire." I quote further from Du Prel. "Mungo Park, who during a trip in Africa was almost exhausted, dreamed without interruption of the fertile valleys and fields of his home. Trenck, tortured by hunger in the redoubt at Magdeburg, likewise saw himself surrounded by wonderful meals, and George Back, who took part in Franklin's first expedition, dreamed regularly and consistently of luxurious meals when, as a result of terrible privations, he was nearly dead of hunger."

A man who feels great thirst at night after enjoying highly seasoned food for supper, often dreams that he is drinking. It is of course impossible to satisfy a rather strong desire for food or drink by means of the dream; from such a dream one awakes thirsty and must now drink real water. The effect of the dream is in this case practically trifling, but it is none the less clear that it was called up for the purpose of maintaining the sleep in spite of the urgent impulse to awake and to act. Dreams of satisfaction often overcome needs of a lesser intensity.

In a like manner, under the influence of sexual stimuli, the dream brings about satisfaction that shows noteworthy peculiarities. As a result of the characteristic of the sexual urge which makes it somewhat less dependent upon its object than hunger and thirst, satisfaction in a dream of pollution may be an actual one, and as a result of difficulties to be mentioned later in connection with the object, it happens especially often that the actual satisfaction is connected with confused or distorted dream content. This peculiarity of the dream of pollution, as O. Rank has observed, makes it a fruitful subject to pursue in the study of dream distortion. Moreover, all dreams of desire of adults usually contain something besides satisfaction, something that has its origin in the sources of the purely psychic stimuli, and which requires interpretation to render it intelligible.

Moreover we shall not maintain that the wish-fulfillment dreams of the infantile kind occur in adults only as reactions to the known imperative desires. We also know of short clear dreams of this sort under the influence of dominating situations that arise from unquestionably psychic sources. As, for example, in dreams of impatience, whenever a person has made preparations for a journey, for a theatrical performance, for a lecture or for a visit, and now dreams of the anticipated fulfillment of his expectations, and so arrives at his goal the night before the actual experience, in the theatre or in conversation with his host. Or the well-named dreams of comfort, when a person who likes to prolong his sleep, dreams that he is already up, is washing himself, or is already in school, while as a matter of fact he continues sleeping, hence would rather get up in a dream than in reality. The desire for sleep which we have recognized as a regular part of the dream structure becomes intense in these dreams and appears in them as the actual shaping force of the dream. The wish for sleep properly takes its place beside other great physical desires.

At this point I refer you to a picture by Schwind, from the Schack Gallery in Munich, so that you may see how rightly the artist has conceived the origin of a dream from a dominating situation. It is the *Dream of a Prisoner,* which can have no other subject than his release. It is a very neat stroke that the release should be effected through the window, for the ray of light that awakens the prisoner comes through the same window. The gnomes standing one above the other probably represent the successive positions which he himself had to take in climbing to the height of the window, and I do not think I am mistaken or that I attribute too much preconcerted design to the artist, by noting that the uppermost of the gnomes, who is filing the grating (and so does what the prisoner would like to do) has the features of the prisoner.

In all other dreams except those of children and those of the infantile type, distortion, as we have said, blocks our way. At the outset we cannot ascertain whether they are also wish fulfillments, as we suspect; from their manifest content we cannot determine from what psychic stimulus they derive their origin, and we cannot prove that they also are occupied in doing away with the stimulus and in satisfying it. They must probably be interpreted, that is, translated; their distortion must be annulled; their manifest content replaced by their latent thought before we can judge whether what we have found in children's dreams may claim a universal application for all dreams.

NINTH LECTURE: THE DREAM

The Dream Censor

WE have learned to know the origin, nature and function of the dream from the study of children's dreams. *Dreams are the removal of sleep-disturbing psychic stimuli by way of hallucinated satisfaction.* Of adults' dreams, to be sure, we could explain only one group, what we characterized as dreams of an infantile type. As to the others we know nothing as yet, nor do we understand them. For the present, however, we have obtained a result whose significance we do not wish to under-estimate. Every time a dream is completely comprehensible to us, it proves to be an hallucinated wish-fulfillment. This coincidence cannot be accidental, nor is it an unimportant matter.

We conclude, on the basis of various considerations and by analogy to the conception of mistakes, that another type of dream is a distorted substitute for an unknown content and that it must first be led back to that content. Our next task is the investigation and the understanding of this dream distortion.

Dream distortion is the thing which makes the dream seem strange and incomprehensible to us. We want to know several things about it; firstly, whence it comes, its dynamics; secondly, what it does; and finally, how it does it. We can say at this point that dream distortion is the product of the dream work, that is, of the mental functioning of which the dream itself is the conscious symptom. Let us describe the dream work and trace it back to the forces which work upon it.

And now I shall ask you to listen to the following dream. It was recorded by a lady of our profession, and according to her, originated with a highly cultivated and respected lady of advanced age. No analysis of this dream was made. Our informant remarks that to a psychoanalyst it needs no interpretation. The dreamer herself did not interpret it, but she judged and condemned it as if she understood its interpretation. For she said concerning it: "That a woman of fifty should dream such abominable, stupid stuff—a woman who has no other thought, day and night, than to care for her child!"

And now follows the dreams of the "*services of love*." "She goes into Military Hospital No. 1, and says to the sentry at the gate, that she must speak to the chief physician ... (she mentions a name which is not familiar to her), as she wants to offer her service to the hospital. She stresses the word 'service,' so love services. Since she is an old lady he lets her pass after some hesitation. But instead of reaching the chief physician, she finds herself in a large somber room in which there are many officers and army doctors sitting and standing around a long table. She turns with her proposal to a staff doctor who, after a few words, soon understands her. The words of her speech in the dream are, 'I and numerous other women and girls of Vienna are ready for the soldiers, troops, and officers, without distinction....' Here in the dream follows a murmuring. That the idea is, however, correctly understood by those present she sees from the semi-embarrassed, somewhat malicious expressions of the officers. The lady then continues, 'I know that our decision sounds strange, but we are in bitter earnest. The soldier in the field is not asked either whether or not he wants to die.' A moment of painful silence follows. The staff doctor puts his arm around her waist and says, 'Madame, let us assume that it really came to that ...' (murmurs). She withdraws from his arm with the thought, 'They are all alike!' and answers, 'My heavens, I am an old woman, and perhaps will never be confronted with that situation; one consideration, moreover, must be kept in mind: the consideration of age, which prevents an older woman from ... with a very young boy ... (murmurs) ... that would be horrible.' The staff doctor, 'I understand perfectly.' Several officers, among them one who had paid court to her in her youth, laugh loudly, and the lady asks to be conducted to the chief physician, whom she knows, so that everything may be arranged. At this she realizes with great dismay that she does not know his name. The staff officer, nevertheless, very politely and respectfully shows her the way to the second story, up a very narrow winding iron stairway which leads to the upper story directly from the door of the room. In going up she hears an officer say, 'That is a tremendous decision irrespective of whether a woman is young or old; all honor to her!'

"With the feeling that she is merely doing her duty, she goes up an endless staircase."

This dream she repeats twice in the course of a few weeks, with—as the lady notices—quite insignificant and very senseless changes.

This dream corresponds in its structure to a day dream. It has few gaps, and many of its individual points might have been elucidated as to content through inquiry, which, as you know, was omitted. The conspicuous and interesting point for us, however, is that the dream shows several gaps, gaps not of recollection, but of original content. In three places the content is apparently obliterated, the speeches in which these gaps occur are interrupted by murmurs. Since we have performed no analysis, we have, strictly speaking, also no right to make any assertion about the meaning of the dream. Yet there are intimations given from which something may be concluded. For example, the phrase "services of love," and above all the bits of speech which immediately precede the murmurs, demand a completion which can have but one meaning. If we interpolate these, then the phantasy yields as its content the idea that the dreamer is ready, as an act of patriotic duty, to offer her person for the satisfaction of the erotic desires of the army, officers as well as troops. That certainly is exceedingly shocking, it is an impudent libidinous phantasy, but—it does not occur in the dream at all. Just at the point where consistency would demand this confession, there is a vague murmur in the manifest dream, something is lost or suppressed.

I hope you will recognize the inevitability of the conclusion that it is the shocking character of these places in the dream that was the motive for their suppression. Yet where do you find a parallel for this state of affairs? In these times you need not seek far. Take up any political paper and you will find that the text is obliterated here and there, and that in its place shimmers the white of the paper. You know that that is the work of the newspaper censor. In these blank spaces something was printed which was not to the liking of the censorship authorities, and for that reason it was crossed out. You think that it is a pity, that it probably was the most interesting part, it was "the best part."

In other places the censorship did not touch the completed sentence. The author foresaw what parts might be expected to meet with the objection of the censor, and for that reason he softened them by way of prevention, modified them slightly, or contented himself with innuendo and allusion to what really wanted to flow from his pen. Thus the sheet, it is true, has no blank spaces, but from certain circumlocutions and obscurities of expression you will be able to guess that thoughts of the censorship were the restraining motive.

Now let us keep to this parallel. We say that the omitted dream speeches, which were disguised by a murmuring, were also sacrifices to a censorship. We actually speak of a *dream censor* to which we may ascribe a contributing part in the dream distortion. Wherever there are gaps in the manifest dream, it is the fault of the dream censor. Indeed, we should go further, and recognize each time as a manifestation of the dream censor, those places at which a dream element is especially faint, indefinitely and doubtfully recalled among other, more clearly delineated portions. But it is only rarely that this censorship manifests itself so undisguisedly, so naively one may say, as in the example of the dream of the "services of love." Far more frequently the censorship manifests itself according to the second type, through the production of weakenings, innuendoes, allusions instead of direct truthfulness.

For a third type of dream censorship I know of no parallel in the practice of newspaper censorship, yet it is just this type that I can demonstrate by the only dream example which we have so far analyzed. You will remember the dream of the "three bad theatre tickets for one florin and a half." In the latent thoughts of this dream, the element "*precipitately, too soon,*" stood in the foreground. It means: "It was foolish to marry so *early*, it was also foolish to buy theatre tickets so *early*, it was ridiculous of the sister-in-law to spend her money so *hastily*, merely to buy an ornament." Nothing of this central element of the dream thought was evident in the manifest dream. In the latter, going to the theatre and getting the tickets were shoved into the foreground. Through this displacement of the emphasis, this regrouping of the elements of the content, the manifest dream becomes so dissimilar from the latent dream thoughts that no one would suspect the latter behind the former. This displacement of emphasis is a favorite device of the dream distortion and gives the dream that strangeness which makes the dreamer himself unwilling to recognize it as his own production.

Omission, modification, regrouping of the material, these, then, are the effects of the dream censor and the devices of dream distortion. The dream censorship itself is the author, or one of the authors, of the dream distortion whose investigation now occupies us. Modification and rearrangement we are already accustomed to summarize as *displacement.*

After these remarks concerning the effects of the dream censor, let us now turn to their dynamics. I hope you will not consider the expression too anthropomorphically, and picture the dream censor as a severe little manikin who lives in a little brain chamber and there performs his duties; nor should you attempt to localize him too much, to think of a brain center from which his censoring influence emanates, and which would cease with the injury or extirpation of this center. For the present, the term "dream censor" is no more than a very convenient phrase for a dynamic relationship. This phrase does not prevent us from asking by what tendencies such influence is exerted and upon which tendencies it works; nor will we be surprised to discover that we have already encountered the dream censor before, perhaps without recognizing him.

For such was actually the case. You will remember that we had a surprising experience when we began to apply our technique of free association. We then began to feel that some sort of a resistance blocked our efforts to proceed from the dream element to the unconscious element for which the former is the substitute. This resistance, we said, may be of varying strength, enormous at one time, quite negligible at another. In the latter case we need cross only a few intermediate steps in our work of interpretation. But when the resistance is strong, then we must go through a long chain of associations, are taken far afield and must overcome all the difficulties which present themselves as critical objections to the association technique. What we met with in the work of interpretation, we must now bring into the dream work as the dream censor. The resistance to interpretation is nothing but the objectivation of the dream censor. The latter proves to us that the force of the censor has not spent itself in causing the dream distortion, has not since been extinguished, but that this censorship continues as a permanent institution with the purpose of preserving the distortion. Moreover, just as in the interpretation the strength of the resistance varied with each element, so also the distortion produced by the censor in the same dream is of varying magnitude for each element. If one compares the manifest with the latent dream one sees that certain isolated latent elements have been practically eliminated, others more or less modified, and still others left unchanged, indeed, have perhaps been taken over into the dream content with additional strength.

But we wanted to discover what purposes the censorship serves and against which tendencies it acts. This question, which is fundamental to the understanding of the dream, indeed perhaps to human life, is easily answered if we look over a series of those dreams which have been analyzed. The tendencies which the censorship exercises are those which are recognized by the waking judgment of the dreamer, those with which he feels himself in harmony. You may rest assured that when you reject an accurate interpretation of a dream of your own, you do so with the same motives with which the dream censor works, the motives with which it produces the dream distortion and makes the interpretation necessary. Recall the dream of our fifty-year old lady. Without having interpreted it, she considers her dream abominable, would have been still more outraged if our informant had told her anything about the indubitable meaning; and it is just on account of this condemnation that the shocking spots in her dream were replaced by a murmur.

The tendencies, however, against which the dream censor directs itself, must now be described from the standpoint of this instance. One can say only that these tendencies are of an objectionable nature throughout, that they are shocking from an ethical, aesthetic and social point of view, that they are things one does not dare even to think, or thinks of only with abhorrence. These censored wishes which have attained to a distorted expression in the dream, are above all expressions of a boundless, reckless egoism. And indeed, the personal ego occurs in every dream to play the major part in each of them, even if it can successfully disguise itself in the manifest content. This *sacro egoismo* of the dream is surely not unconnected with the sleep-inducing cessation of psychic activity which consists, it should be noted, in the withdrawal of interest from the entire external world.

The ego which has been freed of all ethical restraints feels itself in accord with all the demands of the sexual striving, with those demands which have long since been condemned by our aesthetic rearing, demands of such a character that they resist all our moral demands for restraint. The pleasure-striving—the libido, as we term it—chooses its objects without inhibitions, and indeed, prefers those that are forbidden. It chooses not only the wife of another, but, above all, those incestuous objects declared sacred by the agreement of mankind—the mother and sister in the man's case, the father and brother in the woman's. Even the dream of our fifty-year old lady is an incestuous one, its libido unmistakably directed toward her son. Desires which we believe to be far from human nature show themselves strong enough to arouse dreams. Hate, too, expends itself without restraint. Revenge and murderous wishes toward those standing closest to the dreamer are not unusual, toward those best beloved in daily life, toward parents, brothers and sisters, toward one's spouse and one's own children. These censored wishes seem to arise from a veritable hell; no censorship seems too harsh to be applied against their waking interpretation.

But do not reproach the dream itself for this evil content. You will not, I am sure, forget that the dream is charged with the harmless, indeed the useful function of guarding sleep from disturbance. This evil content, then, does not lie in the nature of the dream. You know also that there are dreams which can be recognized as the satisfaction of justified wishes and urgent bodily needs. These, to be sure, undergo no dream distortion. They need none. They can satisfy their function without offending the ethical and aesthetic tendencies of the ego. And will you also keep in mind the fact that the amount of dream distortion is proportional to two factors. On the one hand, the worse the censorable wish, the greater the distortion; on the other hand, however, the stricter the censor himself is at any particular time the greater the distortion will be also. A young, strictly reared and prudish girl will, by reason of those factors, disfigure with an inexorable censorship those dream impulses which we physicians, for example, and which the dreamer herself ten years later, would recognize as permissible, harmless, libidinous desires.

Besides, we are far from being at the point where we can allow ourselves to be shocked by the results of our work of interpretation. I think we are not yet quite adept at it; and above all there lies upon us the obligation to secure it against certain attacks. It is not at all difficult to "find a hitch" in it. Our dream interpretations were made on the hypotheses we accepted a little while ago, that the dream has some meaning, that from the hypnotic to the normal sleep one may carry over the idea of the existence at such times of an unconscious psychic activity, and that all associations are predetermined. If we had come to plausible results on the basis of these hypotheses, we would have been justified in concluding that the hypotheses were correct. But what is to be done when the results are what I have just pictured them to be? Then it surely is natural to say, "These results are impossible, foolish, at least very improbable, hence there must have been something wrong with the hypotheses. Either the dream is no psychic phenomenon after all, or there is no such thing as unconscious mental activity in the normal condition, or our technique has a gap in it somewhere. Is that not a simpler and more satisfying conclusion than the abominations which we pretend to have disclosed on the basis of our suppositions?"

Both, I answer. It is a simpler as well as a more satisfying conclusion, but not necessarily more correct for that reason. Let us take our time, the matter is not yet ripe for judgment. Above all we can strengthen the criticism against our dream interpretation still further. That its conclusions are so unpleasant and unpalatable is perhaps of secondary importance. A stronger argument is the fact that the dreamers to whom we ascribe such wish-tendencies from the interpretation of their dreams reject the interpretations most emphatically, and with good reason. "What," says the one, "you want to prove to me by this dream that I begrudged the sums which I spent for my sister's trousseau and my brother's education? But indeed that can't be so. Why I work only for my sister, I have no interest in life but to fulfill my duties toward her, as being the oldest child, I promised our blessed mother I would." Or a woman says of her dream, "You mean to say that I wish my husband were dead! Why, that is simply revolting, nonsense. It isn't only that we have the happiest possible married life, you probably won't believe me when I tell you so, but his death would deprive me of everything else that I own in the world." Or another will tell us, "You mean that I have sensual desires toward my sister? That is ridiculous. I am not in the least fond of her. We don't get along and I haven't exchanged a word with her in years." We might perhaps ignore this sort of thing if the dreamers did not confirm or deny the tendencies ascribed to them; we could say that they are matters which the dreamers do not know about themselves. But that the dreamers should feel the exact opposite of the ascribed wish, and should be able to prove to us the dominance of the opposite tendency—this fact must finally disconcert us. Is it not time to lay aside the whole work of the dream interpretation as something whose results reduce it to absurdity?

By no means; this stronger argument breaks down when we attack it critically. Assuming that there are unconscious tendencies in the psychic life, nothing is proved by the ability of the subject to show that their opposites dominate his conscious life. Perhaps there is room in the psychic life even for antithetical tendencies, for contradictions which exist side by side, yes, possibly it is just the dominance of the one impulse which is the necessary condition for the unconsciousness of its opposite. The first two objections raised against our work hold merely that the results of dream interpretation are not simple, and very unpleasant. In answer to the first of these, one may say that for all your enthusiasm for the simple solution, you cannot thereby solve a single dream problem. To do so you must make up your mind to accept the fact of complicated relationships. And to the second of these objections one may say that you are obviously wrong to use a preference or a dislike as the basis for a scientific judgment. What difference does it make if the results of the dream interpretation seem unpleasant, even embarrassing and disgusting to you? "That doesn't prevent them from existing," as I used to hear my teacher Charcot say in similar cases, when I was a young doctor. One must be humble, one must keep personal preferences and antipathies in the background, if one wishes to discover the realities of the world. If a physicist can prove to you that the organic life of this planet must, within a short period of time, become completely extinct, do you also venture to say to him, "That cannot be so. This prospect is too unpleasant." On the contrary, you will be silent until another physicist proves some error in the assumptions or calculations of the first. If you reject the unpleasant, you are repeating the mechanism of dream construction instead of understanding and mastering it.

Perhaps you will promise to overlook the repulsive character of the censored dream-wishes, and will take refuge in the argument that it is improbable, after all, that so wide a field be given over to the evil in the constitution of man. But does your own experience justify you in saying that? I will not discuss the question of how you may estimate yourselves, but have you found so much good will among your superiors and rivals, so much chivalry among your enemies, so little envy in their company, that you feel yourselves in duty bound to enter a protest against the part played by the evil of egoism in human nature? Are you ignorant of how uncontrolled and undependable the average human being is in all the affairs of sex life? Or do you not know that all the immoralities and excesses of which we dream nightly are crimes committed daily by waking persons? What else does psychoanalysis do here but confirm the old saying of Plato, that the good people are those who content themselves with dreaming what the others, the bad people, really do?

And now turn your attention from the individual case to the great war devastating Europe. Think of the amount of brutality, the cruelty and the lies allowed to spread over the civilized world. Do you really believe that a handful of conscienceless egoists and corruptionists could have succeeded in setting free all these evil spirits, if the millions of followers did not share in the guilt? Do you dare under these circumstances to break a lance for the absence of evil from the psychic constitution of mankind?

You will reproach me with judging the war one-sidedly, you will say that it has also brought forth all that is most beautiful and noble in mankind, its heroic courage, its self-sacrifice, its social feeling. Certainly, but do not at this point allow yourselves to become guilty of the injustice which has so often been perpetrated against psychoanalysis, of reproaching it with denying one thing because it was asserting another. It is not our intention to deny the noble strivings of human nature, nor have we ever done anything to deprecate their value. On the contrary, I show you not only the censored evil dream-wishes, but also the censor which suppresses them and renders them unrecognizable. We dwell on the evil in mankind with greater emphasis only because others deny it, a method whereby the psychic life of mankind does not become better, but merely incomprehensible. When, however, we give up this one-sided ethical estimate, we shall surely be able to find a more accurate formula for the relationship of the evil to the good in human nature.

And thus the matter stands. We need not give up the conclusions to which our labors in dream interpretation lead us even though we must consider those conclusions strange. Perhaps we can approach their understanding later by another path. For the present, let us repeat: dream distortion is a consequence of the censorship practised by accredited tendencies of the ego against those wish-impulses that are in any way shocking, impulses which stir in us nightly during sleep. Why these wish-impulses come just at night, and whence they come—these are questions which will bear considerable investigation.

It would be a mistake, however, to omit to mention, with fitting emphasis, another result of these investigations. The dream wishes which try to disturb our sleep are not known to us, in fact we learn of them first through the dream interpretation. Therefore, they may be described as "at that time" unconscious in the sense above defined. But we can go beyond this and say that they are more than merely "at that time" unconscious. The dreamer to be sure denies their validity, as we have seen in so many cases, even after he has learned of their existence by means of the interpretation. The situation is then repeated which we first encountered in the interpretation of the tongue slip "hiccough" where the toastmaster was outraged and assured us that neither then nor ever before had he been conscious of disrespectful impulse toward his chief. This is repeated with every interpretation of a markedly distorted dream, and for that reason attains a significance for our conception. We are now prepared to conclude that there are processes and tendencies in the psychic life of which one knows nothing at all, has known nothing for some time, might, in fact, perhaps never have known anything. The unconscious thus receives a new meaning for us; the idea of "at present" or "at a specific time" disappears from its conception, for it can also mean *permanently* unconscious, not merely *latent at the time*. Obviously we shall have to learn more of this at another session.

TENTH LECTURE: THE DREAM

Symbolism in the Dream

WE have discovered that the distortion of dreams, a disturbing element in our work of understanding them, is the result of a censorious activity which is directed against the unacceptable of the unconscious wish-impulses. But, of course, we have not maintained that censorship is the only factor which is to blame for the dream distortion, and we may actually make the discovery in a further study of the dream that other items play a part in this result. That is, even if the dream censorship were eliminated we might not be in a position to understand the dreams; the actual dream still might not be identical with the latent dream thought.

This other item which makes the dream unintelligible, this new addition to dream distortion, we discover by considering a gap in our technique. I have already admitted that for certain elements of the dream, no associations really occur to the person being analyzed. This does not happen so often as the dreamers maintain; in many cases the association can be forced by persistence. But still there are certain instances in which no association is forthcoming, or if forced does not furnish what we expected. When this happens in the course of a psychoanalytic treatment, then a particular meaning may be attached thereto, with which we have nothing to do here. It also occurs, however, in the interpretation of the dreams of a normal person or in interpreting one's own dreams. Once a person is convinced that in these cases no amount of forcing of associations will avail, he will finally make the discovery that the unwished-for contingency occurs regularly in certain dream elements, and he will begin to recognize a new order of things there, where at first he believed he had come across a peculiar exception to our technique.

In this way we are tempted to interpret these silent dream elements ourselves, to undertake their translation by the means at hand. The fact that every time we trust to this substitution we obtain a satisfactory meaning is forced upon us; until we resolve upon this decision the dream remains meaningless, its continuity is broken. The accumulation of many similar cases tends to give the necessary certainty to our first timid attempts.

I am expounding all this in rather a schematic manner, but this is permissible for purposes of instruction, and I am not trying to misstate, but only to simplify matters. In this manner we derive constant translations for a whole series of dream elements just as constant translations are found in our popular dream books for all the things we dream. But do not forget that in our association technique we never discover constant substitutes for the dream elements.

You will say at once that this road to interpretation appears far more uncertain and open to objection than the former methods of free association. But a further fact is to be taken into consideration. After one has gathered a sufficient number of such constant substitutes empirically, he will say that of his own knowledge he should actually have denied that these items of dream interpretation could really be understood without the associations of the dreamer. The facts that force us to recognize their meaning will appear in the second half of our analysis.

We call such a constant relationship between a dream element and its interpretation *symbolic*. The dream element is itself a *symbol* of the unconscious dream thought. You will remember that previously, when we were investigating the relationship between dream elements and their actuality, I drew three distinctions, viz., that of the part of the whole, that of the allusion, and that of the imagery. I then announced that there was a fourth, but did not name it. This fourth is the symbolic relationship here introduced. Very interesting discussions center about this, and we will now consider them before we express our own particular observations on symbolism. Symbolism is perhaps the most noteworthy chapter of dream study.

In the first place, since symbols are permanent or constant translations, they realize, in a certain measure, the ideal of ancient as well as popular dream interpretation, an ideal which by means of our technique we had left behind. They permit us in certain cases to interpret a dream without questioning the dreamer who, aside from this, has no explanation for the symbol. If the interpreter is acquainted with the customary dream symbols and, in addition, with the dreamer himself, the conditions under which the latter lives and the impressions he received before having the dream, it is often possible to interpret a dream without further information—to translate it "right off the bat." Such a trick flatters the interpreter and impresses the dreamer; it stands out as a pleasurable incident in the usual arduous course of cross-examining the dreamer. But do not be misled. It is not our function to perform tricks. Interpretation based on a knowledge of symbols is not a technique that can replace the associative technique, or even compare with it. It is a supplement to the associative technique, and furnishes the latter merely with transplanted, usable results. But as regards familiarity with the dreamer's psychic situation, you must consider the fact that you are not limited to interpreting the dreams of acquaintances; that as a rule you are not acquainted with the daily occurrences which act as the stimuli for the dreams, and that the associations of the subject furnish you with a knowledge of that very thing we call the psychic situation.

Furthermore, it is very extraordinary, particularly in view of circumstances to be mentioned later, that the most vehement opposition has been voiced against the existence of the symbolic relationship between the dream and the unconscious. Even persons of judgment and position, who have otherwise made great progress in psychoanalysis, have discontinued their support at this point. This is the more remarkable since, in the first place, symbolism is neither peculiar to the dream nor characteristic of it, and since in the second place, symbolism in the dream was not discovered through psychoanalysis, although the latter is not poor otherwise in making startling discoveries. The discoverer of dream symbolism, if we insist on a discovery in modern times, was the philosopher K. A. Scherner (1861). Psychoanalysis affirmed Scherner's discovery and modified it considerably.

Now you will want to know something of the nature of dream symbolism, and to hear some examples. I shall gladly impart to you what I know, but I admit that our knowledge is not so complete as we could desire it to be.

The nature of the symbol relationship is a comparison, but not any desired comparison. One suspects a special prerequisite for this comparison, but is unable to say what it is. Not everything to which we are able to compare an object or an occurrence occurs in the dream as its symbol; on the other hand, the dream does not symbolize anything we may choose, but only specific elements of the dream thought. There are limitations on both sides.

It must be admitted that the idea of the symbol cannot be sharply delimited at all times—it mingles with the substitution, dramatization, etc., even approaches the allusion. In one series of symbols the basic comparison is apparent to the senses. On the other hand, there are other symbols which raise the question of where the similarity, the "something intermediate" of this suspected comparison is to be sought. We may discover it by more careful consideration, or it may remain hidden to us. Furthermore, it is extraordinary, if the symbol is a comparison, that this comparison is not revealed by the association, that the dreamer is not acquainted with the comparison, that he makes use of it without knowing of its existence. Indeed, the dreamer does not even care to admit the validity of this comparison when it is pointed out to him. So you see, a symbolic relationship is a comparison of a very special kind, the origin of which is not yet clearly understood by us. Perhaps later we may find references to this unknown factor.

The number of things that find symbolic representation in the dream is not great—the human body as a whole, parents, children, brothers and sisters, birth, death, nakedness and a few others. The only typical, that is, regular representation of the human person as a whole is in the form of a *house*, as was recognized by Scherner who, indeed, wished to credit this symbol with an overwhelming significance which it does not deserve. It occurs in dreams that a person, now lustful, now frightened, climbs down the fronts of houses. Those with entirely smooth walls are men; but those which are provided with projections and balconies to which one can hold on, are women. Parents appear in the dream as *king* and *queen*, or other persons highly respected. The dream in this instance is very pious. It treats children, and brothers and sisters, less tenderly; they are symbolized as *little animals* or *vermin*. Birth is almost regularly represented by some reference to *water*; either one plunges into the water or climbs out of it, or rescues someone from the water, or is himself rescued from it, i.e., there is a mother-relation to the person. Death is replaced in the dream by *taking a journey, riding in a train; being dead, by various darksome, timid suggestions; nakedness, by clothes* and *uniforms*. You see here how the lines between symbolic and suggestive representation merge one into another.

In contrast to the paucity of this enumeration, it is a striking fact that the objects and subject matter of another sphere are represented by an extraordinarily rich symbolism. This is the sphere of the sexual life, the genitals, the sex processes and sexual intercourse. The great majority of symbols in the dream are sex symbols. A remarkable disproportion results from this fact. The designated subject matters are few, their symbols extraordinarily profuse, so that each of these objects can be expressed by any number of symbols of almost equal value. In the interpretation something is disclosed that arouses universal objection. The symbol interpretations, in contrast to the many-sidedness of the dream representations, are very monotonous—this displeases all who deal with them; but what is one to do?

Since this is the first time in these lectures that we speak of the sexual life, I must tell you the manner in which I intend to handle the subject. Psychoanalysis sees no reason for hiding matters or treating them by innuendo, finds no necessity of being ashamed of dealing with this important subject, believes it is proper and decent to call everything by its correct name, and hopes most effectively in this manner to ward off disturbing or salacious thoughts. The fact that I am talking before a mixed audience can make no difference on this point. Just as there is no special knowledge either for the Delphic oracle or for flappers, so the ladies present among you have, by their appearance in this lecture hall, made it clear that they wish to be considered on the same basis as the men.

The dream has a number of representations for the male genital that may be called symbolic, and in which the similarity of the comparison is, for the most part, very enlightening. In the first place, the holy figure 3 is a symbolical substitute for the entire male genital. The more conspicuous and more interesting part of the genital to both sexes, the male organ, has symbolical substitute in objects of like form, those which are long and upright, such as *sticks, umbrellas, poles, trees*, etc. It is also symbolized by objects that have the characteristic, in common with it, of penetration into the body and consequent injury, hence pointed *weapons* of every type, *knives, daggers, lances, swords*, and in the same manner *firearms, guns, pistols* and the *revolver*, which is so suitable because of its shape. In the troubled dream of the young girl, pursuit by a man with a knife or a firearm plays a big role. This, probably the most frequent dream symbolism, is easily translatable. Easily comprehensible, too, is the substitution for the male member of objects out of which water flows: *faucets, water cans, fountains*, as well as its representation by other objects that have the power of elongation, such as *hanging lamps, collapsible pencils*, etc. That *pencils, quills, nail files, hammers* and other *instruments* are undoubtedly male symbols is a fact connected with a conception of the organ, which likewise is not far to seek.

The extraordinary characteristic of the member of being able to raise itself against the force of gravity, one of the phenomena of erection, leads to symbolic representations by *balloons, aeroplanes*, and more recently, *Zeppelins*. The dream has another far more expressive way of symbolizing erection. It makes the sex organ the essential part of the whole person and pictures the person himself as *flying*. Do not feel disturbed because the dreams of flying, often so beautiful, and which we all have had, must be interpreted as dreams of general sexual excitement, as erection dreams. P. Federn, among the psychoanalytical students, has confirmed this interpretation beyond any doubt, and even Mourly Vold, much praised for his sobriety, who carried on his dream experiments with artificial positions of the arms and legs, and who was really opposed to psychoanalysis—perhaps knew nothing about psychoanalysis—has come to the same conclusion as a result of his research. It is no objection to this conclusion that women may have the same dreams of flying. Remember that our dreams act as wish-fulfillments, and that the wish to be a man is often present in women, consciously or unconsciously. And the fact that it is possible for a woman to realize this wish by the same sensation as a man does, will not mislead anyone acquainted with anatomy. There is a small organ in the genitals of a woman similar to that of the male, and this small organ, the clitoris, even in childhood, and in the years before sexual intercourse, plays the same role as does the large organ of the male.

To the less comprehensible male sex-symbols belong certain *reptiles* and *fish*, notably the famous symbol of the *snake*. Why *hats* and *cloaks* should have been turned to the same use is certainly difficult to discover, but their symbolic meaning leaves no room for doubt. And finally the question may be raised whether possibly the substitution of some other member as a representation for the male organ may not be regarded as symbolic. I believe that one is forced to this conclusion by the context and by the female counterparts.

The female genital is symbolically represented by all those objects which share its peculiarity of enclosing a space capable of being filled by something—viz., by *pits*, *caves*, and *hollows*, by *pitchers* and *bottles*, by *boxes* and *trunks*, *jars*, *cases*, *pockets*, etc. The *ship*, too, belongs in this category. Many symbols represent the womb of the mother rather than the female genital, as *wardrobes*, *stoves*, and primarily a *room*. The room-symbolism is related to the house-symbol, *doors* and *entrances* again become symbolic of the genital opening. But materials, too, are symbols of the woman—*wood*, *paper*, and objects that are made of these materials, such as *tables* and *books*. Of animals, at least the *snail* and *mussel* are unmistakably recognizable as symbols for the female; of parts of the body the *mouth* takes the place of the genital opening, while *churches* and *chapels* are structural symbolisms. As you see, all of these symbols are not equally comprehensible.

The breasts must be included in the genitals, and like the larger hemispheres of the female body are represented by *apples*, *peaches* and *fruits* in general. The pubic hair growth of both sexes appears in the dream as *woods* and *bushes*. The complicated topography of the female genitals accounts for the fact that they are often represented as scenes with *cliffs*, *woods* and *water*, while the imposing mechanism of the male sex apparatus leads to the use of all manner of very complicated *machinery*, difficult to describe.

A noteworthy symbol of the female genital is also the *jewel-casket*; *jewels* and *treasure* are also representatives of the beloved person in the dream; *sweets* frequently occur as representatives of sexual delights. The satisfaction in one's own genital is suggested by all types of *play*, in which may be included *piano-playing*. Exquisite symbolic representations of *onanism* are *sliding* and *coasting* as well as *tearing off a branch*. A particularly remarkable dream symbol is that of having *one's teeth fall out*, or *having them pulled*. Certainly its most immediate interpretation is castration as a punishment for onanism. Special representations for the relations of the sexes are less numerous in the dream than we might have expected from the foregoing. Rhythmic activities, such as *dancing*, *riding* and *climbing* may be mentioned, also harrowing experiences, such as *being run over*. One may include certain *manual activities*, and, of course, *being threatened with weapons*.

You must not imagine that either the use or the translation of these symbols is entirely simple. All manner of unexpected things are continually happening. For example, it seems hardly believable that in these symbolic representations the sex differences are not always sharply distinguished. Many symbols represent a genital in general, regardless of whether male or female, e.g., the *little child*, the *small son* or *daughter*. It sometimes occurs that a predominantly male symbol is used for a female genital, or vice versa. This is not understood until one has acquired an insight into the development of the sexual representations of mankind. In many instances this double meaning of symbols may be only apparent; the most striking of the symbols, such as *weapons*, *pockets* and *boxes* are excluded from this bisexual usage.

I should now like to give a summary, from the point of view of the symbols rather than of the thing represented, of the field out of which the sex symbols are for the most part taken, and then to make a few remarks about the symbols which have points in common that are not understood. An obscure symbol of this type is the *hat*, perhaps headdress on the whole, and is usually employed as a male representation, though at times as a female. In the same way the *cloak* represents a man, perhaps not always the genital aspect. You are at liberty to ask, why? The *cravat*, which is suspended and is not worn by women, is an unmistakable male symbol. *White laundry*, all *linen*, in fact, is female. *Dresses*, *uniforms* are, as we have already seen, substitutes for nakedness, for body-formation; the *shoe* or *slipper* is a female genital. *Tables* and *wood* have already been mentioned as puzzling but undoubtedly female symbols. *Ladders*, *ascents*, *steps* in relation to their mounting, are certainly symbols of sexual intercourse. On closer consideration we see that they have the rhythm of walking as a common characteristic; perhaps, too, the heightening of excitement and the shortening of the breath, the higher one mounts.

We have already spoken of *natural scenery* as a representation of the female genitals. *Mountains* and *cliffs* are symbols of the male organ; the *garden* a frequent symbol of the female genitals. *Fruit* does not stand for the child, but for the breasts. *Wild animals* signify sensually aroused persons, or further, base impulses, passions. *Blossoms* and *flowers* represent the female genitals, or more particularly, virginity. Do not forget that the blossoms are really the genitals of the plants.

We already know the *room* as a symbol. The representation may be extended in that the windows, entrances and exits of the room take on the meaning of the body openings. Whether the room is *open* or *closed* is a part of this symbolism, and the *key* that opens it is an unmistakable male symbol.

This is the material of dream symbolism. It is not complete and might be deepened as well as extended. But I am of the opinion it will seem more than enough to you, perhaps will make you reluctant. You will ask, "Do I really live in the midst of sex symbols? Are all the objects that surround me, all the clothes I put on, all the things that I touch, always sex symbols, and nothing else?" There really are sufficient grounds for such questions, and the first is, "Where, in fact, are we to find the meaning of these dream symbols if the dreamer himself can give no information concerning them, or at best can give only incomplete information?"

My answer is: "From many widely different sources, from fairy tales and myths, jokes and farces, from folklore, that is, the knowledge of the customs, usages, sayings and songs of peoples, from the poetic and vulgar language. Everywhere we find the same symbolism and in many of these instances we understand them without further information. If we follow up each of these sources separately we shall find so many parallels to the dream symbolism that we must believe in the correctness of our interpretations."

The human body, we have said, is, according to Scherner, frequently symbolized in the dream by the house. Continuing this representation, the windows, doors and entrances are the entrances into the body cavities, the facades are smooth or provided with balconies and projections to which to hold. The same symbolism is to be found in our daily speech when we greet a good friend as "*old house*" or when we say of someone, "We'll hit him in the *belfry*," or maintain of another that he's not quite right in the *upper story*. In anatomy the body openings are sometimes called the *body-portals*.

The fact that we meet our parents in the dream as imperial or royal persons is at first surprising. But it has its parallel in the fairy tale. Doesn't it begin to dawn upon us that the many fairy tales which begin "Once upon a time there was a *king* and a *queen*" intend nothing else than, "Once there was a *father* and a *mother*?" In our families we refer to our children as *princes*, the eldest as the *crown-prince*. The king usually calls himself the *father of the country*. We playfully designate little children as *worms*, and say, sympathetically, "*poor little worm.*"

Let us return to the symbolism of the house. When we use the projections of the house to hold ourselves on to in the dream, are we not reminded of the familiar colloquialism about persons with well-developed breasts: "She has something to *hold onto*"? The folk express this in still another way when it says, "there's lots of *wood in front of her house*"; as though it wished to come to the aid of our interpretation that wood is a feminine, maternal symbol.

In addition to wood there are others. We might not understand how this material has come to be a substitute for the maternal, the feminine. Here our comparison of languages may be helpful. The German word *Holz* (wood) is said to be from the same stem as the Greek word, νλη, which means stuff, raw material. This is an example of the case, not entirely unusual, where a general word for material finally is exclusively used for some special material. There is an island in the ocean, known by the name of Madeira. The Portuguese gave it this name at the time of its discovery because it was at that time entirely covered with forests, for in the language of the Portuguese, Madeira means *wood*. You will recognize, however, that Madeira, is nothing else than the slightly changed Latin word *materia* which again has the general meaning of *material* Material is derived from *mater*, mother. The material out of which something is made, is at the same time its mother-part. In the symbolic use of wood for woman, mother, this ancient conception still lives.

Birth is regularly expressed in dreams by some connection with water; one plunges into the water, or comes out of the water, which means one gives birth to, or is born. Now let us not forget that this symbol may refer in two ways to the truths of evolutionary history. Not alone have all land-mammals, including the ancestors of man, developed out of water animals—this is the ultimate fact—but every single mammal, every human being, lived the first part of his existence in the water—namely, lived in the body of his mother as an embryo in the amniotic fluid and came out of the water at the time of his birth. I do not wish to maintain that the dreamer knows this, on the contrary I hold that he does not have to know. The dreamer very likely knows some things because of the fact that he was told about them in his childhood, and for that very reason I maintain that this knowledge has played no part in the construction of his symbols. He was told in childhood that the stork brought him—but where did it get him? Out of a lake, out of the well—again, out of the water. One of my patients to whom such information had been given, a little count, disappeared for a whole afternoon. Finally he was discovered lying at the edge of the palace lake, his little face bent above the water and earnestly peering into it to see if he could not see the little children at the bottom.

In the myths of the birth of the hero, which O. Rank submitted to comparative examination,—the oldest is that of King Sargon of Agade, about 2800 B.C.—exposure in the water and rescue from water play a predominating role. Rank has recognized that these are representations of birth, analogous to those customary in dreams. When a person in his dream rescues another from the water, the latter becomes his mother, or just plainly mother; in the myth a person who rescues a child out of the water professes herself as the real mother of the child. In a well-known joke the intelligent Jewish boy is asked who was the mother of Moses. He answered without hesitation, the Princess. But no, he is told, she only took him out of the water. "That's what *she says*," is his reply, and thereby he shows that he has found the correct interpretation of the myth.

Leaving on a trip represents death in the dream. Likewise it is the custom in the nursery when a child asks where someone who has died, and whom he misses, may be, to say to him that the absent one has taken a trip. Again I should like to deny the truth of the belief that the dream symbol originates in this evasion used for the benefit of children. The poet makes use of the same symbol when he speaks of the Hereafter as "that undiscovered bourne from which no *traveler* returns." Even in everyday speech it is customary to refer to the last journey. Every person acquainted with ancient rite knows how seriously, for example, the Egyptians considered the portrayal of a journey to the land of the dead. There still exist many copies of the "death book" which was given to the mummy for this journey as a sort of Baedeker. Since the burial places have been separated from the living quarters, the last journey of the dead person has become a reality.

In the same manner the genital symbolism is just as little peculiar to the dream alone. Every one of you has perhaps at some time or other been so unkind as to call some woman an "*old casket*" without perhaps being aware that he was using a genital symbol. In the New Testament one may read "Woman is a weak *vessel*." The Holy Scriptures of the Jews, so nearly poetic in their style, are filled with sex-symbolic expressions which have not always been correctly understood, and the true construction of which, in the *Song of Songs*, for example, has led to many misunderstandings. In the later Hebraic literature the representation of woman as a house, the door taking the place of the sex opening, is very widespread. The man complains, for instance, when he discovers a lack of virginity, that he has found *the door open*. The symbol of the table for woman is also known to this literature. The woman says of her husband, "I set the table for him, *but he upset it*." Lame children are supposed to result from the fact that the man has *overturned the table*. I take these examples from a work by L. Levy of Brünn, *The Sexual Symbolism of the Bible and the Talmud.*

That ships, too, represent women in dreams is a belief derived from the etymologists, who maintain "ship" was originally the name of an earthen vessel and is the same word as *Schaff* (to create). The Greek myth of Periander of Corinth and his wife Melissa is proof that the stove or oven is a woman, and a womb. When, according to Herodotus, the tyrant entreated the shade of his beloved wife, whom, however, he had murdered in a fit of jealousy, for some sign of its identity, the deceased identified herself by the reminder that he, *Periander, had thrust his bread into a cold oven,* as a disguise for an occurrence that could have been known to no other person. In the *Anthropophyteia* published by F. S. Krauss, an indispensable source book for everything that has to do with the sex life of nations, we read that in a certain German region it is commonly said of a woman who has just been delivered of a child, "*Her oven has caved in.*" The making of a fire and everything connected therewith is filled through and through with sex symbolism. The flame is always the male genital, the fireplace, the hearth, is the womb of the woman.

If you have often wondered why it is that landscapes are so often used to represent the female genitals in the dream, then let the mythologist teach you the role Mother Earth has played in the symbolisms and cults of ancient times. You may be tempted to say that a room represents a woman in the dream because of the German colloquialism which uses the term *Frauenzimmer* instead of *Frau*, in other words, it substitutes for the human person the idea of that room that is set aside for her exclusive use. In like manner we speak of the *Sublime Porte*, and mean the Sultan and his government; furthermore, the name of the ancient Egyptian ruler, Pharaoh, means nothing other than "great court room." (In the ancient Orient the court yards between the double gates of the town were the gathering places of the people, in the same manner as the market place was in the classical world.) What I mean is, this derivation is far too superficial. It seems more probable to me that the room, as the space surrounding man, came to be the symbol of woman. We have seen that the house is used in such a representation; from mythology and poetry we may take the *city, fortress, palace, citadel,* as further symbols of woman. The question may easily be decided by the dreams of those persons who do not speak German and do not understand it. In the last few years my patients have been predominantly foreign-language speaking, and I think I can recall that in their dreams as well the room represents woman, even where they had no analogous usages in their languages. There are still other signs which show that the symbolization is not limited by the bounds of language, a fact that even the old dream investigator, Schubert (1862) maintained. Since none of my dreamers were totally ignorant of German I must leave this differentiation to those psychoanalysts who can gather examples in other lands where the people speak but one language.

Among the symbol-representations of the male genital there is scarcely one that does not recur in jokes or in vulgar or poetical usage, especially among the old classical poets. Not alone do those symbols commonly met with in dreams appeal here, but also new ones, e.g., the working materials of various performances, foremost of which is the incantation. Furthermore, we approach in the symbolic representation of the male a very extended and much discussed province, which we shall avoid for economic reasons. I should like to make a few remarks, however, about one of the unclassified symbols—the figure 3. Whether or not this figure derives its holiness from its symbolic meaning may remain undecided. But it appears certain that many objects which occur in nature as three-part things derive their use as coats-of-arms and emblems from such symbolic meaning, e.g., the clover, likewise the three-part French lily, (fleur-de-lys), and the extraordinary coats-of-arms of two such widely separated islands as Sicily and the Isle of Man, where the Triskeles (three partly bended knees, emerging from a central point) are merely said to be the portrayal in a different form of the male genitals. Copies of the male member were used in antiquity as the most powerful charms (*Apotropaea*) against evil influences, and this is connected with the fact that the lucky amulets of our own time may one and all be recognized as genital or sex-symbols. Let us study such a collection, worn in the form of little silver pendants: the four-leaf clover, a pig, a mushroom, a horse-shoe, a ladder, a chimney-sweep. The four-leaf clover, it seems, has usurped the place of the three-leaf clover, which is really more suitable as a symbol; the pig is an ancient symbol of fertility; the mushroom is an unquestionable penis symbol—there are mushrooms that derive their systematic names from their unmistakable similarity to the male member (Phallus impudicus); the horseshoe recalls the contour of the female genital opening; and the chimney sweep who carries a ladder belongs in this company because he carries on that trade with which the sex-intercourse is vulgarly compared (*cf.* the *Anthropophyteia*). We have already become acquainted with his ladder as a sex symbol in the dream; the German usage is helpful here, it shows us how the verb "to mount"(steigen) is made use of in an exquisite sexual sense. We use the expressions "*to run after women*," which literally translated would be "*to climb after women*," and "*an old climber*" (den Frauen nachsteigen," and "ein alter Steiger) In French, where "*step*" is "*la marche*" we find that the analogous expression for a man about town is "*un vieux marcheur.*" It is apparently not unknown in this connection that the sexual intercourse of many of the larger animals requires a mounting, *a climbing upon* the female.

The tearing off of a branch as the symbolic representation of onanism is not alone in keeping with the vulgar representation of the fact of onanism, but has far-reaching mythological parallels. Especially noteworthy, however, is the representation of onanism, or rather the punishment therefor, castration, by the falling out or pulling out of teeth, because there is a parallel in folk-lore which is probably known to the fewest dreamers. It does not seem at all questionable to me that the practice of circumcision common among so many peoples is an equivalent and a substitute for castration. And now we are informed that in Australia certain primitive tribes practice circumcision as a rite of puberty (the ceremony in honor of the boy's coming of age), while others, living quite near, have substituted for this act the striking out of a tooth.

I end my exposition with these examples. They are only examples. We know more about these matters, and you may well imagine how much richer and how much more interesting such a collection would appear if made, not by amateurs like ourselves, but by real experts in mythology, anthropology, philology and folk-lore. We are compelled to draw a few conclusions which cannot be exhaustive, but which give us much food for thought.

In the first place, we are faced by the fact that the dreamer has at his disposal a symbolic means of expression of which he is unconscious while awake, and does not recognize when he sees. That is as remarkable as if you should make the discovery that your chambermaid understands Sanskrit, although you know she was born in a Bohemian village and never learned the language. It is not easy to harmonize this fact with our psychological views. We can only say that the dreamer's knowledge of symbolism is unconscious, that it is a part of his unconscious mental life. We make no progress with this assumption. Until now it was only necessary to admit of unconscious impulses, those about which one knew nothing, either for a period of time or at all times. But now we deal with something more; indeed, with unknown knowledge, with thought relationships, comparisons between unlike objects which lead to this, that one constant may be substituted for another. These comparisons are not made anew each time, but they lie ready, they are complete for all time. That is to be concluded from the fact of their agreement in different persons, agreement despite differences in language.

But whence comes the knowledge of these symbol-relationships? The usages of language cover only a small part of them. The dreamer is for the most part unacquainted with the numerous parallels from other sources; we ourselves must first laboriously gather them together. Secondly, these symbolic representations are peculiar neither to the dreamer nor to the dream work by means of which they become expressed. We have learned that mythology and fairy-tales make use of the same symbolism, as well as do the people in their sayings and songs, the ordinary language of every day, and poetic phantasy. The field of symbolism is an extraordinarily large one, and dream symbolism is but a small part thereof. It is not even expedient to approach the whole problem from the dream side. Many of the symbols that are used in other places do not occur in the dream at all, or at best only very seldom. Many of the dream symbols are to be found in other fields only very rarely, as you have seen. One gets the impression that he is here confronted with an ancient but no longer existent method of expression, of which various phases, however, continue in different fields, one here, one there, a third, perhaps in a slightly altered form, in several fields. I am reminded of the phantasy of an interesting mental defective, who had imagined a fundamental language, of which all these symbolic representations were the remains.

Thirdly, you must have noticed that symbolism in these other fields is by no means sex symbolism solely, while in the dream the symbols are used almost entirely to express sexual objects and processes. Nor is this easily explained. Is it possible that symbols originally sexual in their meaning later came to have other uses, and that this was the reason perhaps for the weakening of the symbolic representation to one of another nature? These questions are admittedly unanswerable if one has dealt only with dream-symbolism. One can only adhere to the supposition that there is an especially intimate connection between true symbols and things sexual.

An important indication of this has been given us recently. A philologist, H. Sperber (Upsala) who works independently of psychoanalysis, advanced the theory that sexual needs have played the largest part in the origin and development of languages. The first sounds served as means of communication, and called the sexual partner; the further development of the roots of speech accompanied the performance of the primitive man's work. This work was communal and progressed to the accompaniment of rhythmically repeated word sounds. In that way a sexual interest was transferred to the work. The primitive man made work acceptable at the same time that he used it as an equivalent and substitute for sex-activity. The word thus called forth by the common labor had two meanings, designating the sex-act as well as the equivalent labor-activity. In time the word became disassociated from its sexual significance and became fixed on this work. Generations later the same thing happened to a new word that once had sexual significance and came to be used for a new type of work. In this manner a number of word-roots were formed, all of sexual origin, and all of which had lost their sexual significance. If the description sketched here approximates the truth, it opens up the possibility for an understanding of the dream symbolism. We can understand how it is that in the dream, which preserves something of these most ancient conditions, there are so extraordinarily many symbols for the sexual, and why, in general, weapons and implements always stand for the male, materials and things manufactured, for the female. Symbolic relationships would be the remnants of the old word-identity; things which once were called by the same names as the genitals can now appear in the dream as symbols for them.

From our parallels to dream symbolization you may also learn to appreciate what is the character of psychoanalysis which makes it a subject of general interest, which is true of neither psychology nor psychiatry. Psychoanalytic work connects with so many other scientific subjects, the investigation of which promises the most pertinent discoveries, with mythology, with folk-lore, with racial psychology and with religion. You will understand how a journal can have grown on psychoanalytic soil, the sole purpose of which is the furtherance of these relationships. This is the *Imago* founded in 1912 and edited by Hanns Sachs and Otto Rank. In all of these relations, psychoanalysis is first and foremost the giving, less often the receiving, part. Indeed it derives benefit from the fact that its unusual teachings are substantiated by their recurrence in other fields, but on the whole it is psychoanalysis that provides the technical procedure and the point of view, the use of which will prove fruitful in those other fields. The psychic life of the human individual provides us, upon psychoanalytic investigation, with explanations with which we are able to solve many riddles in the life of humanity, or at least show these riddles in their proper light. Furthermore, I have not even told you under what conditions we are able to get the deepest insight into that suppositious "fundamental language," or from which field we gain the most information. So long as you do not know this you cannot appreciate the entire significance of the subject. This field is the neurotic, its materials, the symptoms and other expressions of the nervous patient, for the explanation and treatment of which psychoanalysis was devised.

My fourth point of view returns to our premise and connects up with our prescribed course. We said, even if there were no such thing as dream censorship, the dream would still be hard to understand, for we would then be confronted with the task of translating the symbol-language of the dream into the thought of our waking hours. Symbolism is a second and independent item of dream distortion, in addition to dream censorship. It is not a far cry to suppose that it is convenient for the dream censorship to make use of symbolism since both lead to the same end, to making the dream strange and incomprehensible.

Whether or not in the further study of the dream we shall hit upon a new item that influences dream distortion, remains to be seen. I should not like to leave the subject of dream symbolism without once more touching upon the curious fact that it arouses such strong opposition in the case of educated persons, in spite of the fact that symbolism in myth, religion, art and speech is undoubtedly so prevalent. Is not this again because of its relationship to sexuality?

ELEVENTH LECTURE: THE DREAM

The Dream-Work

IF you have mastered dream censorship and symbolic representation, you are, to be sure, not yet adept in dream distortion, but you are nevertheless in a position to understand most dreams. For this you employ two mutually supplementary methods, call up the associations of the dreamer until you have penetrated from the substitute to the actual, and from your own knowledge supply the meaning for the symbol. Later we shall discuss certain uncertainties which show themselves in this process.

We are now in a position to resume work which we attempted, with very insufficient means at an earlier stage, when we studied the relation between the manifest dream elements and their latent actualities, and in so doing established four such main relationships: that of a part of the whole, that of approach or allusion, the symbolic relationship and plastic word representation. We shall now attempt the same on a larger scale, by comparing the manifest dream content as a whole, with the latent dream which we found by interpretation.

I hope you will never again confuse these two. If you have achieved this, you have probably accomplished more in the understanding of the dream than the majority of the readers of my *Interpretation of Dreams*. Let me remind you once more that this process, which changes the latent into the manifest dream, is called *dream-work*. Work which proceeds in the opposite direction, from the manifest dream to the latent, is our *work of interpretation*. The work of interpretation attempts to undo the dream-work. Infantile dreams that are recognized as evident wish fulfillments nevertheless have undergone some dream-work, namely, the transformation of the wish into reality, and generally, too, of thoughts into visual pictures. Here we need no interpretation, but only a retracing of these transformations. Whatever dream-work has been added to other dreams, we call *dream distortion*, and this can be annulled by our work of interpretation.

The comparison of many dream interpretations has rendered it possible for me to give you a coherent representation of what the dream-work does with the material of the latent dream. I beg of you, however, not to expect to understand too much of this. It is a piece of description that should be listened to with calm attention.

The first process of the dream-work is *condensation*. By this we understand that the manifest dream has a smaller content than the latent one, that is, it is a sort of abbreviated translation of the latter. Condensation may occasionally be absent, but as a rule it is present, often to a very high degree. The opposite is never true, that is, it never occurs that the manifest dream is more extensive in scope and content than the latent. Condensation occurs in the following ways: 1. Certain latent elements are entirely omitted; 2. only a fragment of the many complexes of the latent dream is carried over into the manifest dream; 3. latent elements that have something in common are collected for the manifest dream and are fused into a whole.

If you wish, you may reserve the term "condensation" for this last process alone. Its effects are particularly easy to demonstrate. From your own dreams you will doubtless recall the fusion of several persons into one. Such a compound person probably looks like A., is dressed like B., does something that one remembers of C., but in spite of this one is conscious that he is really D. By means of this compound formation something common to all four people is especially emphasized. One can make a compound formation of events and of places in the same way as of people, provided always that the single events and localities have something in common which the latent dream emphasizes. It is a sort of new and fleeting concept of formation, with the common element as its kernel. This jumble of details that has been fused together regularly results in a vague indistinct picture, as though you had taken several pictures on the same film.

The shaping of such compound formations must be of great importance to the dream-work, for we can prove, (by the choice of a verbal expression for a thought, for instance) that the common elements mentioned above are purposely manufactured where they originally do not exist. We have already become acquainted with such condensation and compound formations; they played an important part in the origin of certain cases of slips of the tongue. You recall the young man who wished to *inscort* a woman. Furthermore, there are jokes whose technique may be traced to such a condensation. But entirely aside from this, one may maintain that this appearance of something quite unknown in the dream finds its counterpart in many of the creations of our imagination which fuse together component parts that do not belong together in experience, as for example the centaurs, and the fabulous animals of old mythology or of Boecklin's pictures. For creative imagination can invent nothing new whatsoever, it can only put together certain details normally alien to one another. The peculiar thing, however, about the procedure of the dream-work is the following: The material at the disposal of the dream-work consists of thoughts, thoughts which may be offensive and unacceptable, but which are nevertheless correctly formed and expressed. These thoughts are transformed into something else by the dream-work, and it is remarkable and incomprehensible that this translation, this rendering, as it were, into another script or language, employs the methods of condensation and combination. For a translation usually strives to respect the discriminations expressed in the text, and to differentiate similar things. The dream-work, on the contrary, tries to fuse two different thoughts by looking, just as the joke does, for an ambiguous word which shall act as a connecting link between the two thoughts. One need not attempt to understand this feature of the case at once, but it may become significant for the conception of the dream-work.

Although condensation renders the dream opaque, one does not get the impression that it is an effect of dream censorship. One prefers to trace it back to mechanical or economic conditions; but censorship undoubtedly has a share in the process.

The results of condensation may be quite extraordinary. With its help, it becomes possible at times to collect quite unrelated latent thought processes into one manifest dream, so that one can arrive at an apparently adequate interpretation, and at the same time conceive a possible further interpretation.

The consequence of condensation for the relation between latent and manifest dreams is the fact that no simple relations can exist between the elements of the one and the other. A manifest element corresponds simultaneously to several latent ones, and vice versa, a latent element may partake of several manifest ones, an interlacing, as it were. In the interpretation of the dream it also becomes evident that the associations to a single element do not necessarily follow one another in orderly sequence. Often we must wait until the entire dream is interpreted.

Dream-work therefore accomplishes a very unusual sort of transcription of dream thoughts, not a translation word for word, or sign for sign, not a selection according to a set rule, as if all the consonants of a word were given and the vowels omitted; nor is it what we might call substitution, namely, the choice of one element to take the place of several others. It is something very different and much more complicated.

The second process of the dream-work is *displacement*. Fortunately we are already prepared for this, since we know that it is entirely the work of dream censorship. The two evidences of this are firstly, that a latent element is not replaced by one of its constituent parts but by something further removed from it, that is, by a sort of allusion; secondly, that the psychic accent is transferred from an important element to another that is unimportant, so that the dream centers elsewhere and seems strange.

Substitution by allusion is known to our conscious thinking also, but with a difference. In conscious thinking the allusion must be easily intelligible, and the substitute must bear a relation to the actual content. Jokes, too, often make use of allusion; they let the condition of content associations slide and replace it by unusual external associations, such as resemblances in sound, ambiguity of words, etc. They retain, however, the condition of intelligibility;

the joke would lose all its effect if the allusion could not be traced back to the actual without any effort whatsoever. The allusion of displacement has freed itself of both these limitations. Its connection with the element which it replaces is most external and remote, is unintelligible for this reason, and if it is retraced, its interpretation gives the impression of an unsuccessful joke or of a forced, far-fetched explanation. For the dream censor has only then accomplished its purpose, when it has made the path of return from the allusion to the original undiscoverable.

The displacement of emphasis is unheard of as a means of expressing thoughts. In conscious thinking we occasionally admit it to gain a comic effect. I can probably give you an idea of the confusion which this produces by reminding you of the story of the blacksmith who had committed a capital crime. The court decided that the penalty for the crime must be paid, but since he was the only blacksmith in the village and therefore indispensable, while there were three tailors, one of the latter was hung in his stead.

The third process of the dream-work is the most interesting from a psychological point of view. It consists of the *translation* of thoughts into visual images. Let us bear in mind that by no means all dream thoughts undergo this translation; many of them retain their form and appear in the manifest dream also as thought or consciousness; moreover, visual images are not the only form into which thoughts are translated. They are, however, the foundation of the dream fabric; this part of the dream work is, as we already know, the second most constant, and for single dream elements we have already learned to know "plastic word representation."

It is evident that this process is not simple. In order to get an idea of its difficulties you must pretend that you have undertaken the task of replacing a political editorial in a newspaper by a series of illustrations, that you have suffered an atavistic return from the use of the alphabet to ideographic writing. Whatever persons or concrete events occur in this article you will be able to replace easily by pictures, perhaps to your advantage, but you will meet with difficulties in the representation of all abstract words and all parts of speech denoting thought relationships, such as particles, conjunctions, etc. With the abstract words you could use all sorts of artifices. You will, for instance, try to change the text of the article into different words which may sound unusual, but whose components will be more concrete and more adapted to representation. You will then recall that most abstract words were concrete before their meaning paled, and will therefore go back to the original concrete significance of these words as often as possible, and so you will be glad to learn that you can represent the "possession" of an object by the actual physical straddling of it. (besitzen," to straddle.) The dream work does the same thing. Under such circumstances you can hardly demand accuracy of representation. You will also have to allow the dream-work to replace an element that is as hard to depict as for instance, broken faith, by another kind of rupture, a broken leg.[13 In this way you will be able to smooth away to some extent the crudity of imagery when the latter is endeavoring to replace word expression.

In the representation of parts of speech that denote thought relations, such as *because, therefore, but*, etc., you have no such aids; these constituent parts of the text will therefore be lost in your translation into images. In the same way, the dream-work resolves the content of the dream thought into its raw material of objects and activities. You may be satisfied if the possibility is vouchsafed you to suggest certain relations, not representable in themselves, in a more detailed elaboration of the image. In quite the same way the dream-work succeeds in expressing much of the content of the latent dream thought in the formal peculiarities of the manifest dream, in its clearness or vagueness, in its division into several parts, etc. The number of fragmentary dreams into which the dream is divided corresponds as a rule to the number of main themes, of thought sequences in the latent dream; a short preliminary dream often stands as an introduction or a motivation to the complementary dream which follows; a subordinate clause in dream thought is represented in the manifest dream as an interpolated change of scene, etc. The form of the dream is itself, therefore, by no means without significance and challenges interpretation. Different dreams of the same night often have the same meaning, and testify to an increasing effort to control a stimulus of growing urgency. In a single dream a particularly troublesome element may be represented by "duplicates," that is, by numerous symbols.

---

13 While revising these pages I chanced upon a newspaper article that I quote here as an unexpected supplement to the above lines.

THE PUNISHMENT OF GOD. A BROKEN ARM FOR BROKEN FAITH

Mrs. Anna M. the wife of a soldier in the reserve accused Mrs. Clementine C. of being untrue to her husband. The accusation reads that Mrs. C. had carried on an illicit relationship with Karl M. while her own husband was on the battlefield, from which he even sent her 70 Kronen a month. Mrs. C. had received *quite a lot of money* from the husband of the plaintiff, while she and her children had to live in *hunger* and in misery. Friends of her husband had told her that Mrs. C. had visited inns with M. and had caroused there until late at night. The accused had even asked the husband of the plaintiff before several infantrymen whether he would not soon get a divorce from his "old woman" and live with her. Mrs. C.'s housekeeper had also repeatedly seen the husband of the plaintiff in her (Mrs. C.'s) apartment, in complete negligée.

Yesterday Mrs. C. *denied* before a judge in Leopoldstadt that she even knew M; there could be no question of intimate relation between them. The witness, Albertine M., however, testified that Mrs. C. had kissed the husband of the plaintiff and that she had surprised them at it.

When M. was called as a witness in an earlier proceeding he had denied any intimate relation to the accused. Yesterday the judge received a *letter* in which the witness retracts the statement he made in the first proceeding and *admits* that he had carried on a love affair with Mrs. C., until last June. He says that he only denied this relationship in the former proceeding for the sake of the accused because before the proceeding she had come to him and begged on her knees that he should save her and not confess. "To-day," wrote the witness, "I felt impelled to make a full confession to the court, since I have *broken my left arm* and this appears to me as the *punishment of God* for my transgression."

The judge maintained the penal offense had already become null and void, whereupon the plaintiff withdrew her accusation and the liberation of the accused followed.

By continually comparing dream thought with the manifest dream that replaces it, we learn all sorts of things for which we were not prepared, as for instance, the fact that even the nonsense and absurdity of the dream have meaning. Yes, on this point the opposition between the medical and psychoanalytic conception of the dream reaches a climax not previously achieved. According to the former, the dream is senseless because the dreaming psychic activity has lost all power of critical judgment; according to our theory, on the other hand, the dream becomes senseless, whenever a critical judgment, contained in the dream thought, wishes to express the opinion: "It is nonsense." The dream which you all know, about the visit to the theatre (three tickets 1 Fl. 50 Kr.) is a good example of this. The opinion expressed here is: "It was *nonsense* to marry so early."

In the same way, we discover in interpretation what is the significance of the doubts and uncertainties so often expressed by the dreamer as to whether a certain element really occurred in the dream; whether it was this or something else. As a rule these doubts and uncertainties correspond to nothing in the latent dream thought; they are occasioned throughout by the working of the dream censor and are equivalent to an unsuccessful attempt at suppression.

One of the most surprising discoveries is the manner in which the dream-work deals with those things which are opposed to one another in the latent dream. We already know that agreements in the latent material are expressed in the manifest dream by condensations. Now oppositions are treated in exactly the same way as agreements and are, with special preference, expressed by the same manifest element. An element in a manifest dream, capable of having an opposite, may therefore represent itself as well as its opposite, or may do both simultaneously; only the context can determine which translation is to be chosen. It must follow from this that the particle "no" cannot be represented in the dream, at least not unambiguously.

The development of languages furnishes us with a welcome analogy for this surprising behavior on the part of the dream work. Many scholars who do research work in languages have maintained that in the oldest languages opposites—such as strong, weak; light, dark; big, little—were expressed by the same root word. (*The Contradictory Sense of Primitive Words.*) In old Egyptian, *ken* originally meant both strong and weak. In conversation, misunderstanding in the use of such ambiguous words was avoided by the tone of voice and by accompanying gestures, in writing by the addition of so-called determinatives, that is, by a picture that was itself not meant to be expressed. Accordingly, if ken meant strong, the picture of an erect little man was placed after the alphabetical signs, if *ken, weak*, was meant, the picture of a cowering man followed. Only later, by slight modifications of the original word, were two designations developed for the opposites which it denoted. In this way, from *ken* meaning both strong and weak, there was derived a *ken*, strong, and a *ken*, weak. It is said that not only the most primitive languages in their last developmental stage, but also the more recent ones, even the living tongues of to-day have retained abundant remains of this primitive opposite meaning. Let me give you a few illustrations of this taken from C. Abel (1884).

In Latin there are still such words of double meaning: *altus*—high, deep, and *sacer*, sacred, accursed. As examples of modifications of the same root, I cite: *clamare*—to scream, *clam*—quiet, still, secret; *siccus*—dry, *succus*—juice. And from the German: *Stimme*—voice, *stumm*—dumb.

The comparison of related tongues yields a wealth of examples:

English: *lock*; German: *Loch*—hole, *Lücke*—gap.

English: *cleave*; German: *kleben*—to stick, to adhere.

The English *without*, is to-day used to mean "not with"; that "with" had the connotation of deprivation as well as that of apportioning, is apparent from the compounds: *withdraw, withhold*. The German *wieder*, again, closely resembles this.

Another peculiarity of dream-work finds it prototype in the development of language. It occurred in ancient Egyptian as well as in other later languages that the sequence of sounds of the words was transposed to denote the same fundamental idea. The following are examples from English and German: *Topf*—*pot*; *boat*—*tub*; *hurry*—*Ruhe* (rest, quiet). *Balken* (beam)—*Kloben* (mallet)—*club*.

From the Latin and the German: *capere* (to seize)—*packen* (to seize, to grasp).

Inversions such as occur here in the single word are effected in a very different way by the dream-work. We already know the inversion of the sense, substitution by the opposite. Besides there are inversions of situations, of relations between two people, and so in dreams we are in a sort of topsy-turvy world. In a dream it is frequently the rabbit that shoots the hunter. Further inversion occurs in the sequence of events, so that in the dream the cause is placed after the effect. It is like a performance in a third-rate theatre, where the hero falls before the shot which kills him is fired from the wings. Or there are dreams in which the whole sequence of the elements is inverted, so that in the interpretation one must take the last first, and the first last, in order to obtain a meaning. You will recall from our study of dream symbolism that to go or fall into the water means the same as to come out of it, namely, to give birth to, or to be born, and that mounting stairs or a ladder means the same as going down. The advantage that dream distortions may gain from such freedom of representation, is unmistakable.

These features of the dream-work may be called *archaic*. They are connected with ancient systems of expression, ancient languages and literatures, and involve the same difficulties which we shall deal with later in a critical connection.

Now for some other aspects of the matter. In the dream-work it is plainly a question of translating the latent thoughts, expressed in words, into psychic images, in the main, of a visual kind. Now our thoughts were developed from such psychic images; their first material and the steps which led up to them were psychic impressions, or to be more exact, the memory images of these psychic impressions. Only later were words attached to these and then combined into thoughts. The dream-work therefore puts the thoughts through a *regressive* treatment, that is, one that retraces the steps in their development. In this regression, all that has been added to the thoughts as a new contribution in the course of the development of the memory pictures must fall away.

This, then, is the dream-work. In view of the processes that we have discovered about it, our interest in the manifest dream was forced into the background. I shall, however, devote a few remarks to the latter, since it is after all the only thing that is positively known to us.

It is natural that the manifest dream should lose its importance for us. It must be a matter of indifference to us whether it is well composed or resolved into a series of disconnected single images. Even when its exterior seems to be significant, we know that it has been developed by means of dream distortion and may have as little organic connection with the inner content of the dream as the facade of an Italian church has with its structure and ground plan. At other times this facade of the dream, too, has its significance, in that it reproduces with little or no distortion an important part of the latent dream thought. But we cannot know this before we have put the dream through a process of interpretation and reached a decision as to what amount of distortion has taken place. A similar doubt prevails when two elements in the dream seem to have been brought into close relations to one another. This may be a valuable hint, suggesting that we may join together those manifest thoughts which correspond to the elements in the latent dream; yet at other times we are convinced that what belongs together in thought has been torn apart in the dream.

As a general rule we must refrain from trying to explain one part of the manifest dream by another, as if the dream were coherently conceived and pragmatically represented. At the most it is comparable to a Breccian stone, produced by the fusion of various minerals in such a way that the markings it shows are entirely different from those of the original mineral constituents. There is actually a part of the dream-work, the so-called *secondary treatment*, whose function it is to develop something unified, something approximately coherent from the final products of the dream-work. In so doing the material is often arranged in an entirely misleading sense and insertions are made wherever it seems necessary.

On the other hand, we must not over-estimate the dream-work, nor attribute too much to it. The processes which we have enumerated tell the full tale of its functioning; beyond condensing, displacing, representing plastically, and then subjecting the whole to a secondary treatment, it can do nothing. Whatever of judgment, of criticism, of surprise, and of deduction are to be found in the dream are not products of the dream-work and are only very seldom signs of afterthoughts about the dream, but are generally parts of the latent dream thought, which have passed over into the manifest dream, more or less modified and adapted to the context. In the matter of composing speeches, the dream-work can also do nothing. Except for a few examples, the speeches in the dream are imitations and combinations of speeches heard or made by oneself during the day, and which have been introduced into the latent thought, either as material or as stimuli for the dream. Neither can the dream pose problems; when these are found in the dream, they are in the main combinations of numbers, semblances of examples that are quite absurd or merely copies of problems in the latent dream thought. Under these conditions it is not surprising that the interest which has attached itself to the dream-work is soon deflected from it to the latent dream thoughts which are revealed in more or less distorted form in the manifest dream. It is not justifiable, however, to have this change go so far that in a theoretical consideration one regularly substitutes the latent dream thought for the dream itself, and maintains of the latter what can hold only for the former. It is odd that the results of psychoanalysis should be misused for such an exchange. "Dream" can mean nothing but the result of the dream-work, that is, the *form* into which the latent dream thoughts have been translated by the dream-work.

Dream-work is a process of a very peculiar sort, the like of which has hitherto not been discovered in psychic life. These condensations, displacements, regressive translations of thoughts into pictures, are new discoveries which richly repay our efforts in the field of psychoanalysis. You will realize from the parallel to the dream-work, what connections psychoanalytic studies will reveal with other fields, especially with the development of speech and thought. You can only surmise the further significance of these connections when you hear that the mechanism of the dream structure is the model for the origin of neurotic symptoms.

I know too that we cannot as yet estimate the entire contribution that this work has made to psychology. We shall only indicate the new proofs that have been given of the existence of unconscious psychic acts—for such are the latent dream thoughts—and the unexpectedly wide approach to the understanding of the unconscious psychic life that dream interpretation opens up to us.

The time has probably come, however, to illustrate separately, by various little examples of dreams, the connected facts for which you have been prepared.

TWELFTH LECTURE: THE DREAM

Analysis of Sample Dreams

I HOPE you will not be disappointed if I again lay before you excerpts from dream analyses instead of inviting you to participate in the interpretation of a beautiful long dream. You will say that after so much preparation you ought to have this right, and that after the successful interpretation of so many thousands of dreams it should long ago have become possible to assemble a collection of excellent dream samples with which we could demonstrate all our assertions concerning dream-work and dream thoughts. Yes, but the difficulties which stand in the way of the fulfillment of your wish are too many.

First of all, I must confess to you that no one practices dream interpretation as his main occupation. When does one interpret dreams? Occasionally one can occupy himself with the dream of some friend, without any special purpose, or else he may work with his own dreams for a time in order to school himself in psychoanalytic method; most often, however, one deals with the dreams of nervous individuals who are undergoing analytic treatment. These latter dreams are excellent material, and in no way inferior to those of normal persons, but one is forced by the technique of the treatment to subordinate dream analysis to therapeutic aims and to pass over a large number of dreams after having derived something from them that is of use in the treatment. Many dreams we meet with during the treatment are, as a matter of fact, impossible of complete analysis. Since they spring from the total mass of psychic material which is still unknown to us, their understanding becomes possible only after the completion of the cure. Besides, to tell you such dreams would necessitate the disclosure of all the secrets concerning a neurosis. That will not do for us, since we have taken the dream as preparation for the study of the neuroses.

I know you would gladly leave this material, and would prefer to hear the dreams of healthy persons, or your own dreams explained. But that is impossible because of the content of these dreams. One can expose neither himself, nor another whose confidence he has won, so inconsiderately as would result from a thorough interpretation of his dreams—which, as you already know, refer to the most intimate things of his personality. In addition to this difficulty, caused by the nature of the material, there is another that must be considered when communicating a dream. You know the dream seems strange even to the dreamer himself, let alone to one who does not know the dreamer. Our literature is not poor in good and detailed dream analyses. I myself have published some in connection with case histories. Perhaps the best example of a dream interpretation is the one published by O. Rank, being two related dreams of a young girl, covering about two pages of print, the analysis covering seventy-six pages. I would need about a whole semester in order to take you through such a task. If we select a longer or more markedly distorted dream, we have to make so many explanations, we must make use of so many free associations and recollections, must go into so many bypaths, that a lecture on the subject would be entirely unsatisfactory and inconclusive. So I must ask you to be content with what is more easily obtained, with the recital of small bits of dreams of neurotic persons, in which we may be able to recognize this or that isolated fact. Dream symbols are the most easily demonstrable, and after them, certain peculiarities of regressive dream representations. This highly technical concept is explained in *The Interpretation of Dreams*, Chap. VII, Sec. (b) pp. 422 et seq.

I shall tell you why I considered each of the following dreams worthy of communication.

1. A dream, consisting of only two brief pictures: "*The dreamer's uncle is smoking a cigarette, although it is Saturday. A woman caresses him as though he were her child.*"

In commenting on the first picture, the dreamer (a Jew) remarks that his uncle is a pious man who never did, and never would do, anything so sinful as smoking on the Sabbath. As to the woman of the second picture, he has no free associations other than his mother. These two pictures or thoughts should obviously be brought into connection with each other, but how? Since he expressly rules out the reality of his uncle's action, then it is natural to interpolate an "if." "*If* my uncle, that pious man, should smoke a cigarette on Saturday, then I could also permit my mother's caresses." This obviously means that the mother's caresses are prohibited, in the same manner as is smoking on Saturday, to a pious Jew. You will recall, I told you that all relations between the dream thoughts disappear in the dream-work, that these relations are broken up into their raw material, and that it is the task of interpretation to re-interpolate the omitted connections.

2. Through my publications on dreams I have become, in certain respects, the public consultant on matters pertaining to dreams, and for many years I have been receiving communications from the most varied sources, in which dreams are related to me or presented to me for my judgment. I am of course grateful to all those persons who include with the story of the dream, enough material to make an interpretation possible, or who give such an interpretation themselves. It is in this category that the following dream

belongs, the dream of a Munich physician in the year 1910. I select it because it goes to show how impossible of understanding a dream generally is before the dreamer has given us what information he has about it. I suspect that at bottom you consider the ideal dream interpretation that in which one simply inserts the meaning of the symbols, and would like to lay aside the technique of free association to the dream elements. I wish to disabuse your minds of this harmful error.

"On July 13, 1910, toward morning, I dreamed *that I was bicycling down a street in Tübingen, when a brown Dachshund tore after me and caught me by the heel. A bit further on I get off, seat myself on a step, and begin to beat the beast, which has clenched its teeth tight. (I feel no discomfort from the biting or the whole scene.) Two elderly ladies are sitting opposite me and watching me with grins on their faces. Then I wake up and, as so often happens to me, the whole dream becomes perfectly clear to me in this moment of transition to the waking state.*"

Symbols are of little use in this case. The dreamer, however, informs us, "I lately fell in love with a girl, just from seeing her on the street, but had no means of becoming acquainted with her. The most pleasant means might have been the Dachshund, since I am a great lover of animals, and also felt that the girl was in sympathy with this characteristic." He also adds that he repeatedly interfered in the fights of scuffling dogs with great dexterity and frequently to the great amazement of the spectators. Thus we learn that the girl, who pleased him, was always accompanied by this particular dog. This girl, however, was disregarded in the manifest dream, and there remained only the dog which he associates with her. Perhaps the elderly ladies who simpered at him took the place of the girl. The remainder of what he tells us is not enough to explain this point. Riding a bicycle in the dream is a direct repetition of the remembered situation. He had never met the girl with the dog except when he was on his bicycle.

3. When anyone has lost a loved one, he produces dreams of a special sort for a long time afterward, dreams in which the knowledge of death enters into the most remarkable compromises with the desire to have the deceased alive again. At one time the deceased is dead and yet continues to live on because he does not know that he is dead, and would die completely only if he knew it; at another time he is half dead and half alive, and each of these conditions has its particular signs. One cannot simply label these dreams nonsense, for to come to life again is no more impossible in the dream than, for example, it is in the fairy story, in which it occurs as a very frequent fate. As far as I have been able to analyze such dreams, I have always found them to be capable of a sensible solution, but that the pious wish to recall the deceased to life goes about expressing itself by the oddest methods. Let me tell you such a dream, which seems queer and senseless enough, and analysis of which will show

you many of the points for which you have been prepared by our theoretical discussions. The dream is that of a man who had lost his father many years previously.

"Father is dead, but has been exhumed and looks badly. He goes on living, and the dreamer does everything to prevent him from noticing that fact." Then the dream goes on to other things, apparently irrelevant.

The father is dead, that we know. That he was exhumed is not really true, nor is the truth of the rest of the dream important. But the dreamer tells us that when he came back from his father's funeral, one of his teeth began to ache. He wanted to treat this tooth according to the Jewish precept, "If thy tooth offend thee, pluck it out," and betook himself to the dentist. But the latter said, "One does not simply pull a tooth out, one must have patience with it. I shall inject something to kill the nerve. Come again in three days and then I will take it out."

"This 'taking it out'," says the dreamer suddenly, "is the exhuming."

Is the dreamer right? It does not correspond exactly, only approximately, for the tooth is not taken out, but something that has died off is taken out of it. But after our other experiences we are probably safe in believing that the dream work is capable of such inaccuracies. It appears that the dreamer condensed, fused into one, his dead father and the tooth that was killed but retained. No wonder then, that in the manifest dream something senseless results, for it is impossible for everything that is said of the tooth to fit the father. What is it that serves as something intermediate between tooth and father and makes this condensation possible?

This interpretation must be correct, however, for the dreamer says that he is acquainted with the saying that when one dreams of losing a tooth it means that one is going to lose a member of his family.

We know that this popular interpretation is incorrect, or at least is correct only in a scurrilous sense. For that reason it is all the more surprising to find this theme thus touched upon in the background of other portions of the dream content.

Without any further urging, the dreamer now begins to tell of his father's illness and death as well as of his relations with him. The father was sick a long time, and his care and treatment cost him, the son, much money. And yet it was never too much for him, he never grew impatient, never wished it might end soon. He boasts of his true Jewish piety toward his father, of rigid adherence to the Jewish precepts. But are you not struck by a contradiction in the thoughts of the dream? He had identified tooth with father. As to the tooth he wanted to follow the Jewish precept that carries out its own judgment, "pull it out if it causes pain and annoyance." He had also been anxious to follow the precept of the law with regard to his father, which in this case, however, tells him to disregard trouble and expense, to take all the burdens upon himself and to let no hostile intent arise toward the object which causes the pain. Would not the agreement be far more compelling if he had really developed feelings toward his father similar to those about his sick tooth; that is, had he wished that a speedy death should put an end to that superfluous, painful and expensive existence?

I do not doubt that this was really his attitude toward his father during the latter's extended illness, and that his boastful assurances of filial piety were intended to distract his attention from these recollections. Under such circumstances, the death-wish directed toward the parent generally becomes active, and disguises itself in phrases of sympathetic consideration such as, "It would really be a blessed release for him." But note well that we have here overcome an obstacle in the latent dream thoughts themselves. The first part of these thoughts was surely unconscious only temporarily, that is to say, during the dream-work, while the inimical feelings toward the father might have been permanently unconscious, dating perhaps from childhood, occasionally slipping into consciousness, shyly and in disguise, during his father's illness. We can assert this with even greater certainty of other latent thoughts which have made unmistakable contributions to the dream content. To be sure, none of these inimical feelings toward the father can be discovered in the dream. But when we search a childhood history for the root of such enmity toward the father, we recollect that fear of the father arises because the latter, even in the earliest years, opposes the boy's sex activities, just as he is ordinarily forced to oppose them again, after puberty, for social motives. This relation to the father applies also to our dreamer; there had been mixed with his love for him much respect and fear, having its source in early sex intimidation.

From the onanism complex we can now explain the other parts of the manifest dream. "*He looks badly*" does, to be sure, allude to another remark of the dentist, that it looks badly to have a tooth missing in that place; but at the same time it refers to the "looking badly" by which the young man betrayed, or feared to betray, his excessive sexual activity during puberty. It was not without lightening his own heart that the dreamer transposed the bad looks from himself to his father in the manifest content, an inversion of the dream work with which you are familiar. "*He goes on living since then*," disguises itself with the wish to have him alive again as well as with the promise of the dentist that the tooth will be preserved. A very subtle phrase, however, is the following: "The dreamer does everything *to prevent him* (*the father*) *from noticing the fact*," a phrase calculated to lead us to conclude that he is dead. Yet the only meaningful conclusion is again drawn from the onanism complex, where it is a matter of course for the young man to do everything in order to hide his sex life from his father. Remember, in conclusion, that we were constantly forced to interpret the so-called toothache dreams as dreams dealing with the subject of onanism and the punishment that is feared.

You now see how this incomprehensible dream came into being, by the creation of a remarkable and misleading condensation, by the fact that all the ideas emerge from the midst of the latent thought process, and by the creation of ambiguous substitute formations for the most hidden and, at the time, most remote of these thoughts.

4. We have tried repeatedly to understand those prosaic and banal dreams which have nothing foolish or repulsive about them, but which cause us to ask: "Why do we dream such unimportant stuff?" So I shall give you a new example of this kind, three dreams belonging together, all of which were dreamed in the same night by a young woman.

(a). "*She it going through the hall of her house and strikes her head against the low-hanging chandelier, so that her head bleeds.*"

She has no reminiscence to contribute, nothing that really happened. The information she gives leads in quite another direction. "You know how badly my hair is falling out. Mother said to me yesterday, 'My child, if it goes on like this, you will have a head like the cheek of a buttock.'" Thus the head here stands for the other part of the body. We can understand the chandelier symbolically without other help; all objects that can be lengthened are symbols of the male organ. Thus the dream deals with a bleeding at the lower end of the body, which results from its collision with the male organ. This might still be ambiguous; her further associations show that it has to do with her belief that menstrual bleeding results from sexual intercourse with a man, a bit of sexual theory believed by many immature girls.

(b). "*She sees a deep hole in the vineyard which she knows was made by pulling out a tree.*" Herewith her remark that "*she misses the tree.*" She means that she did not see the tree in the dream, but the same phrase serves to express another thought which symbolic interpretation makes completely certain. The dream deals with another bit of the infantile sex theory, namely, with the belief that girls originally had the same genitals as boys and that the later conformation resulted from castration (pulling out of a tree).

(c). "*She is standing in front of the drawer of her writing table, with which she is so familiar that she knows immediately if anybody has been through it.*" The writing-table drawer, like every drawer, chest, or box, stands for the female genital. She knows that one can recognize from the genital the signs of sexual intercourse (and, as she thinks, even of any contact at all) and she has long been afraid of such a conviction. I believe that the accent in all these dreams is to be laid upon the idea of *knowing*. She is reminded of the time of her childish sexual investigations, the results of which made her quite proud at the time.

5. Again a little bit of symbolism. But this time I must first describe the psychic situation in a short preface. A man who spent the night with a woman describes his partner as one of those motherly natures whose desire for a child irresistibly breaks through during intercourse. The circumstances of their meeting, however, necessitated a precaution whereby the fertilizing discharge of semen is kept away from the womb. Upon awaking after this night, the woman tells the following dream:

"An officer with a red cap follows her on the street. She flees from him, runs up the staircase, and he follows after her. Breathlessly she reaches her apartment and slams and locks the door behind her. He remains outside and as she looks through a peephole she sees him sitting outside on a bench and weeping."

You undoubtedly recognize in the pursuit by an officer with a red cap, and the breathless stair climbing, the representation of the sexual act. The fact that the dreamer locks herself in against the pursuer may serve as an example of that inversion which is so frequently used in dreams, for in reality it was the man who withdrew before the completion of the act. In the same way her grief has been transposed to the partner, it is he who weeps in the dream, whereby the discharge of the semen is also indicated.

You must surely have heard that in psychoanalysis it is always maintained that all dreams have a sexual meaning. Now you yourselves are in a position to form a judgment as to the incorrectness of this reproach. You have become acquainted with the wish-fulfillment dreams, which deal with the satisfying of the plainest needs, of hunger, of thirst, of longing for freedom, the dreams of convenience and of impatience and likewise the purely covetous and egoistic dreams. But that the markedly distorted dreams preponderantly—though again not exclusively—give expression to sex wishes, is a fact you may certainly keep in mind as one of the results of psychoanalytical research.

6. I have a special motive for piling up examples of the use of symbols in dreams. At our first meeting I complained of how hard it is, when lecturing on psychoanalysis, to demonstrate the facts in order to awaken conviction; and you very probably have come to agree with me since then. But the various assertions of psychoanalysis are so closely linked that one's conviction can easily extend from one point to a larger part of the whole. We might say of psychoanalysis that if we give it our little finger it promptly demands the whole hand. Anyone who was convinced by the explanation of errors can no longer logically disbelieve in all the rest of psychoanalysis. A second equally accessible point of approach is furnished by dream symbolism. I shall give you a dream, already published, of a peasant woman, whose husband is a watchman and who has certainly never heard anything about dream symbolism and psychoanalysis. You may then judge for yourselves whether

its explanation with the help of sex symbols can be called arbitrary and forced.

"Then someone broke into her house and she called in fright for a watchman. But the latter had gone companionably into a church together with two 'beauties.' A number of steps led up to the church. Behind the church was a hill, and on its crest a thick forest. The watchman was fitted out with a helmet, gorget and a cloak. He had a full brown beard. The two were going along peacefully with the watchman, had sack-like aprons bound around their hips. There was a path from the church to the hill. This was overgrown on both sides with grass and underbrush that kept getting thicker and that became a regular forest on the crest of the hill."

You will recognize the symbols without any difficulty. The male genital is represented by a trinity of persons, the female by a landscape with a chapel, hill and forest. Again you encounter steps as the symbol of the sexual act. That which is called a hill in the dream has the same name in anatomy, namely, *mons veneris*, the mount of Venus.

7. I have another dream which can be solved by means of inserting symbols, a dream that is remarkable and convincing because the dreamer himself translated all the symbols, even though he had had no preliminary knowledge of dream interpretation. This situation is very unusual and the conditions essential to its occurrence are not clearly known.

"He is going for a walk with his father in some place which must be the Prater (main street of Vienna) for one can see the rotunda and before it a smaller building to which is anchored a captive balloon, which, however, seems fairly slack. His father asks him what all that is for; he wonders at it himself but explains it to his father. Then they come to a courtyard in which there lies spread out a big sheet of metal. His father wants to break off a big piece of it for himself but first looks about him to see if anyone might see him. He says to him that all he needs to do is to tell the inspector and then he can take some without more ado. There are steps leading from this courtyard down into a pit, the walls of which are upholstered with some soft material rather like a leather arm chair. At the end of this pit is a longish platform and then a new pit begins...."

The dreamer himself interprets as follows: "The rotunda is my genital, the balloon in front of it is my penis, of whose slackness I have been complaining." Thus one may translate in more detail, that the rotunda is the posterior—a part of the body which the child regularly considers as part of the genital—while the smaller building before it is the scrotum. In the dream his father asks him what all that is for; that is to say, he asks the object and function of the genitals. It is easy to turn this situation around so that the dreamer is the one who does the asking. Since no such questioning of the father ever took place in real life, we must think of the thought of this dream as a wish or consider it in the light of a supposition, "If I had asked father for sexual enlightenment." We will find the continuation of this idea in another place shortly.

The courtyard, in which the sheet metal lies spread out, is not to be considered primarily as symbolical but refers to the father's place of business. For reasons of discretion I have substituted the "sheet metal" for another material with which the father deals, without changing anything in the literal wording of the dream. The dreamer entered his father's business and took great offense at the rather dubious practices upon which the profits depended to a large extent. For this reason the continuation of the above idea of the dream might be expressed as "if I had asked him, he would only have deceived me as he deceives his customers." The dreamer himself gives us the second meaning of "breaking off the metal," which serves to represent the commercial dishonesty. He says it means masturbation. Not only have we long since become familiar with this symbol, but the fact also is in agreement. The secrecy of masturbation is expressed by means of its opposite—"It can be safely done openly." Again our expectations are fulfilled by the fact that masturbatory activity is referred to as the father's, just as the questioning was in the first scene of the dream. Upon being questioned he immediately gives the interpretation of the pit as the vagina on account of the soft upholstering of its walls. I will add arbitrarily that the "going down" like the more usual "going up" is meant to describe the sexual intercourse in the vagina.

Such details as the fact that the first pit ends in a platform and then a new one begins, he explains himself as having been taken from his own history. He practiced intercourse for a while, then gave it up on account of inhibitions, and now hopes to be able to resume it as a result of the treatment.

8. The two following dreams are those of a foreigner, of very polygamous tendencies, and I give them to you as proof for the claim that one's ego appears in every dream, even in those in which it is disguised in the manifest content. The trunks in the dream are a symbol for woman.

(a). "*He is to take a trip, his luggage is placed on a carriage to be taken to the station, and there are many trunks piled up, among which are two big black ones like sample trunks. He says, consolingly, to someone, 'Well, they are only going as far as the station with us.'*"

In reality he does travel with a great deal of luggage, but he also brings many tales of women with him when he comes for treatment. The two black trunks stand for two dark women who play the chief part in his life at present. One of them wanted to travel to Vienna after him, but he telegraphed her not to, upon my advice.

(b). A scene at the customs house: "*A fellow traveler opens his trunk and says indifferently while puffing a cigarette, 'There's nothing in here.' The customs official seems to believe him but delves into the trunk once more and finds something particularly forbidden. The traveler then says resignedly, 'Well, there's no help for it.'"*

He himself is the traveler, I the customs official. Though otherwise very frank in his confessions, he has on this occasion tried to conceal from me a new relationship which he had struck up with a lady whom he was justified in believing that I knew. The painful situation of being convicted of this is transposed into a strange person so that he himself apparently is not present in the dream.

9. The following is an example of a symbol which I have not yet mentioned: *"He meets his sister in company with two friends who are themselves sisters. He extends his hand to both of them but not to his sister."*

This is no allusion to a real occurrence. His thoughts instead lead him back to a time when his observations made him wonder why a girl's breasts develop so late. The two sisters, therefore, are the breasts. He would have liked to touch them if only it had not been his sister.

10. Let me add an example of a symbol of death in a dream:

"He is walking with two persons whose name he knows but has forgotten. By the time he is awake, over a very high, steep iron bridge. Suddenly the two people are gone and he sees a ghostly man with a cap, and clad in white. He asks this man whether he is the telegraph messenger.... No. Or is he a coachman? No. Then he goes on," and even in the dream he is in great fear. After waking he continues the dream by a phantasy in which the iron bridge suddenly breaks, and he plunges into the abyss.

When the dreamer emphasizes the fact that certain individuals in a dream are unknown, that he has forgotten their names, they are generally persons standing in very close relationship to the dreamer. This dreamer has two sisters; if it be true, as his dream indicates, that he wished these two dead, then it would only be justice if the fear of death fell upon him for so doing. In connection with the telegraph messenger he remarks that such people always bring bad news. Judged by his uniform he might also have been the lamplighter, who, however, also extinguishes the lamps—in other words, as the spirit of death extinguishes the flame of life. The coachman reminds him of Uhland's poem of King Karl's ocean voyage and also of a dangerous lake trip with two companions in which he played the role of the king in the poem. In connection with the iron bridge he remembers a recent accident and the stupid saying "Life is a suspension bridge."

11. The following may serve as another example of the representation of death in a dream: *"An unknown man leaves a black bordered visiting card for him."*

12. The following dream will interest you for several reasons, though it is one arising from a neurotic condition among other things:

"*He is traveling in a train. The train stops in an open field. He thinks it means that there is going to be an accident, that he must save himself, and he goes through all the compartments of the train and strikes dead everyone whom he meets, conductors, engine drivers, etc.*"

In connection with this he tells a story that one of his friends told him. An insane man was being transported in a private compartment in a certain place in Italy, but through some mistake another traveler was put in the same compartment. The insane man murdered his fellow passenger. Thus he identifies himself with this insane person and bases his right so to do upon a compulsive idea which was then torturing him, namely, he must "do away with all persons who knew of his failings." But then he himself finds a better motivation which gave rise to the dream. The day before, in the theatre, he again saw the girl whom he had expected to marry but whom he had left because she had given him cause for jealousy. With a capacity for intense jealousy such as he has, he would really be insane if he married. In other words, he considers her so untrustworthy that out of jealousy he would have to strike dead all the persons who stood in his way. Going through a series of rooms, of compartments in this case, we have already learned to recognize as the symbol of marriage (the opposite of monogamy).

In connection with the train stopping in the open country and his fear of an accident, he tells the following: Once, when he was traveling in a train and it came to a sudden stop outside of a station, a young lady in the compartment remarked that perhaps there was going to be a collision, and that in that case the best precaution would be to pull one's legs up. But this "legs up" had also played a role in the many walks and excursions into the open which he had taken with the girl in that happy period in their first love. Thus it is a new argument for the idea that he would have to be crazy in order to marry her now. But from my knowledge of the situation I can assume with certainty that the wish to be as crazy as that nevertheless exists in him.

THIRTEENTH LECTURE: THE DREAM

Archaic Remnants and Infantilism in the Dream

LET us revert to our conclusion that the dream-work, under the influence of the dream censorship, transforms the latent dream thoughts into some other form of expression. The latent thoughts are no other than the conscious thoughts known to us in our waking hours; the new mode of expression is incomprehensible to us because of its many-sided features. We have said it extends back to conditions of our intellectual development which we have long progressed beyond, to the language of pictures, the symbol-representations, perhaps to those conditions which were in force before the development of our language of thought. So we called the mode of expression of the dream-work the archaic or regressive.

You may conclude that as a result of the deeper study of the dream-work we gain valuable information about the rather unknown beginnings of our intellectual development. I trust this will be true, but this work has not, up to the present time, been undertaken. The antiquity into which the dream-work carries us back is of a double aspect, firstly, the individual antiquity, childhood; and, secondly (in so far as every individual in his childhood lives over again in some more or less abbreviated manner the entire development of the human race), also this antiquity, the phylogenetic. That we shall be able to differentiate which part of the latent psychic proceeding has its source in the individual, and which part in the phylogenetic antiquity is not improbable. In this connection it appears to me, for example, that the symbolic relations which the individual has never learned are ground for the belief that they should be regarded as a phylogenetic inheritance.

However, this is not the only archaic characteristic of the dream. You probably all know from your own experiences the peculiar amnesia, that is, loss of memory, concerning childhood. I mean the fact that the first years, to the fifth, sixth or eighth, have not left the same traces in our memory as have later experiences. One meets with individual persons, to be sure, who can boast of a continuous memory from the very beginning to the present day, but the other condition, that of a gap in the memory, is far more frequent. I believe we have not laid enough stress on this fact. The child is able to speak well at the age of two, it soon shows that it can become adjusted to the most complicated psychic situations, and makes remarks which years later are retold to it, but which it has itself entirely forgotten. Besides, the memory in the early years is more facile, because it is less burdened than in later years. Nor is there any reason for considering the memory-function as a particularly high or difficult psychic performance; in fact, the contrary is true, and you can find a good memory in persons who stand very low intellectually.

As a second peculiarity closely related to the first, I must point out that certain well-preserved memories, for the most part formatively experienced, stand forth in this memory-void which surrounds the first years of childhood and do not justify this hypothesis. Our memory deals selectively with its later materials, with impressions which come to us in later life. It retains the important and discards the unimportant. This is not true of the retained childhood memories. They do not bespeak necessarily important experiences of childhood, not even such as from the viewpoint of the child need appear of importance. They are often so banal and intrinsically so meaningless that we ask ourselves in wonder why just these details have escaped being forgotten. I once endeavored to approach the riddle of childhood amnesia and the interrupted memory remnants with the help of analysis, and I arrived at the conclusion that in the case of the child, too, only the important has remained in the memory, except that by means of the process of condensation already known to you, and especially by means of distortion, the important is represented in the memory by something that appears unimportant. For this reason I have called these childhood memories "disguise-memories," memories used to conceal; by means of careful analysis one is able to develop out of them everything that is forgotten.

In psychoanalytic treatment we are regularly called upon to fill out the infantile memory gaps, and in so far as the cure is to any degree successful, we are able again to bring to light the content of the childhood years thus clouded in forgetfulness. These impressions have never really been forgotten, they have only been inaccessible, latent, have belonged to the unconscious. But sometimes they bob up out of the unconscious spontaneously, and, as a matter of fact, this is what happens in dreams. It is apparent that the dream life knows how to find the entrance to these latent, infantile experiences. Beautiful examples of this occur in literature, and I myself can present such an example. I once dreamed in a certain connection of a person who must have performed some service for me, and whom I clearly saw. He was a one-eyed man, short in stature, stout, his head deeply sunk into his neck. I concluded from the content that he was a physician. Luckily I was able to ask my mother, who was still living, how the physician in my birth-place, which I left when I was three years old, looked, and I learned from her that he had one eye, was short and stout, with his head sunk into his neck, and also learned at what forgotten mishap he had been of service to me. This control over the forgotten material of childhood years is, then, a further archaic tendency of the dream.

The same information may be made use of in another of the puzzles that have presented themselves to us. You will recall how astonished people were when we came to the conclusion that the stimuli which gave rise to dreams were extremely bad and licentious sexual desires which have made dream-censorship and dream-distortion necessary. After we have interpreted such a dream for the dreamer and he, in the most favorable circumstances does not attack the interpretation itself, he almost always asks the question whence such a wish comes, since it seems foreign to him and he feels conscious of just the opposite sensations. We need not hesitate to point out this origin. These evil wish-impulses have their origin in the past, often in a past which is not too far away. It can be shown that at one time they were known and conscious, even if they no longer are so. The woman, whose dream is interpreted to mean that she would like to see her seventeen-year old daughter dead, discovers under our guidance that she in fact at one time entertained this wish. The child is the fruit of an unhappy marriage, which early ended in a separation. Once, while the child was still in the womb, and after a tense scene with her husband, she beat her body with her fists in a fit of anger, in order to kill the child. How many mothers who to-day love their children tenderly, perhaps too tenderly, received them unwillingly, and at the time wished that the life within them would not develop further; indeed, translated this wish into various actions, happily harmless. The later death-wish against some loved one, which seems so strange, also has its origin in early phases of the relationship to that person.

The father, the interpretation of whose dream shows that he wishes for the death of his eldest and favorite child, must be reminded of the fact that at one time this wish was no stranger to him. While the child was still a suckling, this man, who was unhappy in his choice of a wife, often thought that if the little being that meant nothing to him would die, he would again be free, and would make better use of his freedom. A like origin may be found for a large number of similar hate impulses; they are recollections of something that belonged to the past, were once conscious and played their parts in the psychic life. You will wish to conclude therefrom that such wishes and such dreams cannot occur if such changes in the relationship to a person have not taken place; if such relationship was always of the same character. I am ready to admit this, only wish to warn you that you are to take into consideration not the exact terms of the dream, but the meaning thereof according to its interpretation. It may happen that the manifest dream of the death of some loved person has only made use of some frightful mask, that it really means something entirely different, or that the loved person serves as a concealing substitute for some other.

But the same circumstances will call forth another, more difficult question. You say: "Granted this death wish was present at some time or other, and is substantiated by memory, yet this is no explanation. It is long outlived, to-day it can be present only in the unconscious and as an empty, emotionless memory, but not as a strong impulse. Why should it be recalled by the dream at all!" This question is justified. The attempt to answer it would lead us far afield and necessitate taking up a position in one of the most important points of dream study. But I must remain within the bounds of our discussion and practice restraint. Prepare yourselves for the temporary abstention. Let us be satisfied with the circumstantial proof that this outlived wish can be shown to act as a dream stimulator and let us continue the investigation to see whether or not other evil wishes admit of the same derivation out of the past.

Let us continue with the removal or death-wish which most frequently can be traced back to the unbounded egoism of the dreamer. Such a wish can very often be shown to be the inciting cause of the dream. As often as someone has been in our way in life—and how often must this happen in the complicated relationships of life—the dream is ready to do away with him, be he father, mother, brother, sister, spouse, etc. We have wondered sufficiently over this evil tendency of human nature, and certainly were not predisposed to accept the authenticity of this result of dream interpretation without question. After it has once been suggested to us to seek the origin of such wishes in the past, we disclose immediately the period of the individual past in which such egoism and such wish-impulses, even as directed against those closest to the dreamer, are no longer strangers. It is just in these first years of childhood which later are hidden by amnesia, that this egoism frequently shows itself in most extreme form, and from which regular but clear tendencies thereto, or real remnants thereof, show themselves. For the child loves itself first, and later learns to love others, to sacrifice something of its ego for another. Even those persons whom the child seems to love from the very beginning, it loves at the outset because it has need of them, cannot do without them, in others words, out of egoistical motives. Not until later does the love impulse become independent of egoism. *In brief, egoism has taught the child to love.*

In this connection it is instructive to compare the child's regard for his brothers and sisters with that which he has for his parents. The little child does not necessarily love his brothers and sisters, often, obviously, he does not love them at all. There is no doubt that in them he hates his rivals and it is known how frequently this attitude continues for many years until maturity, and even beyond, without interruption. Often enough this attitude is superseded by a more tender feeling, or rather let us say glossed over, but the hostile feeling appears regularly to have been the earlier. It is most noticeable in children of from two and one-half to four or five years of age, when a new little brother or sister arrives. The latter is usually received in a far from friendly manner. Expressions such as "I don't want him! Let the stork take him away again," are very usual. Subsequently every opportunity is made use of to disparage the new arrival, and even attempts to do him bodily harm, direct attacks, are not unheard of. If the difference in age is less, the child learns of the existence of the rival with intense psychic activity, and accommodates himself to the new situation. If the difference in age is greater, the new child may awaken certain sympathies as an interesting object, as a sort of living doll, and if the difference is eight years or more, motherly impulses, especially in the case of girls, may come into play. But to be truthful, when we disclose in a dream the wish for the death of a mother or sister we need seldom find it puzzling and may trace its origin easily to early childhood, often enough, also, to the propinquity of later years.

Probably no nurseries are free from mighty conflicts among the inhabitants. The motives are rivalry for the love of the parents, articles owned in common, the room itself. The hostile impulses are called forth by older as well as younger brothers and sisters. I believe it was Bernard Shaw who said: "If there is anyone who hates a young English lady more than does her mother, it is her elder sister." There is something about this saying, however, that arouses our antipathy. We can, at a pinch, understand hatred of brothers and sisters, and rivalry among them, but how may feelings of hatred force their way into the relationship between daughter and mother, parents and children?

This relationship is without doubt the more favorable, even when looked at from the viewpoint of the child. This is in accord with our expectation; we find it much more offensive for love between parents and children to be lacking than for love between brothers and sisters. We have, so to speak, made something holy in the first instance which in the other case we permitted to remain profane. But daily observation can show us how frequently the feelings between parents and their grown children fail to come up to the ideal established by society, how much enmity exists and would find expression did not accumulations of piety and of tender impulse hold them back. The motives for this are everywhere known and disclose a tendency to separate those of the same sex, daughter from mother, father from son. The daughter finds in her mother the authority that hems in her will and that is entrusted with the task of causing her to carry out the abstention from sexual liberty which society demands; in certain cases also she is the rival who objects to being displaced. The same type of thing occurs in a more glaring manner between father and son. To the son the father is the embodiment of every social restriction, borne with such great opposition; the father bars the way to freedom of will, to early sexual satisfaction, and where there is family property held in common, to the enjoyment thereof. Impatient waiting for the death of the father grows to heights approximating tragedy in the case of a successor to the throne. Less strained is the relationship between father and daughter, mother and son. The latter affords the purest examples of an unalterable tenderness, in no way disturbed by egoistical considerations.

Why do I speak of these things, so banal and so well known? Because there is an unmistakable disposition to deny their significance in life, and to set forth the ideal demanded by society as a fulfilled thing much oftener than it really is fulfilled. But it is preferable for psychology to speak the truth, rather than that this task should be left to the cynic. In any event, this denial refers only to actual life. The arts of narrative and dramatic poetry are still free to make use of the motives that result from a disturbance of this ideal.

It is not to be wondered at that in the case of a large number of people the dream discloses the wish for the removal of the parents, especially the parent of the same sex. We may conclude that it is also present during waking hours, and that it becomes conscious even at times when it is able to mask itself behind another motive, as in the case of the dreamer's sympathy for his father's unnecessary sufferings in example 3. It is seldom that the enmity alone controls the relationship; much more often it recedes behind more tender impulses, by which it is suppressed, and must wait until a dream isolates it. That which the dream shows us in enlarged form as a result of such isolation, shrinks together again after it has been properly docketed in its relation to life as a result of our interpretation (H. Sachs). But we also find this dream wish in places where it has no connection with life, and where the adult, in his waking hours, would never recognize it. The reason for this is that the deepest and most uniform motive for becoming unfriendly, especially between persons of the same sex, has already made its influence felt in earliest childhood.

I mean the love rivalry, with the especial emphasis of the sex character. The son, even as a small child, begins to develop an especial tenderness for his mother, whom he considers as his own property, and feels his father to be a rival who puts into question his individual possession. In the same manner the daughter sees in her mother a disturbing element in her tender relationship with her father, and who occupies a position that she could very well fill herself. One learns from these observations to what early years these ideas extend back—ideas which we designate as the *Oedipus-complex*, because this myth realizes with a very slightly weakened effect the two extreme wishes which grow out of the situation of the son—to kill his father and take his mother to wife. I do not wish to maintain that the Oedipus-complex covers entirely the relation of the child to its parents; this relation can be much more complicated. Furthermore, the Oedipus-complex is more or less well-developed; it may even experience a reversal, but it is a customary and very important factor in the psychic life of the child; and one tends rather to underestimate than to overestimate its influence and the developments which may follow from it. In addition, children frequently react to the Oedipus-idea through stimulation by the parents, who in the placing of their affection are often led by sex-differences, so that the father prefers the daughter, the mother the son; or again, where the marital affection has cooled, and this love is substituted for the outworn love.

One cannot maintain that the world was very grateful to psychoanalytic research for its discovery of the Oedipus-complex. On the contrary, it called forth the strongest resistance on the part of adults; and persons who had neglected to take part in denying this proscribed or tabooed feeling-relationship later made good the omission by taking all value from the complex through false interpretations. According to my unchanged conviction there is nothing to deny and nothing to make more palatable. One should accept the fact, recognized by the Greek myth itself, as inevitable destiny. On the other hand, it is interesting that this Oedipus-complex, cast out of life, was yielded up to poetry and given the freest play. O. Rank has shown in a careful study how this very Oedipus-complex has supplied dramatic literature with a large number of motives in unending variations, derivations and disguises, also in distorted forms such as we recognize to be the work of a censor. We may also ascribe this Oedipus-complex to those dreamers who were so fortunate as to escape in later life these conflicts with their parents, and intimately associated therewith we find what we call the *castration complex*, the reaction to sexual intimidation or restriction, ascribed to the father, of early infantile sexuality.

By applying our former researches to the study of the psychic life of the child, we may expect to find that the origin of other forbidden dream-wishes, of excessive sexual impulses, may be explained in the same manner. Thus we are moved to study the development of sex-life in the child also, and we discover the following from a number of sources: In the first place, it is a mistake to deny that the child has a sexual life, and to take it for granted that sexuality commences with the ripening of the genitals at the time of puberty. On the contrary—the child has from the very beginning a sexual life rich in content and differing in numerous respects from that which is later considered normal. What we call "perverse" in the life of the adult, differs from the normal in the following respects: first, in disregard for the dividing line of species (the gulf between man and animal); second, being insensible to the conventional feeling of disgust; third, the incest-limitation (being prohibited from seeking sexual satisfaction with near blood-relations); fourth, homosexuality, and fifth, transferring the role of the genitals to other organs and other parts of the body. None of these limitations exist in the beginning, but are gradually built up in the course of development and education. The little child is free from them. He knows no unbridgeable chasm between man and animal; the arrogance with which man distinguishes himself from the animal is a later acquisition. In the beginning he is not disgusted at the sight of excrement, but slowly learns to be so disgusted under the pressure of education; he lays no special stress on the difference between the sexes, rather accredits to both the same genital formation; he directs his earliest sexual desires and his curiosity toward those persons closest to him, and who are dear to him for various reasons—his parents, brothers and sisters, nurses; and finally, you may observe in him that which later breaks through again, raised now to a love attraction, viz., that he does not expect pleasure from his sexual organs alone, but that many other parts of the body portray the same sensitiveness, are the media of analogous sensations, and are able to play the role of the genitals. The child may, then, be called "polymorphus perverse," and if he makes but slight use of all these impulses, it is, on the one hand, because of their lesser intensity as compared to later life, and on the other hand, because the bringing up of the child immediately and energetically suppresses all his sexual expressions. This suppression continues in theory, so to say, since the grown-ups are careful to control part of the childish sex-expressions, and to disguise another part by misrepresenting its sexual nature until they can deny the whole business. These are often the same persons who discourse violently against all the sexual faults of the child and then at the writing table defend the sexual purity of the same children. Where children are left to themselves or are under the influence of corruption, they often are capable of really conspicuous performances of perverse sexual activity. To be sure, the grown-ups are right in looking upon these things as "childish performances," as "play," for the child is not to be judged as mature and answerable either before the bar of custom or before the law, but these things do exist, they have their significance as indications of innate characteristics as well as causes and furtherances of later developments, they give us an insight into childhood sex-life and thereby into the sex life of man. When we rediscover in the background of our distorted dreams all these perverse wish-impulses, it means only that the dream has in this field traveled back to the infantile condition.

Especially noteworthy among these forbidden wishes are those of incest, i.e., those directed towards sexual intercourse with parents and brothers and sisters. You know what antipathy society feels toward such intercourse, or at least pretends to feel, and what weight is laid on the prohibitions directed against it. The most monstrous efforts have been made to explain this fear of incest. Some have believed that it is due to evolutionary foresight on the part of nature, which is psychically represented by this prohibition, because inbreeding would deteriorate the race-character; others maintained that because of having lived together since early childhood the sexual desire is diverted from the persons under consideration. In both cases, furthermore, the incest-avoidance would be automatically assured, and it would be difficult to understand the need of strict prohibitions, which rather point to the presence of a strong desire. Psychoanalytic research has incontrovertibly shown that the incestuous love choice is rather the first and most customary choice, and that not until later is there any resistance, the source of which probably is to be found in the individual psychology.

Let us sum up what our plunge into child psychology has given us toward the understanding of the dream. We found not only that the materials of forgotten childhood experiences are accessible to the dream, but we saw also that the psychic life of children, with all its peculiarities, its egoism, its incestuous love-choice, etc., continues, for the purposes of the dream, in the unconscious, and that the dream nightly leads us back to this infantile stage. Thus it becomes more certain *that the unconscious in our psychic life is the infantile*. The estranging impression that there is so much evil in man, begins to weaken. This frightful evil is simply the original, primitive, infantile side of psychic life, which we may find in action in children, which we overlook partly because of the slightness of its dimensions, partly because it is lightly considered, since we demand no ethical heights of the child. Since the dream regresses to this stage, it seems to have made apparent the evil that lies in us.

But it is only a deceptive appearance by which we have allowed ourselves to be frightened. We are not so evil as we might suspect from the interpretation of dreams.

If the evil impulses of the dream are merely infantilism, a return to the beginnings of our ethical development, since the dream simply makes children of us again in thinking and in feeling, we need not be ashamed of these evil dreams if we are reasonable. But being reasonable is only a part of psychic life. Many things are taking place there that are not reasonable, and so it happens that we are ashamed of such dreams, and unreasonably. We turn them over to the dream-censorship, are ashamed and angry if one of these dreams has in some unusual manner succeeded in penetrating into consciousness in an undistorted form, so that we must recognize it—in fact, we are at times just as ashamed of the distorted dream as we would be if we understood it. Just think of the scandalized opinion of the fine old lady about her uninterpreted dream of "services of love." The problem is not yet solved, and it is still possible that upon further study of the evil in the dream we shall come to some other decision and arrive at another valuation of human nature.

As a result of the whole investigation we grasp two facts, which, however, disclose only the beginnings of new riddles, new doubts. First: the regression of dream-work is not only formal, it is also of greater import. It not only translates our thoughts into a primitive form of expression, but it reawakens the peculiarities of our primitive psychic life, the ancient predominance of the ego, the earliest impulses of our sexual life, even our old intellectual property, if we may consider the symbolic relations as such. And second: We must accredit all these infantilisms which once were governing, and solely governing, to the unconscious, about which our ideas now change and are broadened. Unconscious is no longer a name for what is at that time latent, the unconscious is an especial psychic realm with wish-impulses of its own, with its own method of expression and with a psychic mechanism peculiar to itself, all of which ordinarily are not in force. But the latent dream-thoughts, which we have solved by means of the dream-interpretation, are not of this realm. They are much more nearly the same as any we may have thought in our waking hours. Still they are unconscious; how does one solve this contradiction? We begin to see that a distinction must be made. Something that originates in our conscious life, and that shares its characteristics—we call it the day-remnants—combines in the dream-fabrication with something else out of the realm of the unconscious. Between these two parts the dream-work completes itself. The influencing of the day-remnants by the unconscious necessitates regression. This is the deepest insight into the nature of the dream that we are able to attain without having searched through further psychic realms. The time will soon come, however, when we shall clothe the unconscious character of the latent dream-thought with another name, which shall differentiate it from the unconscious out of the realm of the infantile.

We may, to be sure, propound the question: what forces the psychological activity during sleep to such regression? Why do not the sleep disturbing psychic stimuli do the job without it? And if they must, because of the dream censorship, disguise themselves through old forms of expression which are no longer comprehensible, what is the use of giving new life to old, long-outgrown psychic stimuli, wishes and character types, that is, why the material regression in addition to the formal? The only satisfactory answer would be this, that only in this manner can a dream be built up, that dynamically the dream-stimulus can be satisfied only in this way. But for the time being we have no right to give such an answer.

FOURTEENTH LECTURE: THE DREAM

Wish Fulfillment

MAY I bring to your attention once more the ground we have already covered? How, when we met with dream distortion in the application of our technique, we decided to leave it alone for the time being, and set out to obtain decisive information about the nature of the dream by way of infantile dreams? How, then, armed with the results of this investigation, we attacked dream distortion directly and, I trust, in some measure overcame it? But we must remind ourselves that the results we found along the one way and along the other do not fit together as well as might be. It is now our task to put these two results together and balance them against one another.

From both sources we have seen that the dream-work consists essentially in the transposition of thoughts into an hallucinatory experience. How that can take place is puzzling enough, but it is a problem of general psychology with which we shall not busy ourselves here. We have learned from the dreams of children that the purpose of the dream-work is the satisfaction of one of the sleep-disturbing psychic stimuli by means of a wish fulfillment. We were unable to make a similar statement concerning distorted dreams, until we knew how to interpret them. But from the very beginning we expected to be able to bring the distorted dreams under the same viewpoint as the infantile. The earliest fulfillment of this expectation led us to believe that as a matter of fact all dreams are the dreams of children and that they all work with infantile materials, through childish psychic stimuli and mechanics. Since we consider that we have conquered dream-distortion, we must continue the investigation to see whether our hypothesis of wish-fulfillment holds good for distorted dreams also.

We very recently subjected a number of dreams to interpretation, but left wish-fulfillment entirely out of consideration. I am convinced that the question again and again occurred to you: "What about wish-fulfillment, which ostensibly is the goal of dream-work?" This question is important. It was, in fact, the question of our lay-critics. As you know, humanity has an instinctive antagonism toward intellectual novelties. The expression of such a novelty should immediately be reduced to its narrowest limits, if possible, comprised in a commonplace phrase. Wish-fulfillment has become that phrase for the new dream-science. The layman asks: "Where is the wish-fulfillment?" Immediately, upon having heard that the dream is supposed to be a wish-fulfillment, and indeed, by the very asking of the question, he answers it with a denial. He is at once reminded of countless dream-experiences of his own, where his aversion to the dream was enormous, so that the proposition of psychoanalytic dream-science seems very improbable to him. It is a simple matter to answer the layman that wish-fulfillment cannot be apparent in distorted dreams, but must be sought out, so that it is not recognized until the dream is interpreted. We know, too, that the wishes in these distorted dreams are prohibited wishes, are wishes rejected by the censor and that their existence lit the very cause of the dream distortion and the reason for the intrusion of the dream censor. But it is hard to convince the lay-critic that one may not seek the wish-fulfillment in the dream before the dream has been interpreted. This is continually forgotten. His sceptical attitude toward the theory of wish-fulfillment is really nothing more than a consequence of dream-censorship, a substitute and a result of the denial of this censored dream-wish.

To be sure, even we shall find it necessary to explain to ourselves why there are so many dreams of painful content, and especially dreams of fear. We see here, for the first time, the problem of the affects in the dream, a problem worthy of separate investigation, but which unfortunately cannot be considered here. If the dream is a wish-fulfillment, painful experiences ought to be impossible in the dream; in that the lay-critics apparently are right. But three complications, not thought of by them, must be taken into consideration.

First: It may be that the dream work has not been successful in creating a wish-fulfillment, so that a part of the painful effect of the dream-thought is left over for the manifest dream. Analysis should then show that these thoughts were far more painful even than the dream which was built out of them. This much may be proved in each instance. We admit, then, that the dream work has not achieved its purpose any more than the drink-dream due to the thirst-stimulus has achieved its purpose of satisfying the thirst. One remains thirsty, and must wake up in order to drink. But it was a real dream, it sacrificed nothing of its nature. We must say: "Although strength be lacking, let us praise the will to do." The clearly recognizable intention, at least, remains praiseworthy. Such cases of miscarriage are not unusual. A contributory cause is this, that it is so much more difficult for the dream work to change affect into content in its own sense; the affects often show great resistance, and thus it happens that the dream work has worked the painful content of the dream-thoughts over into a wish-fulfillment, while the painful affect continues in its unaltered form. Hence in dreams of this type the affect does not fit the content at all, and our critics may say the dream is so little a wish-fulfillment that a harmless content may be experienced as painful. In answer to this unintelligible remark we say that the wish-fulfillment tendency in the dream-work appears most prominent, because isolated, in just such dreams. The error is due to the fact that he who does not know neurotics imagines the connection between content and affect as all too intimate, and cannot, therefore, grasp the fact that a content may be altered without any corresponding change in the accompanying affect-expression.

A second, far more important and more extensive consideration, equally disregarded by the layman, is the following: A wish-fulfillment certainly must bring pleasure—but to whom? Naturally, to him who has the wish. But we know from the dreamer that he stands in a very special relationship to his wishes. He casts them aside, censors them, he will have none of them. Their fulfillment gives him no pleasure, but only the opposite. Experience then shows that this opposite, which must still be explained, appears in the form of fear. The dreamer in his relation to his dream-wishes can be compared only to a combination of two persons bound together by some strong common quality. Instead of further explanations I shall give you a well-known fairy tale, in which you will again find the relationships I have mentioned. A good fairy promises a poor couple, husband and wife, to fulfill their first three wishes. They are overjoyed, and determine to choose their three wishes with great care. But the woman allows herself to be led astray by the odor of cooking sausages emanating from the next cottage, and wishes she had a couple of such sausages. Presto! they are there. This is the first wish-fulfillment. Now the husband becomes angry, and in his bitterness wishes that the sausages might hang from the end of her nose. This, too, is accomplished, and the sausages cannot be removed from their new location. So this is the second wish-fulfillment, but the wish is that of the husband. The wife is very uncomfortable because of the fulfillment of this wish. You know how the fairy tale continues. Since both husband and wife are fundamentally one, the third wish must be that the sausages be removed from the nose of the wife. We could make use of this fairy tale any number of times in various connections; here it serves only as an illustration of the possibility that the wish-fulfillment for the one personality may lead to an aversion on the part of the other, if the two do not agree with one another.

It will not be difficult now to come to a better understanding of the anxiety-dream. We shall make one more observation, then we shall come to a conclusion to which many things lead. The observation is that the anxiety dreams often have a content which is entirely free from distortion and in which the censorship is, so to speak, eluded. The anxiety dream is ofttimes an undisguised wish-fulfillment, not, to be sure, of an accepted, but of a discarded wish. The anxiety development has stepped into the place of the censorship. While one may assert of the infantile dream that it is the obvious fulfillment of a wish that has gained admittance, and of the distorted dream that it is the disguised fulfillment of a suppressed wish, he must say of the anxiety dream that the only suitable formula is this, that it is the obvious fulfillment of a suppressed wish. Anxiety is the mark which shows that the suppressed wish showed itself stronger than the censorship, that it put through its wish-fulfillment despite the censorship, or was about to put it through. We understand that what is wish-fulfillment for the suppressed wish is for us, who are on the side of the dream-censor, only a painful sensation and a cause for antagonism. The anxiety which occurs in dreams is, if you wish, anxiety because of the strength of these otherwise suppressed wishes. Why this antagonism arises in the form of anxiety cannot be discovered from a study of the dream alone; one must obviously study anxiety from other sources.

What holds true for the undistorted anxiety dream we may assume to be true also of those dreams which have undergone partial distortion, and of the other dreams of aversion whose painful impressions very probably denote approximations of anxiety. The anxiety dream is usually also a dream that causes waking; we habitually interrupt sleep before the suppressed wish of the dream has accomplished its entire fulfillment in opposition to the censorship. In this case the execution of the dream is unsuccessful, but this does not change its nature. We have likened the dream to the night watchman or sleep-defender who wishes to protect our sleep from being disturbed. The night watchman, too, sometimes wakes the sleeper when he feels himself too weak to drive away the disturbance or danger all by himself. Yet we are often able to remain asleep, even when the dream begins to become suspicious, and begins to assume the form of anxiety. We say to ourselves in our sleep: "It's only a dream," and we sleep on.

When does it happen that the dream-wish is in a position to overpower this censorship? The conditions for this may be just as easily furnished by the dream-wish as by the dream-censorship. The wish may, for unknown reasons, become irresistible; but one gets the impression that more frequently the attitude of the dream censorship is to blame for this disarrangement in the relations of the forces. We have already heard that the censorship works with varying intensity in each single instance, that it handles each element with a different degree of strictness; now we should like to add the proposition that it is an extremely variable thing and does not exert equal force on every occasion against the same objectionable element. If on occasion the censorship feels itself powerless with respect to a dream-wish which threatens to over-ride it, then, instead of distortion, it makes use of the final means at its disposal, it destroys the sleep condition by the development of anxiety.

And now it occurs to us that we know absolutely nothing yet as to why these evil, depraved wishes are aroused just at night, in order that they may disturb our sleep. The answer can only be an assumption which is based on the nature of the condition of sleep. During the day the heavy pressure of a censorship weighs upon these wishes, making it impossible, as a rule, for them to express themselves in any manner. At night, evidently, this censorship is withdrawn for the benefit of the single sleep-wish, in the same manner as are all the other interests of psychic life, or at least placed in a position of very minor importance. The forbidden wishes must thank this nocturnal deposition of the censor for being able to raise their heads again. There are nervous persons troubled with insomnia who admit that their sleeplessness was in the beginning voluntary. They did not trust themselves to fall asleep, because they were afraid of their dreams, that is, of the results due to a slackening of the censorship. So you can readily see that this withdrawal of the censor does not in itself signify rank carelessness. Sleep weakens our power to move; our evil intentions, even if they do begin to stir, can accomplish nothing but a dream, which for practical purposes is harmless, and the highly sensible remark of the sleepers, a night-time remark indeed, but not a part of the dream life, "it is only a dream," is reminiscent of this quieting circumstance. So let us grant this, and sleep on.

If, thirdly, you recall the concept that the dreamer, struggling against his wishes, is to be compared to a summation of two separate persons, in some manner closely connected, you will be able to grasp the further possibility of how a thing which is highly unpleasant, namely, punishment, may be accomplished by wish-fulfillment. Here again the fairy tale of the three wishes can be of service to us: the sausages on the plate are the direct wish-fulfillment of the first person, the woman; the sausages at the end of her nose are the wish-fulfillment of the second person, the husband, but at the same time the punishment for the stupid wish of the woman. Among the neurotics we find again the motivation of the third wish, which remains in fairy tales only. There are many such punishment-tendencies in the psychic life of man; they are very powerful, and we may make them responsible for some of our painful dreams. Perhaps you now say that at this rate, not very much of the famed wish-fulfillment is left. But upon closer view you will admit that you are wrong. In contrast to the many-sided to be discussed, of what the dream might be—and, according to numerous authors, is—the solution (wish-fulfillment, anxiety-fulfillment, punishment-fulfillment) is indeed very restricted. That is why anxiety is the direct antithesis of the wish, why antitheses are so closely allied in association and why they occur together in the unconscious, as we have heard; and that is why punishment, too, is a wish-fulfillment of the other, the censoring person.

On the whole, then, I have made no concessions to your protestation against the theory of wish-fulfillment. We are bound, however, to establish wish-fulfillment in every dream no matter how distorted, and we certainly do not wish to withdraw from this task. Let us go back to the dream, already interpreted, of the three bad theatre tickets for 1 Fl. 50 Kr. from which we have already learned so much. I hope you still remember it. A lady who tells her husband during the day that her friend Elise, only three months younger than herself, has become engaged, dreams she is in the theatre with her husband. Half the parquet is empty. Her husband says, "Elise and her fiancé wanted to go to the theatre, too, but couldn't because they could get only poor seats, three for one gulden and a half." She was of the opinion that that wasn't so unfortunate. We discovered that the dream-thought originated in her discontent at having married too soon, and the fact that she was dissatisfied with her husband. We may be curious as to the manner in which these thoughts have been worked over into a wish-fulfillment, and where their traces may be found in the manifest content. Now we know that the element "too soon, premature" is eliminated from the dream by the censor. The empty parquet is a reference to it. The puzzling "three for 1 Fl. 50 Kr." is now, with the help of symbolism which we have since learned, more understandable.[14 The "3" really means a husband, and the manifest element is easy to translate: to buy a husband for her dowry ("I could have bought one ten times better for my dowry"). The marriage is obviously replaced by going into the theatre. "Buying the tickets too soon" directly takes the place of the premature marriage. This substitution is the work of the wish-fulfillment. Our dreamer was not always so dissatisfied with her early marriage as she was on the day she received news of the engagement of her friend. At the time she was proud of her marriage and felt herself more favored than her friend. Naive girls have frequently confided to their friends after their engagement that soon they, too, will be able to go to all the plays hitherto forbidden, and see everything. The desire to see plays, the curiosity that makes its appearance here, was certainly in the beginning directed towards sex matters, the sex-life, especially the sex-life of the parents, and then became a strong motive which impelled the girl to an early marriage. In this way the visit to the theatre becomes an obvious representative substitute for being

---

14 I do not mention another obvious interpretation of this "3" in the case of this childless woman, because it is not material to this analysis.

married. In the momentary annoyance at her early marriage she recalls the time when it was a wish-fulfillment for her, because she had satisfied her curiosity; and now replaces the marriage, guided by the old wish-impulse, with the going to the theatre.

We may say that we have not sought out the simplest example as proof of a hidden wish-fulfillment. We would have to proceed in analogous manner with other distorted dreams. I cannot do that for you, and simply wish to express the conviction that it will be successful everywhere. But I wish to continue along this theoretical line. Experience has taught me that it is one of the most dangerous phases of the entire dream science, and that many contradictions and misunderstandings are connected therewith. Besides, you are perhaps still under the impression that I have retracted a part of my declaration, in that I said that the dream is a fulfilled wish or its opposite, an actualized anxiety or punishment, and you will think this is the opportunity to compel further reservations of me. I have also heard complaints that I am too abrupt about things which appear evident to me, and that for that reason I do not present the thing convincingly enough.

If a person has gone thus far with us in dream-interpretation, and accepted everything that has been offered, it is not unusual for him to call a halt at wish-fulfillment, and say, "Granted that in every instance the dream has a meaning, and that this meaning can be disclosed by psychoanalytic technique, why must this dream, despite all evidence to the contrary, always be forced into the formula of wish-fulfillment? Why might not the meaning of this nocturnal thought be as many-sided as thought is by day; why may not the dream in one case express a fulfilled wish, in another, as you yourself say, the opposite thereof, an actualized anxiety; or why may it not correspond to a resolution, a warning, a reflection with its pro's and con's, a reproach, a goad to conscience, an attempt to prepare oneself for a contemplated performance, etc? Why always nothing more than a wish, or at best, its opposite?"

One might maintain that a difference of opinion on these points is of no great importance, so long as we are at one otherwise. We might say that it is enough to have discovered the meaning of the dream, and the way to recognize it; that it is a matter of no importance, if we have too narrowly limited this meaning. But this is not so. A misunderstanding of this point strikes at the nature of our knowledge of the dream, and endangers its worth for the understanding of neuroses. Then, too, that method of approach which is esteemed in the business world as genteel is out of place in scientific endeavors, and harmful.

My first answer to the question why the dream may not be many-sided in its meaning is the usual one in such instances: I do not know why it should not be so. I would not be opposed to such a state of affairs. As far as I am concerned, it could well be true. Only one small matter prevents this broader and more comfortable explanation of the dream—namely, that as a matter of fact it isn't so. My second answer emphasizes the fact that the assumption that the dream corresponds to numerous forms of thought and intellectual operations is no stranger to me. In a story about a sick person I once reported a dream that occurred three nights running and then stopped, and I explained this suppression by saying that the dream corresponded to a resolution which had no reason to recur after having been carried out. More recently I published a dream which corresponded to a confession. How is it possible for me to contradict myself, and maintain that the dream is always only a fulfilled wish?

I do that, because I do not wish to admit a stupid misunderstanding which might cost us the fruits of all our labors with regard to the dream, one which confuses the dream with the latent dream-thought and affirms of the dream something that applies specifically and solely to the latter. For it is entirely correct that the dream can represent, and be replaced by all those things we enumerated: a resolution, a warning, reflection, preparation, an attempt to solve a problem, etc. But if you look closely, you will recognize that all these things are true only of the latent dream thoughts, which have been changed about in the dream. You learn from the interpretation of the dreams that the person's unconscious thinking is occupied with such resolutions, preparations, reflections, etc., out of which the dream-work then builds the dream. If you are not at the time interested in the dream-work, but are very much interested in the unconscious thought-work of man, you eliminate the dream-work, and say of the dream, for all practical purposes quite correctly, that it corresponds to a warning, a resolution, etc. This often happens in psychoanalytic activity. People endeavor for the most part only to destroy the dream form, and to substitute in its place in the sequence the latent thoughts out of which the dream was made.

Thus we learn, from the appreciation of the latent dream-thoughts, that all the highly complicated psychic acts we have enumerated can go on unconsciously, a result as wonderful as it is confusing. But to return, you are right only if you admit that you have made use of an abbreviated form of speech, and if you do not believe that you must connect the many-sidedness we have mentioned with the essence of the dream. When you speak of the dream you must mean either the manifest dream, i.e., the product of the dream-work, or at most the dream-work itself—that psychic occurrence which forms the manifest dream out of the latent dream thought. Any other use of the word is a confusion of concept that can only cause trouble. If your assertions refer to the latent thoughts back of the dream, say so, and do not cloud the problem of the dream by using such a faulty means of expression. The latent dream thoughts are the material which the dream-work remolds into the manifest dream. Why do you insist upon confusing the material with the work that makes use of it? Are you any better off than those who knew only the product of this work, and could explain neither where it came from nor how it was produced?

The only essential thing in the dream is the dream-work that has had its influence upon the thought-material. We have no right to disregard it theoretically even if, in certain practical situations, we may fail to take it into account. Analytic observation, too, shows that the dream-work never limits itself to translating these thoughts in the archaic or regressive mode of expression known to you. Rather it regularly adds something which does not belong to the latent thoughts of waking, but which is the essential motive of dream-formation. This indispensable ingredient is at the same time the unconscious wish, for the fulfillment of which the dream content is rebuilt. The dream may be any conceivable thing, if you take into account only the thoughts represented by it, warning, resolution, preparation, etc.; it is also always the fulfillment of an unknown wish, and it is this only if you look upon it as the result of the dream-work. A dream is never itself a resolution, a warning, and no more—but always a resolution, etc., translated into an archaic form of expression with the help of the unconscious wish, and changed about for the purpose of fulfilling this wish. The one characteristic, wish-fulfillment, is constant; the other may vary; it may itself be a wish at times, so that the dream, with the aid of an unconscious wish, presents as fulfilled a latent wish out of waking hours.

I understand all this very well, but I do not know whether or not I shall be successful in making you understand it as well. I have difficulties, too, in proving it to you. This cannot be done without, on the one hand, careful analysis of many dreams, and on the other hand this most difficult and most important point of our conception of the dream cannot be set forth convincingly without reference to things to follow. Can you, in fact, believe that taking into consideration the intimate relationship of all things, one is able to penetrate deeply into the nature of one thing without having carefully considered other things of a very similar nature? Since we know nothing as yet about the closest relatives of the dream, neurotic symptoms, we must once again content ourselves with what has already been accomplished. I want to explain one more example to you, and propose a new viewpoint.

Let us again take up that dream to which we have several times recurred, the dream of the three theatre tickets for 1 Fl. 50 Kr. I can assure you that I took this example quite unpremeditatedly at first. You are acquainted with the latent dream thoughts: annoyance, upon hearing that her friend had just now become engaged, at the thought that she herself had hurried so to be married; contempt for her husband; the idea that she might have had a better one had she waited. We also know the wish, which made a dream out of these thoughts—it is "curiosity to see," being permitted to go to the theatre, very likely a derivation from the old curiosity finally to know just what happens when one is married. This curiosity, as is well known, regularly directs itself in the case of children to the sex-life of the parents. It is an impulse of childhood, and in so far as it persists later, an impulse whose roots reach back into the infantile. But that day's news played no part in awaking the curiosity, it awoke only annoyance and regret. This wish impulse did not have anything to do immediately with the latent dream thoughts, and we could fit the result of the dream interpretation into the analysis without considering the wish impulse at all. But then, the annoyance itself was not capable of producing the dream; a dream could not be derived from the thought: "It was stupid to marry so soon," except by reviving the old wish finally to see what happens when one is married. The wish then formed the dream content, in that it replaced marriage by going to the theatre, and gave it the form of an earlier wish-fulfillment: "so now I may go to the theatre and see all the forbidden things, and you may not. I am married and you must wait." In such a manner the present situation was transposed into its opposite, an old triumph put into the place of the recent defeat. Added thereto was a satisfied curiosity amalgamated with a satisfied egoistic sense of rivalry. This satisfaction determines the manifest dream content in which she really is sitting in the theatre, and her friend was unable to get tickets. Those bits of dream content are affixed to this satisfaction situation as unfitting and inexplicable modifications, behind which the latent dream thoughts still hide. Dream interpretation must take into consideration everything that serves toward the representation of the wish-fulfillment and must reconstruct from these suggestions the painful latent dream-thought.

The observation I now wish to make is for the purpose of drawing your attention to the latent, dream thoughts, now pushed to the fore. I beg of you not to forget first, that the dreamer is unconscious of them, second, they are entirely logical and continuous, so that they may be understood as a comprehensible reaction to the dream occasion, third, that they may have the value of any desired psychic impulse or intellectual operation. I shall now designate these thoughts more forcibly than before as "day-remnants"; the dreamer may acknowledge them or not. I now separate day-remnants and latent dream thoughts in accordance with our previous usage of calling everything that we discover in interpreting the dream "latent dream thoughts," while the day-remnants are only a part of the latent dream thoughts. Then our conception goes to show that something additional has been added to the day-remnants, something which also belonged to the unconscious, a strong but suppressed wish impulse, and it is this alone that has made possible the dream fabrication. The influence of this wish impulse on the day-remnants creates the further participation of the latent dream thoughts, thoughts which no longer appear rational and understandable in relation to waking life.

In explaining the relationship of the day-remnants to the unconscious wish I have made use of a comparison which I can only repeat here. Every undertaking requires a capitalist, who defrays the expenses, and an entrepreneur, who has the idea and understands how to carry it out. The role of the capitalist in the dream fabrication is always played by the unconscious wish; it dispenses the psychic energy for dream-building. The actual worker is the day-remnant, which determines how the expenditure is to be made. Now the capitalist may himself have the idea and the particularized knowledge, or the entrepreneur may have the capital. This simplifies the practical situation, but makes its theoretical comprehension more difficult. In economics we always distinguish between the capitalist and the entrepreneur aspect in a single person, and thus we reconstruct the fundamental situation which was the point of departure for our comparison. In dream-fabrication the same variations occur. I shall leave their further development to you.

We can go no further here, for you have probably long been disturbed by a reflection which deserves to be heard. Are the day-remnants, you ask, really unconscious in the same sense as the unconscious wish which is essential to making them suitable for the dream? You discern correctly. Here lies the salient point of the whole affair. They are not unconscious in the same sense. The dream wish belongs to a different unconsciousness, that which we have recognized as of infantile origin, fitted out with special mechanisms. It is entirely appropriate to separate these two types of unconsciousness and give them different designations. But let us rather wait until we have become acquainted with the field of neurotic symptoms. If people say one unconsciousness is fantastic, what will they say when we acknowledge that we arrived at our conclusions by using two kinds of unconsciousness?

I stop here. Once more you have heard something incomplete; but is there not hope in the thought that this science has a continuation which will be brought to light either by ourselves or by those to follow? And have not we ourselves discovered a sufficient number of new and surprising things?

FIFTEENTH LECTURE: THE DREAM

Doubtful Points and Criticism

LET us not leave the subject of dreams before we have touched upon the most common doubts and uncertainties which have arisen in connection with the new ideas and conceptions we have discussed up to this point. The more attentive members of the audience probably have already accumulated some material bearing upon this.

1. You may have received the impression that the results of our work of interpretation of the dream have left so much that is uncertain, despite our close adherence to technique, that a true translation of the manifest dream into the latent dream thoughts is thereby rendered impossible. In support of this you will point out that in the first place, one never knows whether a specific element of the dream is to be taken literally or symbolically, since those elements which are used symbolically do not, because of that fact, cease to be themselves. But if one has no objective standard by which to decide this, the interpretation is, as to this point, left to the discretion of the dream interpreter. Moreover, because of the way in which the dream work combines opposites, it is always uncertain whether a specific dream element is to be taken in the positive or the negative sense, whether it is to be understood as itself or as its opposite. Hence this is another opportunity for the exercise of the interpreter's discretion. In the third place, in consequence of the frequency with which every sort of inversion is practised in the dream, the dream interpreter is at liberty to assume such an inversion at any point of the dream he pleases. And finally you will say, you have heard that one is seldom sure that the interpretation which is found is the only possible one. There is danger of overlooking a thoroughly admissible second interpretation of the same dream. Under these circumstances, you will conclude there is a scope left for the discretion of the interpreter, the breadth of which seems incompatible with the objective accuracy of the results. Or you may also conclude that the fault does not rest with the dream but that the inadequacies of our dream interpretation result from errors in our conceptions and hypotheses.

All your material is irreproachable, but I do not believe that it justifies your conclusions in two directions, namely, that dream interpretation as we practice it is sacrificed to arbitrariness and that the deficiency of our results makes the justification of our method doubtful. If you will substitute for the arbitrariness of the interpreter, his skill, his experience, his comprehension, I agree with you. We shall surely not be able to dispense with some such personal factor, particularly not in difficult tasks of dream interpretation. But this same state of affairs exists also in other scientific occupations. There is no way in which to make sure that one man will not wield a technique less well, or utilize it more fully, than another. What might, for example, impress you as arbitrariness in the interpretation of symbols, is compensated for by the fact that as a rule the connection of the dream thoughts among themselves, the connection of the dream with the life of the dreamer, and the whole psychic situation in which the dream occurs, chooses just one of the possible interpretations advanced and rejects the others as useless for its purposes. The conclusion drawn from the inadequacies of dream interpretation, that our hypotheses are wrong, is weakened by an observation which shows that the ambiguity and indefiniteness of the dream is rather characteristic and necessarily to be expected.

Recollect that we said that the dream work translates the dream thoughts into primitive expressions analogous to picture writing. All these primitive systems of expression are, however, subject to such indefiniteness and ambiguities, but it does not follow that we are justified in doubting their usefulness. You know that the fusion of opposites by the dream-work is analogous to the so-called "antithetical meaning of primitive words," in the oldest languages. The philologist, R. Abel (1884), whom we have to thank for this point of view, admonishes us not to believe that the meaning of the communication which one person made to another when using such ambiguous words was necessarily unclear. Tone and gesture used in connection with the words would have left no room for doubt as to which of the two opposites the speaker intended to communicate. In writing, where gesture is lacking, it was replaced by a supplementary picture sign not intended to be spoken, as for example by the picture of a little man squatting lazily or standing erect, according to whether the ambiguous hieroglyphic was to mean "weak" or "strong." It was in this way that one avoided any misunderstanding despite the ambiguity of the sounds and signs.

We recognize in the ancient systems of expression, e.g., the writings of those oldest languages, a number of uncertainties which we would not tolerate in our present-day writings. Thus in many Semitic writings only the consonants of words are indicated. The reader had to supply the omitted vowels according to his knowledge and the context. Hieroglyphic writing does not proceed in exactly this way, but quite similarly, and that is why the pronunciation of old Egyptian has remained unknown to us. The holy writings of the Egyptians contain still other uncertainties. For example, it is left to the discretion of the writer whether or not he shall arrange the pictures from right to left or from left to right. To be able to read we have to follow the rule that we must depend upon the faces of the figures, birds, and the like. The writer, however, could also arrange the picture signs in vertical rows, and in inscriptions on small objects he was guided by considerations of beauty and proportion further to change the order of the signs. Probably the most confusing feature of hieroglyphic writing is to be found in the fact that there is no space between words. The pictures stretch over the page at uniform distances from one another, and generally one does not know whether a sign belongs to what has gone before or is the beginning of a new word. Persian cuneiform writing, on the other hand, makes use of an oblique wedge sign to separate the words.

The Chinese tongue and script is exceedingly old, but still used by four hundred million people. Please do not think I understand anything about it. I have only informed myself concerning it because I hoped to find analogies

149

to the indefinite aspects of the dream. Nor was I disappointed. The Chinese language is filled with so many vagaries that it strikes terror into our hearts. It consists, as is well known, of a number of syllable sounds which are spoken singly or are combined in twos. One of the chief dialects has about four hundred such sounds. Now since the vocabulary of this dialect is estimated at about four thousand words, it follows that every sound has on an average of ten different meanings, some less but others, consequently, more. Hence there are a great number of ways of avoiding a multiplicity of meaning, since one cannot guess from the context alone which of the ten meanings of the syllable sound the speaker intended to convey to the hearer. Among them are the combining of two sounds into a compounded word and the use of four different "tones" with which to utter these syllables. For our purposes of comparison, it is still more interesting to note that this language has practically no grammar. It is impossible to say of a one-syllable word whether it is a noun, a verb, or an adjective, and we find none of those changes in the forms of the words by means of which we might recognize sex, number, ending, tense or mood. The language, therefore, might be said to consist of raw material, much in the same manner as our thought language is broken up by the dream work into its raw materials when the expressions of relationship are left out. In the Chinese, in all cases of vagueness the decision is left to the understanding of the hearer, who is guided by the context. I have secured an example of a Chinese saying which, literally translated, reads: "Little to be seen, much to wonder at." That is not difficult to understand. It may mean, "The less a man has seen, the more he finds to wonder at," or, "There is much to admire for the man who has seen little." Naturally, there is no need to choose between these two translations, which differ only in grammar. Despite these uncertainties, we are assured, the Chinese language is an extraordinarily excellent medium for the expression of thought. Vagueness does not, therefore, necessarily lead to ambiguity.

Now we must certainly admit that the condition of affairs is far less favorable in the expression-system of the dream than in these ancient languages and writings. For, after all, these latter are really designed for communication, that is to say, they were always intended to be understood, no matter in what way and with what aids. But it is just this characteristic which the dream lacks. The dream does not want to tell anyone anything, it is no vehicle of communication, it is, on the contrary, constructed so as not to be understood. For that reason we must not be surprised or misled if we should discover that a number of the ambiguities and vagaries of the dream do not permit of determination. As the one specific gain of our comparison, we have only the realization that such uncertainties as people tried to make use of in objecting to the validity of our dream interpretation, are rather the invariable characteristic of all primitive systems of expression.

How far the dream can really be understood can be determined only by practice and experience. My opinion is, that that is very far indeed, and the comparison of results which correctly trained analysts have gathered confirms my view. The lay public, even that part of the lay public which is interested in science, likes, in the face of the difficulties and uncertainties of a scientific task, to make what I consider an unjust show of its superior scepticism. Perhaps not all of you are acquainted with the fact that a similar situation arose in the history of the deciphering of the Babylonian-Assyrian inscriptions. There was a period then when public opinion went far in declaring the decipherors of cuneiform writing to be visionaries and the whole research a "fraud." But in the year 1857 the Royal Asiatic Society made a decisive test. It challenged the four most distinguished decipherors of cuneiform writing, Rawlinson, Hincks, Fox Talbot and Oppert, each to send to it in a sealed envelope his independent translation of a newly discovered inscription, and the Society was then able to testify, after having made a comparison of the four readings, that their agreement was sufficiently marked to justify confidence in what already had been accomplished, and faith in further progress. At this the mockery of the learned lay world gradually came to an end and the confidence in the reading of cuneiform documents has grown appreciably since then.

2. A second series of objections is firmly grounded in the impression from which you too probably are not free, that a number of the solutions of dream interpretations which we find it necessary to make seem forced, artificial, far-fetched, in other words, violent or even comical or jocose. These comments are so frequent that I shall choose at random the latest example which has come to my attention. Recently, in free Switzerland, the director of a boarding-school was relieved of his position on account of his active interest in psychoanalysis. He raised objections and a Berne newspaper made public the judgment of the school authorities. I quote from that article some sentences which apply to psychoanalysis: "Moreover, we are surprised at the many far-fetched and artificial examples as found in the aforementioned book of Dr. Pfister of Zurich.... Thus, it certainly is a cause of surprise when the director of a boarding-school so uncritically accepts all these assertions and apparent proofs." These observations are offered as the decisions of "one who judges calmly." I rather think this calm is "artificial." Let us examine these remarks more closely in the hope that a little reflection and knowledge of the subject can be no detriment to calm judgment.

It is positively refreshing to see how quickly and unerringly some individuals can judge a delicate question of abstruse psychology by first impressions. The interpretations seem to them far-fetched and forced, they do not please them, so the interpretations are wrong and the whole business of interpretation amounts to nothing. No fleeting thought ever brushes the other possibility, that these interpretations must appear as they are for good reasons, which would give rise to the further question of what these good reasons might be.

The content thus judged generally relates to the results of displacement, with which you have become acquainted as the strongest device of the dream censor. It is with the help of displacements that the dream censor creates substitute-formations which we have designated as allusions. But they are allusions which are not easily recognized as such, and from which it is not easy to find one's way back to the original and which are connected with this original by means of the strangest, most unusual, most superficial associations. In all of these cases, however, it is a question of matters which are to be hidden, which were intended for concealment; this is what the dream censor aims to do. We must not expect to find a thing that has been concealed in its accustomed place in the spot where it belongs. In this respect the Commissions for the Surveillance of Frontiers now in office are more cunning than the Swiss school authorities. In their search for documents and maps they are not content to search through portfolios and letter cases but they also take into account the possibility that spies and smugglers might carry such severely proscribed articles in the most concealed parts of their clothing, where they certainly do not belong, as for example between the double soles of their boots. If the concealed objects are found in such a place, they certainly are very far-fetched, but nevertheless they have been "fetched."

If we recognize that the most remote, the most extraordinary associations between the latent dream element and its manifest substitute are possible, associations appearing ofttimes comical, ofttimes witty, we follow in so doing a wealth of experience derived from examples whose solutions we have, as a rule, not found ourselves. Often it is not possible to give such interpretations from our own examples. No sane person could guess the requisite association. The dreamer either gives us the translation with one stroke by means of his immediate association—he can do this, for this substitute formation was created by his mind—or he provides us with so much material that the solution no longer demands any special astuteness but forces itself upon us as inevitable. If the dreamer does not help us in either of these two ways, then indeed the manifest element in question remains forever incomprehensible to us. Allow me to give you one more such example of recent occurrence. One of my patients lost her father during the time that she was undergoing treatment. Since then she has made use of every opportunity to bring him back to life in her dreams. In one of her dreams her father appears in a certain connection, of no further importance here, and says, "*It is a quarter past eleven, it is half past eleven, it is quarter of twelve.*" All she can think of in connection with this curious incident is the recollection that her father liked to see his grown-up children appear punctually at the general meal hour. That very thing probably had some connection with the dream element, but permitted of no conclusion as to its source. Judging from the situation of the treatment at that time, there was a justified suspicion that a carefully suppressed critical rebellion against her loved and respected father played its part in this dream. Continuing her associations, and apparently far afield from topics relevant to the dream, the dreamer relates that yesterday many things of a psychological nature had been discussed in her presence, and that a relative made the remark: "The cave man (*Urmensch*) continues to live in all of us." Now we think we understand. That gave her an excellent opportunity of picturing her father as continuing to live. So in the dream she made of him a clockman (*Uhrmensch*) by having him announce the quarter-hours at noon time.

You may not be able to disregard the similarity which this examples bears to a pun, and it really has happened frequently that the dreamer's pun is attributed to the interpreter. There are still other examples in which it is not at all easy to decide whether one is dealing with a joke or a dream. But you will recall that the same doubt confronted us when we were dealing with slips of the tongue. A man tells us a dream of his, that his uncle, while they were sitting in the latter's *auto*mobile, gave him a kiss. He very quickly supplies the interpretation himself. It means "*auto*-eroticism," (a term taken from the study of the libido, or love impulse, and designating satisfaction of that impulse without an external object). Did this man permit himself to make fun of us and give out as a dream a pun that occurred to him? I do not believe so; he really dreamed it. Whence comes the astounding similarity? This question at one time led me quite a ways from my path, by making it necessary for me to make a thorough investigation of the problem of humor itself. By so doing I came to the conclusion that the origin of wit lies in a foreconscious train of thought which is left for a moment to unconscious manipulation, from which it then emerges as a joke. Under the influence of the unconscious it experiences the workings of the mechanisms there in force, namely, of condensation and displacement, that is, of the same processes which we found active in the dream work, and it is to this agreement that we are to ascribe the similarity between wit and the dream, wherever it occurs. The unintentional "dream joke" has, however, none of the pleasure-giving quality of the ordinary joke. Why that is so, greater penetration into the study of wit may teach you. The "dream joke" seems a poor joke to us, it does not make us laugh, it leaves us cold.

Here we are also following in the footsteps of ancient dream interpretation, which has left us, in addition to much that is useless, many a good example of dream interpretation we ourselves cannot surpass. I am now going to tell you a dream of historical importance which Plutarch and Artemidorus of Daldis both tell concerning Alexander the Great, with certain variations. When the King was engaged in besieging the city of Tyre (322 B.C.), which was being stubbornly defended, he once dreamed that he saw a dancing satyr. Aristandros, his dream interpreter, who accompanied the army, interpreted this dream for him by making of the word *Satyros*, σὰ Τύρος, "Thine is Tyre," and thus promising him a triumph over the city. Alexander allowed himself to be influenced by this interpretation to continue the siege, and finally captured Tyre. The interpretation, which seems artificial enough, was without doubt the correct one.

3. I can imagine that it will make a special impression on you to hear that objections to our conception of the dream have been raised also by persons who, as psychoanalysts, have themselves been interested in the interpretation of dreams. It would have been too extraordinary if so pregnant an opportunity for new errors had remained unutilized, and thus, owing to comprehensible confusions and unjustified generalizations, there have been assertions made which, in point of incorrectness are not far behind the medical conception of dreams. One of these you already know. It is the declaration that the dream is occupied with the dreamer's attempts at adaptation to his present environment, and attempts to solve future problems, in other words, that the dream follows a "prospective tendency" (A. Maeder). We have already shown that this assertion is based upon a confusion of the dream with the latent thoughts of the dream, that as a premise it overlooks the existence of the dream-work. In characterizing that psychic activity which is unconscious and to which the latent thoughts of the dream belong, the above assertion is no novelty, nor is it exhaustive, for this unconscious psychic activity occupies itself with many other things besides preparation for the future. A much worse confusion seems to underlie the assurance that back of every dream one finds the "death-clause," or death-wish. I am not quite certain what this formula is meant to indicate, but I suppose that back of it is a confusion of the dream with the whole personality of the dreamer.

An unjustified generalization, based on few good examples, is the pronouncement that every dream permits of two interpretations, one such as we have explained, the so-called psychoanalytic, and another, the so-called anagogical or mystical, which ignores the instinctive impulses and aims at a representation of the higher psychic functions (V. Silberer). There are such dreams, but you will try in vain to extend this conception to even a majority of the dreams. But after everything you have heard, the statement will seem very incomprehensible that all dreams can be interpreted bisexually, that is, as the concurrence of two tendencies which may be designated as male and female (A. Adler). To be sure, there are a few such dreams, and you may learn later that these are built up in the manner of certain hysterical symptoms. I mention all these newly discovered general characteristics of the dream in order to warn you against them or at least in order not to leave you in doubt as to how I judge them.

4. At one time the objective value of dream research was called into question by the observation that patients undergoing analysis accommodate the content of their dreams to the favorite theories of their physicians, so that some dream predominantly of sexual impulses, others of the desire for power and still others even of rebirth (W. Stekel). The weight of this observation is diminished by the consideration that people dreamed before there was such a thing as a psychoanalytic treatment to influence their dreams, and that those who are now undergoing treatment were also in the habit of dreaming before the treatment was commenced. The meaning of this novel discovery can soon be recognized as a matter of course and as of no consequence for the theory of the dream. Those day-remnants which give rise to the dream are the overflow from the strong interest of the waking life. If the remarks of the physician and the stimuli which he gives have become significant to the patient under analysis, then they become a part of the day's remnants, can serve as psychic stimuli for the formation of a dream along with other, emotionally-charged, unsolved interests of the day, and operate much as do the somatic stimuli which act upon the sleeper during his sleep. Just like these other incitors of the dream, the sequence of ideas which the physician sets in motion may appear in the manifest content, or may be traced in the latent content of the dream. Indeed, we know that one can produce dreams experimentally, or to speak more accurately, one can insert into the dream a part of the dream material. Thus the analyst in influencing his patients, merely plays the role of an experimenter in the manner of Mourly Vold, who places the limbs of his subjects in certain positions.

One can often influence the dreamer as to the *subject-matter* of his dream, but one can never influence *what he will dream* about it. The mechanism of the dream-work and the unconscious wish that is hidden in the dream are beyond the reach of all foreign influences. We already realized, when we evaluated the dreams caused by bodily stimuli, that the peculiarity and self-sufficiency of the dream life shows itself in the reaction with which the dream retorts to the bodily or physical stimuli which are presented. The statement here discussed, which aims to throw doubt upon the objectivity of dream research, is again based on a confusion—this time of the whole dream with the dream material.

This much, ladies and gentlemen, I wanted to tell you concerning the problems of the dream. You will suspect that I have omitted a great deal, and have yourselves discovered that I had to be inconclusive on almost all points. But that is due to the relation which the phenomena of the dream have to those of the neuroses. We studied the dream by way of introduction to the study of the neuroses, and that was surely more correct than the reverse would have been. But just as the dream prepares us for the understanding of the neuroses, so in turn the correct evaluation of the dream can only be gained after a knowledge of neurotic phenomena has been won.

I do not know what you will think about this, but I must assure you that I do not regret having taken so much of your interest and of your available time for the problems of the dream. There is no other field in which one can so quickly become convinced of the correctness of the assertions by which psychoanalysis stands or falls. It will take the strenuous labor of many months, even years, to show that the symptoms in a case of neurotic breakdown have their meaning, serve a purpose, and result from the fortunes of the patient. On the other hand, the efforts of a few hours suffice in proving the same content in a dream product which at first seems incomprehensibly confused, and thereby to confirm all the hypotheses of psychoanalysis, the unconsciousness of psychic processes, the special mechanism which they follow, and the motive forces which manifest themselves in them. And if we associate the thorough analogy in the construction of the dream and the neurotic symptom with the rapidity of transformation which makes of the dreamer an alert and reasonable individual, we gain the certainty that the neurosis also is based only on a change in the balance of the forces of psychic life.

PART III. GENERAL THEORY OF THE NEUROSES

SIXTEENTH LECTURE. GENERAL THEORY OF THE NEUROSES

Psychoanalysis and Psychiatry

I AM very glad to welcome you back to continue our discussions. I last lectured on the psychoanalytic treatment of errors and of the dream. Today I would like to introduce you to an understanding of neurotic phenomena, which, as you soon will discover, have much in common with those topics. But I shall tell you in advance that I cannot leave you to take the same attitude toward me that you had before. At that time I was anxious to take no step without complete reference to your judgment. I discussed much with you, I listened to your objections, in short, I deferred to you and to your "normal common sense." That is no longer possible, and for a very simple reason. As phenomena, the dream and errors were not strange to you. One might say that you had as much experience as I, or that you could easily acquire as much. But neuroses are foreign to you; since you are not doctors you have had access to them only through what I have told you. Of what use is the best judgment if it is not supported by familiarity with the material in question?

Do not, however, understand this as an announcement of dogmatic lectures which demand your unconditional belief. That would be a gross misunderstanding. I do not wish to convince you. I am out to stimulate your interest and shake your prejudices. If, in consequence of not knowing the facts, you are not in a position to judge, neither should you believe nor condemn. Listen and allow yourselves to be influenced by what I tell you. One cannot be so easily convinced; at least if he comes by convictions without effort, they soon prove to be valueless and unable to hold their own. He only has a right to conviction who has handled the same material for many years and who in so doing has gone through the same new and surprising experiences again and again. Why, in matters of intellect these lightning conversions, these momentary repulsions? Do you not feel that a *coup de foudre*, that love at first sight, originates in quite a different field, namely, in that of the emotions? We do not even demand that our patients should become convinced of and predisposed to psychoanalysis. When they do, they seem suspicious to us. The attitude we prefer in them is one of benevolent scepticism. Will you not also try to let the psychoanalytic conception develop in your mind beside the popular or "psychiatric"? They will influence each other, mutually measure their strength, and some day work themselves into a decision on your part.

On the other hand, you must not think for a moment that what I present to you as the psychoanalytic conception is a purely speculative system. Indeed, it is a sum total of experiences and observations, either their direct expression or their elaboration. Whether this elaboration is done adequately and whether the method is justifiable will be tested in the further progress of the science. After two and a half decades, now that I am fairly advanced in years, I may say that it was particularly difficult, intensive and all-absorbing work which yielded these observations. I have often had the impression that our opponents were unwilling to take into consideration this objective origin of our statements, as if they thought it were only a question of subjective ideas arising haphazard, ideas to which another may oppose his every passing whim. This antagonistic behavior is not entirely comprehensible to me. Perhaps the physician's habit of steering clear of his neurotic patients and listening so very casually to what they have to say allows him to lose sight of the possibility of deriving anything valuable from his patients' communications, and therefore, of making penetrating observations on them. I take this opportunity of promising you that I shall carry on little controversy in the course of my lectures, least of all with individual controversialists. I have never been able to convince myself of the truth of the saying that controversy is the father of all things. I believe that it comes down to us from the Greek sophist philosophy and errs as does the latter through the overvaluation of dialectics. To me, on the contrary, it seems as if the so-called scientific criticism were on the whole unfruitful, quite apart from the fact that it is almost always carried on in a most personal spirit. For my part, up to a few years ago, I could even boast that I had entered into a regular scientific dispute with only one scholar (Lowenfeld, of Munich). The end of this was that we became friends and have remained friends to this day. But I did not repeat this attempt for a long time, because I was not certain that the outcome would be the same.

Now you will surely judge that so to reject the discussion of literature must evidence stubborness, a very special obtuseness against objections, or, as the kindly colloquialisms of science have it, "a complete personal bias." In answer, I would say that should you attain to a conviction by such hard labor, you would thereby derive a certain right to sustain it with some tenacity. Furthermore, I should like to emphasize the fact that I have modified my views on certain important points in the course of my researches, changed them and replaced them by new ones, and that I naturally made a public statement of that fact each time. What has been the result of this frankness? Some paid no attention at all to my self-corrections and even to-day criticize me for assertions which have long since ceased to have the same meaning for me. Others reproach me for just this deviation, and on account of it declare me unreliable. For is anyone who has changed his opinions several times still trustworthy; is not his latest assertion, as well, open to error? At the same time he who holds unswervingly to what he has once said, or cannot be made to give it up quickly enough, is called stubborn and biased. In the face of these contradictory criticisms, what else can one do but be himself and act according to his own dictates? That is what I have decided to do, and I will not allow myself to be restrained from modifying and adapting my theories as the progress of my experience demands. In the basic ideas I have hitherto found nothing to change, and I hope that such will continue to be the case.

Now I shall present to you the psychoanalytic conception of neurotic manifestations. The natural thing for me to do is to connect them to the phenomena we have previously treated, for the sake of their analogy as well as their contrast. I will select as symptomatic an act of frequent occurrence in my office hour. Of course, the analyst cannot do much for those who seek him in his medical capacity, and lay the woes of a lifetime before him in fifteen minutes. His deeper knowledge makes it difficult for him to deliver a snap decision as do other physicians—"There is nothing wrong with you"—and to give the advice, "Go to a watering-place for a while." One of our colleagues, in answer to the question as to what he did with his office patients, said, shrugging his shoulders, that he simply "fines them so many kronen for their mischief-making." So it will not surprise you to hear that even in the case of very busy analysts, the hours for consultation are not very crowded. I have had the ordinary door between my waiting room and my office doubled and strengthened by a covering of felt. The purpose of this little arrangement cannot be doubted. Now it happens over and over again that people who are admitted from my waiting room omit to close the door behind them; in fact, they almost always leave both doors open. As soon as I have noticed this I insist rather gruffly that he or she go back in order to rectify the omission, even though it be an elegant gentleman or a lady in all her finery. This gives an impression of misapplied pedantry. I have, in fact, occasionally discredited myself by such a demand, since the individual concerned was one of those who cannot touch even a door knob, and prefer as well to have their attendants spared this contact. But most frequently I was right, for he who conducts himself in this way, and leaves the door from the waiting room into the physician's consultation room open, belongs to the rabble and deserves to be received inhospitably. Do not, I beg you, defend him until you have heard what follows. For the fact is that this negligence of the patient's only occurs when he has been alone in the waiting room and so leaves an empty room behind him, never when others, strangers, have been waiting with him. If that latter is the case, he knows very well that it is in his interest not to be listened to while he is talking to the physician, and never omits to close both the doors with care.

This omission of the patient's is so predetermined that it becomes neither accidental nor meaningless, indeed, not even unimportant, for, as we shall see, it throws light upon the relation of this patient to the physician. He is one of the great number of those who seek authority, who want to be dazzled, intimidated. Perhaps he had inquired by telephone as to what time he had best call, he had prepared himself to come on a crowd of suppliants somewhat like those in front of a branch milk station. He now enters an empty waiting room which is, moreover, most modestly furnished, and he is disappointed. He must demand reparation from the physician for the wasted respect that he had tendered him, and so he omits to close the door between the reception room and the office. By this, he means to say to the physician: "Oh, well, there is no one here anyway, and probably no one will come as long as I am here." He would also be quite unmannerly and supercilious during the consultation if his presumption were not at once restrained by a sharp reminder.

You will find nothing in the analysis of this little symptomatic act which was not previously known to you. That is to say, it asserts that this act is not accidental, but has a motive, a meaning, a purpose, that it has its assignable connections psychologically, and that it serves as a small indication of a more important psychological process. But above all it implies that the process thus intimated is not known to the consciousness of the individual in whom it takes place, for none of the patients who left the two doors open would have admitted that they meant by this omission to show me their contempt. Some could probably recall a slight sense of disappointment at entering an empty waiting room, but the connection between this impression and the symptomatic act which followed—of these, his consciousness was surely not aware.

Now let us place, side by side with this small analysis of a symptomatic act, an observation on a pathological case. I choose one which is fresh in my mind and which can also be described with relative brevity. A certain measure of minuteness of detail is unavoidable in any such account.

A young officer, home on a short leave of absence, asked me to see his mother-in-law who, in spite of the happiest circumstances, was embittering her own and her people's existence by a senseless idea. I am introduced to a well preserved lady of fifty-three with pleasant, simple manners, who gives the following account without any hesitation: She is most happily married and lives in the country with her husband, who operates a large factory. She cannot say enough for the kind thoughtfulness of her husband. They had married for love thirty years ago, and since then there had never been a shadow, a quarrel or cause for jealousy. Now, even though her two children are well married, the husband and father does not yet want to retire, from a feeling of duty. A year ago there happened the incredible thing, incomprehensible to herself as well. She gave complete credence to an anonymous letter which accused her excellent husband of having an affair with a young girl—and since then her happiness is destroyed. The more detailed circumstances were somewhat as follows: She had a chambermaid with whom she had perhaps too often discussed intimate matters. This girl pursued another young woman with positively malicious enmity because the latter had progressed so much further in life, despite the fact that she was of no better origin. Instead of going into domestic service, the girl had obtained a business training, had entered the factory and in consequence of the short-handedness due to the drafting of the clerks into the army had advanced to a good position. She now lives in the factory itself, meets all the gentlemen socially, and is even addressed as "Miss." The girl who had remained behind in life was of course ready to speak all possible evil of her one-time schoolmate. One day our patient and her chambermaid were talking of an old gentleman who had been visiting at the house, and of whom it was known that he did not live with his wife, but kept another woman as his mistress. She does not know how it happened that she suddenly remarked, "That would be the most awful thing that could happen to me, if I should ever hear that my good husband also had a mistress." The next day she received an anonymous letter through the mail which, in a disguised handwriting, carried this very communication which she had conjured up. She concluded—it seems justifiably—that the letter was the handiwork of her malignant chambermaid, for the letter named as the husband's mistress the self-same woman whom the maid persecuted with her hatred. Our patient, in spite of the fact that she immediately saw through the intrigue and had seen enough in her town to know how little credence such cowardly denunciations deserve, was nevertheless at once prostrated by the letter. She became dreadfully excited and promptly sent for her husband in order to heap the bitterest reproaches upon him. Her husband laughingly denied the accusation and did the best that could be done. He called in the family physician, who was as well the doctor in attendance at the factory, and the latter added his efforts to quiet the unhappy woman. Their further procedure was also entirely reasonable. The chambermaid was dismissed, but the pretended rival was not. Since then, the patient claims she has repeatedly so far calmed herself as no longer to believe the contents of the anonymous letter, but this relief was neither thoroughgoing nor lasting. It was enough to hear the name of the young lady spoken or to meet her on the street in order to precipitate a new attack of suspicion, pain and reproach.

This, now, is the case history of this good woman. It does not need much psychiatric experience to understand that her portrayal of her own case was, if anything, rather too mild in contrast to other nervous patients. The picture, we say, was dissimulated; in reality she had never overcome her belief in the accusation of the anonymous letter.

What position does a psychiatrist take toward such a case? We already know what he would do in the case of the symptomatic act of the patient who does not close the doors to the waiting room. He declares it an accident without psychological interest, with which he need not concern himself. But this attitude cannot be maintained toward the pathological case of the jealous woman. The symptomatic act seems no great matter, but the symptom itself claims attention by reason of its gravity. It is bound up with intense subjective suffering while objectively it threatens to break up a home; therefore its claim to psychiatric interest cannot be put aside. The first endeavor of the psychiatrist is to characterize the symptom by some distinctive feature. The idea with which this woman torments herself cannot in itself be called nonsensical, for it does happen that elderly married men have affairs with young girls. But there is something else about it that is nonsensical and incredible. The patient has no reason beyond the declaration in the anonymous letter to believe that her tender and faithful husband belongs to this sort of married men, otherwise not uncommon. She knows that this letter in itself carries no proof; she can satisfactorily explain its origin; therefore she ought to be able to persuade herself that she has no reason to be jealous. Indeed she does this, but in spite of it she suffers every bit as much as she would if she acknowledged this jealousy as fully justified. We are agreed to call ideas of this sort, which are inaccessible to arguments based on logic or on facts, "*obsessions*." Thus the good lady suffers from an "*obsession of jealousy*" that is surely a distinctive characterization for this pathological case.

Having reached this first certainty, our psychiatric interest will have become aroused. If we cannot do away with a delusion by taking reality into account, it can hardly have arisen from reality. But the delusion, what is its origin? There are delusions of the most widely varied content. Why is it that in our case the content should be jealousy? In what types of persons are obsessions liable to occur, and, in particular, obsessions of jealousy? We would like to turn to the psychiatrist with such questions, but here he leaves us in the lurch. There is only one of our queries which he heeds. He will examine the family history of this woman and *perhaps* will give us the answer: "The people who develop obsessions are those in whose families similar and other psychic disturbances have repeatedly occurred." In other words, if this lady develops an obsession she does so because she was predisposed to it by reason of her heredity. That is certainly something, but is it all that we want to know? Is it all that was effective in causing this breakdown? Shall we be content to assume that it is immaterial, accidental and inexplicable why the obsession of jealousy develops rather than any other? And may we also accept this sentence about the dominance of the influence of heredity in its negative meaning, that is, that no matter what experiences came to this human being she was predestined to develop some kind of obsession? You will want to know why scientific psychiatry will give no further explanation. And I reply, "He is a rascal who gives more than he owns." The psychiatrist does not know of any path that leads him further in the explanation of such a case, and must content with the diagnosis and a prognosis which, despite a wealth of experience is uncertain.

Yet, can psychoanalysis do more at this point? Indeed yes! I hope to show you that even in so inaccessible a case as this it can discover something which makes the further understanding possible. May I ask you first to note the apparently insignificant fact that the patient actually provoked the anonymous letter which now supports her delusion. The day before, she announces to the intriguing chambermaid that if her husband were to have an affair with a young girl it would be the worst misfortune that could befall her. By so doing she really gave the maid the idea of sending her the anonymous letter. The obsession thus attains a certain independence from the letter; it existed in the patient beforehand—perhaps as a dread; or was it a wish? Consider, moreover, these additional details yielded by an analysis of only two hours. The patient was indeed most helpful when, after telling her story, she was urged to communicate her further thoughts, ideas and recollections. She declared that nothing came to her mind, that she had already told everything. After two hours the undertaking had really to be given up because she announced that she already felt cured and was sure that the morbid idea would not return. Of course, she said this because of this resistance and her fear of continuing the analysis. In these two hours, however, she had let fall certain remarks which made possible definite interpretation, indeed made it incontestable; and this interpretation throws a clear light on the origin of her obsession of jealousy. Namely, she herself was very much infatuated with a certain young man, the very same son-in-law upon whose urging she had come to consult me professionally. She knew nothing of this infatuation, or at least only a very little. Because of the existing relationship, it was very easy for this infatuation to masquerade under the guise of harmless tenderness. With all our further experience it is not difficult to feel our way toward an understanding of the psychic life of this honest woman and good mother. Such an infatuation, a monstrous, impossible thing, could not be allowed to become conscious. But it continued to exist and unconsciously exerted a heavy pressure. Something had to happen, some sort of relief had to be found and the mechanism of displacement which so constantly takes part in the origin of obsessional jealousy offered the most immediate mitigation. If not only she, old woman that she was, was in love with a young man but if also her old husband had an affair with a young girl, then she would be freed from the voice of her conscience which accused her of infidelity. The phantasy of her husband's infidelity was thus like a cooling salve on her burning wound. Of her own love she never became conscious, but the reflection of it, which would bring her such advantages, now became compulsive, obsessional and conscious. Naturally all arguments directed against the obsession were of no avail since they were directed only to the reflection, and not to the original force to which it owed its strength and which, unimpeachable, lay buried in the unconscious.

Let us now piece together these fragments to see what a short and impeded psychoanalysis can nevertheless contribute to the understanding of this case. It is assumed of course that our inquiries were carefully conducted, a point which I cannot at this place submit to your judgment. In the first place, the obsession becomes no longer nonsensical nor incomprehensible, it is full of meaning, well motivated and an integral part of the patient's emotional experience. Secondly, it is a necessary reaction toward an unconscious psychological process, revealed in other ways, and it is to this very circumstance that it owes its obsessional nature, that is, its resistance to arguments based on logic or fact. In itself the obsession is something wished for, a kind of consolation. Finally, the experiences underlying the condition are such as unmistakably determine an obsession of jealousy and no other. You will also recognize the part played by the two important analogies in the analysis of the symptomatic act with reference to its meaning and intent and also to its relation to an unconscious factor in the situation.

Naturally, we have not yet answered all the questions which may arise on this case. Rather the case bristles with further problems of a kind which we have not yet been able to solve in any way, and of others which could not be solved because of the disadvantage of the circumstances under which we were working. For example: why is this happily married woman open to an infatuation for her son-in-law, and why does the relief which could have been obtained in other ways come to her by way of this mirror-image, this projection of her own condition upon her husband? I trust you will not think that it is idle and wanton to open such problems. Already we have much material at our disposal for their possible solution. This woman is in that critical age when her sexual needs undergo a sudden and unwelcome exaggeration. This might in itself be sufficient. In addition, her good and faithful mate may for many years have been lacking in that sufficient sexual capacity which the well-preserved woman needs for her satisfaction. We have learned by experience to know that those very men whose faithfulness is thus placed beyond a doubt are most gentle in their treatment of their wives and unusually forbearing toward their nervous complaints. Furthermore, the fact that it was just the young husband of a daughter who became the object of her abnormal infatuation is by no means insignificant. A strong erotic attachment to the daughter, which in the last analysis leads back to the mother's sexual constitution, will often find a way to live on under such a disguise. May I perhaps remind you in this connection that the relationship between mother and son-in-law has seemed particularly delicate since all time and is one which among primitive peoples gave rise to very powerful taboos and avoidances (compare Freud's *Totem and Taboo*) It often transgresses our cultural standards positively as well as negatively. I cannot tell you of course which of these three factors were at work in our case; or if only two of them or all cooperated, for as you know I did not have the opportunity to continue the analysis beyond two hours.

I realize at this point, ladies and gentlemen, that I have been speaking entirely of things for which your understanding was not prepared. I did this in order to carry through the comparison of psychiatry and psychoanalysis. May I now ask, have you noticed any contradiction between them? Psychiatry does not apply the technical methods of psychoanalysis, and neglects to look for any significance in the content of the obsession. Instead of first seeking out more specific and immediate causes, psychiatry refers us to the very general and remote source—heredity. But does this imply a contradiction, a conflict between them? Do they not rather supplement one another? For does the hereditary factor deny the significance of the experience, is it not rather true that both operate together in the most effective way? You must admit that there is nothing in the nature of psychiatric work which must repudiate psychoanalytic research. Therefore, it is the psychiatrists who oppose psychoanalysis, not psychiatry itself. Psychoanalysis stands in about the

164

same relation to psychiatry as does histology to anatomy. The one studies the outer forms of organs, the other the closer structure of tissues and cells. A contradiction between two types of study, where one simplifies the other, is not easily conceivable. You know that anatomy to-day forms the basis of scientific medicine, but there was a time when the dissection of human corpses to learn the inner structure of the body was as much frowned upon as the practice of psychoanalysis, which seeks to ascertain the inner workings of the human soul, seems proscribed to-day. And presumably a not too distant time will bring us to the realization that a psychiatry which aspires to scientific depth is not possible without a real knowledge of the deeper unconscious processes in the psychic life.

Perhaps this much-attacked psychoanalysis has now found some friends among you who are anxious to see it justify itself as well from another aspect, namely, the therapeutic side. You know that the therapy of psychiatry has hitherto not been able to influence obsessions. Can psychoanalysis perhaps do so, thanks to its insight into the mechanism of these symptoms? No, ladies and gentlemen, it cannot; for the present at least it is just as powerless in the face of these maladies as every other therapy. We can understand what it was that happened within the patient, but we have no means of making the patient himself understand this. In fact, I told you that I could not extend the analysis of the obsession beyond the first steps. Would you therefore assert that analysis is objectionable in such cases because it remains without result? I think not. We have the right, indeed we have the duty to pursue scientific research without regard to an immediate practical effect. Some day, though we do not know when or where, every little scrap of knowledge will have been translated into skill, even into therapeutic skill. If psychoanalysis were as unsuccessful in all other forms of nervous and psychological disease as it is in the case of the obsession, it would nevertheless remain fully justified as an irreplaceable method of scientific research. It is true that we would then not be in a position to practice it, for the human subjects from which we must learn, live and will in their own right; they must have motives of their own in order to assist in the work, but they would deny themselves to us. Therefore let me conclude this session by telling you that there are comprehensive groups of nervous diseases concerning which our better understanding has actually been translated into therapeutic power; moreover, that in disturbances which are most difficult to reach we can under certain conditions secure results which are second to none in the field of internal therapeutics.

SEVENTEENTH LECTURE. GENERAL THEORY OF THE NEUROSES

The Meaning of the Symptoms

IN the last lecture I explained to you that clinical psychiatry concerns itself very little with the form under which the symptoms appear or with the burden they carry, but that it is precisely here that psychoanalysis steps in and shows that the symptom carries a meaning and is connected with the experience of the patient. The meaning of neurotic symptoms was first discovered by J. Breuer in the study and felicitous cure of a case of hysteria which has since become famous (1880-82). It is true that P. Janet independently reached the same result; literary priority must in fact be accorded to the French scholar, since Breuer published his observations more than a decade later (1893-95) during his period of collaboration with me. On the whole it may be of small importance to us who is responsible for this discovery, for you know that every discovery is made more than once, that none is made all at once, and that success is not meted out according to deserts. America is not named after Columbus. Before Breuer and Janet, the great psychiatrist Leuret expressed the opinion that even for the deliria of the insane, if we only understood how to interpret them, a meaning could be found. I confess that for a considerable period of time I was willing to estimate very highly the credit due to P. Janet in the explanation of neurotic symptoms, because he saw in them the expression of subconscious ideas (*idées inconscientes*) with which the patients were obsessed. But since then Janet has expressed himself most conservatively, as though he wanted to confess that the term "subconscious" had been for him nothing more than a mode of speech, a shift, "*une façon de parler*," by the use of which he had nothing definite in mind. I now no longer understand Janet's discussions, but I believe that he has needlessly deprived himself of high credit.

The neurotic symptoms then have their meaning just like errors and the dream, and like these they are related to the lives of the persons in whom they appear. The importance of this insight into the nature of the symptom can best be brought home to you by way of examples. That it is borne out always and in all cases, I can only assert, not prove. He who gathers his own experience will be convinced of it. For certain reasons, however, I shall draw my instances not from hysteria, but from another fundamentally related and very curious neurosis concerning which I wish to say a few introductory words to you. This so-called compulsion neurosis is not so popular as the widely known hysteria; it is, if I may use the expression, not so noisily ostentatious, behaves more as a private concern of the patient, renounces bodily manifestations almost entirely and creates all its symptoms psychologically. Compulsion neurosis and hysteria are those forms of neurotic disease by the study of which psychoanalysis has been built up, and in whose treatment as well the therapy celebrates its triumphs. Of these the compulsion neurosis, which does not take that mysterious leap from the psychic to the physical, has through psychoanalytic research become more intimately comprehensible and transparent to us than hysteria, and we have come to understand that it reveals far more vividly certain extreme characteristics of the neuroses.

The chief manifestations of compulsion neurosis are these: the patient is occupied by thoughts that in reality do not interest him, is moved by impulses that appear alien to him, and is impelled to actions which, to be sure, afford him no pleasure, but the performance of which he cannot possibly resist. The thoughts may be absurd in themselves or thoroughly indifferent to the individual, often they are absolutely childish and in all cases they are the result of strained thinking, which exhausts the patient, who surrenders himself to them most unwillingly. Against his will he is forced to brood and speculate as though it were a matter of life or death to him. The impulses, which the patient feels within himself, may also give a childish or ridiculous impression, but for the most part they bear the terrifying aspect of temptations to fearful crimes, so that the patient not only denies them, but flees from them in horror and protects himself from actual execution of his desires through inhibitory renunciations and restrictions upon his personal liberty. As a matter of fact he never, not a single time, carries any of these impulses into effect; the result is always that his evasion and precaution triumph. The patient really carries out only very harmless trivial acts, so-called compulsive acts, for the most part repetitions and ceremonious additions to the occupations of every-day life, through which its necessary performances—going to bed, washing, dressing, walking—become long-winded problems of almost insuperable difficulty. The abnormal ideas, impulses and actions are in nowise equally potent in individual forms and cases of compulsion neurosis; it is the rule, rather, that one or the other of these manifestations is the dominating factor and gives the name to the disease; that all these forms, however, have a great deal in common is quite undeniable.

Surely this means violent suffering. I believe that the wildest psychiatric phantasy could not have succeeded in deriving anything comparable, and if one did not actually see it every day, one could hardly bring oneself to believe it. Do not think, however, that you give the patient any help when you coax him to divert himself, to put aside these stupid ideas and to set himself to something useful in the place of his whimsical occupations. This is just what he would like of his own accord, for he possesses all his senses, shares your opinion of his compulsion symptoms, in fact volunteers it quite readily. But he cannot do otherwise; whatever activities actually are released under compulsion neurosis are carried along by a driving energy, such as is probably never met with in normal psychic life. He has only one remedy—to transfer and change. In place of one stupid idea he can think of a somewhat milder absurdity, he can proceed from one precaution and prohibition to another, or carry through another ceremonial. He may shift, but he cannot annul the compulsion. One of the chief characteristics of the sickness is the instability of the symptoms; they can be shifted very far from their original form. It is moreover striking that the contrasts present in all psychological experience are so very sharply drawn in this condition. In addition to the compulsion of positive and negative content, an intellectual doubt makes itself felt that gradually attacks the most ordinary and assured certainties. All these things merge into steadily increasing uncertainty, lack of energy, curtailment of personal liberty, despite the fact that the patient suffering from compulsion neurosis is originally a most energetic character, often of extraordinary obstinacy, as a rule intellectually gifted above the average. For the most part he has attained a desirable stage of ethical development, is overconscientious and more than usually correct. You can imagine that it takes no inconsiderable piece of work to find one's way through this maze of contradictory characteristics and symptoms. Indeed, for the present our only object is to understand and to interpret some symptoms of this disease.

Perhaps in reference to our previous discussions, you would like to know the position of present-day psychiatry to the problems of the compulsion neurosis. This is covered in a very slim chapter. Psychiatry gives names to the various forms of compulsion, but says nothing further concerning them. Instead it emphasizes the fact that those who show these symptoms are degenerates. That yields slight satisfaction, it is an ethical judgment, a condemnation rather than an explanation. We are led to suppose that it is in the unsound that all these peculiarities may be found. Now we do believe that persons who develop such symptoms must differ fundamentally from other people. But we would like to ask, are they more "degenerate" than other nervous patients, those suffering, for instance, from hysteria or other diseases of the mind? The characterization is obviously too general. One may even doubt whether it is at all justified, when one learns that such symptoms occur in excellent men and women of especially great and universally recognized ability. In general we glean very little intimate knowledge of the great men who serve us as models. This is due both to their own discretion and to the lying propensities of their biographers. Sometimes, however, a man is a fanatic disciple of truth, such as Emile Zola, and then we hear from him the strange compulsion habits from which he suffered all his life.[15]

Psychiatry has resorted to the expedient of speaking of "superior degenerates." Very well—but through psychoanalysis we have learned that these peculiar compulsion symptoms may be permanently removed just like any other disease of normal persons. I myself have frequently succeeded in doing this.

I will give you two examples only of the analysis of compulsion symptoms, one, an old observation, which cannot be replaced by anything more

---

[15] E. Toulouse, Emile Zola—*Enquête medico-psychologique*, Paris, 1896.

complete, and one a recent study. I am limiting myself to such a small number because in an account of this nature it is necessary to be very explicit and to enter into every detail.

A lady about thirty years old suffered from the most severe compulsions. I might indeed have helped her if caprice of fortune had not destroyed my work—perhaps I will yet have occasion to tell you about it. In the course of each day the patient often executed, among others, the following strange compulsive act. She ran from her room into an adjoining one, placed herself in a definite spot beside a table which stood in the middle of the room, rang for her maid, gave her a trivial errand to do, or dismissed her without more ado, and then ran back again. This was certainly not a severe symptom of disease, but it still deserved to arouse curiosity. Its explanation was found, absolutely without any assistance on the part of the physician, in the very simplest way, a way to which no one can take exception. I hardly know how I alone could have guessed the meaning of this compulsive act, or have found any suggestion toward its interpretation. As often as I had asked the patient: "Why do you do this? Of what use is it?" she had answered, "I don't know." But one day after I had succeeded in surmounting a grave ethical doubt of hers she suddenly saw the light and related the history of the compulsive act. More than ten years prior she had married a man far older than herself, who had proved impotent on the bridal night. Countless times during the night he had run from his room to hers to repeat the attempt, but each time without success. In the morning he said angrily: "It is enough to make one ashamed before the maid who does the beds," and took a bottle of red ink that happened to be in the room, and poured its contents on the sheet, but not on the place where such a stain would have been justifiable. At first I did not understand the connection between this reminiscence and the compulsive act in question, for the only agreement I could find between them was in the running from one room into another,—possibly also in the appearance of the maid. Then the patient led me to the table in the second room and let me discover a large spot on the cover. She explained also that she placed herself at the table in such a way that the maid could not miss seeing the stain. Now it was no longer possible to doubt the intimate relation of the scene after her bridal night and her present compulsive act, but there were still a number of things to be learned about it.

In the first place, it is obvious that the patient identifies herself with her husband, she is acting his part in her imitation of his running from one room into the other. We must then admit—if she holds to this role—that she replaces the bed and sheet by table and cover. This may seem arbitrary, but we have not studied dream symbolism in vain. In dreams also a table which must be interpreted as a bed, is frequently seen. "Bed and board" together represent married life, one may therefore easily be used to represent the other.

The evidence that the compulsive act carries meaning would thus be plain; it appears as a representation, a repetition of the original significant scene. However, we are not forced to stop at this semblance of a solution; when we examine more closely the relation between these two people, we shall probably be enlightened concerning something of wider importance, namely, the purpose of the compulsive act. The nucleus of this purpose is evidently the summoning of the maid; to her she wishes to show the stain and refute her husband's remark: "It is enough to shame one before the maid." He—whose part she is playing—therefore feels no shame before the maid, hence the stain must be in the right place. So we see that she has not merely repeated the scene, rather she has amplified it, corrected it and "turned it to the good." Thereby, however, she also corrects something else,—the thing which was so embarrassing that night and necessitated the use of the red ink—impotence. The compulsive act then says: "No, it is not true, he did not have to be ashamed before the maid, he was not impotent." After the manner of a dream she represents the fulfillment of this wish in an overt action, she is ruled by the desire to help her husband over that unfortunate incident.

Everything else that I could tell you about this case supports this clue more specifically; all that we otherwise know about her tends to strengthen this interpretation of a compulsive act incomprehensible in itself. For years the woman has lived separated from her husband and is struggling with the intention to obtain a legal divorce. But she is by no means free from him; she forces herself to remain faithful to him, she retires from the world to avoid temptation; in her imagination she excuses and idealizes him. The deepest secret of her malady is that by means of it she shields her husband from malicious gossip, justifies her separation from him, and renders possible for him a comfortable separate life. Thus the analysis of a harmless compulsive act leads to the very heart of this case and at the same time reveals no inconsiderable portion of the secret of the compulsion neurosis in general. I shall be glad to have you dwell upon this instance, as it combines conditions that one can scarcely demand in other cases. The interpretation of the symptoms was discovered by the patient herself in one flash, without the suggestion or interference of the analyst. It came about by the reference to an experience, which did not, as is usually the case, belong to the half-forgotten period of childhood, but to the mature life of the patient, in whose memory it had remained unobliterated. All the objections which critics ordinarily offer to our interpretation of symptoms fail in this case. Of course, we are not always so fortunate.

And one thing more! Have you not observed how this insignificant compulsive act initiated us into the intimate life of the invalid? A woman can scarcely relate anything more intimate than the story of her bridal night, and is it without further significance that we just happened to come on the intimacies of her sexual life? It might of course be the result of the selection I have made in this instance. Let us not judge too quickly and turn our attention to the second instance, one of an entirely different kind, a sample of a frequently occurring variety, namely, the sleep ritual.

A nineteen-year old, well-developed, gifted girl, an only child, who was superior to her parents in education and intellectual activity, had been wild and mischievous in her childhood, but has become very nervous during the last years without any apparent outward cause. She is especially irritable with her mother, always discontented, depressed, has a tendency toward indecision and doubt, and is finally forced to confess that she can no longer walk alone on public squares or wide thoroughfares. We shall not consider at length her complicated condition, which requires at least two diagnoses—agoraphobia and compulsion neurosis. We will dwell only upon the fact that this girl has also developed a sleep ritual, under which she allows her parents to suffer much discomfort. In a certain sense, we may say that every normal person has a sleep ritual, in other words that he insists on certain conditions, the absence of which hinders him from falling asleep; he has created certain observances by which he bridges the transition from waking to sleeping and these he repeats every evening in the same manner. But everything that the healthy person demands in order to obtain sleep is easily understandable and, above all, when external conditions necessitate a change, he adapts himself easily and without loss of time. But the pathological ritual is rigid, it persists by virtue of the greatest sacrifices, it also masks itself with a reasonable justification and seems, in the light of superficial observation, to differ from the normal only by exaggerated pedantry. But under closer observation we notice that the mask is transparent, for the ritual covers intentions that go far beyond this reasonable justification, and other intentions as well that are in direct contradiction to this reasonable justification. Our patient cites as the motive of her nightly precautions that she must have quiet in order to sleep; therefore she excludes all sources of noise. To accomplish this, she does two things: the large clock in her room is stopped, all other clocks are removed; not even the wrist watch on her night-table is suffered to remain. Flowerpots and vases are placed on her desk so that they cannot fall down during the night, and in breaking disturb her sleep. She knows that these precautions are scarcely justifiable for the sake of quiet; the ticking of the small watch could not be heard even if it should remain on the night-table, and moreover we all know that the regular ticking of a clock is conducive to sleep rather than disturbing. She does admit that there is not the least probability that flowerpots and vases left in place might of their own accord fall and break during the night. She drops the pretense of quiet for the other practice of this sleep ritual. She seems on the contrary to release a source of disturbing noises by the demand that the door between her own room and that of her parents remain half open, and she insures this condition by placing various objects in front of the open door. The most important observances concern the bed itself. The large pillow at the head of the bed may not touch the wooden back of the bed. The small pillow for her head must lie on the large pillow to form a rhomb; she then places her head exactly upon the diagonal of the rhomb. Before covering herself, the featherbed must be shaken so that its foot end becomes quite flat, but she never omits to press this down and redistribute the thickness.

Allow me to pass over the other trivial incidents of this ritual; they would teach us nothing new and cause too great digression from our purpose. Do not overlook, however, the fact that all this does not run its course quite smoothly. Everything is pervaded by the anxiety that things have not been done properly; they must be examined, repeated. Her doubts seize first on one, then on another precaution, and the result is that one or two hours elapse during which the girl cannot and the intimidated parents dare not sleep.

These torments were not so easily analyzed as the compulsive act of our former patient. In the working out of the interpretations I had to hint and suggest to the girl, and was met on her part either by positive denial or mocking doubt. This first reaction of denial, however, was followed by a time when she occupied herself of her own accord with the possibilities that had been suggested, noted the associations they called out, produced reminiscences, and established connections, until through her own efforts she had reached and accepted all interpretations. In so far as she did this, she desisted as well from the performance of her compulsive rules, and even before the treatment had ended she had given up the entire ritual. You must also know that the nature of present-day analysis by no means enables us to follow out each individual symptom until its meaning becomes clear. Rather it is necessary to abandon a given theme again and again, yet with the certainty that we will be led back to it in some other connection. The interpretation of the symptoms in this case, which I am about to give you, is a synthesis of results, which, with the interruptions of other work, needed weeks and months for their compilation.

Our patient gradually learns to understand that she has banished clocks and watches from her room during the night because the clock is the symbol of the female genital. The clock, which we have learned to interpret as a symbol for other things also, receives this role of the genital organ through its relation to periodic occurrences at equal intervals. A woman may for instance be found to boast that her menstruation is as regular as clockwork. The special fear of our patient, however, was that the ticking of the clock would disturb her in her sleep. The ticking of the clock may be compared to the throbbing of the clitoris during sexual excitement. Frequently she had actually been awakened by this painful sensation and now this fear of an erection of the clitoris caused her to remove all ticking clocks during the night. Flowerpots and vases are, as are all vessels, also female symbols. The precaution, therefore, that they should not fall and break at night, was not without meaning. We know the widespread custom of breaking a plate or dish when an engagement is celebrated. The fragment of which each guest possesses himself symbolizes his renunciation of his claim to the bride, a renunciation which we may assume as based on the monogamous marriage law. Furthermore, to this part of her ceremonial our patient adds a reminiscence and several associations. As a child she had slipped once and fallen with a bowl of glass or clay, had cut her finger, and bled violently. As she grew up and learned the facts of sexual intercourse, she developed the fear that she might not bleed during her bridal night and so not prove to be a virgin. Her precaution against the breaking of vases was a rejection of the entire virginity complex, including the bleeding connected with the first cohabitation. She rejected both the fear to bleed and the contradictory fear not to bleed. Indeed her precautions had very little to do with a prevention of noise.

One day she guessed the central idea of her ceremonial, when she suddenly understood her rule not to let the pillow come in contact with the bed. The pillows always had seemed a woman to her, the erect back of the bed a man. By means of magic, we may say, she wished to keep apart man and wife; it was her parents she wished to separate, so to prevent their marital intercourse. She had sought to attain the same end by more direct methods in earlier years, before the institution of her ceremonial. She had simulated fear or exploited a genuine timidity in order to keep open the door between the parents' bedroom and the nursery. This demand had been retained in her present ceremonial. Thus she had gained the opportunity of overhearing her parents, a proceeding which at one time subjected her to months of sleeplessness. Not content with this disturbance to her parents, she was at that time occasionally able to gain her point and sleep between father and mother in their very bed. Then "pillow" and "wooden wall" could really not come in contact. Finally when she became so big that her presence between the parents could no longer be borne comfortably, she consciously simulated fear and actually succeeded in changing places with her mother and taking her place at her father's side. This situation was undoubtedly the starting point for the phantasies, whose after-effects made themselves felt in her ritual.

If a pillow represented a woman, then the shaking of the featherbed till all the feathers were lumped at one end, rounding it into a prominence, must have its meaning also. It meant the impregnation of the wife; the ceremonial, however, never failed to provide for the annulment, of this pregnancy by the flattening down of the feathers. Indeed, for years our patient had feared that the intercourse between her parents might result in another child which would be her rival. Now, where the large pillow represents a woman, the mother, then the small pillow could be nothing but the daughter. Why did this pillow have to be placed so as to form a rhomb; and why did the girl's head have to rest exactly upon the diagonal? It was easy to remind the patient that the rhomb on all walls is the rune used to represent the open female genital. She herself then played the part of the man, the father, and her head took the place of the male organ. (Cf. the symbol of beheading to represent castration.)

Wild ideas, you will say, to run riot in the head of a virgin girl. I admit it, but do not forget that I have not created these ideas but merely interpreted them. A sleep ritual of this kind is itself very strange, and you cannot deny the correspondence between the ritual and the phantasies that yielded us the interpretation. For my part I am most anxious that you observe in this connection that no single phantasy was projected in the ceremonial, but a number of them had to be integrated,—they must have their nodal points somewhere in space. Observe also that the observance of the ritual reproduce the sexual desire now positively, now negatively, and serve in part as their rejection, again as their representation.

It would be possible to make a better analysis of this ritual by relating it to other symptoms of the patient. But we cannot digress in that direction. Let the suggestion suffice that the girl is subject to an erotic attachment to her father, the beginning of which goes back to her earliest childhood. That perhaps is the reason for her unfriendly attitude toward her mother. Also we cannot escape the fact that the analysis of this symptom again points to the sexual life of the patient. The more we penetrate to the meaning and purpose of neurotic symptoms, the less surprising will this seem to us.

By means of two selected illustrations I have demonstrated to you that neurotic symptoms carry just as much meaning as do errors and the dream, and that they are intimately connected with the experience of the patient. Can I expect you to believe this vitally significant statement on the strength of two examples? No. But can you expect me to cite further illustrations until you declare yourself convinced? That too is impossible, since considering the explicitness with which I treat each individual case, I would require a five-hour full semester course for the explanation of this one point in the theory of the neuroses. I must content myself then with having given you one proof for my assertion and refer you for the rest to the literature of the subject, above all to the classical interpretation of symptoms in Breuer's first case (hysteria) as well as to the striking clarification of obscure symptoms in the so-called dementia praecox by C. G. Jung, dating from the time when this scholar was still content to be a mere psychoanalyst—and did not yet want to be a prophet; and to all the articles that have subsequently appeared in our periodicals. It is precisely investigations of this sort which are plentiful. Psychoanalysts have felt themselves so much attracted by the analysis, interpretation and translation of neurotic symptoms, that by contrast they seem temporarily to have neglected other problems of neurosis.

Whoever among you takes the trouble to look into the matter will undoubtedly be deeply impressed by the wealth of evidential material. But he will also encounter difficulties. We have learned that the meaning of a symptom is found in its relation to the experience of the patient. The more highly individualized the symptom is, the sooner we may hope to establish these relations. Therefore the task resolves itself specifically into the discovery for every nonsensical idea and useless action of a past situation wherein the idea had been justified and the action purposeful. A perfect example for this kind of symptom is the compulsive act of our patient who ran to the table and rang for the maid. But there are symptoms of a very different nature which are by no means rare. They must be called typical symptoms of the disease, for they are approximately alike in all cases, in which the individual differences disappear or shrivel to such an extent that it is difficult to connect them with the specific experiences of the patient and to relate them to the particular situations of his past. Let us again direct our attention to the compulsion neurosis. The sleep ritual of our second patient is already quite typical, but bears enough individual features to render possible what may be called an *historic* interpretation. But all compulsive patients tend to repeat, to isolate their actions from others and to subject them to a rhythmic sequence. Most of them wash too much. Agoraphobia (topophobia, fear of spaces), a malady which is no longer grouped with the compulsion neurosis, but is now called anxiety hysteria, invariably shows the same pathological picture; it repeats with exhausting monotony the same feature, the patient's fear of closed spaces, of large open squares, of long stretched streets and parkways, and their feeling of safety when acquaintances accompany them, when a carriage drives after them, etc. On this identical groundwork, however, the individual differences between the patients are superimposed—moods one might almost call them, which are sharply contrasted in the various cases. The one fears only narrow streets, the other only wide ones, the one can go out walking only when there are few people abroad, the other when there are many. Hysteria also, aside from its wealth of individual features, has a superfluity of common typical symptoms that appear to resist any facile historical methods of tracing them. But do not let us forget that it is by these typical symptoms that we get our bearings in reaching a diagnosis. When, in one case of hysteria we have finally traced back a typical symptom to an experience or a series of similar experiences, for instance followed back an hysterical vomiting to its origin in a succession of disgust impressions, another case of vomiting will confuse us by revealing an entirely different chain of experiences, seemingly just as effective. It seems almost as though hysterical patients must vomit for some reason as yet unknown, and that the historic factors, revealed by analysis, are chance pretexts, seized on as opportunity best offered to serve the purposes of a deeper need.

Thus we soon reach the discouraging conclusion that although we can satisfactorily explain the individual neurotic symptom by relating it to an experience, our science fails us when it comes to the typical symptoms that occur far more frequently. In addition, remember that I am not going into all the detailed difficulties which come up in the course of resolutely hunting down an historic interpretation of the symptom. I have no intention of doing this, for though I want to keep nothing from you, and so paint everything in its true colors, I still do not wish to confuse and discourage you at the very outset of our studies. It is true that we have only begun to understand the interpretation of symptoms, but we wish to hold fast to the results we have achieved, and struggle forward step by step toward the mastery of the still unintelligible data. I therefore try to cheer you with the thought that a fundamental between the two kinds of symptoms can scarcely be assumed. Since the individual symptoms are so obviously dependent upon the experience of the patient, there is a possibility that the typical symptoms revert to an experience that is in itself typical and common to all humanity. Other regularly recurring features of neurosis, such as the repetition and doubt of the compulsion neurosis, may be universal reactions which are forced upon the patient by the very nature of the abnormal change. In short, we have no reason to be prematurely discouraged; we shall see what our further results will yield.

We meet a very similar difficulty in the theory of dreams, which in our previous discussion of the dream I could not go into. The manifest content of dreams is most profuse and individually varied, and I have shown very explicitly what analysis may glean from this content. But side by side with these dreams there are others which may also be termed "typical" and which occur similarly in all people. These are dreams of identical content which offer the same difficulties for their interpretation as the typical symptom. They are the dreams of falling, flying, floating, swimming, of being hemmed in, of nakedness, and various other anxiety dreams that yield first one and then another interpretation for the different patients, without resulting in an explanation of their monotonous and typical recurrence. In the matter of these dreams also, we see a fundamental groundwork enriched by individual additions. Probably they as well can be fitted into the theory of dream life, built up on the basis of other dreams,—not however by straining the point, but by the gradual broadening of our views.

EIGHTEENTH LECTURE. GENERAL THEORY OF THE NEUROSES

Traumatic Fixation—The Unconscious

I SAID last time that we would not continue our work from the standpoint of our doubts, but on the basis of our results. We have not even touched upon two of the most interesting conclusions, derived equally from the same two sample analyses.

In the first place, both patients give us the impression of being *fixated* upon some very definite part of their past; they are unable to free themselves therefrom, and have therefore come to be completely estranged both from the present and the future. They are now isolated in their ailment, just as in earlier days people withdrew into monasteries there to carry along the burden of their unhappy fates. In the case of the first patient, it is her marriage with her husband, really abandoned, that has determined her lot. By means of her symptoms she continues to deal with her husband; we have learned to understand those voices which plead his case, which excuse him, exalt him, lament his loss. Although she is young and might be coveted by other men, she has seized upon all manner of real and imaginary (magic) precautions to safeguard her virtue for him. She will not appear before strangers, she neglects her personal appearance; furthermore, she cannot bring herself to get up readily from any chair on which she has been seated. She refuses to give her signature, and finally, since she is motivated by her desire not to let anyone have anything of hers, she is unable to give presents.

In the case of the second patient, the young girl, it is an erotic attachment for her father that had established itself in the years prior to puberty, which plays the same role in her life. She also has arrived at the conclusion that she may not marry so long as she is sick. We may suspect she became ill in order that she need not marry, and that she might stay with her father.

It is impossible to evade the question of how, in what manner, and driven by what motives, an individual may come by such a remarkable and unprofitable attitude toward life. Granted of course that this bearing is a general characteristic of neurosis, and not a special peculiarity of these two cases, it is nevertheless a general trait in every neurosis of very great importance in practice. Breuer's first hysterical patient was fixated in the same manner upon the time when she nursed her very sick father. In spite of her recuperation she has, in certain respects, since that time, been done with life; although she remained healthy and able, she did not enter on the normal life of women. In every one of our patients we may see, by the use of analysis, that in his disease-symptoms and their results he has gone back again into a definite period of his past. In the majority of cases he even chooses a very early phase of his life, sometime a childhood phase, indeed, laughable as it may appear, a phase of his very suckling existence.

The closest analogies to these conditions of our neurotics are furnished by the types of sickness which the war has just now made so frequent—the so-called traumatic neuroses. Even before the war there were such cases after railroad collisions and other frightful occurrences which endangered life. The traumatic neuroses are, fundamentally, not the same as the spontaneous neuroses which we have been analysing and treating; moreover, we have not yet succeeded in bringing them within our hypotheses, and I hope to be able to make clear to you wherein this limitation lies. Yet on one point we may emphasize the existence of a complete agreement between the two forms. The traumatic neuroses show clear indications that they are grounded in a fixation upon the moment of the traumatic disaster. In their dreams these patients regularly live over the traumatic situation; where there are attacks of an hysterical type, which permit of an analysis, we learn that the attack approximates a complete transposition into this situation. It is as if these patients had not yet gotten through with the traumatic situation, as if it were actually before them as a task which was not yet mastered. We take this view of the matter in all seriousness; it shows the way to an *economic* view of psychic occurrences. For the expression "traumatic" has no other than an economic meaning, and the disturbance permanently attacks the management of available energy. The traumatic experience is one which, in a very short space of time, is able to increase the strength of a given stimulus so enormously that its assimilation, or rather its elaboration, can no longer be effected by normal means.

This analogy tempts us to classify as traumatic those experiences as well upon which our neurotics appear to be fixated. Thus the possibility is held out to us of having found a simple determining factor for the neurosis. It would then be comparable to a traumatic disease, and would arise from the inability to meet an overpowering emotional experience. As a matter of fact this reads like the first formula, by which Breuer and I, in 1893-1895, accounted theoretically for our new observations. A case such as that of our first patient, the young woman separated from her husband, is very well explained by this conception. She was not able to get over the unfeasibility of her marriage, and has not been able to extricate herself from this trauma. But our very next, that of the girl attached to her father, shows us that the formula is not sufficiently comprehensive. On the one hand, such baby love of a little girl for her father is so usual, and so often outlived that the designation "traumatic" would carry no significance; on the other hand, the history of the patient teaches us that this first erotic fixation apparently passed by harmlessly at the time, and did not again appear until many years later in the symptoms of the compulsion neurosis. We see complications before us, the existence of a greater wealth of determining factors in the disease, but we also suspect that the traumatic viewpoint will not have to be given up as wrong; rather it will have to subordinate itself when it is fitted into a different context.

Here again we must leave the road we have been traveling. For the time being, it leads us no further and we have many other things to find out before we can go on again. But before we leave this subject let us note that the fixation on some particular phase of the past has bearings which extend far beyond the neurosis. Every neurosis contains such a fixation, but every fixation does not lead to a neurosis, nor fall into the same class with neuroses, nor even set the conditions for the development of a neurosis. Mourning is a type of emotional fixation on a theory of the past, which also brings with it the most complete alienation from the present and the future. But mourning is sharply distinguished from neuroses that may be designated as pathological forms of mourning.

It also happens that men are brought to complete deadlock by a traumatic experience that has so completely shaken the foundations on which they have built their lives that they give up all interest in the present and future, and become completely absorbed in their retrospections; but these unhappy persons are not necessarily neurotic. We must not overestimate this one feature as a diagnostic for a neurosis, no matter how invariable and potent it may be.

Now let us turn to the second conclusion of our analysis, which however we will hardly need to limit subsequently. We have spoken of the senseless compulsive activities of our first patient, and what intimate memories she disclosed as belonging to them; later we also investigated the connection between experience and symptom and thus discovered the purpose hidden behind the compulsive activity. But we have entirely omitted one factor that deserves our whole attention. As long as the patient kept repeating the compulsive activity she did not know that it was in any way related with the experience in question. The connection between the two was hidden from her, she truthfully answered that she did not know what compelled her to do this. Once, suddenly, under the influence of the cure, she hit upon the connection and was able to tell it to us. But still she did not know of the end in the service of which she performed the compulsive activities, the purpose to correct a painful part of the past and to place the husband, still loved by her, upon a higher level. It took quite a long time and a great deal of trouble for her to grasp and admit to me that such a motive alone could have been the motive force of the compulsive activity.

The relation between the scene after the unhappy bridal night and the tender motive of the patient yield what we have called the meaning of the compulsive activity. But both the "whence" and the "why" remained hidden from her as long as she continued to carry out the compulsive act. Psychological processes had been going on within her for which the compulsive act found an expression. She could, in a normal frame of mind, observe their effect, but none of the psychological antecedents of her action had come to the knowledge of her consciousness. She had acted in just the same manner as a hypnotized person to whom Bernheim had given the injunction that five minutes after his awakening in the ward he was to open an umbrella, and he had carried out this order on awakening, but could give no motive for his so doing. We have exactly such facts in mind when we speak of the existence of *unconscious psychological processes*. Let anyone in the world account for these facts in a more correct scientific manner, and we will gladly withdraw completely our assumption of unconscious psychological processes. Until then, however, we shall continue to use this assumption, and when anyone wants to bring forward the objection that the unconscious can have no reality for science and is a mere makeshift, (*une façon de parler*), we must simply shrug our shoulders and reject his incomprehensible statement resignedly. A strange unreality which can call out such real and palpable effects as a compulsion symptom!

In our second patient we meet with fundamentally the same thing. She had created a decree which she must follow: the pillow must not touch the head of the bed; yet she does not know how it originated, what its meaning is, nor to what motive it owes the source of its power. It is immaterial whether she looks upon it with indifference or struggles against it, storms against it, determines to overcome it. She must nevertheless follow it and carry out its ordinance, though she asks herself, in vain, why. One must admit that these symptoms of compulsion neurosis offer the clearest evidence for a special sphere of psychological activity, cut off from the rest. What else could be back of these images and impulses, which appear from one knows not where, which have such great resistance to all the influences of an otherwise normal psychic life; which give the patient himself the impression that here are super-powerful guests from another world, immortals mixing in the affairs of mortals. Neurotic symptoms lead unmistakably to a conviction of the existence of an unconscious psychology, and for that very reason clinical psychiatry, which recognizes only a conscious psychology, has no explanation other than that they are present as indications of a particular kind of degeneration. To be sure, the compulsive images and impulses are not themselves unconscious—no more so than the carrying out of the compulsive-acts escapes conscious observation. They would not have been symptoms had they not penetrated through into consciousness. But their psychological antecedents as disclosed by the analysis, the associations into which we place them by our interpretations, are unconscious, at least until we have made them known to the patient during the course of the analysis.

Consider now, in addition, that the facts established in our two cases are confirmed in all the symptoms of all neurotic diseases, that always and everywhere the meaning of the symptoms is unknown to the sufferer, that analysis shows without fail that these symptoms are derivatives of unconscious experiences which can, under various favorable conditions, become conscious. You will understand then that in psychoanalysis we cannot do without this unconscious psyche, and are accustomed to deal with it as with something tangible. Perhaps you will also be able to understand how those who know the unconscious only as an idea, who have never analyzed, never interpreted dreams, or never translated neurotic symptoms into meaning and purpose, are most ill-suited to pass an opinion on this subject. Let us express our point of view once more. Our ability to give meaning to neurotic symptoms by means of analytic interpretation is an irrefutable indication of the existence of unconscious psychological processes—or, if you prefer, an irrefutable proof of the necessity for their assumption.

But that is not all. Thanks to a second discovery of Breuer's, for which he alone deserves credit and which appears to me to be even more far-reaching, we are able to learn still more concerning the relationship between the unconscious and the neurotic symptom. Not alone is the meaning of the symptoms invariably hidden in the unconscious; but the very existence of the symptom is conditioned by its relation to this unconscious. You will soon understand me. With Breuer I maintain the following: Every time we hit upon a symptom we may conclude that the patient cherishes definite unconscious experiences which withhold the meaning of the symptoms. Vice versa, in order that the symptoms may come into being, it is also essential that this meaning be unconscious. Symptoms are not built up out of conscious experiences; as soon as the unconscious processes in question become conscious, the symptom disappears. You will at once recognize here the approach to our therapy, a way to make symptoms disappear. It was by these means that Breuer actually achieved the recovery of his patient, that is, freed her of her symptoms; he found a technique for bringing into her consciousness the unconscious experiences that carried the meaning of her symptoms, and the symptoms disappeared.

This discovery of Breuer's was not the result of a speculation, but of a felicitous observation made possible by the cooperation of the patient. You should therefore not trouble yourself to find things you already know to which you can compare these occurrences, rather you should recognize herein a new fundamental fact which in itself is capable of much wider application. Toward this further end permit me to go over this ground again in a different way.

The symptom develops as a substitution for something else that has remained suppressed. Certain psychological experiences should normally have become so far elaborated that consciousness would have attained knowledge of them. This did not take place, however, but out of these interrupted and disturbed processes, imprisoned in the unconscious, the symptom arose. That is to say, something in the nature of an interchange had been effected; as often as therapeutic measures are successful in again reversing this transposition, psychoanalytic therapy solves the problem of the neurotic symptom.

Accordingly, Breuer's discovery still remains the foundation of psychoanalytic therapy. The assertion that the symptoms disappear when one has made their unconscious connections conscious, has been borne out by all subsequent research, although the most extraordinary and unexpected complications have been met with in its practical execution. Our therapy does its work by means of changing the unconscious into the conscious, and is effective only in so far as it has the opportunity of bringing about this transformation.

Now we shall make a hasty digression so that you do not by any chance imagine that this therapeutic work is too easy. From all we have learned so far, the neurosis would appear as the result of a sort of ignorance, the incognizance of psychological processes that we should know of. We would thus very closely approximate the well-known Socratic teachings, according to which evil itself is the result of ignorance. Now the experienced physician will, as a rule, discover fairly readily what psychic impulses in his several patients have remained unconscious. Accordingly it would seem easy for him to cure the patient by imparting this knowledge to him and freeing him of his ignorance. At least the part played by the unconscious meaning of the symptoms could easily be discovered in this manner, and it would only be in dealing with the relationship of the symptoms to the experiences of the patient that the physician would be handicapped. In the face of these experiences, of course, he is the ignorant one of the two, for he did not go through these experiences, and must wait until the patient remembers them and tells them to him. But in many cases this difficulty could be readily overcome. One can question the relatives of the patient concerning these experiences, and they will often be in a position to point out those that carry any traumatic significance; they may even be able to inform the analyst of experiences of which the patient knows nothing because they occurred in the very early years of his life. By a combination of such means it would seem that the pathogenic ignorance of the patient could be cleared up in a short time and without much trouble.

If only that were all! We have made discoveries for which we were at first unprepared. Knowing and knowing is not always the same thing; there are various kinds of knowing that are psychologically by no means comparable. "*Il y a fagots et fagots*," (There are fagots and fagots) as Molière says. The knowledge of the physician is not the same as that of the patient and cannot bring about the same results. The physician can gain no results by transferring his knowledge to the patient in so many words. This is perhaps putting it incorrectly, for though the transference does not result in dissolving the symptoms, it does set the analysis in motion, and calls out an energetic denial, the first sign usually that this has taken place. The patient has learned something that he did not know up to that time, the meaning of his symptoms, and yet he knows it as little as before. So we discover there is more than one kind of ignorance. It will require a deepening of our psychological insight to make clear to us wherein the difference lies. But our assertion nevertheless remains true that the symptoms disappear with the knowledge of their meaning. For there is only one limiting condition; the knowledge must be founded on an inner change in the patient which can be attained only through psychic labors directed toward a definite end. We have here been confronted by problems which will soon lead us to the elaboration of a dynamics of symptom formation.

I must stop to ask you whether this is not all too vague and too complicated? Do I not confuse you by so often retracting my words and restricting them, spinning out trains of thought and then rejecting them? I should be sorry if this were the case. However, I strongly dislike simplification at the expense of truth, and am not averse to having you receive the full impression of how many-sided and complicated the subject is. I also think that there is no harm done if I say more on every point than you can at the moment make use of. I know that every hearer and reader arranges what is offered him in his own thoughts, shortens it, simplifies it and extracts what he wishes to retain. Within a given measure it is true that the more we begin with the more we have left. Let me hope that, despite all the by-play, you have clearly grasped the essential parts of my remarks, those about the meaning of symptoms, about the unconscious, and the relation between the two. You probably have also understood that our further efforts are to take two directions: first, the clinical problem—to discover how persons become sick, how they later on accomplish a neurotic adaptation toward life; secondly, a problem of psychic dynamics, the evolution of the neurotic symptoms themselves from the prerequisites of the neuroses. We will undoubtedly somewhere come on a point of contact for these two problems.

I do not wish to go any further to-day, but since our time is not yet up I intend to call your attention to another characteristic of our two analyses, namely, the memory gaps or amnesias, whose full appreciation will be possible later. You have heard that it is possible to express the object of psychoanalytic treatment in a formula: all pathogenic unconscious experience must be transposed into consciousness. You will perhaps be surprised to learn that this formula can be replaced by another: all the memory gaps of the patient must be filled out, his amnesias must be abolished. Practically this amounts to the same thing. Therefore an important role in the development of his symptoms must be accredited to the amnesias of the neurotic. The analysis of our first case, however, will hardly justify this valuation of the amnesia. The patient has not forgotten the scene from which the compulsion act derives—on the contrary, she remembers it vividly, nor is there any other forgotten factor which comes into play in the development of these symptoms. Less clear, but entirely analogous, is the situation in the case of our second patient, the girl with the compulsive ritual. She, too, has not really forgotten the behavior of her early years, the fact that she insisted that the door between her bedroom and that of her parents be kept open, and that she banished her mother out of her place in her parents' bed. She recalls all this very clearly, although hesitatingly and unwillingly. Only one factor stands out strikingly in our first case, that though the patient carries out her compulsive act innumerable times, she is not once reminded of its similarity with the experience after the bridal-night; nor was this memory even suggested when by direct questions she was asked to search for its motivation. The same is true of the girl, for in her case not only her ritual, but the situation which provoked it, is repeated identically night after night. In neither case is there any actual amnesia, no lapse of memory, but an association is broken off which should have called out a reproduction, a revival in the memory. Such a disturbance is enough to bring on a compulsion neurosis. Hysteria, however, shows a different picture, for it is usually characterized by most grandiose amnesias. As a rule, in the analysis of each hysterical symptom, one is led back to a whole chain of impressions which, upon their recovery, are expressly designated as forgotten up to the moment. On the one hand this chain extends back to the earliest years of life, so that the hysterical amnesias may be regarded as the direct continuation of the infantile amnesias, which hides the beginnings of our psychic life from those of us who are normal. On the other hand, we discover with surprise that the most recent experiences of the patient are blurred by these losses of memory—that especially the provocations which favored or brought on the illness are, if not entirely wiped out by the amnesia, at least partially obliterated. Without fail important details have disappeared from the general picture of such a recent memory, or are placed by false memories. Indeed it happens almost regularly that just before the completion of an analysis, certain memories of recent experiences suddenly come to light. They had been held back all this time, and had left noticeable gaps in the context.

We have pointed out that such a crippling of the ability to recall is characteristic of hysteria. In hysteria symptomatic conditions also arise (hysterical attacks) which need leave no trace in the memory. If these things do not occur in compulsion-neuroses, you are justified in concluding that these amnesias exhibit psychological characteristics of the hysterical change, and not a general trait of the neuroses. The significance of this difference will be more closely limited by the following observations. We have combined two things as the meaning of a symptom, its "whence," on the one hand, and its "whither" or "why," on the other. By these we mean to indicate the impressions and experiences whence the symptom arises, and the purpose the symptom serves. The "whence" of a symptom is traced back to impressions which have come from without, which have therefore necessarily been conscious at some time, but which may have sunk into the unconscious—that is, have been forgotten. The "why" of the symptom, its tendency, is in every case an endopsychic process, developed from within, which may or may not have become conscious at first, but could just as readily never have entered consciousness at all and have been unconscious from its inception. It is, after all, not so very significant that, as happens in the hysterias, amnesia has covered over the "whence" of the symptom, the experience upon which it is based; for it is the "why," the tendency of the symptom, which establishes its dependence on the unconscious, and indeed no less so in the compulsion neuroses than in hysteria. In both cases the "why" may have been unconscious from the very first.

By thus bringing into prominence the unconscious in psychic life, we have raised the most evil spirits of criticism against psychoanalysis. Do not be surprised at this, and do not believe that the opposition is directed only against the difficulties offered by the conception of the unconscious or against the relative inaccessibility of the experiences which represent it. I believe it comes from another source. Humanity, in the course of time, has had to endure from the hands of science two great outrages against its naive self-love. The first was when humanity discovered that our earth was not the center of the universe, but only a tiny speck in a world-system hardly conceivable in its magnitude. This is associated in our minds with the name "Copernicus," although Alexandrian science had taught much the same thing. The second occurred when biological research robbed man of his apparent superiority under special creation, and rebuked him with his descent from the animal kingdom, and his ineradicable animal nature. This re-valuation, under the influence of Charles Darwin, Wallace and their predecessors, was not accomplished without the most violent opposition of their contemporaries. But the third and most irritating insult is flung at the human mania of greatness by present-day psychological research, which wants to prove to the "I" that it is not even master in its own home, but is dependent upon the most scanty information concerning all that goes on unconsciously

185

in its psychic life. We psychoanalysts were neither the first, nor the only ones to announce this admonition to look within ourselves. It appears that we are fated to represent it most insistently and to confirm it by means of empirical data which are of importance to every single person. This is the reason for the widespread revolt against our science, the omission of all considerations of academic urbanity, and emancipation of the opposition from all restraints of impartial logic. We were compelled to disturb the peace of the world, in addition, in another manner, of which you will soon come to know.

NINETEENTH LECTURE. GENERAL THEORY OF THE NEUROSES

Resistance and Suppression

IN order to progress in our understanding of the neuroses, we need new experiences and we are about to obtain two. Both are very remarkable and were at the time of their discovery, very surprising. You are, of course, prepared for both from our discussions of the past semester.

In the first place: When we undertake to cure a patient, to free him from the symptoms of his malady, he confronts us with a vigorous, tenacious resistance that lasts during the whole time of the treatment. That is so peculiar a fact that we cannot expect much credence for it. The best thing is not to mention this fact to the patient's relatives, for they never think of it otherwise than as a subterfuge on our part in order to excuse the length or the failure of our treatment. The patient, moreover, produces all the phenomena of this resistance without even recognizing it as such; it is always a great advance to have brought him to the point of understanding this conception and reckoning with it. Just consider, this patient suffers from his symptoms and causes those about him to suffer with him. He is willing, moreover, to take upon himself so many sacrifices of time, money, effort and self-denial in order to be freed. And yet he struggles, in the very interests of his malady, against one who would help him. How improbable this assertion must sound! And yet it is so, and if we are reproached with its improbability, we need only answer that this fact is not without its analogies. Whoever goes to a dentist with an unbearable toothache may very well find himself thrusting away the dentist's arm when the man makes for his sick tooth with a pair of pincers.

The resistance which the patient shows is highly varied, exceedingly subtle, often difficult to recognize, Protean-like in its manifold changes of form. It means that the doctor must become suspicious and be constantly on his guard against the patient. In psychoanalytic therapy we make use, as you know, of that technique which is already familiar to you from the interpretation of dreams. We tell the patient that without further reflection he should put himself into a condition of calm self-observation and that he must then communicate whatever results this introspection gives him—feelings, thoughts, reminiscences, in the order in which they appear to his mind. At the same time, we warn him expressly against yielding to any motive which would induce him to choose or exclude any of his thoughts as they arise, in whatever way the motive may be couched and however it may excuse him from telling us the thought: "that is too unpleasant," or "too indiscreet" for him to tell; or "it is too unimportant," or "it does not belong here," "it is nonsensical." We impress upon him the fact that he must skim only across the surface of his consciousness and must drop the last vestige of a critical attitude toward that which he finds. We finally inform him that the result of the treatment and above all its length is dependent on the conscientiousness with which he follows this basic rule of the analytic technique. We know, in fact, from the technique of interpreting dreams, that of all the random notions which may occur, those against which such doubts are raised are invariably the ones to yield the material which leads to the uncovering of the unconscious.

The first reaction we call out by laying down this basic technical rule is that the patient directs his entire resistance against it. The patient tries in every way to escape its requirements. First he will declare that he cannot think of anything, then, that so much comes to his mind that it is impossible to seize on anything definite. Then we discover with no slight displeasure that he has yielded to this or that critical objection, for he betrays himself by the long pauses which he allows to occur in his speaking. He then confesses that he really cannot bring himself to this, that he is ashamed to; he prefers to let this motive get the upper hand over his promise. He may say that he did think of something but that it concerns someone else and is for that reason exempt. Or he says that what he just thought of is really too trivial, too stupid and too foolish. I surely could not have meant that he should take such thoughts into account. Thus it goes on, with untold variations, in the face of which we continually reiterate that "telling everything" really means telling everything.

One can scarcely find a patient who does not make the attempt to reserve some province for himself against the intrusion of the analysis. One patient, whom I must reckon among the most highly intelligent, thus concealed an intimate love relation for weeks; and when he was asked to explain this infringement of our inviolable rule, he defended his action with the argument that he considered this one thing was his private affair. Naturally, analytic treatment cannot countenance such right of sanctuary. One might as well try in a city like Vienna to allow an exception to be made of great public squares like the Hohe Markt or the Stephans Platz and say that no one should be arrested in those places—and then attempt to round up some particular wrong-doer. He will be found nowhere but in those sanctuaries. I once brought myself around to permit such an exception in the case of a man on whose capacity for work a great deal depended, and who was bound by his oath of service, which forbade him to tell anyone of certain things. To be sure, he was satisfied with the results—but not I; I resolved never to repeat such an attempt under these conditions.

Compulsion neurotics are exceedingly adept at making this technical rule almost useless by bringing to bear all their over-conscientiousness and their doubts upon it. Patients suffering from anxiety-hysteria sometimes succeed in reducing it to absurdity by producing only notions so remote from the thing sought for that analysis is quite unprofitable. But it is not my intention to go into the way in which these technical difficulties may be met. It is enough to know that finally, by means of resolution and perseverance, we do succeed in wresting a certain amount of obedience from the patient toward this basic rule of the technique; the resistance then makes itself felt in other ways. It appears in the form of an intellectual resistance, battles by means of arguments, and makes use of all difficulties and improbabilities which a normal yet uninstructed thinking is bound to find in the theory of analysis. Then we hear from one voice alone the same criticisms and objections which thunder about us in mighty chorus in the scientific literature. Therefore the critics who shout to us from outside cannot tell us anything new. It is a veritable tempest in a teapot. Still the patient can be argued with, he is anxious to persuade us to instruct him, to teach him, to lead him to the literature, so that he may continue working things out for himself. He is very ready to become an adherent of psychoanalysis on condition that analysis spare him personally. But we recognize this curiosity as a resistance, as a diversion from our special objects, and we meet it accordingly. In those patients who suffer from compulsion neuroses, we must expect the resistance to display special tactics. They frequently allow the analysis to take its way, so that it may succeed in throwing more and more light on the problems of the case, but we finally begin to wonder how it is that this clearing up brings with it no practical progress, no diminution of the symptom. Then we may discover that the resistance has entrenched itself in the doubts of the compulsion neurosis itself and in this position is able successfully to resist our efforts. The patient has said something like this to himself: "This is all very nice and interesting. And I would be glad to continue it. It would affect my malady considerably if it were true. But I don't believe that it is true and as long as I don't believe it, it has nothing to do with my sickness." And so it may go on for a long time until one finally has shaken this position itself; it is then that the decisive battle takes place.

The intellectual resistances are not the worst, one can always get ahead of them. But the patient can also put up resistances, within the limits of the analysis, whose conquest belongs to the most difficult tasks of our technique. Instead of recalling, he actually goes again through the attitudes and emotions of his previous life which, by means of the so-called "transference," can be utilized as resistances to the physician and the treatment. If the patient is a man, he takes this material as a rule from his relations to his father, in whose place he now puts the physician, and in so doing constructs a resistance out of his struggle for independence of person and opinion; out of his ambition to equal or to excel his father; out of his unwillingness to assume the burden of gratitude a second time in his life. For long times at a stretch one receives the impression that the patient desires to put the physician in the wrong and to let him feel his helplessness by triumphing over him, and that this desire has completely replaced his better intention of making an end to his sickness. Women are adepts at exploiting, for the purposes of the resistance, a tender, erotically tinged transference to the physician. When this leaning attains a certain intensity, all interest for the actual situation of the treatment is lost, together with every sense of the responsibility which was assumed by undertaking it. The never-failing jealousy as well as the embitterment over the inevitable repudiation, however gently effected, all must serve to spoil the personal understanding between patient and physician and thus to throw out one of the most powerful propelling forces of the analysis.

Resistances of this sort must not be narrow-mindedly condemned. They contain so much of the most important material of the patient's past and reproduce it in such a convincing manner, that they become of the greatest aid to the analysis, if a skillful technique is able to turn them in the right direction. It is only remarkable that this material is at first always in the service of the resistance, for which it serves as a barrier against the treatment. One can also say that here are traits of character, adjustments of the ego which were mobilized in order to defeat the attempted change. We are thus able to learn how these traits arose under the conditions of the neurosis, as a reaction to its demands, and to see features more clearly in this character which could otherwise not have shown up so clearly or at least not to this extent, and which one may therefore designate as latent. You must also not get the impression that we see an unforeseen endangering of the analytic influence in the appearance of these resistances. On the contrary, we know that these resistances must come to light; we are dissatisfied only when we do not provoke them in their full strength and so make them plain to the patient Indeed, we at last understand that overcoming these resistances is the essential achievement of analysis and is that portion of the work which alone assures us that we have accomplished something with the patient.

You must also take into account the fact that any accidental occurrences which arise during the treatment will be made use of by the patient as a disturbance—every diverting incident, every statement about analysis from an inimical authority in his circle, any chance illness or any organic affection which complicates the neurosis; indeed, he even uses every improvement of his condition as a motive for abating his efforts. You will then have gained an approximate, though still an incomplete picture of the forms and devices of the resistance which must be met and overcome in the course of every analysis. I have given this point such detailed consideration because I am about to inform you that our dynamic conception of the neurosis is based on this experience with the resistance of neurotic patients against the banishment of their symptoms. Breuer and I both originally practiced psycho-therapy by means of hypnosis. Breuer's first patient was treated throughout under a condition of hypnotic suggestibility, and I at first followed his example. I admit that my work at that time progressed easily and agreeably and also took much less time. But the results were capricious and not permanent; therefore I finally gave up hypnotism. Then only did I realize that no insight into the forces which produce these diseases was possible as long as one used hypnotism. The condition of hypnosis could prevent the physician from realizing the existence of a resistance. Hypnosis drives back the resistance and frees a certain field for the work of analysis, but similarly to the doubt in the compulsion neurosis, in so doing it clogs the boundaries of this field till they become impenetrable. That is why I can say that true psychoanalysis began when the help of hypnotism was renounced.

But if the establishment of the resistance thus becomes a matter of such importance, then surely we must give our caution full rein, and follow up any doubts as to whether we are not all too ready in our assumption of their existence. Perhaps there really are neurotic cases in which associations appear for other reasons, perhaps the arguments against our hypothesis really deserve more consideration and we are unjustified in conveniently rejecting all intellectual criticisms of analysis as a resistance. Indeed, ladies and gentlemen, but our judgment was by no means readily arrived at. We had opportunity to observe every critical patient from the first sign of the resistance till after its disappearance. In the course of the treatment, the resistance is moreover constantly changing in intensity. It is always on the increase as we approach a new theme, is strongest at the height of its elaboration, and dies down again when this theme has been abandoned. Furthermore, unless we have made some unusual and awkward technical error, we never have to deal with the full measure of resistance of which the patient is capable. We could therefore convince ourselves that the same man took up and discarded his critical attitude innumerable times in the course of the analysis. Whenever we are on the point of bringing before his consciousness some piece of unconscious material which is especially painful to him, then he is critical in the extreme. Even though he had previously understood and accepted a great deal, nevertheless all record of these gains seems now to have been wiped out. He may, in his desire to resist at any cost, present a picture of veritable emotional feeblemindedness. If one succeeds in helping him to overcome this new resistance, then he regains his insight and his understanding. Thus his criticism is not an independent function to be respected as such; it plays the role of handy-man to his emotional attitude and is guided by his resistance. If something displeases him, he can defend himself against it very ingeniously and appear most critical. But if something strikes his fancy, then he may show himself easily convinced. Perhaps none of us are very different, and the patient under analysis shows this dependence of the intellect on the emotional life so plainly only because, under the analysis, he is so hard pressed.

In what way shall we now account for the observation that the patient so energetically resists our attempts to rid him of his symptoms and to make his psychic processes function in a normal way? We tell ourselves that we have here come up against strong forces which oppose any change in the condition; furthermore, that these forces must be identical with those which originally brought about the condition. Some process must have been functional in the building up of these symptoms, a process which we can now reconstruct by means of our experiences in solving the meaning of the symptoms. We already know from Breuer's observations that the existence of a symptom presupposes that some psychic process was not carried to its normal conclusion, so that it could not become conscious. The symptom is the substitute for that which did not take place. Now we know where the forces whose existence we suspect must operate. Some violent antagonism must have been aroused to prevent the psychic process in question from reaching consciousness, and it therefore remained unconscious. As an unconscious thought it had the power to create a symptom. The same struggle during the analytic treatment opposes anew the efforts to carry this unconscious thought over into consciousness. This process we felt as a resistance. That pathogenic process which is made evident to us through the resistance, we will name *repression.*

We are now ready to obtain a more definite idea of this process of repression. It is the preliminary condition for the formation of symptoms; it is also a thing for which we have no parallel. If we take as prototype an impulse, a psychological process which is striving to convert itself into action, we know that it may succumb before a rejection, which we call "repudiation" or "condemnation." In the course of this struggle, the energy which the impulse had at its disposal was withdrawn from it, it becomes powerless; yet it may subsist in the form of a memory. The whole process of decision occurs with the full knowledge of the ego. The state of affairs is very different if we imagine that this same impulse has been subjected to repression. In that case, it would retain its energy and there would be no memory of it left; in addition, the process of repression would be carried out without the knowledge of the ego. Through this comparison, however, we have come no nearer understanding the nature of repression.

I now go into the theoretical ideas which alone have shown themselves useful in making the conception of repression more definite. It is above all necessary that we progress from a purely descriptive meaning of the word "unconscious" to its more systematic meaning; that is, we come to a point where we must call the consciousness or unconsciousness of a psychic process only one of its attributes, an attribute which is, moreover, not necessarily unequivocal. If such a process remained unconscious, then this separation from consciousness is perhaps only an indication of the fate to which it has submitted and not this fate itself. To bring this home to us more vividly, let us assume that every psychological process—with one exception, which I will go into later—first exists in an unconscious state or phase and only goes over from this into a conscious phase, much as a photographic picture is first a negative and then becomes a picture by being printed. But not every negative need become a positive, and just as little is it necessary that every unconscious psychological process should be changed into a conscious one. We find it advantageous to express ourselves as follows: Any particular process belongs in the first place to the psychological system of the unconscious; from this system it can under certain conditions go over into the system of the conscious. The crudest conception of these systems is the one which is most convenient for us, namely, a representation in space. We will compare the system of the unconscious to a large ante-chamber, in which the psychic impulses rub elbows with one another, as separate beings. There opens out of this ante-chamber another, a smaller room, a sort of parlor, which consciousness occupies. But on the threshold between the two rooms there stands a watchman; he passes on the individual psychic impulses, censors them, and will not let them into the parlor if they do not meet with his approval. You see at once that it makes little difference whether the watchman brushes a single impulse away from the threshold, or whether he drives it out again after it has already entered the parlor. It is a question here only of the extent of his watchfulness, and the timeliness of his judgment. Still working with this simile, we proceed to a further elaboration of our nomenclature. The impulses in the ante-chamber of the unconscious cannot be seen by the conscious, which is in the other room; therefore for the time being they must remain unconscious. When they have succeeded in pressing forward to the threshold, and have been sent back by the watchman, then they are unsuitable for consciousness and we call them *suppressed*. Those impulses, however, which the watchman has permitted to cross the threshold have not necessarily become conscious; for this can happen only if they have been successful in attracting to themselves the glance of the conscious. We therefore justifiably call this second room the system of the *fore-conscious*.

In this way the process of becoming conscious retains its purely descriptive sense. Suppression then, for any individual impulse, consists in not being able to get past the watchman from the system of the unconscious to that of the fore-conscious. The watchman himself is long since known to us; we have met him as the resistance which opposed us when we attempted to release the suppression through analytic treatment.

Now I know you will say that these conceptions are as crude as they are fantastic, and not at all permissible in a scientific discussion. I know they are crude—indeed, we even know that they are incorrect, and if we are not very much mistaken we have a better substitute for them in readiness. Whether they will continue then to appear so fantastic to you I do not know. For the time being, they are useful conceptions, similar to the manikin *Ampère* who swims in the stream of the electric current. In so far as they are helpful in the understanding of our observation, they are by no means to be despised. I should like to assure you that these crude assumptions go far in approximating the actual situation—the two rooms, the watchman on the threshold between the two, and consciousness at the end of the second room in the role of an onlooker. I should also like to hear you admit that our designations—*unconscious, fore-conscious,* and *conscious* are much less likely to arouse prejudice, and are easier to justify than others that have been used or suggested—such as *sub-conscious, inter-conscious, between-conscious,* etc.

This becomes all the more important to me if you should warn me that this arrangement of the psychic apparatus, such as I have assumed in the explanation of neurotic symptoms, must be generally applicable and must hold for normal functioning as well. In that, of course, you are right. We cannot follow this up at present, but our interest in the psychology of the development of the symptom must be enormously increased if through the study of pathological conditions we have the prospect of finding a key to the normal psychic occurrences which have been so well concealed.

You will probably recognize what it is that supports our assumptions concerning these two systems and their relation to consciousness. The watchman between the unconscious and the fore-conscious is none other than the censor under whose control we found the manifest dream to obtain its form. The residue of the day's experiences, which we found were the stimuli which set off the dream, are fore-conscious materials which at night, during sleep, had come under the influence of unconscious and suppressed wishes. Borne along by the energy of the wish, these stimuli were able to build the latent dream. Under the control of the unconscious system this material was worked over, went through an elaboration and displacement such as the normal psychic life or, better said, the fore-conscious system, either does not know at all or tolerates only exceptionally. In our eyes the characteristics of each of the two systems were betrayed by this difference in their functioning. The dependent relation between the fore-conscious and the conscious was to us only an indication that it must belong to one of the two systems. The dream is by no means a pathological phenomenon; it may appear in every healthy person under the conditions of sleep. Any assumption as to the structure of the psychic apparatus which covers the development of both the dream and the neurotic symptom has also an undeniable claim to be taken into consideration in any theory of normal psychic life.

So much, then, for suppression. It is, however, only a prerequisite for the evolution of the symptom. We know that the symptom serves as a substitute for a process kept back by suppression. Yet it is no simple matter to bridge this gap between the suppression and the evolution of the substitute. We have first to answer several questions on other aspects of the problem concerning the suppression and its substantiation: What kind of psychological stimuli are at the basis of the suppression; by what forces is it achieved; for what motives? On these matters we have only one insight that we can go by. We learned in the investigation of resistance that it grows out of the forces of the "I," in other words from obvious and latent traits of character. It must be from the same traits also that suppression derived support; at least they played a part in its development. All further knowledge is still withheld from us.

A second observation, for which I have already prepared, will help us further at this point. By means of analysis we can assign one very general purpose to the neurotic symptom. This is of course nothing new to you. I have already shown it to you in the two cases of neuroses. But, to be sure, what is the significance of two cases! You have the right to demand that it be shown to you innumerable times. But I am unable to do this. Here again your own experience must step in, or your belief, which may in this matter rely upon the unanimous account of all psychoanalysts.

You will remember that in these two cases, whose symptoms we subjected to searching investigation, the analysis introduced us to the most intimate sexual life of these patients. In the first case, moreover, we could identify with unusual clearness the purpose or tendency of the symptoms under investigation. Perhaps in the second case it was slightly covered by another factor—one we will consider later. Now, the same thing that we saw in these two examples we would see in all other cases that we subjected to analysis. Each time, through analysis, we would be introduced to the sexual wishes and experiences of the patient, and every time we would have to conclude that their symptoms served the same purpose. This purpose shows itself to be the satisfaction of sexual wishes; the symptoms serve as a sexual satisfaction for the patient, they are a substitute for such satisfactions as they miss in reality.

Recall the compulsive act of our first patient. The woman longs for her intensely beloved husband, with whom she cannot share her life because of his shortcoming and weaknesses. She feels she must remain true to him, she can give his place to no one else. Her compulsive symptom affords her that for which she pines, ennobles her husband, denies and corrects his weaknesses,—above all, his impotence. This symptom is fundamentally a wish-fulfillment, exactly as is a dream; moreover, it is what a dream not always is, an erotic wish-fulfillment. In the case of our second patient you can see that one of the component purposes of her ceremonial was the prevention of the intercourse of her parents or the hindrance of the creation of a new child thereby. You have perhaps also guessed that essentially she strove to put herself in the place of her mother. Here again we find the removal of disturbances to sexual satisfaction and the fulfillment of personal sexual wishes. We shall soon turn to the complications of whose existence we have given you several indications.

I do not want to make reservations as to the universal applicability of these declarations later on, and therefore I wish to call to your attention the fact that everything that I say here about suppression, symptom-development and symptom-interpretation has been learned from three types of neuroses—anxiety-hysteria, conversion-hysteria, and compulsion-neuroses—and for the time being is relevant to these forms only. These three conditions, which we are in the habit of combining into one group under the name of "*transference neuroses*," also limit the field open to psychoanalytic therapy. The other neuroses have not been nearly so well studied by psychoanalysis,—in one group, in fact, the impossibility of therapeutic influence has been the reason for the neglect. But you must not forget that psychoanalysis is still a very young science, that it demands much time and care in preparation for it, that not long ago it was still in the cradle, so to speak. Yet at all points we are about to penetrate into the understanding of those other conditions which are not transference neuroses. I hope I shall still be able to speak to you of the developments that our assumptions and results have undergone by being correlated with this new material, and to show you that these further studies have not led to contradictions but rather to the production of still greater uniformity. Granted that everything, then, that has been said here, holds good for the three transference neuroses, allow me to add a new bit of information to the evaluation of its symptoms. A comparative investigation into the causes of the disease discloses a result that may be confined into the formula: in some way or other these patients fell ill through *self-denial* when reality withheld from them the satisfaction of their sexual wishes. You recognize how excellently well these two results are found to agree. The symptoms must be understood, then, as a substitute satisfaction for that which is missed in life.

To be sure, there are all kinds of objections possible to the declaration that neurotic symptoms are substitutes for sexual satisfaction. I shall still go into two of them today. If you yourself have analytically examined a fairly large number of neurotics you will perhaps gravely inform me that in one class of cases this is not at all applicable, the symptoms appear rather to have the opposite purpose, to exclude sexual satisfaction, or discontinue it. I shall not deny the correctness of your interpretation. The psychoanalytic content has a habit of being more complicated than we should like to have it. Had it been so simple, perhaps we should have had no need for psychoanalysis to bring it to light. As a matter of fact, some of the traits of the ceremonial of our second patient may be recognized as of this ascetic nature, inimical to sexual satisfaction; for example, the fact that she removes the clocks, which have the magic qualities of preventing nightly erections, or that she tries to prevent the falling and breaking of vessels, which symbolizes a protection of her virginity. In other cases of bed-ceremonials which I was able to analyze, this negative character was far more evident; the ceremonial might consist throughout of protective regulations against sexual recollections and temptations. On the other hand, we have often discovered in psychoanalysis that opposites do not mean contradictions. We might extend our assertion and say the symptoms purpose either a sexual satisfaction or a guard against it; that in hysteria the positive wish-fulfillment takes precedence, while in the compulsion neuroses the negative, ascetic characteristics have the ascendancy. We have not yet been able to speak of that aspect of the mechanism of the symptoms, their two-sidedness, or polarity, which enables them to serve this double purpose, both the sexual satisfaction and its opposite. The symptoms are, as we shall see, compromise results, arising from the integration of two opposed tendencies; they represent not only the suppressed force but also the suppressing factor, which was originally potent in bringing about the negation. The result may then favor either one side or the other, but seldom is one of the influences entirely lacking. In cases of hysteria, the meeting of the two purposes in the same symptom is most often achieved. In compulsion-neuroses, the two parts often become distinct; the symptom then has a double meaning, it consists of two actions, one following the other, one releasing the other. It will not be so easy to put aside a further misgiving. If you should look over a large number of symptom-interpretations, you would probably judge offhand that the conception of a sexual substitute-satisfaction has been stretched to its utmost limits in these cases. You will not hesitate to emphasize that these symptoms offer nothing in the way of actual satisfaction, that often enough they are limited to giving fresh life to sensations or phantasies from some sexual complex. Further, you will declare that the apparent sexual satisfaction so often shows a childish and unworthy character, perhaps approximates an act of onanism, or is reminiscent of filthy naughtiness, habits that are already forbidden and broken in childhood. Finally, you will express your surprise that one should designate as a sexual satisfaction appetites which can only be described as horrible or ghastly, even unnatural. As to these last points, we shall come to no agreement until we have submitted man's sexual life to a thorough investigation, and thus ascertained what one is justified in calling sexual.

TWENTIETH LECTURE. GENERAL THEORY OF THE NEUROSES

The Sexual Life of Man

ONE might think we could take for granted what we are to understand by the term "sexual." Of course, the sexual is the indecent, which we must not talk about. I have been told that the pupils of a famous psychiatrist once took the trouble to convince their teacher that the symptoms of hysteria very frequently represent sexual matters. With this intention they took him to the bedside of a woman suffering from hysteria, whose attacks were unmistakable imitations of the act of delivery. He, however, threw aside their suggestion with the remark, "a delivery is nothing sexual." Assuredly, a delivery need not under all circumstances be indecent.

I see that you take it amiss that I jest about such serious matters. But this is not altogether a jest. In all seriousness, it is not altogether easy to define the concept "sexual." Perhaps the only accurate definition would be everything that is connected with the difference between the two sexes; but this you may find too general and too colorless. If you emphasize the sexual act as the central factor, you might say that everything is sexual which seeks to obtain sensual excitement from the body and especially from the sexual organs of the opposite sex, and which aims toward the union of the genitals and the performance of the sexual act. But then you are really very close to the comparison of sexual and indecent, and the act of delivery is not sexual. But if you think of the function of reproduction as the nucleus of sexuality you are in danger of excluding a number of things that do not aim at reproduction but are certainly sexual, such as onanism or even kissing. But we are prepared to realize that attempts at definition always lead to difficulties; let us give up the attempt to achieve the unusual in our particular case. We may suspect that in the development of the concept "sexual" something occurred which resulted in a false disguise. On the whole, we are quite well oriented as to what people call sexual.

The inclusion of the following factors in our concept "sexual" amply suffices for all practical purposes in ordinary life: the contrast between the sexes, the attainment of sexual excitement, the function of reproduction, the characteristic of an indecency that must be kept concealed. But this is no longer satisfactory to science. For through careful examinations, rendered possible only by the sacrifices and the unselfishness of the subjects, we have come in contact with groups of human beings whose sexual life deviates strikingly from the average. One group among them, the "perverse," have, as it were, crossed off the difference between the sexes from their program. Only the same sex can arouse their sexual desires; the other sex, even the sexual parts, no longer serve as objects for their sexual desires, and in extreme cases, become a subject for disgust. They have to that extent, of course, foregone any participation in reproduction. We call such persons homosexual or inverted. Often, though not always, they are men and women of high physical, intellectual and ethical development, who are affected only with this one portentous abnormality. Through their scientific leaders they proclaim themselves to be a special species of mankind, "a third sex," which shares equal rights with the two other sexes. Perhaps we shall have occasion to examine their claims critically. Of course they are not, as they would like to claim, the "elect" of humanity, but comprise just as many worthless second-rate individuals as those who possess a different sexual organization.

At any rate, this type among the perverse seek to achieve the same ends with the object of their desires as do normal people. But in the same group there exists a long succession of abnormal individuals whose sexual activities are more and more alien to what seems desirable to the sensible person. In their manifold strangeness they seem comparable only to the grotesque freaks that P. Breughel painted as the temptation of Saint Anthony, or the forgotten gods and believers that G. Flaubert pictures in the long procession that passes before his pious penitent. This ill-assorted array fairly clamors for orderly classification if it is not to bewilder our senses. We first divide them, on the one hand, into those whose sexual object has changed, as is the case with homosexualists, and, on the other, those whose sexual aim has changed. Those of the first group have dispensed with the mutual union of the genital organs, and have, as one of the partners of the act, replaced the genitals by another organ or part of the body; they have thus overcome both the short-comings of organic structure and the usual disgust involved. There are others of this group who still retain the genitals as their object, but not by virtue of their sexual function; they participate for anatomic reasons or rather by reason of their proximity. By means of these individuals we realize that the functions of excretion, which in the education of the child are hushed away as indecent, still remain capable of drawing complete sexual interest on themselves. There are still others who have relinquished the genitals entirely as an objective, have raised another part of the body to serve as the goal of their desire; the woman's breast, the foot, the tress of hair. There are also the fetishists, to whom the body part means nothing, who are gratified by a garment, a piece of white linen, a shoe. And finally there are persons who seek the whole object but with certain peculiar or horrible demands: even those who covet a defenseless corpse for instance, which they themselves must criminally compel to satisfy their desire. But enough of these horrors.

Foremost in the second grouping are those perverted ones who have placed as the end of their sexual desire performances normally introductory or preparatory to it. They satisfy their desire by their eyes and hands. They watch or attempt to watch the other individual in his most intimate doings, or uncover those portions of their own bodies which they should conceal in the vague expectation of being rewarded by a similar procedure on the other person's part. Here also belong the enigmatic sadists, whose affectionate strivings know no other goal than to cause their object pain and agony, varying all the way from humiliating suggestions to the harshest physical ill-treatment. As if to balance the scale, we have on the other hand the masochists, whose sole satisfaction consists in suffering every variety of humiliation and torture, symbolic and real, at the hands of the beloved one. There are still others who combine and confuse a number of these abnormal conditions. Moreover, in both these groups there are those who seek sexual satisfaction in reality, and others who are content merely to imagine such gratification, who need no actual object at all, but can supplant it by their own fantastic creations.

There can be not the least doubt that the sexual activities of these individuals are actually found in the absurdities, caprices and horrors that we have examined. Not only do they themselves conceive them as adequate substitutes, but we must recognize that they take the same place in their lives that normal sex gratification occupies in ours, and for which they bring the same sacrifices, often incommensurate with their ends. It is perfectly possible to trace along broad lines as well as in detail in what way these abnormalities follow the normal procedure and how they diverge from it. You will also find the characteristic of indecency which belongs to the sexual act in these vagaries, only that it is therein magnified to the disreputable.

Ladies and gentlemen, what attitude are we to assume to these unusual varieties of sex gratification? Nothing at all is achieved by the mere expression of indignation and personal disgust and by the assurance that we do not share these lusts. That is not our concern. We have here a field of observation like any other. Moreover, the evasion that these persons are merely rarities, curiosities, is easily refuted. On the contrary, we are dealing with very frequent and widespread phenomena. If, however, we are told that we must not permit them to influence our views on sexual life, since they are all aberrations of the sexual instinct, we must meet this with a serious answer. If we fail to understand these abnormal manifestations of sexuality and are unable to relate them to the normal sexual life, then we cannot understand normal sexuality. It is, in short, our unavoidable task to account theoretically for all the potentialities of the perversions we have gone over and to explain their relation to the so-called normal sexuality.

A penetrating insight due to Ivan Bloch and two new experimental results will help us in this task. Bloch takes exception to the point of view which sees in a perversion a "sign of degeneration"; he proves that such deviations from the aim of the sexual instinct, such loose relations to the object of sexuality, have occurred at all times, among the most primitive and the most highly civilized peoples, and have occasionally achieved toleration and general recognition. The two experimental results were obtained in the course of psychoanalytic investigations of neurotics; they will undoubtedly exert a decided influence on our conceptions of sexual perversion.

We have stated that the neurotic symptoms are substitutions for sexual satisfactions, and I have given you to understand that the proof of this assertion by means of the analysis of symptoms encounters many difficulties. For this statement is only justifiable if, under the term "sexual satisfactions," we include the so-called perverse sexual ends, since with surprising frequency we find symptoms which can be interpreted only in the light of their activity. The claim of rareness made by the homosexualists or the inverted immediately collapses when we learn that in the case of no single neurotic do we fail to obtain evidence of homosexual tendencies, and that in a considerable number of symptoms we find the expression of this latent inversion. Those who call themselves homosexualists are the conscious and manifest inverts, but their number is as nothing before the latent homosexualists. We are forced to regard the desire for an object of one's own sex as a universal aberration of erotic life and to cede increasing importance to it. Of course the differences between manifest homosexuality and the normal attitude are not thus erased; their practical importance persists, but their theoretic value is greatly decreased. Paranoia, a disturbance which cannot be counted among the transference-neuroses, must in fact be assumed as arising regularly from the attempt to ward off powerful homosexual tendencies. Perhaps you will recall that one of our patients under her compulsive symptoms acted the part of a man, namely that of her own estranged husband; the production of such symptoms, impersonating the actions of men, is very common to neurotic women. Though this cannot be ascribed directly to homosexuality, it is certainly concerned with its prerequisites.

You are probably acquainted with the fact that the neurosis of hysteria may manifest its symptoms in all organic systems and may therefore disturb all functions. Analysis shows that in these symptoms there are expressed all those tendencies termed perverse, which seek to represent the genitals through other organs. These organs behave as substitute genitals; through the study of hysteric symptoms we have come to the conclusion that aside from their functional activities, the organs of the body have a sexual significance, and that the performance of their functions is disturbed if the sexual factor claims too much attention. Countless sensations and innervations, which appear as symptoms of hysteria, in organs apparently not concerned with sexuality, are thus discovered as bound up with the fulfillment of perverse sexual desires through the transference of sex instincts to other organs. These symptoms bring home to us the extent to which the organs used in the consumption of food and in excretion may become the bearers of sexual excitement. We see repeated here the same picture which the perversions have openly and unmistakably lain before us; in hysteria, however, we must make the detour of interpreting symptoms, and in this case the perverse sexual tendencies must be ascribed not to the conscious but to the unconscious life of the individual.

Among the many symptoms manifested in compulsion neurosis, the most important are those produced by too powerful sadistic tendencies, i.e., sexual tendencies with perverted aim. These symptoms, in accordance with the structure of compulsion neurosis, serve primarily as a rejection of these desires, or they express a struggle between satisfaction and rejection. In this struggle, the satisfaction is never excessively curtailed; it achieves its results in the patient's behavior in a roundabout way, by preference turning against his own person in self-inflicted torture. Other forms of neurosis, characterized by intensive worry, are the expression of an exaggerated sexualization of acts that are ordinarily only preparatory to sexual satisfactions; such are the desires to see, to touch, to investigate. Here is thus explained the great importance of the fear of contact and also of the compulsion to wash. An unbelievably large portion of compulsion acts may, in the form of disguised repetitions and modifications, be traced back to onanism, admittedly the only uniform action which accompanies the most varied flights of the sexual imagination.

It would cost me very little effort to interweave far more closely the relation between perversion and neurosis, but I believe that what I have said is sufficient for our purposes. We must avoid the error of overestimating the frequency and intensity of perverse inclinations in the light of these interpretations of symptoms. You have heard that a neurosis may develop from the denial of normal sexual satisfactions. Through this actual denial the need is forced into the abnormal paths of sex excitement. You will later obtain a better insight into the way this happens. You certainly understand, that through such "*collateral*" hindrance, the perverse tendencies must become more powerful than they would have been if no actual obstacle had been put in the way of a normal sexual satisfaction. As a matter of fact, a similar influence may be recognized in manifest perversions. In many cases, they are provoked or motivated by the fact that too great difficulties stand in the way of normal sexual satisfactions, owing to temporary circumstances or to the permanent institutions of society. In other cases, to be sure, the perverse tendencies are entirely independent of such conditions; they are, as it were, the normal kind of sexual life for the individual in question.

Perhaps you are momentarily under the impression that we have confused rather than clarified the relation between normal and perverse sexuality. But keep in mind this consideration. If it is true that a hindrance or withholding of normal sexual satisfaction will bring out perverse tendencies in persons who have not previously shown them, we must assume that these persons must have harbored tendencies akin to perversities—or, if you will, perversities in latent form. This brings us to the second experimental conclusion of which I spoke, namely, that psychoanalytic investigation found it necessary to concern itself with the sexual life of the child, since, in the analysis of symptoms, reminiscences and ideas reverted to the early years of childhood. Whatever we revealed in this manner was corroborated point by point through the direct observation of children. The result was the recognition that all inclinations to perversion have their origin in childhood, that children have tendencies toward them all and practice them in a measure corresponding to their immaturity. Perverse sexuality, in brief, is nothing more than magnified infantile sexuality divided into its separate tendencies.

Now you will certainly see these perversions in another light and no longer ignore their relation to the sexual life of man, at the cost, I do not doubt, of surprises and incongruities painful to your emotions. At first you will undoubtedly be disposed to deny everything—the fact that children have something which may be termed sexual life, the truth of our observations and the justification of our claim to see in the behavior of children any relation to what is condemned in later years as perversity. Permit me first to explain to you the cause of your reluctance and then to present to you the sum of our observations. It is biologically improbable, even absurd, to assume that children have no sexual life—sexual excitements, desires, and some sort of satisfaction—but that they develop it suddenly between the ages of twelve and fourteen. This would be just as improbable from the viewpoint of biology as to say that they were not born with genitals but developed them only in the period of puberty. The new factor which becomes active in them at the time is the function of reproduction, which avails itself for its own purposes of all the physical and psychic material already present. You commit the error of confusing sexuality with reproduction and thereby block the road to the understanding of sexuality, and of perversions and neuroses as well. This error is a prejudice. Oddly enough its source is the fact that you yourselves were children, and as children succumbed to the influence of education. One of the most important educational tasks which society must assume is the control, the restriction of the sexual instinct when it breaks forth as an impulse toward reproduction; it must be subdued to an individual will that is identical with the mandates of society. In its own interests, accordingly, society would postpone full development until the child has reached a certain stage of intellectual maturity, for education practically ceases with the complete emergence of the sexual impulse. Otherwise the instinct would burst all bounds and the work of culture, achieved with such difficulty, would be shattered. The task of restraining this sexuality is never easy; it succeeds here too poorly and there too well. The motivating force of human society is fundamentally economic; since there is not sufficient nourishment to support its members without work on their part, the number of these members must be limited and their energies diverted from sexual activity to labor. Here, again, we have the eternal struggle for life that has persisted from prehistoric times to the present.

Experience must have shown educators that the task of guiding the sexual will of the new generation can be solved only by influencing the early sexual life of the child, the period preparatory to puberty, not by awaiting the storm of puberty. With this intention almost all infantile sex activities are forbidden to the child or made distasteful to him; the ideal goal has been to render the life of the child asexual. In the course of time it has really come to be considered asexual, and this point of view has actually been proclaimed by science. In order not to contradict our belief and intentions, we ignore the sexual activity of the child—no slight thing, at that—or are content to interpret it differently. The child is supposed to be pure and innocent, and whoever says otherwise may be condemned as a shameless blasphemer of the tender and sacred feelings of humanity.

The children are the only ones who do not join in carrying out these conventions, who assert their animal rights, who prove again and again that the road to purity is still before them. It is strange that those who deny the sexuality of children, do not therefore slacken in their educational efforts but rather punish severely the manifestations of the very thing they maintain does not exist, and call it "childish naughtiness." Theoretically it is highly interesting to observe that the period of life which offers most striking evidence against the biased conception of asexual childhood, is the time up to five or six years of age; after that everything is enveloped by a veil of amnesia, which is rent apart only by thorough scientific investigation; it may previously have given way partially in certain forms of dreams.

Now I shall present to you what is most easily recognizable in the sexual life of the child. At first, for the sake of convenience let me explain to you the conception of the libido. Libido, analogous to hunger, is the force through which the instinct, here the sex instinct (as in the case of hunger it is the instinct to eat) expresses itself. Other conceptions, such as sexual excitement and satisfaction, require no elucidation. You will easily see that interpretation plays the greatest part in disclosing the sexuality of the suckling; in fact you will probably cite this as an objection. These interpretations proceed from a foundation of analytic investigation that trace backwards from a given symptom. The suckling reveals the first sexual impulses in connection with other functions necessary for life. His chief interest, as you know, is directed toward the taking in of food; when it has fallen asleep at its mother's breast, fully satisfied, it bears the expression of blissful content that will come back again in later life after the experience of the sexual orgasm. That of course would be too slight evidence to form the basis of a conclusion. But we observe that the suckling wishes to repeat the act of taking in food without actually demanding more food; he is therefore no longer urged by hunger. We say he is sucking, and the fact that after this he again falls asleep with a blissful expression shows us that the act of sucking in itself has yielded him satisfaction. As you know, he speedily arranges matters so that he cannot fall asleep without sucking. Dr. Lindner, an old pediatrist in Budapest, was the first one to ascertain the sexual nature of this procedure. Persons attending to the child, who surely make no pretensions to a theoretic attitude, seem to judge sucking in a similar manner. They do not doubt that it serves a pleasurable satisfaction, term it naughty, and force the child to relinquish it against his will, and if he will not do so of his own accord, through painful measures. And so we learn that the suckling performs actions that have no object save the obtaining of a sensual gratification. We believe that this gratification is first experienced during the taking in of food, but that he speedily learns to separate it from this condition. The gratification can only be attributed to the excitation of the mouth and lips, hence we call these parts of the body *erogenous zones* and the pleasure derived from sucking, *sexual*. Probably we shall have to discuss the justification of this name.

If the suckling could express himself, he would probably recognize the act of sucking at his mother's breast as the most important thing in life. He is not so far wrong, for in this one act he satisfies two great needs of life. With no small degree of surprise we learn through psychoanalysis how much of the physical significance of this act is retained through life. The sucking at the mother's breast becomes the term of departure for all of sexual life, the unattained ideal of later sex gratification, to which the imagination often reverts in times of need. The mother's breast is the first object for the sexual instinct; I can scarcely bring home to you how significant this object is for centering on the sexual object in later life, what profound influence it exerts upon the most remote domains of psychic life through evolution and substitution. The suckling, however, soon relinquishes it and fills its place by a part of his own body. The child sucks his thumb or his own tongue. Thereby he renders himself independent of the consent of the outer world in obtaining his sensual satisfactions, and moreover increases the excitement by including a second zone of his body. The erogenous zones are not equally satisfactory; it is therefore an important experience when, as Dr. Lindner puts it, the child while touching his own body discovers the especially excitable genitals, and so finds the way from sucking to onanism.

Through the evaluation of sucking we become acquainted with two decisive characteristics of infantile sexuality. It arises in connection with the satisfaction of great organic needs and behaves *auto-erotically*, that is to say, it seeks and finds it objects on its own body. What is most clearly discernible during the taking in of food is partially repeated during excretion. We conclude that the nursling experiences pleasure during the excretion of urine and the contents of the intestine and that he soon strives to arrange these acts in a way to secure the greatest possible amount of satisfaction by the corresponding excitement of the erogenous membrane zones. Lou Andreas, with her delicate perceptions, has shown how at this point the outer world first intervenes as a hindrance, hostile to the child's desire for satisfaction—the first vague suggestion of outer and inner conflicts. He may not let his excretions pass from him at a moment agreeable to him, but only when other persons set the time. To induce him to renounce these sources of satisfaction, everything relating to these functions is declared indecent and must be concealed. Here, for the first time, he is to exchange pleasure for social dignity. His own relation to his excretions is originally quite different. He experiences no disgust toward his faeces, values them as a part of his body from which he does not part lightly, for he uses them as the first "present" he can give to persons he esteems particularly. Even after education has succeeded in alienating him from these tendencies, he transfers the evaluation of the faeces to the "present" and to "money." On the other hand, he appears to regard his achievements in urination with especial pride.

I know that you have been wanting to interrupt me for a long time and to cry: "Enough of these monstrosities! Excretion a source of sexual gratification that even the suckling exploits! Faeces a valuable substance! The anus a sort of genital! We do not believe it, but we understand why children's physicians and pedagogues have decidedly rejected psychoanalysis and its results." No, you have merely forgotten that it was my intention to present to you infantile sexuality in connection with the facts of sexual perversion. Why should you not know that in the case of many grown-ups, homosexuals as well as heterosexuals, the locus of intercourse is transferred from the normal to a more remote portion of the body. And that there are many individuals who confess to a pleasurable sensation of no slight degree in the emptying of the bowels during their entire lives! Children themselves will confirm their interest in the act of defecation and the pleasure in watching the defecation of another, when they are a few years older and capable of giving expression to their feelings. Of course, if these children have previously been systematically intimidated, they will understand all too well the wisdom of preserving silence on the subject. As for the other things that you do not wish to believe, let me refer you to the results of analysis and the direct observation of children, and you will realize that it is difficult not to see these things or to see them in a different light. I do not even object to making the relation between child-sexuality and sexual perversion quite obvious to you. It is really only natural; if the child has sexual life at all, it must necessarily be perverse, because aside from a few hazy illusions, the child does not know how sexuality gives rise to reproduction. The common characteristic of all perversions, on the other hand, is that they have abandoned reproduction as their aim. We term sexual activity perverse when it has renounced the aim of reproduction and follows the pursuit of pleasure as an independent goal. And so you realize that the turning point in the development of sexual life lies in its subjugation to the purpose of reproduction. Everything this side of the turning point, everything that has given up this purpose and serves the pursuit of pleasure alone, must carry the term "perverse" and as such be regarded with contempt.

Permit me, therefore, to continue with my brief presentation of infantile sexuality. What I have told you about two organic systems I could supplement by a discussion of all the others. The sexual life of the child exhausts itself in the exercise of a series of partial instincts which seek, independently of one another, to gain satisfaction from his own body or from an external object. Among these organs the genitals speedily predominate. There are persons who continue the pursuit of satisfaction by means of their own genitals, without the aid of another genital or object, uninterruptedly from the onanism of the suckling to the onanism of necessity which arises in puberty, and even indefinitely beyond that. The theme of onanism alone would occupy us for a long period of time; it offers material for diverse observations.

In spite of my inclination to shorten the theme, I must tell you something about the sexual curiosity of children. It is most characteristic for child sexuality and significant for the study of neurotic symptoms. The sexual curiosity of children begins very early, sometimes before the third year. It is not connected with the differences of sexes, which means nothing to the child, since the boy, at any rate, ascribes the same male genital to both sexes. When the boy first discovers the primary sexual structure of the female, he tries at first to deny the evidence of his senses, for he cannot conceive a human being who lacks the part of his body that is of such importance to him. Later he is terrified at the possibility revealed to him and he feels the influence of all the former threats, occasioned by his intensive preoccupation with his little organ. He becomes subject to the domination of the castration complex, the formation of which plays an important part in the development of his character, provided he remains healthy; of his neurosis, if he becomes diseased; of his resistance, if he is treated analytically. We know that the little girl feels injured on account of her lack of a large, visible penis, envies the boy his possession, and primarily from this motive desires to be a man. This wish manifests itself subsequently in neurosis, arising from some failure in her role as a woman. During childhood, the clitoris of the girl is the equivalent of the penis; it is especially excitable, the zone where auto-erotic satisfaction is achieved. In the transition to womanhood it is most important that the sensations of the clitoris are completely transferred at the right time to the entrance of the vagina. In cases of so-called sexual anesthesia of women the clitoris has obstinately retained its excitability.

The sexual interest of children generally turns first to the mystery of birth—the same problem that is the basis of the questions asked by the sphinx of Thebes. This curiosity is for the most part aroused by the selfish fear of the arrival of a new child. The answer which the nursery has ready for the child, that the stork brings children, is doubted far more frequently than we imagine, even by very young children. The feeling that he has been cheated out of the truth by grown-ups, contributes greatly to the child's sense of solitude and to his independent development. But the child is not capable of solving this problem unaided. His undeveloped sexual constitution restricts his ability to understand. At first he assumes that children are produced by a special substance in one's food and does not know that only women can bear children. Later he learns of this limitation and relinquishes the derivation of children from food—a supposition retained in the fairy-tale. The growing child soon notices that the father plays some part in reproduction, but what it is he cannot guess. If, by chance, he is witness of a sexual act, he sees in it an attempt to subjugate, a scuffle, the sadistic miscomprehension of coitus; he does not however relate this act immediately to the evolution of the child. When he discovers traces of blood on the bedsheets or on the clothing of his mother, he considers them the proof of an injury inflicted by the father. During the latter part of childhood, he imagines that the sexual organ of the man plays an important part in the evolution of children, but can ascribe only the function of urination to that part of his body.

From the very outset children unite in believing that the birth of the child takes place through the anus; that the child therefore appears as a ball of faeces. After anal interests have been proven valueless, he abandons this theory and assumes that the navel opens or that the region between the two breasts is the birthplace of the child. In this way the curious child approaches the knowledge of sexual facts, which, clouded by his ignorance, he often fails to see. In the years prior to puberty he generally receives an incomplete, disparaging explanation which often causes traumatic consequences.

You have probably heard that the conception "sexual" is unduly expanded by psychoanalysis in order that it may maintain the hypothesis that all neuroses are due to sexual causes and that the meaning of the symptoms is sexual. You are now in a position to judge whether or not this expansion is unjustifiable. We have expanded the conception sexual only to include the sexual life of children and of perverse persons. That is to say, we have reestablished its proper boundaries. Outside of psychoanalysis sexuality means only a very limited thing: normal sexual life in the service of reproduction.

TWENTY-FIRST LECTURE. GENERAL THEORY OF THE NEUROSES

Development of the Libido and Sexual Organizations

I AM under the impression that I did not succeed in convincing you of the significance of perversions for our conception of sexuality. I would like then to clarify and add as much as I can.

It was not only perversions that necessitated an alteration of our conception of sexuality, which aroused such vehement contradiction. The study of infantile sexuality did a great deal more along that line, and its close correspondence to the perversions became decisive for us. But the origin of the expressions of infantile sexuality, unmistakable as they are in later years of childhood, seem to be lost in obscurity. Those who disregard the history of evolution and analytic coherence, will dispute the potency of the sexual factor and will infer the agency of generalized forces. Do not forget that as yet we have no generally acknowledged criterion for identifying the sexual nature of an occurrence, unless we assume that we can find it in a relation to the functions of reproduction, and this we must reject as too narrow. The biological criteria, such as the periodicities of twenty-three and twenty-eight days, suggested by W. Fliess, are by no means established; the specific chemical nature which we can possibly assume for sexual occurrences is still to be discovered. The sexual perversions of adults, on the other hand, are tangible and unambiguous. As their generally accepted nomenclature shows, they are undoubtedly sexual in character; whether we designate them as signs of degeneration, or otherwise, no one has yet had the courage to place them outside the phenomena of sex. They alone justify the assertion that sexuality and reproduction are not coincident, for it is clear that all of them disavow the goal of reproduction.

This brings me to an interesting parallel. While "conscious" and "psychic" were generally considered to be identical, we had to make an essay to widen our conception of the "psychic" to recognize as psychic something that was not conscious. Analogously, when "sexual" and "related to reproduction" (or, in shorter form, "genital") has been generally considered identical, psychoanalysis must admit as "sexual" such things as are not "genital," things which have nothing to do with reproduction. It is only a formal analogy, but it does not lack a deeper basis.

But if the existence of sexual perversions is such a compelling argument, why has it not long ago had its effect, and settled the question? I really am unable to say. It appears to be because the sexual perversions are subject to a peculiar ban that extends even into theory, and stands in the way of their scientific appreciation. It seems as if no one could forget that they are not only revolting, but even unnatural, dangerous; as if they had a seductive influence and that at bottom one had to stifle a secret envy of those who enjoyed them. As the count who passes judgment in the famous Tannhauser parody admits:

"And in the mount of Venus, his honor slipped his mind,

It's odd that never happens to people of our kind."

Truthfully speaking, the perverts are rather poor devils who atone most bitterly for the satisfaction they attain with such difficulty.

What makes the perverse activity unmistakably sexual, despite all the strangeness of its object, is that the act in perverse satisfaction most frequently is accompanied by a complete orgasm, and by an ejaculation of the genital product. Of course, this is only true in the case of adults; with children orgasms and genital excretions are hardly possible; they are replaced by rudiments which, again, are not recognized as truly sexual.

In order to complete the appreciation of sexual perversions, I have something to add. Condemned as they are, sharply as they are contrasted with the normal sexual activity, simple observation shows that rarely is normal sex-life entirely free from one or another of the perverse traits. Even the kiss can be claimed to be perverse, for it consists in the union of two erogenous mouth zones in place of the respective genitals. But no one outlaws it as perverse, it is, on the contrary, admitted in theatrical performances as a modified suggestion of the sexual act. This very kissing may easily become a complete perversion if it results in such intensity that it is immediately followed by an emission and orgasm—a thing that is not at all unusual. Further, we can learn that handling and gazing upon the object becomes an essential prerequisite to sexual pleasure; that some, in the height of sexual excitation, pinch and bite, that the greatest excitation is not always called forth in lovers by the genitals, but rather by other parts of the body, and so forth. There is no sense in considering persons with single traits of this kind abnormal, and counting them among the perverts. Rather, we recognize more and more clearly that the essential nature of perversion does not consist in overstepping the sexual aim, nor in a substitution for the genitals, not even in the variety of objects, but simply in the exclusiveness with which these deviations are carried out and by means of which the sexual act that serves reproduction is pushed aside. When the perverse activities serve to prepare or heighten the normal sexual act, they are really no longer perversions. To be sure, the chasm between normal and perverse sexuality is practically bridged by such facts. The natural result is that normal sexuality takes its origin from something existing prior to it, since certain components of this material are thrown out and others are combined in order to make them subject to a new aim—that of reproduction.

Before we make use of our knowledge of perversions to concentrate anew and with clearer perspective on the study of infantile sexuality, I must call your attention to an important difference between the two. Perverse sexuality is as a rule extraordinarily centralized, its whole action is directed toward one, usually an isolated, goal. A partial instinct has the upper hand. It is either the only one that can be demonstrated or it has subjected the others to its purposes. In this respect there is no difference between normal and perverse sexuality other than that the ruling partial instincts, and with them the sexual goals, are different. In the one case as well as in the other there is, so to say, a well organized tyranny, excepting that here one family and there another has appropriated all the power to itself. Infantile sexuality, on the other hand, is on the whole devoid of such centralization and organization, its individual component impulses are of equal power, and each independently goes in search of the acquisition of pleasurable excitement. The lack as well as the presence of centralization fit in well with the fact that both the perverse and the normal sexuality originated from the infantile. There are also cases of perverse sexuality that have much more similarity with the infantile, where, independently of one another, numerous partial instincts have forced their way, insisted on their aims, or rather perpetuated them. In these cases it is more correct to speak of infantilism of sexual life than of perversions.

Thus prepared we can consider a question which we certainly shall not be spared. People will say to us: "Why are you so set on including within sexuality those manifestations of childhood, out of which the sexual later develops, but which, according to your own admission, are of uncertain origin? Why are you not satisfied rather with the physiological description, and simply say that even in the suckling one may notice activities, such as sucking objects or holding back excrements, which show us that he strives towards an *organic pleasure*? In that way you would have avoided the estranging conception of sexual life in the tiniest child." I have nothing to say against organic pleasure; I know that the most extreme excitement of the sexual union is only an organic pleasure derived from the activity of the genitals. But can you tell me when this organic pleasure, originally not differentiated, acquires the sexual character that it undoubtedly does possess in the later phases of development? Do you know more about the "organic pleasure" than about sexuality? You will answer, the sexual character is acquired when the genitals begin to play their role; sexual means genital. You will even reject the contrary evidence of the perversions by confronting me with the statement that in most perversions it is a matter of achieving the genital orgasm, although by other means than a union of the genitals. You would really command a much better position if you did not regard as characteristic of the sexual that untenable relation to reproduction seen in the perversions, if you replaced it by activity of the genitals. Then we no longer differ very widely; the genital organs merely replace other organs. What do you make of the numerous practices which show you that the genitals may be represented by other organs in the attainment of gratification, as is the case in the normal kiss, or the perverse practices of "fast life," or the symptoms of hysteria? In these neuroses it is quite usual for stimulations, sensations and innervations, even the process of erection, which is localized in the genitals, to be transferred to other distant parts of the body, so that you have nothing to which you can hold as characteristics of the sexual. You will have to decide to follow my example and expand the designation "sexual" to include the strivings of early childhood toward organic pleasure.

Now, for my justification, I should like you to give me the time for two more considerations. As you know, we call the doubtful and indefinable pleasure activities of earliest childhood sexual because our analysis of the symptoms leads us to them by way of material that is undeniably sexual. We admit that it need not for that reason in itself be sexual. But take an analogous case. Suppose there were no way to observe the development of two dicotyledonous plants from their seeds—the apple tree and the bean. In both cases, however, imagine it possible to follow their evolution from the fully developed plant backwards to the first seedling with two leaf-divisions. The two little leaves are indistinguishable, in both cases they look exactly alike. Shall I conclude from this that they really are the same and that the specific differences between an apple tree and bean plant do not appear until later in the history of the plant? Or is it biologically more correct to believe that this difference is already present in the seedling, although the two little leaves show no differences? We do the same thing when we term as sexual the pleasure derived from the activities of the suckling. Whether each and every organic enjoyment may be called sexual, or if besides the sexual there is another that does not deserve this name, is a matter I cannot discuss here. I know too little about organic pleasure and its conditions, and will not be at all surprised if the retrogressive character of the analysis leads us back finally to a generalized factor.

One thing more. You have on the whole gained very little for what you are so anxious to maintain, the sexual purity of the child, even when you can convince me that the activities of the suckling had better not be called sexual. For from the third year on, there is no longer any doubt concerning the presence of a sexual life in the child. At this time the genitals already begin to become active; there is perhaps regularly a period of infantile masturbation, in other words, a gratification by means of the genitals. The psychic and social expressions of the sexual life are no longer absent; choice of an object, affectionate preference for certain persons, indeed, a leaning toward one of the two sexes, jealousy—all these have been established independently by unprejudiced observation, prior to the advent of psychoanalysis, and confirmed by every careful observer. You will say that you had no doubt as to the early awakening of affection, you will take issue only with its sexual nature. Children between the ages of three and eight have already learned to hide these things, but if you look sharply you can always gather sufficient evidence of the "sexual" purpose of this affection. What escapes you will be amply supplied by investigation. The sexual goals of this period of life are most intimately connected with the contemporaneous sexual theories, of which I have given you some examples. The perverse nature of some of these goals is the result of the constitutional immaturity of the child, who has not yet discovered the goal of the act of copulation.

From about the sixth or the eighth year on a pause in, and reversion of, sexual development is noticeable, which in the cases that reach the highest cultural standard deserves the name of a latent period. The latent period may also fail to appear and there need not be an interruption of sexual activity and sexual interests at any period. Most of the experiences and impulses prior to the latent period then fall victim to the infantile amnesia, the forgetting we have already discussed, which cloaks our earliest childhood and makes us strangers to it. In every psychoanalysis we are confronted with the task of leading this forgotten period of life back into memory; one cannot resist the supposition that the beginning of sexual life it contains furnishes the motive for this forgetting, namely, that this forgetting is a result of suppression.

The sexual life of the child shows from the third year that it has much in common with that of the adult; it is distinguished from the latter, as we already know, by the lack of stable organization under the primacy of the genitals, by the unavoidable traits of perversion, and, naturally, by the far lesser intensity of the whole impulse. Theoretically the most interesting phases of the sexual development or, as we would rather say, the libido-development, so far as theory is concerned, lie back of this period. This development is so rapidly gone through that perhaps it would never have been possible for direct observation to grasp its fleeting pictures. Psychoanalytic investigation of the neuroses has for the first time made it possible to discover more remote phases of the libido-development. These are, to be sure, nothing but constructions, but if you wish to carry on psychoanalysis in a practical way you will find that they are necessary and valuable constructions. You will soon understand why pathology may disclose conditions which we would have overlooked in the normal object.

We can now declare what form the sexual life of the child takes before the primacy of the genitals is established. This primacy is prepared in the first infantile epoch prior to the latent period, and is continuously organized from puberty on. There is in this early period a sort of loose organization, which we shall call *pre-genital*. In the foreground of this phase, however, the partial instincts of the genitals are not prominent, rather the *sadistic* and *anal*. The contrast between *masculine* and *feminine* plays no part as yet, its place is taken by the contrast between *active* and *passive*, which we may designate as the forerunner of sexual polarity, with which it is later fused. That which appears masculine to us in the activity of this phase, observed from the standpoint of the later genital stage, is the expression of an instinct to mastery, which may border on cruelty. Impulses with passive goals attach themselves to the erogenous zone of the rectal opening. Most important at this time, curiosity and the instinct to watch are powerful. The genital really takes part in the sexual life only in its role as excretory organ for the bladder. Objects are not lacking to the partial impulses of this period, but they do not necessarily combine into a single object. The sadistico-anal organization is the step antecedent to the phase of genital primacy. A more penetrating study furnishes proof how much of this is retained for the later and final form, and in what ways its partial instincts are forced into line under the new genital organization. Back of the sadistico-anal phase of libido-development, we get a view of an earlier, even more primitive phase of organization, in which the erogenous mouth-zone plays the chief role. You may surmise that the sexual activity of sucking belongs to it, and may wonder at the intuition of the ancient Egyptians, whose art characterized the child, as well as the god Horus, with the finger in his month. Abraham only recently published material concerning the traces which this primitive oral phase has left upon the sexual life of later years.

I can surmise that these details about sexual organization have burdened your mind more than they have informed you. Perhaps I have again gone into detail too much. But be patient; what you have heard will become more valuable through the uses to which it is later put. Keep well in mind the impression that sexual life, as we call it, the function, of the libido, does not make its appearance as a completed whole, nor does it develop in its own image, but goes through a series of successive phases which are not similar to each other. In fact, it is a developmental sequence, like that from the grub to the butterfly. The turning point of the development is the subordination of all sexual partial-instincts to the primacy of the genitals, and thereby the subjection of sexuality to the function of reproduction. Originally it is a diffused sexual life, one which consists of independent activities of single partial instincts which strive towards organic gratification. This anarchy is modified by approaches to pre-genital organization, first of all the sadistico-anal phase, prior to this the oral phase, which is perhaps the most primitive. Added to this there are the various processes, as yet not well known, which carry over one organization level to the later and more advanced phase. The significance, for the understanding of the neuroses, of the long evolutionary path of the libido which carries it over so many grades we shall discuss on another occasion.

Today we shall look at another angle of the development, namely the relation of the partial instinct to the object. We shall make a hurried survey of this development in order to spend more time upon a relatively later product. Some of the components of the sex instincts have had an object from the very beginning and hold fast to it; such are the instinct to mastery (sadism), curiosity, and the impulse to watch. Other impulses which are more clearly attached to specific erogenous zones of the body have this object only in the beginning, as long as they adhere to the functions which are not sexual; they release this object when they free themselves from these non-sexual functions. The first object of the oral component of the sexual impulse is the mother's breast, which satisfies the hunger of the infant. By the act of sucking, the erotic component which is also satisfied by the sucking becoming independent, it gives up the foreign object and replaces it by some part of its own body. The oral impulse becomes *auto-erotic*, just as the anal and other erogenous impulses are from the very beginning. Further development, to express it most briefly, has two goals—first, to give up auto-eroticism, and, again, to substitute for the object of one's own body a foreign object; second, to unify the different objects into a single impulse, replace them by a single object. To be sure, that can happen only if this single object is itself complete, a body similar to one's own. Nor can it be consummated without leaving behind as useless a large number of the auto-erotic instinctive impulses.

The processes of finding the object are rather involved, and have as yet had no comprehensive exposition. For our purpose, let us emphasize the fact that when the process has come to a temporary cessation in the childhood years, before the latent period, the object it has found is seen to be practically identical with the first object derived from its relation to the object of the oral pleasure impulse. It is, if not the mother's breast, the mother herself. We call the mother the first *object of love*. For we speak of love when we emphasize the psychic side of sex-impulses, and disregard or for a moment wish to forget the fundamental physical or "sensual" demands of the instincts. At the time when the mother becomes the object of love, the psychic work of suppression which withdraws the knowledge of a part of his sexual goal from his consciousness has already begun in the child. The selection of the mother as the object of love involves everything we understand by the Oedipus complex which has come to have such great significance in the psychoanalytic explanation of neuroses, and which has had no small part in arousing opposition to psychoanalysis.

Here is a little experience which took place during the present war: A brave young disciple of psychoanalysis is a doctor at the German front somewhere in Poland, and attracts the attention of his colleagues by the fact that he occasionally exercises an unexpected influence in the case of a patient. Upon being questioned he admits that he works by means of psychoanalysis and is finally induced to impart his knowledge to his colleagues. Every evening the physicians of the corps, colleagues and superiors, gather in order to listen to the inmost secrets of analysis. For a while this goes on nicely, but after he has told his audience of the Oedipus-complex, a superior rises and says he does not believe it, that it is shameful for the lecturer to tell such things to them, brave men who are fighting for their fatherland, and who are the fathers of families, and he forbade the continuation of the lectures. This was the end.

Now you will be impatient to discover what this frightful Oedipus-complex consists of. The name tells you. You all know the Greek myth of King Oedipus, who is destined by the fates to kill his father, and take his mother to wife, who does everything to escape the oracle and then does penance by blinding himself when he discovers that he has, unknowingly, committed these two sins. I trust many of you have yourselves experienced the profound effect of the tragedy in which Sophocles handles this material. The work of the Attic poet presents the manner in which the deed of Oedipus, long since accomplished, is finally brought to light by an artistically prolonged investigation, continuously fed with new evidence; thus far it has a certain similarity to the process of psychoanalysis. In the course of the dialogue it happens that the infatuated mother-wife, Jocasta, opposes the continuation of the investigation. She recalls that many men have dreamed that they have cohabited with their mothers, but one should lay little stress on dreams. We do not lay little stress on dreams, least of all typical dreams such as occur to many men, and we do not doubt that this dream mentioned by Jocasta is intimately connected with the strange and frightful content of the myth.

It is surprising that Sophocles' tragedy does not call forth much greater indignation and opposition on the part of the audience, a reaction similar to, and far more justified, than the reaction to our simple military physician. For it is a fundamentally immoral play, it dispenses with the moral responsibility of men, it portrays godlike powers as instigators of guilt, and shows the helplessness of the moral impulses of men which contend against sin. One might easily suppose that the burden of the myth purposed accusation against the gods and Fate, and in the hands of the critical Euripides, always at odds with the gods, it would probably have become such an accusation. But there is no trace of this in the work of the believer Sophocles. A pious sophistry which asserts that the highest morality is to bow to the will of the gods, even if they command a crime, helps him over the difficulty. I do not think that this moral constitutes the power of the drama, but so far as the effect goes, that is unimportant; the listener does not react to it, but to the secret meaning and content of the myth. He reacts as though through self-analysis he had recognized in himself the Oedipus-complex, and had unmasked the will of the gods, as well as the oracle, as sublime disguises of his own unconsciousness. It is as though he remembered the wish to remove his father, and in his place to take his mother to wife, and must be horrified at his own desires. He also understands the voice of the poet as if it were telling him: "You revolt in vain against your responsibility, and proclaim in vain the efforts you have made to resist these criminal purposes. In spite of these efforts, you are guilty, for you have not been able to destroy the criminal purposes, they will persist unconsciously in you." And in that there is psychological truth. Even if man has relegated his evil impulses to the unconscious, and would tell himself that he is no longer answerable for them, he will still be compelled to experience this responsibility as a feeling of guilt which he cannot trace to its source.

It is not to be doubted for a moment that one may recognize in the Oedipus-complex one of the most important sources for the consciousness of guilt with which neurotics are so often harassed. But furthermore, in a study of the origins of religion and morality of mankind which I published in 1913, under the title of *Totem and Taboo*, the idea was brought home to me that perhaps mankind as a whole has, at the beginning of its history, come by its consciousness of guilt, the final source of religion and morality, through the Oedipus-complex. I should like to say more on this subject, but perhaps I had better not. It is difficult to turn away from this subject now that I have begun speaking of it, but we must return to individual psychology.

What does direct observation of the child at the time of the selection of its object, before the latent period, show us concerning the Oedipus-complex? One may easily see that the little man would like to have the mother all to himself, that he finds the presence of his father disturbing, he becomes irritated when the latter permits himself to show tenderness towards the mother, and expresses his satisfaction when the father is away or on a journey. Frequently he expresses his feelings directly in words, promises the mother he will marry her. One may think this is very little in comparison with the deeds of Oedipus, but it is actually enough, for it is essentially the same thing. The observation is frequently clouded by the circumstance that the same child at the same time, on other occasions, gives evidence of great tenderness towards its father; it is only that such contradictory, or rather, *ambivalent* emotional attitudes as would lead to a conflict in the case of an adult readily take their place side by side in a child, just as later on they permanently exist in the unconscious. You might wish to interpose that the behavior of the child springs from egoistic motives and does not justify the setting up of an erotic complex. The mother provides for all the necessities of the child, and it is therefore to the child's advantage that she troubles herself for no one else. This, too, is correct, but it will soon be clear that in this, as in similar situations, the egoistic interest offers only the opportunity upon which the erotic impulse seizes. If the little one shows the most undisguised sexual curiosity about his mother, if he wants to sleep with her at night, insists upon being present while she is dressing, or attempts to caress her, as the mother can so often ascertain and laughingly relates, it is undoubtedly due to the erotic nature of the attachment to his mother. We must not forget that the mother shows the same care for her little daughter without achieving the same effect, and that the father often vies with her in caring for the boy without being able to win the same importance in his eyes as the mother. In short, it is clear that the factor of sex-preference cannot be eliminated from the situation by any kind of criticism. From the standpoint of egoistic interest it would merely be stupid of the little fellow not to tolerate two persons in his services rather than only one.

I have, as you will have noticed, described only the relation of the boy to his father and mother. As far as the little girl is concerned, the process is the same with the necessary modifications. The affectionate devotion to the father, the desire to set aside the mother as superfluous and to take her place, a coquetry which already works with all the arts of later womanhood, give such a charming picture, especially in the baby girl, that we are apt to forget its seriousness, and the grave consequences which may result from this infantile situation. Let us not fail to add that frequently the parents themselves exert a decisive influence over the child in the wakening of the Oedipus attitude, in that they themselves follow a sex preference when there are a number of children. The father in the most unmistakable manner shows preference for the daughter, while the mother is most affectionate toward the son. But even this factor cannot seriously undermine the spontaneous character of the childish Oedipus-complex. The Oedipus-complex expands and becomes a family-complex when other children appear. It becomes the motive force, revived by the sense of personal injury, which causes the child to receive its brothers and sisters with aversion and to wish to remove them without more ado. It is much more frequent for the children to express these feelings of hatred than those arising from the parent-complex. If such a wish is fulfilled, and death takes away the undesired increase in the family, after a short while we may discover through analysis what an important experience this death was for the child, even though he had not remembered it. The child forced into second place by the birth of a little brother or sister, and for the first time practically isolated from his mother, is loathe to forgive her for this;

feelings which we would call extreme bitterness in an adult are aroused in him and often become the basis of a lasting estrangement. We have already mentioned that sexual curiosity with all its consequences usually grows out of these experiences of the child. With the growing up of these brothers and sisters the relation to them undergoes the most significant changes. The boy may take his sister as the object for his love, to replace his faithless mother; situations of dangerous rivalry, which are of vast importance for later life, arise even in the nursery among numerous brothers who court the affection of a younger sister. A little girl finds in her older brother a substitute for her father, who no longer acts towards her with the same affection as in former years, or she takes a younger sister as a substitute for the child that she vainly wished of her father.

Such things, and many more of a similar character, are shown by the direct observation of children and the consideration of their vivid childish recollections, which are not influenced by the analysis. You will conclude, among other things, that the position of a child in the sequence of his brothers and sisters is of utmost importance for the entire course of his later life, a factor which should be considered in every biography. In the face of these explanations that are found with so little effort, you will hardly recall without smiling the scientific explanations for the prohibition of incest. What inventions! By living together from early childhood the sexual attraction must have been diverted from these members of the family who are of opposite sex, or a biological tendency against in-breeding finds its psychic equivalent in an innate dread of incest! In this no account is taken of the fact that there would be no need of so unrelenting a prohibition by law and morality if there were any natural reliable guards against the temptation of incest. Just the opposite is true. The first choice of an object among human beings is regularly an incestuous one, in the man directed toward the mother and sister, and the most stringent laws are necessary to prevent this persisting infantile tendency from becoming active. Among the primitive races the prohibitions against incest are much more stringent than ours, and recently Th. Reik showed in a brilliant paper that the puberty-rites of the savages, which represent a rebirth, have the significance of loosing the incestuous bonds of the boy to his mother, and of establishing the reconciliation with the father.

Mythology teaches that incest, apparently so abhorred by men, is permitted to the gods without further thought, and you may learn from ancient history that incestuous marriage with his sister was holy prescript for the person of the ruler (among the ancient Pharaohs and the Incas of Peru). We have here a privilege denied the common herd.

Incest with his mother is one of the sins of Oedipus, patricide the other. It might also be mentioned that these are the two great sins which the first social-religious institution of mankind, totemism, abhors. Let us turn from the direct observation of the child to analytic investigation of the adult neurotic. What does analysis yield to the further knowledge of the Oedipus-complex? This is easily told. It shows the patient up in the light of the myth; it shows that each of these neurotics was himself an Oedipus or, what amounts to the same thing, became a Hamlet in the reaction to the complex. To be sure, the analytic representation of the Oedipus-complex enlarges upon and is a coarser edition of the infantile sketch. The hatred of the father, the death-wish with regard to him, are no longer timidly suggested, the affection for the mother recognizes the goal of possessing her for a wife. Dare we really accredit these horrible and extreme feelings to those tender childhood years, or does analysis deceive us by bringing in some new element? It is not difficult to discover this. Whenever an account of past events is given, be it written even by a historian, we must take into account the fact that inadvertently something has been interpolated from the present and from intervening times into the past; so that the entire picture is falsified. In the case of the neurotic it is questionable whether this interpolation is entirely unintentional or not; we shall later come to learn its motives and must justify the fact of "imagining back" into the remote past. We also easily discover that hatred of the father is fortified by numerous motives which originate in later times and circumstances, since the sexual wishes for the mother are cast in forms which are necessarily foreign to the child. But it would be a vain endeavor to explain the whole of the Oedipus-complex by "imagining back," and as related to later times. The infantile nucleus and more or less of what has been added to it continues to exist and may be verified by the direct observation of the child.

The clinical fact which we meet with in penetrating the form of the Oedipus-complex as established by analysis, is of the greatest practical importance. We learn that at the period of puberty, when the sexual instinct first asserts its demands in full strength, the old incestuous and familiar objects are again taken up and seized anew by the libido. The infant's choice of an object was feeble, but it nevertheless set the direction for the choice of an object in puberty. At that time very intense emotional experiences are brought into play and directed towards the Oedipus-complex, or utilized in the reaction to it. However, since their presuppositions have become unsupportable, they must in large part remain outside of consciousness. From this time on the human individual must devote himself to the great task of freeing himself from his parents, and only after he has freed himself can he cease to be a child, and become a member of the social community. The task confronting the son consists of freeing himself from his libidinous wishes towards his mother and utilizing them in the quest for a really foreign object for his love. He must also effect a reconciliation with his father, if he has stayed hostile to him, or if in the reaction to his infantile opposition he has become subject to his domination, he must now free himself from this pressure. These tasks are set for every man; it is noteworthy how seldom their solution is ideally achieved, i.e., how seldom the solution is psychologically as well as socially correct. Neurotics, however, find no solution whatever; the son remains during his whole life subject to the authority of his father, and is not able to transfer his libido to a foreign sexual object. Barring the difference in the specific relation, the same fate may befall the daughter. In this sense the Oedipus-complex is correctly designated as the nucleus of the neurosis.

You can imagine how rapidly I am reviewing a great number of conditions which are associated with the Oedipus-complex, of practical as well as of theoretical importance. I cannot enter upon their variations or possible inversions. Of its less immediate relations I only wish to indicate the influence which the Oedipus-complex has been found to exert on literary production. In a valuable book, Otto Rank has shown that the dramatists of all times have taken their materials principally from the Oedipus-and incest-complexes, with their variations and disguises. Moreover, we will not forget to mention that the two guilty wishes of Oedipus were recognized long before the time of psychoanalysis as the true representatives of the unrestrained life of impulses. Among the writings of the encyclopedist Diderot we find a famous dialogue, *The Nephew of Ramau*, which no less a person than Goethe has translated into German. In this you may read the remarkable sentence: "*If the little savage were left to himself he would preserve all his imbecility, he would unite the passions of a man of thirty to the unreasonableness of the child in the cradle; he would twist his father's neck and bed with his mother.*"

There is also one other thing of which I must needs speak. The mother-wife of Oedipus shall not have reminded us of the dream in vain. Do you still remember the result of our dream analysis, that the wishes out of which the dream is constructed so frequently are of a perverse, incestuous nature, or disclose an enmity toward near and beloved relatives the existence of which had never been suspected? At the time we did not trace the sources of these evil impulses. Now you may see them for yourselves. They represent the disposition made in early infancy of the libidinous energy, with the objects, long since given up in conscious life, to which it had once clung, which are now shown at night to be still present and in a certain sense capable of activity. But since all people have such perverse, incestuous and murderous dreams, and not the neurotics alone, we may conclude that even those who are normal have passed through the same evolutionary development, through the perversions and the direction of the libidio toward the objects of the Oedipus-complex. This, then, is the way of normal development, upon which the neurotics merely enlarge. They show in cruder form what dream analysis exposes in the healthy dreamer as well. Accordingly here is one of the motives which led us to deal with the study of the dream before we considered the neurotic symptom.

TWENTY-SECOND LECTURE. GENERAL THEORY OF THE NEUROSES

Theories of Development and Regression—Etiology

WE have learned that the libido goes through an extensive development before it can enter the service of reproduction in a way which may be regarded as normal. Now I wish to present to you what importance this fact possesses for the causation of neuroses.

I believe we are in harmony with the teachings of general pathology in assuming that this development involves two dangers, inhibition and regression. In other words, with the universal tendency of biological processes toward variation, it must necessarily happen that not all preparatory phases of a given function are equally well passed through or accomplished with comparable thoroughness. Certain components of a function may be permanently held back in an early stage of development and the complete development is therefore retarded to a certain extent.

Let us seek analogies for these processes from other fields. If a whole people leaves its dwellings to seek a new home, as frequently happened in the early periods of the history of mankind, their entire number will certainly not reach the new destination. Setting aside other losses, small groups or associations of these wandering peoples would stop on the way, and, while the majority passes on, they would settle down at these way-stations. Or, to seek a more appropriate comparison: You know that in the most highly evolved mammals, the male seminal glands, which originally are located in the far depths of the abdominal cavity, begin to wander during a certain period of intra-uterine life until they reach a position almost immediately under the skin of the pelvic extremity. In the case of a number of male individuals, one of the paired glands may as a result of this wandering remain in the pelvic cavity, or may be permanently located in the canal through which both glands must pass in their journey, or finally the canal itself may stay open permanently instead of growing together with the seminal glands after the change of position has taken place normally. When, as a young student, I was doing my first piece of scientific research under the direction of von Brücke, I was working on the dorsal nerve-roots in the spinal cord of a small fish very archaic in form. I discovered that the nerve ganglia of these roots grow out from large cells which lie in the grey matter of the dorsal column, a condition no longer true of other vertebrates. But I soon discovered that such nerve cells are found outside the grey matter all the way to the so-called spinal ganglion of the dorsal root. From this I concluded that the cells of this group of ganglia had traveled from the spinal cord to the roots of the nerves. This same result is attested by embryology. In this little fish, however, the entire path of the journey was traceable by the cells that had remained behind. Closer observation will easily reveal to you the weak points of these comparisons. Therefore let me simply say that with reference to every single sexual impulse, I consider it possible for several of its components to be held back in the earlier stages of development while other components have worked themselves out to completion. You will realize that we think of every such impulse as a current continuously driving on from the very beginning of life, and that our resolving it into individual movements which follow separately one upon the other is to a certain extent artificial. Your impression that these concepts require further clarification is correct, but an attempt would lead to too great digression. Before we pass on, however, let us agree to call this arrest of a partial impulse in an early stage of development, a *fixation* of the instinct.

Regression is the second danger of this development by stages. Even those components which have achieved a degree of progress may readily turn backward to these earlier stages. Having attained to this later and more highly developed form, the impulse is forced to a regression when it encounters great external difficulties in the exercise of its function, and accordingly cannot reach the goal which will satisfy its strivings. We can obviously assume that fixation and regression are not independent of each other. The stronger the fixations in the process of development prove to be, the more readily will the function evade external difficulties by a regression back to those fixations, and the less capable will the fully developed function be to withstand the hindrances that stand in the way of its exercise. Remember that if a people in its wandering has left large groups at certain way-stations, it is natural for those who have gone on to return to these stations if they are beaten or encounter a mighty foe. The more they have left on the way, however, the greater is their chance of defeat.

For your comprehension of the neuroses it is necessary to keep in mind this connection between fixation and regression. This will give you a secure hold upon the question of the cause of neuroses—of the etiology of neuroses— which we shall soon consider.

For the present we have still to discuss various aspects of regression. With the knowledge you have gained concerning the development of the function of libido, you must expect two kinds of regression: incestuous return to the first libidinous objects and return of the entire sexual organization to an earlier stage of development. Both occur in the transference neuroses and play an important part in its mechanism. Especially is the return to the first incestuous objects of libido a feature that the neurotic exhibits with positively tiresome regularity. We could say far more about regression of libido if we took into consideration another group of neuroses: neurotic narcism. But we cannot do this now. These conditions give us a clue to other stages of development of the function of libido, which have not been mentioned previously, and correspondingly show new kinds of regression. But I think the most important task before me at this point is to warn you not to confuse *regression* and *suppression*, and aid you to see clearly the connection between the two processes. Suppression, as you know, is the process by which an act capable of becoming conscious, in other words, an act that belongs to the fore-conscious system, is rendered unconscious and accordingly is thrust back into the unconscious system. Similarly we speak of suppression when the unconscious psychic act never has been admitted into the adjoining fore-conscious system but is arrested by the censor at the threshold. Kindly observe that the conception of suppression has nothing to do with sexuality. It describes a purely psychological process, which could better be characterized by terming it *localized*. By that we mean that it is concerned with the spatial relationships within the psyche, or if we drop this crude metaphor, with building up the psychological apparatus out of separate, psychic systems.

Through these comparisons we observe that up to this point we have not used the word regression in its general, but in a very special sense. If you accord it the general meaning of return from a higher to a lower stage of development you must include suppression as a form of regression, for suppression may also be described as the reversion to an earlier and lower stage in the development of a psychic act. Only in regard to suppression, this tendency to revert is not necessarily involved, for when a psychic act is held back in the early unconscious stage we also term it suppression in a dynamic sense. Suppression is a localized and dynamic conception, regression purely descriptive. What up this point we have called regression and considered in its relation to fixation, was only the return of libido to former stages of its development. The nature of this latter conception is entirely distinct and independent of suppression. We cannot call the libido regressions purely psychical processes and do not know what localization in the psychological apparatus we should assign to them. Even though the libido exerts a most powerful influence on psychic life, its organic significance is still the most conspicuous.

Discussions of this sort, gentlemen, are bound to be somewhat dry. To render them more vivid and impressive, let us return to clinical illustrations. You know that hysteria and compulsion-neurosis are the two chief factors in the group of transference neuroses. In hysteria, libidinous return to primary, incestuous sexual objects is quite regular, but regression to a former stage of sexual organization very rare. In the mechanism of hysteria suppression plays the chief part. If you will permit me to supplement our previous positive knowledge of this neurosis by a constructive suggestion, I could describe the state of affairs in this manner: the union of the partial instincts under the domination of the genitals is accomplished, but its results encounter the opposition of the fore-conscious system which, of course, is bound up with consciousness. Genital organization, therefore, may stand for the unconscious but not for the fore-conscious. Through this rejection on the part of the fore-conscious, a situation arises which in certain aspects is similar to the condition existing before the genitals had attained their primacy. Of the two libido regressions, the regression to a former stage of sexual organization is by far the more conspicuous. Since it is lacking in hysteria and our entire conception of the neuroses is still too much dominated by the study of hysteria which preceded it in point of time, the meaning of libido regression became clearer to us much later than that of repression. Let us be prepared to widen and change our attitude still more when we consider other narcistic neuroses besides compulsion-neurosis and hysteria in our discussion.

In contrast to this, regression of libido in compulsion-neurosis turns back most conspicuously to the earlier sadistico-anal organization, which accordingly becomes the most significant factor expressed by the symptoms. Under these conditions the love impulse must mask itself as a sadistic impulse. The compulsion idea must therefore be reinterpreted. Isolated from other superimposed factors, which though they are not accidental are also indispensable, it no longer reads: "I want to murder you"; rather it says "I want to enjoy you in love." Add to this, that simultaneously regression of the object has also set in, so that this impulse is invariably directed toward the nearest and dearest persons, and you can imagine with what horror the patient thinks of these compulsion ideas and how alien they appear to his conscious perception. In the mechanism of these neuroses, suppression, too, assumes an important part, which it is not easy to explain in a superficial discussion of this sort. Regression of the libido without suppression would never result in neurosis but would finally end in perversion. This makes it obvious that suppression is the process most characteristic of neurosis, and typifies it most perfectly. Perhaps I shall at some future time have the opportunity of presenting to you our knowledge of the mechanism of perversions and then you will see that here also things do not work themselves out as simply as we should best like to construe them.

You will most readily reconcile yourself with these elucidations of fixation and regression, when you consider them as a preface to the investigation of the etiology of neuroses. Towards this I have only advanced a single fact: that people become neurotically ill when the possibility of satisfying their libido is removed, ill with "denial," as I expressed myself, and that their symptoms are the substitutes for the denied gratification. Of course, that does not mean that every denial of libidinous satisfaction makes every person neurotic, but merely that in all cases known of neurosis, the factor of denial was traceable. The syllogism therefore cannot be reversed. You also understand, I trust, that this statement is not supposed to reveal the entire secret of the etiology of neurosis, but only emphasizes an important and indispensable condition.

Now, we do not know, in the further discussion of this statement, whether to emphasize the nature of denial or the individuality of the person affected by it. Denial is very rarely complete and absolute; to cause a pathological condition, the specific gratification desired by the particular person in question must be withheld, the certain satisfaction of which he alone is capable. On the whole there are many ways of enduring abstinence from libidinous gratification without succumbing to a neurosis by reason thereof. Above all we know of people who are able to endure abstinence without doing themselves injury; they are not happy under the circumstances, they are filled with yearning, but they do not become ill. Furthermore, we must take into consideration that the impulses of the sex instinct are extraordinarily *plastic*, if I may use that term in this connection. One thing may take the place of the other; one may assume the other's intensity; if reality refuses the one gratification, the satisfaction of another may offer full compensation. The sexual impulses are like a network of communicating channels filled with fluids; they are this in spite of their subjugation to the primacy of the genitals, though I realize it is difficult to unite these two ideas in one conception. The component impulses of sexuality as well as the total sexual desire, which represents their aggregate, show a marked ability to change their object, to exchange it, for instance, for one more easily attainable. This displacement and the readiness to accept substitutes must exert powerful influences in opposition to the pathological effect of abstinence. Among these processes which resist the ill effects of abstinence, one in particular has won cultural significance. Sexual desire relinquishes either its goal of partial gratification of desire, or the goal of desire toward reproduction, and adopts another aim, genetically related to the abandoned one, save that it is no longer sexual but must be termed social. This process is called "sublimation," and in adopting this process we subscribe to the general standard which places social aims above selfish sexual desires. Sublimation is, as a matter of fact, only a special case of the relation of sexual to non-sexual desires. We shall have occasion to talk more about this later in another connection.

Now your impression will be that abstinence has become an insignificant factor, since there are so many methods of enduring it. Yet this is not the case, for its pathological power is unimpaired. The remedies are generally not sufficient. The measure of unsatisfied libido which the average human being can stand is limited. The plasticity and freedom of movement of libido is by no means retained to the same extent by all individuals; sublimation can, moreover, never account for more than a certain small fraction of the libido, and finally most people possess the capacity for sublimation only to a very slight degree. The most important of these limitations clearly lies in the adaptability of the libido, as it renders the gratification of the individual dependent upon the attainment of only a very few aims and objects. Kindly recall that incomplete development of the libido leaves extensive and possibly even numerous libido fixations in earlier developmental phases of the processes of sexual organization and object-finding, and that these phases are usually not capable of affording a real gratification. You will then recognize libido fixation as the second powerful factor which together with abstinence constitutes the causative factors of the illness. We may abbreviate schematically and say that libido fixation represents the internal disposing factor, abstinence the accidental external factor of the etiology of neurosis.

I seize the opportunity to warn you of taking sides in a most unnecessary conflict. In scientific affairs it is a popular proceeding to emphasize a part of the truth in place of the whole truth and to combat all the rest, which has lost none of its verity, in the name of that fraction. In this way various factions have already separated out from the movement of psychoanalysis; one faction recognizes only the egoistic impulses and denies the sexual, another appreciates the influence of objective tasks in life, but ignores the part played by the individual past, and so on. Here is occasion for a similar antithesis and subject for dispute: are neuroses *exogenous* or *endogenous* diseases, are they the inevitable results of a special constitution or the product of certain harmful (traumatic) impressions; in particular, are they called forth by libido fixation (and the sexual constitution which goes with this) or through the pressure of forbearance? This dilemma seems to me no whit wiser than another I could present to you: is the child created through the generation of the father or the conception of the mother? Both factors are equally essential, you will answer very properly. The conditions which cause neuroses are very similar if not precisely the same. For the consideration of the causes of neuroses, we may arrange neurotic diseases in a series, in which two factors, sexual constitution and experience, or, if you wish, libido-fixation and self-denial, are represented in such a way that one increases as the other decreases. At one end of the series are the extreme cases, of which you can say with full conviction: These persons would have become ill because of the peculiar development of their libido, no matter what they might have experienced, no matter how gently life might have treated them. At the other end are cases which would call forth the reversed judgment, that the patients would undoubtedly have escaped illness if life had not thrust certain conditions upon them. But in the intermediate cases of the series, predisposing sexual constitution and subversive demands of life combine. Their sexual constitution would not have given rise to neurosis if the victims had not had such experiences, and their experiences would not have acted upon them traumatically if the conditions of the libido had been otherwise. Within this series I may grant a certain preponderance to the weight carried by the predisposing factors, but this admission, too, depends upon the boundaries within which you wish to delimit nervousness.

Allow me to suggest that you call such series *complementary series*. We shall have occasion to establish other series of this sort.

The tenacity with which the libido clings to certain tendencies and objects, the so-called *adhesiveness* of the libido, appears to us as an independent factor, individually variable, the determining conditions of which are completely unknown to us, but the importance of which for the etiology of the neuroses we can no longer underestimate. At the same time we must not overestimate the closeness of this interrelation. A similar adhesiveness of the libido occurs—for unknown reasons—in normal persons under various conditions, and is a determining factor in the perverse, who are in a certain sense the opposite of nervous. Before the period of psychoanalysis, it was known (Binet) that the anamnesia of the perverse is often traced back to an early impression—an abnormality in the tendency of the instinct or its choice of object—and it is to this that the libido of the individual has clung for life. Frequently it is hard to say how such an impression becomes capable of attracting the libido so intensively. I shall give you a case of this kind which I observed myself. A man, to whom the genital and all other sex stimuli of woman now mean nothing, who in fact can only be thrown into an irresistible sexual excitation by the sight of a shoe on a foot of a certain form, is able to recall an experience he had in his sixth year, which proved decisive for the fixation of his libido. One day he sat on a stool beside his governess, who was to give him an English lesson. She was an old, shriveled, unbeautiful girl with washed-out blue eyes and a pug nose, who on this day, because of some injury, had put a velvet slipper on her foot and stretched it out on a footstool; the leg itself she had most decorously covered. After a diffident attempt at normal sexual activity, undertaken during puberty, such a thin sinewy foot as his governess' had become the sole object of his sexuality; and the man was irresistibly carried away if other features, reminiscent of the English governess, appeared in conjunction with the foot. Through this fixation of the libido the man did not become neurotic but perverse, a foot fetishist, as we say. So you see that, although exaggerated and premature fixation of the libido is indispensable for the causation of neuroses, its sphere of action exceeds the limits of neuroses immeasurably. This condition also, taken by itself, is no more decisive than abstinence.

And so the problem of the cause of neuroses seems to become more complicated. Psychoanalytic investigation does, in fact, acquaint us with a new factor, not considered in our etiological series, which is recognized most easily in those cases where permanent well-being is suddenly disturbed by an attack of neurosis. These individuals regularly show signs of contradiction between their wishes, or, as we are wont to say, indication of psychic *conflict*. A part of their personality represents certain wishes, another rebels against them and resists them. A neurosis cannot come into existence without such conflict. This may seem to be of small significance. You know that our psychic life is continually agitated by conflicts for which we must find a solution. Certain conditions, therefore, must exist to make such a conflict pathological. We want to know what these conditions are, what psychic powers form the background for these pathological conflicts, what relation the conflict bears to the causative factors.

I hope I shall be able to give you satisfactory answers to these questions even if I must make them schematically brief. Self-denial gives rise to conflict, for libido deprived of its gratification is forced to seek other means and ends. A pathogenic conflict arises when these other means and ends arouse the disfavor of one part of the personality, and a veto ensues which makes the new mode of gratification impossible for the time being. This is the point of departure for the development of the symptoms, a process which we shall consider later. The rejected libidinous desires manage to have their own way, through circuitous byways, but not without catering to the objections through the observance of certain symptom-formation; the symptoms are the new or substitute satisfaction which the condition of self-denial has made necessary.

We can express the significance of the psychic conflict in another way, by saying: the *outer* self-denial, in order to become pathological, must be supplemented by an *inner* self-denial. Outer denial removes one possibility of gratification, inner denial would like to exclude another possibility, and it is this second possibility which becomes the center of the ensuing conflict. I prefer this form of presentation because it possesses secret content. It implies the probability that the inner impediment found its origin in the prehistoric stage of human development in real external hindrances.

What powers are these which interpose objections to libidinous desire, who are the other parties to the pathological conflict? They are, in the widest sense, the non-sexual impulses. We call them comprehensively the "ego impulses"; psychoanalysis of transference neuroses does not grant us ready access to their further investigation, but we learn to know them, in a measure, through the resistance they offer to analysis. The pathological struggle is waged between ego-impulses and sexual impulses. In a series of cases it appears as though conflict could exist between various purely sexual desires; but that is really the same thing, for of the two sexual desires involved in the conflict, one is always considerate of the ego, while the other demands that the ego be denied, and so it remains a conflict between the ego and sexuality.

Again and again when psychoanalysis claimed that psychological event was the result of sexual impulses, indignant protest was raised that in psychic life there were other impulses and interests besides the sexual, that everything could not be derived from sexuality, etc. Well, it is a great pleasure to share for once the opinion of one's opponents. Psychoanalysis never forgot that non-sexual impulses exist. It insisted on the decided distinction between sexual and ego-impulses and maintained in the face of every objection not that neuroses arise from sexuality, but that they owe their origin to the conflict between sexuality and the ego. Psychoanalysis can have no reasonable motive for denying the existence or significance of ego-impulses, even though it investigates the influence sexual impulses play in illness and in life. Only it has been destined to deal primarily with sexual impulses, because transference neuroses have furnished the readiest access to their investigation, and because it had become obligatory to study what others had neglected.

It does not follow, either, that psychoanalysis has never occupied itself at all with the non-sexual side of personality. The very distinction of the ego from sexuality has shown most clearly that the ego-impulses also pass through a significant development, which is by no means entirely independent of the development of the libido, nor does it fail to exert a reaction upon it. To be sure, we know much less about the evolution of the ego than about libido development, for so far only the study of narcistic neuroses has promised to throw light on the structure of the ego. There is extant the notable attempt of Ferenczi to construct theoretically the stages of ego development, and furthermore we already possess two fixed points from which to proceed in our evolution of this development. We do not dream of asserting that the libidinous interests of a person are from the outset opposed to the interests of self-preservation; in every stage, rather, the ego will strive to remain in harmony with its sexual organization at that time, and accommodate itself thereto. The succession of the separate phases of development of libido probably follows a prescribed program; but we cannot deny that this sequence can be influenced by the ego, and that a certain parallelism of the phases of development of the ego and the libido may also be assumed. Indeed, the disturbance of this parallelism could become a pathological factor. One of the most important insights we have to gain is the nature of the attitude which the ego exhibits when an intensive fixation of its libido is left behind in one stage of its development. It may countenance the fixation and accordingly become perverse or, what amounts to the same thing, become infantile. Or it may be averse to this attachment of the libido, the result of which is that wherever the libido is subject to *fixation*, there the ego undergoes *suppression*.

In this way we reach the conclusion that the third factor of the etiology of neuroses is the tendency to *conflict*, upon which the development both of the ego and libido are dependent. Our insight into the causation of the neuroses has therefore been amplified. First, the most generalized factor, self-denial, then the fixation of the libido, by which it is forced into certain directions, and thirdly, the tendency to conflict in the development of the ego, which has rejected libidinous impulses of this kind. The state of affairs is therefore not so confused and difficult to see through, as you may have imagined it to be in the course of my explanation. But of course we are to discover that we have not, as yet, reached the end. We must add still a new factor and further analyze one we already know.

To show you the influence of ego development in the formation of a conflict, and so to give an illustration of the causation of neuroses, I should like to cite an example which, although it is entirely imaginary, is not far removed from probability in any respect. Drawing upon the title of a farce by Nestroy, I shall label this example "On the ground floor and in the first story." The janitor lives on the ground floor, while the owner of the house, a rich, distinguished man, occupies the first story. Both have children, and we shall assume that the owner permits his little daughter to play unwatched with the child of the people. Then it may easily happen that the games of the children become "naughty," that is, they assume a sexual character; they play "father and mother," watch each other in the performance of intimate performances and mutually stimulate their genitals. The janitor's daughter, who, in spite of her five or six years of age, has had occasion to make observations on the sexuality of adults, probably played the part of the seducer. These experiences, even though they be of short duration, are sufficient to set in motion certain sexual impulses in both children, which continue in the form of onanism for several years after the common games have ceased. So far the consequences are similar; the final result will be very different. The janitor's daughter will continue onanism possibly to the commencement of her periods, abandon it then without difficulty, not many years later find a lover, perhaps bear a child, choose this or that path of life, which may likely enough make of her a popular artist who ends as an aristocrat. Perhaps the outcome will be less brilliant, but at any rate she will work out her life, free from neurosis, unharmed by her premature sexual activity. Very different is the effect on the other child. Even while she is very young she will realize vaguely that she has done wrong. In a short while, perhaps only after a violent struggle, she will renounce the gratification of onanism, yet still retain an undercurrent of depression in her attitude. If, during her early childhood, she chances to learn something about sexual intercourse, she will turn away in explicable disgust and seek to remain innocent. Probably she is at the time subjected anew to an irresistible impulse to onanism, of which she does not dare to complain. When the time arrives for her to find favor in the eyes of a man, a neurosis will suddenly develop and cheat her out of marriage and the joy of life. When analysis succeeds in gaining insight into this neurosis, it will reveal that this well-bred, intelligent girl of high ideals, has completely suppressed her sexual desires, but that unconsciously they cling to the meager experiences she had with the friend of her childhood.

The difference of these two destinies, arising from the same experience, is due to the fact that one ego has experienced development while the other has not. The janitor's daughter in later years looks upon sexual intercourse as the same natural and harmless thing it had seemed in her childhood. The owner's daughter had experienced the influence of education and had recognized its claims. Thus stimulated, her ego had forged its ideals of womanly purity and lack of desire which, however, could not agree with any sexual activity; her intellectual development had made unworthy her interest in the woman's part she was to play. This higher moral and intellectual evolution of her ego was in conflict with the claims of her sexuality.

I should like to consider today one more point in the development of the ego, partly because it opens wide vistas, partly because it will justify the sharp, perhaps unnatural line of division we are wont to draw between sexual and ego impulses. In estimating the several developments of ego and of libido, we must emphasize an aspect which has not frequently been appreciated heretofore. Both the ego and the libido are fundamentally heritages, abbreviated repetitions of an evolution which mankind has, in the course of long periods of time, traversed from primeval ages. The libido shows its phylogenetic origin most readily, I should say. Recall, if you please, that in one class of animals the genital apparatus is closely connected with the mouth, that in another it cannot be separated from the excretory apparatus, and in others it is attached to organs of locomotion. Of all these things you will find a most fascinating description in the valuable book of W. Bölsche. Animals portray, so to speak, all kinds of perversions which have become set as their permanent sexual organizations. In man this phylogenetic aspect is partly clouded by the circumstance that these activities, although fundamentally inherited, are achieved anew in individual development, presumably because the same conditions still prevail and still continue to exert their influence on each personality. I should say that originally they served to call forth an activity, where they now serve only as a stimulus for recollection. There is no doubt that in addition the course of development in each individual, which has been innately determined, may be disturbed or altered from without by recent influences. That power which has forced this development upon mankind, and which today maintains the identical pressure, is indeed known to us: it is the same self-denial enforced by the realities—or, given its big and actual name, *Necessity*, the struggle for existence, the 'Ανάγχη. This has been a severe teacher, but under him we have become potent. The neurotics are those children upon whom this severity has had a bad effect—but there is risk in all education. This appreciation of the struggle of life as the moving force of development need not prejudice us against the importance of "innate tendencies in evolution" if their existence can be proved.

It is worth noting that sexual instincts and instincts of self-preservation do not behave similarly when they are confronted with the necessities of actuality. It is easier to educate the instincts of self-preservation and everything that is connected with them; they speedily learn to adapt themselves to necessity and to arrange their development in accordance with the mandates of fact. That is easy to understand, for they cannot procure the objects they require in any other way; without these objects the individual must perish. The sex instincts are more difficult to educate because at the outset they do not suffer from the need of an object. As they are related almost parasitically to the other functions of the body and gratify themselves auto-erotically by way of their own body, they are at first withdrawn from the educational influence of real necessity. In most people, they maintain themselves in some way or other during the entire course of life as those characteristics of obstinacy and inaccessibility to influence which are generally collectively called unreasonableness. The education of youth generally comes to an end when the sexual demands are aroused to their full strength. Educators know this and act accordingly; but perhaps the results of psychoanalysis will influence them to transfer the greatest emphasis to the education of the early years, of childhood, beginning with the suckling. The little human being is frequently a finished product in his fourth or fifth year, and only reveals gradually in later years what has long been ready within him.

To appreciate the full significance of the aforementioned difference between the two groups of instincts, we must digress considerably and introduce a consideration which we must needs call *economic*. Thereby we enter upon one of the most important but unfortunately one of the most obscure domains of psychoanalysis. We ask ourselves whether a fundamental purpose is recognizable in the workings of our psychological apparatus, and answer immediately that this purpose is the pursuit of pleasurable excitement. It seems as if our entire psychological activity were directed toward gaining pleasurable stimulation, toward avoiding painful ones; that it is regulated automatically by the *principle of pleasure*. Now we should like to know, above all, what conditions cause the creation of pleasure and pain, but here we fall short. We may only venture to say that pleasurable excitation *in some way* involves lessening, lowering or obliterating the amount of stimuli present in the psychic apparatus. This amount, on the other hand, is increased by pain. Examination of the most intense pleasurable excitement accessible to man, the pleasure which accompanies the performance of the sexual act, leaves small doubt on this point. Since such processes of pleasure are concerned with the destinies of quantities of psychic excitation or energy, we call considerations of this sort economic. It thus appears that we can describe the tasks and performances of the psychic apparatus in different and more generalized terms than by the emphasis of the pursuit of pleasure. We may say that the psychic apparatus serves the purpose of mastering and bringing to rest the mass of stimuli and the stimulating forces which approach it. The sexual instincts obviously show their aim of pleasurable excitement from the beginning to the end of their development; they retain this original function without much change. The ego instincts strive at first for the same thing. But through the influence of their teacher, necessity, the ego instincts soon learn to adduce some qualification to the principle of pleasure. The task of avoiding pain becomes an objective almost comparable to the gain of pleasure; the ego learns that its direct gratification is unavoidably withheld, the gain of pleasurable excitement postponed, that always a certain amount of pain must be borne and certain sources of pleasure entirely relinquished. This educated ego has become "reasonable." It is no longer controlled by the principle of pleasure, but by the *principle of fact*, which at bottom also aims at pleasure, but pleasure which is postponed and lessened by considerations of fact.

The transition from the pleasure principle to that of fact is the most important advance in the development of the ego. We already know that the sexual instincts pass through this stage unwillingly and late. We shall presently learn the consequence to man of the fact that his sexuality admits of such a loose relation to the external realities of his life. Yet one more observation belongs here. Since the ego of man has, like the libido, its history of evolution, you will not be surprised to hear that there are "ego-regressions," and you will want to know what role this return of the ego to former phases of development plays in neurotic disease.

TWENTY-THIRD LECTURE. GENERAL THEORY OF THE NEUROSES

The Development of the Symptoms

IN the layman's eyes the symptom shows the nature of the disease, and cure means removal of symptoms. The physician, however, finds it important to distinguish the symptoms from the disease and recognizes that doing away with the symptoms is not necessarily curing the disease. Of course, the only tangible thing left over after the removal of the symptoms is the capacity to build new symptoms. Accordingly, for the time being, let us accept the layman's viewpoint and consider the understanding of the symptoms as equivalent to the understanding of the sickness.

The symptoms,—of course, we are dealing here with psychic (or psychogenic) symptoms, and psychic illness—are acts which are detrimental to life as a whole, or which are at least useless; frequently they are obnoxious to the individual who performs them and are accompanied by distaste and suffering. The principal injury lies in the psychic exertion which they cost, and in the further exertion needed to combat them. The price these efforts exact may, when there is an extensive development of the symptoms, bring about an extraordinary impoverishment of the personality of the patient with respect to his available psychic energy, and consequently cripple him in all the important tasks of life. Since such an outcome is dependent on the amount of energy so utilized, you will readily understand that "being sick" is essentially a practical concept. But if you take a theoretical standpoint and disregard these quantitative relations, you can readily say that we are all sick, or rather neurotic, since the conditions favorable to the development of symptoms are demonstrable also among normal persons.

As to the neurotic symptoms, we already know that they are the result of a conflict aroused by a new form of gratifying the libido. The two forces that have contended against each other meet once more in the symptom; they become reconciled through the compromise of a symptom development. That is why the symptom is capable of such resistance; it is sustained from both sides. We also know that one of the two partners to the conflict is the unsatisfied libido, frustrated by reality, which must now seek other means for its satisfaction. If reality remains inflexible even where the libido is prepared to take another object in place of the one denied it, the libido will then finally be compelled to resort to regression and to seek gratification in one of the earlier stages in its organizations already out-lived, or by means of one of the objects given up in the past. Along the path of regression the libido is enticed by fixations which it has left behind at these stages in its development.

Here the development toward perversion branches off sharply from that of the neuroses. If the regressions do not awaken the resistance of the ego, then a neurosis does not follow and the libido arrives at some actual, even if abnormal, satisfaction. The ego, however, controls not alone consciousness, but also the approaches to motor innervation, and hence the realization of psychic impulses. If the ego then does not approve this regression, the conflict takes place. The libido is locked out, as it were, and must seek refuge in some place where it can find an outlet for its fund of energy, in accordance with the controlling demands for pleasurable gratification. It must withdraw from the ego. Such an evasion is offered by the fixations established in the course of its evolution and now traversed regressively, against which the ego had, at the time, protected itself by suppressions. The libido, streaming back, occupies these suppressed positions and thus withdraws from before the ego and its laws. At the same time, however, it throws off all the influences acquired under its tutelage. The libido could be guided so long as there was a possibility of its being satisfied; under the double pressure of external and internal denial it becomes unruly and harks back to former and more happy times. Such is its character, fundamentally unchangeable. The ideas which the libido now takes over in order to hold its energy belong to the system of the unconscious, and are therefore subject to its peculiar processes, especially elaboration and displacement. Conditions are set up here which are entirely comparable to those of dream formation. Just as the latent dream, the fulfillment of a wish-phantasy, is first built up in the unconsciousness, but must then pass through conscious processes before, censored and approved, it can enter into the compromise construction of the manifest dream, so the ideas representing the libido in the unconscious must still contend against the power of the fore-conscious ego. The opposition that has arisen against it in the ego follows it down by a "counter-siege" and forces it to choose such an expression as will serve at the same time to express itself. Thus, then, the symptom comes into being as a much distorted offshoot from the unconscious libidinous wish-fulfillment, an artificially selected ambiguity— with two entirely contradictory meanings. In this last point alone do we realize a difference between dream and symptom development, for the only fore-conscious purpose in dream formation is the maintenance of sleep, the exclusion from consciousness of anything which may disturb sleep; but it does not necessarily oppose the unconscious wish impulse with an insistent "No." Quite the contrary; the purpose of the dream may be more tolerant, because the situation of the sleeper is a less dangerous one. The exit to reality is closed only through the condition of sleep.

You see, this evasion which the libido finds under the conditions of the conflict is possible only by virtue of the existing fixations. When these fixations are taken in hand by the regression, the suppression is side-tracked and the libido, which must maintain itself under the conditions of the compromise, is led off or gratified. By means of such a detour by way of the unconscious and the old fixations, the libido has at last succeeded in breaking its way through to some sort of gratification, however extraordinarily limited this may seem and however unrecognizable any longer as a genuine satisfaction. Now allow me to add two further remarks concerning this final result. In the first place, I should like you to take note of the intimate connection between the libido and the unconscious on the one hand, and on the other of the ego, consciousness, and reality. The connection that is evidenced here, however, does not indicate that originally they in any way belong together. I should like you to bear continually in mind that everything I have said here, and all that will follow, pertains only to the symptom development of hysterical neurosis.

Where, now, can the libido find the fixations which it must have in order to force its way through the suppressions? In the activities and experiences of infantile sexuality, in its abandoned component-impulses, its childish objects which have been given up. The libido again returns to them. The significance of this period of childhood is a double one; on the one hand, the instinctive tendencies which were congenital in the child first showed themselves at this time; secondly, at the same time, environmental influences and chance experiences were first awakening his other instincts. I believe our right to establish this bipartite division cannot be questioned. The assertion that the innate disposition plays a part is hardly open to criticism, but analytic experience actually makes it necessary for us to assume that purely accidental experiences of childhood are capable of leaving fixations of the libido. I do not see any theoretical difficulties here. Congenital tendencies undoubtedly represent the after-effects of the experiences of an earlier ancestry; they must also have once been acquired; without such acquired characters there could be no heredity. And is it conceivable that the inheritance of such acquired characters comes to a standstill in the very generation that we have under observation? The significance of infantile experience, however, should not, as is so often done, be completely ignored as compared with ancestral experiences or those of our adult years; on the contrary, they should meet with an especial appreciation. They have such important results because they occur in the period of uncompleted development, and because of this very fact are in a position to cause a traumatic effect. The researches on the mechanics of development by Roux and others have shown us that a needle prick into an embryonic cell mass which is undergoing division results in most serious developmental disturbances. The same injury to a larva or a completed animal can be borne without injury.

The libido fixation of adults, which we have referred to as representative of the constitutional factor in the etiological comparison of the neuroses, can be thought of, so far as we are concerned, as divisible into two separate factors, the inherited disposition and the tendency acquired in early childhood. We know that a schematic representation is most acceptable to the student. Let us combine these relations as follows:

Cause of the neurosis   ==

Disposition as determined by libido fixation   accidental experiences
(traumatic element)

Sexual constitution (pre-historic experience)   Infantile experience

The hereditary sexual constitution provides us with manifold tendencies, varying with the special emphasis given one or the other component of the instinct, either individually or in combination. With the factor of infantile experience, there is again built up a complementary series within the sexual constitution which is perfectly comparable with our first series, namely, the gradations between disposition and the chance experiences of the adult. Here again we find the same extreme cases and similar relations in the matter of substitution. At this point the question becomes pertinent as to whether the most striking regressions of the libido, those which hark back to very early stages in sexual organization, are not essentially conditioned by the hereditary constitutional factor. The answer to this question, however, may best be put off until we are in a position to consider a wider range in the forms of neurotic disease.

Let us devote a little time to the consideration of the fact that analytic investigation of neurotics shows the libido to be bound up with the infantile sexual experiences of these persons. In this light they seem of enormous importance for both the life and health of mankind. With respect to therapeutic work their importance remains undiminished. But when we do not take this into account we can herein readily recognize the danger of being misled by the situation as it exists in neurotics into adopting a mistaken and one-sided orientation toward life. In figuring the importance of the infantile experiences we must also subtract the influences arising from the fact that the libido has returned to them by regression, after having been forced out of its later positions. Thus we approach the opposite conclusion, that experiences of the libido had no importance whatever in their own time, but rather acquired it at the time of regression. You will remember that we were led to a similar alternative in the discussion of the Oedipus-complex.

A decision on this matter will hardly be difficult for us. The statement is undoubtedly correct that the hold which the infantile experiences have on the libido—with the pathogenic influences this involves—is greatly augmented by the regression; still, to allow them to become definitive would nevertheless be misleading. Other considerations must be taken into account as well. In the first place, observation shows, in a way that leaves no room for doubt, that infantile experiences have their particular significance which is evidenced already during childhood. There are, furthermore, neuroses in children in which the factor of displacement in time is necessarily greatly minimized or is entirely lacking, since the illness follows as an immediate consequence of the traumatic experience. The study of these infantile neuroses keeps us from many dangerous misunderstandings of adult neuroses, just as the dreams of children similarly serve as the key to the understanding of the dreams of adults. As a matter of fact, the neuroses of children are very frequent, far more frequent than is generally believed. They are often overlooked, dismissed as signs of badness or naughtiness, and often suppressed by the authority of the nursery; in retrospect, however, they may be easily recognized later. They occur most frequently in the form of *anxiety hysteria*. What this implies we shall learn upon another occasion. When a neurosis breaks out in later life, analysis regularly shows that it is a direct continuation of that infantile malady which had perhaps developed only obscurely and incipiently. However, there are cases, as already stated, in which this childish nervousness continues, without any interruption, as a lifelong affliction. We have been able to analyze a very few examples of such neuroses during childhood, while they were actually going on; much more often we had to be satisfied with obtaining our insight into the childhood neurosis subsequently, when the patient is already well along in life, under conditions in which we are forced to work with certain corrections and under definite precautions.

Secondly, we must admit that the universal regression of the libido to the period of childhood would be inexplicable if there were nothing there which could exert an attraction for it. The fixation which we assume to exist towards specific developmental phases, conveys a meaning only if we think of it as stabilizing a definite amount of libidinous energy. Finally, I am able to remind you that here there exists a complementary relationship between the intensity and the pathogenic significance of the infantile experiences to the later ones which is similar to that studied in previous series. There are cases in which the entire causal emphasis falls upon the sexual experiences of childhood, in which these impressions take on an effect which is unmistakably traumatic and in which no other basis exists for them beyond what the average sexual constitution and its immaturity can offer. Side by side with these there are others in which the whole stress is brought to bear by the later conflicts, and the emphasis the analysis places on childhood impressions appears entirely as the work of regression. There are also extremes of "retarded development" and "regression," and between them every combination in the interaction of the two factors.

These relations have a certain interest for that pedagogy which assumes as its object the prevention of neuroses by an early interference in the sexual development of the child. So long as we keep our attention fixed essentially on the infantile sexual experiences, we readily come to believe we have done everything for the prophylaxis of nervous afflictions when we have seen to it that this development is retarded, and that the child is spared this type of experience. Yet we already know that the conditions for the causation of neuroses are more complicated and cannot in general be influenced through one single factor. The strict protection in childhood loses its value because it is powerless against the constitutional factor; furthermore, it is more difficult to carry out than the educators imagine, and it brings with it two new dangers that cannot be lightly dismissed. It accomplishes too much, for it favors a degree of sexual suppression which is harmful for later years, and it sends the child into life without the power to resist the violent onset of sexual demands that must be expected during puberty. The profit, therefore, which childhood prophylaxis can yield is most dubious; it seems, indeed, that better success in the prevention of neuroses can be gained by attacking the problem through a changed attitude toward facts.

Let us return to the consideration of the symptoms. They serve as substitutes for the gratification which has been forborne, by a regression of the libido to earlier days, with a return to former development phases in their choice of object and in their organization. We learned some time ago that the neurotic is held fast somewhere in his past; we now know that it is a period of his past in which his libido did not miss the satisfaction which made him happy. He looks for such a time in his life until he has found it, even though he must hark back to his suckling days as he retains them in his memory or as he reconstructs them in the light of later influences. The symptom in some way again yields the old infantile form of satisfaction, distorted by the censoring work of the conflict. As a rule it is converted into a sensation of suffering and fused with other causal elements of the disease. The form of gratification which the symptom yields has much about it that alienates one's sympathy. In this we omit to take into account, however, the fact that the patients do not recognize the gratification as such and experience the apparent satisfaction rather as suffering, and complain of it. This transformation is part of the psychic conflict under the pressure of which the symptom must be developed. What was at one time a satisfaction for the individual must now awaken his antipathy or disgust. We know a simple but instructive example for such a change of feeling. The same child that sucked the milk with such voracity from its mother's breast is apt to show a strong antipathy for milk a few years later, which is often difficult to overcome. This antipathy increases to the point of disgust when the milk, or any substituted drink, has a little skin over it. It is rather hard to throw out the suggestion that this skin calls up the memory of the mother's breast, which was once so intensely coveted. In the meantime, to be sure, the traumatic experience of weaning has intervened.

There is something else that makes the symptoms appear remarkable and inexplicable as a means of libidinous satisfaction. They in no way recall anything from which we normally are in the habit of expecting satisfaction. They usually require no object, and thereby give up all connection with external reality. We understand this to be a result of turning away from fact and of returning to the predominance of pleasurable gratification. But it is also a return to a sort of amplified autoeroticism, such as was yielded the sex impulse in its earliest satisfactions. In the place of a modification in the outside world, we have a physical change, in other words, an internal reaction in place of an external one, an adjustment instead of an activity. Viewed from a phylogenetic standpoint, this expresses a very significant regression. We will grasp this better when we consider it in connection with a new factor

239

which we are still to discover from the analytic investigation of symptom development. Further, we recall that in symptom formation the same processes of the unconscious have been at work as in dream formation—elaboration and displacement. Similarly to the dream, the symptom represents a fulfillment, a satisfaction after the manner of the infantile; by the utmost elaboration this satisfaction can be compressed into a single sensation or innervation, or by extreme displacement it may be restricted to a tiny element of the entire libidinous complex. It is no wonder that we often have difficulties in recognizing in the symptom the libidinous satisfaction which we anticipate and always find verified.

I have indicated that we must still become familiar with a new factor. It is something really surprising and confusing. You know that by analysis of the symptoms we arrive at a knowledge of the infantile experiences upon which the libido is fixated and out of which the symptoms are formed. Well, the surprising thing is this, that these infantile scenes are not always true. Indeed, in the majority of cases they are untrue, and in some instances they are directly contrary to historical truth. You see that this discovery, as no other, serves either to discredit the analysis which has led to such a result, or to discredit the patients upon whose testimony the analysis, as well as the whole understanding of neuroses, is built up. In addition there is something else utterly confusing about it. If the infantile experiences, revealed by analysis, were in every case real, we should have the feeling of walking on sure ground; if they were regularly falsified, disclosed themselves as inventions or phantasies of the patients, we should have to leave this uncertain ground and find a surer footing elsewhere. But it is neither the one nor the other, for when we look into the matter we find that the childhood experiences which are recalled or reconstructed in the course of the analysis may in some in some instances be false, in others undeniably true, and in the majority of cases a mixture of truth and fiction. The symptoms then are either the representation of actual experiences to which we may ascribe an influence in the fixation of the libido, or the representation of phantasies of the patient which, of course, can be of no etiological significance. It is hard to find one's way here. The first foothold is given perhaps by an analogous discovery, namely, that the same scattered childhood memories that individuals always have had and have been conscious of prior to an analysis may be falsified as well, or at least may contain a generous mixture of true and false. Evidence of error very seldom offers difficulties, and we at least gain the satisfaction of knowing that the blame for this unexpected disappointment is not to be laid at the door of analysis, but in some way upon the patients.

After reflecting a bit we can easily understand what is so confusing in this matter. It is the slight regard for reality, the neglect to keep fact distinct from phantasy. We are apt to feel insulted that the patient has wasted our time with invented tales. There is an enormous gap in our thinking between reality and invention and we accord an entirely different valuation to reality. The patient, too, takes this same viewpoint in his normal thinking. When he offers the material which, by way of the symptom, leads back to the wish situations which are modeled upon the childhood experiences, we are at first, to be sure, in doubt whether we are dealing with reality or with phantasy. Later certain traits determine this decision; we are confronted with the task of acquainting the patient with them. This can never be accomplished without difficulty. If at the outset we tell him that he is going to reveal phantasies with which he has veiled his childhood history, just as every people weaves myths around its antiquity, we notice (to our comfort) that his interest in the further pursuit of the subject suddenly diminishes. He, too, wants to discover realities, and despises all "notions." But if until this is accomplished we allow him to believe that we are investigating the actual occurrences of his childhood, we run the risk of later being charged with error and with our apparent gullibility. For a long time he is unable to reconcile himself to the idea of considering phantasy and reality on equal terms and he tends, with reference to the childish experiences to be explained, to neglect for the time being the difference between the real and the imaginary. And yet this is obviously the only correct attitude toward these psychological products because they are, in a sense, real. It is a fact that the patient is able to create such phantasies for himself, and this is of scarcely less importance for his neurosis than if he had really undergone the experience which he imagines. These phantasies possess *psychological* reality in contrast to *physical* reality, and so we gradually come to understand that *in the realm of neuroses the psychological reality is the determining factor*.

Among the experiences which recur continually in the early history of neurotics and, in fact, are never lacking, some are of particular significance and accordingly I consider them worthy of special treatment. I shall enumerate a few examples of this species: observation of the parental intercourse, seduction by an adult, and the threat of castration. It would be a grievous error to assume that physical reality can never be accorded them; this may often be proved beyond doubt by the testimony of adult relatives. So, for example, it is not at all unusual if the little boy who begins to play with his penis, and does not yet know that one must conceal this, is threatened by his parents or nurse with the cutting off of the organ or the guilty hand. Parents often admit upon questioning that they thought they had done the right thing by this intimidation; many individuals retain a correct, conscious memory of these threats, especially if it has occurred in later childhood. When the mother or some other woman makes the threat she usually delegates the responsibility of executing it to the father or to the doctor. In the famous *Struwelpeter* by the pediatrist Hoffman, of Frankfort, rhymes which owe their popularity to his very fine understanding of the sexual and other complexes of childhood, you find a milder substitute for castration in the cutting off of the thumbs as a punishment for insistent sucking. But it is highly improbable that the threat of castration is actually made as often as it occurs in the analyses of neurotics. We are content to understand that the child imaginatively constructs this threat for himself from suggestions, from the knowledge that auto-erotic satisfaction is forbidden, and from the impression of castration he has received in discovering the female genital. It is, moreover, in no way impossible that the little child, so long as he is not credited with any understanding or memory, will, even in families outside the proletariat, become a witness to the sexual act between his parents or some other group-ups, and it cannot be disproved that the child *subsequently* understands this impression, and may react upon it. But when this intercourse is described with minute details which could hardly have been observed, or if it turns out to be, as it so frequently does, an intercourse which was not face to face, *more ferarum*, there is no longer any doubt that this phantasy is derived from the observation of the intercourse of animals (dogs) and the unsatisfied curiosity of the child in his period of puberty. The greatest feat of the imagination is the phantasy of having witnessed the coitus of the parents while still unborn in the mother's womb. Of especial interest is the phantasy of having been seduced, because so often it is not a phantasy at all, but a real memory. But luckily it is not real so often as first appears from the results of analysis. Seduction by older children, or children of the same age, is much more frequent than seduction by adults, and if, in the case of little girls, the father quite regularly appears as the seducer in the occurrences which they relate, neither the fantastic nature of this accusation nor its motive can be doubted. The child as a rule covers the autoerotic period of his sexual activity, where there has been no actual seduction, with the seduction-phantasy. He spares himself the shame of onanism by imagining the presence of an object for his desires in that early period. As a matter of fact, you must not be misled in attributing sexual misuse of the child by its nearest male relatives solely and always to phantasy. Most analysts have probably treated cases in which such relations were real and could be proved beyond doubt, with the qualification that in such cases they belong to the later years of childhood and were transposed to an earlier time.

We cannot avoid the impression that such experiences of childhood are in some way necessary to the neurosis, that they are claimed by its iron rule. If they exist in reality, then well and good, but if reality has withheld them they are constructed from suggestions and supplemented by the imagination. The result is the same, and to this day we have been unable to trace any difference in the results, whether fancy or fact played the larger part in these childish occurrences. Here again we encounter one of the complementary relationships so frequently met with; it is, to be sure, the most estranging of all those we have become acquainted with. Whence comes the need for these phantasies, and the material for them? There can be no doubt as to the sources of the impulse, but we must explain why the same phantasies are always created with the same content. I have an answer in readiness which I know you will think very far-fetched. I am of the opinion that these *primal phantasies*—so I should like to term these, and certainly some others also—are a phylogenetic possession. In them the individual reaches out beyond his own life, into the experiences of antiquity, where his own experience has become all too rudimentary. It seems very possible to me that everything which is obtained during an analysis in the guise of phantasy, the seduction of children, the release of sexual excitement by watching parental intercourse, the threat of castration—or rather castration itself—were once realities in the primeval existence of mankind and that the imaginative child is merely filling in the gaps of individual truth with prehistoric truth. We have again and again suspected that the psychology of neuroses stores up more of the antiquities of human development than all other sources.

What we have just discussed makes it necessary for us to enter further into the origin and significance of that mental activity that is called imagination. As you well know, it enjoys universal esteem, although we have never clearly understood its place in the psychic life. I have this much to say about it. As you know, the ego of man is slowly educated by the influence of external necessity to an appreciation of reality and a pursuit of the principle of reality, and must therefore renounce temporarily or permanently various objects and goals of its strivings for satisfaction, sexual and otherwise. But renunciation of gratification has always been difficult for man. He cannot accomplish it without something in the nature of compensation. Accordingly he has reserved for himself a psychological activity wherein all these abandoned sources of pleasures and means of pleasurable gratification are granted a further existence, a form of existence in which they are freed from the requirements of reality and what we like to call the test of reality. Every impulse is soon transformed into the form of its own fulfillment. There is no doubt that dwelling on the imagined fulfillment of a given wish affords some satisfaction, although the realization that it is unreal is unobscured. In the activity of the imagination, man enjoys that freedom from external compulsion that he has long since renounced. He has made it possible to be alternately a pleasure-seeking animal and a reasoning human being. He finds that the scant satisfaction that he can force out of reality is not enough. "There is no getting along without auxiliary-constructions," Th. Fontaine once said. The creation of the psychic realm of fancy has its complete counterpart in the establishment of "preserves" and "conservation projects" in those places where the demands of husbandry, traffic and industry threaten quickly to change the original face of the earth into something unrecognizable. The national reserves maintain this old condition of things, which otherwise has everywhere been regretfully sacrificed to necessity. Everything may grow and spread there as it will, even that which is useless and harmful. The psychic realm of phantasy is such a reservation withdrawn from the principles of reality.

The best known productions of phantasy are the so-called "day dreams," which we already know, pictured satisfactions of ambitious, of covetous and erotic wishes, which flourish the more grandly the more reality admonishes them to modesty and patience. There is unmistakably shown in them the nature of imaginative happiness, the restoration of the independence of pleasurable gratification from the acquiescence of reality. We know such day dreams are nuclei and models for the dreams of night. The night dream is essentially nothing but a day dream, distorted by the nocturnal forms of psychological activity, and made available by the freedom which the night gives to instinctive impulses. We have already become acquainted with the idea that a day dream is not necessarily conscious, that there are also unconscious day dreams. Such unconscious day dreams are as much the source of night dreams as of neurotic symptoms.

The significance of phantasy for the development of symptoms will become clear to you by the following: We have said that in a case of renunciation, the libido occupies regressively the positions once abandoned by it, to which, nevertheless, it has clung in certain ways. We shall neither retract this statement nor correct it, but we shall insert a missing link. How does the libido find its way to these points of fixation? Well, every object and tendency of the libido that has been abandoned, is not abandoned in every sense of the word. They, or their derivatives, are still held in presentations of the phantasy, with a certain degree of intensity. The libido need only retire to the imagination in order to find from them the open road to all suppressed fixations. These phantasies were happy under a sort of tolerance, there was no conflict between them and the ego, no matter how acute the contrast, so long as a certain condition was observed—a condition *quantitative* in nature that is now disturbed by the flowing back of the libido to the phantasies. By this addition the accumulation of energy in the phantasies is heightened to such a degree that they become assertive and develop a pressure in the direction of realization. But that makes a conflict between them and the ego inevitable. Whether formerly conscious or unconscious, they now are subject to suppression by the ego and are victims to the attraction of the unconscious. The libido wanders from phantasies now unconscious to their sources in unconsciousness, and back to its own points of fixation.

The return of the libido to phantasy is an intermediate step on the road to symptom development and well deserves a special designation. C. G. Jung coined for it the very appropriate name of *introversion*, but inappropriately he also lets it stand for other things. Let us therefore retain the idea that introversion signifies the turning aside of the libido from the possibilities of actual satisfaction and the excessive accumulation of the phantasies hitherto tolerated as harmless. An introvert is not yet a neurotic, but he finds himself in a labile situation; he must develop symptoms at the next dislocation of forces, if he does not find other outlets for his pent-up libido. The intangible nature of neurotic satisfaction and the neglect of the difference between imagination and reality are already determined by arrest in the phase of introversion.

You have certainly noticed that in the last discussions I have introduced a new factor into the structure of the etiological chain, namely, the quantity, the amount of energy that comes under consideration. We must always take this factor into account. Purely qualitative analysis of the etiological conditions is not sufficient. Or, to put it in another way, a *dynamic* conception alone of these psychic processes is not enough; there is need of an *economic* viewpoint. We must say to ourselves that the conflict between two impulses is not released before certain occupation-intensities have been reached, even though the qualitative conditions have long been potent. Similarly, the pathogenic significance of the constitutional factors is guided by how much *more* of a given component impulse is present in the predisposition over and above that of another; one can even conceive the predispositions of all men to be qualitatively the same and to be differentiated only by these quantitative conditions. The quantitative factor is no less important for the power of resistance against neurotic ailments. It depends upon *what amount* of unused libido a person can hold freely suspended, and upon *how large a fraction* of the libido he is able to direct from the sexual path to the goal of sublimation. The final goal of psychological activity, which may be described qualitatively as striving towards pleasure-acquisition and avoidance of unpleasantness, presents itself in the light of economic considerations as the task of overcoming the gigantic stimuli at work in the psychological apparatus, and to prevent those obstructions which cause unpleasantness. So much I wanted to tell you about symptom development in the neuroses. Yes, but do not let me neglect to emphasize this especially: everything I have said here relates to the symptom development in hysteria. Even in compulsion neuroses, which retain the same fundamentals, much is found that is different. The counter-siege directed against the claims of the instincts, of which we have spoken in connection with hysteria, press to the fore in compulsion neuroses, and control the clinical picture by means of so-called "reaction-formations." The same kind and more far-reaching variations are discoverable among the other neuroses, where the investigations as to the mechanism of symptom development have in no way been completed.

Before I leave you today I should like to have your attention for a while for an aspect of imaginative life which is worthy of the most general interest. For there is a way back from imagination to reality and that is—art. The artist is an incipient introvert who is not far from being a neurotic. He is impelled by too powerful instinctive needs. He wants to achieve honor, power, riches, fame and the love of women. But he lacks the means of achieving these satisfactions. So like any other unsatisfied person, he turns away from reality, and transfers all his interests, his libido, too, to the elaboration of his imaginary wishes, all of which might easily point the way to neurosis. A great many factors must combine to present this termination of his development; it is well known how often artists especially suffer from a partial inhibition of their capacities through neurosis. Apparently their constitutions are strongly endowed with an ability to sublimize and to shift the suppression determining their conflicts. The artist finds the way back to reality in this way. He is not the only one who has a life of imagination. The twilight-realm of phantasy is upheld by the sanction of humanity and every hungry soul looks here for help and sympathy. But for those who are not artists, the ability to obtain satisfaction from imaginative sources is very restricted. Their relentless suppressions force them to be satisfied with the sparse day dreams which may become conscious. If one is a real artist he has more at his disposal. In the first place, he understands how to elaborate his day dreams so that they lose their essentially personal element, which would repel strangers, and yield satisfaction to others as well. He also knows how to disguise them so that they do not easily disclose their origin in their despised sources. He further possesses the puzzling ability of molding a specific material into a faithful image of the creatures of his imagination, and then he is able to attach to this representation of his unconscious phantasies so much pleasurable gratification that, for a time at least, it is able to outweigh and release the suppressions. If he is able to accomplish all this, he makes it possible for others, in their return, to obtain solace and consolation from their own unconscious sources of gratification which had become inaccessible. He wins gratitude and admiration for himself and so, by means of his imagination, achieves the very things which had at first only an imaginary existence for him: honor, power, and the love of women.

TWENTY-FOURTH LECTURE. GENERAL THEORY OF THE NEUROSES

Ordinary Nervousness

IN our last discussion we accomplish a difficult task. Now I shall temporarily leave our subject and address myself to you.

For I know quite well that you are dissatisfied. You thought that an introduction to psychoanalysis would be quite a different matter. You expected to hear vivid illustrations instead of theories. You will tell me that when I gave you the illustration of "on the ground floor in the first story," you had grasped something of the causation of neurosis, only of course this should have been a real observation and not an imaginary story. Or, when in the beginning I described two symptoms (not imaginary also, let us hope) whose analysis revealed a close connection with the life of the patient, you first came to grasp the meaning of the symptoms and you hoped that I would proceed in the same way. Instead I have given you theories—lengthy, difficult to see in perspective and incomplete, to which something new was constantly being added. I worked with conceptions that I had not previously presented to you, abandoned descriptive for dynamic conceptions, and these in turn for economic ones. I made it hard for you to understand how many of the artificial terms I made use of still carry the same meaning and are used interchangeably only for the sake of euphony. Finally, I allowed broad conceptions to pass in review before you: the principles of pleasure and of fact and their phylogenetically inherited possession; and then, instead of introducing you to definite facts, I allowed them to become increasingly vague till they seemed to fade into dim distances.

Why did I not begin my introduction to the theory of neurosis with the facts that you yourselves know about nervousness, with something that has always aroused your interest, with the peculiar temperament of nervous people, their incomprehensible reactions to external influences, to human intercourse, their irritability, their uselessness? Why did I not lead you step by step from the understanding of simple, everyday forms to the problems of mysterious and extreme manifestations of nervousness?

I cannot even say that you are wrong. I am not so infatuated with my art of representation as to see some special attraction in every blemish. I myself believe that I could have proceeded differently, to your better advantage, and this indeed had been my intention. But one cannot always carry out one's sensible intentions. The nature of the subject matter issues its own commands, and easily modifies our plans. Even so usual a performance as the organization of well-known material is not entirely subject to the particular purposes of the author. It forms itself as it will and later one wonders why it turned out so and not otherwise.

Probably one of the reasons is that the title, *A General Introduction to Psychoanalysis*, no longer applies to this part, which deals with the neuroses. The introduction to psychoanalysis is found in the study of errors and the dream; the theory of neurosis is psychoanalysis itself. I do not think that in so short a time I could have given you a knowledge of the theory of neurosis other than in concentrated form. It was necessary to present to you connectedly the meaning and interpretation of the symptoms, their external and internal conditions and their bearing on the mechanism of symptom formation. This I have attempted to do; it is practically the nucleus of the material that modern psychoanalysis is able to offer. We had to say quite a good deal concerning the libido and its development, and something as well concerning the development of the ego. The introduction had already prepared you for the presuppositions of our technique, for the large aspects of the unconscious and of suppression (resistance). In a subsequent lecture you will learn from what points psychoanalysis proceeds organically. For the present I have not sought to hide from you the fact that all our results are based on the study of a single group of nervous affections, the so-called transference neuroses. Though you have gained no positive knowledge and have not retained every detail, still I hope that you have a fair picture of the methods, the problems and the results of psychoanalysis.

I have assumed that it was your wish for me to begin my presentation of neuroses with a description of nervous behavior, the nature of neurotic suffering, and the way in which the nervous meet the conditions of their illness and adapt themselves to these. Such subject matter is certainly interesting and well worth knowing. It is moreover not very hard to handle, yet it is not wise to begin with its consideration. There is danger of not discovering the unconscious, of overlooking the great significance of the libido, of judging all conditions as they appear to the ego of the nervous person. It is obvious that this ego is neither a reliable nor an impartial authority. For this very ego is the force that denies and suppresses the unconscious; when the unconscious is concerned, how then could we expect justice to be done? The rejected claims of sexuality stand first in the line of these suppressions; it is natural that from the standpoint of the ego we can never learn their extent and significance. As soon as we attain to the point of view of suppression, we are sufficiently warned not to make one of the contending factions, above all not to make the victor judge of the struggle. We are prepared to find that the testimony of the ego may lead us astray. If one is to believe the evidence of the ego, it would appear to have been active all along, all its symptoms would have been actively willed and formed. Yet we know that it has passively allowed a great deal to occur, a fact which it subsequently seeks to conceal and to palliate. To be sure, it does not always attempt this; in the case of the symptoms of compulsion neurosis it must admit that it is being opposed by something alien, which it can resist only with difficulty.

Whoever does not heed these warnings not to mistake the prevarications of the ego for truth, has clear sailing; he avoids all the resistances which oppose the psychoanalytic emphasis upon the unconscious, on sexuality, and on the passiveness of the ego. He will assert with Alfred Adler that the "nervous character" is the cause instead of the result of the neurosis, but he will not be able to explain a single detail of symptom formation or to interpret a single dream.

You will ask: Is it not possible to do justice to the part the ego plays in nervousness and in symptom formation without crudely neglecting the factors revealed by psychoanalysis? I answer you: Surely it must be possible and at some time or other it will take place; but the methods by which we organize the work of psychoanalysis do not favor our beginning with just this task. We can foresee the time when this task will claim the attention of psychoanalysis. There are forms of neuroses, the so-called narcistic neuroses, in which the ego is far more deeply involved than in anything we have studied heretofore. The analytic investigation of these conditions will enable us to judge reliably and impartially the part that the ego plays in neurotic illness.

One of the relations which the ego bears to its neurosis is so obvious that it must be considered at the very outset. In no case does it seem to be absent, and it is most clearly recognizable in the traumatic neuroses, conditions which we do not as yet clearly understand. You must know that in the causation and mechanisms of all possible forms of neurosis, the same factors are active again and again; it is only the emphasis that is shifted from one to the other of these factors in symptom formation. The members of a company of actors each have certain parts to play—hero, villain, confidant, etc.—yet each will select a different drama for his benefit. Thus the phantasies which undergo conversion into symptoms are especially easy to detect in hysteria; compulsion neuroses are essentially dominated by the reactionary formations, or counter-seizures of the ego; what we designate as *secondary elaboration* in dreams dominates paranoia in the form of delusions, etc.

In traumatic neuroses, particularly if they are caused by the horrors of war, we are especially impressed by a selfish ego-impulse which seeks protection and personal advantage. This in itself is not a sufficient cause for illness, but it can favor its beginning and also feed its needs once it has been established. This motive serves to protect the ego from the dangers whose imminence precipitated the disease, and does not permit convalescence until the recurrence of these dangers seems impossible, or until compensation has been obtained for the danger that has been undergone.

But the ego betrays similar interest in the origin and maintenance of all other neuroses. We have already said that the ego suffers the symptom to exist, because one of its phases gratifies the egoistic tendency toward suppression. Besides, the ending of the conflict by means of symptom development is the path of least resistance, and a most convenient solution for the principle of pleasure. Through symptom formation the ego is undoubtedly spared a severe and unpleasant inner task. There are cases where even the physician must admit that the resolution of the conflict into neurosis is the most harmless outcome and one most easily tolerated by society. Do not be surprised, then, to learn that occasionally even the physician takes the part of the illness he is battling against. He does not have to restrict himself to the role of the fanatic warrior for health in all situations of life. He knows that the world contains not only neurotic misery, but also real, incurable suffering. He knows that necessity may even require a human being to sacrifice his health, and he learns that by this sacrifice on the part of one individual untold wretchedness may be spared for many others. So if we say that the neurotic escapes the conflict *by taking refuge in illness*, we must admit that in some cases this escape is justifiable, and the physician who has diagnosed the state of affairs will retire silently and tactfully.

But let us not consider these special cases in our further discussion. In average cases the ego, by having recourse to neurosis, obtains a certain inner *advantage from the disease*. Under certain conditions of life, there may also be derived a tangible external advantage, more or less valuable in reality. Let me direct your attention to the most frequent occurrences of this sort. Women who are brutally treated and mercilessly exploited by their husbands almost always adopt the evasion of the neurosis, provided that their predisposition permits this. This usually follows when the woman is too cowardly or too virtuous to seek secret solace in the arms of another, or when she dare not separate from her husband in the face of all opposition, when she has no prospect of maintaining herself or of finding a better husband and especially when her sexual emotions still bind her to this brutal man. Her illness becomes a weapon in her struggle with him, one that she can use for self-protection and misuse for purposes of vengeance. She probably dare not complain of her marriage, but she can complain of her illness. The doctor becomes her assistant. She forces her inconsiderate husband to spare her, to attend to her wishes, to permit her absence from the house and thus free her from the oppressions of her married life. Wherever such external or accidental gain through illness is considerable and can find no substitute in fact, you can prophesy that the possibility of influencing neurosis through therapy is very slight.

You will tell me that what I have said about the advantage gained from the disease speaks entirely for the hypothesis I have rejected, namely, that the ego itself wills and creates the neurosis. Just a moment! It probably does not mean more than that the ego passively suffers the neurosis to exist, which it is unable to prevent anyway. It makes the most of the neurosis, if anything can be made of it at all. This is only one side of the question, the advantageous side. The ego is willing to endure the advantages of the neurosis, but there are not only advantages. As a rule it soon appears that the ego has made a poor deal in accepting the neurosis. It has paid too high a price for the mitigation of the conflict; and the sensations of suffering which the symptoms bring with them are perhaps every bit as bad as the agonies of conflict, usually they cause even greater discomfort. The ego wants to rid itself of the pain of the symptoms without relinquishing the gain of illness, and that is impossible. Thus the ego is discovered as by no means so active as it had thought itself to be, and this we want to keep in mind.

If you were to come into contact with neurotics as a physician, you would soon cease to expect that those who complain most woefully of their illness are the ones who will oppose its therapy with the least resistance or who will welcome any help. On the contrary, you would readily understand that everything contributing to the advantage derived from the disease will strengthen the resistance to the suppression and heighten the difficulty of the therapy. We must also add another and later advantage to the gain of illness which is born with the symptom. If a psychic organization, such as this illness, has persisted for a long time, it finally behaves as an independent unit, it expresses something like self-preservation, attains a kind of *modus vivendi* between itself and other parts of psychic life, even those that are fundamentally hostile to it. And occasions will probably arise where it can prove again to be both useful and valuable, by which it will attain a *secondary function*, which gives strength to its existence. Instead of an illustration from pathology take a striking example from everyday life. An efficient workman who earns his living is crippled for his occupation by some disaster; his work is over for him. After a while, however, he receives a small accident insurance, and learns to exploit his injury by begging. His new existence, though most undesirable, is based upon the very thing that robbed him of his former maintenance. If you could cure his defect, he would be without a means of subsistence, he would have no livelihood. The question would arise: Is he capable of resuming his former work? That which corresponds to such secondary exploitation of illness in neurosis we may add to the primary benefit derived therefrom and may term it a *secondary* advantage of disease.

In general I should like to warn you not to underestimate the practical significance of the advantage from illness and yet not to be too much impressed by it theoretically. Aside from the previously recognized exceptions, I am always reminded of Oberländer's pictures on "the intelligence of animals" which appeared in the *Fliegende Blätter*. An Arab is riding a camel on a narrow path cut through a steep mountain side. At a turn of the trail he is suddenly confronted by a lion who makes ready to spring. He sees no way out, on one side the precipice, on the other the abyss; retreat and flight—both are impossible; he gives himself up as lost. Not so the camel. He leaps into the abyss with his rider—and the lion is left in the lurch. The help of neurosis is as a rule no kinder to the rider. It may be due to the fact that the settlement of the conflict through symptom development is nevertheless an automatic process, not able to meet the demands of life, and for whose sake man renounces the use of his best and loftiest powers. If it were possible to choose, it were indeed best to perish in an honorable struggle with destiny.

I still owe you further explanation as to why, in my presentation of the theory of neurosis, I did not proceed from ordinary nervousness as a starting point. You may assume that, had I done this, the proof of the sexual origin of neurosis would have been more difficult for me, and so I refrained. There you are mistaken. In transference neurosis we must work at interpretations of the symptoms to arrive at this conclusion. In the ordinary forms of the so-called true neuroses, however, the etiological significance of sexual life is a crude fact open to observation. I discovered it twenty years ago when I asked myself one day why we regularly barred out questions concerning sexual activity in examining nervous patients. At that time I sacrificed my popularity among my patients to my investigations, yet after a brief effort I could state that no neurosis, no true neurosis at least, is present with a normal sexual life. Of course, this statement passes too lightly over the individual differences, it is unclear through the vagueness with which it uses the term "normal," but even to-day it retains its value for purposes of rough orientation. At that time I reached the point of drawing comparisons between certain forms of nervousness and sexual abnormalities, and I do not doubt that I could repeat the same observations now, if similar material were at my disposal. I frequently noticed that a man who contented himself with incomplete sexual gratification, with manual ononism, for instance, would suffer from a true neurosis, and that this neurosis would promptly give way to another form, if another sexual regime no less harmful were substituted. From the change in the condition of the patient I was able to guess the change in the mode of his sexual life. At that time I learned to hold obstinately to my conjectures until I had overcome the patient's prevarications and had forced him to confirm my suppositions. To be sure, then he preferred to consult other physicians who did not inquire so insistently into his sexual life.

At that time it did not escape my notice that the origin of the disease could not always be traced back to sexual life; sexual abnormality would cause the illness in one person, while another would fall ill because he had lost his fortune or had suffered an exhausting organic disease. We gained insight into this variation by means of the interrelations between the ego and the libido, and the more profound our insight became, the more satisfactory were the results. A person begins to suffer from neurosis when his ego has lost the capacity of accommodating the libido. The stronger the ego, the easier the solution of the problem; a weakening of the ego from any cause whatsoever has the same effect as a superlative increase of the claims of the libido. There are other and more intimate relations between the ego and the libido which I shall not discuss, as we are not concerned with them here. To us it is of enlightening significance that in every case, regardless of the way in which the illness was caused, the symptoms of neurosis were opposed by the libido and thus gave evidence for its abnormal use.

Now, however, I want to draw your attention to the difference between the symptoms of the true neuroses and the psychoneuroses, the first group of which, the transference neurosis, has occupied us considerably. In both cases the symptoms proceed from the libido. They are accordingly abnormal uses of it, substitutes for gratification. But the symptoms of the true neurosis—such as pressure in the head, sensations of pain, irritability of an organ, weakening or inhibition of a function—these have no meaning, no psychic significance. They are manifested not only in the body, as for instance hysteric symptoms, but are in themselves physical processes whose creation is devoid of all the complicated psychic mechanism with which we have become acquainted. They really embody the character that has so long been attributed to the psychoneurotic symptom. But how can they then correspond to uses of the libido, which we have come to know as a psychological force? That is quite simple. Let me recall one of the very first objections that was made to psychoanalysis. It was stated that psychoanalysis was concerned with a purely psychological theory of neurotic manifestations; that this was a hopeless outlook since psychological theories could never explain illness. The objectors chose to forget that the sexual function is neither purely psychic nor merely somatic. It influences physical as well as psychic life. In the symptoms of the psychoneuroses we have recognized the expression of a disturbance in psychic processes. And so we shall not be surprised to discover that the true neuroses are the direct somatic consequences of sexual disturbances.

The medical clinic gives us a valuable suggestion (observed by many research workers) for the comprehension of the true neuroses. In all the details of their symptomatology, and as well in their characteristic power to influence all organic systems and all functions, the true neuroses reveal a marked similarity to the conditions of those diseases which originate through the chronic influence of foreign poisons and as well through their acute diminution; with conditions prevalent in intoxication and abstinence. The two groups of conditions are brought still closer together by the relation of intermediate conditions, which, following M. Basedowi, we have learned to attribute to the influence of toxic substances, but of toxins, however, which are not introduced into the body from without, but arise in its own metabolism. These analogies, I think, lead us directly to the consideration of these neuroses as disturbances in sexual metabolism. It may be that more sexual toxins are produced than the individual can dispose of, or that inner, even psychic conditions, stand in the way of the proper elaboration of these substances. The language of the people has always favored such assumptions as to the nature of sexual desires. It calls love an "intoxication"; it will have love-madness aroused through potions, and thus sees the motive force removed, as it were, to the outer world. For the rest, the phrase "sexual metabolism" or "chemism of sexuality" is a chapter-head without content. We know nothing about it and cannot even decide whether we are to assume two sexual substances, the male and the female, or, if there is only *one* sexual toxin, which to consider the carrier of all the stimulating power of the libido. The structure of psychoanalysis that we have erected is really only a superstructure which at some future time must be placed upon its organic foundation; but what this is we do not know as yet.

Psychoanalysis is characterized as a science, not by reason of the subject matter it handles but by the technique it employs. This can be employed in dealing with the history of civilization, the science of religion or mythology, as well as with the theory of neurosis, without altering its character. The revealing of the unconscious in psychic life is all it aims to accomplish. The problems of the true neuroses, whose symptoms probably originate in direct toxic damage, yield no point of attack to psychoanalysis. Psychoanalysis can do little for their elucidation, and must leave the task to biological-medical research. Perhaps you understand now why I did not choose to organize my material differently. If I had given to you an *Introduction to the Theory of the Neuroses* as you wished, it would unquestionably have been correct to proceed from the simple forms of the true neuroses to those complex illnesses caused by a disturbance of the libido. In discussing the true neuroses I would have had to bring together the facts we have gleaned from various quarters and present what we think we know of them. Only later, under the psychoneuroses, would psychoanalysis have been discussed as the most important technical aid for insight into these conditions. I had, however, intended and announced *A General Introduction to Psychoanalysis*, and it seemed to me more important to give you an idea of psychoanalysis than to present certain positive facts about neuroses; and so I could not place the true neuroses into the foreground, for they prove sterile for the purposes of psychoanalysis. I believe that I have made the wiser choice for you, since psychoanalysis deserves the interest of every educated person because of its profound hypotheses and far-reaching connections. The theory of neurosis, on the other hand, is a chapter of medicine like any other.

You are, however, justified in expecting some interest on our part in the true neuroses. Because of their intimate connection with psychoneuroses we find this decidedly necessary. I shall tell you then that we distinguish three pure forms of true neuroses: *neurasthenia, anxiety neurosis* and *hypochondria*. Even this classification has not remained uncontradicted. The terms are all widely used, but their connotation is vague and uncertain. Besides, there are in this world of confusion physicians who object to any distinctions between manifestations, any emphasis of clinical detail, who do not even recognize the separation of true neuroses and psychoneuroses. I think they have gone too far and have not chosen the road which leads to progress. The types of neuroses we have mentioned occur occasionally in pure form; more often they are blended with one another or with a psychoneurotic condition. This need not discourage us to the extent of abandoning the task of distinction. Think of the difference between the study of minerals and that of ores in mineralogy. Minerals are described as individuals; frequently of course they occur as crystals, separated sharply from their surroundings. Ores consist of an aggregate of minerals which have coalesced not accidentally, but as a result of the conditions of their origin. We understand too little of the process of development of neuroses, to create anything similar to the study of ores. But we are surely working in the right direction when we isolate the known clinical factors, comparable to the separate minerals, from the great mass.

A noteworthy connection between the symptoms of the true neuroses and the psychoneuroses adds a valuable contribution to our knowledge of symptom formation in the latter. The symptom in the true neuroses is frequently the nucleus and incipient stage of development of the psychoneurotic symptom. Such a connection is most easily observed between neurasthenia and the transference neuroses, which are termed conversion hysteria, between anxiety neurosis and anxiety hysteria, but also between hypochondria and paraphrenia (dementia praecox and paranoia), forms of neuroses of which we shall speak subsequently. Let us take as an illustration the hysteric headache or backache. Analysis shows that through elaboration and displacement this pain has become the gratification substitute for a whole series of libidinous phantasies or reminiscences. But once upon a time this pain was real, a direct sexual toxic symptom, the physical expression of libidinous excitation. We do not wish to assert, by any means, that all hysteric symptoms can be traced to such a nucleus, but it is true that this is frequently the case, and that all influences upon the body through libidinous excitation, whether normal or pathological, are especially significant for the symptom development in hysteria. They play the part of the grain of sand which the mollusc has enveloped in mother-of-pearl. In the same way passing signs of sexual excitation, which accompany the sexual act, are used by psychoneurosis as the most convenient and appropriate material for symptom formation.

A similar procedure is of diagnostic and therapeutic interest especially. People disposed to be neurotic, without suffering from a flourishing neurosis, frequently set in motion the work of symptom development as the result of an abnormal physical change—often an inflammation or an injury. This development rapidly makes the symptom given by reality the representative of the unconscious phantasies that had been lurking for an opportunity to seize means of expression. In such a case the physician will try different ways of therapy. Either he will try to do away with the organic basis without bothering about its noisy neurotic elaboration, or he will struggle with the neurosis brought out by the occasion, and ignore its organic cause. The result will justify now one, now the other method of procedure; no general laws can be laid down for such mixed cases.

TWENTY-FIFTH LECTURE. GENERAL THEORY OF THE NEUROSES

Fear and Anxiety

PROBABLY you will term what I told you about ordinary nervousness in my last lecture most fragmentary and unsatisfactory information. I know this, and I think you were probably most surprised that I did not mention fear, which most nervous people complain of and describe as their greatest source of suffering. It can attain a terrible intensity which may result in the wildest enterprises. But I do not wish to fall short of your expectations in this matter. I intend, on the contrary, to treat the problem of the fear of nervous people with great accuracy and to discuss it with you at some length.

Fear itself needs no introduction; everyone has at some time or other known this sensation or, more precisely, this effect. It seems to me that we never seriously inquired why the nervous suffered so much more and so much more intensely under this condition. Perhaps it was thought a matter of course; it is usual to confuse the words "nervous" and "anxious" as though they meant the same thing. That is unjustifiable; there are anxious people who are not nervous, and nervous people who suffer from many symptoms, but not from the tendency to anxiety.

However that may be, it is certain that the problem of fear is the meeting point of many important questions, an enigma whose complete solution would cast a flood of light upon psychic life. I do not claim that I can furnish you with this complete solution, but you will certainly expect psychoanalysis to deal with this theme in a manner different from that of the schools of medicine. These schools seem to be interested primarily in the anatomical cause of the condition of fear. They say the medulla oblongata is irritated, and the patient learns that he is suffering from neurosis of the nervus vague. The medulla oblongata is a very serious and beautiful object. I remember exactly how much time and trouble I devoted to the study of it, years ago. But today I must say that I know of nothing more indifferent to me for the psychological comprehension of fear, than knowledge of the nerve passage through which these sensations must pass.

One can talk about fear for a long time without even touching upon nervousness. You will understand me without more ado, when I term this fear *real* fear in contrast to *neurotic* fear. Real fear seems quite rational and comprehensible to us. We may testify that it is a reaction to the perception of external danger, viz., harm that is expected and foreseen. It is related to the flight reflex and may be regarded as an expression of the instinct of self-preservation. And so the occasions, viz., the objects and situations which arouse fear, will depend largely on our knowledge of and our feeling of power over the outer world. We deem it quite a matter of course that the savage fears a cannon or an eclipse of the sun, while the white man, who can handle the instrument and prophesy the phenomenon, does not fear these things. At other times superior knowledge promulgates fear, because it recognizes the danger earlier. The savage, for instance, will recoil before a footprint in the woods, meaningless to the uninstructed, which reveals to him the proximity of an animal of prey; the experienced sailor will notice a little cloud, which tells him of a coming hurricane, with terror, while to the passenger it seems insignificant.

After further consideration, we must say to ourselves that the verdict on real fear, whether it be rational or purposeful, must be thoroughly revised. For the only purposeful behavior in the face of imminent danger would be the cool appraisal of one's own strength in comparison with the extent of the threatening danger, and then decide which would presage a happier ending: flight, defense, or possibly even attack. Under such a proceeding fear has absolutely no place; everything that happens would be consummated just as well and better without the development of fear. You know that if fear is too strong, it proves absolutely useless and paralyzes every action, even flight. Generally the reaction against danger consists in a mixture of fear and resistance. The frightened animal is afraid and flees. But the purposeful factor in such a case is not fear but flight.

We are therefore tempted to claim that the development of fear is never purposeful. Perhaps closer examination will give us greater insight into the fear situation. The first factor is the expectancy of danger which expresses itself in heightened sensory attention and in motor tension. This expectancy is undoubtedly advantageous; its absence may be responsible for serious consequences. On the one hand, it gives rise to motor activity, primarily to flight, and on a higher plane to active defense; on the other hand, it gives rise to something which we consider the condition of fear. In so far as the development is still incipient, and is restricted to a mere signal, the more undisturbed the conversion of the readiness to be afraid into action the more purposeful the entire proceeding. The readiness to be afraid seems to be the purposeful aspect; evolution of fear itself, the element that defeats its own object.

I avoid entering upon a discussion as to whether our language means the same or distinct things by the words anxiety, fear or fright. I think that anxiety is used in connection with a condition regardless of any objective, while fear is essentially directed toward an object. Fright, on the other hand, seems really to possess a special meaning, which emphasizes the effects of a danger which is precipitated without any expectance or readiness of fear. Thus we might say that anxiety protects man from fright.

You have probably noticed the ambiguity and vagueness in the use of the word "anxiety." Generally one means a subjective condition, caused by the perception that an "evolution of fear" has been consummated. Such a condition may be called an emotion. What is an emotion in the dynamic sense? Certainly something very complex. An emotion, in the first place, includes indefinite motor innervations or discharges; secondly, definite sensations which moreover are of two kinds, the perception of motor activities that have already taken place, and the direct sensations of pleasure and pain, which give the effect of what we call its feeling tone. But I do not think that the true nature of the emotion has been fathomed by these enumerations. We have gained deeper insight into some emotions and realize that the thread which binds together such a complex as we have described is the repetition of a certain significant experience. This experience might be an early impression of a very general sort, which belongs to the antecedent history of the species rather than to that of the individual. To be more clear: the emotional condition has a structure similar to that of an hysterical attack; it is the upshot of a reminiscence. The hysteric attack, then, is comparable to a newly formed individual emotion, the normal emotion to an hysteria which has become a universal heritage.

Do not assume that what I have said here about emotions is derived from normal psychology. On the contrary, these are conceptions that have grown up with and are at home only in psychoanalysis. What psychology has to say about emotions—the James-Lange theory, for instance—is absolutely incomprehensible for us psychoanalysts, and cannot be discussed. Of course, we do not consider our knowledge about emotions very certain; it is a preliminary attempt to become oriented in this obscure region. To continue: We believe we know the early impression which the emotion of fear repeats. We think it is birth itself which combines that complex of painful feelings, of a discharge of impulses, of physical sensations, which has become the prototype for the effect of danger to life, and is ever after repeated within us as a condition of fear. The tremendous heightening of irritability through the interruption of the circulation (internal respiration) was at the time the cause of the experience of fear; the first fear was therefore toxic. The name anxiety—angustial—narrowness, emphasizes the characteristic tightening of the breath, which was at the time a consequence of an actual situation and is henceforth repeated almost regularly in the emotion. We shall also recognize how significant it is that this first condition of fear appeared during the separation from the mother. Of course, we are convinced that the tendency to repetition of the first condition of fear has been so deeply ingrained in the organism through countless generations, that not a single individual can escape the emotion of fear; not even the mythical Macduff who was "cut out of his mother's womb," and therefore did not experience birth itself. We do not know the prototype of the condition of fear in the case of other mammals, and so we do not know the complex of emotions that in them is the equivalent of our fear.

Perhaps it will interest you to hear how the idea that birth is the source and prototype of the emotion of fear, happened to occur to me. Speculation plays the smallest part in it; I borrowed it from the native train of thought of the people. Many years ago we were sitting around the dinner table—a number of young physicians—when an assistant in the obstetrical clinic told a jolly story of what had happened in the last examination for midwives. A candidate was asked what it implied if during delivery the feces of the newborn was present in the discharge of waters, and she answered promptly "the child is afraid." She was laughed at and "flunked." But I silently took her part and began to suspect that the poor woman of the people had, with sound perception, revealed an important connection.

Proceeding now to neurotic fear, what are its manifestations and conditions? There is much to be described. In the first place we find a general condition of anxiety, a condition of free-floating fear as it were, which is ready to attach itself to any appropriate idea, to influence judgment, to give rise to expectations, in fact to seize any opportunity to make itself felt. We call this condition "expectant fear" or "anxious expectation." Persons who suffer from this sort of fear always prophesy the most terrible of all possibilities, interpret every coincidence as an evil omen, and ascribe a dreadful meaning to all uncertainty. Many persons who cannot be termed ill show this tendency to anticipate disaster. We blame them for being over-anxious or pessimistic. A striking amount of expectant fear is characteristic of a nervous condition which I have named "anxiety neurosis," and which I group with the true neuroses.

A second form of fear in contrast to the one we have just described is psychologically more circumscribed and bound up with certain objects or situations. It is the fear of the manifold and frequently very peculiar phobias. Stanley Hall, the distinguished American psychologist, has recently taken the trouble to present a whole series of these phobias in gorgeous Greek terminology. They sound like the enumeration of the ten Egyptian plagues, except that their number exceeds ten, by far. Just listen to all the things which may become the objects of contents of a phobia: Darkness, open air, open squares, cats, spiders, caterpillars, snakes, mice, thunder-storms, sharp points, blood, enclosed spaces, crowds, solitude, passing over a bridge, travel on land and sea, etc. A first attempt at orientation in this chaos leads readily to a division into three groups. Some of the fearful objects and situations have something gruesome for normal people too, a relation to danger, and so, though they are exaggerated in intensity, they do not seem incomprehensible to us. Most of us, for instance, experience a feeling of repulsion in the presence of a snake. One may say that snakephobia is common to all human beings, and Charles Darwin has described most impressively how he was unable to control his fear of a snake pointing for him, though he knew he was separated from it by a thick pane of glass. The second group consists of cases which still bear a relation to danger, but this is of a kind which we are disposed to belittle rather than to overestimate. Most of the situation-phobia belong here. We know that by taking a railroad journey we entail greater chance of disaster than by staying at home. A collision, for instance, may occur, or a ship sink, when as a rule we must drown; yet we do not think of these dangers, and free from fear we travel on train and boat. We cannot deny that if a bridge should collapse at the moment we are crossing it, we would fall into the river, but that is such a rare occurrence that we do not take the danger into account. Solitude too has its dangers and we avoid it under certain conditions; but it is by no means a matter of being unable to suffer it for a single moment. The same is true for the crowd, the enclosed space, the thunder-storm, etc. It is not at all the content but the intensity of these neurotic phobias that appears strange to us. The fear of the phobia cannot even be described. Sometimes we almost receive the impression that the neurotic is not really afraid of the same things and situations that can arouse fear in us, and which he calls by the same name.

There remains a third group of phobias which is entirely unintelligible to us. When a strong, adult man is afraid to cross a street or a square of his own home town, when a healthy, well-developed woman becomes almost senseless with fear because a cat has brushed the hem of her dress or a mouse has scurried through the room—how are we to establish the relation to danger that obviously exists under the phobia? In these animal phobias it cannot possibly be a question of the heightening of common human antipathies. For, as an illustration of the antithesis, there are numerous persons who cannot pass a cat without calling and petting it. The mouse of which women are so much afraid, is at the same time a first class pet name. Many a girl who has been gratified to have her lover call her so, screams when she sees the cunning little creature itself. The behavior of the man who is afraid to cross the street or the square can only be explained by saying that he acts like a little child. A child is really taught to avoid a situation of this sort as dangerous, and our agoraphobist is actually relieved of his fear if some one goes with him across the square or street.

The two forms of fear that have been described, free-floating fear and the fear which is bound up with phobias, are independent of one another. The one is by no means a higher development of the other; only in exceptional cases, almost by accident, do they occur simultaneously. The strongest condition of general anxiety need not manifest itself in phobias; and persons whose entire life is hemmed in by agoraphobia can be entirely free of pessimistic expectant fear. Some phobias, such as the fear of squares or of trains, are acquired only in later life, while others, the fear of darkness, storms and animals, exist from the very beginning. The former signify serious illness, the latter appear rather as peculiarities, moods. Yet whoever is burdened with fear of this second kind may be expected to harbor other and similar phobias. I must add that we group all these phobias under *anxiety hysteria*, and therefore regard it as a condition closely related to the well-known conversion hysteria.

The third form of neurotic fear confronts us with an enigma; we loose sight entirely of the connection between fear and threatening danger. This anxiety occurs in hysteria, for instance, as the accompaniment of hysteric symptoms, or under certain conditions of excitement, where we would expect an emotional manifestation, but least of all of fear, or without reference to any known circumstance, unintelligible to us and to the patient. Neither far nor near can we discover a danger or a cause which might have been exaggerated to such significance. Through these spontaneous attacks we learn that the complex which we call the condition of anxiety can be resolved into its components. The whole attack may be represented by a single intensively developed symptom, such as a trembling, dizziness, palpitation of the heart, or tightening of breath; the general undertone by which we usually recognize fear may be utterly lacking or vague. And yet these conditions, which we describe as "anxiety equivalents," are comparable to anxiety in all its clinical and etiological relations.

Two questions arise. Can we relate neurotic fear, in which danger plays so small a part or none at all, to real fear, which is always a reaction to danger? And what can we understand as the basis of neurotic fear? For the present we want to hold to our expectations: "Wherever there is fear, there must be a cause for it."

Clinical observation yields several suggestions for the comprehension of neurotic fear, the significance of which I shall discuss with you.

1. It is not difficult to determine that expectant fear or general anxiety is closely connected with certain processes in sexual life, let us say with certain types of libido. Utilization, the simplest and most instructive case of this kind, results when persons expose themselves to frustrated excitation, viz., if their sexual excitation does not meet with sufficient relief and is not brought to a satisfactory conclusion, in men, during the time of their engagement to

marry, for instance, or in women whose husbands are not sufficiently potent or who, from caution, execute the sexual act in a shortened or mutilated form. Under these circumstances libidinous excitement disappears and anxiety takes its place, both in the form of expectant fear and in attacks and anxiety equivalents. The cautious interruption of the sexual act, when practiced as the customary sexual regime, so frequently causes the anxiety neurosis in men, and especially in women, that physicians are wise in such cases to examine primarily this etiology. On innumerable occasions we have learned that anxiety neurosis vanishes when the sexual misuse is abandoned.

So far as I know, the connection between sexual restraint and conditions of anxiety is no longer questioned even by physicians who have nothing to do with psychoanalysis. But I can well imagine that they do not desist from reversing the connection and saying that these persons have exhibited a tendency to anxiety from the outset and therefore practice reserve in sexual matters. The behavior of women whose sexual conduct is passive, viz., is determined by the treatment of the husband, contradicts this supposition. The more temperamental, that is, the more disposed toward sexual intercourse and capable of gratification is the woman, the more will she react to the impotence of the man, or to the *coitus interruptus*, by anxiety manifestations. In anaesthetic or only slightly libidinous women, such misuse will not carry such consequences.

Sexual abstinence, recommended so warmly by the physicians of to-day, has the same significance in the development of conditions of anxiety only when the libido, to which satisfactory relief is denied, is sufficiently strong and not for the most part accounted for by sublimation. The decision whether illness is to result always depends upon the quantitative factors. Even where character formation and not disease is concerned, we easily recognize that sexual constraint goes hand in hand with a certain anxiety, a certain caution, while fearlessness and bold daring arise from free gratification of sexual desires. However much these relations are altered by various influences of civilization, for the average human being it is true that anxiety and sexual constraint belong together.

I have by no means mentioned all the observations that speak for the genetic relation of the libido to fear. The influence on the development of neurotic fear of certain phases of life, such as puberty and the period of menopause, when the production of libido is materially heightened, belongs here too. In some conditions of excitement we may observe the mixture of anxiety and libido and the final substitution of anxiety for libido. These facts give us a twofold impression, first that we are concerned with an accumulation of libido, which is diverted from its normal channel, second that we are working with somatic processes. Just how anxiety originates from the libido we do not know; we can only ascertain that the libido is in abeyance, and that we observe anxiety in its place.

2. We glean a second hint from the analysis of the psychoneuroses, especially of hysteria. We have heard that in addition to the symptoms, fear frequently accompanies this condition; this, however, is free floating fear, which is manifested either as an attack or becomes a permanent condition. The patients cannot tell what they are afraid of and connect their fear, through an unmistakable secondary elaboration, with phobias nearest at hand; death, insanity, paralysis. When we analyze the situation which gave rise to the anxiety or to symptoms accompanied by it, we can generally tell which normal psychologic process has been omitted and has been replaced by the phenomenon of fear. Let me express it differently: we reconstruct the unconscious process as though it had not experienced suppression and had continued its way into consciousness uninterruptedly. Under these conditions as well this process would have been accompanied by an emotion, and we now learn with surprise that when suppression has occurred the emotion accompanying the normal process has been replaced by fear, regardless of its original quality. In hysteric conditions of fear, its unconscious correlative may be either an impulse of similar character, such as fear, shame, embarrassment or positive libidinous excitation, or hostile and aggressive emotion such as fury or rage. Fear then is the common currency for which all emotional impulses can be exchanged, provided that the idea with which it has been associated has been subject to suppression.

3. Patients suffering from compulsive acts are remarkably devoid of fear. They yield us the data for our third point. If we try to hinder them in the performance of their compulsive acts, of their washing or their ceremonials, or if they themselves dare to give up one of their compulsions, they are seized with terrible fear that again exacts obedience to the compulsion. We understand that the compulsive act had veiled fear and had been performed only to avoid it. In compulsion neurosis then, fear, which would otherwise be present, is replaced by symptom development. Similar results are yielded by hysteria. Following the process of suppression we find the development, either of anxiety alone or of anxiety and symptom development, or finally a more complete symptom development and no anxiety. In an abstract sense, then, it would be correct to say that symptoms are formed only to evade development of fear, which otherwise could not be escaped. According to this conception, fear is seen to occupy the center of the stage in the problems of neurosis.

Our observations on anxiety neuroses led to the conclusion that when the libido was diverted from its normal use and anxiety thus released, it occurred on the basis of somatic processes. The analyses of hysteria and compulsion neuroses furnish the correlative observations that similar diversion with similar results may also be the consequence of a constraint of psychic forces. Such then is our knowledge of the origin of neurotic fear; it still sounds rather vague. But as yet I know no path that would lead us further. The second task we have set ourselves is still more difficult to accomplish. It is the establishment of a connection between neurotic fear, which is misused libido, and real fear, which is a reaction to danger. You may believe that these things are quite distinct and yet we have no criterion for distinguishing the sensations of real and neurotic fear.

The desired connection is brought about by presupposing the antithesis of the ego to libido that is so frequently claimed. We know that the development of fear is the ego's reaction to danger, the signal for preparation for flight, and from this we are led to believe that in neurotic fear the ego attempts to escape the claims of its libido, and treats this inner danger as though it came from without. Accordingly our expectation that where there is fear there must be something to be afraid of, is fulfilled. But the analogy admits of further application. Just as the attempt to flee external danger is relieved by standing one's ground, and by appropriate steps toward defense, so the development of neurotic fear is arrested as fast as the symptom develops, for by means of it the fear is held in check.

Our difficulties in understanding now lie elsewhere. The fear, which represents flight of the ego before the libido, is supposed to have sprung from the libido itself. That is obscure and warns us not to forget that the libido of a person belongs fundamentally to him and cannot confront him as an external force. The localized dynamics of fear development are still unintelligible; we do not know what psychic energies are released or from what psychic systems they are derived. I cannot promise to solve this problem, but we still have two trails to follow which lead us to direct observations and analytic investigation which can aid our speculations. We turn to the origin of fear in the child, and to the source of neurotic fear which attaches itself to phobias.

Fear in children is quite common and it is very hard to tell whether it is neurotic or real fear. Indeed, the value of this distinction is rendered questionable by the behavior of children. On the one hand we are not surprised that the child fears all strange persons, new situations and objects, and we explain this reaction very easily by his weakness and ignorance. We ascribe to the child a strong disposition to real fear and would consider it purposeful if this fear were in fact a heritage. Herein the child would only repeat the behavior of prehistoric man and of the primitive man of today who, on account of his ignorance and helplessness, fears everything that is new, and much that is familiar, all of which can no longer inspire us with fear. If the phobias of the child were at least partially such as might be attributed to that primeval period of human development, this would tally entirely with our expectations.

On the other hand, we cannot overlook the fact that not all children are equally afraid, and that those very children who express particular timidity toward all possible objects and situations subsequently prove to be nervous. Thus the neurotic disposition reveals itself by a decided tendency to real fear; anxiety rather than nervousness appears to be primary. We therefore arrive at the conclusion that the child (and later the adult) fears the power of his libido because he is anxious in the face of everything. The derivation of anxiety from the libido is hence put aside. Any investigation of the conditions of real fear consistently leads to the conclusion that consciousness of one's own weakness and helplessness—inferiority, in the terminology of A. Adler—when it is able to persist from childhood to maturity, is the cause underlying the neuroses.

This sounds so simple and convincing that it has a claim upon our attention. To be sure, it would result in our shifting the basis of nervousness. The persistence of the feeling of inferiority, and its prerequisite condition of anxiety and its subsequent development of symptoms, is so firmly established that it is rather the exceptional case, when health is the outcome, which requires an explanation. What can be learned from careful observation of the fear of children? The little child is primarily afraid of strange people; situations wax important only because they involve people, and objects become influential much later. But the child does not fear these strange persons because he attributes evil intentions to them, because he compares his weakness with their strength or recognizes them as dangerous to his existence, his safety and freedom from pain. Such a child, suspicious, afraid of the aggressive impulse which dominates the world, would prove a sad theoretic construction. The child is afraid of a stranger because he is adjusted to a dear, beloved person, his mother. His disappointment and longing are transformed into fear, his unemployed libido, which cannot yet be held suspended, is diverted by fear. It cannot be termed a coincidence that this situation, which is a typical example of all childish fear, is a repetition of the first condition of fear during birth, viz., separation from the mother.

The first situation phobias of children are darkness and solitude; the former often persists throughout life; common to both is the absence of the dear nurse, the mother. I once heard a child, who was afraid of the dark, call into an adjoining room, "Auntie, talk to me, I am afraid." "But what good will that do you? You cannot see me!" Whereupon the child answered, "If someone speaks, it is brighter." The yearning felt in darkness is converted into the fear of darkness. Far from saying that neurotic fear is only a secondary, a special case of real fear, we observe in little children something that resembles the behavior of real fear and has in common with neurotic fear, this characteristic feature: origin from unemployed libido. The child seems to bring very little real fear into the world. In all situations which may later become the conditions of phobias, on elevations, narrow bridges across water, on railroad and boat trips, the child exhibits no fear. And the more ignorant he is, the less fear he feels. It would be most desirable to have a greater heritage of such life-preservative instincts; the task of supervision, which is to hinder him from exposing himself to one danger after another, would be lessened. In reality the child at first overestimates his powers and behaves fearlessly because he does not recognize dangers. He will run to the water's edge, mount the window sill, play with fire or with sharp utensils, in short, he will do everything that would harm him and alarm his guardians. The awakening of real fear is the result of education, since we may not permit him to pass through the instructive experience himself.

If there are children who meet this education to fear half way, and who discover dangers of which they have not been warned, the explanation suffices that their constitution contains a greater measure of libidinous need or that they have been spoiled early through libidinous gratification. No wonder that those persons who are nervous in later life are recruited from the ranks of these children. We know that the creation of neurosis is made easy by the inability to endure a considerable amount of pent-up libido for any length of time. You see that here too we must do justice to the constitutional factor, whose rights we never wish to question. We fight shy of it only when others neglect all other claims for this, and introduce the constitutional factor where it does not belong according to the combined results of observation and analysis, or where it must be the last consideration.

Let us extract the sum of our observations on the anxiety of children: Infantile fear has very little to do with real fear, but is closely related to the neurotic fear of adults. It originates in unemployed libido and replaces the object of love that is lacking by an external object or situation.

Now you will be glad to hear that the analysis of phobias cannot teach much more that is new. The same thing occurs in them as in the fear of children; unemployed libido is constantly being converted into real fear and so a tiny external danger takes the place of the demands of the libido. This coincidence is not strange, for infantile phobias are not only the prototypes but the direct prerequisite and prelude to later phobias, which are grouped with the anxiety hysterias. Every hysteria phobia can be traced to childish fear of which it is a continuation, even if it has another content and must therefore receive a different name. The difference between the two conditions lies in their mechanism. In the adult the fact that the libido has momentarily become useless in the form of longing, is not sufficient to effect the transformation of fear into libido. He has long since learned to maintain such libido in a suspended state or to use it differently. But when the libido is part of a psychic impulse which has experienced suppression, similar conditions to those of the child, who cannot distinguish the conscious from the unconscious, are reestablished. The regression to infantile phobia is the bridge where the transformation of libido into fear is conveniently effected. We have, as you know, spoken a great deal about suppression, but we have always followed the fate of the conception that was to be suppressed, because this was easier to recognize and to present. We have always omitted from our consideration what happened to the emotion that clung to the suppressed idea; and only now we learn that whatever quality this emotion might have manifested under normal conditions, its fate is a transformation into fear. This transformation of emotion is by far the more important part of the suppression process. It is not so easy to discuss, because we cannot assert the existence of unconscious emotions in the same sense as unconscious ideas. With one difference, an idea remains the same whether it is conscious or unconscious; we can give an account of what corresponds to an unconscious idea. But an emotion is a release and must be judged differently from an idea. Without a deeper reflection and clarification of our hypotheses of psychic processes, we cannot tell what corresponds to its unconscious stage. We cannot undertake this here. But we want to retain the impression we have gained, that the development of anxiety is closely connected with the unconscious system.

I said that the transformation into fear, rather a discharge in the form of fear, is the immediate fate of suppressed libido. Not the only or final fate, I must add. These neuroses are accompanied by processes that strive to restrain the development of fear, and succeed in various ways. In phobias, for instance, two phases of the neurotic process can be clearly distinguished. The first effects the suppression of libido and its transition to fear, which is joined to an external danger. The second consists in building up all those precautions and safety devices which are to prevent contact with this danger which is dealt with as an external fact. Suppression corresponds to the ego's flight from the libido, which it regards dangerous. The phobia is comparable to a fortification against outer danger, which is represented by the much feared libido. The weakness of the phobias' system of defense lies in the fact that the fort has been strengthened from without and has remained vulnerable within. The projection of peril from the libido into the environment is never very successful. In other neuroses, therefore, other systems of defense are used against the possibility of fear development. That is an interesting aspect of the psychology of neurosis. Unfortunately its study would lead us to digress too far, and presupposes a more thorough and special knowledge of the subject. I shall add only one thing more. I have already spoken to you of the counter siege by which the ego imprisons the suppression and which it must maintain permanently for the suppression to subsist. The task of this counter siege is to carry out diverse forms of defense against the fear development which follows the suppression.

To return to the phobias, I may now say that you realize how insufficient it would be to explain only their content, to be interested only in knowing that this or that object or situation is made the subject of a phobia. The content of the phobia has about the same importance for it as the manifest dream facade has for the dream. With some necessary restrictions, we admit that among the contents of the phobias are some that are especially qualified to be objects of fear through phylogenetic inheritance, as Stanley Hall has emphasized. In harmony with this is the fact that many of these objects of fear can establish connections with danger only by symbolic relations.

And so we are convinced of the central position that the problem of fear assumes in the questions of the neurotic psychology. We are deeply impressed with how closely the development of fear is interwoven with the fate of the libido and the unconscious system. There is only one disconnected point, one inconsistency in our hypothesis: the indisputable fact that real fear must be considered an expression of the ego's instincts of self-preservation.

TWENTY-SIXTH LECTURE. GENERAL THEORY OF THE NEUROSES

The Libido Theory and Narcism

REPEATEDLY in the past and more recently we have dealt with the distinction between the ego instincts and the sexual instincts. At first, suppression taught us that the two may be flatly opposed to each other, that in the struggle the sexual instincts suffer apparent defeat and are forced to obtain satisfaction by other regressive methods, and so find the compensation for defeat in their invulnerability. After that we learned that at the outset both have a different relation to the educator, Necessity, so that they do not develop in the same manner and do not enter into the same relationship with the principle of reality. We come to realize that the sexual instincts are much more closely allied to the emotional condition of fear than the ego instincts. This result appears incomplete only in one respect, which, however, is most important. For further evidence we shall mention the significant fact that non-satisfaction of hunger and thirst, the two most elementary instincts of self-preservation, never result in their reversal into anxiety, while the transformation of unsatisfied libido into fear is, as we have heard, one of the best known and most frequently observed phenomena.

No one can contest our perfect justification in separating the ego from sexual instincts. It is affirmed by the existence of sexual desire, which is a very special activity of the individual. The only question is, what significance shall we give to this distinction, how decisive is it? The answer will depend upon the results of our observations; on how far the sexual instincts, in their psychological and somatic manifestations, behave differently from the others that are opposed to them; on how important are the consequences which result from these differences. We have, of course, no motive whatever for insisting upon a certain intangible difference in the character of the two groups of instincts. Both are only designations of the sources of energy of the individual. The discussion as to whether they are fundamentally of the same or of a different character, and if the same, when it was that they separated from one another, cannot profit by the conceptions, but must deal rather with the underlying biological facts. At present we know very little about this, and even if we knew more it would not be relevant to our analytic task.

Obviously, we should gain slight profit if, following the example of Jung, we were to emphasize the original unity of all instincts, and were to call the energy expressed in all of them "libido." Since the sexual function cannot be eliminated from psychic life by any device, we are forced to speak of sexual and asexual libido. As in the past, we rightly retain the name libido for the instincts of sexual life. I believe, therefore, that the question, how far the justifiable distinction of the instincts of sex and of self-preservation may be carried, is of little importance for psychoanalysis; and psychoanalysis is moreover not competent to deal with it. From a biological standpoint there are, to be sure, various reasons for believing that this distinction is significant. Sexuality is the only function of the living organism which extends beyond the individual and sees to his kinship with the species. It is undeniable that its practice does not always benefit the individual as do his other performances. For the price of ecstatic pleasures it involves him in dangers which threaten his life and frequently cause death. Probably peculiar metabolic processes, different from all others, are required to maintain a part of the individual life for its progeny. The individual who places himself in the foreground and regards his sexuality as a means to his gratification is, from a biological point of view, only an episode in a series of generations, a transient appendage to a germ-plasm which is virtually endowed with immortality, just as though he were the temporary partner in a corporation which continues to persist after his death.

For psychoanalytic explanation of neuroses, however, there is no need to enter upon these far-reaching implications. By separate observation of the sexual and the ego instincts, we have gained the key to the understanding of transference-neuroses. We were able to trace them back to the fundamental situation where the sexual instinct and the instinct of self-preservation had come in conflict with one another, or biologically although not so accurately, expressed where the part played by the ego, that of independent individuality, was opposed to the other, that of a link in a series of generations. Only human beings are capable of such conflict, and therefore, taken all in all, neurosis is the prerogative of man, and not of animals. The excessive development of his libido and the elaboration of a varied and complicated psychic life thus made possible, appear to have created the conditions prerequisite for conflict. It is clear that these conditions are also responsible for the great progress that man has made beyond his kinship with animals. The capacity for neurosis is really only the reverse side of his talents and gifts. But these are only speculations, which divert us from our task.

Until now we worked with the impulse that we can distinguish the ego and the sexual instincts from one another by their manifestations. We could do this without difficulty in the transference neuroses. We called the accumulation of energy which the ego directed towards the object of its sexual striving libido and all others, which proceeded from the instincts of self-preservation, interest. We were able to achieve our first insight into the workings of psychic forces by observing the accumulation of the libido, its transformations and its final destiny. The transference neuroses furnished the best material for this. But the ego, composed from various organizations, their construction and functioning, remained hidden and we were led to believe that only the analysis of other neurotic disturbances would raise the veil.

Very soon we began to extend these psychoanalytic conceptions to other conditions. As early as 1908, K. Abraham asserted, after a discussion with me, that the principal characteristic of dementia praecox (which may be considered one of the psychoses) is *that there is no libidinous occupation of objects* (*The Psycho-sexual Differences between Hysteria and Dementia Praecox*). But then the question arose, what happens to the libido of the demented, which is diverted from its objects? Abraham did not hesitate to give the answer, "It is turned back upon the ego, and *this reflected turning back is the source of the megalomania* in dementia praecox." This hallucination of greatness is exactly comparable to the well-known over-estimation of the objects habitual to lovers. So, for the first time, we gained an understanding of psychotic condition by comparing it with the normal course of love.

These first interpretations of Abraham's have been maintained in psychoanalysis, and have become the basis of our attitude towards the psychoses. Slowly we familiarized ourselves with the idea that the libido, which we find attached to certain objects, which expresses a striving to attain gratification from these objects, may also forsake them and put in their place the person's own ego. Gradually these ideas were developed more and more consistently. The name for this placing of the libido—narcism—was borrowed from one of the perversions described by P. Naecke. In it the grown individual lavishes upon his own body all the affection usually devoted to some foreign sex object.

We reflected that if such a fixation of libido on one's own body and person instead of on some external object exists, this cannot be an exceptional or trivial occurrence. It is much more probable that this narcism is the general and original condition, out of which the love for an object later develops, without however necessarily causing narcism to disappear. From the evolutionary history of object-libido we remembered that in the beginning many sex instincts seek auto-erotic gratification, and that this capacity for auto-eroticism forms the basis for the retardation of sexuality in its education to conformity with fact. And so, auto-eroticism was the sexual activity of the narcistic stage in the placing of the libido.

To be brief: We represented the relation of the ego-libido to the object-libido in a way which I can explain by an analogy from zoology. Think of the simplest forms of life, which consist of a little lump of protoplasmic substance which is only slightly differentiated. They stretch out protrusions, known as pseudopia, into which the protoplasm flows. But they can withdraw these protrusions and assume their original shape. Now we compare the stretching out of these processes with the radiation of libido to the objects, while the central mass of libido can remain in the ego, and we assume that under normal conditions ego-libido can be changed into object-libido, and this can again be taken up into the ego, without any trouble.

With the help of this representation we can now explain a great number of psychic conditions, or to express it more modestly, describe them, in the language of the libido theory; conditions that we must accredit to normal life, such as the psychic attitude during love, during organic sickness, during sleep. We assumed that the conditions of sleep rest upon withdrawal from the outer world and concentration upon the wish to sleep. The nocturnal psychic activity expressed in the dream we found in the service of a wish to sleep and, moreover, governed by wholly egoistic motives. Continuing in the sense of libido theory: sleep is a condition in which all occupations of objects, the libidinous as well as the egoistic, are given up, and are withdrawn into the ego. Does this not throw a new light upon recovery during sleep, and upon the nature of exhaustion in general? The picture of blissful isolation in the intra-uterine life, which the sleeper conjures up night after night, thus also completes the picture from the psychic side. In the sleeper the original condition of libido division is again restored, a condition of complete narcism in which libido and ego-interest are still united and live indistinguishably in the self-sufficient ego.

We must observe two things: First, how can the conceptions of narcism and egoism be distinguished? I believe narcism is the libidinous complement of egoism. When we speak of egoism we mean only the benefits to the individual; if we speak of narcism we also take into account his libidinous satisfaction. As practical motives the two can be followed up separately to a considerable degree. One can be absolutely egoistic, and still have strong libidinous occupation of objects, in so far as the libidinous gratification by way of the object serves the needs of the ego. Egoism will then take care that the striving for the object results in no harm to the ego. One can be egoistic and at the same time excessively narcistic, i.e., have very slight need of an object. This need may be for direct sexual satisfaction or even for those higher desires, derived from need, which we are in the habit of calling love as opposed to sensuality. In all of these aspects, egoism is the self-evident, the constant, and narcism the variable element. The antithesis of egoism, *altruism*, is not the same as the conception of libidinous occupation of objects. Altruism differs from it by the absence of desire for sexual satisfaction. But in the state of being completely in love, altruism and libidinous occupation with an object clash. The sex object as a rule draws upon itself a part of the narcism of the ego. This is generally called "sexual over-estimation" of the object. If the altruistic transformation from egoism to the sex object is added, the sex object becomes all powerful; it has virtually sucked up the ego.

I think you will find it a pleasant change if after the dry phantasy of science I present to you a poetic representation of the economic contrast between narcism and being in love. I take it from the *Westostliche Divans* of Goethe:

SULEIKA:

Conqueror and serf and nation; They proclaim it joyously;

Mankind's loftiest elation, Shines in personality.

Life's enchantment lures and lingers, Of yourself is not afar,

All may slip through passive fingers, If you tarry as you are.

HATEM:

Never could I be thus ravished, Other thoughts are in my mind,

All the gladness earth has lavished, In Suleika's charms I find.

When I cherish her, then only, Dearer to myself I grow,

If she turned to leave me lonely, I should lose the self I know.

Hatem's happiness were over,—But his changeling soul would glide

Into any favored lover, Whom she fondles at her side.

The second observation is supplementary to the dream theory. We cannot explain the origin of the dream unless we assume that the suppressed unconscious has achieved a certain independence of the ego. It does not conform to the wish for sleep and retains its hold on the energies that have seized it, even when all the occupations with objects dependent upon the ego have been released for the benefit of sleep. Not until then can we understand how this unconscious can take advantage of the nocturnal discontinuance or deposition of the censor, and can seize control of fragments left over from the day to fashion a forbidden dream wish from them. On the other hand, it is to the already existing connections with these supposed elements that these fragments owe a part of the resistance directed against the withdrawal of the libido, and controlled by the wish for sleep. We also wish to supplement our conception of dream formation with this trait of dynamic importance.

Organic diseases, painful irritations, inflammation of the organs create a condition which clearly results in freeing the libido of its objects. The withdrawn libido again finds itself in the ego and occupies the diseased part of the part. We may even venture to assert that under these conditions the withdrawal of the libido from its objects is more conspicuous than the withdrawal of egoistic interest from the outside world. This seems to open the way to an understanding of hypochondria, where an organ occupies the ego in a similar way without being diseased, according to our conception. I shall resist the temptation of continuing along this line, or of discussing other situations which we can understand or represent through the assumption that the object libido travels to the ego. For I am eager to meet two objections, which I know are absorbing your attention. In the first place, you want to call me to account for my insistence upon distinguishing in sleep, in sickness and in similar situations between libido and interest, sexual instincts and ego instincts, since throughout the observations can be explained by assuming a single and uniform energy, which, freely mobile, occupies now the object, now the ego, and enters into the services of one or the other of these impulses. And, secondly, how can I venture to treat the freeing of libido from its object as the source of a pathological condition, since such transformation of object-libido into ego-libido—or more generally, ego-energy—belongs to the normal, daily and nightly repeated occurrences of psychic dynamics?

The answer is: Your first objection sounds good. The discussion of the conditions of sleep, of sickness and of being in love would in themselves probably never have led to a distinction between ego-libido and object-libido, or between libido and interest. But you do not take into account the investigations from which we have set out, in the light of which we now regard the psychic situations under discussion. The necessity of distinguishing between libido and interest, that is, between sexual instincts and those of self-preservation, is forced upon us by our insight into the conflict out of which the transference neuroses emerge. We can no longer reckon without it. The assumption that object-libido can change into the ego-libido, in other words, that we must reckon with an ego-libido, appeared to us the only possible one wherewith to solve the riddle of the so-called narcistic neuroses—for instance, dementia praecox—or to justify the similarities and differences in a comparison of hysteria and compulsion. We now apply to sickness, sleep and love that which we found undeniably affirmed elsewhere. We may proceed with such applications as far as they will go. The only assertion that is not a direct refutation of our analytic experience is that libido remains libido whether it is directed towards objects or toward the ego itself, and is never transferred into egoistic interest, and vice-versa. But this assertion is of equal weight with the distinction of sex and ego instincts which we have already critically appraised, and which we will maintain from methodological motives until it may possibly be disproved.

Your second objection, too, raises a justified question, but it points in a wrong direction. To be sure the retreat of object-libido into the ego is not purely pathogenic; we see that it occurs each time before going to sleep, only to be released again upon awaking. The little protoplasmic animal draws in its protrusions, only to send them out again on a later occasion. But it is quite another matter when a specific, very energetic process compels the withdrawal of libido from the object. The libido has become narcistic and cannot find its way back to the object, and this hindrance to the mobility of the libido certainly becomes pathogenic. It appears that an accumulation of narcistic libido cannot be borne beyond a certain point. We can imagine that the reason for occupation with the object is that the ego found it necessary to send out its libido in order not to become diseased because it was pent up. If it were our plan to go further into the subject of dementia praecox, I would show you that this process which frees the libido from the objects and bars the way back to them, is closely related to the process of suppression, and must be considered as its counterpart. But above all you would recognize familiar ground, for the conditions of these processes are practically identical, as far as we can now see, with those of suppression. The conflict appears to be the same, and to take place between the same forces. The reason for a result as different as, for instance, the result in hysteria, can be found only in a difference of dispositions. The vulnerable point in the libido development of these patients lies in another phase; the controlling fixation, which, as you will remember, permits the breach resulting in the formation of symptoms, is in another place probably in the stage of primitive narcism, to which dementia praecox returns in its final stage. It is noteworthy that for all the narcistic neuroses, we must assume fixation points of the libido which reach back into far earlier phases of development than in cases of hysteria or compulsion neuroses. But you have heard that the conceptions obtained in our study of transference neuroses are sufficient to orient us in the narcistic neuroses, which present far greater practical difficulties. The similarities are considerable; it is fundamentally the same field of observation. But you can easily imagine how hopeless the explanations of these conditions, which belong to psychiatry, appear to him who is not equipped for this task with an analytic knowledge of transference neuroses.

The picture given by the symptoms of dementia praecox, which, moreover, is highly variable, is not exclusively determined by the symptoms. These result from forcing the libido away from the objects and accumulating it in the ego in the form of narcistic libido. A large space is occupied by other phenomena, which result from the impulses of the libido to regain the objects, and so show an attempt toward restitution and healing. These symptoms are in fact the more conspicuous, the more clamorous; they show an unquestionable similarity to those of hysteria, or less often to those of compulsion neurosis, and yet they are different in every respect. It appears that in dementia praecox the libido in its endeavor to return to the objects, i.e., to the images of the objects, really captures something, but only their shadows—I mean, the verbal images belonging to them. This is not the place to discuss this matter, but I believe that these reversed impulses of the libido have permitted us an insight into what really determines the difference between a conscious and an unconscious representation.

I have now brought you into the field where we may expect the further progress of analytic work. Since we can now employ the conception of ego-libido, the narcistic neuroses have become accessible to us. We are confronted with the problem of finding a dynamic explanation of these conditions and at the same time of enlarging our knowledge of psychic life by an understanding of the ego. The ego psychology, which we strive to understand, must not be founded upon introspective data, but rather, as in the libido, upon analysis of the disturbances and decompositions of the ego. When this greater task is accomplished we shall probably disparage our previous knowledge of the fate of the libido which we gained from our study of the transference neuroses. But there is still much to be said in this matter. Narcistic neuroses can scarcely be approached by the same technique which served us in the transference neuroses. Soon you will hear why. After forging ahead a little in the study of narcistic neuroses we always seem to come to a wall which impedes progress. You know that in the transference neuroses we also encountered such barriers of resistance, but we were able to break them down piece by piece. In narcistic neuroses the resistance is insuperable; at best we are permitted to cast a curious glance over the wall to spy out what is taking place on the other side. Our technical methods must be replaced by others; we do not yet know whether or not we shall be able to find such a substitute. To be sure, even these patients furnish us with ample material. They do say many things, though not in answer to our questions, and for the time being we are forced to interpret these utterances through the understanding we have gained from the symptoms of transference neuroses. The coincidence is sufficiently great to assure us a good beginning. How far this technique will go, remains to be seen.

There are additional difficulties that impede our progress. The narcistic conditions and the psychoses related to them can only be solved by observers who have schooled themselves in analytic study of transference neuroses. But our psychiatrists do not study psychoanalysis and we psychoanalysts see too few psychiatric cases. A race of psychiatrists that has gone through the school of psychoanalysis as a preparatory science most first grow up. The beginnings of this are now being made in America, where many leading psychiatrists explain the teachings of psychoanalysis to their students, and where many owners of sanatoriums and directors of institutes for the insane take pains to observe their patients in the light of these teachings. But even here we have occasionally been successful in casting a glance over the narcistic wall and I shall tell you a few things that we think we have discovered.

The disease of paranoia, chronic systematic insanity, is given a very uncertain position by the attempts at classification of present-day psychiatry. There is no doubt of its close relationship to dementia praecox. I once was so bold as to propose that paranoia and dementia praecox could be classed together under the common name of paraphrenia. The types of paranoia are described according to their content as: megalomania, the mania of persecution, eroto mania, mania of jealousy, etc. From psychiatry we do not expect attempts at explanation. As an example of such an attempt, to be sure an antiquated and not entirely valid example, I might mention the attempt to develop one symptom directly out of another by means of an intellectual rationalization, as: the patient who primarily believes he is being persecuted draws the conclusion from this persecution that he must be an extraordinarily important personality and thus develops megalomania. In our analytical conception megalomania is the immediate outcome of exaggeration of the ego, which results from the drawing-in of libidinous occupation with objects, a secondary narcism as a recurrence of the originally early infantile form. In cases of the mania of persecution we have noticed a few things that lead us to follow a definite track. In the first place, we observed that in the great majority of cases the persecutor was of the same sex as the persecuted. This could still be explained in a harmless way, but in a few carefully studied cases it was clearly shown that the person of the same sex, who was most loved in normal times, became the persecutor after the malady set in. A further development is made possible by the fact that one loved person is replaced by another, according to familiar affinities, e.g., the father by the teacher or the superior. We concluded from such ever-increasing experiences, that paranoia persecutoria is the form in which the individual guards himself against a homosexual tendency that has become too powerful. The change from affection to hate, which notoriously may take the form of serious threats against the life of the loved and hated person, expresses the transformation of libidinous impulse into fear, which is a regularly recurring result of the process of suppression. As an illustration

I shall cite the last case in which I made observations on this subject. A young physician had to be sent away from his home town because he had threatened the life of the son of a university professor, who up to that time had been his best friend. He ascribed truly devilish intentions to his erstwhile friend and credited him with power of a demon. He was to blame for all the misfortunes that had in recent years befallen the family of the patient, for all his personal and social ill-luck. But this was not enough. The wicked friend, and his father the professor, had been the cause of the war and had called the Russians into the land. He had forfeited his life a thousand times and our patient was convinced that with the death of the culprit all misfortune would come to an end. And yet his old affection for his friend was so great that it had paralyzed his hand when he had had the opportunity of shooting down the enemy at close quarters. In my short consultations with the patient, I discovered that the friendship between the two dated back to early school-life. Once at least the bonds of friendship had been over-stepped; a night spent together had been the occasion for complete sexual intercourse. Our patient never felt attracted to women, as would have been natural to his age or his charming personality. At one time he was engaged to a beautiful and distinguished young girl, but she broke off the engagement because she found so little affection in her fiancé. Years later his malady broke out just at that moment when for the first time he had succeeded in giving complete gratification to a woman. When this woman embraced him, full of gratitude and devotion, he suddenly felt a strange pain which cut around his skull like a sharp incision. His later interpretation of this sensation was that an incision such as is used to expose a part of the brain had been performed upon him, and since his friend had become a pathological anatomist, he gradually came to the conclusion that he alone could have sent him this last woman as a temptation. From that time on his eyes were also opened to the other persecutions in which he was to be the victim of the intrigues of his former friend.

But how about those cases where the persecutor is not of the same sex as the persecuted, where our explanation of a guard against homosexual libido is apparently contradicted? A short time ago I had occasion to investigate such a case and was able to glean corroboration from this apparent contradiction. A young girl thought she was followed by a man, with whom she had twice had intimate relations. She had, as a matter of fact, first laid these maniacal imputations at the door of a woman, whom we may consider as having played the part of a mother-substitute in her psychic life. Only after the second meeting did she progress to the point of diverting this maniacal idea from the woman and of transferring it to the man. The condition that the persecutor must be of the same sex was also originally maintained in this instance. In her claim before the lawyer and the physician, this patient did not mention this first stage of her mania, and this caused the appearance of a contradiction to our theory of paranoia.

Homosexual choice of object is originally more natural to narcism than the heterosexual. If it is a matter of thwarting a strong and undesirable homosexual impulse, the way back to narcism is made especially easy. Until now I have had very little opportunity of speaking to you about the fundamental conditions of love-life, so far as we know them, and now I cannot make up for lost time. I only want to point out that the choice of an object, that progress in the development of the libido which comes after the narcistic stage, can proceed according to two different types—either according to the *narcistic* type, which puts a very similar personality in the place of the personal ego, or according to the *dependent* type, which chooses those persons who have become valuable by satisfying needs of life other than as objects of the libido. We also accredit a strong fixation of the libido to the narcistic type of object-choice when there is a disposition toward manifest homosexuality.

You will recall that in our first meeting of this semester I told you about the case of a woman who suffered from the mania of jealousy. Since we are so near the end you certainly will be glad to hear the psychoanalytic explanation of a maniacal idea. But I have less to say about it than you expect. The maniacal idea as well as the compulsion idea cannot be assailed by logical arguments or actual experience. This is explained by their relation to the unconscious, which is represented by the maniacal idea or the compulsion idea, and held down by whichever is effective. The difference between the two is based upon respective localization and dynamic relations of the two conditions.

As in paranoia, so also in melancholia, of which, moreover, very different clinical forms are described. We have discovered a point of vantage which will yield us an insight into the inner structure of the condition. We realize that the self-accusations with which these melancholic patients torture themselves in the most pitiless way, really apply to another person, namely, the sex object which they have lost, or which through some fault has lost value for them. From this we may conclude that the melancholic has withdrawn his libido from the object. Through a process which we designate as "narcistic identification" the object is built up within the ego itself, is, so to say, projected upon the ego. Here I can give you only a descriptive representation, as yet without reference to the topical and dynamic relations. The personal ego is now treated in the same manner as the abandoned object, and suffers all the aggression and expressions of revenge which were planned for the object. Even the suicidal tendencies of melancholia are more comprehensible when we consider that this bitterness of the patient falls alike on the ego itself and on the object of its love and hate. In melancholia as well as in other narcistic conditions a feature of emotional life is strikingly shown which, since the time of Bleuler, we have been accustomed to designate as *ambivalence*. By this we mean that hostile and affectionate feelings are directed against one and the same person. I have, in the course of these discussions, unfortunately not been in a position to tell you more about this emotional ambivalence.

We have, in addition to narcistic identification, an hysterical identification as well, which moreover has been known to us for a much longer time. I wish it were possible to determine clearly the difference between the two. Of the periodic and cyclic forms of melancholia I can tell you something that you will certainly be glad to hear, for it is possible, under favorable circumstances—I have twice had the experience—to prevent these emotional conditions (or their antitheses) by means of analytic treatment in the free intervals between the attacks. We learn that in melancholia as well as in mania, it is a matter of finding a special way for solving the conflict, the prerequisites for which entirely coincide with those of other neuroses. You can imagine how much there still is for psychoanalysis to learn in this field.

I told you, too, that we hoped to gain a knowledge of the structure of the ego, and of the separate factors out of which it is built by means of the analysis of narcistic conditions. In one place we have already made a beginning. From the analysis of the maniacal delusion of being watched we concluded that in the ego there is really an agent which continually watches, criticizes and compares the other part of the ego and thus opposes it. We believe that the patient imparts to us a truth that is not yet sufficiently appreciated, when he complains that all his actions are spied upon and watched, all his thoughts recorded and criticized. He errs only in transferring this distressing force to something alien, outside of himself. He feels the dominance of a factor in his ego, which compares his actual ego and all of its activities to an *ideal ego* that he has created in the course of his development. We also believe that the creation of this ideal ego took place with the purpose of again establishing that self-satisfaction which is bound up with the original infantile narcism, but which since then has experienced so many disturbances and disparagements. In this self-observing agent we recognize the ego-censor, the conscience; it is the same factor which at night exercises dream-censorship, and which creates the suppressions against inadmissible wish-impulses. Under analysis in the maniacal delusion of being watched it reveals its origin in the influence of parents, tutors and social environment and in the identification of the ego with certain of these model individuals.

These are some of the conclusions which the application of psychoanalysis to narcistic conditions has yielded us. They are certainly all too few, and they often lack that accuracy which can only be acquired in a new field with the attainment of absolute familiarity. We owe them all to the exploitation of the conception of ego-libido or narcistic libido, by the aid of which we have extended to narcistic neuroses those observations which were confirmed in the transference neuroses. But now you will ask, is it possible for us to succeed in subordinating all the disturbances of narcistic conditions and the psychoses to the libido theory in such a way that in every case we recognize the libidinous factor of psychic life as the cause of the malady, and never make an abnormality in the functioning of the instincts of self-preservation answerable? Ladies and gentlemen, this conclusion does not seem urgent to me, and above all not ripe for decision. We can best leave it calmly to the progress of the science. I should not be surprised to find that the power to exert a pathogenic influence is really an exclusive prerogative of the libidinous impulses, and that the libido theory will celebrate its triumphs along the whole line from the simplest true neurosis to the most difficult psychotic derangement of the individual. For we know it to be a characteristic of the libido that it is continually struggling against subordinating itself to the realities of the world. But I consider it most probable that the ego instincts are indirectly swept along by the pathogenic excitations of the libido and forced into a functional disturbance. Moreover, I cannot see any defeat for our trend of investigation when we are confronted with the admission that in difficult psychoses the ego impulses themselves are fundamentally led astray; the future will teach us—or at least it will teach you. Let me return for one moment more to fear, in order to eliminate one last ambiguity that we have left. We have said that the relation between fear and the libido, which in other respects seems clearly defined, does not fit in with the assumption that in the face of danger real fear should become the expression of the instinct of self-preservation. This, however, can hardly be doubted. But suppose the emotion of fear is not contested by the egoistic ego impulse, but rather by the ego-libido? The condition of fear is in all cases purposeless and its lack of purpose is obvious when it reaches a higher level. It then disturbs the action, be it flight or defense, which alone is purposeful, and which serves the ends of self-preservation. If we accredit the emotional component of actual fear to the ego-libido, and the accompanying activity to the egoistic instinct to self-preservation, we have overcome every theoretical difficulty. Furthermore, you do not really believe that we flee *because* we experience fear? On the contrary, we first are afraid *and then* take to flight from the same motive that is awakened by the realization of danger. Men who have survived the endangering of their lives tell us that they were not at all afraid, they only acted. They turned the weapon against the wild animal, and that was in fact the most purposeful thing to do.

TWENTY-SEVENTH LECTURE. GENERAL THEORY OF THE NEUROSES

Transference

WE are nearing the close of our discussions, and you probably cherish certain expectations, which shall not be disappointed. You think, I suppose, that I have not guided you through thick and thin of psychoanalytic subject matter to dismiss you without a word about therapy, which furnishes the only possibility of carrying on psychoanalysis. I cannot possibly omit this subject, for the observation of some of its aspects will teach you a new fact, without which the understanding of the diseases we have examined would be most incomplete.

I know that you do not expect any guidance in the technique of practising analysis for therapeutic purposes. You wish to know only along what general lines psychoanalytic therapy works and approximately what it accomplishes. And you have an undeniable right to know this. I shall not actually tell you, however, but shall insist that you guess it yourselves.

Only think! You know everything essential, from the conditions which precipitate the illness to all the factors at work within. Where is there room for therapeutic influence? In the first place, there is hereditary disposition; we do not speak of it often because it is strongly emphasized from another quarter, and we have nothing new to say about it. But do not think that we underestimate it. Just because we are therapeutists, we feel its power distinctly. At any rate, we cannot change it; it is a given fact which erects a barrier to our efforts. In the second place, there is the influence of the early experiences of childhood, which are in the habit of becoming sharply emphasized under analysis; they belong to the past and we cannot undo them. And then everything that we include in the term "actual forbearance"— misfortunes of life out of which privations of love arise, poverty, family discord, unfortunate choice in marriage, unfavorable social conditions and the severity of moral claims. These would certainly offer a foothold for very effectual therapy. But it would have to be the kind of therapy which, according to the Viennese folk-tale, Emperor Joseph practiced: the beneficial interference of a potentate, before whose will men bow and difficulties vanish. But who are we, to include such charity in the methods of our therapy? Poor as we are, powerless in society, forced to earn our living by practicing medicine, we are not even in a position to treat free of charge those patients who are unable to pay, as physicians who employ other methods of treatment can do. Our therapy is too long drawn-out, too extended for that. But perhaps you are still holding to one of the factors already mentioned, and think that you have found a factor through which our influence may be effective. If the restrictions of morality which are imposed by society have a share in the privation forced upon the patient, treatment might give him the courage, or possibly even the prescription itself, to cross these barriers, might tell him how gratification and health can be secured in the renunciation of that ideal which society has held up to us but often disregards. One grows healthy then, by giving one's sexuality full reign. Such analytic treatment, however, would be darkened by a shadow; it does not serve our recognized morality. The gain to the individual is a loss to society.

But, ladies and gentlemen, who has misinformed you to this degree? It is inconceivable that the advice to give one's sexuality full reign can play a part in analytic therapy, if only from the circumstance we have ourselves described, that there is going on within the patient a bitter conflict between libidinous impulse and sexual suppression, between sensual and ascetic tendencies. This conflict is not abolished by giving one of these tendencies the victory over its opponent. We see that in the case of the nervous, asceticism has retained the upper hand. The consequence of this is that the suppressed sexual desire gains breathing space by the development of symptoms. If, on the other hand, we were to give the victory to sexuality, symptoms would have to replace the sexual suppression, which has been pushed aside. Neither of the two decisions can end the inner conflict, one part always remains unsatisfied. There are only a few cases wherein the conflict is so labile, that a factor such as the intervention of the physician could be decisive, and these cases really require no analytic treatment. Persons who can be so much influenced by a physician would have found some solution without him. You know that when an abstinent young man decides upon illegitimate sex-intercourse, or when an unsatisfied woman seeks compensation from another man, they have generally not waited for the permission of a physician, far less of an analyst, to do this.

In studying the situation, one essential point is generally overlooked, that the pathogenic conflict of the neurotic must not be confused with normal struggles between psychic impulses of which all have their root in the same psychological soil. The neurotic struggle is a strife of forces, one of which has attained the level of the fore-conscious and the conscious, while the other has been held back in the unconscious stage. That is why the conflict can have no outcome; the struggling parties approach each other as little as in the well-known instance of the polar-bear and the whale. A real decision can be reached only if both meet on the same ground. To accomplish this is, I believe, the sole task of therapy.

Moreover, I assure you that you are misinformed if you assume that advice and guidance in the affairs of life is an integral part of the analytic influence. On the contrary, we reject this role of the mentor as far as possible. Above all, we wish to attain independent decisions on the part of the patient. With this intention in mind, we require him to postpone all vital resolutions such as choice of a career, marriage or divorce, until the close of the treatment. You must confess that this is not what you had imagined. It is only in the case of certain very young or entirely helpless persons that we cannot insist upon the desired limitation. Here we must combine the function of physician and educator; we are well aware of the responsibility and behave with the necessary precaution.

Judging from the zeal with which I defend myself against the accusation that analytic treatment urges the nervous person to give his sexuality full reign, you must not gather that we influence him for the benefit of conventional morality. We are just as far removed from that. We are no reformers, it is true, only observers, but we cannot help observing with critical eyes, and we have found it impossible to take the part of conventional sex morality, or to estimate highly the way in which society has tried to regulate the problems of sexual life in practice. We can prove to society mathematically that its code of ethics has exacted more sacrifices than is its worth, and that its procedure rests neither on veracity nor wisdom. We cannot spare our patients the task of listening to this criticism. We accustom them to weigh sexual matters, as well as others, without prejudice; and when, after the completion of the cure, they have become independent and choose some intermediate course between unrestrained sexuality and asceticism, our conscience is not burdened by the consequences. We tell ourselves: whoever has been successfully educated in being true to himself is permanently protected against the danger of immorality, even if his moral standard diverges from that of society. Let us, moreover, be careful not to overestimate the significance of the problem of abstinence with respect to its influence on neuroses. Only the minority of pathogenic situations of forbearance, with a subsequent condition of pent-up libido, can be resolved without more ado by such sexual intercourse as can be procured with little trouble.

And so you cannot explain the therapeutic influence of psychoanalysis by saying that it simply recommends giving full sway to sexuality. You must seek another solution. I think that while I was refuting this supposition of yours, one of my remarks put you on the right track. Our usefulness consists in replacing the unconscious by the conscious, in translating the unconscious into the conscious. You are right; that is exactly it. By projecting the unconscious into the conscious, we do away with suppressions, we remove conditions of symptom formation and transform a pathogenic into a normal conflict which can be decided in some way or other. This is the only psychic change we produce in our patients; its extent is the extent of our helpfulness. Wherever no suppression and no analogous psychic process can be undone, there is no place for our therapy.

We can express the aim of our efforts by various formulae of rendering the unconscious conscious, removing suppressions, filling out amnestic gaps—it all amounts to the same thing. But perhaps this admission does not satisfy you. You imagined that when a nervous person became cured something very different happened, that after having been subjected to the laborious process of psychoanalysis, he was transformed into a different human being. And now I tell you that the entire result is only that he has a little less of the unconscious, a little more of the conscious within him. Well, you probably underestimate the significance of such an inner change. The person cured of neurosis has really become another human being. Fundamentally, of course, he has remained the same. That is to say, he has only become what he might have been under the most favorable conditions. But that is saying a great deal. When you learn all that has to be done, the effort required to effect apparently so slight a change in psychic life, the significance of such a difference in the psychic realm will be credible to you.

I shall digress for a moment to ask whether you know what is meant by a causal therapy? This name is given to the procedure which does not take the manifestations of disease for its point of departure, but seeks to remove the causes of disease. Is our psychoanalytical therapy causal or not? The answer is not simple, but perhaps it will give us the opportunity of convincing ourselves that this point of departure is comparatively fruitless. In so far as analytical therapy does not concern itself immediately with the removal of symptoms, it may be termed causal. Yet in another respect, you might say this would hardly follow. For we have followed the causal chain back far beyond the suppressions to the instinctive tendencies and their relative intensity as given by the constitution of the patient, and finally the nature of the digression in the abnormal process of its development. Assume for a moment that it were possible to influence these functions chemically, to increase or to decrease the quantity of the libido that happens to be present, to strengthen one impulse at the expense of another. This would be causal therapy in its true sense and our analysis would have furnished the indispensable preparatory work of reconnaissance. You know that there is as yet no possibility of so influencing the processes of the libido. Our psychic therapy interposes elsewhere, not exactly at those sources of the phenomena which have been disclosed to us, but sufficiently far beyond the symptoms, at an opening in the structure of the disease which has become accessible to us by means of peculiar conditions.

What must we do in order to replace the unconscious by the conscious in our patient? At one time we thought this was quite simple, that all we had to do was to reconstruct the unconscious and then tell the patient about it. But we already know this was a shortsighted error. Our knowledge of the unconscious has not the same value as his; if we communicate our knowledge to him it will not stand *in place of* the unconscious within him, but will exist *beside* it, and only a very small change will have been effected. We must rather think of the unconscious as *localized,* and must seek it in memory at the point where it came into existence by means of a suppression. This suppression must be removed before the substitution of the conscious for the unconscious can be successfully effected. How can such a suppression be removed? Here our task enters a second phase. First to find the suppression, then to remove the resistance by which this suppression is maintained.

How can we do away with resistance? In the same way—by reconstructing it and confronting the patient with it. For resistance arises from suppression, from the very suppression which we are trying to break up, or from an earlier one. It has been established by the counter-attack that was instigated to suppress the offensive impulse. And so now we do the very thing we intended at the outset: interpret, reconstruct, communicate—but now we do it in the right place. The counter-seizure of the idea or resistance is not part of the unconscious but of the ego, which is our fellow-worker. This holds true even if resistance is not conscious. We know that the difficulty arises from the ambiguity of the word "unconscious," which may connote either a phenomenon or a system. That seems very difficult, but it is only a repetition, isn't it? We were prepared for it a long time ago. We expect resistance to be relinquished, the counter-siege to collapse, when our interpretation has enabled the ego to recognize it. With what impulses are we able to work in such a case? In the first place, the patient's desire to become well, which has led him to accommodate himself to co-operate with us in the task of the cure; in the second place, the help of his intelligence, which is supported by the interpretation we offer him. There is no doubt that after we have made clear to him what he may expect, the patient's intelligence can identify resistances, and find their translation into the suppressions more readily. If I say to you, "Look up into the sky, you can see a balloon there," you will find it more readily than if I had just asked you to look up to see whether you could discover anything. And unless the student who for the first time works with a microscope is told by his teacher what he may look for, he will not see anything, even if it is present and quite visible.

And now for the fact! In a large number of forms of nervous illness, in hysteria, conditions of anxiety and compulsion neuroses, one hypothesis is correct. By finding the suppression, revealing resistance, interpreting the thing suppressed, we really succeed in solving the problem, in overcoming resistance, in removing suppression, in transforming the unconscious into the conscious. While doing this we gain the clearest impression of the violent struggle that takes place in the patient's soul for the subjugation of resistance—a normal psychological struggle, in one psychic sphere between the motives that wish to maintain the counter-siege and those which are willing to give it up. The former are the old motives that at one time effected suppression; among the latter are those that have recently entered the conflict, to decide it, we trust, in the sense we favor. We have succeeded in reviving the old conflict of the suppression, in reopening the case that had already been decided. The new material we contribute consists in the first place of the warning, that the former solution of the conflict had led to illness, and the promise that another will pave the way to health; secondly, the powerful change of all conditions since the time of that first rejection. At that time the ego had been weak, infantile and may have had reason to denounce the claims of the libido as if they were dangerous. Today it is strong, experienced and is supported by the assistance of the physician. And so we may expect to guide the revived conflict to a better issue than a suppression, and in hysteria, fear and compulsion neuroses, as I have said before, success justifies our claims.

There are other forms of illness, however, in which our therapeutic procedure never is successful, even though the causal conditions are similar. Though this may be characterized topically in a different way, in them there was also an original conflict between the ego and libido, which led to suppression. Here, too, it is possible to discover the occasions when suppressions occurred in the life of the patient. We employ the same procedure, are prepared to furnish the same promises, give the same kind of help. We again present to the patient the connections we expect him to discover, and we have in our favor the same interval in time between the treatment and these suppressions favoring a solution of the conflict; yet in spite of these conditions, we are not able to overcome the resistance, or to remove the suppression. These patients, suffering from paranoia, melancholia, and dementia praecox, remain untouched on the whole, and proof against psychoanalytic therapy. What is the reason for this? It is not lack of intelligence; we require, of course, a certain amount of intellectual ability in our patients; but those suffering from paranoia, for instance, who effect such subtle combinations of facts, certainly are not in want of it. Nor can we say that other motive forces are lacking. Patients suffering from melancholia, in contrast to those afflicted with paranoia, are profoundly conscious of being ill, of suffering greatly, but they are not more accessible. Here we are confronted with a fact we do not understand, which bids us doubt if we have really understood all the conditions of success in other neuroses.

In the further consideration of our dealings with hysterical and compulsion neurotics we soon meet with a second fact, for which we were not at all prepared. After a while we notice that these patients behave toward us in a very peculiar way. We thought that we had accounted for all the motive forces that could come into play, that we had rationalized the relation between the patient and ourselves until it could be as readily surveyed as an example in arithmetic, and yet some force begins to make itself felt that we had not considered in our calculations. This unexpected something is highly variable. I shall first describe those of its manifestations which occur frequently and are easy to understand.

We see our patient, who should be occupying himself only with finding a way out of his painful conflicts, become especially interested in the person of the physician. Everything connected with this person is more important to him than his own affairs and diverts him from his illness. Dealings with him are very pleasant for the time being. He is especially cordial, seeks to show his gratitude wherever he can, and manifests refinements and merits of character that we hardly had expected to find. The physician forms a very favorable opinion of the patient and praises the happy chance that permitted him to render assistance to so admirable a personality. If the physician has the opportunity of speaking to the relatives of the patient he hears with pleasure that this esteem is returned. At home the patient never tires of praising the physician, of prizing advantages which he constantly discovers. "He adores you, he trusts you blindly, everything you say is a revelation to him," the relatives say. Here and there one of the chorus observes more keenly and remarks, "It is a positive bore to hear him talk, he speaks only of you; you are his only subject of conversation."

Let us hope that the physician is modest enough to ascribe the patient's estimation of his personality to the encouragement that has been offered him and to the widening of his intellectual horizon through the astounding and liberating revelations which the cure entails. Under these conditions analysis progressed splendidly. The patient understands every suggestion, he concentrates on the problems that the treatment requires him to solve, reminiscences and ideas flood his mind. The physician is surprised by the certainty and depth of these interpretations and notices with satisfaction how willingly the sick man receives the new psychological facts which are so hotly contested by the healthy persons in the world outside. An objective improvement in the condition of the patient, universally admitted, goes hand in hand with this harmonious relation of the physician to the patient under analysis.

But we cannot always expect to have fair weather. There comes a day when the storm breaks. Difficulties turn up in the treatment. The patient asserts that he can think of nothing more. We are under the impression that he is no longer interested in the work, that he lightly passes over the injunction that, heedless of any critical impulse, he must say everything that comes to his mind. He behaves as though he were not under treatment, as though he had closed no agreement with the physician; he is clearly obsessed by something he does not wish to divulge. This is a situation which endangers the success of the treatment. We are distinctly confronted with a tremendous resistance. What can have happened?

Provided we are able once more to clarify the situation, we recognize the cause of the disturbance to have been intense affectionate emotions, which the patient has transferred to the physician. This is certainly not justified either by the behavior of the physician or by the relations the treatment has created. The way in which this affection is manifested and the goals it strives for will depend on the personal affiliations of the two parties involved. When we have here a young girl and a man who is still young we receive the impression of normal love. We find it quite natural that a girl should fall in love with a man with whom she is alone a great deal, with whom she discusses intimate matters, who appears to her in the advantageous light of a beneficent adviser. In this we probably overlook the fact that in a neurotic girl we should rather presuppose a derangement in her capacity to love. The more the personal relations of physician and patient diverge from this hypothetical case, the more are we puzzled to find the same emotional relation over and over again. We can understand that a young woman, unhappy in her marriage, develops a serious passion for her physician, who is still free; that she is ready to seek divorce in order to belong to him, or even does not hesitate to enter into a secret love affair, in case the conventional obstacles loom too large. Similar things are known to occur outside of psychoanalysis. Under these circumstances, however, we are surprised to hear women and girls make remarks that reveal a certain attitude toward the problems of the cure. They always knew that love alone could cure them, and from the very beginning of their treatment they anticipated that this relationship would yield them what life had denied. This hope alone has spurred them on to exert themselves during the treatments, to overcome all the difficulties in communicating their disclosures. We add on our own account—"and to understand so easily everything that is generally most difficult to believe." But we are amazed by such a confession; it upsets our calculations completely. Can it be that we have omitted the most important factor from our hypothesis?

And really, the more experience we gain, the less we can deny this correction, which shames our knowledge. The first few times we could still believe that the analytic cure had met with an accidental interruption, not inherent to its purpose. But when this affectionate relation between physician and patient occurs regularly in every new case, under the most unfavorable conditions and even under grotesque circumstances; when it occurs in the case of the elderly woman, and is directed toward the grey-beard, or to one in whom, according to our judgment, no seductive attractions exist, we must abandon the idea of an accidental interruption, and realize that we are dealing with a phenomenon which is closely interwoven with the nature of the illness.

The new fact which we recognize unwillingly is termed *transference*. We mean a transference of emotions to the person of the physician, because we do not believe that the situation of the cure justifies the genesis of such feelings. We rather surmise that this readiness toward emotion originated elsewhere, that it was prepared within the patient, and that the opportunity given by analytic treatment caused it to be transferred to the person of the physician. Transference may occur as a stormy demand for love or in a more moderate form; in place of the desire to be his mistress, the young girl may wish to be adopted as the favored daughter of the old man, the libidinous desire may be toned down to a proposal of inseparable but ideal and platonic friendship. Some women understand how to sublimate the transference, how to modify it until it attains a kind of fitness for existence; others manifest it in its original, crude and generally impossible form. But fundamentally it is always the same and can never conceal that its origin is derived from the same source.

Before we ask ourselves how we can accommodate this new fact, we must first complete its description. What happens in the case of male patients? Here we might hope to escape the troublesome infusion of sex difference and sex attraction. But the answer is pretty much the same as with women patients. The same relation to the physician, the same over-estimation of his qualities, the same abandon of interest toward his affairs, the same jealousy toward all those who are close to him. The sublimated forms of transference are more frequent in men, the direct sexual demand is rarer to the extent to which manifest homosexuality retreats before the methods by which these instinct components may be utilized. In his male patients more often than in his women patients, the physician observes a manifestation of transference which at first sight seems to contradict everything previously described: a hostile or *negative* transference.

In the first place, let us realize that the transference occurs in the patient at the very outset of the treatment and is, for a time, the strongest impetus to work. We do not feel it and need not heed it as long as it acts to the advantage of the analysis we are working out together. When it turns into resistance, however, we must pay attention to it. Then we discover that two contrasting conditions have changed their relation to the treatment. In the first place there is the development of an affectionate inclination, clearly revealing the signs of its origin in sexual desire which becomes so strong as to awaken an inner resistance against it. Secondly, there are the hostile instead of the tender impulses. The hostile feelings generally appear later than the affectionate impulses or succeed them. When they occur simultaneously they exemplify the ambivalence of emotions which exists in most of the intimate relations between all persons. The hostile feelings connote an emotional attachment just as do the affectionate impulses, just as defiance signifies dependence as well as does obedience, although the activities they call out are opposed. We cannot doubt but that the hostile feelings toward the physician deserve the name of transference, since the situation which the treatment creates certainly could not give sufficient cause for their origin. This necessary interpretation of negative transference assures us that we have not mistaken the positive or affectionate emotions that we have similarly named.

The origin of this transference, the difficulties it causes us, the means of overcoming it, the use we finally extract from it—these matters must be dealt with in the technical instruction of psychoanalysis, and can only be touched upon here. It is out of the question to yield to those demands of the patient which take root from the transference, while it would be unkind to reject them brusquely or even indignantly. We overcome transference by proving to the patient that his feelings do not originate in the present situation, and are not intended for the person of the physician, but merely repeat what happened to him at some former time. In this way we force him to transform his repetition into a recollection. And so transference, which whether it be hostile or affectionate, seems in every case to be the greatest menace of the cure, really becomes its most effectual tool, which aids in opening the locked compartments of the psychic life. But I should like to tell you something which will help you to overcome the astonishment you must feel at this unexpected phenomenon. We must not forget that this illness of the patient which we have undertaken to analyze is not consummated or, as it were, congealed; rather it is something that continues its development like a living being. The beginning of the treatment does not end this development. When the cure, however, first has taken possession of the patient, the productivity of the illness in this new phase is concentrated entirely on one aspect: the relation of the patient to the physician. And so transference may be compared to the cambrium layer between the wood and the bark of a tree, from which the formation of new tissues and the growth of the trunk proceed at the same time. When the transference has once attained this significance the work upon the recollections of the patient recedes into the background. At that point it is correct to say that we are no longer concerned with the patient's former illness, but with a newly created, transformed neurosis, in place of the former. We followed up this new edition of an old condition from the very beginning, we saw it originate and grow; hence we understand it especially well, because we ourselves are the center of it, its object. All the symptoms of the patient have lost their original meaning and have adapted themselves to a new meaning, which is determined by its relation to transference. Or, only such symptoms as are capable of this transformation have persisted. The control of this new, artificial neurosis coincides with the removal of the illness for which treatment was sought in the first place, namely, with the solution of our therapeutic problem. The human being who, by means of his relations to the physician, has freed himself from the influences of suppressed impulses, becomes and stays free in his individual life, when the influence of the physician is subsequently removed.

Transference has attained extraordinary significance, has become the centre of the cure, in the conditions of hysteria, anxiety and compulsion neuroses. Their conditions therefore are properly included under the term transference neuroses. Whoever in his analytic experience has come into contact with the existence of transference can no longer doubt the character of those suppressed impulses that express themselves in the symptoms of these neuroses and requires no stronger proof of their libidinous character. We may say that our conviction that the meaning of the symptoms is substituted libidinous gratification was finally confirmed by this explanation of transference.

Now we have every reason to correct our former dynamic conception of the healing process, and to bring it into harmony with our new discernment. If the patient is to fight the normal conflict that our analysis has revealed against the suppressions, he requires a tremendous impetus to influence the desirable decision which will lead him back to health. Otherwise he might decide for a repetition of the former issue and allow those factors which have been admitted to consciousness to slip back again into suppression. The deciding vote in this conflict is not given by his intellectual penetration—which is neither strong nor free enough for such an achievement—but only by his relation to the physician. Inasmuch as his transference carries a positive sign, it invests the physician with authority and is converted into faith for his communications and conceptions. Without transference of this sort, or without a negative transfer, he would not even listen to the physician and to his arguments. Faith repeats the history of its own origin; it is a derivative of love and at first requires no arguments. When they are offered by a beloved person, arguments may later be admitted and subjected to critical reflection. Arguments without such support avail nothing, and never mean anything in life to most persons. Man's intellect is accessible only in so far as he is capable of libidinous occupation with an object, and accordingly we have good ground to recognize and to fear the limit of the patient's capacity for being influenced by even the best analytical technique, namely, the extent of his narcism.

The capacity for directing libidinous occupation with objects towards persons as well must also be accorded to all normal persons. The inclination to transference on the part of the neurotic we have mentioned, is only an extraordinary heightening of this common characteristic. It would be strange indeed if a human trait so wide-spread and significant had never been noticed and turned to account. But that has been done. Bernheim, with unerring perspicacity, based his theory of hypnotic manifestations on the statement that all persons are open to suggestion in some way or other. Suggestibility in his sense is nothing more than an inclination to transference, bounded so narrowly that there is no room for any negative transfer. But Bernheim could never define suggestion or its origin. For him it was a fundamental fact, and he could never tell us anything regarding its origin. He did not recognize the dependence of suggestibility upon sexuality and the activity of the libido. We, on the other hand, must realize that we have excluded hypnosis from our technique of neurosis only to rediscover suggestion in the shape of transference.

But now I shall pause and let you put in a word. I see that an objection is looming so large within you that if it were not voiced you would be unable to listen to me. "So at last you confess that like the hypnotists, you work with the aid of suggestion. That is what we have been thinking for a long time. But why choose the detour over reminiscences of the past, revealing of the unconscious, interpretation and retranslation of distortions, the tremendous expenditure of time and money, if the only efficacious thing is suggestion? Why do you not use suggestion directly against symptoms, as the others do, the honest hypnotists? And if, furthermore, you offer the excuse that by going your way you have made numerous psychological discoveries which are not revealed by direct suggestion, who shall vouch for their accuracy? Are not they, too, a result of suggestion, that is to say, of unintentional suggestion? Can you not, in this realm also, thrust upon the patient whatever you wish and whatever you think is so?"

Your objections are uncommonly interesting, and must be answered. But I cannot do it now for lack of time. Till the next time, then. You shall see, I shall be accountable to you. Today I shall only end what I have begun. I promised to explain, with the aid of the factor of transference, why our therapeutic efforts have not met with success in narcistic neuroses.

This I can do in a few words and you will see how simply the riddle can be solved, how well everything harmonizes. Observation shows that persons suffering from narcistic neuroses have no capacity for transference, or only insufficient remains of it. They reject the physician not with hostility, but with indifference. That is why he cannot influence them. His words leave them cold, make no impression, and so the mechanism of the healing process, which we are able to set in motion elsewhere, the renewal of the pathogenic conflict and the overcoming of the resistance to the suppression, cannot be reproduced in them. They remain as they are. Frequently they are known to attempt a cure on their own account, and pathological results have ensued. We are powerless before them.

On the basis of our clinical impressions of these patients, we asserted that in their case libidinous occupation with objects must have been abandoned, and object-libido must have been transformed into ego-libido. On the strength of this characteristic we had separated it from the first group of neurotics (hysteria, anxiety and compulsion neuroses). Their behavior under attempts at therapy confirms this supposition. They show no neurosis. They, therefore, are inaccessible to our efforts and we cannot cure them.

TWENTY-EIGHTH LECTURE. GENERAL THEORY OF THE NEUROSES

Analytical Therapy

YOU know our subject for today. You asked me why we do not make use of direct suggestion in psychoanalytic therapy, when we admit that our influence depends substantially upon transference, i.e., suggestion, for you have come to doubt whether or not we can answer for the objectivity of our psychological discoveries in the face of such a predominance of suggestion. I promised to give you a comprehensive answer.

Direct suggestion is suggestion directed against the expression of the symptoms, a struggle between your authority and the motives of the disease. You pay no attention during this process to the motives, but only demand of the patient that he suppress their expression in symptoms. So it makes no difference in principle whether you hypnotize the patient or not. Bernheim, with his usual perspicacity, asserted that suggestion is the essential phenomenon underlying hypnotism, that hypnotism itself is already a result of suggestion, is a suggested condition. Bernheim was especially fond of practising suggestion upon a person in the waking state, and could achieve the same results as with suggestion under hypnosis.

What shall I deal with first, the evidence of experience or theoretic considerations?

Let us begin with our experiences. I was a pupil of Bernheim's, whom I sought out in Nancy in 1889, and whose book on suggestion I translated into German. For years I practised hypnotic treatment, at first by means of prohibitory suggestions alone, and later by this method in combination with investigation of the patient after the manner of Breuer. So I can speak from experience about the results of hypnotic or suggestive therapy. If we judge Bernheim's method according to the old doctor's password that an ideal therapy must be rapid, reliable and not unpleasant for the patient, we find it fulfills at least two of these requirements. It can be carried out much more rapidly, indescribably more rapidly than the analytic method, and it brings the patient neither trouble nor discomfort. In the long run it becomes monotonous for the physician, since each case is exactly the same; continually forbidding the existence of the most diverse symptoms under the same ceremonial, without being able to grasp anything of their meaning or their significance. It is second-rate work, not scientific activity, and reminiscent of magic, conjuring and hocus-pocus; yet in the face of the interest of the patient this cannot be considered. The third requisite, however, was lacking. The procedure was in no way reliable. It might succeed in one case, and fail with the next; sometimes much was accomplished, at other times little, one knew not why. Worse than this capriciousness of the technique was the lack of permanency of the results. After a short time, when the patient was again heard from, the old malady had reappeared, or it had been replaced by a new malady. We could start in again to hypnotize. At the same time we had been warned by those who were experienced that by frequent repetitions of hypnotism we would deprive the patient of his self-reliance and accustom him to this therapy as though it were a narcotic. Granted that we did occasionally succeed as well as one could wish; with slight trouble we achieved complete and permanent results. But the conditions for such a favorable outcome remained unknown. I have had it happen that an aggravated condition which I had succeeded in clearing up completely by a short hypnotic treatment returned unchanged when the patient became angry and arbitrarily developed ill feeling against me. After a reconciliation I was able to remove the malady anew and with even greater thoroughness, yet when she became hostile to me a second time it returned again. Another time a patient whom I had repeatedly helped through nervous conditions by hypnosis, during the treatment of an especially stubborn attack, suddenly threw her arms around my neck. This made it necessary to consider the question, whether one wanted to or not, of the nature and source of the suggestive authority.

So much for experience. It shows us that in renouncing direct suggestion we have given up nothing that is not replaceable. Now let us add a few further considerations. The practice of hypnotic therapy demands only a slight amount of work of the patient as well as of the physician. This therapy fits in perfectly with the estimation of neuroses to which the majority of physicians subscribe. The physician says to the neurotic, "There is nothing the matter with you; you are only nervous, and so I can blow away all your difficulties with a few words in a few minutes." But it is contrary to our dynamic conceptions that we should be able to move a great weight by an inconsiderable force, by attacking it directly and without the aid of appropriate preparations. So far as conditions are comparable, experience shows us that this performance does not succeed with the neurotic. But I know this argument is not unassailable; there are also "redeeming features."

In the light of the knowledge we have gained from psychoanalysis we can describe the difference between hypnotic and psychoanalytic suggestion as follows: Hypnotic therapy seeks to hide something in psychic life, and to gloss it over; analytic therapy seeks to lay it bare and to remove it. The first method works cosmetically, the other surgically. The first uses suggestion in order to prevent the appearance of the symptoms, it strengthens suppression, but leaves unchanged all other processes that have led to symptom development. Analytic therapy attacks the illness closer to its sources, namely in the conflicts out of which the symptoms have emerged, it makes use of suggestion to change the solution of these conflicts. Hypnotic therapy leaves the patient inactive and unchanged, and therefore without resistance to every new occasion for disease. Analytic treatment places upon the physician, as well as upon the patient, a difficult responsibility; the inner resistance of the patient must be abolished. The psychic life of the patient is permanently changed by overcoming these resistances, it is lifted upon a higher plane of development and remains protected against new possibilities of disease. The work of overcoming resistance is the fundamental task of the analytic cure. The patient, however, must take it on himself to accomplish this, while the physician, with the aid of suggestion, makes it possible for him to do so. The suggestion works in the nature of an *education*. We are therefore justified in saying that analytic treatment is a sort of *after-education*.

I hope I have made it clear to you wherein our technique of using suggestion differs therapeutically from the only use possible in hypnotic therapy. With your knowledge of the relation between suggestion and transference you will readily understand the capriciousness of hypnotic therapy which attracted our attention, and you will see why, on the other hand, analytic suggestion can be relied upon to its limits. In hypnosis we depend on the condition of the patient's capacity for transference, yet we are unable to exert any influence on this capacity. The transference of the subject may be negative, or, as is most frequent, ambivalent; the patient may have protected himself against suggestion by very special adjustments, yet we are unable to learn anything concerning them. In psychoanalysis we work with the transference itself, we do away with the forces opposing it, prepare the instrument with which we are to work. So it becomes possible to derive entirely new uses from the power of suggestion; we are able to control it, the patient does not work himself into any state of mind he pleases, but in so far as we are able to influence him at all, we can guide the suggestion.

Now you will say, regardless of whether we call the driving force of our analysis transference or suggestion, there is still the danger that through our influence on the patient the objective certainty of our discoveries becomes doubtful. That which becomes a benefit to therapy works harm to the investigation. This objection is most often raised against psychoanalysis, and it must be admitted that even if it does not hit the mark, it cannot be waved aside as stupid. But if it were justified, psychoanalysis would be nothing more than an extraordinarily well disguised and especially workable kind of treatment by suggestion, and we may lay little weight upon all its assertions concerning the influences of life, psychic dynamics, and the unconscious. This is in fact the opinion held by our opponents; we are supposed especially to have "balked into" the patients everything that supports the importance of sexual experiences, and often the experiences themselves, after the combinations themselves have grown up in our degenerate imaginations. We can refute these attacks most easily by calling on the evidence of experience rather than by resorting to theory. Anyone who has himself performed a psychoanalysis has been able to convince himself innumerable times that it is impossible thus to suggest anything to the patient. There is no difficulty, of course, in making the patient a disciple of any one theory, and thus causing him to share the possible error of the physician. With respect to this he behaves just like any other person, like a student, but he has influenced only his intelligence, not his disease. The solving of his conflicts and the overcoming of his resistances succeeds only if we have aroused in him representations of such expectations as can agree with reality. What was inapplicable in the assumptions of the physician falls away during the course of the analysis; it must be withdrawn and replaced by something more nearly correct. By employing a careful technique we seek to prevent the occurrence of temporary results arising out of suggestion, yet there is no harm if such temporary results occur, for we are never satisfied with early successes. We do not consider the analysis finished until all the obscurities of the case are cleared up, all amnestic gaps filled out and the occasions which originally called out the suppressions discovered. We see in results that are achieved too quickly a hindrance rather than a furtherance of analytic work and repeatedly we undo these results again by purposely breaking up the transference upon which they rest. Fundamentally it is this feature which distinguishes analytical treatment from the purely suggestive technique and frees analytic results from the suspicion of having been suggested. Under every other suggestive treatment the transference itself is most carefully upheld and the influence left unquestioned; in analytic treatment, however, the transference becomes the subject of treatment and is subject to criticism in whatever form it may appear. At the end of an analytic cure the transference itself must be abolished; therefore the effect of the treatment, whether positive or negative, must be founded not upon suggestion but upon the overcoming of inner resistances, upon the inner change achieved in the patient, which the aid of suggestion has made possible.

Presumably the creation of the separate suggestions is counteracted, in the course of the cure, by our being continually forced to attack resistances which have the ability to change themselves into negative (hostile)

296

transferences. Furthermore, let me call your attention to the fact that a large number of results of analysis, otherwise perhaps subject to the suspicion that they are products of suggestion, can be confirmed from other unquestionable sources. As authoritative witnesses in this case we refer to the testimony of dements and paranoiacs, who are, naturally far removed from any suspicion of suggestive influence. Whatever these patients can tell us about symbolic translations and phantasies which have forced their way into their consciousness agrees faithfully with the results of our investigations upon the unconscious of transference-neurotics, and this gives added weight to the objective correctness of our interpretations which are so often doubted. I believe you will not go wrong if you give your confidence to analysis with reference to these factors.

We now want to complete our statement concerning the mechanism of healing, by including it within the formulae of the libido theory. The neurotic is incapable both of enjoyment and work; first, because his libido is not directed toward any real object, and second because he must use up a great deal of his former energy to keep his libido suppressed and to arm himself against its attacks. He would become well if there could be an end to the conflict between his ego and his libido, and if his ego could again have the libido at its disposal. The task of therapy, therefore, consists of freeing the libido from its present bonds, which have estranged it from the ego, and furthermore to bring it once more into the service of the ego. Where is the libido of the neurotics? It is easy to find; it is bound to the symptoms which at that time furnish it with the only available substitute satisfaction. We have to become master of the symptoms, and abolish them, which is of course exactly what the patient asks us to do. To abolish the symptoms it becomes necessary to go back to their origin, to renew the conflict out of which they emerged, but this time with the help of motive forces that were originally not available, to guide it toward a new solution. This revision of the process of suppression can be accomplished only in part by following the traces in memory of the occurrences which led to the suppression. The decisive part of the cure is accomplished by means of the relationship to the physician, the transference, by means of which new editions of the old conflict are created. Under this situation the patient would like to behave as he had behaved originally, but by summoning all his available psychic power we compel him to reach a different decision. Transference, then, becomes the battlefield on which all the contending forces are to meet.

The full strength of the libido, as well as the entire resistance against it, is concentrated in this relationship to the physician; so it is inevitable that the symptoms of the libido should be laid bare. In place of his original disturbance the patient manifests the artificially constructed disturbance of transference; in place of heterogeneous unreal objects for the libido you now have only the person of the physician, a single object, which, however, is also fantastic. The new struggle over this object is, however, raised to the highest psychic level with the aid of the physician's suggestions, and proceeds as a normal psychic conflict. By avoiding a new suppression the estrangement between the ego and the libido comes to an end, the psychic unity of the personality is restored. When the libido again becomes detached from the temporary object of the physician it cannot return to its former objects, but is now at the disposal of the ego. The forces we have overcome in the task of therapy are on the one hand the aversion of the ego for certain directions of the libido, which had expressed itself as a tendency to suppression, and on the other hand the tenacity of the libido, which is loathe to leave an object which it has once occupied.

Accordingly the work of therapy falls into two phases: first, all the libido is forced from the symptoms into the transference, and concentrated there; secondly, the struggle over this new object is carried on and the libido set free. The decisive change for the better in this renewed conflict is the throwing out of the suppression, so that the libido cannot this time again escape the ego by fleeing into the unconscious. This is accomplished by the change in the ego under the influence of the physician's suggestion. In the course of the work of interpretation, which translates unconscious into conscious, the ego grows at the expense of the unconscious; it learns forgiveness toward the libido, and becomes inclined to permit some sort of satisfaction for it. The ego's timidity in the face of the demands of the libido is now lessened by the prospect of occupying some of the libido through sublimation. The more the processes of the treatment correspond to this theoretic description the greater will be the success of psychoanalytic therapy. It is limited by the lack of mobility of the libido, which can stand in the way of releasing its objects, and by the obstinate narcism which will not permit the object-transference to effect more than just so much. Perhaps we shall obtain further light on the dynamics of the healing process by the remark that we are able to gather up the entire libido which has become withdrawn from the control of the ego by drawing a part of it to ourselves in the process of transference.

It is to be remembered that we cannot reach a direct conclusion as to the disposition of the libido during the disease from the distributions of the libido which are effected during and because of the treatment. Assuming that we have succeeded in curing the case by means of the creation and destruction of a strong father-transference to the physician, it would be wrong to conclude that the patient had previously suffered from a similar and unconscious attachment of his libido to his father. The father-transference is merely the battlefield upon which we were able to overcome the libido; the patient's libido had been concentrated here from its other positions. The battlefield need not necessarily have coincided with the most important fortresses of the enemy. Defense of the hostile capital need not take place before its very gates. Not until we have again destroyed the transference can we begin to reconstruct the distribution of the libido that existed during the illness.

From the standpoint of the libido theory we might say a last word in regard to the dream. The dreams of neurotics, as well as their errors and haphazard thoughts, help us in finding the meaning of the symptoms and in discovering the disposition of the libido. In the form of the wish fulfillment they show us what wish impulses have been suppressed, and to what objects the libido, withdrawn from the ego, has been attached. That is why interpretation of dreams plays a large role in psychoanalytic treatment, and is in many cases, for a long time, the most important means with which we work. We already know that the condition of sleep itself carries with it a certain abatement of suppressions. Because of this lessening of the pressure upon it, it becomes possible for the suppressed impulse to create in the dream a much clearer expression than the symptom can furnish during the day. So dream-study is the easiest approach to a knowledge of the libidinous suppressed unconscious which has been withdrawn from the ego.

Dreams of neurotics differ in no essential point from the dreams of normal persons; you might even say they cannot be distinguished. It would be unreasonable to explain the dreams of the nervous in any way which could not be applied to the dreams of the normal. So we must say the difference between neurosis and health applies only during the day, and does not continue in dream life. We find it necessary to attribute to the healthy numerous assumptions which have grown out of the connections between the dreams and the symptoms of the neurotic. We are not in a position to deny that even a healthy man possesses those factors in his psychic life which alone make possible the development of the dream and of the symptom as well. We must conclude, therefore, that the healthy have also made use of suppressions and are put to a certain amount of trouble to keep those impulses under control; the system of their unconscious, too, conceals impulses which are suppressed, yet are still possessed of energy, and *a part of their libido is also withdrawn from the control of their ego*. So the healthy man is virtually a neurotic, but dreams are apparently the only symptoms which he can manifest. Yet if we subject our waking hours to a more penetrating analysis we discover, of course, that they refute this appearance and that this seemingly healthy life is shot through with a number of trivial, practically unimportant symptom formations.

The difference between nervous health and neurosis is entirely a practical one which is determined by the available capacity for enjoyment and accomplishment retained by the individual. It varies presumably with the relative proportion of the energy totals which have remained free and those which have been bound by suppressions, and is quantitative rather than qualitative. I do not have to remind you that this conception is the theoretical basis for the certainty that neuroses can be cured, despite their foundation in constitutional disposition.

This is accordingly what we may make out of the identity between the dreams of the healthy and those of the neurotic for the definition of health. As regards the dream itself, we must note further that we cannot separate it from its relation to neurotic symptoms. We must recognize that it is not completely defined as a translation of thoughts into an archaic form of expression, that is, we must assume it discloses a disposition of libido and of object-occupations which have actually taken place.

We have about come to the end. Perhaps you are disappointed that I have dealt only with theory in this chapter on psychoanalytic therapy, and have said nothing concerning the conditions under which the cure is undertaken, or of the successes which it achieves. But I shall omit both. I shall omit the first because I had intended no practical training in the practice of psychoanalysis, and I shall neglect the second for numerous reasons. At the beginning of our talks I emphasized the fact that under favorable circumstances we attain results which can be favorably compared with the happiest achievements in the field of internal therapy, and, I may add, these results could not have been otherwise achieved. If I were to say more I might be suspected of wishing to drown the voices of disparagement, which have become so loud, by advertising our claims. We psychoanalysts have repeatedly been threatened by our medical colleagues, even in open congresses, that the eyes of the suffering public must be opened to the worthlessness of this method of treatment by a statistical collection of analytic failures and injuries. But such a collection, aside from the biased, denunciatory character of its purpose, would hardly be able to give a correct picture of the therapeutic values of analysis. Analytic therapy is, as you know, still young; it took a long time to establish the technique, and this could be done only during the course of the work and under the influence of accumulating experience. As a result of the difficulties of instruction the physician who begins the practice of psychoanalysis is more dependent upon his capacity to develop on his own account than is the ordinary specialist, and the results he achieves in his first years can never be taken as indicative of the possibilities of analytic therapy.

Many attempts at treatment failed in the early years of analysis because they were made on cases that were not at all suited to the procedure, and which today we exclude by our classification of symptoms. But this classification could be made only after practice. In the beginning we did not know that paranoia and dementia praecox are, in their fully developed phases, inaccessible, and we were justified in trying out our method on all kinds of conditions. Besides, the greatest number of failures in those first years were not due to the fault of the physician or because of unsuitable choice of subjects, but rather to the unpropitiousness of external conditions. We have hitherto spoken only of internal resistances, those of the patient, which are necessary and may be overcome. External resistances to psychoanalysis, due to the circumstances of the patient and his environment, have little theoretical interest, but are of great practical importance. Psychoanalytic treatment may be compared to a surgical operation, and has the right to be undertaken under circumstances favorable to its success. You know what precautions the surgeon is accustomed to take: a suitable room, good light, assistance, exclusion of relatives, etc. How many operations would be successful, do you think, if they had to be performed in the presence of all the members of the family, who would put their fingers into the field of operation and cry aloud at every cut of the knife? The interference of relatives in psychoanalytical treatment is a very great danger, a danger one does not know how to meet. We are armed against the internal resistances of the patient which we recognize as necessary, but how are we to protect ourselves against external resistance? It is impossible to approach the relatives of the patient with any sort of explanation, one cannot influence them to hold aloof from the whole affair, and one cannot get into league with them because we then run the danger of losing the confidence of the patient, who rightly demands that we in whom he confides take his part. Besides, those who know the rifts that are often formed in family life will not be surprised as analysts when they discover that the patient's nearest relatives are less interested in seeing him cured than in having him remain as he is. Where, as is so often the case, the neurosis is connected with conflicts with members of the family, the healthy member does not hesitate long in the choice between his own interest and that of the cure of the patient. It is not surprising if a husband looks with disfavor upon a treatment in which, as he may correctly suspect, the register of his sins is unrolled; nor are we surprised, and surely we cannot take the blame, when our efforts remain fruitless and are prematurely broken off because the resistance of the husband is added to that of the sick wife. We had only undertaken something which, under the existing circumstance, was impossible to carry out.

Instead of many cases, I shall tell you of just one in which, because of professional precautions, I was destined to play a sad role. Many years ago I treated a young girl who for a long time was afraid to go on the street, or to remain at home alone. The patient hesitatingly admitted that her phantasy had been caused by accidentally observing affectionate relations between her mother and a well-to-do friend of the family. But she was so clumsy—or perhaps so sly—as to give her mother a hint of what had been discussed during the analysis, and changed her behavior toward her mother, insisting that no one but her mother should protect her against the fear of being alone, and anxiously barring the way when her mother wished to leave the house. The mother had previously been very nervous herself, but had been cured years before in a hydropathic sanatorium. Let us say, in that institution she made the acquaintance of the man with whom she was to enter upon the relationship which was able to satisfy her in every respect. Becoming suspicious of the stormy demands of the girl, the mother *suddenly* realized the meaning of her daughter's fear. She must have made herself sick to imprison her mother and to rob her of the freedom she needed to maintain relations with her lover. Immediately the mother made an end to the harmful treatment. The girl was put into a sanatorium for the nervous and exhibited for many years as "a poor victim of psychoanalysis." For just as long a period I was pursued by evil slander, due to the unfavorable outcome of this case. I maintained silence because I thought myself bound by the rules of professional discretion. Years later I learned from a colleague who had visited the institution, and had seen the agoraphobic girl there, that the relationship between the mother and the wealthy friend of the family was known all over town, and apparently connived at by the husband and father. It was to this "secret" that our treatment had been sacrificed.

In the years before the war, when the influx of patients from all parts made me independent of the favor or disfavor of my native city, I followed the rule of not treating anyone who was not *sui juris*, was not independent of all other persons in his essential relations of life. Every psychoanalyst cannot do this. You may conclude from my warning against the relatives of patients that for purposes of psychoanalysis we should take the patients away from their families, and should limit this therapy to the inmates of sanatoriums. I should not agree with you in this; it is much more beneficial for the patients, if they are not in a stage of great exhaustion, to continue in the same circumstances under which they must master the tasks set for them during the treatment. But the relatives ought not to counteract this advantage by their behavior, and above all, they should not antagonize and oppose the endeavors of the physician. But how are we to contend against these influences which are so inaccessible to us! You see how much the prospects of a treatment are determined by the social surroundings and the cultural conditions of a family.

This offers a sad outlook indeed for the effectiveness of psychoanalysis as a therapy, even if we can explain the great majority of our failures by putting the blame on such disturbing external factors! Friends of analysis have advised us to counterbalance such a collection of failures by means of a statistical compilation on our part of our successful cases. Yet I could not try myself to do this. I tried to explain that statistics would be worthless if the collected cases were not comparable, and in fact, the various neuroses which we have undertaken to treat could, as a matter of fact, hardly be compared on the same basis, since they differed in many fundamental respects. Besides, the period of time over which we could report was too short to permit us to judge the permanency of our cures, and concerning certain cases we could not have given any information whatever. They related to persons who had kept their ailments, as well as their treatment, secret, and whose cure must necessarily be kept secret as well. The strongest hindrance, however, lay in the knowledge that men behave most irrationally in matters of therapy, and that we have no prospect of attaining anything by an appeal to reason. A therapeutic novelty is received either with frenzied enthusiasm, as was the case when Koch first made public his tuberculin against tuberculosis, or it is treated with abysmal distrust, as was the really blessed vaccination of Jenner, which even today retains implacable opponents. There was a very obvious prejudice against psychoanalysis. When we had cured a very difficult case we would hear it said: "That is no proof, he would have become well by himself in all this time." Yet when a patient who had already gone through four cycles of depression and mania came into my care during a temporary cessation in the melancholia, and three weeks later found herself in the beginnings of a new attack, all the members of the family as well as the high medical authorities called into consultation, were convinced that the new attack could only be the result of the attempted analysis. Against prejudice we are powerless; you see it again in the prejudices that one group of warring nations has developed against the other. The most sensible thing for us to do is to wait and allow time to wear it away. Some day the same persons think quite differently about the same things than before. Why they formerly thought otherwise remains the dark secret.

It may be possible that the prejudice against psychoanalysis is already on the wane. The continual spread of psychoanalytic doctrine, the increase of the number of physicians in many lands who treat analytically, seems to vouch for it. When I was a young physician I was caught in just such a storm of outraged feeling of the medical profession toward hypnosis, treatment by suggestion, which today is contrasted with psychoanalysis by "sober" men. Hypnotism did not, however, as a therapeutic agent, live up to its promises; we psychoanalysts may call ourselves its rightful heirs, and we have not forgotten the large amount of encouragement and theoretical explanation we owe to it. The injuries blamed upon psychoanalysis are limited essentially to temporary aggravation of the conflict when the analysis is clumsily handled, or when it is broken off unfinished. You have heard our justification for our form of treatment, and you can form your own opinion as to whether or not our endeavors are likely to lead to lasting injury. Misuse of psychoanalysis is possible in various ways; above all, transference is a dangerous remedy in the hands of an unconscientious physician. But no professional method of procedure is protected from misuse; a knife that is not sharp is of no use in effecting a cure.

I have thus reached the end, ladies and gentlemen. It is more than the customary formal speech when I admit that I am myself keenly depressed over the many faults in the lectures I have just delivered. First of all, I am sorry that I have so often promised to return to a subject only slightly touched upon at the time, and then found that the context has not made it possible to keep my word. I have undertaken to inform you concerning an unfinished thing, still in the process of development, and my brief exposition itself was an incomplete thing. Often I presented the evidence and then did not myself draw the conclusion. But I could not endeavor to make you masters of the subject. I tried only to give you some explanation and stimulation.

THE END

BOOK TWO
THREE CONTRIBUTIONS TO THE THEORY OF SEX

INTRODUCTION TO TRANSLATION

The somewhat famous "Three Essays," which Dr. Brill is here bringing to the attention of an English-reading public, occupy—brief as they are—an important position among the achievements of their author, a great investigator and pioneer in an important line. It is not claimed that the facts here gathered are altogether new. The subject of the sexual instinct and its aberrations has long been before the scientific world and the names of many effective toilers in this vast field are known to every student. When one passes beyond the strict domains of science and considers what is reported of the sexual life in folkways and art-lore and the history of primitive culture and in romance, the sources of information are immense. Freud has made considerable additions to this stock of knowledge, but he has done also something of far greater consequence than this. He has worked out, with incredible penetration, the part which this instinct plays in every phase of human life and in the development of human character, and has been able to establish on a firm footing the remarkable thesis that psychoneurotic illnesses never occur with a perfectly normal sexual life. Other sorts of emotions contribute to the result, but some aberration of the sexual life is always present, as the cause of especially insistent emotions and repressions.

The instincts with which every child is born furnish desires or cravings which must be dealt with in some fashion. They may be refined ("sublimated"), so far as is necessary and desirable, into energies of other sorts—as happens readily with the play-instinct—or they may remain as the source of perversions and inversions, and of cravings of new sorts substituted for those of the more primitive kinds under the pressure of a conventional civilization. The symptoms of the functional psychoneuroses represent, after a fashion, some of these distorted attempts to find a substitute for the imperative cravings born of the sexual instincts, and their form often depends, in part at least, on the peculiarities of the sexual life in infancy and early childhood. It is Freud's service to have investigated this inadequately chronicled period of existence with extraordinary acumen. In so doing he made it plain that the "perversions" and "inversions," which reappear later under such striking shapes, belong to the normal sexual life of the young child and are seen, in veiled forms, in almost every case of nervous illness.

It cannot too often be repeated that these discoveries represent no fanciful deductions, but are the outcome of rigidly careful observations which any one who will sufficiently prepare himself can verify. Critics fret over the amount of "sexuality" that Freud finds evidence of in the histories of his patients, and assume that he puts it there. But such criticisms are evidences of misunderstandings and proofs of ignorance.

Freud had learned that the amnesias of hypnosis and of hysteria were not absolute but relative and that in covering the lost memories, much more, of unexpected sort, was often found. Others, too, had gone as far as this, and stopped. But this investigator determined that nothing but the absolute impossibility of going further should make him cease from urging his patients into an inexorable scrutiny of the unconscious regions of their memories and thoughts, such as never had been made before. Every species of forgetfulness, even the forgetfulness of childhood's years, was made to yield its hidden stores of knowledge; dreams, even though apparently absurd, were found to be interpreters of a varied class of thoughts, active, although repressed as out of harmony with the selected life of consciousness; layer after layer, new sets of motives underlying motives were laid bare, and each patient's interest was strongly enlisted in the task of learning to know himself in order more truly and wisely to "sublimate" himself. Gradually other workers joined patiently in this laborious undertaking, which now stands, for those who have taken pains to comprehend it, as by far the most important movement in psychopathology.

It must, however, be recognized that these essays, of which Dr. Brill has given a translation that cannot but be timely, concern a subject which is not only important but unpopular. Few physicians read the works of v. Krafft-Ebing, Magnus Hirschfeld, Moll, and others of like sort. The remarkable volumes of Havelock Ellis were refused publication in his native England. The sentiments which inspired this hostile attitude towards the study of the sexual life are still active, though growing steadily less common. One may easily believe that if the facts which Freud's truth-seeking researches forced him to recognize and to publish had not been of an unpopular sort, his rich and abundant contributions to observational psychology, to the significance of dreams, to the etiology and therapeutics of the psychoneuroses, to the interpretation of mythology, would have won for him, by universal acclaim, the same recognition among all physicians that he has received from a rapidly increasing band of followers and colleagues.

May Dr. Brill's translation help toward this end.

There are two further points on which some comments should be made. The first is this, that those who conscientiously desire to learn all that they can from Freud's remarkable contributions should not be content to read any one of them alone. His various publications, such as "The Selected Papers on

Hysteria and Other Psychoneuroses," "The Interpretation of Dreams," "The Psychopathology of Everyday Life," "Wit and its Relation to the Unconscious," the analysis of the case of the little boy called Hans, the study of Leonardo da Vinci, and the various short essays in the four Sammlungen kleiner Schriften, not only all hang together, but supplement each other to a remarkable extent. Unless a course of study such as this is undertaken many critics may think various statements and inferences in this volume to be far fetched or find them too obscure for comprehension.

The other point is the following: One frequently hears the psychoanalytic method referred to as if it was customary for those practicing it to exploit the sexual experiences of their patients and nothing more, and the insistence on the details of the sexual life, presented in this book, is likely to emphasize that notion. But the fact is, as every thoughtful inquirer is aware, that the whole progress of civilization, whether in the individual or the race, consists largely in a "sublimation" of infantile instincts, and especially certain portions of the sexual instinct, to other ends than those which they seemed designed to serve. Art and poetry are fed on this fuel and the evolution of character and mental force is largely of the same origin. All the forms which this sublimation, or the abortive attempts at sublimation, may take in any given case, should come out in the course of a thorough psychoanalysis. It is not the sexual life alone, but every interest and every motive, that must be inquired into by the physician who is seeking to obtain all the data about the patient, necessary for his reeducation and his cure. But all the thoughts and emotions and desires and motives which appear in the man or woman of adult years were once crudely represented in the obscure instincts of the infant, and among these instincts those which were concerned directly or indirectly with the sexual emotions, in a wide sense, are certain to be found in every case to have been the most important for the end-result.

JAMES J. PUTNAM.

BOSTON, August 23, 1910.

AUTHOR'S PREFACE TO THE SECOND EDITION

Although the author is fully aware of the gaps and obscurities contained in this small volume, he has, nevertheless, resisted a temptation to add to it the results obtained from the investigations of the last five years, fearing that thus its unified and documentary character would be destroyed. He accordingly reproduces the original text with but slight modifications, contenting himself with the addition of a few footnotes. For the rest, it is his ardent wish that this book may speedily become antiquated—to the end that the new material brought forward in it may be universally accepted, while the shortcomings it displays may give place to juster views.

VIENNA, December, 1909.

AUTHOR'S PREFACE TO THE THIRD EDITION

After watching for ten years the reception accorded to this book and the effect it has produced, I wish to provide the third edition of it with some prefatory remarks dealing with the misunderstandings of the book and the demands, insusceptible of fulfillment, made against it. Let me emphasize in the first place that whatever is here presented is derived entirely from every-day medical experience which is to be made more profound and scientifically important through the results of psychoanalytic investigation. The "Three Contributions to the Theory of Sex" can contain nothing except what psychoanalysis obliges them to accept or what it succeeds in corroborating. It is therefore excluded that they should ever be developed into a "theory of sex," and it is also quite intelligible that they will assume no attitude at all towards some important problems of the sexual life. This should not however give the impression that these omitted chapters of the great theme were unfamiliar to the author, or that they were neglected by him as something of secondary importance.

The dependence of this work on the psychoanalytic experiences which have determined the writing of it, shows itself not only in the selection but also in the arrangement of the material. A certain succession of stages was observed, the occasional factors are rendered prominent, the constitutional ones are left in the background, and the ontogenetic development receives greater consideration than the phylogenetic. For the occasional factors play the principal rôle in analysis, and are almost completely worked up in it, while the constitutional factors only become evident from behind as elements which have been made functional through experience, and a discussion of these would lead far beyond the working sphere of psychoanalysis.

A similar connection determines the relation between ontogenesis and phylogenesis. Ontogenesis may be considered as a repetition of phylogenesis insofar as the latter has not been varied by a more recent experience. The phylogenetic disposition makes itself visible behind the ontogenetic process. But fundamentally the constitution is really the precipitate of a former experience of the species to which the newer experience of the individual being is added as the sum of the occasional factors.

Beside its thoroughgoing dependence on psychoanalytic investigation I must emphasize as a character of this work of mine its intentional independence of biological investigation. I have carefully avoided the inclusion of the results of scientific investigation in general sex biology or of particular species of animals in this study of human sexual functions which is made possible by the technique of psychoanalysis. My aim was indeed to find out how much of the biology of the sexual life of man can be discovered by means of psychological investigation; I was able to point to additions and agreements which resulted from this examination, but I did not have to become confused if the psychoanalytic methods led in some points to views and results which deviated considerably from those merely based on biology.

I have added many passages in this edition, but I have abstained from calling attention to them, as in former editions, by special marks. The scientific work in our sphere has at present been retarded in its progress, nevertheless some supplements to this work were indispensable if it was to remain in touch with our newer psychoanalytic literature.

VIENNA, October, 1914.

I. THE SEXUAL ABERRATIONS [16]

The fact of sexual need in man and animal is expressed in biology by the assumption of a "sexual impulse." This impulse is made analogous to the impulse of taking nourishment, and to hunger. The sexual expression

---

[16] The facts contained in the first "Contribution" have been gathered from the familiar publications of Krafft-Ebing, Moll, Moebius, Havelock Ellis, Schrenk-Notzing, Löwenfeld, Eulenberg, J. Bloch, and M. Hirschfeld, and from the later works published in the "Jahrbuch für sexuelle Zwischenstufen." As these publications also mention the other literature bearing on this subject I may forbear giving detailed references. The conclusions reached through the investigation of sexual inverts are all based on the reports of J. Sadger and on my own experience.

corresponding to hunger not being found colloquially, science uses the expression "libido."[17]

Popular conception makes definite assumptions concerning the nature and qualities of this sexual impulse. It is supposed to be absent during childhood and to commence about the time of and in connection with the maturing process of puberty; it is supposed that it manifests itself in irresistible attractions exerted by one sex upon the other, and that its aim is sexual union or at least such actions as would lead to union. But we have every reason to see in these assumptions a very untrustworthy picture of reality. On closer examination they are found to abound in errors, inaccuracies and hasty conclusions.

If we introduce two terms and call the person from whom the sexual attraction emanates the *sexual object*, and the action towards which the impulse strives the *sexual aim*, then the scientifically examined experience shows us many deviations in reference to both sexual object and sexual aim, the relations of which to the accepted standard require thorough investigation.

1. DEVIATION IN REFERENCE TO THE SEXUAL OBJECT

The popular theory of the sexual impulse corresponds closely to the poetic fable of dividing the person into two halves—man and woman—who strive to become reunited through love. It is therefore very surprising to hear that there are men for whom the sexual object is not woman but man, and that there are women for whom it is not man but woman. Such *persons* are called contrary sexuals, or better, inverts; the *condition*, that of inversion. The number of such individuals is considerable though difficult of accurate determination.[18]

A. Inversion

The Behavior of Inverts.—The above-mentioned persons behave in many ways quite differently.

(*a*) They are absolutely inverted; *i.e.*, their sexual object must be always of the same sex, while the opposite sex can never be to them an object of sexual longing, but leaves them indifferent or may even evoke sexual

---

[17] For general use the word "libido" is best translated by "craving." (Prof. James J. Putnam, Journal of Abnormal Psychology, Vol. IV, 6.)

[18] For the difficulties entailed in the attempt to ascertain the proportional number of inverts compare the work of M. Hirschfeld in the Jahrbuch für sexuelle Zwischenstufen, 1904. Cf. also Brill, The Conception of Homosexuality, Journal of the A.M.A., August 2, 1913.

repugnance. As men they are unable, on account of this repugnance, to perform the normal sexual act or miss all pleasure in its performance.

(b) They are amphigenously inverted (psychosexually hermaphroditic); i.e., their sexual object may belong indifferently to either the same or to the other sex. The inversion lacks the character of exclusiveness.

(c) They are occasionally inverted; i.e., under certain external conditions, chief among which are the inaccessibility of the normal sexual object and initiation, they are able to take as the sexual object a person of the same sex and thus find sexual gratification.

The inverted also manifest a manifold behavior in their judgment about the peculiarities of their sexual impulse. Some take the inversion as a matter of course, just as the normal person does regarding his libido, firmly demanding the same rights as the normal. Others, however, strive against the fact of their inversion and perceive in it a morbid compulsion.[19]

Other variations concern the relations of time. The characteristics of the inversion in any individual may date back as far as his memory goes, or they may become manifest to him at a definite period before or after puberty[20]The character is either retained throughout life, or it occasionally recedes or represents an episode on the road to normal development. A periodical fluctuation between the normal and the inverted sexual object has also been observed. Of special interest are those cases in which the libido changes, taking on the character of inversion after a painful experience with the normal sexual object.

These different categories of variation generally exist independently of one another. In the most extreme cases it can regularly be assumed that the inversion has existed at all times and that the person feels contented with his peculiar state.

Many authors will hesitate to gather into a unit all the cases enumerated here and will prefer to emphasize the differences rather than the common characters of these groups, a view which corresponds with their preferred judgment of inversions. But no matter what divisions may be set up, it cannot be overlooked that all transitions are abundantly met with, so that the formation of a series would seem to impose itself.

Conception of Inversion.—The first attention bestowed upon inversion gave rise to the conception that it was a congenital sign of nervous degeneration. This harmonized with the fact that doctors first met it among

---

[19] Such a striving against the compulsion to inversion favors cures by suggestion of psychoanalysis.

[20] Many have justly emphasized the fact that the autobiographic statements of inverts, as to the time of the appearance of their tendency to inversion, are untrustworthy as they may have repressed from memory any evidences of heterosexual feelings.

Psychoanalysis has confirmed this suspicion in all cases of inversion accessible, and has decidedly changed their anamnesis by filling up the infantile amnesias.

the nervous, or among persons giving such an impression. There are two elements which should be considered independently in this conception: the congenitality, and the degeneration.

Degeneration.—This term *degeneration* is open to the objections which may be urged against the promiscuous use of this word in general. It has in fact become customary to designate all morbid manifestations not of traumatic or infectious origin as degenerative. Indeed, Magnan's classification of degenerates makes it possible that the highest general configuration of nervous accomplishment need not exclude the application of the concept of degeneration. Under the circumstances, it is a question what use and what new content the judgment of "degeneration" still possesses. It would seem more appropriate not to speak of degeneration: (1) Where there are not many marked deviations from the normal; (2) where the capacity for working and living do not in general appear markedly impaired.[21]

That the inverted are not degenerates in this qualified sense can be seen from the following facts:

1. The inversion is found among persons who otherwise show no marked deviation from the normal.

2. It is found also among persons whose capabilities are not disturbed, who on the contrary are distinguished by especially high intellectual development and ethical culture.[22]

3. If one disregards the patients of one's own practice and strives to comprehend a wider field of experience, he will in two directions encounter facts which will prevent him from assuming inversions as a degenerative sign.

(*a*) It must be considered that inversion was a frequent manifestation among the ancient nations at the height of their culture. It was an institution endowed with important functions. (*b*) It is found to be unusually prevalent among savages and primitive races, whereas the term degeneration is generally limited to higher civilization (I. Bloch). Even among the most civilized nations of Europe, climate and race have a most powerful influence on the distribution of, and attitude toward, inversion.[23]

Innateness.—Only for the first and most extreme class of inverts, as can be imagined, has innateness been claimed, and this from their own assurance

---

[21] With what reserve the diagnosis of degeneration should be made and what slight practical significance can be attributed to it can be gathered from the discussions of Moebius (Ueber Entartung; Grenzfragen des Nerven- und Seelenlebens, No. III, 1900). He says: "If we review the wide sphere of degeneration upon which we have here turned some light we can conclude without further ado that it is really of little value to diagnose degeneration."

[22] We must agree with the spokesman of "Uranism" that some of the most prominent men known have been inverts and perhaps absolute inverts.

[23] In the conception of inversion the pathological features have been Separated from the anthropological. For this credit is due to I. Bloch (Beiträge zur Ätiologie der Psychopathia Sexualis, 2 Teile, 1902-3), who has also brought into prominence the existence of inversion in the old civilized nations.

that at no time in their life has their sexual impulse followed a different course. The fact of the existence of two other classes, especially of the third, is difficult to reconcile with the assumption of its being congenital. Hence, the propensity of those holding this view to separate the group of absolute inverts from the others results in the abandonment of the general conception of inversion. Accordingly in a number of cases the inversion would be of a congenital character, while in others it might originate from other causes.

In contradistinction to this conception is that which assumes inversion to be an *acquired* character of the sexual impulse. It is based on the following facts. (1) In many inverts (even absolute ones) an early affective sexual impression can be demonstrated, as a result of which the homosexual inclination developed. (2) In many others outer influences of a promoting and inhibiting nature can be demonstrated, which in earlier or later life led to a fixation of the inversion—among which are exclusive relations with the same sex, companionship in war, detention in prison, dangers of hetero-sexual intercourse, celibacy, sexual weakness, etc. (3) Hypnotic suggestion may remove the inversion, which would be surprising in that of a congenital character.

In view of all this, the existence of congenital inversion can certainly be questioned. The objection may be made to it that a more accurate examination of those claimed to be congenitally inverted will probably show that the direction of the libido was determined by a definite experience of early childhood, which has not been retained in the conscious memory of the person, but which can be brought back to memory by proper influences (Havelock Ellis). According to that author inversion can be designated only as a frequent variation of the sexual impulse which may be determined by a number of external circumstances of life.

The apparent certainty thus reached is, however, overthrown by the retort that manifestly there are many persons who have experienced even in their early youth those very sexual influences, such as seduction, mutual onanism, without becoming inverts, or without constantly remaining so. Hence, one is forced to assume that the alternatives congenital and acquired are either incomplete or do not cover the circumstances present in inversions.

Explanation of Inversion.—The nature of inversion is explained neither by the assumption that it is congenital nor that it is acquired. In the first case, we need to be told what there is in it of the congenital, unless we are satisfied with the roughest explanation, namely, that a person brings along a congenital sexual impulse connected with a definite sexual object. In the second case it is a question whether the manifold accidental influences suffice to explain the acquisition unless there is something in the individual to meet them half way. The negation of this last factor is inadmissible according to our former conclusions.

The Relation of Bisexuality.—Since the time of Frank Lydston, Kiernan, and Chevalier, a new series of ideas has been introduced for the explanation of the possibility of sexual inversion. This contains a new contradiction to the popular belief which assumes that a human being is either a man or a woman. Science shows cases in which the sexual characteristics appear blurred and thus the sexual distinction is made difficult, especially on an anatomical basis. The genitals of such persons unite the male and female characteristics (hermaphroditism). In rare cases both parts of the sexual apparatus are well developed (true hermaphroditism), but usually both are stunted.[24]

The importance of these abnormalities lies in the fact that they unexpectedly facilitate the understanding of the normal formation. A certain degree of anatomical hermaphroditism really belongs to the normal. In no normally formed male or female are traces of the apparatus of the other sex lacking; these either continue functionless as rudimentary organs, or they are transformed for the purpose of assuming other functions.

The conception which we gather from this long known anatomical fact is the original predisposition to bisexuality, which in the course of development has changed to monosexuality, leaving slight remnants of the stunted sex.

It was natural to transfer this conception to the psychic sphere and to conceive the inversion in its aberrations as an expression of psychic hermaphroditism. In order to bring the question to a decision, it was only necessary to have one other circumstance, viz., a regular concurrence of the inversion with the psychic and somatic signs of hermaphroditism.

But this second expectation was not realized. The relations between the assumed psychical and the demonstrable anatomical androgyny should never be conceived as being so close. There is frequently found in the inverted a diminution of the sexual impulse (H. Ellis) and a slight anatomical stunting of the organs. This, however, is found frequently but by no means regularly or preponderantly. Thus we must recognize that inversion and somatic hermaphroditism are totally independent of each other.

Great importance has also been attached to the so-called secondary and tertiary sex characters and their aggregate occurrence in the inverted has been emphasized (H. Ellis). There is much truth in this but it should not be forgotten that the secondary and tertiary sex characteristics very frequently manifest themselves in the other sex, thus indicating androgyny without, however, involving changes in the sexual object in the sense of an inversion.

Psychic hermaphroditism would gain in substantiality if parallel with the inversion of the sexual object there should be at least a change in the other

---

[24] Compare the last detailed discussion of somatic hermaphroditism (Taruffi, Hermaphroditismus und Zeugungsunfähigkeit, German edit. by R. Teuscher, 1903), and the works of Neugebauer in many volumes of the Jahrbuch für sexuelle Zwischenstufen.

psychic qualities, such as in the impulses and distinguishing traits characteristic of the other sex. But such inversion of character can be expected with some regularity only in inverted women; in men the most perfect psychic manliness may be united with the inversion. If one firmly adheres to the hypothesis of a psychic hermaphroditism, one must add that in certain spheres its manifestations allow the recognition of only a very slight contrary determination. The same also holds true in the somatic androgyny. According to Halban, the appearance of individual stunted organs and secondary sex characters are quite independent of each other.[25]

A spokesman of the masculine inverts stated the bisexual theory in its crudest form in the following words: "It is a female brain in a male body." But we do not know the characteristics of a "female brain." The substitution of the anatomical for the psychological is as frivolous as it is unjustified. The tentative explanation by v. Krafft-Ebing seems to be more precisely formulated than that of Ulrich but does not essentially differ from it. v. Krafft-Ebing thinks that the bisexual predisposition gives to the individual male and female brain centers as well as somatic sexual organs. These centers develop first towards puberty mostly under the influence of the independent sex glands. We can, however, say the same of the male and female "centers" as of the male and female brains; and, moreover, we do not even know whether we can assume for the sexual functions separate brain locations ("centers") such as we may assume for language.

After this discussion, two notions, at all events, persist; first, that a bisexual predisposition is to be presumed for the inversion also, only we do not know of what it consists beyond the anatomical formations; and, second, that we are dealing with disturbances which are experienced by the sexual impulse during its development.[26]

---

[25] J. Halban, "Die Entstehung der Geschlechtscharaktere," Arch. für Gynäkologie, Bd. 70, 1903. See also there the literature on the subject.

[26] According to a report in Vol. 6 of the Jahrbuch f. sexuelle Zwischenstufen, E. Gley is supposed to have been the first to mention bisexuality as an explanation of inversion. He published a paper (Les Abérrations de l'instinct Sexuel) in the Revue Philosophique as early as January, 1884. It is moreover noteworthy that the majority of authors who trace the inversion to bisexuality assume this factor not only for the inverts but also for those who have developed normally, and justly interpret the inversion as a result of a disturbance in development. Among these authors are Chevalier (Inversion Sexuelle, 1893), and v. Krafft-Ebing ("Zur Erklärung der konträren Sexualempfindung," Jahrbücher f. Psychiatrie u. Nervenheilkunde, XIII), who states that there are a number of observations "from which at least the virtual and continued existence of this second center (of the underlying sex) results." A Dr. Arduin (Die Frauenfrage und die sexuellen Zwischenstufen, 2d vol. of the Jahrbuch f. sexuelle Zwischenstufen, 1900) states that "in every man there exist male and female elements." See also the same Jahrbuch, Bd. I, 1899 ("Die objektive Diagnose der Homosexualitat," by M. Hirschfeld, pp. 8-9). In the determination of sex, as far as heterosexual persons are concerned, some are disproportionately more strongly developed than others. G. Herman is firm in his belief "that in every woman there are male, and in every man there are female germs and qualities" (Genesis, das Gesetz der Zeugung, 9 Bd., Libido und Manie, 1903). As recently as 1906 W. Fliess (Der Ablauf des Lebens) has claimed ownership of the idea of bisexuality (in the sense of double sex). Psychoanalytic investigation very strongly opposes the attempt to separate homosexuals from other persons as a group of a special nature. By also studying sexual excitations other than the manifestly open ones it

The Sexual Object of Inverts.—The theory of psychic hermaphroditism presupposed that the sexual object of the inverted is the reverse of the normal. The inverted man, like the woman, succumbs to the charms emanating from manly qualities of body and mind; he feels himself like a woman and seeks a man.

But however true this may be for a great number of inverts, it by no means indicates the general character of inversion. There is no doubt that a great part of the male inverted have retained the psychic character of virility, that proportionately they show but little of the secondary characters of the other sex, and that they really look for real feminine psychic features in their sexual object. If that were not so it would be incomprehensible why masculine prostitution, in offering itself to inverts, copies in all its exterior, to-day as in antiquity, the dress and attitudes of woman. This imitation would otherwise be an insult to the ideal of the inverts. Among the Greeks, where the most manly men were found among inverts, it is quite obvious that it was not the masculine character of the boy which kindled the love of man, but it was his physical resemblance to woman as well as his feminine psychic qualities, such as shyness, demureness, and the need of instruction and help. As soon as the boy himself became a man he ceased to be a sexual object for men and in turn became a lover of boys. The sexual object in this case as in many others is therefore not of the like sex, but it unites both sex characters, a compromise

---

discovers that all men are capable of homosexual object selection and actually accomplish this in the unconscious. Indeed the attachments of libidinous feelings to persons of the same sex play no small rôle as factors in normal psychic life, and as causative factors of disease they play a greater rôle than those belonging to the opposite sex. According to psychoanalysis, it rather seems that it is the independence of the object, selection of the sex of the object, the same free disposal over male and female objects, as observed in childhood, in primitive states and in prehistoric times, which forms the origin from which the normal as well as the inversion types developed, following restrictions in this or that direction. In the psychoanalytic sense the exclusive sexual interest of the man for the woman is also a problem requiring an explanation, and is not something that is self-evident and explainable on the basis of chemical attraction. The determination as to the definite sexual behavior does not occur until after puberty and is the result of a series of as yet not observable factors, some of which are of a constitutional, while some are of an accidental nature. Certainly some of these factors can turn out to be so enormous that by their character they influence the result. In general, however, the multiplicity of the determining factors is reflected by the manifoldness of the outcomes in the manifest sexual behavior of the person. In the inversion types it can be ascertained that they are altogether controlled by an archaic constitution and by primitive psychic mechanisms. The importance of the *narcissistic object selection* and the *clinging* to the erotic significance of the *anal* zone seem to be their most essential characteristics. But one gains nothing by separating the most extreme inversion types from the others on the basis of such constitutional peculiarities. What is found in the latter as seemingly an adequate determinant can also be demonstrated only in lesser force in the constitution of transitional types and in manifestly normal persons. The differences in the results may be of a qualitative nature, but analysis shows that the differences in the determinants are only quantitative. As a remarkable factor among the accidental influences of the object selection, we found the sexual rejection or the early sexual intimidation, and our attention was also called to the fact that the existence of both parents plays an important rôle in the child's life. The disappearance of a strong father in childhood not infrequently favors the inversion. Finally, one might demand that the inversion of the sexual object should notionally be strictly separated from the mixing of the sex characteristics in the subject. A certain amount of independence is unmistakable also in this relation.

316

between the impulses striving for the man and for the woman, but firmly conditioned by the masculinity of body (the genitals).[27]

The conditions in the woman are more definite; here the active inverts, with special frequency, show the somatic and psychic characters of man and desire femininity in their sexual object; though even here greater variation will be found on more intimate investigation.

The Sexual Aim of Inverts.—The important fact to bear in mind is that no uniformity of the sexual aim can be attributed to inversion. Intercourse per anum in men by no means goes with inversion; masturbation is just as frequently the exclusive aim; and the limitation of the sexual aim to mere effusion of feelings is here even more frequent than in hetero-sexual love. In women, too, the sexual aims of the inverted are manifold, among which contact with the mucous membrane of the mouth seems to be preferred.

Conclusion.—Though from the material on hand we are by no means in a position satisfactorily to explain the origin of inversion, we can say that through this investigation we have obtained an insight which can become of greater significance to us than the solution of the above problem. Our attention is called to the fact that we have assumed a too close connection between the sexual impulse and the sexual object. The experience gained from the so called abnormal cases teaches us that a connection exists between the sexual impulse and the sexual object which we are in danger of overlooking in the uniformity of normal states where the impulse seems to bring with it the object. We are thus instructed to separate this connection between the impulse and the object. The sexual impulse is probably entirely independent of its object and is not originated by the stimuli proceeding from the object.

B. The Sexually Immature and Animals as Sexual Objects

Whereas those sexual inverts whose sexual object does not belong to the normally adapted sex, appear to the observer as a collective number of perhaps otherwise normal individuals, the persons who choose for their sexual object the sexually immature (children) are apparently from the first

---

[27] Although psychoanalysis has not yet given us a full explanation for the origin of inversion, it has revealed the psychic mechanism of its genesis and has essentially enriched the problems in question. In all the cases examined we have ascertained that the later inverts go through in their childhood a phase of very intense but short-lived fixation on the woman (usually on the mother) and after overcoming it they identify themselves with the woman and take themselves as the sexual object; that is, proceeding on a narcissistic basis, they look for young men resembling themselves in persons whom they wish to love as their mother has loved them. We have, moreover, frequently found that alleged inverts are by no means indifferent to the charms of women, but the excitation evoked by the woman is always transferred to a male object. They thus repeat through life the mechanism which gave origin to their inversion. Their obsessive striving for the man proves to be determined by their restless flight from the woman.

sporadic aberrations. Only exceptionally are children the exclusive sexual objects. They are mostly drawn into this rôle by a faint-hearted and impotent individual who makes use of such substitutes, or when an impulsive urgent desire cannot at the time secure the proper object. Still it throws some light on the nature of the sexual impulse, that it should suffer such great variation and depreciation of its object, a thing which hunger, adhering more energetically to its object, would allow only in the most extreme cases. The same may be said of sexual relations with animals—a thing not at all rare among farmers—where the sexual attraction goes beyond the limits of the species.

For esthetic reasons one would fain attribute this and other excessive aberrations of the sexual impulse to the insane, but this cannot be done. Experience teaches that among the latter no disturbances of the sexual impulse can be found other than those observed among the sane, or among whole races and classes. Thus we find with gruesome frequency sexual abuse of children by teachers and servants merely because they have the best opportunities for it. The insane present the aforesaid aberration only in a somewhat intensified form; or what is of special significance is the fact that the aberration becomes exclusive and takes the place of the normal sexual gratification.

This very remarkable relation of sexual variations ranging from the normal to the insane gives material for reflection. It seems to me that the fact to be explained would show that the impulses of the sexual life belong to those which even normally are most poorly controlled by the higher psychic activities. He who is in any way psychically abnormal, be it in social or ethical conditions, is, according to my experience, regularly so in his sexual life. But many are abnormal in their sexual life who in every other respect correspond to the average; they have followed the human cultural development, but sexuality remained as their weak point.

As a general result of these discussions we come to see that, under numerous conditions and among a surprising number of individuals, the nature and value of the sexual object steps into the background. There is something else in the sexual impulse which is the essential and constant.[28]

---

[28] The most pronounced difference between the sexual life (Liebesleben) of antiquity and ours lies in the fact that the ancients placed the emphasis on the impulse itself, while we put it on its object. The ancients extolled the impulse and were ready to ennoble through it even an inferior object, while we disparage the activity of the impulse as such and only countenance it on account of the merits of the object.

2. DEVIATION IN REFERENCE TO THE SEXUAL AIM

The union of the genitals in the characteristic act of copulation is taken as the normal sexual aim. It serves to loosen the sexual tension and temporarily to quench the sexual desire (gratification analogous to satisfaction of hunger). Yet even in the most normal sexual process those additions are distinguishable, the development of which leads to the aberrations described as *perversions*. Thus certain intermediary relations to the sexual object connected with copulation, such as touching and looking, are recognized as preliminary to the sexual aim. These activities are on the one hand themselves connected with pleasure and on the other hand they enhance the excitement which persists until the definite sexual aim is reached. One definite kind of contiguity, consisting of mutual approximation of the mucous membranes of the lips in the form of a kiss, has received among the most civilized nations a sexual value, though the parts of the body concerned do not belong to the sexual apparatus but form the entrance to the digestive tract. This therefore supplies the factors which allow us to bring the perversions into relation with the normal sexual life, and which are available also for their classification. The perversions are either (*a*) anatomical *transgressions* of the bodily regions destined for sexual union, or (*b*) a *lingering* at the intermediary relations to the sexual object which should normally be rapidly passed on the way to the definite sexual aim.

(a) Anatomical Transgression

Overestimation of the Sexual Object.—The psychic estimation in which the sexual object as a goal of the sexual impulse shares is only in the rarest cases limited to the genitals; generally it embraces the whole body and tends to include all sensations emanating from the sexual object. The same overestimation spreads over the psychic sphere and manifests itself as a logical blinding (diminished judgment) in the face of the psychic attainments and perfections of the sexual object, as well as a blind obedience to the judgments issuing from the latter. The full faith of love thus becomes an important, if not the primordial source of authority.[29]

It is this sexual overvaluation, which so ill agrees with the restriction of the sexual aim to the union of the genitals only, that assists other parts of the

---

[29]: I must mention here that the blind obedience evinced by the hypnotized subject to the hypnotist causes me to think that the nature of hypnosis is to be found in the unconscious fixation of the libido on the person of the hypnotizer (by means of the masochistic component of the sexual impulse). Ferenczi connects this character of suggestibility with the "parent complex" (Jahrbuch für Psychoanalytische und psychopathologische Forschungen, I, 1909).

body to participate as sexual aims. [30] In the development of this most manifold anatomical overestimation there is an unmistakable desire towards variation, a thing denominated by Hoche as "excitement-hunger" (Reiz-hunger).[31]

Sexual Utilization of the Mucous Membrane of the Lips and Mouth.—The significance of the factor of sexual overestimation can be best studied in the man, in whom alone the sexual life is accessible to investigation, whereas in the woman it is veiled in impenetrable darkness, partly in consequence of cultural stunting and partly on account of the conventional reticence and dishonesty of women.

The employment of the mouth as a sexual organ is considered as a perversion if the lips (tongue) of the one are brought into contact with the genitals of the other, but not when the mucous membrane of the lips of both touch each other. In the latter exception we find the connection with the normal. He who abhors the former as perversions, though these since antiquity have been common practices among mankind, yields to a distinct *feeling of loathing* which protects him from adopting such sexual aims. The limit of such loathing is frequently purely conventional; he who kisses fervently the lips of a pretty girl will perhaps be able to use her tooth brush only with a sense of loathing, though there is no reason to assume that his own oral cavity for which he entertains no loathing is cleaner than that of the girl. Our attention is here called to the factor of loathing which stands in the way of the libidinous overestimation of the sexual aim, but which may in turn be vanquished by the libido. In the loathing we may observe one of the forces which have brought about the restrictions of the sexual aim. As a rule these forces halt at the genitals; there is, however, no doubt that even the genitals of the other sex themselves may be an object of loathing. Such behavior is characteristic of all hysterics, especially women. The force of the sexual impulse prefers to occupy itself with the overcoming of this loathing (see below).

Sexual Utilization of the Anal Opening.—It is even more obvious than in the former case that it is the loathing which stamps as a perversion the use of the anus as a sexual aim. But it should not be interpreted as espousing a cause when I observe that the basis of this loathing—namely, that this part of the body serves for the excretion and comes in contact with the loathsome excrement—is not more plausible than the basis which hysterical

---

[30] Moreover, it is to be noted that sexual overvaluation does not become pronounced in all mechanisms of object selection, and that we shall later learn to know another and more direct explanation for the sexual rôle of the other parts of the body.

[31] Further investigations lead to the conclusion that I. Bloch has overestimated the factor of excitement-hunger (Reizhunger). The various roads upon which the libido moves behave to each other from the very beginning like communicating pipes; the factor of collateral streaming must also be considered.

girls have for the disgust which they entertain for the male genital because it serves for urination.

The sexual rôle of the mucous membrane of the anus is by no means limited to intercourse between men; its preference has nothing characteristic of the inverted feeling. On the contrary, it seems that the *pedicatio* of the man owes its rôle to the analogy with the act in the woman, whereas among inverts it is mutual masturbation which is the most common sexual aim.

The Significance of Other Parts of the Body.—Sexual infringement on the other parts of the body, in all its variations, offers nothing new; it adds nothing to our knowledge of the sexual impulse which herein only announces its intention to dominate the sexual object in every way. Besides the sexual overvaluation, a second and generally unknown factor may be mentioned among the anatomical transgressions. Certain parts of the body, like the mucous membrane of the mouth and anus, which repeatedly appear in such practices, lay claim as it were to be considered and treated as genitals. We shall hear how this claim is justified by the development of the sexual impulse, and how it is fulfilled in the symptomatology of certain morbid conditions.

Unfit Substitutes for the Sexual Object. Fetichism.—We are especially impressed by those cases in which for the normal sexual object another is substituted which is related to it but which is totally unfit for the normal sexual aim. According to the scheme of the introduction we should have done better to mention this most interesting group of aberrations of the sexual impulse among the deviations in reference to the sexual object, but we have deferred mention of these until we became acquainted with the factor of sexual overestimation, upon which these manifestations, connected with the relinquishing of the sexual aim, depend.

The substitute for the sexual object is generally a part of the body but little adapted for sexual purposes, such as the foot, or hair, or an inanimate object which is in demonstrable relation with the sexual person, and preferably with the sexuality of the same (fragments of clothing, white underwear). This substitution is not unjustly compared with the fetich in which the savage sees the embodiment of his god.

The transition to the cases of fetichism, with a renunciation of a normal or of a perverted sexual aim, is formed by cases in which a fetichistic determination is demanded in the sexual object if the sexual aim is to be attained (definite color of hair, clothing, even physical blemishes). No other variation of the sexual impulse verging on the pathological claims our interest as much as this one, owing to the peculiarity occasioned by its manifestations. A certain diminution in the striving for the normal sexual aim may be presupposed in all these cases (executive weakness of the sexual apparatus).

[32]The connection with the normal is occasioned by the psychologically necessary overestimation of the sexual object, which inevitably encroaches upon everything associatively related to it (sexual object). A certain degree of such fetichism therefore regularly belong to the normal, especially during those stages of wooing when the normal sexual aim seems inaccessible or its realization deferred.

"Get me a handkerchief from her bosom—a garter of my love." —FAUST.

The case becomes pathological only when the striving for the fetich fixes itself beyond such determinations and takes the place of the normal sexual aim; or again, when the fetich disengages itself from the person concerned and itself becomes a sexual object. These are the general determinations for the transition of mere variations of the sexual impulse into pathological aberrations.

The persistent influence of a sexual impress mostly received in early childhood often shows itself in the selection of a fetich, as Binet first asserted, and as was later proven by many illustrations,—a thing which may be placed parallel to the proverbial attachment to a first love in the normal ("On revient toujours à ses premiers amours"). Such a connection is especially seen in cases with only fetichistic determinations of the sexual object. The significance of early sexual impressions will be met again in other places.

In other cases it was mostly a symbolic thought association, unconscious to the person concerned, which led to the replacing of the object by means of a fetich. The paths of these connections can not always be definitely demonstrated. The foot is a very primitive sexual symbol already found in myths.[33] Fur is used as a fetich probably on account of its association with the hairiness of the mons veneris. Such symbolism seems often to depend on sexual experiences in childhood.[34]

(b) Fixation of Precursory Sexual Aims

---

[32] This weakness corresponds to the constitutional predisposition. The early sexual intimidation which pushes the person away from the normal sexual aim and urges him to seek a substitute, has been demonstrated by psychoanalysis, as an accidental determinant.

[33] The shoe or slipper is accordingly a symbol for the female genitals.

[34] Psychoanalysis has filled up the gap in the understanding of fetichisms by showing that the selection of the fetich depends on a coprophilic smell-desire which has been lost by repression. Feet and hair are strong smelling objects which are raised to fetiches after the renouncing of the now unpleasant sensation of smell. Accordingly, only the filthy and ill-smelling foot is the sexual object in the perversion which corresponds to the foot fetichism. Another contribution to the explanation of the fetichistic preference of the foot is found in the Infantile Sexual Theories (see later). The foot replaces the penis which is so much missed in the woman. In some cases of foot fetichism it could be shown that the desire for looking originally directed to the genitals, which wished to reach its object from below, was stopped on the way by prohibition and repression, and therefore adhered to the foot or shoe as a fetich. In conformity with infantile expectation, the female genital was hereby imagined as a male genital.

The Appearance of New Intentions.—All the outer and inner determinations which impede or hold at a distance the attainment of the normal sexual aim, such as impotence, costliness of the sexual object, and dangers of the sexual act, will conceivably strengthen the inclination to linger at the preparatory acts and to form them into new sexual aims which may take the place of the normal. On closer investigation it is always seen that the ostensibly most peculiar of these new intentions have already been indicated in the normal sexual act.

Touching and Looking.—At least a certain amount of touching is indispensable for a person in order to attain the normal sexual aim. It is also generally known that the touching of the skin of the sexual object causes much pleasure and produces a supply of new excitement. Hence, the lingering at the touching can hardly be considered a perversion if the sexual act is proceeded with.

The same holds true in the end with looking which is analogous to touching. The manner in which the libidinous excitement is frequently awakened is by the optical impression, and selection takes account of this circumstance—if this teleological mode of thinking be permitted—by making the sexual object a thing of beauty. The covering of the body, which keeps abreast with civilization, serves to arouse sexual inquisitiveness, which always strives to restore for itself the sexual object by uncovering the hidden parts. This can be turned into the artistic ("sublimation") if the interest is turned from the genitals to the form of the body.[35] The tendency to linger at this intermediary sexual aim of the sexually accentuated looking is found to a certain degree in most normals; indeed it gives them the possibility of directing a certain amount of their libido to a higher artistic aim. On the other hand, the fondness for looking becomes a perversion (*a*) when it limits itself entirely to the genitals; (*b*) when it becomes connected with the overcoming of loathing (voyeurs and onlookers at the functions of excretion); and (*c*) when instead of preparing for the normal sexual aim it suppresses it. The latter, if I may draw conclusions from a single analysis, is in a most pronounced way true of exhibitionists, who expose their genitals so as in turn to bring to view the genitals of others.

In the perversion which consists in striving to look and be looked at we are confronted with a very remarkable character which will occupy us even more intensively in the following aberration. The sexual aim is here present in twofold formation, in an *active* and a *passive* form.

The force which is opposed to the peeping mania and through which it is eventually abolished is *shame* (like the former loathing).

---

[35] I have no doubt that the conception of the "beautiful" is rooted in the soil of sexual excitement and originally signified the sexual excitant. The more remarkable, therefore, is the fact that the genitals, the sight of which provokes the greatest sexual excitement, can really never be considered "beautiful."

Sadism and Masochism.—The desire to cause pain to the sexual object and its opposite, the most frequent and most significant of all perversions, was designated in its two forms by v. Krafft-Ebing as sadism or the active form, and masochism or the passive form. Other authors prefer the narrower term algolagnia which emphasizes the pleasure in pain and cruelty, whereas the terms selected by v. Krafft-Ebing place the pleasure secured in all kinds of humility and submission in the foreground.

The roots of active algolagnia, sadism, can be readily demonstrable in the normal. The sexuality of most men shows a taint of *aggression*, it is a propensity to subdue, the biological significance of which lies in the necessity of overcoming the resistance of the sexual object by actions other than mere *courting*. Sadism would then correspond to an aggressive component of the sexual impulse which has become independent and exaggerated and has been brought to the foreground by displacement.

The conception of sadism fluctuates in the usage of language from a mere active or impetuous attitude towards the sexual object to the exclusive attachment of the gratification to the subjection and maltreatment of the object. Strictly speaking only the last extreme case has a claim to the name of perversion.

Similarly, the designation of masochism comprises all passive attitude to the sexual life and to the sexual object; in its most extreme form the gratification is connected with suffering of physical or mental pain at the hands of the sexual object. Masochism as a perversion seems to be still more remote from the normal sexual life by forming a contrast to it; it may be doubted whether it ever appears as a primary form or whether it does not more regularly originate through transformation from sadism. It can often be recognized that the masochism is nothing but a continuation of the sadism turning against one's own person in which the latter at first takes the place of the sexual object. Analysis of extreme cases of masochistic perversions show that there is a cooperation of a large series of factors which exaggerate and fix the original passive sexual attitude (castration complex, conscience).

The pain which is here overcome ranks with the loathing and shame which were the resistances opposed to the libido.

Sadism and masochism occupy a special place among the perversions, for the contrast of activity and passivity lying at their bases belong to the common traits of the sexual life.

That cruelty and sexual impulse are most intimately connected is beyond doubt taught by the history of civilization, but in the explanation of this connection no one has gone beyond the accentuation of the aggressive factors of the libido. The aggression which is mixed with the sexual impulse is according to some authors a remnant of cannibalistic lust, a participation on the part of the domination apparatus (Bemächtigungsapparatus), which served also for the gratification of the great wants of the other, ontogenetically the older impulse.[36] It has also been claimed that every pain contains in itself the possibility of a pleasurable sensation. Let us be satisfied with the impression that the explanation of this perversion is by no means satisfactory and that it is possible that many psychic efforts unite themselves into one effect.

The most striking peculiarity of this perversion lies in the fact that its active and passive forms are regularly encountered together in the same person. He who experiences pleasure by causing pain to others in sexual relations is also able to experience the pain emanating from sexual relations as pleasure. A sadist is simultaneously a masochist, though either the active or the passive side of the perversion may be more strongly developed and thus represent his preponderate sexual activity.[37]

We thus see that certain perverted propensities regularly appear in *contrasting pairs*, a thing which, in view of the material to be produced later, must claim great theoretical value. It is furthermore clear that the existence of the contrast, sadism and masochism, can not readily be attributed to the mixture of aggression. On the other hand one may be tempted to connect such simultaneously existing contrasts with the united contrast of male and female in bisexuality, the significance of which is reduced in psychoanalysis to the contrast of activity and passivity.

3. GENERAL STATEMENTS
APPLICABLE TO ALL PERVERSIONS

Variation and Disease.—The physicians who at first studied the *perversions* in pronounced cases and under peculiar conditions were naturally inclined to attribute to them the character of a morbid or degenerative sign similar to the *inversions*. This view, however, is easier to refute in this than in the former case. Everyday experience has shown that most of these transgressions, at least the milder ones, are seldom wanting as components in the sexual life of normals who look upon them as upon other intimacies. Wherever the conditions are favorable such a perversion may for

---

[36] Cf. here the later communication on the pregenital phases of the sexual development, in which this view is confirmed. See below, "Ambivalence."

[37] Instead of substantiating this statement by many examples I will merely cite Havelock Ellis (The Sexual Impulse, 1903): "All known cases of sadism and masochism, even those cited by v. Krafft-Ebing, always show (as has already been shown by Colin, Scott, and Féré) traces of both groups of manifestations in the same individual."

a long time be substituted by a normal person for the normal sexual aim or it may be placed near it. In no normal person does the normal sexual aim lack some designable perverse element, and this universality suffices in itself to prove the inexpediency of an opprobrious application of the name perversion. In the realm of the sexual life one is sure to meet with exceptional difficulties which are at present really unsolvable, if one wishes to draw a sharp line between the mere variations within physiological limits and morbid symptoms.

Nevertheless, the quality of the new sexual aim in some of these perversions is such as to require special notice. Some of the perversions are in content so distant from the normal that we cannot help calling them "morbid," especially those in which the sexual impulse, in overcoming the resistances (shame, loathing, fear, and pain) has brought about surprising results (licking of feces and violation of cadavers). Yet even in these cases one ought not to feel certain of regularly finding among the perpetrators persons of pronounced abnormalities or insane minds. We can not lose sight of the fact that persons who otherwise behave normally are recorded as sick in the realm of the sexual life where they are dominated by the most unbridled of all impulses. On the other hand, a manifest abnormality in any other relation in life generally shows an undercurrent of abnormal sexual behavior.

In the majority of cases we are able to find the morbid character of the perversion not in the content of the new sexual aim but in its relation to the normal. It is morbid if the perversion does not appear beside the normal (sexual aim and sexual object), where favorable circumstances promote it and unfavorable impede the normal, or if it has under all circumstances repressed and supplanted the normal; *the exclusiveness* and *fixation* of the perversion justifies us in considering it a morbid symptom.

The Psychic Participation in the Perversions.— Perhaps it is precisely in the most abominable perversions that we must recognize the most prolific psychic participation for the transformation of the sexual impulse. In these cases a piece of psychic work has been accomplished in which, in spite of its gruesome success, the value of an idealization of the impulse can not be disputed. The omnipotence of love nowhere perhaps shows itself stronger than in this one of her aberrations. The highest and the lowest everywhere in sexuality hang most intimately together. ("From heaven through the world to hell.")

Two Results.—In the study of perversions we have gained an insight into the fact that the sexual impulse has to struggle against certain psychic forces, resistances, among which shame and loathing are most prominent. We may presume that these forces are employed to confine the impulse within the accepted normal limits, and if they have become developed in the individual before the sexual impulse has attained its full strength, it is really they which have directed it in the course of development.[38]

We have furthermore remarked that some of the examined perversions can be comprehended only by assuming the union of many motives. If they are amenable to analysis—disintegration—they must be of a composite nature. This may give us a hint that the sexual impulse itself may not be something simple, that it may on the contrary be composed of many components which detach themselves to form perversions. Our clinical observation thus calls our attention to *fusions* which have lost their expression in the uniform normal behavior.

4. THE SEXUAL IMPULSE IN NEUROTICS

Psychoanalysis.—A proper contribution to the knowledge of the sexual impulse in persons who are at least related to the normal can be gained only from one source, and is accessible only by one definite path. There is only one way to obtain a thorough and unerring solution of problems in the sexual life of so-called psychoneurotics (hysteria, obsessions, the wrongly-named neurasthenia, and surely also dementia præcox, and paranoia), and that is by subjecting them to the psychoanalytic investigations propounded by J. Breuer and myself in 1893, which we called the "cathartic" treatment.

I must repeat what I have said in my published work, that these psychoneuroses, as far as my experience goes, are based on sexual motive powers. I do not mean that the energy of the sexual impulse merely contributes to the forces supporting the morbid manifestations (symptoms), but I wish distinctly to maintain that this supplies the only constant and the most important source of energy in the neurosis, so that the sexual life of such persons manifests itself either exclusively, preponderately, or partially in these symptoms. As I have already stated in different places, the symptoms are the sexual activities of the patient. The proof for this assertion I have obtained from the psychoanalysis of hysterics and other neurotics during a period of twenty years, the results of which I hope to give later in a detailed account.

---

[38] On the other hand the restricting forces of the sexual evolution—disgust, shame, morality—must also be looked upon as historic precipitates of the outer inhibitions which the sexual impulse experienced in the psychogenesis of humanity. One can observe that they appear in their time during the development of the individual almost spontaneously at the call of education and influence.

Psychoanalysis removes the symptoms of hysteria on the supposition that they are the substitutes—the transcriptions as it were—for a series of emotionally accentuated psychic processes, wishes, and desires, to which a passage for their discharge through the conscious psychic activities has been cut off by a special process (repression). These thought formations which are restrained in the state of the unconscious strive for expression, that is, for *discharge*, in conformity to their affective value, and find such in hysteria through a process of *conversion* into somatic phenomena—the hysterical symptoms. If, *lege artis*, and with the aid of a special technique, retrogressive transformations of the symptoms into the affectful and conscious thoughts can be effected, it then becomes possible to get the most accurate information about the nature and origin of these previously unconscious psychic formations.

Results of Psychoanalysis.—In this manner it has been discovered that the symptoms represent the equivalent for the strivings which received their strength from the source of the sexual impulse. This fully concurs with what we know of the character of hysterics, which we have taken as models for all psycho-neurotics, before they have become diseased, and with what we know concerning the causes of the disease. The hysterical character evinces a part of sexual repression which reaches beyond the normal limits, an exaggeration of the resistances against the sexual impulse which we know as shame and loathing. It is an instinctive flight from intellectual occupation with the sexual problem, the consequence of which in pronounced cases is a complete sexual ignorance, which is preserved till the age of sexual maturity is attained.[39]

This feature, so characteristic of hysteria, is not seldom concealed in crude observation by the existence of the second constitutional factor of hysteria, namely, the enormous development of the sexual craving. But the psychological analysis will always reveal it and solves the very contradictory enigma of hysteria by proving the existence of the contrasting pair, an immense sexual desire and a very exaggerated sexual rejection.

The provocation of the disease in hysterically predisposed persons is brought about if in consequence of their progressive maturity or external conditions of life they are earnestly confronted with the real sexual demand. Between the pressure of the craving and the opposition of the sexual rejection an outlet for the disease results, which does not remove the conflict but seeks to elude it by transforming the libidinous strivings into symptoms. It is an exception only in appearance if a hysterical person, say a man, becomes subject to some banal emotional disturbance, to a conflict in the center of which there is no sexual interest. Psychoanalysis will regularly show that it is

---

[39] Studien über Hysterie, 1895, J. Breuer tells of the patient on whom he first practiced the cathartic method: "The sexual factor was surprisingly undeveloped."

the sexual components of the conflict which make the disease possible by withdrawing the psychic processes from normal adjustment.

Neurosis and Perversion.—A great part of the opposition to my assertion is explained by the fact that the sexuality from which I deduce the psychoneurotic symptoms is thought of as coincident with the normal sexual impulse. But psychoanalysis teaches us better than this. It shows that the symptoms do not by any means result at the expense only of the so called normal sexual impulse (at least not exclusively or preponderately), but they represent the converted expression of impulses which in a broader sense might be designated as *perverse* if they could manifest themselves directly in phantasies and acts without deviating from consciousness. The symptoms are therefore partially formed at the cost of abnormal sexuality. *The neurosis is, so to say, the negative of the perversion.*[40]

The sexual impulse of the psychoneurotic shows all the aberrations which we have studied as variations of the normal and as manifestations of morbid sexual life.

(*a*) In all the neurotics without exception we find feelings of inversion in the unconscious psychic life, fixation of libido on persons of the same sex. It is impossible, without a deep and searching discussion, adequately to appreciate the significance of this factor for the formation of the picture of the disease; I can only assert that the unconscious propensity to inversion is never wanting and is particularly of immense service in explaining male hysteria.[41]

(*b*) All the inclinations to anatomical transgression can be demonstrated in psychoneurotics in the unconscious and as symptom-creators. Of special frequency and intensity are those which impart to the mouth and the mucous membrane of the anus the rôle of genitals.

(*c*) The partial desires which usually appear in contrasting pairs play a very prominent rôle among the symptom-creators in the psychoneuroses. We have learned to know them as carriers of new sexual aims, such as peeping mania, exhibitionism, and the actively and passively formed impulses of cruelty. The contribution of the last is indispensable for the understanding of the morbid nature of the symptoms; it almost regularly controls some portion of the social behavior of the patient. The transformation of love into hatred, of tenderness into hostility, which is characteristic of a large number of

---

[40] The well-known fancies of perverts which under favorable conditions are changed into contrivances, the delusional fears of paranoiacs which are in a hostile manner projected on others, and the unconscious fancies of hysterics which are discovered in their symptoms by psychoanalysis, agree as to content in the minutest details.

[41] A psychoneurosis very often associates itself with a manifest inversion in which the heterosexual feeling becomes subjected to complete repression.—It is but just to state that the necessity of a general recognition of the tendency to inversion in psychoneurotics was first imparted to me personally by Wilh. Fliess, of Berlin, after I had myself discovered it in some cases.

neurotic cases and apparently of all cases of paranoia, takes place by means of the union of cruelty with the libido.

The interest in these deductions will be more heightened by certain peculiarities of the diagnosis of facts.

α. There is nothing in the unconscious streams of thought of the neuroses which would correspond to an inclination towards fetichism; a circumstance which throws light on the psychological peculiarity of this well understood perversion.

β. Wherever any such impulse is found in the unconscious which can be paired with a contrasting one, it can regularly be demonstrated that the latter, too, is effective. Every active perversion is here accompanied by its passive counterpart. He who in the unconscious is an exhibitionist is at the same time a voyeur, he who suffers from sadistic feelings as a result of repression will also show another reinforcement of the symptoms from the source of masochistic tendencies. The perfect concurrence with the behavior of the corresponding positive perversions is certainly very noteworthy. In the picture of the disease, however, the preponderant rôle is played by either one or the other of the opposing tendencies.

γ. In a pronounced case of psychoneurosis we seldom find the development of one single perverted impulse; usually there are many and regularly there are traces of all perversions. The individual impulse, however, on account of its intensity, is independent of the development of the others, but the study of the positive perversions gives us the accurate counterpart to it.

PARTIAL IMPULSES AND EROGENOUS ZONES

Keeping in mind what we have learned from the examination of the positive and negative perversions, it becomes quite obvious that they can be referred to a number of "partial impulses," which are not, however, primary but are subject to further analysis. By an "impulse" we can understand in the first place nothing but the psychic representative of a continually flowing internal somatic source of excitement, in contradistinction to the "stimulus" which is produced by isolated excitements coming from without. The impulse is thus one of the concepts marking the limits between the psychic and the physical. The simplest and most obvious assumption concerning the nature of the impulses would be that in themselves they possess no quality but are only taken into account as a measure of the demand for effort in the psychic life. What distinguishes the impulses from one another and furnishes them with specific attributes is their relation to their somatic *sources* and to their *aims*. The source of the impulse is an exciting process in an organ, and the immediate aim of the impulse lies in the elimination of this organic stimulus.

Another preliminary assumption in the theory of the impulse which we cannot relinquish, states that the bodily organs furnish two kinds of excitements which are determined by differences of a chemical nature. One of these forms of excitement we designate as the specifically sexual and the concerned organ as the *erogenous zone*, while the sexual element emanating from it is the partial impulse. (It is not easy to justify here this assumption which was taken from a definite class of neurotic diseases. On the other hand, it would be impossible to assert anything definite concerning the impulses if one did not take the trouble of mentioning these presuppositions.)

In the perversions which claim sexual significance for the oral cavity and the anal opening the part played by the erogenous zone is quite obvious. It behaves in every way like a part of the sexual apparatus. In hysteria these parts of the body, as well as the tracts of mucous membrane proceeding from them, become the seat of new sensations and innervating changes in a manner similar to the real genitals when under the excitement of normal sexual processes.

The significance of the erogenous zones in the psychoneuroses, as additional apparatus and substitutes for the genitals, appears to be most prominent in hysteria though that does not signify that it is of lesser validity in the other morbid forms. It is not so recognizable in compulsion neurosis and paranoia because here the symptom formation takes place in regions of the psychic apparatus which lie at a great distance from the central locations for bodily control. The more remarkable thing in the compulsion neurosis is the significance of the impulses which create new sexual aims and appear independently of the erogenous zones. Nevertheless, the eye corresponds to an erogenous zone in the looking and exhibition mania, while the skin takes on the same part in the pain and cruelty components of the sexual impulse. The skin, which in special parts of the body becomes differentiated as sensory organs and modified by the mucous membrane, is the erogenous zone, κατ ex ogen. (One should here think of Moll's assertion, who divides the sexual impulse into the impulses of contrectation and detumescence. Contrectation signifies a desire to touch the skin.)

EXPLANATION OF THE MANIFEST PREPONDERANCE OF SEXUAL

PERVERSIONS IN THE
PSYCHONEUROSES

The sexuality of psychoneurotics has perhaps been placed in a false light by the above discussions. It appears that the sexual behavior of the psychoneurotic approaches in predisposition to the pervert and deviates by just so much from the normal. Nevertheless, it is very possible that the constitutional disposition of these patients besides containing an immense amount of sexual repression and a predominant force of sexual impulse also possesses an unusual tendency to perversions in the broadest sense. However, an examination of milder cases shows that the last assumption is not an absolute requisite, or at least that in pronouncing judgment on the morbid effects one ought to discount the effect of one of the factors. In most psychoneurotics the disease first appears after puberty following the demands of the normal sexual life. Against these the repression above all directs itself. Or the disease comes on later, owing to the fact that the libido is unable to attain normal sexual gratification. In both cases the libido behaves like a stream the principal bed of which is dammed; it fills the collateral roads which until now perhaps have been empty. Thus the manifestly great (though to be sure negative) tendency to perversion in psychoneurotics may be collaterally conditioned; at any rate, it is certainly collaterally increased. The fact of the matter is that the sexual repression has to be added as an inner factor to such external ones as restriction of freedom, inaccessibility to the normal sexual object, dangers of the normal sexual act, etc., which cause the origin of perversions in individuals who might have otherwise remained normal.

In individual cases of neurosis the behavior may be different; now the congenital force of the tendency to perversion may be more decisive and at other times more influence may be exerted by the collateral increase of the same through the deviation of the libido from the normal sexual aim and object. It would be unjust to construe a contrast where a cooperation exists. The greatest results will always be brought about by a neurosis if constitution and experience cooperate in the same direction. A pronounced constitution may perhaps be able to dispense with the assistance of daily impressions, while a profound disturbance in life may perhaps bring on a neurosis even in an average constitution. These views similarly hold true in the etiological significance of the congenital and the accidental experiences in other spheres.

If, however, preference is given to the assumption that an especially formed tendency to perversions is characteristic of the psychoneurotic constitution, there is a prospect of being able to distinguish a multiformity of such constitutions in accordance with the congenital preponderance of this or that erogenous zone, or of this or that partial impulse. Whether there is a special relationship between the predisposition to perversions and the selection of the morbid picture has not, like many other things in this realm, been investigated.

REFERENCE TO THE INFANTILISM OF SEXUALITY

By demonstrating the perverted feelings as symptomatic formations in psychoneurotics, we have enormously increased the number of persons who can be added to the perverts. This is not only because neurotics represent a very large proportion of humanity, but we must consider also that the neuroses in all their gradations run in an uninterrupted series to the normal state. Moebius was quite justified in saying that we are all somewhat hysterical. Hence, the very wide dissemination of perversions urged us to assume that the predisposition to perversions is no rare peculiarity but must form a part of the normally accepted constitution.

We have heard that it is a question whether perversions should be referred to congenital determinations or whether they originate from accidental experiences, just as Binet showed in fetichisms. Now we are forced to the conclusion that there is indeed something congenital at the basis of perversions, but it is something *which is congenital in all persons*, which as a predisposition may fluctuate in intensity and is brought into prominence by influences of life. We deal here with congenital roots in the constitution of the sexual impulse which in one series of cases develop into real carriers of sexual activity (perverts); while in other cases they undergo an insufficient suppression (repression), so that as morbid symptoms they are enabled to attract to themselves in a round-about way a considerable part of the sexual energy; while again in favorable cases between the two extremes they originate the normal sexual life through effective restrictions and other elaborations. But we must also remember that the assumed constitution which shows the roots of all perversions will be demonstrable only in the child, though all impulses can be manifested in it only in moderate intensity. If we are led to suppose that neurotics conserve the infantile state of their sexuality or return to it, our interest must then turn to the sexual life of the child, and we will then follow the play of influences which control the processes of development of the infantile sexuality up to its termination in a perversion, a neurosis or a normal sexual life.

II. THE INFANTILE SEXUALITY

It is a part of popular belief about the sexual impulse that it is absent in childhood and that it first appears in the period of life known as puberty. This, though a common error, is serious in its consequences and is chiefly due to our present ignorance of the fundamental principles of the sexual life. A comprehensive study of the sexual manifestations of childhood would probably reveal to us the existence of the essential features of the sexual impulse, and would make us acquainted with its development and its composition from various sources.

The Neglect of the Infantile.—It is remarkable that those writers who endeavor to explain the qualities and reactions of the adult individual have given so much more attention to the ancestral period than to the period of the individual's own existence—that is, they have attributed more influence to heredity than to childhood. As a matter of fact, it might well be supposed that the influence of the latter period would be easier to understand, and that it would be entitled to more consideration than heredity.[42] To be sure, one occasionally finds in medical literature notes on the premature sexual activities of small children, about erections and masturbation and even actions resembling coitus, but these are referred to merely as exceptional occurrences, as curiosities, or as deterring examples of premature perversity. No author has to my knowledge recognized the normality of the sexual impulse in childhood, and in the numerous writings on the development of the child the chapter on "Sexual Development" is usually passed over.[43]

Infantile Amnesia.—This remarkable negligence is due partly to conventional considerations, which influence the writers on account of their own bringing up, and partly to a psychic phenomenon which has thus far

---

[42] This assertion on revision seemed even to myself so bold that I decided to test its correctness by again reviewing the literature. The result of this second review did not warrant any change in my original statement. The scientific elaboration of the physical as well as the psychic phenomena of the infantile sexuality is still in its initial stages. One author (S. Bell, "A Preliminary Study of the Emotions of Love Between the Sexes," American Journal of Psychology, XIII, 1902) says: "I know of no scientist who has given a careful analysis of the emotion as it is seen in the adolescent." The only attention given to somatic sexual manifestations occurring before the age of puberty was in connection with degenerative manifestations, and these were referred to as a sign of degeneration. A chapter on the sexual life of children is not to be found in all the representative psychologies of this age which I have read. Among these works I can mention the following: Preyer; Baldwin (The Development of the Mind in the Child and in the Race, 1898); Pérez (L'enfant de 3-7 ans, 1894); Strümpel (Die pädagogische Pathologie, 1899); Karl Groos (Das Seelenleben des Kindes, 1904); Th. Heller (Grundriss der Heilpädagogic, 1904); Sully (Observations Concerning Childhood, 1897). The best impression of the present situation of this sphere can be obtained from the journal Die Kinderfehler (issued since 1896). On the other hand one gains the impression that the existence of love in childhood is in no need of demonstration. Pérez (l.c.) speaks for it; K. Groos (Die Spiele der Menschen, 1899) states that some children are very early subject to sexual emotions, and show a desire to touch the other sex (p. 336); S. Bell observed the earliest appearance of sex-love in a child during the middle part of its third year. See also Havelock Ellis, The Sexual Impulse, Appendix II.

[43] For it is really impossible to have a correct knowledge of the part belonging to heredity without first understanding the part belonging to the infantile.

remained unexplained. I refer to the peculiar amnesia which veils from most people (not from all!) the first years of their childhood, usually the first six or eight years. So far it has not occurred to us that this amnesia ought to surprise us, though we have good reasons for surprise. For we are informed that in those years from which we later obtain nothing except a few incomprehensible memory fragments, we have vividly reacted to impressions, that we have manifested pain and pleasure like any human being, that we have evinced love, jealousy, and other passions as they then affected us; indeed we are told that we have uttered remarks which proved to grown-ups that we possessed understanding and a budding power of judgment. Still we know nothing of all this when we become older. Why does our memory lag behind all our other psychic activities? We really have reason to believe that at no time of life are we more capable of impressions and reproductions than during the years of childhood.[44]

On the other hand we must assume, or we may convince ourselves through psychological observations on others, that the very impressions which we have forgotten have nevertheless left the deepest traces in our psychic life, and acted as determinants for our whole future development. We conclude therefore that we do not deal with a real forgetting of infantile impressions but rather with an amnesia similar to that observed in neurotics for later experiences, the nature of which consists in their being detained from consciousness (repression). But what forces bring about this repression of the infantile impressions? He who can solve this riddle will also explain hysterical amnesia. We shall not, however, hesitate to assert that the existence of the infantile amnesia gives us a new point of comparison between the psychic states of the child and those of the psychoneurotic. We have already encountered another point of comparison when confronted by the fact that the sexuality of the psychoneurotic preserves the infantile character or has returned to it. May there not be an ultimate connection between the infantile and the hysterical amnesias?

The connection between the infantile and the hysterical amnesias is really more than a mere play of wit. The hysterical amnesia which serves the repression can only be explained by the fact that the individual already possesses a sum of recollections which have been withdrawn from conscious disposal and which by associative connection now seize that which is acted upon by the repelling forces of the repression emanating from

---

[44] One cannot understand the mechanism of repression when one takes into consideration only one of the two cooperating processes. As a comparison one may think of the way the tourist is despatched to the top of the great pyramid of Gizeh; he is pushed from one side and pulled from the other.

consciousness.[45] We may say that without infantile amnesia there would be no hysterical amnesia.

I believe that the infantile amnesia which causes the individual to look upon his childhood as if it were a *prehistoric* time and conceals from him the beginning of his own sexual life—that this amnesia is responsible for the fact that one does not usually attribute any value to the infantile period in the development of the sexual life. One single observer cannot fill the gap which has been thus produced in our knowledge. As early as 1896 I had already emphasized the significance of childhood for the origin of certain important phenomena connected with the sexual life, and since then I have not ceased to put into the foreground the importance of the infantile factor for sexuality.

THE SEXUAL LATENCY PERIOD OF CHILDHOOD AND ITS INTERRUPTIONS

The extraordinary frequent discoveries of apparently abnormal and exceptional sexual manifestations in childhood, as well as the discovery of infantile reminiscences in neurotics, which were hitherto unconscious, allow us to sketch the following picture of the sexual behavior of childhood.[46]

It seems certain that the newborn child brings with it the germs of sexual feelings which continue to develop for some time and then succumb to a progressive suppression, which is in turn broken through by the proper advances of the sexual development and which can be checked by individual idiosyncrasies. Nothing is known concerning the laws and periodicity of this oscillating course of development. It seems, however, that the sexual life of the child mostly manifests itself in the third or fourth year in some form accessible to observation.[47]

---

[45] I have attempted to solve the problems presented by earliest infantile recollections in "Über Deckerinnerungen" (Monatsschrift für Psychiatrie und Neurologie VI, 1899) Cf. also The Psychopathology of Everyday Life

[46] The above-mentioned judgment concerning the literature of infantile sexuality no longer holds true since the appearance of the great and important work of G. Stanley Hall (Adolescence, Its Psychology and its Relation to Physiology, Anthropology, Sociology, Sex, Crime, Religion, and Education, 2 vols., New York, 1908). The recent book of A. Moll, Das Sexualleben des Kindes, Berlin, 1909, offers no occasion for such a modification. See, on the other hand, Bleuler, Sexuelle abnormitäten der Kinder (Jahrbuch der Schweizerischen Gesellschaft für Schulgesundheitspflege, IX, 1908). A book by Mrs. Dr. H.v. Hug-Hellmuth, Aus dem Seelenleben des Kindes (1913), has taken full account of the neglected sexual factors. [Translated in Monograph Series.]

The use of the latter material is justified by the fact that the years of childhood of those who are later neurotics need not necessarily differ from those who are later normal except in intensity and distinctness.

[47] An anatomic analogy to the behavior of the infantile sexual function formulated by me is perhaps given by Bayer (Deutsches Archiv für klinische Medizin, Bd. 73) who claims that the internal genitals (uterus) are regularly larger in newborn than in older children. However, Halban's conception, that after birth there is also an involution of the other parts of the sexual apparatus, has

The Sexual Inhibition.—It is during this period of total or at least partial latency that the psychic forces develop which later act as inhibitions on the sexual life, and narrow its direction like dams. These psychic forces are loathing, shame, and moral and esthetic ideal demands. We may gain the impression that the erection of these dams in the civilized child is the work of education; and surely education contributes much to it. In reality, however, this development is organically determined and can occasionally be produced without the help of education. Indeed education remains properly within its assigned realm only if it strictly follows the path of the organic determinant and impresses it somewhat cleaner and deeper.

Reaction Formation and Sublimation.—What are the means that accomplish these very important constructions so significant for the later personal culture and normality? They are probably brought about at the cost of the infantile sexuality itself, the influx of which has not stopped even in this latency period—the energy of which indeed has been turned away either wholly or partially from sexual utilization and conducted to other aims. The historians of civilization seem to be unanimous in the opinion that such deviation of sexual motive powers from sexual aims to new aims, a process which merits the name of *sublimation*, has furnished powerful components for all cultural accomplishments. We will therefore add that the same process acts in the development of every individual, and that it begins to act in the sexual latency period.[48]

We can also venture an opinion about the mechanisms of such sublimation. The sexual feelings of these infantile years on the one hand could not be utilizable, since the procreating functions are postponed,—this is the chief character of the latency period; on the other hand, they would in themselves be perverse, as they would emanate from erogenous zones and would be born of impulses which in the individual's course of development could only evoke a feeling of displeasure. They therefore awaken contrary forces (feelings of reaction), which in order to suppress such displeasure, build up the above mentioned psychic dams: loathing, shame, and morality.[49]

The Interruptions of the Latency Period.—Without deluding ourselves as to the hypothetical nature and deficient clearness of our understanding regarding the infantile period of latency and delay, we will return to reality and state that such a utilization of the infantile sexuality represents an ideal bringing up from which the development of the individual usually deviates in some measure and often very considerably. A portion of

---

not been verified. According to Halban (Zeitschrift für Geburtshilfe u. Gynäkologie, LIII, 1904) this process of involution ends after a few weeks of extra-uterine life.

[48] The expression "sexual latency period" (sexuelle latenz-periode) I have borrowed from W. Fliess.

[49] In the case here discussed the sublimation of the sexual motive powers proceed on the road of reaction formations. But in general it is necessary to separate from each other sublimation and reaction formation as two diverse processes. Sublimation may also result through other and simpler mechanisms.

the sexual manifestation which has withdrawn from sublimation occasionally breaks through, or a sexual activity remains throughout the whole duration of the latency period until the reinforced breaking through of the sexual impulse in puberty. In so far as they have paid any attention to infantile sexuality the educators behave as if they shared our views concerning the formation of the moral forces of defence at the cost of sexuality, and as if they knew that sexual activity makes the child uneducable; for the educators consider all sexual manifestations of the child as an "evil" in the face of which little can be accomplished. We have, however, every reason for directing our attention to those phenomena so much feared by the educators, for we expect to find in them the solution of the primitive formation of the sexual impulse.

THE MANIFESTATIONS OF THE INFANTILE SEXUALITY

For reasons which we shall discuss later we will take as a model of the infantile sexual manifestations thumbsucking (pleasure-sucking), to which the Hungarian pediatrist, Lindner, has devoted an excellent essay.[50]

Thumbsucking.—Thumbsucking, which manifests itself in the nursing baby and which may be continued till maturity or throughout life, consists in a rhythmic repetition of sucking contact with the mouth (the lips), wherein the purpose of taking nourishment is excluded. A part of the lip itself, the tongue, which is another preferable skin region within reach, and even the big toe—may be taken as objects for sucking. Simultaneously, there is also a desire to grasp things, which manifests itself in a rhythmical pulling of the ear lobe and which may cause the child to grasp a part of another person (generally the ear) for the same purpose. The pleasure-sucking is connected with an entire exhaustion of attention and leads to sleep or even to a motor reaction in the form of an orgasm.[51] Pleasure-sucking is often combined with a rubbing contact with certain sensitive parts of the body, such as the breast and external genitals. It is by this road that many children go from thumbsucking to masturbation.

Lindner himself has recognized the sexual nature of this action and openly emphasized it. In the nursery thumbsucking is often treated in the same way as any other sexual "naughtiness" of the child. A very strong objection was raised against this view by many pediatrists and neurologists

---

[50] Jahrbuch für Kinderheilkunde, N.F., XIV, 1879.
[51] This already shows what holds true for the whole life, namely, that sexual gratification is the best hypnotic. Most nervous insomnias are traced to lack of sexual gratification. It is also known that unscrupulous nurses calm crying children to sleep by stroking their genitals.

which in part is certainly due to the confusion of the terms "sexual" and "genital." This contradiction raises the difficult question, which cannot be rejected, namely, in what general traits do we wish to recognize the sexual manifestations of the child. I believe that the association of the manifestations into which we gained an insight through psychoanalytic investigation justify us in claiming thumbsucking as a sexual activity and in studying through it the essential features of the infantile sexual activity.

Autoerotism.—It is our duty here to arrange this state of affairs differently. Let us insist that the most striking character of this sexual activity is that the impulse is not directed against other persons but that it gratifies itself on its own body; to use the happy term invented by Havelock Ellis, we will say that it is autoerotic.[52]

It is, moreover, clear that the action of the thumbsucking child is determined by the fact that it seeks a pleasure which has already been experienced and is now remembered. Through the rhythmic sucking on a portion of the skin or mucous membrane it finds the gratification in the simplest way. It is also easy to conjecture on what occasions the child first experienced this pleasure which it now strives to renew. The first and most important activity in the child's life, the sucking from the mother's breast (or its substitute), must have acquainted it with this pleasure. We would say that the child's lips behaved like an *erogenous zone*, and that the excitement through the warm stream of milk was really the cause of the pleasurable sensation. To be sure, the gratification of the erogenous zone was at first united with the gratification of taking nourishment. He who sees a satiated child sink back from the mother's breast, and fall asleep with reddened cheeks and blissful smile, will have to admit that this picture remains as typical of the expression of sexual gratification in later life. But the desire for repetition of the sexual gratification is separated from the desire for taking nourishment; a separation which becomes unavoidable with the appearance of the teeth when the nourishment is no longer sucked in but chewed. The child does not make use of a strange object for sucking but prefers its own skin because it is more convenient, because it thus makes itself independent of the outer world which it cannot yet control, and because in this way it creates for itself, as it were, a second, even if an inferior, erogenous zone. The inferiority of this second region urges it later to seek the same parts, the lips of another person. ("It is a pity that I cannot kiss myself," might be attributed to it.)

Not all children suck their thumbs. It may be assumed that it is found only in children in whom the erogenous significance of the lip-zone is constitutionally reënforced. Children in whom this is retained are habitual

---

[52] Ellis spoils, however, the sense of his invented term by comprising under the phenomena of autoerotism the whole of hysteria and masturbation in its full extent.

kissers as adults and show a tendency to perverse kissing, or as men they have a marked desire for drinking and smoking. But if repression comes into play they experience disgust for eating and evince hysterical vomiting. By virtue of the community of the lip-zone the repression encroaches upon the impulse of nourishment. Many of my female patients showing disturbances in eating, such as hysterical globus, choking sensations, and vomiting, have been energetic thumbsuckers during infancy.

In the thumbsucking or pleasure-sucking we have already been able to observe the three essential characters of an infantile sexual manifestation. The latter has its origin in conjunction with a bodily function which is very important for life, it does not yet know any sexual object, it is *autoerotic* and its sexual aim is under the control of an *erogenous zone*. Let us assume for the present that these characters also hold true for most of the other activities of the infantile sexual impulse.

THE SEXUAL AIM OF THE INFANTILE SEXUALITY

The Characters of the Erogenous Zones.—From the example of thumbsucking we may gather a great many points useful for the distinguishing of an erogenous zone. It is a portion of skin or mucous membrane in which the stimuli produce a feeling of pleasure of definite quality. There is no doubt that the pleasure-producing stimuli are governed by special determinants which we do not know. The rhythmic characters must play some part in them and this strongly suggests an analogy to tickling. It does not, however, appear so certain whether the character of the pleasurable feeling evoked by the stimulus can be designated as "peculiar," and in what part of this peculiarity the sexual factor exists. Psychology is still groping in the dark when it concerns matters of pleasure and pain, and the most cautious assumption is therefore the most advisable. We may perhaps later come upon reasons which seem to support the peculiar quality of the sensation of pleasure.

The erogenous quality may adhere most notably to definite regions of the body. As is shown by the example of thumbsucking, there are predestined erogenous zones. But the same example also shows that any other region of skin or mucous membrane may assume the function of an erogenous zone; it must therefore carry along a certain adaptability. The production of the sensation of pleasure therefore depends more on the quality of the stimulus than on the nature of the bodily region. The thumbsucking child looks around on his body and selects any portion of it for pleasure-sucking, and becoming accustomed to it, he then prefers it. If he accidentally strikes upon a predestined region, such as breast, nipple or genitals, it naturally has the preference. A quite analogous tendency to displacement is again found in the symptomatology of hysteria. In this neurosis the repression mostly concerns the genital zones proper; these in turn transmit their excitation to the other erogenous zones, usually dormant in mature life, which then behave exactly like genitals. But besides this, just as in thumbsucking, any other region of the body may become endowed with the excitation of the genitals and raised to an erogenous zone. Erogenous and hysterogenous zones show the same characters.[53]

The Infantile Sexual Aim.—The sexual aim of the infantile impulse consists in the production of gratification through the proper excitation of this or that selected erogenous zone. In order to leave a desire for its repetition this gratification must have been previously experienced, and we may be sure that nature has devised definite means so as not to leave this occurrence to mere chance. The arrangement which has fulfilled this purpose for the lip-zone we have already discussed; it is the simultaneous connection of this part of the body with the taking of nourishment. We shall also meet other similar mechanisms as sources of sexuality. The state of desire for repetition of gratification can be recognized through a peculiar feeling of tension which in itself is rather of a painful character, and through a centrally-determined feeling of itching or sensitiveness which is projected into the peripheral erogenous zone. The sexual aim may therefore be formulated as follows: the chief object is to substitute for the projected feeling of sensitiveness in the erogenous zone that outer stimulus which removes the feeling of sensitiveness by evoking the feeling of gratification. This external stimulus consists usually in a manipulation which is analogous to sucking.

It is in full accord with our physiological knowledge if the desire happens to be awakened also peripherally through an actual change in the erogenous zone. The action is puzzling only to some extent as one stimulus for its suppression seems to want another applied to the same place.

---

[53] Further reflection and observation lead me to attribute the quality of erogenity to all parts of the body and inner organs. See later on narcism.

THE MASTURBATIC SEXUAL MANIFESTATIONS[54]

It is a matter of great satisfaction to know that there is nothing further of greater importance to learn about the sexual activity of the child after the impulse of one erogenous zone has become comprehensible to us. The most pronounced differences are found in the action necessary for the gratification, which consists in sucking for the lip zone and which must be replaced by other muscular actions according to the situation and nature of the other zones.

The Activity of the Anal Zone.—Like the lip zone the anal zone is, through its position, adapted to conduct the sexuality to the other functions of the body. It should be assumed that the erogenous significance of this region of the body was originally very large. Through psychoanalysis one finds, not without surprise, the many transformations that are normally undertaken with the usual excitations emanating from here, and that this zone often retains for life a considerable fragment of genital irritability.[55] The intestinal catarrhs so frequent during infancy produce intensive irritations in this zone, and we often hear it said that intestinal catarrh at this delicate age causes "nervousness." In later neurotic diseases they exert a definite influence on the symptomatic expression of the neurosis, placing at its disposal the whole sum of intestinal disturbances. Considering the erogenous significance of the anal zone which has been retained at least in transformation, one should not laugh at the hemorrhoidal influences to which the old medical literature attached so much weight in the explanation of neurotic states.

Children utilizing the erogenous sensitiveness of the anal zone can be recognized by their holding back of fecal masses until through accumulation there result violent muscular contractions; the passage of these masses through the anus is apt to produce a marked irritation of the mucus membrane. Besides the pain this must produce also a sensation of pleasure. One of the surest premonitions of later eccentricity or nervousness is when an infant obstinately refuses to empty his bowel when placed on the chamber by the nurse and reserves this function at its own pleasure. It does not concern him that he will soil his bed; all he cares for is not to lose the subsidiary pleasure while defecating. The educators have again the right

---

[54] Compare here the very comprehensive but confusing literature on onanism, *e.g.*, Rohleder, Die Masturbation, 1899. Cf. also the pamphlet, "Die Onanie," which contains the discussion of the Vienna Psychoanalytic Society, Wiesbaden, 1912.

[55] Compare here the essay on "Charakter und Analerotic" in the Sammlung kleiner Schriften zur Neurosenlehre, Zweite Folge, 1909. Cf. also Brill, Psychanalysis, Chap. XIII, Anal Eroticism and Character, W.B. Saunders, Philadelphia.

inkling when they designate children who withhold these functions as bad. The content of the bowel which is an exciting object to the sexually sensitive surface of mucous membrane behaves like the precursor of another organ which does not become active until after the phase of childhood. In addition it has other important meanings to the nursling. It is evidently treated as an additional part of the body, it represents the first "donation," the disposal of which expresses the pliability while the retention of it can express the spite of the little being towards its environment. From the idea of "donation" he later gains the meaning of the "babe" which according to one of the infantile sexual theories is acquired through eating and is born through the bowel.

The retention of fecal masses, which is at first intentional in order to utilize them, as it were, for masturbatic excitation of the anal zone, is at least one of the roots of constipation so frequent in neuropaths. The whole significance of the anal zone is mirrored in the fact that there are but few neurotics who have not their special scatologic customs, ceremonies, etc., which they retain with cautious secrecy. Real masturbatic irritation of the anal zone by means of the fingers, evoked through either centrally or peripherally supported itching, is not at all rare in older children.

The Activity of the Genital Zone.—Among the erogenous zones of the child's body there is one which certainly does not play the main rôle, and which cannot be the carrier of earliest sexual feeling—which, however, is destined for great things in later life. In both male and female it is connected with the voiding of urine (penis, clitoris), and in the former it is enclosed in a sack of mucous membrane, probably in order not to miss the irritations caused by the secretions which may arouse the sexual excitement at an early age. The sexual activities of this erogenous zone, which belongs to the real genitals, are the beginning of the later normal sexual life.

Owing to the anatomical position, the overflowing of secretions, the washing and rubbing of the body, and to certain accidental excitements (the wandering of intestinal worms in the girl), it happens that the pleasurable feeling which these parts of the body are capable of producing makes itself noticeable to the child even during the sucking age, and thus awakens desire for its repetition. When we review all the actual arrangements, and bear in mind that the measures for cleanliness have the same effect as the uncleanliness itself, we can then scarcely mistake nature's intention, which is to establish the future primacy of these erogenous zones for the sexual activity through the infantile onanism from which hardly an individual escapes. The action of removing the stimulus and setting free the gratification consists in a rubbing contiguity with the hand or in a certain previously-formed pressure reflex effected by the closure of the thighs. The latter procedure seems to be the more primitive and is by far the more common in girls. The preference for the hand in boys already indicates what an important part of the male sexual activity will be accomplished in the future by the impulse to mastery (Bemächtigungstrieb).[56] It can only help towards clearness if I state that the infantile masturbation should be divided into three phases. The first phase belongs to the nursing period, the second to the short flourishing period of sexual activity at about the fourth year, only the third corresponds to the one which is often considered exclusively as onanism of puberty.

The infantile onanism seems to disappear after a brief time, but it may continue uninterruptedly till puberty and thus represent the first marked deviation from the development desirable for civilized man. At some time during childhood after the nursing period, the sexual impulse of the genitals reawakens and continues active for some time until it is again suppressed, or it may continue without interruption. The possible relations are very diverse and can only be elucidated through a more precise analysis of individual cases. The details, however, of this *second* infantile sexual activity leave behind the profoundest (unconscious) impressions in the person's memory; if the individual remains healthy they determine his character and if he becomes sick after puberty they determine the symptomatology of his neurosis.[57] In the latter case it is found that this sexual period is forgotten and the conscious reminiscences pointing to them are displaced; I have already mentioned that I would like to connect the normal infantile amnesia with this infantile sexual activity. By psychoanalytic investigation it is possible to bring to consciousness the forgotten material, and thereby to remove a compulsion which emanates from the unconscious psychic material.

The Return of the Infantile Masturbation.—The sexual excitation of the nursing period returns during the designated years of childhood as a centrally determined tickling sensation demanding onanistic gratification, or as a pollution-like process which, analogous to the pollution of maturity, may attain gratification without the aid of any action. The latter case is more frequent in girls and in the second half of childhood; its determinants are not well understood, but it often, though not regularly, seems to have as a basis a period of early active onanism. The symptomatology of this sexual manifestation is poor; the genital apparatus is still undeveloped and all signs are therefore displayed by the urinary apparatus which is, so to say, the guardian of the genital apparatus. Most of the so-called bladder disturbances of this period are of a sexual nature; whenever the enuresis nocturna does not represent an epileptic attack it corresponds to a pollution.

---

[56] : Unusual techniques in the performance of onanism seem to point to the influence of a prohibition against onanism which has been overcome.

[57] Why neurotics, when conscience stricken, regularly connect it with their onanistic activity, as was only recently recognized by Bleuler, is a problem which still awaits an exhaustive analysis.

The return of the sexual activity is determined by inner and outer causes which can be conjectured from the formation of the symptoms of neurotic diseases and definitely revealed by psychoanalytic investigations. The internal causes will be discussed later, the accidental outer causes attain at this time a great and permanent significance. As the first outer cause we have the influence of seduction which prematurely treats the child as a sexual object; under conditions favoring impressions this teaches the child the gratification of the genital zones, and thus usually forces it to repeat this gratification in onanism. Such influences can come from adults or other children. I cannot admit that I overestimated its frequency or its significance in my contributions to the etiology of hysteria, [58]though I did not know then that normal individuals may have the same experiences in their childhood, and hence placed a higher value on seductions than on the factors found in the sexual constitution and development.[59] It is quite obvious that no seduction is necessary to awaken the sexual life of the child, that such an awakening may come on spontaneously from inner sources.

Polymorphous-perverse Disposition.—It is instructive to know that under the influence of seduction the child may become polymorphous-perverse and may be misled into all sorts of transgressions. This goes to show that it carries along the adaptation for them in its disposition. The formation of such perversions meets but slight resistance because the psychic dams against sexual transgressions, such as shame, loathing and morality—which depend on the age of the child—are not yet erected or are only in the process of formation. In this respect the child perhaps does not behave differently from the average uncultured woman in whom the same polymorphous-perverse disposition exists. Such a woman may remain sexually normal under usual conditions, but under the guidance of a clever seducer she will find pleasure in every perversion and will retain the same as her sexual activity. The same polymorphous or infantile disposition fits the prostitute for her professional activity, and in the enormous number of prostitutes and of women to whom we must attribute an adaptation for prostitution, even if they do not follow this calling, it is absolutely impossible not to recognize in their uniform disposition for all perversions the universal and primitive human.

---

[58] Freud, Selected Papers on Hysteria and Other Psychoneuroses, 3d edition, translated by A.A. Brill, N.Y. Nerv. and Ment. Dis. Pub. Co. Nervous and Mental Disease Monograph, Series No. 4.
[59] Havelock Ellis, in an appendix to his study on the Sexual Impulse, 1903, gives a number of autobiographic reports of normal persons treating their first sexual feelings in childhood and the causes of the same. These reports naturally show the deficiency due to infantile amnesia; they do not cover the prehistoric time in the sexual life and therefore must be supplemented by psychoanalysis of individuals who became neurotic. Notwithstanding this these reports are valuable in more than one respect, and information of a similar nature has urged me to modify my etiological assumption as mentioned in the text.

Partial Impulses.—For the rest, the influence of seduction does not aid us in unravelling the original relations of the sexual impulse, but rather confuses our understanding of the same, inasmuch as it prematurely supplies the child with the sexual object at a time when the infantile sexual impulse does not yet evince any desire for it. We must admit, however, that the infantile sexual life, though mainly under the control of erogenous zones, also shows components in which from the very beginning other persons are regarded as sexual objects. Among these we have the impulses for looking and showing off, and for cruelty, which manifest themselves somewhat independently of the erogenous zones and which only later enter into intimate relationship with the sexual life; but along with the erogenous sexual activity they are noticeable even in the infantile years as separate and independent strivings. The little child is above all shameless, and during its early years it evinces definite pleasure in displaying its body and especially its sexual organs. A counterpart to this desire which is to be considered as perverse, the curiosity to see other persons' genitals, probably appears first in the later years of childhood when the hindrance of the feeling of shame has already reached a certain development. Under the influence of seduction the looking perversion may attain great importance for the sexual life of the child. Still, from my investigations of the childhood years of normal and neurotic patients, I must conclude that the impulse for looking can appear in the child as a spontaneous sexual manifestation. Small children, whose attention has once been directed to their own genitals—usually by masturbation—are wont to progress in this direction without outside interference, and to develop a vivid interest in the genitals of their playmates. As the occasion for the gratification of such curiosity is generally afforded during the gratification of both excrementitious needs, such children become *voyeurs* and are zealous spectators at the voiding of urine and feces of others, After this tendency has been repressed, the curiosity to see the genitals of others (one's own or those of the other sex) remains as a tormenting desire which in some neurotic cases furnishes the strongest motive power for the formation of symptoms.

The cruelty component of the sexual impulse develops in the child with still greater independence of those sexual activities which are connected with erogenous zones. Cruelty is especially near the childish character, since the inhibition which restrains the impulse to mastery before it causes pain to others—that is, the capacity for sympathy—develops comparatively late. As we know, a thorough psychological analysis of this impulse has not as yet been successfully accomplished; we may assume that the cruel feelings emanate from the impulse to mastery and appear at a period in the sexual life before the genitals have taken on their later rôle. It then dominates a phase of the sexual life, which we shall later describe as the pregenital organization. Children who are distinguished for evincing especial cruelty to animals and playmates may be justly suspected of intensive and premature sexual activity in the erogenous zones; and in a simultaneous prematurity of all sexual impulses, the erogenous sexual activity surely seems to be primary. The absence of the barrier of sympathy carries with it the danger that the connections between cruelty and the erogenous impulses formed in childhood cannot be broken in later life.

An erogenous source of the passive impulse for cruelty (masochism) is found in the painful irritation of the gluteal region which is familiar to all educators since the confessions of J.J. Rousseau. This has justly caused them to demand that physical punishment, which usually concerns this part of the body, should be withheld from all children in whom the libido might be forced into collateral roads by the later demands of cultural education.[60]

THE INFANTILE SEXUAL INVESTIGATION

Inquisitiveness.—At the same time when the sexual life of the child reaches its first bloom, from the age of three to the age of five, it also evinces the beginning of that activity which is ascribed to the impulse for knowledge and investigation. The desire for knowledge can neither be added to the elementary components of the impulses nor can it be altogether subordinated

---

[60] The above-mentioned assertions concerning the infantile sexuality were justified in 1905, in the main through the results of psychoanalytic investigations in adults. Direct observation of the child could not at the time be utilized to its full extent and resulted only in individual indications and valuable confirmations. Since then it has become possible through the analysis of some cases of nervous disease in the delicate age of childhood to gain a direct understanding of the infantile psychosexuality (Jahrbuch für psychoanalytische und psychopathologische Forschungen, Bd. 1, 2, 1909). I can point with satisfaction to the fact that direct observation has fully confirmed the conclusion drawn from psychoanalysis, and thus furnishes good evidence for the reliability of the latter method of investigation.

Moreover, the "Analysis of a Phobia in a Five-year-old Boy" (Jahrbuch, Bd. 1) has taught us something new for which psychoanalysis had not prepared us, to wit, that sexual symbolism, the representation of the sexual by non-sexual objects and relations—reaches back into the years when the child is first learning to master the language. My attention has also been directed to a deficiency in the above-cited statement which for the sake of clearness described any conceivable separation between the two phases of autoerotism and object love as a temporal separation. From the cited analysis (as well as from the above-mentioned work of Bell) we learn that children from three to five are capable of evincing a very strong object-selection which is accompanied by strong affects.

under sexuality. Its activity corresponds on the one hand to a sublimating mode of acquisition and on the other hand it labors with the energy of the desire for looking. Its relations to the sexual life, however, are of particular importance, for we have learned from psychoanalysis that the inquisitiveness of children is attracted to the sexual problems unusually early and in an unexpectedly intensive manner, indeed it perhaps may first be awakened by the sexual problems.

The Riddle of the Sphinx.—It is not theoretical but practical interests which start the work of the investigation activity in the child. The threat to the conditions of his existence through the actual or expected arrival of a new child, the fear of the loss in care and love which is connected with this event, cause the child to become thoughtful and sagacious. Corresponding with the history of this awakening, the first problem with which it occupies itself is not the question as to the difference between the sexes, but the riddle: from where do children come? In a distorted form, which can easily be unraveled, this is the same riddle which was given by the Theban Sphinx. The fact of the two sexes is usually first accepted by the child without struggle and hesitation. It is quite natural for the male child to presuppose in all persons it knows a genital like his own, and to find it impossible to harmonize the lack of it with his conception of others.

The Castration Complex.—This conviction is energetically adhered to by the boy and tenaciously defended against the contradictions which soon result, and are only given up after severe internal struggles (castration complex). The substitutive formations of this lost penis of the woman play a great part in the formation of many perversions.

The assumption of the same (male) genital in all persons is the first of the remarkable and consequential infantile sexual theories. It is of little help to the child when biological science agrees with his preconceptions and recognizes the feminine clitoris as the real substitute for the penis. The little girl does not react with similar refusals when she sees the differently formed genital of the boy. She is immediately prepared to recognize it, and soon becomes envious of the penis; this envy reaches its highest point in the consequentially important wish that she also should be a boy.

Birth Theories.—Many people can remember distinctly how intensely they interested themselves, in the prepubescent period, in the question where children came from. The anatomical solutions at that time read very differently; the children come out of the breast or are cut out of the body, or the navel opens itself to let them out. Outside of analysis one only seldom remembers the investigation corresponding to the early childhood years; it had long merged into repression but its results were thoroughly uniform. One gets children by eating something special (as in the fairy tale) and they are born through the bowel like a passage. These infantile theories recall the structures in the animal kingdom, especially do they recall the cloaca of the types which stand lower than the mammals.

Sadistic Conception of the Sexual Act.—If children of so delicate an age become spectators of the sexual act between grown-ups, for which an occasion is furnished by the conviction of the grown-ups that little children cannot understand anything sexual, they cannot help conceiving the sexual act as a kind of maltreating or overpowering, that is, it impresses them in a sadistic sense. Psychoanalysis also teaches us that such an early childhood impression contributes much to the disposition for a later sadistic displacement of the sexual aim. Besides this children also occupy themselves with the problem of what the sexual act consists in or, as they grasp it, of what marriage consists, and seek the solution of the mystery mostly in an association to which the functions of urination and defecation give occasion.

The Typical Failure of the Infantile Sexual Investigation.—It can be stated in general about the infantile sexual theories that they are reproductions of the child's own sexual constitution, and that despite their grotesque mistakes they evince more understanding of the sexual processes than is credited to their creators. Children also perceive the pregnancy of the mother and know how to interpret it correctly; the stork fable is very often related before auditors who confront it with a deep, but mostly mute suspicion. But as two elements remain unknown to the infantile sexual investigation, namely, the rôle of the propagating semen and the female genital opening—precisely the same points in which the infantile organization is still backward—the effort of the infantile investigator regularly remains fruitless, and ends in a renunciation which not infrequently leaves a lasting injury to the desire for knowledge. The sexual investigation of these early childhood years is always conducted alone, it signifies the first step towards independent orientation in the world, and causes a marked estrangement between the child and the persons of his environment who formerly enjoyed its full confidence.

The Phases of Development of the Sexual Organization.—As characteristics of the infantile sexuality we have hitherto emphasized the fact that it is essentially autoerotic (it finds its object in its own body), and that its individual partial impulses, which on the whole are unconnected and independent of one another, are striving for the acquisition of pleasure. The end of this development forms the so-called normal sexual life of the adult in which the acquisition of pleasure has been put into the service of the function of propagation, and the partial impulses, under the primacy of one single erogenous zone, have formed a firm organization for the attainment of the sexual aim in a strange sexual object.

Pregenital Organizations.—The study, with the help of psychoanalysis, of the inhibitions and disturbances in this course of development now permits us to recognize additions and primary stages of such organization of the partial impulses which likewise furnish a sort of sexual regime. These phases of the sexual organization normally will pass over smoothly and will only be recognizable by slight indications. Only in pathological cases do they become active and discernible to coarse observation.

Organizations of the sexual life in which the genital zones have not yet assumed the dominating rôle we would call the *pregenital* phase. So far we have become acquainted with two of them which recall reversions to early animal states.

One of the first of such pregenital sexual organizations is the *oral*, or if we wish, the cannibalistic. Here the sexual activity is not yet separated from the taking of nourishment, and the contrasts within the same not yet differentiated. The object of the one activity is also that of the other, the sexual aim consists in the *incorporating* into one's own body of the object, it is the prototype of that which later plays such an important psychic rôle as *identification*. As a remnant of this fictitious phase of organization forced on us by pathology we can consider thumbsucking. Here the sexual activity became separated from the nourishment activity and the strange object was given up in favor of one from his own body.

A second pregenital phase is the sadistic-anal organization. Here the contrasts which run through the whole sexual life are already developed, but cannot yet be designated as *masculine* and *feminine*, but must be called *active* and *passive*. The activity is supplied by the musculature of the body through the mastery impulse; the erogenous mucous membrane of the bowel manifests itself above all as an organ with a passive sexual aim, for both strivings there are objects present, which however do not merge together. Besides them there are other partial impulses which are active in an autoerotic manner. The sexual polarity and the strange object can thus already be demonstrated in this phase. The organization and subordination under the function of propagation are still lacking.

Ambivalence.—This form of the sexual organization could be retained throughout life and continue to draw to itself a large part of the sexual activity. The prevalence of sadism and the rôle of the cloaca of the anal zone stamps it with an exquisitely archaic impression. As another characteristic belonging to it we can mention the fact that the contrasting pair of impulses are developed in almost the same manner, a behavior which was designated by Bleuler with the happy name of *ambivalence*.

The assumption of the pregenital organizations of the sexual life is based on the analysis of the neuroses and hardly deserves any consideration without a knowledge of the same. We may expect that continued analytic efforts will furnish us with still more disclosures concerning the structure and development of the normal sexual function.

To complete the picture of the infantile sexual life one must add that frequently or regularly an object selection takes place even in childhood which is as characteristic as the one we have represented for the phase of development of puberty. This object selection proceeds in such a manner that all the sexual strivings proceed in the direction of one person in whom they wish to attain their aim. This is then the nearest approach to the definitive formation of the sexual life after puberty, that is possible in childhood. It differs from the latter only in the fact that the collection of the partial impulses and their subordination to the primacy of the genitals is very imperfectly or not at all accomplished in childhood. The establishment of this primacy in the service of propagation is therefore the last phase through which the sexual organization passes.

The Two Periods of Object Selection.—That the object selection takes place in two periods, or in two shifts, can be spoken of as a typical occurrence. The first shift has its origin between the age of three and five years, and is brought to a stop or to retrogression by the latency period; it is characterized by the infantile nature of its sexual aims. The second shift starts with puberty and determines the definitive formation of the sexual life.

The fact of the double object selection which is essentially due to the effect of the latency period, becomes most significant for the disturbance of this terminal state. The results of the infantile object selection reach into the later period; they are either preserved as such or are even refreshed at the time of puberty. But due to the development of the repression which takes place between the two phases they turn out as unutilizable. The sexual aims have become softened and now represent what we can designate as the *tender* streams of the sexual life. Only psychoanalytic investigation can demonstrate that behind this tenderness, such as honoring and esteeming, there is concealed the old sexual strivings of the infantile partial impulses which have now become useless. The object selection of the pubescent period must renounce the infantile objects and begin anew as a sensuous stream. The fact that the two streams do not meet often enough has as a result that one of the ideals of the sexual life, namely, the union of all desires in one object, can not be attained.

THE SOURCES OF THE INFANTILE SEXUALITY

In our effort to follow up the origins of the sexual impulse, we have thus far found that the sexual excitement originates (*a*) as an imitation of a gratification which has been experienced in conjunction with other organic processes; (*b*) through the appropriate peripheral stimulation of erogenous zones; (*c*) and as an expression of some "impulse," like the looking and cruelty impulses, the origin of which we do not yet fully understand. The psychoanalytic investigation of later life which leads back to childhood and the contemporary observation of the child itself coöperate to reveal to us still other regularly-flowing sources of the sexual excitement. The observation of childhood has the disadvantage of treating easily misunderstood material, while psychoanalysis is made difficult by the fact that it can reach its objects and conclusions only by great detours; still the united efforts of both methods achieve a sufficient degree of positive understanding.

In investigating the erogenous zones we have already found that these skin regions merely show the special exaggeration of a form of sensitiveness which is to a certain degree found over the whole surface of the skin. It will therefore not surprise us to learn that certain forms of general sensitiveness in the skin can be ascribed to very distinct erogenous action. Among these we will above all mention the temperature sensitiveness; this will perhaps prepare us for the understanding of the therapeutic effects of warm baths.

Mechanical Excitation.—We must, moreover, describe here the production of sexual excitation by means of rhythmic mechanical shaking of the body. There are three kinds of exciting influences: those acting on the sensory apparatus of the vestibular nerves, those acting on the skin, and those acting on the deep parts, such as the muscles and joints. The sexual excitation produced by these influences seems to be of a pleasurable nature—it is worth emphasizing that for some time we shall continue to use indiscriminately the terms "sexual excitement" and "gratification" leaving the search for an explanation of the terms to a later time—and that the pleasure is produced by mechanical stimulation is proved by the fact that children are so fond of play involving passive motion, like swinging or flying in the air, and repeatedly demand its repetition. (Some can recall that the contact of the moving air in swinging caused them direct sexual pleasure in the genitals.) As we know, rocking is regularly used in putting restless children to sleep. The shaking sensation experienced in wagons and railroad trains exerts such a fascinating influence on older children, that all boys, at least at one time in their lives, want to become conductors and drivers. They are wont to ascribe to railroad activities an extraordinary and mysterious interest, and during the age of phantastic activity (shortly before puberty) they utilize these as a nucleus for exquisite sexual symbolisms. The desire to connect railroad travelling with sexuality apparently originates from the pleasurable character of the sensation of motion. When the repression later sets in and changes so many of the childish likes into their opposites, these same persons as adolescents and adults then react to the rocking and rolling with nausea and become terribly exhausted by a railroad journey, or they show a tendency to attacks of anxiety during the journey, and by becoming obsessed with railroad phobia they protect themselves against a repetition of the painful experiences.

This also fits in with the not as yet understood fact that the concurrence of fear with mechanical shaking produces the severest hysterical forms of traumatic neurosis. It may at least be assumed that inasmuch as even a slight intensity of these influences becomes a source of sexual excitement, the action of an excessive amount of the same will produce a profound disorder in the sexual mechanism.

Muscular Activity.—It is well known that the child has need for strong muscular activity, from the gratification of which it draws extraordinary pleasure. Whether this pleasure has anything to do with sexuality, whether it includes in itself sexual satisfaction? or can be the occasion of sexual excitement; all this may be refuted by critical consideration, which will probably be directed also to the position taken above that the pleasure in the sensations of passive movement are of sexual character or that they are sexually exciting. The fact remains, however, that a number of persons report that they experienced the first signs of excitement in their genitals during fighting or wrestling with playmates, in which situation, besides the general muscular exertion, there is an intensive contact with the opponent's skin which also becomes effective. The desire for muscular contest with a definite person, like the desire for word contest in later years, is a good sign that the object selection has been directed toward this person. "Was sich liebt, das neckt sich."(Those who love each other tease each other.") In the promotion of sexual excitement through muscular activity we might recognize one of the sources of the sadistic impulse. The infantile connection between fighting and sexual excitement acts in many persons as a determinant for the future preferred course of their sexual impulse.[61]

Affective Processes.—The other sources of sexual excitement in the child are open to less doubt. Through contemporary observations, as well as later investigations, it is easy to ascertain that all more intensive affective processes, even excitements of a terrifying nature, encroach upon sexuality; this can at all events furnish us with a contribution to the understanding of the pathogenic action of such emotions. In the school child, fear of a coming examination or exertion expended in the solution of a difficult task can

---

[61] The analyses of neurotic disturbances of walking and of agoraphobia remove all doubt as to the sexual nature of the pleasure of motion. As everybody knows modern cultural education utilizes sports to a great extent in order to turn away the youth from sexual activity; it would be more proper to say that it replaces the sexual pleasure by motion pleasure, and forces the sexual activity back upon one of its autoerotic components.

become significant for the breaking through of sexual manifestations as well as for his relations to the school, inasmuch as under such excitements a sensation often occurs urging him to touch the genitals, or leading to a pollution-like process with all its disagreeable consequences. The behavior of children at school, which is so often mysterious to the teacher, ought surely to be considered in relation with their germinating sexuality. The sexually-exciting influence of some painful affects, such as fear, shuddering, and horror, is felt by a great many people throughout life and readily explains why so many seek opportunities to experience such sensations, provided that certain accessory circumstances (as under imaginary circumstances in reading, or in the theater) suppress the earnestness of the painful feeling.

If we might assume that the same erogenous action also reaches the intensive painful feelings, especially if the pain be toned down or held at a distance by a subsidiary determination, this relation would then contain the main roots of the masochistic-sadistic impulse, into the manifold composition of which we are gaining a gradual insight.

Intellectual Work.—Finally, it is evident that mental application or the concentration of attention on an intellectual accomplishment will result, especially often in the young, but also in older persons, in a simultaneous sexual excitement, which may be looked upon as the only justified basis for the otherwise so doubtful etiology of nervous disturbances from mental "overwork."

If we now, in conclusion, review the evidences and indications of the sources of the infantile sexual excitement, which have been reported neither completely nor exhaustively, we may lay down the following general laws as suggested or established. It seems to be provided in the most generous manner that the process of sexual excitement—the nature of which certainly remains quite mysterious to us—should be set in motion. The factor making this provision in a more or less direct way is the excitation of the sensible surfaces of the skin and sensory organs, while the most immediate exciting influences are exerted on certain parts which are designated as erogenous zones. The criterion in all these sources of sexual excitement is really the quality of the stimuli, though the factor of intensity (in pain) is not entirely unimportant. But in addition, there are arrangements in the organism which induce sexual excitement as a subsidiary action in a large number of inner processes as soon as their intensity has risen above certain quantitative limits. What we have designated as the partial impulses of sexuality are either directly derived from these inner sources of sexual excitation or composed of contributions from such sources and from erogenous zones. It is possible that nothing of any considerable significance occurs in the organism that does not contribute its components to the excitement of the sexual impulse.

It seems to me at present impossible to shed more light and certainty on these general propositions, and for this I hold two factors responsible; first, the novelty of this manner of investigation, and secondly, the fact that the nature of the sexual excitement is entirely unfamiliar to us. Nevertheless, I will not forbear speaking about two points which promise to open wide prospects in the future.

Diverse Sexual Constitutions.—(*a*) We have considered above the possibility of establishing the manifold character of congenital sexual constitutions through the diverse formation of the erogenous zones; we may now attempt to do the same in dealing with the indirect sources of sexual excitement. We may assume that, although these different sources furnish contributions in all individuals, they are not all equally strong in all persons; and that a further contribution to the differentiation of the diverse sexual constitution will be found in the preferred developments of the individual sources of sexual excitement.

The Paths of Opposite Influences.—(*b*) Since we are now dropping the figurative manner of expression hitherto employed, by which we spoke of *sources* of sexual excitement, we may now assume that all the connecting ways leading from other functions to sexuality must also be passable in the reverse direction. For example, if the lip zone, the common possession of both functions, is responsible for the fact that the sexual gratification originates during the taking of nourishment, the same factor offers also an explanation for the disturbances in the taking of nourishment if the erogenous functions of the common zone are disturbed. As soon as we know that concentration of attention may produce sexual excitement, it is quite natural to assume that acting on the same path, but in a contrary direction, the state of sexual excitement will be able to influence the availability of the voluntary attention. A good part of the symptomatology of the neuroses which I trace to disturbance of sexual processes manifests itself in disturbances of the other non-sexual bodily functions, and this hitherto incomprehensible action becomes less mysterious if it only represents the counterpart of the influences controlling the production of the sexual excitement.

However the same paths through which sexual disturbances encroach upon the other functions of the body must in health be supposed to serve another important function. It must be through these paths that the attraction of the sexual motive-powers to other than sexual aims, the sublimation of sexuality, is accomplished. We must conclude with the admission that very little is definitely known concerning the paths beyond the fact that they exist, and that they are probably passable in both directions.

III. THE TRANSFORMATION OF PUBERTY

With the beginning of puberty the changes set in which transform the infantile sexual life into its definite normal form. Hitherto the sexual impulse has been preponderantly autoerotic; it now finds the sexual object. Thus far it has manifested itself in single impulses and in erogenous zones seeking a certain pleasure as a single sexual aim. A new sexual aim now appears for the production of which all partial impulses coöperate, while the erogenous zones subordinate themselves to the primacy of the genital zone.[62] As the new sexual aim assigns very different functions to the two sexes their sexual developments now part company. The sexual development of the man is more consistent and easier to understand, while in the woman there even appears a form of regression. The normality of the sexual life is guaranteed only by the exact concurrence of the two streams directed to the sexual object and sexual aim. It is like the piercing of a tunnel from opposite sides.

The new sexual aim in the man consists in the discharging of the sexual products; it is not contradictory to the former sexual aim, that of obtaining pleasure; on the contrary, the highest amount of pleasure is connected with this final act in the sexual process. The sexual impulse now enters into the service of the function of propagation; it becomes, so to say, altruistic. If this transformation is to succeed its process must be adjusted to the original dispositions and all the peculiarities of the impulses.

Just as on every other occasion where new connections and compositions are to be formed in complicated mechanisms, here, too, there is a possibility for morbid disturbance if the new order of things does not get itself established. All morbid disturbances of the sexual life may justly be considered as inhibitions of development.

THE PRIMACY OF THE GENITAL ZONES AND THE FORE-PLEASURE

From the course of development as described we can clearly see the issue and the end aim. The intermediary transitions are still quite obscure and many a riddle will have to be solved in them.

The most striking process of puberty has been selected as its most characteristic; it is the manifest growth of the external genitals which have shown a relative inhibition of growth during the latency period of childhood. Simultaneously the inner genitals develop to such an extent as to be able to furnish sexual products or to receive them for the purpose of forming a new

---

[62] The differences will be emphasized in the schematic representation given in the text. To what extent the infantile sexuality approaches the definitive sexual organization through its object selection has been discussed before.

living being. A most complicated apparatus is thus formed which waits to be claimed.

This apparatus can be set in motion by stimuli, and observation teaches that the stimuli can affect it in three ways: from the outer world through the familiar erogenous zones; from the inner organic world by ways still to be investigated; and from the psychic life, which merely represents a depository of external impressions and a receptacle of inner excitations. The same result follows in all three cases, namely, a state which can be designated as "sexual excitation" and which manifests itself in psychic and somatic signs. The psychic sign consists in a peculiar feeling of tension of a most urgent character, and among the manifold somatic signs the many changes in the genitals stand first. They have a definite meaning, that of readiness; they constitute a preparation for the sexual act (the erection of the penis and the glandular activity of the vagina).

The Sexual Tension—The character of the tension of sexual excitation is connected with a problem the solution of which is as difficult as it would be important for the conception of the sexual process. Despite all divergence of opinion regarding it in psychology, I must firmly maintain that a feeling of tension must carry with it the character of displeasure. For me it is conclusive that such a feeling carries with it the impulse to alter the psychic situation, and acts incitingly, which is quite contrary to the nature of perceived pleasure. But if we ascribe the tension of the sexual excitation to the feelings of displeasure we encounter the fact that it is undoubtedly pleasurably perceived. The tension produced by sexual excitation is everywhere accompanied by pleasure; even in the preparatory changes of the genitals there is a distinct feeling of satisfaction. What relation is there between this unpleasant tension and this feeling of pleasure?

Everything relating to the problem of pleasure and pain touches one of the weakest spots of present-day psychology. We shall try if possible to learn something from the determinations of the case in question and to avoid encroaching on the problem as a whole. Let us first glance at the manner in which the erogenous zones adjust themselves to the new order of things. An important rôle devolves upon them in the preparation of the sexual excitation. The eye which is very remote from the sexual object is most often in position, during the relations of object wooing, to become attracted by that particular quality of excitation, the motive of which we designate as beauty in the sexual object. The excellencies of the sexual object are therefore also called "attractions." This attraction is on the one hand already connected with pleasure, and on the other hand it either results in an increase of the sexual excitation or in an evocation of the same where it is still wanting. The effect is the same if the excitation of another erogenous zone, *e.g.*, the touching hand, is added to it. There is on the one hand the feeling of pleasure which soon becomes enhanced by the pleasure from the preparatory changes, and on the other hand there is a further increase of the sexual tension which soon changes into a most distinct feeling of displeasure if it cannot proceed to more pleasure. Another case will perhaps be clearer; let us, for example, take the case where an erogenous zone, like a woman's breast, is excited by touching in a person who is not sexually excited at the time. This touching in itself evokes a feeling of pleasure, but it is also best adapted to awaken sexual excitement which demands still more pleasure. How it happens that the perceived pleasure evokes the desire for greater pleasure, that is the real problem.

Fore-pleasure Mechanism.—But the rôle which devolves upon the erogenous zones is clear. What applies to one applies to all. They are all utilized to furnish a certain amount of pleasure through their own proper excitation, which increases the tension, and which is in turn destined to produce the necessary motor energy in order to bring to a conclusion the sexual act. The last part but one of this act is again a suitable excitation of an erogenous zone; *i.e.*, the genital zone proper of the glans penis is excited by the object most fit for it, the mucous membrane of the vagina, and through the pleasure furnished by this excitation it now produces reflexly the motor energy which conveys to the surface the sexual substance. This last pleasure is highest in its intensity, and differs from the earliest ones in its mechanism. It is altogether produced through discharge, it is altogether gratification pleasure and the tension of the libido temporarily dies away with it.

It does not seem to me unjustified to fix by name the distinction in the nature of these pleasures, the one through the excitation of the erogenous zones, and the other through the discharge of the sexual substance. In contradistinction to the end-pleasure, or pleasure of gratification of sexual activity, we can properly designate the first as *fore-pleasure*. The fore-pleasure is then the same as that furnished by the infantile sexual impulse, though on a reduced scale; while the *end-pleasure* is new and is probably connected with determinations which first appear at puberty. The formula for the new function of the erogenous zones reads as follows: they are utilized for the purpose of making possible the production of the greater pleasure of gratification by means of the fore-pleasure which is gained from them as in infantile life.

I have recently been able to elucidate another example from a quite different realm of the psychic life, in which likewise a greater feeling of pleasure is achieved by means of a lesser feeling of pleasure which thereby acts as an alluring premium. We had there also the opportunity of entering more deeply into the nature of pleasure.[63]

Dangers of the Fore-pleasure.—However the connection of fore-pleasure with the infantile life is strengthened by the pathogenic rôle which may devolve upon it. In the mechanism through which the fore-pleasure is expressed there exists an obvious danger to the attainment of the normal sexual aim. This occurs if it happens that there is too much fore-pleasure and too little tension in any part of the preparatory sexual process. The motive power for the further continuation of the sexual process then escapes, the whole road becomes shortened, and the preparatory action in question takes the place of the normal sexual aim. Experience shows that such a hurtful condition is determined by the fact that the erogenous zone concerned or the corresponding partial impulse has already contributed an unusual amount of pleasure in infantile life. If other factors favoring fixation are added a compulsion readily results for the later life which prevents the fore-pleasure from arranging itself into a new combination. Indeed, the mechanism of many perversions is of such a nature; they merely represent a lingering at a preparatory act of the sexual process.

The failure of the function of the sexual mechanism through the fault of the fore-pleasure is generally avoided if the primacy of the genital zones has also already been sketched out in infantile life. The preparations of the second half of childhood (from the eighth year to puberty) really seem to favor this. During these years the genital zones behave almost as at the age of maturity; they are the seat of exciting sensations and of preparatory changes if any kind of pleasure is experienced through the gratification of other erogenous zones; although this effect remains aimless, *i.e.*, it contributes nothing towards the continuation of the sexual process. Besides the pleasure of gratification a certain amount of sexual tension appears even in infancy, though it is less constant and less abundant. We can now understand also why in the discussion of the sources of sexuality we had a perfectly good reason for saying that the process in question acts as sexual gratification as well as sexual excitement. We note that on our way towards the truth we have at first enormously exaggerated the distinctions between the infantile and the mature sexual life, and we therefore supplement what has been said with a correction. The infantile manifestations of sexuality determine not only the deviations from the normal sexual life but also the normal formations of the same.

---

[63] See my work, Wit and its Relation to the Unconscious, translated by A.A. Brill, Moffat Yard Pub. Co., New York: "The fore-pleasure gained by the technique of wit is utilized for the purpose of setting free a greater pleasure by the removal of inner inhibitions."

THE PROBLEM OF SEXUAL EXCITEMENT

It remains entirely unexplained whence the sexual tension comes which originates simultaneously with the gratification of erogenous zones and what is its nature. The obvious supposition that this tension originates in some way from the pleasure itself is not only improbable in itself but untenable, inasmuch as during the greatest pleasure which is connected with the voiding of sexual substance there is no production of tension but rather a removal of all tension. Hence, pleasure and sexual tension can be only indirectly connected.

The Rôle of the Sexual Substance.—Aside from the fact that only the discharge of the sexual substance can normally put an end to the sexual excitement, there are other essential facts which bring the sexual tension into relation with the sexual products. In a life of continence the sexual activity is wont to discharge the sexual substance at night during pleasurable dream hallucinations of a sexual act, this discharge coming at changing but not at entirely capricious intervals; and the following interpretation of this process—the nocturnal pollution—can hardly be rejected, viz., that the sexual tension which brings about a substitute for the sexual act by the short hallucinatory road is a function of the accumulated semen in the reservoirs for the sexual products. Experiences with the exhaustibility of the sexual mechanism speak for the same thing. Where there is no stock of semen it is not only impossible to accomplish the sexual act, but there is also a lack of excitability in the erogenous zones, the suitable excitation of which can evoke no pleasure. We thus discover incidentally that a certain amount of sexual tension is itself necessary for the excitability of the erogenous zones.

One would thus be forced to the assumption, which if I am not mistaken is quite generally adopted, that the accumulation of sexual substance produces and maintains the sexual tension. The pressure of these products on the walls of their receptacles acts as an excitant on the spinal center, the state of which is then perceived by the higher centers which then produce in consciousness the familiar feeling of tension. If the excitation of erogenous zones increases the sexual tension, it can only be due to the fact that the erogenous zones are connected with these centers by previously formed anatomical connections. They increase there the tone of the excitation, and with sufficient sexual tension they set in motion the sexual act, and with insufficient tension they merely stimulate a production of the sexual substance.

The weakness of the theory which one finds adopted, *e.g.*, in v. Krafft-Ebing's description of the sexual process, lies in the fact that it has been formed for the sexual activity of the mature man and pays too little heed to three kinds of relations which should also have been elucidated. We refer to the relations as found in the child, in the woman, and in the castrated male. In none of the three cases can we speak of an accumulation of sexual products in the same sense as in the man, which naturally renders difficult the general application of this scheme; still it may be admitted without any further ado that ways can be found to justify the subordination of even these cases. Nevertheless one should be cautious about burdening the factor of accumulation of sexual products with actions which it seems incapable of supporting.

Overestimation of the Internal Genitals.—That sexual excitement can be independent to a considerable extent of the production of sexual substance seems to be shown by observations on castrated males, in whom the libido sometimes escapes the injury caused by the operation, although the opposite behavior, which is really the motive for the operation, is usually the rule. It is therefore not at all surprising, as C. Rieger puts it, that the loss of the male germ glands in maturer age should exert no new influence on the psychic life of the individual. The germ glands are really not the sexuality, and the experience with castrated males only verifies what we had long before learned from the removal of the ovaries, namely that it is impossible to do away with the sexual character by removing the germ glands. To be sure, castration performed at a tender age, before puberty, comes nearer to this aim, but it would seem in this case that besides the loss of the sexual glands we must also consider the inhibition of development and other factors which are connected with that loss.

Chemical Theories.—The truth remains, however, that we are unable to give any information about the nature of the sexual excitement for the reason that we do not know with what organ or organs sexuality is connected, since we have seen that the sexual glands have been overestimated in this significance. Since surprising discoveries have taught us the important rôle of the thyroid gland in sexuality, we may assume that the knowledge of the essential factors of sexuality are still withheld from us. One who feels the need of filling up the large gap in our knowledge with a preliminary assumption may formulate for himself the following theory based on the active substances found in the thyroid. Through the appropriate excitement of erogenous zones, as well as through other conditions under which sexual excitement originates, a material which is universally distributed in the organism becomes disintegrated, the decomposing products of which supply a specific stimulus to the organs of reproduction or to the spinal center connected with them. Such a transformation of a toxic stimulus in a particular organic stimulus we are already familiar with from other toxic products introduced into the body from without. To treat, if only hypothetically, the complexities of the pure toxic and the physiologic stimulations which result in the sexual processes is not now our appropriate task. To be sure, I attach no value to this special assumption and I shall be quite ready to give it up in favor of another, provided its original character, the emphasis on the sexual chemism, were preserved. For this apparently arbitrary statement is supported by a fact which, though little heeded, is most noteworthy. The neuroses which can be traced only to disturbances of the sexual life show the greatest clinical resemblance to the phenomena of intoxication and abstinence which result from the habitual introduction of pleasure-producing poisonous substances (alkaloids.)

THE THEORY OF THE LIBIDO

These assumptions concerning the chemical basis of the sexual excitement are in full accord with the auxiliary conception which we formed for the purpose of mastering the psychic manifestations of the sexual life. We have determined the concept of *libido* as that of a force of variable quantity which has the capacity of measuring processes and transformations in the spheres of sexual excitement. This libido we distinguished from the energy which is to be generally adjudged to the psychic processes with reference to its special origin and thus we attribute to it also a qualitative character. In separating libidinous from other psychic energy we give expression to the assumption that the sexual processes of the organism are differentiated from the nutritional processes through a special chemism. The analyses of perversions and psychoneuroses have taught us that this sexual excitement is furnished not only from the so-called sexual parts alone but from all organs of the body. We thus formulate for ourselves the concept of a libido-quantum whose psychic representative we designate as the ego-libido; the production, increase, distribution and displacement of this ego-libido will offer the possible explanation for the observed psycho-sexual phenomena.

But this ego-libido becomes conveniently accessible to psychoanalytic study only when the psychic energy is employed on sexual objects, that is when it becomes object libido. Then we see it as it concentrates and fixes itself on objects, or as it leaves those objects and passes over to others from which positions it directs the individual's sexual activity, that is, it leads to partial and temporary extinction of the libido. Psychoanalysis of the so-called transference neuroses (hysteria and compulsion neurosis) offers us here a reliable insight.

Concerning the fates of the object libido we also state that it is withdrawn from the object, that it is preserved floating in special states of tension and is finally taken back into the ego, so that it again becomes ego-libido. In contradistinction to the object-libido we also call the ego-libido narcissistic libido. From psychoanalysis we look over the boundary which we are not permitted to pass into the activity of the narcissistic libido and thus form an idea of the relations between the two. The narcissistic or ego-libido appears to us as the great reservoir from which the energy for the investment of the object is sent out and into which it is drawn back again, while the narcissistic libido investment of the ego appears to us as the realized primitive state in the first childhood, which only becomes hidden by the later emissions of the libido, and is retained at the bottom behind them.

The task of a theory of libido of neurotic and psychotic disturbances would have for its object to express in terms of the libido-economy all observed phenomena and disclosed processes. It is easy to divine that the greater significance would attach thereby to the destinies of the ego-libido, especially where it would be the question of explaining the deeper psychotic disturbances. The difficulty then lies in the fact that the means of our investigation, psychoanalysis, at present gives us definite information only concerning the transformation of the object-libido, but cannot distinguish without further study the ego-libido from the other effective energies in the ego.[64]

DIFFERENTIATION BETWEEN MAN AND WOMAN

It is known that the sharp differentiation of the male and female character originates at puberty, and it is the resulting difference which, more than any other factor, decisively influences the later development of personality. To be sure, the male and female dispositions are easily recognizable even in infantile life; thus the development of sexual inhibitions (shame, loathing, sympathy, etc.) ensues earlier and with less resistance in the little girl than in the little boy. The tendency to sexual repression certainly seems much greater, and where partial impulses of sexuality are noticed they show a

---

[64] Cf. Zur Einführung des Narzismus, Jahrbuch der Psychoanalyse, VI, 1913.

preference for the passive form. But, the autoerotic activity of the erogenous zones is the same in both sexes, and it is this agreement that removes the possibility of a sex differentiation in childhood as it appears after puberty. In respect to the autoerotic and masturbatic sexual manifestations, it may be asserted that the sexuality of the little girl has entirely a male character. Indeed, if one could give a more definite content to the terms "masculine and feminine," one might advance the opinion that *the libido is regularly and lawfully of a masculine nature, whether in the man or in the woman; and if we consider its object, this may be either the man or the woman.*[65]

Since becoming acquainted with the aspect of bisexuality I hold this factor as here decisive, and I believe that without taking into account the factor of bisexuality it will hardly be possible to understand the actually observed sexual manifestations in man and woman.

The Leading Zones in Man and Woman.—Further than this I can only add the following. The chief erogenous zone in the female child is the clitoris, which is homologous to the male penis. All I have been able to discover concerning masturbation in little girls concerned the clitoris and not those other external genitals which are so important for the later sexual functions. With few exceptions I myself doubt whether the female child can be seduced to anything but clitoris masturbation. The frequent spontaneous discharges of sexual excitement in little girls manifest themselves in a twitching of the clitoris, and its frequent erections enable the girl to understand correctly even without any instruction the sexual manifestations of the other sex; they simply transfer to the boys the sensations of their own sexual processes.

If one wishes to understand how the little girl becomes a woman, he must follow up the further destinies of this clitoris excitation. Puberty, which brings to the boy a great advance of libido, distinguishes itself in the girl by a new wave of repression which especially concerns the clitoris sexuality. It is

---

[65] It is necessary to make clear that the conceptions "masculine" and "feminine," whose content seems so unequivocal to the ordinary meaning, belong to the most confused terms in science and can be cut up into at least three paths. One uses masculine and feminine at times in the sense of activity and passivity, again, in the biological sense, and then also in the sociological sense. The first of these three meanings is the essential one and the only one utilizable in psychoanalysis. It agrees with the masculine designation of the libido in the text above, for the libido is always active even when it is directed to a passive aim. The second, the biological significance of masculine and feminine, is the one which permits the clearest determination. Masculine and feminine are here characterized by the presence of semen or ovum and through the functions emanating from them. The activity and its secondary manifestations, like stronger developed muscles, aggression, a greater intensity of libido, are as a rule soldered to the biological masculinity but not necessarily connected with it, for there are species of animals in whom these qualities are attributed to the female. The third, the sociological meaning, receives its content through the observation of the actual existing male and female individuals. The result of this in man is that there is no pure masculinity or feminity either in the biological or psychological sense. On the contrary every individual person shows a mixture of his own biological sex characteristics with the biological traits of the other sex and a union of activity and passivity; this is the case whether these psychological characteristic features depend on the biological or whether they are independent of it.

a part of the male sexual life that sinks into repression. The reënforcement of the sexual inhibitions produced in the woman by the repression of puberty causes a stimulus in the libido of the man and forces it to increase its capacity; with the height of the libido there is a rise in the overestimation of the sexual, which can be present in its full force only when the woman refuses and denies her sexuality. If the sexual act is finally submitted to and the clitoris becomes excited its rôle is then to conduct the excitement to the adjacent female parts, and in this it acts like a chip of pine wood which is utilized to set fire to the harder wood. It often takes some time for this transference to be accomplished; during which the young wife remains anesthetic. This anesthesia may become permanent if the clitoris zone refuses to give up its excitability; a condition brought on by abundant activities in infantile life. It is known that anesthesia in women is often only apparent and local. They are anesthetic at the vaginal entrance but not at all unexcitable through the clitoris or even through other zones. Besides these erogenous causes of anesthesia there are also psychic causes likewise determined by the repression.

If the transference of the erogenous excitability from the clitoris to the vagina has succeeded, the woman has thus changed her leading zone for the future sexual activity; the man on the other hand retains his from childhood. The main determinants for the woman's preference for the neuroses, especially for hysteria, lie in this change of the leading zone as well as in the repression of puberty. These determinants are therefore most intimately connected with the nature of femininity.

THE OBJECT-FINDING

While the primacy of the genital zones is being established through the processes of puberty, and the erected penis in the man imperiously points towards the new sexual aim, *i.e.*, towards the penetration of a cavity which excites the genital zone, the object-finding, for which also preparations have been made since early childhood, becomes consummated on the psychic side. While the very incipient sexual gratifications are still connected with the taking of nourishment, the sexual impulse has a sexual object outside its own body in his mother's breast. This object it loses later, perhaps at the very time when it becomes possible for the child to form a general picture of the person to whom the organ granting him the gratification belongs. The sexual impulse later regularly becomes autoerotic, and only after overcoming the latency period is there a resumption of the original relation. It is not without good reason that the suckling of the child at its mother's breast has become a model for every amour. The object-finding is really a re-finding.[66]

The Sexual Object of the Nursing Period.—However, even after the separation of the sexual activity from the taking of nourishment, there still remains from this first and most important of all sexual relations an important share, which prepares the object selection and assists in reestablishing the lost happiness. Throughout the latency period the child learns to love other persons who assist it in its helplessness and gratify its wants; all this follows the model and is a continuation of the child's infantile relations to his wet nurse. One may perhaps hesitate to identify the tender feelings and esteem of the child for his foster-parents with sexual love; I believe, however, that a more thorough psychological investigation will establish this identity beyond any doubt. The intercourse between the child and its foster-parents is for the former an inexhaustible source of sexual excitation and gratification of erogenous zones, especially since the parents— or as a rule the mother—supplies the child with feelings which originate from her own sexual life; she pats it, kisses it, and rocks it, plainly taking it as a substitute for a full-valued sexual object.[67]The mother would probably be terrified if it were explained to her that all her tenderness awakens the sexual impulse of her child and prepares its future intensity. She considers her actions as asexually "pure" love, for she carefully avoids causing more irritation to the genitals of the child than is indispensable in caring for the body. But as we know the sexual impulse is not awakened by the excitation of genital zones alone. What we call tenderness will some day surely manifest its influence on the genital zones also. If the mother better understood the high significance of the sexual impulse for the whole psychic life and for all ethical and psychic activities, the enlightenment would spare her all reproaches. By teaching the child to love she only fulfills her function; for the child should become a fit man with energetic sexual needs, and accomplish in life all that the impulse urges the man to do. Of course, too much parental tenderness becomes harmful because it accelerates the sexual maturity, and also because it "spoils" the child and makes it unfit to temporarily renounce love or be satisfied with a smaller amount of love in later life. One of the surest premonitions of later nervousness is the fact that the child shows itself insatiable in its demands for parental tenderness; on the other hand, neuropathic parents, who usually display a boundless tenderness, often with their caressing awaken in the child a disposition for neurotic diseases. This

---

[66] Psychoanalysis teaches that there are two paths of object-finding; the first is the one discussed in the text which is guided by the early infantile prototypes. The second is the narcissistic which seeks its own ego and finds it in the other. The latter is of particularly great significance for the pathological outcomes, but does not fit into the connection treated here.

[67] Those to whom this conception appears "wicked" may read Havelock Ellis's treatise on the relations between mother and child which expresses almost the same ideas (The Sexual Impulse, p. 16).

example at least shows that neuropathic parents have nearer ways than inheritance by which they can transfer their disturbances to their children.

Infantile Fear.—The children themselves behave from their early childhood as if their attachment to their foster-parents were of the nature of sexual love. The fear of children is originally nothing but an expression for the fact that they miss the beloved person. They therefore meet every stranger with fear, they are afraid of the dark because they cannot see the beloved person, and are calmed if they can grasp that person's hand. The effect of childish fears and of the terrifying stories told by nurses is overestimated if one blames the latter for producing the fear in children. Children who are predisposed to fear absorb these stories, which make no impression whatever upon others; and only such children are predisposed to fear whose sexual impulse is excessive or prematurely developed, or has become exigent through pampering. The child behaves here like the adult, that is, it changes its libido into fear when it cannot bring it to gratification, and the grown-up who becomes neurotic on account of ungratified libido behaves in his anxiety like a child; he fears when he is alone, *i.e.*, without a person of whose love he believes himself sure, and who can calm his fears by means of the most childish measures.[68]

Incest Barriers.—If the tenderness of the parents for the child has luckily failed to awaken the sexual impulse of the child prematurely, *i.e.*, before the physical determinations for puberty appear, and if that awakening has not gone so far as to cause an unmistakable breaking through of the psychic excitement into the genital system, it can then fulfill its task and direct the child at the age of maturity in the selection of the sexual object. It would, of course, be most natural for the child to select as the sexual object that person whom it has loved since childhood with, so to speak, a suppressed libido.[69] But owing to the delay of sexual maturity time has been gained for the erection beside the sexual inhibitions of the incest barrier, that moral prescription which explicitly excludes from the object selection the beloved person of infancy or blood relation. The observance of this barrier is above all a demand of cultural society which must guard against the absorption by the family of those interests which it needs for the production of higher social units. Society, therefore, uses every means to loosen those family ties in

---

[68] For the explanation of the origin of the infantile fear I am indebted to a three-year-old boy whom I once heard calling from a dark room: "Aunt, talk to me, I am afraid because it is dark." "How will that help you," answered the aunt; "you cannot see anyhow." "That's nothing," answered the child; "if some one talks then it becomes light."—He was, as we see, not afraid of the darkness but he was afraid because he missed the person he loved, and he could promise to calm down as soon as he was assured of her presence.

[69] Cf. here what was said on page 83 concerning the object selection of the child; the "tender stream."

every individual, especially in the boy, which are authoritative in childhood only.[70]

The object selection, however, is first accomplished in the imagination, and the sexual life of the maturing youth has hardly any escape except indulgence in phantasies or ideas which are not destined to be brought to execution. In the phantasies of all persons the infantile inclinations, now reënforced by somatic emphasis, reappear, and among them one finds in regular frequency and in the first place the sexual feeling of the child for the parents. This has usually already been differentiated by the sexual attraction, the attraction of the son for the mother and of the daughter for the father. [71]Simultaneously with the overcoming and rejection of these distinctly incestuous phantasies there occurs one of the most important as well as one of the most painful psychic accomplishments of puberty; it is the breaking away from the parental authority, through which alone is formed that opposition between the new and old generations which is so important for cultural progress. Many persons are detained at each of the stations in the course of development through which the individual must pass; and accordingly there are persons who never overcome the parental authority and never, or very imperfectly, withdraw their affection from their parents. They are mostly girls, who, to the delight of their parents, retain their full infantile love far beyond puberty, and it is instructive to find that in their married life these girls are incapable of fulfilling their duties to their husbands. They make cold wives and remain sexually anesthetic. This shows that the apparently non-sexual love for the parents and the sexual love are nourished from the same source, i.e., that the first merely corresponds to an infantile fixation of the libido.

The nearer we come to the deeper disturbances of the psychosexual development the more easily we can recognize the evident significance of the incestuous object-selection. As a result of sexual rejection there remains in the unconscious of the psychoneurotic a great part or the whole of the psychosexual activity for object finding. Girls with an excessive need for affection and an equal horror for the real demands of the sexual life experience an uncontrollable temptation on the one hand to realize in life the ideal of the asexual love and on the other hand to conceal their libido under an affection which they may manifest without self reproach; this they do by clinging for life to the infantile attraction for their parents or brothers or

---

[70] The incest barrier probably belongs to the historical acquisitions of humanity and like other moral taboos it must be fixed in many individuals through organic heredity. (Cf. my work, Totem and Taboo, 1913.) Psychoanalytic studies show, however, how intensively the individual struggles with the incest temptations during his development and how frequently he puts them into phantasies and even into reality.

[71] Compare the description concerning the inevitable relation in the Oedipus legend (The Interpretation of Dreams, p. 222, translated by A.A. Brill, The Macmillan Co., New York, and Allen & Unwin, London).

sisters which has been repressed in puberty. With the help of the symptoms and other morbid manifestations, psychoanalysis can trace their unconscious thoughts and translate them into the conscious, and thus easily show to such persons that they are in love with their consanguinous relations in the popular meaning of the term. Likewise when a once healthy person falls sick after an unhappy love affair, the mechanism of the disease can distinctly be explained as a return of his libido to the persons preferred in his infancy.

The After Effects of the Infantile Object Selection.—Even those who have happily eluded the incestuous fixation of their libido have not completely escaped its influence. It is a distinct echo of this phase of development that the first serious love of the young man is often for a mature woman and that of the girl for an older man equipped with authority—*i.e.,* for persons who can revive in them the picture of the mother and father. Generally speaking object selection unquestionably takes place by following more freely these prototypes. The man seeks above all the memory picture of his mother as it has dominated him since the beginning of childhood; this is quite consistent with the fact that the mother, if still living, strives against this, her renewal, and meets it with hostility. In view of this significance of the infantile relation to the parents for the later selection of the sexual object, it is easy to understand that every disturbance of this infantile relation brings to a head the most serious results for the sexual life after puberty. Jealousy of the lover, too, never lacks the infantile sources or at least the infantile reinforcement. Quarrels between parents and unhappy marital relations between the same determine the severest predispositions for disturbed sexual development or neurotic diseases in the children.

The infantile desire for the parents is, to be sure, the most important, but not the only trace revived in puberty which points the way to the object selection. Other dispositions of the same origin permit the man, still supported by his infancy, to develop more than one single sexual series and to form different determinations for the object selection.[72]

Prevention of Inversion.—One of the tasks imposed in the object selection consists in not missing the opposite sex. This, as we know, is not solved without some difficulty. The first feelings after puberty often enough go astray, though not with any permanent injury. Dessoir has called attention to the normality of the enthusiastic friendships formed by boys and girls with their own sex. The greatest force which guards against a permanent inversion of the sexual object is surely the attraction exerted by the opposite sex characters on each other. For this we can give no explanation in connection with this discussion. This factor, however, does not in itself suffice to exclude

---

[72] Innumerable peculiarities of the human love-life as well as the compulsiveness of being in love itself can surely only be understood through a reference to childhood or as an effective remnant of the same.

the inversion; besides this there are surely many other supporting factors. Above all, there is the authoritative inhibition of society; experience shows that where the inversion is not considered a crime it fully corresponds to the sexual inclinations of many persons. Moreover, it may be assumed that in the man the infantile memories of the mother's tenderness, as well as that of other females who cared for him as a child, energetically assist in directing his selection to the woman, while the early sexual intimidation experienced through the father and the attitude of rivalry existing between them deflects the boy from the same sex. Both factors also hold true in the case of the girl whose sexual activity is under the special care of the mother. This results in a hostile relation to the same sex which decisively influences the object selection in the normal sense. The bringing up of boys by male persons (slaves in the ancient times) seems to favor homosexuality; the frequency of inversion in the present day nobility is probably explained by their employment of male servants, and by the scant care that mothers of that class give to their children. It happens in some hysterics that one of the parents has disappeared (through death, divorce, or estrangement), thus permitting the remaining parent to absorb all the love of the child, and in this way establishing the determinations for the sex of the person to be selected later as the sexual object; thus a permanent inversion is made possible.

SUMMARY

It is now time to attempt a summing-up. We have started from the aberrations of the sexual impulse in reference to its object and aim and have encountered the question whether these originate from a congenital predisposition, or whether they are acquired in consequence of influences from life. The answer to this question was reached through an examination of the relations of the sexual life of psychoneurotics, a numerous group not very remote from the normal. This examination has been made through psychoanalytic investigations. We have thus found that a tendency to all perversions might be demonstrated in these persons in the form of unconscious forces revealing themselves as symptom creators and we could say that the neurosis is, as it were, the negative of the perversion. In view of the now recognized great diffusion of tendencies to perversion the idea forced itself upon us that the disposition to perversions is the primitive and universal disposition of the human sexual impulse, from which the normal sexual behavior develops in consequence of organic changes and psychic inhibitions in the course of maturity. We hoped to be able to demonstrate the original disposition in the infantile life; among the forces restraining the direction of the sexual impulse we have mentioned shame, loathing and sympathy, and the social constructions of morality and authority. We have thus been forced to perceive in every fixed aberration from the normal sexual life a fragment of inhibited development and infantilism. The significance of the variations of the original dispositions had to be put into the foreground, but between them and the influences of life we had to assume a relation of coöperation and not of opposition. On the other hand, as the original disposition must have been a complex one, the sexual impulse itself appeared to us as something composed of many factors, which in the perversions becomes separated, as it were, into its components. The perversions, thus prove themselves to be on the one hand inhibitions, and on the other dissociations from the normal development. Both conceptions became united in the assumption that the sexual impulse of the adult due to the composition of the diverse feelings of the infantile life became formed into one unit, one striving, with one single aim.

We also added an explanation for the preponderance of perversive tendencies in the psychoneurotics by recognizing in these tendencies collateral fillings of side branches caused by the shifting of the main river bed through repression, and we then turned our examination to the sexual life of the infantile period.[73] We found it regrettable that the existence of a sexual life in infancy has been disputed, and that the sexual manifestations which have been often observed in children have been described as abnormal occurrences. It rather seemed to us that the child brings along into the world germs of sexual activity and that even while taking nourishment it at the same time also enjoys a sexual gratification which it then seeks again to procure for itself through the familiar activity of "thumbsucking." The sexual activity of the child, however, does not develop in the same measure as its other functions, but merges first into the so-called latency period from the age of three to the age of five years. The production of sexual excitation by no means ceases at this period but continues and furnishes a stock of energy, the greater part of which is utilized for aims other than sexual; namely, on the one hand for the delivery of sexual components for social feelings, and on the other hand (by means of repression and reaction formation) for the erection of the future sexual barriers. Accordingly, the forces which are destined to hold the sexual impulse in certain tracks are built up in infancy at the expense of the greater part of the perverse sexual feelings and with the assistance of education. Another part of the infantile sexual manifestations escapes this

---

[73] This was true not only of the "negative" tendencies to perversion appearing in the neurosis, but also of the so-called positive perversions. The latter are not only to be attributed to the fixation of the infantile tendencies, but also to regression to these tendencies owing to the misplacement of other paths of the sexual stream. Hence the positive perversions are also accessible to psychoanalytic therapy. (Cf. the works of Sadger, Ferenczi, and Brill.)

utilization and may manifest itself as sexual activity. It can then be discovered that the sexual excitation of the child flows from diverse sources. Above all gratifications originate through the adapted sensible excitation of so-called erogenous zones. For these probably any skin region or sensory organ may serve; but there are certain distinguished erogenous zones the excitation of which by certain organic mechanisms is assured from the beginning. Moreover, sexual excitation originates in the organism, as it were, as a by-product in a great number of processes, as soon as they attain a certain intensity; this especially takes place in all strong emotional excitements even if they be of a painful nature. The excitations from all these sources do not yet unite, but they pursue their aim individually—this aim consisting merely in the gaining of a certain pleasure. The sexual impulse of childhood is therefore objectless or *autoerotic*.

Still during infancy the erogenous zone of the genitals begins to make itself noticeable, either by the fact that like any other erogenous zone it furnishes gratification through a suitable sensible stimulus, or because in some incomprehensible way the gratification from other sources causes at the same time the sexual excitement which has a special connection with the genital zone. We found cause to regret that a sufficient explanation of the relations between sexual gratification and sexual excitement, as well as between the activity of the genital zone and the remaining sources of sexuality, was not to be attained.

We were unable to state what amount of sexual activity in childhood might be designated as normal to the extent of being incapable of further development. The character of the sexual manifestation showed itself to be preponderantly masturbatic. We, moreover, verified from experience the belief that the external influences of seduction, might produce premature breaches in the latency period leading as far as the suppression of the same, and that the sexual impulse of the child really shows itself to be polymorphous-perverse; furthermore, that every such premature sexual activity impairs the educability of the child.

Despite the incompleteness of our examinations of the infantile sexual life we were subsequently forced to attempt to study the serious changes produced by the appearance of puberty. We selected two of the same as criteria, namely, the subordination of all other sources of the sexual feeling to the primacy of the genital zones, and the process of object finding. Both of them are already developed in childhood. The first is accomplished through the mechanism of utilizing the fore-pleasure, whereby all other independent sexual acts which are connected with pleasure and excitement become preparatory acts for the new sexual aim, the voiding of the sexual products, the attainment of which under enormous pleasure puts an end to the sexual feeling. At the same time we had to consider the differentiation of the sexual nature of man and woman, and we found that in order to become a woman a new repression is required which abolishes a piece of infantile masculinity, and prepares the woman for the change of the leading genital zones. Lastly, we found the object selection, tracing it through infancy to its revival in puberty; we also found indications of sexual inclinations on the part of the child for the parents and foster-parents, which, however, were turned away from these persons to others resembling them by the incest barriers which had been erected in the meantime. Let us finally add that during the transition period of puberty the somatic and psychic processes of development proceed side by side, but separately, until with the breaking through of an intense psychic love-stimulus for the innervation of the genitals, the normally demanded unification of the erotic function is established.

The Factors Disturbing the Development.—As we have already shown by different examples, every step on this long road of development may become a point of fixation and every joint in this complicated structure may afford opportunity for a dissociation of the sexual impulse. It still remains for us to review the various inner and outer factors which disturb the development, and to mention the part of the mechanism affected by the disturbance emanating from them. The factors which we mention here in a series cannot, of course, all be in themselves of equal validity and we must expect to meet with difficulties in the assigning to the individual factors their due importance.

Constitution and Heredity.—In the first place, we must mention here the congenital *variation of the sexual constitution*, upon which the greatest weight probably falls, but the existence of which, as may be easily understood, can be established only through its later manifestations and even then not always with great certainty. We understand by it a preponderance of one or another of the manifold sources of the sexual excitement, and we believe that such a difference of disposition must always come to expression in the final result, even if it should remain within normal limits. Of course, we can also imagine certain variations of the original disposition that even without further aid must necessarily lead to the formation of an abnormal sexual life. One can call these "degenerative" and consider them as an expression of hereditary deterioration. In this connection I have to report a remarkable fact. In more than half of the severe cases of hysteria, compulsion neuroses, etc., which I have treated by psychotherapy, I have succeeded in positively demonstrating that their fathers have gone through an attack of syphilis before marriage; they have either suffered from tabes or general paresis, or there was a definite history of lues. I expressly add that the children who were later neurotic showed absolutely no signs of hereditary lues, so that the abnormal sexual constitution was to be considered as the last off-shoot of the

373

luetic heredity. As far as it is now from my thoughts to put down a descent from syphilitic parents as a regular and indispensable etiological determination of the neuropathic constitution, I nevertheless maintain that the coincidence observed by me is not accidental and not without significance.

The hereditary relations of the positive perverts are not so well known because they know how to avoid inquiry. Still there is reason to believe that the same holds true in the perversions as in the neuroses. We often find perversions and psychoneuroses in the different sexes of the same family, so distributed that the male members, or one of them, is a positive pervert, while the females, following the repressive tendencies of their sex, are negative perverts or hysterics. This is a good example of the substantial relations between the two disturbances which I have discovered.

Further Elaboration.—It cannot, however, be maintained that the structure of the sexual life is rendered finally complete by the addition of the diverse components of the sexual constitution. On the contrary, qualifications continue to appear and new possibilities result, depending upon the fate experienced by the sexual streams originating from the individual sources. This *further elaboration* is evidently the final and decisive one while the constitution described as uniform may lead to three final issues. If all the dispositions assumed to be abnormal retain their relative proportion, and are strengthened with maturity, the ultimate result can only be a perverse sexual life. The analysis of such abnormally constituted dispositions has not yet been thoroughly undertaken, but we already know cases that can be readily explained in the light of these theories. Authors believe, for example, that a whole series of fixation perversions must necessarily have had as their basis a congenital weakness of the sexual impulse. The statement seems to me untenable in this form, but it becomes ingenious if it refers to a constitutional weakness of one factor in the sexual impulse, namely, the genital zone, which later in the interests of propagation accepts as a function the sum of the individual sexual activities. In this case the summation which is demanded in puberty must fail and the strongest of the other sexual components continues its activity as a perversion.[74]

Repression.—Another issue results if in the course of development certain powerful components experience a *repression*—which we must carefully note is not a suspension. The excitations in question are produced as usual but are prevented from attaining their aim by psychic hindrances, and are driven off into many other paths until they express themselves in a symptom. The result can be an almost normal sexual life—usually a limited

---

[74] Here one often sees that at first a normal sexual stream begins at the age of puberty, but owing to its inner weakness it breaks down at the first outer hindrance and then changes from regression, to perverse fixation.

one—but supplemented by psychoneurotic disease. It is these cases that become so familiar to us through the psychoanalytic investigation of neurotics. The sexual life of such persons begins like that of perverts, a considerable part of their childhood is filled up with perverse sexual activity which occasionally extends far beyond the period of maturity, but owing to inner reasons a repressive change then results—usually before puberty, but now and then even much later—and from this point on without any extinction of the old feelings there appears a neurosis instead of a perversion. One may recall here the saying, "Junge Hure, alte Betschwester,"—only here youth has turned out to be much too short. The relieving of the perversion by the neurosis in the life of the same person, as well as the above mentioned distribution of perversion and hysteria in different persons of the same family, must be placed side by side with the fact that the neurosis is the negative of the perversion.

Sublimation.—The third issue in abnormal constitutional dispositions is made possible by the process of "sublimation," through which the powerful excitations from individual sources of sexuality are discharged and utilized in other spheres, so that a considerable increase of psychic capacity results from an, in itself dangerous, predisposition. This forms one the sources of artistic activity, and, according as such sublimation is complete or incomplete, the analysis of the character of highly gifted, especially of artistically disposed persons, will show any proportionate, blending between productive ability, perversion, and neurosis. A sub-species of sublimation is the suppression through *reaction-formation*, which, as we have found, begins even in the latency period of infancy, only to continue throughout life in favorable cases. What we call the *character* of a person is built up to a great extent from the material of sexual excitations; it is composed of impulses fixed since infancy and won through sublimation, and of such constructions as are destined to suppress effectually those perverse feelings which are recognized as useless. The general perverse sexual disposition of childhood can therefore be esteemed as a source of a number of our virtues, insofar as it incites their creation through the formation of reactions.[75]

Accidental Experiences.—All other influences lose in significance when compared with the sexual discharges, shifts of repressions, and sublimations; the inner determinations for the last two processes are totally unknown to us. He who includes repressions and sublimations among constitutional predispositions, and considers them as the living manifestations of the same, has surely the right to maintain that the final structure of the sexual life is above all the result of the congenital

---

[75] That keen observer of human nature, E. Zola, describes a girl in his book, La Joie de vivre, who in cheerful self renunciation offers all she has in possession or expectation, her fortune and her life's hopes to those she loves without thought of return. The childhood of this girl was dominated by an insatiable desire for love which whenever she was depreciated caused her to merge into a fit of cruelty.

constitution. No intelligent person, however, will dispute that in such a cooperation of factors there is also room for the modifying influences of occasional factors derived from experience in childhood and later on.

It is not easy to estimate the effectiveness of the constitutional and of the occasional factors in their relation to each other. Theory is always inclined to overestimate the first while therapeutic practice renders prominent the significance of the latter. By no means should it be forgotten that between the two there exists a relation of cooperation and not of exclusion. The constitutional factor must wait for experiences which bring it to the surface, while the occasional needs the support of the constitutional factor in order to become effective. For the majority of cases one can imagine a so-called "etiological group" in which the declining intensities of one factor become balanced by the rise in the others, but there is no reason to deny the existence of extremes at the ends of the group.

It would be still more in harmony with psychoanalytic investigation if the experiences of early childhood would get a place of preference among the occasional factors. The one etiological group then becomes split up into two which may be designated as the dispositional and the definitive groups. Constitution and occasional infantile experiences are just as cooperative in the first as disposition and later traumatic experiences in the second group. All the factors which injure the sexual development show their effect in that they produce a *regression*, or a return to a former phase of development.

We may now continue with our task of enumerating the factors which have become known to us as influential for the sexual development, whether they be active forces or merely manifestations of the same.

Prematurity.—Such a factor is the spontaneous sexual *prematurity* which can be definitely demonstrated at least in the etiology of the neuroses, though in itself it is as little adequate for causation as the other factors. It manifests itself in a breaking through, shortening, or suspending of the infantile latency period and becomes a cause of disturbances inasmuch as it provokes sexual manifestations which, either on account of the unready state of the sexual inhibitions or because of the undeveloped state of the genital system, can only carry along the character of perversions. These tendencies to perversion may either remain as such, or after the repression sets in they may become motive powers for neurotic symptoms; at all events, the sexual prematurity renders difficult the desirable later control of the sexual impulse by the higher psychic influences, and enhances the compulsive-like character which even without this prematurity would be claimed by the psychic representatives of the impulse. Sexual prematurity often runs parallel with premature intellectual development; it is found as such in the infantile history of the most distinguished and most productive individuals, and in such connection it does not seem to act as pathogenically as when appearing isolated.

Temporal Factors.—Just like prematurity, other factors, which under the designation of *temporal* can be added to prematurity, also demand consideration. It seems to be phylogenetically established in what sequence the individual impulsive feelings become active, and how long they can manifest themselves before they succumb to the influence of a newly appearing active impulse or to a typical repression. But both in this temporal succession as well as in the duration of the same, variations seem to occur, which must exercise a definite influence on the experience. It cannot be a matter of indifference whether a certain stream appears earlier or later than its counterstream, for the effect of a repression cannot be made retrogressive; a temporal deviation in the composition of the components regularly produces a change in the result. On the other hand impulsive feelings which appear with special intensity often come to a surprisingly rapid end, as in the case of the heterosexual attachment of the later manifest homosexuals. The strivings of childhood which manifest themselves most impetuously do not justify the fear that they will lastingly dominate the character of the grown-up; one has as much right to expect that they will disappear in order to make room for their counterparts. (Harsh masters do not rule long.) To what one may attribute such temporal confusions of the processes of development we are hardly able to suggest. A view is opened here to a deeper phalanx of biological, and perhaps also historical problems, which we have not yet approached within fighting distance.

Adhesion.—The significance of all premature sexual manifestations is enhanced by a psychic factor of unknown origin which at present can be put down only as a psychological preliminary. I believe that it is the *heightened adhesion* or *fixedness* of these impressions of the sexual life which in later neurotics, as well as in perverts, must be added for the completion of the other facts; for the same premature sexual manifestations in other persons cannot impress themselves deeply enough to repeat themselves compulsively and to succeed in prescribing the way for the sexual impulse throughout later life. Perhaps a part of the explanation for this adhesion lies in another psychic factor which we cannot miss in the causation of the neuroses, namely, in the preponderance which in the psychic life falls to the share of memory traces as compared with recent impressions. This factor is apparently dependent on the intellectual development and grows with the growth of personal culture. In contrast to this the savage has been characterized as "the unfortunate child of the moment."[76]Owing to the oppositional relation existing between culture and the free development of sexuality, the results of which may be traced far

---

[76] It is possible that the heightened adhesion is only the result of a special intensive somatic sexual manifestation of former years.

into the formation of our life, the problem how the sexual life of the child evolves is of very little importance for the later life in the lower stages of culture and civilization, and of very great importance in the higher.

Fixation.—The influence of the psychic factors just mentioned favored the development of the accidentally experienced impulses of the infantile sexuality. The latter (especially in the form of seductions through other children or through adults) produce the material which, with the help of the former, may become fixed as a permanent disturbance. A considerable number of the deviations from the normal sexual life observed later have been thus established in neurotics and perverts from the beginning through the impressions received during the alleged sexually free period of childhood. The causation is produced by the responsiveness of the constitution, the prematurity, the quality of heightened adhesion, and the accidental excitement of the sexual impulse through outside influence.

The unsatisfactory conclusions which have resulted from this investigation of the disturbances of the sexual life is due to the fact that we as yet know too little concerning the biological processes in which the nature of sexuality consists to form from our isolated examinations a satisfactory theory for the explanation of either the normal or the pathological.

THE END

BOOK THREE.
TOTEM AND TABOO

RESEMBLANCES BETWEEN THE PSYCHIC LIVES OF SAVAGES AND NEUROTICS

AUTHOR'S PREFACE

THESE essays appeared under the subtitle of this book in the first numbers of the periodical *Imago* edited by me. They represent my first efforts to apply view-points and results of psychoanalysis to unexplained problems of racial psychology. In method this book contrasts with that of W. Wundt and the works of the Zurich Psychoanalytic School. The former tries to accomplish the same object through assumptions and procedures from non-analytic psychology, while the latter follow the opposite course and strive to settle problems of individual psychology by referring to material of racial psychology.[77]

I am pleased to say that the first stimulus for my own works came from these two sources.

I am fully aware of the shortcomings in these essays. I shall not touch upon those which are characteristic of first efforts at investigation. The others, however, demand a word of explanation. The four essays which are here collected will be of interest to a wide circle of educated people, but they can only be thoroughly understood and judged by those who are really acquainted with psychoanalysis as such. It is hoped that they may serve as a bond between students of ethnology, philology, folklore and of the allied sciences, and psychoanalysts; they cannot, however, supply both groups the entire requisites for such co-operation. They will not furnish the former with sufficient insight into the new psychological technique, nor will the psychoanalysts acquire through them an adequate command over the material to be elaborated. Both groups will have to content themselves with whatever attention they can stimulate here and there and with the hope that frequent meetings between them will not remain unproductive for science.

The two principal themes, totem and taboo, which give the name to this small book are not treated alike here. The problem of taboo is presented more exhaustively, and the effort to solve it is approached with perfect confidence. The investigation of totemism may be modestly expressed as: "This is all that psychoanalytic study can contribute at present to the elucidation of the

---

[77] Jung: *Wandlungen and Symbole der Libido* (Transformations and Symbols of the Libido.

problem of totemism." This difference in the treatment of the two subjects is due to the fact that taboo still exists in our midst. To be sure, it is negatively conceived and directed to different contents, but according to its psychological nature, it is still nothing else than Kant's 'Categorical Imperative', which tends to act compulsively and rejects all conscious motivations. On the other hand, totemism is a religio-social institution which is alien to our present feelings; it has long been abandoned and replaced by new forms. In the religions, morals, and customs of the civilized races of to-day it has left only slight traces, and even among those races where it is still retained, it has had to undergo great changes. The social and material progress of the history of mankind could obviously change taboo much less than totemism.

In this book the attempt is ventured to find the original meaning of totemism through its infantile traces, that is, through the indications in which it reappears in the development of our own children. The close connection between totem and taboo indicates the further paths to the hypothesis maintained here. And although this hypothesis leads to somewhat improbable conclusions, there is no reason for rejecting the possibility that it comes more or less near to the reality which is so hard to reconstruct.

I. THE SAVAGE'S FEAR OF INCEST

PRIMITIVE man is known to us by the stages of development through which he has passed: that is, through the inanimate monuments and implements which he has left behind for us, through our knowledge of his art, his religion and his attitude towards life, which we have received either directly or through the medium of legends, myths and fairy tales; and through the remnants of his ways of thinking that survive in our own manners and customs. Moreover, in a certain sense he is still our contemporary: there are people whom we still consider more closely related to primitive man than to ourselves, in whom we therefore recognize the direct descendants and representatives of earlier man. We can thus judge the so-called savage and semi-savage races; their psychic life assumes a peculiar interest for us, for we can recognize in their psychic life a well-preserved, early stage of our own development.

If this assumption is correct, a comparison of the 'Psychology of Primitive Races' as taught by folklore, with the psychology of the neurotic as it has become known through psychoanalysis will reveal numerous points of correspondence and throw new light on subjects that are more or less familiar to us.

For outer as well as for inner reasons, I am choosing for this comparison those tribes which have been described by ethnographists as being most backward and wretched: the aborigines of the youngest continent, namely Australia, whose fauna has also preserved for us so much that is archaic and no longer to be found elsewhere.

The aborigines of Australia are looked upon as a peculiar race which shows neither physical nor linguistic relationship with its nearest neighbours, the Melanesian, Polynesian and Malayan races. They do not build houses or permanent huts; they do not cultivate the soil or keep any domestic animals except dogs; and they do not even know the art of pottery. They live exclusively on the flesh of all sorts of animals which they kill in the chase, and on the roots which they dig. Kings or chieftains are unknown among them, and all communal affairs are decided by the elders in assembly. It is quite doubtful whether they evince any traces of religion in the form of worship of higher beings. The tribes living in the interior who have to contend with the greatest vicissitudes of life owing to a scarcity of water, seem in every way more primitive than those who live near the coast.

We surely would not expect that these poor naked cannibals should be moral in their sex life according to our ideas, or that they should have imposed a high degree of restriction upon their sexual impulses. And yet we learn that they have considered it their duty to exercise the most searching care and the most painful rigour in guarding against incestuous sexual relations. In fact their whole social organization seems to serve this object or to have been brought into relation with its attainment.

Among the Australians the system of *Totemism* takes the place of all religious and social institutions. Australian tribes are divided into smaller *septs* or clans, each taking the name of its *totem*. Now what is a totem? As a rule it is an animal, either edible and harmless, or dangerous and feared; more rarely the totem is a plant or a force of nature (rain, water), which stands in a peculiar relation to the whole clan. The totem is first of all the tribal ancestor of the clan, as well as its tutelary spirit and protector; it sends oracles and, though otherwise dangerous, the totem knows and spares its children. The members of a totem are therefore under a sacred obligation not to kill (destroy) their totem, to abstain from eating its meat or from any other enjoyment of it. Any violation of these prohibitions is automatically punished. The character of a totem is inherent not only in a single animal or a single being but in all the members of the species. From time to time festivals are held at which the members of a totem represent or imitate, in ceremonial dances, the movements and characteristics of their totems. The totem is hereditary either through the maternal or the paternal line; (maternal transmission probably always preceded and was only later supplanted by the paternal). The attachment to a totem is the foundation of all the social obligations of an Australian: it extends on the one hand beyond the tribal relationship, and on the other hand it supersedes consanguineous relationship. (Frazer, *Totemism and Exogamy*, Vol. I, p. 53. "The totem bond is stronger than the bond of blood or family in the modern sense."

The totem is not limited to district or to locality; the members of a totem may live separated from one another and on friendly terms with adherents of other totems[78].

And now, finally, we must consider that peculiarity of the totemic system which attracts the interest of the psychoanalyst. Almost everywhere the totem prevails there also exists the law that *the members of the same totem are not allowed to enter into sexual*

---

[78] This very brief extract of the totemic system cannot be left without some elucidation and without discussing its limitations. The name Totem or Totam was first learned from the North American Indians by the Englishman, J. Long, in 1791. The subject has gradually acquired great scientific interest and has called forth a copious literature. I refer especially to *Totemism and Exogamy* by J. G. Frazer, 4 vols., 1910, and the books and articles of Andrew Lang (*The Secret of Totem*, 1905). The credit for having recognized the significance of totemism for the ancient history of man belongs to the Scotchman, J. Ferguson MacLennan (*Fortnightly Review*, 1869-70). Exterior to Australia, totemic institutions were found and are still observed among North American Indians, as well as among the races of the Polynesian Islands group, in East India, and in a large part of Africa. Many traces and survivals otherwise hard to interpret lead to the conclusion that totemism also once existed among the aboriginal Aryan and Semitic races of Europe, so that many investigators are inclined to recognize in totemism a necessary phase of human development through which every race has passed.

How then did prehistoric man come to acquire a totem; that is, how did he come to make his descent from this or that animal foundation of his social duties and, as we shall hear, of his sexual restrictions as well? Many different theories have been advanced to explain this, a review of which the reader may find in Wundt's *Voelkerpsychologie* (Vol. II: *Mythus und Religion*). I promise soon to make the problem of totemism a subject of special study in which an effort will be made to solve it by applying the psychoanalytic method. (Cf. The fourth chapter of this work.)

Not only is the theory of totemism controversial, but the very facts concerning it are hardly to be expressed in such general statements as were attempted above. There is hardly an assertion to which one would not have to add exceptions and contradictions. But it must not be forgotten that even the most primitive and conservative races are, in a certain sense, old, and have a long period behind them during which whatsoever was aboriginal with them has undergone much development and distortion. Thus among those races who still evince it, we find totemism to-day in the most manifold states of decay and disintegration; we observe that fragments of it have passed over to other social and religious institutions; or it may exist in fixed forms but far removed from its original nature. The difficulty then consists in the fact that it is not altogether easy to decide what in the actual conditions is to be taken as a faithful copy of the significant past and what is to be considered as a secondary distortion of it.

relations with each other; that is, that they cannot marry each other. This represents the *exogamy* which is associated with the totem.

This sternly maintained prohibition is very remarkable. There is nothing to account for it in anything that we have hitherto learned from the conception of the totem or from any of its attributes; that is, we do not understand how it happened to enter the system of totemism. We are therefore not astonished if some investigators simply assume that at first exogamy—both as to its origin and to its meaning—had nothing to do with totemism, but that it was added to it at some time without any deeper association, when marriage restrictions proved necessary. However that may be, the association of totemism and exogamy exists, and proves to be very strong.

Let us elucidate the meaning of this prohibition through further discussion.

(*a*) The violation of the prohibition is not left to what is, so to speak, an automatic punishment, as is the case with other violations of the prohibitions of the totem (e.g., not to kill the totem animal), but is most energetically avenged by the whole tribe as if it were a question of warding off a danger that threatens the community as a whole or a guilt that weighs upon all. A few sentences from Frazer's book (*l.c.*, p. 54.) will show how seriously such trespasses are treated by these savages who, according to our standard are otherwise very immoral.

"In Australia the regular penalty for sexual intercourse with a person of a forbidden clan is death. It matters not whether the woman is of the same local group or has been captured in war from another tribe; a man of the wrong clan who uses her as his wife is hunted down and killed by his clansmen, and so is the woman; though in some cases, if they succeed in eluding capture for a certain time, the offence may be condoned. In the Ta-Ta-thi tribe, New South Wales, in the rare cases which occur, the man is killed, but the woman is only beaten or speared, or both, till she is nearly dead; the reason given for not actually killing her being that she was probably coerced. Even in casual amours the clan prohibitions are strictly observed; any violations of these prohibitions 'are regarded with the utmost abhorrence and are punished by death' (Howitt)."

(*b*) As the same severe punishment is also meted out for temporary love affairs which have not resulted in childbirth, the assumption of other motives, perhaps of a practical nature, becomes improbable.

(*c*) As the totem is hereditary and is not changed by marriage, the results of the prohibition, for instance in the case of maternal heredity, are easily perceived. If, for example, the man belongs to a clan with the totem of the Kangaroo and marries a woman of the Emu totem, the children, both boys and girls, are all Emu. According to the totem law incestuous relations with his mother and his sister, who are Emu like himself, are therefore made impossible for a son of this marriage[79].

(*d*) But we need only a reminder to realize that the exogamy connected with the totem accomplishes more; that is, aims at more than the prevention of incest with the mother or the sisters. It also makes it impossible for the man to have sexual union with all the women of his own group, with a number of females, therefore, who are not consanguineously related to him, by treating all these women like blood relations. The psychological justification for this extraordinary restriction, which far exceeds anything comparable to it among civilized races, is not, at first, evident. All we seem to understand is that the rôle of the totem (the animal) as ancestor is taken very seriously. Everybody descended from the same totem is consanguineous; that is, of one family; and in this family the most distant grades of relationship are recognized as an absolute obstacle to sexual union.

Thus these savages reveal to us an unusually high grade of incest dread or incest sensitiveness, combined with the peculiarity, which we do not very well understand, of substituting the totem relationship for the real blood relationship. But we must not exaggerate this contradiction too much, and let us bear in mind that the totem prohibitions include real incest as a special case.

In what manner the substitution of the totem group for the actual family has come about remains a riddle, the solution of which is

---

[79] But the father, who is a Kangaroo, is free—at least under this prohibition—to commit incest with his daughters, who are Emu. In the case of paternal inheritance of the totem the father would be Kangaroo as well as the children; then incest with the daughters would be forbidden to the father and incest with the mother would be left open to the son. These consequences of the totem prohibition seem to indicate that the maternal inheritance is older than the paternal one, for there are grounds for assuming that the totem prohibitions are directed first of all against the incestuous desires of the son

perhaps bound up with the explanation of the totem itself. Of course it must be remembered that with a certain freedom of sexual intercourse, extending beyond the limitations of matrimony, the blood relationship, and with it also the prevention of incest, becomes so uncertain that we cannot dispense with some other basis for the prohibition. It is therefore not superfluous to note that the customs of Australians recognize social conditions and festive occasions at which the exclusive conjugal right of a man to a woman is violated.

The linguistic customs of these tribes, as well as of most totem races, reveals a peculiarity which undoubtedly is pertinent in this connection. For the designations of relationship of which they make use do not take into consideration the relationship between two individuals, but between an individual and his group; they belong, according to the expression of L. H. Morgan, to the 'classifying' system. That means that a man calls not only his begetter 'father' but also every other man who, according to the tribal regulations, might have married his mother and thus become his father; he calls 'mother' not only the woman who bore him but also every other woman who might have become his mother without violation of the tribal laws; he calls 'brothers' and 'sisters' not only the children of his real parents, but also the children of all the persons named who stand in the parental group relation with him, and so on. The kinship names which two Australians give each other do not, therefore, necessarily point to a blood relationship between them, as they would have to according to the custom of our language; they signify much more the social than the physical relations. An approach to this classifying system is perhaps to be found in our nursery, when the child is induced to greet every male and female friend of the parents as 'uncle' and 'aunt', or it may be found in a transferred sense when we speak of 'Brothers in Apollo', or 'Sisters in Christ'.

The explanation of this linguistic custom, which seems so strange to us, is simple if looked upon as a remnant and indication of those marriage institutions which the Rev. L. Fison has called 'group marriage', characterized by a number of men exercising conjugal rights over a number of women. The children of this group marriage would then rightly look upon each other as brothers and sisters although not born of the same mother, and would take all the men of the group for their fathers.

Although a number of authors, as, for instance, B. Westermarck in his *History of Human Marriage*, oppose the conclusions which others have drawn from the existence of group-relationship names, the best authorities on the Australian savages are agreed that the classificatory relationship names must be considered as survivals from the period of group marriages. And, according to Spencer and Gillen[*The Native Tribes of Central Australia* (London, 1899)], a certain form of group marriage can be established as still existing to-day among the tribes of the Urabunna and the Dieri. Group marriage therefore preceded individual marriage among these races, and did not disappear without leaving distinct traces in language and custom.

But if we replace individual marriage, we can then grasp the apparent excess of cases of incest shunning which we have met among these same races. The totem exogamy, or prohibition of sexual intercourse between members of the same clan, seemed the most appropriate means for the prevention of group incest; and this totem exogamy then became fixed and long survived its original motivation.

Although we believe we understand the motives of the marriage restrictions among the Australian savages, we have still to learn that the actual conditions reveal a still more bewildering complication. For there are only few tribes in Australia which show no other prohibition besides the totem barrier. Most of them are so organized that they fall into two divisions which have been called marriage classes, or phratries. Each of these marriage groups is exogamous and includes a majority of totem groups. Usually each marriage group is again divided into two subclasses (subphratries), and the whole tribe is therefore divided into four classes; the subclasses thus standing between the phratries and the totem groups.

The typical and very often intricate scheme of organization of an Australian tribe therefore looks as follows:

The twelve totem groups are brought under four subclasses and two main classes. All the divisions are exogamous (The number of totems is arbitrarily chosen). The subclass c forms an exogamous unit with e, and the subclass d with f. The success or the tendency of these arrangements is quite obvious; they serve as a further restriction on the marriage choice and on sexual freedom. If there were only these twelve totem groups—assuming the same number of people in each group—every member of a group would have 11/12 of all the women of the tribe to choose from. The existence of the two phratries reduces this number to 6/12 or ½; a man of the totem α can only marry a woman from the groups 1 to 6. With the introduction of the two subclassess the selection sinks to 3/12 or ¼; a man of the totem α must limit his marriage choice to a woman of the totems 4, 5, 6.

The historical relations of the marriage classes—of which there are found as many as eight in some tribes—are quite unexplained. We only see that these arrangements seek to attain the same object as the totem exogamy, and even strive for more. But whereas the totem exogamy makes the impression of a sacred statute which sprang into existence, no one knows how, and is therefore a custom, the complicated institutions of the marriage classes, with their sub-divisions and the conditions attached to them, seem to spring from legislation with a definite aim in view. They have perhaps taken up afresh the task of incest prohibition because the influence of the totem was on the wane. And while the totem system is, as we know, the basis of all other social obligations and moral restrictions of the tribe, the importance of the phratries generally ceases when the regulation of the marriage choice at which they aimed has been accomplished.

In the further development of the classification of the marriage system there seems to be a tendency to go beyond the prevention of natural and group incest, and to prohibit marriage between more distant group relations, in a manner similar to the Catholic church, which extended the marriage prohibitions always in force for brother and sisters, to cousins, and invented for them the grades of spiritual kinship (Article *Totemism* in *Encyclopedia Britannica*, eleventh edition, 1911 (A. Lang)).

It would hardly serve our purpose to go into the extraordinarily intricate and unsettled discussion concerning the origin and significance of the marriage classes, or to go more deeply into their relation to totemism. It is sufficient for our purposes to point out the great care expended by the Australians as well as by other savage people to prevent incest[80]. We must say that these savages are even more sensitive to incest than we, perhaps because they are more

---

[80] Storfer has recently drawn special attention to this point in his monograph: *Parricide as a Special Case. Papers on Applied Psychic Investigation*, No. 12 (Vienna, 1911).

subject to temptations than we are, and hence require more extensive protection against it.

But the incest dread of these races does not content itself with the creation of the institutions described, which, in the main, seem to be directed against group incest. We must add a series of 'customs' which watch over the individual behaviour to near relatives in our sense, which are maintained with almost religious severity and of whose object there can hardly be any doubt. These customs or custom prohibitions may be called 'avoidances'. They spread far beyond the Australian totem races. But here again I must ask the reader to be content with a fragmentary excerpt from the abundant material.

Such restrictive prohibitions are directed in Melanesia against the relations of boys with their mothers and sisters. Thus, for instance, on Lepers Island, one of the New Hebrides, the boy leaves his maternal home at a fixed age and moves to the 'clubhouse', where he there regularly sleeps and takes his meals. He may still visit his home to ask for food; but if his sister is at home he must go away before he has eaten; if no sister is about he may sit down to eat near the door. If brother and sister meet by chance in the open, she must run away or turn aside and conceal herself. If the boy recognizes certain footprints in the sand as his sister's he is not to follow them, nor is she to follow his. He will not even mention her name and will guard against using any current word if it forms part of her name. This avoidance, which begins with the ceremony of puberty, is strictly observed for life. The reserve between mother and son increases with age and generally is more obligatory on the mother's side. If she brings him something to eat she does not give it to him herself but puts it down before him, nor does she address him in the familiar manner of mother and son, but uses the formal address. Similar customs obtain in New Caledonia. If brother and sister meet, she flees into the bush and he passes by without turning his head toward her[81].

On the Gazella Peninsula in New Britain a sister, beginning with her marriage, may no longer speak with her brother, nor does she utter his name but designates him by means of a circumlocution (Frazer, l.c., II, p. 124).

---

[81] R. H. Codrington, *The Melanesians*, also Frazer *Totemism and Exogamy*, Vol. I, p. 77.

In New Mecklenburg some cousins are subject to such restrictions, which also apply to brothers and sisters. They may neither approach each other, shake hands, nor give each other presents, though they may talk to each other at a distance of several paces. The penalty for incest with a sister is death through hanging (Frazer, *l.c.*, II, p. 131).

These rules of avoidance are especially severe in the Fiji Islands where they concern not only consanguineous sisters but group sisters as well.

To hear that these savages hold sacred orgies in which persons of just these forbidden degrees of kinship seek sexual union would seem still more peculiar to us, if we did not prefer to make use of this contradiction to explain the prohibition instead of being astonished at it (Frazer, *l.c.*, II, p. 147, according to the Rev. L. Fison.).

Among the Battas of Sumatra these laws of avoidance affect all near relationships. For instance, it would be most offensive for a Battan to accompany his own sister to an evening party. A brother will feel most uncomfortable in the company of his sister even when other persons are also present. If either comes into the house, the other prefers to leave. Nor will a father remain alone in the house with his daughter any more than the mother with her son. The Dutch missionary who reported these customs added that unfortunately he had to consider them well founded. It is assumed without question by these races that a man and a woman left alone together will indulge in the most extreme intimacy, and as they expect all kinds of punishments and evil consequences from consanguineous intercourse they do quite right to avoid all temptations by means of such prohibitions (Frazer, *l.c.*, II. p. 189)

Among the Barongos in Delagoa Bay, in Africa, the most rigorous precautions are directed, curiously enough, against the sister-in-law, the wife of the brother of one's own wife. If a man meets this person who is so dangerous to him, he carefully avoids her. He does not dare to eat out of the same dish with her; he speaks only timidly to her, does not dare to enter her hut, and greets her only with a trembling voice (Frazer, *l.c.*, II, p. 388, according to Junod).

Among the Akamba (or Wakamba) in British East Africa, a law of avoidance is in force which one would have expected to encounter more frequently. A girl must carefully avoid her own father between the time of her puberty and her marriage. She hides herself if she meets him on the street and never attempts to sit down next to him, behaving in this way right up to her engagement. But after her marriage no further obstacle is put in the way of her social intercourse with her father (Frazer, *l.c.*, II, p. 424)

The most widespread and strictest avoidance, which is perhaps the most interesting one for civilized races is that which restricts the social relations between a man and his mother-in-law. It is quite general in Australia, but it is also in force among the Melanesian, Polynesian and Negro races of Africa as far as the traces of totemism and group relationship reach, and probably further still. Among some of these races similar prohibitions exist against the harmless social intercourse of a wife with her father-in-law, but these are by far not so constant or so serious. In a few cases both parents-in-law become objects of avoidance.

As we are less interested in the ethnographic dissemination than in the substance and the purpose of the mother-in-law avoidance, I will here also limit myself to a few examples.

On the Banks Island these prohibitions are very severe and painfully exact. A man will avoid the proximity of his mother-in-law as she avoids his. If they meet by chance on a path, the woman steps aside and turns her back until he is passed, or he does the same.

In Vanna Lava (Port Patterson) a man will not even walk behind his mother-in-law along the beach until the rising tide has washed away the trace of her footsteps. But they may talk to each other at a certain distance. It is quite out of the question that he should ever pronounce the name of his mother-in-law, or she his (Frazer, *l.c.*, II, p. 76).

On the Solomon Islands, beginning with his marriage, a man must neither see nor speak with his mother-in-law. If he meets her he acts as if he did not know her and runs away as fast as he can in order to hide himself (Frazer, *l.c.*, II, p. 113). Among the Zulu Kaffirs custom demands that a man should be ashamed of his mother-in-law and that he should do everything to avoid her company. He does not enter a hut in which she is, and when they meet he or she goes aside, she perhaps hiding behind a bush while he holds his shield before his face. If they cannot avoid each other and the woman has nothing with which to cover herself, she at least binds a bunch of grass around her head in order to satisfy the ceremonial requirements. Communication between them must either be made through a third person or else they may shout at each other at a considerable distance if they have some barrier between them as, for instance, the enclosure of a kraal. Neither may utter the other's name (Frazer, l.c., II, p. 385.)

Among the Basogas, a negro tribe living in the region of the Nile sources, a man may talk to his mother-in-law only if she is in another room of the house and is not visible to him. Moreover, this race abominates incest to such an extent as not to let it go unpunished even among domestic animals (Frazer, l.c., II, p. 461)

Whereas all observers have interpreted the purpose and meaning of the avoidances between near relatives as protective measures against incest, different interpretations have been given for those prohibitions which concern the relationship with the mother-in-law. It was quite incomprehensible why all these races should manifest such great fear of temptation on the part of the man for an elderly woman, old enough to be his mother(v. Crawley: *The Mystic Rose*, p. 405)

The same objection was also raised against the conception of Fison who called attention to the fact that certain marriage class systems show a gap in that they make marriage between a man and his mother-in-law theoretically not impossible and that a special guarantee was therefore necessary to guard against this possibility.

Sir J. Lubbock, in his book *The Origin of Civilization*, traces back the behaviour of the mother-in-law toward the son-in-law to the former 'marriage by capture'. "As long as the capture of women actually took place, the indignation of the parents was probably serious enough. When nothing but symbols of this form of marriage survived, the indignation of the parents was also symbolized and this custom continued after its origin had been forgotten." Crawley has found it easy to show how little this tentative explanation agrees with the details of actual observation.

E. B. Tylor thinks that the treatment of the son-in-law on the part of the mother-in-law is nothing more than a form of 'cutting' on the part of the woman's family. The man counts as a stranger, and this continues until the first child is born. But even if no account is taken of cases in which this last condition does not remove the prohibition, this explanation is subject to the objection that it does not throw any light on the custom dealing with the relation between mother-in-law and son-in-law, thus overlooking the sexual factor, and that it does not take into account the almost sacred loathing which finds expression in the laws of avoidance (Crawley, *l.c.*, p. 407.)

A Zulu woman who was asked about the basis for this prohibition showed great delicacy of feeling in her answer: "It is not right that he should see the breasts which nursed his wife."

It is known that also among civilized races the relation of son-in-law and mother-in-law belongs to one of the most difficult sides of family organization. Although laws of avoidance no longer exist in the society of the white races of Europe and America, much quarrelling and displeasure would often be avoided if they did exist and did not have to be re-established by individuals. Many a European will see an act of high wisdom in the laws of avoidance which savage races have established to preclude any understanding between two persons who have become so closely related. There is hardly any doubt that there is something in the psychological situation of mother-in-law and son-in-law which furthers hostilities between them and renders living together difficult. The fact that the witticisms of civilized races show such a preference for this very mother-in-law theme seems to me to point to the fact that the emotional relations between mother-in-law and son-in-law are controlled by components which stand in sharp contrast to each other. I mean that the relation is really 'ambivalent', that is, it is composed of conflicting feelings of tenderness and hostility.

A certain part of these feelings is evident. The mother-in-law is unwilling to give up the possession of her daughter; she distrusts the stranger to whom her daughter has been delivered, and shows a tendency to maintain the dominating position, to which she became accustomed at home. On the part of the man, there is the determination not to subject himself any longer to any foreign will, his jealousy of all persons who preceded him in the possession of his wife's tenderness, and, last but not least, his aversion to being disturbed in his illusion of sexual over-valuation. As a rule such a disturbance emanates for the most part from his mother-in-law who reminds him of her daughter through so many common traits but who lacks all the charm of youth, such as beauty and that psychic spontaneity which makes his wife precious to him.

The knowledge of hidden psychic feelings which psychoanalytic investigation of individuals has given us, makes it possible to add other motives to the above. Where the psycho-sexual needs of the woman are to be satisfied in marriage and family life, there is always the danger of dissatisfaction through the premature termination of the conjugal relation, and the monotony in the wife's emotional life. The ageing mother protects herself against this by living through the lives of her children, by identifying herself with them and making their emotional experiences her own. Parents are said to remain young with their children, and this is, in fact, one of the most valuable psychic benefits which parents derive from their children. Childlessness thus eliminates one of the best means to endure the necessary resignation imposed upon the individual through marriage. This emotional identification with the daughter may easily go so far with the mother that she also falls in love with the man her daughter loves, which leads, in extreme cases, to severe forms of neurotic ailments on account of the violent psychic resistance against this emotional predisposition. At all events the tendency to such infatuation is very frequent with the mother-in-law, and either this infatuation itself or the tendency opposed to it joins the conflict of contending forces in the psyche of the mother-in-law. Very often it is just this harsh and sadistic component of the love emotion which is turned against the son-in-law in order better to suppress the forbidden tender feelings.

The relation of the husband to his mother-in-law is complicated through similar feelings which, however, spring from other sources. The path of object selection has normally led him to his love object through the image of his mother and perhaps of his sister; in consequence of the incest barriers his preference for these two beloved persons of his childhood has been deflected and he is then able to find their image in strange objects. He now sees the mother-in-law taking the place of his own mother and of his sister's mother, and there develops a tendency to return to the primitive selection, against which everything in him resists. His incest dread demands that he should not be reminded of the genealogy of his love selection; the actuality of his mother-in-law, whom he had not known all his life like his mother so that her picture can be preserved unchanged in his unconscious, facilitates this rejection. An added mixture of irritability and animosity in his feelings leads us to suspect that the mother-in-law actually represents an incest temptation for the son-in-law, just as it not infrequently happens that a man falls in love with his subsequent mother-in-law before his inclination is transferred to her daughter.

I see no objection to the assumption that it is just this incestuous factor of the relationship which motivates the avoidance between son- and mother-in-law among savages. Among the explanations for the 'avoidances' which these primitive races observe so strictly, we would therefore give preference to the opinion originally expressed by Fison, who sees nothing in these regulations but a protection against possible incest. This would also hold good for all the other avoidances between those related by blood or by marriage. There is only one difference, namely, in the first case the incest is direct, so that the purpose of the prevention might be conscious; in the other case, which includes the mother-in-law relation, the incest would be a phantasy temptation brought about by unconscious intermediary links.

We have had little opportunity in this exposition to show that the facts of folk-psychology can be seen in a new light through the application of the psychoanalytic point of view, for the incest dread of savages has long been known as such, and is in need of no further interpretation. What we can add to the further appreciation of incest dread is the statement that it is a subtle infantile trait and is in striking agreement with the psychic life of the neurotic. Psychoanalysis has taught us that the first object selection of the boy is of an incestuous nature and that it is directed to the forbidden objects, the mother and the sister; psychoanalysis has taught us also the methods through which the maturing individual frees himself from these incestuous attractions. The neurotic, however, regularly presents to us a piece of psychic infantilism; he has either not been able to free himself from the childlike conditions of psychosexuality, or else he has returned to them (inhibited development and regression). Hence the incestuous fixations of the libido still play or again are playing the main rôle in his unconscious psychic life. We have gone so far as to declare that the relation to the parents instigated by incestuous longings is the central complex of the neurosis. This discovery of the significance of incest for the neurosis naturally meets with the most general incredulity on the part of the grown-up, normal man; a similar rejection will also meet the researches of Otto Rank, which show in even larger scope to what extent the incest theme stands in the centre of poetical interest and how it forms the material of poetry in countless variations and distortions. We are forced to believe that such a rejection is above all the product of man's deep aversion to his former incest wishes which have since succumbed to repression. It is therefore of importance to us to be able to show that man's incest wishes, which later are destined to become unconscious, are still felt to be dangerous by savage races who consider them worthy of the most severe defensive measures.

II. TABOO AND THE AMBIVALENCE OF EMOTIONS

1

TABOO is a Polynesian word, the translation of which provides difficulties for us because we no longer possess the idea which it connotes. It was still current with the ancient Romans: their word 'sacer' was the same as the taboo of the Polynesians. The ἄγος of the Greeks and the Kodaush of the Hebrews must also have signified the same thing which the Polynesians express through their word taboo and what many races in America, Africa (Madagascar), North and Central Asia express through analogous designations.

For us the meaning of taboo branches off into two opposite directions. On the one hand it means to us sacred, consecrated: but on the other hand it means, uncanny, dangerous, forbidden, and unclean. The opposite for taboo is designated in Polynesian by the word *noa* and signifies something ordinary and generally accessible. Thus something like the concept of reserve inheres in taboo; taboo expresses itself essentially in prohibitions and restrictions. Our combination of 'holy dread' would often express the meaning of taboo.

The taboo restrictions are different from religious or moral prohibitions. They are not traced to a commandment of a god but really they themselves impose their own prohibitions; they are differentiated from moral prohibitions by failing to be included in a system which declares abstinences in general to be necessary and gives reasons for this necessity. The taboo prohibitions lack all justification and are of unknown origin. Though incomprehensible to us they are taken as a matter of course by those who are under their dominance.

Wundt (*Voelkerpsychologie*, II. Band: *Mythus und Religion*, 1906, II, p. 308) calls taboo the oldest unwritten code of law of humanity. It is generally assumed that taboo is older than the gods and goes back to the pre-religious age.

As we are in need of an impartial presentation of the subject of taboo before subjecting it to psychoanalytic consideration I shall now cite an excerpt from the article *Taboo* in the *Encyclopedia Britannica*, Eleventh Edition, written by the anthropologist Northcote W. Thomas:

"Properly speaking taboo includes only (a) the sacred (or unclean) character of persons or things, (b) the kind of prohibition which results from this character, and (c) the sanctity (or uncleanliness) which results from a violation of the prohibition. The converse of taboo in Polynesia is 'noa' and allied forms which mean 'general' or 'common' ...

"Various classes of taboo in the wider sense may be distinguished: 1. natural or direct, the result of 'mana' mysterious (power) inherent in a person or thing; 2. communicated or indirect, equally the result of 'mana' but (*a*) acquired or (*b*) imposed by a priest, chief or other person; 3. intermediate, where both factors are present, as in the appropriation of a wife to her husband. The term taboo is also applied to ritual prohibitions of a different nature; but its use in these senses is better avoided. It might be argued that the term should be extended to embrace cases in which the sanction of the prohibition is the creation of a god or spirit, i.e., to religious interdictions as distinguished from magical, but there is neither automatic action nor contagion in such a case, and a better term for it is religious interdiction.

"The objects of the taboo are many: 1. direct taboos aim at (*a*) protection of important persons—chiefs, priests, etc.—and things against harm; (*b*) safeguarding of the weak—women children and common people generally—from the powerful mana (magical influence) of chiefs and priests; (*c*) providing against the dangers incurred by handling or coming in contact with corpses, by eating certain food, etc.; (*d*) guarding the chief acts of life—births, initiation, marriage and sexual functions—against interference; (*e*) securing human beings against the wrath or power of gods and spirits[This application of the taboo can be omitted as not originally belonging in this connection]; (*f*) securing unborn infants and young children who stand in a specially sympathetic relation with their parents, from the consequence of certain actions, and more especially from the communication of qualities supposed to be derived from certain foods. 2. Taboos are imposed in order to secure against thieves the property of an individual, his fields, tools, etc."

Other parts of the article may be summarized as follows. Originally the punishment for the violation of a taboo was probably left to an inner, automatic arrangement. The violated taboo avenged itself. Wherever the taboo was related to ideas of gods and demons an automatic punishment was expected from the power of the godhead. In other cases, probably as a result of a further development of the idea, society took over the punishment of the offender, whose action has endangered his companions. Thus man's first systems of punishment are also connected with taboo.

"The violation of a taboo makes the offender himself taboo." The author goes on to say that certain dangers resulting from the violation of a taboo may be exercised through acts of penance and ceremonies of purification.

A peculiar power inherent in persons and ghosts, which can be transmitted from them to inanimate objects is regarded as the source of the taboo. This part of the article reads as follows: "Persons or things which are regarded as taboo may be compared to objects charged with electricity; they are the seat of tremendous power which is transmissible by contact, and may be liberated with destructive effect if the organisms which provoke its discharge are too weak to resist it; the result of a violation of a taboo depends partly on the strength of the magical influence inherent in the taboo object or person, partly on the strength of the opposing mana of the violator of the taboo. Thus, kings and chiefs are possessed of great power, and it is death for their subjects to address them directly; but a minister or other person of greater *mana* than common, can approach them unharmed, and can in turn be approached by their inferiors without risk.... So, too, indirect taboos depend for their strength on the mana of him who opposes them; if it is a chief or a priest, they are more powerful than those imposed by a common person."

The fact that a taboo is transmissible has surely given rise to the effort of removing it through expiatory ceremonies.

The author states that there are permanent and temporary taboos. The former comprise priests and chiefs as well as the dead and everything that has belonged to them. Temporary taboos attach themselves to certain conditions such as menstruation and child-bed, the status of the warrior before and after the expedition, the activities of fishing and of the chase, and similar activities. A general taboo may also be imposed upon a large district like an ecclesiastical interdict, and may then last for years.

If I judge my readers' impressions correctly, I dare say that after hearing all that was said about taboo they are far from knowing what to understand by it and where to store it in their minds. This is surely due to the insufficient information I have given and to the omission of all discussions concerning the relation of taboo to superstition, to belief in the soul, and to religion. On the other hand I fear that a more detailed description of what is known about taboo would be still more confusing; I can therefore assure the reader that the state of affairs is really far from clear. We may say, however, that we deal with a series of restrictions which these primitive races impose upon themselves; this and that is forbidden without any apparent reason; nor does it occur to them to question this matter, for they subject themselves to these restrictions as a matter of course and are convinced that any transgression will be punished automatically in the most severe manner. There are reliable reports that innocent transgressions of such prohibitions have actually been punished automatically. For instance, the innocent offender who had eaten from a forbidden animal became deeply depressed, expected his death and then actually died. The prohibitions mostly concern matters which are capable of enjoyment such as freedom of movement and unrestrained intercourse; in some cases they appear very ingenious, evidently representing abstinences and renunciations; in other cases their content is quite incomprehensible, they seem to concern themselves with trifles and give the impression of ceremonials. Something like a theory seems to underlie all these prohibitions, it seems as if these prohibitions are necessary because some persons and objects possess a dangerous power which is transmitted by contact with the object so charged, almost like a contagion. The quantity of this dangerous property is also taken into consideration. Some persons or things have more of it than others and the danger is precisely in accordance with the charge. The most peculiar part of it is that any one who has violated such a prohibition assumes the nature of the forbidden object as if he had absorbed the whole dangerous charge. This power is inherent in all persons who are more or less prominent, such as kings, priests and the newly born, in all exceptional physical states such as menstruation, puberty and birth, in everything sinister like illness and death and in everything connected with these conditions by virtue of contagion or dissemination.

However, the term 'taboo' includes all persons, localities, objects and temporary conditions which are carriers or sources of this mysterious attribute. The prohibition derived from this attribute is also designated as taboo, and lastly taboo, in the literal sense, includes everything that is sacred, above the ordinary, and at the same time dangerous, unclean and mysterious.

Both this word and the system corresponding to it express a fragment of psychic life which really is not comprehensible to us. And indeed it would seem that no understanding of it could be possible without entering into the study of the belief in spirits and demons which is so characteristic of these low grades of culture.

Now why should we take any interest at all in the riddle of taboo? Not only, I think, because every psychological problem is well worth the effort of investigation for its own sake, but for other reasons as well. It may be surmised that the taboo of Polynesian savages is after all not so remote from us as we were at first inclined to believe; the moral and customary prohibitions which we ourselves obey may have some essential relation to this primitive taboo the explanation of which may in the end throw light upon the dark origin of our own 'categorical imperative.'

We are therefore inclined to listen with keen expectations when an investigator like W. Wundt gives his interpretation of taboo, especially as he promises to "go back to the very roots of the taboo concepts"[*Voelkerpsychologie*, Vol. II: *Religion und Mythus*, p. 300].

Wundt states that the idea of taboo "includes all customs which express dread of particular objects connected with cultic ideas or of actions having reference to them"[*l.c.*, p. 237].

On another occasion he says: "In accordance with the general sense of the word we understand by taboo every prohibition laid down in customs or manners or in expressly formulated laws, not to touch an object or to take it for one's own use, or to make use of certain proscribed words...." Accordingly there would not be a single race or stage of culture which had escaped the injurious effects of taboo.

Wundt then shows why he finds it more practical to study the nature of taboo in the primitive states of Australian savages rather than in the higher culture of the Polynesian races. In the case of the Australians he divides taboo prohibitions into three classes according as they concern animals, persons or other objects. The animal taboo, which consists essentially of the taboo against killing and eating, forms the nucleus of Totemism [Comp. Chapter I]. The taboo of the second class, which has human beings for its object, is of an essentially different nature. To begin with it is restricted to conditions which bring about an unusual situation in life for the person tabooed. Thus young men at the feast of initiation, women during menstruation and immediately after delivery, newly born children, the deceased and especially the dead, are all taboo. The constantly used property of any person, such as his clothes, tools and weapons, is permanently taboo for everybody else. In Australia the new name which a youth receives at his initiation into manhood becomes part of his most personal property, it is taboo and must be kept secret. The taboos of the third class, which apply to trees, plants, houses and localities, are more variable and seem only to follow the rule that anything which for any reason arouses dread or is mysterious, becomes subject to taboo.

Wundt himself has to acknowledge that the changes which taboo undergoes in the richer culture of the Polynesians and in the Malayan Archipelago are not very profound. The greater social differentiation of these races manifests itself in the fact that chiefs, kings and priests exercise an especially effective taboo and are themselves exposed to the strongest taboo compulsion.

But the real sources of taboo lie deeper than in the interests of the privileged classes: "They begin where the most primitive and at the same time the most enduring human impulses have their origin, namely, *in the fear of the effect of demonic powers*"[l.c., p. 307]. "The taboo, which originally was nothing more than the objectified fear of the demonic power thought to be concealed in the tabooed object, forbids the irritation of this power and demands the placation of the demon whenever the taboo has been knowingly or unknowingly violated."

The taboo then gradually became an autonomous power which has detached itself from demonism. It becomes the compulsion of custom and tradition and finally of the law. "But the commandment concealed behind taboo prohibitions which differ materially according to place and time, had originally the meaning: Beware of the wrath of the demons."

Wundt therefore teaches that taboo is the expression and evolution of the belief of primitive races in demonic powers, and that later taboo has dissociated itself from this origin and has remained a power simply because it was one by virtue of a kind of a psychic persistence and in this manner it became the root of our customs and laws. As little as one can object to the first part of this statement I feel, however, that I am only voicing the impression of many of my readers if I call Wundt's explanation disappointing. Wundt's explanation is far from going back to the sources of taboo concepts or to their deepest roots. For neither fear nor demons can be accepted in psychology as finalities defying any further deduction. It would be different if demons really existed; but we know that, like gods, they are only the product of the psychic powers of man; they have been created from and out of something.

Wundt also expresses a number of important though not altogether clear opinions about the double meaning of taboo. According to him the division between *sacred* and *unclean* does not yet exist in the first primitive stages of taboo. For this reason these conceptions entirely lack the significance which they could only acquire later on when they came to be contrasted. The animal, person or place on which there is a taboo is demonic, that is, not sacred, and therefore not yet, in the later sense, unclean. The expression taboo is particularly suitable for this undifferentiated and intermediate meaning of the demonic, in the sense of something which may not be touched, since it emphasizes a characteristic which finally adheres both to what is sacred and to the unclean, namely, the dread of contact. But the fact that this important characteristic is permanently held in common points to the existence of an original agreement here between these two spheres which gave way to a differentiation only as the result of further conditions through which both finally developed into opposites.

The belief associated with the original taboo, according to which a demonic power concealed in the object avenges the touching of it or its forbidden use by bewitching the offender was still an entirely objectified fear. This had not yet separated into the two forms which it assumed at a more developed stage, namely, awe and aversion.

How did this separation come about? According to Wundt [p. 313], this was done through the transference of taboo prohibitions from the sphere of demons to that of theistic conceptions. The antithesis of sacred and unclean coincides with the succession of two mythological stages the first of which did not entirely disappear when the second was reached but continued in a state of greatly lowered esteem which gradually turned into contempt. It is a general law in mythology that a preceding stage, just because it has been overcome and pushed back by a higher stage, maintains itself next to it in a debased form so that the objects of its veneration become objects of aversion.

Wundt's further elucidations refer to the relation of taboo to lustration and sacrifice.

2

He who approaches the problem of taboo from the field of psychoanalysis, which is concerned with the study of the unconscious part of the individual's psychic life, needs but a moment's reflection to realize that these phenomena are by no means foreign to him. He knows people who have individually created such taboo prohibitions for themselves, which they follow as strictly as savages observe the taboos common to their tribe or society. If he were not accustomed to call these individuals 'compulsion neurotics' he would find the term 'taboo disease' quite appropriate for their malady. Psychoanalytic investigation has taught him the clinical etiology and the essential part of the psychological mechanism of this compulsion disease, so that he cannot resist applying what he has learnt there to explain corresponding manifestations in folk psychology.

There is one warning to which we shall have to give heed in making this attempt. The similarity between taboo and compulsion disease may be purely superficial, holding good only for the manifestations of both without extending into their deeper characteristics. Nature loves to use identical forms in the most widely different biological connections, as, for instance, for coral stems and plants and even for certain crystals or for the formation of certain chemical precipitates. It would certainly be both premature and unprofitable to base conclusions relating to inner relationships upon the correspondence of merely mechanical conditions. We shall bear this warning in mind without, however, giving up our intended comparison on account of the possibility of such confusions.

The first and most striking correspondence between the compulsion prohibitions of neurotics and taboo lies in the fact that the origin of these prohibitions is just as unmotivated and enigmatic. They have appeared at some time or other and must now be retained on account of an unconquerable anxiety. An external threat of punishment is superfluous, because an inner certainty (a conscience) exists that violation will be followed by unbearable disaster. The very most that compulsion patients can tell us is the vague premonition that some person of their environment will suffer harm if they should violate the prohibition. Of what the harm is to consist is not known, and this inadequate information is more likely to be obtained during the later discussions of the expiatory and defensive actions than when the prohibitions themselves are being discussed.

As in the case of taboo the nucleus of the neurotic prohibition is the act of touching, whence we derive the name 'touching phobia' or *délire de toucher*. The prohibition extends not only to direct contact with the body but also to the figurative use of the phrase as 'to come into contact' or 'be in touch with some one or something'. Anything that leads the thoughts to what is prohibited and thus calls forth mental contact is just as much prohibited as immediate bodily contact; this same extension is also found in taboo.

Some prohibitions are easily understood from their purpose but others strike us as incomprehensible, foolish and senseless. We designate such commands as 'ceremonials' and we find that taboo customs show the same variations.

Obsessive prohibitions possess an extraordinary capacity for displacement; they make use of almost any form of connection to extend from one object to another and then in turn make this new object 'impossible', as one of my patients aptly puts it. This impossibility finally lays an embargo upon the whole world. The compulsion neurotics act as if the 'impossible' persons and things were the carriers of a dangerous contagion which is ready to displace itself through contact to all neighbouring things. We have already emphasized the same characteristics of contagion and transference in the description of taboo prohibitions. We also know that any one who has violated a taboo by touching something which is taboo becomes taboo himself, and no one may come into contact with him.

I shall put side by side two examples of transference or, to use a better term, displacement, one from the life of the Maori, and the other from my observation of a woman suffering from a compulsion neurosis:

"For a similar reason a Maori chief would not blow on a fire with his mouth; for his sacred breath would communicate its sanctity to the fire, which would pass it on to the meat in the pot, which would pass it on to the man who ate the meat which was in the pot, which stood on the fire, which was breathed on by the chief; so that the eater, infected by the chiefs breath conveyed through these intermediaries, would surely die"[Frazer, *The Golden Bough*, II: *Taboo and the Perils of the Soul*, 1911, p. 136)

My patient demanded that a utensil which her husband had purchased and brought home should be removed lest it make the place where she lives impossible. For she has heard that this object was bought in a store which is situated, let us say, in Stag Street. But as the word 'stag' is the name of a friend now in a distant city, whom she has known in her youth under her maiden name and whom she now finds 'impossible', that is taboo, the object bought in Vienna is just as taboo as this friend with whom she does not want to come into contact.

Compulsion prohibitions, like taboo prohibitions, entail the most extraordinary renunciations and restrictions of life, but a part of these can be removed by carrying out certain acts which now also must be done because they have acquired a compulsive character (obsessive acts); there is no doubt that these acts are in the nature of penances, expiations, defence reactions, and purifications. The most common of these obsessive acts is washing with water (washing obsession). A part of the taboo prohibitions can also be replaced in this way, that is to say, their violation can be made good through such a 'ceremonial', and here too lustration through water is the preferred way.

Let us now summarize the points in which the correspondence between taboo customs and the symptoms of compulsion neurosis are most clearly manifested: 1. In the lack of motivation of the commandments, 2. in their enforcement through an inner need, 3. in their capacity of displacement and in the danger of contagion from what is prohibited, 4. and in the causation of ceremonial actions and commandments which emanate from the forbidden.

However, psychoanalysis has made us familiar with the clinical history as well as the psychic mechanism of compulsion neurosis. Thus the history of a typical case of touching phobia reads as follows: In the very beginning, during the early period of childhood, the person manifested a strong pleasure in touching himself, the object of which was much more specialized than one would be inclined to suspect. Presently the carrying out of this very pleasurable act of touching was opposed by a prohibition from without[82].

The prohibition was accepted because it was supported by strong inner forces[83]; it proved to be stronger than the impulse which wanted to manifest itself through this act of touching. But due to the primitive psychic constitution of the child this prohibition did not succeed in abolishing the impulse. Its only success lay in repressing the impulse (the pleasure of touching) and banishing it into the unconscious. Both the prohibition and the impulse remained; the impulse because it had only been repressed and not abolished, the prohibition, because if it had ceased the impulse would have broken through into consciousness and would have been carried out. An unsolved situation, a psychic fixation, had thus been created and now everything else emanated from the continued conflict between prohibition and impulse.

The main characteristic of the psychic constellation which has thus gone under fixation lies in what one might call the ambivalent behaviour (to use an excellent term coined by Bleuler) of the individual to the object, or rather to an action regarding it. The individual constantly

---

[82] Both the pleasure and the prohibition referred to touching one's own genitals
[83] The relation to beloved persons who impose the prohibition

wants to carry out this action (the act of touching), he sees in it the highest pleasure, but he may not carry it out, and he even abominates it. The opposition between these two streams cannot be easily adjusted because—there is no other way to express it—they are so localized in the psychic life that they cannot meet. The prohibition becomes fully conscious, while the surviving pleasure of touching remains unconscious, the person knowing nothing about it. If this psychological factor did not exist the ambivalence could neither maintain itself so long nor lead to such subsequent manifestations.

In the clinical history of the case we have emphasized the appearance of the prohibition in early childhood as the determining factor; but for the further elaboration of the neurosis this rôle is played by the repression which appears at this age. On account of the repression which has taken place, which is connected with forgetting (amnesia), the motivation of the prohibition that has become conscious remains unknown, and all attempts to unravel it intellectually must fail, as the point of attack cannot be found. The prohibition owes its strength—its compulsive character—to its association with its unknown counterpart, the hidden and unabated pleasure, that is to say, to an inner need into which conscious insight is lacking. The transferability and reproductive power of the prohibition reflect a process which harmonizes with the unconscious pleasure and is very much facilitated through the psychological determinants of the unconscious. The pleasure of the impulse constantly undergoes displacement in order to escape the blocking which it encounters and seeks to acquire surrogates for the forbidden in the form of substitutive objects and actions. For the same reason the prohibition also wanders and spreads to the new aims of the proscribed impulse. Every new advance of the repressed libido is answered by the prohibition with a new severity. The mutual inhibition of these two contending forces creates a need for discharge and for lessening the existing tension, in which we may recognize the motivation for the compulsive acts. In the neurosis there are distinctly acts of compromise which on the one hand may be regarded as proofs of remorse and efforts to expiate and similar actions; but on the other hand they are at the same time substitutive actions which recompense the impulse for what has been forbidden. It is a law of neurotic diseases that these obsessive acts serve the impulse more and more and come nearer and nearer to the original and forbidden act.

We may now make the attempt to study taboo as if it were of the same nature as the compulsive prohibitions of our patients. It must naturally be clearly understood that many of the taboo prohibitions which we shall study are already secondary, displaced and distorted, so that we shall have to be satisfied if we can shed some light upon the earliest and most important taboo prohibitions. We must also remember that the differences in the situation of the savage and of the neurotic may be important enough to exclude complete correspondence and prevent a point by point transfer from one to the other such as would be possible if we were dealing with exact copies.

First of all it must be said that it is useless to question savages as to the real motivation of their prohibitions or as to the genesis of taboo. According to our assumption they must be incapable of telling us anything about it since this motivation is 'unconscious' to them. But following the model of the compulsive prohibition we shall construct the history of taboo as follows: Taboos are very ancient prohibitions which at one time were forced upon a generation of primitive people from without, that is, they probably were forcibly impressed upon them by an earlier generation. These prohibitions concerned actions for which there existed a strong desire. The prohibitions maintained themselves from generation to generation, perhaps only as the result of a tradition set up by paternal and social authority. But in later generations they have perhaps already become 'organized' as a piece of inherited psychic property. Whether there are such 'innate ideas' or whether these have brought about the fixation of the taboo by themselves or by co-operating with education no one could decide in the particular case in question. The persistence of taboo teaches, however, one thing, namely, that the original pleasure to do the forbidden still continues among taboo races. They therefore assume an *ambivalent attitude* toward their taboo prohibitions; in their unconscious they would like nothing better than to transgress them but they are also afraid to do it; they are afraid just because they would like to transgress, and the fear is stronger than the pleasure. But in every individual of the race the desire for it is unconscious, just as in the neurotic.

The oldest and most important taboo prohibitions are the two basic laws of *totemism*: namely not to kill the totem animal, and to avoid sexual intercourse with totem companions of the other sex.

It would therefore seem that these must have been the oldest and strongest desires of mankind. We cannot understand this and therefore we cannot use these examples to test our assumptions as long as the meaning and the origin of the totemic system is so wholly unknown to us. But the very wording of these taboos and the fact that they occur together will remind any one who knows the results of the psychoanalytic investigation of individuals, of something quite definite which psychoanalysts call the central point of the infantile wish life and the nucleus of the later neurosis (See Chapter IV; *Totemism, etc.*)

All other varieties of taboo phenomena which have led to the attempted classifications noted above become unified if we sum them up in the following sentence. The basis of taboo is a forbidden action for which there exists a strong inclination in the unconscious.

We know, without understanding it, that whoever does what is prohibited and violates the taboo, becomes himself taboo. But how can we connect this fact with the other, namely that the taboo adheres not only to persons who have done what is prohibited but also to persons who are in exceptional circumstances, to these circumstances themselves, and to impersonal things? What can this dangerous attribute be which always remains the same under all these different conditions? Only one thing, namely, the propensity to arouse the ambivalence of man and to tempt him to violate the prohibition.

An individual who has violated a taboo becomes himself taboo because he has the dangerous property of tempting others to follow his example. He arouses envy; why should he be allowed to do what is prohibited to others? He is therefore really *contagious*, in so far as every example incites to imitation and therefore he himself must be avoided.

But a person may become permanently or temporarily taboo without having violated any taboos, for the simple reason that he is in a condition which has the property of inciting the forbidden desires of others and of awakening the ambivalent conflict in them. Most of the exceptional positions and conditions have this character and possess this dangerous power. The king or chieftain rouses envy of his prerogatives; everybody would perhaps like to be king. The dead, the newly born, and women when they are incapacitated all act as incitements on account of their peculiar helplessness, while the individual who has just reached sexual maturity tempts through the promise of a new pleasure. Therefore all these persons and all these conditions are taboo, for one must not yield to the temptations which they offer.

Now, too, we understand why the forces inherent in the 'mana' of various persons can neutralize one another so that the mana of one individual can partly cancel that of the other. The taboo of a king is too strong for his subject because the social difference between them is too great. But a minister, for example, can become the harmless mediator between them. Translated from the language of taboo into the language of normal psychology this means: the subject who shrinks from the tremendous temptation which contact with the king creates for him can brook the intercourse of an official, whom he does not have to envy so much and whose position perhaps seems attainable to him. The minister, on his part, can moderate his envy of the king by taking into consideration the power that has been granted to him. Thus smaller differences in the magic power that lead to temptation are less to be feared than exceptionally big differences.

It is equally clear how the violation of certain taboo prohibitions becomes a social danger which must be punished or expiated by all the members of society lest it harm them all. This danger really exists if we substitute the known impulses for the unconscious desires. It consists in the possibility of imitation, as a result of which society would soon be dissolved. If the others did not punish the violation they would perforce become aware that they want to imitate the evil doer.

Though the secret meaning of a taboo prohibition cannot possibly be of so special a nature as in the case of a neurosis, we must not be astonished to find that touching plays a similar rôle in taboo prohibition as in the *délire de toucher*. To touch is the beginning of every act of possession, of every attempt to make use of a person or thing.

We have interpreted the power of contagion which inheres in the taboo as the property of leading into temptation, and of inciting to imitation. This does not seem to be in accord with the fact that the contagiousness of the taboo is above all manifested in the transference to objects which thus themselves become carriers of the taboo.

This transferability of the taboo reflects what is found in the neurosis, namely, the constant tendency of the unconscious impulse to become displaced through associative channels upon new objects. Our attention is thus drawn to the fact that the dangerous magic power of the 'mana' corresponds to two real faculties, the capacity of reminding man of his forbidden wishes, and the apparently more important one of tempting him to violate the prohibition in the service of these wishes. Both functions reunite into one, however, if we assume it to be in accord with a primitive psychic life that with the awakening of a memory of a forbidden action there should also be combined the awakening of the tendency to carry out the action. Memory and temptation then again coincide. We must also admit that if the example of a person who has violated a prohibition leads another to the same action, the disobedience of the prohibition has been transmitted like a contagion, just as the taboo is transferred from a person to an object, and from this to another.

If the violation of a taboo can be condoned through expiation or penance, which means, of course, a *renunciation* of a possession or a liberty, we have the proof that the observance of a taboo regulation was itself a renunciation of something really wished for. The omission of one renunciation is cancelled through a renunciation at some other point. This would lead us to conclude that, as far as taboo ceremonials are concerned, penance is more primitive than purification.

Let us now summarize what understanding we have gained of taboo through its comparison with the compulsive prohibition of the neurotic. Taboo is a very primitive prohibition imposed from without (by an authority) and directed against the strongest desires of man. The desire to violate it continues in the unconscious; persons who obey the taboo have an ambivalent feeling toward what is affected by the taboo. The magic power attributed to taboo goes back to its ability to lead man into temptation; it behaves like a contagion, because the example is contagious, and because the prohibited desire becomes displacing in the unconscious upon something else. The expiation for the violation of a taboo through a renunciation proves that a renunciation is at the basis of the observance of the taboo.

3

We may ask what we have gained from the comparison of taboo with compulsion neurosis and what value can be claimed for the interpretation we have given on the basis of this comparison? Our intrepretation is evidently of no value unless it affords an advantage not to be had in any other way and unless it affords a better understanding of taboo than was otherwise possible. We might claim that we have already given proof of its usefulness in what has been said above; but we shall have to try to strengthen our proof by continuing the explanation of taboo prohibitions and customs in detail.

But we can avail ourselves of another method. We can shape our investigation so as to ascertain whether a part of the assumptions which we have transferred from the neurosis to the taboo, or the conclusions at which we have thereby arrived can be demonstrated directly in the phenomena of taboo. We must decide, however, what we want to look for. The assertion concerning the genesis of taboo, namely, that it was derived from a primitive prohibition which was once imposed from without, cannot, of course, be proved. We shall therefore seek to confirm those psychological conditions for taboo with which we have become acquainted in the case of compulsion neurosis. How did we gain our knowledge of these psychological factors in the case of neurosis? Through the analytical study of the symptoms, especially the compulsive actions, the defence reactions and the obsessive commands. These mechanisms gave every indication of having been derived from *ambivalent* impulses or tendencies, they either represented simultaneously the wish and counter-wish or they served preponderantly one of the two contrary tendencies. If we should now succeed in showing that ambivalence, i.e., the sway of contrary tendencies, exists also in the case of taboo regulations or if we should find among taboo mechanisms some which like neurotic obsessions give simultaneous expression to both currents, we would have established what is practically the most important point in the psychological correspondence between taboo and compulsion neurosis.

We have already mentioned that the two fundamental taboo prohibitions are inaccessible to our analysis because they belong to totemism; another part of the taboo rules is of secondary origin and cannot be used for our purpose. For among these races taboo has become the general form of law giving and has helped to promote social tendencies which are certainly younger; than taboo itself, as for instance, the taboos imposed by chiefs and priests to insure their property and privileges. But there still remains a large group of laws which we may undertake to investigate. Among these I lay stress on those taboos which are attached (*a*) to enemies, (*b*) to chiefs, and (*c*) to the dead; the material for our investigation is taken from the excellent collection of J. G. Frazer in his great work, *The Golden Bough* (Part II: *Taboo and the Perils of the Soul*, 1911).

(*A*) THE TREATMENT OF ENEMIES

Inclined as we may have been to ascribe to savage and semi-savage races uninhibited and remorseless cruelty towards their enemies, it is of great interest to us to learn that with them, too, the killing of a person compels the observation of a series of rules which are associated with taboo customs. These rules are easily brought under four groups; they demand 1. reconciliation with the slain enemy, 2. restrictions, 3. acts of expiation, and purifications of the manslayer, and 4. certain ceremonial rites. The incomplete reports do not allow us to decide with certainty how general or how isolated such taboo customs may be among these races, but this is a matter of indifference as far as our interest in these occurrences is concerned. Still, it may be assumed that we are dealing with widespread customs and not with isolated peculiarities.

The reconciliation customs practised on the island of Timor, after a victorious band of warriors has returned with the severed heads of the vanquished enemy, are especially significant because the leader of the expedition is subject to heavy additional restrictions. "At the solemn entry of the victors, sacrifices are made to conciliate the souls of the enemy; otherwise one would have to expect harm to come to the victors. A dance is given and a song is sung in which the slain enemy is mourned and his forgiveness is implored: 'Be not angry', they say 'because your head is here with us; had we been less lucky, our heads might have been exposed in your village. We have offered the sacrifice to appease you. Your spirit may now rest and leave us at peace. Why were you our enemy? Would it not have been better that we should remain friends? Then your blood would not have been spilt and your head would not have been cut off"[Frazer, *l.c.*, p. 166.].

Similar customs are found among the Palu in Celebes; the Gallas sacrifice to the spirits of their dead enemies before they return to their home villages [Paulitschke, *Ethnography of North-east Africa*].

Other races have found methods of making friends, guardians and protectors out of their former enemies after they are dead. This consists in the tender treatment of the severed heads, of which many wild tribes of Borneo boast. When the See-Dayaks of Sarawak bring home a head from a war expedition, they treat it for months with the greatest kindness and courtesy and address it with the most endearing names in their language. The best morsels from their meals are put into its mouth, together with titbits and cigars. The dead enemy is repeatedly entreated to hate his former friends and to bestow his love upon his new hosts because he has now become one of them. It would be a great mistake to think that any derision is attached to this treatment, horrible though it may seem to us[84].

Observers have been struck by the mourning for the enemy after he is slain and scalped, among several of the wild tribe of North America. When a Choctaw had killed an enemy he began a month's mourning during which he submitted himself to serious restrictions. The Dakota Indians mourned in the same way. One authority mentions that the Osaga Indians after mourning for their own dead mourned for their foes as if they had been friends[85].

Before proceeding to the other classes of taboo customs for the treatment of enemies, we must define our position in regard to a pertinent objection. Both Frazer as well as other authorities may well be quoted against us to show that the motive for these rules of reconciliation is quite simple and has nothing to do with 'ambivalence.' These races are dominated by a superstitious fear of the spirits of the slain, a fear which was also familiar to classical antiquity, and which the great British dramatist brought upon the stage in the

---

[84] Frazer, *Adonis, Attis, Osiris*, p. 248, 1907. According to Hugh Low, *Sarawak* (London, 1848).
[85] J. O. Dorsay, see Frazer, *Taboo*, etc., p. 181.

413

hallucinations of Macbeth and Richard the Third. From this superstition all the reconciliation rules as well as the restrictions and expiations which we shall discuss later can be logically deduced; moreover, the ceremonies included in the fourth group also argue for this interpretation, since the only explanation of which they admit is the effort to drive away the spirits of the slain which pursue the manslayers [86] Besides, the savages themselves directly admit their fear for the spirits of their slain foes and trace back the taboo customs under discussion to this fear.

This objection is certainly pertinent and if it were adequate as well we would gladly spare ourselves the trouble of our attempt to find a further explanation. We postpone the consideration of this objection until later and for the present merely contrast it to the interpretation derived from our previous discussion of taboo. All these rules of taboo lead us to conclude that other impulses besides those that are merely hostile find expression in the behaviour towards enemies. We see in them manifestations of repentance, of regard for the enemy, and of a bad conscience for having slain him. It seems that the commandment, Thou shalt not slay, which could not be violated without punishment, existed also among these savages, long before any legislation was received from the hands of a god.

We now return to the remaining classes of taboo rules. The *restrictions* laid upon the victorious manslayer are unusually frequent and are mostly of a serious nature. In Timor (compare the reconciliation customs mentioned above) the leader of the expedition cannot return to his house under any circumstances. A special hut is erected for him in which he spends two months engaged in the observance of various rules of purification. During this period he may not see his wife or nourish himself; another person must put his food in his mouth. Among some Dayak tribes warriors returning from a successful expedition must remain sequestered for several days and abstain from certain foods; they may not touch iron and must remain away from their wives. In Logea, an island near New Guinea, men who have killed an enemy or have taken part in the killing, lock themselves up in their houses for a week. They avoid every intercourse with their wives and friends, they do not touch their victuals with their hands and

---

[86] Frazer, *Taboo*, pp. 166-174. These ceremonies consist of hitting shields, shouting, bellowing and making noises with various instruments, etc.)

414

live on nothing but vegetable foods which are cooked for them in special dishes. As a reason for this last restriction it is alleged that they must smell the blood of the slain, otherwise they would sicken and die. Among the Toaripi-or Motumotu-tribes in New Guinea a manslayer must not approach his wife and must not touch his food with his fingers. A second person must feed him with special food. This continues until the next new moon.

I avoid the complete enumeration of all the cases of restrictions of the victorious slayer mentioned by Frazer, and emphasize only such cases in which the character of taboo is especially noticeable or where the restriction appears in connection with expiation, purification and ceremonial.

Among the Monumbos in German New Guinea a man who has killed an enemy in combat becomes 'unclean', the same word being employed which is applied to women during menstruation or confinement. For a considerable period he is not allowed to leave the men's club-house, while the inhabitants of his village gather about him and celebrate his victory with songs and dances. He must not touch any one, not even his wife and children; if he did so they would be afflicted with boils. He finally becomes clean through washing and other ceremonies.

Among the Natchez in North America young warriors who had procured their first scalp were bound for six months to the observance of certain renunciations. They were not allowed to sleep with their wives or to eat meat, and received only fish and maize pudding as nourishment. When a Choctaw had killed and scalped an enemy he began a period of mourning for one month, during which he was not allowed to comb his hair. When his head itched he was not allowed to scratch it with his hand but used a small stick for this purpose.

After a Pima Indian had killed an Apache he had to submit himself to severe ceremonies of purification and expiation. During a fasting period of sixteen days he was not allowed to touch meat or salt, to look at a fire or to speak to any one. He lived alone in the woods, where he was waited upon by an old woman who brought him a small allowance of food; he often bathed in the nearest river, and carried a lump of clay on his head as a sign of mourning. On the seventeenth day there took place a public ceremony through which he and his weapons were solemnly purified. As the Pima Indians took the manslayer taboo much more seriously than their enemies and, unlike them, did not postpone expiation and purification until the end of the expedition, their prowess in war suffered very much through their moral severity or what might be called their piety. In spite of their extraordinary bravery they proved to be unsatisfactory allies to the Americans in their wars against the Apaches.

The detail and variations of these expiatory and purifying ceremonies after the killing of an enemy would be most interesting for purposes of a more searching study, but I need not enumerate any more of them here because they cannot furnish us with any new points of view. I might mention that the temporary or permanent isolation of the professional executioner, which was maintained up to our time, is a case in point. The position of the 'free-holder' in mediæval society really conveys a good idea of the 'taboo' of savages (Frazer, *Taboo*, p. 165-170, "Manslayers Tabooed.").

The current explanation of all these rules of reconciliation, restriction, expiation and purification, combines two principles, namely, the extension of the taboo of the dead to everything that has come into contact with him, and the fear of the spirit of the slain. In what combination these two elements are to explain the ceremonial, whether they are to be considered as of equal value or whether one of them is primary and the other secondary, and which one, is nowhere stated, nor would this be an easy matter to decide. In contradistinction to all this we emphasize the unity which our interpretation gains by deducing all these rules from the ambivalence of the emotion of savages towards their enemies.

(B) THE TABOO OF RULERS

The behaviour of primitive races towards their chiefs, kings, and priests, is controlled by two principles which seem rather to supplement than to contradict each other. They must both be guarded and be guarded against. (Frazer, *Taboo*, p. 132)

Both objects are accomplished through innumerable rules of taboo. Why one must guard against rulers is already known to us; because they are the bearers of that mysterious and dangerous magic power which communicates itself by contact, like an electric charge, bringing death and destruction to any one not protected by a similar charge. All direct or indirect contact with this dangerous sacredness is therefore avoided, and where it cannot be avoided a ceremonial has been found to ward off the dreaded consequences. The Nubas in East Africa, for instance, believe that they must die if they enter the house of their priest-king, but that they escape this danger if, on entering, they bare the left shoulder and induce the king to touch it with his hand. Thus we have the remarkable case of the king's touch becoming the healing and protective measure against the very dangers that arise from contact with the king; but it is probably a question of the healing power of the intentional touching on the king's part in contradistinction to the danger of touching him, in other words, of the opposition between passivity and activity towards the king.

Where the healing power of the royal touch is concerned we do not have to look for examples among savages. In comparatively recent times the kings of England exercised this power upon scrofula, whence it was called 'The King's Evil'. Neither Queen Elizabeth nor any of her successors renounced this part of the royal prerogative. Charles I is said to have healed a hundred sufferers at one time, in the year 1633. Under his dissolute son Charles II, after the great English revolution had passed, royal healings of scrofula attained their greatest vogue.

This king is said to have touched close to a hundred thousand victims of scrofula in the course of his reign. The crush of those seeking to be cured used to be so great that on one occasion six or seven patients suffered death by suffocation instead of being healed. The sceptical king of Orange, William III, who became king of England after the banishment of the Stuarts, refused to exercise the spell; on the one occasion when he consented to practise the touch, he did so with words: "May God give you better health and more sense"[Frazer, *The Magic Art*, I, p. 368].

The following account will bear witness to the terrible effect of touching by virtue of which a person, even though unintentionally, becomes active against his king or against what belongs to him. A chief of high rank and great holiness in New Zealand happened to leave the remains of his meal by the roadside. A young slave came along, a strong healthy fellow, who saw what was left over and started to eat it. Hardly had he finished when a horrified spectator informed him of his offence in eating the meal of the chief. The man had been a strong,

417

brave warrior, but as soon as he heard this he collapsed and was afflicted by terrible convulsions, from which he died towards sunset of the following day[87] A Maori woman ate a certain fruit and then learned that it came from a place on which there was a taboo. She cried out that the spirit of the chief whom she had thus offended would surely kill her. This incident occurred in the afternoon, and on the next day at twelve o'clock she was dead[88]. The tinder box of a Maori chief once cost several persons their lives. The chief had lost it, and those who found it used it to light their pipes. When they learned whose property the tinder box was they all died of fright.(*Frazer, l.c.*)

It is hardly astonishing that the need was felt to isolate dangerous persons like chiefs and priests, by building a wall around them which made them inaccessible to others. We surmise that this wall, which originally was constructed out of taboo rules, still exists to-day in the form of court ceremony. But probably the greater part of this taboo of the rulers cannot be traced back to the need of guarding against them. The other point of view in the treatment of privileged persons, the need of guarding them from dangers with which they are threatened, has had a distinct share in the creation of taboo and therefore of the origin of court etiquette.

The necessity of guarding the king from every conceivable danger arises from his great importance for the weal and woe of his subjects. Strictly speaking, he is a person who regulates the course of the world; his people have to thank him not only for rain and sunshine, which allow the fruits of the earth to grow, but also for the wind which brings the ships to their shores and for the solid ground on which they set their feet[Frazer, *Taboo. The Burden of Royalty*, p. 7].

These savage kings are endowed with a wealth of power and an ability to bestow happiness which only gods possess; certainly in later stages of civilization none but the most servile courtiers would play the hypocrite to the extent of crediting their sovereigns with the possession of attributes similar to these.

It seems like an obvious contradiction that persons of such perfection of power should themselves require the greatest care to guard them against threatening dangers, but this is not the only contradiction revealed in the treatment of royal persons on the part of

---

[87] *Old New Zealand*, by a Pakeha Maori (London, 1884), see Frazer, *Taboo*, p. 135.
[88] W. Brown, *New Zealand and Its Aborigines* (London, 1845) *Frazer, l.c*

savages. These races consider it necessary to watch over their kings to see that they use their powers in the right way; they are by no means sure of their good intentions or of their conscientiousness. A strain of mistrust is mingled with the motivation of the taboo rules for the king. "The idea that early kingdoms are despotisms", says Frazer[*l.c.*, p. 7.), "in which the people exist only for the sovereign, is wholly inapplicable to the monarchies we are considering. On the contrary, the sovereign in them exists only for his subjects: his life is only valuable so long as he discharges the duties of his position by ordering the course of nature for his people's benefit. So soon as he fails to do so, the care, the devotion, the religious homage which they had hitherto lavished on him cease and are changed into hatred and contempt; he is ignominiously dismissed and may be thankful if he escapes with his life. Worshipped as a god one day, he is killed as a criminal the next. But in this changed behaviour of the people there is nothing capricious or inconsistent. On the contrary, their conduct is quite consistent. If their king is their god he is or should be, also their preserver; and if he will not preserve them he must make room for another who will. So long, however, as he answers their expectations, there is no limit to the care which they take of him, and which they compel him to take of himself. A king of this sort lives hedged in by ceremonious etiquette, a network of prohibitions and observances, of which the intention is not to contribute to his dignity, much less to his comfort, but to restrain him from conduct which, by disturbing the harmony of nature, might involve himself, his people, and the universe in one common catastrophe. Far from adding to his comfort, these observances, by trammelling his every act, annihilate his freedom and often render the very life, which it is their object to preserve, a burden and sorrow to him."

One of the most glaring examples of thus fettering and paralysing a holy ruler through taboo ceremonial seems to have been reached in the life routine of the Mikado of Japan, as it existed in earlier centuries. A description which is now over two hundred years old[89] relates: "He thinks that it would be very prejudicial to his dignity and holiness to touch the ground with his feet; for this reason when he intends to go anywhere, he must be carried thither on men's shoulders. Much less will they suffer that he should expose his sacred person to the open air,

---

[89] Kaempfer, *History of Japan*, see in Frazer, *l.c.*, p. 3.

and the sun is not thought worthy to shine on his head. There is such a holiness ascribed to all the parts of his body that he dares to cut off neither his hair, nor his beard, nor his nails. However, lest he should grow too dirty, they may clean him in the night when he is asleep; because they say that what is taken from his body at that time, hath been stolen from him, and that such a theft does not prejudice his holiness or dignity. In ancient times, he was obliged to sit on the throne for some hours every morning, with the imperial crown on his head; but to sit altogether like a statue without stirring either hands or feet, head or eyes, nor indeed any part of his body, because by this means it was thought that he could preserve peace and tranquillity in his empire; for if unfortunately, he turned himself on one side or other, or if he looked a good while towards any part of his dominion, it was apprehended that war, famine, fire or some other great misfortune was near at hand to desolate the country."

Some of the taboos to which barbarian kings are subject vividly recall the restrictions placed on murderers. On Shark Point at Cape Padron in Lower Guinea (West Africa), a priest-king called Kukulu lives alone in a woods. He is not allowed to touch a woman or to leave his house and cannot even rise out of his chair, in which he must sleep in a sitting position. If he should lie down the wind would cease and shipping would be disturbed. It is his function to keep storms in check, and in general, to see to an even, healthy condition of the atmosphere[90]. The more powerful a king of Loango is, says Bastian, the more taboos he must observe. The heir to the throne is also bound to them from childhood on; they accumulate about him while he is growing up, and by the time of his accession he is suffocated by them.

Our interest in the matter does not require us to take up more space to describe more fully the taboos that cling to royal and priestly dignity. We merely add that restrictions as to freedom of movement and diet play the main rôle among them. But two examples of taboo ceremonial taken from civilized nations, and therefore from much higher stages of culture, will indicate to what an extent association with these privileged persons tends to preserve ancient customs.

The Flamen *Dialis*, the high-priest of Jupiter in Rome, had to observe an extraordinarily large number of taboo rules. He was not

---

[90] Bastian, *The German Expedition to the Coast of Loango* (Jena 1874), cited by Frazer, *l.c.*, p. 5

allowed to ride, to see a horse or an armed man, to wear a ring that was not broken, to have a knot in his garments, to touch wheat flour or leaven, or even to mention by name a goat, a dog, raw meat, beans and ivy; his hair could only be cut by a free man and with a bronze knife, his hair combings and nail parings had to be buried under a lucky tree; he could not touch the dead, go into the open with bare head, and similar prohibitions. His wife, the Flaminica, also had her own prohibitions: she was not allowed to ascend more than three steps on a certain kind of stairs and on certain holidays she could not comb her hair; the leather for her shoes could not be taken from any animal that had died a natural death but only from one that had been slaughtered or sacrificed; when she heard thunder she was unclean until she had made an expiatory sacrifice[Frazer, l.c., p. 13.].

The old kings of Ireland were subject to a series of very curious restrictions, the observance of which was expected to bring every blessing to the country while their violation entailed every form of evil. The complete description of these taboos is given in the *Book of Rights*, of which the oldest manuscript copies bear the dates 1890 and 1418. The prohibitions are very detailed and concern certain activities at specified places and times; in some cities, for instance, the king cannot stay on a certain day of the week, while at some specified hour this or that river may not be crossed, or again there is a plane on which he cannot camp a full nine days, etc.[Frazer, l.c., p. 11.]

Among many savage races the severity of the taboo restrictions for the priest-kings has had results of historic importance which are especially interesting from our point of view. The honour of being a priest-king ceased to be desirable; the person in line for the succession often used every means to escape it. Thus in Combodscha, where there is a fire and water king, it is often necessary to use force to compel the successor to accept the honour. On Niue or Savage Island, a coral island in the Pacific Ocean, monarchy actually came to an end because nobody was willing to undertake the responsible and dangerous office. In some parts of West Africa a general council is held after the death of the king to determine upon the successor. The man on whom the choice falls is seized, tied and kept in custody in the fetish house until he has declared himself willing to accept the crown. Sometimes the presumptive successor to the throne finds ways and means to avoid the intended honour; thus it is related of a certain chief that he used to go armed day and night and resist by force every attempt to place him on the throne. Among the negroes of Sierra Leone the resistance against accepting the kingly honour was so great that most of the tribes were compelled to make strangers their kings.

Frazer makes these conditions responsible for the fact that in the development of history a separation of the original priest-kingship into a spiritual and a secular power finally took place. Kings, crushed by the burden of their holiness, became incapable of exercising their power over real things and had to leave this to inferior but executive persons who were willing to renounce the honours of royal dignity. From these there grew up the secular rulers, while the spiritual over-lordship, which was now of no practical importance, was left to the former taboo kings. It is well known to what extent this hypothesis finds confirmation in the history of old Japan.

A survey of the picture of the relations of primitive peoples to their rulers gives rise to the expectation that our advance from description to psychoanalytic understanding will not be difficult. These relations are of an involved nature and are not free from contradictions. Rulers are granted great privileges which are practically cancelled by taboo prohibitions in regard to other privileges. They are privileged persons, they can do or enjoy what is withheld from the rest through taboo. But in contrast to this freedom they are restricted by other taboos which do not affect the ordinary individual. Here, therefore, is the first contrast, which amounts almost to a contradiction, between an excess of freedom and an excess of restriction as applied to the same persons. They are credited with extraordinary magic powers, and contact with their person or their property is therefore feared, while on the other hand the most beneficial effect is expected from these contacts. This seems to be a second and an especially glaring contradiction; but we have already learned that it is only apparent. The king's touch, exercised by him with benevolent intention, heals and protects; it is only when a common man touches the king or his royal effects that the contact becomes dangerous, and this is probably because the act may recall aggressive tendencies. Another contradiction which is not so easily solved is expressed in the fact that great power over the processes of nature is ascribed to the ruler and yet the obligation is felt to guard him with especial care against threatening dangers, as if his own power, which can do so much, were incapable of accomplishing this. A further difficulty in the relation arises because there is no confidence that the ruler will use his tremendous power to the advantage of his subjects as well as for his own protection; he is therefore distrusted and surveillance over him is considered to be justified. The taboo etiquette, to which the life of the king is subject, simultaneously serves all these objects of exercising a tutelage over the king, of guarding him against dangers and of guarding his subjects against danger which he brings to them.

We are inclined to give the following explanation of the complicated and contradictory relation of the primitive peoples to their rulers. Through superstition as well as through other motives, various tendencies find expression in the treatment of kings, each of which is developed to the extreme without regard to the other. As a result of this, contradictions arise at which the intellect of savages takes no more offence than a highly civilized person would as long as it is only a question of religious matters or of 'loyalty'.

That would be so far so good; but the psychoanalytic technique may enable us to penetrate more deeply into the matter and to add something about the nature of these various tendencies. If we subject the facts as stated to analysis, just as if they formed the symptoms of a neurosis, our first attention would be directed to the excess of anxious worry which is said to be the cause of the taboo ceremonial. The occurrence of such excessive tenderness is very common in the neurosis and especially in the compulsion neurosis upon which we are drawing primarily for our comparison. We now thoroughly understand the origin of this tenderness. It occurs wherever, besides the predominant tenderness, there exists a contrary but unconscious stream of hostility, that is to say, wherever the typical case of an ambivalent affective attitude is realized. The hostility is then cried down by an excessive increase of tenderness which is expressed as anxiety and becomes compulsive because otherwise it would not suffice for its task of keeping the unconscious opposition in a state of repression. Every psychoanalyst knows how infallibly this anxious excess of tenderness can be resolved even under the most improbable circumstances, as for instance, when it appears between mother and child, or in the case of affectionate married people. Applied to the treatment of privileged persons this theory of an ambivalent feeling would reveal that their veneration, their very deification, is opposed in the unconscious by an intense hostile tendency, so that, as we had expected, the situation of an ambivalent feeling is here realized. The distrust which certainly seems to contribute to the motivation of the royal taboo, would be another direct manifestation of the same unconscious hostility. Indeed the ultimate issues of this conflict show such a diversity among different races that we would not be at a loss for examples in which the proof of such hostility would be much easier. We learn from Frazer (*l.c.*, p. 18) that the savage Timmes of Sierra Leone reserve the right to administer a beating to their elected king on the evening before his coronation, and that they make use of this constitutional right with such thoroughness that the unhappy ruler sometimes does not long survive his accession to the throne; for this reason the leaders of the race have made it a rule to elect some man against whom they have a particular grudge. Nevertheless, even in such glaring cases the hostility is not acknowledged as such, but is expressed as if it were a ceremonial.

Another trait in the attitude of primitive races towards their rulers recalls a mechanism which is universally present in mental disturbances, and is openly revealed in the so-called delusions of persecution. Here the importance of a particular person is extraordinarily heightened and his omnipotence is raised to the improbable in order to make it easier to attribute to him the responsibility for everything painful which happens to the patient. Savages really do not act differently towards their rulers when they ascribe to them power over rain and shine, wind and weather, and then dethrone or kill them because nature has disappointed their expectation of a good hunt or a ripe harvest. The prototype which the paranoiac reconstructs in his persecution mania, is found in the relation of the child to its father. Such omnipotence is regularly attributed to the father in the imagination of the son, and distrust of the father has been shown to be intimately connected with the highest esteem for him. When a paranoiac names a person of his acquaintance as his 'persecutor', he thereby elevates him to the paternal succession and brings him under conditions which enable him to make him responsible for all the misfortune which he experiences. Thus this second analogy between the savage and the neurotic may allow us to surmise how much in the relation of the savage to his ruler arises from the infantile attitude of the child to its father.

But the strongest support for our point of view, which seeks to compare taboo prohibitions with neurotic symptoms, is to be found in the taboo ceremonial itself, the significance of which for the status of kinship has already been the subject of our previous discussion. This ceremonial unmistakably reveals its double meaning and its origin from ambivalent tendencies if only we are willing to assume that the effects it produces are those which it intended from the very beginning. It not only distinguishes kings and elevates them above all ordinary mortals, but it also makes their life a torture and an unbearable burden and forces them into a thraldom which is far worse than that of their subjects. It would thus be the correct counterpart to the compulsive action of the neurosis, in which the suppressed impulse and the impulse which suppresses it meet in mutual and simultaneous satisfaction. The compulsive action is nominally a protection against the forbidden action; but we would say that actually it is a repetition of what is forbidden. The word 'nominally' is here applied to the conscious whereas the word 'actually' applies to the unconscious instance of the psychic life. Thus also the taboo ceremonial of kings is nominally an expression of the highest veneration and a means of guarding them; actually it is the punishment for their elevation, the revenge which their subjects take upon them. The experiences which Cervantes makes Sancho Panza undergo as governor on his island have evidently made him recognize this interpretation of courtly ceremonial as the only correct one. It is very possible that this point would be corroborated if we could induce kings and rulers of to-day to express themselves on this point.

Why the emotional attitude towards rulers should contain such a strong unconscious share of hostility is a very interesting problem which, however, exceeds the scope of this book. We have already referred to the infantile father-complex; we may add that an investigation of the early history of kingship would bring the decisive explanations. Frazer has an impressive discussion of the theory that the first kings were strangers who, after a short reign, were destined to be sacrificed at solemn festivals as representatives of the deity; but Frazer (*The Magic Art and the Evolution of Kings*) himself does not consider his facts altogether convincing. Christian myths are said to have been still influenced by the after-effects of this evolution of kings.

(C) THE TABOO OF THE DEAD

We know that the dead are mighty rulers: we may be surprised to learn that they are regarded as enemies.

Among most primitive people the taboo of the dead displays, if we may keep to our infection analogy, a peculiar virulence. It manifests itself in the first place, in the consequences which result from contact with the dead, and in the treatment of the mourners for the dead. Among the Maori any one who had touched a corpse or who had taken part in its interment, became extremely unclean and was almost cut off from intercourse with his fellow beings; he was, as we say, boycotted. He could not enter a house, or approach persons or objects without infecting them with the same properties. He could not even touch his food with his own hands, which were now unclean and therefore quite useless to him. His food was put on the ground and he had no alternative except to seize it as best he could, with his lips and teeth, while he held his hands behind on his back. Occasionally he could be fed by another person who helped him to his food with outstretched arms so as not to touch the unfortunate one himself, but this assistant was then in turn subjected to almost equally oppressive restrictions. Almost every village contained some altogether disreputable individual, ostracized by society, whose wretched existence depended upon people's charity. This creature alone was allowed within arm's length of a person who had fulfilled the last duty towards the deceased. But as soon as the period of segregation was over and the person rendered unclean through the corpse could again mingle with his fellow-beings, all the dishes which he had used during the dangerous period were broken and all his clothing was thrown away.

The taboo customs after bodily contact with the dead are the same all over Polynesia, in Melanesia, and in a part of Africa; their most constant feature is the prohibition against handling one's food and the consequent necessity of being fed by somebody else. It is noteworthy that in Polynesia, or perhaps only in Hawaii[Frazer, *Taboo*, p. 148], priest-kings were subject to the same restrictions during the exercise of holy functons. In the taboo of the dead on the Island of Tonga the abatement and gradual abolition of the prohibitions through the individual's own taboo power are clearly shown. A person who touched the corpse of a dead chieftain was unclean for ten months; but if he was himself a chief, he was unclean for only three, four, or five months, according to the rank of the deceased; if it was the corpse of the idolized head-chief even the greatest chiefs became taboo for ten months. These savages are so certain that any one who violates these taboo rules must become seriously ill and die, that according to the opinion of an observer, they have never yet dared to convince themselves of the contrary[W. Mariner, *The Natives of the Tonga Islands*, 1818; see *Frazer*, *l.c.*, p. 140].

The taboo restrictions imposed upon persons whose contact with the dead is to be understood in the transferred sense, namely the mourning relatives such as widows and widowers, are essentially the same as those mentioned above, but they are of greater interest for the point we are trying to make. In the rules hitherto mentioned we see only the typical expression of the virulence and power of diffusion of the taboo; in those about to be cited we catch a gleam of the motives, including both the ostensible ones and those which may be regarded as the underlying and genuine motives.

Among the Shuswap in British-Columbia widows and widowers have to remain segregated during their period of mourning; they must not use their hands to touch the body or the head and all utensils used by them must not be used by any one else. No hunter will want to approach the hut in which such mourners live, for that would bring misfortune; if the shadow of one of the mourners should fall on him he would become ill. The mourners sleep on thorn bushes, with which they also surround their beds. This last precaution is meant to keep off the spirit of the deceased; plainer still is the reported custom of other North American tribes where the widow, after the death of her husband, has to wear a kind of trousers of dried grass in order to make herself inaccessible to the approach of the spirit. Thus it is quite obvious that touching 'in the transferred sense' is after all understood only as bodily contact, since the spirit of the deceased does not leave his kin and does not desist from 'hovering about them', during the period of mourning.

Among the Agutainos, who live on Palawan, one of the Philippine Islands, a widow may not leave her hut for the first seven or eight days after her husband's death, except at night, when she need not expect encounters. Whoever sees her is in danger of immediate death and therefore she herself warns others of her approach by hitting the trees with a wooden stick with every step she takes; these trees all wither. Another observation explains the nature of the danger inherent in a widow. In the district of Mekeo, British New Guinea, a widower forfeits all civil rights and lives like an outlaw. He may not tend a garden, or show himself in public, or enter the village or go on the street. He slinks about like an animal, in the high grass or in the bushes, and must hide in a thicket if he sees anybody, especially a woman, approaching. This last hint makes it easy for us to trace back the danger of the widower or widow to the danger of temptation. The husband who has lost his wife must evade the desire for a substitute; the widow has to contend with the same wish, and beside this, she may arouse the desire of other men because she is without a master. Every such satisfaction through a substitute runs contrary to the intention of mourning and would cause the anger of the spirit to flare up[69[91]].

One of the most surprising, but at the same time one of the most instructive taboo customs of mourning among primitive races is the prohibition against pronouncing the *name* of the deceased. This is very widespread, and has been subjected to many modifications with important consequences.

Aside from the Australians and the Polynesians, who usually show us taboo customs in their best state of preservation, we also find this prohibition among races so far apart and unrelated to each other as the Samojedes in Siberia and the Todas in South India, the Mongolians of Tartary and the Tuaregs of the Sahara, the Aino of Japan and the Akamba and Nandi in Central Africa, the Tinguanes in the Philippines and the inhabitants of the Nikobari Islands and of Madagascar and Borneo[Frazer, p. 353]. Among some of these races the prohibition and its consequences hold good only for the period of mourning while in others it remains permanent; but in all cases it seems to diminish with the lapse of time after the death.

The avoidance of the name of the deceased is as a rule kept up with extraordinary severity. Thus, among many South American tribes, it is considered the gravest insult to the survivors to pronounce the name of the deceased in their presence, and the penalty set for it is no less

---

[91] The same patient whose 'impossibilities' I have correlated with taboo (see above, p. 47) acknowledged that she always became indignant when she met anybody on the street who was dressed in mourning. "Such people should be forbidden to go out!" she said.

than that for the slaying itself[Frazer, p. 352]. At first it is not easy to guess why the mention of the name should be so abominated, but the dangers associated with it have called into being a whole series of interesting and important expedients to avoid this. Thus the Masai in Africa have hit upon the evasion of changing the name of the deceased immediately upon his death; he may now be mentioned without dread by this new name, while all the prohibitions remain attached to the old name. It seems to be assumed that the ghost does not know his new name and will not find it out. The Australian tribes on Adelaide and Encounter Bay are so consistently cautious that when a death occurs almost every person who has the same name as the deceased or a very similar one, exchanges it for another. Sometimes by a further extension of the same idea as seen among several tribes in Victoria and in North America all the relatives of the deceased change their names regardless of whether their names resemble the name of the deceased in sound. Among the Guaycuru in Paraguay the chief used to give new names to all the members of the tribe, on such sad occasions, which they then remembered as if they had always had them[Frazer, l.c., p. 357].

Furthermore, if the deceased had the same name as an animal or object, etc., some of the races just enumerated thought it necessary to give these animals and objects new names, in order not to be reminded of the deceased when they mentioned them. Through this there must have resulted a never ceasing change of vocabulary, which caused a good deal of difficulty for the missionaries, especially where the interdiction upon a name was permanent. In the seven years which the missionary Dobrizhofer spent among the Abipons in Paraguay, the name for jaguar was changed three times and the words for crocodile, thorns and animal slaughter underwent a similar fate[Frazer, l.c., p. 360]. But the dread of pronouncing a name which has belonged to a deceased person extends also to the mention of everything in which the deceased had any part, and a further important result of this process of suppression is that these races have no tradition or any historical reminiscences, so that we encounter the greatest difficulties in investigating their past history. Among a number of these primitive races compensating customs have also been established in order to re-awaken the names of the deceased after a long period of mourning; they are bestowed upon children who were regarded as reincarnations of the dead.

The strangeness of this taboo on names diminishes if we bear in mind that the savage looks upon his name as an essential part and an important possession of his personality, and that he ascribes the full significance of things to words. Our children do the same, as I have shown elsewhere, and therefore they are never satisfied with accepting a meaningless verbal similarity, but consistently conclude that when two things have identical names a deeper correspondence between them must exist. Numerous peculiarities of normal behaviour may lead civilized man to conclude that he too is not yet as far removed as he thinks from attributing the importance of things to mere names and feeling that his name has become peculiarly identified with his person. This is corroborated by psychoanalytic experiences, where there is much occasion to point out the importance of names in unconscious thought activity [Stekel, *Abraham*]. As was to be expected, the compulsion neurotics behave just like savages in regard to names. They show the full 'complex sensitiveness' towards the utterance and hearing of special words (as do also other neurotics) and derive a good many, often serious, inhibitions from their treatment of their own name. One of these taboo patients whom I knew, had adopted the avoidance of writing down her name for fear that it might get into somebody's hands who thus would come into possession of a piece of her personality. In her frenzied faithfulness, which she needed to protect herself against the temptations of her phantasy, she had created for herself the commandment, 'not to give away anything of her personality'. To this belonged first of all her name, then by further application her hand-writing, so that she finally gave up writing.

Thus it no longer seems strange to us that savages should consider a dead person's name as a part of his personality and that it should be subjected to the same taboo as the deceased. Calling a dead person by name can also be traced back to contact with him, so that we can turn our attention to the more inclusive problem of why this contact is visited with such a severe taboo.

The nearest explanation would point to the natural horror which a corpse inspires, especially in view of the changes so soon noticeable after death. Mourning for a dead person must also be considered as a sufficient motive for everything which has reference to him. But horror of the corpse evidently does not cover all the details of taboo rules, and mourning can never explain to us why the mention of the dead is a severe insult to his survivors. On the contrary, mourning loves to preoccupy itself with the deceased, to elaborate his memory, and preserve it for the longest possible time. Something besides mourning must be made responsible for the peculiarities of taboo customs, something which evidently serves a different purpose. It is this very taboo on names which reveals this still unknown motive, and if the customs did not tell us about it we would find it out from the statements of the mourning savages themselves.

For they do not conceal the fact that they fear the presence and the return of the spirit of a dead person; they practise a host of ceremonies to keep him off and banish him[92]. They look upon the mention of his name as a conjuration which must result in his immediate presence[93]. They therefore consistently do everything to avoid conjuring and awakening a dead person. They disguise themselves in order that the spirit may not recognize them[On the Nikobar Islands, Frazer, p. 382], they distort either his name or their own, and become infuriated when a ruthless stranger incites the spirit against his survivors by mentioning his name. We can hardly avoid the conclusion that they suffer, according to Wundt's expression, from the fear of "his soul now turned into a demon,"[Wundt, *Religion and Myth*, Vol. II, p. 49].

With this understanding we approach Wundt's conception who, as we have heard, sees the nature of taboo in the fear of demons.

The assumption which this theory makes, namely, that immediately after death the beloved member of a family becomes a demon, from whom the survivors have nothing but hostility to expect, so that they must protect themselves by every means from his evil desires, is so peculiar that our first impulse is not to believe it. Yet almost all competent authors agree as to this interpretation of primitive races. Westermarck[94], who, in my opinion, gives altogether too little consideration to taboo, makes this statement: "On the whole

---

[92] Frazer, *l.c.*, p. 353, cites the Tuaregs of the Sahara as an example of such an acknowledgment.

[93] Perhaps this condition is to be added: as long as any part of his physical remains exist. Frazer, *l.c.*, p. 372

[94] *The Origin and Development of Moral Conceptions*, see section entitled "Attitude Towards the Dead," Vol. II, p. 424. Both the notes and the text show an abundance of corroborating, and often very characteristic testimony, e.g., the Maori believed that "the nearest and most beloved relatives changed their nature after death and bore ill-will even to their former favourites." The Austral negroes believe that every dead person is for a long time malevolent; the closer the relationship the greater the fear. The Central Eskimos are dominated by the idea that the dead come to rest very late and that at first they are to be feared as mischievous spirits who frequently hover about the village to spread illness, death and other evils. (Boas.)

facts lead me to conclude that the dead are more frequently regarded as enemies than as friends and that Jevons and Grant Allen are wrong in their assertion that it was formerly believed that the malevolence of the dead was as a rule directed only against strangers, while they were paternally concerned about the life and welfare of their descendants and the members of their clan."

R. Kleinpaul has written an impressive book, *The Living and the Dead in Folklore, Religion and Myth,* in which he makes use of the remnants of the old belief in souls among civilized races to show the relation between the living and the dead. According to him too, this relation culminates in the conviction that the dead, thirsting for blood, draw the living after them. The living did not feel themselves safe from the persecutions of the dead until a body of water had been put between them. That is why it was preferred to bury the dead on islands or to bring them to the other side of a river: the expressions 'here' and 'beyond' originated in this way. Later moderation has restricted the malevolence of the dead to those categories where a peculiar right to feel rancour had to be admitted, such as the murdered who pursue their murderer as evil spirits, and those who, like brides, had died with their longings unsatisfied. Kleinpaul believes that originally, however, the dead were all vampires, who bore ill-will to the living, and strove to harm them and deprive them of life. It was the corpse that first furnished the conception of an evil spirit.

The hypothesis that those whom we love best turn into demons after death obviously allows us to put a further question. What prompted primitive races to ascribe such a change of sentiment to the beloved dead? Why did they make demons out of them? According to Westermarck this question is easily answered [l.c., p. 426]. "As death is usually considered the worst calamity that can overtake man, it is believed that the deceased are very dissatisfied with their lot. Primitive races believe that death comes only through being slain, whether by violence or by magic, and this is considered already sufficient reason for the soul to be vindictive and irritable. The soul presumably envies the living and longs for the company of its former kin; we can therefore understand that the soul should seek to kill with them diseases in order to be re-united with them....

" ...A further explanation of the malevolence ascribed to souls lies in the instinctive fear of them, which is itself the result of the fear of death."

Our study of psychoneurotic disturbances points to a more comprehensive explanation, which includes that of Westermarck.

When a wife loses her husband, or a daughter her mother, it not infrequently happens that the survivor is afflicted with tormenting scruples, called 'obsessive reproaches' which raises the question whether she herself has not been guilty through carelessness or neglect, of the death of the beloved person. No recalling of the care with which she nursed the invalid, or direct refutation of the asserted guilt can put an end to the torture, which is the pathological expression of mourning and which in time slowly subsides. Psychoanalytic investigation of such cases has made us acquainted with the secret mainsprings of this affliction. We have ascertained that these obsessive reproaches are in a certain sense justified and therefore are immune to refutation or objections. Not that the mourner has really been guilty of the death or that she has really been careless, as the obsessive reproach asserts; but still there was something in her, a wish of which she herself was unaware, which was not displeased with the fact that death came, and which would have brought it about sooner had it been strong enough. The reproach now reacts against this unconscious wish after the death of the beloved person. Such hostility, hidden in the unconscious behind tender love, exists in almost all cases of intensive emotional allegiance to a particular person, indeed it represents the classic case, the prototype of the ambivalence of human emotions. There is always more or less of this ambivalence in everybody's disposition; normally it is not strong enough to give rise to the obsessive reproaches we have described. But where there is abundant predisposition for it, it manifests itself in the relation to those we love most, precisely where you would least expect it. The disposition to compulsion neurosis which we have so often taken for comparison with taboo problems, is distinguished by a particularly high degree of this original ambivalence of emotions.

We now know how to explain the supposed demonism of recently departed souls and the necessity of being protected against their hostility through taboo rules. By assuming a similar high degree of ambivalence in the emotional life of primitive races such as psychoanalysis ascribes to persons suffering from compulsion neurosis, it becomes comprehensible that the same kind of reaction against the hostility latent in the unconscious behind the obsessive reproaches of the neurotic should also be necessary here after the painful loss has occurred. But this hostility which is painfully felt in the unconscious in the form of satisfaction with the demise, experiences a different fate in the case of primitive man: the defence against it is accomplished by displacement upon the object of hostility, namely the dead. We call this defence process, frequent both in normal and diseased psychic life, a *projection*. The survivor will deny that he has ever entertained hostile impulses toward the beloved dead; but now the soul of the deceased entertains them and will try to give vent to them during the entire period of mourning. In spite of the successful defence through projection, the punitive and remorseful character of this emotional reaction manifests itself in being afraid, in self-imposed renunciations and in subjection to restrictions which are partly disguised as protective measures against the hostile demon. Thus we find again that taboo has grown out of the soil of an ambivalent emotional attitude. The taboo of the dead also originates from the opposition between the conscious grief and the unconscious satisfaction at death. If this is the origin of the resentment of spirits it is self-evident that just the nearest and formerly most beloved survivors have to fear it most.

As in neurotic symptoms, the taboo regulations also evince opposite feelings. Their restrictive character expresses mourning, while they also betray very clearly what they are trying to conceal, namely, the hostility towards the dead, which is now motivated as self-defence. We have learnt to understand part of the taboo regulations as temptation fears. A dead person is defenceless, which must act as an incitement to satisfy hostile desires entertained against him; this temptation has to be opposed by the prohibition.

But Westermarck is right in not admitting any difference in the savage's conception between those who have died by violence and those who have died a natural death. As will be shown later[Cf. Chap. III], in the unconscious mode of thinking even a natural death is perceived as murder; the person was killed by evil wishes. Any one interested in the origin and meaning of dreams dealing with the death of dear

434

relatives such as parents and brothers and sisters will find that the same feeling of ambivalence is responsible for the fact that the dreamer, the child, and the savage all have the same attitude towards the dead [*see The Interpretation of Dreams.*].

A little while ago we challenged Wundt's conception, who explains the nature of taboo through the fear of demons, and yet we have just agreed with the explanation which traces back the taboo of the dead to a fear of the soul of the dead after it has turned into a demon. This seems like a contradiction, but it will not be difficult for us to explain it. It is true that we have accepted the idea of demons, but we know that this assumption is not something final which psychology cannot resolve into further elements. We have, as it were, exposed the demons by recognizing them as mere projections of hostile feelings which the survivor entertains towards the dead.

The double feeling—tenderness and hostility—against the deceased, which we consider well founded, endeavours to assert itself at the time of bereavement as mourning and satisfaction. A conflict must ensue between these contrary feelings, and as one of them, namely the hostility, is altogether or for the greater part unconscious, the conflict cannot result in a conscious difference in the form of hostility or tenderness as, for instance, when we forgive an injury inflicted upon us by some one we love. The process usually adjusts itself through a special psychic mechanism, which is designated in psychoanalysis as *projection*. This unknown hostility, of which we are ignorant and of which we do not wish to know, is projected from our inner perception into the outer world and is thereby detached from our own person and attributed to the other. Not we, the survivors, rejoice because we are rid of the deceased, on the contrary, we mourn for him; but now, curiously enough, he has become an evil demon who would rejoice in our misfortune and who seeks our death. The survivors must now defend themselves against this evil enemy; they are freed from inner oppression, but they have only succeeded in exchanging it for an affliction from without.

It is not to be denied that this process of projection, which turns the dead into malevolent enemies, finds some support in the real hostilities of the dead which the survivors remember and with which they really can reproach the dead. These hostilities are harshness, the desire to dominate, injustice, and whatever else forms the background of even the most tender relations between men. But the process cannot be so simple that this factor alone could explain the origin of demons by projection. The offences of the dead certainly motivate in part the hostility of the survivors, but they would have been ineffective if they had not given rise to this hostility and the occasion of death would surely be the least suitable occasion for awakening the memory of the reproaches which justly could have been brought against the deceased. We cannot dispense with the unconscious hostility as the constant and really impelling motive. This hostile tendency towards those nearest and dearest could remain latent during their lifetime, that is to say, it could avoid betraying itself to consciousness either directly or indirectly through any substitutive formation. However, when the person who was simultaneously loved and hated died, this was no longer possible, and the conflict became acute. The mourning originating from the enhanced tenderness, became on the one hand more intolerant of the latent hostility, while on the other hand it could not tolerate that the latter should not give origin to a feeling of pure gratification. Thus there came about the repression of the unconscious hostility through projection, and the formation of the ceremonial in which fear of punishment by demons finds expression. With the termination of the period of mourning, the conflict also loses its acuteness so that the taboo of the dead can be abated or sink into oblivion.

4

Having thus explained the basis on which the very instructive taboo of the dead has grown up, we must not miss the opportunity of adding a few observations which may become important for the understanding of taboo in general.

The projection of unconscious hostility upon demons in the taboo of the dead is only a single example from a whole series of processes to which we must grant the greatest influence in the formation of primitive psychic life. In the foregoing case the mechanism of projection is used to settle an emotional conflict; it serves the same purpose in a large number of psychic situations which lead to neuroses. But projection is not specially created for the purpose of defence, it also comes into being where there are no conflicts. The projection of inner perceptions to the outside is a primitive mechanism which, for instance, also influences our sense-perceptions, so that it normally has the greatest share in shaping our outer world. Under conditions that have not yet been sufficiently determined even inner perceptions of ideational and emotional processes are projected outwardly, like sense perceptions, and are used to shape the outer world, whereas they ought to remain in the inner world. This is perhaps genetically connected with the fact that the function of attention was originally directed not towards the inner world, but to the stimuli streaming in from the outer world, and only received reports of pleasure and pain from the endopsychic processes. Only with the development of the language of abstract thought through the association of sensory remnants of word representations with inner processes, did the latter gradually become capable of perception. Before this took place primitive man had developed a picture of the outer world through the outward projection of inner perceptions, which we, with our reinforced conscious perception, must now translate back into psychology.

The projection of their own evil impulses upon demons is only a part of what has become the world system ('Weltanschauung') of primitive man which we shall discuss later as 'animism'. We shall then have to ascertain the psychological nature of such a system formation and the points of support which we shall find in the analysis of these system formations will again bring us face to face with the neurosis. For the present we merely wish to suggest that the 'secondary elaboration' of the dream content is the prototype of all these system formations [see *The Interpretation of Dreams*]. And let us not forget that beginning at the stage of system formation there are two origins for every act judged by consciousness, namely the systematic, and the real but unconscious origin.[95]

Wundt [*Myth and Religion*, p. 129] remarks that "among the influences which myth everywhere ascribes to demons the evil ones preponderate, so that according to the religions of races evil demons are evidently older than good demons." Now it is quite possible that the whole conception of demons was derived from the extremely important relation to the dead. In the further course of human

---

[95] (The projection creations of primitive man resemble the personifications through which the poet projects his warring impulses out of himself, as separated individuals.)

development the ambivalence inherent in this relation then manifested itself by allowing two altogether contrary psychic formations to issue from the same root, namely, the fear of demons and of *ghosts*, and the reverence for ancestors[96]. Nothing testifies so much to the influence of mourning on the origin of belief in demons as the fact that demons were always taken to be the spirits of persons not long dead. Mourning has a very distinct psychic task to perform, namely, to detach the memories and expectations of the survivors from the dead. When this work is accomplished the grief, and with it the remorse and reproach, lessens, and therefore also the fear of the demon. But the very spirits which at first were feared as demons now serve a friendlier purpose; they are revered as ancestors and appealed to for help in times of distress.

If we survey the relation of survivors to the dead through the course of the ages, it is very evident that the ambivalent feeling has extraordinarily abated. We now find it easy to suppress whatever unconscious hostility towards the dead there may still exist without any special psychic effort on our part. Where formerly satisfied hate and painful tenderness struggled with each other, we now find piety, which appears like a cicatrice and demands: *De mortuis nil nisi bene.* Only neurotics still blur the mourning for the loss of their dear ones with attacks of compulsive reproaches which psychoanalysis reveals as the old ambivalent emotional feeling. How this change was brought about, and to what extent constitutional changes and real improvement of familiar relations share in causing the abatement of the ambivalent feeling, need not be discussed here. But this example would lead us to assume *that the psychic impulses of primitive man possessed a higher degree of ambivalence than is found at present among civilized human beings. With the decline of this ambivalence the taboo, as the compromise symptom of the ambivalent conflict, also slowly disappeared.* Neurotics who are compelled to reproduce this conflict, together with the taboo resulting from it, may be said to have brought with them an atavistic remnant in the form of an archaic constitution the compensation of which in the interest of cultural demands entails the most prodigious psychic efforts on their part.

---

[96] In the psychoanalysis of neurotic persons who suffer, or have suffered, in their childhood from the fear of ghosts, it is often not difficult to expose these ghosts as the parents. Compare also in this connection the communication of P. Haeberlin, *Sexual Ghosts* (*Sexual Problems*, Feb. 1912), a question of another erotically accentuated person, but where the father was dead.

At this point we may recall the confusing information which Wundt offered us about the double meaning of the word taboo, namely, holy and unclean (see above). It was supposed that originally the word taboo did not yet mean holy and unclean but signified something demonic, something which may not be touched, thus emphasizing a characteristic common to both extremes of the later conception; this persistent common trait proves, however, that an original correspondence existed between what was holy and what was unclean, which only later became differentiated.

In contrast to this, our discussion readily shows that the double meaning in question belonged to the word taboo from the very beginning and that it serves to designate a definite ambivalence as well as everything which has come into existence on the basis of this ambivalence. Taboo is itself an ambivalent word and by way of supplement we may add that the established meaning of this word might of itself have allowed us to guess what we have found as the result of extensive investigation, namely, that the taboo prohibition is to be explained as the result of an emotional ambivalence. A study of the oldest languages has taught us that at one time there were many such words which included their own contrasts so that they were in a certain sense ambivalent, though perhaps not exactly in the same sense as the word taboo[97]. Slight vocal modifications of this primitive word containing two opposite meanings later served to create a separate linguistic expression for the two opposites originally united in one word.

The word taboo has had a different fate; with the diminished importance of the ambivalence which it connotes it has itself disappeared, or rather, the words analogous to it have vanished from the vocabulary. In a later connection I hope to be able to show that a tangible historic change is probably concealed behind the fate of this conception; that the word at first was associated with definite human relations which were characterized by great emotional ambivalence from which it expanded to other analogous relations.

Unless we are mistaken, the understanding of taboo also throws light upon the nature and origin of *conscience*. Without stretching

---

[97] Compare my article on Abel's *Gegensinn der Urworte* in the *Jahrbuch für Psychoanalytische und Psychopathologische Forschungen*, Bd. II, 1910.

ideas we can speak of a taboo conscience and a taboo sense of guilt after the violation of a taboo. Taboo conscience is probably the oldest form in which we meet the phenomenon of conscience. For what is 'conscience'? According to linguistic testimony it belongs to what we know most surely; in some languages its meaning is hardly to be distinguished from consciousness.

Conscience is the inner perception of objections to definite wish impulses that exist in us; but the emphasis is put upon the fact that this rejection does not have to depend on anything else, that it is sure of itself. This becomes even plainer in the case of a guilty conscience, where we become aware of the inner condemnation of such acts which realized some of our definite wish impulses. Confirmation seems superfluous here; whoever has a conscience must feel in himself the justification of the condemnation, and the reproach for the accomplished action. But this same character is evinced by the attitude of savages towards taboo. Taboo is a command of conscience, the violation of which causes a terrible sense of guilt which is as self-evident as its origin is unknown[98].

It is therefore probable that conscience also originates on the basis of an ambivalent feeling from quite definite human relations which contain this ambivalence. It probably originates under conditions which are in force both for taboo and the compulsion neurosis, that is, one component of the two contrasting feelings is unconscious and is kept repressed by the compulsive domination of the other component. This is confirmed by many things which we have learned from our analysis of neurosis. In the first place the character of compulsion neurotics shows a predominant trait of painful conscientiousness which is a symptom of reaction against the temptation which lurks in the unconscious, and which develops into the highest degrees of guilty conscience as their illness grows worse. Indeed, one may venture the assertion that if the origin of guilty conscience could not be discovered through compulsion neurotic patients, there would be no prospect of ever discovering it. This task is successfully solved in the case of the

---

[98] It is an interesting parallel that the sense of guilt resulting from the violation of a taboo is in no way diminished if the violation took place unwittingly (see examples above), and that even in the Greek myth the guilt of Oedipus is not cancelled by the fact that it was incurred without his knowledge and will and even against them.

individual neurotic, and we are confident of finding a similar solution in the case of races.

In the second place we cannot help noticing that the sense of guilt contains much of the nature of anxiety; without hesitation it may be described as 'conscience phobia'. But fear points to unconscious sources. The psychology of the neuroses taught us that when wish feelings undergo repression their libido becomes transformed into anxiety. In addition we must bear in mind that the sense of guilt also contains something unknown and unconscious, namely the motivation for the rejection. The character of anxiety in the sense of guilt corresponds to this unknown quantity.

If taboo expresses itself mainly in prohibitions it may well be considered self-evident, without remote proof from the analogy with neurosis that it is based on a positive, desireful impulse. For what nobody desires to do does not have to be forbidden, and certainly whatever is expressly forbidden must be an object of desire. If we applied this plausible theory to primitive races we would have to conclude that among their strongest temptations were desires to kill their kings and priests, to commit incest, to abuse their dead and the like. That is not very probable. And if we should apply the same theory to those cases in which we ourselves seem to hear the voice of conscience most clearly we would arouse the greatest contradiction. For there we would assert with the utmost certainty that we did not feel the slightest temptation to violate any of these commandments, as for example, the commandment: Thou shalt not kill, and that we felt nothing but repugnance at the very idea. But if we grant the testimony of our conscience the importance it claims, then the prohibition—the taboo as well as our moral prohibitions—becomes superfluous, while the existence of a conscience, in turn, remains unexplained and the connection between conscience, taboo and neurosis disappears. The net result of this would then be our present state of understanding unless we view the problem psychoanalytically.

But if we take into account the following results of psychoanalysis, our understanding of the problem is greatly advanced. The analysis of dreams of normal individuals has shown that our own temptation to kill others is stronger and more frequent than we had suspected and that it produces psychic effects even where it does not reveal itself to our consciousness. And when we have learnt that the obsessive rules of certain neurotics are nothing but measures of self-reassurance and self-punishment erected against the reinforced impulse to commit murder, we can return with fresh appreciation to our previous hypothesis that every prohibition must conceal a desire. We can then assume that this desire to murder actually exists and that the taboo as well as the moral prohibition are psychologically by no means superfluous but are, on the contrary, explained and justified through our ambivalent attitude towards the impulse to slay.

The nature of this ambivalent relation so often emphasized as fundamental, namely, that the positive underlying desire is unconscious, opens the possibility of showing further connections and explaining further problems. The psychic processes in the unconscious are not entirely identical with those known to us from our conscious psychic life, but have the benefit of certain notable liberties of which the latter are deprived. An unconscious impulse need not have originated where we find it expressed, it can spring from an entirely different place and may originally have referred to other persons and relations, but through the mechanism of *displacement*, it reaches the point where it comes to our notice. Thanks to the indestructibility of unconscious processes and their inaccessibility to correction, the impulse may be saved over from earlier times to which it was adapted to later periods and conditions in which its manifestations must necessarily seem foreign. These are all only hints, but a careful elaboration of them would show how important they may become for the understanding of the development of civilization.

In closing these discussions we do not want to neglect to make an observation that will be of use for later investigations. Even if we insist upon the essential similarity between taboo and moral prohibitions we do not dispute that a psychological difference must exist between them. A change in the relations of the fundamental ambivalence can be the only reason why the prohibition no longer appears in the form of a taboo.

In the analytical consideration of taboo phenomena we have hitherto allowed ourselves to be guided by their demonstrable agreements with compulsion neurosis; but as taboo is not a neurosis but a social creation we are also confronted with the task of showing wherein lies the essential difference between the neurosis and a product of culture like the taboo.

Here again I will take a single fact as my starting point. Primitive races fear a punishment for the violation of a taboo, usually a serious disease or death. This punishment threatens only him who has been guilty of the violation. It is different with the compulsion neurosis. If the patient wants to do something that is forbidden to him he does not fear punishment for himself, but for another person. This person is usually indefinite, but, by means of analysis, is easily recognized as some one very near and dear to the patient. The neurotic therefore acts as if he were altruistic, while primitive man seems egotistical. Only if retribution fails to overtake the taboo violator spontaneously does a collective feeling awaken among savages that they are all threatened through the sacrilege, and they hasten to inflict the omitted punishment themselves. It is easy for us to explain the mechanism of this solidarity. It is a question of fear of the contagious example, the temptation to imitate, that is to say, of the capacity of the taboo to infect. If some one has succeeded in satisfying the repressed desire, the same desire must manifest itself in all his companions; hence, in order to keep down this temptation, this envied individual must be despoiled of the fruit of his daring. Not infrequently the punishment gives the executors themselves an opportunity to commit the same sacrilegious act by justifying it as an expiation. This is really one of the fundamentals of the human code of punishment which rightly presumes the same forbidden impulses in the criminal and in the members of society who avenge his offence.

Psychoanalysis here confirms what the pious were wont to say, that we are all miserable sinners. How then shall we explain the unexpected nobility of the neurosis which fears nothing for itself and everything for the beloved person? Psychoanalytic investigation shows that this nobility is not primary. Originally, that is to say at the beginning of the disease, the threat of punishment pertained to one's own person; in every case the fear was for one's own life; the fear of death being only later displaced upon another beloved person. The process is somewhat complicated but we have a complete grasp of it. An evil impulse—a death wish—towards the beloved person is always at the basis of the formation of a prohibition. This is repressed through a prohibition, and the prohibition is connected with a certain act which by displacement usually substitutes the hostile for the beloved person, and the execution of this act is threatened with the penalty of death. But the process goes further and the original wish for the death of the beloved other person is then replaced by fear for his death. The tender altruistic trait of the neurosis therefore merely *compensates* for the opposite attitude of brutal egotism which is at the basis of it. If we designate as social those emotional impulses which are determined through regard for another person who is not taken as a sexual object, we can emphasize the withdrawal of these social factors as an essential feature of the neurosis, which is later disguised through overcompensation.

Without lingering over the origin of these social impulses and their relation to other fundamental impulses of man, we will bring out the second main characteristic of the neurosis by means of another example. The form in which taboo manifests itself has the greatest similarity to the touching phobia of neurotics, the *Délire de toucher*. As a matter of fact this neurosis is regularly concerned with the prohibition of sexual touching and psychoanalysis has quite generally shown that the motive power which is deflected and displaced in the neurosis is of sexual origin. In taboo the forbidden contact has evidently not only sexual significance but rather the more, general one of attack, of acquisition and of personal assertion. If it is prohibited to touch the chief or something that was in contact with him it means that an inhibition should be imposed upon the same impulse which on other occasions expresses itself in suspicious surveillance of the chief and even in physical ill-treatment of him before his coronation (see above). *Thus the preponderance of sexual components of the impulse over the social components is the determining factor of the neurosis.* But the social impulses themselves came into being through the union of egotistical and erotic components into special entities.

From this single example of a comparison between taboo and compulsion neurosis it is already possible to guess the relation between individual forms of the neurosis and the creations of culture, and in what respect the study of the psychology of the neurosis is important for the understanding of the development of culture.

In one way the neuroses show a striking and far-reaching correspondence with the great social productions of art, religion and philosophy, while again they seem like distortions of them. We may say that hysteria is a caricature of an artistic creation, a compulsion neurosis, a caricature of a religion, and a paranoic delusion, a caricature of a philosophic system. In the last analysis this deviation goes back to the fact that the neuroses are asocial formations; they seek to accomplish by private means what arose in society through collective labour. In analysing the impulse of the neuroses one learns that motive powers of sexual origin exercise the determining influence in them, while the corresponding cultural creations rest upon social impulses and on such as have issued from the combination of egotistical and sexual components. It seems that the sexual need is not capable of uniting men in the same way as the demands of self preservation; sexual satisfaction is in the first place the private concern of the individual.

Genetically the asocial nature of the neurosis springs from its original tendency to flee from a dissatisfying reality to a more pleasurable world of phantasy. This real world which neurotics shun is dominated by the society of human beings and by the institutions created by them; the estrangement from reality is at the same time a withdrawal from human companionship.

III. ANIMISM, MAGIC AND THE OMNIPOTENCE OF THOUGHT

1

IT is a necessary defect of studies which seek to apply the point of view of psychoanalysis to the mental sciences that they cannot do justice to either subject. They therefore confine themselves to the rôle of incentives and make suggestions to the expert which he should take into consideration in his work. This defect will make itself felt most strongly in an essay such as this which tries to treat of the enormous sphere called animism.[99] Animism in the narrower sense is the theory of psychic concepts, and in the wider sense, of spiritual beings in general. Animatism, the animation theory of seemingly inanimate nature, is a further subdivision which also includes animatism and

---

[99] The necessary crowding of the material also compels us to dispense with a thorough bibliography. Instead of this the reader is referred to the well-known works of Herbert Spencer, J. G. Frazer, A. Lang, E. B. Tylor and W. Wundt, from which all the statements concerning animism and magic are taken. The independence of the author can manifest itself only in the choice of the material and of opinions.

animism. The name animism, formerly applied to a definite philosophic system, seems to have acquired its present meaning through E. B. Tylor[100].

What led to the formulation of these names is the insight into the very remarkable conceptions of nature and the world of those primitive races known to us from history and from our own times. These races populate the world with a multitude of spiritual beings which are benevolent or malevolent to them, and attribute the causation of natural processes to these spirits and demons; they also consider that not only animals and plants, but inanimate things as well are animated by them. A third and perhaps the most important part of this primitive 'nature philosophy' seems far less striking to us because we ourselves are not yet far enough removed from it, though we have greatly limited the existence of spirits and to-day explain the processes of nature by the assumption of impersonal physical forces. For primitive people believe in a similar 'animation' of human individuals as well. Human beings have souls which can leave their habitation and enter into other beings; these souls are the bearers of spiritual activities and are, to a certain extent, independent of the 'bodies'. Originally souls were thought of as being very similar to individuals; only in the course of a long evolution did they lose their material character and attain a high degree of 'spiritualization'[101].

Most authors incline to the assumption that these soul conceptions are the original nucleus of the animistic system, that spirits merely correspond to souls that have become independent, and that the souls of animals, plants and things were formed after the analogy of human souls.

How did primitive people come to the peculiarly dualistic fundamental conceptions on which this animistic system rests? Through the observation, it is thought, of the phenomena of sleep (with dreams) and death which resemble sleep, and through the effort to explain these conditions, which affect each individual so intimately. Above all, the problem of death must have become the starting point of the formation of the theory. To primitive man the continuation of life—immortality—would be self-evident. The conception of death is

---

[100] E. B. Tylor, *Primitive Culture*, Vol. I, p. 425, fourth ed., 1903. W. Wundt, *Myth and Religion*, Vol. II, p. 173, 1906.
[101] Wundt *l.c.*, Chapter IV: *Die Seelenvorstellungen*.

something accepted later, and only with hesitation, for even to us it is still devoid of content and unrealizable. Very likely discussions have taken place over the part which may have been played by other observations and experiences in the formation of the fundamental animistic conceptions such as dream imagery, shadows and reflections, but these have led to no conclusion[102].

If primitive man reacted to the phenomena that stimulated his reflection with the formation of conceptions of the soul, and then transferred these to objects of the outer world, his attitude will be judged to be quite natural and in no way mysterious. In view of the fact that animistic conceptions have been shown to be similar among the most varied races and in all periods, Wundt states that these "are the necessary psychological product of the myth-forming consciousness, and primitive animism may be looked upon as the spiritual expression of man's natural state in so far as this is at all accessible to our observation"[103]. Hume has already justified the animation of the inanimate in his *Natural History of Religions*, where he said: "There is a universal tendency among mankind to conceive all beings like themselves and to transfer to every object those qualities with which they are familiarly acquainted and of which they are intimately conscious"[104].

Animism is a system of thought, it gives not only the explanation of a single phenomenon, but makes it possible to comprehend the totality of the world from one point, as a continuity. Writers maintain that in the course of time three such systems of thought, three great world systems came into being: the animistic (mythological), the religious, and the scientific. Of these animism, the first system is perhaps the most consistent and the most exhaustive, and the one which explains the nature of the world in its entirety. This first world system, of mankind is now a psychological theory. It would go beyond our scope to show how much of it can still be demonstrated in the life of to-day, either as a worthless survival in the form of superstition, or in living form, as the foundation of our language, our belief, and our philosophy.

---

[102] Compare, besides Wundt and H. Spencer and the instructive article in the *Encyclopedia Britannica*, 1911 (*Animism, Mythology*, and so forth).
[103] *l.c.*, p. 154

It is in reference to the successive stages of these three world systems that we say that animism in itself was not yet a religion but contained the prerequisites from which religions were later formed. It is also evident that myths are based upon animistic foundations, but the detailed relation of myths to animism seem unexplained in some essential points.

2

Our psychoanalytic work will begin at a different point. It must not be assumed that mankind came to create its first world system through a purely speculative thirst for knowledge. The practical need of mastering the world must have contributed to this effort. We are therefore not astonished to learn that something else went hand in hand with the animistic system, namely the elaboration of directions for making oneself master of men, animals and things, as well as of their spirits. S. Reinach[105] wants to call these directions, which are known under the names of 'sorcery and magic', the strategy of animism; With Mauss and Hubert, I should prefer to compare them to a technique[106].

Can the conceptions of sorcery and magic be separated? It can be done if we are willing on our own authority to put ourselves above the vagaries of linguistic usage. Then sorcery is essentially the art of influencing spirits by treating them like people under the same circumstances, that is to say by appeasing them, reconciling them, making them more favourably disposed to one, by intimidating them, by depriving them of their power and by making them subject to one's will; all that is accomplished through the same methods that have been found effective with living people. Magic, however, is something else; it does not essentially concern itself with spirits, and uses special means, not the ordinary psychological method. We can easily guess that magic is the earlier and the more important part of animistic technique, for among the means with which spirits are to be treated there are also found the magic kind[107], and magic is also applied where

---

105 See Tylor, *Primitive Culture*, Vol. I, p. 477.
105] *Cultes, Mythes et Religions*, T. II: *Introduction*, p. XV, 1909
106 *Année Sociologique*, Seventh Vol, 1904.
107] To frighten away a ghost with noise and cries is a form of pure sorcery; to force him to do something by taking his name is to employ magic against him

spiritualization of nature has not yet, as it seems to us, been accomplished.

Magic must serve the most varied purposes. It must subject the processes of nature to the will of man, protect the individual against enemies and dangers, and give him the power to injure his enemies. But the principles on whose assumptions the magic activity is based, or rather the principle of magic, is so evident that it was recognized by all authors. If we may take the opinion of E. B. Tylor at its face value it can be most tersely expressed in his words: "mistaking an ideal connection for a real one". We shall explain this characteristic in the case of two groups of magic acts.

One of the most widespread magic procedures for injuring an enemy consists of making an effigy of him out of any kind of material. The likeness counts for little, in fact any object may be 'named' as his image. Whatever is subsequently done to this image will also happen to the hated prototype; thus if the effigy has been injured in any place he will be afflicted by a disease in the corresponding part of the body. This same magic technique, instead of being used for private enmity can also be employed for pious purposes and can thus be used to aid the gods against evil demons. I quote Frazer[The Magic Art, II. p. 67]: "Every night when the sun-god Ra in ancient Egypt sank to his home in the glowing west he was assailed by hosts of demons under the leadership of the archfiend Apepi. All night long he fought them, and sometimes by day the powers of darkness sent up clouds even into the blue Egyptian sky to obscure his light and weaken his power. To aid the sun-god in this daily struggle, a ceremony was daily performed in his temple at Thebes. A figure of his foe Apepi, represented as a crocodile with a hideous face or a serpent with many coils, was made of wax, and on it the demon's name was written in green ink. Wrapt in a papyrus case, on which another likeness of Apepi had been drawn in green ink, the figure was then tied up with black hair, spat upon, hacked with a stone knife and cast on the ground. There the priest trod on it with his left foot again and again, and then burned it in a fire made of a certain plant or grass. When Apepi himself had thus been effectively disposed of, waxen effigies of each of his principle demons, and of their fathers, mothers, and children, were made and burnt in the same way. The service accompanied by the recitation of certain prescribed spells, was repeated not merely morning, noon and night, but whenever a storm was raging or heavy rain had set in, or black clouds were stealing across the sky to hide the sun's bright disk. The fiends of darkness, clouds and rain, felt the injury inflicted on their images as if it had been done to themselves; they passed away, at least for a time, and the beneficent sun-god shone out triumphant once more"[108].

There is a great mass of magic actions which show a similar motivation, but I shall lay stress upon only two, which have always played a great rôle among primitive races and which have been partly preserved in the myths and cults of higher stages of evolution: the art of causing rain and fruitfulness by magic. Rain is produced by magic means, by imitating it, and perhaps also by imitating the clouds and storm which produce it. It looks as if they wanted to 'play rain'. The Ainos of Japan, for instance, make rain by pouring out water through a big sieve, while others fit out a big bowl with sails and oars as if it were a ship, which is then dragged about the village and gardens. But the fruitfulness of the soil was assured by magic means by showing it the spectacle of human sexual intercourse. To cite one out of many examples; in some part of Java, the peasants used to go out into the fields at night for sexual intercourse when the rice was about to blossom in order to stimulate the rice to fruitfulness through their example[*The Magic Art*, II, p. 98]. At the same time it was feared that proscribed incestuous relationships would stimulate the soil to grow weeds and render it unfruitful[109].

Certain negative rules, that is to say magic precautions, must be put into this first group. If some of the inhabitants of a Dayak village had set out on a hunt for wild-boars, those remaining behind were in the meantime not permitted to touch either oil or water with their hands, as such acts would soften the hunters' fingers and would let the quarry slip through their hands[*The Magic Art*, p. 120.]. Or when a Gilyak hunter was pursuing game in the woods, his children were forbidden to make drawings on wood or in the sand, as the paths in the thick woods might become as intertwined as the lines of the drawing and the hunter would not find his way home[*l.c.*, p. 122].

---

[108] The Biblical prohibition against making an image of anything living hardly sprang from any fundamental rejection of plastic art, but was probably meant to deprive magic, which the Hebraic religion proscribed, of one of its instruments. Frazer, p. 87.
[109] An echo of this is to be found in the *Oedipus Rex* of Sophocles.

The fact that in these as in a great many other examples of magic influence, distance plays no part, telepathy is taken as a matter of course—will cause us no difficulties in grasping the peculiarity of magic.

There is no doubt about what is considered the effective force in all these examples. It is the *similarity* between the performed action and the expected happening. Frazer therefore calls this kind of magic *imitative* or*homœopathic*. If I want it to rain I only have to produce something that looks like rain or recalls rain. In a later phase of cultural development, instead of these magic conjurations of rain, processions are arranged to a house of god, in order to supplicate the saint who dwells there to send rain. Finally also this religious technique will be given up and instead an effort will be made to find out what would influence the atmosphere to produce rain.

In another group of magic actions the principle of similarity is no longer involved, but in its stead there is another principle the nature of which is well brought out in the following examples.

Another method may be used to injure an enemy. You possess yourself of his hair, his nails, anything that he has discarded, or even a part of his clothing, and do something hostile to these things. This is just as effective as if you had dominated the person himself, and anything that you do to the things that belong to him must happen to him too. According to the conception of primitive men a name is an essential part of a personality; if therefore you know the name of a person or a spirit you have acquired a certain power over its bearer. This explains the remarkable precautions and restrictions in the use of names which we have touched upon in the essay on taboo[See preceding chapter]. In these examples similarity is evidently replaced by relationship.

The cannibalism of primitive races derives its more sublime motivation in a similar manner. By absorbing parts of the body of a person through the act of eating we also come to possess the properties which belonged to that person. From this there follow precautions and restrictions as to diet under special circumstances. Thus a pregnant woman will avoid eating the meat of certain animals because their undesirable properties, for example, cowardice, might thus be transferred to the child she is nourishing. It makes no difference to the magic influence whether the connection is already abolished or whether it had consisted of only one very important contact. Thus, for instance, the belief in a magic bond which links the fate of a wound with the weapon which caused it can be followed unchanged through thousands of years. If a Melanesian gets possession of the bow by which he was wounded he will carefully keep it in a cool place in order thus to keep down the inflammation of the wound. But if the bow has remained in the possession of the enemy it will certainly be kept in close proximity to a fire in order that the wound may burn and become thoroughly inflamed. Pliny, in his *Natural History*, XXVIII, advises spitting on the hand which has caused the injury if one regrets having injured some one; the pain of the injured person will then immediately be eased. Francis Bacon, in his *Natural History*, mentions the generally accredited belief that putting a salve on the weapon which has made a wound will cause this wound to heal of itself. It is said that even to-day English peasants follow this prescription, and that if they have cut themselves with a scythe they will from that moment on carefully keep the instrument clean in order that the wound may not fester. In June, 1902, a local English weekly reported that a woman called Matilde Henry of Norwich accidentally ran an iron nail into the sole of her foot. Without having the wound examined or even taking off her stocking she bade her daughter to oil the nail thoroughly in the expectation that then nothing could happen to her. She died a few days later of tetanus[*The Magic Art*, pp. 201-3] in consequence of postponed antisepsis.

The examples from this last group illustrate Frazer's distinction between *contagious* magic and *imitative* magic. What is considered as effective in these examples is no longer the similarity, but the association in space, the contiguity, or at least the imagined contiguity, or the memory of its existence. But since similarity and contiguity are the two essential principles of the processes of association of ideas, it must be concluded that the dominance of associations of ideas really explains all the madness of the rules of magic. We can see how true Tylor's quoted characteristic of magic: "mistaking an ideal connection for a real one", proves to be. The same may be said of Frazer's idea, who has expressed it in almost the same terms: "men mistook the order of their ideas for the order of nature, and hence imagined that the control which they have, or seem to have, over their thoughts, permitted them to have a corresponding control over things"[*The Magic Art*, p. 420].

It will at first seem strange that this illuminating explanation of magic could have been rejected by some authors as unsatisfactory[110]. But on closer consideration we must sustain the objection that the association theory of magic merely explains the paths that magic travels, and not its essential nature, that is, it does not explain the misunderstanding which bids it put psychological laws in place of natural ones. We are apparently in need here of a dynamic factor; but while the search for this leads the critics of Frazer's theory astray, it will be easy to give a satisfactory explanation of magic by carrying its association theory further and by entering more deeply into it.

First let us examine the simpler and more important case of imitative magic. According to Frazer (p. 54) this may be practised by itself, whereas contagious magic as a rule presupposes the imitative. The motives which impel one to exercise magic are easily recognized; they are the wishes of men. We need only assume that primitive man had great confidence in the power of his wishes. At bottom everything which he accomplished by magic means must have been done solely because he wanted it. Thus in the beginning only his wish is accentuated.

In the case of the child which finds itself under analogous psychic conditions, without being as yet capable of motor activity, we have elsewhere advocated the assumption that it at first really satisfies its wishes by means of hallucinations, in that it creates the satisfying situation through centrifugal excitements of its sensory organs[111]. The adult primitive man knows another way. A motor impulse, the will, clings to his wish and this will which later will change the face of the earth in the service of wish fulfilment is now used to represent the gratification so that one may experience it, as it were, through motor hallucination. Such a *representation* of the gratified wish is altogether comparable to the *play* of children, where it replaces the purely sensory technique of gratification. If play and imitative representation suffice for the child and for primitive man, it must not be taken as a

---

[110] Compare the article *Magic* (N. T. W.), in the *Encyclopedia Britannica*, 11th Ed

[111] Formulation of two principles of psychic activity, *Jahrb. für Psychoanalyt. Forschungen*, Vol. III, 1912, p. 2.

sign of modesty, in our sense, or of resignation due to the realization of their impotence, on the contrary; it is the very obvious result of the excessive valuation of their wish, of the will which depends upon the wish and of the paths the wish takes. In time the psychic accent is displaced from the motives of the magic act to its means, namely to the act itself. Perhaps it would be more correct to say that primitive man does not become aware of the over-valuation of his psychic acts until it becomes evident to him through the means employed. It would also seem as if it were the magic act itself which compels the fulfilment of the wish by virtue of its similarity to the object desired. At the stage of animistic thinking there is as yet no way of demonstrating objectively the true state of affairs, but this becomes possible at later stages when, though such procedures are still practised, the psychic phenomenon of scepticism already manifests itself as a tendency to repression. At that stage men will acknowledge that the conjuration of spirits avails nothing unless accompanied by belief, and that the magic effect of prayer fails if there is no piety behind it[112]].

The possibility of a contagious magic which depends upon contiguous association will then show us that the psychic valuation of the wish and the will has been extended to all psychic acts which the will can command. We may say that at present there is a general over-valuation of all psychic processes, that is to say there is an attitude towards the world which according to our understanding of the relation of reality to thought must appear like an over-estimation of the latter. Objects as such are over-shadowed by the ideas representing them; what takes place in the latter must also happen to the former, and the relations which exist between ideas are also postulated as to things. As thought does not recognize distances and easily brings together in one act of consciousness things spatially and temporally far removed, the magic world also puts itself above spatial distance by telepathy, and treats a past association as if it were a present one. In the animistic age the reflection of the inner world must obscure that other picture of the world which we believe we recognize.

Let us also point out that the two principles of association, similarity and contiguity, meet in the higher unity of contact. Association by contiguity is contact in the direct sense, and association

---

[112] The King in *Hamlet* (Act III, Scene 4): "My words fly up, my thoughts remain below, Words without thoughts never to heaven go."

by similarity is contact in the transferred sense. Another identity in the psychic process which has not yet been grasped by us is probably concealed in the use of the same word for both kinds of associations. It is the same range of the concept of contact which we have found in the analysis of taboo[Compare Chapter II].

In summing up we may now say that the principle which controls magic, and the technique of the animistic method of thought, is 'Omnipotence of Thought'.

3

I have adopted the term 'Omnipotence of Thought' from a highly intelligent man, a former sufferer from compulsion neurosis, who, after being cured through psychoanalytic treatment, was able to demonstrate his efficiency and good sense[113]. He had coined this phrase to designate all those peculiar and uncanny occurrences which seemed to pursue him just as they pursue others afflicted with his malady. Thus if he happened to think of a person, he was actually confronted with this person as if he had conjured him up; if he inquired suddenly about the state of health of an acquaintance whom he had long missed he was sure to hear that this acquaintance had just died, so that he could believe that the deceased had drawn his attention to himself by telepathic means; if he uttered a half meant imprecation against a stranger, he could expect to have him die soon thereafter and burden him with the responsibility for his death. He was able to explain most of these cases in the course of the treatment, he could tell how the illusion had originated, and what he himself had contributed towards furthering his superstitious expectations[114]. All compulsion neurotics are superstitious in this manner and often against their better judgment.

The existence of omnipotence of thought is most clearly seen in compulsion neurosis, where the results of this primitive method of thought are most often found or met in consciousness. But we must guard against seeing in this a distinguishing characteristic of this

---

[113] Remarks upon a case of Compulsion Neurosis, *Jahrb. für Psychoanalyt. und Psychopath. Forschungen*, Vol. I, 1909.
[114] We seem to attribute the character of the 'uncanny' to all such impressions which seek to confirm the omnipotence of thought and the animistic method of thought in general, though our judgment has long rejected it. .

neurosis, for analytic investigation reveals the same mechanism in the other neuroses. In every one of the neuroses it is not the reality of the experience but the reality of the thought which forms the basis for the symptom formation. Neurotics live in a special world in which, as I have elsewhere expressed it, only the 'neurotic standard of currency' counts, that is to say, only things intensively thought of or affectively conceived are effective with them, regardless of whether these things are in harmony with outer reality. The hysteric repeats in his attacks and fixates through his symptoms, occurrences which have taken place only in his phantasy, though in the last analysis they go back to real events or have been built up from them. The neurotic's guilty conscience is just as incomprehensible if traced to real misdeeds. A compulsion neurotic may be oppressed by a sense of guilt which is appropriate to a wholesale murderer, while at the same time he acts towards his fellow beings in a most considerate and scrupulous manner, a behaviour which he evinced since his childhood. And yet his sense of guilt is justified; it is based upon intensive and frequent death wishes which unconsciously manifest themselves towards his fellow beings. It is motivated from the point of view of unconscious thoughts, but not of intentional acts. Thus the omnipotence of thought, the over-estimation of psychic processes as opposed to reality, proves to be of unlimited effect in the neurotic's affective life and in all that emanates from it. But if we subject him to psychoanalytic treatment, which makes his unconscious thoughts conscious to him he refuses to believe that thoughts are free and is always afraid to express evil wishes lest they be fulfilled in consequence of his utterance. But through this attitude as well as through the superstition which plays an active part in his life he reveals to us how close he stands to the savage who believes he can change the outer world by a mere thought of his.

The primary obsessive actions of these neurotics are really altogether of a magical nature. If not magic they are at least anti-magic and are destined to ward off the expectation of evil with which the neurosis is wont to begin. Whenever I was able to pierce these secrets it turned out that the content of this expectation of evil was death. According to Schopenhauer the problem of death stands at the beginning of every philosophy; we have heard that the formation of the soul conception and of the belief in demons which characterize animism, are also traced back to the impression which death makes upon man. It is hard to decide whether these first compulsive and protective actions follow the principle of similarity, or of contrast, for under the conditions of the neurosis they are usually distorted through displacement upon some trifle, upon some action which in itself is quite insignificant[115]. The protective formulæ of the compulsion neurosis also have a counterpart in the incantations of magic. But the evolution of compulsive actions may be described by pointing out how these actions begin as a spell against evil wishes which are very remote from anything sexual, only to end up as a substitute for forbidden sexual activity, which they imitate as faithfully as possible.

If we accept the evolution of man's conceptions of the universe mentioned above, according to which the *animistic* phase is *succeeded* by the *religious*, and this in turn by the *scientific*, we have no difficulty in following the fortunes of the 'omnipotence of thought' through all these phases. In the animistic stage man ascribes omnipotence to himself; in the religious he has ceded it to the gods, but without seriously giving it up, for he reserves to himself the right to control the gods by influencing them in some way or other in the interest of his wishes. In the scientific attitude towards life there is no longer any room for man's omnipotence; he has acknowledged his smallness and has submitted to death as to all other natural necessities in a spirit of resignation. Nevertheless, in our reliance upon the power of the human spirit which copes with the laws of reality, there still lives on a fragment of this primitive belief in the omnipotence of thought.

In retracing the development of libidinous impulses in the individual from its mature form back to its first beginnings in childhood, we at first found an important distinction which is stated in the *Three Contributions to the Theory of Sex* [*see previous book in this collection*]. The manifestations of sexual impulses can be recognized from the beginning, but at first they are not yet directed to any outer object. Each individual component of the sexual impulse works for a gain in pleasure and finds its gratification in its own body. This stage is called *autoerotism* and is distinguished from the stage of object selection.

In the course of further study it proved to be practical and really necessary to insert a third stage between these two or, if one prefers,

---

[115] The following discussions will yield a further motive for this displacement upon a trivial action

to divide the first stage of autoerotism into two. In this intermediary stage, the importance of which increases the more we investigate it, the sexual impulses which formerly were separate, have already formed into a unit and have also found an object; but this object is not external and foreign to the individual, but is his own ego, which is formed at this period. This new stage is called *narcism*, in view of the pathological fixation of this condition which may be observed later on. The individual acts as if he were in love with himself; for the purposes of our analysis the ego impulses and the libidinous wishes cannot yet be separated from each other.

Although this narcistic stage, in which the hitherto dissociated sexual impulses combine into a unity and take the ego as their object, cannot as yet be sharply differentiated, we can already surmise that the narcistic organization is never altogether given up again. To a certain extent man remains narcistic, even after he had found outer subjects for his libido, and the objects on which he bestows it represent, as it were, emanations of the libido which remain with his ego and which can be withdrawn into it. The state of being in love, so remarkable psychologically, and the normal prototype of the psychoses, corresponds to the highest stage of these emanations, in contrast to the state of self-love.

This high estimation of psychic acts found among primitives and neurotics, which we feel to be an overestimation, may now appropriately be brought into relation to narcism, and interpreted as an essential part of it. We would say that among primitive people thinking is still highly sexualized and that this accounts for the belief in the omnipotence of thought, the unshaken confidence in the capacity to dominate the world and the inaccessibility to the obvious facts which could enlighten man as to his real place in the world. In the case of neurotics a considerable part of this primitive attitude had remained as a constitutional factor, while on the other hand the sexual repression occurring in them has brought about a new sexualization of the processes of thought. In both cases, whether we deal with an original libidinous investment of thought or whether the same process has been accomplished regressively, the psychic results are the same, namely, intellectual narcism and omnipotence of thought[116].

If we may take the now established omnipotence of thought among primitive races as a proof of their narcism, we may venture to compare the various evolutionary stages of man's conception of the universe with the stages of the libidinous evolution of the individual. We find that the animistic phase corresponds in time as well as in content with narcism, the religious phase corresponds to that stage of object finding which is characterized by dependence on the parents, while the scientific stage has its full counterpart in the individual's stage of maturity where, having renounced the pleasure principle and having adapted himself to reality, he seeks his object in the outer world[117].

Only in one field has the omnipotence of thought been retained in our own civilization, namely in art. In art alone it still happens that man, consumed by his wishes, produces something similar to the gratification of these wishes, and this playing, thanks to artistic illusion, calls forth effects as if it were something real. We rightly speak of the magic of art and compare the artist with a magician. But this comparison is perhaps more important than it claims to be. Art, which certainly did not begin as art for art's sake, originally served tendencies which to-day have for the greater part ceased to exist. Among these we may suspect various magic intentions[118].

4

---

[116] It is almost an axiom with writers on this subject that a sort of 'Solipsism or Berkleianism' (as Professor Sully terms it as he finds it in the child) operates in the savage to make him refuse to recognize death as a fact.—Marett, *Pre-animistic Religion, Folklore*, Vol. XI, 1900, p. 178.

[117] We merely wish to indicate here that the original narcism of the child is decisive for the interpretation of its character development and that it precludes the assumption of a primitive feeling of inferiority for the child.

[118]] S. Reinach, *L'Art et la Magie*, in the collection *Cultes, Mythes et Religions*, Vol. I, pp. 125-136. Reinach thinks that the primitive artists who have left us the scratched or painted animal pictures in the caves of France did not want to 'arouse' pleasure, but to 'conjure things'. He explains this by showing that these drawings are in the darkest and most inaccessible part of the caves and that representations of feared beasts of prey are absent. "Les modernes parlent souvent, par hyperbole, de la magie du pinceau ou du ciseau d'un grand artiste et, en général, de la magie de l'art. Entendu en sense propre, qui est celui d'une constrainte mystique exercée par la volonté de l'homme sur d'autres volontés ou sur les choses, cette expression n'est plus admissible; mais nous avons vu qu'elle était autrefois rigoureusement, vraie, du moins dans l'opinion des artistes" (p. 136).

Animism, the first conception of the world which man succeeded in evolving, was therefore psychological. It did not yet require any science to establish it, for science sets in only after we have realized that we do not know the world and that we must therefore seek means of getting to know it. But animism was natural and self-evident to primitive man; he knew how the things of the world were constituted, and as man conceived himself to be. We are therefore prepared to find that primitive man transferred the structural relations of his own psyche to the outer world [recognized through so-called endopsychic perceptions.], and on the other hand we may make the attempt to transfer back into the human soul what animism teaches about the nature of things.

Magic, the technique of animism, clearly and unmistakably shows the tendency of forcing the laws of psychic life upon the reality of things, under conditions where spirits did not yet have to play any rôle, and could still be taken as objects of magic treatment. The assumptions of magic are therefore of older origin than the spirit theory, which forms the nucleus of animism. Our psychoanalytic view here coincides with a theory of R. R. Marett, according to which animism is preceded by a pre-animistic stage the nature of which is best indicated by the name Animatism (the theory of general animation). We have practically no further knowledge of pre-animism, as no race has yet been found without conceptions of spirits[119].

While magic still retains the full omnipotence of ideas, animism has ceded part of this omnipotence to spirits and thus has started on the way to form a religion. Now what could have moved primitive man to this first act of renunciation? It could hardly have been an insight into the incorrectness of his assumptions, for he continued to retain the magic technique.

As pointed out elsewhere, spirits and demons were nothing but the projection of primitive man's emotional impulses[120]; he personified the things he endowed with effects, populated the world with them and then rediscovered his inner psychic processes outside himself, quite like the ingenious paranoiac Schreber, who found the fixations and

---

[119]] R. R. Marett, *Pre-animistic Religion, Folklore*, Vol. XI, No. 2, 1900.—Comp. Wundt, *Myth and Religion*, Vol. II, p. 171.
[120] We assume that in this early narcistic stage feelings from libidinous and other sources of excitement are perhaps still indistinguishably combined with each other.

detachments of his libido reflected in the fates of the 'God-rays' which he invented[121].

As on a former occasion[122], we want to avoid the problem as to the origin of the tendency to project psychic processes into the outer world. It is fair to assume, however, that this tendency becomes stronger where the projection into the outer world offers psychic relief. Such a state of affairs can with certainty be expected if the impulses struggling for omnipotence have come into conflict with each other, for then they evidently cannot all become omnipotent. The morbid process in paranoia actually uses the mechanism of projection to solve such conflicts which arise in the psychic life. However, it so happens that the model case of such a conflict between two parts of an antithesis is the ambivalent attitude which we have analysed in detail in the situation of the mourner at the death of one dear to him. Such a case appeals to us especially fitted to motivate the creation of projection formations. Here again we are in agreement with those authors who declare that evil spirits were the first born among spirits, and find the origin of soul conceptions in the impression which death makes upon the survivors. We differ from them only in not putting the intellectual problem which death imposes upon the living into the foreground, instead of which we transfer the force which stimulates inquiry to the conflict of feelings into which this situation plunges the survivor.

The first theoretical accomplishment of man, the creation of spirits would therefore spring from the same source as the first moral restrictions to which he subjects himself, namely, the rules of taboo. But the fact that they have the same source should not prejudice us in favour of a simultaneous origin. If it really were the situation of the survivor confronted by the dead which first caused primitive man to reflect, so that he was compelled to surrender some of his omnipotence to spirits and to sacrifice a part of the free will of his actions, these cultural creations would be a first recognition of the ἀνάγκη, which opposes man's narcism. Primitive man would bow to the superior power of death with the same gesture with which he seems to deny it.

---

[121] Schreber, *Denkwürdigkeiten eines Nervenkranken*, 1903.—Freud, Psychoanalytic Observations concerning an autobiographically described case of Paranoia, *Jahrbuch für Psychoanalyt. Forsch.* Vol. III, 1911.

[122] Compare the latest communication about the Schreber case, p. 59

If we have the courage to follow our assumptions further, we may ask what essential part of our psychological structure is reflected and reviewed in the projection formation of souls and spirits. It is then difficult to dispute that the primitive conception of the soul, though still far removed from the later and wholly immaterial soul, nevertheless shares its nature and therefore looks upon a person or a thing as a duality, over the two elements of which the known properties and changes of the whole are distributed. This origin duality, we have borrowed the term from Herbert Spencer[*Principles of Sociology*, Vol. I, p. 179], is already identical with the dualism which manifests itself in our customary separation of spirit from body, and whose indestructible linguistic manifestations we recognize, for instance, in the description of a person who faints or raves as one who is 'beside himself.'

The thing which we, just like primitive man, project in outer reality, can hardly be anything else than the recognition of a state in which a given thing is present to the senses and to consciousness, next to which another state exists in which the thing is *latent*, but can reappear, that is to say, the co-existence of perception and memory, or, to generalize it, the existence of unconscious psychic processes next to conscious ones[123]. It might be said that in the last analysis the 'spirit' of a person or thing is the faculty of remembering and representing the object, after he or it was withdrawn from conscious perception.

Of course we must not expect from either the primitive or the current conception of the 'soul' that its line of demarcation from other parts should be as marked as that which contemporary science draws between conscious and unconscious psychic activity. The animistic soul, on the contrary, unites determinants from both sides. Its flightiness and mobility, its faculty of leaving the body, of permanently or temporarily taking possession of another body, all these are characteristics which remind us unmistakably of the nature of consciousness. But the way in which it keeps itself concealed behind the personal appearance reminds us of the unconscious; to-day we no longer ascribe its unchangeableness and indestructibility to conscious but to unconscious processes and look upon these as the real bearers of psychic activity.

---

[123] Compare my short paper: *A Note on the Unconscious in Psychoanalysis*, in the *Proceedings of the Society for Psychical Research*, Part LXVI, Vol. XXVI, 1912

We said before that animism is a system of thought, the first complete theory of the world; we now want to draw certain inferences through psychoanalytic interpretation of such a system. Our everyday experience is capable of constantly showing us the main characteristics of the 'system'. We dream during the night and have learnt to interpret the dream in the daytime. The dream can, without being untrue to its nature, appear confused and incoherent; but on the other hand it can also imitate the order of impressions of an experience, infer one occurrence from another, and refer one part of its contents to another. The dream succeeds more or less in this, but hardly ever succeeds so completely that an absurdity or a gap in the structure does not appear somewhere. If we subject the dream to interpretation we find that this unstable and irregular order of its components is quite unimportant for our understanding of it. The essential part of the dream are the dream thoughts, which have, to be sure, a significant, coherent, order. But their order is quite different from that which we remember from the manifest content of the dream. The coherence of the dream thoughts has been abolished and may either remain altogether lost or can be replaced by the new coherence of the dream content. Besides the condensation of the dream elements there is almost regularly a re-grouping of the same which is more or less independent of the former order. We say in conclusion, that what the dream-work has made out of the material of the dream thoughts has been subjected to a new influence, the so-called secondary elaboration, the object of which evidently is to do away with the incoherence and incomprehensibility caused by the dream-work, in favour of a new 'meaning'. This new meaning which has been brought about by the secondary elaboration is no longer the meaning of the dream thoughts.

The secondary elaboration of the product of the dream-work is an excellent example of the nature and the pretensions of a system. An intellectual function in us demands the unification, coherence and comprehensibility of everything perceived and thought of, and does not hesitate to construct a false connexion if, as a result of special circumstances, it cannot grasp the right one. We know such system formation not only from the dream, but also from phobias, from compulsive thinking and from the types of delusions. The system formation is most ingenious in delusional states (paranoia) and dominates the clinical picture, but it also must not be overlooked in other forms of neuropsychoses. In every case we can show that a re-arrangement of the psychic material takes place, which may often be quite violent, provided it seems comprehensible from the point of view of the system. The best indication that a system has been formed then lies in the fact that each result of it can be shown to have at least two motivations one of which springs from the assumptions of the system and is therefore eventually delusional,—and a hidden one which, however, we must recognize as the real and effective motivation.

An example from a neurosis may serve as illustration. In the chapter on taboo I mentioned a patient whose compulsive prohibitions correspond very neatly to the taboo of the Maori. The neurosis of this woman was directed against her husband and culminated in the defence against the unconscious wish for his death. But her manifest systematic phobia concerned the mention of death in general, in which her husband was altogether eliminated and never became the object of conscious solicitude. One day she heard her husband give an order to have his dull razors taken to a certain shop to have them sharpened. Impelled by a peculiar unrest she went to the shop herself, and on her return from this reconnoitre she asked her husband to lay the razors aside for good because she had discovered that there was a warehouse of coffins and funeral accessories next to the shop he mentioned. She claimed that he had intentionally brought the razors into permanent relation with the idea of death. This was then the systematic motivation of the prohibition, but we may be sure that the patient would have brought home the prohibition relating to the razors even if she had not discovered this warehouse in the neighbourhood. For it would have been sufficient if on her way to the shop she had met a hearse, a person in mourning, or somebody carrying a wreath. The net of determinants was spread out far enough to catch the prey in any case, it was simply a question whether she should pull it in or not. It could be established with certainty that she did not mobilize the determinants of the prohibition in other circumstances. She would then have said it had been one of her 'better days'. The real reason for the prohibition of the razor was, of course, as we can easily guess, her resistance against a pleasurably accentuated idea that her husband might cut his throat with the sharpened razors.

In much the same way a motor inhibition, an abasia or an agoraphobia, becomes perfected and detailed if the symptom once succeeds in representing an unconscious wish and of imposing a defence against it. All the patient's remaining unconscious phantasies and effective reminiscences strive for symptomatic expression through this outlet, when once it has been opened, and range themselves appropriately in the new order within the sphere of the disturbance of gait. It would therefore be a futile and really foolish way to begin to try to understand the symptomatic structure, and the details of, let us say, an agoraphobia, in terms of its basic assumptions. For the whole logic and strictness of connexion is only apparent. Sharper observation can reveal, as in the formation of the façade in the dream, the greatest inconsistency and arbitrariness in the symptom formation. The details of such a systematic phobia take their real motivation from concealed determinants which must have nothing to do with the inhibition in gait; it is for this reason that the form of such a phobia varies so and is so contradictory in different people.

If we now attempt to retrace the system of animism with which we are concerned, we may conclude from our insight into other psychological systems that 'superstition' need not be the only and actual motivation of such a single rule or custom even among primitive races, and that we are not relieved of the obligation of seeking for concealed motives. Under the dominance of an animistic system it is absolutely essential that each rule and activity should receive a systematic motivation which we to-day call 'superstitious'. But 'superstition', like 'anxiety', 'dreams', and 'demons', is one of the preliminaries of psychology which have been dissipated by psychoanalytic investigation. If we get behind these structures, which like a screen conceal understanding, we realize that the psychic life and the cultural level of savages have hitherto been inadequately appreciated.

If we regard the repression of impulses as a measure of the level of culture attained, we must admit that under the animistic system too, progress and evolution have taken place, which unjustly have been under-estimated on account of their superstitious motivation. If we hear that the warriors of a savage tribe impose the greatest chastity and cleanliness upon themselves as soon as they go upon the war-path [Frazer, *Taboo and the Perils of the Soul*, p. 158], the obvious explanation is that they dispose of their refuse in order that the enemy may not come into possession of this part of their person in order to harm them by magical means, and we may surmise analogous superstitious motivations for their abstinence. Nevertheless the fact remains that the impulse is renounced and we probably understand the case better if we assume that the savage warrior imposes such restrictions upon himself in compensation, because he is on the point of allowing himself the full satisfaction of cruel and hostile impulses otherwise forbidden. The same holds good for the numerous cases of sexual restriction while he is preoccupied with difficult or responsible tasks [*l.c.*, p. 200]. Even if the basis of these prohibitions can be referred to some association with magic, the fundamental conception of gaining greater strength by foregoing gratification of desires nevertheless remains unmistakable, and besides the magic rationalization of the prohibition, one must not neglect its hygienic root. When the men of a savage tribe go away to hunt, fish, make war, or collect valuable plants, the women at home are in the meantime subjected to numerous oppressive restrictions which, according to the savages themselves, exert a sympathetic effect upon the success of the far away expedition. But it does not require much acumen to guess that this element acting at a distance is nothing but a thought of home, the longing of the absent, and that these disguises conceal the sound psychological insight that the men will do their best only if they are fully assured of the whereabouts of their guarded women. On other occasions the thought is directly expressed without magic motivation that the conjugal infidelity of the wife thwarts the absent husband's efforts.

The countless taboo rules to which the women of savages are subject during their menstrual periods are motivated by the superstitious dread of blood which in all probability actually determines it. But it would be wrong to overlook the possibility that this blood dread also serves æsthetic and hygienic purposes which in every case have to be covered by magic motivations.

We are probably not mistaken in assuming that such attempted explanations expose us to the reproach of attributing a most improbable delicacy of psychic activities to contemporary savages.

But I think that we may easily make the same mistake with the psychology of these races who have remained at the animistic stage that we made with the psychic life of the child, which we adults

466

understood no better and whose richness and fineness of feeling we have therefore so greatly undervalued.

I want to consider another group of hitherto unexplained taboo rules because they admit of an explanation with which the psychoanalyst is familiar. Under certain conditions it is forbidden to many savage races to keep in the house sharp weapons and instruments for cutting[*l.c.*, p. 237]. Frazer sites a German superstition that a knife must not be left lying with the edge pointing upward because God and the angels might injure themselves with it. May we not recognize in this taboo a premonition of certain 'symptomatic actions'[Freud, *Psychopathology of Everyday Life*, p. 215] for which the sharp weapon might be used by unconscious evil impulses?

IV. THE INFANTILE RECURRENCE OF TOTEMISM

THE reader need not fear that psychoanalysis, which first revealed the regular over-determination of psychic acts and formations, will be tempted to derive anything so complicated as religion from a single source. If it necessarily seeks, as in duty bound, to gain recognition for one of the sources of this institution, it by no means claims exclusiveness for this source or even first rank among the concurring factors. Only a synthesis from various fields of research can decide what relative importance in the genesis of religion is to be assigned to the mechanism which we are to discuss; but such a task exceeds the means as well as the intentions of the psychoanalyst.

1

The first chapter of this book made us acquainted with the conception of totemism. We heard that totemism is a system which takes the place of religion among certain primitive races in Australia, America, and Africa, and furnishes the basis of social organization. We know that in 1869 the Scotchman MacLennan attracted general interest to the phenomena of totemism, which until then had been considered merely as curiosities, by his conjecture that a large number of customs and usages in various old as well as modern societies were to be taken as remnants of a totemic epoch. Science has since then fully recognized this significance of totemism. I quote a passage from the *Elements of the Psychology of Races* by W. Wundt (1912), as the latest utterance on this question[p. 139]: 'Taking all this together it becomes highly probable that a totemic culture was at one time the preliminary stage of every later evolution as well as a transition stage between the state of primitive man and the age of gods and heroes.'

It is necessary for the purposes of this chapter to go more deeply into the nature of totemism. For reasons that will be evident later I here give preference to an outline by S. Reinach, who in the year 1900 sketched the following *Code du Totémisme* in twelve articles, like a catechism of the totemic religion[124]:

1. Certain animals must not be killed or eaten, but men bring up individual animals of these species and take care of them.

2. An animal that dies accidentally is mourned and buried with the same honours as a member of the tribe.

3. The prohibition as to eating sometimes refers only to a certain part of the animal.

4. If pressure of necessity compels the killing of an animal usually spared, it is done with excuses to the animal and the attempt is made to mitigate the violation of the taboo, namely the killing, through various tricks and evasions.

5. If the animal is sacrificed by ritual, it is solemnly mourned.

6. At specified solemn occasions, like religious ceremonies, the skins of certain animals are donned. Where totemism still exists, these are totem animals.

7. Tribes and individuals assume the names of totem animals.

8. Many tribes use pictures of animals as coats of arms and decorate their weapons with them; the men paint animal pictures on their bodies or have them tattooed.

9. If the totem is one of the feared and dangerous animals it is assumed that the animal will spare the members of the tribe named after it.

10. The totem animal protects and warns the members of the tribe.

---

[124] *Revue Scientifique*, October, 1900, reprinted in the four volume work of the author, *Cultes, Mythes et Religions*, 1908, Tome I, p. 17

11. The totem animal foretells the future to those faithful to it and serves as their leader.

12. The members of a totem tribe often believe that they are connected with the totem animal by the bond of common origin.

The value of this catechism of the totem religion can be more appreciated if one bears in mind that Reinach has here also incorporated all the signs and clews which lead to the conclusion that the totemic system had once existed. The peculiar attitude of this author to the problem is shown by the fact that to some extent he neglects the essential traits of totemism, and we shall see that of the two main tenets of the totemistic catechism he has forced one into the background and completely lost sight of the other.

In order to get a more correct picture of the characteristics of totemism we turn to an author who has devoted four volumes to the theme, combining the most complete collection of the observations in question with the most thorough discussion of the problems they raise. We shall remain indebted to J. G. Frazer, the author of *Totemism and Exogamy*, for the pleasure and information he affords, even though psychoanalytic investigation may lead us to results which differ widely from his[125].

"A totem," wrote Frazer in his first essay *Totemism*, "is a class of material objects which a savage regards with superstitious respect, believing that there exists between him and every member of the class

---

[125] But it may be well to show the reader beforehand how difficult it is to establish the facts in this field. In the first place those who collect the observations are not identical with those who digest and discuss them; the first are travellers and missionaries, while the others are scientific men who perhaps have never seen the objects of their research.—It is not easy to establish an understanding with savages. Not all the observers were familiar with the languages but had to use the assistance of interpreters or else had to communicate with the people they questioned in the auxiliary language of pidgin-English. Savages are not communicative about the most intimate affairs of their culture and unburden themselves only to those foreigners who have passed many years in their midst. From various motives they often give wrong or misleading information, (Compare Frazer, *The Beginnings of Religion and Totemism Among the Australian Aborigines*; *Fortnightly Review*, 1905; *Totemism and Exogamy*, Vol. I, p. 150).—It must not be forgotten that primitive races are not young races but really are as old as the most civilized, and that we have no right to expect that they have preserved their original ideas and institutions for our information without any evolution or distortion. It is certain, on the contrary, that far-reaching changes in all directions have taken place among primitive races, so that we can never unhesitatingly decide which of their present conditions and opinions have preserved the original past, having remained petrified, as it were, and which represent a distortion and change of the original. It is due to this that one meets the many disputes among authors as to what proportion of the peculiarities of a primitive culture is to be taken as a primary, and what as a later and secondary manifestation. To establish the original conditions, therefore, always remains a matter of construction. Finally, it is not easy to adapt oneself to the ways of thinking of primitive races. For like children, we easily misunderstand them, and are always inclined to interpret their acts and feelings according to our own psychic constellations.

an intimate and altogether special relation. The connexion between a person and his totem is mutually beneficent; the totem protects the man and the man shows his respect for the totem in various ways, by not killing it if it be an animal, and not cutting or gathering it if it be a plant. As distinguished from a fetich, a totem is never an isolated individual but always a class of objects, generally a species of animals or of plants, more rarely a class of inanimate natural objects, very rarely a class of artificial objects."

At least three kinds of totem can be distinguished:

1. The tribal totem which a whole tribe shares and which is hereditary from generation to generation,

2. The sex totem which belongs to all the masculine or feminine members of a tribe to the exclusion of the opposite sex, and

3. The individual totem which belongs to the individual and does not descend to his successors.

The last two kinds of totem are comparatively of little importance compared to the tribal totem. Unless we are mistaken they are recent formations and of little importance as far as the nature of the taboo is concerned.

The tribal totem (clan totem) is the object of veneration of a group of men and women who take their name from the totem and consider themselves consanguineous offspring of a common ancestor, and who are firmly associated with each other through common obligations towards each other as well as by the belief in their totem.

Totemism is a religious as well as a social system. On its religious side it consists of the relations of mutual respect and consideration between a person and his totem, and on its social side it is composed of obligations of the members of the clan towards each other and towards other tribes. In the later history of totemism these two sides show a tendency to part company; the social system often survives the religious and conversely remnants of totemism remain in the religion of countries in which the social system based upon totemism had disappeared. In the present state of our ignorance about the origin of totemism we cannot say with certainty how these two sides were originally combined. But there is on the whole a strong probability that in the beginning the two sides of totemism were indistinguishable from each other. In other words, the further we go back the clearer it becomes that a member of a tribe looks upon himself as being of the same genus as his totem and makes no distinction between his attitude towards the totem and his attitude towards his tribal companions.

In the special description of totemism as a religious system, Frazer lays stress on the fact that the members of a tribe assume the name of their totem and also as a *rule believe that they are descended from it*. It is due to this belief that they do not hunt the totem animal or kill or eat it, and that they deny themselves every other use of the totem if it is not an animal. The prohibitions against killing or eating the totem are not the only taboos affecting it; sometimes it is also forbidden to touch it and even to look at it; in a number of cases the totem must not be called by its right name. Violation of the taboo prohibitions which protect the totem is punished automatically by serious disease or death[Compare the chapter on Taboo].

Specimens of the totem animals are sometimes raised by the clan and taken care of in captivity[126]. A totem animal found dead is mourned and buried like a member of the clan. If a totem animal had to be killed it was done with a prescribed ritual of excuses and ceremonies of expiation.

The tribe expected protection and forbearance from its totem. If it was a dangerous animal (a beast of prey or a poisonous snake), it was assumed that it would not harm, and where this assumption did not come true the person attacked was expelled from the tribe. Frazer thinks that oaths were originally ordeals, many tests as to descent and genuineness being in this way left to the decision of the totem. The totem helps in case of illness and gives the tribe premonitions and warnings. The appearance of the totem animal near a house was often looked upon as an announcement of death. The totem had come to get its relative.[127]

A member of a clan seeks to emphasize his relationship to the totem in various significant ways; he imitates an exterior similarity by dressing himself in the skin of the totem animal, by having the picture of it tattooed upon himself, and in other ways. On the solemn occasions of birth, initiation into manhood or funeral obsequies this

---

[126] Just as to-day we still have the wolves in a cage at the steps of the Capitol in Rome and the bears in the pit at Berne
[127] Like the legend of the white woman in many noble families

identification with the totem is carried out in deeds and words. Dances in which all the members of the tribe disguise themselves as their totem and act like it, serve various magic and religious purposes. Finally there are the ceremonies at which the totem animal is killed in a solemn manner (*Frazer* p. 35.—See the discussion of sacrifice further on).

The social side of totemism is primarily expressed in a sternly observed commandment and in a tremendous restriction. The members of a totem clan are brothers and sisters, pledged to help and protect each other; if a member of the clan is slain by a stranger the whole tribe of the slayer must answer for the murder and the clan of the slain man shows its solidarity in the demand for expiation for the blood that has been shed. The ties of the totem are stronger than our ideas of family ties, with which they do not altogether coincide, since the transfer of the totem takes place as a rule through maternal inheritance, paternal inheritance possibly not counting at all in the beginning.

But the corresponding taboo restriction consists in the prohibition against members of the same clan marrying each other or having any kind of sexual intercourse whatsoever with each other. This is the famous and enigmatic *exogamy* connexion with totemism. We have devoted the whole first chapter of this book to it, and therefore need only mention here that this exogamy springs from the intensified incest dread of primitive races, that it becomes entirely comprehensible as a security against incest in group marriages, and that at first it accomplishes the avoidance of incest for the younger generation and only in the course of further development becomes a hindrance to the older generation as well. [See Chapter I.].

To this presentation of totemism by Frazer, one of the earliest in the literature on the subject, I will now add a few excerpts from one of the latest summaries. In the *Elements of the Psychology of Races*, which appeared in 1912, W. Wundt says (p.116): "The totem animal is considered the ancestral animal. 'Totem' is therefore both a group name and a birth name and in the latter aspect this name has at the same time a mythological meaning. But all these uses of the conception play into each other and the particular meanings may recede so that in some cases the totems have become almost a mere nomenclature of the tribal divisions, while in others the idea of the descent or else the cultic meaning of the totem remains in the foreground.... The conception of the totem determines the *tribal* arrangement and the *tribal organization*. These norms and their establishment in the belief and feelings of the members of the tribe account for the fact that originally the totem animal was certainly not considered merely a name for a group division but that it usually was considered the progenitor of the corresponding division.... This accounted for the fact that these animal ancestors enjoyed a cult.... This animal cult expresses itself primarily in the attitude towards the totem animal, quite aside from special ceremonies and ceremonial festivities: not only each individual animal but every representative of the same species was to a certain degree a sanctified animal; the member of the totem was forbidden to eat the flesh of the totem animal or he was allowed to eat it only under special circumstances. This is in accord with the significant contradictory phenomenon found in this connexion, namely, that under certain conditions there was a kind of ceremonial consumption of the totem flesh...."

" ...But the most important social side of this totemic tribal arrangement consists in the fact that it was connected with certain rules of conduct for the relations of the groups with each other. The most important of these were the rules of conjugal relations. This tribal division is thus connected with an important phenomenon which first made its appearance in the totemic age, namely with exogamy."

If we wish to arrive at the characteristics of the original totemism by sifting through everything that may correspond to later development or decline, we find the following essential facts: *The totems were originally only animals and were considered the ancestors of single tribes. The totem was hereditary only through the female line; it was forbidden to kill the totem* (or to eat it, which under primitive conditions amounts to the same thing); *members of a totem were forbidden to have sexual intercourse with each other*[128].

---

[128] The conclusion which Frazer draws about totemism in his second work on the subject (*The Origin of Totemism; Fortnightly Review*, 1899) agrees with this text: "Thus, totemism has commonly been treated as a primitive system both of religion and of society. As a system of religion it embraces the mystic union of the savage with his totem; as a system of society it comprises the relations in which men and women of the same totem stand to each other and to the members of other totemic groups. And corresponding to these two sides of the system are two rough-and-ready tests or canons of totemism: first, the rule that a man may not kill or eat his totem animal or plant, and second, the rule that he may not marry or cohabit with a woman of the same totem" (p. 101). Frazer then adds something which takes us into the midst of the discussion about totemism: "Whether the two sides—the religious and the social—have always coexisted or are essentially independent, is a question which has been variously answered."

It may now seem strange to us that in the *Code du totémisme* which Reinach has drawn up the one principal taboo, namely exogamy, does not appear at all while the assumption of the second taboo, namely the descent from the totem animal, is only casually mentioned. Yet Reinach is an author to whose work in this field we owe much and I have chosen his presentation in order to prepare us for the differences of opinion among the authors, which will now occupy our attention.

2

The more convinced we became that totemism had regularly formed a phase of every culture, the more urgent became the necessity of arriving at an understanding of it and of casting light upon the riddle of its nature. To be sure, everything about totemism is in the nature of a riddle; the decisive questions are the origin of the totem, the motivation of exogamy (or rather of the incest taboo which it represents) and the relation between the two, the totem organization and the incest prohibition. The understanding should be at once historical and psychological; it should inform us under what conditions this peculiar institution developed and to what psychic needs of man it has given expression.

The reader will certainly be astonished to hear from how many different points of view the answer to these questions has been attempted and how far the opinions of expert investigators vary. Almost everything that might be asserted in general about totemism is doubtful; even the above statement of it, taken from an article by Frazer in 1887, cannot escape the criticism that it expresses an arbitrary preference of the author and would be challenged to-day by Frazer himself, who has repeatedly changed his view on the subject.[129]

---

[129] In connexion with such a change of opinion Frazer made this excellent statement: "That my conclusions on these difficult questions are final, I am not so foolish as to pretend. I have changed my views repeatedly, and I am resolved to change them again with every change of the evidence, for like a chameleon the inquirer should shift his colours with the shifting colours of the ground he treads." Preface to Vol. I, *Totemism and Exogamy*, 1910.

It is quite obvious that the nature of totemism and exogamy could be most readily grasped if we could get into closer touch with the origin of both institutions. But in judging the state of affairs we must not forget the remark of Andrew Lang, that even primitive races have not preserved these original forms and the conditions of their origin, so that we are altogether dependent upon hypotheses to take the place of the observation we lack[130]. Among the attempted explanations some seem inadequate from the very beginning in the judgment of the psychologist. They are altogether too rational and do not take into consideration the effective character of what they are to explain. Others rest on assumptions which observation fails to verify; while still others appeal to facts which could better be subjected to another interpretation. The refutation of these various opinions as a rule hardly presents any difficulties; the authors are, as usual, stronger in the criticism which they practice on each other than in their own work. The final result as regards most of the points treated is a *non liquet*. It is therefore not surprising that most of the new literature on the subject, which we have largely omitted here, shows the unmistakable effort to reject a general solution of totemic problems as unfeasible. (See, for instance, B. Goldenweiser in the *Journal of American Folklore* XXIII, 1910. Reviewed in the *Brittanica Year Book*, 1913.) I have taken the liberty of disregarding the chronological order in stating these contradictory hypotheses.

(a) THE ORIGIN OF TOTEMISM

The question of the origin of totemism can also be formulated as follows: How did primitive people come to select the names of animals, plants and inanimate objects for themselves and their tribes?[At first probably only animals]

The Scotchman, MacLennan, who discovered totemism and exogamy for science[131], refrained from publishing his views of the origin of totemism. According to a communication of Andrew Lang (*The Secret of the Totem*, p. 34] he was for a time inclined to trace totemism back to the custom of tattooing. I shall divide the accepted theories of

---

[130] By the nature of the case, as the origin of totemism lies far beyond our powers of historical examination or of experiment, we must have recourse as regards this matter, to conjecture," Andrew Lang, *Secret of the Totem*, p. 27.—"Nowhere do we see absolutely primitive man, and a totemic system in the making," p. 29.
[131] *The Worship of Animals and Plants* (*Fortnightly Review*, 1869-1870). *Primitive Marriage*, 1865; both works reprinted in *Studies in Ancient History*, 1876; second edition, 1886.

the derivation of totemism into three groups, (α) nominalistic, β) sociological, (γ) psychological.

(α) *The Nominalistic Theories*

The information about these theories will justify their summation under the headings I have used. Garcilaso de La Vega, a descendant of the Peruvian Inkas, who wrote the history of his race in the seventeenth century, is already said to have traced back what was known to him about totemic phenomena to the need of the tribes to differentiate themselves from each other by means of names[*Ibid*]. The same idea appears centuries later in the *Ethnology* of A. K. Keane where totems are said to be derived from heraldic badges through which individuals, families and tribes wanted to differentiate themselves[*Ibid*].

Max Müller expresses the same opinion about the meaning of the totem in his *Contributions to the Science of Mythology* [According to Andrew Lang]. A totem is said to be, 1. a mark of the clan, 2. a clan name, 3. the name of the ancestor of the clan, 4. the name of the object which the clan reveres. J. Pikler wrote later, in 1899, that men needed a permanent name for communities and individuals that could be preserved in writing.... Thus totemism arises, not from a religious, but from a prosaic everyday need of mankind. The giving of names, which is the essence of totemism, is a result of the technique of primitive writing. The totem is of the nature of an easily represented writing symbol. But if savages first bore the name of an animal they deduced the idea of relationship from this animal[132].

Herbert Spencer[133], also, thought that the origin of totemism was to be found in the giving of names. The attributes of certain individuals, he showed, had brought about their being named after animals so that they had come to have names of honour or nicknames which continued in their descendants. As a result of the indefiniteness and incomprehensibility of primitive languages, these names are said to have been taken by later generations as proof of their descent from the animals themselves. Totemism would thus be the result of a mistaken reverence for ancestors.

---

[132] Pikler and Somló, *The Origin of Totemism*, 1901. The authors rightly call their attempt at explanation a "Contribution to the materialistic theory of History."

[133] *The Origin of Animal Worship* (*Fortnightly Review*, 1870). *Principles of Psychology*, Vol. I, §§ 169 to 176.

Lord Avebury (better known under his former name, Sir John Lubbock) has expressed himself quite similarly about the origin of totemism, though without emphasizing the misunderstanding. If we want to explain the veneration of animals we must not forget how often human names are borrowed from animals. The children and followers of a man who was called bear or lion naturally made this their ancestral name. In this way it came about that the animal itself came to be respected and finally venerated.

Fison has advanced what seems an irrefutable objection to such a derivation of the totem name from the names of individuals[134]. He shows from conditions in Australia that the totem is always the mark of a group of people and never of an individual. But if it were otherwise, if the totem was originally the name of a single individual, it could never, with the system of maternal inheritance, descend to his children.

The theories thus far stated are evidently inadequate. They may explain how animal names came to be applied to primitive tribes but they can never explain the importance attached to the giving of names which constitutes the totemic system. The most noteworthy theory of this group has been developed by Andrew Lang in his books, *Social Origins*, 1903, and *The Secret of the Totem*, 1905. This theory still makes naming the centre of the problem, but it uses two interesting psychological factors and thus may claim to have contributed to the final solution of the riddle of totemism.

Andrew Lang holds that it does not make any difference how clans acquired their animal names. It might be assumed that one day they awoke to the consciousness that they had them without being able to account from where they came. *The origin of these names had been forgotten.* In that case they would seek to acquire more information by pondering over their names, and with their conviction of the importance of names they necessarily came to all the ideas that are contained in the totemic system. For primitive men, as for savages of to-day and even for our children (See chapter on Taboo), a name is not indifferent and conventional as it seems to us, but is something important and essential. A man's name is one of the main constituents of his person and perhaps a part of his psyche. The fact that they had

---

[134] *Kamilaroi and Kurmai*, p. 165, 1880 (Lang, *Secret of the Totem*, etc.).

the same names as animals must have led primitive men to assume a secret and important bond between their persons and the particular animal species. What other bond than consanguinity could it be? But if the similarity of names once led to this assumption it could also account directly for all the totemic prohibitions of the blood taboo, including exogamy.

"No more than these three things—a group animal name of unknown origin; belief in a transcendental connexion between all bearers, human and bestial, of the same name; and belief in the blood superstitions—were needed to give rise to all the totemic creeds and practices, including exogamy" (*Secret of the Totem*, p. 126).

Lang's explanation extends over two periods. It derives the totemic system of psychological necessity from the totem names, on the assumption that the origin of the naming has been forgotten. The other part of the theory now seeks to clear up the origin of these names. We shall see that it bears an entirely different stamp.

This other part of the Lang theory is not markedly different from those which I have called 'nominalistic'. The practical need of differentiation compelled the individual tribes to assume names and therefore they tolerated the names which every tribe ascribed to the other. This 'naming from without' is the peculiarity of Lang's construction. The fact that the names which thus originated were borrowed from animals is not further remarkable and need not have been felt by primitive men as abuse or derision. Besides, Lang has cited numerous cases from later epochs of history in which names given from without that were first meant to be derisive were accepted by those nicknamed and voluntarily borne (The Guises, Whigs and Tories). The assumption that the origin of these names was forgotten in the course of time connects this second part of the Lang theory with the first one just mentioned.

(β) *The Sociological Theories*

S. Reinach (Vol. I, p. 41.), who successfully traced the relics of the totemic system in the cult and customs of later periods, though attaching from the very beginning only slight value to the factor of descent from the totem animal, once made the casual remark that totemism seemed to him to be nothing but "*une hypertrophie de l'instinct social.*"

The same interpretation seems to permeate the new work of E. Durkheim, *Les Formes Élémentaires de la Vie Religieuse; Le Système Totémique en Australie*, 1912. The totem is the visible representative of the social religion of these races. It embodies the community, which is the real object of veneration.

Other authors have sought a more intimate reason for the share which social impulses have played in the formation of totemic institutions. Thus A. C. Haddon has assumed that every primitive tribe originally lived on a particular plant or animal species and perhaps also traded with this food and exchanged it with other tribes. It then was inevitable that a tribe should become known to other tribes by the name of the animal which played such weighty rôle with it. At the same time this tribe would develop a special familiarity with this animal, and a kind of interest for it which, however, was based upon the psychic motive of man's most elementary and pressing need, namely, hunger[135].

The objections against this most rational of all the totem theories are that such a state of the food supply is never found among primitive men and probably never existed. Savages are the more omnivorous the lower they stand in the social scale. Besides, it is incomprehensible how such an exclusive diet could have developed an almost religious relation to the totem, culminating in an absolute abstention from the referred food.

The first of the three theories about the origin of totemism which Frazer stated was a psychological one. We shall report it elsewhere.

Frazer's second theory, which we will discuss here, originated under the influence of an important publication by two investigators of the inhabitants of Central Australia.[136]

Spencer and Gillen describe a series of peculiar institutions, customs, and opinions of a group of tribes, the so-called Arunta nation, and Frazer subscribes to their opinion that these peculiarities are to be looked upon as characteristics of a primary state and that they can explain the first and real meaning of totemism.

---

[135] *Address to the Anthropological Section, British Association*, Belfast, 1902. According to Frazer, *l.c.*, Vol. IV, p. 50.
[136] *The Native Tribes of Central Australia*, by Baldwin Spencer and H. J. Gillen, London, 1891.

In the Arunta tribe itself (a part of the Arunta nation) these peculiarities are as follows:

1. They have the division into totem clans but the totem is not hereditary but is individually determined (as will be shown later).

2. The totem clans are not exogamous, and the marriage restrictions are brought about by a highly developed division into marriage classes which have nothing to do with the totems.

3. The function of the totem clan consists of carrying out a ceremony which in a subtle magic manner brings about an increase of the edible totem. (This ceremony is called *Intichiuma*.)

4. The Aruntas have a peculiar theory about conception and re-birth. They assume that the spirits of the dead who belonged to their totem wait for their re-birth in definite localities and penetrate into the bodies of the women who pass such a spot. When a child is born the mother states at which spirit abode she thinks she conceived her child. This determines the totem of the child. It is further assumed that the spirits (of the dead as well as of the re-born) are bound to peculiar stone amulets, called *Churinga*, which are found in these places.

Two factors seem to have induced Frazer to believe that the oldest form of totemism had been found in the institution of the Aruntas. In the first place the existence of certain myths which assert that the ancestors of the Aruntas always lived on their totem animal, and that they married no other women except those of their own totem. Secondly, the apparent disregard of the sexual act in their theory of conception. People who have not yet realized that conception was the result of the sexual act might well be considered the most backward and primitive people living to-day.

Frazer, in having recourse to the *Intichiuma* ceremony to explain totemism, suddenly saw the totemic system in a totally different light as a thoroughly practical organization for accomplishing the most natural needs of man. (Compare Haddon above[137].) The system was simply an extraordinary piece of 'co-operative magic'. Primitive men formed what might be called a magic production and consumption

---

[137] There is nothing vague or mystical about it, nothing of that metaphysical haze which some writers love to conjure up over the humblest beginnings of human speculation but which is utterly foreign to the simple, sensuous, and concrete modes of the savage. (*Totemism and Exogamy*, I., p. 117.)

club. Each totem clan undertook to see to the cleanliness of a certain article of food. If it were a question of inedible totems like harmful animals, rain, wind, or similar objects, it was the duty of the totem clan to dominate this part of nature and to ward off its injuriousness. The efforts of each clan were for the good of all the others. As the clan could not eat its totem or could eat only a very little of it, it furnished this valuable product for the rest and was in turn furnished with what these had to take care of as their social totem duty. In the light of this interpretation furnished by the *Intichiuma* ceremony, it appeared to Frazer as if the prohibition against eating the totem had misled observers to neglect the more important side of the relation, namely the commandment to supply as much as possible of the edible totem for the needs of others.

Frazer accepted the tradition of the Aruntas that each totem clan had originally lived on its totem without any restriction. It then became difficult to understand the evolution that followed through which savages were satisfied to ensure the totem for others while they themselves abstained from eating it. He then assumed that this restriction was by no means the result of a kind of religious respect, but came about through the observation that no animal devoured its own kind, so that this break in the identification with the totem was injurious to the power which savages sought to acquire over the totem. Or else it resulted from the endeavour to make the being favourably disposed by sparing it. Frazer did not conceal the difficulties of this explanation from himself[*l.c.*, p. 120.], nor did he dare to indicate in what way the habit of marrying within the totem, which the myths of the Aruntas proclaimed, was converted into exogamy.

Frazer's theory based on the *Intichiuma*, stands or falls with the recognition of the primitive nature of the Arunta institutions. But it seems impossible to hold to this in the fact of the objections advanced by Durkheim[138] and Lang.[139] The Aruntas seem on the contrary to be the most developed of the Australian tribes and to represent rather a dissolution stage of totemism than its beginning. The myths that made such an impression on Frazer because they emphasize, in contrast to prevailing institutions of to-day, that the Aruntas are free to eat the totem and to marry within it, easily explain themselves to us as wish

---

[138] *L'année Sociologique*, Vol. I, V, VIII, and elsewhere. See especially the chapter, *Sur le Totémisme*, Vol. V, 1901.
[139] *Social Origins and the Secret of the Totem*

phantasies, which are projected into the past, like the myths of the Golden Age.

(γ) *The Psychological Theories*

Frazer's first psychological theories, formed before his acquaintance with the observations of Spencer and Gillen, were based upon the belief in an 'outward soul'[*The Golden Bough*, II, p. 332.]. The totem was meant to represent a safe place of refuge where the soul is deposited in order to avoid the dangers which threaten it. After primitive man had housed his soul in his totem he himself became invulnerable and he naturally took care himself not to harm the bearer of his soul. But as he did not know which individual of the species in question was the bearer of his soul he was concerned in sparing the whole species. Frazer himself later gave up this derivation of totemism from the belief in souls.

When he became acquainted with the observations of Spencer and Gillen he set up the other social theory which has just been stated, but he himself then saw that the motive from which he had derived totemism was altogether too 'rational' and that he had assumed a social organization for it which was altogether too complicated to be called primitive[140]. The magic co-operative companies now appeared to him rather as the fruit than as the germ of totemism. He sought a simpler factor for the derivation of totemism in the shape of a primitive superstition behind these forms. He then found this original factor in the remarkable conception theory of the Aruntas.

As already stated, the Aruntas establish no connexion between conception and the sexual act. If a woman feels herself to be a mother it means that at that moment one of the spirits from the nearest spirit abode who has been watching for a re-birth, has penetrated into her body and is born as her child. This child has the same totem as all the spirits that lurk in that particular locality. But if we are willing to go back a step further and assume that the woman originally believed that the animal, plant, stone, or other object which occupied her fancy at the moment when she first felt herself pregnant had really penetrated

---

[140] It is unlikely that a community of savages should deliberately parcel out the realm of nature into provinces, assign each province to a particular band of magicians, and bid all the bands to work their magic and weave their spells for the common good." *Totemism and Exogamy*, Vol. IV, p. 57.

into her and was being born through her in human form, then the identity of a human being with his totem would really be founded on the belief of the mother, and all the other totem commandments (with the exception of exogamy) could easily be derived from this belief. Men would refuse to eat the particular animal or plant because it would be just like eating themselves. But occasionally they would be impelled to eat some of their totem in a ceremonial manner because they could thus strengthen their identification with the totem, which is the essential part of totemism. W. H. R. Rivers' observations among the inhabitants of the Bank Islands seemed to prove men's direct identification with their totems on the basis of such a conception theory.

The ultimate sources of totemism would then be the ignorance of savages as to the process of procreation among human beings and animals; especially their ignorance as to the rôle which the male plays in fertilization. This ignorance must be facilitated by the long interval which is interposed between the fertilizing act and the birth of the child or the sensation of the child's first movements. Totemism is therefore a creation of the feminine mind and not of the masculine. The sick fancies of the pregnant woman are the roots of it. Anything indeed that struck a woman at that mysterious moment of her life when she first knows herself to be a mother might easily be identified by her with the child in her womb. Such maternal fancies, so natural and seemingly so universal, appear to be the root of totemism[*Totemism and Exogamy*, Vol. IV, p. 63].

The main objection to this third theory of Frazer's is the same which has already been advanced against his second, sociological theory. The Aruntas seem to be far removed from the beginnings of totemism. Their denial of fatherhood does not apparently rest upon primitive ignorance; in many cases they even have paternal inheritance. They seem to have sacrificed fatherhood to a kind of a speculation which strives to honour the ancestral spirits.[141] Though they raise the myth of immaculate conception through a spirit to a general theory of conception, we cannot for that reason credit them

---

[141] That belief is a philosophy far from primitive", Andrew Lang, *Secret of the Totem*, p. 192.

with ignorance as to the conditions of procreation any more than we could the old races who lived during the rise of the Christian myths.

Another psychological theory of the origin of totemism has been formulated by the Dutch writer, G. A. Wilcken. It establishes a connexion between totemism and the migration of souls. "The animal into which, according to general belief, the souls of the dead passed, became a blood relative, an ancestor, and was revered as such." But the belief in the soul's migration to animals is more readily derived from totemism than inversely [Frazer, *Totemism and Exogamy*, Vol. IV, p. 45].

Still another theory of totemism is advanced by the excellent American ethnologists, Franz Boas, Hill-Tout, and others. It is based on observations of totemic Indian tribes and asserts that the totem is originally the guardian spirit of an ancestor who has acquired it through a dream and handed it on to his descendants. We have already heard the difficulties which the derivation of totemism through inheritance from a single individual offers; besides, the Australian observations seem by no means to support the tracing back of the totem to the guardian spirit [Frazer, *l.c.*, p. 48.].

Two facts have become decisive for the last of the psychological theories as stated by Wundt; in the first place, that the original and most widely known totem object was an animal, and secondly, that the earliest totem animals corresponded to animals which had a soul[Wundt, *Elemente der Völker-Psychologie*, p. 190]. Such animals as birds, snakes, lizards, mice are fitted by their extreme mobility, their flight through the air, and by other characteristics which arouse surprise and fear, to become the bearers of souls which leave their bodies. The totem animal is a descendant of the animal transformations of the spirit-soul. Thus with Wundt totemism is directly connected with the belief in souls or with animism.

(b) and (c) THE ORIGIN OF EXOGAMY AND ITS RELATION TO TOTEMISM

I have put forth the theories of totemism with considerable detail and yet I am afraid that I have not made them clear enough on account of the condensation that was constantly necessary. In the interest of the reader I am taking the liberty of further condensing the other questions that arise. The discussions about the exogamy of totem races become especially complicated and untractable, one might even say confused, on account of the nature of the material used. Fortunately the object of this treatise permits me to limit myself to pointing out several guide-posts and referring to the frequently quoted writings of experts in the field for a more thorough pursuit of the subject.

The attitude of an author to the problems of exogamy is of course not independent of the stand he has taken toward one or the other of the totem theories. Some of these explanations of totemism lack all connexion with exogamy so that the two institutions are entirely separated. Thus we find here two opposing views, one of which clings to the original likelihood that exogamy is an essential part of the totemic system while the other disputes such a connection and believes in an accidental combination of these two traits of the most ancient cultures. In his later works Frazer has emphatically stood for this latter point of view.

"I must request the reader to bear constantly in mind that the two institutions of totemism and exogamy are fundamentally distinct in origin and nature though they have accidentally crossed and blended in many tribes." (*Totemism and Exogamy* I, Preface XII.)

He warns directly against the opposite view as being a source of endless difficulties and misunderstandings. In contrast to this, many authors have found a way of conceiving exogamy as a necessary consequence of the basic views on totemism. Durkheim [*L'année Sociologique*, 1898-1904] has shown in his writings how the taboo, which is attached to the totem, must have entailed the prohibition against putting a woman of the same totem to sexual uses. The totem is of the same blood as the human being and for this reason the blood bann (in reference to defloration and menstruation) forbids sexual intercourse with a woman of the same totem[142]. Andrew Lang, who here agrees with Durkheim, goes so far as to believe that the blood taboo was not necessary to bring about the prohibition in regard to the women of the same tribe[*Secret*, etc., p. 125.]. The general totem taboo which, for instance, forbids any one to sit in the shadow of the totem tree, would have sufficed. Andrew Lang also contends for another derivation of exogamy (see below) and leaves it in doubt how these two explanations are related to each other.

---

[142] See Frazer's *Criticism of Durkheim, Totemism and Exogamy*, p. 101.

As regards the temporal relations, the majority of authors subscribe to the opinion that totemism is the older institution and that exogamy came later[143].

Among the theories which seek to explain exogamy independently of totemism only a few need be mentioned in so far as they illustrate different attitudes of the authors towards the problem of incest.

MacLennan in *Primitive Marriage* had ingeniously guessed that exogamy resulted from the remnants of customs pointing to earlier forms of female rape. He assumed that it was the general custom in ancient times to procure women from strange tribes so that marriage with a woman from the same tribe gradually became "improper because it was unusual". He sought the motive for the exogamous habit in the scarcity of women among these tribes, which had resulted from the custom of killing most female children at birth. We are not concerned here with investigation whether actual conditions corroborate MacLennan's assumptions. We are more interested in the argument that these premises still leave it unexplained why the male members of the tribe should have made these few women of their blood inaccessible to themselves, as well as in the manner in which the incest problem is here entirely neglected[Frazer, *l.c.*, p. 73 to 92].

Other writers have on the contrary assumed, and evidently with more right, that exogamy is to be interpreted as an institution for the prevention of incest[Compare Chapter I].

If we survey the gradually increasing complication of Australian marriage restrictions we can hardly help agreeing with the opinion of Morgan Frazer, Hewitt and Baldwin Spencer[144], that these institutions bear the stamp of 'deliberate design', as Frazer puts it, and that they were meant to do what they have actually accomplished. "In no other way does it seem possible to explain in all its details a system at once so complex and so regular"[Frazer, *l.c.*, p. 106].

It is of interest to point out that the first restrictions which the introduction of marriage classes brought about affected the sexual freedom of the younger generation, in other words, incest between brothers and sisters and between sons and mothers, while incest

---

[143] See Frazer, *l.c.*, Vol. IV, p. 75: "The totemic clan is a totally different social organism from the exogamous class, and we have good grounds for thinking that it is far older."
[144] Morgan, *Ancient Society*, 1877.—Frazer, *Totemism and Exogamy*, Vol. IV, p. 105.

between father and daughter was only abrogated by more sweeping measures.

However, to trace back exogamous sexual restrictions to legal intentions does not add anything to the understanding of the motive which created these institutions. From what source, in the final analysis, springs the dread of incest which must be recognized as the root of exogamy? It evidently does not suffice to appeal to an instinctive aversion against sexual intercourse with blood relatives, that is to say, to the fact of incest dread, in order to explain the dread of incest, if social experience shows that, in spite of this instinct, incest is not a rare occurrence even in our society, and if the experience of history can acquaint us with cases in which incestuous marriage of privileged persons was made the rule.

Westermarck[145] advanced the following to explain the dread of incest: "that an innate aversion against sexual intercourse exists between persons who live together from childhood and that this feeling, since such persons are as a rule consanguineous, finds a natural expression in custom and law through the abhorrence of sexual intercourse between those closely related." Though Havelock Ellis disputed the instinctive character of this aversion in the *Studies in the Psychology of Sex*, he otherwise supported the same explanation in its essentials by declaring: "The normal absence of the manifestation of the pairing instinct where brothers and sisters or boys and girls living together from childhood are concerned, is a purely negative phenomenon due to the fact that under these circumstances the antecedent conditions for arousing the mating instinct must be entirely lacking.... For persons who have grown up together from childhood habit has dulled the sensual attraction of seeing, hearing and touching and has led it into a channel of quiet attachment, robbing it of its power to call forth the necessary erethistic excitement required to produce sexual tumescence."

It seems to me very remarkable that Westermarck looks upon this innate aversion to sexual intercourse with persons with whom we have shared childhood as being at the same time a psychic representative of the biological fact that inbreeding means injury to the species. Such a

---

[145] *Origin and Development of Moral Conceptions*, Vol. II: Marriage (1909). See also there the author's defence against familiar objections.

biological instinct would hardly go so far astray in its psychological manifestation as to affect the companions of home and hearth which in this respect are quite harmless, instead of the blood relatives which alone are injurious to procreation. And I cannot resist citing the excellent criticism which Frazer opposes to Westermarck's assertion. Frazer finds it incomprehensible that sexual sensibility to-day is not at all opposed to sexual intercourse with companions of the hearth and home while the dread of incest, which is said to be nothing but an offshoot of this reluctance, has nowadays grown to be so overpowering. But other remarks of Frazer's go deeper and I set them down here in unabbreviated form because they are in essential agreement with the arguments developed in my chapter on taboo.

"It is not easy to see why any deep human instinct should need reinforcement through law. There is no law commanding men to eat and drink, or forbidding them to put their hands in the fire. Men eat and drink and keep their hands out of the fire instinctively, for fear of natural, not legal penalties, which would be entailed by violence done to these instincts. The law only forbids men to do what their instincts incline them to do; what nature itself prohibits and punishes it would be superfluous for the law to prohibit and punish. Accordingly we may always safely assume that crimes forbidden by law are crimes which many men have a natural propensity to commit. If there were no such propensity there would be no such crimes, and if no such crimes were committed, what need to forbid them? Instead of assuming therefore, from the legal prohibition of incest, that there is a natural aversion to incest we ought rather to assume that there is a natural instinct in favour of it, and that if the law represses it, it does so because civilized men have come to the conclusion that the satisfaction of these natural instincts is detrimental to the general interests of society"[Frazer p. 97.].

To this valuable argument of Frazer's I can add that the experiences of psychoanalysis make the assumption of such an innate aversion to incestuous relations altogether impossible. They have taught, on the contrary, that the first sexual impulses of the young are regularly of an incestuous nature and that such repressed impulses play a rôle which can hardly be overestimated as the motive power of later neuroses.

The interpretation of incest dread as an innate instinct must therefore be abandoned. The same holds true of another derivation of the incest prohibition which counts many supporters, namely the assumption that primitive races very soon observed the dangers with which inbreeding threatened their race and that they therefore had decreed the incest prohibition with a conscious purpose. The objections to this attempted explanation crowd upon each other[146]. Not only must the prohibition of incest be older than all breeding of domestic animals from which men could derive experience of the effect of inbreeding upon the characteristics of the breed, but the harmful consequences of inbreeding are not established beyond all doubt even to-day and in man they can be shown only with difficulty. Besides, everything that we know about contemporaneous savages makes it very improbable that the thoughts of their far-removed ancestors should already have been occupied with preventing injury to their later descendants. It sounds almost ridiculous to attribute hygienic and eugenic motives such as have hardly yet found consideration in our culture, to these children of the race who lived without thought of the morrow[147].

And finally it must be pointed out that a prohibition against inbreeding as an element weakening to the race, which is imposed from practical hygienic motives, seems quite inadequate to explain the deep abhorrence which our society feels against incest. This dread of incest, as I have shown in Chapter 1, seems to be even more active and stronger among primitive races living to-day than among the civilized.

In inquiring into the origin of incest dread it could be expected that here also there is the choice between possible explanations of a sociological, biological, and psychological nature in which the psychological motives might have to be considered as representative of biological forces. Still, in the end, one is compelled to subscribe to Frazer's resigned statement, namely, that we do not know the origin of incest dread and do not even know how to guess at it. None of the solutions of the riddle thus far advanced seems satisfactory to us[148].

---

[146] Compare Durkheim, *La Prohibition de l'Inceste* (*L'année Sociologique*, I, 1896-7)

[147] Charles Darwin says about savages: "They are not likely to reflect on distant evils to their progeny."

[148] Thus the ultimate origin of exogamy and with it the law of incest—since exogamy was devised to prevent incest—remains a problem nearly as dark as ever."—*Totemism and Exogamy*, I, p. 165.

I must mention another attempt to explain the origin of incest dread which is of an entirely different nature from those considered up to now. It might be called an historic explanation.

This attempt is associated with a hypothesis of Charles Darwin about the primal social state of man. From the habits of the higher apes Darwin concluded that man, too, lived originally in small hordes in which the jealousy of the oldest and strongest male prevented sexual promiscuity. "We may indeed conclude from what we know of the jealousy of all male quadrupeds, armed, as many of them are, with special weapons for battling with their rivals, that promiscuous intercourse in a state of nature is extremely improbable.... If we therefore look back far enough into the stream of time and judging from the social habits of man as he now exists, the most probable view is that he originally lived in small communities, each with a single wife, or if powerful with several, whom he jealously defended against all other men. Or he may not have been a social animal and yet have lived with several wives, like the gorilla; for all the natives agree that only the adult male is seen in a band; when the young male grows up a contest takes place for mastery, and the strongest, by killing and driving out the others, establishes himself as the head of the community (Dr Savage in the Boston *Journal of Natural History*, Vol. V, 1845-7). The younger males being thus driven out and wandering about would also, when at last successful in finding a partner, prevent too close breeding within the limits of the same family".[149]

Atkinson[150] seems to have been the first to recognize that these conditions of the Darwinian primal horde would in practice bring about the exogamy of the young men. Each one of those driven away could found a similar horde in which, thanks to jealousy of the chief, the same prohibition as to sexual intercourse obtained, and in the course of time these conditions would have brought about the rule which is now known as law: no sexual intercourse with the members of the horde. After the advent of totemism the rule would have changed into a different form: no sexual intercourse within the totem.

Andrew Lang in *Secret of the Totem* (pp. 114, 143) declared himself in agreement with this explanation of exogamy. But in the same book he

---

[149] *The Origin of Man*, Vol. II, Chap. 20, pp. 603-4.
[150] *Primal Law*, London, 1903 (with Andrew Lang, *Social Origins*).

advocates the other theory of Durkheim which explains exogamy as a consequence of the totem laws. It is not altogether easy to combine the two interpretations; in the first case exogamy would have existed before totemism; in the second case it would be a consequence of it[151]

3

Into this darkness psychoanalytic experience throws one single ray of light.

The relation of the child to animals has much in common with that of primitive man. The child does not yet show any trace of the pride which afterwards moves the adult civilized man to set a sharp dividing line between his own nature and that of all other animals. The child unhesitatingly attributes full equality to animals; he probably feels himself more closely related to the animal than to the undoubtedly mysterious adult, in the freedom with which he acknowledges his needs.

Not infrequently a curious disturbance manifests itself in this excellent understanding between child and animal. The child suddenly begins to fear a certain animal species and to protect himself against seeing or touching any individual of this species. There results the clinical picture of *animal phobia*, which is one of the most frequent among the psychoneurotic diseases of this age and perhaps the earliest form of such an ailment. The phobia is as a rule in regard to animals for which the child has until then shown the liveliest interest and has nothing to do with the individual animal. In cities the choice of animals which can become the object of phobia is not great. They are horses, dogs, cats, more seldom birds, and strikingly often very small animals like bugs and butterflies. Sometimes animals which are known to the child only from picture books and fairy stories become objects of the

---

[151] If it be granted that exogamy existed in practice, on the lines of Mr. Darwin's theory, before the totem beliefs lent to the practice a *sacred* sanction, our task is relatively easy. The first practical rule would be that of the jealous sire: 'No males to touch the females in my camp,' with expulsion of adolescent sons. *In efflux of time that rule, becoming habitual,* would be, 'No marriages within the local group.' Next let the local groups receive names such as Emus, Crows, Opossums, Snipes, and the rule becomes, 'No marriage within the local group of animal name; no Snipe to marry a Snipe.' But, if the primal groups were not exogamous they would become so as soon as totemic myths and taboos were developed out of the animal, vegetable, and other names of small local groups."—'*Secret of the Totem*', p. 143. (The italics above are mine).—In his last expression on the subject (*Folklore*, December, 1911), Andrew Lang states, however, that he has given up the derivation of exogamy out of the "general totemic" taboo

senseless and inordinate anxiety which is manifested with these phobias; it is seldom possible to learn the manner in which such an unusual choice of anxiety has been brought about. I am indebted to Dr Karl Abraham for the report of a case in which the child itself explained its fear of wasps by saying that the colour and the stripes of the body of the wasp had made it think of the tiger of which, from all that it had heard, it might well be afraid.

The animal phobias have not yet been made the object of careful analytical investigation, although they very much merit it. The difficulties of analysing children of so tender an age have probably been the motive of such neglect. It cannot therefore be asserted that the general meaning of these illnesses is known, and I myself do not think that it would turn out to be the same in all cases. But a number of such phobias directed against larger animals have proved accessible to analysis and have thus betrayed their secret to the investigator. In every case it was the same: the fear at bottom was of the father, if the children examined were boys, and was merely displaced upon the animal.

Every one of any experience in psychoanalysis has undoubtedly seen such cases and has received the same impression from them. But I can refer to only a few detailed reports on the subject. This is an accident of the literature of such cases, from which the conclusion should not be drawn that our general assertion is based on merely scattered observation. For instance I mention an author, M. Wulff of Odessa, who has very intelligently occupied himself with the neuroses of childhood. He tells, in relating the history of an illness, that a nine year old boy suffered from a dog phobia at the age of four. "When he saw a dog running by on the street he wept and cried: 'Dear dog, don't touch me, I will be good.'" By "being good" he meant "not to play violin any more" (to practice onanism)[152]

The same author later sums up as follows: "His dog phobia is really his fear of the father displaced upon the dog, for his peculiar expression: 'Dog, I will be good'—that is to say, I will not masturbate— really refers to the father who has forbidden masturbation." He then adds something in a note which fully agrees with my experience and at

---

[152] M. Wulff, *Contributions to Infantile Sexuality*, Zentralbl. f. Psychoanalyze, 1912, II, No. I, p. 15.

the same time bears witness to the abundance of such experiences: "such phobias (of horses, dogs, cats, chickens and other domestic animals) are, I think, at least as prevalent as *pavor nocturnus* in childhood, and usually reveal themselves in the analysis as a displacement of fear from one of the parents to animals. I am not prepared to assert that the wide-spread mouse and rat phobia has the same mechanism."

I reported the "Analysis of the Phobia of a five-year-old Boy"[153] which the father of the little patient had put at my disposal. It was a fear of horses as a result of which the boy refused to go on the street. He expressed his apprehension that the horse would come into the room and bite him. It proves that this was meant to be the punishment for his wish that the horse should fall over (die). After assurances had relieved the boy of his fear of his father, it proved that he was fighting against wishes whose content was the absence (departure or death) of the father. He indicated only too plainly that he felt the father to be his rival for the favour of the mother, upon whom his budding sexual wishes were by dark premonitions directed. He therefore had the typical attitude of the male child to its parents which we call the 'Oedipus complex' in which we recognize the central complex of the neuroses in general. Through the analysis, of 'little John' we have learnt a fact which is very valuable in relation to totemism, namely, that under such conditions the child displaces a part of its feelings from the father upon some animal.

Analysis showed the paths of association, both significant and accidental in content, along which such a displacement took place. It also allowed one to guess the motives for the displacement. The hate which resulted from the rivalry for the mother could not permeate the boy's psychic life without being inhibited; he had to contend with the tenderness and admiration which he had felt for his father from the beginning, so that the child assumed a double or ambivalent emotional attitude towards the father and relieved himself of this ambivalent conflict by displacing his hostile and anxious feelings upon a substitute for the father. The displacement could not, however, relieve the conflict by bringing about a smooth division between the tender and the hostile feelings. On the contrary, the conflict was continued in

---

[153] *Little Hans*, trans. by A. A. Brill (Moffat, Yard & Co., N.Y.).

reference to the object to which displacement has been made and to which also the ambivalence spreads. There was no doubt that little John had not only fear, but respect and interest for horses. As soon as his fear was moderated he identified himself with the feared animal; he jumped around like a horse, and now it was he who bit the father[l.c., p. 41]. In another stage of solution of the phobia he did not scruple to identify his parents with other large animals. (The Phantasy of the Giraffe,' l.c., p. 30.)

We may venture the impression that certain traits of totemism return as a negative expression in these animal phobias of children. But we are indebted to S. Ferenczi for a beautiful individual observation of what must be called a case of positive totemism in the child.[154]

It is true that with the little Arpád, whom Ferenczi reports, the totemic interests do not awaken in direct connexion with the Oedipus complex, but on the basis of a narcistic premise, namely, the fear of castration. But whoever looks attentively through the history of little John will also find there abundant proof that the father was admired as the possessor of large genitals and was feared as threatening the child's own genitals. In the Oedipus as well as in the castration complex the father plays the same rôle of feared opponent to the infantile sexual interests. Castration and its substitute through blinding is the punishment he threatens.[155]

When little Arpád was two and a half years old he once tried, while at a summer resort, to urinate into the chicken coop, and on this occasion a chicken bit his penis or snapped at it. When he returned to the same place a year later he became a chicken himself, was interested only in the chicken coop and in everything that occurred there, and gave up human speech for cackling and crowing. During the period of observation, at the age of five, he spoke again, but his speech was exclusively about chickens and other fowl. He played with no other toy and sang only songs in which there was something about poultry. His behaviour towards his totem animal was subtly ambivalent, expressing itself in immoderate hating and loving. He loved best to

---

[154] S. Ferenczi, *Contributions to Psychoanalysis*, p. 204, translated by Ernest Jones (Badger, Boston, 1916).
[155] Compare the communications of Reitler, Ferenczi, Rank, and Eder about the substitution of blindness in the Oedipus myth for castration. *Intern. Zeitschrift f. ärtzl. Psychoanalyze*, 1913, I, No. 2.

play killing chickens. "The slaughtering of poultry was quite a festival for him. He could dance around the animals' bodies for hours at a time in a state of intense excitement[Ferenczi, p. 209]." But then he kissed and stroked the slaughtered animal, and cleaned and caressed the chicken effigies which he himself had ill-used.

Arpád himself saw to it that the meaning of his curious activity could not remain hidden. At times he translated his wishes from the totemic method, of expression back into that of everyday life. "Now I am small, now I am a chicken. When I get bigger I shall be a fowl. When I am bigger still, I shall be a cock." On another occasion he suddenly expressed the wish to eat a "potted mother" (by analogy, potted fowl). He was very free with open threats of castration against others, just as he himself had received them on account of onanistic preoccupation with his penis.

According to Ferenczi (p. 212) there was no doubt as to the source of his interest in the activities of the chicken yard: "The continual sexual activity between cock and hen, the laying of eggs and the creeping out of the young brood" satisfied his sexual curiosity which really was directed towards human family life. His object wishes have been formed on the model of chicken life when we find him saying to a woman neighbour: "I am going to marry you and your sister and my three cousins and the cook; no, instead of the cook I'll marry my mother."

We shall be able to complete our consideration of these observations later; at present we will only point out two traits that show a valuable correspondence with totemism: the complete identification with the totem animal[156], and the ambivalent affective attitude towards it. In view of these observations we consider ourselves justified in substituting the father for the totem animal in the male's formula of totemism. We then notice that in doing so we have taken no new or especially daring step. For primitive men say it themselves and, as far as the totemic system is still in effect to-day, the totem is called ancestor and primal father. We have only taken literally an expression of these races which ethnologists did not know what to do with and were therefore inclined to put it into the background.

---

[156] Frazer finds that the essence of totemism is in this identification: "Totemism is an identification of a man with his totem." *Totemism and Exogamy*, IV, p. 5.

Psychoanalysis warns us, on the contrary, to emphasize this very point and to connect it with the attempt to explain totemism[157].

The first result of our substitution is very remarkable. If the totem animal is the father, then the two main commandments of totemism, the two taboo rules which constitute its nucleus,—not to kill the totem animal and not to use a woman belonging to the same totem for sexual purposes,—agree in content with the two crimes of Oedipus, who slew his father and took his mother to wife, and also with the child's two primal wishes whose insufficient repression or whose re-awakening forms the nucleus of perhaps all neuroses. If this similarity is more than a deceptive play of accident it would perforce make it possible for us to shed light upon the origin of totemism in prehistoric times. In other words, we should succeed in making it probable that the totemic system resulted from the conditions underlying the Oedipus complex, just as the animal phobia of 'little John' and the poultry perversion of 'little Arpád' resulted from it. In order to trace this possibility we shall in what follows study a peculiarity of the totemic system or, as we may say, of the totemic religion, which until now could hardly be brought into the discussion.

4

W. Robertson Smith, who died in 1894, was a physicist, philologist, Bible critic, and archæologist, a many-sided as well as keen and free-thinking man, expressed the assumption in his work, *The Religion of the Semites*, published in 1889, that a peculiar ceremony, the so-called *totem feast*, had, from the very beginning, formed an integral part of the totemic system. For the support of this supposition he had at his disposal at that time only a single description of such an act from the year 500 A.D.; he knew, however, how to give a high degree of probability to his assumption through his analysis of the nature of sacrifice among the old Semites. As sacrifice assumes a godlike person we are dealing here with an inference from a higher phase of religious rite to its lowest phase in totemism.

---

[157] I am indebted to Otto Rank for the report of a case of dog phobia in an intelligent young man whose explanation of how he acquired his ailment sounds remarkably like the totem theory of the Aruntas mentioned above. He had heard from his father that his mother at one time during her pregnancy had been frightened by a dog.

I shall now cite from Robertson Smith's excellent book *The Religion of the Semites* those statements about the origin and meaning of the sacrificial right which are of great interest to us; I shall omit the only too numerous tempting details as well as the parts dealing with all later developments. In such an excerpt it is quite impossible to give the reader any sense of the lucidity or of the argumentative force of the original.

Robertson Smith shows that sacrifice at the altar was the essential part of the rite of old religions. It plays the same rôle in all religions, so that its origin must be traced back to very general causes whose effects were everywhere the same.

But the sacrifice—the holy action κατεξογη (sacrificium ἱερουργία)—originally meant something different from what later times understood by it: the offering to the deity in order to reconcile him or to incline him to be favourable. The profane use of the word was afterwards derived from the secondary sense of self-denial. As is demonstrated the first sacrifice was nothing else than "an act of social fellowship between the deity and his worshipper".

Things to eat and drink were brought as sacrifice; man offered to his god the same things as those on which he himself lived, flesh, cereals, fruits, wine and oil. Only in regard to sacrificial flesh did there exist restrictions and exceptions. The god partakes of the animal sacrifices with his worshippers while the vegetable sacrifices are left to him alone. There is no doubt that animal sacrifices are older and at one time were the only forms of sacrifice. The vegetable sacrifices resulted from the offering of the first-fruits and correspond to a tribute to the lord of the soil and the land. But animal sacrifice is older than agriculture.

Linguistic survivals make it certain that the part of the sacrifice destined for the god was looked upon as his real food. This conception became offensive with the progressive dematerialization of the deity, and was avoided by offering the deity only the liquid part of the meal. Later the use of fire, which made the sacrificial flesh ascend in smoke from the altar, made it possible to prepare human food in such a way that it was more suitable for the deity. The drink sacrifice was originally the blood of the sacrificed animals; wine was used later as a substitute for the blood. Primitive man looked upon wine as the "blood of the grape", as our poets still call it.

The oldest form of sacrifice, older than the use of fire and the knowledge of agriculture, was therefore the sacrifice of animals, whose flesh and blood the god and his worshippers ate together. It was essential that both participants should receive their shares of the meal.

Such a sacrifice was a public ceremony, the celebration of a whole clan. As a matter of fact all religion was a public affair; religious duty was a part of the social obligation. Sacrifice and festival go together among all races; each sacrifice entails a holiday and no holiday can be celebrated without a sacrifice. The sacrificial festival was an occasion for joyously transcending one's own interests and emphasizing social community and community with god.

The ethical power of the public sacrificial feast was based upon primal conceptions of the meaning of eating and drinking in common. To eat and drink with some one was at the same time a symbol and a confirmation of social community and of the assumption of mutual obligations; the sacrificial eating gave direct expression to the fact that the god and his worshippers are communicants, thus confirming all their other relations. Customs that to-day still are in force among the Arabs of the desert prove that the binding force resulting from the common meal is not a religious factor but that the subsequent mutual obligations are due to the act of eating itself. Whoever has shared the smallest bite with such a Bedouin, or has taken a swallow of his milk, need not fear him any longer as an enemy, but may be sure of his protection and help. Not indeed, forever, strictly speaking this lasts only while it may be assumed that the food partaken remains in the body. So realistically is the bond of union conceived; it requires repetition to strengthen it and make it endure.

But why is this binding power ascribed to eating and drinking in common? In the most primitive societies there is only one unconditional and never failing bond, that of kinship. The members of a community stand by each other jointly and severally, a kin is a group of persons whose life is so bound into a physical unity that they can be considered as parts of a common life. In case of the murder of one of this kin they therefore do not say: the blood of so and so has been spilt, but our blood has been spilt. The Hebraic phrase by which the tribal relation is acknowledged is: "Thou art my bone and my flesh". Kinship therefore signifies having part in a general substance. It is natural then that it is based not only upon the fact that we are a part of the substance of our mother who has borne us, and whose milk nourished us, but also that the food eaten later through which the body is renewed, can acquire and strengthen kinship. If one shared a meal with one's god the conviction was thus expressed that one was of the same substance as he; no meal was therefore partaken with any one recognized as a stranger.

The sacrificial repast was therefore originally a feast of the kin, following the rule that only those of kin could eat together. In our society the meal unites the members of the family; but the sacrificial repast has nothing to do with the family. Kinship is older than family life; the oldest families known to us regularly comprised persons who belonged to various bonds of kinship. The men married women of strange clans and the children inherited the clan of the mother; there was no kinship between the man and the rest of the members of the family. In such a family there was no common meal. Even to-day savages eat apart and alone, and the religious prohibitions of totemism as to eating often make it impossible for them to eat with their wives and children.

Let us now turn to the sacrificial animal. There was, as we have heard, no meeting of the kin without animal sacrifice, but, and this is significant, no animal was slaughtered except for such a solemn occasion. Without any hesitation the people ate fruits, game and the milk of domestic animals, but religious scruples made it impossible for the individual to kill a domestic animal for his own use. There is not the least doubt, says Robertson Smith, that every sacrifice was originally a clan sacrifice, and that the *killing of a sacrificial animal* originally belonged to those acts which were *forbidden to the individual and were only justified if the whole kin assumed the responsibility.* Primitive men had only one class of actions, which were thus characterized, namely, actions which touched the holiness of the kin's common blood. A life which no individual might take and which could be sacrificed only through the consent and participation of all the members of the clan was on the same plane as the life of a member of the kin. The rule that every guest of the sacrificial repast must partake of the flesh of the sacrificial animal, had the same meaning as the rule that the execution of a guilty member of the kin must be performed by the whole kin. In other words: the sacrificial animal was treated like one of kin; *the sacrificing community, its god, and the sacrificial animal were of the same blood,* and the members of a clan.

On the basis of much evidence Robertson Smith identifies the sacrificial animal with the old totem animal. In a later age there were two kinds of sacrifices, those of domestic animals which usually were also eaten, and the unusual sacrifice of animals which were forbidden as being unclean. Further investigation then shows that these unclean animals were holy and that they were sacrificed to the gods to whom they were holy, that these animals were originally identified with the gods themselves and that at the sacrifice the worshippers in some way emphasized their blood relationship to the god and to the animal. But this difference between usual and 'mystic' sacrifices does not hold good for still earlier times. Originally all animals were holy, their meat was forbidden and might be eaten only on solemn occasions, with the participation of the whole kin. The slaughter of the animal amounted to the spilling of the kin's blood and had to be done with the same precautions and assurances against reproach.

The taming of domestic animals and the rise of cattle-breeding seems everywhere to have put an end to the pure and rigorous totemism of earliest times[158]. But such holiness as still clung to domestic animals in what was now a 'pastoral' religion, is sufficiently distinct for us to recognize its totemic character. Even in late classical times the rite in several localities prescribed flight for the sacrificer after the sacrifice, as if to escape revenge. In Greece the idea must once have been general that the killing of an ox was really a crime. At the Athenian festival of the Bouphonia a formal trial, to which all the participants were summoned, was instituted after the sacrifice. Finally it was agreed to put the blame for the murder upon the knife, which was then cast into the sea.

In spite of the dread which protects the life of the animal as being of kin, it became necessary to kill it from time to time in solemn

---

[158] The inference is that the domestication to which totemism leads (when there are any animals capable of domestication) is fatal to totemism." Jevons, *Introduction to the History of Religion,* 1911, fifth edition, p. 120.

conclave, and to divide its flesh and blood among the members of the clan. The motive which commands this act reveals the deepest meaning of the essence of sacrifice. We have heard that in later times every eating in common, the participation in the same substance which entered into their bodies, established a holy bond between the communicants; in oldest time this meaning seemed to be attached only to participation in the substance of a holy sacrifice. *The holy mystery of the sacrificial death was justified in that only in this way could the holy bond be established which united the participants with each other and with their god[l.cp.313].*

This bond was nothing else than the life of the sacrificial animal which lived on its flesh and blood and was shared by all the participants by means of the sacrificial feast. Such an idea was the basis of all the *blood bonds* through which men in still later times became pledged to each other. The thoroughly realistic conception of consanguinity as an identity of substance makes comprehensible the necessity of renewing it from time to time through the physical process of the sacrificial repast.

We will now stop quoting from Robertson Smith's train of thought in order to give a condensed summary of what is essential in it. When the idea of private property came into existence sacrifice was conceived as a gift to the deity, as a transfer from the property of man to that of the god. But this interpretation left all the peculiarities of the sacrificial ritual unexplained. In oldest times the sacrificial animal itself had been holy and its life inviolate; it could be taken only in the presence of the god, with the whole tribe taking part and sharing the guilt in order to furnish the holy substance through the eating of which the members of the clan assured themselves of their material identity with each other and with the deity. The sacrifice was a sacrament, and the sacrificial animal itself was one of the kin. In reality it was the old totem animal, the primitive god himself through the slaying and eating of whom the members of the clan revived and assured their similarity with the god.

From this analysis of the nature of sacrifice Robertson Smith drew the conclusion that the periodic killing and eating of the totem before the period when the *anthropomorphic deities were venerated* was an important part of totem religion. The ceremonial of such a totem feast was preserved for us, he thought, in the description of a sacrifice in later times. Saint Nilus tells of a sacrificial custom of the Bedouins in the desert of Sinai towards the end of the fourth century A.D. The victim, a camel, was bound and laid upon a rough altar of stones; the leader of the tribe made the participants walk three times around the altar to the accompaniment of song, inflicted the first wound upon the animal and greedily drank the spurting blood; then the whole community threw itself upon the sacrifice, cut off pieces of the palpitating flesh with their swords and ate them raw in such haste that in a short interval between the rise of the morning star, for whom this sacrifice was meant, and its fading before the rays of the sun, the whole sacrificial animal, flesh, skin, bones, and entrails, were devoured. According to every testimony this barbarous rite, which speaks of great antiquity, was not a rare custom but the general original form of the totem sacrifice, which in later times underwent the most varied modifications.

Many authors have refused to grant any weight to this conception of the totem feast because it could not be strengthened by direct observation at the stage of totemism. Robertson Smith himself has referred to examples in which the sacramental meaning of sacrifices seems certain, such as the human sacrifices of the Aztecs and others which recall the conditions of the totem feast, the bear sacrifices of the bear tribe of the *Ouataouaks* in America, and the bear festival of the Ainus in Japan. Frazer has given a full account of these and similar cases in the two divisions of his great work that have last appeared[159]. An Indian tribe in California which reveres the buzzard, a large bird of prey, kills it once a year with solemn ceremony, whereupon the bird is mourned and its skin and feathers preserved. The Zuni Indians in New Mexico do the same thing with their holy turtle.

In the *Intichiuma* ceremonies of Central Australian tribes a trait has been observed which fits in excellently with the assumptions of Robertson Smith. Every tribe that practises magic for the increase of its totem, which it cannot eat itself, is bound to eat a part of its totem at the ceremony before it can be touched by the other tribes. According to Frazer the best example of the sacramental consumption of the

---

[159] *The Golden Bough*, Part V; *Spirits of the Corn and of the Wild*, in the chapters: "Eating the God and Killing the Divine Animal."

otherwise forbidden totem is to be found among the Bini in West Africa, in connexion with the burial ceremony of this tribe[160].

But we shall follow Robertson Smith in the assumption that the sacramental killing and the common consumption of the otherwise forbidden totem animal was an important trait of the totem religion.[161]

5

Let us now envisage the scene of such a totem meal and let us embellish it further with a few probable features which could not be adequately considered before. Thus we have the clan, which on a solemn occasion kills its totem in a cruel manner and eats it raw, blood, flesh, and bones. At the same time the members of the clan disguised in imitation of the totem, mimic it in sound and movement as if they wanted to emphasize their common identity. There is also the conscious realization that an action is being carried out which is forbidden to each individual and which can only be justified through the participation of all, so that no one is allowed to exclude himself from the killing and the feast. After the act is accomplished the murdered animal is bewailed and lamented. The death lamentation is compulsive, being enforced by the fear of a threatening retribution, and its main purpose is, as Robertson Smith remarks on an analogous occasion, to exculpate oneself from responsibility for the slaying[162].

But after this mourning there follows loud festival gaiety accompanied by the unchaining of every impulse and the permission of every gratification. Here we find an easy insight into the nature of the *holiday.*

A holiday is permitted, or rather a prescribed excess, a solemn violation of a prohibition. People do not commit the excesses which at all times have characterized holidays, as a result of an order to be in a holiday mood, but because in the very nature of a holiday there is

---

[160] Frazer, *Totem and Exogamy*, Vol. II, p. 590.
[161] I am not ignorant of the objections to this theory of sacrifice as expressed by Marillier, Hubert, Mauss and others, but they have not essentially impaired the theories of Robertson Smith.
[162] *Religion of the Semites*, 2nd Edition, 1907, p. 412

excess; the holiday mood is brought about by the release of what is otherwise forbidden.

But what has mourning over the death of the totem animal to do with the introduction of this holiday spirit? If men are happy over the slaying of the totem, which is otherwise forbidden to them, why do they also mourn it?

We have heard that members of a clan become holy through the consumption of the totem and thereby also strengthen their identification with it and with each other. The fact that they have absorbed the holy life with which the substance of the totem is charged may explain the holiday mood and everything that results from it.

Psychoanalysis has revealed to us that the totem animal is really a substitute for the father, and this really explains the contradiction that it is usually forbidden to kill the totem animal, that the killing of it results in a holiday and that the animal is killed and yet mourned. The ambivalent emotional attitude which to-day still marks the father complex in our children and so often continues into adult life also extended to the father substitute of the totem animal.

But if we associate the translation of the totem as given by psychoanalysis, with the totem feast and the Darwinian hypothesis about the primal state of human society, a deeper understanding becomes possible and a hypothesis is offered which may seem fantastic but which has the advantage of establishing an unexpected unity among a series of hitherto separated phenomena.

The Darwinian conception of the primal horde does not, of course, allow for the beginning of totemism. There is only a violent, jealous father who keeps all the females for himself and drives away the growing sons. This primal state of society has nowhere been observed. The most primitive organization we know, which to-day is still in force with certain tribes, is *associations of men* consisting of members with equal rights, subject to the restrictions of the totemic system, and founded on matriarchy, or descent through the mother. Can the one have resulted from the other, and how was this possible?

By basing our argument upon the celebration of the totem we are in a position to give an answer: One day[163] the expelled brothers joined forces, slew and ate the father, and thus put an end to the father horde. Together they dared and accomplished what would have remained impossible for them singly. Perhaps some advance in culture, like the use of a new weapon, had given them the feeling of superiority. Of course these cannibalistic savages ate their victim. This violent primal father had surely been the envied and feared model for each of the brothers. Now they accomplished their identification with him by devouring him and each acquired a part of his strength. The totem feast, which is perhaps mankind's first celebration, would be the repetition and commemoration of this memorable, criminal act with which so many things began, social organization, moral restrictions and religion[164].

In order to find these results acceptable, quite aside from our supposition, we need only assume that the group of brothers banded

---

[163] The reader will avoid the erroneous impression which this exposition may call forth by taking into consideration the concluding sentence of the subsequent chapter.

[164] The seemingly monstrous assumption that the tyrannical father was overcome and slain by a combination of the expelled sons has also been accepted by Atkinson as a direct result of the conditions of the Darwinian primal horde. "A youthful band of brothers living together in forced celibacy, or at most in polyandrous relation with some single female captive. A horde as yet weak in their impubescence they are, but they would, when strength was gained with time, inevitably wrench by combined attacks, renewed again and again, both wife and life from the paternal tyrant" (*Primal Law*, pp. 220-1). Atkinson, who spent his life in New Caledonia and had unusual opportunities to study the natives, also refers to the fact that the conditions of the primal horde which Darwin assumes can easily be observed among herds of wild cattle and horses and regularly lead to the killing of the father animal. He then assumes further that a disintegration of the horde took place after the removal of the father through embittered fighting among the victorious sons, which thus precluded the origin of a new organization of society; "An ever recurring violent succession to the solitary paternal tyrant by sons, whose parricidal hands were so soon again clenched in fratricidal strife" (p. 228). Atkinson, who did not have the suggestions of psychoanalysis at his command and did not know the studies of Robertson Smith, finds a less violent transition from the primal horde to the next social stage in which many men live together in peaceful accord. He attributes it to maternal love that at first only the youngest sons and later others too remain in the horde, who in return for this toleration acknowledge the sexual prerogative of the father by the restraint which they practise towards the mother and towards their sisters.

So much for the very remarkable theory of Atkinson, its essential correspondence with the theory here expounded, and its point of departure which makes it necessary to relinquish so much else.

I must ascribe the indefiniteness, the disregard of time interval, and the crowding of the material in the above exposition to a restraint which the nature of the subject demands. It would be just as meaningless to strive for exactness in this material as it would be unfair to demand certainty here.

together were dominated by the same contradictory feelings towards the father which we can demonstrate as the content of ambivalence of the father complex in all our children and in neurotics. They hated the father who stood so powerfully in the way of their sexual demands and their desire for power, but they also loved and admired him. After they had satisfied their hate by his removal and had carried out their wish for identification with him, the suppressed tender impulses had to assert themselves[165]. This took place in the form of remorse, a sense of guilt was formed which coincided here with the remorse generally felt. The dead now became stronger than the living had been, even as we observe it to-day in the destinies of men. What the fathers' presence had formerly prevented they themselves now prohibited in the psychic situation of 'subsequent obedience', which we know so well from psychoanalysis. They undid their deed by declaring that the killing of the father substitute, the totem, was not allowed, and renounced the fruits of their deed by denying themselves the liberated women. Thus they created the two fundamental taboos of totemism out of the *sense of guilt of the son*, and for this very reason these had to correspond with the two repressed wishes of the Oedipus complex. Whoever disobeyed became guilty of the two only crimes which troubled primitive society[166].

The two taboos of totemism with which the morality of man begins are psychologically not of equal value. One of them, the sparing of the totem animal, rests entirely upon emotional motives; the father had been removed and nothing in reality could make up for this. But the other, the incest prohibition, had, besides, a strong practical foundation. Sexual need does not unite men; it separates them. Though the brothers had joined forces in order to overcome the father, each was the other's rival among the women. Each one wanted to have them all to himself like the father, and in the fight of each against the other the new organization would have perished. For there was no longer any one stronger than all the rest who could have successfully

---

[165] This new emotional attitude must also have been responsible for the fact that the deed could not bring full satisfaction to any of the perpetrators. In a certain sense it had been in vain. For none of the sons could carry out his original wish of taking the place of the father. But failure is, as we know, much more favourable to moral reaction than success.

[166] Murder and incest, or offences of like kind against the sacred law of blood are in primitive society the only crimes of which the community as such takes cognizance ..." *Religion of the Semites*, p. 419

assumed the rôle of the father. Thus there was nothing left for the brothers, if they wanted to live together, but to erect the incest prohibition—perhaps after many difficult experiences—through which they all equally renounced the women whom they desired, and on account of whom they had removed the father in the first place. Thus they saved the organization which had made them strong and which could be based upon the homo-sexual feelings and activities which probably manifested themselves among them during the time of their banishment. Perhaps this situation also formed the germ of the institution of the mother right discovered by Bachofen, which was then abrogated by the patriarchal family arrangement.

On the other hand the claim of totemism to be considered the first attempt at a religion is connected with the other taboo which protects the life of the totem animal. The feelings of the sons found a natural and appropriate substitute for the father in the animal, but their compulsory treatment of it expressed more than the need of showing remorse. The surrogate for the father was perhaps used in the attempt to assuage the burning sense of guilt, and to bring about a kind of reconciliation with the father. The totemic system was a kind of agreement with the father in which the latter granted everything that the child's phantasy could expect from him, protection, care, and forbearance, in return for which the pledge was given to honour his life, that is to say, not to repeat the act against the totem through which the real father had perished. Totemism also contained an attempt at justification, "If the father had treated us like the totem we should never have been tempted to kill him." Thus totemism helped to gloss over the real state of affairs and to make one forget the event to which it owed its origin.

In this connexion some features were formed which henceforth determined the character of every religion. The totem religion had issued from the sense of guilt of the sons as an attempt to palliate this feeling and to conciliate the injured father through subsequent obedience. All later religions prove to be attempts to solve the same problem, varying only in accordance with the stage of culture in which they are attempted and according to the paths which they take; they are all, however, reactions aiming at the same great event with which culture began and which ever since has not let mankind come to rest.

There is still another characteristic faithfully preserved in religion which already appeared in totemism at this time. The ambivalent strain was probably too great to be adjusted by any arrangement, or else the psychological conditions are entirely unfavourable to any kind of settlement of these contradictory feelings. It is certainly noticeable that the ambivalence attached to the father complex also continues in totemism and in religions in general. The religion of totemism included not only manifestations of remorse and attempts at reconciliation, but also serves to commemorate the triumph over the father. The gratification obtained thereby creates the commemorative celebration of the totem feast at which the restrictions of subsequent obedience are suspended, and makes it a duty to repeat the crime of parricide through the sacrifice of the totem animal as often as the benefits of this deed, namely, the appropriation of the father's properties, threaten to disappear as a result of the changed influences of life. We shall not be surprised to find that a part of the son's defiance also reappears, often in the most remarkable disguises and inversions, in the formation of later religions.

If thus far we have followed, in religion and moral precepts—but little differentiated in totemism—the consequences of the tender impulses towards the father as they are changed into remorse, we must not overlook the fact that for the most part the tendencies which have impelled to parricide have retained the victory. The social and fraternal feelings on which this great change is based, henceforth for long periods exercises the greatest influence upon the development of society. They find expression in the sanctification of the common blood and in the emphasis upon the solidarity of life within the clan. In thus ensuring each other's lives the brothers express the fact that no one of them is to be treated by the other as they all treated the father. They preclude a repetition of the fate of the father. The socially established prohibition against fratricide is now added to the prohibition against killing the totem, which is based on religious grounds. It will still be a long time before the commandment discards the restriction to members of the tribe and assumes the simple phraseology: Thou shalt not kill. At first the *brother clan* has taken the place of the *father horde* and was guaranteed by the blood bond. Society is now based on complicity in the common crime, religion on the sense of guilt and the consequent remorse, while morality is based partly on the necessities of society and partly on the expiation which this sense of guilt demands.

Thus psychoanalysis, contrary to the newer conceptions of the totemic system and more in accord with older conceptions, bids us argue for an intimate connexion between totemism and exogamy as well as for their simultaneous origin.

6

I am under the influence of many strong motives which restrain me from the attempt to discuss the further development of religions from their beginning in totemism up to their present state. I shall follow out only two threads as I see them appearing in the weft with especial distinctness: the motive of the totem sacrifice and the relation of the son to the father.[167]

Robertson Smith has shown us that the old totem feast returns in the original form of sacrifice. The meaning of the rite is the same: sanctification through participation in the common meal. The sense of guilt, which can only be allayed through the solidarity of all the participants, has also been retained. In addition to this there is the tribal deity in whose supposed presence the sacrifice takes place, who takes part in the meal like a member of the tribe, and with whom identification is effected by the act of eating the sacrifice. How does the god come into this situation which originally was foreign to him?

The answer might be that the idea of god had meanwhile appeared,—no one knows whence—and had dominated the whole religious life, and that the totem feast, like everything else that wished to survive, had been forced to fit itself into the new system. However, psychoanalytic investigation of the individual teaches with especial emphasis that god is in every case modelled after the father and that our personal relation to god is dependent upon our relation to our physical, fluctuating and changing with him, and that god at bottom is nothing but an exalted father. Here also, as in the case of totemism,

---

[167] Compare Jung's *Transformations and Symbols of the Libido*, in which some dissenting points of view are represented.

psychoanalysis advises us to believe the faithful, who call god father just as they called the totem their ancestor. If psychoanalysis deserves any consideration at all, then the share of the father in the idea of a god must be very important, quite aside from all the other origins and meanings of god upon which psychoanalysis can throw no light. But then the father would be represented twice in primitive sacrifice, first as god, and secondly as the totem-animal sacrifice, and we must ask, with all due regard for the limited number of solutions which psychoanalysis offers, whether this is possible and what the meaning of it may be.

We know that there are a number of relations of the god to the holy animal (the totem and the sacrificial animal): 1. Usually one animal is sacred to every god, sometimes even several animals. 2. In certain, especially holy, sacrifices, the so-called 'mystical' sacrifices, the very animal which had been sanctified through the god was sacrificed to him[168]. 3. The god was often revered in the form of an animal, or from another point of view, animals enjoyed a godlike reverence long after the period of totemism. 4. In myths the god is frequently transformed into an animal, often into the animal that is sacred to him. From this the assumption was obvious that the god himself was the animal, and that he had evolved from the totem animal at a later stage of religious feeling. But the reflection that the totem itself is nothing but a substitute for the father relieves us of all further discussion. Thus the totem may have been the first form of the father substitute and the god a later one in which the father regained his human form. Such a new creation from the root of all religious evolution, namely, the longing for the father, might become possible if in the course of time an essential change had taken place in the relation to the father and perhaps also to the animal.

Such changes are easily divined even if we disregard the beginning of a psychic estrangement from the animal as well as the disintegration of totemism through animal domestication. The situation created by the removal of the father contained an element which in the course of time must have brought about an extraordinary increase of longing for the father. For the brothers who had joined forces to kill the father had each been animated by the wish to become like the father and had

---

[168] Robertson Smith, *Religion of the Semites*, Second Edition, 1907.

given expression to this wish by incorporating parts of the substitute for him in the totem feast. In consequence of the pressure which the bonds of the brother clan exercised upon each member, this wish had to remain unfulfilled. No one could or was allowed to attain the father's perfection of power, which was the thing they had all sought. Thus the bitter feeling against the father which had incited to the deed could subside in the course of time, while the longing for him grew, and an ideal could arise having as a content the fullness of power and the freedom from restriction of the conquered primal father, as well as the willingness to subject themselves to him. The original democratic equality of each member of the tribe could no longer be retained on account of the interference of cultural changes; in consequence of which there arose a tendency to revive the old father ideal in the creation of gods through the veneration of those individuals who had distinguished themselves above the rest. That a man should become a god and that a god should die, which to-day seems to us an outrageous presumption, was still by no means offensive to the conceptions of classical antiquity[169]. But the deification of the murdered father from whom the tribe now derived its origin, was a much more serious attempt at expiation than the former covenant with the totem.

In this evolution I am at a loss to indicate the place of the great maternal deities who perhaps everywhere preceded the paternal deities. But it seems certain that the change in the relation to the father was not restricted to religion but logically extended to the other side of human life influenced by the removal of the father, namely, the social organization. With the institution of paternal deities the fatherless society gradually changed into a patriarchal one. The family was a reconstruction of the former primal horde and also restored a great part of their former rights to the fathers. Now there were patriarchs again but the social achievements of the brother clan had not been given up and the actual difference between the new family patriarchs and the unrestricted primal father was great enough to ensure the

---

[169] To us moderns, for whom the breach which divides the human and divine has deepened into an impassable gulf, such mimicry may appear impious, but it was otherwise with the ancients. To their thinking gods and men were akin, for many families traced their descent from a divinity, and the deification of a man probably seemed as little extraordinary to them as the canonization of a saint seems to a modern Catholic." Frazer, *The Golden Bough*, I; *The Magic Art and the Evolution of Kings*, II, p. 177.

continuation of the religious need, the preservation of the unsatisfied longing for the father.

The father therefore really appears twice in the scene of sacrifice before the tribal god, once as the god and again as the totem-sacrificial-animal. But in attempting to understand this situation we must beware of interpretations which superficially seek to translate it as an allegory, and which forget the historical stages in the process. The twofold presence of the father corresponds to the two successive meanings of the scene. The ambivalent attitude towards the father as well as the victory of the son's tender emotional feelings over his hostile ones, have here found plastic expression. The scene of vanquishing the father, his greatest degradation, furnishes here the material to represent his highest triumph. The meaning which sacrifice has quite generally acquired is found in the fact that in the very same action which continues the memory of this misdeed it offers satisfaction to the father for the ignominy put upon him.

In the further development the animal loses its sacredness and the sacrifice its relation to the celebration of the totem; the rite becomes a simple offering to the deity, a self-deprivation in favour of the god. God himself is now so exalted above man that he can be communicated with only through a priest as intermediary. At the same time the social order produces godlike kings who transfer the patriarchal system to the state. It must be said that the revenge of the deposed and reinstated father has been very cruel; it culminated in the dominance of authority. The subjugated sons have used the new relation to disburden themselves still more of their sense of guilt. Sacrifice, as it is now constituted, is entirely beyond their responsibility. God himself has demanded and ordained it. Myths in which the god himself kills the animal that is sacred to him, which he himself really is, belong to this phase. This is the greatest possible denial of the great misdeed with which society and the sense of guilt began. There is an unmistakable second meaning in this sacrificial demonstration. It expresses satisfaction at the fact that the earlier father substitute has been abandoned in favour of the higher conception of god. The superficial allegorical translation of the scene here roughly corresponds with its psychoanalytic interpretation by saying that god is represented as overcoming the animal part of his nature.[170]

But it would be erroneous to believe that in this period of renewed patriarchal authority the hostile impulses which belong to the father complex had entirely subsided. On the contrary, the first phases in the domination of the two new substitutive formations for the father, those of gods and kings, plainly show the most energetic expression of that ambivalence which is characteristic of religion.

In his great work, *The Golden Bough*, Frazer has expressed the conjecture that the first kings of the Latin tribes were strangers who played the part of a deity and were solemnly sacrificed in this rôle on specified holidays. The yearly sacrifice (self-sacrifice is a variant) of a god seems to have been an important feature of Semitic religions. The ceremony of human sacrifice in various parts of the inhabited world makes it certain that these human beings ended their lives as representatives of the deity. This sacrificial custom can still be traced in later times in the substitution of an inanimate imitation (doll) for the living person. The theanthropic god sacrifice into which unfortunately I cannot enter with the same thoroughness with which the animal sacrifice has been treated throws the clearest light upon the meaning of the older forms of sacrifice. It acknowledges with unsurpassable candour that the object of the sacrificial action has always been the same, being identical with what is now revered as a god, namely with the father. The question as to the relation of animal to human sacrifice can now be easily solved. The original animal sacrifice was already a substitute for a human sacrifice, for the solemn killing of the father, and when the father substitute regained its human form, the animal substitute could also be retransformed into a human sacrifice.

Thus the memory of that first great act of sacrifice had proved to be indestructible despite all attempts to forget it, and just at the moment when men strove to get as far away as possible from its

---

[170] It is known that the overcoming of one generation of gods by another in mythology represents the historical process of the substitution of one religious system by another, either as the result of conquest by a strange race or by means of a psychological development. In the latter case the myth approaches the "functional phenomena" in H. Silberer's sense. That the god who kills the animal is a symbol of the libido, as asserted by C. G. Jung (*l.c.*), presupposes a different conception of the libido from that hitherto held, and at any rate seems to me questionable.

motives, the undistorted repetition of it had to appear in the form of the god sacrifice. I need not fully indicate here the developments of religious thought which made this return possible in the form of rationalizations. Robertson Smith who is, of course, far removed from the idea of tracing sacrifice back to this great event of man's primal history, says that the ceremony of the festivals in which the old Semites celebrated the death of a deity were interpreted as "a commemoration of a mythical tragedy" and that the attendant lament was not characterized by spontaneous sympathy, but displayed a compulsive character, something that was imposed by the fear of a divine wrath[171]. We are in a position to acknowledge that this interpretation was correct, the feelings of the celebrants being well explained by the basic situation.

We may now accept it as a fact that in the further development of religions these two inciting factors, the son's sense of guilt and his defiance, were never again extinguished. Every attempted solution of the religious problem and every kind of reconciliation of the two opposing psychic forces gradually falls to the ground, probably under the combined influence of cultural changes, historical events, and inner psychic transformations.

The endeavour of the son to put himself in place of the father god, appeared with greater and greater distinctness. With the introduction of agriculture the importance of the son in the patriarchal family increased. He was emboldened to give new expression to his incestuous libido which found symbolic satisfaction in labouring over mother earth. There came into existence figures of gods like Attis, Adonis, Tammuz, and others, spirits of vegetation as well as youthful divinities who enjoyed the favours of maternal deities and committed incest with the mother in defiance of the father. But the sense of guilt which was not allayed through these creations, was expressed in myths which visited these youthful lovers of the maternal goddesses with short life and punishment through castration or through the wrath of the father god appearing in animal form. Adonis was killed by the boar, the sacred animal of Aphrodite; Attis, the lover of Kybele, died of

---

[171]] *Religion of the Semites*, pp. 412-413. "The mourning is not a spontaneous expression of sympathy with the divine tragedy, but obligatory and enforced by fear of supernatural anger. And a chief object of the mourners is *to disclaim responsibility for the god's death*—a point which has already come before us in connexion with theanthropic sacrifices, such as the 'ox-murder at Athens.'"

castration[172]. The lamentation for these gods and the joy at their resurrection have gone over into the ritual of another son which divinity was destined to survive long.

When Christianity began its entry into the ancient world it met with the competition of the religion of Mithras and for a long time it was doubtful which deity was to be the victor.

The bright figure of the youthful Persian god has eluded our understanding. Perhaps we may conclude from the illustrations of Mithras slaying the steers that he represented the son who carried out the sacrifice of the father by himself and thus released the brothers from their oppressing complicity in the deed. There was another way of allaying this sense of guilt and this is the one that Christ took. He sacrificed his own life and thereby redeemed the brothers from primal sin.

The theory of primal sin is of Orphic origin; it was preserved in the mysteries and thence penetrated into the philosophic schools of Greek antiquity[173]. Men were the descendants of Titans, who had killed and dismembered the young Dionysos-Zagreus; the weight of this crime oppressed them. A fragment of Anaximander says that the unity of the world was destroyed by a primordial crime and everything that issued from it must carry on the punishment for this crime[174]. Although the features of banding together, killing, and dismembering as expressed in the deed of the Titans very clearly recall the totem sacrifice described by St Nilus—as also many other myths of antiquity, for example, the death of Orpheus himself—we are nevertheless disturbed here by the variation according to which a youthful god was murdered.

---

[172] The fear of castration plays an extraordinarily big rôle in disturbing the relations to the father in the case of our youthful neurotics. In Ferenczi's excellent study we have seen how the boy recognized his totem in the animal which snaps at his little penis. When children learn about ritual circumcision they identify it with castration. To my knowledge the parallel in the psychology of races to this attitude of our children has not yet been drawn. The circumcision which was so frequent in primordial times among primitive races belongs to the period of initiation in which its meaning is to be found; it has only secondarily been relegated to an earlier time of life. It is very interesting that among primitive men circumcision is combined with or replaced by the cutting off of the hair and the drawing of teeth, and that our children, who cannot know anything about this, really treat these two operations as equivalents to castration when they display their fear of them.

[173] Reinach, *Cultes, Mythes, et Religions*, II, p. 75."

[174] Une sorte de péché proethnique," *l.c.*, p. 76

In the Christian myth man's original sin is undoubtedly an offence against God the Father, and if Christ redeems mankind from the weight of original sin by sacrificing his own life, he forces us to the conclusion that this sin was murder. According to the law of retaliation which is deeply rooted in human feeling, a murder can be atoned only by the sacrifice of another life; the self-sacrifice points to a blood-guilt.[175] And if this sacrifice of one's own life brings about a reconciliation with god, the father, then the crime which must be expiated can only have been the murder of the father.

Thus in the Christian doctrine mankind most unreservedly acknowledges the guilty deed of primordial times because it now has found the most complete expiation for this deed in the sacrificial death of the son. The reconciliation with the father is the more thorough because simultaneously with this sacrifice there follows the complete renunciation of woman, for whose sake mankind rebelled against the father. But now also the psychological fatality of ambivalence demands its rights. In the same deed which offers the greatest possible expiation to the father, the son also attains the goal of his wishes against the father. He becomes a god himself beside or rather in place of his father. The religion of the son succeeds the religion of the father. As a sign of this substitution the old totem feast is revived again in the form of communion in which the band of brothers now eats the flesh and blood of the son and no longer that of the father, the sons thereby identifying themselves with him and becoming holy themselves. Thus through the ages we see the identity of the totem feast with the animal sacrifice, the theanthropic human sacrifice, and the Christian eucharist, and in all these solemn occasions we recognize the after-effects of that crime which so oppressed men but of which they must have been so proud. At bottom, however, the Christian communion is a new setting aside of the father, a repetition of the crime that must be expiated. We see how well justified is Frazer's dictum that "the Christian communion has absorbed within itself a sacrament which is doubtless far older than Christianity"[176].

---

[175] The suicidal impulses of our neurotics regularly prove to be self-punishments for death wishes directed against others.

[176] *Eating the God*, p. 51.... Nobody familiar with the literature on this subject will assume that the tracing back of the Christian communion to the totem feast is an idea of the author of this book

7

A process like the removal of the primal father by the band of brothers must have left ineradicable traces in the history of mankind and must have expressed itself the more frequently in numerous substitutive formations the less it itself was to be remembered.[177] I am avoiding the temptation of pointing out these traces in mythology, where they are not hard to find, and am turning to another field in following a hint of S. Reinach in his suggestive treatment of the death of Orpheus[178].

There is a situation in the history of Greek art which is strikingly familiar even if profoundly divergent, to the scene of a totem feast discovered by Robertson Smith. It is the situation of the oldest Greek tragedy. A group of persons, all of the same name and dressed in the same way, surround a single figure upon whose words and actions they are dependent, to represent the chorus and the original single impersonator of the hero. Later developments created a second and a third actor in order to represent opponents in playing, and off-shoots of the hero, but the character of the hero as well as his relation to the chorus remains unchanged. The hero of the tragedy had to suffer; this is to-day still the essential content of a tragedy. He had taken upon himself the so-called 'tragic guilt', which is not always easy to explain; it is often not a guilt in the ordinary sense. Almost always it consisted of a rebellion against a divine or human authority and the chorus accompanied the hero with their sympathies, trying to restrain and warn him, and lamented his fate after he had met with what was considered fitting punishment for his daring attempt.

But why did the hero of the tragedy have to suffer, and what was the meaning of his 'tragic' guilt? We will cut short the discussion by a prompt answer. He had to suffer because he was the primal father, the hero of that primordial tragedy the repetition of which here serves a certain tendency, and the tragic guilt is the guilt which he had to take

---

[177] Ariel in *The Tempest*:

Full fathom five thy father lies; Of his bones are coral made;
Those are pearls that were his eyes; Nothing of him that doth fade
But doth suffer a sea-change Into something rich and strange....

[178] La Mort d'Orphée, *Cultes, Mythes, et Religions*, Vol. II, p. 100.

upon himself in order to free the chorus of theirs. The scene upon the stage came into being through purposive distortion of the historical scene or, one is tempted to say, it was the result of refined hypocrisy. Actually, in the old situation, it was the members of the chorus themselves who had caused the suffering of the hero; here, on the other hand, they exhaust themselves in sympathy and regret, and the hero himself is to blame for his suffering. The crime foisted upon him, namely, presumption and rebellion against a great authority, is the same as that which in the past oppressed the colleagues of the chorus, namely, the band of brothers. Thus the tragic hero, though still against his will, is made the redeemer of the chorus.

When one bears in mind the suffering of the divine goat Dionysos in the performance of the Greek tragedy and the lament of the retinue of goats who identified themselves with him, one can easily understand how the almost extinct drama was reviewed in the Middle Ages in the Passion of Christ.

In closing this study, which has been carried out in extremely condensed form, I want to state the conclusion that the beginnings of religion, ethics, society, and art meet in the Oedipus complex. This is in entire accord with the findings of psychoanalysis, namely, that the nucleus of all neuroses as far as our present knowledge of them goes is the Oedipus complex. It comes as a great surprise to me that these problems of racial psychology can also be solved through a single concrete instance, such as the relation to the father. Perhaps another psychological problem must be included here. We have so frequently had occasion to show the ambivalence of emotions in its real sense, that is to say the coincidence of love and hate towards the same object, at the root of important cultural formations. We know nothing about the origin of this ambivalence. It may be assumed to be a fundamental phenomenon of our emotional life. But the other possibility seems to me also worthy of consideration: that ambivalence, originally foreign to our emotional life was acquired by mankind from the father complex (That is to say, the parent complex), where psychoanalytic investigation of the individual to-day still reveals the strongest expression of it[179].

---

[179] I am used to being misunderstood and therefore do not think it superfluous to state clearly that in giving these deductions I am by no means oblivious of the complex nature of the

Before closing we must take into account that the remarkable convergence reached in these illustrations, pointing to a single inclusive relation, ought not to blind us to the uncertainties of our assumptions and to the difficulties of our conclusions. Of these difficulties I will point out only two which must have forced themselves upon many readers.

In the first place it can hardly have escaped any one that we base everything upon the assumption of a psyche of the mass in which psychic processes occur as in the psychic life of the individual. Moreover, we let the sense of guilt for a deed survive for thousands of years, remaining effective in generations which could not have known anything of this deed. We allow an emotional process such as might have arisen among generations of sons that had been ill-treated by their fathers, to continue to new generations which had escaped such treatment by the very removal of the father. These seem indeed to be weighty objections and any other explanation which can avoid such assumptions would seem to merit preference.

But further consideration shows that we ourselves do not have to carry the whole responsibility for such daring. Without the assumption of a mass psyche, or a continuity in the emotional life of mankind which permits us to disregard the interruptions of psychic acts through the transgression of individuals, social psychology could not exist at all. If psychic processes of one generation did not continue in the next, if each had to acquire its attitude towards life afresh, there would be no progress in this field and almost no development. We are now confronted by two new questions: how much can be attributed to this psychic continuity within the series of generations, and what ways and means does a generation use to transfer its psychic states to the next generation? I do not claim that these problems have been sufficiently explained or that direct communication and tradition, of which one immediately thinks, are adequate for the task. Social psychology is in general little concerned with the manner in which the required continuity in the psychic life of succeeding generations is established.

---

phenomena which give rise to them; the only claim made is that a new factor has been added to the already known or still unrecognized origins of religion, morality, and society, which was furnished through psychoanalytic experience. The synthesis of the whole explanation must be left to another. But it is in the nature of this new contribution that it could play none other than the central rôle in such a synthesis, although it will be necessary to overcome great affective resistances before such importance will be conceded to it.

A part of the task seems to be performed by the inheritance of psychic dispositions which, however, need certain incentives in the individual life in order to become effective. This may be the meaning of the poet's words: "Strive to possess yourself of what you have inherited from your ancestors." The problem would appear more difficult if we could admit that there are psychic impulses which can be so completely suppressed that they leave no traces whatsoever behind them. But that does not exist. The greatest suppression must leave room for distorted substitutions and their resulting reactions. But in that case we may assume that no generation is capable of concealing its more important psychic processes from the next. For psychoanalysis has taught us that in his unconscious psychic activity every person possesses an apparatus which enables him to interpret the reactions of others, that is to say, to straighten out the distortions which the other person has affected in the expression of his feelings. By this method of unconscious understanding of all customs, ceremonies, and laws which the original relation to the primal father had left behind, later generations may also have succeeded in taking over this legacy of feelings.

There is another objection which the analytic method of thought itself might raise.

We have interpreted the first rules of morality and moral restrictions of primitive society as reactions to a deed which gave the authors of it the conception of crime. They regretted this deed and decided that it should not be repeated and that its execution must bring no gain. This creative sense of guilt has not become extinct with us. We find its asocial effects in neurotics producing new rules of morality and continued restrictions, in expiation for misdeeds committed, or as precautions against misdeeds to be committed(Compare Chapter II).

But when we examine these neurotics for the deeds which have called forth such reactions, we are disappointed. We do not find deeds, but only impulses and feelings which sought evil but which were restrained from carrying it out. Only psychic realities and not actual ones are at the basis of the neurotics' sense of guilt. It is characteristic of the neurosis to put a psychic reality above an actual one and to react as seriously to thoughts as the normal person reacts only towards realities.

May it not be true that the case was somewhat the same with primitive men? We are justified in ascribing to them an extraordinary over-valuation of their psychic acts as a partial manifestation of their narcistic organization (See Chapter III). According to this the mere impulses of hostility towards the father and the existence of the wish phantasy to kill and devour him may have sufficed to bring about the moral reaction which has created totemism and taboo. We should thus escape the necessity of tracing back the beginning of our cultural possession, of which we rightly are so proud, to a horrible crime which wounds all our feelings. The causal connexion, which stretches from that beginning to the present time, would not be impaired, for the psychic reality would be of sufficient importance to account for all those consequences. It may be agreed that a change has really taken place in the form of society from the father horde to the brother clan. This is a strong argument, but it is not conclusive. The change might have been accomplished in a less violent manner and still have conditioned the appearance of the moral reaction. As long as the pressure of the primal father was felt the hostile feelings against him were justified and repentance at these feelings had to wait for another opportunity. Of as little validity is the second objection, that everything derived from the ambivalent relation to the father, namely taboos, and rules of sacrifice, is characterized by the highest seriousness and by complete reality. The ceremonials and inhibitions of compulsion neurotics exhibit this characteristic too and yet they go back to a merely psychic reality, to resolution and not to execution. We must beware of introducing the contempt for what is merely thought or wished which characterizes our sober world where there are only material values, into the world of primitive man and the neurotic, which is full of inner riches only.

We face a decision here which is really not easy. But let us begin by acknowledging that the difference which may seem fundamental to others does not, in our judgment, touch the most important part of the subject. If wishes and impulses have the full value of fact for primitive man, it is for us to follow such a conception intelligently instead of correcting it according to our standard. But in that case we must scrutinize more closely the prototype of the neurosis itself which is responsible for having raised this doubt. It is not true that compulsion neurotics, who to-day are under the pressure of over-morality, defend themselves only against the psychic reality of temptations and punish themselves for impulses which they have only felt. A piece of historic reality is also involved; in their childhood these persons had nothing but evil impulses and as far as their childish impotence permitted they put them into action. Each of these over-good persons had a period of badness in his childhood, and a perverse phase as a fore-runner and a premise of the latter over morality. The analogy between primitive men and neurotics is therefore much more fundamentally established if we assume that with the former, too, the psychic reality, concerning whose structure there is no doubt, originally coincided with the actual reality, and that primitive men really did what according to all testimony they intended to do.

But we must not let our judgment about primitive men be influenced too far by the analogy with neurotics. Differences must also be taken into account. Of course the sharp division between thinking and doing as we draw it does not exist either with savages or with neurotics. But the neurotic is above all inhibited in his actions; with him the thought is a complete substitute for the deed. Primitive man is not inhibited, the thought is directly converted into the deed, the deed is for him so to speak rather a substitute for the thought, and for that reason I think we may well assume in the case we are discussing, though without vouching for the absolute certainty of the decision, that "In the beginning was the deed".

THE END

BOOK FOUR.
DREAM PSYCHOLOGY:
PSYCHOANALYSIS FOR BEGINNERS

INTRODUCTION

The medical profession is justly conservative. Human life should not be considered as the proper material for wild experiments.

Conservatism, however, is too often a welcome excuse for lazy minds, loath to adapt themselves to fast changing conditions.

Remember the scornful reception which first was accorded to Freud's discoveries in the domain of the unconscious.

When after years of patient observations, he finally decided to appear before medical bodies to tell them modestly of some facts which always recurred in his dream and his patients' dreams, he was first laughed at and then avoided as a crank.

The words "dream interpretation" were and still are indeed fraught with unpleasant, unscientific associations. They remind one of all sorts of childish, superstitious notions, which make up the thread and woof of dream books, read by none but the ignorant and the primitive.

The wealth of detail, the infinite care never to let anything pass unexplained, with which he presented to the public the result of his investigations, are impressing more and more serious-minded scientists, but the examination of his evidential data demands arduous work and presupposes an absolutely open mind.

This is why we still encounter men, totally unfamiliar with Freud's writings, men who were not even interested enough in the subject to attempt an interpretation of their dreams or their patients' dreams, deriding Freud's theories and combatting them with the help of statements which he never made.

Some of them, like Professor Boris Sidis, reach at times conclusions which are strangely similar to Freud's, but in their ignorance of psychoanalytic literature, they fail to credit Freud for observations antedating theirs.

Besides those who sneer at dream study, because they have never looked into the subject, there are those who do not dare to face the facts revealed by dream study. Dreams tell us many an unpleasant biological truth about ourselves and only very free minds can thrive on such a diet. Self-deception is a plant which withers fast in the pellucid atmosphere of dream investigation.

The weakling and the neurotic attached to his neurosis are not anxious to turn such a powerful searchlight upon the dark corners of their psychology.

Freud's theories are anything but theoretical.

He was moved by the fact that there always seemed to be a close connection between his patients' dreams and their mental abnormalities, to collect thousands of dreams and to compare them with the case histories in his possession.

He did not start out with a preconceived bias, hoping to find evidence which might support his views. He looked at facts a thousand times "until they began to tell him something."

His attitude toward dream study was, in other words, that of a statistician who does not know, and has no means of foreseeing, what conclusions will be forced on him by the information he is gathering, but who is fully prepared to accept those unavoidable conclusions.

This was indeed a novel way in psychology. Psychologists had always been wont to build, in what Bleuler calls "autistic ways," that is through methods in no wise supported by evidence, some attractive hypothesis, which sprung from their brain, like Minerva from Jove's brain, fully armed.

After which, they would stretch upon that unyielding frame the hide of a reality which they had previously killed.

It is only to minds suffering from the same distortions, to minds also autistically inclined, that those empty, artificial structures appear acceptable molds for philosophic thinking.

The pragmatic view that "truth is what works" had not been as yet expressed when Freud published his revolutionary views on the psychology of dreams.

Five facts of first magnitude were made obvious to the world by his interpretation of dreams.

First of all, Freud pointed out a constant connection between some part of every dream and some detail of the dreamer's life during the previous waking state. This positively establishes a relation between sleeping states and waking states and disposes of the widely prevalent view that dreams are purely nonsensical phenomena coming from nowhere and leading nowhere.

Secondly, Freud, after studying the dreamer's life and modes of thought, after noting down all his mannerisms and the apparently insignificant details of his conduct which reveal his secret thoughts, came to the conclusion that there was in every dream the attempted or successful gratification of some wish, conscious or unconscious.

Thirdly, he proved that many of our dream visions are symbolical, which causes us to consider them as absurd and unintelligible; the universality of those symbols, however, makes them very transparent to the trained observer.

Fourthly, Freud showed that sexual desires play an enormous part in our unconscious, a part which puritanical hypocrisy has always tried to minimize, if not to ignore entirely.

Finally, Freud established a direct connection between dreams and insanity, between the symbolic visions of our sleep and the symbolic actions of the mentally deranged.

There were, of course, many other observations which Freud made while dissecting the dreams of his patients, but not all of them present as much interest as the foregoing nor were they as revolutionary or likely to wield as much influence on modern psychiatry.

Other explorers have struck the path blazed by Freud and leading into man's unconscious. Jung of Zurich, Adler of Vienna and Kempf of Washington, D.C., have made to the study of the unconscious, contributions which have brought that study into fields which Freud himself never dreamt of invading.

One fact which cannot be too emphatically stated, however, is that but for Freud's wishfulfillment theory of dreams, neither Jung's "energic theory," nor Adler's theory of "organ inferiority and compensation," nor Kempf's "dynamic mechanism" might have been formulated.

Freud is the father of modern abnormal psychology and he established the psychoanalytical point of view. No one who is not well grounded in Freudian lore can hope to achieve any work of value in the field of psychoanalysis.

On the other hand, let no one repeat the absurd assertion that Freudism is a sort of religion bounded with dogmas and requiring an act of faith. Freudism as such was merely a stage in the development of psychoanalysis, a stage out of which all but a few bigoted camp followers, totally lacking in originality, have evolved. Thousands of stones have been added to the structure erected by the Viennese physician and many more will be added in the course of time.

But the new additions to that structure would collapse like a house of cards but for the original foundations which are as indestructible as Harvey's statement as to the circulation of the blood.

Regardless of whatever additions or changes have been made to the original structure, the analytic point of view remains unchanged. That point of view is not only revolutionising all the methods of diagnosis and treatment of mental derangements, but compelling the intelligent, up-to-date physician to revise entirely his attitude to almost every kind of disease.

The insane are no longer absurd and pitiable people, to be herded in asylums till nature either cures them or relieves them, through death, of their misery. The insane who have not been made so by actual injury to their brain or nervous system, are the victims of unconscious forces which cause them to do abnormally things which they might be helped to do normally.

Insight into one's psychology is replacing victoriously sedatives and rest cures.

Physicians dealing with "purely" physical cases have begun to take into serious consideration the "mental" factors which have predisposed a patient to certain ailments.

Freud's views have also made a revision of all ethical and social values unavoidable and have thrown an unexpected flood of light upon literary and artistic accomplishment.

But the Freudian point of view, or more broadly speaking, the psychoanalytic point of view, shall ever remain a puzzle to those who, from laziness or indifference, refuse to survey with the great Viennese the field over which he carefully groped his way. We shall never be convinced until we repeat under his guidance all his laboratory experiments.

We must follow him through the thickets of the unconscious, through the land which had never been charted because academic philosophers, following the line of least effort, had decided *a priori* that it could not be charted.

Ancient geographers, when exhausting their store of information about distant lands, yielded to an unscientific craving for romance and, without any evidence to support their day dreams, filled the blank spaces left on their maps by unexplored tracts with amusing inserts such as "Here there are lions."

Thanks to Freud's interpretation of dreams the "royal road" into the unconscious is now open to all explorers. They shall not find lions, they shall find man himself, and the record of all his life and of his struggle with reality.

And it is only after seeing man as his unconscious, revealed by his dreams, presents him to us that we shall understand him fully. For as Freud said to Putnam: "We are what we are because we have been what we have been."

Not a few serious-minded students, however, have been discouraged from attempting a study of Freud's dream psychology.

The book in which he originally offered to the world his interpretation of dreams was as circumstantial as a legal record to be pondered over by scientists at their leisure, not to be assimilated in a few hours by the average alert reader. In those days, Freud could not leave out any detail likely to make his extremely novel thesis evidentially acceptable to those willing to sift data.

Freud himself, however, realized the magnitude of the task which the reading of his *magnum opus* imposed upon those who have not been prepared for it by long psychological and scientific training and he abstracted from that gigantic work the parts which constitute the essential of his discoveries.

The publishers of the present book deserve credit for presenting to the reading public the gist of Freud's psychology in the master's own words, and in a form which shall neither discourage beginners, nor appear too elementary to those who are more advanced in psychoanalytic study.

Dream psychology is the key to Freud's works and to all modern psychology. With a simple, compact manual such as *Dream Psychology* there shall be no longer any excuse for ignorance of the most revolutionary psychological system of modern times.

ANDRE TRIDON. 121 Madison Avenue, New York. November, 1920.

I. DREAMS HAVE A MEANING

In what we may term "prescientific days" people were in no uncertainty about the interpretation of dreams. When they were recalled after awakening they were regarded as either the friendly or hostile manifestation of some higher powers, demoniacal and Divine. With the rise of scientific thought the whole of this expressive mythology was transferred to psychology; to-day there is but a small minority among educated persons who doubt that the dream is the dreamer's own psychical act.

But since the downfall of the mythological hypothesis an interpretation of the dream has been wanting. The conditions of its origin; its relationship to our psychical life when we are awake; its independence of disturbances which, during the state of sleep, seem to compel notice; its many peculiarities repugnant to our waking thought; the incongruence between its images and the feelings they engender; then the dream's evanescence, the way in which, on awakening, our thoughts thrust it aside as something bizarre, and our reminiscences mutilating or rejecting it—all these and many other problems have for many hundred years demanded answers which up till now could never have been satisfactory. Before all there is the question as to the meaning of the dream, a question which is in itself double-sided. There is, firstly, the psychical significance of the dream, its position with regard to the psychical processes, as to a possible biological function; secondly, has the dream a meaning—can sense be made of each single dream as of other mental syntheses?

Three tendencies can be observed in the estimation of dreams. Many philosophers have given currency to one of these tendencies, one which at the same time preserves something of the dream's former over-valuation. The foundation of dream life is for them a peculiar state of psychical activity, which they even celebrate as elevation to some higher state. Schubert, for instance, claims: "The dream is the liberation of the spirit from the pressure of external nature, a detachment of the soul from the fetters of matter." Not all go so far as this, but many maintain that dreams have their origin in real spiritual excitations, and are the outward manifestations of spiritual powers whose free movements have been hampered during the day ("Dream Phantasies," Scherner, Volkelt). A large number of observers acknowledge that dream life is capable of extraordinary achievements—at any rate, in certain fields ("Memory").

In striking contradiction with this the majority of medical writers hardly admit that the dream is a psychical phenomenon at all. According to them dreams are provoked and initiated exclusively by stimuli proceeding from the senses or the body, which either reach the sleeper from without or are accidental disturbances of his internal organs. The dream has no greater claim to meaning and importance than the sound called forth by the ten fingers of a person quite unacquainted with music running his fingers over the keys of an instrument. The dream is to be regarded, says Binz, "as a physical process always useless, frequently morbid." All the peculiarities of dream life are explicable as the incoherent effort, due to some physiological stimulus, of certain organs, or of the cortical elements of a brain otherwise asleep.

But slightly affected by scientific opinion and untroubled as to the origin of dreams, the popular view holds firmly to the belief that dreams really have got a meaning, in some way they do foretell the future, whilst the meaning can be unravelled in some way or other from its oft bizarre and enigmatical content. The reading of dreams consists in replacing the events of the dream, so far as remembered, by other events. This is done either scene by scene, *according to some rigid key*, or the dream as a whole is replaced by something else of which it was a *symbol*. Serious-minded persons laugh at these efforts—"Dreams are but sea-foam!"

One day I discovered to my amazement that the popular view grounded in superstition, and not the medical one, comes nearer to the truth about dreams. I arrived at new conclusions about dreams by the use of a new method of psychological investigation, one which had rendered me good service in the investigation of phobias, obsessions, illusions, and the like, and which, under the name "psycho-analysis," had found acceptance by a whole school of investigators. The manifold analogies of dream life with the most diverse conditions of psychical disease in the waking state have been rightly insisted upon by a number of medical observers. It seemed, therefore, *a priori*, hopeful to apply to the interpretation of dreams methods of investigation which had been tested in psychopathological processes. Obsessions and those peculiar sensations of haunting dread remain as strange to normal consciousness as do dreams to our waking consciousness; their origin is as unknown to consciousness as is that of dreams. It was practical ends that impelled us, in these diseases, to fathom their origin and formation. Experience had shown us that a cure and a consequent mastery of the obsessing ideas did result when once those thoughts, the connecting links between the morbid ideas and the rest of the psychical content, were revealed which were heretofore veiled from consciousness. The procedure I employed for the interpretation of dreams thus arose from psychotherapy.

This procedure is readily described, although its practice demands instruction and experience. Suppose the patient is suffering from intense morbid dread. He is requested to direct his attention to the idea in question, without, however, as he has so frequently done, meditating upon it. Every impression about it, without any exception, which occurs to him should be imparted to the doctor. The statement which will be perhaps then made, that he cannot concentrate his attention upon anything at all, is to be countered by assuring him most positively that such a blank state of mind is utterly impossible. As a matter of fact, a great number of impressions will soon occur, with which others will associate themselves. These will be invariably accompanied by the expression of the observer's opinion that they have no meaning or are unimportant. It will be at once noticed that it is this self-criticism which prevented the patient from imparting the ideas, which had indeed already excluded them from consciousness. If the patient can be induced to abandon this self-criticism and to pursue the trains of thought which are yielded by concentrating the attention, most significant matter will be obtained, matter which will be presently seen to be clearly linked to the morbid idea in question. Its connection with other ideas will be manifest, and later on will permit the replacement of the morbid idea by a fresh one, which is perfectly adapted to psychical continuity.

This is not the place to examine thoroughly the hypothesis upon which this experiment rests, or the deductions which follow from its invariable success. It must suffice to state that we obtain matter enough for the resolution of every morbid idea if we especially direct our attention to the *unbidden* associations *which disturb our thoughts*—those which are otherwise put aside by the critic as worthless refuse. If the procedure is exercised on oneself, the best plan of helping the experiment is to write down at once all one's first indistinct fancies.

I will now point out where this method leads when I apply it to the examination of dreams. Any dream could be made use of in this way. From certain motives I, however, choose a dream of my own, which appears confused and meaningless to my memory, and one which has the advantage of brevity. Probably my dream of last night satisfies the requirements. Its content, fixed immediately after awakening, runs as follows:

"Company; at table or table d'hôte.... Spinach is served. Mrs. E.L., sitting next to me, gives me her undivided attention, and places her hand familiarly upon my knee. In defence I remove her hand. Then she says: 'But you have always had such beautiful eyes.'.... I then distinctly see something like two eyes as a sketch or as the contour of a spectacle lens...."

This is the whole dream, or, at all events, all that I can remember. It appears to me not only obscure and meaningless, but more especially odd. Mrs. E.L. is a person with whom I am scarcely on visiting terms, nor to my knowledge have I ever desired any more cordial relationship. I have not seen her for a long time, and do not think there was any mention of her recently. No emotion whatever accompanied the dream process.

Reflecting upon this dream does not make it a bit clearer to my mind. I will now, however, present the ideas, without premeditation and without criticism, which introspection yielded. I soon notice that it is an advantage to break up the dream into its elements, and to search out the ideas which link themselves to each fragment.

Company; at table or table d'hôte. The recollection of the slight event with which the evening of yesterday ended is at once called up. I left a small party in the company of a friend, who offered to drive me home in his cab. "I prefer a taxi," he said; "that gives one such a pleasant occupation; there is always something to look at." When we were in the cab, and the cab-driver turned the disc so that the first sixty hellers were visible, I continued the jest. "We have hardly got in and we already owe sixty hellers. The taxi always reminds me of the table d'hôte. It makes me avaricious and selfish by continuously reminding me of my debt. It seems to me to mount up too quickly, and I am always afraid that I shall be at a disadvantage, just as I cannot resist at table d'hôte the comical fear that I am getting too little, that I must look after myself." In far-fetched connection with this I quote:

"To earth, this weary earth, ye bring us, To guilt ye let us heedless go."

Another idea about the table d'hôte. A few weeks ago I was very cross with my dear wife at the dinner-table at a Tyrolese health resort, because she was not sufficiently reserved with some neighbors with whom I wished to have absolutely nothing to do. I begged her to occupy herself rather with me than with the strangers. That is just as if I had *been at a disadvantage at the table d'hôte.* The contrast between the behavior of my wife at the table and that of Mrs. E.L. in the dream now strikes me: *"Addresses herself entirely to me."*

Further, I now notice that the dream is the reproduction of a little scene which transpired between my wife and myself when I was secretly courting her. The caressing under cover of the tablecloth was an answer to a wooer's passionate letter. In the dream, however, my wife is replaced by the unfamiliar E.L.

Mrs. E.L. is the daughter of a man to whom I *owed money*! I cannot help noticing that here there is revealed an unsuspected connection between the dream content and my thoughts. If the chain of associations be followed up which proceeds from one element of the dream one is soon led back to another of its elements. The thoughts evoked by the dream stir up associations which were not noticeable in the dream itself.

Is it not customary, when some one expects others to look after his interests without any advantage to themselves, to ask the innocent question satirically: "Do you think this will be done *for the sake of your beautiful eyes?*" Hence Mrs. E.L.'s speech in the dream. "You have always had such beautiful eyes," means nothing but "people always do everything to you for love of you; you have had *everything for nothing.*" The contrary is, of course, the truth; I have always paid dearly for whatever kindness others have shown me. Still, the fact that *I had a ride for nothing* yesterday when my friend drove me home in his cab must have made an impression upon me.

In any case, the friend whose guests we were yesterday has often made me his debtor. Recently I allowed an opportunity of requiting him to go by. He has had only one present from me, an antique shawl, upon which eyes are painted all round, a so-called Occhiale, as a *charm* against the *Malocchio*. Moreover, he is an *eye specialist*. That same evening I had asked him after a patient whom I had sent to him for *glasses.*

As I remarked, nearly all parts of the dream have been brought into this new connection. I still might ask why in the dream it was *spinach* that was served up. Because spinach called up a little scene which recently occurred at our table. A child, whose *beautiful eyes* are really deserving of praise, refused to eat spinach. As a child I was just the same; for a long time I loathed *spinach*, until in later life my tastes altered, and it became one of my favorite dishes. The mention of this dish brings my own childhood and that of my child's near together. "You should be glad that you have some spinach," his mother had said to the little gourmet. "Some children would be very glad to get spinach." Thus I am reminded of the parents' duties towards their children. Goethe's words—

"To earth, this weary earth, ye bring us, To guilt ye let us heedless go"—

take on another meaning in this connection.

Here I will stop in order that I may recapitulate the results of the analysis of the dream. By following the associations which were linked to the single elements of the dream torn from their context, I have been led to a series of thoughts and reminiscences where I am bound to recognize interesting expressions of my psychical life. The matter yielded by an analysis of the dream stands in intimate relationship with the dream content, but this relationship is so special that I should never have been able to have inferred the new discoveries directly from the dream itself. The dream was passionless, disconnected, and unintelligible. During the time that I am unfolding the thoughts at the back of the dream I feel intense and well-grounded emotions. The thoughts themselves fit beautifully together into chains logically bound together with certain central ideas which ever repeat themselves. Such ideas not represented in the dream itself are in this instance the antitheses *selfish, unselfish, to be indebted, to work for nothing*. I could draw closer the threads of the web which analysis has disclosed, and would then be able to show how they all run together into a single knot; I am debarred from making this work public by considerations of a private, not of a scientific, nature. After having cleared up many things which I do not willingly acknowledge as mine, I should have much to reveal which had better remain my secret. Why, then, do not I choose another dream whose analysis would be more suitable for publication, so that I could awaken a fairer conviction of the sense and cohesion of the results disclosed by analysis? The answer is, because every dream which I investigate leads to the same difficulties and places me under the same need of discretion; nor should I forgo this difficulty any the more were I to analyze the dream of some one else. That could only be done when opportunity allowed all concealment to be dropped without injury to those who trusted me.

The conclusion which is now forced upon me is that the dream is a *sort of substitution* for those emotional and intellectual trains of thought which I attained after complete analysis. I do not yet know the process by which the dream arose from those thoughts, but I perceive that it is wrong to regard the dream as psychically unimportant, a purely physical process which has arisen from the activity of isolated cortical elements awakened out of sleep.

I must further remark that the dream is far shorter than the thoughts which I hold it replaces; whilst analysis discovered that the dream was provoked by an unimportant occurrence the evening before the dream.

Naturally, I would not draw such far-reaching conclusions if only one analysis were known to me. Experience has shown me that when the associations of any dream are honestly followed such a chain of thought is revealed, the constituent parts of the dream reappear correctly and sensibly linked together; the slight suspicion that this concatenation was merely an accident of a single first observation must, therefore, be absolutely relinquished. I regard it, therefore, as my right to establish this new view by a proper nomenclature. I contrast the dream which my memory evokes with the dream and other added matter revealed by analysis: the former I call the dream's *manifest content*; the latter, without at first further subdivision, its *latent content*. I arrive at two new problems hitherto unformulated: (1)

What is the psychical process which has transformed the latent content of the dream into its manifest content? (2) What is the motive or the motives which have made such transformation exigent? The process by which the change from latent to manifest content is executed I name the *dream-work*. In contrast with this is the *work of analysis*, which produces the reverse transformation. The other problems of the dream—the inquiry as to its stimuli, as to the source of its materials, as to its possible purpose, the function of dreaming, the forgetting of dreams—these I will discuss in connection with the latent dream-content.

I shall take every care to avoid a confusion between the *manifest* and the *latent content*, for I ascribe all the contradictory as well as the incorrect accounts of dream-life to the ignorance of this latent content, now first laid bare through analysis.

The conversion of the latent dream thoughts into those manifest deserves our close study as the first known example of the transformation of psychical stuff from one mode of expression into another. From a mode of expression which, moreover, is readily intelligible into another which we can only penetrate by effort and with guidance, although this new mode must be equally reckoned as an effort of our own psychical activity. From the standpoint of the relationship of latent to manifest dream-content, dreams can be divided into three classes. We can, in the first place, distinguish those dreams which have a *meaning* and are, at the same time, *intelligible*, which allow us to penetrate into our psychical life without further ado. Such dreams are numerous; they are usually short, and, as a general rule, do not seem very noticeable, because everything remarkable or exciting surprise is absent. Their occurrence is, moreover, a strong argument against the doctrine which derives the dream from the isolated activity of certain cortical elements. All signs of a lowered or subdivided psychical activity are wanting. Yet we never raise any objection to characterizing them as dreams, nor do we confound them with the products of our waking life.

A second group is formed by those dreams which are indeed self-coherent and have a distinct meaning, but appear strange because we are unable to reconcile their meaning with our mental life. That is the case when we dream, for instance, that some dear relative has died of plague when we know of no ground for expecting, apprehending, or assuming anything of the sort; we can only ask ourself wonderingly: "What brought that into my head?" To the third group those dreams belong which are void of both meaning and intelligibility; they are *incoherent, complicated, and meaningless*. The overwhelming number of our dreams partake of this character, and this has given rise to the contemptuous attitude towards dreams and the medical theory of their limited psychical activity. It is especially in the longer and more complicated dream-plots that signs of incoherence are seldom missing.

The contrast between manifest and latent dream-content is clearly only of value for the dreams of the second and more especially for those of the third class. Here are problems which are only solved when the manifest dream is replaced by its latent content; it was an example of this kind, a complicated and unintelligible dream, that we subjected to analysis. Against our expectation we, however, struck upon reasons which prevented a complete cognizance of the latent dream thought. On the repetition of this same experience we were forced to the supposition that there is an *intimate bond, with laws of its own, between the unintelligible and complicated nature of the dream and the difficulties attending communication of the thoughts connected with the dream.* Before investigating the nature of this bond, it will be advantageous to turn our attention to the more readily intelligible dreams of the first class where, the manifest and latent content being identical, the dream work seems to be omitted.

The investigation of these dreams is also advisable from another standpoint. The dreams of *children* are of this nature; they have a meaning, and are not bizarre. This, by the way, is a further objection to reducing dreams to a dissociation of cerebral activity in sleep, for why should such a lowering of psychical functions belong to the nature of sleep in adults, but not in children? We are, however, fully justified in expecting that the explanation of psychical processes in children, essentially simplified as they may be, should serve as an indispensable preparation towards the psychology of the adult.

I shall therefore cite some examples of dreams which I have gathered from children. A girl of nineteen months was made to go without food for a day because she had been sick in the morning, and, according to nurse, had made herself ill through eating strawberries. During the night, after her day of fasting, she was heard calling out her name during sleep, and adding: "*Tawberry, eggs, pap.*" She is dreaming that she is eating, and selects out of her menu exactly what she supposes she will not get much of just now.

The same kind of dream about a forbidden dish was that of a little boy of twenty-two months. The day before he was told to offer his uncle a present of a small basket of cherries, of which the child was, of course, only allowed one to taste. He woke up with the joyful news: "Hermann eaten up all the cherries."

A girl of three and a half years had made during the day a sea trip which was too short for her, and she cried when she had to get out of the boat. The next morning her story was that during the night she had been on the sea, thus continuing the interrupted trip.

A boy of five and a half years was not at all pleased with his party during a walk in the Dachstein region. Whenever a new peak came into sight he asked if that were the Dachstein, and, finally, refused to accompany the party to the waterfall. His behavior was ascribed to fatigue; but a better explanation was forthcoming when the next morning he told his dream: *he had ascended the Dachstein*. Obviously he expected the ascent of the Dachstein to be the object of the excursion, and was vexed by not getting a glimpse of the mountain. The dream gave him what the day had withheld. The dream of a girl of six was similar; her father had cut short the walk before reaching the promised objective on account of the lateness of the hour. On the way back she noticed a signpost giving the name of another place for excursions; her father promised to take her there also some other day. She greeted her father next day with the news that she had dreamt that *her father had been with her to both places*.

What is common in all these dreams is obvious. They completely satisfy wishes excited during the day which remain unrealized. They are simply and undisguisedly realizations of wishes.

The following child-dream, not quite understandable at first sight, is nothing else than a wish realized. On account of poliomyelitis a girl, not quite four years of age, was brought from the country into town, and remained over night with a childless aunt in a big—for her, naturally, huge—bed. The next morning she stated that she had dreamt that *the bed was much too small for her, so that she could find no place in it*. To explain this dream as a wish is easy when we remember that to be "big" is a frequently expressed wish of all children. The bigness of the bed reminded Miss Little-Would-be-Big only too forcibly of her smallness. This nasty situation became righted in her dream, and she grew so big that the bed now became too small for her.

Even when children's dreams are complicated and polished, their comprehension as a realization of desire is fairly evident. A boy of eight dreamt that he was being driven with Achilles in a war-chariot, guided by Diomedes. The day before he was assiduously reading about great heroes. It is easy to show that he took these heroes as his models, and regretted that he was not living in those days.

From this short collection a further characteristic of the dreams of children is manifest—*their connection with the life of the day*. The desires which are realized in these dreams are left over from the day or, as a rule, the day previous, and the feeling has become intently emphasized and fixed during the day thoughts. Accidental and indifferent matters, or what must appear so to the child, find no acceptance in the contents of the dream.

Innumerable instances of such dreams of the infantile type can be found among adults also, but, as mentioned, these are mostly exactly like the manifest content. Thus, a random selection of persons will generally respond to thirst at night-time with a dream about drinking, thus striving to get rid of the sensation and to let sleep continue. Many persons frequently have these comforting *dreams* before waking, just when they are called. They then dream that they are already up, that they are washing, or already in school, at the office, etc., where they ought to be at a given time. The night before an intended journey one not infrequently dreams that one has already arrived at the destination; before going to a play or to a party the dream not infrequently anticipates, in impatience, as it were, the expected pleasure. At other times the dream expresses the realization of the desire somewhat indirectly; some connection, some sequel must be known—the first step towards recognizing the desire. Thus, when a husband related to me the dream of his young wife, that her monthly period had begun, I had to bethink myself that the young wife would have expected a pregnancy if the period had been absent. The dream is then a sign of pregnancy. Its meaning is that it shows the wish realized that pregnancy should not occur just yet. Under unusual and extreme circumstances, these dreams of the infantile type become very frequent. The leader of a polar expedition tells us, for instance, that during the wintering amid the ice the crew, with their monotonous diet and slight rations, dreamt regularly, like children, of fine meals, of mountains of tobacco, and of home.

It is not uncommon that out of some long, complicated and intricate dream one specially lucid part stands out containing unmistakably the realization of a desire, but bound up with much unintelligible matter. On more frequently analyzing the seemingly more transparent dreams of adults, it is astonishing to discover that these are rarely as simple as the dreams of children, and that they cover another meaning beyond that of the realization of a wish.

It would certainly be a simple and convenient solution of the riddle if the work of analysis made it at all possible for us to trace the meaningless and intricate dreams of adults back to the infantile type, to the realization of some intensely experienced desire of the day. But there is no warrant for such an expectation. Their dreams are generally full of the most indifferent and bizarre matter, and no trace of the realization of the wish is to be found in their content.

Before leaving these infantile dreams, which are obviously unrealized desires, we must not fail to mention another chief characteristic of dreams, one that has been long noticed, and one which stands out most clearly in this class. I can replace any of these dreams by a phrase expressing a desire. If the sea trip had only lasted longer; if I were only washed and dressed; if I had only been allowed to keep the cherries instead of giving them to my uncle. But the dream gives something more than the choice, for here the desire is already realized; its realization is real and actual. The dream presentations consist chiefly, if not wholly, of scenes and mainly of visual sense images. Hence a kind of transformation is not entirely absent in this class of dreams, and this may be fairly designated as the dream work. *An idea merely existing in the region of possibility is replaced by a vision of its accomplishment.*

II. THE DREAM MECHANISM

We are compelled to assume that such transformation of scene has also taken place in intricate dreams, though we do not know whether it has encountered any possible desire. The dream instanced at the commencement, which we analyzed somewhat thoroughly, did give us occasion in two places to suspect something of the kind. Analysis brought out that my wife was occupied with others at table, and that I did not like it; in the dream itself *exactly the opposite* occurs, for the person who replaces my wife gives me her undivided attention. But can one wish for anything pleasanter after a disagreeable incident than that the exact contrary should have occurred, just as the dream has it? The stinging thought in the analysis, that I have never had anything for nothing, is similarly connected with the woman's remark in the dream: "You have always had such beautiful eyes." Some portion of the opposition between the latent and manifest content of the dream must be therefore derived from the realization of a wish.

Another manifestation of the dream work which all incoherent dreams have in common is still more noticeable. Choose any instance, and compare the number of separate elements in it, or the extent of the dream, if written down, with the dream thoughts yielded by analysis, and of which but a trace can be refound in the dream itself. There can be no doubt that the dream working has resulted in an extraordinary compression or *condensation*. It is not at first easy to form an opinion as to the extent of the condensation; the more deeply you go into the analysis, the more deeply you are impressed by it. There will be found no factor in the dream whence the chains of associations do not lead in two or more directions, no scene which has not been pieced together out of two or more impressions and events. For instance, I once dreamt about a kind of swimming-bath where the bathers suddenly separated in all directions; at one place on the edge a person stood bending towards one of the bathers as if to drag him out. The scene was a composite one, made up out of an event that occurred at the time of puberty, and of two pictures, one of which I had seen just shortly before the dream. The two pictures were The Surprise in the Bath, from Schwind's Cycle of the Melusine (note the bathers suddenly separating), and The Flood, by an Italian master. The little incident was that I once witnessed a lady, who had tarried in the swimming-bath until the men's hour, being helped out of the water by the swimming-master. The scene in the dream which was selected for analysis led to a whole group of reminiscences, each one of which had contributed to the dream content. First of all came the little episode from the time of my courting, of which I have already spoken; the pressure of a hand under the table gave rise in the dream to the "under the table," which I had subsequently to find a place for in my recollection. There was, of course, at the time not a word about "undivided attention." Analysis taught me that this factor is the realization of a desire through its contradictory and related to the behavior of my wife at the table d'hôte. An exactly similar and much more important episode of our courtship, one which separated us for an entire day, lies hidden behind this recent recollection. The intimacy, the hand resting upon the knee, refers to a quite different connection and to quite other persons. This element in the dream becomes again the starting-point of two distinct series of reminiscences, and so on.

The stuff of the dream thoughts which has been accumulated for the formation of the dream scene must be naturally fit for this application. There must be one or more common factors. The dream work proceeds like Francis Galton with his family photographs. The different elements are put one on top of the other; what is common to the composite picture stands out clearly, the opposing details cancel each other. This process of reproduction partly explains the wavering statements, of a peculiar vagueness, in so many elements of the dream. For the interpretation of dreams this rule holds good: When analysis discloses *uncertainty*, as to *either—or* read *and, taking* each section of the apparent alternatives as a separate outlet for a series of impressions.

When there is nothing in common between the dream thoughts, the dream work takes the trouble to create a something, in order to make a common presentation feasible in the dream. The simplest way to approximate two dream thoughts, which have as yet nothing in common, consists in making such a change in the actual expression of one idea as will meet a slight responsive recasting in the form of the other idea. The process is analogous to that of rhyme, when consonance supplies the desired common factor. A good deal of the dream work consists in the creation of those frequently very witty, but often exaggerated, digressions. These vary from the common presentation in the dreamcontent to dream thoughts which are as varied as are the causes in form and essence which give rise to them. In the analysis of our example of a dream, I find a like case of the transformation of a thought in order that it might agree with another essentially foreign one. In following out the analysis I struck upon the thought: *I should like to have something for nothing.* But this formula is not serviceable to the dream. Hence it is replaced by another one: "I should like to enjoy something free of cost."[180]

---

[180] "Ich möchte gerne etwas geniessen ohne 'Kosten' zu haben." A a pun upon the word "kosten," which has two meanings—"taste" and "cost." In "Die Traumdeutung," third edition, p. 71 footnote, Professor Freud remarks that "the finest example of dream interpretation left us by the ancients is based upon a pun" (from "The Interpretation of Dreams," by Artemidorus

The word "kost" (taste), with its double meaning, is appropriate to a table d'hôte; it, moreover, is in place through the special sense in the dream. At home if there is a dish which the children decline, their mother first tries gentle persuasion, with a "Just taste it." That the dream work should unhesitatingly use the double meaning of the word is certainly remarkable; ample experience has shown, however, that the occurrence is quite usual.

Through condensation of the dream certain constituent parts of its content are explicable which are peculiar to the dream life alone, and which are not found in the waking state. Such are the composite and mixed persons, the extraordinary mixed figures, creations comparable with the fantastic animal compositions of Orientals; a moment's thought and these are reduced to unity, whilst the fancies of the dream are ever formed anew in an inexhaustible profusion. Every one knows such images in his own dreams; manifold are their origins. I can build up a person by borrowing one feature from one person and one from another, or by giving to the form of one the name of another in my dream. I can also visualize one person, but place him in a position which has occurred to another. There is a meaning in all these cases when different persons are amalgamated into one substitute. Such cases denote an "and," a "just like," a comparison of the original person from a certain point of view, a comparison which can be also realized in the dream itself. As a rule, however, the identity of the blended persons is only discoverable by analysis, and is only indicated in the dream content by the formation of the "combined" person.

The same diversity in their ways of formation and the same rules for its solution hold good also for the innumerable medley of dream contents, examples of which I need scarcely adduce. Their strangeness quite disappears when we resolve not to place them on a level with the objects of perception as known to us when awake, but to remember that they represent the art of dream condensation by an exclusion of unnecessary detail. Prominence is given to the common character of the combination. Analysis must also generally supply the common features. The dream says simply: *All these things have an "x" in common.* The decomposition of these mixed images by analysis is often the quickest way to an interpretation of the dream. Thus I once dreamt that I was sitting with one of my former university tutors on a bench, which was undergoing a rapid continuous movement amidst other benches. This was a combination of lecture-room and moving staircase. I will not pursue the further result of the thought. Another time I was sitting in a carriage, and on my lap an object in shape like a top-hat, which, however, was made of transparent glass. The scene at once brought to my mind the

---

Daldianus). "Moreover, dreams are so intimately bound up with language that Ferenczi truly points out that every tongue has its own language of dreams. A dream is as a rule untranslatable into other languages."—TRANSLATOR

proverb: "He who keeps his hat in his hand will travel safely through the land." By a slight turn the *glass hat* reminded me of *Auer's light,* and I knew that I was about to invent something which was to make me as rich and independent as his invention had made my countryman, Dr. Auer, of Welsbach; then I should be able to travel instead of remaining in Vienna. In the dream I was traveling with my invention, with the, it is true, rather awkward glass top-hat. The dream work is peculiarly adept at representing two contradictory conceptions by means of the same mixed image. Thus, for instance, a woman dreamt of herself carrying a tall flower-stalk, as in the picture of the Annunciation (Chastity-Mary is her own name), but the stalk was bedecked with thick white blossoms resembling camellias (contrast with chastity: La dame aux Camelias).

A great deal of what we have called "dream condensation" can be thus formulated. Each one of the elements of the dream content is *overdetermined* by the matter of the dream thoughts; it is not derived from one element of these thoughts, but from a whole series. These are not necessarily interconnected in any way, but may belong to the most diverse spheres of thought. The dream element truly represents all this disparate matter in the dream content. Analysis, moreover, discloses another side of the relationship between dream content and dream thoughts. Just as one element of the dream leads to associations with several dream thoughts, so, as a rule, the *one dream thought represents more than one dream element.* The threads of the association do not simply converge from the dream thoughts to the dream content, but on the way they overlap and interweave in every way.

Next to the transformation of one thought in the scene (its "dramatization"), condensation is the most important and most characteristic feature of the dream work. We have as yet no clue as to the motive calling for such compression of the content.

In the complicated and intricate dreams with which we are now concerned, condensation and dramatization do not wholly account for the difference between dream contents and dream thoughts. There is evidence of a third factor, which deserves careful consideration.

When I have arrived at an understanding of the dream thoughts by my analysis I notice, above all, that the matter of the manifest is very different from that of the latent dream content. That is, I admit, only an apparent difference which vanishes on closer investigation, for in the end I find the whole dream content carried out in the dream thoughts, nearly all the dream thoughts again represented in the dream content. Nevertheless, there does remain a certain amount of difference.

The essential content which stood out clearly and broadly in the dream must, after analysis, rest satisfied with a very subordinate rôle among the dream thoughts. These very dream thoughts which, going by my feelings, have a claim to the greatest importance are either not present at all in the dream content, or are represented by some remote allusion in some obscure region of the dream. I can thus describe these phenomena: *During the dream work the psychical intensity of those thoughts and conceptions to which it properly pertains flows to others which, in my judgment, have no claim to such emphasis.* There is no other process which contributes so much to concealment of the dream's meaning and to make the connection between the dream content and dream ideas irrecognizable. During this process, which I will call *the dream displacement,* I notice also the psychical intensity, significance, or emotional nature of the thoughts become transposed in sensory vividness. What was clearest in the dream seems to me, without further consideration, the most important; but often in some obscure element of the dream I can recognize the most direct offspring of the principal dream thought.

I could only designate this dream displacement as the *transvaluation of psychical values.* The phenomena will not have been considered in all its bearings unless I add that this displacement or transvaluation is shared by different dreams in extremely varying degrees. There are dreams which take place almost without any displacement. These have the same time, meaning, and intelligibility as we found in the dreams which recorded a desire. In other dreams not a bit of the dream idea has retained its own psychical value, or everything essential in these dream ideas has been replaced by unessentials, whilst every kind of transition between these conditions can be found. The more obscure and intricate a dream is, the greater is the part to be ascribed to the impetus of displacement in its formation.

The example that we chose for analysis shows, at least, this much of displacement—that its content has a different center of interest from that of the dream ideas. In the forefront of the dream content the main scene appears as if a woman wished to make advances to me; in the dream idea the chief interest rests on the desire to enjoy disinterested love which shall "cost nothing"; this idea lies at the back of the talk about the beautiful eyes and the far-fetched allusion to "spinach."

If we abolish the dream displacement, we attain through analysis quite certain conclusions regarding two problems of the dream which are most disputed—as to what provokes a dream at all, and as to the connection of the dream with our waking life. There are dreams which at once expose their links with the events of the day; in others no trace of such a connection can be found. By the aid of analysis it can be shown that every dream, without any exception, is linked up with our impression of the day, or perhaps it would be more correct to say of the day previous to the dream. The impressions which have incited the dream may be so important that we are not surprised at our being occupied with them whilst awake; in this case we are right in saying that the dream carries on the chief interest of our waking life. More usually, however, when the dream contains anything relating to the impressions of the day, it is so trivial, unimportant, and so deserving of oblivion, that we can only recall it with an effort. The dream content appears, then, even when coherent and intelligible, to be concerned with those indifferent trifles of thought undeserving of our waking interest. The depreciation of dreams is largely due to the predominance of the indifferent and the worthless in their content.

Analysis destroys the appearance upon which this derogatory judgment is based. When the dream content discloses nothing but some indifferent impression as instigating the dream, analysis ever indicates some significant event, which has been replaced by something indifferent with which it has entered into abundant associations. Where the dream is concerned with uninteresting and unimportant conceptions, analysis reveals the numerous associative paths which connect the trivial with the momentous in the psychical estimation of the individual. *It is only the action of displacement if what is indifferent obtains recognition in the dream content instead of those impressions which are really the stimulus, or instead of the things of real interest.* In answering the question as to what provokes the dream, as to the connection of the dream, in the daily troubles, we must say, in terms of the insight given us by replacing the manifest latent dream content: *The dream does never trouble itself about things which are not deserving of our concern during the day, and trivialities which do not trouble us during the day have no power to pursue us whilst asleep.*

What provoked the dream in the example which we have analyzed? The really unimportant event, that a friend invited me to a *free ride in his cab.* The table d'hôte scene in the dream contains an allusion to this indifferent motive, for in conversation I had brought the taxi parallel with the table d'hôte. But I can indicate the important event which has as its substitute the trivial one. A few days before I had disbursed a large sum of money for a member of my family who is very dear to me. Small wonder, says the dream thought, if this person is grateful to me for this—this love is not cost-free. But love that shall cost nothing is one of the prime thoughts of the dream. The fact that shortly before this I had had several *drives* with the relative in question puts the one drive with my friend in a position to recall the connection with the other person. The indifferent impression which, by such ramifications, provokes the dream is subservient to another condition which is not true of the real source of the dream—the impression must be a recent one, everything arising from the day of the dream.

I cannot leave the question of dream displacement without the consideration of a remarkable process in the formation of dreams in which condensation and displacement work together towards one end. In condensation we have already considered the case where two conceptions in the dream having something in common, some point of contact, are replaced in the dream content by a mixed image, where the distinct germ corresponds to what is common, and the indistinct secondary modifications to what is distinctive. If displacement is added to condensation, there is no formation of a mixed image, but a *common mean* which bears the same relationship to the individual elements as does the resultant in the parallelogram of forces to its components. In one of my dreams, for instance, there is talk of an injection with *propyl*. On first analysis I discovered an indifferent but true incident where *amyl* played a part as the excitant of the dream. I cannot yet vindicate the exchange of amyl for propyl. To the round of ideas of the same dream, however, there belongs the recollection of my first visit to Munich, when the *Propylœa* struck me. The attendant circumstances of the analysis render it admissible that the influence of this second group of conceptions caused the displacement of amyl to propyl. *Propyl* is, so to say, the mean idea between *amyl* and *propylœa*; it got into the dream as a kind of *compromise* by simultaneous condensation and displacement.

The need of discovering some motive for this bewildering work of the dream is even more called for in the case of displacement than in condensation.

Although the work of displacement must be held mainly responsible if the dream thoughts are not refound or recognized in the dream content (unless the motive of the changes be guessed), it is another and milder kind of transformation which will be considered with the dream thoughts which leads to the discovery of a new but readily understood act of the dream work. The first dream thoughts which are unravelled by analysis frequently strike one by their unusual wording. They do not appear to be expressed in the sober form which our thinking prefers; rather are they expressed symbolically by allegories and metaphors like the figurative language of the poets. It is not difficult to find the motives for this degree of constraint in the expression of dream ideas. The dream content consists chiefly of visual scenes; hence the dream ideas must, in the first place, be prepared to make use of these forms of presentation. Conceive that a political leader's or a barrister's address had to be transposed into pantomime, and it will be easy to understand the transformations to which the dream work is constrained by regard for this *dramatization of the dream content*.

Around the psychical stuff of dream thoughts there are ever found reminiscences of impressions, not infrequently of early childhood—scenes which, as a rule, have been visually grasped. Whenever possible, this portion of the dream ideas exercises a definite influence upon the modelling of the dream content; it works like a center of crystallization, by attracting and rearranging the stuff of the dream thoughts. The scene of the dream is not infrequently nothing but a modified repetition, complicated by interpolations of events that have left such an impression; the dream but very seldom reproduces accurate and unmixed reproductions of real scenes.

The dream content does not, however, consist exclusively of scenes, but it also includes scattered fragments of visual images, conversations, and even bits of unchanged thoughts. It will be perhaps to the point if we instance in the briefest way the means of dramatization which are at the disposal of the dream work for the repetition of the dream thoughts in the peculiar language of the dream.

The dream thoughts which we learn from the analysis exhibit themselves as a psychical complex of the most complicated superstructure. Their parts stand in the most diverse relationship to each other; they form backgrounds and foregrounds, stipulations, digressions, illustrations, demonstrations, and protestations. It may be said to be almost the rule that one train of thought is followed by its contradictory. No feature known to our reason whilst awake is absent. If a dream is to grow out of all this, the psychical matter is submitted to a pressure which condenses it extremely, to an inner shrinking and displacement, creating at the same time fresh surfaces, to a selective interweaving among the constituents best adapted for the construction of these scenes. Having regard to the origin of this stuff, the term *regression* can be fairly applied to this process. The logical chains which hitherto held the psychical stuff together become lost in this transformation to the dream content. The dream work takes on, as it were, only the essential content of the dream thoughts for elaboration. It is left to analysis to restore the connection which the dream work has destroyed.

The dream's means of expression must therefore be regarded as meager in comparison with those of our imagination, though the dream does not renounce all claims to the restitution of logical relation to the dream thoughts. It rather succeeds with tolerable frequency in replacing these by formal characters of its own.

By reason of the undoubted connection existing between all the parts of dream thoughts, the dream is able to embody this matter into a single scene. It upholds a *logical connection* as *approximation in time and space*, just as the painter, who groups all the poets for his picture of Parnassus who, though they have never been all together on a mountain peak, yet form ideally a community. The dream continues this method of presentation in individual dreams, and often when it displays two elements close together in the dream content it warrants some special inner connection between what they represent in the dream thoughts. It should be, moreover, observed that all the dreams of one night prove on analysis to originate from the same sphere of thought.

The causal connection between two ideas is either left without presentation, or replaced by two different long portions of dreams one after the other. This presentation is frequently a reversed one, the beginning of the dream being the deduction, and its end the hypothesis. The direct *transformation* of one thing into another in the dream seems to serve the relationship of *cause* and *effect*.

The dream never utters the *alternative "either-or,"* but accepts both as having equal rights in the same connection. When "either-or" is used in the reproduction of dreams, it is, as I have already mentioned, to be replaced by "*and.*"

Conceptions which stand in opposition to one another are preferably expressed in dreams by the same element.[181] There seems no "not" in dreams. Opposition between two ideas, the relation of conversion, is represented in dreams in a very remarkable way. It is expressed by the reversal of another part of the dream content just as if by way of appendix. We shall later on deal with another form of expressing disagreement. The common dream sensation of *movement checked* serves the purpose of representing disagreement of impulses—a *conflict of the will.*

Only one of the logical relationships—that of *similarity, identity, agreement*—is found highly developed in the mechanism of dream formation. Dream work makes use of these cases as a starting-point for condensation, drawing together everything which shows such agreement to a *fresh unity.*

These short, crude observations naturally do not suffice as an estimate of the abundance of the dream's formal means of presenting the logical relationships of the dream thoughts. In this respect, individual dreams are worked up more nicely or more carelessly, our text will have been followed more or less closely, auxiliaries of the dream work will have been taken more or less into consideration. In the latter case they appear obscure, intricate, incoherent. When the dream appears openly absurd, when it contains an obvious paradox in its content, it is so of purpose. Through its apparent disregard of all logical claims, it expresses a part of the intellectual content of

---

[181] It is worthy of remark that eminent philologists maintain that the oldest languages used the same word for expressing quite general antitheses. In C. Abel's essay, "Ueber den Gegensinn der Urworter" (1884, the following examples of such words in England are given: "gleam—gloom"; "to lock—loch"; "down—The Downs"; "to step—to stop." In his essay on "The Origin of Language" ("Linguistic Essays," p. 240), Abel says: "When the Englishman says 'without,' is not his judgment based upon the comparative juxtaposition of two opposites, 'with' and 'out'; 'with' itself originally meant 'without,' as may still be seen in 'withdraw.' 'Bid' includes the opposite sense of giving and of proffering." Abel, "The English Verbs of Command," "Linguistic Essays," p. 104; see also Freud, "Ueber den Gegensinn der Urworte"; *Jahrbuch für Psychoanalytische und Psychopathologische Forschungen*, Band II., part i., p. 179).— TRANSLATOR.

the dream ideas. Absurdity in the dream denotes *disagreement, scorn, disdain* in the dream thoughts. As this explanation is in entire disagreement with the view that the dream owes its origin to dissociated, uncritical cerebral activity, I will emphasize my view by an example:

"One of my acquaintances, Mr. M____, has been attacked by no less a person than Goethe in an essay with, we all maintain, unwarrantable violence. Mr. M____ has naturally been ruined by this attack. He complains very bitterly of this at a dinner-party, but his respect for Goethe has not diminished through this personal experience. I now attempt to clear up the chronological relations which strike me as improbable. Goethe died in 1832. As his attack upon Mr. M____ must, of course, have taken place before, Mr. M____ must have been then a very young man. It seems to me plausible that he was eighteen. I am not certain, however, what year we are actually in, and the whole calculation falls into obscurity. The attack was, moreover, contained in Goethe's well-known essay on 'Nature.'"

The absurdity of the dream becomes the more glaring when I state that Mr. M____ is a young business man without any poetical or literary interests. My analysis of the dream will show what method there is in this madness. The dream has derived its material from three sources:

1. Mr. M____, to whom I was introduced at a dinner-party, begged me one day to examine his elder brother, who showed signs of mental trouble. In conversation with the patient, an unpleasant episode occurred. Without the slightest occasion he disclosed one of his brother's *youthful escapades*. I had asked the patient the *year of his birth* (*year of death* in dream), and led him to various calculations which might show up his want of memory.

2. A medical journal which displayed my name among others on the cover had published a *ruinous* review of a book by my friend F____ of Berlin, from the pen of a very *juvenile* reviewer. I communicated with the editor, who, indeed, expressed his regret, but would not promise any redress. Thereupon I broke off my connection with the paper; in my letter of resignation I expressed the hope that our *personal relations would not suffer from this*. Here is the real source of the dream. The derogatory reception of my friend's work had made a deep impression upon me. In my judgment, it contained a fundamental biological discovery which only now, several years later, commences to find favor among the professors.

3. A little while before, a patient gave me the medical history of her brother, who, exclaiming *"Nature, Nature!"* had gone out of his mind. The doctors considered that the exclamation arose from a study of *Goethe's* beautiful essay, and indicated that the patient had been overworking. I expressed the opinion that it seemed more *plausible* to me that the exclamation "Nature!" was to be taken in that sexual meaning known also to the less educated in our country. It seemed to me that this view had

something in it, because the unfortunate youth afterwards mutilated his genital organs. The patient was eighteen years old when the attack occurred.

The first person in the dream-thoughts behind the ego was my friend who had been so scandalously treated. *"I now attempted to clear up the chronological relation."* My friend's book deals with the chronological relations of life, and, amongst other things, correlates *Goethe's* duration of life with a number of days in many ways important to biology. The ego is, however, represented as a general paralytic (*"I am not certain what year we are actually in"*). The dream exhibits my friend as behaving like a general paralytic, and thus riots in absurdity. But the dream thoughts run ironically. "Of course he is a madman, a fool, and you are the genius who understands all about it. But shouldn't it be the *other way round*?" This inversion obviously took place in the dream when Goethe attacked the young man, which is absurd, whilst any one, however young, can to-day easily attack the great Goethe.

I am prepared to maintain that no dream is inspired by other than egoistic emotions. The ego in the dream does not, indeed, represent only my friend, but stands for myself also. I identify myself with him because the fate of his discovery appears to me typical of the acceptance of *my own*. If I were to publish my own theory, which gives sexuality predominance in the ætiology of psychoneurotic disorders (see the allusion to the eighteen-year-old patient—*"Nature, Nature!"*), the same criticism would be leveled at me, and it would even now meet with the same contempt.

When I follow out the dream thoughts closely, I ever find only *scorn* and *contempt* as *correlated with the dream's absurdity*. It is well known that the discovery of a cracked sheep's skull on the Lido in Venice gave Goethe the hint for the so-called vertebral theory of the skull. My friend plumes himself on having as a student raised a hubbub for the resignation of an aged professor who had done good work (including some in this very subject of comparative anatomy), but who, on account of *decrepitude*, had become quite incapable of teaching. The agitation my friend inspired was so successful because in the German Universities an *age limit* is not demanded for academic work. *Age is no protection against folly.* In the hospital here I had for years the honor to serve under a chief who, long fossilized, was for decades notoriously *feebleminded*, and was yet permitted to continue in his responsible office. A trait, after the manner of the find in the Lido, forces itself upon me here. It was to this man that some youthful colleagues in the hospital adapted the then popular slang of that day: "No Goethe has written that," "No Schiller composed that," etc.

We have not exhausted our valuation of the dream work. In addition to condensation, displacement, and definite arrangement of the psychical matter, we must ascribe to it yet another activity—one which is, indeed, not shared by every dream. I shall not treat this position of the dream work exhaustively; I will only point out that the readiest way to arrive at a conception of it is to take for granted, probably unfairly, that it *only subsequently influences the dream content which has already been built up.* Its mode of action thus consists in so coördinating the parts of the dream that these coalesce to a coherent whole, to a dream composition. The dream gets a kind of façade which, it is true, does not conceal the whole of its content. There is a sort of preliminary explanation to be strengthened by interpolations and slight alterations. Such elaboration of the dream content must not be too pronounced; the misconception of the dream thoughts to which it gives rise is merely superficial, and our first piece of work in analyzing a dream is to get rid of these early attempts at interpretation.

The motives for this part of the dream work are easily gauged. This final elaboration of the dream is due to a *regard for intelligibility*—a fact at once betraying the origin of an action which behaves towards the actual dream content just as our normal psychical action behaves towards some proffered perception that is to our liking. The dream content is thus secured under the pretense of certain expectations, is perceptually classified by the supposition of its intelligibility, thereby risking its falsification, whilst, in fact, the most extraordinary misconceptions arise if the dream can be correlated with nothing familiar. Every one is aware that we are unable to look at any series of unfamiliar signs, or to listen to a discussion of unknown words, without at once making perpetual changes through *our regard for intelligibility,* through our falling back upon what is familiar.

We can call those dreams *properly made up* which are the result of an elaboration in every way analogous to the psychical action of our waking life. In other dreams there is no such action; not even an attempt is made to bring about order and meaning. We regard the dream as "quite mad," because on awaking it is with this last-named part of the dream work, the dream elaboration, that we identify ourselves. So far, however, as our analysis is concerned, the dream, which resembles a medley of disconnected fragments, is of as much value as the one with a smooth and beautifully polished surface. In the former case we are spared, to some extent, the trouble of breaking down the super-elaboration of the dream content.

All the same, it would be an error to see in the dream façade nothing but the misunderstood and somewhat arbitrary elaboration of the dream carried out at the instance of our psychical life. Wishes and phantasies are not infrequently employed in the erection of this façade, which were already fashioned in the dream thoughts; they are akin to those of our waking life— "day-dreams," as they are very properly called. These wishes and phantasies, which analysis discloses in our dreams at night, often present themselves as repetitions and refashionings of the scenes of infancy. Thus the dream façade may show us directly the true core of the dream, distorted through admixture with other matter.

Beyond these four activities there is nothing else to be discovered in the dream work. If we keep closely to the definition that dream work denotes the transference of dream thoughts to dream content, we are compelled to say that the dream work is not creative; it develops no fancies of its own, it judges nothing, decides nothing. It does nothing but prepare the matter for condensation and displacement, and refashions it for dramatization, to which must be added the inconstant last-named mechanism—that of explanatory elaboration. It is true that a good deal is found in the dream content which might be understood as the result of another and more intellectual performance; but analysis shows conclusively every time that these *intellectual operations were already present in the dream thoughts, and have only been taken over by the dream content.* A syllogism in the dream is nothing other than the repetition of a syllogism in the dream thoughts; it seems inoffensive if it has been transferred to the dream without alteration; it becomes absurd if in the dream work it has been transferred to other matter. A calculation in the dream content simply means that there was a calculation in the dream thoughts; whilst this is always correct, the calculation in the dream can furnish the silliest results by the condensation of its factors and the displacement of the same operations to other things. Even speeches which are found in the dream content are not new compositions; they prove to be pieced together out of speeches which have been made or heard or read; the words are faithfully copied, but the occasion of their utterance is quite overlooked, and their meaning is most violently changed.

It is, perhaps, not superfluous to support these assertions by examples: 1. *A seemingly inoffensive, well-made dream of a patient. She was going to market with her cook, who carried the basket. The butcher said to her when she asked him for something: "That is all gone," and wished to give her something else, remarking; "That's very good." She declines, and goes to the greengrocer, who wants to sell her a peculiar vegetable which is bound up in bundles and of a black color. She says: "I don't know that; I won't take it."*

The remark "That is all gone" arose from the treatment. A few days before I said myself to the patient that the earliest reminiscences of childhood *are all gone* as such, but are replaced by transferences and dreams. Thus I am the butcher.

The second remark, *"I don't know that"* arose in a very different connection. The day before she had herself called out in rebuke to the cook (who, moreover, also appears in the dream): *"Behave yourself properly*; I don't know*that"*—that is, "I don't know this kind of behavior; I won't have it."

The more harmless portion of this speech was arrived at by a displacement of the dream content; in the dream thoughts only the other portion of the speech played a part, because the dream work changed an imaginary situation into utter irrecognizability and complete inoffensiveness (while in a certain sense I behave in an unseemly way to the lady). The situation resulting in this phantasy is, however, nothing but a new edition of one that actually took place.

2. A dream apparently meaningless relates to figures. *"She wants to pay something; her daughter takes three florins sixty-five kreuzers out of her purse; but she says: 'What are you doing? It only cost twenty-one kreuzers.'"*

The dreamer was a stranger who had placed her child at school in Vienna, and who was able to continue under my treatment so long as her daughter remained at Vienna. The day before the dream the directress of the school had recommended her to keep the child another year at school. In this case she would have been able to prolong her treatment by one year. The figures in the dream become important if it be remembered that time is money. One year equals 365 days, or, expressed in kreuzers, 365 kreuzers, which is three florins sixty-five kreuzers. The twenty-one kreuzers correspond with the three weeks which remained from the day of the dream to the end of the school term, and thus to the end of the treatment. It was obviously financial considerations which had moved the lady to refuse the proposal of the directress, and which were answerable for the triviality of the amount in the dream.

3. A lady, young, but already ten years married, heard that a friend of hers, Miss Elise L____, of about the same age, had become engaged. This gave rise to the following dream: *She was sitting with her husband in the theater; the one side of the stalls was quite empty. Her husband tells her, Elise L____ and her fiancé had intended coming, but could only get some cheap seats, three for one florin fifty kreuzers, and these they would not take. In her opinion, that would not have mattered very much.*

The origin of the figures from the matter of the dream thoughts and the changes the figures underwent are of interest. Whence came the one florin fifty kreuzers? From a trifling occurrence of the previous day. Her sister-in-law had received 150 florins as a present from her husband, and had quickly got rid of it by buying some ornament. Note that 150 florins is one hundred times one florin fifty kreuzers. For the *three* concerned with the tickets, the only link is that Elise L____ is exactly three months younger than the dreamer. The scene in the dream is the repetition of a little adventure for which she has often been teased by her husband. She was once in a great hurry to get tickets in time for a piece, and when she came to the theater *one side of the stalls was almost empty*. It was therefore quite unnecessary for

550

her to have been in *such a hurry*. Nor must we overlook the absurdity of the dream that two persons should take three tickets for the theater.

Now for the dream ideas. It was *stupid* to have married so early; I *need not* have been *in so great a hurry*. Elise L_____'s example shows me that I should have been able to get a husband later; indeed, one a *hundred times better* if I had but waited. I could have bought *three* such men with the money (dowry).

III. WHY THE DREAM DISGUISES THE DESIRES

In the foregoing exposition we have now learnt something of the dream work; we must regard it as a quite special psychical process, which, so far as we are aware, resembles nothing else. To the dream work has been transferred that bewilderment which its product, the dream, has aroused in us. In truth, the dream work is only the first recognition of a group of psychical processes to which must be referred the origin of hysterical symptoms, the ideas of morbid dread, obsession, and illusion. Condensation, and especially displacement, are never-failing features in these other processes. The regard for appearance remains, on the other hand, peculiar to the dream work. If this explanation brings the dream into line with the formation of psychical disease, it becomes the more important to fathom the essential conditions of processes like dream building. It will be probably a surprise to hear that neither the state of sleep nor illness is among the indispensable conditions. A whole number of phenomena of the everyday life of healthy persons, forgetfulness, slips in speaking and in holding things, together with a certain class of mistakes, are due to a psychical mechanism analogous to that of the dream and the other members of this group.

Displacement is the core of the problem, and the most striking of all the dream performances. A thorough investigation of the subject shows that the essential condition of displacement is purely psychological; it is in the nature of a motive. We get on the track by thrashing out experiences which one cannot avoid in the analysis of dreams. I had to break off the relations of my dream thoughts in the analysis of my dream on p. 8 because I found some experiences which I do not wish strangers to know, and which I could not relate without serious damage to important considerations. I added, it would be no use were I to select another instead of that particular dream; in every dream where the content is obscure or intricate, I should hit upon dream thoughts which call for secrecy. If, however, I continue the analysis for myself, without regard to those others, for whom, indeed, so personal an event as my dream cannot matter, I arrive finally at ideas which surprise me, which I have not known to be mine, which not only appear *foreign* to me, but which are *unpleasant*, and which I would like to oppose vehemently, whilst the chain of ideas running through the analysis intrudes upon me inexorably. I can only take these circumstances into account by admitting that these thoughts are actually part of my psychical life, possessing a certain psychical intensity or energy. However, by virtue of a particular psychological condition, the *thoughts could not become conscious to me*. I call this particular condition "*Repression*." It is therefore impossible for me not to recognize some casual relationship between the obscurity of the dream content and this state of repression—this *incapacity of consciousness*. Whence I conclude that the cause of the obscurity is *the desire to conceal these thoughts*. Thus I arrive at the conception of the *dream distortion* as the deed of the dream work, and of *displacement* serving to disguise this object.

I will test this in my own dream, and ask myself, What is the thought which, quite innocuous in its distorted form, provokes my liveliest opposition in its real form? I remember that the free drive reminded me of the last expensive drive with a member of my family, the interpretation of the dream being: I should for once like to experience affection for which I should not have to pay, and that shortly before the dream I had to make a heavy disbursement for this very person. In this connection, I cannot get away from the thought *that I regret this disbursement*. It is only when I acknowledge this feeling that there is any sense in my wishing in the dream for an affection that should entail no outlay. And yet I can state on my honor that I did not hesitate for a moment when it became necessary to expend that sum. The regret, the counter-current, was unconscious to me. Why it was unconscious is quite another question which would lead us far away from the answer which, though within my knowledge, belongs elsewhere.

If I subject the dream of another person instead of one of my own to analysis, the result is the same; the motives for convincing others is, however, changed. In the dream of a healthy person the only way for me to enable him to accept this repressed idea is the coherence of the dream thoughts. He is at liberty to reject this explanation. But if we are dealing with a person suffering from any neurosis—say from hysteria—the recognition of these repressed ideas is compulsory by reason of their connection with the symptoms of his illness and of the improvement resulting from exchanging the symptoms for the repressed ideas. Take the patient from whom I got the last dream about the three tickets for one florin fifty kreuzers. Analysis shows that she does not think highly of her husband, that she regrets having married him, that she would be glad to change him for some one else. It is true that she maintains that she loves her husband, that her emotional life knows nothing about this depreciation (a hundred times better!), but all her symptoms lead to the same conclusion as this dream. When her repressed memories had rewakened a certain period when she was conscious that she did not love her husband, her symptoms disappeared, and therewith disappeared her resistance to the interpretation of the dream.

This conception of repression once fixed, together with the distortion of the dream in relation to repressed psychical matter, we are in a position to give a general exposition of the principal results which the analysis of dreams supplies. We learnt that the most intelligible and meaningful dreams are unrealized desires; the desires they pictured as realized are known to consciousness, have been held over from the daytime, and are of absorbing interest. The analysis of obscure and intricate dreams discloses something very similar; the dream scene again pictures as realized some desire which regularly proceeds from the dream ideas, but the picture is unrecognizable, and is only cleared up in the analysis. The desire itself is either one repressed, foreign to consciousness, or it is closely bound up with repressed ideas. The formula for these dreams may be thus stated: *They are concealed realizations of repressed desires*. It is interesting to note that they are right who regard the dream as foretelling the future. Although the future which the dream shows us is not that which will occur, but that which we would like to occur. Folk psychology proceeds here according to its wont; it believes what it wishes to believe.

Dreams can be divided into three classes according to their relation towards the realization of desire. Firstly come those which exhibit a *non-repressed, non-concealed desire*; these are dreams of the infantile type, becoming ever rarer among adults. Secondly, dreams which express in *veiled* form some *repressed desire*; these constitute by far the larger number of our dreams, and they require analysis for their understanding. Thirdly, these dreams where repression exists, but *without* or with but slight concealment. These dreams are invariably accompanied by a feeling of dread which brings the dream to an end. This feeling of dread here replaces dream displacement; I regarded the dream work as having prevented this in the dream of the second class. It is not very difficult to prove that what is now present as intense dread in the dream was once desire, and is now secondary to the repression.

There are also definite dreams with a painful content, without the presence of any anxiety in the dream. These cannot be reckoned among dreams of dread; they have, however, always been used to prove the unimportance and the psychical futility of dreams. An analysis of such an example will show that it belongs to our second class of dreams—a *perfectly concealed* realization of repressed desires. Analysis will demonstrate at the same time how excellently adapted is the work of displacement to the concealment of desires.

A girl dreamt that she saw lying dead before her the only surviving child of her sister amid the same surroundings as a few years before she saw the first child lying dead. She was not sensible of any pain, but naturally combatted the view that the scene represented a desire of hers. Nor was that view necessary. Years ago it was at the funeral of the child that she had last seen and spoken to the man she loved. Were the second child to die, she would be sure to meet this man again in her sister's house. She is longing to meet him, but struggles against this feeling. The day of the dream she had taken a ticket for a lecture, which announced the presence of the man she always loved. The dream is simply a dream of impatience common to those which happen before a journey, theater, or simply anticipated pleasures. The longing is concealed by the shifting of the scene to the occasion when any joyous feeling were out of place, and yet where it did once exist. Note, further, that the emotional behavior in the dream is adapted, not to the displaced, but to the real but suppressed dream ideas. The scene anticipates the long-hoped-for meeting; there is here no call for painful emotions.

There has hitherto been no occasion for philosophers to bestir themselves with a psychology of repression. We must be allowed to construct some clear conception as to the origin of dreams as the first steps in this unknown territory. The scheme which we have formulated not only from a study of dreams is, it is true, already somewhat complicated, but we cannot find any simpler one that will suffice. We hold that our psychical apparatus contains two procedures for the construction of thoughts. The second one has the advantage that its products find an open path to consciousness, whilst the activity of the first procedure is unknown to itself, and can only arrive at consciousness through the second one. At the borderland of these two procedures, where the first passes over into the second, a censorship is established which only passes what pleases it, keeping back everything else. That which is rejected by the censorship is, according to our definition, in a state of repression. Under certain conditions, one of which is the sleeping state, the balance of power between the two procedures is so changed that what is repressed can no longer be kept back. In the sleeping state this may possibly occur through the negligence of the censor; what has been hitherto repressed will now succeed in finding its way to consciousness. But as the censorship is never absent, but merely off guard, certain alterations must be conceded so as to placate it. It is a compromise which becomes conscious in this case—a compromise between what one procedure has in view and the demands of the other. *Repression, laxity of the censor, compromise*—this is the foundation for the origin of many another psychological process, just as it is for the dream. In such compromises we can observe the processes of condensation, of displacement, the acceptance of superficial associations, which we have found in the dream work.

It is not for us to deny the demonic element which has played a part in constructing our explanation of dream work. The impression left is that the formation of obscure dreams proceeds as if a person had something to say which must be agreeable for another person upon whom he is dependent to hear. It is by the use of this image that we figure to ourselves the conception of the *dream distortion* and of the censorship, and ventured to crystallize our impression in a rather crude, but at least definite, psychological theory. Whatever explanation the future may offer of these first and second procedures, we shall expect a confirmation of our correlate that the second procedure commands the entrance to consciousness, and can exclude the first from consciousness.

Once the sleeping state overcome, the censorship resumes complete sway, and is now able to revoke that which was granted in a moment of weakness. That the *forgetting* of dreams explains this in part, at least, we are convinced by our experience, confirmed again and again. During the relation of a dream, or during analysis of one, it not infrequently happens that some fragment of the dream is suddenly forgotten. This fragment so forgotten invariably contains the best and readiest approach to an understanding of the dream. Probably that is why it sinks into oblivion—*i.e.*, into a renewed suppression.

Viewing the dream content as the representation of a realized desire, and referring its vagueness to the changes made by the censor in the repressed matter, it is no longer difficult to grasp the function of dreams. In fundamental contrast with those saws which assume that sleep is disturbed by dreams, we hold the *dream as the guardian of sleep*. So far as children's dreams are concerned, our view should find ready acceptance.

The sleeping state or the psychical change to sleep, whatsoever it be, is brought about by the child being sent to sleep or compelled thereto by fatigue, only assisted by the removal of all stimuli which might open other objects to the psychical apparatus. The means which serve to keep external stimuli distant are known; but what are the means we can employ to depress the internal psychical stimuli which frustrate sleep? Look at a mother getting her child to sleep. The child is full of beseeching; he wants another kiss; he wants to play yet awhile. His requirements are in part met, in part drastically put off till the following day. Clearly these desires and needs, which agitate him, are hindrances to sleep. Every one knows the charming story of the bad boy (Baldwin Groller's) who awoke at night bellowing out, "*I want the rhinoceros.*" A really good boy, instead of bellowing, would have *dreamt* that he was playing with the rhinoceros. Because the dream which realizes his desire is believed during sleep, it removes the desire and makes sleep possible. It cannot be denied that this belief accords with the dream image, because it is arrayed in the psychical appearance of probability; the child is without the capacity which it will acquire later to distinguish hallucinations or phantasies from reality.

The adult has learnt this differentiation; he has also learnt the futility of desire, and by continuous practice manages to postpone his aspirations, until they can be granted in some roundabout method by a change in the external world. For this reason it is rare for him to have his wishes realized during sleep in the short psychical way. It is even possible that this never happens, and that everything which appears to us like a child's dream demands a much more elaborate explanation. Thus it is that for adults—for every sane person without exception—a differentiation of the psychical matter has been fashioned which the child knew not. A psychical procedure has been reached which, informed by the experience of life, exercises with jealous power a dominating and restraining influence upon psychical emotions; by its relation to consciousness, and by its spontaneous mobility, it is endowed with the greatest means of psychical power. A portion of the infantile emotions has been withheld from this procedure as useless to life, and all the thoughts which flow from these are found in the state of repression.

Whilst the procedure in which we recognize our normal ego reposes upon the desire for sleep, it appears compelled by the psycho-physiological conditions of sleep to abandon some of the energy with which it was wont during the day to keep down what was repressed. This neglect is really harmless; however much the emotions of the child's spirit may be stirred, they find the approach to consciousness rendered difficult, and that to movement blocked in consequence of the state of sleep. The danger of their disturbing sleep must, however, be avoided. Moreover, we must admit that even in deep sleep some amount of free attention is exerted as a protection against sense-stimuli which might, perchance, make an awakening seem wiser than the continuance of sleep. Otherwise we could not explain the fact of our being always awakened by stimuli of certain quality. As the old physiologist Burdach pointed out, the mother is awakened by the whimpering of her child, the miller by the cessation of his mill, most people by gently calling out their names. This attention, thus on the alert, makes use of the internal stimuli arising from repressed desires, and fuses them into the dream, which as a compromise satisfies both procedures at the same time. The dream creates a form of psychical release for the wish which is either suppressed or formed by the aid of repression, inasmuch as it presents it as realized. The other procedure is also satisfied, since the continuance of the sleep is assured. Our ego here gladly behaves like a child; it makes the dream pictures believable, saying, as it were, "Quite right, but let me sleep." The contempt which, once awakened, we bear the dream, and which rests upon the absurdity and apparent illogicality of the dream, is probably nothing but the reasoning of our sleeping ego on the feelings about what was repressed; with greater right it should rest upon the incompetency of this disturber of our sleep. In sleep we are now and then aware of this contempt; the dream content transcends the censorship rather too much, we think, "It's only a dream," and sleep on.

It is no objection to this view if there are borderlines for the dream where its function, to preserve sleep from interruption, can no longer be maintained—as in the dreams of impending dread. It is here changed for another function—to suspend the sleep at the proper time. It acts like a conscientious night-watchman, who first does his duty by quelling disturbances so as not to waken the citizen, but equally does his duty quite properly when he awakens the street should the causes of the trouble seem to him serious and himself unable to cope with them alone.

This function of dreams becomes especially well marked when there arises some incentive for the sense perception. That the senses aroused during sleep influence the dream is well known, and can be experimentally verified; it is one of the certain but much overestimated results of the medical investigation of dreams. Hitherto there has been an insoluble riddle connected with this discovery. The stimulus to the sense by which the investigator affects the sleeper is not properly recognized in the dream, but is intermingled with a number of indefinite interpretations, whose determination appears left to psychical free-will. There is, of course, no such psychical free-will. To an external sense-stimulus the sleeper can react in many ways. Either he awakens or he succeeds in sleeping on. In the latter case he can make use of the dream to dismiss the external stimulus, and this, again, in more ways than one. For instance, he can stay the stimulus by dreaming of a scene which is absolutely intolerable to him. This was the means used by one who was troubled by a painful perineal abscess. He dreamt that he was on horseback, and made use of the poultice, which was intended to alleviate his pain, as a saddle, and thus got away from the cause of the trouble. Or, as is more frequently the case, the external stimulus undergoes a new rendering, which leads him to connect it with a repressed desire seeking its realization, and robs him of its reality, and is treated as if it were a part of the psychical matter. Thus, some one dreamt that he had written a comedy which embodied a definite *motif*; it was being performed; the first act was over amid enthusiastic applause; there was great clapping. At this moment the dreamer must have succeeded in prolonging his sleep despite the disturbance, for when he woke he no longer heard the noise; he concluded rightly that some one must have been beating a carpet or bed. The dreams which come with a loud noise just before waking have all attempted to cover the stimulus to waking by some other explanation, and thus to prolong the sleep for a little while.

Whosoever has firmly accepted this *censorship* as the chief motive for the distortion of dreams will not be surprised to learn as the result of dream interpretation that most of the dreams of adults are traced by analysis to erotic desires. This assertion is not drawn from dreams obviously of a sexual nature, which are known to all dreamers from their own experience, and are the only ones usually described as "sexual dreams." These dreams are ever sufficiently mysterious by reason of the choice of persons who are made the objects of sex, the removal of all the barriers which cry halt to the dreamer's sexual needs in his waking state, the many strange reminders as to details of what are called perversions. But analysis discovers that, in many other dreams in whose manifest content nothing erotic can be found, the work of interpretation shows them up as, in reality, realization of sexual desires; whilst, on the other hand, that much of the thought-making when awake, the thoughts saved us as surplus from the day only, reaches presentation in dreams with the help of repressed erotic desires.

Towards the explanation of this statement, which is no theoretical postulate, it must be remembered that no other class of instincts has required so vast a suppression at the behest of civilization as the sexual, whilst their mastery by the highest psychical processes are in most persons soonest of all relinquished. Since we have learnt to understand *infantile sexuality*, often so vague in its expression, so invariably overlooked and misunderstood, we are justified in saying that nearly every civilized person has retained at some point or other the infantile type of sex life; thus we understand that repressed infantile sex desires furnish the most frequent and most powerful impulses for the formation of dreams.(Freud, "Three Contributions to Sexual Theory,")

If the dream, which is the expression of some erotic desire, succeeds in making its manifest content appear innocently asexual, it is only possible in one way. The matter of these sexual presentations cannot be exhibited as such, but must be replaced by allusions, suggestions, and similar indirect means; differing from other cases of indirect presentation, those used in dreams must be deprived of direct understanding. The means of presentation which answer these requirements are commonly termed "symbols." A special interest has been directed towards these, since it has been observed that the dreamers of the same language use the like symbols—indeed, that in certain cases community of symbol is greater than community of speech. Since the dreamers do not themselves know the meaning of the symbols they use, it remains a puzzle whence arises their relationship with what they replace and denote. The fact itself is undoubted, and becomes of importance for the technique of the interpretation of dreams, since by the aid of a knowledge of this symbolism it is possible to understand the meaning of the elements of a dream, or parts of a dream, occasionally even the whole dream itself, without having to question the dreamer as to his own ideas. We thus come near to the popular idea of an interpretation of dreams, and, on the other hand, possess again the technique of the ancients, among whom the interpretation of dreams was identical with their explanation through symbolism.

Though the study of dream symbolism is far removed from finality, we now possess a series of general statements and of particular observations which are quite certain. There are symbols which practically always have the same meaning: Emperor and Empress (King and Queen) always mean the parents; room, a woman, and so on. The sexes are represented by a great variety of symbols, many of which would be at first quite incomprehensible had not the clews to the meaning been often obtained through other channels.

There are symbols of universal circulation, found in all dreamers, of one range of speech and culture; there are others of the narrowest individual significance which an individual has built up out of his own material. In the first class those can be differentiated whose claim can be at once recognized by the replacement of sexual things in common speech (those, for instance, arising from agriculture, as reproduction, seed) from others whose sexual references appear to reach back to the earliest times and to the obscurest depths of our image-building. The power of building symbols in both these special forms of symbols has not died out. Recently discovered things, like the airship, are at once brought into universal use as sex symbols.

It would be quite an error to suppose that a profounder knowledge of dream symbolism (the "Language of Dreams") would make us independent of questioning the dreamer regarding his impressions about the dream, and would give us back the whole technique of ancient dream interpreters. Apart from individual symbols and the variations in the use of what is general, one never knows whether an element in the dream is to be understood symbolically or in its proper meaning; the whole content of the dream is certainly not to be interpreted symbolically. The knowledge of dream symbols will only help us in understanding portions of the dream content, and does not render the use of the technical rules previously given at all superfluous. But it must be of the greatest service in interpreting a dream just when the impressions of the dreamer are withheld or are insufficient.

Dream symbolism proves also indispensable for understanding the so-called "typical" dreams and the dreams that "repeat themselves." Dream symbolism leads us far beyond the dream; it does not belong only to dreams, but is likewise dominant in legend, myth, and saga, in wit and in folklore. It compels us to pursue the inner meaning of the dream in these productions. But we must acknowledge that symbolism is not a result of the dream work, but is a peculiarity probably of our unconscious thinking, which furnishes to the dream work the matter for condensation, displacement, and dramatization.

IV. DREAM ANALYSIS

Perhaps we shall now begin to suspect that dream interpretation is capable of giving us hints about the structure of our psychic apparatus which we have thus far expected in vain from philosophy. We shall not, however, follow this track, but return to our original problem as soon as we have cleared up the subject of dream-disfigurement. The question has arisen how dreams with disagreeable content can be analyzed as the fulfillment of wishes. We see now that this is possible in case dream-disfigurement has taken place, in case the disagreeable content serves only as a disguise for what is wished. Keeping in mind our assumptions in regard to the two psychic instances, we may now proceed to say: disagreeable dreams, as a matter of fact, contain something which is disagreeable to the second instance, but which at the same time fulfills a wish of the first instance. They are wish dreams in the sense that every dream originates in the first instance, while the second instance acts towards the dream only in repelling, not in a creative manner. If we limit ourselves to a consideration of what the second instance contributes to the dream, we can never understand the dream. If we do so, all the riddles which the authors have found in the dream remain unsolved.

That the dream actually has a secret meaning, which turns out to be the fulfillment of a wish, must be proved afresh for every case by means of an analysis. I therefore select several dreams which have painful contents and attempt an analysis of them. They are partly dreams of hysterical subjects, which require long preliminary statements, and now and then also an examination of the psychic processes which occur in hysteria. I cannot, however, avoid this added difficulty in the exposition.

When I give a psychoneurotic patient analytical treatment, dreams are always, as I have said, the subject of our discussion. It must, therefore, give him all the psychological explanations through whose aid I myself have come to an understanding of his symptoms, and here I undergo an unsparing criticism, which is perhaps not less keen than that I must expect from my colleagues. Contradiction of the thesis that all dreams are the fulfillments of wishes is raised by my patients with perfect regularity. Here are several examples of the dream material which is offered me to refute this position.

"You always tell me that the dream is a wish fulfilled," begins a clever lady patient. "Now I shall tell you a dream in which the content is quite the opposite, in which a wish of mine is *not* fulfilled. How do you reconcile that with your theory? The dream is as follows: *I want to give a supper, but having nothing at hand except some smoked salmon, I think of going marketing, but I remember that it is Sunday afternoon, when all the shops are closed. I next try to telephone to some caterers, but the telephone is out of order.... Thus I must resign my wish to give a supper.*"

I answer, of course, that only the analysis can decide the meaning of this dream, although I admit that at first sight it seems sensible and coherent, and looks like the opposite of a wish-fulfillment. "But what occurrence has given rise to this dream?" I ask. "You know that the stimulus for a dream always lies among the experiences of the preceding day."

Analysis.—The husband of the patient, an upright and conscientious wholesale butcher, had told her the day before that he is growing too fat, and that he must, therefore, begin treatment for obesity. He was going to get up early, take exercise, keep to a strict diet, and above all accept no more invitations to suppers. She proceeds laughingly to relate how her husband at an inn table had made the acquaintance of an artist, who insisted upon painting his portrait because he, the painter, had never found such an expressive head. But her husband had answered in his rough way, that he was very thankful for the honor, but that he was quite convinced that a portion of the backside of a pretty young girl would please the artist better than his whole face[182]. She said that she was at the time very much in love with her husband, and teased him a good deal. She had also asked him not to send her any caviare. What does that mean?

As a matter of fact, she had wanted for a long time to eat a caviare sandwich every forenoon, but had grudged herself the expense. Of course, she would at once get the caviare from her husband, as soon as she asked him for it. But she had begged him, on the contrary, not to send her the caviare, in order that she might tease him about it longer.

This explanation seems far-fetched to me. Unadmitted motives are in the habit of hiding behind such unsatisfactory explanations. We are reminded of subjects hypnotized by Bernheim, who carried out a posthypnotic order, and who, upon being asked for their motives, instead of answering: "I do not know why I did that," had to invent a reason that was obviously inadequate. Something similar is probably the case with the caviare of my patient. I see that she is compelled to create an unfulfilled wish in life. Her dream also shows the reproduction of the wish as accomplished. But why does she need an unfulfilled wish?

The ideas so far produced are insufficient for the interpretation of the dream. I beg for more. After a short pause, which corresponds to the overcoming of a resistance, she reports further that the day before she had made a visit to a friend, of whom she is really jealous, because her husband is always praising this woman so much. Fortunately, this friend is very lean and thin, and her husband likes well-rounded figures. Now of what did this lean friend speak? Naturally of her wish to become somewhat stouter. She

---

[182] To sit for the painter. Goethe: "And if he has no backside, how can the nobleman sit?"

also asked my patient: "When are you going to invite us again? You always have such a good table."

Now the meaning of the dream is clear. I may say to the patient: "It is just as though you had thought at the time of the request: 'Of course, I'll invite you, so you can eat yourself fat at my house and become still more pleasing to my husband. I would rather give no more suppers.' The dream then tells you that you cannot give a supper, thereby fulfilling your wish not to contribute anything to the rounding out of your friend's figure. The resolution of your husband to refuse invitations to supper for the sake of getting thin teaches you that one grows fat on the things served in company." Now only some conversation is necessary to confirm the solution. The smoked salmon in the dream has not yet been traced. "How did the salmon mentioned in the dream occur to you?" "Smoked salmon is the favorite dish of this friend," she answered. I happen to know the lady, and may corroborate this by saying that she grudges herself the salmon just as much as my patient grudges herself the caviare.

The dream admits of still another and more exact interpretation, which is necessitated only by a subordinate circumstance. The two interpretations do not contradict one another, but rather cover each other and furnish a neat example of the usual ambiguity of dreams as well as of all other psychopathological formations. We have seen that at the same time that she dreams of the denial of the wish, the patient is in reality occupied in securing an unfulfilled wish (the caviare sandwiches). Her friend, too, had expressed a wish, namely, to get fatter, and it would not surprise us if our lady had dreamt that the wish of the friend was not being fulfilled. For it is her own wish that a wish of her friend's—for increase in weight—should not be fulfilled. Instead of this, however, she dreams that one of her own wishes is not fulfilled. The dream becomes capable of a new interpretation, if in the dream she does not intend herself, but her friend, if she has put herself in the place of her friend, or, as we may say, has identified herself with her friend.

I think she has actually done this, and as a sign of this identification she has created an unfulfilled wish in reality. But what is the meaning of this hysterical identification? To clear this up a thorough exposition is necessary. Identification is a highly important factor in the mechanism of hysterical symptoms; by this means patients are enabled in their symptoms to represent not merely their own experiences, but the experiences of a great number of other persons, and can suffer, as it were, for a whole mass of people, and fill all the parts of a drama by means of their own personalities alone. It will here be objected that this is well-known hysterical imitation, the ability of hysteric subjects to copy all the symptoms which impress them when they occur in others, as though their pity were stimulated to the point of reproduction. But this only indicates the way in which the psychic process is discharged in hysterical imitation; the way in which a psychic act proceeds and the act itself are two different things. The latter is slightly more complicated than one is apt to imagine the imitation of hysterical subjects to be: it corresponds to an unconscious concluded process, as an example will show. The physician who has a female patient with a particular kind of twitching, lodged in the company of other patients in the same room of the hospital, is not surprised when some morning he learns that this peculiar hysterical attack has found imitations. He simply says to himself: The others have seen her and have done likewise: that is psychic infection. Yes, but psychic infection proceeds in somewhat the following manner: As a rule, patients know more about one another than the physician knows about each of them, and they are concerned about each other when the visit of the doctor is over. Some of them have an attack to-day: soon it is known among the rest that a letter from home, a return of lovesickness or the like, is the cause of it. Their sympathy is aroused, and the following syllogism, which does not reach consciousness, is completed in them: "If it is possible to have this kind of an attack from such causes, I too may have this kind of an attack, for I have the same reasons." If this were a cycle capable of becoming conscious, it would perhaps express itself in *fear* of getting the same attack; but it takes place in another psychic sphere, and, therefore, ends in the realization of the dreaded symptom. Identification is therefore not a simple imitation, but a sympathy based upon the same etiological claim; it expresses an "as though," and refers to some common quality which has remained in the unconscious.

Identification is most often used in hysteria to express sexual community. An hysterical woman identifies herself most readily—although not exclusively—with persons with whom she has had sexual relations, or who have sexual intercourse with the same persons as herself. Language takes such a conception into consideration: two lovers are "one." In the hysterical phantasy, as well as in the dream, it is sufficient for the identification if one thinks of sexual relations, whether or not they become real. The patient, then, only follows the rules of the hysterical thought processes when she gives expression to her jealousy of her friend (which, moreover, she herself admits to be unjustified, in that she puts herself in her place and identifies herself with her by creating a symptom—the denied wish). I might further clarify the process specifically as follows: She puts herself in the place of her friend in the dream, because her friend has taken her own place relation to her husband, and because she would like to take her friend's place in the esteem of her husband.[183]

---

[183] I myself regret the introduction of such passages from the psychopathology of hysteria, which, because of their fragmentary representation and of being torn from all connection with the subject, cannot have a very enlightening influence. If these passages are capable of throwing

The contradiction to my theory of dreams in the case of another female patient, the most witty among all my dreamers, was solved in a simpler manner, although according to the scheme that the non-fulfillment of one wish signifies the fulfillment of another. I had one day explained to her that the dream is a wish of fulfillment. The next day she brought me a dream to the effect that she was traveling with her mother-in-law to their common summer resort. Now I knew that she had struggled violently against spending the summer in the neighborhood of her mother-in-law. I also knew that she had luckily avoided her mother-in-law by renting an estate in a far-distant country resort. Now the dream reversed this wished-for solution; was not this in the flattest contradiction to my theory of wish-fulfillment in the dream? Certainly, it was only necessary to draw the inferences from this dream in order to get at its interpretation. According to this dream, I was in the wrong. *It was thus her wish that I should be in the wrong, and this wish the dream showed her as fulfilled.* But the wish that I should be in the wrong, which was fulfilled in the theme of the country home, referred to a more serious matter. At that time I had made up my mind, from the material furnished by her analysis, that something of significance for her illness must have occurred at a certain time in her life. She had denied it because it was not present in her memory. We soon came to see that I was in the right. Her wish that I should be in the wrong, which is transformed into the dream, thus corresponded to the justifiable wish that those things, which at the time had only been suspected, had never occurred at all.

Without an analysis, and merely by means of an assumption, I took the liberty of interpreting a little occurrence in the case of a friend, who had been my colleague through the eight classes of the Gymnasium. He once heard a lecture of mine delivered to a small assemblage, on the novel subject of the dream as the fulfillment of a wish. He went home, dreamt *that he had lost all his suits*—he was a lawyer—and then complained to me about it. I took refuge in the evasion: "One can't win all one's suits," but I thought to myself: "If for eight years I sat as Primus on the first bench, while he moved around somewhere in the middle of the class, may he not naturally have had a wish from his boyhood days that I, too, might for once completely disgrace myself?"

In the same way another dream of a more gloomy character was offered me by a female patient as a contradiction to my theory of the wish-dream. The patient, a young girl, began as follows: "You remember that my sister has now only one boy, Charles: she lost the elder one, Otto, while I was still at her house. Otto was my favorite; it was I who really brought him up. I like the other little fellow, too, but of course not nearly as much as the dead one. Now

---

light upon the intimate relations between the dream and the psychoneuroses, they have served the purpose for which I have taken them up.

I dreamt last night that *I saw Charles lying dead before me. He was lying in his little coffin, his hands folded: there were candles all about, and, in short, it was just like the time of little Otto's death, which shocked me so profoundly.* Now tell me, what does this mean? You know me: am I really bad enough to wish my sister to lose the only child she has left? Or does the dream mean that I wish Charles to be dead rather than Otto, whom I like so much better?"

I assured her that this interpretation was impossible. After some reflection I was able to give her the interpretation of the dream, which I subsequently made her confirm.

Having become an orphan at an early age, the girl had been brought up in the house of a much older sister, and had met among the friends and visitors who came to the house, a man who made a lasting impression upon her heart. It looked for a time as though these barely expressed relations were to end in marriage, but this happy culmination was frustrated by the sister, whose motives have never found a complete explanation. After the break, the man who was loved by our patient avoided the house: she herself became independent some time after little Otto's death, to whom her affection had now turned. But she did not succeed in freeing herself from the inclination for her sister's friend in which she had become involved. Her pride commanded her to avoid him; but it was impossible for her to transfer her love to the other suitors who presented themselves in order. Whenever the man whom she loved, who was a member of the literary profession, announced a lecture anywhere, she was sure to be found in the audience; she also seized every other opportunity to see him from a distance unobserved by him. I remembered that on the day before she had told me that the Professor was going to a certain concert, and that she was also going there, in order to enjoy the sight of him. This was on the day of the dream; and the concert was to take place on the day on which she told me the dream. I could now easily see the correct interpretation, and I asked her whether she could think of any event which had happened after the death of little Otto. She answered immediately: "Certainly; at that time the Professor returned after a long absence, and I saw him once more beside the coffin of little Otto." It was exactly as I had expected. I interpreted the dream in the following manner: "If now the other boy were to die, the same thing would be repeated. You would spend the day with your sister, the Professor would surely come in order to offer condolence, and you would see him again under the same circumstances as at that time. The dream signifies nothing but this wish of yours to see him again, against which you are fighting inwardly. I know that you are carrying the ticket for to-day's concert in your bag. Your dream is a dream of impatience; it has anticipated the meeting which is to take place to-day by several hours."

In order to disguise her wish she had obviously selected a situation in which wishes of that sort are commonly suppressed—a situation which is so filled with sorrow that love is not thought of. And yet, it is very easily probable that even in the actual situation at the bier of the second, more dearly loved boy, which the dream copied faithfully, she had not been able to suppress her feelings of affection for the visitor whom she had missed for so long a time.

A different explanation was found in the case of a similar dream of another female patient, who was distinguished in her earlier years by her quick wit and her cheerful demeanors and who still showed these qualities at least in the notion, which occurred to her in the course of treatment. In connection with a longer dream, it seemed to this lady that she saw her fifteen-year-old daughter lying dead before her in a box. She was strongly inclined to convert this dream-image into an objection to the theory of wish-fulfillment, but herself suspected that the detail of the box must lead to a different conception of the dream.[184] In the course of the analysis it occurred to her that on the evening before, the conversation of the company had turned upon the English word "box," and upon the numerous translations of it into German, such as box, theater box, chest, box on the ear, &c. From other components of the same dream it is now possible to add that the lady had guessed the relationship between the English word "box" and the German *Büchse*, and had then been haunted by the memory that *Büchse* (as well as "box") is used in vulgar speech to designate the female genital organ. It was therefore possible, making a certain allowance for her notions on the subject of topographical anatomy, to assume that the child in the box signified a child in the womb of the mother. At this stage of the explanation she no longer denied that the picture of the dream really corresponded to one of her wishes. Like so many other young women, she was by no means happy when she became pregnant, and admitted to me more than once the wish that her child might die before its birth; in a fit of anger following a violent scene with her husband she had even struck her abdomen with her fists in order to hit the child within. The dead child was, therefore, really the fulfillment of a wish, but a wish which had been put aside for fifteen years, and it is not surprising that the fulfillment of the wish was no longer recognized after so long an interval. For there had been many changes meanwhile.

The group of dreams to which the two last mentioned belong, having as content the death of beloved relatives, will be considered again under the head of "Typical Dreams." I shall there be able to show by new examples that in spite of their undesirable content, all these dreams must be interpreted as wish-fulfillments. For the following dream, which again was told me in order to deter me from a hasty generalization of the theory of wishing in dreams, I am indebted, not to a patient, but to an intelligent jurist of my acquaintance.

---

[184] Something like the smoked salmon in the dream of the deferred supper.

"*I dream,*" my informant tells me, "*that I am walking in front of my house with a lady on my arm. Here a closed wagon is waiting, a gentleman steps up to me, gives his authority as an agent of the police, and demands that I should follow him. I only ask for time in which to arrange my affairs.* Can you possibly suppose this is a wish of mine to be arrested?" "Of course not," I must admit. "Do you happen to know upon what charge you were arrested?" "Yes; I believe for infanticide." "Infanticide? But you know that only a mother can commit this crime upon her newly born child?" "That is true."[185] "And under what circumstances did you dream; what happened on the evening before?" "I would rather not tell you that; it is a delicate matter." "But I must have it, otherwise we must forgo the interpretation of the dream." "Well, then, I will tell you. I spent the night, not at home, but at the house of a lady who means very much to me. When we awoke in the morning, something again passed between us. Then I went to sleep again, and dreamt what I have told you." "The woman is married?" "Yes." "And you do not wish her to conceive a child?" "No; that might betray us." "Then you do not practice normal coitus?" "I take the precaution to withdraw before ejaculation." "Am I permitted to assume that you did this trick several times during the night, and that in the morning you were not quite sure whether you had succeeded?" "That might be the case." "Then your dream is the fulfillment of a wish. By means of it you secure the assurance that you have not begotten a child, or, what amounts to the same thing, that you have killed a child. I can easily demonstrate the connecting links. Do you remember, a few days ago we were talking about the distress of matrimony (Ehenot), and about the inconsistency of permitting the practice of coitus as long as no impregnation takes place, while every delinquency after the ovum and the semen meet and a fœtus is formed is punished as a crime? In connection with this, we also recalled the mediæval controversy about the moment of time at which the soul is really lodged in the fœtus, since the concept of murder becomes admissible only from that point on. Doubtless you also know the gruesome poem by Lenau, which puts infanticide and the prevention of children on the same plane." "Strangely enough, I had happened to think of Lenau during the afternoon." "Another echo of your dream. And now I shall demonstrate to you another subordinate wish-fulfillment in your dream. You walk in front of your house with the lady on your arm. So you take her home, instead of spending the night at her house, as you do in actuality. The fact that the wish-fulfillment, which is the essence of the dream, disguises itself in such an unpleasant form, has perhaps more than one reason. From my essay on the etiology of anxiety neuroses, you will see that I note interrupted coitus as one

---

[185] It often happens that a dream is told incompletely, and that a recollection of the omitted portions appear only in the course of the analysis. These portions subsequently fitted in, regularly furnish the key to the interpretation. *Cf.* below, about forgetting in dreams.

of the factors which cause the development of neurotic fear. It would be consistent with this that if after repeated cohabitation of the kind mentioned you should be left in an uncomfortable mood, which now becomes an element in the composition of your dream. You also make use of this unpleasant state of mind to conceal the wish-fulfillment. Furthermore, the mention of infanticide has not yet been explained. Why does this crime, which is peculiar to females, occur to you?" "I shall confess to you that I was involved in such an affair years ago. Through my fault a girl tried to protect herself from the consequences of a *liaison* with me by securing an abortion. I had nothing to do with carrying out the plan, but I was naturally for a long time worried lest the affair might be discovered." "I understand; this recollection furnished a second reason why the supposition that you had done your trick badly must have been painful to you."

A young physician, who had heard this dream of my colleague when it was told, must have felt implicated by it, for he hastened to imitate it in a dream of his own, applying its mode of thinking to another subject. The day before he had handed in a declaration of his income, which was perfectly honest, because he had little to declare. He dreamt that an acquaintance of his came from a meeting of the tax commission and informed him that all the other declarations of income had passed uncontested, but that his own had awakened general suspicion, and that he would be punished with a heavy fine. The dream is a poorly-concealed fulfillment of the wish to be known as a physician with a large income. It likewise recalls the story of the young girl who was advised against accepting her suitor because he was a man of quick temper who would surely treat her to blows after they were married.

The answer of the girl was: "I wish he *would* strike me!" Her wish to be married is so strong that she takes into the bargain the discomfort which is said to be connected with matrimony, and which is predicted for her, and even raises it to a wish.

If I group the very frequently occurring dreams of this sort, which seem flatly to contradict my theory, in that they contain the denial of a wish or some occurrence decidedly unwished for, under the head of "counter wish-dreams," I observe that they may all be referred to two principles, of which one has not yet been mentioned, although it plays a large part in the dreams of human beings. One of the motives inspiring these dreams is the wish that I should appear in the wrong. These dreams regularly occur in the course of my treatment if the patient shows a resistance against me, and I can count with a large degree of certainty upon causing such a dream after I have once explained to the patient my theory that the dream is a wish-fulfillment.[186] I may even expect this to be the case in a dream merely in order to fulfill the wish that I may appear in the wrong. The last dream which I shall tell from those occurring in the course of treatment again shows this very thing. A young girl who has struggled hard to continue my treatment, against the will of her relatives and the authorities whom she had consulted, dreams as follows: *She is forbidden at home to come to me any more. She then reminds me of the promise I made her to treat her for nothing if necessary, and I say to her: "I can show no consideration in money matters."*

It is not at all easy in this case to demonstrate the fulfillment of a wish, but in all cases of this kind there is a second problem, the solution of which helps also to solve the first. Where does she get the words which she puts into my mouth? Of course I have never told her anything like that, but one of her brothers, the very one who has the greatest influence over her, has been kind enough to make this remark about me. It is then the purpose of the dream that this brother should remain in the right; and she does not try to justify this brother merely in the dream; it is her purpose in life and the motive for her being ill.

The other motive for counter wish-dreams is so clear that there is danger of overlooking it, as for some time happened in my own case. In the sexual make-up of many people there is a masochistic component, which has arisen through the conversion of the aggressive, sadistic component into its opposite. Such people are called "ideal" masochists, if they seek pleasure not in the bodily pain which may be inflicted upon them, but in humiliation and in chastisement of the soul. It is obvious that such persons can have counter wish-dreams and disagreeable dreams, which, however, for them are nothing but wish-fulfillment, affording satisfaction for their masochistic inclinations. Here is such a dream. A young man, who has in earlier years tormented his elder brother, towards whom he was homosexually inclined, but who had undergone a complete change of character, has the following dream, which consists of three parts: (1) *He is "insulted" by his brother.* (2) *Two adults are caressing each other with homosexual intentions.* (3) *His brother has sold the enterprise whose management the young man reserved for his own future.* He awakens from the last-mentioned dream with the most unpleasant feelings, and yet it is a masochistic wish-dream, which might be translated: It would serve me quite right if my brother were to make that sale against my interest, as a punishment for all the torments which he has suffered at my hands.

I hope that the above discussion and examples will suffice—until further objection can be raised—to make it seem credible that even dreams with a

---

painful content are to be analyzed as the fulfillments of wishes. Nor will it seem a matter of chance that in the course of interpretation one always happens upon subjects of which one does not like to speak or think. The disagreeable sensation which such dreams arouse is simply identical with the antipathy which endeavors—usually with success—to restrain us from the treatment or discussion of such subjects, and which must be overcome by all of us, if, in spite of its unpleasantness, we find it necessary to take the matter in hand. But this disagreeable sensation, which occurs also in dreams, does not preclude the existence of a wish; every one has wishes which he would not like to tell to others, which he does not want to admit even to himself. We are, on other grounds, justified in connecting the disagreeable character of all these dreams with the fact of dream disfigurement, and in concluding that these dreams are distorted, and that the wish-fulfillment in them is disguised until recognition is impossible for no other reason than that a repugnance, a will to suppress, exists in relation to the subject-matter of the dream or in relation to the wish which the dream creates. Dream disfigurement, then, turns out in reality to be an act of the censor. We shall take into consideration everything which the analysis of disagreeable dreams has brought to light if we reword our formula as follows: *The dream is the (disguised) fulfillment of a (suppressed, repressed) wish.*

Now there still remain as a particular species of dreams with painful content, dreams of anxiety, the inclusion of which under dreams of wishing will find least acceptance with the uninitiated. But I can settle the problem of anxiety dreams in very short order; for what they may reveal is not a new aspect of the dream problem; it is a question in their case of understanding neurotic anxiety in general. The fear which we experience in the dream is only seemingly explained by the dream content. If we subject the content of the dream to analysis, we become aware that the dream fear is no more justified by the dream content than the fear in a phobia is justified by the idea upon which the phobia depends. For example, it is true that it is possible to fall out of a window, and that some care must be exercised when one is near a window, but it is inexplicable why the anxiety in the corresponding phobia is so great, and why it follows its victims toan extent so much greater than is warranted by its origin. The same explanation, then, which applies to the phobia applies also to the dream of anxiety. In both cases the anxiety is only superficially attached to the idea which accompanies it and comes from another source.

On account of the intimate relation of dream fear to neurotic fear, discussion of the former obliges me to refer to the latter. In a little essay on "The Anxiety Neurosis,"[187] I maintained that neurotic fear has its origin in the

---

[187] 6: See *Selected Papers on Hysteria and other Psychoneuroses*, p. 133, translated by A.A. Brill, *Journal of Nervous and Mental Diseases*, Monograph Series.

sexual life, and corresponds to a libido which has been turned away from its object and has not succeeded in being applied. From this formula, which has since proved its validity more and more clearly, we may deduce the conclusion that the content of anxiety dreams is of a sexual nature, the libido belonging to which content has been transformed into fear.

V. SEX IN DREAMS

The more one is occupied with the solution of dreams, the more willing one must become to acknowledge that the majority of the dreams of adults treat of sexual material and give expression to erotic wishes. Only one who really analyzes dreams, that is to say, who pushes forward from their manifest content to the latent dream thoughts, can form an opinion on this subject— never the person who is satisfied with registering the manifest content (as, for example, Näcke in his works on sexual dreams). Let us recognize at once that this fact is not to be wondered at, but that it is in complete harmony with the fundamental assumptions of dream explanation. No other impulse has had to undergo so much suppression from the time of childhood as the sex impulse in its numerous components, from no other impulse have survived so many and such intense unconscious wishes, which now act in the sleeping state in such a manner as to produce dreams. In dream interpretation, this significance of sexual complexes must never be forgotten, nor must they, of course, be exaggerated to the point of being considered exclusive.

Of many dreams it can be ascertained by a careful interpretation that they are even to be taken bisexually, inasmuch as they result in an irrefutable secondary interpretation in which they realize homosexual feelings—that is, feelings that are common to the normal sexual activity of the dreaming person. But that all dreams are to be interpreted bisexually, seems to me to be a generalization as indemonstrable as it is improbable, which I should not like to support. Above all I should not know how to dispose of the apparent fact that there are many dreams satisfying other than—in the widest sense— erotic needs, as dreams of hunger, thirst, convenience, &c. Likewise the similar assertions "that behind every dream one finds the death sentence" (Stekel), and that every dream shows "a continuation from the feminine to the masculine line" (Adler), seem to me to proceed far beyond what is admissible in the interpretation of dreams.

We have already asserted elsewhere that dreams which are conspicuously innocent invariably embody coarse erotic wishes, and we might confirm this by means of numerous fresh examples. But many dreams which appear indifferent, and which would never be suspected of any particular significance, can be traced back, after analysis, to unmistakably sexual wish-feelings, which are often of an unexpected nature. For example, who would suspect a sexual wish in the following dream until the interpretation had been worked out? The dreamer relates: *Between two stately palaces stands a little house, receding somewhat, whose doors are closed. My wife leads me a little way along the street up to the little house, and pushes in the door, and then I slip quickly and easily into the interior of a courtyard that slants obliquely upwards.*

Any one who has had experience in the translating of dreams will, of course, immediately perceive that penetrating into narrow spaces, and opening locked doors, belong to the commonest sexual symbolism, and will easily find in this dream a representation of attempted coition from behind (between the two stately buttocks of the female body). The narrow slanting passage is of course the vagina; the assistance attributed to the wife of the dreamer requires the interpretation that in reality it is only consideration for the wife which is responsible for the detention from such an attempt. Moreover, inquiry shows that on the previous day a young girl had entered the household of the dreamer who had pleased him, and who had given him the impression that she would not be altogether opposed to an approach of this sort. The little house between the two palaces is taken from a reminiscence of the Hradschin in Prague, and thus points again to the girl who is a native of that city.

If with my patients I emphasize the frequency of the Oedipus dream—of having sexual intercourse with one's mother—I get the answer: "I cannot remember such a dream." Immediately afterwards, however, there arises the recollection of another disguised and indifferent dream, which has been dreamed repeatedly by the patient, and the analysis shows it to be a dream of this same content—that is, another Oedipus dream. I can assure the reader that veiled dreams of sexual intercourse with the mother are a great deal more frequent than open ones to the same effect.

There are dreams about landscapes and localities in which emphasis is always laid upon the assurance: "I have been there before." In this case the locality is always the genital organ of the mother; it can indeed be asserted with such certainty of no other locality that one "has been there before."

A large number of dreams, often full of fear, which are concerned with passing through narrow spaces or with staying, in the water, are based upon fancies about the embryonic life, about the sojourn in the mother's womb, and about the act of birth. The following is the dream of a young man who in his fancy has already while in embryo taken advantage of his opportunity to spy upon an act of coition between his parents.

"He is in a deep shaft, in which there is a window, as in the Semmering Tunnel. At first he sees an empty landscape through this window, and then he composes a picture into it, which is immediately at hand and which fills

572

out the empty space. *The picture represents a field which is being thoroughly harrowed by an implement, and the delightful air, the accompanying idea of hard work, and the bluish-black clods of earth make a pleasant impression. He then goes on and sees a primary school opened ... and he is surprised that so much attention is devoted in it to the sexual feelings of the child, which makes him think of me.*"

Here is a pretty water-dream of a female patient, which was turned to extraordinary account in the course of treatment.

At her summer resort at the ... Lake, she hurls herself into the dark water at a place where the pale moon is reflected in the water.

Dreams of this sort are parturition dreams; their interpretation is accomplished by reversing the fact reported in the manifest dream content; thus, instead of "throwing one's self into the water," read "coming out of the water," that is, "being born." The place from which one is born is recognized if one thinks of the bad sense of the French "la lune." The pale moon thus becomes the white "bottom" (Popo), which the child soon recognizes as the place from which it came. Now what can be the meaning of the patient's wishing to be born at her summer resort? I asked the dreamer this, and she answered without hesitation: "Hasn't the treatment made me as though I were born again?" Thus the dream becomes an invitation to continue the cure at this summer resort, that is, to visit her there; perhaps it also contains a very bashful allusion to the wish to become a mother herself.[188]

Another dream of parturition, with its interpretation, I take from the work of E. Jones. "*She stood at the seashore watching a small boy, who seemed to be hers, wading into the water. This he did till the water covered him, and she could only see his head bobbing up and down near the surface. The scene then changed to the crowded hall of a hotel. Her husband left her, and she 'entered into conversation with' a stranger.*" The second half of the dream was discovered in the analysis to represent a flight from her husband, and the entering into intimate relations with a third person, behind whom was plainly indicated Mr. X.'s brother mentioned in a former dream. The first part of the dream was a fairly evident birth phantasy. In dreams as in mythology, the delivery of a child *from* the uterine waters is commonly presented by distortion as the entry of the child *into* water; among many others, the births of Adonis, Osiris, Moses, and Bacchus are well-known illustrations of this. The bobbing up and down of the head in the water at once

---

[188] It is only of late that I have learned to value the significance of fancies and unconscious thoughts about life in the womb. They contain the explanation of the curious fear felt by so many people of being buried alive, as well as the profoundest unconscious reason for the belief in a life after death which represents nothing but a projection into the future of this mysterious life before birth. *The act of birth, moreover, is the first experience with fear, and is thus the source and model of the emotion of fear.*

recalled to the patient the sensation of quickening she had experienced in her only pregnancy. Thinking of the boy going into the water induced a reverie in which she saw herself taking him out of the water, carrying him into the nursery, washing him and dressing him, and installing him in her household.

The second half of the dream, therefore, represents thoughts concerning the elopement, which belonged to the first half of the underlying latent content; the first half of the dream corresponded with the second half of the latent content, the birth phantasy. Besides this inversion in order, further inversions took place in each half of the dream. In the first half the child *entered* the water, and then his head bobbed; in the underlying dream thoughts first the quickening occurred, and then the child left the water (a double inversion). In the second half her husband left her; in the dream thoughts she left her husband.

Another parturition dream is related by Abraham of a young woman looking forward to her first confinement. From a place in the floor of the house a subterranean canal leads directly into the water (parturition path, amniotic liquor). She lifts up a trap in the floor, and there immediately appears a creature dressed in a brownish fur, which almost resembles a seal. This creature changes into the younger brother of the dreamer, to whom she has always stood in maternal relationship.

Dreams of "saving" are connected with parturition dreams. To save, especially to save from the water, is equivalent to giving birth when dreamed by a woman; this sense is, however, modified when the dreamer is a man.

Robbers, burglars at night, and ghosts, of which we are afraid before going to bed, and which occasionally even disturb our sleep, originate in one and the same childish reminiscence. They are the nightly visitors who have awakened the child to set it on the chamber so that it may not wet the bed, or have lifted the cover in order to see clearly how the child is holding its hands while sleeping. I have been able to induce an exact recollection of the nocturnal visitor in the analysis of some of these anxiety dreams. The robbers were always the father, the ghosts more probably corresponded to feminine persons with white night-gowns.

When one has become familiar with the abundant use of symbolism for the representation of sexual material in dreams, one naturally raises the question whether there are not many of these symbols which appear once and for all with a firmly established significance like the signs in stenography; and one is tempted to compile a new dream-book according to the cipher method. In this connection it may be remarked that this symbolism does not belong peculiarly to the dream, but rather to unconscious thinking, particularly that of the masses, and it is to be found in greater perfection in the folklore, in the myths, legends, and manners of speech, in the proverbial sayings, and in the current witticisms of a nation than in its dreams.

The dream takes advantage of this symbolism in order to give a disguised representation to its latent thoughts. Among the symbols which are used in this manner there are of course many which regularly, or almost regularly, mean the same thing. Only it is necessary to keep in mind the curious plasticity of psychic material. Now and then a symbol in the dream content may have to be interpreted not symbolically, but according to its real meaning; at another time the dreamer, owing to a peculiar set of recollections, may create for himself the right to use anything whatever as a sexual symbol, though it is not ordinarily used in that way. Nor are the most frequently used sexual symbols unambiguous every time.

After these limitations and reservations I may call attention to the following: Emperor and Empress (King and Queen) in most cases really represent the parents of the dreamer; the dreamer himself or herself is the prince or princess. All elongated objects, sticks, tree-trunks, and umbrellas (on account of the stretching-up which might be compared to an erection! all elongated and sharp weapons, knives, daggers, and pikes, are intended to represent the male member. A frequent, not very intelligible, symbol for the same is a nail-file (on account of the rubbing and scraping?). Little cases, boxes, caskets, closets, and stoves correspond to the female part. The symbolism of lock and key has been very gracefully employed by Uhland in his song about the "Grafen Eberstein," to make a common smutty joke. The dream of walking through a row of rooms is a brothel or harem dream. Staircases, ladders, and flights of stairs, or climbing on these, either upwards or downwards, are symbolic representations of the sexual act. Smooth walls over which one is climbing, façades of houses upon which one is letting oneself down, frequently under great anxiety, correspond to the erect human body, and probably repeat in the dream reminiscences of the upward climbing of little children on their parents or foster parents. "Smooth" walls are men. Often in a dream of anxiety one is holding on firmly to some projection from a house. Tables, set tables, and boards are women, perhaps on account of the opposition which does away with the bodily contours. Since "bed and board" (*mensa et thorus*) constitute marriage, the former are often put for the latter in the dream, and as far as practicable the sexual presentation complex is transposed to the eating complex. Of articles of dress the woman's hat may frequently be definitely interpreted as the male genital. In dreams of men one often finds the cravat as a symbol for the penis; this indeed is not only because cravats hang down long, and are characteristic of the man, but also because one can select them at pleasure, a freedom which is prohibited by nature in the original of the symbol. Persons who make use of this symbol in the dream are very extravagant with cravats, and possess regular collections of them. All complicated machines and apparatus in dream are very probably genitals, in the description of which dream symbolism shows itself to be as tireless as the activity of wit. Likewise many

575

landscapes in dreams, especially with bridges or with wooded mountains, can be readily recognized as descriptions of the genitals. Finally where one finds incomprehensible neologisms one may think of combinations made up of components having a sexual significance. Children also in the dream often signify the genitals, as men and women are in the habit of fondly referring to their genital organ as their "little one." As a very recent symbol of the male genital may be mentioned the flying machine, utilization of which is justified by its relation to flying as well as occasionally by its form. To play with a little child or to beat a little one is often the dream's representation of onanism. A number of other symbols, in part not sufficiently verified are given by Stekel, who illustrates them with examples. Right and left, according to him, are to be conceived in the dream in an ethical sense. "The right way always signifies the road to righteousness, the left the one to crime. Thus the left may signify homosexuality, incest, and perversion, while the right signifies marriage, relations with a prostitute, &c. The meaning is always determined by the individual moral view-point of the dreamer." Relatives in the dream generally play the rôle of genitals. Not to be able to catch up with a wagon is interpreted by Stekel as regret not to be able to come up to a difference in age. Baggage with which one travels is the burden of sin by which one is oppressed. Also numbers, which frequently occur in the dream, are assigned by Stekel a fixed symbolical meaning, but these interpretations seem neither sufficiently verified nor of general validity, although the interpretation in individual cases can generally be recognized as probable. In a recently published book by W. Stekel, *Die Sprache des Traumes*, which I was unable to utilize, there is a list of the most common sexual symbols, the object of which is to prove that all sexual symbols can be bisexually used. He states: "Is there a symbol which (if in any way permitted by the phantasy) may not be used simultaneously in the masculine and the feminine sense!" To be sure the clause in parentheses takes away much of the absoluteness of this assertion, for this is not at all permitted by the phantasy. I do not, however, think it superfluous to state that in my experience Stekel's general statement has to give way to the recognition of a greater manifoldness. Besides those symbols, which are just as frequent for the male as for the female genitals, there are others which preponderately, or almost exclusively, designate one of the sexes, and there are still others of which only the male or only the female signification is known. To use long, firm objects and weapons as symbols of the female genitals, or hollow objects (chests, pouches, &c.), as symbols of the male genitals, is indeed not allowed by the fancy.

It is true that the tendency of the dream and the unconscious fancy to utilize the sexual symbol bisexually betrays an archaic trend, for in childhood a difference in the genitals is unknown, and the same genitals are attributed to both sexes.

These very incomplete suggestions may suffice to stimulate others to make a more careful collection.

I shall now add a few examples of the application of such symbolisms in dreams, which will serve to show how impossible it becomes to interpret a dream without taking into account the symbolism of dreams, and how imperatively it obtrudes itself in many cases.

1. The hat as a symbol of the man (of the male genital): (a fragment from the dream of a young woman who suffered from agoraphobia on account of a fear of temptation).

"I am walking in the street in summer, I wear a straw hat of peculiar shape, the middle piece of which is bent upwards and the side pieces of which hang downwards (the description became here obstructed), and in such a fashion that one is lower than the other. I am cheerful and in a confidential mood, and as I pass a troop of young officers I think to myself: None of you can have any designs upon me."

As she could produce no associations to the hat, I said to her: "The hat is really a male genital, with its raised middle piece and the two downward hanging side pieces." I intentionally refrained from interpreting those details concerning the unequal downward hanging of the two side pieces, although just such individualities in the determinations lead the way to the interpretation. I continued by saying that if she only had a man with such a virile genital she would not have to fear the officers—that is, she would have nothing to wish from them, for she is mainly kept from going without protection and company by her fancies of temptation. This last explanation of her fear I had already been able to give her repeatedly on the basis of other material.

It is quite remarkable how the dreamer behaved after this interpretation. She withdrew her description of the hat, and claimed not to have said that the two side pieces were hanging downwards. I was, however, too sure of what I had heard to allow myself to be misled, and I persisted in it. She was quiet for a while, and then found the courage to ask why it was that one of her husband's testicles was lower than the other, and whether it was the same in all men. With this the peculiar detail of the hat was explained, and the whole interpretation was accepted by her. The hat symbol was familiar to me long before the patient related this dream. From other but less transparent cases I believe that the hat may also be taken as a female genital.

2. The little one as the genital—to be run over as a symbol of sexual intercourse (another dream of the same agoraphobic patient).

"Her mother sends away her little daughter so that she must go alone. She rides with her mother to the railroad and sees her little one walking directly upon the tracks, so that she cannot avoid being run over. She hears the bones crackle. (From this she experiences a feeling of discomfort but no real horror.) She then looks out through the car window to see whether the parts cannot be seen behind. She then reproaches her mother for allowing the little one to go out alone." Analysis. It is not an easy matter to give here a complete interpretation of the dream. It forms part of a cycle of dreams, and can be fully understood only in connection with the others. For it is not easy to get the necessary material sufficiently isolated to prove the symbolism. The patient at first finds that the railroad journey is to be interpreted historically as an allusion to a departure from a sanatorium for nervous diseases, with the superintendent of which she naturally was in love. Her mother took her away from this place, and the physician came to the railroad station and handed her a bouquet of flowers on leaving; she felt uncomfortable because her mother witnessed this homage. Here the mother, therefore, appears as a disturber of her love affairs, which is the rôle actually played by this strict woman during her daughter's girlhood. The next thought referred to the sentence: "She then looks to see whether the parts can be seen behind." In the dream façade one would naturally be compelled to think of the parts of the little daughter run over and ground up. The thought, however, turns in quite a different direction. She recalls that she once saw her father in the bath-room naked from behind; she then begins to talk about the sex differentiation, and asserts that in the man the genitals can be seen from behind, but in the woman they cannot. In this connection she now herself offers the interpretation that the little one is the genital, her little one (she has a four-year-old daughter) her own genital. She reproaches her mother for wanting her to live as though she had no genital, and recognizes this reproach in the introductory sentence of the dream; the mother sends away her little one so that she must go alone. In her phantasy going alone on the street signifies to have no man and no sexual relations (coire = to go together), and this she does not like. According to all her statements she really suffered as a girl on account of the jealousy of her mother, because she showed a preference for her father.

The "little one" has been noted as a symbol for the male or the female genitals by Stekel, who can refer in this connection to a very widespread usage of language.

The deeper interpretation of this dream depends upon another dream of the same night in which the dreamer identifies herself with her brother. She was a "tomboy," and was always being told that she should have been born a boy. This identification with the brother shows with special clearness that "the little one" signifies the genital. The mother threatened him (her) with castration, which could only be understood as a punishment for playing with the parts, and the identification, therefore, shows that she herself had masturbated as a child, though this fact she now retained only in memory concerning her brother. An early knowledge of the male genital which she later lost she must have acquired at that time according to the assertions of this second dream. Moreover the second dream points to the infantile sexual theory that girls originate from boys through castration. After I had told her of this childish belief, she at once confirmed it with an anecdote in which the boy asks the girl: "Was it cut off?" to which the girl replied, "No, it's always been so."

The sending away of the little one, of the genital, in the first dream therefore also refers to the threatened castration. Finally she blames her mother for not having been born a boy.

That "being run over" symbolizes sexual intercourse would not be evident from this dream if we were not sure of it from many other sources.

3. Representation of the genital by structures, stairways, and shafts. (Dream of a young man inhibited by a father complex.)

"He is taking a walk with his father in a place which is surely the Prater, for the *Rotunda* may be seen in front of which there is a small front structure to which is attached a captive balloon; the balloon, however, seems quite collapsed. His father asks him what this is all for; he is surprised at it, but he explains it to his father. They come into a court in which lies a large sheet of tin. His father wants to pull off a big piece of this, but first looks around to see if any one is watching. He tells his father that all he needs to do is to speak to the watchman, and then he can take without any further difficulty as much as he wants to. From this court a stairway leads down into a shaft, the walls of which are softly upholstered something like a leather pocketbook. At the end of this shaft there is a longer platform, and then a new shaft begins...."

Analysis. This dream belongs to a type of patient which is not favorable from a therapeutic point of view. They follow in the analysis without offering any resistances whatever up to a certain point, but from that point on they remain almost inaccessible. This dream he almost analyzed himself. "The Rotunda," he said, "is my genital, the captive balloon in front is my penis, about the weakness of which I have worried." We must, however, interpret in greater detail; the Rotunda is the buttock which is regularly associated by the child with the genital, the smaller front structure is the scrotum. In the dream his father asks him what this is all for—that is, he asks him about the purpose and arrangement of the genitals. It is quite evident that this state of affairs should be turned around, and that he should be the questioner. As such a questioning on the side of the father has never taken place in reality, we must conceive the dream thought as a wish, or take it conditionally, as follows: "If I had only asked my father for sexual enlightenment." The continuation of this thought we shall soon find in another place.

The court in which the tin sheet is spread out is not to be conceived symbolically in the first instance, but originates from his father's place of business. For discretionary reasons I have inserted the tin for another

579

material in which the father deals, without, however, changing anything in the verbal expression of the dream. The dreamer had entered his father's business, and had taken a terrible dislike to the questionable practices upon which profit mainly depends. Hence the continuation of the above dream thought ("if I had only asked him") would be: "He would have deceived me just as he does his customers." For the pulling off, which serves to represent commercial dishonesty, the dreamer himself gives a second explanation—namely, onanism. This is not only entirely familiar to us, but agrees very well with the fact that the secrecy of onanism is expressed by its opposite ("Why one can do it quite openly"). It, moreover, agrees entirely with our expectations that the onanistic activity is again put off on the father, just as was the questioning in the first scene of the dream. The shaft he at once interprets as the vagina by referring to the soft upholstering of the walls. That the act of coition in the vagina is described as a going down instead of in the usual way as a going up, I have also found true in other instances[189].

The details that at the end of the first shaft there is a longer platform and then a new shaft, he himself explains biographically. He had for some time consorted with women sexually, but had then given it up because of inhibitions and now hopes to be able to take it up again with the aid of the treatment. The dream, however, becomes indistinct toward the end, and to the experienced interpreter it becomes evident that in the second scene of the dream the influence of another subject has begun to assert itself; in this his father's business and his dishonest practices signify the first vagina represented as a shaft so that one might think of a reference to the mother.

4. The male genital symbolized by persons and the female by a landscape.

(Dream of a woman of the lower class, whose husband is a policeman, reported by B. Dattner.)

... Then some one broke into the house and anxiously called for a policeman. But he went with two tramps by mutual consent into a church,[190] to which led a great many stairs;[191] behind the church there was a mountain,[192] on top of which a dense forest.[193] The policeman was furnished with a helmet, a gorget, and a cloak.[194] The two vagrants, who went along with the policeman quite peaceably, had tied to their loins sack-like aprons.[195] A road led from the church to the mountain. This road was overgrown on each

---

[189] Cf. *Zentralblatt für psychoanalyse*, I.

[190] Or chapel—vagina.

[191] Symbol of coitus.

[192] Mons veneris.

[193] Crines pubis.

[194] Demons in cloaks and capucines are, according to the explanation of a man versed in the subject, of a phallic nature.

[195] The two halves of the scrotum.

side with grass and brushwood, which became thicker and thicker as it reached the height of the mountain, where it spread out into quite a forest.

5. A stairway dream. (Reported and interpreted by Otto Rank.)

For the following transparent pollution dream, I am indebted to the same colleague who furnished us with the dental-irritation dream.

"I am running down the stairway in the stair-house after a little girl, whom I wish to punish because she has done something to me. At the bottom of the stairs some one held the child for me. (A grown-up woman?) I grasp it, but do not know whether I have hit it, for I suddenly find myself in the middle of the stairway where I practice coitus with the child (in the air as it were). It is really no coitus, I only rub my genital on her external genital, and in doing this I see it very distinctly, as distinctly as I see her head which is lying sideways. During the sexual act I see hanging to the left and above me (also as if in the air) two small pictures, landscapes, representing a house on a green. On the smaller one my surname stood in the place where the painter's signature should be; it seemed to be intended for my birthday present. A small sign hung in front of the pictures to the effect that cheaper pictures could also be obtained. I then see myself very indistinctly lying in bed, just as I had seen myself at the foot of the stairs, and I am awakened by a feeling of dampness which came from the pollution."

Interpretation. The dreamer had been in a book-store on the evening of the day of the dream, where, while he was waiting, he examined some pictures which were exhibited, which represented motives similar to the dream pictures. He stepped nearer to a small picture which particularly took his fancy in order to see the name of the artist, which, however, was quite unknown to him.

Later in the same evening, in company, he heard about a Bohemian servant-girl who boasted that her illegitimate child "was made on the stairs." The dreamer inquired about the details of this unusual occurrence, and learned that the servant-girl went with her lover to the home of her parents, where there was no opportunity for sexual relations, and that the excited man performed the act on the stairs. In witty allusion to the mischievous expression used about wine-adulterers, the dreamer remarked, "The child really grew on the cellar steps."

These experiences of the day, which are quite prominent in the dream content, were readily reproduced by the dreamer. But he just as readily reproduced an old fragment of infantile recollection which was also utilized by the dream. The stair-house was the house in which he had spent the greatest part of his childhood, and in which he had first become acquainted with sexual problems. In this house he used, among other things, to slide down the banister astride which caused him to become sexually excited. In the dream he also comes down the stairs very rapidly—so rapidly that, according to his own distinct assertions, he hardly touched the individual stairs, but rather "flew" or "slid down," as we used to say. Upon reference to this infantile experience, the beginning of the dream seems to represent the factor of sexual excitement. In the same house and in the adjacent residence the dreamer used to play pugnacious games with the neighboring children, in which he satisfied himself just as he did in the dream.

If one recalls from Freud's investigation of sexual symbolism[196] that in the dream stairs or climbing stairs almost regularly symbolizes coitus, the dream becomes clear. Its motive power as well as its effect, as is shown by the pollution, is of a purely libidinous nature. Sexual excitement became aroused during the sleeping state (in the dream this is represented by the rapid running or sliding down the stairs) and the sadistic thread in this is, on the basis of the pugnacious playing, indicated in the pursuing and overcoming of the child. The libidinous excitement becomes enhanced and urges to sexual action (represented in the dream by the grasping of the child and the conveyance of it to the middle of the stairway). Up to this point the dream would be one of pure, sexual symbolism, and obscure for the unpracticed dream interpreter. But this symbolic gratification, which would have insured undisturbed sleep, was not sufficient for the powerful libidinous excitement. The excitement leads to an orgasm, and thus the whole stairway symbolism is unmasked as a substitute for coitus. Freud lays stress on the rhythmical character of both actions as one of the reasons for the sexual utilization of the stairway symbolism, and this dream especially seems to corroborate this, for, according to the express assertion of the dreamer, the rhythm of a sexual act was the most pronounced feature in the whole dream.

Still another remark concerning the two pictures, which, aside from their real significance, also have the value of "Weibsbilder" (literally *woman-pictures*, but idiomatically *women*). This is at once shown by the fact that the dream deals with a big and a little picture, just as the dream content presents a big (grown up) and a little girl. That cheap pictures could also be obtained points to the prostitution complex, just as the dreamer's surname on the little picture and the thought that it was intended for his birthday, point to the parent complex (to be born on the stairway—to be conceived in coitus).

The indistinct final scene, in which the dreamer sees himself on the staircase landing lying in bed and feeling wet, seems to go back into childhood even beyond the infantile onanism, and manifestly has its prototype in similarly pleasurable scenes of bed-wetting.

6. A modified stair-dream.

To one of my very nervous patients, who was an abstainer, whose fancy was fixed on his mother, and who repeatedly dreamed of climbing stairs

---

[196] See *Zentralblatt für Psychoanalyse*, vol. i., p. 2.

accompanied by his mother, I once remarked that moderate masturbation would be less harmful to him than enforced abstinence. This influence provoked the following dream:

"His piano teacher reproaches him for neglecting his piano-playing, and for not practicing the *Etudes* of Moscheles and Clementi's *Gradus ad Parnassum*." In relation to this he remarked that the *Gradus* is only a stairway, and that the piano itself is only a stairway as it has a scale.

It is correct to say that there is no series of associations which cannot be adapted to the representation of sexual facts. I conclude with the dream of a chemist, a young man, who has been trying to give up his habit of masturbation by replacing it with intercourse with women.

Preliminary statement.—On the day before the dream he had given a student instruction concerning Grignard's reaction, in which magnesium is to be dissolved in absolutely pure ether under the catalytic influence of iodine. Two days before, there had been an explosion in the course of the same reaction, in which the investigator had burned his hand.

Dream I. *He is to make phenylmagnesium-bromid; he sees the apparatus with particular clearness, but he has substituted himself for the magnesium. He is now in a curious swaying attitude. He keeps repeating to himself, "This is the right thing, it is working, my feet are beginning to dissolve and my knees are getting soft." Then he reaches down and feels for his feet, and meanwhile (he does not know how) he takes his legs out of the crucible, and then again he says to himself, "That cannot be.... Yes, it must be so, it has been done correctly." Then he partially awakens, and repeats the dream to himself, because he wants to tell it to me. He is distinctly afraid of the analysis of the dream. He is much excited during this semi-sleeping state, and repeats continually, "Phenyl, phenyl."*

II. *He is in ....ing with his whole family; at half-past eleven. He is to be at the Schottenthor for a rendezvous with a certain lady, but he does not wake up until half-past eleven. He says to himself, "It is too late now; when you get there it will be half-past twelve." The next instant he sees the whole family gathered about the table—his mother and the servant girl with the soup-tureen with particular clearness. Then he says to himself, "Well, if we are eating already, I certainly can't get away."*

Analysis: He feels sure that even the first dream contains a reference to the lady whom he is to meet at the rendezvous (the dream was dreamed during the night before the expected meeting). The student to whom he gave the instruction is a particularly unpleasant fellow; he had said to the chemist: "That isn't right," because the magnesium was still unaffected, and the latter answered as though he did not care anything about it: "It certainly isn't right." He himself must be this student; he is as indifferent towards his analysis as the student is towards his synthesis; the *He* in the dream, however, who

583

accomplishes the operation, is myself. How unpleasant he must seem to me with his indifference towards the success achieved!

Moreover, he is the material with which the analysis (synthesis) is made. For it is a question of the success of the treatment. The legs in the dream recall an impression of the previous evening. He met a lady at a dancing lesson whom he wished to conquer; he pressed her to him so closely that she once cried out. After he had stopped pressing against her legs, he felt her firm responding pressure against his lower thighs as far as just above his knees, at the place mentioned in the dream. In this situation, then, the woman is the magnesium in the retort, which is at last working. He is feminine towards me, as he is masculine towards the woman. If it will work with the woman, the treatment will also work. Feeling and becoming aware of himself in the region of his knees refers to masturbation, and corresponds to his fatigue of the previous day.... The rendezvous had actually been set for half-past eleven. His wish to oversleep and to remain with his usual sexual objects (that is, with masturbation) corresponds with his resistance.

VI. THE WISH IN DREAMS

That the dream should be nothing but a wish-fulfillment surely seemed strange to us all—and that not alone because of the contradictions offered by the anxiety dream.

After learning from the first analytical explanations that the dream conceals sense and psychic validity, we could hardly expect so simple a determination of this sense. According to the correct but concise definition of Aristotle, the dream is a continuation of thinking in sleep (in so far as one sleeps). Considering that during the day our thoughts produce such a diversity of psychic acts—judgments, conclusions, contradictions, expectations, intentions, &c.—why should our sleeping thoughts be forced to confine themselves to the production of wishes? Are there not, on the contrary, many dreams that present a different psychic act in dream form, e.g., a solicitude, and is not the very transparent father's dream mentioned above of just such a nature? From the gleam of light falling into his eyes while asleep the father draws the solicitous conclusion that a candle has been upset and may have set fire to the corpse; he transforms this conclusion into a dream by investing it with a senseful situation enacted in the present tense. What part is played in this dream by the wish-fulfillment, and which are we to suspect—the predominance of the thought continued from, the waking state or of the thought incited by the new sensory impression?

All these considerations are just, and force us to enter more deeply into the part played by the wish-fulfillment in the dream, and into the significance of the waking thoughts continued in sleep.

It is in fact the wish-fulfillment that has already induced us to separate dreams into two groups. We have found some dreams that were plainly wish-fulfillments; and others in which wish-fulfillment could not be recognized, and was frequently concealed by every available means. In this latter class of dreams we recognized the influence of the dream censor. The undisguised wish dreams were chiefly found in children, yet fleeting open-hearted wish dreams *seemed*(I purposely emphasize this word) to occur also in adults.

We may now ask whence the wish fulfilled in the dream originates. But to what opposition or to what diversity do we refer this "whence"? I think it is to the opposition between conscious daily life and a psychic activity remaining unconscious which can only make itself noticeable during the night. I thus find a threefold possibility for the origin of a wish. Firstly, it may have been incited during the day, and owing to external circumstances failed to find gratification, there is thus left for the night an acknowledged but unfulfilled wish. Secondly, it may come to the surface during the day but be rejected, leaving an unfulfilled but suppressed wish. Or, thirdly, it may have no relation to daily life, and belong to those wishes that originate during the night from the suppression. If we now follow our scheme of the psychic apparatus, we can localize a wish of the first order in the system Forec. We may assume that a wish of the second order has been forced back from the Forec. system into the Unc. system, where alone, if anywhere, it can maintain itself; while a wish-feeling of the third order we consider altogether incapable of leaving the Unc. system. This brings up the question whether wishes arising from these different sources possess the same value for the dream, and whether they have the same power to incite a dream.

On reviewing the dreams which we have at our disposal for answering this question, we are at once moved to add as a fourth source of the dream-wish the actual wish incitements arising during the night, such as thirst and sexual desire. It then becomes evident that the source of the dream-wish does not affect its capacity to incite a dream. That a wish suppressed during the day asserts itself in the dream can be shown by a great many examples. I shall mention a very simple example of this class. A somewhat sarcastic young lady, whose younger friend has become engaged to be married, is asked throughout the day by her acquaintances whether she knows and what she thinks of the fiancé. She answers with unqualified praise, thereby silencing her own judgment, as she would prefer to tell the truth, namely, that he is an ordinary person. The following night she dreams that the same question is put to her, and that she replies with the formula: "In case of subsequent orders it will suffice to mention the number." Finally, we have learned from numerous analyses that the wish in all dreams that have been subject to distortion has been derived from the unconscious, and has been unable to come to perception in the waking state. Thus it would appear that all wishes are of the same value and force for the dream formation.

I am at present unable to prove that the state of affairs is really different, but I am strongly inclined to assume a more stringent determination of the dream-wish. Children's dreams leave no doubt that an unfulfilled wish of the day may be the instigator of the dream. But we must not forget that it is, after all, the wish of a child, that it is a wish-feeling of infantile strength only. I have a strong doubt whether an unfulfilled wish from the day would suffice to create a dream in an adult. It would rather seem that as we learn to control our impulses by intellectual activity, we more and more reject as vain the formation or retention of such intense wishes as are natural to childhood. In this, indeed, there may be individual variations; some retain the infantile type of psychic processes longer than others. The differences are here the same as those found in the gradual decline of the originally distinct visual imagination.

In general, however, I am of the opinion that unfulfilled wishes of the day are insufficient to produce a dream in adults. I readily admit that the wish instigators originating in conscious like contribute towards the incitement of dreams, but that is probably all. The dream would not originate if the foreconscious wish were not reinforced from another source.

That source is the unconscious. I believe that *the conscious wish is a dream inciter only if it succeeds in arousing a similar unconscious wish which reinforces it.* Following the suggestions obtained through the psychoanalysis of the neuroses, I believe that these unconscious wishes are always active and ready for expression whenever they find an opportunity to unite themselves with an emotion from conscious life, and that they transfer their greater intensity to the lesser intensity of the latter.[197] It may therefore seem that the conscious wish alone has been realized in a dream; but a slight peculiarity in the formation of this dream will put us on the track of the powerful helper from the unconscious. These ever active and, as it were, immortal wishes from the unconscious recall the legendary Titans who from time immemorial have borne the ponderous mountains which were once rolled upon them by the victorious gods, and which even now quiver from

---

[197] They share this character of indestructibility with all psychic acts that are really unconscious—that is, with psychic acts belonging to the system of the unconscious only. These paths are constantly open and never fall into disuse; they conduct the discharge of the exciting process as often as it becomes endowed with unconscious excitement To speak metaphorically they suffer the same form of annihilation as the shades of the lower region in the *Odyssey*, who awoke to new life the moment they drank blood. The processes depending on the foreconscious system are destructible in a different way. The psychotherapy of the neuroses is based on this difference.

time to time from the convulsions of their mighty limbs; I say that these wishes found in the repression are of themselves of an infantile origin, as we have learned from the psychological investigation of the neuroses. I should like, therefore, to withdraw the opinion previously expressed that it is unimportant whence the dream-wish originates, and replace it by another, as follows: *The wish manifested in the dream must be an infantile one.* In the adult it originates in the Unc., while in the child, where no separation and censor as yet exist between Forec. and Unc., or where these are only in the process of formation, it is an unfulfilled and unrepressed wish from the waking state. I am aware that this conception cannot be generally demonstrated, but I maintain nevertheless that it can be frequently demonstrated, even when it was not suspected, and that it cannot be generally refuted.

The wish-feelings which remain from the conscious waking state are, therefore, relegated to the background in the dream formation. In the dream content I shall attribute to them only the part attributed to the material of actual sensations during sleep. If I now take into account those other psychic instigations remaining from the waking state which are not wishes, I shall only adhere to the line mapped out for me by this train of thought. We may succeed in provisionally terminating the sum of energy of our waking thoughts by deciding to go to sleep. He is a good sleeper who can do this; Napoleon I. is reputed to have been a model of this sort. But we do not always succeed in accomplishing it, or in accomplishing it perfectly. Unsolved problems, harassing cares, overwhelming impressions continue the thinking activity even during sleep, maintaining psychic processes in the system which we have termed the foreconscious. These mental processes continuing into sleep may be divided into the following groups: 1, That which has not been terminated during the day owing to casual prevention; 2, that which has been left unfinished by temporary paralysis of our mental power, *i.e.* the unsolved; 3, that which has been rejected and suppressed during the day. This unites with a powerful group (4) formed by that which has been excited in our Unc. during the day by the work of the foreconscious. Finally, we may add group (5) consisting of the indifferent and hence unsettled impressions of the day.

We should not underrate the psychic intensities introduced into sleep by these remnants of waking life, especially those emanating from the group of the unsolved. These excitations surely continue to strive for expression during the night, and we may assume with equal certainty that the sleeping state renders impossible the usual continuation of the excitement in the foreconscious and the termination of the excitement by its becoming conscious. As far as we can normally become conscious of our mental processes, even during the night, in so far we are not asleep. I shall not venture to state what change is produced in the Forec. system by the sleeping state, but there is no doubt that the psychological character of sleep is essentially due to the change of energy in this very system, which also dominates the approach to motility, which is paralyzed during sleep. In contradistinction to this, there seems to be nothing in the psychology of the dream to warrant the assumption that sleep produces any but secondary changes in the conditions of the Unc. system. Hence, for the nocturnal excitation in the Force, there remains no other path than that followed by the wish excitements from the Unc. This excitation must seek reinforcement from the Unc., and follow the detours of the unconscious excitations. But what is the relation of the foreconscious day remnants to the dream? There is no doubt that they penetrate abundantly into the dream, that they utilize the dream content to obtrude themselves upon consciousness even during the night; indeed, they occasionally even dominate the dream content, and impel it to continue the work of the day; it is also certain that the day remnants may just as well have any other character as that of wishes; but it is highly instructive and even decisive for the theory of wish-fulfillment to see what conditions they must comply with in order to be received into the dream.

Let us pick out one of the dreams cited above as examples, *e.g.*, the dream in which my friend Otto seems to show the symptoms of Basedow's disease. My friend Otto's appearance occasioned me some concern during the day, and this worry, like everything else referring to this person, affected me. I may also assume that these feelings followed me into sleep. I was probably bent on finding out what was the matter with him. In the night my worry found expression in the dream which I have reported, the content of which was not only senseless, but failed to show any wish-fulfillment. But I began to investigate for the source of this incongruous expression of the solicitude felt during the day, and analysis revealed the connection. I identified my friend Otto with a certain Baron L. and myself with a Professor R. There was only one explanation for my being impelled to select just this substitution for the day thought. I must have always been prepared in the Unc. to identify myself with Professor R., as it meant the realization of one of the immortal infantile wishes, viz. that of becoming great. Repulsive ideas respecting my friend, that would certainly have been repudiated in a waking state, took advantage of the opportunity to creep into the dream, but the worry of the day likewise found some form of expression through a substitution in the dream content. The day thought, which was no wish in itself but rather a worry, had in some way to find a connection with the infantile now unconscious and suppressed wish, which then allowed it, though already properly prepared, to "originate" for consciousness. The more dominating this worry, the stronger must be the connection to be established; between the contents of the wish and that of the worry there need be no connection, nor was there one in any of our examples.

We can now sharply define the significance of the unconscious wish for the dream. It may be admitted that there is a whole class of dreams in which the incitement originates preponderatingly or even exclusively from the remnants of daily life; and I believe that even my cherished desire to become at some future time a "professor extraordinarius" would have allowed me to slumber undisturbed that night had not my worry about my friend's health been still active. But this worry alone would not have produced a dream; the motive power needed by the dream had to be contributed by a wish, and it was the affair of the worriment to procure for itself such wish as a motive power of the dream. To speak figuratively, it is quite possible that a day thought plays the part of the contractor (*entrepreneur*) in the dream. But it is known that no matter what idea the contractor may have in mind, and how desirous he may be of putting it into operation, he can do nothing without capital; he must depend upon a capitalist to defray the necessary expenses, and this capitalist, who supplies the psychic expenditure for the dream is invariably and indisputably *a wish from the unconscious*, no matter what the nature of the waking thought may be.

In other cases the capitalist himself is the contractor for the dream; this, indeed, seems to be the more usual case. An unconscious wish is produced by the day's work, which in turn creates the dream. The dream processes, moreover, run parallel with all the other possibilities of the economic relationship used here as an illustration. Thus, the entrepreneur may contribute some capital himself, or several entrepreneurs may seek the aid of the same capitalist, or several capitalists may jointly supply the capital required by the entrepreneur. Thus there are dreams produced by more than one dream-wish, and many similar variations which may readily be passed over and are of no further interest to us. What we have left unfinished in this discussion of the dream-wish we shall be able to develop later.

The "tertium comparationis" in the comparisons just employed—*i.e.* the sum placed at our free disposal in proper allotment—admits of still finer application for the illustration of the dream structure. We can recognize in most dreams a center especially supplied with perceptible intensity. This is regularly the direct representation of the wish-fulfillment; for, if we undo the displacements of the dream-work by a process of retrogression, we find that the psychic intensity of the elements in the dream thoughts is replaced by the perceptible intensity of the elements in the dream content. The elements adjoining the wish-fulfillment have frequently nothing to do with its sense, but prove to be descendants of painful thoughts which oppose the wish. But, owing to their frequently artificial connection with the central element, they have acquired sufficient intensity to enable them to come to expression. Thus, the force of expression of the wish-fulfillment is diffused over a certain sphere of association, within which it raises to expression all elements, including those that are in themselves impotent. In dreams having several strong wishes we can readily separate from one another the spheres of the individual wish-fulfillments; the gaps in the dream likewise can often be explained as boundary zones.

Although the foregoing remarks have considerably limited the significance of the day remnants for the dream, it will nevertheless be worth our while to give them some attention. For they must be a necessary ingredient in the formation of the dream, inasmuch as experience reveals the surprising fact that every dream shows in its content a connection with some impression of a recent day, often of the most indifferent kind. So far we have failed to see any necessity for this addition to the dream mixture. This necessity appears only when we follow closely the part played by the unconscious wish, and then seek information in the psychology of the neuroses. We thus learn that the unconscious idea, as such, is altogether incapable of entering into the foreconscious, and that it can exert an influence there only by uniting with a harmless idea already belonging to the foreconscious, to which it transfers its intensity and under which it allows itself to be concealed. This is the fact of transference which furnishes an explanation for so many surprising occurrences in the psychic life of neurotics.

The idea from the foreconscious which thus obtains an unmerited abundance of intensity may be left unchanged by the transference, or it may have forced upon it a modification from the content of the transferring idea. I trust the reader will pardon my fondness for comparisons from daily life, but I feel tempted to say that the relations existing for the repressed idea are similar to the situations existing in Austria for the American dentist, who is forbidden to practise unless he gets permission from a regular physician to use his name on the public signboard and thus cover the legal requirements. Moreover, just as it is naturally not the busiest physicians who form such alliances with dental practitioners, so in the psychic life only such foreconscious or conscious ideas are chosen to cover a repressed idea as have not themselves attracted much of the attention which is operative in the foreconscious. The unconscious entangles with its connections preferentially either those impressions and ideas of the foreconscious which have been left unnoticed as indifferent, or those that have soon been deprived of this attention through rejection. It is a familiar fact from the association studies confirmed by every experience, that ideas which have formed intimate connections in one direction assume an almost negative attitude to whole groups of new connections. I once tried from this principle to develop a theory for hysterical paralysis.

If we assume that the same need for the transference of the repressed ideas which we have learned to know from the analysis of the neuroses makes its influence felt in the dream as well, we can at once explain two riddles of the dream, viz. that every dream analysis shows an interweaving of a recent impression, and that this recent element is frequently of the most indifferent character. We may add what we have already learned elsewhere, that these recent and indifferent elements come so frequently into the dream content as a substitute for the most deep-lying of the dream thoughts, for the further reason that they have least to fear from the resisting censor. But while this freedom from censorship explains only the preference for trivial elements, the constant presence of recent elements points to the fact that there is a need for transference. Both groups of impressions satisfy the demand of the repression for material still free from associations, the indifferent ones because they have offered no inducement for extensive associations, and the recent ones because they have had insufficient time to form such associations.

We thus see that the day remnants, among which we may now include the indifferent impressions when they participate in the dream formation, not only borrow from the Unc. the motive power at the disposal of the repressed wish, but also offer to the unconscious something indispensable, namely, the attachment necessary to the transference. If we here attempted to penetrate more deeply into the psychic processes, we should first have to throw more light on the play of emotions between the foreconscious and the unconscious, to which, indeed, we are urged by the study of the psychoneuroses, whereas the dream itself offers no assistance in this respect.

Just one further remark about the day remnants. There is no doubt that they are the actual disturbers of sleep, and not the dream, which, on the contrary, strives to guard sleep. But we shall return to this point later.

We have so far discussed the dream-wish, we have traced it to the sphere of the Unc., and analyzed its relations to the day remnants, which in turn may be either wishes, psychic emotions of any other kind, or simply recent impressions. We have thus made room for any claims that may be made for the importance of conscious thought activity in dream formations in all its variations. Relying upon our thought series, it would not be at all impossible for us to explain even those extreme cases in which the dream as a continuer of the day work brings to a happy conclusion and unsolved problem possess an example, the analysis of which might reveal the infantile or repressed wish source furnishing such alliance and successful strengthening of the efforts of the foreconscious activity. But we have not come one step nearer a solution of the riddle: Why can the unconscious furnish the motive power for the wish-fulfillment only during sleep? The answer to this question must throw light on the psychic nature of wishes; and it will be given with the aid of the diagram of the psychic apparatus.

We do not doubt that even this apparatus attained its present perfection through a long course of development. Let us attempt to restore it as it existed in an early phase of its activity. From assumptions, to be confirmed elsewhere, we know that at first the apparatus strove to keep as free from excitement as possible, and in its first formation, therefore, the scheme took the form of a reflex apparatus, which enabled it promptly to discharge through the motor tracts any sensible stimulus reaching it from without. But this simple function was disturbed by the wants of life, which likewise furnish the impulse for the further development of the apparatus. The wants of life first manifested themselves to it in the form of the great physical needs. The excitement aroused by the inner want seeks an outlet in motility, which may be designated as "inner changes" or as an "expression of the emotions." The hungry child cries or fidgets helplessly, but its situation remains unchanged; for the excitation proceeding from an inner want requires, not a momentary outbreak, but a force working continuously. A change can occur only if in some way a feeling of gratification is experienced—which in the case of the child must be through outside help—in order to remove the inner excitement. An essential constituent of this experience is the appearance of a certain perception (of food in our example), the memory picture of which thereafter remains associated with the memory trace of the excitation of want.

Thanks to the established connection, there results at the next appearance of this want a psychic feeling which revives the memory picture of the former perception, and thus recalls the former perception itself, *i.e.* it actually re-establishes the situation of the first gratification. We call such a feeling a wish; the reappearance of the perception constitutes the wish-fulfillment, and the full revival of the perception by the want excitement constitutes the shortest road to the wish-fulfillment. We may assume a primitive condition of the psychic apparatus in which this road is really followed, *i.e.* where the wishing merges into an hallucination, This first psychic activity therefore aims at an identity of perception, *i.e.* it aims at a repetition of that perception which is connected with the fulfillment of the want.

This primitive mental activity must have been modified by bitter practical experience into a more expedient secondary activity. The establishment of the identity perception on the short regressive road within the apparatus does not in another respect carry with it the result which inevitably follows the revival of the same perception from without. The gratification does not take place, and the want continues. In order to equalize the internal with the external sum of energy, the former must be continually maintained, just as actually happens in the hallucinatory psychoses and in the deliriums of hunger which exhaust their psychic capacity in clinging to the object desired. In order to make more appropriate use of the psychic force, it becomes necessary to inhibit the full regression so as to prevent it from extending beyond the image of memory, whence it can select other paths leading ultimately to the establishment of the desired identity from the outer world. This inhibition and consequent deviation from the excitation becomes the task of a second system which dominates the voluntary motility, *i.e.* through whose activity the expenditure of motility is now devoted to previously recalled purposes. But this entire complicated mental activity which works its way from the memory picture to the establishment of the perception identity from the outer world merely represents a detour which has been forced upon the wish-fulfillment by experience.[198] Thinking is indeed nothing but the equivalent of the hallucinatory wish; and if the dream be called a wish-fulfillment this becomes self-evident, as nothing but a wish can impel our psychic apparatus to activity. The dream, which in fulfilling its wishes follows the short regressive path, thereby preserves for us only an example of the primary form of the psychic apparatus which has been abandoned as inexpedient. What once ruled in the waking state when the psychic life was still young and unfit seems to have been banished into the sleeping state, just as we see again in the nursery the bow and arrow, the discarded primitive weapons of grown-up humanity. *The dream is a fragment of the abandoned psychic life of the child.* In the psychoses these modes of operation of the psychic apparatus, which are normally suppressed in the waking state, reassert themselves, and then betray their inability to satisfy our wants in the outer world.

The unconscious wish-feelings evidently strive to assert themselves during the day also, and the fact of transference and the psychoses teach us that they endeavor to penetrate to consciousness and dominate motility by the road leading through the system of the foreconscious. It is, therefore, the censor lying between the Unc. and the Forec., the assumption of which is forced upon us by the dream, that we have to recognize and honor as the guardian of our psychic health. But is it not carelessness on the part of this guardian to diminish its vigilance during the night and to allow the suppressed emotions of the Unc. to come to expression, thus again making possible the hallucinatory regression? I think not, for when the critical guardian goes to rest—and we have proof that his slumber is not profound— he takes care to close the gate to motility. No matter what feelings from the otherwise inhibited Unc. may roam about on the scene, they need not be interfered with; they remain harmless because they are unable to put in motion the motor apparatus which alone can exert a modifying influence upon the outer world. Sleep guarantees the security of the fortress which is

---

[198] Le Lorrain justly extols the wish-fulfilment of the dream: "Sans fatigue sérieuse, sans être obligé de recourir à cette lutte opinâtre et longue qui use et corrode les jouissances poursuivies."

under guard. Conditions are less harmless when a displacement of forces is produced, not through a nocturnal diminution in the operation of the critical censor, but through pathological enfeeblement of the latter or through pathological reinforcement of the unconscious excitations, and this while the foreconscious is charged with energy and the avenues to motility are open. The guardian is then overpowered, the unconscious excitations subdue the Forec.; through it they dominate our speech and actions, or they enforce the hallucinatory regression, thus governing an apparatus not designed for them by virtue of the attraction exerted by the perceptions on the distribution of our psychic energy. We call this condition a psychosis.

We are now in the best position to complete our psychological construction, which has been interrupted by the introduction of the two systems, Unc. and Forec. We have still, however, ample reason for giving further consideration to the wish as the sole psychic motive power in the dream. We have explained that the reason why the dream is in every case a wish realization is because it is a product of the Unc., which knows no other aim in its activity but the fulfillment of wishes, and which has no other forces at its disposal but wish-feelings. If we avail ourselves for a moment longer of the right to elaborate from the dream interpretation such far-reaching psychological speculations, we are in duty bound to demonstrate that we are thereby bringing the dream into a relationship which may also comprise other psychic structures. If there exists a system of the Unc.—or something sufficiently analogous to it for the purpose of our discussion—the dream cannot be its sole manifestation; every dream may be a wish-fulfillment, but there must be other forms of abnormal wish-fulfillment beside this of dreams. Indeed, the theory of all psychoneurotic symptoms culminates in the proposition *that they too must be taken as wish-fulfillments of the unconscious*. Our explanation makes the dream only the first member of a group most important for the psychiatrist, an understanding of which means the solution of the purely psychological part of the psychiatric problem. But other members of this group of wish-fulfillments, *e.g.*, the hysterical symptoms, evince one essential quality which I have so far failed to find in the dream. Thus, from the investigations frequently referred to in this treatise, I know that the formation of an hysterical symptom necessitates the combination of both streams of our psychic life. The symptom is not merely the expression of a realized unconscious wish, but it must be joined by another wish from the foreconscious which is fulfilled by the same symptom; so that the symptom is at least doubly determined, once by each one of the conflicting systems. Just as in the dream, there is no limit to further over-determination. The determination not derived from the Unc. is, as far as I can see, invariably a stream of thought in reaction against the unconscious wish, *e.g.*, a self-punishment. Hence I may say, in general, that *an hysterical symptom originates only where two contrasting wish-fulfillments, having*

594

their source in different psychic systems, are able to combine in one expression. (Compare my latest formulation of the origin of the hysterical symptoms in a treatise published by the *Zeitschrift für Sexualwissenschaft*, by Hirschfeld and others, 1908). Examples on this point would prove of little value, as nothing but a complete unveiling of the complication in question would carry conviction. I therefore content myself with the mere assertion, and will cite an example, not for conviction but for explication. The hysterical vomiting of a female patient proved, on the one hand, to be the realization of an unconscious fancy from the time of puberty, that she might be continuously pregnant and have a multitude of children, and this was subsequently united with the wish that she might have them from as many men as possible. Against this immoderate wish there arose a powerful defensive impulse. But as the vomiting might spoil the patient's figure and beauty, so that she would not find favor in the eyes of mankind, the symptom was therefore in keeping with her punitive trend of thought, and, being thus admissible from both sides, it was allowed to become a reality. This is the same manner of consenting to a wish-fulfillment which the queen of the Parthians chose for the triumvir Crassus. Believing that he had undertaken the campaign out of greed for gold, she caused molten gold to be poured into the throat of the corpse. "Now hast thou what thou hast longed for." As yet we know of the dream only that it expresses a wish-fulfillment of the unconscious; and apparently the dominating foreconscious permits this only after it has subjected the wish to some distortions. We are really in no position to demonstrate regularly a stream of thought antagonistic to the dream-wish which is realized in the dream as in its counterpart. Only now and then have we found in the dream traces of reaction formations, as, for instance, the tenderness toward friend R. in the "uncle dream." But the contribution from the foreconscious, which is missing here, may be found in another place. While the dominating system has withdrawn on the wish to sleep, the dream may bring to expression with manifold distortions a wish from the Unc., and realize this wish by producing the necessary changes of energy in the psychic apparatus, and may finally retain it through the entire duration of sleep.[199]

This persistent wish to sleep on the part of the foreconscious in general facilitates the formation of the dream. Let us refer to the dream of the father who, by the gleam of light from the death chamber, was brought to the conclusion that the body has been set on fire. We have shown that one of the psychic forces decisive in causing the father to form this conclusion, instead of being awakened by the gleam of light, was the wish to prolong the life of the child seen in the dream by one moment. Other wishes proceeding from

---

[199] This idea has been borrowed from *The Theory of Sleep* by Liébault, who revived hypnotic investigation in our days. (*Du Sommeil provoqué*, etc.; Paris, 1889.)

the repression probably escape us, because we are unable to analyze this dream. But as a second motive power of the dream we may mention the father's desire to sleep, for, like the life of the child, the sleep of the father is prolonged for a moment by the dream. The underlying motive is: "Let the dream go on, otherwise I must wake up." As in this dream so also in all other dreams, the wish to sleep lends its support to the unconscious wish. We reported dreams which were apparently dreams of convenience. But, properly speaking, all dreams may claim this designation. The efficacy of the wish to continue to sleep is the most easily recognized in the waking dreams, which so transform the objective sensory stimulus as to render it compatible with the continuance of sleep; they interweave this stimulus with the dream in order to rob it of any claims it might make as a warning to the outer world. But this wish to continue to sleep must also participate in the formation of all other dreams which may disturb the sleeping state from within only. "Now, then, sleep on; why, it's but a dream"; this is in many cases the suggestion of the Forec. to consciousness when the dream goes too far; and this also describes in a general way the attitude of our dominating psychic activity toward dreaming, though the thought remains tacit. I must draw the conclusion that *throughout our entire sleeping state we are just as certain that we are dreaming as we are certain that we are sleeping*. We are compelled to disregard the objection urged against this conclusion that our consciousness is never directed to a knowledge of the former, and that it is directed to a knowledge of the latter only on special occasions when the censor is unexpectedly surprised. Against this objection we may say that there are persons who are entirely conscious of their sleeping and dreaming, and who are apparently endowed with the conscious faculty of guiding their dream life. Such a dreamer, when dissatisfied with the course taken by the dream, breaks it off without awakening, and begins it anew in order to continue it with a different turn, like the popular author who, on request, gives a happier ending to his play. Or, at another time, if placed by the dream in a sexually exciting situation, he thinks in his sleep: "I do not care to continue this dream and exhaust myself by a pollution; I prefer to defer it in favor of a real situation."

VII. THE FUNCTION OF THE DREAM

Since we know that the foreconscious is suspended during the night by the wish to sleep, we can proceed to an intelligent investigation of the dream process. But let us first sum up the knowledge of this process already gained. We have shown that the waking activity leaves day remnants from which the sum of energy cannot be entirely removed; or the waking activity revives during the day one of the unconscious wishes; or both conditions occur simultaneously; we have already discovered the many variations that may take place. The unconscious wish has already made its way to the day remnants, either during the day or at any rate with the beginning of sleep, and has effected a transference to it. This produces a wish transferred to the recent material, or the suppressed recent wish comes to life again through a reinforcement from the unconscious. This wish now endeavors to make its way to consciousness on the normal path of the mental processes through the foreconscious, to which indeed it belongs through one of its constituent elements. It is confronted, however, by the censor, which is still active, and to the influence of which it now succumbs. It now takes on the distortion for which the way has already been paved by its transference to the recent material. Thus far it is in the way of becoming something resembling an obsession, delusion, or the like, *i.e.* a thought reinforced by a transference and distorted in expression by the censor. But its further progress is now checked through the dormant state of the foreconscious; this system has apparently protected itself against invasion by diminishing its excitements. The dream process, therefore, takes the regressive course, which has just been opened by the peculiarity of the sleeping state, and thereby follows the attraction exerted on it by the memory groups, which themselves exist in part only as visual energy not yet translated into terms of the later systems. On its way to regression the dream takes on the form of dramatization. The subject of compression will be discussed later. The dream process has now terminated the second part of its repeatedly impeded course. The first part expended itself progressively from the unconscious scenes or phantasies to the foreconscious, while the second part gravitates from the advent of the censor back to the perceptions. But when the dream process becomes a content of perception it has, so to speak, eluded the obstacle set up in the Forec. by the censor and by the sleeping state. It succeeds in drawing attention to itself and in being noticed by consciousness. For consciousness, which means to us a sensory organ for the reception of psychic qualities, may receive stimuli from two sources—first, from the periphery of the entire apparatus, viz. from the perception system, and, secondly, from the pleasure and pain stimuli, which constitute the sole psychic quality produced in the transformation of energy within the apparatus. All other processes in the system, even those in the foreconscious, are devoid of any psychic quality, and are therefore not objects of consciousness inasmuch as they do not furnish pleasure or pain for perception. We shall have to assume that those liberations of pleasure and pain automatically regulate the outlet of the occupation processes. But in order to make possible more delicate functions, it was later found necessary to render the course of the presentations more independent of the manifestations of pain. To accomplish this the Forec. system needed some qualities of its own which could attract consciousness, and most probably received them through the connection of the foreconscious processes with the memory system of the signs of speech, which is not devoid of qualities. Through the qualities of this system, consciousness, which had hitherto been a sensory organ only for the perceptions, now becomes also a sensory organ for a part of our mental processes. Thus we have now, as it were, two sensory surfaces, one directed to perceptions and the other to the foreconscious mental processes.

I must assume that the sensory surface of consciousness devoted to the Forec. is rendered less excitable by sleep than that directed to the P-systems. The giving up of interest for the nocturnal mental processes is indeed purposeful. Nothing is to disturb the mind; the Forec. wants to sleep. But once the dream becomes a perception, it is then capable of exciting consciousness through the qualities thus gained. The sensory stimulus accomplishes what it was really destined for, namely, it directs a part of the energy at the disposal of the Forec. in the form of attention upon the stimulant. We must, therefore, admit that the dream invariably awakens us, that is, it puts into activity a part of the dormant force of the Forec. This force imparts to the dream that influence which we have designated as secondary elaboration for the sake of connection and comprehensibility. This means that the dream is treated by it like any other content of perception; it is subjected to the same ideas of expectation, as far at least as the material admits. As far as the direction is concerned in this third part of the dream, it may be said that here again the movement is progressive.

To avoid misunderstanding, it will not be amiss to say a few words about the temporal peculiarities of these dream processes. In a very interesting discussion, apparently suggested by Maury's puzzling guillotine dream, Goblet tries to demonstrate that the dream requires no other time than the transition period between sleeping and awakening. The awakening requires time, as the dream takes place during that period. One is inclined to believe that the final picture of the dream is so strong that it forces the dreamer to awaken; but, as a matter of fact, this picture is strong only because the dreamer is already very near awakening when it appears. "Un rêve c'est un réveil qui commence."

It has already been emphasized by Dugas that Goblet was forced to repudiate many facts in order to generalize his theory. There are, moreover, dreams from which we do not awaken, e.g., some dreams in which we dream that we dream. From our knowledge of the dream-work, we can by no means admit that it extends only over the period of awakening. On the contrary, we must consider it probable that the first part of the dream-work begins during the day when we are still under the domination of the foreconscious. The second phase of the dream-work, viz. the modification through the censor, the attraction by the unconscious scenes, and the penetration to perception must continue throughout the night. And we are probably always right when we assert that we feel as though we had been dreaming the whole night, although we cannot say what. I do not, however, think it necessary to assume that, up to the time of becoming conscious, the dream processes really follow the temporal sequence which we have described, viz. that there is first the transferred dream-wish, then the distortion of the censor, and consequently the change of direction to regression, and so on. We were forced to form such a succession for the sake of *description*; in reality, however, it is much rather a matter of simultaneously trying this path and that, and of emotions fluctuating to and fro, until finally, owing to the most expedient distribution, one particular grouping is secured which remains. From certain personal experiences, I am myself inclined to believe that the dream-work often requires more than one day and one night to produce its result; if this be true, the extraordinary art manifested in the construction of the dream loses all its marvels. In my opinion, even the regard for comprehensibility as an occurrence of perception may take effect before the dream attracts consciousness to itself. To be sure, from now on the process is accelerated, as the dream is henceforth subjected to the same treatment as any other perception. It is like fireworks, which require hours of preparation and only a moment for ignition.

Through the dream-work the dream process now gains either sufficient intensity to attract consciousness to itself and arouse the foreconscious, which is quite independent of the time or profundity of sleep, or, its intensity being insufficient it must wait until it meets the attention which is set in motion immediately before awakening. Most dreams seem to operate with relatively slight psychic intensities, for they wait for the awakening. This, however, explains the fact that we regularly perceive something dreamt on being suddenly aroused from a sound sleep. Here, as well as in spontaneous awakening, the first glance strikes the perception content created by the dream-work, while the next strikes the one produced from without.

But of greater theoretical interest are those dreams which are capable of waking us in the midst of sleep. We must bear in mind the expediency elsewhere universally demonstrated, and ask ourselves why the dream or the unconscious wish has the power to disturb sleep, *i.e.* the fulfillment of the foreconscious wish. This is probably due to certain relations of energy into which we have no insight. If we possessed such insight we should probably find that the freedom given to the dream and the expenditure of a certain amount of detached attention represent for the dream an economy in energy, keeping in view the fact that the unconscious must be held in check at night just as during the day. We know from experience that the dream, even if it interrupts sleep, repeatedly during the same night, still remains compatible with sleep. We wake up for an instant, and immediately resume our sleep. It is like driving off a fly during sleep, we awake *ad hoc*, and when we resume our sleep we have removed the disturbance. As demonstrated by familiar examples from the sleep of wet nurses, &c., the fulfillment of the wish to sleep is quite compatible with the retention of a certain amount of attention in a given direction.

But we must here take cognizance of an objection that is based on a better knowledge of the unconscious processes. Although we have ourselves described the unconscious wishes as always active, we have, nevertheless, asserted that they are not sufficiently strong during the day to make themselves perceptible. But when we sleep, and the unconscious wish has shown its power to form a dream, and with it to awaken the foreconscious, why, then, does this power become exhausted after the dream has been taken cognizance of? Would it not seem more probable that the dream should continually renew itself, like the troublesome fly which, when driven away, takes pleasure in returning again and again? What justifies our assertion that the dream removes the disturbance of sleep?

That the unconscious wishes always remain active is quite true. They represent paths which are passable whenever a sum of excitement makes use of them. Moreover, a remarkable peculiarity of the unconscious processes is the fact that they remain indestructible. Nothing can be brought to an end in the unconscious; nothing can cease or be forgotten. This impression is most strongly gained in the study of the neuroses, especially of hysteria. The unconscious stream of thought which leads to the discharge through an attack becomes passable again as soon as there is an accumulation of a sufficient amount of excitement. The mortification brought on thirty years ago, after having gained access to the unconscious affective source, operates during all these thirty years like a recent one. Whenever its memory is touched, it is revived and shows itself to be supplied with the excitement which is discharged in a motor attack. It is just here that the office of psychotherapy begins, its task being to bring about adjustment and forgetfulness for the unconscious processes. Indeed, the fading of memories and the flagging of affects, which we are apt to take as self-evident and to explain as a primary influence of time on the psychic memories, are in reality secondary changes brought about by painstaking work. It is the foreconscious that accomplishes this work; and the only course to be pursued by psychotherapy is the subjugate the Unc, to the domination of the Forec.

There are, therefore, two exits for the individual unconscious emotional process. It is either left to itself, in which case it ultimately breaks through somewhere and secures for once a discharge for its excitation into motility; or it succumbs to the influence of the foreconscious, and its excitation becomes confined through this influence instead of being discharged. It is the latter process that occurs in the dream. Owing to the fact that it is directed by the conscious excitement, the energy from the Forec., which confronts the dream when grown to perception, restricts the unconscious excitement of the dream and renders it harmless as a disturbing factor. When the dreamer wakes up for a moment, he has actually chased away the fly that has threatened to disturb his sleep. We can now understand that it is really more expedient and economical to give full sway to the unconscious wish, and clear its way to regression so that it may form a dream, and then restrict and adjust this dream by means of a small expenditure of foreconscious labor, than to curb the unconscious throughout the entire period of sleep. We should, indeed, expect that the dream, even if it was not originally an expedient process, would have acquired some function in the play of forces of the psychic life. We now see what this function is. The dream has taken it upon itself to bring the liberated excitement of the Unc. back under the domination of the foreconscious; it thus affords relief for the excitement of the Unc. and acts as a safety-valve for the latter, and at the same time it insures the sleep of the foreconscious at a slight expenditure of the waking state. Like the other psychic formations of its group, the dream offers itself as a compromise serving simultaneously both systems by fulfilling both wishes in so far as they are compatible with each other. A glance at Robert's "elimination theory," will show that we must agree with this author in his main point, viz. in the determination of the function of the dream, though we differ from him in our hypotheses and in our treatment of the dream process.

The above qualification—in so far as the two wishes are compatible with each other—contains a suggestion that there may be cases in which the function of the dream suffers shipwreck. The dream process is in the first instance admitted as a wish-fulfillment of the unconscious, but if this tentative wish-fulfillment disturbs the foreconscious to such an extent that the latter can no longer maintain its rest, the dream then breaks the compromise and fails to perform the second part of its task. It is then at once broken off, and replaced by complete wakefulness. Here, too, it is not really the fault of the dream, if, while ordinarily the guardian of sleep, it is here compelled to appear as the disturber of sleep, nor should this cause us to entertain any doubts as to its efficacy. This is not the only case in the organism in which an otherwise efficacious arrangement became inefficacious and disturbing as soon as some element is changed in the conditions of its origin; the disturbance then serves at least the new purpose of announcing the change, and calling into play against it the means of adjustment of the organism. In this connection, I naturally bear in mind the case of the anxiety dream, and in order not to have the appearance of trying to exclude this testimony against the theory of wish-fulfillment wherever I encounter it, I will attempt an explanation of the anxiety dream, at least offering some suggestions.

That a psychic process developing anxiety may still be a wish-fulfillment has long ceased to impress us as a contradiction. We may explain this occurrence by the fact that the wish belongs to one system (the Unc.), while by the other system (the Forec.), this wish has been rejected and suppressed. The subjection of the Unc. by the Forec. is not complete even in perfect psychic health; the amount of this suppression shows the degree of our psychic normality. Neurotic symptoms show that there is a conflict between the two systems; the symptoms are the results of a compromise of this conflict, and they temporarily put an end to it. On the one hand, they afford the Unc. an outlet for the discharge of its excitement, and serve it as a sally port, while, on the other hand, they give the Forec. the capability of dominating the Unc. to some extent. It is highly instructive to consider, *e.g.*, the significance of any hysterical phobia or of an agoraphobia. Suppose a neurotic incapable of crossing the street alone, which we would justly call a "symptom." We attempt to remove this symptom by urging him to the action which he deems himself incapable of. The result will be an attack of anxiety, just as an attack of anxiety in the street has often been the cause of establishing an agoraphobia. We thus learn that the symptom has been constituted in order to guard against the outbreak of the anxiety. The phobia is thrown before the anxiety like a fortress on the frontier.

Unless we enter into the part played by the affects in these processes, which can be done here only imperfectly, we cannot continue our discussion. Let us therefore advance the proposition that the reason why the suppression of the unconscious becomes absolutely necessary is because, if the discharge of presentation should be left to itself, it would develop an affect in the Unc. which originally bore the character of pleasure, but which, since the appearance of the repression, bears the character of pain. The aim, as well as the result, of the suppression is to stop the development of this pain. The suppression extends over the unconscious ideation, because the liberation of pain might emanate from the ideation. The foundation is here laid for a very definite assumption concerning the nature of the affective development. It is regarded as a motor or secondary activity, the key to the innervation of which is located in the presentations of the Unc. Through the domination of the Forec. these presentations become, as it were, throttled and inhibited at the exit of the emotion-developing impulses. The danger, which is due to the fact that the Forec. ceases to occupy the energy, therefore consists in the fact that the unconscious excitations liberate such an affect as—in consequence of the repression that has previously taken place—can only be perceived as pain or anxiety.

This danger is released through the full sway of the dream process. The determinations for its realization consist in the fact that repressions have taken place, and that the suppressed emotional wishes shall become sufficiently strong. They thus stand entirely without the psychological realm of the dream structure. Were it not for the fact that our subject is connected through just one factor, namely, the freeing of the Unc. during sleep, with the subject of the development of anxiety, I could dispense with discussion of the anxiety dream, and thus avoid all obscurities connected with it.

As I have often repeated, the theory of the anxiety belongs to the psychology of the neuroses. I would say that the anxiety in the dream is an anxiety problem and not a dream problem. We have nothing further to do with it after having once demonstrated its point of contact with the subject of the dream process. There is only one thing left for me to do. As I have asserted that the neurotic anxiety originates from sexual sources, I can subject anxiety dreams to analysis in order to demonstrate the sexual material in their dream thoughts.

For good reasons I refrain from citing here any of the numerous examples placed at my disposal by neurotic patients, but prefer to give anxiety dreams from young persons.

Personally, I have had no real anxiety dream for decades, but I recall one from my seventh or eighth year which I subjected to interpretation about thirty years later. The dream was very vivid, and showed me *my beloved mother, with peculiarly calm sleeping countenance, carried into the room and laid on the bed by two (or three) persons with birds' beaks*. I awoke crying and screaming, and disturbed my parents. The very tall figures—draped in a peculiar manner—with beaks, I had taken from the illustrations of Philippson's bible; I believe they represented deities with heads of sparrowhawks from an Egyptian tomb relief. The analysis also introduced the reminiscence of a naughty janitor's boy, who used to play with us children on the meadow in front of the house; I would add that his name was Philip. I feel that I first heard from this boy the vulgar word signifying sexual intercourse, which is replaced among the educated by the Latin "coitus," but to which the dream distinctly alludes by the selection of the birds' heads. I must have suspected the sexual significance of the word from the facial expression of my worldly-wise teacher. My mother's features in the dream were copied from the countenance of my grandfather, whom I had seen a few days before his death snoring in the state of coma. The interpretation of the secondary elaboration in the dream must therefore have been that my mother was dying; the tomb relief, too, agrees with this. In this anxiety I awoke, and could not calm myself until I had awakened my parents. I remember that I suddenly became calm on coming face to face with my mother, as if I needed the assurance that my mother was not dead. But this secondary interpretation of the dream had been effected only under the influence of the developed anxiety. I was not frightened because I dreamed that my mother was dying, but I interpreted the dream in this manner in the foreconscious elaboration because I was already under the domination of the anxiety. The latter, however, could be traced by means of the repression to an obscure obviously sexual desire, which had found its satisfying expression in the visual content of the dream.

A man twenty-seven years old who had been severely ill for a year had had many terrifying dreams between the ages of eleven and thirteen. He thought that a man with an ax was running after him; he wished to run, but felt paralyzed and could not move from the spot. This may be taken as a good example of a very common, and apparently sexually indifferent, anxiety dream. In the analysis the dreamer first thought of a story told him by his uncle, which chronologically was later than the dream, viz. that he was attacked at night by a suspicious-looking individual. This occurrence led him to believe that he himself might have already heard of a similar episode at the time of the dream. In connection with the ax he recalled that during that period of his life he once hurt his hand with an ax while chopping wood. This immediately led to his relations with his younger brother, whom he used to maltreat and knock down. In particular, he recalled an occasion when he struck his brother on the head with his boot until he bled, whereupon his mother remarked: "I fear he will kill him some day." While he was seemingly thinking of the subject of violence, a reminiscence from his ninth year suddenly occurred to him. His parents came home late and went to bed while he was feigning sleep. He soon heard panting and other noises that appeared strange to him, and he could also make out the position of his parents in bed. His further associations showed that he had established an analogy between this relation between his parents and his own relation toward his younger brother. He subsumed what occurred between his parents under the conception "violence and wrestling," and thus reached a sadistic conception of the coitus act, as often happens among children. The fact that he often noticed blood on his mother's bed corroborated his conception.

That the sexual intercourse of adults appears strange to children who observe it, and arouses fear in them, I dare say is a fact of daily experience. I have explained this fear by the fact that sexual excitement is not mastered by their understanding, and is probably also inacceptable to them because their parents are involved in it. For the same son this excitement is converted into fear. At a still earlier period of life sexual emotion directed toward the parent of opposite sex does not meet with repression but finds free expression, as we have seen before.

For the night terrors with hallucinations (*pavor nocturnus*) frequently found in children, I would unhesitatingly give the same explanation. Here, too, we are certainly dealing with the incomprehensible and rejected sexual feelings, which, if noted, would probably show a temporal periodicity, for an enhancement of the sexual *libido* may just as well be produced accidentally through emotional impressions as through the spontaneous and gradual processes of development.

I lack the necessary material to sustain these explanations from observation. On the other hand, the pediatrists seem to lack the point of view which alone makes comprehensible the whole series of phenomena, on the somatic as well as on the psychic side. To illustrate by a comical example how one wearing the blinders of medical mythology may miss the understanding of such cases I will relate a case which I found in a thesis on *pavor nocturnus* by *Debacker*, 1881. A thirteen-year-old boy of delicate health began to become anxious and dreamy; his sleep became restless, and about once a week it was interrupted by an acute attack of anxiety with hallucinations. The memory of these dreams was invariably very distinct. Thus, he related that the *devil* shouted at him: "Now we have you, now we have you," and this was followed by an odor of sulphur; the fire burned his skin. This dream aroused him, terror-stricken. He was unable to scream at first; then his voice returned, and he was heard to say distinctly: "No, no, not me; why, I have done nothing," or, "Please don't, I shall never do it again." Occasionally, also, he said: "Albert has not done that." Later he avoided undressing, because, as he said, the fire attacked him only when he was undressed. From amid these evil dreams, which menaced his health, he was sent into the country, where he recovered within a year and a half, but at the age of fifteen he once confessed: "Je n'osais pas l'avouer, mais j'éprouvais continuellement des picotements et des surexcitations aux *parties*; à la fin, cela m'énervait tant que plusieurs fois, j'ai pensé me jeter par la fenêtre au dortoir."

It is certainly not difficult to suspect: 1, that the boy had practiced masturbation in former years, that he probably denied it, and was threatened with severe punishment for his wrongdoing (his confession: Je ne le ferai plus; his denial: Albert n'a jamais fait ça). 2, That under the pressure of puberty the temptation to self-abuse through the tickling of the genitals was reawakened. 3, That now, however, a struggle of repression arose in him, suppressing the *libido* and changing it into fear, which subsequently took the form of the punishments with which he was then threatened.

Let us, however, quote the conclusions drawn by our author. This observation shows:

1, That the influence of puberty may produce in a boy of delicate health a condition of extreme weakness, and that it may lead to a *very marked cerebral anæmia.*

2. This cerebral anæmia produces a transformation of character, demonomaniacal hallucinations, and very violent nocturnal, perhaps also diurnal, states of anxiety.

3. Demonomania and the self-reproaches of the day can be traced to the influences of religious education which the subject underwent as a child.

4. All manifestations disappeared as a result of a lengthy sojourn in the country, bodily exercise, and the return of physical strength after the termination of the period of puberty.

5. A predisposing influence for the origin of the cerebral condition of the boy may be attributed to heredity and to the father's chronic syphilitic state.

The concluding remarks of the author read: "Nous avons fait entrer cette observation dans le cadre des délires apyrétiques d'inanition, car c'est à l'ischémie cérébrale que nous rattachons cet état particulier."

VIII. THE PRIMARY AND SECONDARY PROCESS—REGRESSION

In venturing to attempt to penetrate more deeply into the psychology of the dream processes, I have undertaken a difficult task, to which, indeed, my power of description is hardly equal. To reproduce in description by a succession of words the simultaneousness of so complex a chain of events, and in doing so to appear unbiassed throughout the exposition, goes fairly beyond my powers. I have now to atone for the fact that I have been unable in my description of the dream psychology to follow the historic development of my views. The view-points for my conception of the dream were reached through earlier investigations in the psychology of the neuroses, to which I am not supposed to refer here, but to which I am repeatedly forced to refer, whereas I should prefer to proceed in the opposite direction, and, starting from the dream, to establish a connection with the psychology of the neuroses. I am well aware of all the inconveniences arising for the reader from this difficulty, but I know of no way to avoid them.

As I am dissatisfied with this state of affairs, I am glad to dwell upon another view-point which seems to raise the value of my efforts. As has been shown in the introduction to the first chapter, I found myself confronted with a theme which had been marked by the sharpest contradictions on the part of the authorities. After our elaboration of the dream problems we found room for most of these contradictions. We have been forced, however, to take decided exception to two of the views pronounced, viz. that the dream is a senseless and that it is a somatic process; apart from these cases we have had to accept all the contradictory views in one place or another of the complicated argument, and we have been able to demonstrate that they had discovered something that was correct. That the dream continues the impulses and interests of the waking state has been quite generally confirmed through the discovery of the latent thoughts of the dream. These thoughts concern themselves only with things that seem important and of momentous interest to us. The dream never occupies itself with trifles. But we have also concurred with the contrary view, viz., that the dream gathers up the indifferent remnants from the day, and that not until it has in some measure withdrawn itself from the waking activity can an important event of the day be taken up by the dream. We found this holding true for the dream content, which gives the dream thought its changed expression by means of disfigurement. We have said that from the nature of the association mechanism the dream process more easily takes possession of recent or indifferent material which has not yet been seized by the waking mental activity; and by reason of the censor it transfers the psychic intensity from the important but also disagreeable to the indifferent material. The hypermnesia of the dream and the resort to infantile material have become main supports in our theory. In our theory of the dream we have attributed to the wish originating from the infantile the part of an indispensable motor for the formation of the dream. We naturally could not think of doubting the experimentally demonstrated significance of the objective sensory stimuli during sleep; but we have brought this material into the same relation to the dream-wish as the thought remnants from the waking activity. There was no need of disputing the fact that the dream interprets the objective sensory stimuli after the manner of an illusion; but we have supplied the motive for this interpretation which has been left undecided by the authorities. The interpretation follows in such a manner that the perceived object is rendered harmless as a sleep disturber and becomes available for the wish-fulfillment. Though we do not admit as special sources of the dream the subjective state of excitement of the sensory organs during sleep, which seems to have been demonstrated by Trumbull Ladd, we are nevertheless able to explain this excitement through the regressive revival of active memories behind the dream. A modest part in our conception has also been assigned to the inner organic sensations which are wont to be taken as the cardinal point in the explanation of the dream. These—the sensation of falling, flying, or inhibition—stand as an ever ready material to be used by the dream-work to express the dream thought as often as need arises.

That the dream process is a rapid and momentary one seems to be true for the perception through consciousness of the already prepared dream content; the preceding parts of the dream process probably take a slow, fluctuating course. We have solved the riddle of the superabundant dream content compressed within the briefest moment by explaining that this is due to the appropriation of almost fully formed structures from the psychic life. That the dream is disfigured and distorted by memory we found to be correct, but not troublesome, as this is only the last manifest operation in the work of disfigurement which has been active from the beginning of the dream-work.

In the bitter and seemingly irreconcilable controversy as to whether the psychic life sleeps at night or can make the same use of all its capabilities as during the day, we have been able to agree with both sides, though not fully with either. We have found proof that the dream thoughts represent a most complicated intellectual activity, employing almost every means furnished by the psychic apparatus; still it cannot be denied that these dream thoughts have originated during the day, and it is indispensable to assume that there is a sleeping state of the psychic life. Thus, even the theory of partial sleep has come into play; but the characteristics of the sleeping state have been found not in the dilapidation of the psychic connections but in the cessation of the psychic system dominating the day, arising from its desire to sleep. The withdrawal from the outer world retains its significance also for our conception; though not the only factor, it nevertheless helps the regression to make possible the representation of the dream. That we should reject the voluntary guidance of the presentation course is uncontestable; but the psychic life does not thereby become aimless, for we have seen that after the abandonment of the desired end-presentation undesired ones gain the mastery. The loose associative connection in the dream we have not only recognized, but we have placed under its control a far greater territory than could have been supposed; we have, however, found it merely the feigned substitute for another correct and senseful one. To be sure we, too, have called the dream absurd; but we have been able to learn from examples how wise the dream really is when it simulates absurdity. We do not deny any of the functions that have been attributed to the dream. That the dream relieves the mind like a valve, and that, according to Robert's assertion, all kinds of harmful material are rendered harmless through representation in the dream, not only exactly coincides with our theory of the twofold wish-fulfillment in the dream, but, in his own wording, becomes even more comprehensible for us than for Robert himself. The free indulgence of the psychic in the play of its faculties finds expression with us in the non-interference with the dream on the part of the foreconscious activity. The "return to the embryonal state of psychic life in the dream" and the observation of Havelock Ellis, "an archaic world of vast emotions and imperfect thoughts," appear to us as happy anticipations of our deductions to the effect that *primitive* modes of work suppressed during the day participate in the formation of the dream; and with us, as with Delage, the *suppressed* material becomes the mainspring of the dreaming.

We have fully recognized the rôle which Scherner ascribes to the dream phantasy, and even his interpretation; but we have been obliged, so to speak, to conduct them to another department in the problem. It is not the dream that produces the phantasy but the unconscious phantasy that takes the greatest part in the formation of the dream thoughts. We are indebted to Scherner for his clew to the source of the dream thoughts, but almost everything that he ascribes to the dream-work is attributable to the activity of the unconscious, which is at work during the day, and which supplies incitements not only for dreams but for neurotic symptoms as well. We have had to separate the dream-work from this activity as being something entirely different and far more restricted. Finally, we have by no means abandoned the relation of the dream to mental disturbances, but, on the contrary, we have given it a more solid foundation on new ground.

Thus held together by the new material of our theory as by a superior unity, we find the most varied and most contradictory conclusions of the authorities fitting into our structure; some of them are differently disposed, only a few of them are entirely rejected. But our own structure is still unfinished. For, disregarding the many obscurities which we have necessarily encountered in our advance into the darkness of psychology, we are now apparently embarrassed by a new contradiction. On the one hand, we have allowed the dream thoughts to proceed from perfectly normal mental operations, while, on the other hand, we have found among the dream thoughts a number of entirely abnormal mental processes which extend likewise to the dream contents. These, consequently, we have repeated in the interpretation of the dream. All that we have termed the "dream-work" seems so remote from the psychic processes recognized by us as correct, that the severest judgments of the authors as to the low psychic activity of dreaming seem to us well founded.

Perhaps only through still further advance can enlightenment and improvement be brought about. I shall pick out one of the constellations leading to the formation of dreams.

We have learned that the dream replaces a number of thoughts derived from daily life which are perfectly formed logically. We cannot therefore doubt that these thoughts originate from our normal mental life. All the qualities which we esteem in our mental operations, and which distinguish these as complicated activities of a high order, we find repeated in the dream thoughts. There is, however, no need of assuming that this mental work is performed during sleep, as this would materially impair the conception of the psychic state of sleep we have hitherto adhered to. These thoughts may just as well have originated from the day, and, unnoticed by our consciousness from their inception, they may have continued to develop until they stood complete at the onset of sleep. If we are to conclude anything from this state of affairs, it will at most prove *that the most complex mental operations are possible without the coöperation of consciousness*, which we have already learned independently from every psychoanalysis of persons suffering from hysteria or obsessions. These dream thoughts are in themselves surely not incapable of consciousness; if they have not become conscious to us during the day, this may have various reasons. The state of becoming conscious depends on the exercise of a certain psychic function, viz. attention, which seems to be extended only in a definite quantity, and which may have been withdrawn from the stream of thought in Question by other aims. Another way in which such mental streams are kept from consciousness is the following:—Our conscious reflection teaches us that when exercising attention we pursue a definite course. But if that course leads us to an idea which does not hold its own with the critic, we discontinue and cease to apply our attention. Now, apparently, the stream of thought thus started and abandoned may spin on without regaining attention unless it reaches a spot of especially marked intensity which forces the return of attention. An initial rejection, perhaps consciously brought about by the judgment on the ground of incorrectness or unfitness for the actual purpose of the mental act, may therefore account for the fact that a mental process continues until the onset of sleep unnoticed by consciousness.

Let us recapitulate by saying that we call such a stream of thought a foreconscious one, that we believe it to be perfectly correct, and that it may just as well be a more neglected one or an interrupted and suppressed one. Let us also state frankly in what manner we conceive this presentation course. We believe that a certain sum of excitement, which we call occupation energy, is displaced from an end-presentation along the association paths selected by that end-presentation. A "neglected" stream of thought has received no such occupation, and from a "suppressed" or "rejected" one this occupation has been withdrawn; both have thus been left to their own emotions. The end-stream of thought stocked with energy is under certain conditions able to draw to itself the attention of consciousness, through which means it then receives a "surplus of energy." We shall be obliged somewhat later to elucidate our assumption concerning the nature and activity of consciousness.

A train of thought thus incited in the Forec. may either disappear spontaneously or continue. The former issue we conceive as follows: It diffuses its energy through all the association paths emanating from it, and throws the entire chain of ideas into a state of excitement which, after lasting for a while, subsides through the transformation of the excitement requiring an outlet into dormant energy.[200] If this first issue is brought about the process has no further significance for the dream formation. But other end-presentations are lurking in our foreconscious that originate from the sources of our unconscious and from the ever active wishes. These may take possession of the excitations in the circle of thought thus left to itself, establish a connection between it and the unconscious wish, and transfer to it the energy inherent in the unconscious wish. Henceforth the neglected or

_____

[200] *Cf.* the significant observations by J. Bueuer in our *Studies on Hysteria*, 1895, and 2nd ed. 1909.

suppressed train of thought is in a position to maintain itself, although this reinforcement does not help it to gain access to consciousness. We may say that the hitherto foreconscious train of thought has been drawn into the unconscious.

Other constellations for the dream formation would result if the foreconscious train of thought had from the beginning been connected with the unconscious wish, and for that reason met with rejection by the dominating end-occupation; or if an unconscious wish were made active for other—possibly somatic—reasons and of its own accord sought a transference to the psychic remnants not occupied by the Forec. All three cases finally combine in one issue, so that there is established in the foreconscious a stream of thought which, having been abandoned by the foreconscious occupation, receives occupation from the unconscious wish.

The stream of thought is henceforth subjected to a series of transformations which we no longer recognize as normal psychic processes and which give us a surprising result, viz. a psychopathological formation. Let us emphasize and group the same.

1. The intensities of the individual ideas become capable of discharge in their entirety, and, proceeding from one conception to the other, they thus form single presentations endowed with marked intensity. Through the repeated recurrence of this process the intensity of an entire train of ideas may ultimately be gathered in a single presentation element. This is the principle of *compression or condensation*. It is condensation that is mainly responsible for the strange impression of the dream, for we know of nothing analogous to it in the normal psychic life accessible to consciousness. We find here, also, presentations which possess great psychic significance as junctions or as end-results of whole chains of thought; but this validity does not manifest itself in any character conspicuous enough for internal perception; hence, what has been presented in it does not become in any way more intensive. In the process of condensation the entire psychic connection becomes transformed into the intensity of the presentation content. It is the same as in a book where we space or print in heavy type any word upon which particular stress is laid for the understanding of the text. In speech the same word would be pronounced loudly and deliberately and with emphasis. The first comparison leads us at once to an example taken from the chapter on "The Dream-Work" (trimethylamine in the dream of Irma's injection). Historians of art call our attention to the fact that the most ancient historical sculptures follow a similar principle in expressing the rank of the persons represented by the size of the statue. The king is made two or three times as large as his retinue or the vanquished enemy. A piece of art, however, from the Roman period makes use of more subtle means to accomplish the same purpose. The figure of the emperor is placed in the center in a firmly erect

posture; special care is bestowed on the proper modelling of his figure; his enemies are seen cowering at his feet; but he is no longer represented a giant among dwarfs. However, the bowing of the subordinate to his superior in our own days is only an echo of that ancient principle of representation.

The direction taken by the condensations of the dream is prescribed on the one hand by the true foreconscious relations of the dream thoughts, an the other hand by the attraction of the visual reminiscences in the unconscious. The success of the condensation work produces those intensities which are required for penetration into the perception systems.

2. Through this free transferability of the intensities, moreover, and in the service of condensation, *intermediary presentations*—compromises, as it were—are formed (*cf.* the numerous examples). This, likewise, is something unheard of in the normal presentation course, where it is above all a question of selection and retention of the "proper" presentation element. On the other hand, composite and compromise formations occur with extraordinary frequency when we are trying to find the linguistic expression for foreconscious thoughts; these are considered "slips of the tongue."

3. The presentations which transfer their intensities to one another are *very loosely connected*, and are joined together by such forms of association as are spurned in our serious thought and are utilized in the production of the effect of wit only. Among these we particularly find associations of the sound and consonance types.

4. Contradictory thoughts do not strive to eliminate one another, but remain side by side. They often unite to produce condensation *as if no contradiction* existed, or they form compromises for which we should never forgive our thoughts, but which we frequently approve of in our actions.

These are some of the most conspicuous abnormal processes to which the thoughts which have previously been rationally formed are subjected in the course of the dream-work. As the main feature of these processes we recognize the high importance attached to the fact of rendering the occupation energy mobile and capable of discharge; the content and the actual significance of the psychic elements, to which these energies adhere, become a matter of secondary importance. One might possibly think that the condensation and compromise formation is effected only in the service of regression, when occasion arises for changing thoughts into pictures. But the analysis and—still more distinctly—the synthesis of dreams which lack regression toward pictures, *e.g.* the dream "Autodidasker—Conversation with Court-Councilor N.," present the same processes of displacement and condensation as the others.

Hence we cannot refuse to acknowledge that the two kinds of essentially different psychic processes participate in the formation of the dream; one forms perfectly correct dream thoughts which are equivalent to normal thoughts, while the other treats these ideas in a highly surprising and incorrect manner. The latter process we have already set apart as the dream-work proper. What have we now to advance concerning this latter psychic process?

We should be unable to answer this question here if we had not penetrated considerably into the psychology of the neuroses and especially of hysteria. From this we learn that the same incorrect psychic processes—as well as others that have not been enumerated—control the formation of hysterical symptoms. In hysteria, too, we at once find a series of perfectly correct thoughts equivalent to our conscious thoughts, of whose existence, however, in this form we can learn nothing and which we can only subsequently reconstruct. If they have forced their way anywhere to our perception, we discover from the analysis of the symptom formed that these normal thoughts have been subjected to abnormal treatment and *have been transformed into the symptom by means of condensation and compromise formation, through superficial associations, under cover of contradictions, and eventually over the road of regression.* In view of the complete identity found between the peculiarities of the dream-work and of the psychic activity forming the psychoneurotic symptoms, we shall feel justified in transferring to the dream the conclusions urged upon us by hysteria.

From the theory of hysteria we borrow the proposition that *such an abnormal psychic elaboration of a normal train of thought takes place only when the latter has been used for the transference of an unconscious wish which dates from the infantile life and is in a state of repression.* In accordance with this proposition we have construed the theory of the dream on the assumption that the actuating dream-wish invariably originates in the unconscious, which, as we ourselves have admitted, cannot be universally demonstrated though it cannot be refuted. But in order to explain the real meaning of the term *repression*, which we have employed so freely, we shall be obliged to make some further addition to our psychological construction.

We have above elaborated the fiction of a primitive psychic apparatus, whose work is regulated by the efforts to avoid accumulation of excitement and as far as possible to maintain itself free from excitement. For this reason it was constructed after the plan of a reflex apparatus; the motility, originally the path for the inner bodily change, formed a discharging path standing at its disposal. We subsequently discussed the psychic results of a feeling of gratification, and we might at the same time have introduced the second assumption, viz. that accumulation of excitement—following certain modalities that do not concern us—is perceived as pain and sets the apparatus in motion in order to reproduce a feeling of gratification in which the diminution of the excitement is perceived as pleasure. Such a current in the apparatus which emanates from pain and strives for pleasure we call a wish. We have said that nothing but a wish is capable of setting the apparatus in motion, and that the discharge of excitement in the apparatus is regulated automatically by the perception of pleasure and pain. The first wish must have been an hallucinatory occupation of the memory for gratification. But this hallucination, unless it were maintained to the point of exhaustion, proved incapable of bringing about a cessation of the desire and consequently of securing the pleasure connected with gratification.

Thus there was required a second activity—in our terminology the activity of a second system—which should not permit the memory occupation to advance to perception and therefrom to restrict the psychic forces, but should lead the excitement emanating from the craving stimulus by a devious path over the spontaneous motility which ultimately should so change the outer world as to allow the real perception of the object of gratification to take place. Thus far we have elaborated the plan of the psychic apparatus; these two systems are the germ of the Unc. and Forec, which we include in the fully developed apparatus.

In order to be in a position successfully to change the outer world through the motility, there is required the accumulation of a large sum of experiences in the memory systems as well as a manifold fixation of the relations which are evoked in this memory material by different end-presentations. We now proceed further with our assumption. The manifold activity of the second system, tentatively sending forth and retracting energy, must on the one hand have full command over all memory material, but on the other hand it would be a superfluous expenditure for it to send to the individual mental paths large quantities of energy which would thus flow off to no purpose, diminishing the quantity available for the transformation of the outer world. In the interests of expediency I therefore postulate that the second system succeeds in maintaining the greater part of the occupation energy in a dormant state and in using but a small portion for the purposes of displacement. The mechanism of these processes is entirely unknown to me; any one who wishes to follow up these ideas must try to find the physical analogies and prepare the way for a demonstration of the process of motion in the stimulation of the neuron. I merely hold to the idea that the activity of the first Ψ-system is directed *to the free outflow of the quantities of excitement*, and that the second system brings about an inhibition of this outflow through the energies emanating from it, *i.e.* it produces a *transformation into dormant energy, probably by raising the level.* I therefore assume that under the control of the second system as compared with the first, the course of the excitement is bound to entirely different mechanical conditions. After the second system has finished its tentative mental work, it removes the inhibition and congestion of the excitements and allows these excitements to flow off to the motility.

An interesting train of thought now presents itself if we consider the relations of this inhibition of discharge by the second system to the regulation through the principle of pain. Let us now seek the counterpart of the primary feeling of gratification, namely, the objective feeling of fear. A perceptive stimulus acts on the primitive apparatus, becoming the source of a painful emotion. This will then be followed by irregular motor manifestations until one of these withdraws the apparatus from perception and at the same time from pain, but on the reappearance of the perception this manifestation will immediately repeat itself (perhaps as a movement of flight) until the perception has again disappeared. But there will here remain no tendency again to occupy the perception of the source of pain in the form of an hallucination or in any other form. On the contrary, there will be a tendency in the primary apparatus to abandon the painful memory picture as soon as it is in any way awakened, as the overflow of its excitement would surely produce (more precisely, begin to produce) pain. The deviation from memory, which is but a repetition of the former flight from perception, is facilitated also by the fact that, unlike perception, memory does not possess sufficient quality to excite consciousness and thereby to attract to itself new energy. This easy and regularly occurring deviation of the psychic process from the former painful memory presents to us the model and the first example of *psychic repression*. As is generally known, much of this deviation from the painful, much of the behavior of the ostrich, can be readily demonstrated even in the normal psychic life of adults.

By virtue of the principle of pain the first system is therefore altogether incapable of introducing anything unpleasant into the mental associations. The system cannot do anything but wish. If this remained so the mental activity of the second system, which should have at its disposal all the memories stored up by experiences, would be hindered. But two ways are now opened: the work of the second system either frees itself completely from the principle of pain and continues its course, paying no heed to the painful reminiscence, or it contrives to occupy the painful memory in such a manner as to preclude the liberation of pain. We may reject the first possibility, as the principle of pain also manifests itself as a regulator for the emotional discharge of the second system; we are, therefore, directed to the second possibility, namely, that this system occupies a reminiscence in such a manner as to inhibit its discharge and hence, also, to inhibit the discharge comparable to a motor innervation for the development of pain. Thus from two starting points we are led to the hypothesis that occupation through the second system is at the same time an inhibition for the emotional discharge, viz. from a consideration of the principle of pain and from the principle of the smallest expenditure of innervation. Let us, however, keep to the fact—this is the key to the theory of repression—that the second system is capable of occupying an idea only when it is in position to check the development of pain emanating from it. Whatever withdraws itself from this inhibition also remains inaccessible for the second system and would soon be abandoned by virtue of the principle of pain. The inhibition of pain, however, need not be complete; it must be permitted to begin, as it indicates to the second system the nature of the memory and possibly its defective adaptation for the purpose sought by the mind.

The psychic process which is admitted by the first system only I shall now call the *primary* process; and the one resulting from the inhibition of the second system I shall call the *secondary* process. I show by another point for what purpose the second system is obliged to correct the primary process. The primary process strives for a discharge of the excitement in order to establish a *perception* identity with the sum of excitement thus gathered; the secondary process has abandoned this intention and undertaken instead the task of bringing about a *thought identity*. All thinking is only a circuitous path from the memory of gratification taken as an end-presentation to the identical occupation of the same memory, which is again to be attained on the track of the motor experiences. The state of thinking must take an interest in the connecting paths between the presentations without allowing itself to be misled by their intensities. But it is obvious that condensations and intermediate or compromise formations occurring in the presentations impede the attainment of this end-identity; by substituting one idea for the other they deviate from the path which otherwise would have been continued from the original idea. Such processes are therefore carefully avoided in the secondary thinking. Nor is it difficult to understand that the principle of pain also impedes the progress of the mental stream in its pursuit of the thought identity, though, indeed, it offers to the mental stream the most important points of departure. Hence the tendency of the thinking process must be to free itself more and more from exclusive adjustment by the principle of pain, and through the working of the mind to restrict the affective development to that minimum which is necessary as a signal. This refinement of the activity must have been attained through a recent over-occupation of energy brought about by consciousness. But we are aware that this refinement is seldom completely successful even in the most normal psychic life and that our thoughts ever remain accessible to falsification through the interference of the principle of pain.

This, however, is not the breach in the functional efficiency of our psychic apparatus through which the thoughts forming the material of the secondary mental work are enabled to make their way into the primary psychic process—with which formula we may now describe the work leading to the dream and to the hysterical symptoms. This case of insufficiency results from the union of the two factors from the history of our evolution; one of which belongs solely to the psychic apparatus and has exerted a determining influence on the relation of the two systems, while the other operates fluctuatingly and introduces motive forces of organic origin into the psychic life. Both originate in the infantile life and result from the transformation which our psychic and somatic organism has undergone since the infantile period.

When I termed one of the psychic processes in the psychic apparatus the primary process, I did so not only in consideration of the order of precedence and capability, but also as admitting the temporal relations to a share in the nomenclature. As far as our knowledge goes there is no psychic apparatus possessing only the primary process, and in so far it is a theoretic fiction; but so much is based on fact that the primary processes are present in the apparatus from the beginning, while the secondary processes develop gradually in the course of life, inhibiting and covering the primary ones, and gaining complete mastery over them perhaps only at the height of life. Owing to this retarded appearance of the secondary processes, the essence of our being, consisting in unconscious wish feelings, can neither be seized nor inhibited by the foreconscious, whose part is once for all restricted to the indication of the most suitable paths for the wish feelings originating in the unconscious. These unconscious wishes establish for all subsequent psychic efforts a compulsion to which they have to submit and which they must strive if possible to divert from its course and direct to higher aims. In consequence of this retardation of the foreconscious occupation a large sphere of the memory material remains inaccessible.

Among these indestructible and unincumbered wish feelings originating from the infantile life, there are also some, the fulfillments of which have entered into a relation of contradiction to the end-presentation of the secondary thinking. The fulfillment of these wishes would no longer produce an affect of pleasure but one of pain; *and it is just this transformation of affect that constitutes the nature of what we designate as "repression," in which we recognize the infantile first step of passing adverse sentence or of rejecting through reason.* To investigate in what way and through what motive forces such a transformation can be produced constitutes the problem of repression, which we need here only skim over. It will suffice to remark that such a transformation of affect occurs in the course of development (one may think of the appearance in infantile life of disgust which was originally absent), and that it is connected with the activity of the secondary system. The memories from which the unconscious wish brings about the emotional discharge have never been accessible to the Forec., and for that reason their emotional discharge cannot be inhibited. It is just on account of this affective development that these ideas are not even now accessible to the foreconscious thoughts to which they have transferred their wishing power. On the contrary, the principle of pain comes into play, and causes the Forec.

to deviate from these thoughts of transference. The latter, left to themselves, are "repressed," and thus the existence of a store of infantile memories, from the very beginning withdrawn from the Forec., becomes the preliminary condition of repression.

In the most favorable case the development of pain terminates as soon as the energy has been withdrawn from the thoughts of transference in the Forec., and this effect characterizes the intervention of the principle of pain as expedient. It is different, however, if the repressed unconscious wish receives an organic enforcement which it can lend to its thoughts of transference and through which it can enable them to make an effort towards penetration with their excitement, even after they have been abandoned by the occupation of the Forec. A defensive struggle then ensues, inasmuch as the Forec. reinforces the antagonism against the repressed ideas, and subsequently this leads to a penetration by the thoughts of transference (the carriers of the unconscious wish) in some form of compromise through symptom formation. But from the moment that the suppressed thoughts are powerfully occupied by the unconscious wish-feeling and abandoned by the foreconscious occupation, they succumb to the primary psychic process and strive only for motor discharge; or, if the path be free, for hallucinatory revival of the desired perception identity. We have previously found, empirically, that the incorrect processes described are enacted only with thoughts that exist in the repression. We now grasp another part of the connection. These incorrect processes are those that are primary in the psychic apparatus; *they appear wherever thoughts abandoned by the foreconscious occupation are left to themselves, and can fill themselves with the uninhibited energy, striving for discharge from the unconscious.* We may add a few further observations to support the view that these processes designated "incorrect" are really not falsifications of the normal defective thinking, but the modes of activity of the psychic apparatus when freed from inhibition. Thus we see that the transference of the foreconscious excitement to the motility takes place according to the same processes, and that the connection of the foreconscious presentations with words readily manifest the same displacements and mixtures which are ascribed to inattention. Finally, I should like to adduce proof that an increase of work necessarily results from the inhibition of these primary courses from the fact that we gain a *comical effect*, a surplus to be discharged through laughter, *if we allow these streams of thought to come to consciousness.*

The theory of the psychoneuroses asserts with complete certainty that only sexual wish-feelings from the infantile life experience repression (emotional transformation) during the developmental period of childhood. These are capable of returning to activity at a later period of development, and then have the faculty of being revived, either as a consequence of the sexual constitution, which is really formed from the original bisexuality, or in consequence of unfavorable influences of the sexual life; and they thus supply the motive power for all psychoneurotic symptom formations. It is only by the introduction of these sexual forces that the gaps still demonstrable in the theory of repression can be filled. I will leave it undecided whether the postulate of the sexual and infantile may also be asserted for the theory of the dream; I leave this here unfinished because I have already passed a step beyond the demonstrable in assuming that thedream-wish invariably originates from the unconscious.[201] Nor will I further investigate the difference in the play of the psychic forces in the dream formation and in the formation of the hysterical symptoms, for to do this we ought to possess a more explicit knowledge of one of the members to be compared. But I regard another point as important, and will here confess that it was on account of this very point that I have just undertaken this entire discussion concerning the two psychic systems, their modes of operation, and the repression. For it is now immaterial whether I have conceived the psychological relations in question with approximate correctness, or, as is easily possible in such a difficult matter, in an erroneous and fragmentary manner. Whatever changes may be made in the interpretation of the psychic censor and of the correct and of the abnormal elaboration of the dream content, the fact nevertheless remains that such processes are active in dream formation, and that essentially they show the closest analogy to the processes observed in the formation of the hysterical symptoms. The dream is not a pathological phenomenon, and it does not leave behind an enfeeblement of the mental faculties. The objection that no deduction can be drawn regarding the dreams of healthy persons from my own dreams and from those of neurotic patients

---

[201] Here, as in other places, there are gaps in the treatment of the subject, which I have left intentionally, because to fill them up would require on the one hand too great effort, and on the other hand an extensive reference to material that is foreign to the dream. Thus I have avoided stating whether I connect with the word "suppressed" another sense than with the word "repressed." It has been made clear only that the latter emphasizes more than the former the relation to the unconscious. I have not entered into the cognate problem why the dream thoughts also experience distortion by the censor when they abandon the progressive continuation to consciousness and choose the path of regression. I have been above all anxious to awaken an interest in the problems to which the further analysis of the dreamwork leads and to indicate the other themes which meet these on the way. It was not always easy to decide just where the pursuit should be discontinued. That I have not treated exhaustively the part played in the dream by the psychosexual life and have avoided the interpretation of dreams of an obvious sexual content is due to a special reason which may not come up to the reader's expectation. To be sure, it is very far from my ideas and the principles expressed by me in neuropathology to regard the sexual life as a "pudendum" which should be left unconsidered by the physician and the scientific investigator. I also consider ludicrous the moral indignation which prompted the translator of Artemidoros of Daldis to keep from the reader's knowledge the chapter on sexual dreams contained in the *Symbolism of the Dreams*. As for myself, I have been actuated solely by the conviction that in the explanation of sexual dreams I should be bound to entangle myself deeply in the still unexplained problems of perversion and bisexuality; and for that reason I have reserved this material for another connection.

may be rejected without comment. Hence, when we draw conclusions from the phenomena as to their motive forces, we recognize that the psychic mechanism made use of by the neuroses is not created by a morbid disturbance of the psychic life, but is found ready in the normal structure of the psychic apparatus. The two psychic systems, the censor crossing between them, the inhibition and the covering of the one activity by the other, the relations of both to consciousness—or whatever may offer a more correct interpretation of the actual conditions in their stead—all these belong to the normal structure of our psychic instrument, and the dream points out for us one of the roads leading to a knowledge of this structure. If, in addition to our knowledge, we wish to be contented with a minimum perfectly established, we shall say that the dream gives us proof that the *suppressed, material continues to exist even in the normal person and remains capable of psychic activity.* The dream itself is one of the manifestations of this suppressed material; theoretically, this is true in *all* cases; according to substantial experience it is true in at least a great number of such as most conspicuously display the prominent characteristics of dream life. The suppressed psychic material, which in the waking state has been prevented from expression and cut off from internal perception *by the antagonistic adjustment of the contradictions*, finds ways and means of obtruding itself on consciousness during the night under the domination of the compromise formations.

"*Flectere si nequeo superos, Acheronta movebo.*"

At any rate the interpretation of dreams is the *via regia* to a knowledge of the unconscious in the psychic life.

In following the analysis of the dream we have made some progress toward an understanding of the composition of this most marvelous and most mysterious of instruments; to be sure, we have not gone very far, but enough of a beginning has been made to allow us to advance from other so-called pathological formations further into the analysis of the unconscious. Disease—at least that which is justly termed functional—is not due to the destruction of this apparatus, and the establishment of new splittings in its interior; it is rather to be explained dynamically through the strengthening and weakening of the components in the play of forces by which so many activities are concealed during the normal function. We have been able to show in another place how the composition of the apparatus from the two systems permits a subtilization even of the normal activity which would be impossible for a single system.

IX. THE UNCONSCIOUS AND CONSCIOUSNESS—REALITY

On closer inspection we find that it is not the existence of two systems near the motor end of the apparatus but of two kinds of processes or modes of emotional discharge, the assumption of which was explained in the psychological discussions of the previous chapter. This can make no difference for us, for we must always be ready to drop our auxiliary ideas whenever we deem ourselves in position to replace them by something else approaching more closely to the unknown reality. Let us now try to correct some views which might be erroneously formed as long as we regarded the two systems in the crudest and most obvious sense as two localities within the psychic apparatus, views which have left their traces in the terms "repression" and "penetration." Thus, when we say that an unconscious idea strives for transference into the foreconscious in order later to penetrate consciousness, we do not mean that a second idea is to be formed situated in a new locality like an interlineation near which the original continues to remain; also, when we speak of penetration into consciousness, we wish carefully to avoid any idea of change of locality. When we say that a foreconscious idea is repressed and subsequently taken up by the unconscious, we might be tempted by these figures, borrowed from the idea of a struggle over a territory, to assume that an arrangement is really broken up in one psychic locality and replaced by a new one in the other locality. For these comparisons we substitute what would seem to correspond better with the real state of affairs by saying that an energy occupation is displaced to or withdrawn from a certain arrangement so that the psychic formation falls under the domination of a system or is withdrawn from the same. Here again we replace a topical mode of presentation by a dynamic; it is not the psychic formation that appears to us as the moving factor but the innervation of the same.

I deem it appropriate and justifiable, however, to apply ourselves still further to the illustrative conception of the two systems. We shall avoid any misapplication of this manner of representation if we remember that presentations, thoughts, and psychic formations should generally not be localized in the organic elements of the nervous system, but, so to speak, between them, where resistances and paths form the correlate corresponding to them. Everything that can become an object of our internal perception is virtual, like the image in the telescope produced by the passage of the rays of light. But we are justified in assuming the existence of the systems, which have nothing psychic in themselves and which never become accessible to our psychic perception, corresponding to the lenses of the telescope which design the image. If we continue this comparison, we may say that the censor between two systems corresponds to the refraction of rays during their passage into a new medium.

Thus far we have made psychology on our own responsibility; it is now time to examine the theoretical opinions governing present-day psychology and to test their relation to our theories. The question of the unconscious, in psychology is, according to the authoritative words of Lipps, less a psychological question than the question of psychology. As long as psychology settled this question with the verbal explanation that the "psychic" is the "conscious" and that "unconscious psychic occurrences" are an obvious contradiction, a psychological estimate of the observations gained by the physician from abnormal mental states was precluded. The physician and the philosopher agree only when bothacknowledge that unconscious psychic processes are "the appropriate and well-justified expression for an established fact." The physician cannot but reject with a shrug of his shoulders the assertion that "consciousness is the indispensable quality of the psychic"; he may assume, if his respect for the utterings of the philosophers still be strong enough, that he and they do not treat the same subject and do not pursue the same science. For a single intelligent observation of the psychic life of a neurotic, a single analysis of a dream must force upon him the unalterable conviction that the most complicated and correct mental operations, to which no one will refuse the name of psychic occurrences, may take place without exciting the consciousness of the person. It is true that the physician does not learn of these unconscious processes until they have exerted such an effect on consciousness as to admit communication or observation. But this effect of consciousness may show a psychic character widely differing from the unconscious process, so that the internal perception cannot possibly recognize the one as a substitute for the other. The physician must reserve for himself the right to penetrate, by a process of deduction, from the effect on consciousness to the unconscious psychic process; he learns in this way that the effect on consciousness is only a remote psychic product of the unconscious process and that the latter has not become conscious as such; that it has been in existence and operative without betraying itself in any way to consciousness.

A reaction from the over-estimation of the quality of consciousness becomes the indispensable preliminary condition for any correct insight into the behavior of the psychic. In the words of Lipps, the unconscious must be accepted as the general basis of the psychic life. The unconscious is the larger circle which includes within itself the smaller circle of the conscious; everything conscious has its preliminary step in the unconscious, whereas the unconscious may stop with this step and still claim full value as a psychic activity. Properly speaking, the unconscious is the real psychic; *its inner nature is just as unknown to us as the reality of the external world, and it is just as imperfectly reported to us through the data of consciousness as is the external world through the indications of our sensory organs.*

A series of dream problems which have intensely occupied older authors will be laid aside when the old opposition between conscious life and dream life is abandoned and the unconscious psychic assigned to its proper place. Thus many of the activities whose performances in the dream have excited our admiration are now no longer to be attributed to the dream but to unconscious thinking, which is also active during the day. If, according to Scherner, the dream seems to play with a symboling representation of the body, we know that this is the work of certain unconscious phantasies which have probably given in to sexual emotions, and that these phantasies come to expression not only in dreams but also in hysterical phobias and in other symptoms. If the dream continues and settles activities of the day and even brings to light valuable inspirations, we have only to subtract from it the dream disguise as a feat of dream-work and a mark of assistance from obscure forces in the depth of the mind (*cf.* the devil in Tartini's sonata dream). The intellectual task as such must be attributed to the same psychic forces which perform all such tasks during the day. We are probably far too much inclined to over-estimate the conscious character even of intellectual and artistic productions. From the communications of some of the most highly productive persons, such as Goethe and Helmholtz, we learn, indeed, that the most essential and original parts in their creations came to them in the form of inspirations and reached their perceptions almost finished. There is nothing strange about the assistance of the conscious activity in other cases where there was a concerted effort of all the psychic forces. But it is a much abused privilege of the conscious activity that it is allowed to hide from us all other activities wherever it participates.

It will hardly be worth while to take up the historical significance of dreams as a special subject. Where, for instance, a chieftain has been urged through a dream to engage in a bold undertaking the success of which has had the effect of changing history, a new problem results only so long as the dream, regarded as a strange power, is contrasted with other more familiar psychic forces; the problem, however, disappears when we regard the dream as a form of expression for feelings which are burdened with resistance during the day and which can receive reinforcements at night from deep emotional sources. But the great respect shown by the ancients for the dream is based on a correct psychological surmise. It is a homage paid to the unsubdued and indestructible in the human mind, and to the demoniacal which furnishes the dream-wish and which we find again in our unconscious.

Not inadvisedly do I use the expression "in our unconscious," for what we so designate does not coincide with the unconscious of the philosophers, nor with the unconscious of Lipps. In the latter uses it is intended to designate only the opposite of conscious. That there are also unconscious psychic processes beside the conscious ones is the hotly contested and energetically defended issue. Lipps gives us the more far-reaching theory that everything psychic exists as unconscious, but that some of it may exist also as conscious. But it was not to prove this theory that we have adduced the phenomena of the dream and of the hysterical symptom formation; the observation of normal life alone suffices to establish its correctness beyond any doubt. The new fact that we have learned from the analysis of the psychopathological formations, and indeed from their first member, viz. dreams, is that the unconscious—hence the psychic—occurs as a function of two separate systems and that it occurs as such even in normal psychic life. Consequently there are two kinds of unconscious, which we do not as yet find distinguished by the psychologists. Both are unconscious in the psychological sense; but in our sense the first, which we call Unc., is likewise incapable of consciousness, whereas the second we term "Forec." because its emotions, after the observance of certain rules, can reach consciousness, perhaps not before they have again undergone censorship, but still regardless of the Unc. system. The fact that in order to attain consciousness the emotions must traverse an unalterable series of events or succession of instances, as is betrayed through their alteration by the censor, has helped us to draw a comparison from spatiality. We described the relations of the two systems to each other and to consciousness by saying that the system Forec. is like a screen between the system Unc. and consciousness. The system Forec. not only bars access to consciousness, but also controls the entrance to voluntary motility and is capable of sending out a sum of mobile energy, a portion of which is familiar to us as attention.

We must also steer clear of the distinctions superconscious and subconscious which have found so much favor in the more recent literature on the psychoneuroses, for just such a distinction seems to emphasize the equivalence of the psychic and the conscious.

What part now remains in our description of the once all-powerful and all-overshadowing consciousness? None other than that of a sensory organ for the perception of psychic qualities. According to the fundamental idea of schematic undertaking we can conceive the conscious perception only as the particular activity of an independent system for which the abbreviated designation "Cons." commends itself. This system we conceive to be similar in its mechanical characteristics to the perception system P, hence excitable by qualities and incapable of retaining the trace of changes, *i.e.* it is devoid of memory. The psychic apparatus which, with the sensory organs of the P-system, is turned to the outer world, is itself the outer world for the sensory organ of Cons.; the teleological justification of which rests on this relationship. We are here once more confronted with the principle of the succession of instances which seems to dominate the structure of the apparatus. The material under excitement flows to the Cons, sensory organ from two sides, firstly from the P-system whose excitement, qualitatively determined, probably experiences a new elaboration until it comes to conscious perception; and, secondly, from the interior of the apparatus itself, the quantitative processes of which are perceived as a qualitative series of pleasure and pain as soon as they have undergone certain changes.

The philosophers, who have learned that correct and highly complicated thought structures are possible even without the coöperation of consciousness, have found it difficult to attribute any function to consciousness; it has appeared to them a superfluous mirroring of the perfected psychic process. The analogy of our Cons. system with the systems of perception relieves us of this embarrassment. We see that perception through our sensory organs results in directing the occupation of attention to those paths on which the incoming sensory excitement is diffused; the qualitative excitement of the P-system serves the mobile quantity of the psychic apparatus as a regulator for its discharge. We may claim the same function for the overlying sensory organ of the Cons. system. By assuming new qualities, it furnishes a new contribution toward the guidance and suitable distribution of the mobile occupation quantities. By means of the perceptions of pleasure and pain, it influences the course of the occupations within the psychic apparatus, which normally operates unconsciously and through the displacement of quantities. It is probable that the principle of pain first regulates the displacements of occupation automatically, but it is quite possible that the consciousness of these qualities adds a second and more subtle regulation which may even oppose the first and perfect the working capacity of the apparatus by placing it in a position contrary to its original design for occupying and developing even that which is connected with the liberation of pain. We learn from neuropsychology that an important part in the functional activity of the apparatus is attributed to such regulations through the qualitative excitation of the sensory organs. The automatic control of the primary principle of pain and the restriction of mental capacity connected with it are broken by the sensible regulations, which in their turn are again automatisms. We learn that the repression which, though originally expedient, terminates nevertheless in a harmful rejection of inhibition and of psychic domination, is so much more easily accomplished with reminiscences than with perceptions, because in the former there is no increase in occupation through the excitement of the psychic sensory organs. When an idea to be rejected has once failed to become conscious because it has succumbed to repression, it can be repressed on other occasions only because it has been withdrawn from conscious perception on other grounds. These are hints employed by therapy in order to bring about a retrogression of accomplished repressions.

The value of the over-occupation which is produced by the regulating influence of the Cons. sensory organ on the mobile quantity, is demonstrated in the teleological connection by nothing more clearly than by the creation of a new series of qualities and consequently a new regulation which constitutes the precedence of man over the animals. For the mental processes are in themselves devoid of quality except for the excitements of pleasure and pain accompanying them, which, as we know, are to be held in check as possible disturbances of thought. In order to endow them with a quality, they are associated in man with verbal memories, the qualitative remnants of which suffice to draw upon them the attention of consciousness which in turn endows thought with a new mobile energy.

The manifold problems of consciousness in their entirety can be examined only through an analysis of the hysterical mental process. From this analysis we receive the impression that the transition from the foreconscious to the occupation of consciousness is also connected with a censorship similar to the one between the Unc. and the Forec. This censorship, too, begins to act only with the reaching of a certain quantitative degree, so that few intense thought formations escape it. Every possible case of detention from consciousness, as well as of penetration to consciousness, under restriction is found included within the picture of the psychoneurotic phenomena; every case points to the intimate and twofold connection between the censor and consciousness. I shall conclude these psychological discussions with the report of two such occurrences.

On the occasion of a consultation a few years ago the subject was an intelligent and innocent-looking girl. Her attire was strange; whereas a woman's garb is usually groomed to the last fold, she had one of her stockings hanging down and two of her waist buttons opened. She complained of pains in one of her legs, and exposed her leg unrequested. Her chief complaint, however, was in her own words as follows: She had a feeling in her body as if something was stuck into it which moved to and fro and made her tremble through and through. This sometimes made her whole body stiff. On hearing this, my colleague in consultation looked at me; the complaint was quite plain to him. To both of us it seemed peculiar that the patient's mother thought nothing of the matter; of course she herself must have been repeatedly in the situation described by her child. As for the girl, she had no idea of the import of her words or she would never have allowed them to pass her lips. Here the censor had been deceived so successfully that under the mask of an innocent complaint a phantasy was admitted to consciousness which otherwise would have remained in the foreconscious.

Another example: I began the psychoanalytic treatment of a boy of fourteen years who was suffering from *tic convulsif*, hysterical vomiting, headache, &c., by assuring him that, after closing his eyes, he would see pictures or have ideas, which I requested him to communicate to me. He answered by describing pictures. The last impression he had received before coming to me was visually revived in his memory. He had played a game of checkers with his uncle, and now saw the checkerboard before him. He commented on various positions that were favorable or unfavorable, on moves that were not safe to make. He then saw a dagger lying on the checker-board, an object belonging to his father, but transferred to the checker-board by his phantasy. Then a sickle was lying on the board; next a scythe was added; and, finally, he beheld the likeness of an old peasant mowing the grass in front of the boy's distant parental home. A few days later I discovered the meaning of this series of pictures. Disagreeable family relations had made the boy nervous. It was the case of a strict and crabbed father who lived unhappily with his mother, and whose educational methods consisted in threats; of the separation of his father from his tender and delicate mother, and the remarrying of his father, who one day brought home a young woman as his new mamma. The illness of the fourteen-year-old boy broke out a few days later. It was the suppressed anger against his father that had composed these pictures into intelligible allusions. The material was furnished by a reminiscence from mythology. The sickle was the one with which Zeus castrated his father; the scythe and the likeness of the peasant represented Kronos, the violent old man who eats his children and upon whom Zeus wreaks vengeance in so unfilial a manner. The marriage of the father gave the boy an opportunity to return the reproaches and threats of his father—which had previously been made because the child played with his genitals (the checkerboard; the prohibitive moves; the dagger with which a person may be killed). We have here long repressed memories and their unconscious remnants which, under the guise of senseless pictures have slipped into consciousness by devious paths left open to them.

I should then expect to find the theoretical value of the study of dreams in its contribution to psychological knowledge and in its preparation for an understanding of neuroses. Who can foresee the importance of a thorough knowledge of the structure and activities of the psychic apparatus when even our present state of knowledge produces a happy therapeutic influence in the curable forms of the psychoneuroses? What about the practical value of such study some one may ask, for psychic knowledge and for the discovering of the secret peculiarities of individual character? Have not the unconscious feelings revealed by the dream the value of real forces in the psychic life? Should we take lightly the ethical significance of the suppressed wishes which, as they now create dreams, may some day create other things?

I do not feel justified in answering these questions. I have not thought further upon this side of the dream problem. I believe, however, that at all events the Roman Emperor was in the wrong who ordered one of his subjects executed because the latter dreamt that he had killed the Emperor. He should first have endeavored to discover the significance of the dream; most probably it was not what it seemed to be. And even if a dream of different content had the significance of this offense against majesty, it would still have been in place to remember the words of Plato, that the virtuous man contents himself with dreaming that which the wicked man does in actual life. I am therefore of the opinion that it is best to accord freedom to dreams. Whether any reality is to be attributed to the unconscious wishes, and in what sense, I am not prepared to say offhand. Reality must naturally be denied to all transition—and intermediate thoughts. If we had before us the unconscious wishes, brought to their last and truest expression, we should still do well to remember that more than one single form of existence must be ascribed to the psychic reality.Action and the conscious expression of thought mostly suffice for the practical need of judging a man's character. Action, above all, merits to be placed in the first rank; for many of the impulses penetrating consciousness are neutralized by real forces of the psychic life before they are converted into action; indeed, the reason why they frequently do not encounter any psychic obstacle on their way is because the unconscious is certain of their meeting with resistances later. In any case it is instructive to become familiar with the much raked-up soil from which our virtues proudly arise. For the complication of human character moving dynamically in all directions very rarely accommodates itself to adjustment through a simple alternative, as our antiquated moral philosophy would have it.

And how about the value of the dream for a knowledge of the future? That, of course, we cannot consider. One feels inclined to substitute: "for a knowledge of the past." For the dream originates from the past in every sense. To be sure the ancient belief that the dream reveals the future is not entirely devoid of truth. By representing to us a wish as fulfilled the dream certainly leads us into the future; but this future, taken by the dreamer as present, has been formed into the likeness of that past by the indestructible wish.

THE END

BOOK FIVE.
LEONARDO DA VINCI

I

WHEN psychoanalytic investigation, which usually contents itself with frail human material, approaches the great personages of humanity, it is not impelled to it by motives which are often attributed to it by laymen. It does not strive "to blacken the radiant and to drag the sublime into the mire"; it finds no satisfaction in diminishing the distance between the perfection of the great and the inadequacy of the ordinary objects. But it cannot help finding that everything is worthy of understanding that can be perceived through those prototypes, and it also believes that none is so big as to be ashamed of being subject to the laws which control the normal and morbid actions with the same strictness.

Leonardo da Vinci (1452-1519) was admired even by his contemporaries as one of the greatest men of the Italian Renaissance, still even then he appeared as mysterious to them as he now appears to us. An all-sided genius, "whose form can only be divined but never deeply fathomed,"[202]he exerted the most decisive influence on his time as an artist; and it remained to us to recognize his greatness as a naturalist which was united in him with the artist. Although he left masterpieces of the art of painting, while his scientific discoveries remained unpublished and unused, the investigator in him has never quite left the artist, often it has severely injured the artist and in the end it has perhaps suppressed the artist altogether. According to Vasari, Leonardo reproached himself during the last hour of his life for having insulted God and men because he has not done his duty to his art.[203] And even if Vasari's story lacks all probability and belongs to those legends which began to be woven about the mystic master while he was still living, it nevertheless retains indisputable value as a testimonial of the judgment of those people and of those times.

What was it that removed the personality of Leonardo from the understanding of his contemporaries? Certainly not the many sidedness of his capacities and knowledge, which allowed him to install himself as a player of the lyre on an instrument invented by himself, in the court of Lodovico Sforza, nicknamed Il Moro, the Duke of Milan, or which allowed him to write to the same person that remarkable letter in which he boasts of his abilities as a civil and military engineer. For the combination of manifold talents in

---

[202] In the words of J. Burckhard, cited by Alexandra Konstantinowa, Die Entwicklung des Madonnentypus by Leonardo da Vinci, Strassburg, 1907.
[203] Vite, etc. LXXXIII. 1550-1584.

the same person was not unusual in the times of the Renaissance; to be sure Leonardo himself furnished one of the most splendid examples of such persons. Nor did he belong to that type of genial persons who are outwardly poorly endowed by nature, and who on their side place no value on the outer forms of life, and in the painful gloominess of their feelings fly from human relations. On the contrary he was tall and symmetrically built, of consummate beauty of countenance and of unusual physical strength, he was charming in his manner, a master of speech, and jovial and affectionate to everybody. He loved beauty in the objects of his surroundings, he was fond of wearing magnificent garments and appreciated every refinement of conduct. In his treatise [204]on the art of painting he compares in a significant passage the art of painting with its sister arts and thus discusses the difficulties of the sculptor: "Now his face is entirely smeared and powdered with marble dust, so that he looks like a baker, he is covered with small marble splinters, so that it seems as if it snowed on his back, and his house is full of stone splinters, and dust. The case of the painter is quite different from that; for the painter is well dressed and sits with great comfort before his work, he gently and very lightly brushes in the beautiful colors. He wears as decorative clothes as he likes, and his house is filled with beautiful paintings and is spotlessly clean. He often enjoys company, music, or some one may read for him various nice works, and all this can be listened to with great pleasure, undisturbed by any pounding from the hammer and other noises."

It is quite possible that the conception of a beaming jovial and happy Leonardo was true only for the first and longer period of the master's life. From now on, when the downfall of the rule of Lodovico Moro forced him to leave Milan, his sphere of action and his assured position, to lead an unsteady and unsuccessful life until his last asylum in France, it is possible that the luster of his disposition became pale and some odd features of his character became more prominent. The turning of his interest from his art to science which increased with age must have also been responsible for widening the gap between himself and his contemporaries. All his efforts with which, according to their opinion, he wasted his time instead of diligently filling orders and becoming rich as perhaps his former classmate Perugino, seemed to his contemporaries as capricious playing, or even caused them to suspect him of being in the service of the "blackart." We who know him from his sketches understand him better. In a time in which the authority of the church began to be substituted by that of antiquity and in which only theoretical investigation existed, he the forerunner, or better the worthy competitor of Bacon and Copernicus, was necessarily isolated. When he dissected cadavers of horses and human beings, and built flying apparatus,

---

[204] Traktat von der Malerei, new edition and introduction by Marie Herzfeld, E. Diederichs, Jena, 1909.

or when he studied the nourishment of plants and their behavior towards poisons, he naturally deviated much from the commentators of Aristotle and came nearer the despised alchemists, in whose laboratories the experimental investigations found some refuge during these unfavorable times.

The effect that this had on his paintings was that he disliked to handle the brush, he painted less and what was more often the case, the things he began were mostly left unfinished; he cared less and less for the future fate of his works. It was this mode of working that was held up to him as a reproach from his contemporaries to whom his behavior to his art remained a riddle.

Many of Leonardo's later admirers have attempted to wipe off the stain of unsteadiness from his character. They maintained that what is blamed in Leonardo is a general characteristic of great artists. They said that even the energetic Michelangelo who was absorbed in his work left many incompleted works, which was as little due to his fault as to Leonardo's in the same case. Besides some pictures were not as unfinished as he claimed, and what the layman would call a masterpiece may still appear to the creator of the work of art as an unsatisfied embodiment of his intentions; he has a faint notion of a perfection which he despairs of reproducing in likeness. Least of all should the artist be held responsible for the fate which befalls his works.

As plausible as some of these excuses may sound they nevertheless do not explain the whole state of affairs which we find in Leonardo. The painful struggle with the work, the final flight from it and the indifference to its future fate may be seen in many other artists, but this behavior is shown in Leonardo to highest degree. Edm. Solmi[205] cites (p. 12) the expression of one of his pupils: "Pareva, che ad ogni ora tremasse, quando si poneva a dipingere, e però no diede mai fine ad alcuna cosa cominciata, considerando la grandezza dell'arte, tal che egli scorgeva errori in quelle cose, che ad altri parevano miracoli." His last pictures, Leda, the Madonna di Saint Onofrio, Bacchus and St. John the Baptist, remained unfinished "come quasi intervenne di tutte le cose sue." Lomazzo,[206] who finished a copy of The Holy Supper, refers in a sonnet to the familiar inability of Leonardo to finish his works:

"Protogen che il penel di sue pitture

Non levava, agguaglio il Vinci Divo,

Di cui opra non è finita pure."

The slowness with which Leonardo worked was proverbial. After the most thorough preliminary studies he painted The Holy Supper for three years in the cloister of Santa Maria delle Grazie in Milan. One of his contemporaries, Matteo Bandelli, the writer of novels, who was then a young monk in the

---

[205] Solmi. La resurrezione dell' opera di Leonardo in the collected work; Leonardo da Vinci. Conferenze Florentine, Milan, 1910.

[206] Scognamiglio Ricerche e Documenti sulla giovinezza di Leonardo da Vinci. Napoli, 1900.

cloister, relates that Leonardo often ascended the scaffold very early in the morning and did not leave the brush out of his hand until twilight, never thinking of eating or drinking. Then days passed without putting his hand on it, sometimes he remained for hours before the painting and derived satisfaction from studying it by himself. At other times he came directly to the cloister from the palace of the Milanese Castle where he formed the model of the equestrian statue for Francesco Sforza, in order to add a few strokes with the brush to one of the figures and then stopped immediately.[207] According to Vasari he worked for years on the portrait of Monna Lisa, the wife of the Florentine de Gioconda, without being able to bring it to completion. This circumstance may also account for the fact that it was never delivered to the one who ordered it but remained with Leonardo who took it with him to France.[208] Having been procured by King Francis I, it now forms one of the greatest treasures of the Louvre.

When one compares these reports about Leonardo's way of working with the evidence of the extraordinary amount of sketches and studies left by him, one is bound altogether to reject the idea that traits of flightiness and unsteadiness exerted the slightest influence on Leonardo's relation to his art. On the contrary one notices a very extraordinary absorption in work, a richness in possibilities in which a decision could be reached only hesitatingly, claims which could hardly be satisfied, and an inhibition in the execution which could not even be explained by the inevitable backwardness of the artist behind his ideal purpose. The slowness which was striking in Leonardo's works from the very beginning proved to be a symptom of his inhibition, a forerunner of his turning away from painting which manifested itself later.[209] It was this slowness which decided the not undeserving fate of The Holy Supper. Leonardo could not take kindly to the art of fresco painting which demands quick work while the background is still moist, it was for this reason that he chose oil colors, the drying of which permitted him to complete the picture according to his mood and leisure. But these colors separated themselves from the background upon which they were painted and which isolated them from the brick wall; the blemishes of this wall and the vicissitudes to which the room was subjected seemingly contributed to the inevitable deterioration of the picture.[210]

The picture of the cavalry battle of Anghiari, which in competition with Michelangelo he began to paint later on a wall of the Sala de Consiglio in Florence and which he also left in an unfinished state, seemed to have

---

[207] W. v. Seidlitz. Leonardo da Vinci, der Wendepunkt der Renaissance, 1909, Bd. I, p. 203.

[208] W. v. Seidlitz, l. c. Bd. II, p. 48

[209] W. Pater. The Renaissance, p. 107, The Macmillan Co., 1910. "But it is certain that at one period of his life he had almost ceased to be an artist."

[210] Cf. v. Seidlitz, Bd. I die Geschichte der Restaurations—und Rettungsversuche.

perished through the failure of a similar technical process. It seems here as if a peculiar interest, that of the experimenter, at first reënforced the artistic, only later to damage the art production.

The character of the man Leonardo evinces still some other unusual traits and apparent contradictions. Thus a certain inactivity and indifference seemed very evident in him. At a time when every individual sought to gain the widest latitude for his activity, which could not take place without the development of energetic aggression towards others, he surprised every one through his quiet peacefulness, his shunning of all competition and controversies. He was mild and kind to all, he was said to have rejected a meat diet because he did not consider it just to rob animals of their lives, and one of his special pleasures was to buy caged birds in the market and set them free. [211]He condemned war and bloodshed and designated man not so much as the king of the animal world, but rather as the worst of the wild beasts.[212] But this effeminate delicacy of feeling did not prevent him from accompanying condemned criminals on their way to execution in order to study and sketch in his notebook their features, distorted by fear, nor did it prevent him from inventing the most cruel offensive weapons, and from entering the service of Cesare Borgia as chief military engineer. Often he seemed to be indifferent to good and evil, or he had to be measured with a special standard. He held a high position in Cesare's campaign which gained for this most inconsiderate and most faithless of foes the possession of the Romagna. Not a single line of Leonardo's sketches betrays any criticism or sympathy of the events of those days. The comparison with Goethe during the French campaign cannot here be altogether rejected.

If a biographical effort really endeavors to penetrate the understanding of the psychic life of its hero it must not, as happens in most biographies through discretion or prudery, pass over in silence the sexual activity or the sex peculiarity of the one examined. What we know about it in Leonardo is very little but full of significance. In a period where there was a constant struggle between riotous licentiousness and gloomy asceticism, Leonardo presented an example of cool sexual rejection which one would not expect in an artist and a portrayer of feminine beauty. Solmi[213] cites the following sentence from Leonardo showing his frigidity: "The act of procreation and everything that has any relation to it is so disgusting that human beings would soon die out if it were not a traditional custom and if there were no pretty faces and sensuous dispositions." His posthumous works which not only treat of the greatest scientific problems but also comprise the most

---

[211] Müntz. Léonard de Vinci, Paris, 1899, p. 18. (A letter of a contemporary from India to a Medici alludes to this peculiarity of Leonardo. Given by Richter: The literary Works of Leonardo da Vinci.)

[212] F. Botazzi. Leonardo biologo e anatomico. Conferenze Florentine, p. 186, 1910.

[213] E. Solmi: Leonardo da Vinci. German Translation by Emmi Hirschberg. Berlin, 1908.

guileless objects which to us do not seem worthy of so great a mind (an allegorical natural history, animal fables, witticisms, prophecies),[214] are chaste to a degree—one might say abstinent—that in a work of *belle lettres* would excite wonder even to-day. They evade everything sexual so thoroughly, as if Eros alone who preserves everything living was no worthy material for the scientific impulse of the investigator.[215] It is known how frequently great artists found pleasure in giving vent to their phantasies in erotic and even grossly obscene representations; in contradistinction to this Leonardo left only some anatomical drawings of the woman's internal genitals, the position of the child in the womb, etc.

It is doubtful whether Leonardo ever embraced a woman in love, nor is it known that he ever entertained an intimate spiritual relation with a woman as in the case of Michelangelo and Vittoria Colonna. While he still lived as an apprentice in the house of his master Verrocchio, he with other young men were accused of forbidden homosexual relations which ended in his acquittal. It seems that he came into this suspicion because he employed as a model a boy of evil repute.[216] When he was a master he surrounded himself with handsome boys and youths whom he took as pupils. The last of these pupils Francesco Melzi, accompanied him to France, remained with him until his death, and was named by him as his heir. Without sharing the certainty of his modern biographers, who naturally reject the possibility of a sexual relation between himself and his pupils as a baseless insult to this great man, it may be thought by far more probable that the affectionate relationships of Leonardo to the young men did not result in sexual activity. Nor should one attribute to him a high measure of sexual activity.

The peculiarity of this emotional and sexual life viewed in connection with Leonardo's double nature as an artist and investigator can be grasped only in one way. Of the biographers to whom psychological viewpoints are often very foreign, only one, Edm. Solmi, has to my knowledge approached the solution of the riddle. But a writer, Dimitri Sergewitsch Merejkowski, who selected Leonardo as the hero of a great historical novel has based his delineation on such an understanding of this unusual man, and if not in dry words he gave unmistakable utterance in plastic expression in the manner of a poet.[217] Solmi judges Leonardo as follows: "But the unrequited

---

[214] Marie Herzfeld: Leonardo da Vinci der Denker, Forscher und Poet. Second edition. Jena, 1906.

[215] His collected witticisms—belle facezie,—which are not translated, may be an exception. Cf. Herzfeld, Leonardo da Vinci, p. 151.

[216] According to Scognamiglio (l. c. p. 49) reference is made to this episode in an obscure and even variously interpreted passage of the Codex Atlanticus: "Quando io feci Domeneddio putto voi mi metteste in prigione, ora s'io lo fo grande, voi mi farete peggio."

[217] Merejkowski: The Romance of Leonardo da Vinci, translated by Herbert Trench, G. P. Putnam Sons, New York. It forms the second of the historical Trilogy entitled Christ and Anti-Christ, of which the first volume is Julian Apostata, and the third volume is Peter the Great and Alexei.

desire to understand everything surrounding him, and with cold reflection to discover the deepest secret of everything that is perfect, has condemned Leonardo's works to remain forever unfinished."[218] In an essay of the Conferenze Fiorentine the utterances of Leonardo are cited, which show his confession of faith and furnish the key to his character.

"*Nessuna cosa si può amare nè odiare, se*
prima no si ha cognition di quella."[219]

That is: One has no right to love or to hate anything if one has not acquired a thorough knowledge of its nature. And the same is repeated by Leonardo in a passage of the Treaties on the Art of Painting where he seems to defend himself against the accusation of irreligiousness:

"But such censurers might better remain silent. For that action is the manner of showing the workmaster so many wonderful things, and this is the way to love so great a discoverer. For, verily great love springs from great knowledge of the beloved object, and if you little know it you will be able to love it only little or not at all."[220]

The value of these utterances of Leonardo cannot be found in that they impart to us an important psychological fact, for what they maintain is obviously false, and Leonardo must have known this as well as we do. It is not true that people refrain from loving or hating until they have studied and became familiar with the nature of the object to whom they wish to give these affects, on the contrary they love impulsively and are guided by emotional motives which have nothing to do with cognition and whose affects are weakened, if anything, by thought and reflection. Leonardo only could have implied that the love practiced by people is not of the proper and unobjectionable kind, one should so love as to hold back the affect and to subject it to mental elaboration, and only after it has stood the test of the intellect should free play be given to it. And we thereby understand that he wishes to tell us that this was the case with himself and that it would be worth the effort of everybody else to treat love and hatred as he himself does.

And it seems that in his case it was really so. His affects were controlled and subjected to the investigation impulse, he neither loved nor hated, but questioned himself whence does that arise, which he was to love or hate, and what does it signify, and thus he was at first forced to appear indifferent to good and evil, to beauty and ugliness. During this work of investigation love and hatred threw off their designs and uniformly changed into intellectual interest. As a matter of fact Leonardo was not dispassionate, he did not lack the divine spark which is the mediate or immediate motive power—*il primo motore*—of all human activity. He only transmuted his passion into

---

[218] Solmi l. c. p. 46.
[219] Filippo Botazzi, l. c. p. 193.
[220] Marie Herzfeld: Leonardo da Vinci, Traktat von der Malerei, Jena, 1909 (Chap. I, 64).

inquisitiveness. He then applied himself to study with that persistence, steadiness, and profundity which comes from passion, and on the height of the psychic work, after the cognition was won, he allowed the long checked affect to break loose and to flow off freely like a branch of a stream, after it has accomplished its work. At the height of his cognition when he could examine a big part of the whole he was seized with a feeling of pathos, and in ecstatic words he praised the grandeur of that part of creation which he studied, or—in religious cloak—the greatness of the creator. Solmi has correctly divined this process of transformation in Leonardo. According to the quotation of such a passage, in which Leonardo celebrated the higher impulse of nature ("O mirabile necessita ... ") he said: "Tale trasfigurazione della scienza della natura in emozione, quasi direi, religiosa, è uno dei tratti caratteristici de manoscritti vinciani, e si trova cento e cento volte espressa...."[221]

Leonardo was called the Italian Faust on account of his insatiable and indefatigable desire for investigation. But even if we disregard the fact that it is the possible retransformation of the desire for investigation into the joys of life which is presupposed in the Faust tragedy, one might venture to remark that Leonardo's system recalls Spinoza's mode of thinking.

The transformation of psychic motive power into the different forms of activity is perhaps as little convertible without loss, as in the case of physical powers. Leonardo's example teaches how many other things one must follow up in these processes. Not to love before one gains full knowledge of the thing loved presupposes a delay which is harmful. When one finally reaches cognition he neither loves nor hates properly; one remains beyond love and hatred. One has investigated instead of having loved. It is perhaps for this reason that Leonardo's life was so much poorer in love than those of other great men and great artists. The storming passions of the soul-stirring and consuming kind, in which others experience the best part of their lives, seem to have missed him.

There are still other consequences when one follows Leonardo's dictum. Instead of acting and producing one just investigates. He who begins to divine the grandeur of the universe and its needs readily forgets his own insignificant self. When one is struck with admiration and becomes truly humble he easily forgets that he himself is a part of that living force, and that according to the measure of his own personality he has the right to make an effort to change that destined course of the world, the world in which the insignificant is no less wonderful and important than the great.

---

[221] "Such transfiguration of science and of nature into emotions, or one might say, religion, is one of the characteristic traits of da Vinci's manuscripts, which one finds expressed hundreds of times." Solmi: La resurrezione, etc, p. 11.

Solmi thinks that Leonardo's investigations started with his art,[222] he tried to investigate the attributes and laws of light, of color, of shades and of perspective so as to be sure of becoming a master in the imitation of nature and to be able to show the way to others. It is probable that already at that time he overestimated the value of this knowledge for the artist. Following the guide-rope of the painter's need, he was then driven further and further to investigate the objects of the art of painting, such as animals and plants, and the proportions of the human body, and to follow the path from their exterior to their interior structure and biological functions, which really also express themselves in their appearance and should be depicted in art. And finally he was pulled along by this overwhelming desire until the connection was torn from the demands of his art, so that he discovered the general laws of mechanics and divined the history of the stratification and fossilization of the Arno-valley, until he could enter in his book with capital letters the cognition: *Il sole non si move* (The sun does not move). His investigations were thus extended over almost all realms of natural science, in every one of which he was a discoverer or at least a prophet or forerunner.[223] However, his curiosity continued to be directed to the outer world, something kept him away from the investigation of the psychic life of men; there was little room for psychology in the "Academia Vinciana," for which he drew very artistic and very complicated emblems.

When he later made the effort to return from his investigations to the art from which he started he felt that he was disturbed by the new paths of his interest and by the changed nature of his psychic work. In the picture he was interested above all in a problem, and behind this one he saw emerging numerous other problems just as he was accustomed in the endless and indeterminable investigations of natural history. He was no longer able to limit his demands, to isolate the work of art, and to tear it out from that great connection of which he knew it formed part. After the most exhausting efforts to bring to expression all that was in him, all that was connected with it in his thoughts, he was forced to leave it unfinished, or to declare it incomplete.

The artist had once taken into his service the investigator to assist him, now the servant was stronger and suppressed his master.

When we find in the portrait of a person one single impulse very forcibly developed, as curiosity in the case of Leonardo, we look for the explanation in a special constitution, concerning its probable organic determination hardly anything is known. Our psychoanalytic studies of nervous people lead us to look for two other expectations which we would like to find verified in

---

[222] La resurrezione, etc., p. 8: "Leonardo placed the study of nature as a precept to painting ... later the passion for study became dominating, he no longer wished to acquire science for art, but science for science' sake."

[223] For an enumeration of his scientific attainments see Marie Herzfeld's interesting introduction (Jena, 1906) to the essays of the Conference Florentine, 1910, and elsewhere.

every case. We consider it probable that this very forcible impulse was already active in the earliest childhood of the person, and that its supreme sway was fixed by infantile impressions; and we further assume that originally it drew upon sexual motive powers for its reënforcement so that it later can take the place of a part of the sexual life. Such person would then, e.g., investigate with that passionate devotion which another would give to his love, and he could investigate instead of loving. We would venture the conclusion of a sexual reënforcement not only in the impulse to investigate, but also in most other cases of special intensity of an impulse.

Observation of daily life shows us that most persons have the capacity to direct a very tangible part of their sexual motive powers to their professional or business activities. The sexual impulse is particularly suited to yield such contributions because it is endowed with the capacity of sublimation, i.e., it has the power to exchange its nearest aim for others of higher value which are not sexual. We consider this process as proved, if the history of childhood or the psychic developmental history of a person shows that in childhood this powerful impulse was in the service of the sexual interest. We consider it a further corroboration if this is substantiated by a striking stunting in the sexual life of mature years, as if a part of the sexual activity had now been replaced by the activity of the predominant impulse.

The application of these assumptions to the case of the predominant investigation-impulse seems to be subject to special difficulties, as one is unwilling to admit that this serious impulse exists in children or that children show any noteworthy sexual interest. However, these difficulties are easily obviated. The untiring pleasure in questioning as seen in little children demonstrates their curiosity, which is puzzling to the grown-up, as long as he does not understand that all these questions are only circumlocutions, and that they cannot come to an end because they replace only one question which the child does not put. When the child becomes older and gains more understanding this manifestation of curiosity suddenly disappears. But psychoanalytic investigation gives us a full explanation in that it teaches us that many, perhaps most children, at least the most gifted ones, go through a period beginning with the third year, which may be designated as the period of *infantile sexual investigation*. As far as we know, the curiosity is not awakened spontaneously in children of this age, but is aroused through the impression of an important experience, through the birth of a little brother or sister, or through fear of the same endangered by some outward experience, wherein the child sees a danger to his egotistic interests. The investigation directs itself to the question whence children come, as if the child were looking for means to guard against such undesired event. We were astonished to find that the child refuses to give credence to the information imparted to it, e.g., it energetically rejects the mythological and so ingenious stork-fable, we were astonished to find that its psychic independence dates from this act of disbelief, that it often feels itself at serious variance with the grown-ups, and never forgives them for having been deceived of the truth on this occasion. It investigates in its own way, it divines that the child is in the mother's womb, and guided by the feelings of its own sexuality, it formulates for itself theories about the origin of children from food, about being born through the bowels, about the rôle of the father which is difficult to fathom, and even at that time it has a vague conception of the sexual act which appears to the child as something hostile, as something violent. But as its own sexual constitution is not yet equal to the task of producing children, his investigation whence come children must also run aground and must be left in the lurch as unfinished. The impression of this failure at the first attempt of intellectual independence seems to be of a persevering and profoundly depressing nature.[224]

If the period of infantile sexual investigation comes to an end through an impetus of energetic sexual repression, the early association with sexual interest may result in three different possibilities for the future fate of the investigation impulse. The investigation either shares the fate of the sexuality, the curiosity henceforth remains inhibited and the free activity of intelligence may become narrowed for life; this is especially made possible by the powerful religious inhibition of thought, which is brought about shortly hereafter through education. This is the type of neurotic inhibition. We know well that the so acquired mental weakness furnishes effective support for the outbreak of a neurotic disease. In a second type the intellectual development is sufficiently strong to withstand the sexual repression pulling at it. Sometimes after the disappearance of the infantile sexual investigation, it offers its support to the old association in order to elude the sexual repression, and the suppressed sexual investigation comes back from the unconscious as compulsive reasoning, it is naturally distorted and not free, but forceful enough to sexualize even thought itself and to accentuate the intellectual operations with the pleasure and fear of the actual sexual processes. Here the investigation becomes sexual activity and often exclusively so, the feeling of settling the problem and of explaining things in the mind is put in place of sexual gratification. But the indeterminate character of the infantile investigation repeats itself also in the fact that this reasoning never ends, and that the desired intellectual feeling of the solution constantly recedes into the distance. By virtue of a special disposition the

---

[224] For a corroboration of this improbable sounding assertion see the "Analysis of the Phobia of a Five-year-old Boy," Jahrbuch für Psychoanalytische und Psychopathologische Forschungen, Bd. I, 1909, and the similar observation in Bd. II, 1910. In an essay concerning "Infantile Theories of Sex" (Sammlungen kleiner Schriften zur Neurosenlehre, p. 167, Second Series, 1909), I wrote: "But this reasoning and doubting serves as a model for all later intellectual work in problems, and the first failure acts as a paralyzer for all times."

third, which is the most rare and most perfect type, escapes the inhibition of thought and the compulsive reasoning. Also here sexual repression takes place, it is unable, however, to direct a partial impulse of the sexual pleasure into the unconscious, but the libido withdraws from the fate of the repression by being sublimated from the beginning into curiosity, and by reënforcing the powerful investigation impulse. Here, too, the investigation becomes more or less compulsive and a substitute of the sexual activity, but owing to the absolute difference of the psychic process behind it (sublimation in place of the emergence from the unconscious) the character of the neurosis does not manifest itself, the subjection to the original complexes of the infantile sexual investigation disappears, and the impulse can freely put itself in the service of the intellectual interest. It takes account of the sexual repression which made it so strong in contributing to it sublimated libido, by avoiding all occupation with sexual themes.

In mentioning the concurrence in Leonardo of the powerful investigation impulse with the stunting of his sexual life which was limited to the so-called ideal homosexuality, we feel inclined to consider him as a model example of our third type. The most essential point of his character and the secret of it seems to lie in the fact, that after utilizing the infantile activity of curiosity in the service of sexual interest he was able to sublimate the greater part of his libido into the impulse of investigation. But to be sure the proof of this conception is not easy to produce. To do this we would have to have an insight into the psychic development of his first childhood years, and it seems foolish to hope for such material when the reports concerning his life are so meager and so uncertain; and moreover, when we deal with information which even persons of our own generation withdraw from the attention of the observer.

We know very little concerning Leonardo's youth. He was born in 1452 in the little city of Vinci between Florence and Empoli; he was an illegitimate child which was surely not considered a great popular stain in that time. His father was Ser Piero da Vinci, a notary and descendant of notaries and farmers, who took their name from the place Vinci; his mother, a certain Caterina, probably a peasant girl, who later married another native of Vinci. Nothing else about his mother appears in the life history of Leonardo, only the writer Merejkowski believed to have found some traces of her. The only definite information about Leonardo's childhood is furnished by a legal document from the year 1457, a register of assessment in which Vinci Leonardo is mentioned among the members of the family as a five-year-old illegitimate child of Ser Piero.[225] As the marriage of Ser Piero with Donna Albiera remained childless the little Leonardo could be brought up in his father's house. He did not leave this house until he entered as apprentice—it is not known what year—in the studio of Andrea del Verrocchio. In 1472

---

[225] Scognamiglio 1. c., p. 15.

Leonardo's name could already be found in the register of the members of the "Compagnia dei Pittori." That is all.

II

As far as I know Leonardo only once interspersed in his scientific descriptions a communication from his childhood. In a passage where he speaks about the flight of the vulture, he suddenly interrupts himself in order to follow up a memory from very early years which came to his mind.

"It seems that it had been destined before that I should occupy myself so thoroughly with the vulture, for it comes to my mind as a very early memory, when I was still in the cradle, a vulture came down to me, he opened my mouth with his tail and struck me a few times with his tail against my lips."[226]

We have here an infantile memory and to be sure of the strangest sort. It is strange on account of its content and account of the time of life in which it was fixed. That a person could retain a memory of the nursing period is perhaps not impossible, but it can in no way be taken as certain. But what this memory of Leonardo states, namely, that a vulture opened the child's mouth with its tail, sounds so improbable, so fabulous, that another conception which puts an end to the two difficulties with one stroke appeals much more to our judgment. The scene of the vulture is not a memory of Leonardo, but a phantasy which he formed later, and transferred into his childhood. The childhood memories of persons often have no different origin, as a matter of fact, they are not fixated from an experience like the conscious memories from the time of maturity and then repeated, but they are not produced until a later period when childhood is already past, they are then changed and disguised and put in the service of later tendencies, so that in general they cannot be strictly differentiated from phantasies. Their nature will perhaps be best understood by recalling the manner in which history writing originated among ancient nations. As long as the nation was small and weak it gave no thought to the writing of its history, it tilled the soil of its land, defended its existence against its neighbors by seeking to wrest land from them and endeavored to become rich. It was a heroic but unhistoric time. Then came another age, a period of self-realization in which one felt rich and powerful, and it was then that one experienced the need to discover whence one originated and how one developed. The history-writing which then continues to register the present events throws also its backward glance to the past, it gathers traditions and legends, it interprets what survived from olden times into customs and uses, and thus creates a history of past ages. It is quite natural that this history of the past ages is more the expressions of

---

[226] Cited by Scognamiglio from the Codex Atlanticus, p. 65.

opinions and desires of the present than a faithful picture of the past, for many a thing escaped the people's memory, other things became distorted, some trace of the past was misunderstood and interpreted in the sense of the present; and besides one does not write history through motives of objective curiosity, but because one desires to impress his contemporaries, to stimulate and extol them, or to hold the mirror before them. The conscious memory of a person concerning the experiences of his maturity may now be fully compared to that of history writing, and his infantile memories, as far as their origin and reliability are concerned will actually correspond to the history of the primitive period of a people which was compiled later with purposive intent.

Now one may think that if Leonardo's story of the vulture which visited him in his cradle is only a phantasy of later birth, it is hardly worth while giving more time to it. One could easily explain it by his openly avowed inclination to occupy himself with the problem of the flight of the bird which would lend to this phantasy an air of predetermined fate. But with this depreciation one commits as great an injustice as if one would simply ignore the material of legends, traditions, and interpretations in the primitive history of a people. Notwithstanding all distortions and misunderstandings to the contrary they still represent the reality of the past; they represent what the people formed out of the experiences of its past age under the domination of once powerful and to-day still effective motives, and if these distortions could be unraveled through the knowledge of all effective forces, one would surely discover the historic truth under this legendary material. The same holds true for the infantile reminiscences or for the phantasies of individuals. What a person thinks he recalls from his childhood, is not of an indifferent nature. As a rule the memory remnants, which he himself does not understand, conceal invaluable evidences of the most important features of his psychic development. As the psychoanalytic technique affords us excellent means for bringing to light this concealed material, we shall venture the attempt to fill the gaps in the history of Leonardo's life through the analysis of his infantile phantasy. And if we should not attain a satisfactory degree of certainty, we will have to console ourselves with the fact that so many other investigations about this great and mysterious man have met no better fate.

When we examine Leonardo's vulture-phantasy with the eyes of a psychoanalyst then it does not seem strange very long; we recall that we have often found similar structures in dreams, so that we may venture to translate this phantasy from its strange language into words that are universally understood. The translation then follows an erotic direction. Tail, "coda," is one of the most familiar symbols, as well as a substitutive designation of the male member which is no less true in Italian than in other languages. The situation contained in the phantasy, that a vulture opened the mouth of the child and forcefully belabored it with its tail, corresponds to the idea of fellatio, a sexual act in which the member is placed into the mouth of the other person. Strangely enough this phantasy is altogether of a passive character; it resembles certain dreams and phantasies of women and of passive homosexuals who play the feminine part in sexual relations.

Let the reader be patient for a while and not flare up with indignation and refuse to follow psychoanalysis because in its very first applications it leads to an unpardonable slander of the memory of a great and pure man. For it is quite certain that this indignation will never solve for us the meaning of Leonardo's childhood phantasy; on the other hand, Leonardo has unequivocally acknowledged this phantasy, and we shall therefore not relinquish the expectation—or if you prefer the preconception—that like every psychic production such as dreams, visions and deliria this phantasy, too, must have some meaning. Let us therefore lend our unprejudiced ears for a while to psychoanalytic work which after all has not yet uttered the last word.

The desire to take the male member into the mouth and suck it, which is considered as one of the most disgusting of sexual perversions, is nevertheless a frequent occurrence among the women of our time—and as shown in old sculptures was the same in earlier times—and in the state of being in love seems to lose entirely its disgusting character. The physician encounters phantasies based on this desire, even in women who did not come to the knowledge of the possibility of such sexual gratification by reading V. Krafft-Ebing's Psychopathia Sexualis or through other information. It seems that it is quite easy for the women themselves to produce such wish-phantasies.[227] Investigation then teaches us that this situation, so forcibly condemned by custom, may be traced to the most harmless origin. It is nothing but the elaboration of another situation in which we all once felt comfort, namely, when we were in the suckling-age ("when I was still in the cradle") and took the nipple of our mother's or wet-nurse's breast into our mouth to suck it. The organic impression of this first pleasure in our lives surely remains indelibly impregnated; when the child later learns to know the udder of the cow, which in function is a breast-nipple, but in shape and in position on the abdomen resembles the penis, it obtains the primary basis for the later formation of that disgusting sexual phantasy.

We now understand why Leonardo displaced the memory of the supposed experience with the vulture to his nursing period. This phantasy conceals nothing more or less than a reminiscence of nursing—or being nursed—at the mother's breast, a scene both human and beautiful, which he

---

[227] Cf. here the "Bruchstück einer Hysterieanalyse," in Neurosenlehre, Second series, 1909.

as well as other artists undertook to depict with the brush in the form of the mother of God and her child. At all events, we also wish to maintain, something we do not as yet understand, that this reminiscence, equally significant for both sexes, was elaborated in the man Leonardo into a passive homosexual phantasy. For the present we shall not take up the question as to what connection there is between homosexuality and suckling at the mother's breast, we merely wish to recall that tradition actually designates Leonardo as a person of homosexual feelings. In considering this, it makes no difference whether that accusation against the youth Leonardo was justified or not. It is not the real activity but the nature of the feeling which causes us to decide whether to attribute to some one the characteristic of homosexuality.

Another incomprehensible feature of Leonardo's infantile phantasy next claims our interest. We interpret the phantasy of being wet-nursed by the mother and find that the mother is replaced by a vulture. Where does this vulture originate and how does he come into this place?

A thought now obtrudes itself which seems so remote that one is tempted to ignore it. In the sacred hieroglyphics of the old Egyptians the mother is represented by the picture of the vulture.[228] These Egyptians also worshiped a motherly deity, whose head was vulture like, or who had many heads of which at least one or two was that of a vulture.[229] The name of this goddess was pronounced *Mut*; we may question whether the sound similarity to our word mother (Mutter) is only accidental? So the vulture really has some connection with the mother, but of what help is that to us? Have we a right to attribute this knowledge to Leonardo when François Champollion first succeeded in reading hieroglyphics between 1790-1832?[230]

It would also be interesting to discover in what way the old Egyptians came to choose the vulture as a symbol of motherhood. As a matter of fact the religion and culture of Egyptians were subjects of scientific interest even to the Greeks and Romans, and long before we ourselves were able to read the Egyptian monuments we had at our disposal some communications about them from preserved works of classical antiquity. Some of these writings belonged to familiar authors like Strabo, Plutarch, Aminianus Marcellus, and some bear unfamiliar names and are uncertain as to origin and time, like the hieroglyphica of Horapollo Nilus, and like the traditional book of oriental priestly wisdom bearing the godly name Hermes Trismegistos. From these sources we learn that the vulture was a symbol of motherhood because it was thought that this species of birds had only female vultures and no

---

[228] Horapollo: Hieroglyphica I, II. Μητέ ρα δέ γρά φοντες ... γὐ πα ζωγραφοὐ σιυ

[229] Roscher: Ausf. Lexicon der griechischen und römischen Mythologie. Artikel Mut, II Bd., 1894-1897.—Lanzone. Dizionario di Mitologia egizia. Torino, 1882.

[230] H. Hartleben, Champollion. Sein Leben und sein Werk, 1906.

males.[231] The natural history of the ancients shows a counterpart to this limitation among the scarebæus beetles which were revered by the Egyptians as godly, no females were supposed to exist.[232]

But how does impregnation take place in vultures if only females exist? This is fully answered in a passage of Horapollo.[233] At a certain time these birds stop in the midst of their flight, open their vagina and are impregnated by the wind.

Unexpectedly we have now reached a point where we can take something as quite probable which only shortly before we had to reject as absurd. It is quite possible that Leonardo was well acquainted with the scientific fable, according to which the Egyptians represented the idea of mother with the picture of the vulture. He was an omnivorous reader whose interest comprised all spheres of literature and knowledge. In the Codex Atlanticus we find an index of all books which he possessed at a certain time,[234] as well as numerous notices about other books which he borrowed from friends, and according to the excerpts which Fr. Richter compiled from his drawings we can hardly overestimate the extent of his reading. Among these books there was no lack of older as well as contemporary works treating of natural history. All these books were already in print at that time, and it so happens that Milan was the principal place of the young art of book printing in Italy.

When we proceed further we come upon a communication which may raise to a certainty the probability that Leonardo knew the vulture fable. The erudite editor and commentator of Horapollo remarked in connection with the text (p. 172) cited before: *Caeterum hanc fabulam de vulturibus cupide amplexi sunt Patres Ecclesiastici, ut ita argumento ex rerum natura petito refutarent eos, qui Virginis partum negabant; itaque apud omnes fere hujus rei mentio occurit.*

Hence the fable of the monosexuality and the conception of the vulture by no means remained as an indifferent anecdote as in the case of the analogous fable of the scarebæus beetles; that church fathers mastered it in order to have it ready as an argument from natural history against those who doubted the sacred history. If according the best information from antiquity the vultures were directed to let themselves be impregnated by the wind, why should the same thing not have happened even once in a human female? On account of this use the church fathers were "almost all" in the habit of relating

---

[231] "γὺ πα δὲ ἀ ρρενα οὐ φασνγέ νεσθαι ποτε, ἀ ιλὰ φηλεί ας ἀ πὰ σας," cited by v. Römer. Über die androgynische Idee des Lebens, Jahrb. f. Sexuelle Zwischenstufen, V, 1903, p. 732.

[232] Plutarch: Veluti scarabaeos mares tantum esse putarunt Aegyptii sic inter vultures mares non inveniri statuerunt

[233] Horapollinis Niloi Hieroglyphica edidit Conradus Leemans Amstelodami, 1835. The words referring to the sex of the vulture read as follows (p. 14): "μητέ ρα μέ ν ἐ πειδὴ ἀ ρρεν ἐ ν τοῦ τω γέ νει τῶ ων οὐ χ ὐ πὰ ρχει."

[234] E. Müntz, 1. c., p. 282.

this vulture fable, and now it can hardly remain doubtful that it also became known to Leonardo through so powerful a source.

The origin of Leonardo's vulture phantasy can be conceived in the following manner: While reading in the writings of a church father or in a book on natural science that the vultures are all females and that they know to procreate without the coöperation of a male, a memory emerged in him which became transformed into that phantasy, but which meant to say that he also had been such a vulture child, which had a mother but no father. An echo of pleasure which he experienced at his mother's breast was added to this in the manner as so old impressions alone can manifest themselves. The allusion to the idea of the holy virgin with the child, formed by the authors, which is so dear to every artist, must have contributed to it to make this phantasy seem to him valuable and important. For this helped him to identify himself with the Christ child, the comforter and savior of not alone this one woman.

When we break up an infantile phantasy we strive to separate the real memory content from the later motives which modify and distort the same. In the case of Leonardo we now think that we know the real content of the phantasy. The replacement of the mother by the vulture indicates that the child missed the father and felt himself alone with his mother. The fact of Leonardo's illegitimate birth fits in with his vulture phantasy; only on account of it was he able to compare himself with a vulture child. But we have discovered as the next definite fact from his youth that at the age of five years he had already been received in his father's home; when this took place, whether a few months following his birth, or a few weeks before the taking of the assessment of taxes, is entirely unknown to us. The interpretation of the vulture phantasy then steps in and wants to tell us that Leonardo did not spend the first decisive years of his life with his father and his step-mother but with his poor, forsaken, real mother, so that he had time to miss his father. This still seems to be a rather meager and rather daring result of the psychoanalytic effort, but on further reflection it will gain in significance. Certainty will be promoted by mentioning the actual relations in Leonardo's childhood. According to the reports, his father Ser Piero da Vinci married the prominent Donna Albiera during the year of Leonardo's birth; it was to the childlessness of this marriage that the boy owed his legalized reception into his father's or rather grandfather's house during his fifth year. However, it is not customary to offer an illegitimate offspring to a young woman's care at the beginning of marriage when she is still expecting to be blessed with children. Years of disappointment must have elapsed before it was decided to adopt the probably handsomely developed illegitimate child as a compensation for legitimate children who were vainly hoped for. It harmonizes best with the interpretation of the vulture-phantasy, if at least three years or perhaps five years of Leonardo's life had elapsed before he changed from his lonely mother to his father's home. But then it had already become too late. In the first three or four years of life impressions are fixed and modes of reactions are formed towards the outer world which can never be robbed of their importance by any later experiences.

If it is true that the incomprehensible childhood reminiscences and the person's phantasies based on them always bring out the most significant of his psychic development, then the fact corroborated by the vulture phantasy, that Leonardo passed the first years of his life alone with his mother must have been a most decisive influence on the formation of his inner life. Under the effect of this constellation it could not have been otherwise than that the child which in his young life encountered one problem more than other children, should have begun to ponder very passionately over this riddle and thus should have become an investigator early in life. For he was tortured by the great questions where do children come from and what has the father to do with their origin. The vague knowledge of this connection between his investigation and his childhood history has later drawn from him the exclamation that it was destined that he should deeply occupy himself with the problem of the bird's flight, for already in his cradle he had been visited by a vulture. To trace the curiosity which is directed to the flight of the bird to the infantile sexual investigation will be a later task which will not be difficult to accomplish.

III

The element of the vulture represents to us the real memory content in Leonardo's childhood phantasy; the association into which Leonardo himself placed his phantasy threw a bright light on the importance of this content for his later life. In continuing the work of interpretation we now encounter the strange problem why this memory content was elaborated into a homosexual situation. The mother who nursed the child, or rather from whom the child suckled was transformed into a vulture which stuck its tail into the child's mouth. We maintain that the "coda" (tail) of the vulture, following the common substituting usages of language, cannot signify anything else but a male genital or penis. But we do not understand how the phantastic activity came to furnish precisely this maternal bird with the mark of masculinity, and in view of this absurdity we become confused at the possibility of reducing this phantastic structure to rational sense.

However, we must not despair. How many seemingly absurd dreams have we not forced to give up their sense! Why should it become more difficult to accomplish this in a childhood phantasy than in a dream!

Let us remember the fact that it is not good to find one isolated peculiarity, and let us hasten to add another to it which is still more striking.

The vulture-headed goddess *Mut* of the Egyptians, a figure of altogether impersonal character, as expressed by Drexel in Roscher's lexicon, was often fused with other maternal deities of living individuality like Isis and Hathor, but she retained besides her separate existence and reverence. It was especially characteristic of the Egyptian pantheon that the individual gods did not perish in this amalgamation. Besides the composition of deities the simple divine image remained in her independence. In most representations the vulture-headed maternal deity was formed by the Egyptians in a phallic manner,[235] her body which was distinguished as feminine by its breasts also bore the masculine member in a state of erection.

The goddess Mut thus evinced the same union of maternal and paternal characteristics as in Leonardo's vulture phantasy. Should we explain this concurrence by the assumption that Leonardo knew from studying his book the androgynous nature of the maternal vulture? Such possibility is more than questionable; it seems that the sources accessible to him contained nothing of remarkable determination. It is more likely that here as there the agreement is to be traced to a common, effective and unknown motive.

Mythology can teach us that the androgynous formation, the union of masculine and feminine sex characteristics, did not belong to the goddess Mut alone but also to other deities such as Isis and Hathor, but in the latter perhaps only insofar as they possessed also a motherly nature and became fused with the goddess Mut.[236] It teaches us further that other Egyptian deities such as Neith of Sais out of whom the Greek Athene was later formed, were originally conceived as androgynous or dihermaphroditic, and that the same held true for many of the Greek gods, especially of the Dionysian circle, as well as for Aphrodite who was later restricted to a feminine love deity. Mythology may also offer the explanation that the phallus which was added to the feminine body was meant to denote the creative primitive force of nature, and that all these hermaphroditic deistic formations express the idea that only a union of the masculine and feminine elements can result in a worthy representation of divine perfection. But none of these observations explain the psychological riddle, namely, that the phantasy of men takes no offense at the fact that a figure which was to embody the essence of the mother should be provided with the mark of the masculine power which is the opposite of motherhood.

The explanation comes from the infantile sexual theories. There really was a time in which the male genital was found to be compatible with the representation of the mother. When the male child first directs his curiosity

---

[235] See the illustrations in Lanzone l. c. T. CXXXVI-VIII.
[236] v. Römer l. c.

to the riddle of the sexual life, he is dominated by the interest for his own genitals. He finds this part of the body too valuable and too important to believe that it would be missing in other persons to whom he feels such a resemblance. As he cannot divine that there is still another equally valuable type of genital formation he must grasp the assumption that all persons, also women, possess such a member as he. This preconception is so firm in the youthful investigator that it is not destroyed even by the first observation of the genitals in little girls. His perception naturally tells him that there is something different here than in him, but he is unable to admit to himself as the content of this perception that he cannot find this member in girls. That this member may be missing is to him a dismal and unbearable thought, and he therefore seeks to reconcile it by deciding that it also exists in girls but it is still very small and that it will grow later.[237] If this expectation does not appear to be fulfilled on later observation he has at his disposal another way of escape. The member also existed in the little girl but it was cut off and on its place there remained a wound. This progress of the theory already makes use of his own painful experience; he was threatened in the meantime that this important organ will be taken away from him if it will form too much of an interest for his occupation. Under the influence of this threat of castration he now interprets his conception of the female genital, henceforth he will tremble for his masculinity, but at the same time he will look with contempt upon those unhappy creatures upon whom, in his opinion, this cruel punishment had already been visited.

Before the child came under the domination of the castration complex, at the time when he still held the woman at her full value, he began to manifest an intensive desire to look as an erotic activity of his impulse. He wished to see the genitals of other persons, originally probably because he wished to compare them with his own. The erotic attraction which emanated from the person of his mother soon reached its height in the longing to see her genital which he believed to be a penis. With the cognition acquired only later that the woman has no penis, this longing often becomes transformed into its opposite and gives place to disgust, which in the years of puberty may become the cause of psychic impotence, of misogyny and of lasting homosexuality. But the fixation on the once so vividly desired object, the penis of the woman, leaves ineradicable traces in the psychic life of the child, which has gone through that fragment of infantile sexual investigation with particular thoroughness. The fetich-like reverence for the feminine foot and shoe seems to take the foot only as a substitutive symbol for the once revered and since then missed member of the woman. The "braid-slashers" without knowing it

---

[237] Cf. the observations in the Jahrbuch für Psychoanalytische und Psychopathologische Forschungen, Vol. I, 1909.

play the part of persons who perform the act of castration on the female genital.

One will not gain any correct understanding of the activities of the infantile sexuality and probably will consider these communications unworthy of belief, as long as one does not relinquishthe attitude of our cultural depreciation of the genitals and of the sexual functions in general. To understand the infantile psychic life one has to look to analogies from primitive times. For a long series of generations we have been in the habit of considering the genitals or *pudenda* as objects of shame, and in the case of more successful sexual repression as objects of disgust. The majority of those living to-day only reluctantly obey the laws of propagation, feeling thereby that their human dignity is being offended and degraded. What exists among us of the other conception of the sexual life is found only in the uncultivated and in the lower social strata; among the higher and more refined types it is concealed as culturally inferior, and its activity is ventured only under the embittered admonition of a guilty conscience. It was quite different in the primitive times of the human race. From the laborious collections of students of civilization one gains the conviction that the genitals were originally the pride and hope of living beings, they enjoyed divine worship, and the divine nature of their functions was transported to all newly acquired activities of mankind. Through sublimation of its essential elements there arose innumerable god-figures, and at the time when the relation of official religions with sexual activity was already hidden from the general consciousness, secret cults labored to preserve it alive among a number of the initiated. In the course of cultural development it finally happened that so much godliness and holiness had been extracted from sexuality that the exhausted remnant fell into contempt. But considering the indestructibility which is in the nature of all psychic impressions one need not wonder that even the most primitive forms of genital worship could be demonstrated until quite recent times, and that language, customs and superstitions of present day humanity contain the remnants of all phases of this course of development.[238]

Important biological analogies have taught us that the psychic development of the individual is a short repetition of the course of development of the race, and we shall therefore not find improbable what the psychoanalytic investigation of the child's psyche asserts concerning the infantile estimation of the genitals. The infantile assumption of the maternal penis is thus the common source of origin for the androgynous formation of the maternal deities like the Egyptian goddess Mut and the vulture's "coda" (tail) in Leonardo's childhood phantasy. As a matter of fact, it is only through misunderstanding that these deistic representations are designated

---

[238] Cf. Richard Payne Knight: The Cult of Priapus.

hermaphroditic in the medical sense of the word. In none of them is there a union of the true genitals of both sexes as they are united in some deformed beings to the disgust of every human eye; but besides the breast as a mark of motherhood there is also the male member, just as it existed in the first imagination of the child about his mother's body. Mythology has retained for the faithful this revered and very early fancied bodily formation of the mother. The prominence given to the vulture-tail in Leonardo's phantasy we can now translate as follows: At that time when I directed my tender curiosity to my mother I still adjudged to her a genital like my own. A further testimonial of Leonardo's precocious sexual investigation, which in our opinion became decisive for his entire life.

A brief reflection now admonishes us that we should not be satisfied with the explanation of the vulture-tail in Leonardo's childhood phantasy. It seems as if it contained more than we as yet understand. For its more striking feature really consisted in the fact that the nursing at the mother's breast was transformed into being nursed, that is into a passive act which thus gives the situation an undoubted homosexual character. Mindful of the historical probability that Leonardo behaved in life as a homosexual in feeling, the question obtrudes itself whether this phantasy does not point to a causal connection between Leonardo's childhood relations to his mother and the later manifest, if only ideal, homosexuality. We would not venture to draw such conclusion from Leonardo's disfigured reminiscence were it not for the fact that we know from our psychoanalytic investigation of homosexual patients that such a relation exists, indeed it really is an intimate and necessary relation.

Homosexual men who have started in our times an energetic action against the legal limitations of their sexual activity are fond of representing themselves through theoretical spokesmen as evincing a sexual variation, which may be distinguished from the very beginning, as an intermediate stage of sex or as "a third sex." In other words, they maintain that they are men who are forced by organic determinants originating in the germ to find that pleasure in the man which they cannot feel in the woman. As much as one would wish to subscribe to their demands out of humane considerations, one must nevertheless exercise reserve regarding their theories which were formulated without regard for the psychic genesis of homosexuality. Psychoanalysis offers the means to fill this gap and to put to test the assertions of the homosexuals. It is true that psychoanalysis fulfilled this task in only a small number of people, but all investigation thus far undertaken brought the same surprising results.[239] In all our male homosexuals there

---

[239] Prominently among those who undertook these investigations are I. Sadger, whose results I can essentially corroborate from my own experience. I am also aware that Stekel of Vienna, Ferenczi of Budapest, and Brill of New York, came to the same conclusions.

was a very intensive erotic attachment to a feminine person, as a rule to the mother, which was manifest in the very first period of childhood and later entirely forgotten by the individual. This attachment was produced or favored by too much love from the mother herself, but was also furthered by the retirement or absence of the father during the childhood period. Sadger emphasizes the fact that the mothers of his homosexual patients were often man-women, or women with energetic traits of character who were able to crowd out the father from the place allotted to him in the family. I have sometimes observed the same thing, but I was more impressed by those cases in which the father was absent from the beginning or disappeared early so that the boy was altogether under feminine influence. It almost seems that the presence of a strong father would assure for the son the proper decision in the selection of his object from the opposite sex.

Following this primary stage, a transformation takes place whose mechanisms we know but whose motive forces we have not yet grasped. The love of the mother cannot continue to develop consciously so that it merges into repression. The boy represses the love for the mother by putting himself in her place, by identifying himself with her, and by taking his own person as a model through the similarity of which he is guided in the selection of his love object. He thus becomes homosexual; as a matter of fact he returns to the stage of autoerotism, for the boys whom the growing adult now loves are only substitutive persons or revivals of his own childish person, whom he loves in the same way as his mother loved him. We say that he finds his love object on the road to narcism, for the Greek legend called a boy Narcissus to whom nothing was more pleasing than his own mirrored image, and who became transformed into a beautiful flower of this name.

Deeper psychological discussions justify the assertion that the person who becomes homosexual in this manner remains fixed in his unconscious on the memory picture or his mother, By repressing the love for his mother he conserves the same in his unconscious and henceforth remains faithful to her. When as a lover he seems to pursue boys, he really thus runs away from women who could cause him to become faithless to his mother. Through direct observation of individual cases we could demonstrate that he who is seemingly receptive only of masculine stimuli is in reality influenced by the charms emanating from women just like a normal person, but each and every time he hastens to transfer the stimulus he received from the woman to a male object and in this manner he repeats again and again the mechanism through which he acquired his homosexuality.

It is far from us to exaggerate the importance of these explanations concerning the psychic genesis of homosexuality. It is quite clear that they are in crass opposition to the official theories of the homosexual spokesmen, but we are aware that these explanations are not sufficiently comprehensive to render possible a final explanation of the problem. What one calls homosexual for practical purposes may have its origin in a variety of psychosexual inhibiting processes, and the process recognized by us is perhaps only one among many, and has reference only to one type of "homosexuality." We must also admit, that the number of cases in our homosexual type which shows the conditions required by us, exceeds by far those cases in which the resulting effect really appears, so that even we cannot reject the supposed coöperation of unknown constitutional factors from which one was otherwise wont to deduce the whole of homosexuality. As a matter of fact there would be no occasion for entering into the psychic genesis of the form of homosexuality studied by us if there were not a strong presumption that Leonardo, from whose vulture-phantasy we started, really belonged to this one type of homosexuality.

As little as is known concerning the sexual behavior of the great artist and investigator, we must still trust to the probability that the testimonies of his contemporaries did not go far astray. In the light of this tradition he appears to us as a man whose sexual need and activity were extraordinarily low, as if a higher striving had raised him above the common animal need of mankind. It may be open to doubt whether he ever sought direct sexual gratification, and in what manner, or whether he could dispense with it altogether. We are justified, however, to look also in him for those emotional streams which imperatively force others to the sexual act, for we cannot imagine a human psychic life in whose development the sexual desire in the broadest sense, the libido, has not had its share, whether the latter has withdrawn itself far from the original aim or whether it was detained from being put into execution.

Anything but traces of unchanged sexual desire we need not expect in Leonardo. These point however to one direction and allow us to count him among homosexuals. It has always been emphasized that he took as his pupils only strikingly handsome boys and youths. He was kind and considerate towards them, he cared for them and nursed them himself when they were ill, just like a mother nurses her children, as his own mother might have cared for him. As he selected them on account of their beauty rather than their talent, none of them—Cesare da Sesto, G. Boltraffio, Andrea Salaino, Francesco Melzi and the others—ever became a prominent artist. Most of them could not make themselves independent of their master and disappeared after his death without leaving a more definite physiognomy to the history of art. The others who by their productions earned the right to call themselves his pupils, as Luini and Bazzi, nicknamed Sodoma, he probably did not know personally.

We realize that we will have to face the objection that Leonardo's behavior towards his pupils surely had nothing to do with sexual motives, and permits no conclusion as to his sexual peculiarity. Against this we wish to assert with all caution that our conception explains some strange features in the master's behavior which otherwise would have remained enigmatical. Leonardo kept a diary; he made entries in his small hand, written from right to left which were meant only for himself. It is to be noted that in this diary he addressed himself with "thou": "Learn from master Lucca the multiplication of roots."[240] "Let master d'Abacco show thee the square of the circle."[241] Or on the occasion of a journey he entered in his diary:

"I am going to Milan to look after the affairs of my garden ... order two pack-sacks to be made. Ask Boltraffio to show thee his turning-lathe and let him polish a stone on it.—Leave the book to master Andrea il Todesco."[242] Or he wrote a resolution of quite different significance: "Thou must show in thy treatise that the earth is a star, like the moon or resembling it, and thus prove the nobility of our world."[243]

In this diary, which like the diaries of other mortals often skim over the most important events of the day with only few words or ignore them altogether, one finds a few entries which on account of their peculiarity are cited by all of Leonardo's biographers. They show notations referring to the master's petty expenses, which are recorded with painful exactitude as if coming from a pedantic and strictly parsimonious family father, while there is nothing to show that he spent greater sums, or that the artist was well versed in household management. One of these notes refers to a new cloak which he bought for his pupil Andrea Salaino:[244]

Silver brocade	Lira	15	Soldi	4		
Crimson velvet for trimming	"	9	"	0		
Braid	"	0	"	9		
Buttons	"	0	"	12		

Another very detailed notice gives all the expenses which he incurred through the bad qualities and the thieving tendencies of another pupil or model: "On 21st day of April, 1490, I started this book and started again the horse.[245] Jacomo came to me on Magdalene day, 1490, at the age of ten years (marginal note: thievish, mendacious, willful, gluttonous). On the second day I ordered for him two shirts, a pair of pants, and a jacket, and as I put the money away to pay for the things named he stole the money from my purse, and it was never possible to make him confess, although I was absolutely sure of it (marginal note: 4 Lira ...)." So the report continues concerning the

---

[240] Edm. Solmi: Leonardo da Vinci, German translation, p. 152.

[241] Solmi, 1. c. p. 203.

[242] Leonardo thus behaves like one who was in the habit of making a daily confession to another person whom he now replaced by his diary. For an assumption as to who this person may have been see Merejkowski, p. 309.

[243] M. Herzfeld: Leonardo da Vinci, 1906, p. 141.

[244] The wording is that of Merejkowski, 1. c. p. 237.

[245] The equestrian monument of Francesco Sforza.

misdeeds of the little boy and concludes with the expense account: "In the first year, a cloak, Lira 2: 6 shirts, Lira 4: 3 jackets, Lira 6: 4 pair of socks, Lira 7, etc."[246]

Leonardo's biographers, to whom nothing was further than to solve the riddle in the psychic life of their hero from these slight weaknesses and peculiarities, were wont to remark in connection with these peculiar accounts that they emphasized the kindness and consideration of the master for his pupils. They forget thereby that it is not Leonardo's behavior that needs an explanation, but the fact that he left us these testimonies of it. As it is impossible to ascribe to him the motive of smuggling into our hands proofs of his kindness, we must assume that another affective motive caused him to write this down. It is not easy to conjecture what this motive was, and we could not give any if not for another account found among Leonardo's papers which throws a brilliant light on these peculiarly petty notices about his pupils' clothes, and others of a kind:[247]

Burial expenses following the death of Caterina		27	florins	
2 pounds wax	18	"		
Cataphalc	12	"		
For the transportation and erection of the cross		4	"	
Pall bearers	8	"		
To 4 priests and 4 clerics		20	"	
Ringing of bells		2	"	
To grave diggers		16	"	
For the approval—to the officials		1	"	
To sum up	108	florins		
Previous expenses:				
To the doctor	4	florins		
For sugar and candles		12	"	
	16	florins		
Sum total	124	florins		

The writer Merejkowski is the only one who can tell us who this Caterina was. From two different short notices he concludes that she was the mother of Leonardo, the poor peasant woman from Vinci, who came to Milan in 1493

---

[246] The full wording is found in M. Herzfeld, 1. c. p. 45.

[247] Merejkowski 1. c.—As a disappointing illustration of the vagueness of the information concerning Leonardo's intimate life, meager as it is, I mention the fact that the same expense account is given by Solmi with considerable variation (German translation, p. 104). The most serious difference is the substitution of florins by soldi. One may assume that in this account florins do not mean the old "gold florins," but those used at a later period which amounted to 1-2/3 lira or 33½ soldi.—Solmi represents Caterina as a servant who had taken care of Leonardo's household for a certain time. The source from which the two representations of this account were taken was not accessible to me.

to visit her son then 41 years old. While on this visit she fell ill and was taken to the hospital by Leonardo, and following her death she was buried by her son with such sumptuous funeral.[248]

This deduction of the psychological writer of romances is not capable of proof, but it can lay claim to so many inner probabilities, it agrees so well with everything we know besides about Leonardo's emotional activity that I cannot refrain from accepting it as correct. Leonardo succeeded in forcing his feelings under the yoke of investigation and in inhibiting their free utterance, but even in him there were episodes in which the suppression obtained expression, and one of these was the death of his mother whom he once loved so ardently. Through this account of the burial expenses he represents to us the mourning of his mother in an almost unrecognizable distortion. We wonder how such a distortion could have come about, and we certainly cannot grasp it when viewed under normal mental processes. But similar mechanisms are familiar to us under the abnormal conditions of neuroses, and especially in the so-called *compulsion neurosis*. Here one can observe how the expressions of more intensive feelings have been displaced to trivial and even foolish performances. The opposing forces succeeded in debasing the expression of these repressed feelings to such an extent that one is forced to estimate the intensity of these feelings as extremely unimportant, but the imperative compulsion with which these insignificant acts express themselves betrays the real force of the feelings which are rooted in the unconscious, which consciousness would wish to disavow. Only by bearing in mind the mechanisms of compulsion neurosis can one explain Leonardo's account of the funeral expenses of his mother. In his unconscious he was still tied to her as in childhood, by erotically tinged feelings; the opposition of the repression of this childhood love which appeared later stood in the way of erecting to her in his diary a different and more dignified monument, but what resulted as a compromise of this neurotic conflict had to be put in operation and hence the account was entered in the diary which thus came to the knowledge of posterity as something incomprehensible.

It is not venturing far to transfer the interpretation obtained from the funeral expenses to the accounts dealing with his pupils. Accordingly we would say that here also we deal with a case in which Leonardo's meager remnants of libidinous feelings compulsively obtained a distorted expression. The mother and the pupils, the very images of his own boyish beauty, would be his sexual objects—as far as his sexual repression dominating his nature would allow such manifestations—and the compulsion to note with painful circumstantiality his expenses on their behalf, would designate the strange betrayal of his rudimentary conflicts. From this we would conclude that Leonardo's love-life really belonged to that type of homosexuality, the psychic

---

[248] "Caterina came in July, 1493."

development of which we were able to disclose, and the appearance of the homosexual situation in his vulture-phantasy would become comprehensible to us, for it states nothing more or less than what we have asserted before concerning that type. It requires the following interpretation: Through the erotic relations to my mother I became a homosexual.[249]

IV

The vulture phantasy of Leonardo still absorbs our interest. In words which only too plainly recall a sexual act ("and has many times struck against my lips with his tail"), Leonardo emphasizes the intensity of the erotic relations between the mother and the child. A second memory content of the phantasy can readily be conjectured from the association of the activity of the mother (of the vulture) with the accentuation of the mouth zone. We can translate it as follows: My mother has pressed on my mouth innumerable passionate kisses. The phantasy is composed of the memories of being nursed and of being kissed by the mother.

A kindly nature has bestowed upon the artist the capacity to express in artistic productions his most secret psychic feelings hidden even to himself, which powerfully affect outsiders who are strangers to the artist without their being able to state whence this emotivity comes. Should there be no evidence in Leonardo's work of that which his memory retained as the strongest impression of his childhood? One would have to expect it. However, when one considers what profound transformations an impression of an artist has to experience before it can add its contribution to the work of art, one is obliged to moderate considerably his expectation of demonstrating something definite. This is especially true in the case of Leonardo.

He who thinks of Leonardo's paintings will be reminded by the remarkably fascinating and puzzling smile which he enchanted on the lips of all his feminine figures. It is a fixed smile on elongated, sinuous lips which is considered characteristic of him and is preferentially designated as "Leonardesque." In the singular and beautiful visage of the Florentine Monna Lisa del Giocondo it has produced the greatest effect on the spectators and even perplexed them. This smile was in need of an interpretation, and received many of the most varied kind but none of them was considered satisfactory. As Gruyer puts it: "It is almost four centuries since Monna Lisa

---

[249] The manner of expression through which the repressed libidio could manifest itself in Leonardo, such as circumstantiality and marked interest in money, belongs to those traits of character which emanate from anal eroticism. Cf. Character und Analerotik in the second series of my Sammlung zur Neurosenlehre, 1909, also Brill's Psychoanalysis, its Theories and Practical Applications, Chap. XIII, Anal Eroticism and Character, Saunders, Philadelphia.

causes all those to lose their heads who have looked upon her for some time."[250]

Muther states:[251] "What fascinates the spectator is the demoniacal charm of this smile. Hundreds of poets and writers have written about this woman, who now seems to smile upon us seductively and now to stare coldly and lifelessly into space, but nobody has solved the riddle of her smile, nobody has interpreted her thoughts. Everything, even the scenery is mysterious and dream-like, trembling as if in the sultriness of sensuality."

The idea that two diverse elements were united in the smile of Monna Lisa has been felt by many critics. They therefore recognize in the play of features of the beautiful Florentine lady the most perfect representation of the contrasts dominating the love-life of the woman which is foreign to man, as that of reserve and seduction, and of most devoted tenderness and inconsiderateness in urgent and consuming sensuality. Müntz[252] expresses himself in this manner: "One knows what indecipherable and fascinating enigma Monna Lisa Gioconda has been putting for nearly four centuries to the admirers who crowd around her. No artist (I borrow the expression of the delicate writer who hides himself under the pseudonym of Pierre de Corlay) has ever translated in this manner the very essence of femininity: the tenderness and coquetry, the modesty and quiet voluptuousness, the whole mystery of the heart which holds itself aloof, of a brain which reflects, and of a personality who watches itself and yields nothing from herself except radiance...." The Italian Angelo Conti[253] saw the picture in the Louvre illumined by a ray of the sun and expressed himself as follows: "The woman smiled with a royal calmness, her instincts of conquest, of ferocity, the entire heredity of the species, the will of seduction and ensnaring, the charm of the deceiver, the kindness which conceals a cruel purpose, all that appears and disappears alternately behind the laughing veil and melts into the poem of her smile.... Good and evil, cruelty and compassion, graceful and cat-like, she laughed...."

Leonardo painted this picture four years, perhaps from 1503 until 1507, during his second sojourn in Florence when he was about the age of fifty years. According to Vasari he applied the choicest artifices in order to divert the lady during the sittings and to hold that smile firmly on her features. Of all the gracefulness that his brush reproduced on the canvas at that time the picture preserves but very little in its present state. During its production it was considered the highest that art could accomplish; it is certain, however, that it did not satisfy Leonardo himself, that he pronounced it as unfinished

---

[250] Seidlitz: Leonardo da Vinci, II Bd., p. 280.
[251] Geschichte der Malerei, Bd. I, p. 314.
[252] l. c. p. 417.
[253] A. Conti: Leonardo pittore, Conferenze Fiorentine, l. c. p. 93.

and did not deliver it to the one who ordered it, but took it with him to France where his benefactor Francis I, acquired it for the Louvre.

Let us leave the physiognomic riddle of Monna Lisa unsolved, and let us note the unequivocal fact that her smile fascinated the artist no less than all the spectators for these 400 years. This captivating smile had thereafter returned in all of his pictures and in those of his pupils. As Leonardo's Monna Lisa was a portrait we cannot assume that he has added to her face a trait of his own so difficult to express which she herself did not possess. It seems, we cannot help but believe, that he found this smile in his model and became so charmed by it that from now on he endowed it on all the free creations of his phantasy. This obvious conception is, e.g., expressed by A. Konstantinowa in the following manner:[254]

"During the long period in which the master occupied himself with the portrait of Monna Lisa del Gioconda, he entered into the physiognomic delicacies of this feminine face with such sympathy of feeling that he transferred these creatures, especially the mysterious smile and the peculiar glance, to all faces which he later painted or drew. The mimic peculiarity of Gioconda can even be perceived in the picture of John the Baptist in the Louvre. But above all they are distinctly recognized in the features of Mary in the picture of St. Anne of the Louvre."

But the case could have been different. The need for a deeper reason for the fascination which the smile of Gioconda exerted on the artist from which he could not rid himself has been felt by more than one of his biographers. W. Pater, who sees in the picture of Monna Lisa the embodiment of the entire erotic experience of modern man, and discourses so excellently on "that unfathomable smile always with a touch of something sinister in it, which plays over all Leonardo's work," leads us to another track when he says:[255]

"Besides, the picture is a portrait. From childhood we see this image defining itself on the fabric of his dream; and but for express historical testimony, we might fancy that this was but his ideal lady, embodied and beheld at last."

Herzfeld surely must have had something similar in mind when stating that in Monna Lisa Leonardo encountered himself and therefore found it possible to put so much of his own nature into the picture, "whose features from time immemorial have been imbedded with mysterious sympathy in Leonardo's soul."[256]

Let us endeavor to clear up these intimations. It was quite possible that Leonardo was fascinated by the smile of Monna Lisa, because it had awakened something in him which had slumbered in his soul for a long time,

---

[254] l. c. p. 45.
[255] W. Pater: The Renaissance, p. 124, The Macmillan Co., 1910.
[256] M. Herzfeld: Leonardo da Vinci, p. 88.

in all probability an old memory. This memory was of sufficient importance to stick to him once it had been aroused; he was forced continually to provide it with new expression. The assurance of Pater that we can see an image like that of Monna Lisa defining itself from Leonardo's childhood on the fabric of his dreams, seems worthy of belief and deserves to be taken literally.

Vasari mentions as Leonardo's first artistic endeavors, "heads of women who laugh."[257] The passage, which is beyond suspicion, as it is not meant to prove anything, reads more precisely as follows:[258] "He formed in his youth some laughing feminine heads out of lime, which have been reproduced in plaster, and some heads of children, which were as beautiful as if modeled by the hands of a master...."

Thus we discover that his practice of art began with the representation of two kinds of objects, which would perforce remind us of the two kinds of sexual objects which we have inferred from the analysis of his vulture phantasy. If the beautiful children's heads were reproductions of his own childish person, then the laughing women were nothing else but reproductions of Caterina, his mother, and we are beginning to have an inkling of the possibility that his mother possessed that mysterious smile which he lost, and which fascinated him so much when he found it again in the Florentine lady.[259]

The painting of Leonardo which in point of time stands nearest to the Monna Lisa is the so-called Saint Anne of the Louvre, representing Saint Anne, Mary and the Christ child. It shows the Leonardesque smile most beautifully portrayed in the two feminine heads. It is impossible to find out how much earlier or later than the portrait of Monna Lisa Leonardo began to paint this picture. As both works extended over years, we may well assume that they occupied the master simultaneously. But it would best harmonize with our expectation if precisely the absorption in the features of Monna Lisa would have instigated Leonardo to form the composition of Saint Anne from his phantasy. For if the smile of Gioconda had conjured up in him the memory of his mother, we would naturally understand that he was first urged to produce a glorification of motherhood, and to give back to her the smile he found in that prominent lady. We may thus allow our interest to glide over from the portrait of Monna Lisa to this other hardly less beautiful picture, now also in the Louvre.

---

[257] Scognamiglio, l. c. p. 32.

[258] L. Schorn, Bd. III, 1843, p. 6.

[259] The same is assumed by Merejkowski, who imagined a childhood for Leonardo which deviates in the essential points from ours, drawn from the results of the vulture phantasy. But if Leonardo himself had displayed this smile, tradition hardly would have failed to report to us this coincidence.

Saint Anne with the daughter and grandchild is a subject seldom treated in the Italian art of painting; at all events Leonardo's representation differs widely from all that is otherwise known. Muther states:[260]

"Some masters like Hans Fries, the older Holbein, and Girolamo dei Libri, made Anne sit near Mary and placed the child between the two. Others like Jakob Cornelicz in his Berlin pictures, represented Saint Anne as holding in her arm the small figure of Mary upon which sits the still smaller figure of the Christ child." In Leonardo's picture Mary sits on her mother's lap, bent forward and is stretching out both arms after the boy who plays with a little lamb, and must have slightly maltreated it. The grandmother has one of her unconcealed arms propped on her hip and looks down on both with a blissful smile. The grouping is certainly not quite unconstrained. But the smile which is playing on the lips of both women, although unmistakably the same as in the picture of Monna Lisa, has lost its sinister and mysterious character; it expresses a calm blissfulness.[261]

On becoming somewhat engrossed in this picture it suddenly dawns upon the spectator that only Leonardo could have painted this picture, as only he could have formed the vulture phantasy. This picture contains the synthesis of the history of Leonardo's childhood, the details of which are explainable by the most intimate impressions of his life. In his father's home he found not only the kind step-mother Donna Albiera, but also the grandmother, his father's mother, Monna Lucia, who we will assume was not less tender to him than grandmothers are wont to be. This circumstance must have furnished him with the facts for the representation of a childhood guarded by a mother and grandmother. Another striking feature of the picture assumes still greater significance. Saint Anne, the mother of Mary and the grandmother of the boy who must have been a matron, is formed here perhaps somewhat more mature and more serious than Saint Mary, but still as a young woman of unfaded beauty. As a matter of fact Leonardo gave the boy two mothers, the one who stretched out her arms after him and another who is seen in the background, both are represented with the blissful smile of maternal happiness. This peculiarity of the picture has not failed to excite the wonder of the authors. Muther, for instance, believes that Leonardo could not bring himself to paint old age, folds and wrinkles, and therefore formed also Anne as a woman of radiant beauty. Whether one can be satisfied with this explanation is a question. Other writers have taken occasion to deny generally the sameness of age of mother and daughter.[262] However, Muther's tentative explanation is sufficient proof for the fact that the impression of Saint Anne's

---

[260] l. c. p. 309.
[261] A. Konstantinowa, l. c., says: "Mary looks tenderly down on her beloved child with a smile that recalls the mysterious expression of la Gioconda." Elsewhere speaking of Mary she says: "The smile of Gioconda floats upon her features."
[262] Cf. v. Seidlitz, l. c. Bd. II, p. 274.

youthful appearance was furnished by the picture and is not an imagination produced by a tendency.

Leonardo's childhood was precisely as remarkable as this picture. He has had two mothers, the first his true mother, Caterina, from whom he was torn away between the age of three and five years, and a young tender step-mother, Donna Albiera, his father's wife. By connecting this fact of his childhood with the one mentioned above and condensing them into a uniform fusion, the composition of Saint Anne, Mary and the Child, formed itself in him. The maternal form further away from the boy designated as grandmother, corresponds in appearance and in spatial relation to the boy, with the real first mother, Caterina. With the blissful smile of Saint Anne the artist actually disavowed and concealed the envy which the unfortunate mother felt when she was forced to give up her son to her more aristocratic rival, as once before her lover.

Our feeling that the smile of Monna Lisa del Gioconda awakened in the man the memory of the mother of his first years of childhood would thus be confirmed from another work of Leonardo. Following the production of Monna Lisa, Italian artists depicted in Madonnas and prominent ladies the humble dipping of the head and the peculiar blissful smile of the poor peasant girl Caterina, who brought to the world the noble son who was destined to paint, investigate, and suffer.

When Leonardo succeeded in reproducing in the face of Monna Lisa the double sense comprised in this smile, namely, the promise of unlimited tenderness, and sinister threat (in the words of Pater), he remained true even in this to the content of his earliest reminiscence. For the love of the mother became his destiny, it determined his fate and the privations which were in store for him. The impetuosity of the caressing to which the vulture phantasy points was only too natural. The poor forsaken mother had to give vent through mother's love to all her memories of love enjoyed as well as to all her yearnings for more affection; she was forced to it, not only in order to compensate herself for not having a husband, but also the child for not having a father who wanted to love it. In the manner of all ungratified mothers she thus took her little son in place of her husband, and robbed him of a part of his virility by the too early maturing of his eroticism. The love of the mother for the suckling whom she nourishes and cares for is something far deeper reaching than her later affection for the growing child. It is of the nature of a fully gratified love affair, which fulfills not only all the psychic wishes but also all physical needs, and when it represents one of the forms of happiness attainable by man it is due, in no little measure, to the possibility of gratifying without reproach also wish feelings which were long repressed and designated as perverse.[263] Even in the happiest recent marriage the father feels that his child, especially the little boy has become his rival, and this gives origin to an antagonism against the favorite one which is deeply rooted in the unconscious.

When in the prime of his life Leonardo re-encountered that blissful and ecstatic smile as it had once encircled his mother's mouth in caressing, he had long been under the ban of an inhibition, forbidding him ever again to desire such tenderness from women's lips. But as he had become a painter he endeavored to reproduce this smile with his brush and furnish all his pictures with it, whether he executed them himself or whether they were done by his pupils under his direction, as in Leda, John, and Bacchus. The latter two are variations of the same type. Muther says: "From the locust eater of the Bible Leonardo made a Bacchus, an Apollo, who with a mysterious smile on his lips, and with his soft thighs crossed, looks on us with infatuated eyes." These pictures breathe a mysticism into the secret of which one dares not penetrate; at most one can make the effort to construct the connection to Leonardo's earlier productions. The figures are again androgynous but no longer in the sense of the vulture phantasy, they are pretty boys of feminine tenderness with feminine forms; they do not cast down their eyes but gaze mysteriously triumphant, as if they knew of a great happy issue concerning which one must remain quiet; the familiar fascinating smile leads us to infer that it is a love secret. It is possible that in these forms Leonardo disavowed and artistically conquered the unhappiness of his love life, in that he represented the wish fulfillment of the boy infatuated with his mother in such blissful union of the male and female nature.

V

Among the entries in Leonardo's diaries there is one which absorbs the reader's attention through its important content and on account of a small formal error. In July, 1504, he wrote:

"Adi 9 Luglio, 1504, mercoledi, a ore 7 mori Ser Piero da Vinci notalio al palazzo del Potestà, mio padre, a ore 7. Era d'età d'anni 80, lasciò 10 figlioli maschi e 2 feminine."[264]

The notice as we see deals with the death of Leonardo's father. The slight error in its form consists in the fact that in the computation of the time "at 7 o'clock" is repeated two times, as if Leonardo had forgotten at the end of the

---

[263] Cf. Three Contributions to the Theory of Sex, translated by A. A. Brill, 2nd edition, 1916,

[264] "On the 9th of July, 1504, Wednesday at 7 o'clock died Ser Piero da Vinci, notary at the palace of the Podesta, my father, at 7 o'clock. He was 80 years old, left 10 sons and 2 daughters." (E. Müntz, l. c. p. 13.)

sentence that he had already written it at the beginning. It is only a triviality to which any one but a psychoanalyst would pay no attention. Perhaps he would not even notice it, or if his attention would be called to it he would say "that can happen to anybody during absent-mindedness or in an affective state and has no further meaning."

The psychoanalyst thinks differently; to him nothing is too trifling as a manifestation of hidden psychic processes; he has long learned that such forgetting or repetition is full of meaning, and that one is indebted to the "absent-mindedness" when it makes possible the betrayal of otherwise concealed feelings.

We would say that, like the funeral account of Caterina and the expense account of the pupils, this notice, too, corresponds to a case in which Leonardo was unsuccessful in suppressing his affects, and the long hidden feeling forcibly obtained a distorted expression. Also the form is similar, it shows the same pedantic precision, the same pushing forward of numbers.[265]

We call such a repetition a perseveration. It is an excellent means to indicate the affective accentuation. One recalls for example Saint Peter's angry speech against his unworthy representative on earth, as given in Dante's Paradiso:[266]

"Quegli ch'usurpa in terra il luoga mio
Il luoga mio, il luogo mio, che vaca
Nella presenza del Figliuol di Dio,
Fatto ha del cimiterio mio cloaca."

Without Leonardo's affective inhibition the entry into the diary could perhaps have read as follows: To-day at 7 o'clock died my father, Ser Piero da Vinci, my poor father! But the displacement of the perseveration to the most indifferent determination of the obituary to dying-hour robs the notice of all pathos and lets us recognize that there was something here to conceal and to suppress.

Ser Piero da Vinci, notary and descendant of notaries, was a man of great energy who attained respect and affluence. He was married four times, the two first wives died childless, and not till the third marriage has he gotten the first legitimate son, in 1476, when Leonardo was 24 years old, and had long ago changed his father's home for the studio of his master Verrocchio. With the fourth and last wife whom he married when he was already in the fifties he begot nine sons and two daughters.[267]

---

[265] I shall overlook a greater error committed by Leonardo in his notice in that he gives his 77-year-old father 80 years.

[266] "He who usurps on earth my place, my place, my place, which is void in the presence of the Son of God, has made out of my cemetery a sewer." Canto XXXVII.

[267] It seems that in that passage of the diary Leonardo also erred in the number of his sisters and brothers, which stands in remarkable contrast to the apparent exactness of the same.

To be sure the father also assumed importance in Leonardo's psychosexual development, and what is more, it was not only in a negative sense, through his absence during the boy's first childhood years, but also directly through his presence in his later childhood. He who as a child desires his mother, cannot help wishing to put himself in his father's place, to identify himself with him in his phantasy and later make it his life's task to triumph over him. As Leonardo was not yet five years old when he was received into his paternal home, the young step-mother, Albiera, certainly must have taken the place of his mother in his feeling, and this brought him into that relation of rivalry to his father which may be designated as normal. As is known, the preference for homosexuality did not manifest itself till near the years of puberty. When Leonardo accepted this preference the identification with the father lost all significance for his sexual life, but continued in other spheres of non-erotic activity. We hear that he was fond of luxury and pretty raiments, and kept servants and horses, although according to Vasari's words "he hardly possessed anything and worked little." We shall not hold his artistic taste entirely responsible for all these special likings; we recognize in them also the compulsion to copy his father and to excel him. He played the part of the great gentleman to the poor peasant girl, hence the son retained the incentive that he also play the great gentleman, he had the strong feeling "to out-herod Herod," and to show his father exactly how the real high rank looks.

Whoever works as an artist certainly feels as a father to his works. The identification with his father had a fateful result in Leonardo's works of art. He created them and then troubled himself no longer about them, just as his father did not trouble himself about him. The later worriments of his father could change nothing in this compulsion, as the latter originated from the impressions of the first years of childhood, and the repression having remained unconscious was incorrigible through later experiences.

At the time of the Renaissance, and even much later, every artist was in need of a gentleman of rank to act as his benefactor. This patron was wont to give the artist commissions for work and entirely controlled his destiny. Leonardo found his patron in Lodovico Sforza, nicknamed Il Moro, a man of high aspirations, ostentations, diplomatically astute, but of an unstable and unreliable character. In his court in Milan, Leonardo spent the best period of his life, while in his service he evinced his most uninhibited productive activity as is evidenced in The Last Supper, and in the equestrian statue of Francesco Sforza. He left Milan before the catastrophe struck Lodovico Moro, who died a prisoner in a French prison. When the news of his benefactor's fate reached Leonardo he made the following entry in his diary: "The duke has lost state, wealth, and liberty, not one of his works will be finished by himself."[268] It is remarkable and surely not without significance that he here raises the same reproach to his benefactor that posterity was to apply to him, as if he wanted to lay the responsibility to a person who substituted his father-series, for the fact that he himself left his works unfinished. As a matter of fact he was not wrong in what he said about the Duke.

However, if the imitation of his father hurt him as an artist, his resistance against the father was the infantile determinant of his perhaps equally vast accomplishment as an artist. According to Merejkowski's beautiful comparison he was like a man who awoke too early in the darkness, while the others were all still asleep. He dared utter this bold principle which contains the justification for all independent investigation: *"Chi dispute allegando l'autorità non adopra l'ingegno ma piuttosto la memoria"* (Whoever refers to authorities in disputing ideas, works with his memory rather than with his reason).[269] Thus he became the first modern natural philosopher, and his courage was rewarded by an abundance of cognitions and suggestions; since the Greek period he was the first to investigate the secrets of nature, relying entirely on his observation and his own judgment. But when he learned to depreciate authority and to reject the imitation of the "ancients" and constantly pointed to the study of nature as the source of all wisdom, he only repeated in the highest sublimation attainable to man, which had already obtruded itself on the little boy who surveyed the world with wonder. To retranslate the scientific abstractions into concrete individual experiences, we would say that the "ancients" and authority only corresponded to the father, and nature again became the tender mother who nourished him. While in most human beings to-day, as in primitive times, the need for a support of some authority is so imperative that their world becomes shaky when their authority is menaced, Leonardo alone was able to exist without such support; but that would not have been possible had he not been deprived of his father in the first years of his life. The boldness and independence of his later scientific investigation presupposes that his infantile sexual investigation was not inhibited by his father, and this same spirit of scientific independence was continued by his withdrawing from sex.

If any one like Leonardo escapes in his childhood his father's intimidation and later throws off the shackles of authority in his scientific investigation, it would be in gross contradiction to our expectation if we found that this same man remained a believer and unable to withdraw from dogmatic religion. Psychoanalysis has taught us the intimate connection between the father complex and belief in God, and daily demonstrates to us how youthful persons lose their religious belief as soon as the authority of the father breaks down. In the parental complex we thus recognize the roots of religious need;

[268] v. Seidlitz, l. c., II, p. 270.
[269] Solmi, Conf. fior, p. 13.

the almighty, just God, and kindly nature appear to us as grand sublimations of father and mother, or rather as revivals and restorations of the infantile conceptions of both parents. Religiousness is biologically traced to the long period of helplessness and need of help of the little child. When the child grows up and realizes his loneliness and weakness in the presence of the great forces of life, he perceives his condition as in childhood and seeks to disavow his despair through a regressive revival of the protecting forces of childhood.

It does not seem that Leonardo's life disproves this conception of religious belief. Accusations charging him with irreligiousness, which in those times was equivalent to renouncing Christianity, were brought against him already in his lifetime, and were clearly described in the first biography given by Vasari.[270] In the second edition of his Vite (1568) Vasari left out this observation. In view of the extraordinary sensitiveness of his age in matters of religion it is perfectly comprehensible to us why Leonardo refrained from directly expressing his position to Christianity in his notes. As investigator he did not permit himself to be misled by the account of the creation of the holy scriptures; for instance, he disputed the possibility of a universal flood, and in geology he was as unscrupulous in calculating with hundred thousands of years as modern investigators.

Among his "prophecies" one finds some things that would perforce offend the sensitive feelings of a religious Christian, e.g. Praying to the images of Saints, reads as follows:[271]

"People talk to people who perceive nothing, who have open eyes and see nothing; they shall talk to them and receive no answer; they shall adore those who have ears and hear nothing; they shall burn lamps for those who do not see."

Or: Concerning mourning on Good Friday (p. 297):

"In all parts of Europe great peoples will bewail the death of one man who died in the Orient."

It was asserted of Leonardo's art that he took away the last remnant of religious attachment from the holy figures and put them into human form in order to depict in them great and beautiful human feelings. Muther praises him for having overcome the feeling of decadence, and for having returned to man the right of sensuality and pleasurable enjoyment. The notices which show Leonardo absorbed in fathoming the great riddles of nature do not lack any expressions of admiration for the creator, the last cause of all these wonderful secrets, but nothing indicates that he wished to hold any personal relation to this divine force. The sentences which contain the deep wisdom of his last years breathe the resignation of the man who subjects himself to the

---

[270] Müntz, l. c., La Religion de Leonardo, p. 292, etc.
[271] Herzfeld, p. 292.

laws of nature and expects no alleviation from the kindness or grace of God. There is hardly any doubt that Leonardo had vanquished dogmatic as well as personal religion, and through his work of investigation he had withdrawn far from the world aspect of the religious Christian.

From our views mentioned before in the development of the infantile psychic life, it becomes clear that also Leonardo's first investigations in childhood occupied themselves with the problems of sexuality. But he himself betrays it to us through a transparent veil, in that he connects his impulse to investigate with the vulture phantasy, and in emphasizing the problem of the flight of the bird as one whose elaboration devolved upon him through special concatenations of fate. A very obscure as well as a prophetically sounding passage in his notes dealing with the flight of the bird demonstrates in the nicest way with how much affective interest he clung to the wish that he himself should be able to imitate, the art of flying: "The human bird shall take his first flight, filling the world with amazement, all writings with his fame, and bringing eternal glory to the nest whence he sprang." He probably hoped that he himself would sometimes be able to fly, and we know from the wish fulfilling dreams of people what bliss one expects from the fulfillment of this hope.

But why do so many people dream that they are able to fly? Psychoanalysis answers this question by stating that to fly or to be a bird in the dream is only a concealment of another wish, to the recognition of which one can reach by more than one linguistic or objective bridge. When the inquisitive child is told that a big bird like the stork brings the little children, when the ancients have formed the phallus winged, when the popular designation of the sexual activity of man is expressed in German by the word "to bird" (vögeln), when the male member is directly called l'uccello (bird) by the Italians, all these facts are only small fragments from a large collection which teaches us that the wish to be able to fly signifies in the dream nothing more or less than the longing for the ability of sexual accomplishment. This is an early infantile wish. When the grown-up recalls his childhood it appears to him as a happy time in which one is happy for the moment and looks to the future without any wishes, it is for this reason that he envies children. But if children themselves could inform us about it they would probably give different reports. It seems that childhood is not that blissful Idyl into which we later distort it, that on the contrary children are lashed through the years of childhood by the wish to become big, and to imitate the grown ups. This wish instigates all their playing. If in the course of their sexual investigation children feel that the grown up knows something wonderful in the mysterious and yet so important realm, what they are prohibited from knowing or doing, they are seized with a violent wish to know it, and dream of it in the form of flying, or prepare this disguise of the wish for their later flying dreams. Thus aviation, which has attained its aim in our times, has also its infantile erotic roots.

By admitting that he entertained a special personal relation to the problem of flying since his childhood, Leonardo bears out what we must assume from our investigation of children of our times, namely, that his childhood investigation was directed to sexual matters. At least this one problem escaped the repression which has later estranged him from sexuality. From childhood until the age of perfect intellectual maturity this subject, slightly varied, continued to hold his interest, and it is quite possible that he was as little successful in his cherished art in the primary sexual sense as in his desires for mechanical matters, that both wishes were denied to him.

As a matter of fact the great Leonardo remained infantile in some ways throughout his whole life; it is said that all great men retain something of the infantile. As a grown up he still continued playing, which sometimes made him appear strange and incomprehensible to his contemporaries. When he constructed the most artistic mechanical toys for court festivities and receptions we are dissatisfied thereby because we dislike to see the master waste his power on such petty stuff. He himself did not seem averse to giving his time to such things. Vasari reports that he did similar things even when not urged to it by request: "There (in Rome) he made a doughy mass out of wax, and when it softened he formed thereof very delicate animals filled with air; when he blew into them they flew in the air, and when the air was exhausted they fell to the ground. For a peculiar lizard caught by the wine-grower of Belvedere Leonardo made wings from skin pulled off from other lizards, which he filled with mercury so that they moved and trembled when it walked; he then made for it eyes, a beard and horns, tamed it and put it in a little box and terrified all his friends with it."[272] Such playing often served him as an expression of serious thoughts: "He had often cleaned the intestines of a sheep so well that one could hold them in the hollow of the hand; he brought them into a big room, and attached them to a blacksmith's bellows which he kept in an adjacent room, he then blew them up until they filled up the whole room so that everybody had to crowd into a corner. In this manner he showed how they gradually became transparent and filled up with air, and as they were at first limited to very little space and gradually became more and more extended in the big room, he compared them to a genius."[273] His fables and riddles evince the same playful pleasure in harmless concealment and artistic investment, the riddles were put into the form of prophecies; almost all are rich in ideas and to a remarkable degree devoid of wit.

---

[272] Vasari, translated by Schorn, 1843.
[273] Ebenda, p. 39.

The plays and jumps which Leonardo allowed his phantasy have in some cases quite misled his biographers who misunderstood this part of his nature. In Leonardo's Milanese manuscripts one finds, for example, outlines of letters to the "Diodario of Sorio (Syria), viceroy of the holy Sultan of Babylon," in which Leonardo presents himself as an engineer sent to these regions of the Orient in order to construct some works. In these letters he defends himself against the reproach of laziness, he furnishes geographical descriptions of cities and mountains, and finally discusses a big elementary event which occurred while he was there.[274]

In 1881, J. P. Richter had endeavored to prove from these documents that Leonardo made these traveler's observations when he really was in the service of the Sultan of Egypt, and that while in the Orient he embraced the Mohammedan religion. This sojourn in the Orient should have taken place in the time of 1483, that is, before he removed to the court of the Duke of Milan. However, it was not difficult for other authors to recognize the illustrations of this supposed journey to the Orient as what they really were, namely, phantastic productions of the youthful artist which he created for his own amusement, and in which he probably brought to expression his wishes to see the world and experience adventures.

A phantastic formation is probably also the "Academia Vinciana," the acceptance of which is due to the existence of five or six most clever and intricate emblems with the inscription of the Academy. Vasari mentions these drawings but not the Academy.[275] Müntz who placed such ornament on the cover of his big work on Leonardo belongs to the few who believe in the reality of an "Academia Vinciana."

It is probable that this impulse to play disappeared in Leonardo's maturer years, that it became discharged in the investigating activity which signified the highest development of his personality. But the fact that it continued so long may teach us how slowly one tears himself away from his infantilism after having enjoyed in his childhood supreme erotic happiness which is later unattainable.

VI

It would be futile to delude ourselves that at present, readers find every pathography unsavory. This attitude is excused with the reproach that from

---

[274] Concerning these letters and the combinations connected with them see Müntz, l. c., p. 82; for the wording of the same and for the notices connected with them see Herzfeld, l. c., p. 223.

[275] Besides, he lost some time in that he even made a drawing of a braided cord in which one could follow the thread from one end to the other, until it formed a perfectly circular figure; a very difficult and beautiful drawing of this kind is engraved on copper, in the center of it one can read the words: "Leonardus Vinci Academia" (p. 8).

a pathographic elaboration of a great man one never obtains an understanding of his importance and his attainments, that it is therefore useless mischief to study in him things which could just as well be found in the first comer. However, this criticism is so clearly unjust that it can only be grasped when viewed as a pretext and a disguise for something. As a matter of fact pathography does not aim at making comprehensible the attainments of the great man; no one should really be blamed for not doing something which one never promised. The real motives for the opposition are quite different. One finds them when one bears in mind that biographers are fixed on their heroes in quite a peculiar manner. Frequently they take the hero as the object of study because, for reasons of their personal emotional life, they bear him a special affection from the very outset. They then devote themselves to a work of idealization which strives to enroll the great men among their infantile models, and to revive through him, as it were, the infantile conception of the father. For the sake of this wish they wipe out the individual features in his physiognomy, they rub out the traces of his life's struggle with inner and outer resistances, and do not tolerate in him anything of human weakness or imperfection; they then give us a cold, strange, ideal form instead of the man to whom we could feel distantly related. It is to be regretted that they do this, for they thereby sacrifice the truth to an illusion, and for the sake of their infantile phantasies they let slip the opportunity to penetrate into the most attractive secrets of human nature.[276]

Leonardo himself, judging from his love for the truth and his inquisitiveness, would have interposed no objections to the effort of discovering the determinations of his psychic and intellectual development from the trivial peculiarities and riddles of his nature. We respect him by learning from him. It does no injury to his greatness to study the sacrifices which his development from the child must have entailed, and to the compile factors which have stamped on his person the tragic feature of failure.

Let us expressly emphasize that we have never considered Leonardo as a neurotic or as a "nervous person" in the sense of this awkward term. Whoever takes it amiss that we should even dare apply to him viewpoints gained from pathology, still clings to prejudices which we have at present justly given up. We no longer believe that health and disease, normal and nervous, are sharply distinguished from each other, and that neurotic traits must be judged as proof of general inferiority. We know to-day that neurotic symptoms are substitutive formations for certain repressive acts which have to be brought about in the course of our development from the child to the cultural man, that we all produce such substitutive formations, and that only the amount, intensity, and distribution of these substitutive formations

---

[276] This criticism holds quite generally and is not aimed at Leonardo's biographers in particular.

justify the practical conception of illness and the conclusion of constitutional inferiority. Following the slight signs in Leonardo's personality we would place him near that neurotic type which we designate as the "compulsive type," and we would compare his investigation with the "reasoning mania" of neurotics, and his inhibitions with the so-called "abulias" of the latter.

The object of our work was to explain the inhibitions in Leonardo's sexual life and in his artistic activity. For this purpose we shall now sum up what we could discover concerning the course of his psychic development.

We were unable to gain any knowledge about his hereditary factors, on the other hand we recognize that the accidental circumstances of his childhood produced a far reaching disturbing effect. His illegitimate birth deprived him of the influence of a father until perhaps his fifth year, and left him to the tender seduction of a mother whose only consolation he was. Having been kissed by her into sexual prematurity, he surely must have entered into a phase of infantile sexual activity of which only one single manifestation was definitely evinced, namely, the intensity of his infantile sexual investigation. The impulse for looking and inquisitiveness were most strongly stimulated by his impressions from early childhood; the enormous mouth-zone received its accentuation which it had never given up. From his later contrasting behavior, as the exaggerated sympathy for animals, we can conclude that this infantile period did not lack in strong sadistic traits.

An energetic shift of repression put an end to this infantile excess, and established the dispositions which became manifest in the years of puberty. The most striking result of this transformation was a turning away from all gross sensual activities. Leonardo was able to lead a life of abstinence and made the impression of an asexual person. When the floods of pubescent excitement came over the boy they did not make him ill by forcing him to costly and harmful substitutive formations; owing to the early preference for sexual inquisitiveness, the greater part of the sexual needs could be sublimated into a general thirst after knowledge and so elude repression. A much smaller portion of the libido was applied to sexual aims, and represented the stunted sexual life of the grown up. In consequence of the repression of the love for the mother this portion assumed a homosexual attitude and manifested itself as ideal love for boys. The fixation on the mother, as well as the happy reminiscences of his relations with her, was preserved in his unconscious but remained for the time in an inactive state. In this manner the repression, fixation, and sublimation participated in the disposal of the contributions which the sexual impulse furnished to Leonardo's psychic life.

From the obscure age of boyhood Leonardo appears to us as an artist, a painter, and sculptor, thanks to a specific talent which was probably enforced by the early awakening of the impulse for looking in the first years of childhood. We would gladly report in what way the artistic activity depends on the psychic primitive forces were it not that our material is inadequate just here. We content ourselves by emphasizing the fact, concerning which hardly any doubt still exists, that the productions of the artist give outlet also to his sexual desire, and in the case of Leonardo we can refer to the information imparted by Vasari, namely, that heads of laughing women and pretty boys, or representations of his sexual objects, attracted attention among his first artistic attempts. It seems that during his flourishing youth Leonardo at first worked in an uninhibited manner. As he took his father as a model for his outer conduct in life, he passed through a period of manly creative power and artistic productivity in Milan, where favored by fate he found a substitute for his father in the duke Lodovico Moro. But the experience of others was soon confirmed in him, to wit, that the almost complete suppression of the real sexual life does not furnish the most favorable conditions for the activity of the sublimated sexual strivings. The figurativeness of his sexual life asserted itself, his activity and ability to quick decisions began to weaken, the tendency to reflection and delay was already noticeable as a disturbance in The Holy Supper, and with the influence of the technique determined the fate of this magnificent work. Slowly a process developed in him which can be put parallel only to the regressions of neurotics. His development at puberty into the artist was outstripped by the early infantile determinant of the investigator, the second sublimation of his erotic impulses turned back to the primitive one which was prepared at the first repression. He became an investigator, first in service of his art, later independently and away from his art. With the loss of his patron, the substitute for his father, and with the increasing difficulties in his life, the regressive displacement extended in dimension. He became *"impacientissimo al pennello"* (most impatient with the brush) as reported by a correspondent of the countess Isabella d'Este who desired to possess at any cost a painting from his hand.[277] His infantile past had obtained control over him. The investigation, however, which now took the place of his artistic production, seems to have born certain traits which betrayed the activity of unconscious impulses; this was seen in his insatiability, his regardless obstinacy, and in his lack of ability to adjust himself to actual conditions.

At the summit of his life, in the age of the first fifties, at a time when the sex characteristics of the woman have already undergone a regressive change, and when the libido in the man not infrequently ventures into an energetic advance, a new transformation came over him. Still deeper strata of his psychic content became active again, but this further regression was of benefit to his art which was in a state of deterioration. He met the woman who awakened in him the memory of the happy and sensuously enraptured

---

[277] Seidlitz II, p. 271.

smile of his mother, and under the influence of this awakening he acquired back the stimulus which guided him in the beginning of his artistic efforts when he formed the smiling woman. He painted Monna Lisa, Saint Anne, and a number of mystic pictures which were characterized by the enigmatic smile. With the help of his oldest erotic feelings he triumphed in conquering once more the inhibition in his art. This last development faded away in the obscurity of the approaching old age. But before this his intellect rose to the highest capacity of a view of life, which was far in advance of his time.

In the preceding chapters I have shown what justification one may have for such representation of Leonardo's course of development, for this manner of arranging his life and explaining his wavering between art and science. If after accomplishing these things I should provoke the criticism from even friends and adepts of psychoanalysis, that I have only written a psychoanalytic romance, I should answer that I certainly did not overestimate the reliability of these results. Like others I succumbed to the attraction emanating from this great and mysterious man, in whose being one seems to feel powerful propelling passions, which after all can only evince themselves so remarkably subdued.

But whatever may be the truth about Leonardo's life we cannot relinquish our effort to investigate it psychoanalytically before we have finished another task. In general we must mark out the limits which are set up for the working capacity of psychoanalysis in biography so that every omitted explanation should not be held up to us as a failure. Psychoanalytic investigation has at its disposal the data of the history of the person's life, which on the one hand consists of accidental events and environmental influences, and on the other hand of the reported reactions of the individual. Based on the knowledge of psychic mechanisms it now seeks to investigate dynamically the character of the individual from his reactions, and to lay bare his earliest psychic motive forces as well as their later transformations and developments. If this succeeds then the reaction of the personality is explained through the coöperation of constitutional and accidental factors or through inner and outer forces. If such an undertaking, as perhaps in the case of Leonardo, does not yield definite results then the blame for it is not to be laid to the faulty or inadequate psychoanalytic method, but to the vague and fragmentary material left by tradition about this person. It is, therefore, only the author who forced psychoanalysis to furnish an expert opinion on such insufficient material, who is to be held responsible for the failure.

However, even if one had at his disposal a very rich historical material and could manage the psychic mechanism with the greatest certainty, a psychoanalytic investigation could not possibly furnish the definite view, if it concerns two important questions, that the individual could turn out only so and not differently. Concerning Leonardo we had to represent the view that the accident of his illegitimate birth and the pampering of his mother exerted the most decisive influence on his character formation and his later fate, through the fact that the sexual repression following this infantile phase caused him to sublimate his libido into a thirst after knowledge, and thus determined his sexual inactivity for his entire later life. The repression, however, which followed the first erotic gratification of childhood did not have to take place, in another individual it would perhaps not have taken place or it would have turned out not nearly as profuse. We must recognize here a degree of freedom which can no longer be solved psychoanalytically. One is as little justified in representing the issue of this shift of repression as the only possible issue. It is quite probable that another person would not have succeeded in withdrawing the main part of his libido from the repression through sublimation into a desire for knowledge; under the same influences as Leonardo another person might have sustained a permanent injury to his intellectual work or an uncontrollable disposition to compulsion neurosis. The two characteristics of Leonardo which remained unexplained through psychoanalytic effort are first, his particular tendency to repress his impulses, and second, his extraordinary ability to sublimate the primitive impulses.

The impulses and their transformations are the last things that psychoanalysis can discern. Henceforth it leaves the place to biological investigation. The tendency to repression, as well as the ability to sublimate, must be traced back to the organic bases of the character, upon which alone the psychic structure springs up. As artistic talent and productive ability are intimately connected with sublimation we have to admit that also the nature of artistic attainment is psychoanalytically inaccessible to us. Biological investigation of our time endeavors to explain the chief traits of the organic constitution of a person through the fusion of male and female predispositions in the material sense; Leonardo's physical beauty as well as his left-handedness furnish here some support. However, we do not wish to leave the ground of pure psychologic investigation. Our aim remains to demonstrate the connection between outer experiences and reactions of the person over the path of the activity of the impulses. Even if psychoanalysis does not explain to us the fact of Leonardo's artistic accomplishment, it still gives us an understanding of the expressions and limitations of the same. It does seem as if only a man with Leonardo's childhood experiences could have painted Monna Lisa and Saint Anne, and could have supplied his works with that sad fate and so obtain unheard of fame as a natural historian; it seems as if the key to all his attainments and failures was hidden in the childhood phantasy of the vulture.

But may one not take offense at the results of an investigation which concede to the accidents of the parental constellation so decisive an influence on the fate of a person, which, for example, subordinates Leonardo's fate to his illegitimate birth and to the sterility of his first step-mother Donna Albiera? I believe that one has no right to feel so; if one considers accident as unworthy of determining our fate, it is only a relapse to the pious aspect of life, the overcoming of which Leonardo himself prepared when he put down in writing that the sun does not move. We are naturally grieved over the fact that a just God and a kindly providence do not guard us better against such influences in our most defenseless age. We thereby gladly forget that as a matter of fact everything in our life is accident from our very origin through the meeting of spermatozoa and ovum, accident, which nevertheless participates in the lawfulness and fatalities of nature, and lacks only the connection to our wishes and illusions. The division of life's determinants into the "fatalities" of our constitution and the "accidents" of our childhood may still be indefinite in individual cases, but taken altogether one can no longer entertain any doubt about the importance of precisely our first years of childhood. We all still show too little respect for nature, which in Leonardo's deep words recalling Hamlet's speech *"is full of infinite reasons which never appeared in experience."*[278] Every one of us human beings corresponds to one of the infinite experiments in which these "reasons of nature" force themselves into experience.

THE END

---

[278] La natura è piena d'infinite ragionè che non furono mai in isperienza, M. Herzfeld, l. c. p. II.

BOOK SIX. PSYCHOPATHOLOGY OF EVERYDAY LIFE

INTRODUCTION

Professor Freud developed his system of psychoanalysis while studying the so-called borderline cases of mental diseases, such as hysteria and compulsion neurosis. By discarding the old methods of treatment and strictly applying himself to a study of the patient's life he discovered that the hitherto puzzling symptoms had a definite meaning, and that there was nothing arbitrary in any morbid manifestation. Psychoanalysis always showed that they referred to some definite problem or conflict of the person concerned. It was while tracing back the abnormal to the normal state that Professor Freud found how faint the line of demarcation was between the normal and neurotic person, and that the psychopathologic mechanisms so glaringly observed in the psychoneuroses and psychoses could usually be demonstrated in a lesser degree in normal persons. This led to a study of the faulty actions of everyday life and later to the publication of the *Psychopathology of Everyday Life*, a book which passed through four editions in Germany and is considered the author's most popular work. With great ingenuity and penetration the author throws much light on the complex problems of human behavior, and clearly demonstrates that the hitherto considered impassable gap between normal and abnormal mental states is more apparent than real.

This translation is made of the fourth German edition, and while the original text was strictly followed, linguistic difficulties often made it necessary to modify or substitute some of the author's cases by examples comprehensible to the English-speaking reader.

I. Forgetting of Proper Names

During the year 1898 I published a short essay *On the Psychic Mechanism of Forgetfulness.*

I shall now repeat its contents and take it as a starting-point for further discussion. I have there undertaken a psychologic analysis of a common case of temporary forgetfulness of proper names, and from a pregnant example of my own observation I have reached the conclusion that this frequent and practically unimportant occurrence of a failure of a psychic function — of memory — admits an explanation which goes beyond the customary utilization of this phenomenon.

If an average psychologist should be asked to explain how it happens that we often fail to recall a name which we are sure we know, he would probably content himself with the answer that proper names are more apt to be forgotten than any other content of memory. He might give plausible reasons for this "forgetting preference" for proper names, but he would not assume any deep determinant for the process.

I was led to examine exhaustively the phenomenon of temporary forgetfulness through the observation of certain peculiarities, which, although not general, can, nevertheless, be seen clearly in some cases. In these there is not only *forgetfulness*, but also false *recollection*: he who strives for the escaped name brings to consciousness others — substitutive names — which, although immediately recognized as false, nevertheless obtrude themselves with great tenacity. The process which should lead to the reproduction of the lost name is, as it were, displaced, and thus brings one to an incorrect substitute.

Now it is my assumption that the displacement is not left to psychic arbitrariness, but that it follows lawful and rational paths. In other words, I assume that the substitutive name (or names) stands in direct relation to the lost name, and I hope, if I succeed in demonstrating this connection, to throw light on the origin of the forgetting of names.

In the example which I selected for analysis in 1898 I vainly strove to recall the name of the master who made the imposing frescoes of the "Last Judgment" in the dome of *Orvieto*. Instead of the lost name — *Signorelli* — two other names of artists — *Botticelli* and *Boltraffio* — obtruded themselves, names which my judgment immediately and definitely rejected as being incorrect. When the correct name was imparted to me by an outsider I recognized it at once without any hesitation. The examination of the influence and association paths which caused the displacement from *Signorelli* to *Botticelli* and *Boltraffio* led to the following results:—

(*a*) The reason for the escape of the name *Signorelli* is neither to be sought in the strangeness in itself of this name nor in the psychologic character of the connection in which it was inserted. The forgotten name was just as familiar to me as one of the substitutive names — *Botticelli* — and somewhat more familiar than the other substitute — *Boltraffio* — of the possessor of which I could hardly say more than that he belonged to the Milanese School. The connection, too, in which the forgetting of the name took place appeared to me harmless, and led to no further explanation. I journeyed by carriage with a stranger from Ragusa, Dalmatia, to a station in Herzegovina. Our conversation drifted to travelling in Italy, and I asked my companion whether he had been in Orvieto and had seen there the famous frescoes of —

(*b*) The forgetting of the name could not be explained until after I had recalled the theme discussed immediately before this conversation. This forgetting then made itself known *as a disturbance of the newly emerging theme caused by the theme preceding it.* In brief, before I asked my travelling companion if he had been in Orvieto we had been discussing the customs of the Turks living in *Bosnia* and *Herzegovina.* I had related what I heard from a colleague who was practising medicine among them, namely, that they show full confidence in the physician and complete submission to fate. When one is compelled to inform them that there is no help for the patient, they answer: "*Sir* (Herr), what can I say? I know that if he could be saved you would save him." In these sentences alone we can find the words and names: *Bosnia, Herzegovina,* and *Herr* (sir), which may be inserted in an association series between *Signorelli, Botticelli,* and *Boltraffio.*

(*c*) I assume that the stream of thoughts concerning the customs of the Turks in Bosnia, etc., was able to disturb the next thought, because I withdrew my attention from it before it came to an end. For I recalled that I wished to relate a second anecdote which was next to the first in my memory. These Turks value the sexual pleasure above all else, and at sexual disturbances merge into an utter despair which strangely contrasts with their resignation at the peril of losing their lives. One of my colleague's patients once told him: "For you know, sir (Herr), if that ceases, life no longer has any charm."

I refrained from imparting this characteristic feature because I did not wish to touch upon such a delicate theme in conversation with a stranger. But I went still further; I also deflected my attention from the continuation of the thought which might have associated itself in me with the theme "Death and Sexuality." I was at that time under the after-effects of a message which I had received a few weeks before, during a brief sojourn in *Trafoi.* A patient on whom I had spent much effort had ended his life on account of an incurable sexual disturbance. I know positively that this sad event, and everything connected with it, did not come to my conscious recollection on that trip in Herzegovina. However, the agreement between *Trafoi* and *Boltraffio* forces me to assume that this reminiscence was at that time brought to activity despite all the intentional deviation of my attention.

(*d*) I can no longer conceive the forgetting of the name Signorelli as an accidental occurrence. I must recognize in this process the influence of a *motive.* There were motives which actuated the interruption in the communication of my thoughts (concerning the customs of the Turks, etc.), and which later influenced me to exclude from my consciousness the thought connected with them, and which might have led to the message concerning the incident in Trafoi — that is, I wanted to forget something, I *repressed* something. To be sure, I wished to forget something other than the name of the master of Orvieto; but this other thought brought about an associative connection between itself and this name, so that my act of volition missed the aim, and I *forgot the one against my will*, while I *intentionally* wished to forget the other. The disinclination to recall directed itself against the one content; the inability to remember appeared in another. The case would have been obviously simpler if this disinclination and the inability to remember had concerned the same content. The substitutive names no longer seem so thoroughly justified as they were before this explanation. They remind me (after the form of a compromise) as much of what I wished to forget as of what I wished to remember, and show me that my object to forget something was neither a perfect success nor a failure.

(*e*) The nature of the association formed between the lost name and the repressed theme (death and sexuality, etc.), containing the names of Bosnia, Herzegovina, and Trafoi, is also very strange. In the scheme inserted here, which originally appeared in 1898, an attempt is made to graphically represent these associations.

The name Signorelli was thus divided into two parts. One pair of syllables (*elli*) returned unchanged in one of the substitutions, while the other had gained, through the translation of *signor* (sir, Herr), many and diverse relations to the name contained in the repressed theme, but was lost through it in the reproduction. Its substitution was formed in a way to suggest that a displacement took place along the same associations — "Herzegovina and Bosnia" — regardless of the sense and acoustic demarcation. The names were therefore treated in this process like the written pictures of a sentence which is to be transformed into a picture-puzzle (rebus). No information was given to consciousness concerning the whole process, which, instead of the name Signorelli, was thus changed to the substitutive names. At first sight no relation is apparent between the theme that contained the name Signorelli and the repressed one which immediately preceded it.

Perhaps it is not superfluous to remark that the given explanation does not contradict the conditions of memory reproduction and forgetting assumed by other psychologists, which they seek in certain relations and dispositions. Only in certain cases have we added another *motive* to the factors long recognized as causative in forgetting names, and have thus laid bare the mechanism of faulty memory. The assumed dispositions are indispensable also in our case, in order to make it possible for the repressed element to associatively gain control over the desired name and take it along into the repression. Perhaps this would not have occurred in another name having more favourable conditions of reproduction. For it is quite probable that a suppressed element continually strives to assert itself in some other way, but attains this success only where it meets with suitable conditions. At other times the suppression succeeds without disturbance of function, or, as we may justly say, without symptoms.

When we recapitulate the conditions for forgetting a name with faulty recollection we find:

(1) a certain disposition to forget the same; (2) a process of suppression which has taken place shortly before; and (3) the possibility of establishing an *outer* association between the concerned name and the element previously suppressed. The last condition will probably not have to be much overrated, for the slightest claim on the association is apt in most cases to bring it about. But it is a different and farther-reaching question whether such outer association can really furnish the proper condition to enable the suppressed element to disturb the reproduction of the desired name, or whether after all a more intimate connection between the two themes is not necessarily required. On superficial consideration one may be willing to reject the latter requirement and consider the temporal meeting in perfectly dissimilar contents as sufficient. But on more thorough examination one finds more and more frequently that the two elements (the repressed and the new one) connected by an outer association, possess besides a connection in content, and this can also be demonstrated in the example *Signorelli*.

The value of the understanding gained through the analysis of the example *Signorelli* naturally depends on whether we must explain this case as a typical or as an isolated process. I must now maintain that the forgetting of a name associated with faulty recollection uncommonly often follows the same process as was demonstrated in the case of *Signorelli*. Almost every time that I observed this phenomenon in myself I was able to explain it in the manner indicated above as being motivated by repression.

I must mention still another view-point in favour of the typical nature of our analysis. I believe that one is not justified in separating the cases of name-forgetting with faulty recollection from those in which incorrect substitutive names have not obtruded themselves. These substitutive names occur spontaneously in a number of cases; in other cases, where they do not come spontaneously, they can be brought to the surface by concentration of attention, and they then show the same relation to the repressed element and the lost name as those that come spontaneously. Two factors seem to play a part in bringing to consciousness the substitutive names: first, the effort of attention, and second, and inner determinant which adheres to the psychic material. I could find the latter in the greater or lesser facility which forms the required outer associations between the two elements. A great many of the cases of name-forgetting without faulty recollection therefore belong to the cases with substitutive name formation, the mechanism of which corresponds to the one in the example *Signorelli*. But I surely shall not venture to assert that all cases of name-forgetting belong to the same group.

There is no doubt that there are cases of name-forgetting that proceed in a much simpler way. We shall represent this state of affairs carefully enough if we assert that *besides the simple forgetting of proper names there is another forgetting which is motivated by repression.*

II. Forgetting of Foreign Words

The ordinary vocabulary of our own language seems to be protected against forgetting within the limits of normal function, but it is quite different with words from a foreign language. The tendency to forget such words extends to all parts of speech. In fact, depending on our own general state and the degree of fatigue, the first manifestation of functional disturbance evinces itself in the irregularity of our control over foreign vocabulary. In a series of cases this forgetting follows the same mechanism as the one revealed in the example *Signorelli.* As a demonstration of this I shall report a single analysis, characterized, however, by valuable features, concerning the forgetting of a word, not a noun, from a Latin quotation. Before proceeding, allow me to give a full and clear account of this little episode.

Last summer, while journeying on my vacation, I renewed the acquaintance of a young man of academic education, who, as I soon noticed, was conversant with some of my works. In our conversation we drifted — I no longer remember how — to the social position of the race to which we both belonged. He, being ambitious, bemoaned the fact that his generation, as he expressed it, was destined to grow crippled, that it was prevented from developing its talents and from gratifying its desires. He concluded his passionately felt speech with the familiar verse from Virgil: *Exoriare. . .* in which the unhappy *Dido* leaves her vengeance upon *Æneas* to posterity. Instead of "concluded," I should have said "wished to conclude," for he could not bring the quotation to an end, and attempted to conceal the open gap in his memory by transposing the words: —

"Exoriar(e) ex nostris ossibus ultor!"

He finally became piqued and said: "Please don't make such a mocking face, as if you were gloating over my embarrassment, but help me. There is something missing in this verse. How does it read in its complete form?"

"With pleasure," I answered, and cited it correctly: —

"Exoriar(e) aliquis nostris ex ossibus ultor!"

"It is too stupid to forget such a word," he said. "By the way, I understand you claim that forgetting is not without its reasons; I should be very curious to find out how I came to forget this indefinite pronoun '*aliquis.*'"

I gladly accepted the challenge, as I hoped to get an addition to my collection, and said, "We can easily do this, but I must ask you to tell me frankly and without any criticism everything that occurs to your mind after you focus your attention, without any particular intention, on the forgotten word."[279]

"Very well, the ridiculous idea comes to me to divide the word in the following way: *a* and *liquis*."

"What does that mean?"

"I don't know."

"What else does that recall to you?"

"The thought goes on to *reliques* — *liquidation* —*liquidity* — *fluid*."

"Does that mean anything to you now?"

"No, not by a long shot."

"Just go ahead."

"I now think," he said, laughing sarcastically, "of Simon of Trent, whose relics I saw two years ago in a church in Trent. I think of the old accusation which has been brought against the Jews again, and of the work of *Kleinpaul*, who sees in these supposed sacrifices reincarnations or revivals, so to speak, of the Saviour."

"This stream of thoughts has some connection with the theme which we discussed before the Latin word escaped you."

"You are right. I now think of an article in an Italian journal which I have recently read. I believe it was entitled: 'What St. Augustine said Concerning Women.' What can you do with this?"

I waited.

"Now I think of something which surely has no connection with the theme."

"Oh, please abstain from all criticism, and — "

"Oh, I know! I recall a handsome old gentleman whom I met on my journey last week. He was really an *original* type. He looked like a big bird of prey. His name, if you care to know, is Benedict."

"Well, at least you give a grouping of saints and Church fathers: *St. Simon, St. Augustine,* and *St. Benedict.* I believe that there was a Church father named *Origines*. Three of these, moreover, are Christian names, like *Paul* in the name *Kleinpaul*."

"Now I think of *St. Januarius* and his blood miracle — I find that the thoughts are running mechanically."

"Just stop a moment; both *St. Januarius* and *St. Augustine* *have* something to do with the calendar. Will you recall to me the blood miracle?"

---

[279] This is the usual way of bringing to consciousness hidden ideas. Cf. *The Interpretation of Dreams*, pp. 83-4, translated by A. A. Brill, The Macmillan Company, New York, and Allen, London.

"Don't you know about it? The blood of St. Januarius is preserved in a phial in a church in Naples, and on a certain holiday a miracle takes place causing it to liquefy. The people think a great deal of this miracle, and become very excited if the liquefying process is retarded, as happened once during the French occupation. The General in command — or Garibaldi, if I am not mistaken — then took the priest aside, and with a very significant gesture pointed out to him the soldiers arrayed without, and expressed his hope that the miracle would soon take place. And it actually took place. . ."

"Well, what else comes to your mind? Why do you hesitate?"

"Something really occurred to me . . . but it is too intimate a matter to impart . . . besides, I see no connection and no necessity for telling it."

"I will take care of the connection. Of course I cannot compel you to reveal what is disagreeable to you, but then you should not have demanded that I tell you why you forgot the word 'aliquis.'"

"Really? Do you think so? Well, I suddenly thought of a woman from whom I could easily get a message that would be very annoying to us both."

"That she missed her courses?"

"How could you guess such a thing?"

"That was not very difficult. You prepared me for it long enough. Just think of the *saints of the calendar, the liquefying of the blood on a certain day, the excitement if the event does not take place, and the distinct threat that the miracle must take place.* . . . Indeed, you have elaborated the miracle of St. Januarius into a clever allusion to the courses of the woman."

"It was surely without my knowledge. And do you really believe that my inability to reproduce the word 'aliquis' was due to this anxious expectation?"

"That appears to me absolutely certain. Don't you recall dividing it into *a-liquis* and the associations: *reliques, liquidation, fluid*? Shall I also add to this connection the fact that St. Simon, to whom you got by way of the *reliques*, was sacrificed as a child?"

"Please stop. I hope you do not take these thoughts — if I really entertained them — seriously. I will, however, confess to you that the lady is Italian, and that I visited Naples in her company. But may not all this be coincidental?"

"I must leave to your own judgment whether you can explain all these connections through the assumption of coincidence. I will tell you, however, that every similar case that you analyze will lead you to just such remarkable 'coincidences!'"

I have more than one reason for valuing this little analysis, for which I am indebted to my traveling companion. First, because in this case I was able to make use of a source which is otherwise inaccessible to me. Most of the examples of psychic disturbances of daily life that I have here compiled I was obliged to take from observation of myself. I endeavoured to evade the far richer material furnished me by my neurotic patients, because I had to preclude the objection that the phenomena in question were only the result and manifestation of the neurosis. It was therefore of special value for my purpose to have a stranger free from a neurosis offer himself as a subject for such examination. This analysis is also important in other respects, inasmuch as it elucidates a case of word-forgetting *without* substitutive recollection, and thus confirms the principle formulated above, namely, that the appearance or nonappearance of incorrect substitutive recollections does not constitute an essential distinction.[280]

But the principal value of the example *aliquis* lies in another of its distinctions from the case *Signorelli*. In the latter example the reproduction of the name becomes disturbed through the after-effects of a stream of thought which began shortly before and was interrupted, but whose content had no distinct relation to the new theme which contained the name Signorelli. Between the repression and the theme of the forgotten name there existed only the relation of temporal contiguity, which reached the other in order that the two should be able to form a connection through an outer association.[281] On the other hand, in the example *aliquis* one can note no trace of such an independent repressed theme which could occupy conscious thought immediately before and then re-echo as a disturbance. The disturbance of the reproduction proceeded here from the inner part of the

---

[280] Finer observation reduces somewhat the contrast between the analyses of *Signorelli* and *aliquis* as far as the substitutive recollections are concerned. Here, too, the forgetting seems to be accompanied by substitutive formations. When I later asked my companion whether in his effort to recall the forgotten word he did not think of some substitution, he informed me that he was at first tempted to put an *ab* into the verse: *nostris ab ossibus* (perhaps the disjointed part of *a-liquis*) and that later the word *exoriare obtruded* itself with particular distinctness and persistency. Being sceptical, he added that it was apparently due to the fact that it was the first word of the verse. But when I asked him to focus his attention on the associations to *exoriare* he gave me the word *exorcism*. *This* makes me think that the reinforcement of *exoriare* in the reproduction has really the value of such substitution. It probably came through the association *exorcism* from the names of the saints. However, those are refinements upon which no value need be laid. It seems now quite possible that the appearance of any kind of substitutive recollection is a constant sign — perhaps only characteristic and misleading — of the purposive forgetting motivated by repression. This substitution might also existing the reinforcement of an element akin to the thing forgotten, even where incorrect substitutive names fail to appear. Thus, in the example Signorelli, as long as the name of the painter remained inaccessible to me, I had more than a clear visual memory of the cycle of his frescoes, and of the picture of himself in the corner; at least it was more intensive than any of my other visual memory traces. In another case, also reported in my essay of 1898, I had hopelessly forgotten the street name and address connected with a disagreeable visit in a strange city, but — as if to mock me —the house number appeared especially vivid, whereas the memory of numbers usually causes me the greatest difficulty.

[281] I am not fully convinced of the lack of an inner connection between the two streams of thought in the case of *Signorelli*. In carefully following the repressed thought concerning the theme of death and sexual life, one does strike an idea which shows a near relation to the theme of the frescoes of *Orvieto*.

theme touched upon, and was brought about by the fact that unconsciously a contradiction arose against the wish-idea represented in the quotation.

The origin must be construed in the following manner: The speaker deplored the fact that the present generation of his people was being deprived of its rights, and like Dido he presaged that a new generation would take upon itself vengeance against the oppressors. He therefore expressed the wish for posterity. In this moment he was interrupted by the contradictory thought: "Do you really wish so much for posterity? That is not true. Just think in what a predicament you would be if you should now receive the information that you must expect posterity from the quarter you have in mind! No, you want no posterity — as much as you need it for your vengeance." This contradiction asserts itself, just as in the example *Signorelli*, by forming an outer association between one of his ideation elements and an element of the repressed wish, but here it is brought about in a most strained manner through what seems an artificial detour of associations. Another important agreement with the example *Signorelli* results from the fact that the contradiction originates from repressed sources and emanates from thoughts which would cause a deviation of attention.

So much for the diversity and the inner relationship of both paradigms of the forgetting of names. We have learned to know a second mechanism of forgetting, namely, the disturbance of thought through an inner contradiction emanating from the repression. In the course of this discussion we shall repeatedly meet with this process, which seems to me to be the more easily understood.

III. Forgetting of Names and Order of Words

Experiences like those mentioned concerning the process of forgetting apart of the order of words from a foreign language may cause one to wonder whether the forgetting of the order of words in one's own language requires an essentially different explanation. To be sure, one is not wont to be surprised if after awhile a formula or poem learned by heart can only be reproduced imperfectly, with variations and gaps. Still, as this forgetting does not affect equally all the things learned together, but seems to pick out therefrom definite parts, it may be worth our effort to investigate analytically some examples of such faulty reproductions.

Brill reports the following example: —

"While conversing one day with a very brilliant young woman she had occasion to quote from Keats. The poem was entitled 'Ode to Apollo,' and she recited the following lines: —

"'In thy western house of gold

Where thou livest in thy state,

Bards, that once sublimely told

Prosaic truths that came too late.'

She hesitated many times during the recitation, being sure that there was something wrong with the last line. To her great surprise, on referring to the book she found that not only was the last line misquoted but that there were many other mistakes. The correct lines read as follows:—

ODE TO APOLLO

"'In thy western *halls* of gold

When thou *sittest* in thy state,

Bards, that *erst* sublimely told

Heroic deeds and sang of fate.'

The words italicized are those that have been forgotten and replaced by others during the recitation.

"She was astonished at her many mistakes, and attributed them to a failure of memory. I could readily convince her, however, that there was no qualitative or quantitative disturbance of memory in her case, and recalled to her our conversation immediately before quoting these lines.

"We were discussing the over-estimation of personality among lovers, and she thought it was Victor Hugo who said that love is the greatest thing in the world because it makes an angel or a god out of a grocery clerk. She continued: "Only when we are in love have we blind faith in humanity; everything is perfect, everything is beautiful, and . . . everything is so poetically unreal. Still, it is a wonderful experience; worth going through, notwithstanding the terrible disappointments that usually follow. It puts us on a level with the gods and incites us to all sorts of artistic activities. We become real poets; we not only memorize and quote poetry, but we often become Apollos ourselves.' She then quoted the lines given above.

"When I asked on what occasion she memorized the lines she could not recall. As a teacher of elocution she was wont to memorize so much and so often that it was difficult to tell just when she had memorized these lines. 'Judging by the conversation,' I suggested, 'it would seem that this poem is intimately associated with the idea of over-estimation of personality of one in love. Have you perhaps memorized this poem when you were in such a state?' She became thoughtful for a while and soon recalled the following facts: Twelve years before, when she was eighteen years old, she fell in love. She met the young man while participating in an amateur theatrical performance. He was at the time studying for the stage, and it was predicated that someday he would be a matinée idol. He was endowed with all the attributes needed for such a calling. He was well built, fascinating, impulsive, very clever, and .

. . very fickle-minded. She was warned against him, but she paid no heed, attributing it all to the envy of her counsellors. Everything went well for a few months, when she suddenly received word that her Apollo, for whom she had memorized these lines, had eloped with and married a very wealthy young woman. A new years later she heard that he was living in a Western city, where he was taking care of his father-in-law's interests.

"The misquoted lines are now quite plain. The discussion about the over-estimation of personality among lovers unconsciously recalled to her a disagreeable experience, when she herself over-estimated the personality of the man she loved. She thought he was a god, but he turned out to be even worse than the average mortal. The episode could not come to the surface because it was determined by very disagreeable and painful thoughts, but the unconscious variations in the poem plainly showed her present mental state. The poetic expressions were not only changed to prosaic ones, but they clearly alluded to the whole episode."

Another example of forgetting the order of words of a poem well known to the person I shall cite from Dr. C. G. Jung,[282] quoting the words of the author: —

"A man wished to recite the familiar poem, 'A Pine-tree Standalone,' etc. In the line 'He felt drowsy' he became hopelessly stuck at the words 'with the white sheet.' This forgetting of such a well-known verse seemed to me rather peculiar, and I therefore asked him to reproduce what came to his mind when he thought of the words 'with the white sheet. 'He gave the following series of associations 'The white sheet makes one think of a white sheet on a corpse — a linen sheet with which one covers dead body — [pause] — now I think of a near friend — his brother died quite recently — he is supposed to have died of heart disease — he was also very corpulent — my friend is corpulent, too, and I thought that he might meet the same fate — probably he doesn't exercise enough — when heard of this death I suddenly became frightened: the same thing might happen to me, as my own family is predisposed to obesity — my grandfather died of heart disease — I, also, am somewhat too corpulent, and for that reason I began an obesity cure a few days ago.'"

Jung remarks: "The man had unconsciously immediately identified himself with the pine-tree which was covered with a white sheet."

For the following example of forgetting the order of words I am indebted to my friend Dr. Ferenczi, of Budapest. Unlike the former examples, it does not refer to a verse taken from poetry, but to a self-coined saying. It may also demonstrate to us the rather unusual case where the forgetting places itself at the disposal of discretion when the latter is in danger of yielding to a momentary desire. The mistake thus advances to a useful function. After we

---

[282] *The Psychology of Dementia Præcox*, translated by F. Peterson and A. A. Brill.

have sobered down we justify that inner striving which at first could manifest itself only by way of inability, as in forgetting or psychic impotence.

"At a social gathering someone quoted, *Tout comprendre c'est tout pardonner*, to which I remarked that the first part of the sentence should suffice, as 'pardoning' is an exemption which must be left to God and the priest. One of the guests thought this observation very good, which in turn emboldened me to remark — probably to ensure myself of the good opinion of the well-disposed critic — that some time ago I thought of something still better. But when I was about to repeat this clever idea was unable to recall it. Thereupon I immediately withdrew from the company and wrote my concealing thoughts. I first recalled the name of the friend who had witnessed the birth of this (desired) thought, and of the street in Budapest where it took place, and then the name of another friend, whose name was Max, whom we usually called Maxie. That led me to the word 'maxim, 'and to the thought that at that time, as in the present case, it was a question of varying a well-known maxim. Strangely enough, I did not recall any maxim but the following sentence: '*God created man in His own image*,' and its changed conception, '*Man created God in his own image*. Immediately I recalled the sought-for recollection.

"My friend said to me at that time in Andrassy Street, '*Nothing human is foreign to me*.' To which I remarked, basing it on psychoanalytic experience, "You should go further and acknowledge *that nothing animal is foreign to you*."

"But after I had finally found the desired recollection I was even then prevented from telling it in this social gathering. The young wife of the friend whom I had reminded of the animality of the unconscious was also among those present, and I was perforce reminded that she was not at all prepared for the reception of such unsympathetic views. The forgetting spared me a number of unpleasant questions from her and a hopeless discussion, and just that must have been the motive of the 'temporary amnesia.'

"It is interesting to note that as a concealing thought there emerged sentence in which the deity is degraded to a human invention, while in the sought-for sentence there was an allusion to the animal in the man. The *capitis diminutio* is therefore common to both. The whole matter was apparently only a continuation of the stream of thought concerning understanding and forgiving which was stimulated by the discussion.

"That the desired thought so rapidly appeared may be also due to the fact that I withdrew into a vacant room, away from the society in which it was censored."

I have since then analysed a large number of cases of forgetting or faulty reproduction of the order of words, and the consistent result of these investigations led me to assume that the mechanisms of forgetting as demonstrated in the examples "*aliquis*" and "*Ode to Apollo,*" are almost of universal validity. It is not always very convenient to report such analyses, for, just as those cited, they usually lead to intimate and painful things in the person analysed; I shall therefore add no more to the number of such examples. What is common to all these cases, regardless of the material, is the fact that the forgotten or distorted material becomes connected through some associative road with an unconscious stream of thought, which gives rise to the influence that comes to light as forgetting.

I am now returning to the forgetting of names, concerning which we have so far considered exhaustively neither the casuistic elements nor the motives. As this form of faulty acts can at times be abundantly observed in myself, I am not at a loss for examples. The slight attacks of migraine, from which I am still suffering, are wont to announce themselves hours before through the forgetting of names, and at the height of the attack, during which I am not forced, however, to give up my work, I am often unable to recall all proper names.

Still, just such cases as mine may furnish the cause for a strong objection to our analytic efforts. Should not one be forced to conclude from such observations that the causation of the forgetfulness, especially the forgetting of names, is to be sought in circulatory or functional disturbances of the brain, and spare himself the trouble of searching for psychological explanations for these phenomena? Not at all; that would mean to interchange the mechanism of a process, which is the same in all cases, with its variations. But instead of an analysis I shall cite a comparison which will settle the argument.

Let us assume that I was so reckless as to take a walk at night in an uninhabited neighbourhood of a big city, and was attacked and robbed of my watch and purse. At the nearest police-station I report the matter in the following words: "I was in this or that street, and was there robbed of my watch and purse by *lonesomeness* and *darkness*." Although these words would not express anything that is incorrect, I would, nevertheless, run the danger of being considered — judging from the wording of this report — as not quite right in the head. To be correct, the state of affairs could only be described by saying that, *favoured* by the lonesomeness of the place and under *cover* of darkness, I was robbed of my valuables by *unknown malefactors*.

Now, then, the state of affairs in forgetting names need not be different. Favoured by exhaustion, circulatory disturbances, and intoxication, I am robbed by an unknown psychic force of the disposal over the proper names belonging to my memory; it is the same force which in other cases may bring about the same failure of memory during perfect health and mental capacity.

When I analyses those cases of name-forgetting occurring in myself, I find almost regularly that the name withheld shows some relation to a theme which concerns my own person, and is apt to provoke in me strong and often painful emotions. Following the convenient and commendable practice of the Zurich School (Bleuler, Jung, Riklin), I might express the same thing in the following form: The name withheld has touched a "personal complex" in me. The relation of the name to my person is an unexpected one, and is mostly brought about through superficial associations (words of double meaning and of similar sounds); it may generally be designated as a side association. A few simple examples will best illustrate the nature of the same: —

(*a*) A patient requested me to recommend to him a sanatorium in the Riviera. I knew of such a place very near Genoa, I also recalled the name of the German colleague who was in charge of the place, but the place itself I could not name, well as I believed I knew it. There was nothing left to do but ask the patient to wait, and to appeal quickly to the women of the family.

"Just what is the name of the place near Genoa where Dr. X. has his small institution in which Mrs. So-and-so remained so long under treatment?"

"Of course you would forget a name of that sort. The name is Nervi."

To be sure, I have enough to do with nerves.

(*b*) Another patient spoke about a neighbouring summer resort, and maintained that besides the two familiar inns there was a third. I disputed the existence of any third inn, and referred to the fact that had spent seven summers in the vicinity and therefore knew more about the place than he. Instigated by my contradiction, he recalled the name. The name of the third inn was "The Hochwartner." Of course, I had to admit it; indeed, I was forced to confess that for seven summers I had lived near this very inn whose existence I had so strenuously denied. But why should I have forgotten the name and the object? I believe because the name sounded very much like that of a Vienna colleague who practised the same specialty as my own. It touched in me the "professional complex."

(*c*) On another occasion, when about to buy a railroad ticket on the Reichenhall Station, I could not recall the very familiar name of the next big railroad station which I had so often passed. I was forced to look it up in the time-table. The name was Rosehome (Rosenheim). I soon discovered through what associations I lost it. An hour earlier I had visited my sister in her home near Reichenhall; my sister's name is Rose, hence also a Rosehome. This name was taken away by my "family complex."

(*d*) This predatory influence of the "family complex" I can demonstrate in a whole series of complexes.

One day I was consulted by a young man, younger brother of one of my female patients, whom I saw any number of times, and whom I used to call by his first name. Later, while wishing to talk about his visit, I forgot his first

691

name, in no way an unusual one, and could not recall it in anyway. I walked into the street to read the business signs and recognized the name as soon as it met my eyes.

The analysis showed that I had formed a parallel between the visitor and my own brother which centred in the question: "Would my brother, in a similar case, have behaved like him or even more contrarily?" Theouter connection between the thoughts concerning the stranger and my own family was rendered possible through the accident that the name of the mothers in each case was the same, Amelia. Subsequently I also understood the substitutive names, Daniel and Frank, which obtruded themselves without any explanation. These names, as well as Amelia, belong to Schiller's play *The Robbers*; they are all connected with a joke of the Vienna pedestrian, Daniel Spitzer.

(*e*) On another occasion I was unable to find a patient's name which had a certain reference to my early life. The analysis had to be followed over a long devious road before the desired name was discovered. The patient expressed his apprehension lest he should lose his eyesight; this recalled a young man who became blind from a gunshot, and this again led to a picture of another youth who shot himself, and the latter bore the same name as my first patient, though not at all related to him. The name became known to me, however, only after the anxious apprehension from these two juvenile cases was transferred to a person of my own family.

Thus an incessant stream of "self-reference" flows through my thoughts concerning which I usually have no inkling, but which betrays itself through such name-forgetting. It seems as if I were forced to compare with my own person all that I hear about strangers, as if my personal complexes became stirred up at every information from others. It seems impossible that this should be an individual peculiarity of my own person; it must, on the contrary, point to the way we grasp outside matters in general. I have reasons to assume that other individuals meet with experiences quite similar to mine.

The best example of this kind was reported to me by a gentleman named Lederer as a personal experience. While on his wedding trip in Venice he came across a man with whom he was but slightly acquainted, and whom he was obliged to introduce to his wife. As he forgot the name of the stranger he got himself out of the embarrassment the first time by mumbling the name unintelligibly. But when he met the man a second time, as is inevitable in Venice, he took him aside and begged him to help him out of the difficulty by telling him his name, which he unfortunately had forgotten. The answer of the stranger pointed to a superior knowledge of human nature: "I readily believe that you did not grasp my name. My name is like yours — Lederer!"

One cannot suppress a slight feeling of unpleasantness on discovering his own name in a stranger. I had recently felt it very plainly when I was consulted during my office hours by a man named S. Freud. However, I am assured by one of my own critics that in this respect he behaves inquire the opposite manner.

(f) The effect of personal relation can be recognized also in the following examples reported by Jung.[283]

"Mr. Y. falls in love with a lady who soon thereafter marries Mr. Ian spite of the fact that Mr. Y. was an old acquaintance of Mr. X., and had business relations with him, he repeatedly forgot the name, and one number of occasions, when wishing to correspond with X., he was obliged to ask other people for his name."

However, the motivation for the forgetting is more evident in this case than in the preceding ones, which were under the constellation of the personal reference. Here the forgetting is manifestly a direct result of the dislike of Y. for the happy rival; he does not wish to know anything about him.

(g) The following case, reported by Ferenczi, the analysis of which is especially instructive through the explanation of the substitutive thoughts (like 'Botticelli-Boltraffio to Signorelli), shows in a somewhat different way how self-reference leads to the forgetting of a name: —

"A lady who heard something about psycho- analysis could not recall the name of the psychiatrist, Young (Jung).

"Instead, the following names occurred to her: K1. (a name) — Wilde— Nietzsche — Hauptmann.

"I did not tell her the name, and requested her to repeat her free associations to every thought.

"To K1. she at once thought of Mrs. K1., that she was an embellished and affected person who looked very well for her age. 'She does not age. 'As a general and principal conception of Wilde and Nietzsche, she gave the association 'mental disease.' She then added jocosely: 'The Freudians will continue looking for the causes of mental diseases until they themselves become insane.' She continued: 'I cannot bear Wilde and Nietzsche. I do not understand them. I hear that they were both homosexual. Wilde has occupied himself with *young* people' (although she uttered in this sentence the correct name she still could not remember it).

"To Hauptmann she associated the words *half* and *youth*, and only after I called her attention to the word *youth* did she become aware that she was looking for the name Young (Jung)."

It is clear that this lady, who had lost her husband at the age of thirty-nine, and had no prospect of marrying a second time, had cause enough to avoid reminiscences recalling youth or old age. The remarkable thing is that

---

[283] *The Psychology of Dementia Præcox*, p. 45.

the concealing thoughts of the desired name came to the surface as simple associations of content without any sound-associations.

(*h*) Still different and very finely motivated is an example of name-forgetting which the person concerned has himself explained.

"While taking an examination in philosophy as a minor subject I was questioned by the examiner about the teachings of Epicurus, and was asked whether I knew who took up his teachings centuries later. I answered that it was Pierre Gassendi, whom two days before while in a café I had happened to hear spoken of as a follower of Epicurus. To the question how I knew this I boldly replied that I had taken an interest in Gassendi fora long time. This resulted in a certificate with a *magna cum laude*, but later, unfortunately, also in a persistent tendency to forget the name Gassendi. I believe that it is due to my guilty conscience that even now I cannot retain this name despite all efforts. I had no business knowing it at that time."

To have a proper appreciation of the intense repugnance entertained by our narrator against the recollection of this examination episode, one must have realized how highly he prizes his doctor's degree, and for how many other things this substitute must stand.

I add here another example of forgetting the name of a city, an instance which is perhaps not as simple as those given before, but which will appear credible and valuable to those more familiar with such investigations. The name of an Italian city withdrew itself from memory on account of its far-reaching sound-similarity to a woman's first name, which was in turn connected with various emotional reminiscences which were surely not exhaustively treated in this report. Dr. S. Ferenczi, who observed this case of forgetting in himself, treated it — quite justly — as an analysis of a dream or an erotic idea.

"To-day I visited some old friends, and the conversation turned to cities of Northern Italy. Someone remarked that they still showed the Austrian influence. A few of these cities were cited. I, too, wished to mention one, but the name did not come to me, although I knew that I had spent two very pleasant days there; this, of course, does not quite concur with Freud's theory of forgetting. Instead of the desired name of the city there obtruded themselves the following thoughts: 'Capua — Brescia — the lion of Brescia.' This lion I saw objectively before me in the form of a marble statue, but I soon noticed that he resembled less the lion of the statue of liberty in Brescia (which I saw only in a picture) than the other marble lion which I saw in Lucerne on the monument in honour of the Swiss Guard fallen in the Toiletries. I finally thought of the desired name: it was Verona.

"I knew at once the cause of this amnesia. No other than a former servant of the family whom I visited at the time. Her name was Veronica; in Hungarian Verona. I felt a great antipathy for her on account of her repulsive physiognomy, as well as her hoarse, shrill voice and her unbearable self-assertion (to which she thought herself entitled on account of her long service). Also the tyrannical way in which she treated the children of the family was insufferable to me. Now I knew the significance of the substitutive thoughts.

"To Capua I immediately associated *caput mortuum*. I had often compared Veronica's head to a skull. The Hungarian word *kapzoi* (greed after money) surely furnished a determinant for the displacement. Naturally I also found those more direct associations which connected Capua and Verona as geographical ideas and as Italian words of the same rhythm.

"The same held true for Brescia; here, too, I found concealed side-tracks of associations of ideas.

"My antipathy at that time was so violent that I thought Veronica very ugly, and have often expressed my astonishment at the fact that any one should love her: 'Why, to kiss her,' I said, 'must provoke nausea.'

"Brescia, at least in Hungary, is very often mentioned not in connection with the lion but with another wild beast. The most hated name in this country, as well as in North Italy, is that of General Haynau, who is briefly referred to as the hyena of Brescia. From the hated tyrant Haynau one stream of thought leads over Brescia to the city of Verona, and the other over the idea of the *grave-digging animal with the hoarse voice* (which corresponds to the thought of a monument to the dead),to the skull, and to the disagreeable organ of Veronica, which was so cruelly insulted in my unconscious mind. Veronica in her time ruled as tyrannically as did the Austrian General after the Hungarian and Italian struggles for liberty.

"Lucerne is associated with the idea of the summer which Veronica spent with her employers in a place near Lucerne. The Swiss Guard again recalls that she tyrannized not only the children but also the adult members of the family, and thus played the part of the 'Garde-Dame.'

"I expressly observe that this antipathy of mine against V. consciously belongs to things long overcome. Since that time she has changed in her appearance and manner, very much to her advantage, so that I am able to meet her with sincere regard (to be sure I hardly find such occasion).As usual, however, my unconscious sticks more tenaciously to those impressions; it is old in its resentment.

"The Tuileries represent an allusion to a second personality, an old French lady who actually 'guarded' the women of the house, and who was in high regard and somewhat feared by everybody. For a long time was her *élève* in French conversation. The word *élève* recalls that when I visited the brother-in-law of my present host in northern Bohemia I had to laugh a great deal because the rural population referred to the *élèves* (pupils) of the school of forestry as *löwen* (lions). Also this jocose recollection might have taken part in the displacement of the hyena by the lion."

(*i*) The following example can also show how a personal complex swaying the person at the time being may by devious ways bring about the forgetting of a name.[284]

Two men, an elder and a younger, who had travelled together in Sicily six months before, exchanged reminiscences of those pleasant and interesting days.

"Let's see, what was the name of that place," asked the younger, "where we passed the night before taking the trip to Selinunt? *Calatafini*, was it not?"

The elder rejected this by saying: "Certainly not; but I have forgotten the name, too, although I can recall perfectly all the details of the place. Whenever I hear someone forget a name it immediately produces forgetfulness in me. Let us look for the name. I cannot think of any other name except *Caltanisetta*, which is surely not correct."

"No," said the younger, "the name begins with, or contains, a *w*."

"But the Italian language contains no *w*," retorted the elder.

"I really meant a *v*, and I said *w* because I am accustomed to interchange them in my mother tongue."

The elder, however, objected to the *v*. He added: "I believe that I have already forgotten many of the Sicilian names. Suppose we try to find out. For example, what is the name of the place situated on a height which was called *Enna* in antiquity?"

"Oh, I know that: *Castrogiovanni*." In the next moment the younger man discovered the lost name. He cried out 'Castelvetrano,' and was pleased to be able to demonstrate the supposed *v*.

For a moment the elder still lacked the feeling of recognition, but after he accepted the name he was able to state why it had escaped him. He thought: "Obviously because the second half, *vetrano*, suggests *veteran*. I am aware that I am not quite anxious to think of ageing, and react peculiarly when I am reminded of it. Thus, *e.g.* ,I had recently reminded a very esteemed friend in most unmistakable terms that he had 'long ago passed the years of youth,' because before this he once remarked in the most flattering manner, 'I am no longer a young man.' That my resistance was directed against the second half of the name *Castelvetrano* is shown by the fact that the initial sound of the same returned in the substitutive name Caltanisetta."

"What about the name Caltanisetta itself?" asked the younger.

"That always seemed to me like a pet name of a young woman," admitted the elder.

---

[284] *Zentralb. t. Psychoanalyse*, I. 9, 1911.

Somewhat later he added: "The name for *Enna* was also only a substitutive name. And now it occurs to me that the name *Castrogiovanni*, which obtruded itself with the aid of a rationalization, alludes as expressly to *giovane*, young, as the last name, *Castelvetrano*, to *veteran*."

The older man believed that he had thus accounted for his forgetting the name. What the motive was that led the young man to this memory failure was not investigated.

In some cases one must have recourse to all the fineness of psychoanalytic technique in order to explain the forgetting of a name. Those who wish to read an example of such work I refer to a communication by Professor E. Jones. [285]

I could multiply the examples of name-forgetting and prolong the discussion very much further if I did not wish to avoid elucidating here almost all the view-points which will be considered in later themes. I shall, however, take the liberty of comprehending in a few sentences the results of the analyses reported here.

The mechanism of forgetting, or rather of losing or temporary forgetting of a name, consists in the disturbance of the intended reproduction of the name through a strange stream of thought unconscious at the time. Between the disturbed name and the disturbing complex there exists a connection either from the beginning or such a connection has been formed – perhaps by artificial means - through superficial (outer) associations.

The self-reference complex (personal, family or professional) proves to be the most effective of the disturbing complexes.

A name which by virtue of its many meanings belongs to a number of thought associations (complexes) is frequently disturbed in its connection to one series of thoughts through a stronger complex belonging to the other associations.

To avoid the awakening of pain through memory is one of the objects among the motives of these disturbances.

In general one may distinguish two principal cases of name-forgetting; when the name itself touches something unpleasant, or when it is brought into connection with other associations which are influenced by such effects. So that names can be disturbed on their own account or on account of their nearer or more remote associative relations in the reproduction.

A review of these general principles readily convinces us that the temporary forgetting of a name is observed as the most frequent faulty action of our mental functions.

---

[285] "Analyse eines Falles von Namenvergessen," *Zentralb.f. Psychoanalyse*, Jahrg. II, Heft 2, 1911.

However, we are far from having described all the peculiarities of this phenomenon. I also wish to call attention to the fact that name-forgetting is extremely contagious. In a conversation between two persons the mere mention of having forgotten this or that name by one often suffices to induce the same memory slip in the other. But whenever the forgetting is induced, the sought for name easily comes to the surface.

There is also a continuous forgetting of names in which whole chains of names are withdrawn from memory. If in the course of endeavoring to discover an escaped name one finds others with which the latter is intimately connected, it often happens that these new names also escape. The forgetting thus jumps from one name to another, as if to demonstrate the existence of a hindrance not to be easily removed.

IV. Childhood and Concealing Memories

In a second essay,[286] I was able to demonstrate the purposive nature of our memories in an unexpected field. I started with the remarkable fact that the earliest recollections of a person often seemed to preserve the unimportant and accidental, whereas (frequently though not universally !) not a trace is found in the adult memory of the weighty and affective impressions of this period. As it is known that the memory exercises a certain selection among the impressions at its disposal, it would seem logical to suppose that this selection follows entirely different principles in childhood than at the time of intellectual maturity. However, close investigation points to the fact that such an assumption is superfluous. The indifferent childhood memories owe their existence to a process of displacement. It be shown by psychoanalysis that in the reproduction they represent the substitute for other really significant impressions, whose reproduction is hindered by some resistance they do not owe their existence to their contents, but to an associative relation of contents to another repressed thought, deserve the title of "concealing memories" which I have designated them.

In the aforementioned essay I only touched upon, but in no way exhausted, the varieties in the relations and meanings of concealed memories. In the given example fully analysed I particularly emphasized a peculiarity in temporal relation between the concealing and the contents of the memory concealed by it. The content of the concealing memory in that example belonged to one of the first of childhood, while the thoughts represents it which remained practically unconscious, belonged to a later period of the individual question. I called this form of displacement a retroactive or *regressive* one. Perhaps more often one finds the reversed

---

[286] Published in the *Monatschrift f. Psychiatrie u. Neurologie.* 1899.

relation — that is, an indifferent impression of the most remote period becomes a concealing memory in consciousness, which simply owes its existence to an association with an earlier experience, against whose direct reproduction there are resistances. We would call these *encroaching* or *interposing* concealing memories. What most concerns memory lies here chronologically beyond concealing memory. Finally, there may be a third possible case, namely, the concealing memory may be connected with the impression it conceals, not only through its contents, just through contiguity of time; this is the *contemporaneous,* or *contiguous* concealing memory.

How large a portion of the sum total of our memory belongs to the category of concealing memories, and what part it plays in various neurotic hidden processes, these are problems into the value of which I have neither inquired nor shall I enter here. I am concerned only with emphasizing the sameness between the forgetting of proper names with faulty recollection and the formation of concealing memories.

At first sight it would seem that the diversities of both phenomena are far more striking than their exact analogies. There we deal with proper names, here with complete impressions experienced either in reality or in thought; there we deal with a manifest failure of the memory function, here with a memory act which appears strange to us. Again, there we are concerned with a momentary disturbance — for the name just forgotten could have been reproduced correctly a hundred times before, and will be so again from tomorrow on; here we deal with lasting possession without a failure, for the indifferent child- hood memories seem to be able to accompany us through a great part of life. In both these cases the riddle seems to be solved in an entirely different way. There it is the forgetting, while here it is the remembering which excites our scientific curiosity.

After deeper reflection one realizes that though there is a diversity in the psychic material and in the duration of time of the two phenomena, yet these are by far outweighed by the conformities between the two. In both cases we deal with the failure of remember what should be correctly reproduced by memory fails to appear, and instead something else comes as a substitute. In the case of getting a name there is no lack of memory function in the form of name substitution. The formation of a concealing memory depends on the forgetting of other important impressions. In both cases we are reminded by an intellectual feeling of the intervention of a disturbance, which in each case takes a different form. In the case of forgetting of names we are aware that the substitutive names are incorrect, in concealing memories we are surprised that we have them at all. Hence, if psychological analysis demonstrates that the substitutive formation in each case is brought about in the same manner — that is, through displacement of a superficial association — we are justified in saying that the diversities in material, in duration of time, and in the centring of both phenomena serve to enhance our expectation, that we have discovered something that is important and of general value. This generality purports that the stopping and straying of the reproducing function indicates more often than we suppose that there is an intervention of a tendency which favours one memory and at the same time works against another. The subject of childhood memories appears to me so important and interesting that I would like to devote to it a few additional remarks which go beyond the views expressed so far.

How far back into childhood do our memories reach? I am familiar with some investigations on this question by V. and C. Henri[287] and Potwin[288]. They assert that such examinations show wide individual variations, inasmuch as some trace their first reminiscences to the sixth month of life, while others can recall nothing of their lives before the end of the sixth or even the eighth year. But what connection is there between these variations in the behaviour of childhood reminiscences, and what signification may be ascribed to them? It seems that it is not enough to procure the material for this question by simple inquiry, but it must be subjected to a study in which the person furnishing the information must participate.

I believe we accept too indifferently the fact of infantile amnesia — that is, the failure of memory for the first years of our lives — and fail to find in it a strange riddle. We forget of what great intellectual accomplishments and of what complicated emotions a child of four years is capable. We really ought to wonder why the memory of later years has, as a rule, retained so little of these psychic processes, especially as we have every reason for assume that these same forgotten childhood activities have not glided off without leaving a trace in the development of the person, but that they have left a definite influence for all future time. Yet in spite of this unparalleled effectiveness were forgotten! This would suggest that there are particularly formed conditions of memory (in the sense of conscious reproduction) have thus far eluded our knowledge. It is possible that the forgetting of childhood give us the key to the understanding of amnesias which, according to our newer studies, lie at the basis of the formation of all neurotic symptoms.

Of these retained childhood reminisces, some appear to us readily comprehensible, while others seem strange or unintelligible. It is not difficult to correct certain errors in regard to both kinds. If the retained reminiscences of a person are subjected to an analytic test, it can be readily ascertained that a guarantee for their correctness does not exist. Some of the memory pictures are surely falsified and incomplete, or displaced in point of time and place. The assertions of persons examined that their first memories reach back perhaps to their second year are evidently unreliable. Motives can soon be

---

[287] "Enquête sur les premiers souvenirs de l'enfance." *L'Année psychologique,* iii., 1897.
[288] "Study of Early Memories,'" *Psychological Review,* 1901.

discovered which explain the disfigurement and the displacement of these experiences, but they also demonstrate that these memory lapses are not the result of a mere unreliable memory. Powerful forces from a later period have moulded the memory capacity of our infantile experiences, and it is probably due to these same forces that the understanding of our childhood is generally so very strange to us.

The recollection of adults, as is known, proceeds through different psychic material. Some recall by means of visual pictures — their memories are of a visual character; other individuals can scarcely reproduce in memory the most paltry sketch of an experience we call such persons *"auditifs"* and *"moteurs"* in contrast to the to *"visuels,"* terms proposed by Charcot. These differences vanish in dreams; all our dreams are preponderatingly visual. But this development is also found in the childhood memories; the latter are plastic and visual, even in those people whose later memory lacks the visual element. The visual memory, therefore preserves the type of the infantile recollections. Only my earliest childhood memories are visual character; they represent plastic depicted scenes, comparable only to stage settings.

In these scenes of childhood, whether they prove true or false, one usually sees his childish person both in contour and dress. This circumstance must excite our wonder, for adults do not see their own persons in their reflections of later experiences. [289] It is, moreover, against our experiences to assume that the child's attention during his experiences is centred on himself rather than exclusively on outside impressions. Various sources force us to assume the so-called earliest childhood recollections are not true memory traces but later elaborate of the same, elaborations which might have been subjected to the influences of many later psychic forces. Thus the, "childhood reminiscences" of individuals altogether advance to the signification of "concealing memories," and thereby form a noteworthy analogy to the childhood remembrances as laid down in the legends and of nations.

Whoever has examined mentally a number of persons by the method of psychoanalysis must have gathered in this work numerous examples of concealing memories of every description. However, owing to the previously discussed nature of the relations of the childhood reminiscences to later life, it becomes extraordinarily difficult to report such examples. For, in order to attach the value of the concealing memory to an infantile reminiscence, it would be often necessary to present the entire life-history of the person concerned. Only seldom is it possible, as in the following good example, to take out from its context and report a single childhood memory.

---

[289] I assert this as a result of certain investigations made by myself.

A twenty-four-year-old man preserved the following picture from the fifth year of his life: In the garden of a summer-house he sat on a stool next to his aunt, who was engaged in teaching him the alphabet. He found difficulty in distinguishing the letter m from n, and he begged his aunt to tell him how to tell one from the other. His aunt called his attention to the fact that the letter *m* had one whole portion (a stroke) more than the letter *n*. There was no reason to dispute the reliability of this childhood recollection; its meaning, however, was discovered only later, when it showed itself to be the symbolic representation of another boyish inquisitiveness. For just as he wanted to know the difference between *m* and *n* at that time so he concerned himself later about the difference between boy and girl, and he would have willing that just this aunt should be his teacher. He also discovered that the difference similar one; that the boy again had one portion more than the girl, and at the time of this recognition his memory awoke to the responding childish inquisitiveness.

I would like to show by one more example the sense that may be gained by a childhood reminiscence through analytic work, although it may seem to contain no sense before. In my forty-third year, when I began to interest myself in what remained in my memory of my own childhood, a scene struck me which for a long time, as I afterwards believed, had repeatedly come to consciousness, and which through reliable identification could be traced to a period before the completion of my third year. I saw myself in front of a chest, the door of which was held open by my half-brother, twenty years my senior. I stood there demanding something and screaming; my mother, pretty and slender then suddenly entered the room, as if returning from the street.

In these words I formulated this scene so vividly seen, which, however, furnished no other clue. Whether my brother wished to open or lock the chest (in the first explanation it was a "cupboard"), why I cried, and what bearing, the arrival of my mother had, all these questions were dim to me; I was tempted to explain to myself that it dealt with the memory of a hoax by my older brother, which was interrupted by my mother. Such misunderstandings of childhood scenes retained in memory are not uncommon; we recall a situation, but it is not centralized; we do not know on which of the elements to place the psychic accent. Analytic effort led me to an entirely unexpected solution of the picture. I missed my mother and began to suspect that she was locked in this cupboard or chest, and therefore demanded that my brother should unlock it. As he obliged me, and I became convinced that she was not in the chest, I began to cry; this is the moment firmly retained in the memory, which was directly followed by the appearance of my mother, who appeased my worry and anxiety.

But how did the child get the idea of looking for the absent mother in the chest? Dreams which occurred at the same time pointed dimly to a nurse, concerning whom other reminiscences were retained; as, for example, that she conscientiously urged me to deliver to her the small coins which I received as gifts, a detail which in itself may lay claim to the value of a concealing memory for later things. I then concluded to facilitate for myself this time the task of interpretation, and asked my now mother about that nurse. I found out all of things, among others the fact that this shrewd but dishonest person had committed extensive robberies during the confinement of my mother and that my half-brother was instrumental bringing her to justice. This information gave me the key to the from childhood, as through a sort of inspiration. The sudden disappearance of the nurse was a matter of indifference to me; I had just asked this brother where she was, probably because I had noticed that he had played a part in disappearance, and he, evasive and witty as he is to this day, answered that she was "boxed in." I understood this answer in the childish way, but asked no more, as there was nothing else to be discovered. When my mother left shortly thereafter I suspected that the naughty brother had treated her in the same way as he did the nurse, and therefore pressed him the chest.

I also understand now why in the translation of the visual childhood scene my mothers slenderness was accentuated; she must struck me as being newly restored. I am and a half years older than the sister born that time, and when I was three years of I was separated from my half-brother.

V. Mistakes in Speech

ALTHOUGH the ordinary material of speech of our mother-tongue seems to be guarded against forgetting, its application, however, more often succumbs to another disturbance which is familiar to us as "slips of the tongue." What we observe in normal persons as slips of the tongue gives the gives same impression as the first step of the so-called "paraphasias" which manifest themselves under pathologic conditions.

I am in the exceptional position of being about to refer to a previous work on the subject. In the year 1895 Meringer and C. Mayer published a study on *Mistakes in Speech and Reading*, with whose view-points I do not agree. One of the authors, who is the spokesman in the text, is a philologist actuated by a linguistic interest to examine the rules governing those slips. He hoped to deduce from these rules the existence "of a definite psychic mechanism," "whereby the Sounds of a word, of a sentence, and even the words themselves, would be associated and connected with one another in a quite peculiar manner" (p. 10).

The authors grouped the examples of speech mistakes collected by them first "accord purely descriptive view-points, such as interchangings *(e.g.,* the Milo of Venus instead of the Venus of Milo), as anticipations (e.g., the shoes made her sorft . . . the shoes made her feet sore), echoes and post positions, as contaminations *(e.g., "I will soon him home,"* instead of I will soon go home and I will see him"), and substitutions (e.g., "he entrusted his money to a "savings crank," instead of "a savings bank.")[290] Besides these principal categories there are so others of lesser importance (or of lesser significance for our purpose). In this grouping makes no difference whether the transposition disfigurement, fusion, etc., affects single sounds of the word or syllables, or whole words of the concerned sentence.

To explain the various forms of mist speech, Meringer assumes a varied psychic value of phonetics. As soon as the innervation the first syllable of a word, or the first word of a sentence, the stimulating process immediately strikes the succeeding sounds, and the following words, and in so far as these innervations are synchronous they may effect some changes in one another. The stimulus of the psychically intensive sound "rings" before or continues echoing, and thus disturbs the less important process of innervation. It is necessary therefore to determine which are the most important sounds of a word. Meringer states: "If one wishes to know which sound of a word possesses the greatest intensity he should examine himself while searching for a forgotten word, for example, a name. That which first returns to consciousness invariably had the greatest intensity prior to the forgetting (p. 160). Thus the most important sounds are the initial sound of the root-syllable and the initial sound of the word itself, as well as one or another of the accentuated vowels (p. 162).

Here I cannot help voicing a contradiction. Whether or not the initial sound of the name belongs to the most important elements of the word, it is surely not true that in the case of the forgetting of the word it first returns to consciousness; the above rule is therefore of no use. When we observe ourselves during the search for a forgotten name we are comparatively often forced to express the opinion that it begins with a certain letter. This conviction proves to be as often unfounded as founded. Indeed, I would even go so far as to assert that in the majority of cases one reproduces a false initial sound. Also in our example *Signorelli* the substitutive name lacked the initial sound, and the principal syl- lables were lost; on the other hand, the important pair of syllables *elli* returned to consciousness in the substitutive name *Botticelli.*

How little substitutive names respect the sound of the lost names may be learned from following case. One day I found it impossible to recall the name of the small country whose capital is Monte Carlo. The substitutive names *follows: Piedmont, Albania, Montevideo, Colico.* In place of Albania *Montenegro* soon appeared and then it struck me that the syllable *Mont* (pronounced *Mon*) occurred in all but the last of the

---

[290] These examples are given by the editor.

substitutive names. It thus became easy for me to find from the name of Prince Albert the forgotten name *Monaco. Colico* practically imitates the syllabic sequence and rhythm of the forgotten name.

If we admit the conjecture that a mechanism similar to that pointed out in the forgetting names may also play a part in the phenomena speech-blunders, we are then led to a better founded judgment of cases of speech-blunders. The speech disturbance which manifests a speech-blunder may in the first place be caused by the influence of another component of same speech that is, through a fore-sound or echo, or through another meaning within the sentence or context which differs from that the speaker wishes to utter. In the second place, however, the disturbance could be brought about analogously to the process in the case *Signorelli,* through influences outside this word, sentence or context, from elements which we did not intend to express, and of whose incitement we became conscious only through the disturbance. In both modes of origin of the mistake in speech the common element lies in the simultaneity of the stimulus, while the differentiating elements lie in the arrangement within or without the same sentence or context.

The difference does not at first appear as wide as when it is taken into consideration in certain conclusions drawn from the symptomatology of speech-mistakes. It is clear, however, that only in the first case is there a prospect of drawing conclusions from the manifestations of speech-blunders concerning a mechanism which connects together sounds and words for the reciprocal influence of their articulation; that is, conclusions such as the philologist hopes to gain from the study of speech-blunders. In the case of disturbance through influence outside of the same sentence or context, it would before all be a question of becoming acquainted with the disturbing elements, and then the question would arise whether the mechanism of this disturbance cannot also suggest the probable laws of the formation of speech.

We cannot maintain that Meringer and Mayer have overlooked the possibility of speech disturbance through "complicated psychic influences," that is, through elements outside of the same word or sentence or the same sequence of words. Indeed, they must have observed that the theory of the psychic variation of sounds applies, strictly speaking, only to the explanation of disturbances as well as to fore-sounds and sounds. Where the word disturbances cannot reduced to sound disturbances, as, for example, the substitutions and contaminations of words they, too, have without hesitation sought the cause of the mistake in speech outside of intended context, and proved this state of affairs by means of fitting examples.[291] According to the author's own understanding it is some similarity between a certain word in the intended sentence and some other not intended, which allows the latter

---

[291] Those who are interested are referred to pp. 62-97 of the author's work.

to assert itself in consciousness by causing a disfigurement, a composition, or a compromise formation (contamination).

Now, in my work on the *Interpretation of Dreams* I have shown the part played by process of condensation in the origin of the called manifest contents of the dream from latent thoughts of the dream. Any similarity of objects or of word-presentations between elements of the unconscious material is taken as a cause for the formation of a third, which is a composite or compromise formation. This element represents both components in the dream content, and in view of this origin it is frequently endowed with numerous contradictory individual determinants. The formation of solutions and contaminations in speech-mistakes is, therefore, the beginning of that work of condensation which we find taking a most active part in the construction of the dream.

In a small essay destined for the general reader,[292] Meringer advanced a theory of very practical significance for certain cases of interchanging of words, especially for such cases where one word is substituted by another of opposite meaning. He says: "We may still recall the manner in which the President of the Austrian House of Deputies opened the session some time ago: ' Honoured Sirs! I announce the presence of so and so many gentlemen, and therefore declare the session as "closed" ' ! " The general merriment first attracted his attention and he corrected his mistake. In the present case the probable explanation is that the President wished himself in a position to close this session, from which he had little good to expect, and the thought broke through at least partially — a frequent manifestation — resulting in his use of "closed" in place of 'opened," that is, the opposite of the statement intended. Numerous observations have taught me, however, that we frequently interchange contrasting words; they are already associated in our speech consciousness; they lie very close together and are easily incorrectly evoked.

Still, not in all cases of contrast substitution it so simple as in the example of the President as to appear plausible that the speech-mistake occurs merely as a contradiction which arises in the inner thought of the speaker opposing the sentence uttered. We have found the analogous mechanism in the analysis of the example *aliquis;* the inner contradiction asserts itself in the form of forgetting a word instead of a substitution through its opposite. But in order to adjust the difference we may remark that the little word *aliquis* is incapable of a contrast similar to "closing" and "opening," and that the word "opening" cannot be subject to forgetting on account of its being a common component of speech.

---

[292] *Neue Freie Presse*, August 23, 1900: "Wie man sich versprechen kann."

Having been shown by the last examples of Merinzer and May that speech disturbance may be caused through the influence of fore-sounds, after-sounds, words from the same sentence that were intended for expression, as well as through the effect of words outside the sentence intended, *the stimulus of which would otherwise not have been suspected,* we shall next wish to discover whether we can definitely separate the two classes of mistakes in speech, and how we can distinguish the example of the one from a case of the other class.

But at this stage of the discussion we must also think of the assertions of Wundt, who deals with the manifestations of speech-mistakes in his recent work on the development of language.[293] Psychic influences, according to Wundt, never lack in these as well as in other phenomena related to them. The uninhibited stream of *sound* and *word associations* stimulated by spoken sounds belongs here in the first place as a positive determinant. This is supported as a negative factor by the relaxation or suppression of the influences of the will which inhibit this stream, and by the active attention which is here a function of volition. Whether that play of association manifests itself in the fact that a coming sound is anticipated or a preceding sound reproduced, or whether a familiar practised sound becomes intercalated between others, or finally, whether it manifests itself in the fact that altogether different sounds associatively related to the spoken sounds act upon these — all these questions designate only differences in the direction, and at most in the play of the occurring associations but not in the general nature of the same. In some cases it may be also doubtful to which form a certain disturbance may be attributed, or whether it would not be more correct to refer such disturbance to a concurrence of motives, *following the principle of the complication of causes*[294] (cf . pp. 380 - 81)."

I consider these observations of Wundt as absolutely justified and very instructive. Perhaps we could emphasize with even greater firmness than Wundt that the positive factor favouring mistakes in speech (the uninhibited stream of associations, and its negative, the relaxation of the inhibiting attention) regularly attain synchronous action, so that both factors only different determinants of the same process. With the relaxation, or, more unequivocal pressed, *through* this relaxation, of the uninhibited attention the uninhibited stream of associations becomes active.

Among the examples of the mistakes in collected by me I can scarcely find one in I would be obliged to attribute the speech disturbance simply and solely to what Wundt calls "contact effect of sound." Almost invariably I discover besides this a disturbing influence something outside of the intended speech. The disturbing element is either a single unconscious

---

[293] Völker psychologie, vol. I., pt. I., p. 371, ect., 1900
[294] Italics are mine.

thought, which comes to light through the special blunder, and can only be brought to consciousness through a searching analysis, or it is a general psychic motive, which directs against the entire speech.

(*Example a*) Seeing my daughter make an unpleasant face while biting into an apple, I wished to quote the following couplet: —

"The ape he is a funny sight,

When in the apple he takes a bite."

But I began: " The apel . . ." This seems to be a contamination of "ape" and "apple" (compromise formation), or it may be also conceived as an anticipation of the prepared "apple." The true state of affairs, however, was this: I began the quotation once before, and made no mistake the first time. I made the mistake only during the repetition, which was necessary because my daughter, having been distracted from another side, did not listen to me. This repetition with the added impatience to disburden myself of the sentence I must include in the motivation of the speech-blunder, which represented itself as a function of condensation.

(*b*) My daughter said, "I wrote to Mrs. Schresinger." The woman's name was Schlesinger. This speech-blunder may depend on the tendency to facilitate articulation. I must state, however, that this mistake was made by my daughter a few moments after I had said *apel,* instead of *ape.* Mistakes in speech are in a great measure contagious; a similar peculiarity was noticed by Meringer and Mayer in the forgetting of names. I know of no reason for this contagiousness.

(*c*) " I *sut* up like a pocket-knife," patient in the beginning of treatment, in "I *shut* up." This suggests a difficulty of articulation which may serve as an excuse for interchanging of sounds. When her attention was called to the speech-blunder, she promptly replied, "Yes, that happened because you said *'earnesht'* instead of *'earnest.'* " As a of fact I received her with the remark, "To-day we shall be in earnest" (because it was the last hour before her discharge from treatment), jokingly changed the word into *earnesht.* In the course of the hour she repeatedly made in mistakes speech, and I finally observed that it only because she imitated me but because she had a special reason in her unconscious to linger on the word earnest (Ernst) as a name.[295]

(*d*) A woman, speaking about a game invented by her children and called by them "the man in the box," said "the manx in the boc." I could readily

---

[295] It turned out that she was under the influence conscious thoughts concerning pregnancy and prevention of conception. With the words "shut up like a knife," which she uttered consciously as a complaint, she meant to describe the position of the child in the womb. The word "earnest" in my remark recalled to her the name (S. Ernst) of the well-known Vienna business firm in Ka¨rthner Strasse, which used to advertise the sale of articles for the prevention of conception.

understand her mistake. It was while analysing her dream, in which her husband is depicted as very generous in money matters — just the reverse of reality — that she made this speech-blunder. The day before she had asked for a new set of furs, which her husband denied her, claiming that he could not afford to spend so much money. She upbraided him for his stinginess, "for putting away so much into the strongbox," and mentioned a friend whose husband has not nearly his income, and yet he presented his wife with a *mink* coat for her birthday. The mistake is now comprehensible. The word *manx (manks)* reduces itself to the "minks" which she longs for, and the *box* refers to her husband's stinginess.

(e) A similar mechanism is shown in the mistake of another patient whose memory deserted her in the midst of a long-forgotten childish reminiscence. Her memory failed to inform her on what part of the body the prying and lustful hand of another had touched her. Soon thereafter she Visited one of her friends, with whom she discussed summer homes. Asked where her cottage in M. was located, she answered, "Near the *mountain loin*" instead of *"mountain lane."*

(f) Another patient, whom I asked at the end of her visit how her uncle was, answered: "I don't know, I only see him now *in flagranti."*

The following day she said, "I am really ashamed of myself for having given you yesterday such a stupid answer. Naturally you must have thought me a very uneducated person always mistakes the meaning of foreign words I wished to say *en passant."* We did not know at the time where she got the incorrectly used foreign words, but during the same session she reproduced a reminiscence as a continuation the theme from the previous day, in which being caught *in flagranti* played the principal part. The mistake of the previous day had therefore anticipated the recollection, which at that had not yet become conscious.

(g) In discussing her summer plans, a patient said, "I shall remain most of the summer in *Elberlon."* She noted her mistake, and asked me to analyse it. The associations to *Elberton* elicited: seashore on the Jersey coast — summer resort — vacation travelling. This recalled travelling in Europe with her cousin, a topic which we had discussed the day before during the analysis of a dream. The dream dealt with her dislike for this cousin, and she admitted that it was due to the fact that the latter was the favourite of the man whom they met together while travelling abroad. During the dream analysis she not recall the name of the city in which they met this man, and I did not make any effort time to bring it to her consciousness, as we were then engrossed in a totally different problem. When asked to focus her attention again on Elberton and reproduce her associations, she said, "It brings to mind *Elberlawn-lawn-field-*and-*Elberfield."Elberleld"* was the lost name of the city in Germany. Here the mistake served to bring to consciousness in a concealed manner a memory which was connected with a painful feeling.

(h) A woman said to me, " If you wish to buy a carpet, go to *Merchant* (Kaufmann) in *Matthew Street* (Mathdusgasse)." I repeated, " Then at Matthew's — I mean at Merchant's —" It would seem that my repeating of one name in place of the other was simply the result of distraction. The woman's remark really did distract me, as she turned my attention to something else much more vital to me than carpet. In Matthew Street stands the house in which my wife lived as a bride, The entrance to the house was in another street, and now I noticed that I had forgotten its name and could only recall it through a roundabout method. The name Matthew, which kept only attention, is thus a substitutive name for the forgotten name of the street. It is more suitable than the name Merchant, for Matthew is exclusively the name of a person, while Merchant is lot. The forgotten street, too, bears the name of a person: *Radetzky.*

(i) A patient consulted me for the first time, and from her history it became apparent that the cause of her nervousness was largely happy married life. Without any encouragement she went into details about her marital troubles. She had not lived with her husband for about six months, and she saw him last at the theatre when she saw the play *Officer 606.* I her attention to the mistake, and she immediately corrected herself, saying that she to say *Officer 666*(the name of a recent popular play). I decided to find out the reason for the mistake, and as the patient came for analytic treatment, I discovered that immediate cause of the rupture between herself and husband was the disease which is treated by "606." [296]

(k) Before calling on me a patient telephone for an appointment, and also wished to be informed about my consultation fee. He was told that the first consultation was ten dollars; after the examination was over he again as what he was to pay, and added: " I don't like to owe money to any one, especially to doctors; I prefer to pay right away." Instead of he said *play*. His last voluntary remarks and his mistake put me on my guard, but after a few more uncalled-for remarks he set me at ease by taking money from his pocket. He counted four paper dollars and was very chagrined and surprised because he had no more money with him, and promised to send me a cheque for the balance. I was sure that his mistake betrayed him, that he was only *playing* with me, but there was nothing to be done. At the end of a few weeks I sent him a bill for the balance, and the letter was returned to me by the post-office authorities marked "Not found."

(l) Miss X. spoke very warmly of Mr. Y., which was rather strange, as before this she had always expressed her indifference, not to say her

---

[296] Similar mistakes dealing with *Officer 666* were reported to me by other psycho-analysts.

contempt, for him. On being asked about this sudden change of heart she said: "I really never had anything against him; he was always nice to me, but I never gave him the chance to cultivate my acquaintance." She said "cuptivate." This neologism was a contamination of *cultivate* and *captivate,* and foretold the coming betrothal.

(m) An illustration of the mechanisms of contamination and condensation will be found in the following *lapsus linguæ.* Speaking of Miss Z., Miss W. depicted her as a very "straitlaced" person who was not given to levities, etc. Miss X. thereupon remarked: "Yes, that is a very characteristic description, she always appealed to me as very *'straicet-brazed.'* " Here the mistake resolved itself into *straitlaced and brazen-laced,* which corresponded to Miss W.'s opinion of Miss Z.

(n) I shall quote a number of example a paper by my colleague, Dr. W. Stekel, which appeared in the Berlin *Tageblaltt* of January 1904, entitled "Unconscious Confessions".

"An unpleasant trick of my unpleasant thoughts was revealed by the following example: To begin with, I may state that in my capacity as a physician I never consider my remuneration: but always keep in view the patient's interest only: this goes without saying. I was visiting a patient who was convalescing from a serious illness. We had passed through hard days and nights. I was happy to find her improved, and I portrayed to her the pleasures of a sojourn in Abbazia, concluding with: 'If, as I hope, you will *not* soon leave your bed.' This obviously came from an unconscious selfish motive, to be able to continue treating wealthy patient, a wish which is entirely foreign to my waking consciousness, and which I would reject with indignation."

(o) Another example (Dr. W. Stekel): My wife engaged a French governess for the afternoons, and later, coming to a satisfactory agreement, wished to retain her testimonials. The governess begged to be allowed to keep them, saying, 'Je cherche encore pour les *après-midis* — pardons, pour les *avant-midis.'* She appar intended to seek another place which would perhaps offer more profitable arrangements — an intention which she carried out."

(p) I was to give a lecture to a woman. Her husband, upon whose request this was done, stood behind the door listening. At the end of my sermonizing, which had made a visible impression, I said: "Good-bye, sir !" To the experienced person I thus betrayed the fact that the words were directed towards the husband; that I had spoken to oblige him.

(q) Dr. Stekel reports about himself that he had under treatment at the same time two patients from Triest, each of whom he always addressed incorrectly. "Good morning, Mr. Peloni!" he would say to Askoli, and to Peloni, " Good morning, Mr. Askoli !" He was at first inclined to attribute no

deeper motive to this mistake, but to explain it through a number of similarities in both persons. However, he easily convinced himself that here the interchange of names bespoke a sort of boast — that is, he was acquainting each of his Italian patients with the fact that neither was the only resident of Triest who came to Vienna in search of his medical advice.

(r) Two women stopped in front of a drugstore, and one said to her companion, "If you will wait a few *moments* I'll soon be back," but she said *movements* instead. She was on her way to buy some castoria for her child.

(s) Mr. L., who is fonder of being called on than of calling, spoke to me through the telephone from a nearby summer resort. He wanted to know when I would pay him a visit. I reminded him that it was his turn to visit me, and called his attention to the fact that, as was the happy possessor of an automobile would be easier for him to call on me. (We were at different summer resorts, separated about one half-hour's railway trip.) He gladly promised to call, and asked: "How about Labour Day (September 1st), will it be convenient for you? "When I answered affirmatively, he said, "Very well, then, put me down for *Election* Day" (November). His mistake was quite plain. He likes to visit me, but it was inconvenient to travel so far. November we would both be in the city. My analysis proved correct.

(t) A friend described to me a nervous patient, and wished to know whether I could benefit him. I remarked: "I believe that in time I can remove all his symptoms by psychoanalysis because it is a *durable* case" wishing to say "curable"!

(u) I repeatedly addressed my patient as Mrs. Smith, her married daughter's name, when her real name is Mrs. James. My attention having been called to it, I soon discovered that I had another patient of the same name who refused to pay for the treatment. Mrs. Smith was also my patient and paid her bills promptly.

(v) A *lapsus linguæ* sometimes stands for a particular characteristic. A young woman, who is the domineering spirit in her home, said of her ailing husband that he had consulted the doctor about a wholesome diet for himself and then added: "The doctor said that diet has nothing to do with his ailments, and that he can eat and drink what *I* want."

(w) I cannot omit this excellent and instructive example, although, according to my authority, it is about twenty years old. A lady once expressed herself in society — the very words show that they were uttered with fervour and under the pressure of a great many secret emotions: "Yes, a woman must be pretty if she is to please the men. A man is much better off. As long as he has *five* straight limbs, he needs no more !"

This example affords us a good insight into the intimate mechanisms of a mistake in speech by means of condensation and contamination (cf. p. 72). It is quite obvious that we have here a fusion of two similar modes of expression: —

"As long as he has his four *straight limbs.*"

" As long as he has all his *five senses.*"

Or the term "straight" may be the common element of the two intended expressions: —

"As long as he has his *straight* limbs."

"All five should be *straight.*"

It may also be assumed that both modes of expression — viz., those of the five senses and those of the straight five — have co-operated to introduce into the sentence about the straight limbs first a number and then the mysterious five instead of the simple four. But this fusion surely would not have succeeded if it had not expressed good sense in the form resulting from the mistake; if it had not expressed a cynical truth which, naturally, could not be uttered unconcealed, coming as it did from a woman.

Finally, we shall not hesitate to call attention to the fact that the woman's saying, following wording, could just as well be an excellent witticism as a jocose speech-blunder. It is simply a question whether she uttered these words with conscious or unconscious intention. The behaviour of the speaker in this case certainly speaks against the conscious intention, and thus excludes wit.

(x) Owing to similarity of material, I add here another case of speech-blunder, the interpretation of which requires less skill. A professor of anatomy strove to explain the nostril, which, as is known, is a very difficult anatomical structure. To his question whether his audience grasped his ideas he received an affirmative reply. The professor, known self-esteem, thereupon remarked: "I can hardly believe this, for the number of people who understand the nostril, even in a city of millions like Vienna, can be counted *on a finger* — pardon me, I meant to say *on the fingers* of a hand."

(y) I am indebted to Dr. Alf. Robitsek, of Vienna, for calling my attention to two speech-blunders from an old French author, which I shall reproduce in the original.

Brantôme (1527-1614), *Vies des Dames galantries,* Discours second: " Si ay-je cogneu une très belle et honneste dame de par le monde, qui, devisant avec un honneste gentilhomme de la cour des affaires de la guerre durant ces civiles, elle luy dit: 'J'ay ouy dire que le roy a faiet rompre tous les c — de ce pays là.' Elle vouloit dire le ponts. Pensez que, venant de coucher d'avec son mary, ou songeant à son amant, elle avoit encor ce nom frais en la bouche; et le gentilhomme s'en eschauffer en amours d'elle pour ce mot.

"Une autre dame que j'ai cogneue, entretenant une autre grand dame plus qu'elle, et luy louant et exaltant ses beautez, elle luy dit après : 'Non, madame, ce que je vous en dis, ce n'est point pour vous *adultérer;* voulant dire *adulater,*comme elle le rhabilla ainsi : pensez qu'elle songeoit à adultérer."

In the psychotherapeutic procedure which I employ in the solution and removal of neurotic symptoms, I am often confronted with the task of discovering from the accidental utterances and fancies of the patient the thought contents, which, though striving for concealment, nevertheless intentionally betray themselves. In doing this the mistakes often perform the most valuable, service, as I can show through most convincing and still most singular examples.

For example, patients speak of an aunt and later, without noting the mistake, call her "my mother, or designate a husband as a "brother." In this way they attract my attention to the fact that they have "identified" these person with each other, that they have placed them same category, which for their emotional life signifies the recurrence of the same type. Or, a young man of twenty years presents himself during my office hours with these words: "I am the father of N. N., whom you have treated — pardon me, I mean the brother; why, he is four years older than I." I understand though this mistake that he wishes to express that, like the brother, he, too, is ill through the fault the father; like his brother, he wishes to be cured, but that the father is the one most need of treatment. At other times an unusual arrangement of words, or a forced expression is sufficient to disclose in the speech of the patient the participation of a repressed thought having a different motive.

Hence, in coarse as well as in finer speech disturbances, which may, nevertheless, be sumed as " speech-blunders," I find that it is not the not the contact effects of the thoughts outside the intended speech, which determine the origin of the speech-blunder, and also suffice to explain the newly formed, mistakes in speech. I do not doubt the laws whereby the sounds produce changes upon one another; but they alone do not appear to me sufficiently forcible to mar the correct execution of speech. In those cases which I have studied and investigated more closely they merely represent the preformed mechanism, which is conveniently utilized by a more remote psychic motive. The latter does not, however, form a part of the sphere of influence of these sound relations. *In a large number of substitutions caused by mistakes in talking there is an entire absence of such phonetic laws.* In this respect I am in full accord with Wundt, who likewise assumes that the conditions underlying speech-blunders are complex and go far beyond the contact effect of the sounds.

If I accept as certain "these more remote psychic influences," following Wundt's expression, there is still nothing to detain me from conceding also that in accelerated speech, with a certain amount of diverted attention, the causes of speech-blunder may be easily limited to the definite law of Meringer

714

and Mayer. However, in a number of examples gathered by these authors a more complicated solution is apparent.

In some forms of speech-blunders we may assume that the disturbing factor is the of striking against obscene words and meanings. The purposive disfigurement and distortion of words and phrases, which is so popular with vulgar persons, aims at nothing else but the employing of a harmless motive as a reminder of the obscene, and this sport is so frequent that it would not be at all remarkable if appeared unintentionally and contrary to the will.

I trust that the readers will not depreciate the value of these interpretations, for which there no proof, and of these examples which I have myself collected and explained by means of analysis. But if secretly I still cherish the expectation that even the apparently simple of speech-blunder will be traced to a disturbance caused by a half-repressed idea cuts the intended context, I am tempted to it noteworthy observation of Meringer. This author asserts that it is remarkable that nobody wishes to admit having made a mistake in speaking. There are many intelligent and honest people who are offended if we tell them that they made a mistake in speaking. I would not risk making this assertion as general as Meringer, using the term "nobody." But the emotional trace which clings to the demonstration of the mistake, which manifestly belongs to the nature of shame, has its significance. It may be classed with the anger displayed- at the inability to recall a forgotten name, and with the surprise at the tenaciousness of an apparently indifferent memory, and it invariably points to the participation of a motive in the formation of the disturbance.

The distorting of names amounts to an insult when done intentionally, and could have the same significance in a whole series of cases where it appears as unintentional speech-blunders. The person who, according to Mayer's report, once said "Freuder" instead of "Freud," because shortly before he pronounced the name "Breuer (p. 38), and who at another time spoke of the Freuer-Breudian" method (p. 28), was certainly not particularly enthusiastic over this method. Later, under the mistakes in writing, I shall report a case of name disfigurement which certainly admits of no other explanation.[297]

---

[297] It may be observed that aristocrats in particular very frequently distort the names of the physicians they consult, from which we may conclude that inwardly they slight them, in spite of the politeness with which they are wont to greet them. I shall cite here some excellent observations concerning the forgetting of names from the works of Professor E. Jones, of Toronto : *Papers on Psycho-analysis*, chap. iii. p. 49 : —

"Few people can avoid feeling a twinge of resentment when they find that their name has been forgotten, particularly if it is by some one with whom they had hoped or expected it would be remembered. They instinctively realize if they had made a greater impression on the person's mind he would certainly have remembered them again, for the name is an integral part of the personality. Similarly, few things are more flattering to most people than to find themselves addressed by name by a great person where they could hardly have anticipated it. Napoleon,

As a disturbing element in these cases there is an intermingling of a criticism which be omitted, because at the time being it does not correspond to the intention of the speaker.

Or it may be just the reverse; the substituted name, or the adoption of the strange name, signifies an appreciation of the same. The identification which is brought about by mistake is equivalent to a recognition which for the moment must remain in the background. An experience of this kind from his schooldays is related by Dr. Ferenczi: —

"While in my first year at college I obliged to recite a poem before the whole class. It was the first experience of the kind in my life, but I was well prepared. As soon as I began my recitation I was dismayed at being disturbed by an outburst of laughter. The professor later explained to me this strange reception. I started by giving the title 'From the Distance,' which was correct, but instead of giving the name of the real author, I mentioned — my own. The name of the poet is Alexander Petöfi. The identity of the first name with my own favoured the interchange of names, but the real reason was surely the fact that I identified myself at that time with the celebrated poet-hero. Even consciously I entertained for him a love and respect which verged on adoration. The whole ambition-complex hides it under this faulty action."

A similar identification was reported to me concerning a young physician who timidly and reverently introduced himself to the celebrated Virchow with the following words: " I am Dr. Virchow." The surprised professor turned to him and asked, "Is your name also Virchow" I do not know how the ambitious young man justified his speech-blunder, whether he thought of the charming excuse that he imagined himself so insignificant next to this big man that his own name slipped from him, or whether I had the courage to admit that he hoped that he too would some day be as great a man Virchow, and that the professor should therefore, not treat him in too disparaging a

---

like most leaders of men, was a master of this art. In the midst of the disastrous campaign of France in 1814, he gave a proof of his memory in this direction. When in a town near Craonne, he recollected that he had met the mayor, De Bussy, over twenty years ago in the La Fère Regiment. The delighted De Bussy at once threw himself into his service with extraordinary zeal. Conversely, there is no surer of affronting some one than by pretending to forget his name; the insinuation is thus conveyed that the person is so unimportant in our eyes that we cannot be bothered to remember his name. This device is often exploited in literature. In Turgentev's *Smoke (p.* 255) the following passage occurs: " 'So you still find Baden entertaining, M'sieur — Litvinov.' Ratmirov always uttered Litvinov's surname with hesitation, every time, as though he had forgotten it, and could not at once recall it. In this way, as well as by the lofty flourish of his hat in saluting him, he meant to insult his pride." The same author, in his *Fathers and Children* (p. 107), writes : "The Governor invited Kirsanov and Bazarov to his ball, and within a few minutes invited them a second time, regarding them as brothers, and calling them Kisarov." Here the forgetting that he had spoken to them, the mistake in the names, and the inability to distinguish between the two young men, constitute a culmination of disparagement. Falsification of a name has the same signification as forgetting it; it is only a step towards complete amnesia."

manner. One or both of these thoughts may have put young man in an embarrassing position during the introduction.

Owing to very personal motives I must it undecided whether a similar interpretation may also apply in the case to be cited. At the International Congress in Amsterdam, in 1907 my theories of hysteria were the subject of a lively discussion. One of my most violent opponents, in his diatribe against me, repeatedly made mistakes in speech in such a manner that he put himself in my place and spoke name. He said, for example, "Breuer and I, as is well known, have demonstrated," etc., when he wished to say "Breuer and Freud." The name of this opponent does not show the slightest sound similarity to my own. From this example, as well as from other cases of interchanging names in speech-blunders, we are reminded of the fact that the speech-blunder can fully forego the facility afforded to it through similar sounds, and can achieve its purpose if only supported in content by concealed relations.

In other and more significant cases it is a self-criticism, an internal contradiction against one's own utterance, which causes the speech-blunder, and even forces a contrasting substitution for the one intended. We then observe with surprise how the wording of an assertion removes the purpose of the same, and how the error in speech lays bare the inner dishonesty. Here the *lapsus linguæ* becomes a mimicking form of expression, often, indeed, for the expression of what one does not wish to say. It is, thus a means of self-betrayal.

Brill, relates: "I had recently been consulted by a woman who showed many paranoid trends, and as she had no relatives who could co-operate with me, I urged her to enter a State hospital as a voluntary patient. She was quite willing to do so, but on the following day she told me that her friends with whom she leased an apartment objected to her going to a hospital as it would interfere with their plans, and so on. I lost patience and said: 'There is no use listening to your friends who know nothing about your mental condition; you are quite *incompetent* to take care of your own affairs.' I meant to say 'competent.' Here the *lapus linguæ* expressed my true opinion."

Favoured by chance the speech material often gives origin to examples of speech-blunders which serve to bring about an overwhelming revelation or a full comic effect, as shown by the following examples reported by Brill: —

"A wealthy but not very generous host invited his friends for an evening dance. Everything went well until about 11:30 P.M., when was an intermission, presumably for supper. To the great disappointment of most of the guests there was no supper; instead, they were regaled with thin sandwiches and lemonade. As it was close to Election day the conversation centered on the different candidates; and as the discussion grew warmer, one of the guests, an ardent admirer of the Progressive Party candidate, marked to the host: 'You may say what please about Teddy, but there is one thing can always be relied upon; he always gives you *a square meal,'* wishing to say *square deal.* The assembled guests burst into a roar of laughter to the great embarrassment of the speaker and the host, who fully understood each other."

"While writing a prescription for a woman who was especially weighed down by the financial burden of the treatment, I was interested to hear her say suddenly: 'Please do not give me *big bills,* because I cannot swallow them.' Of course she meant to say *pills.* "

The following example illustrates a rather serious case of self-betrayal through a mistake in talking. Some accessory details justify, full reproduction as first printed by Dr. A. A. Brill.[298]

"While walking one night with Dr. Frink we accidentally met a colleague, Dr. P., whom I had not seen for years, and of whose private life I knew nothing. We were naturally very pleased to meet again, and on my invitation he accompanied us to a café, where we spent about two hours in pleasant conversation. To my question as to whether he was married he gave a negative answer, and added, 'Why should a man like me marry?'

"On leaving the cafe, he suddenly turned to me and said: 'I should like to know what you would do in a case like this: I know a nurse who was named as co-respondent in a divorce case. The wife sued the husband for divorce and named her as co-respondent, and *he* got the divorce.' I interrupted him, saying, 'You mean *she* got the divorce.' He immediately corrected himself, saying, 'Yes, she got the divorce,' and continued to tell how the excitement of the trial had affected this nurse to such an extent that she became nervous and took to drink. He wanted me to advise him how to treat her.

"As soon as I had corrected his mistake I asked him to explain it, but, as is usually the case he was surprised at my question. He wanted to know whether a person had no right, to make mistakes in talking. I explained to him that there is a reason for every mistake and that if he had not told me that he was unmarried, I would say that he was the hero of the divorce case in question, and that the mistake showed that he wished he had obtained the divorce instead of his wife, so as not to obliged to pay alimony and to be permitted marry again in New York State.

"He stoutly denied my interpretation, but his emotional agitation, followed by loud laughter only strengthened my suspicions. To my appeal that he should tell the truth 'for science' sake he said, 'Unless you wish me to lie you must believe that I was never married, and hence your psychoanalytic interpretation is all wrong.' He, however, added that it was dangerous to be

---

[298] *Zentralb. f. Psychoanalyse,* ii., Jahrg. I. Cf. also Brill's *Psychanalysis: Its Theories and Practical Application,* p. 202. Saunders, Philadelphia and London.

with a person who paid attention to such little things. Then he suddenly remembered that he had another appointment and left us.

"Both Dr. Frink and I were convinced that my interpretation of his *lapsus linguæ* was correct, and I decided to corroborate or disprove it by further investigation. The next day I found a neighbour and old friend of Dr. P., who confirmed my interpretation in every particular. The divorce was granted to Dr. P.'s wife a few weeks before, and a nurse was named as co-respondent. A few weeks later I met Dr. P., and he told me that he was thoroughly convinced of the Freudian mechanisms."

The self-betrayal is just as plain in the following case reported by Otto Rank: —

A father who was devoid of all patriotic feeling and desirous of educating his children to be just as free from this superfluous sentiment, reproached his sons for participating in a patriotic demonstration, and rejected their reference to a similar behaviour of their uncle with these words: "You are not obliged to imitate him; why, he is an *idiot.*" The astonished features of the children at their father's unusual tone aroused him to the fact that he had made a mistake, and he remarked apologetically, "Of course I wished to say *patriot.*" When such a speech-blunder occurs in a serious squabble and reverses the intended meaning of one of the disputants, it at once puts him at a disadvantage with his adversary a disadvantage which the latter seldom fails to utilize.

This clearly shows that although people are unwilling to accept the theory of my conception and are not inclined to forego the convenience that is connected with the tolerance of a faulty action, they nevertheless interpret speech-blunders and other faulty acts in a manner similar to the one presented in this book. The merriment and derision which are sure to be evoked at the decisive moment through such linguistic mistakes speak conclusively against the generally accepted convention that such a speech-blunder is a *lapsus lingæ* and, psychologically of no importance. It was no less a man than the German Chancellor, Prince Bullow, who endeavoured to save the situation through such a protest when the wording of his defence of his Emperor (November 1907) turned into the opposite through speech-blunder.

"Concerning the present, the new epoch of Emperor Wilhelm II, I can only repeat what I said a year ago, that *it would be unfair and unjust to speak of a coterie of responsible advisers around our Emperor* (loud calls, 'Irresponsible !) — to speak of *irresponsible advisers*. Pardon the *lapsus linguæ*" (hilarity).

A nice example of speech-blunder, which aims not so much at the betrayal of the speaker as at the enlightenment of the listener outside the scene, is found in Wallenstein *(Piccolomini,* Act I, Scene 5), and shows us that the poet who here uses this means is well versed in the mechanism and intent of speech-blunders. In the preceding scene Max Piccolomini was passionately in favour of the ducal party, and was enthusiastic over the blessings of the peace which became known to him in the course of a journey while accompanying Wallenstein's daughter to the encampment. He leaves his father and the Court ambassador, Questenberg, in great consternation. The scene proceeds as follows: —

QUESTENBERG. Woe unto us! Are matters thus? Friend, should we allow him to go there with this false opinion, and not recall him at once in order to open his eyes instantly.

OCTAVIO *(rousing himself from profound meditation)*. He has already opened mine, and I see more than pleases me.

QUESTENBERG. What is it, friend ?

OCTAVIO. A curse on that journey!

QUESTENBERG. Why? What is it?

OCTAVIO. Come! I must immediately follow the unlucky trail, must see with my own eyes - come — *(Wishes to lead him away.)*

QUESTENBERG. What is the matter? Where ?

OCTAVIO *(urging)*. To *her!*

QUESTENBERG. To — ?

OCTAVIO *(corrects himself)*. To the duke! Let us go, etc,

The slight speech-blunder *to her* in place of *to him* is meant to betray to us the fact that the father has seen through his son's motive for espousing the other cause, while the courtier complains that "he speaks to him altogether in riddles."

Another example wherein a poet makes use of a speech-blunder was discovered by Otto Rank in Shakespeare. I quote Rank's report from the *Zentralblatt für Psychoanalyse,* I. 3." A poetic speech-blunder, very delicately motivated and technically remarkably utilized, which, like the one pointed out by Freud in Wallenstein *(Zur Psychopathologie des Alltagslebens,* 2nd Edition, p. 48), not only shows that poets knew the mechanism and sense of this error, but also presupposes an understanding of it on the part of the hearer, can be found in Shakespeare's *Merchant of Venice* (Act Ill, Scene 2). By the will of her fathers Portia was bound to select a husband through a lottery. She escaped all her distasteful suitors by lucky chance. When she finally found in Bassanio the suitor after her own heart, she had cause to fear lest he, too, should draw the unlucky lottery.' In the scene she would to tell him that even if he chose the wrong casket, he might, nevertheless, be sure of love. But she is hampered by her vow. In this mental conflict the poet puts these words in her mouth, which were directed to the welcome suitor: —

"There is something tells me (but it is not love),
I would not lose you; and you know yourself
Hate counsels not in such a quality.
But lest you should not understand me well
(And yet a maiden hath no tongue but thought),
I would detain you here some month or two,
Before you venture for me. I could teach you
How to choose right, but then I am forsworn
So will I never be; so may you miss me;
But if you do, you'll make me wish a sin,
That I had been forsworn. Beshrew your eyes,
They have overlooked me, and divided me:
One half of me is yours, the other half yours —
Mine own, I would say; but if mine, then yours —
And so all yours."

"Just the very thing which she would like to hint to him gently, because really she should keep it from him, namely, that even before the choice she is wholly his — that she loves him, the poet, with admirable psychologic sensitiveness, allows to come to the surface in the speech-blunder. It is through this artifice that he manages to allay the intolerable uncertainty of the lover as well as the like tension of the hearer concerning the outcome of the choice."

The interest merited by the confirmation of our conception of speech-blunders through the great poets justifies the citation of a third example which was reported by Dr. E. Jones in *Papers on Psycho-analysis,* p. 60.

"Our great novelist, George Meredith, in his masterpiece, *The Egoist,* shows an even finer understanding of the mechanism. The plot of the novel is, shortly, as follows: Sir Willoughby Patterne, an aristocrat greatly admired by his circle, becomes engaged to a Miss Constantia Durham. She discovers in him an intense egoism, which he skilfully conceals from the world, and to escape the marriage she elopes with a Captain Oxford. Some years later Patterne becomes engaged to a Miss Middleton, and most of the book is taken up with a detailed description of the conflict that arises in her mind on also discovering his egotism. External circumstances and her conception of honour hold her to her pledge, while he becomes more and more distasteful in her eyes. She partly confided in his cousin and secretary, Vernon Whitford, the man whom she ultimately marries, but from a mixture of motives stands aloof.

"In the soliloquy Clara speaks as follows: 'If some noble gentleman could see me as I am and not disdain to aid me! Oh I to be caught out of this prison

721

of thorns and brambles I cannot tear my own way out. I am a coward. A beckoning of a finger would change me, I believe. I could fly bleeding and through hootings to a comrade. . . . Constantia met a soldier. Perhaps she prayed and her prayer was answered. She did ill. But, oh, how I love her for it! His name was Harry Oxford. . . . She did not waver, she cut the links, she signed herself over. Oh, brave girl, what do you think of me? But I have no Harry Whitford; I am alone. . . .' The sudden consciousness that she had put another name for Oxford struck her a buffet, drowning her in crimson.

"The fact that both men's names end in 'ford' evidently renders the confounding of them more easy, and would by many be regarded as an adequate cause for this, but the real underlying motive for it is plainly indicated by the author. In another passage the same *lapsus* occurs, and is followed by the hesitation and change of subject that one is familiar with in psychoanalysis when a half-conscious complex is touched. Sir Willoughby patronizingly says of Whitford: 'False alarm. The resolution to do anything unaccustomed is quite beyond poor old Vernon.' Clara replies: 'But if Mr. Oxford — Whitford . . . your swans, coming sailing up the lake; how beautiful they look when they are indignant! I was going to ask you, surely men witnessing a marked admiration for some one else will naturally be discouraged? ' Sir Willoughby stiffened with sudden enlightenment.

In still another passage Clara, by another *lapsus,* betrays her secret wish that she was on a more intimate footing with Vernon Whitford. Speaking to a boy friend, she says, 'Tell Mr. Vernon — tell Mr. Whitford.' "

The conception of speech-blunders here defended can be readily verified in the smallest details. I have been able to demonstrate repeatedly that the most insignificant and most natural cases of speech-blunders have their good sense, and admit of the same interpretation as the more striking examples. A patient who, contrary to my wishes but with firm personal motives, decided upon a short trip to Budapest justified herself by saying that she was for only three days, but she blundered said for only three weeks. She, betrayed her secret feeling that, to spite me, she preferred spending three weeks to three days in that society which I considered unfit for her.

One evening, wishing to excuse myself for not having called for my wife at the theatre, I said: "I was at the theatre at ten minutes after ten." I was corrected: "You meant to say ten o'clock." Naturally I wanted to say before ten. After ten would certainly be no excuse. I had been told that the theatre programme read, "Finished before ten o'clock." We arrived at the theatre I found the foyer dark and the theatre empty. Evidently the performance was over earlier and my wife did not wait me. When I looked at the clock it still wanted five minutes to ten. I determined to make my case more favourable at home, and say that it was ten minutes to ten. Unfortunately, the speech-blunder spoiled the intent and laid bare my dishonesty, in which I acknowledged more than there really was to confess.

This leads us to those speech disturbances which can no longer be described as speech-blunders, for they do not injure the individual word., but affect the rhythm and execution of the entire speech, as, for example, the stammering and stuttering of embarrassment. But here, as in the former cases, it is the inner conflict that is betrayed to us through the disturbance in speech. I really do not believe that any one will make mistakes in talking in an audience with His Majesty, in a serious love declaration, or in defending one's name and honour before a jury; in short, people make no mistakes where *they are all there* as the saying goes. Even in criticizing an author's style we are allowed and accustomed to follow the principle of explanation, which we cannot miss in the origin of a single speech-blunder. A clear and unequivocal manner of writing shows us that here the author is in harmony with himself, but where we find a forced and involved expression aiming at more target, as appropriately expressed, we can thereby recognize the participation of an unfinished and complicated thought, or we can hear through it the stifle voice of the author's self-criticism. [299]

VI. Mistakes in Reading and Writing

That the same view-points and observation should hold true for mistakes in reading and writing as for lapses in speech is not at all surprising when one remembers the inner relation of these functions. I shall here confine myself to the reports of several carefully analysed examples and shall make no attempt to include all of the phenomena.

A. LAPSES IN READING.

(*a*) While looking over a number of the *Leipziger Illustrierten*, which I was holding obliquely, I read as the title of the front-page picture, "A Wedding Celebration in the Odyssey." Astonished and with my attention aroused, I moved the page into the proper position only to read correctly, "A Wedding Celebration in the Ostsee (Baltic Sea)." How did this senseless mistake in reading come about?

Immediately my thoughts turned to a book by Ruth, *Experimental Investigations of "Music Phantoms,"* etc., with which I had recently been

---

[299] "Ce qu'on conçoit bien
Sénonce clairement,
Et les mots pour le dire
Arrivent aisément."
Boileau, *Art Poétique.*

much occupied, as it closely touched the psychologic problems that are of interest to me. The author promised a work in the near future to be called *Analysis and Principles of Dream Phenomena.* No wonder that I, having just published an *Interpretation of Dreams*, awaited the appearance of this book with the most intense interest. In Ruth's work concerning music phantoms I found an announcement in the beginning of the table of contents of the detailed inductive proof that the old Hellenic myths and traditions originated mainly from slumber and music phantoms, from dream phenomena and from deliria. Thereupon I had immediately plunged into the text in order to find out whether he was also aware that the scene where Odysseus appears before Nausicaa was based upon the common dream of nakedness. One of my friends called my attention to the clever passage in G. Keller's *Grünem Heinrich*, which explains this episode in the Odyssey as an objective representation of the dream of the mariner straying far from home. I added to it the reference to the exhibition dream of nakedness.[300]

(*b*) A woman who is very anxious to get children always reads *storks* instead of *stocks*.

(*c*) One day I received a letter which contained very disturbing news. I immediately called my wife and informed her that poor Mrs. Wm. H. was seriously ill and was given up by the doctors. There must have been a false ring to the words in which I expressed my sympathy, as my wife grew suspicious, asked to see the letter, and expressed her opinion that it could not read as stated by me, because no one calls the wife byte husband's name. Moreover, the correspondent was well acquainted with the Christian name of the woman concerned. I defended my assertion obstinately and referred to the customary visiting-cards, on which a woman designates herself by the Christian name of her husband. I was finally compelled to take up the letter, and, as a matter of fact, we read therein "Poor W.M." What is more, I had even overlooked "Poor Dr. W. M." My mistake in reading signified a spasmodic effort, so to speak, to turn the sad news from the man towards the woman. The title between the adjective and the name did not go well with my claim that the woman must have been meant. That is why it was omitted in the reading. The motive for this falsifying was not that the woman was less an object of my sympathy than the man, but the fate of this poor man had excited my fears regarding another and nearer person who, I was aware, had the same disease.

(*d*) Both irritating and laughable is a lapse in reading to which I am frequently subject when I walk through the streets of a strange city during my vacation. I then read *antiquities* on every shop sign that shows the slightest resemblance to the word; this displays the questing spirit of the collector.

---

[300] *The Interpretation of Dreams*, p. 208.

(*e*) In his important work[301] Bleuler relates: "While reading I once had the intellectual feeling of seeing my name towlines below. To my astonishment I found only the words blood corpuscles. Of the many thousands of lapses in reading in the peripheral as well as in the central field of vision that I have analysed, this was the most striking case. Whenever I imagined that I saw my name, the word that induced this illusion usually showed a greater resemblance to my name than the word *blood corpuscles*. In most cases all the letters of my name had to be close together before I could commit such an error. In this case, however, I could readily explain the delusion of reference and the illusion. What I had just read was the end of a statement concerning a form of bad style in scientific works, a tendency from which I am not entirely free."

B. LAPSES IN WRITING.

(*a*) On a sheet of paper containing principally short daily notes of business interest, I found, to my surprise, the incorrect date, "Thursday, October 20th," bracketed under the correct date of the month of September. It was not difficult to explain this anticipation as the expression of a wish. A few days before I had returned fresh from my vacation and felt ready for any amount of professional work, but as yet there were few patients. On my arrival I had found a letter from a patient announcing her arrival on the 20th of October. As I wrote the same date in September may certainly have thought "X. ought to be here already; what a pity about that whole month!" and with this thought I pushed the current data month ahead. In this case the disturbing thought can scarcely be called unpleasant; therefore after noticing this lapse in writing, I immediately knew the solution. In the fall of the following year I experienced an entirely analogous and similarly motivated lapse in writing. E. Jones has made a study of similar cases, and found that most mistakes in writing dates are motivated.

(*b*) I received the proof sheets of my contribution to the annual report on neurology and psychiatry, and I was naturally obliged to review with special care the names of authors, which, because of the many different nationalities represented, offer the greatest difficulties to the compositor. As a matter of fact, I found some strange-sounding names still in need of correction; but, oddly enough, the compositor had corrected one single name in my manuscript, and with very good reason. I had written *Buckrhard*, which the compositor guessed to be *Burckhard*. I had praised the treatise of this obstetrician entitled *The Influence of Birth on the Origin of Infantile Paralysis*, and I was not conscious of the least enmity toward him. But an

---

[301] Bleuler, *Affektivität Suggestibilität,Paranoia*, p. 121, Halle. Marhold, 1906.

author in Vienna, who had angered me by an adverse criticism of my *Traumdeutung*, bears the same name. It was as if in writing the name Burckhard, meaning the obstetrician, a wicked thought concerning the other B. had obtruded itself. The twisting of the name, as I have already stated in regard to lapses in speech, often signifies a depreciation.[302]

(c) The following is seemingly a serious case of *lapsus calami*, which it would be equally correct to describe as an erroneously carried out action. I intended to withdraw from the postal savings bank the sum of 300 crowns, which I wished to send to an absent relative to enable him to take treatment at a watering-place. I noted that my account was 4,380 crowns, and I decided to bring it down to the round sum of 4,000 crowns, which was not to be touched in the near future. After making out the regular cheque I suddenly noticed that I had written not 380 crowns, as I had intended, but exactly 438 crowns. I was frightened at the untrustworthiness of my action. I soon realized that my fear was groundless, as I had not grown poorer than I was before. But I had to reflect for quite a while in order to discover what influence diverted me from my first intention without making itself known to my consciousness.

First I got on a wrong track: I subtracted 380 from 438, but after that I did not know what to do with the difference. Finally an idea occurred to me which showed me the true connection. 438 is exactly 10 per cent. of the entire account of 4,380 crowns! But the bookseller, too, gives a 10 per cent. discount! I recalled that a few days before I had selected several books, in which I was no longer interested, in order to offer them to the bookseller for 300 crowns. He thought the price demanded too high, but promised to give me a final answer within the next few days. If he should accept my first offer he would replace the exact sum that I waste spend on the sufferer. There is no doubt that I was sorry about this expenditure. The emotion at the realization of my mistakes can be more easily understood as a fear of growing poor through such outlays. But both the sorrow over this expense and the fear of poverty connected with it were entirely foreign to my consciousness; I did not regret this expense when I promised the sum, and would have laughed at the idea of any such underlying motive. I should probably not have assigned such feelings to myself had not my psychoanalytic practice made me quite familiar with the repressed elements of psychic life, and if I had not had a dream few days before which brought forth the same solution.

(d) Although it is usually difficult to find the person responsible for printers' errors, the psychological mechanisms underlying them are the same

---

[302] A similar situation occurs in *Julius Cæsar*, iii. 3:
"CINNA. Truly, my name is Cinna.
"BURGHER. Tear him to pieces! he is a conspirator.
"CINNA. I am Cinna the poet! not Cinna the conspirator.
"BURGHER. No matter; his name is Cinna; tear the name out of his heartand let him go."

as in other mistakes. Typographical errors also well demonstrate the fact that people are not at all indifferent to such trivialities as "mistakes, "and, judging by the indignant reactions of the parties concerned, one is forced to the conclusion that mistakes are not treated by the public at large as mere accidents. This state of affairs is very well summed up in the following editorial from the *New York Times* of April 14, 1913 Not the least interesting are the comments of the keen-witted editor, who seems to share our views: —

"A BLUNDER TRULY UNFORTUNATE.

"Typographical errors come only too frequently from even the best-regulated newspaper presses. They are always humiliating, often a cause of anger, and occasionally dangerous, but now and then they are distinctly amusing. This latter quality they are most apt to have when they are made in the office of a journalistic neighbour, a fact that probably explains why we can read with smiling composure an elaborate editorial apology which appears in the *Hartford Courant*.

"Its able political commentator tried the other day to say that, *unfortunately* for Connecticut, 'J. H. is no longer a Member of Congress. Printer and proof-reader combined to deprive the adverb of its negative particle. 'At least, the able political commentator so declares, and we wouldn't question his veracity for the world; but sorrowful experience has taught most of us that it's safer to get that sort of editorial disclaimer of responsibility into print before looking up the copy, and perhaps — just perhaps — the world-enlightener, who *knows* that he wrote *unfortunate*, because that is what he intended to write, didn't rashly chance the discovery of his own guilt before he convicted the composing-room of it.

"Be that as it may, the meaning of the sentence was cruelly changed, and a friend was grieved or offended. Not so long ago a more astonishing error than this one crept into a book review of ours — a very solemn and scientific book. It consisted of the substitution of the word 'caribou' for the word 'carbon' in a paragraph dealing with the chemical composition of the stars. In that case the writer's fierce self-exculpation is at least highly plausible, as it seems hardly possible that he wrote 'caribou' when he intended to write 'carbon,' but even he was cautious enough to make no deep inquiry into the matter."

(*e*) I cite the following case contributed by Dr. W. Stekel, forth authenticity of which I can vouch: "An almost unbelievable example of miswriting and misreading occurred in the editing of a widely circulated weekly. It concerned an article of defence and vindication which was written with much warmth and great pathos. The editor-in-chief of the paper read the article, while the author himself naturally read it from the manuscript and proof-sheets more than once. Everybody was satisfied, when the printer's reader suddenly noticed a slight error which had escaped the attention of all. There it was, plainly enough: 'Our readers will bear witness tithe fact that we have always acted in a *selfish* manner for the good of the community.' It is quite evident that it was meant to read *unselfish*. The real thoughts, however, broke through the pathetic speech with elemental force."

(*f*) The following example of misprinting is taken from a Western gazette: The teacher was giving an instruction paper on mathematical methods, and spoke of a plan "for the instruction of youth that might be carried out *ad libidinem*."

(*g*) Even the Bible did not escape misprints. Thus we have the "Wicked Bible," so called from the fact that the negative was left out of the seventh commandment. This authorized edition of the Bible was published in London in 1631, and it is said that the printer had to pay a fine of two thousand pounds for the omission.

Another biblical misprint dates back to the year 1580, and is found in the Bible of the famous library of Wolfenbuttel, in Hesse. In the passage in Genesis where God tells Eve that Adam shall be her master and shall rule over her, the German translation is "*Und er soll dein Herr sein.*"The word *Herr* (master) was substituted by *Narr*, which means fool. Newly discovered evidence seems to show that the error was a conscious machination of the printer's suffragette wife, who refused to be ruled by her husband.

(*h*) Dr. Ernest Jones reports the following case concerning A. A. Brill: "Although by custom almost a teetotaler, he yielded to a friend's importunity one evening, in order to avoid offending him, and took a little wine. During the next morning an exacerbation of an eye-strain headache gave him cause to regret this slight indulgence, and his reflection on the subject found expression in the following slip of the pen. Having occasion to write the name of a girl mentioned by a patient, he wrote not Ethel but Ethyl.[303] It happened that the girl in question was rather too fond of drink, and in Dr. Brill's mood at the time this characteristic of hers stood out with conspicuous significance."[304]

(*i*) A woman wrote to her sister, felicitating her on the occasion of taking possession of a new and spacious residence. A friend who was present noticed that the writer put the wrong address on the letter, and what was still more remarkable was the fact that she did not address it to the previous residence, but to one long ago given up, but which her sister had occupied when she first

---

[303] Ethyl alcohol is, of course, the chemical namefor ordinary alcohol.
[304] Jones, *Psycho-analysis*, p. 66.

married. When the friend called her attention to it the writer remarked, "You are right; but what in the world made me do this?" to which her friend replied: "Perhaps you begrudge her the nice big apartment into which she has just moved because you yourself are cramped for space, and for that reason you put her back into her first residence, where she was no better off than yourself." "Of course I begrudge her the new apartment," she honestly admitted. As an afterthought she added, "It is a pity that one is so mean in such matters."

(*k*) Ernest Jones reports the following example given to him by Dr. A. A. Brill. In a letter to Dr. Brill a patient tried to attribute his nervousness to business worries and excitement during the cotton crisis. He went on to say: "My trouble is all due to that d — frigid wave; there isn't even any seed to be obtained for new crops." He referred to a cold wave which had destroyed the cotton crops, but instead of writing "wave" he wrote "wife." In the bottom of his heart he entertained reproaches against his wife on account of her marital frigidity and childlessness, and he was not far from the cognition that the enforced abstinence played no little part in the causation of his malady.

Omissions in writing are naturally explained in the same manner as mistakes in writing. A remarkable example of omission which is of historic importance was reported by Dr. B. Dattner[305]. In one of the legal articles dealing with the financial obligations of both countries, which was drawn up in the year 1867 during the readjustment between Austria and Hungary, the word "effective" was accidentally omitted in the Hungarian translation. Dattner thinks it probable that the unconscious desire of the Hungarian law-makers to grant Austria the least possible advantages had something to do with this omission.

Another example of omission is the following related by Brill: "A prospective patient, who had corresponded with me relative to treatment, finally wrote for an appointment for a certain day. Instead of keeping his appointment he sent regrets which began as follows: 'Owing to *foreseen* circumstances I am unable to keep my appointment.' He naturally meant to write *unforeseen*. He finally came to me months later, and in the course of the analysis I discovered that my suspicions at the time were justified; there were no unforeseen circumstances to prevent his coming at that time; he was advised not to come to me. The unconscious does not lie."

Wundt gives a most noteworthy proof for the easily ascertained fact that we more easily make mistakes in writing than in speaking (*loc. cit.*, p. 374). He states: "In the course of normal conversation the inhibiting function of the will is constantly directed toward bringing into harmony the course of ideation with the movement of articulation. If the articulation following the

---

[305] *Zentralbl. f. Psychoanalyse,* i. 12.

ideas becomes retarded through mechanical causes, as in writing, such anticipations then readily make their appearance."

Observation of the determinants which favour lapses in reading gives rise to doubt, which I do not like to leave unmentioned, because I am of the opinion that it may become the starting-point of a fruitful investigation. It is a familiar fact that in reading aloud the attention of the reader often wanders from the text and is directed toward his own thoughts. The results of this deviation of attention are often such that when interrupted and questioned he cannot even state what he had read. In other words, he has read automatically, although the reading was nearly always correct. I do not think that such conditions favour any noticeable increase in the mistakes. We are accustomed to assume concerning a whole series of functions that they are most precisely performed when done automatically, with scarcely any conscious attention. This argues that the conditions governing attention in mistakes in speaking, writing, and reading must be differently determined than assumed by Wundt (cessation or diminution of attention). The examples which we have subjected to analysis have really not given us the right to take for granted a quantitative diminution of attention. We found what is probably not exactly the same thing, a disturbance of the attention through a strange obtruding thought.

VII. Forgetting of Impressions and Resolutions

If any one should be inclined to overrate the state of our present knowledge of mental life, all that would be needed to force him to assume a modest attitude would be to remind him of the function of memory. No psychologic theory has yet been able to account for the connection between the fundamental phenomena of remembering and forgetting; indeed, even the complete analysis of that which one can actually observe has as yet scarcely been grasped. To-day forgetting has perhaps grown more puzzling than remembering, especially since we have learned from the study of dreams and pathologic states that even what for a long time we believed forgotten may suddenly return to consciousness.

To be sure, we are in possession of some view-points which we hope will receive general recognition. Thus we assume that forgetting is a spontaneous process to which we may ascribe a certain temporal discharge. We emphasize the fact that, just as among the units of every impression or experience, in forgetting, too, a certain selection takes place among the existing impressions. We are acquainted with some of the conditions that underlie the tenaciousness of memory and the awakening of that which would otherwise remain forgotten. Nevertheless, we can observe in innumerable cases of daily life how unreliable and unsatisfactory our knowledge of the mechanism is. Thus we may listen to two persons exchanging reminiscences concerning the same outward impressions, say of a journey that they have taken together some time before. What remains most firmly in the memory of the one is often forgotten by the other, as if it had never occurred, even when there is not the slightest reason to assume that this impression is of greater psychic importance for the one than for the other. A great many of those factors which determine the selective power of memory are obviously still beyond our ken.

With the purpose of adding some small contribution to the knowledge of the conditions of forgetting, I was wont to subject to a psychologic analysis those cases in which forgetting concerned me personally. As a rule I took up only a certain group of those cases, namely, those in which the forgetting astonished me, because, in my opinion, I should have remembered the experience in question. I wish further to remark that I am generally not inclined to forgetfulness (of things experienced, not of things learned), and that for a short period of my youth I was able to perform extraordinary feats of memory. When I was a schoolboy it was quite natural for me to be able to repeat from memory the page of a book which I had read; and shortly before I entered the University I could write down practically verbatim the popular lectures on scientific subjects directly after hearing them. In the tension before the final medical examination I must have made use of the remnant of this ability, for in certain subjects I gave the examiners apparently automatic answers, which proved to be exact reproductions of the text-book, which I had skimmed through but once and then in greatest haste.

Since those days I have steadily lost control over my memory; of late, however, I became convinced that with the aid of a certain artifice I can recall far more than I would otherwise credit myself with remembering. For example, when, during my office hours, a patient states that I have seen him before and I cannot recall either the fact or the time, then I help myself by guessing — that is, I allow a number of years, beginning from the present time, to come to my mind quickly. Whenever this could be controlled by records of definite information from the patient, it was always shown that in over ten years[306] I have seldom missed it by more than six months. The same thing happens when I meet a casual acquaintance and, from politeness, inquire about his small child. When he tells of its progress I try to fancy how old the child now is. I control my estimate by the information given by the father, and at most I make a mistake of a month, and in older children of three months. I cannot state, however, what basis I have for this estimate. Of late I have grown so bold that I always offer my estimate spontaneously, and still run no risk of grieving the father by displaying my ignorance in regard to his offspring. Thus I extend my conscious memory by invoking my larger unconscious memory.

---

[306] In the course of the conference the details of the previous first visit return to consciousness.

I shall report some *striking* examples of forgetting which for the most part I have observed in myself. I distinguish forgetting of impressions and experiences, that is, the forgetting of knowledge, from forgetting of resolutions, that is, the forgetting of omissions. The uniform result of the entire series of observations I can formulate as follows: *The forgetting in all cases is proved to be founded on a motive of displeasure.*

A. FORGETTING OF IMPRESSIONS AND KNOWLEDGE.

(*a*) During the summer my wife once made me very angry, although the cause in itself was trifling. We sat in a restaurant opposite a gentleman from Vienna whom I knew, and who had cause to know me, and whose acquaintance I had reasons for not wishing to renew. My wife, who had heard nothing to the disrepute of the man opposite her, showed by her actions that she was listening to his conversation with his neighbours, for from time to time she asked me questions which took up the thread of their discussion. I became impatient and finally irritated. A few weeks later I complained to a relative about this behaviour on the part of my wife, but I was not able to recall even a single word of the conversation of the gentleman in the case. As I am usually rather resentful and cannot forget a single incident of an episode that has annoyed me, my amnesia in this case was undoubtedly determined by respect for my wife.

A short time ago I had a similar experience. I wished to make merry with an intimate friend over a statement made by my wife only a few hours earlier, but I found myself hindered by the noteworthy fact that I had entirely forgotten the statement. I had first to beg my wife to recall it to me. It is easy to understand that my forgetting in this case may be analogous to the typical disturbance of judgment which dominates us when it concerns those nearest to us.

(*b*) To oblige a woman who was a stranger in Vienna I had undertaken to procure a small iron safe for the preservation of documents and money. When I offered my services, the image of an establishment in the heart of the city where I was sure I had seen such safes floated before me with extraordinary visual vividness. To be sure, I could not recall the name of the street, but I felt certain that I would discover the store in a walk through the city, for my memory told me that I had passed it countless times. To my chagrin I could not find this establishment with the safes, though I walked through the inner part of the city in every direction. I concluded that the only thing left to do was to search through a business directory, and if that failed, to try to identify the establishment in a second round of the city. It did not, however, require so much effort; among the addresses in the directory I found one which immediately presented itself as that which had been forgotten. It was true that I had passed the show window countless times, each time, however, when I had gone to visit the M. family, who have lived a great many years in this identical building. After this intimate friendship had turned to an absolute estrangement, I had taken care to avoid the neighbourhood as well as the house, though without ever thinking of the reason for my action. In my walk through the city searching for the safe in the show window I had traversed every street in the neighbourhood but the right one, and I had avoided this as if it were forbidden ground.

The motive of displeasure which was at the bottom of my disorientation is thus comprehensible. But the mechanism of forgetting is no longer so simple as in the former example. Here my aversion naturally does not extend to the vendor of safes, but to another person, concerning whom I wish to know nothing, and later transfers itself from the latter to this incident where it brings about the forgetting. Similarly, in the case of *Burckhard* mentioned above, the grudge against the one brought about the error in writing the name of the other. The similarity of names which here established a connection between two essentially different streams of thought was accomplished in the showcase window instance by the contiguity of space and the inseparable environment. Moreover, this latter case was more closely knit together, for money played a great part in the causation of the estrangement from the family living in this house.

(c) The B. and R. Company requested me to pay a professional call on one of their officers. On my way to him I was engrossed in the thought that I must already have been in the building occupied by the firm. It seemed as if I used to see their signboard in a lower story while my professional visit was taking me to a higher story. I could not recall, however, which house it was nor when I had called there. Although the entire matter was indifferent and of no consequence, I nevertheless occupied myself with it, and at last learned in the usual roundabout way, by collecting the thoughts that occurred to me in this connection, that one story above the floor occupied by the firm B. and R. was the *Pension Fischer*, where I had frequently visited patients. Then I remembered the building which sheltered both the company and the *pension*.

I was still puzzled, however, as to the motive that entered into play in this forgetting. I found nothing disagreeable in my memory concerning the firm itself or the *Pension Fischer*, or the patients living there. I was also aware that it could not deal with anything very painful, otherwise I hardly would have been successful in tracing the thing forgotten in a roundabout way without resorting to external aid, as happened in the preceding example. Finally it occurred to me that a little before, while starting on my way to a new patient, a gentleman whom I had difficulty in recalling greeted me in the street. Some months previously I had seen this man in an apparently serious condition and had made the diagnosis of general paresis, but later I had learned of his recovery, consequently my judgment had been incorrect. Was it not possible that we had in this case a remission, which one usually finds in *dementia paralytica*? In that contingency my diagnosis would still be justified. The influence emanating from this meeting caused me to forget the neighbourhood of the B. and R. Company, and my interest to discover the thing forgotten was transferred from this case of disputed diagnosis. But the associative connection in this loose inner relation was effected by means of a similarity of names: the man who recovered, contrary to expectation, was also an officer of a large company that recommends patients to me. And the physician with whom I had seen the supposed paretic bore the name of Fischer, the name of the *pension* in the house which I had forgotten.

(*d*) Mislaying a thing really has the same significance as forgetting where we have placed it. Like most people delving in pamphlets and books, I am well oriented about my desk, and can produce what I want with one lunge. What appears to others as disorder has become for me perfect order. Why, then, did I mislay a catalogue which was sent to me not long ago so that it could not be found? What is more, it had been my intention to order a book which I found announced therein, entitled *Ueber die Sprache*, because it was written by an author whose spirited, vivacious style I like, whose insight into psychology and whose knowledge of the cultural world I have learned to appreciate. I believe that was just why I mislaid the catalogue. It was my habit to lend the books of this author among my friends for their enlightenment, and a few days before, on returning one, somebody had said: "His style reminds me altogether of yours, and his way of thinking is identical." The speaker did not know what he was stirring up with this remark. Years ago, when I was younger and in greater need of forming alliances, I was told practically the same thing by an older colleague, to whom I had recommended the writings of a familiar medical author. To put it in his words, "It is absolutely your style and manner." I was so influenced by these remarks that I wrote a letter to this author with the object of bringing about a closer relation, but a rather cool answer put me back "in my place." Perhaps still earlier discouraging experiences conceal themselves behind this last one, for I did not find the mislaid catalogue. Through this premonition I was actually prevented from ordering the advertised book, although the disappearance of the catalogue formed no real hindrance, as I remembered well both the name of the book and the author.

(*e*) Another case of mislaying merits our interest on account of the conditions under which the mislaid object was rediscovered. A younger man narrates as follows: "Several years ago there were some misunderstandings between me and my wife. I found her too cold, and though I fully appreciated her excellent qualities, we lived together without evincing any tenderness for each other. One day on her return from a walk she gave me a book which she had bought because she thought it would interest me. I thanked her for this mark of 'attention,' promised to read the book, put it away, and did not find it again. So months passed, during which I occasionally remembered the lost book, and also tried in vain to find it.

"About six months later my beloved mother, who was not living with us, became ill. My wife left home to nurse her mother-in-law. The patient's condition became serious and gave my wife the opportunity to show the best side of herself. One evening I returned home full of enthusiasm over what my wife had accomplished, and felt very grateful to her. I stepped to my desk and, without definite intention but with the certainty of a somnambulist, I opened a certain drawer, and in the very top of it I found the long-missing, mislaid book."

The following example of "misplacing" belongs to a type well known to every psychoanalyst. I must add that the patient who experienced this misplacing has himself found the solution of it.

This patient, whose psychoanalytic treatment had to be interrupted through the summer vacation when he was in a state of resistance and ill-health, put away his keys in the evening in their usual place, or so he thought. He then remembered that he wished to take some things from his desk, where he also had put the money which he needed on the journey. He was to depart the next day, which was the last day of treatment and the date when the doctor's fee was due. But the keys had disappeared.

He began a thorough and systematic search through his small apartment. He became more and more excited over it, but his search was unsuccessful. As he recognized this "misplacement" as a symptomatic act — that is, as being intentional — he aroused his servant in order to continue his search with the help of an " unprejudiced" person. After another hour he gave up the search and feared that he had lost the keys. The next morning he ordered new keys from the desk factory, which were hurriedly made for him. Two acquaintances who had been with him in a cab even recalled hearing something fall to the ground as he stepped out of the cab, and he was therefore convinced that the keys had slipped from his pocket. They were found lying between a thick book and a thin pamphlet, the latter a work of one of my pupils, which he wished to take along as reading matter for his vacation; and they were so skilfully placed that no one would have supposed that they were there. He himself was unable to replace the keys in such a position as to render them invisible. The unconscious skill with which an object is misplaced on account of secret but strong motives reminds one of "somnambulistic sureness." The motive was naturally ill-humour over the interruption of the treatment and the secret rage over the fact that he had to pay such a high fee when he felt so ill.

(*g*) Brill relates:[307] "A man was urged by his wife to attend a social function in which he really took no interest. Yielding to his wife's entreaties, he began to take his dress-suit from the trunk when he suddenly thought of shaving. After accomplishing this he returned to the trunk and found it locked. Despite a long, earnest search the key could not be found. A locksmith could not be found on Sunday evening, so that the couple had to send their regrets. On having the trunk opened the next morning the lost key was found within. The husband had absentmindedly dropped the key into the trunk and sprung the lock. He assured me that this was wholly unintentional and unconscious, but we know that he did not wish to go to this social affair. The mislaying of the key therefore lacked no motive."

Ernest Jones noticed in himself that he was in the habit of mislaying his pipe whenever he suffered from the effects of over-smoking. The pipe was then found in some unusual place where it did not belong and which it normally did not occupy.

If one looks over the cases of mislaying it will be difficult to assume that mislaying is anything other than the result of an unconscious intention.

(*h*) In the summer of 1901 I once remarked to a friend with whom I was then actively engaged in exchanging ideas on scientific questions: "These neurotic problems can be solved only if we take the position of absolutely accepting an original bi-sexuality in every individual." To which he replied: "I told you that two and a half years ago while we were taking an evening walk in Br. At that time you wouldn't listen to it."

It is truly painful to be thus requested to renounce one's originality. I could neither recall such a conversation nor my friend's revelation. One of us must be mistaken; and according to the principle of the question *cui prodest?* I must be the one. Indeed, in the course of the following weeks everything came back to me just as my friend had recalled it. I myself remembered that at that time I gave the answer: "I have not yet got so far, and I do not care to discuss it." But since this incident I have grown more tolerant when I miss any mention of my name in medical literature in connection with ideas for which I deserve credit.

It is scarcely accidental that the numerous examples of forgetting which have been collected without any selection should require for their solution the introduction of such painful themes as exposing of one's wife; a friendship that has turned into the opposite; a mistake in medical diagnosis; enmity on account of similar pursuits, or the borrowing of somebody's ideas. I am rather inclined to believe that every person who will undertake an inquiry into the

---

[307] Brill, *loc. cit.*, p. 197.

motives underlying his forgetting will be able to fill up a similar sample card of vexatious circumstances. The tendency to forget the disagreeable seems to me to be quite general; the capacity for it is naturally differently developed in different persons. Certain *denials* which we encounter in medical practice can probably be ascribed to *forgetting*.[308] Our conception of such forgetting confines the distinction between this and that behaviour to purely psychologic relations, and permits us to see in both forms of reaction the expression of the same motive. Of the numerous examples of denials of unpleasant recollection which I have observed in kinsmen of patients, one remains in my memory as especially singular.

A mother telling me of the childhood of her nervous son, now in his puberty, made the statement that, like his brothers and sisters, he was subject to bed-wetting throughout his childhood, a symptom which certainly has some significance in a history of a neurotic patient. Some weeks later, while seeking information regarding the treatment, I had occasion to call her attention to signs of a constitutional morbid predisposition in the young man, and at the same time referred to the bed-wetting recounted in the anamnesis. To my surprise she contested this fact concerning him, denying it as well for the other children, and asked me how I could possibly know this. Finally I let her know that she herself had told me a short time before what she had thus forgotten.[309]

---

[308] If we inquire of a person whether he suffered from luetic infection ten or fifteen years ago, we are only too apt to forget that psychically the patient has looked upon this disease in an entirely different manner than on, let us say, an acute attack of rheumatism. In the anamneses which parents give about their neurotic daughters, it is hardly possible to distinguish with any degree of certainty the portion forgotten from that hidden, for anything that stands in the way of the girl's future marriage is systematically set aside by the parents, that is, it becomes repressed. A man who had recently lost his beloved wife from an affection of the lungs reported to me the following case of misleading the doctor, which can only be explained by the theory of such forgetting. "As my poor wife's pleuritis had not disappeared after many weeks, Dr. P. was called in consultation. While taking the history he asked among others the customary questions whether there were any cases of lung trouble in my wife's family. My wife denied any such cases, and even I myself could not remember any. While Dr. P. was taking leave the conversation accidentally turned to excursions, and my wife said: 'Yes, even to Landgersdorf, where my poor brother lies buried, is a long journey.' This brother died about fifteen years ago, after having suffered for years from tuberculosis. My wife was very fond of him, and often spoke about him. Indeed, I recall that when her malady was diagnosed as pleurisy she was very worried and sadly remarked: 'My brother also died of lung trouble.' But the memory was so very repressed that even after the above-cited conversation about the trip to L. she found no occasion to correct her information concerning the diseases in her family. I myself was struck by this forgetting at the very moment she began to talk about Landgersdorf." A perfectly analogous experience is related by Ernest Jones in his work. A physician whose wife suffered from some obscure abdominal malady remarked to her: "It is comforting to think that there has been no tuberculosis in your family." She turned to him very astonished and said, "Have you forgotten that my mother died of tuberculosis, and that my sister recovered from it only after having been given up by the doctors?"

[309] During the days when I was first writing these pages the following almost incredible case of forgetting happened to me. On the 1st of January I examined my notes so that I could send out my bills. In the month of June I came across the name M ——l, and could not recall the person to whom it belonged. My surprise increased when I observed from my books that I

737

One also finds abundant indications which show that even in healthy, not neurotic, persons resistances are found against the memory of disagreeable impressions and the idea of painful thoughts.[310] But the full significance of this fact can be estimated only when we enter into the psychology of neurotic persons. One is forced to make such elementary defensive striving against ideas which can awaken painful feelings, a striving which can be put side by side only with the flight-reflex in painful stimuli, as the main pillar of the mechanism which carries the hysterical symptoms. One need not offer any objection to the acceptance of such defensive tendency on the ground that we frequently find it impossible to rid ourselves of painful memories which cling to us, or to banish such painful emotions as remorse and reproaches of conscience. No one maintains that this defensive tendency invariably gains the upper hand, that in the play of psychic forces it may not strike against factors which stir up the contrary feeling for other purposes and bring it about in spite of it.

As the architectural principle of the psychic apparatus we may conjecture a certain stratification or structure of instances deposited in strata. And it is quite possible that this defensive tendency belongs to a lower psychic instance, and

is inhibited by higher instances. At all events, it speaks for the existence and force of this defensive tendency, when we can trace it to processes such as those found in our examples of forgetting. We see then that something is forgotten for its own sake, and where this is not possible the defensive tendency misses the target and causes something else to be forgotten — something less significant, but which has fallen into associative connection with the disagreeable material.

---

treated the case in a sanatorium, and that for weeks I had called on the patient daily. A patient treated under such conditions is rarely forgotten by a physician in six months. I asked myself if it could have been a man — a paretic — a case without interest? Finally, the note about the fee received brought to my memory all the knowledge which strove to elude it. M ——l was a fourteen- year-old girl, the most remarkable case of my latter years, a case which taught me a lesson I am not likely ever to forget, a case whose upshot gave me many painful hours. The child became afflicted with an unmistakable hysteria, which quickly and thoroughly improved under my care. After this improvement the child was taken away from me by the parents. She still complained of abdominal pains which had played the part in the hysterical symptoms. Two months later she died of sarcoma of the abdominal glands. The hysteria, to which she was greatly predisposed, took the tumour-formation as a provocative agent, and I, fascinated by the tumultuous but harmless manifestations of hysteria, perhaps overlooked the first sign of the insidious and incurable disease.

[310] A. Pick ("Zur Psychologie des Vergessens bei Geistesund Nervenkranken," *Archiv. f. Kriminal-Anthropologie u. Kriminalistik*, von H. Gross) has recently collected a number of authors who realize the value of the influence of the affective factors on memory, and who more or less clearly recognize that a defensive striving against pain can lead to forgetting. But none of us has been able to represent this phenomenon and its psychologic determination as exhaustively, and at the same time as effectively, as Nietzsche in one of his aphorisms (*Fenseits von Gut und Bosen*, ii., *Haupstuck* 68) : "'I have done that,' says my Memory. 'I could not have done that,' says my Pride, and remains inexorable. Finally, my Memory yields."

The views here developed, namely, that painful memories merge into motivated forgetting with special ease, merits application in many spheres where as yet it has found no, or scarcely any, recognition. Thus it seems to me that it has not yet been strongly enough emphasized in the estimation of testimony taken in court,[311] where the putting of a witness under oath obviously leads us to place too great a trust on the purifying influence of his psychic play of forces. It is universally admitted that in the origin of the traditions and folklore of a people care must be taken to eliminate from memory such a motive as would be painful to the national feeling. Perhaps on closer investigation it may be possible to form a perfect analogy between the manner of development of national traditions and infantile reminiscences of the individual. The great Darwin has formulated a "golden rule" for the scientific worker from his insight into this pain-motive of forgetting.[312]

Almost exactly as in the forgetting of names, faulty recollections can also appear in the forgetting of impressions, and when finding credence they may be designated as delusions of memory. The memory disturbance in pathologic cases (in paranoia it actually plays the rôle of a constituting factor in the formation of delusions) has brought to light an extensive literature in which there is no reference whatever to its being motivated. As this theme also belongs to the psychology of the neuroses it goes beyond our present treatment. Instead, I will give from my own experience a curious example of memory disturbance showing clearly enough its determination through unconscious repressed material and its connection with this material.

While writing the latter chapters of my volume on the interpretation of dreams, I happened to be in a summer resort without access to libraries and reference books, so that I was compelled to introduce into the manuscript all kinds of references and citations from memory. These I naturally reserved for future correction. In the chapter on day-dreams I thought of the distinguished figure of the poor book-keeper in Alphonse Daudet's *Nabab*, through whom the author probably described his own day-dreams. I imagined that I distinctly remembered one fantasy of this man, whom I called Mr. Jocelyn, which he hatched while walking the streets of Paris, and I began to reproduce it from memory. This fantasy described how Mr. Jocelyn boldly hurled himself at a runaway horse and brought it to a standstill; how the carriage door opened and a great personage stepped from the coupé, pressed

---

[311] Cf. Hans Gross, *Kriminal Psychologie*, 1898.

[312] Darwin on forgetting. In Darwin's autobiography one finds the following passage that does equal credit to his scientific honesty and his psychologic acumen: "I had during many years followed a golden rule, namely, that whenever a published fact, a new observation or thought, came across me which was opposed to my general results, to make a memorandum of it without fail and at once; for I had found by experience that such facts and thoughts were far more apt to escape from the memory than favourable ones" (quoted by Jones, *loc. cit.*, p. 38).

Mr. Jocelyn's hand and said: "You are my saviour — I owe my life to you! What can I do for you?"

I assured myself that casual inaccuracies in the rendition of this fantasy could readily be corrected at home on consulting the book. But when I perused *Nabab* in order to compare it with my manuscript, I found to my very great shame and consternation that there was nothing to suggest such a dream by Mr. Jocelyn; indeed, the poor book-keeper did not even bear this name — he was called Mr. Joyeuse.

This second error then furnished the key for the solution of the first mistake, the faulty reminiscence. Joyeux, of which Joyeuse is the feminine form, was the only possible word which would translate my own name *Freud* into French. Whence, therefore, came this falsely remembered fantasy which I had attributed to Daudet? It could only be a product of my own, a day-dream which I myself had spun, and which did not become conscious, or which was once conscious and had since been absolutely forgotten. Perhaps I invented it myself in Paris, where frequently enough I walked the streets alone, and full of longing for a helper and protector, until Charcot took me into his circle. I had often met the author of *Nabab* in Charcot's house. But the provoking part of it all is the fact that there is scarcely anything to which I am so hostile as the thought of being some one's protégé. What we see of this sort of thing in our country spoils all desire for it, and my character is little suited to the rôle of a protected child. I have always entertained an immense desire to "be the strong man myself." And it had to happen that I should be reminded of such a, to be sure, never fulfilled, day-dream! Besides, this incident is a good example of how the restraint relation to one's ego, which breaks forth triumphantly in paranoia, disturbs and entangles us in the objective grasp of things.

Another case of faulty recollection which can be satisfactorily explained resembles the *fausse reconnaissance* to be discussed later. I related to one of my patients, an ambitious and very capable man, that a young student had recently gained admittance into the circle of my pupils by means of an interesting work, *Der Künstler, Versuch einer Sexualpsychologie.* When, a year and a quarter later, this work lay before me in print, my patient maintained that he remembered with certainty having read somewhere, perhaps in a bookseller's advertisement, the announcement of the same book even before I first mentioned it to him. He remembered that this announcement came to his mind at that time, and he ascertained besides that the author had changed the title, that it no longer read "*Versuch*" but "*Ansätze zu einer Sexualpsychologie.*"

Careful inquiry of the author and comparison of all dates showed conclusively that my patient was trying to recall the impossible. No notice of this work had appeared anywhere before its publication, certainly not a year and a quarter before it went to print. However, I neglected to seek a solution for this false recollection until the same man brought about an equally valuable renewal of it. He thought that he had recently noticed a work on "agoraphobia" in the show window of a bookshop, and as he was now looking for it in all available catalogues I was able to explain to him why his effort must remain fruitless. The work on agoraphobia existed only in his fantasy as an unconscious resolution to write such a book himself. His ambition to emulate that young man, and through such a scientific work to become one of my pupils, had led him to the first as well as to the second false recollection. He also recalled later that the bookseller's announcement which had occasioned his false reminiscence dealt with a work entitled *Genesis, Das Gesetz der* Zeugung ("Genesis, The Law of Generation"). But the change in the title as mentioned by him was really instigated by me; I recalled that I myself have perpetrated the same inaccuracy in the repetition of the title by saying "*Ansätze*" in place of "*Versuch*."

B. FORGETTING OF INTENTIONS.

No other group of phenomena is better qualified to demonstrate the thesis that lack of attention does not in itself suffice to explain faulty acts as the forgetting of intentions. An intention is an impulse for an action which has already found approbation, but whose execution is postponed for a suitable occasion. Now, in the interval thus created sufficient change may take place in the motive to prevent the intention from coming to execution. It is not, however, forgotten, it is simply revised and omitted.

We are naturally not in the habit of explaining the forgetting of intentions which we daily experience in every possible situation as being due to a recent change in the adjustment of motives. We generally leave it unexplained, or we seek a psychologic explanation in the assumption that at the time of execution the required attention for the action, which was an indispensable condition for the occurrence of the intention, and was then at the disposal of the same action, no longer exists. Observation of our normal behaviour towards intentions urges us to reject this tentative explanation as arbitrary. If I resolve in the morning to carry out a certain intention in the evening, I may be reminded of it several times in the course of the day, but it is not at all necessary that it should become conscious throughout the day. As the time for its execution approaches it suddenly occurs to me and induces me to make the necessary preparation for the intended action. If I go walking and take a letter with me to be posted, it is not at all necessary that I, as a normal not nervous individual, should carry it in my hand and continually look for a letter-box. As a matter of fact I am accustomed to put it in my pocket and give my thoughts free rein on my way, feeling confident that the first letter-box will attract my attention and cause me to put my hand in my pocket and draw out the letter.

This normal behaviour in a formed intention corresponds perfectly with the experimentally produced conduct of persons who are under a so-called "post-hypnotic suggestion" to perform something after a certain time.[313] We are accustomed to describe the phenomenon in the following manner: the suggested intention slumbers in the person concerned until the time for its execution approaches. Then it awakes and excites the action.

In two positions of life even the layman is cognizant of the fact that forgetting referring to intended purposes can in no wise claim consideration as an elementary phenomenon no further reducible, but realizes that it ultimately depends on unadmitted motives. I refer to affairs of love and military service. A lover who is late at the appointed place will vainly tell his sweetheart that unfortunately he has entirely forgotten their rendezvous. She will not hesitate to answer him: "A year ago you would not have forgotten. Evidently you no longer care for me" Even if he should grasp the above cited psychologic explanation, and should wish to excuse his forgetting on the plea of important business, he would only elicit the answer from the woman, who has become as keen-sighted as the physician in the psychoanalytic treatment, "How remarkable that such business disturbances did not occur before!" Of course the woman does not wish to deny the possibility of forgetting; but she believes, and not without reason, that practically the same inference of a certain unwillingness may be drawn from the unintentional forgetting as from a conscious subterfuge.

Similarly, in military service no distinction is recognized between an omission resulting from forgetting and one in consequence of intentional neglect. And rightly so. The soldier dares forget nothing that military service demands of him. If he forgets in spite of this, even when he is acquainted with the demands, then it is due to the fact that the motives which urge the fulfilment of the military exactions are opposed by contrary motives. Thus the one year's volunteer[314] who at inspection pleads forgetting as an excuse for not having polished his buttons is sure to be punished. But this punishment is small in comparison to the one he courts if he admits to his superiors that the motive for his negligence is because "this miserable menial service is altogether disgusting to me." Owing to this saving of punishment for economic reasons, as it were, he makes use of forgetting as an excuse, or it comes about as a compromise.

The service of women (as well as the military service of the State) demands that nothing relating to that service be subject to forgetting. Thus it

---

[313] Cf. Bernheim, *Neue Studien über Hypnotismus, Suggetion und Psychotherapie*, 1892.
[314] Young men of education who can pass the examination and pay for their maintenance serve one instead of two years' compulsory service.

but suggests that forgetting is permissible in unimportant matters, but in weighty matters its occurrence is an indication that one wishes to treat weighty matters as unimportant: that is, that their importance is disputed.[315] The view-point of psychic validity is in fact not to be contested here. No person forgets to carry out actions that seem important to himself without exposing himself to the suspicion of being a sufferer from mental weakness. Our investigations therefore can extend only to the forgetting of more or less secondary intentions, for no intention do we deem absolutely indifferent, otherwise it would certainly never have been formed.

As in the preceding functional disturbances, I have collected the cases of neglect through forgetting which I have observed in myself, and endeavoured to explain them. I have found that they could invariably be traced to some interference of unknown and unadmitted motives — or, as may be said, they were due to a counter- will. In a number of these cases I found myself in a position similar to that of being in some distasteful service: I was under a constraint to which I had not entirely resigned myself, so that I showed my protest in the form of forgetting. This accounts for the fact that I am particularly prone to forget to send congratulations on such occasions as birthdays, jubilees, wedding celebrations, and promotions to higher rank. I continually make new resolutions, but I am more than ever convinced that I shall not succeed. I am now on the point of giving it up altogether, and to admit consciously the striving motives. In a period of transition, I told a friend who asked me to send a congratulatory telegram for him, at a certain time when I was to send one myself, that I would probably forget both. It was not surprising that the prophecy came true. It is undoubtedly due to painful experiences in life that I am unable to manifest sympathy where this manifestation must necessarily appear exaggerated, for the small amount of my feeling does not admit the corresponding expression. Since I have learned that I often mistook the pretended sympathy of others for real, I am in rebellion against the conventions of expressing sympathy, the social expediency of which I naturally acknowledge. Condolences in cases of death are excepted from this double treatment; once I determine to send them I do not neglect them. Where my emotional participation has nothing more to do with social duty, its expression is never inhibited by forgetting

Cases in which we forget to carry out actions which we have promised to do as a favour for others can similarly be explained as antagonism to conventional duty and as an unfavourable inward opinion. Here it regularly proves correct, inasmuch as the only person appealed to believes in the

---

315 In Bernard Shaw's *Cæsar and Cleopatra*, Cæsar's indifference to Cleopatra is depicted by his being vexed on leaving Egypt at having forgotten to do something. He finally recollected what he had forgotten — to take leave of Cleopatra — this, to be sure, is in full accord with historical truth. How little Cæsar thought of the little Egyptian princess! Cited from Jones, *loc. cit.*, p. 50.

excusing power of forgetfulness, while the one requesting the favour has no doubt about the right answer: he has no interest in this matter, otherwise he would not have forgotten it.

There are some who are noted as generally forgetful, and we excuse their lapses in the same manner as we excuse those who are short-sighted when they do not greet us in the street.[316] Such persons forget all small promises which they have made; they leave unexecuted all orders which they have received; they prove themselves unreliable in little things; and at the same time demand that we shall not take these slight offences amiss — that is, they do not want us to attribute these failings to personal characteristics but to refer them to an organic peculiarity.[317] I am not one of these people myself, and have had no opportunity to analyse the actions of such a person in order to discover from the selection of forgetting the motive underlying the same. I cannot forego, however, the conjecture *per analogiam*, that here the motive is an unusual large amount of unavowed disregard for others which exploits the constitutional factor for its purpose.[318]

In other cases the motives for forgetting are less easy to discover, and when found excite greater astonishment. Thus, in former years I observed that of a great number of professional calls I only forgot those that I was to make on patients whom I treated gratis or on colleagues. The mortification caused by this discovery led me to the habit of noting every morning the calls of the day in a form of resolution. I do not know if other physicians have come to the same practice by a similar road. Thus we get an idea of what causes the so-called neurasthenic to make a memorandum of the communications he wishes to make to the doctor. He apparently lacks confidence in the reproductive capacity of his memory. This is true, but the scene usually proceeds in this manner. The patient has recounted his various complaints and inquiries at considerable length. After he has finished he pauses for a

---

[316] Women, with their fine understanding of unconscious mental processes, are, as a rule, more apt to take offence when we do not recognize them in the street, and hence do not greet them, than to accept the most obvious explanation, namely, that the dilatory one is short-sighted or so engrossed in thought that he did not see them. They conclude that they surely would have been noticed if they had been considered of any consequence.

[317] Dr. Ferenczi reports that he was a distracted person himself, and was considered peculiar by his friends on account of the frequency and strangeness of his failing. But the signs of this inattention have almost all disappeared since he began to practise psychoanalysis with patients, and was forced to turn his attention to the analysis of his own ego. He believes that one renounces these failings when one learns to extend by so much one's own responsibilities. He therefore justly maintains that distractedness is a state which depends on unconscious complexes, and is curable by psychoanalysis. One day he was reproaching himself for having committed a technical error in the psychoanalysis of a patient, and on this day all his former distractions reappeared. He stumbled while walking in the street (a representation of that *faux pas* in the treatment), he forgot his pocket-book at home, he was a penny short in his car fare, he did not properly button his clothes, etc.

[318] E. Jones remarks regarding this: "Often the resistance is of a general order. Thus a busy man forgets to mail a letter entrusted to him — to his slight annoyance — by his wife, just as he may 'forget' to carry out her shopping orders.

moment, then he pulls out the memorandum, and says apologetically, "I have made some notes because I cannot remember anything." As a rule he finds nothing new on the memorandum. He repeats each point and answers it himself: "Yes, I have already asked about that." By means of the memorandum he probably only demonstrates one of his symptoms, the frequency with which his resolutions are disturbed through the interference of obscure motives.

I am touching, moreover, on an affliction to which even most of my healthy acquaintances are subject, when I admit that especially in former years I had the habit of easily forgetting for a long time to return borrowed books, also that it very often happened that I deferred payments through forgetfulness. One morning not long ago I left the tobacco-shop where I make my daily purchase of cigars without paying. It was a most harmless omission, as I am known there and could therefore expect to be reminded of my debt the next morning. But this slight neglect, the attempt to contract a debt, was surely not unconnected with reflections concerning the budget with which I had occupied myself throughout the preceding day. Even among the so-called respectable people one can readily demonstrate a double behaviour when it concerns the theme of money and possession. The primitive greed of the suckling which wishes to seize every object (in order to put it in its mouth) has generally been only imperfectly subdued through culture and training.[319]

I fear that in all the examples thus far given I have grown quite commonplace. But it can be only a pleasure to me if I happen upon familiar matters which every one understands, for my main object is to collect everyday material and utilize it scientifically. I cannot conceive why wisdom, which is, so to speak, the sediment of everyday experiences, should be denied admission among the acquisitions of knowledge. For it is not the diversity of objects but the stricter method of verification and the striving for far-reaching connections which make up the essential character of scientific work.

---

[319]   For the sake of the unity of the theme I may here digress from the accepted classification, and add that the human memory evinces a particular partiality in regard to money matters. False reminiscences of having already paid something are often very obstinate, as I know from personal experience. When free sway is given to avaricious intent outside of the serious interests of life, when it is indulged in in the spirit of fun, as in card playing, we then find that the most honourable men show an inclination to errors, mistakes in memory and accounts, and without realizing how, they even find themselves involved in small frauds. Such liberties depend in no small part also on the psychically refreshing character of the play. The saying that in play we can learn a person's character may be admitted if we can add "the repressed character." If waiters ever make unintentional mistakes they are apparently due to the same mechanism. Among merchants we can frequently observe a certain delay in the paying out of sums of money, in payments of bills and the like, which brings the owner no profit and can be only understood psychologically as the expression of a counter-will against giving out money. Brill sums it up with epigrammatic keenness: "We are more apt to mislay letters containing bills than cheques" (Brill, *Psychoanalysis, its Theories and Practical Application*, p. 197).

We have invariably found that intentions of some importance are forgotten when obscure motives arise to disturb them. In still less important intentions we find a second mechanism of forgetting. Here a counter-will becomes transferred to the resolution from something else after an external association has been formed between the latter and the content of the resolution. The following example reported by Brill illustrates this: "A patient found that she had suddenly became very negligent in her correspondence. She was naturally punctual and took pleasure in letter-writing, but for the last few weeks she simply could not bring herself to write a letter without exerting the greatest amount of effort. The explanation was quite simple. Some weeks before she had received an important letter calling for a categorical answer. She was undecided what to say, and therefore did not answer it at all. This indecision in the form of inhibition was unconsciously transferred to other letters and caused the inhibition against letter-writing in general."

Direct counter-will and more remote motivation are found together in the following example of delaying: I had written a short treatise on the dream for the series *Grenzfragen des Nerven und* Seelenlebens, in which I gave an abstract of my book, *The Interpretation of Dreams*. Bergmann, the publisher, had sent me the proof sheets and asked for a speedy return of the same as he wished to issue the pamphlet before Christmas. I corrected the sheets the same night, and placed them on my desk in order to take them to the post office the next morning. In the morning I forgot all about it, and only thought of it in the afternoon at the sight of the paper cover on my desk. In the same way I forgot the proofs that evening and the following morning, and until the afternoon of the second day, when I quickly took them to a letter-box, wondering what might be the basis of this procrastination. Obviously I did not want to send them off, although I could find no explanation for such an attitude.

After posting the letter I entered the shop of my Vienna publisher, who put out my *Interpretation of Dreams*. I left a few orders; then, as if impelled by a sudden thought, said, "You undoubtedly know that I have written the 'Dream' book a second time?" "Ah!" he exclaimed, "then I must ask you to — —" "Calm yourself," I interposed; "it is only a short treatise for the Löwenfeld-Kurella collection." But still he was not satisfied; he feared that the abstract would hurt the sale of the book. I disagreed with him, and finally asked: "If I had come to you before, would you have objected to the publication?" "No; under no circumstances," he answered.

Personally I believe I acted within my full rights and did nothing contrary to the general practice; still it seems certain to me that a thought similar to that entertained by the publisher was the motive for my procrastination in dispatching the proof sheets.

This reflection leads back to a former occasion when another publisher raised some difficulties because I was obliged to take out several pages of the text from an earlier work on cerebral infantile paralysis, and put them unchanged into a work on the same theme in Nothnagel's handbook. There again the reproach received no recognition; that time also I had loyally informed my first publisher (the same who published *The Interpretation of Dreams*) of my intention.

However, if this series of recollections is followed back still farther it brings to light a still earlier occasion relating to a translation from the French, in which I really violated the property rights that should be considered in a publication. I had added notes to the text without asking the author's permission, and some years later I had cause to think that the author was dissatisfied with this arbitrary action.

There is a proverb which indicates the popular knowledge that the forgetting of intentions is not accidental. It says: "What one forgets once he will often forget again."

Indeed, we sometimes cannot help feeling that no matter what may be said about forgetting and faulty actions, the whole subject is already known to everybody as something self-evident. It is strange enough that it is still necessary to push before consciousness such well-known facts. How often I have heard people remark: "Please do not ask me to do this, I shall surely forget it." The coming true of this prophecy later is surely nothing mysterious in itself. He who speaks thus perceives the inner resolution not to carry out the request, and only hesitates to acknowledge it to himself.

Much light is thrown, moreover, on the forgetting of resolutions through something which could be designated as "forming false resolutions." I had once promised a young author to write a review of his short work, but on account of inner resistances, not unknown to me, I promised him that it would be done the same evening. I really had serious intentions of doing so, but I had forgotten that I had set aside that evening for the preparation of an expert testimony that could not be deferred. After I thus recognized my resolution as false, I gave up the struggle against my resistances and refused the author's request.

VIII. Erroneously Carried-Out Actions

I shall give another passage from the above-mentioned work of Meringer and Mayer (p. 981):

"Lapses in speech do not stand entirely alone. They resemble the errors which often occur in our other activities and are quite foolishly termed 'forgetfulness.'"

I am therefore in no way the first to presume that there is a sense and purpose behind the slight functional disturbances of the daily life of healthy people.[320]

If the lapse in speech, which is without doubt a motor function, admits of such a conception, it is quite natural to transfer to the lapses of our other motor functions the same expectation. I have here formed two groups of cases; all these cases in which the faulty effect seems to be the essential element — that is, the deviation from the intention — I denote as erroneously carried-out actions (*Vergreifen*); the others, in which the entire action appears rather inexpedient, I call "symptomatic and chance actions. But no distinct line of demarcation can be formed; indeed, we are forced to conclude that all divisions used in this treatise are or only descriptive significance and contradict the inner unity of the sphere of manifestation.

The psychologic understanding of erroneous actions apparently gains little in clearness when we place it under the head of "ataxia," and especially under "cortical ataxia." Let us rather try to trace the individual examples to their proper determinants. To do this I shall again resort to personal observations, the opportunities for which I could not very frequently find in myself .

(*a*) In former years, when I made more calls at the homes of patients than I do at present, it often happened, when I stood before a door where I should have knocked or rung the bell, that I would pull the key of my own house from my pocket, only to replace it, quite abashed. When I investigated in what patients' homes this occurred, I had to admit that the faulty action — taking out my key instead of ringing the bell — signified paying a certain tribute to the house where the error occurred. It was equivalent to the thought "Here I feel at home," as it happened only where I possessed the patient's regard. (Naturally, I never rang my own bell.)

The faulty action was therefore a symbolic representation of a definite thought which was not accepted consciously as serious; for in reality the neurologist is well aware that the patient seeks him only so long as he expects to be benefited by him and that his own excessively warm interest for his patient is evinced only as a means of psychic treatment.

An almost identical repetition of my experience is described by A. Maeder ("Contrib. à la psychopathologie de la vie quotidienne," *Arch.de Psychol.*, vi., 1906): " Il est arrivè a chacun de sortir son trousseau, ·en arrivant à la porte d'un ami particulièrement cher, de se surprendre pour ainsi dire, en train d'ouvrir avec sa clé comme chez soi. C'est un retard, puisqu'il faut sonner

---

[320] A second publication of Meringer has later shown me how very unjust I was to this author when I attributed to him so much understanding.

malgré tout, mais c'est une preuve qu'on se sent — ou qu'on voudrait se sentir — comme chez soi, auprès de cet ami."

Jones speaks as follows about the use of keys [321] "The use of keys is a fertile source of occurrences of this kind, of which two examples may be given. If I am disturbed in the midst of some engrossing work at home by having to go to the hospital to carry out some routine work, I am very apt to find myself trying to open the door of my laboratory there with the key of my desk at home, although the two keys are quite unlike each other. The mistake unconsciously demonstrates where I would rather be at the moment.

"Some years ago I was acting in a subordinate position at a certain institution, the front door of which was kept locked, so that it was necessary to ring for admission. On several occasions I found myself making serious attempts to open the door with my house key. Each one of the permanent visiting staff, of which I aspired to be a member, was provided with a key to avoid the trouble of having to wait at the door. My mistake thus expressed the desire to be on a similar footing and to be quite 'at home' there."

A similar experience is reported by Dr. Hans Sachs of Vienna: "I always carry two keys with me, one for the door of my office and one for my residence. They are not by any means easily interchanged, as the office key is at least three times as big as my house key. Besides, I carry the first in my trouser pocket and the other in my vest pocket. Yet it often happened that I noticed on reaching the door that while ascending the stairs I had taken out the wrong key. I decided to undertake a statistical examination; as I was daily in about the same emotional state when I stood before both doors, I thought that the interchanging of the two keys must show a regular tendency, if they were differently determined psychically. Observation of later occurrences showed that I regularly took out my house key before the office door. Only on one occasion was this reversed: I came home tired, knowing that I would find there a guest. I made an attempt to unlock the door with the, naturally too big, office key."

(b) At a certain time twice a day for six years I was accustomed to wait for admission before a door in the second story of the same house, and during this long period of time it happened twice (within a short interval) that I climbed a story higher. On the first of these occasions I was in an ambitious day-dream, which allowed me to "mount always higher and higher." In fact, at that time I heard the door in question open as I put my foot on the first step of the third flight. On the other occasion I again went too far "engrossed in thought." As soon as I became aware of it, I turned back and sought to snatch the dominating fantasy; I found that I was irritated over a criticism of

---

[321] Jones, *loc. cit.*, p. 79.

my works, in which the reproach was made that I "always went too far," which I replaced by the less respectful expression "climbed too high."

(c) For many years a reflex hammer and a tuning-fork lay side by side on my desk. One day I hurried off at the close of my office hours, as I wished to catch a certain train, and, despite broad daylight, put the tuning-fork in my coat pocket in place of the reflex hammer. My attention was called to the mistake through the weight of the object drawing down my pocket. Any one unaccustomed to reflect on such slight occurrences would without hesitation explain the faulty action by the hurry of the moment, and excuse it. In spite of that, I preferred to ask myself why I took the tuning-fork instead of the hammer. The haste could just as well have been a motive for carrying out the action properly in order not to waste time over the correction.

"Who last grasped the tuning-fork? " was the question which immediately flashed through my mind. It happened that only a few days ago an idiotic child, whose attention to sensory impressions I was testing, had been so fascinated by the tuning-fork that I found it difficult to tear it away from him. Could it mean, therefore, that I was an idiot? To be sure, so it would seem, as the next thought which associated itself with the hammer was *chamer* (Hebrew for "ass").

But what was the meaning of this abusive language? We must here inquire into the situation. I hurried to a consultation at a place on the Western railroad to see a patient who, according to the anamnesis which I received by letter, had fallen from a balcony some months before, and since then had been unable to walk. The physician who invited me wrote that he was still unable to say whether he was dealing with a spinal injury or traumatic neurosis — hysteria. That was what I was to decide. This could therefore be a reminder to be particularly careful in this delicate differential diagnosis. As it is, my colleagues think that hysteria is diagnosed far too carelessly where more serious matters are concerned. But the abuse is not yet justified. Yes, the next association was that the small railroad station is the same place in which, some years previous, I saw a young man who, after a certain emotional experience, could not walk properly. At that time I diagnosed his malady as hysteria, and later put him under psychic treatment; but it afterward turned out that my diagnosis was neither incorrect nor correct. A large number of the patient's symptoms were hysterical, and they promptly disappeared in the course of treatment. But back of these there was a visible remnant that could not be reached by therapy, and could be referred only to a multiple sclerosis. Those who saw the patient after me had no difficulty in recognizing the organic affection. I could scarcely have acted or judged differently, still the impression was that of a serious mistake; the promise of a cure which I had given him could naturally not be kept.

The mistake in grasping the tuning-fork instead of the hammer could therefore be translated into the following words: "You fool, you ass, get yourself together this time, and be careful not to diagnose again a case of hysteria where there is an incurable disease, as you did in this place years ago in the case of the poor man !" And fortunately for this little analysis, even if unfortunately for my mood, this same man, now having a very spastic gait, had been to my office a few days before, one day after the examination of the idiotic child.

We observe that this time it is the voice of self-criticism which makes itself perceptible through the mistake in grasping. The erroneously carried-out action is specially suited to express self-reproach. The present mistake attempts to represent the mistake which was committed elsewhere.

(d) It is quite obvious that grasping the wrong thing may also serve a whole series of other obscure purposes. Here is a first example: It is very seldom that I break anything. I am not particularly dexterous, but by virtue of the anatomic integrity of my nervous and muscular apparatus there are apparently no grounds in me for such awkward movements with undesirable results. I can recall no object in my home the counterpart of which I have ever broken. Owing to the narrowness of my study it has often been necessary for me to work in the most uncomfortable position among my numerous antique clay and stone objects, of which I have a small collection. So much is this true that onlookers have expressed fear lest I topple down something and shatter it. But it never happened. Then why did I brush to the floor the cover of my simple inkwell so that it broke into pieces? My inkstand is made of a flat piece of marble which is hollowed out for the reception of the glass inkwell; the inkwell has a marble cover with a knob of the same stone. A circle of bronze statuettes with small terra-cotta figures is set behind this inkstand. I seated myself at the desk to write, I made a remarkably awkward outward movement with the hand holding the pen-holder, and so swept the cover of the ink-stand, which already lay on the desk, to the floor.

It is not difficult to find the explanation. Some hours before my sister had been in the room to look at some of my new acquisitions. She found them very pretty, and then remarked: "Now the desk really looks very well, only the inkstand does not match. You must get a prettier one." I accompanied my sister out and did not return for several hours. But then, as it seems, I performed the execution of the condemned inkstand.

Did I perhaps conclude from my sister's words that she intended to present me with a prettier inkstand on the next festive occasion, and did I shatter the unsightly old one in order to force her to carry out her signified intention? If that be so, then my swinging motion was only apparently awkward; in reality it was most skilful and designed, as it understood how to avoid all the valuable objects located near it.

I actually believe that we must accept this explanation of the whole series of seemingly accidental awkward movements. It is true that on the surface these seem to show something violent and irregular, similar to spastic-ataxic movements, but on examination they seem to be dominated by some intention, and they accomplish their aim with a certainty that cannot be generally credited to conscious arbitrary motions. In both characteristics, the force as well as the sure aim, they show besides a resemblance to the motor manifestations of the hysterical neurosis, and in part also to the motor accomplishments of somnambulism, which here as well as there point to the same unfamiliar modification of the functions of innervation.

In latter years, since I have been collecting such observations, it has happened several times that I have shattered and broken objects of some value, but the examination of these cases convinced me that it was never the result of accident or of my unintentional awkwardness. Thus, one morning while in my bath-robe and straw slippers I followed a sudden impulse as I passed a room, and hurled a slipper from my foot against the wall so that it brought down a beautiful little marble Venus from its bracket. As it fell to pieces I recited quite unmoved the following verse from Busch:—

"Ach ! Die Venus ist perdü — [322]

Klickeradoms! — von Medici!"

This crazy action and my calmness at the sight of the damage is explained in the then existing situation. We had a very sick person in the family, of whose recovery I had personally despaired. That morning I had been informed that there was a great improvement; I know that I had said to myself, "After all she will live." My attack of destructive madness served therefore as the expression of a grateful feeling toward fate, and afforded me the opportunity of performing an "act of sacrifice," just as if I had vowed, "If she gets well I will give this or that as a sacrifice," That I chose the Venus of Medici as this sacrifice was only gallant homage to the convalescent. But even to-day it is still incomprehensible to me that I decided so quickly, aimed so accurately, and struck no other object in close proximity.

Another breaking, in which I utilized a penholder falling from my hand, also signified a sacrifice, but this time it was a pious offering to avert some evil. I had once allowed myself to reproach a true and worthy friend for no other reason than certain manifestations which I interpreted from his unconscious activity. He took it amiss and wrote me a letter in which he bade me not to treat my friends by psychoanalysis. I had to admit that he was right and appeased him with my answer. While writing this letter I had before me my latest acquisition-a small, handsome glazed Egyptian figure. I broke it in the manner mentioned, and then immediately knew that I had caused this

---

[322] Alas! the Venus of Medici is lost!

mischief to avert a greater one. Luckily, both the friendship and the figure could be so cemented that the break would not be noticed.

A third case of breaking had a less serious connection; it was only a disguised "execution," to use an expression from Th. Vischer's *Auch Einer*, of an object that no longer suited my taste. For quite a while I had carried a cane with a silver handle; through no fault of mine the thin silver plate was once damaged and poorly repaired. Soon after the cane was returned I mirthfully used the handle to angle for the leg of one of my children. In that way it naturally broke, and I got rid of it.

The indifference with which we accept the resulting damage in all these cases may certainly be taken as evidence for the existence of an unconscious purpose in their execution.

(*e*) As can sometimes be demonstrated by, analysis, the dropping of objects or the overturning and breaking of the same are very frequently utilized as the expression of unconscious streams of thought, but more often they serve to represent the superstitious or odd significances connected therewith in popular sayings. The meanings attached to the spilling of salt, the overturning of a wineglass, the sticking of a knife dropped to the floor, and so on, are well known. I shall discuss later the right to investigate such superstitious interpretations ; here I shall simply, observe that the individual awkward acts do not by any means always have the same meaning, but, depending on the circumstances, they serve to represent now this or that purpose.

Recently we passed through a period in my house during which an unusual number of glass and china dishes were broken. I myself largely contributed to this damage. This little endemic was readily explained by the fact that it preceded the public betrothal of my eldest daughter. On such festivities it is customary to break some dishes and utter at the same time some felicitating expression. This custom may signify a sacrifice or express any other symbolic sense.

When servants destroy fragile objects through dropping them, we certainly do not think in the first place of a psychologic motive for it; still, some obscure motives are not improb- able even here. Nothing lies farther from the uneducated than the appreciation of art and works of art. Our servants are dominated by a foolish hostility against these productions, especially when the objects, whose worth they do not realize ,become a source of a great deal of work for them. On the other hand, persons of the same education and origin employed in scientific institutions often distinguish themselves by great dexterity and reliability in the handling of delicate objects, as soon as they begin to identify themselves with their masters and consider themselves an essential part of the staff.

I shall here add the report of a young mechanical engineer, which gives some insight into the mechanism of damaging things. "Some time ago I worked with many others in the laboratory of the High School on a series of complicated experiments on the subject of elasticity. It was a work that we undertook of our own volition, but it turned out that it took up more of our time than we expected. One day, while going to the laboratory with F., he complained of losing so much time, especially on this day, when he had so many other things to do at home. I could only agree with him, and he added half jokingly, alluding to an incident of the previous week, 'Let us hope that the machine will refuse to work, so that we can interrupt the experiment and go home earlier.'

"In arranging the work, it happened that F. was assigned to the regulation of the pressure valve, that is, it was his duty to carefully open the valve and let the fluid under pressure flow from the accumulator into the cylinder of the hydraulic press. The leader of the experiment stood at the manometer and called a loud 'Stop!' when the maximum pressure was reached. At this command F. grasped the valve and turned it with all his force — to the left (all valves, without any exception, are closed to the right). This caused a sudden full pressure in the accumulator of the press, and as there was no outlet, the connecting pipe burst. This was quite a trifling accident to the machine, but enough to force us to stop our work for the day and go home.

"It is characteristic, moreover, that some time later, on discussing this occurrence, my friend F. could not recall the remark that I positively remember his having made."

Similarly, to fall, to make a misstep, or to slip need not always be interpreted as an entirely accidental miscarriage of a motor action. The linguistic double meaning of these expressions points to diverse hidden fantasies, which may present themselves through the giving up of bodily equilibrium. I recall a number of lighter nervous ailments in women and girls which made their appearance after falling without injury, and which were conceived as traumatic hysteria as a result of the shock of the fall. At that time I already entertained the impression that these conditions had a different connection, that the fall was already a preparation of the neurosis, and an expression of the same unconscious fantasies of sexual content which may be taken as the moving forces behind the symptoms. Was not this very thing meant in the proverb which says, "When a maiden falls, she falls on her back!"

We can also add to these mistakes the case of one who gives a beggar a gold piece in place of a copper or a silver coin. The solution of such mishandling is simple: it is an act of sacrifice designed to mollify fate, to avert evil, and so on. If we hear a tender mother or aunt express concern regarding the health of a child, directly before taking a walk during which she displays her charity, contrary to her usual habit, we can no longer doubt the sense of this apparently undesirable accident. In this manner our faulty acts make possible the practice of all those pious and superstitious customs which must shun the light of consciousness, because of the strivings against them of our unbelieving reason.

(f) That accidental actions are really intentional will find no greater credence in any other sphere than in sexual activity, where the border between the intention and accident hardly seems discernible, That an apparently clumsy movement may be utilized in a most refined way for sexual purposes I can verify by; a nice example from my own experience. In a friend's house I met a young girl visitor who excited in me a feeling of fondness which I had long believed extinct, thus putting me in a jovial, loquacious, and complaisant mood. At that time I endeavoured to find out how this came about, as a year before this same girl made no impression on me.

As the girl's uncle, a very old man, entered the room, we both jumped to our feet to bring him a chair which stood in the corner. She was more agile than I and also nearer the object, so that she was the first to take possession of the chair. She carried it with its back to her, holding both hands on the edge of the seat. As I got there later and did not give up the claim to carrying the chair, I suddenly stood directly back of her, and with both my arms was embracing her from behind, and for a moment my hands touched her lap. I naturally solved the situation as quickly as it came about. Nor did it occur to anybody how dexterously I had taken advantage of this awkward movement.

Occasionally I have had to admit to myself that the annoying, awkward stepping aside on the street, whereby for some seconds one steps here and there, yet always in the same direction as the other person, until finally both stop facing each other, that this "barring one's way" repeats an ill-mannered, provoking conduct of earlier times and conceals erotic purposes under the mask of awkwardness. From my psychoanalysis of neurotics I know that the so-called naïveté of young people and children is frequently only such a mask, employed in order that the subject may say or do the indecent without restraint.

W. Stekel has reported similar observations in regard to himself: "I entered a house and offered my right hand to the hostess. In a most remarkable way I thereby loosened the bow which held together her loose morning-gown. I was conscious of no dishonourable intent, still I executed this awkward movement with the agility of a juggler."

(g) The effects which result from mistakes of normal persons are, as a rule, of a most harmless nature. Just for this reason it would be particularly interesting to find out whether mistakes of considerable importance, which could be followed by serious results, as, for example, those of physicians or druggists, fall within the range of our point of view.

As I am seldom in a position to deal with active medical matters, I can only, report one mistake from my own experience. I treated a very old woman, whom I visited twice daily for several years. My medical activities were limited to two acts, which I performed during my morning visits: I dropped a few drops of an eye lotion into her eyes and gave her a hypodermic injection of morphine. I prepared regularly two bottles — a blue one, containing the eye lotion, and a white one, containing the morphine solution. While performing these duties my thoughts were mostly occupied with something else, for they had been repeated so often that the attention acted as if free. One morning I noticed that the automaton worked wrong; I had put the dropper into the white instead of into the blue bottle, and had dropped into the eyes the morphine instead of the lotion. I was greatly frightened, but then calmed myself through the reflection that a few drops of a *two per cent.* solution of morphine would not likely do any harm even if left in the conjunctival sac. The cause of the fright manifestly belonged elsewhere .

In attempting to analyse the slight mistake I first thought of the phrase, "to seize the old woman by mistake," which pointed out the short way to the solution. I had been impressed by a dream which a young man had told me the previous evening, the contents of which could be explained only on the basis of sexual inter- course with his own mother.[323] The strangeness of the fact that the Oedipus legend takes no offence at the age of Queen Jocasta seemed to me to agree with the assumption that in being in love with one's mother we never deal with the present personality, but with her youthful memory picture carried over from our childhood. Such incongruities always show themselves where one fantasy fluctuating between two periods is made conscious, and is then bound to one definite period.

Deep in thoughts of this kind, I came to my patient of over ninety; I must have been well on the way to grasp the universal character of the Oedipus fable as the correlation of the fate which the oracle pronounces, for I made a blunder in reference to or on the old woman. Here, again, the mistake was harmless; of the two possible errors, taking the morphine solution for the eye, or the eye lotion for the injection, I chose the one by far the least harmful. The question still remains open whether in mistakes in handling things which may cause serious harm we can assume an unconscious intention as in the cases here discussed.

The following case from Brill's experience corroborates the assumption that even serious mistakes are determined by unconscious intentions: "A physician received a telegram informing him that his aged uncle was very sick. In spite of important family affairs at home he at once repaired to that

---

[323] The Oedipus dream as I was wont to call it, because it contains the key to the understanding of the legend of King Oedipus. In the text of Sophocles the relation of such a dream is put in the mouth of Jocasta (cf. *The Interpretation of Dreams*, pp. 222-4, etc.).

distant town because his uncle was really his father, who had cared for him since he was one and a half years old, when his own father had died. On reaching there he found his uncle suffering from pneumonia, and, as the old man was an octogenarian, the doctors held out no hope for his recovery. 'It was simply a question of a day or two,' was the local doctor's verdict. Although a prominent physician in a big city, he refused to co-operate in the treatment, as he found that the case was properly managed by the local doctor, and he could not suggest anything to improve matters.

"Since death was daily expected, he decided to remain to the end. He waited a few days, but the sick man struggled hard, and although there was no question of any recovery, because of the many new complications which had arisen, death seemed to be deferred for a while. One night before retiring he went into the sick-room and took his uncle's pulse. As it was quite weak, he decided not to wait for the doctor, and administered a hypodermic injection. The patient grew rapidly worse and died within a few hours.

There was something strange in the last symptoms, and on later attempting to replace the tube of hypodermic tablets into the case, he found to his consternation that he had taken out the wrong tube, and instead of a small dose of digitalis he had given a large dose of hyoscine.

"This case was related to me by the doctor after he read my paper on the Oedipus Complex.[324] We agreed that this mistake was determined not only by his impatience to get home to his sick child, but also by an old resentment and unconscious hostility toward his uncle (father)."

It is known that in the more serious cases of psychoneuroses one sometimes finds self-mutilations as symptoms of the disease. That the psychic conflict may end in suicide can never be excluded in these cases. Thus I know from experience, which some day I shall support with convincing examples, that many apparently accidental injuries happening to such patients are really self-inflicted. This is brought about by the fact that there is a constantly lurking tendency to self-punishment, usually expressing itself in self-reproach, or contributing to the formation of a symptom, which skilfully makes use of an external situation. The required external situation may accidentally present itself or the punishment tendency may assist it until the way is open for the desired injurious effect.

Such occurrences are by no means rare even in cases of moderate severity, and they betray the portion of unconscious intention through a series of special features — for example, through the striking presence of mind which the patients show in the pretended accidents. [325]

---

[324] *New York Medical Journal*, September, 1912. Reprinted in large form as Chapter X of *Psychoanalysis*, etc., Saunders. Philadelphia.

[325] The self-inflicted injury which does not entirely tend toward self-annihilation has, moreover, no other choice in our present state of civilization than to hide itself behind the

I will report exhaustively one in place of many such examples from my professional experience. A young woman broke her leg below the knee in a carriage accident so that she was bedridden for weeks. The striking part of it was the lack of any manifestation of pain and the calmness with which she bore her misfortune. This calamity ushered in a long and serious neurotic illness, from which she was finally cured by psychotherapy. During the treatment I discovered the circumstances surrounding the accident, as well as certain impressions which preceded it. The young woman with her jealous husband spent some time on the farm of her married sister, in company with her numerous other brothers and sisters with their wives and husbands. One evening she gave an exhibition of one of her talents before this intimate circle; she danced artistically the "cancan," to the great delight of her relatives, but to the great annoyance of her husband, who afterward whispered to her, "Again you have behaved like a prostitute." The words took effect; we will leave it undecided whether it was just on account of the dance. That night she was restless in her sleep, and the next forenoon she decided to go out driving. She chose the horses herself refusing one team and demanding another. Her youngest sister wished to have her baby with its nurse accompany her, but she opposed this vehemently. During the drive she was nervous; she reminded the coachman that the horses were getting skittish, and as the fidgety animals really produced a momentary difficulty she jumped from the carriage in fright and broke her leg, while those remaining; in the carriage were uninjured. Although after the disclosure of these details we can hardly doubt that this accident was really contrived, we cannot fail to admire the skill which forced the accident to mete out a punishment so suitable to the crime. For as it happened "cancan" dancing with her became impossible for a long time.

Concerning self-inflicted injuries of my own experience, I cannot report anything in calm times, but under extraordinary: conditions I do not believe myself incapable of such acts. When a member of my family complains that he or she has bitten his tongue, bruised her finger, and so on, instead of the expected sympathy I put the question, "Why did you do that?" But I have most painfully squeezed my thumb, after a youthful patient acquainted me during the treatment with his intention (naturally not to be taken seriously) of marrying my eldest daughter, while I knew that she was then in a private hospital in extreme danger of losing her life.

One of my boys, whose vivacious temperament was wont to put difficulties in the management of nursing him in his illness, had a fit of anger one morning because he was ordered to remain in bed during the forenoon,

---

accidental, or to break through in a simulation of spontaneous illness. Formerly, it was a customary sign of mourning, at other times it expressed itself in ideas of piety and renunciation of the world.

and threatened to kill himself a way out suggested to him by the newspapers. In the evening he showed me a swelling on the side of his chest which was the result of bumping against the door knob. To my ironical question why he did it, and what he meant by, it, the eleven-year-old child explained, "That was my attempt at suicide which I threatened this morning." However, I do not believe that my views on self-inflicted wounds were accessible to my children at that time.

Whoever believes in the occurrence of semi-intentional self-inflicted injury — if this awkward expression be permitted — will become prepared to accept through it the fact that aside from conscious intentional suicide there also exists semi-intentional annihilation — with unconscious intention — which is capable of aptly utilizing a threat against life and masking it as a casual mishap. Such mechanism is by no means rare. For the tendency to self-destruction exists to a certain degree in many more persons than in those who bring it to completion. Self-inflicted injuries are, as a rule, a compromise between this impulse and the forces working against it, and even where it really comes to suicide the inclination has existed for a long time with less strength or as an unconscious and repressed tendency.

Even suicide consciously committed chooses its time, means, and opportunity; it is quite natural that unconscious suicide should wait for a motive to take upon itself one part of the causation and thus free it from its oppression by taking up the defensive forces of the person.[326] These are in no way idle discussions which I here bring up; more than one case of apparently accidental misfortune (on a horse or out of a carriage) has become known to me whose surrounding circumstances justified the suspicion of suicide.

For example, during an officers' horse-race one of the riders fell from his horse and was so seriously injured that a few days later he succumbed to his injuries. His behaviour after regaining consciousness was remarkable in more than one way, and his conduct previous to the accident was still more remarkable. He had been greatly depressed by the death of his beloved mother, had crying spells in the society of his comrades, and to his trusted friend had spoken of the *tædium vitæ*. He had wished to quit the service in

---

[326] The case is then identical with a sexual attack on a woman, in whom the attack of the man cannot be warded off through the full muscular strength of the woman because a portion of the unconscious feelings of the one attacked meets it with ready acceptance. To be sure, it is said that such a situation paralyses the strength of a woman; we need only add the reasons for this paralysis. Insofar the clever sentence of Sancho Panza, which he pronounced as governor of his island, is psychologically unjust (*Don Quixote*, vol. ii. chap. xlv). A woman hauled before the judge a man who was supposed to have robbed her of her honour by force of violence. Sancho indemnified her with a full purse which he took from the accused, but after the departure of the woman he gave the accused permission to follow her and snatch the purse from her. Both returned wrestling, the woman priding herself that the villain was unable to possess himself of the purse. Thereupon Sancho spoke: "Had you shown yourself so stout and valiant to defend your body (nay, but half so much) as you have done to defend your purse, the strength of Hercules could not have forced you."

759

order to take part in a war in Africa which had no interest for him.[327] Formerly a keen rider, he had later evaded riding whenever possible. Finally, before the horse-race, from which he could not withdraw, he expressed a sad foreboding, which most expectedly in the light of our conception came true. It may be contended that it is quite comprehensible without any further cause that a person in such a state of nervous depression cannot manage a horse as well as on normal days. I quite agree with that, only, I should like to look for the mechanism of this motor inhibition through "nervousness" in the intention of self-destruction here emphasized.

Dr. Ferenczi has left to me for publication the analysis of an apparently accidental injury by shooting which he explained as an unconscious attempt at suicide. I can only agree with his deduction:

"J. Ad., 22 years old, carpenter, visited me on the 18th of January, 1908. He wished to know whether the bullet which pierced his left temple March 20, 1907, could or should be removed by operation. Aside from occasional, not very severe, headaches, he felt quite well, also the objective examination showed nothing besides the characteristic powder wound on the left temple, so that I advised against an operation. When questioned concerning the circumstances of the case he asserted that he injured himself accidentally. He was playing with his brother's revolver, and *believing that it was not loaded* he pressed it with his left hand: against the left temple (he is not left-handed), put his finger on the trigger, and the shot went off. *There were three bullets in the six-shooter.*

"I asked him how he came to carry the revolver, and he answered that it was at the time of his army conscription, that he took it to the inn the evening before because he feared fights. At the army examination he was considered unfit for service on account of varicose veins, which caused him much mortification. He went home and played with the revolver. He had no intention of hurting himself, but the accident occurred. On further questioning, whether he was otherwise satisfied with his fortune, he answered with a sigh, and related a love affair with a girl who loved him in return, but nevertheless left him. She emigrated to America out of sheer avariciousness. He wanted to follow her, but his parents prevented him. His lady-love left on the 20th of January, 1907, just two months before the accident.

"Despite all these suspicious elements the patient insisted that the shot was an 'accident.' I was firmly convinced, however, that the neglect to find out whether the revolver was loaded before he began to play with it, as well

---

[327] It is evident that the situation of a battlefield is such as to meet the requirement of conscious suicidal intent which, nevertheless, shuns the direct way. Cf. in *Wallenstein* the words of the Swedish captain concerning the death of Max Piccolomini: "They say he wished to die."

as the self-inflicted injury, were psychically determined. He was still under the depressing effects of the unhappy love affair, and apparently wanted 'to forget everything' in the army. When this hope, too, was taken away from him he resorted to playing with the weapon — that is, to an unconscious attempt at suicide. The fact that he did not hold the revolver in the right but in the left hand speaks conclusively in favour of the fact that he was really only 'playing' — that is, he did not wish consciously to commit suicide."

Another analysis of an apparently accidental self-inflicted wound, detailed to me by an observer, recalls the saying, "He who digs a pit for others falls in himself."[328]

"Mrs. X., belonging to a good middle-class family, is married and has three children. She is somewhat nervous, but never needed any strenuous treatment, as she could sufficiently adapt herself to life. One day she sustained a rather striking though transitory disfigurement of her face in the following manner: She stumbled in a street that was in process of repair and struck her face against the house wall. The whole face was bruised, the eyelids blue and oedematous, and as she feared that something might happen to her eyes she sent for the doctor. After she was calmed I asked her, 'But why did you fall in such a manner? She answered that just before this accident she wanted her husband, who had been suffering for some months from a joint affection, to be very careful in the street, and she often had the experience that in some remarkable way those things occurred to her against which she warned others.

"I was not satisfied with this as the determination of her accident, and asked her whether she had not something else to tell me. 'Yes, just before the accident she noticed a nice picture in a shop on the other side or the street, which she suddenly desired as an ornament for her nursery, and wished to buy it at once. She thereupon walked across to the shop without looking at the street, stumbled over a heap of stones, and fell with her face against the wall without making the slightest effort to shield herself with her hands. The intention to buy the .picture was immediately forgotten, and she walked home in haste.'

"'But why were you not more careful?' I asked.

"'Oh!' she answered, 'perhaps it was only a punishment for that episode which I confided to you!'

"'Has this episode still bothered you?'

"'Yes, later I regretted it very much; I considered myself wicked, criminal, and immoral, but at the time I was almost crazy with nervousness.'

---

[328] "Selbstbestrafung wegen Abortus von Dr. J. E. G. van Emden," Haag (Holland), *Zentralb. f. Psychoanalyse*, ii, 12.

"She referred to an abortion which was started by a quack and had to be brought to completion by a gynecologist. This abortion was initiated with the consent of her husband, as both wished, on account of their pecuniary circumstances, to be spared from being additionally blessed with children.

"She said: 'I had often reproached myself with the words, "You really had your child killed," and I feared that such a crime could not remain unpunished. Now that you have assured me that there is nothing seriously wrong with my eyes I am quite assured I have already been sufficiently punished.'

"This accident, therefore, was, on the one hand, a retribution for her sin, but, on the other hand, it may have served as an escape from a more dire punishment which she had feared for many months. In the moment that she ran to the shop to buy the picture the memory of this whole history, with its fears (already quite active in her unconscious at the time she warned her husband), became overwhelming and could perhaps find expression in words like these: 'But why do you want an ornament for the nursery? — you who had your child killed! You are a murderer! The great punishment is surely approaching!'

"This thought did not become conscious, but instead of it she made use of the situation — I might say of the psychologic moment — to utilize in a commonplace manner the heap of stones to inflict upon herself this punishment. It was for this reason that she did not even attempt to put out her arms while falling and was not much frightened. The second, and probably lesser, determinant of her accident was obviously the self-punishment for her unconscious wish to be rid of her husband, who was an accessory to the crime in this affair. This was betrayed by her absolutely superfluous warning to be very careful in the street on account of the stones. For, just because her husband had a weak leg, he was very careful in walking."

If such a rage against one's own integrity and one's own life can be hidden behind apparently accidental awkwardness and motor insufficiency then it is not a big step forward to grasp the possibility of transferring the same conception to mistakes which seriously endanger the life and health of others. What I can put forward as evidence for the validity of this conception was taken from my experience with neurotics, and hence does not fully meet the demands of this situation. I will report a case in which it was not an erroneously carried-out action, but what may be more aptly termed a symbolic or chance action that gave me the clue which later made possible the solution of the patient's conflict.

I once undertook to improve the marriage relations of a very intelligent man, whose differences with his tenderly attached young wife could surely be traced to real causes, but as he himself admitted could not be altogether explained through them. He continually occupied himself with the thought of a separation, which he repeatedly rejected because he dearly loved his two small children. In spite of this he always returned to that resolution and sought no means to make the situation bearable to himself. Such an unsettlement of a conflict served to prove to me that there were unconscious and repressed motives which enforced the conflicting conscious thoughts, and in such cases I always undertake to end the conflict by psychic analysis. One day the man related to me a slight occurrence which had extremely frightened him. He was sporting with the older child, by far his favourite. He tossed it high in the air and repeated this tossing till finally he thrust it so high that its head almost struck the massive gas chandelier. Almost, but not quite, or say "just about!" Nothing happened to the child except that it became dizzy from fright. The father stood transfixed with the child in his arms, while the mother merged into an hysterical attack. The particular facility of this careless movement, with the violent reaction in the parents, suggested to me to look upon this accident as a symbolic action which gave expression to an evil intention toward the beloved child.

I could remove the contradiction of the actual tenderness of this father for his child by referring the impulse to injure it to the time when it was the only one, and so small that as yet the father had no occasion for tender interest in it. Then it was easy to assume that this man, so little pleased with his wife at that time, might have thought: "If this small being for whom I have no regard whatever should die, I would be free and could separate from my wife." The wish for the death of this much loved being must therefore have continued unconsciously. From here it was easy to find the way to the unconscious fixation of this wish.

There was indeed a powerful determinant in a memory from the patient's childhood: it referred to the death of a little brother, which the mother laid to his father's negligence, and which led to serious quarrels with threats of separation between the parents. The continued course of my patient's life, as well as the therapeutic success confirmed my analysis.

IX. Symptomatic and Chance Actions

The actions described so far, in which we recognize the execution of an unconscious intention, appeared as disturbances of other unintended actions, and hid themselves under the pretext of awkwardness. Chance actions, which we shall now discuss, differ from erroneously carried out actions only in that they disdain the support of a conscious intention and really need no pretext. They appear independently and are accepted because one does not credit them with any aim or purpose. We execute them "without thinking anything of them," "by mere chance," "just to keep the hands busy," and we feel confident that such information will be quite sufficient should one inquire as to their significance. In order to enjoy the advantage of this exceptional position these actions which no longer claim awkwardness as an excuse must fulfil certain conditions: they must not be striking, and their effects must be insignificant.

I have collected a large number of such "chance actions" from myself and others, and after thoroughly investigating the individual examples, I believe that the name "symptomatic actions" is more suitable. They give expression to something which the actor himself does not suspect in them, and which as a rule he has no intention of imparting to others, but aims to keep to himself. Like the other phenomena considered so far, they thus play the part of symptoms.

The richest output of such chance or symptomatic actions is above all obtained in the psychoanalytic treatment of neurotics. I cannot deny myself the pleasure of showing by two examples of this nature how far and how delicately the determination of these plain occurrences are swayed by unconscious thoughts. The line of demarcation between the symptomatic actions and the erroneously carried out actions is so indefinite that I could have disposed of these examples in the preceding chapter.

(*a*) During the analysis a young woman reproduced this idea which suddenly occurred to her. Yesterday while cutting her nails "she had cut into the flesh while engaged in trimming the cuticle." This is of so little interest that we ask in astonishment why it is at all remembered and mentioned, and therefore come to the conclusion that we deal with a symptomatic action. It was really the finger upon which the wedding-ring is worn which was injured through this slight awkwardness. It happened, moreover, on her wedding-day, which thus gives to the injury of the delicate skin a very definite and easily guessed meaning. At the same time she, also related a dream which alluded to the awkwardness of her husband and her anesthesia as a woman. But why did she injure the ring finger of her left hand when the wedding-ring is worn on the right? Her husband is a jurist, a "Doctor of Laws" (*Doktor der Rechte*, literally a Doctor of Rights), and her secret affection as a girl belonged to a physician who was jokingly called *Doktor der Linke* (literally, Doctor of Left). Incidentally a left-handed marriage has a definite meaning.

(b) A single young woman relates: "Yesterday, quite unintentionally, I tore a hundred-dollar note in two pieces and gave half to a woman who was visiting me. Is that, too, a symptomatic action?" After closer investigation the matter of the hundred-dollar note elicited the following associations: She dedicated a part of her time and her fortune to charitable work. Together with another woman she was taking care of the rearing of an orphan. The hundred dollars was the contribution sent her by that woman, which she enclosed in an envelope and provisionally deposited on her writing-desk.

The visitor was a prominent woman with whom she was associated in another act of charity. This woman wished to note the names of a number of persons to whom she could apply for charitable aid. There was no paper, so my patient grasped the envelope from her desk, and without thinking of its contents tore it in two pieces, one of which she kept, in order to have a duplicate list of names, and gave the other to her visitor.

Note the harmlessness of this aimless occurrence. It is known that a hundred-dollar note suffers no loss in value when it is torn, provided all the pieces are produced. That the woman would not throw away the piece of paper was assumed by the importance of the names on it, and there was just as little doubt that she would return the valuable content as soon as she noticed it.

But to what unconscious thought should this chance action, which was made possible through forgetfulness, give expression? The visitor in this case had a very definite relation to my patient and myself. It was she who at one time had recommended me as physician to the suffering girl, and if I am, not mistaken my patient considered herself indebted for this advice. Should this halved hundred-dollar note perhaps represent a fee for her mediation? That still remained enigmatic.

But other material was added to this beginning. Several days before a woman mediator of a different sort had inquired of a relative whether the gracious young lady wished to make the acquaintance of a certain gentleman, and that morning, some hours before the woman's visit, the wooing letter of the suitor arrived, giving occasion for much mirth. When therefore the visitor opened the conversation with inquiries regarding the health of my patient, the latter could well have thought: "You certainly found me the right doctor, but if you could assist me in obtaining the right husband (and a child) I should be still more grateful."

Both mediators became fused into one in this repressed thought, and she handed the visitor the fee which her fantasy was ready to give the other. This resolution became perfectly convincing when I add that I had told her of such chance or symptomatic actions only the previous evening. She then took advantage of the next occasion to produce an analogous action.

We can undertake a grouping of these extremely frequent chance and symptomatic actions according to their occurrence as habitual, regular under certain circumstances, and as isolated ones. The first group (such as playing with the watch-chain, fingering one's beard, and so on), which can almost serve as a characteristic of the person concerned, is related to the numerous tic movements, and certainly deserves to be dealt with in connection with the latter. In the second group I place the playing with one's cane, the scribbling with one's pencil, the jingling of coins in one's pocket, kneading dough and other plastic materials, all sorts of handling of one's clothing, and many other actions of the same order.

These playful occupations during psychic treatment regularly conceal sense and meaning to which other expression is denied. Generally the person in question knows nothing about it; he is unaware whether he is doing the same thing or whether he has imitated certain modifications in his customary playing, and he also fails to see or hear the effects of these actions. For example, he does not hear the noise which is produced by the jingling of coins, and he is astonished and incredulous when his attention is called to it. Of equal significance to the physician, and worthy of his observation, is everything that one does with his clothing often without noticing it. Every change in the customary attire, every little negligence, such as an unfastened button, every trace of exposure means to express something that the wearer of the apparel does not wish to say directly, usually he is entirely unconscious of it.

The interpretation of these trifling chance actions, as well as the proof for their interpretation, can be demonstrated every time with sufficient certainty from the surrounding circumstances during the treatment, from the themes under discussion, and from the ideas that come to the surface when attention is directed to the seeming accident. Because of this connection I will refrain from supporting my assertions by reporting examples with their analyses; but I mention these matters because I believe that they have the same meaning in normal persons as in my patients.

I cannot, however, refrain from showing by at least one example how closely an habitually accomplished symbolic action may be connected with the most intimate and important part of the life of a normal individual.[329]

"As Professor Freud has taught us, the symbolism in the infantile life of the normal plays a greater role than was expected from earlier psychoanalytic experiences. In view of this the following brief analysis may be of general interest, especially on account of its medical aspects.

"A doctor on rearranging his furniture in a new house came across a straight, wooden stethoscope, and, after pausing to decide where he should put it, was impelled to place it on the side of his writing-desk in such a position that it stood exactly between his chair and the one reserved for his patients. The act in itself was certainly odd, for in the first place the straight stethoscope served no purpose, as he invariably used a binaural one; and in the second place all his medical apparatus and instruments were always kept in drawers, with the sole exception of this one. However, he gave no thought to the matter until one day it was brought to his notice by a patient who had never seen a wooden stethoscope, asking him what it was. On being told, she

[329] "Beitrag zur Symbolik im Alltag von Ernest Jones," *Zentralb. f. Psychoanalyse,* i. 3, 1911.

asked why he kept it there. He answered in an offhand way that that place was as good as any other. This, however, started him thinking, and he wondered whether there had been an unconscious motive in his action. Being interested in the psychoanalytic method, he asked me to investigate the matter.

"The first memory that occurred to him was the fact that when a medical student he had been struck by the habit his hospital interne had of always carrying in his hand a wooden stethoscope on his ward visits, although he never used it. He greatly admired this interne, and was much attached to him. Later on, when he himself became an interne he contracted the same habit, and would feel very uncomfortable if by mistake he left the room without having the instrument to swing in his hand. The aimlessness of the habit was shown, not only by the fact that the only stethoscope he ever used was a binaural one, which he carried in his pocket, but also in that it was continued when he was a surgical interne and never needed any stethoscope at all.

"From this it was evident that the idea of the instrument in question had in some way or other become invested with a greater psychic significance than normally belongs to it — in other words, that to the subject it stood for more than it does for other people. The idea must have got unconsciously associated with some other one, which it symbolized, and from which it derived its additional fulness of meaning. I will forestall the rest of the analysis by saying what this secondary idea was — namely, a phallic one; the way in which this curious association had been formed will presently be related. The discomfort he experienced in hospital on missing the instrument, and the relief and assurance the presence of it gave him, was related to what is known as a 'castration-complex' — namely, a childhood fear, often continued in a disguised form into adult life, lest a private part of his body should be taken away from him, just as playthings so often were. The fear was due to paternal threats that it would be cut off if he were not a good boy, particularly in a certain direction. This is a very common complex, and accounts for a great deal of general nervousness and lack of confidence in later years.

"Then came a number of childhood memories relating to his family doctor. He had been strongly attached to this doctor as a child, and during the analysis long-buried memories were recovered of a double phantasy he had in his fourth year concerning the birth of a younger sister — namely, that she was the child (1) of himself and his mother, the father being relegated to the background, and (2) of the doctor and himself; in this he thus played both a masculine and feminine part.[330] At the time, when his curiosity was being aroused by the event, he could not help noticing; the prominent share taken

---

[330] Psychoanalytic research, with the penetration of infantile amnesia, has shown that this apparent precocity is a less abnormal occurrence than was previously supposed.

by the doctor in the proceedings, and the subordinate position occupied by the father: the significance of this for his later life will presently be pointed out.

"The stethoscope association was formed through many connections. In the first place, the physical appearance of the instrument —a straight, rigid, hollow tube, having a small bulbous summit at one extremity and a broad base at the other — and the fact of its being the essential part of the medical paraphernalia, the instrument with which the doctor performed his magical and interesting feats, were matters that attracted his boyish attention. He had had his chest repeatedly examined by the doctor at the age of six, and distinctly recollected the voluptuous sensation of feeling the latter's head near him pressing the wooden stethoscope into his chest, and of the rhythmic to-and-fro respiratory movement. He had been struck by the doctor's habit of carrying his stethoscope inside his hat; he found it interesting that the doctor should carry his chief instrument concealed about his person, always handy when he went to see patients, and that he only had to take off his hat (i.e., a part of his clothing) and 'pull it out.' At the age of eight he was impressed by being told by an older boy that it was the doctor's custom to get into bed with his women patients. It is certain that the doctor, who was young and handsome, was extremely popular among the women of the neighbourhood, including the subject's own mother. The doctor and his 'instrument' were therefore the objects of great interest throughout his boyhood.

"It is probable that, as in many other cases, unconscious identification with the family doctor had been a main motive in determining the subject's choice of profession. It was here doubly conditioned (1) by the superiority of the doctor on certain interesting occasions to the father, of whom the subject was very jealous, and (2) by the doctor's knowledge of forbidden topics[331] and his opportunity for illicit indulgence. The subject admitted that he had on several occasions experienced erotic temptations in regard to his women patients; he had twice fallen in love with one, and finally had married one.

"The next memory was of a dream, plainly of a homosexual-masochistic nature; in it a man, who proved to be a replacement figure of the family doctor, attacked the subject with a 'sword.' The idea of a sword, as is so frequently the case in dreams, represented the same idea that was mentioned above to be associated with that of a wooden stethoscope. The thought of a sword reminded the subject of the passage in the *Nibelung Saga*, where Sigurd sleeps with his naked sword (*Gram*) between him and Brunhilda, an incident that had always greatly struck his imagination.

---

[331] The term " medical questions" is a common periphrasis for " sexual questions."

"The meaning of the symptomatic act now at last became clear. The subject had placed his wooden stethoscope between him and his patients, just as Sigurd had placed his sword (an equivalent symbol) between him and the maiden he was not to touch. The act was a compromise-formation; it served both to gratify in his imagination the repressed wish to enter into nearer relations with an attractive patient (interposition of phallus), and at the same time to remind him that this wish was not to become a reality (interposition of sword). It was, so to speak, a charm against yielding to temptation.

"I might add that the following passage from Lord Lytton's *Richelieu* made a great impression on the boy:—

'Beneath the rule of men entirely great
The pen is mightier than the sword,' [332]

and that he became a prolific writer and uses an unusually large fountain-pen. When I asked him what need he had of this pen, he replied in a characteristic manner, 'I have so much to express.'

"This analysis again reminds us of the profound views that are afforded us in the psychic life through the 'harmless' and 'senseless' actions, and how early in life the tendency to symbolization develops."

I can also relate an experience from my psychotherapeutic practice in which the hand, playing with a mass of bread-crumbs, gave evidence of an eloquent declaration. My patient was a boy not yet thirteen years of age, who had been very hysterical for two years. I finally took him for psychoanalytic treatment, after a lengthy stay at a hydrotherapeutic institution had proved futile. My supposition was that he must have had sexual experiences, and that, corresponding to his age, he had been troubled by sexual questions; but I was cautious about helping him with explanations as I wished to test further my assumption. I was therefore curious as to the manner in which the desired material would evince itself in him.

One day it struck me that he was rolling something between the fingers of his right hand; he would thrust it into his pocket and there continue playing with it, then would draw it out again, and so on. I did not ask what he had in his hand; but as he suddenly opened his hand he showed it to me. It was bread-crumbs kneaded into a mass. At the next session he again brought along a mass, and in the course of our conversation, although his eyes were closed, modelled a figure with an incredible rapidity which excited my interest. Without doubt it was a manikin like the crudest prehistoric idols, with a head, two arms, two legs, and an appendage between the legs which he drew out to a long point.

This was scarcely completed when he kneaded the manikin together again: later he allowed it to remain, but modelled an identical appendage on

---

[332] Cf. Oldham's "I wear my pen as others do their sword."

the flat of the back and on other parts in order to veil the meaning of the first. I wished to show him that I had understood him, but at the same time I wanted to deprive him of the evasion that he had thought of nothing while actively forming these figures. With this intention I suddenly asked him whether he remembered the story of the Roman king who gave his son's envoy a pantomimic answer in his garden.

The boy did not wish to recall what he must have learned so much more recently than I. He asked if that was the story of the slave on whose bald skull the answer was written. I told him, " No, that belonged to Greek history," and related the following: "King Tarquinius Superbus had induced his son Sextus to steal into a Latin city. The son, who had later obtained a foothold in the city, sent a messenger to the king asking what steps he should take next. The king gave no answer, but went into his garden, had the question repeated there, and silently struck off the heads of the largest and most beautiful poppies. All that the messenger could do was to report this to Sextus, who understood his father, and caused the most distinguished citizens of the city to be removed by assassination."

While I was speaking the boy stopped kneading, and as I was relating what the king did in his garden, I noticed that at the words "silently struck" he tore off the head of the manikin with a movement as quick as lightning. He therefore understood me, and showed that he was also understood by me. Now I could question him directly, and gave him the information that he desired, and in a short time the neurosis came to an end.

The symptomatic actions which: we observe in inexhaustible abundance in healthy as well as in nervous people are worthy of our interest for more than one reason. To the physician they often serve as valuable indications for orienting himself in new or unfamiliar conditions; to the keen observer they often betray everything, occasionally even more than he cares to know. He who is familiar with its application sometimes feels like King Solomon, who, according to the Oriental legend, understood the language of animals.

One day I was to examine a strange young man at his mother's home. As he came towards me I was attracted by a large stain on his trousers, which by its peculiar stiff edges I recognized as one produced by albumen. After a moment's embarrassment the young man excused this stain by remarking that he was hoarse and therefore drank a raw egg, and that some of the slippery white of the egg had probably fallen on his clothes. To confirm his statements he showed the eggshell which could still be seen on a small plate in the room. The suspicious spot was thus explained in this harmless way; but as his mother left us alone I thanked him for having so greatly facilitated the diagnosis for me, and without further procedure I took as the topic of our discussion his confession that he was suffering from the effects of masturbation.

Another time I called on a woman as rich as she was miserly and foolish, who was in the habit of giving the physician the task of working his way through a heap of her complaints before he could reach the simple cause of her condition. As I entered she was sitting at a small table engaged in arranging silver dollars in little piles as she rose she tumbled some of the pieces of money to the floor. I helped her pick them up, but interrupted the recitation of her misery by remarking: "Has your good son-in-law been spending so much of your money again? " She bitterly denied this, only to relate a few moments later the lamentable story of the aggravation caused by her son-in-law's extravagances. And she has not sent for me since. I cannot maintain that one always makes friends of those to whom he tells the meaning of their symptomatic actions.

He who observes his fellow-men while at table will be able to verify in them the nicest and most instructive symptomatic actions.

Dr. Hans Sachs relates the following:—

"I happened to be present when an elderly, couple related to me partook of their supper. The lady had stomach trouble and was forced to follow a strict diet. A roast was put before the husband, and he requested his wife, who was not allowed to partake of this food, to give him the mustard. The wife opened the closet and took out the small bottle of stomach drops, and placed it on the table before her husband. Between the barrel-shaped mustard-glass and the small drop-bottle there was naturally no similarity through which the mishandling could be explained; yet the wife only noticed the mistake after her husband laughingly called her attention to it. The sense of this symptomatic action needs no explanation."

For an excellent example of this kind which was very skilfully utilized by the observer, I am indebted to Dr. Bernh. Dattner (Vienna):—

"I dined in a restaurant with my colleague H., a doctor of philosophy. He spoke about the injustice done to probationary students, and added that even before he finished his studies he was placed as secretary to the ambassador, or rather the extraordinary plenipotentiary Minister to Chili [*sic*]. 'But,' he added, 'the minister was afterwards transferred, and I did not make any effort to meet the newly appointed.' While uttering the last sentence he was lifting a piece of pie to his mouth, but he let it drop as if out of awkwardness. I immediately grasped the hidden sense of this symptomatic action, and remarked to my colleague, who was unacquainted with psychoanalysis, 'You really allowed a very choice morsel to slip from you.' He did not realize, however, that my words could equally refer to his symptomatic action, and he repeated the same words I uttered with a peculiarly agreeable and surprising vividness, as if I had actually -taken the words from his mouth: 'It was really a very choice morsel that I allowed to get away from me.' He then followed this remark with a detailed description of his clumsiness, which has cost him this very remunerative position.

"The sense of this symbolic action becomes clearer if we remember that my colleague had scruples about telling me, almost a perfect stranger, concerning his precarious material situation, and his repressed thought took on the mask of symptomatic action which expressed symbolically what was meant to be concealed, and the speaker thus got relief from his unconscious."

That the taking away or taking along things without any apparent intention may prove to be senseful [sic] may be shown by the following examples .

1. Dr. B. Dattner relates: "An acquaintance paid the first after-marriage visit to a highly regarded lady friend of his youth. He told me of this visit and expressed his surprise at the fact that he failed in his resolution to visit with her only a short time, and then reported to me a rather strange faulty act which happened to him there.

"The husband of this friend, who took part in the conversation, was looking for a box of matches which he was sure was on the table when he came there. My acquaintance, too, looked through his pockets to ascertain whether he had not put it in his pocket, but without avail. Some time later he actually found it in his pocket, and was struck by the fact that there was only one match in the box.

"A dream a few days later showing the box symbolism in reference to the friend of his youth confirmed my explanation. With the symptomatic action my acquaintance meant to announce his priority-right and the exclusiveness of his possession (it contained only one match)."

Dr. Hans Sachs relates the following: "Our cook is very fond of a certain kind of pie. There is no possible doubt about this, as it is the only kind of pastry which she always prepares well. One Sunday she brought this pie to the table, took it off the pie-plate, and proceeded to remove the dishes used in the former course, but on the top of this pile she placed the pie, and disappeared with it into the kitchen.

We first thought that she had something to improve on the pie, but as she failed to appear my wife rang the bell and asked, 'Betty, what happened to the pie?' to which the girl answered, without comprehending the question, 'How is that?' We had to call her attention to the fact that she carried the pie back to the kitchen. She had put it on the pile of dishes, taken it out, and put it away 'without noticing it.'

"The next day, when we were about to consume the rest of the pie, my wife noticed that there was as much of it as we had left the day before — that is, the girl had disdained to eat the portion of her favourite dish which was rightly hers. Questioned why she did not eat the pie, she answered, somewhat embarrassed, that she did not care for it.

"The infantile attitude is distinctly noticeable on both occasions — first the childish insatiableness in refusing to share with anybody the object of her wishes, then the reaction of spite which is just as childish: 'If you grudge it to me, keep it for yourself, I want nothing of it.' "

Chance or symptomatic actions occurring in affairs of married life have often a most serious significance, and could lead those who do not concern themselves with the psychology of the unconscious to a belief in omens. It is not an auspicious beginning if a young woman loses her wedding-ring on her wedding-tour, even if it were only mislaid and soon found.

I know a woman, now divorced, who in the management of her business affairs frequently signed her maiden name many years before she actually resumed it.

Once I was the guest of a newly married couple and heard the young woman laughingly relate her latest experience, how, on the day succeeding her return from the wedding tour she had sought out her single sister in order to go shopping with her as in former times, while her husband was attending business. Suddenly she noticed a man on the opposite side of the street; nudging her sister she said, "Why, that is surely Mr. L." She forgot that for some weeks this man had been her husband. I was chilled at this tale, but I did not dare draw any inferences. The little story came back to me only several years later, after this marriage had ended most unhappily .

The following observation, which could as well have found a place among the examples of forgetting, was taken from a noteworthy work published in French by A. Maeder.[333]

"Une dame nous racontait récement qu'elle avait oublie d'essayer sa robe de noce et s'en souvint la veille du marriage, à huit heur du soir, la couturière désespérait de voir sa cliente. Ce détail suffit à montrer que la fiancée ne se sentait pas très hereuse de porter une robe d'épouse, elle cherchait à oublier cette représentation pénible. Elle est aujourd'hui . . . divorcée."

A friend who has learned to observe signs related to me that the great actress Eleanora Duse introduces a symptomatic action into one of her rôles which shows very nicely from what depth she draws her acting. It is a drama dealing with adultery; she has just been discussing with her husband and now stands soliloquizing before the seducer makes his appearance. During this short interval she plays with her wedding-ring, she pulls it off, replaces it, and finally takes it off again. She is now ready for the other.

I know of an elderly man who married a young girl, and instead of starting at once on his wedding tour he decided to spend the night in a hotel. Scarcely had they reached the hotel, when he noticed with fright that he was without

---

[333] Maeder, "Contribution a la psychologie de la vie quotidienne," *Arch. des psychologie,* T. vi. 1906.

his wallet, in which he had the entire sum of money for the wedding tour; he must have mislaid or lost it. He was still able to reach his servant by telephone; the latter found the missing article in the coat discarded for the travelling clothes and brought it to the hotel to the waiting bridegroom, who had thus entered upon his marriage without means.

It is consoling to think that the "losing of objects" by people is merely an unsuspected extension of a symptomatic action, and is thus welcome at least to the secret intention of the loser. Often it is only an expression of slight appreciation of the lost article, a secret dislike for the same, or perhaps for the person from whom it came, or the desire to lose this object was transferred to it from other and more important objects through symbolic association. The loss of valuable articles serves as an expression of diverse feelings; it may either symbolically represent a repressed thought — that is, it may bring back a memory which one would rather not hear — of it may represent a sacrifice to the obscure forces of fate, the worship of which is not yet entirely extinct even with us. [334]

---

[334] Here is another small collection of various symptomatic actions in normal and neurotic persons. An elderly colleague who does not like to lose at cards had to pay one evening a large sum of money in consequence of his losses; he did this without complaint, but with a peculiar constrained temper. After his departure it was discovered that he had left at this place practically everything he had with him, spectacles, cigar-case, and handkerchief. That would be readily translated into the words: "You robbers, you have nicely plundered me." A man who suffers from occasional sexual impotence, which has its origin in the intimacy of his infantile relations to his mother, relates that he is in the habit of embellishing pamphlets and notes with an S, the initial of his mother's name. He cannot bear the idea of having letters from home come in contact with other unsanctified correspondence, and therefore finds it necessary to keep the former separate. A young woman suddenly flings open the door of the consulting-room while her predecessor is still present. She excused herself on the ground of "thoughtlessness"; it soon came to light that she demonstrated her curiosity which caused her at an earlier time to intrude into the bedroom of her parents. Girls who are proud of their beautiful hair know so well how to manipulate combs and hairpins, that in the midst of conversation their hair becomes loosened. During the treatment (in a reclining position) some men scatter change from their pockets and thus pay for the hour of treatment; the amount scattered is in proportion to their estimation of the work. Whoever forgets articles in the doctor's office, such as eye-glasses, gloves, handbags, generally indicates that he cannot tear himself away and is anxious to return soon. Ernest Jones says: "One can almost measure the success with which a physician is practising psychotherapy, for instance, by the size of the collection of umbrellas, handkerchiefs, purses, and so on, that he could make in a month. The slightest habits and acts performed with a minimum of attention, such as the winding of a clock before retiring to sleep, the putting out of lights before leaving the room, and similar actions, are occasionally subject to disturbances which clearly demonstrate the influence of the unconscious complex, and what is thought to be the strongest "habits." In the journal *Coenobium*, Maeder relates about a hospital physician who, on account of an important matter, desired to get to the city that evening, although he was on duty and had no right to leave the hospital. On his return he noticed to his surprise that there was a light in his room. On leaving the room he had forgotten to put it out, something that had never happened before. But he soon grasped the motive of this forgetting. The hospital superintendent who lived in the same house must have concluded from the light in the room that he was at home. A man overburdened with worries and subject to occasional depressions assured me that he regularly forgot to wind his watch on those evenings when life seemed too hard and unfriendly. In this omission to wind his watch he symbolically expressed that it was a matter of indifference to him whether he lived to see the next day. Another man who was personally unknown to me wrote: "Having been struck by a terrible misfortune, life appeared

The following examples will illustrate these statements concerning the losing of objects:—

Dr. B. Dattner states: "A colleague related to me that he lost his steel pencil which he had had for over two years, and which, on account of its superior quality, was highly prized by him. Analysis elicited the following facts: The day before he had received a very disagreeable letter from his brother-in-law, the concluding sentence of which read: 'At present I have neither the desire nor the time to assist you in your carelessness and laziness.' The effect connected with this letter was so powerful that the next day he promptly sacrificed the pencil which was a present from this brother-in-law in order not to be burdened with his favours."

Brill reports the following example: "A doctor took exception to the following statement in my book, 'We never lose what we really want' (*Psychanalysis, its Theories and Practical Application*, p. 214). His wife, who is very interested in psychologic subjects, read with him the chapter on "Psychopathology of Everyday Life "; they were both very much impressed with the novelty of the ideas, and so on, and were very willing to accept most of the statements. He could not, however, agree with the above-given statement because, as he said to his wife, 'I surely did not wish to lose my knife.' He referred to a valuable knife given to him by his wife, which he highly prized, the loss of which caused him much pain.

"It did not take his wife very long to discover the solution for this loss in a manner to convince them both of the accuracy of my statement. When she presented him with this knife he was a bit loath to accept it. Although he considered himself quite emancipated, he nevertheless entertained some superstition about giving or accepting a knife as a gift, because it is said that a knife cuts friendship. He even remarked this to his wife, who only laughed at his superstition. He had the knife for years before it disappeared.

"Analysis brought out the fact that the disappearance of the knife was directly connected with a period when there were violent quarrels between himself and his wife, which threatened to end in separation. They lived happily together until his step-daughter (it was his second marriage) came to

---

so harsh and unsympathetic, that I imagined that I had not sufficient strength to live to see the next day. I then noticed that almost every day I forgot to wind my watch, something that I never omitted before. I had been in the habit of doing it regularly before retiring in an almost mechanical and unconscious manner. It was only very seldom that I thought of it, and that happened when I had something important for the next day which held my interest. "Should this be considered a symptomatic action? I really cannot explain it." Whoever will take the trouble, like Jung (*The Psychology of Dementia Præcox*, translated by Peterson and Brill), or Maeder ("Une voie nouvelle en Psychologie — Freud et son ecole," *Coenobium*, Lugano, 1906), to pay attention to melodies which one hums to himself aimlessly and unconsciously, will regularly discover the relation of the melody's text to a theme which occupies the person at that time.

live with them. His daughter was the cause of many misunderstandings, and it was at the height of these quarrels that he lost the knife.

"The unconscious activity is very nicely shown in this symptomatic action. In spite of his apparent freedom from superstition, he still unconsciously believed that a donated knife may cut friendship between the persons concerned. The losing of it was simply an unconscious defence against losing his wife, and by sacrificing the knife he made the superstitious ban impotent."

In a lengthy discussion and with the aid of dream analysis[335] Otto Rank made clear the sacrificial tendency with its deep-reaching motivation. It must be said that just such symptomatic actions often give us access to the understanding of the intimate psychic life of the person.

Of the many isolated chance-actions, I will relate one example which showed a deeper meaning even without analysis. This example clearly explains the conditions under which such symptoms may be produced most casually, and also shows that an observation of practical importance may be attached to it. During a summer tour it happened that I had to wait several days at a certain place for the arrival of my travelling companions. In the meantime I made the acquaintance of a young man, who also seemed lonely and was quite willing to join me. As we lived at the same hotel it was quite natural that we should take all our meals and our walks together.

On the afternoon of the third day he suddenly informed me that he expected his wife to arrive on that evening's express train. My psychologic interest was now aroused, as it had already struck me that morning that my companion rejected my proposal to make a long excursion, and in our short walk he objected to a certain path as too steep and dangerous. During our afternoon walk he suddenly thought that I must be hungry and insisted that I should not delay my evening meal on his account, that he would not sup before his wife's arrival. I understood the hint and seated myself at the table while he went to the station.

The next morning we met in the foyer of the hotel. He presented me to his wife, and added, "Of course, you will breakfast with us? " I had to attend first to a small matter in the next street, but assured him that I would return shortly. Later, as I entered the breakfast-room, I noticed that the couple were at a small table near the window, both seated on the same side of it. On the opposite side there was only one chair, which was covered, however, with a man's large and heavy coat. I understood well the meaning of this unintentional, none the less expressive, disposition of the coat. It meant this: "There is no room for you here, you are superfluous now."

---

[335] Das Verlieren als Symptom-handlung," *Zentralb. f. Psychoanalyse,* i. 10-11.

The man did not notice that I remained standing before the table, being unable to take the seat, but his wife noticed it, and quickly nudged her husband and whispered: "Why, you have covered the gentleman's place with your coat."

These as well as other similar experiences have caused me to think that the actions executed unintentionally must inevitably become the source of misunderstanding in human relations. The perpetrator of the act, who is unaware of any associated intention, takes no account of it, and does not hold himself responsible for it. On the other hand, the second party, having regularly utilized even such acts as those of his partner to draw conclusions as to the purpose and meaning, recognizes more of the stranger's psychic processes than the latter is ready either to admit or believe that he has imparted. He becomes indignant when these conclusions drawn from his symptomatic actions are held up to him; he declares them baseless because he does not see any conscious intention in their execution, and complains of being misunderstood by the other. Close examination shows that such misunderstandings are based on the fact that the person is too fine an observer and understands too much. The more "nervous" two persons are the more readily will they give each other cause for disputes, which are based on the fact that one as definitely denies about his own person what he is sure to accept about the other.

And this is, indeed, the punishment for the inner dishonesty to which people grant expression under the guise of "forgetting," of erroneous actions and accidental emotions, a feeling which they would do better to confess to themselves and others when they can no longer control it. As a matter of fact it can be generally affirmed that every one is continually practising psychoanalysis on his neighbours, and consequently learns to know them better than each individual knows himself. The road following the admonition γ ν ω θ ι σ ε α υ τ ο ν leads through study of one's own apparently casual commissions and omissions.

X. Errors

Errors of memory are distinguished from forgetting and false recollections through one feature only, namely, that the error false recollection) is not recognized as such but finds credence. However, the use of the expression "error" seems to depend on still another condition. We speak of "erring·" instead of "falsely recollecting where the character of the objective reality is emphasized in the psychic material to be reproduced — that is, where something other than a fact of my own psychic life is to be remembered, or rather something that mat be confirmed or refuted through the memory of others. The reverse of the error in memory in this sense is formed by ignorance.

In my book *The Interpretation of Dreams,* I was responsible for a series of errors in historical, and above all, in material facts, which I was astonished to discover after the appearance of the book. On closer examination I found that they did not originate from my ignorance, but could be traced to errors of memory explainable by means of analysis.

(*a*) On page 361 I indicated as *Schiller's* birthplace the city of *Marburg,* a name which recurs in *Styria.* The error is found in the analysis of a dream during a night journey from which I was awakened by the conductor calling out the name of the station *Marburg.* In the contents of the dream inquiry is made concerning a book by *Schiller.* But *Schiller* was not born in the university town of *Marburg* but in the Swabian city *Marbach.* I maintain that I always knew this.

(*b*) On page 165 *Hannibal's* father is called *Hasdrubal.* This error was particularly annoying to me, but it was most corroborative of my conception of such errors. Few readers of the book are better posted on the history of the *Barkides* than the author who wrote this error and overlooked it in three proofs. The name of Hannibal's father was *Hamilcar Barkas*; *Hasdrubal* was the name of *Hannibal's* brother as well as that of his brother-in-law and predecessor in command.

(*c*) On pages 217 and 492 I assert that *Zeus* emasculates his father *Kronos,* and hurls him from the throne. This horror I have erroneously advanced by a generation; according to Greek mythology it was *Kronos* who committed this on his father *Uranos.* (*This is not a perfect error. According to the orphic version of the myth the emasculation was performed by Zeus on his father Kronos.*)

How is it to be explained that my memory furnished me with false material on these points, while it usually places the most remote and unusual material at my disposal, as the readers of my books can verify? And, what is more, in three carefully executed proof-readings I passed over these errors as if struck blind.

Goethe said of Lichtenberg: "Where he cracks a joke, there lies a concealed problem." Similarly we can affirm of these passages cited from my book: back of every error is a repression. More accurately stated: the error conceals a falsehood, disfigurement which is ultimately based on repressed material. In the analysis of the dreams there reported, I was compelled by the very nature of the theme to which the dream thoughts related, on the one hand, to break off the analysis in some places before it had reached its completion, and on the other hand, to remove an indiscreet detail through a slight disfigurement of its outline. I could not act differently, and had no other choice if I was at all to offer examples and illustrations. My constrained position was necessarily brought about by the peculiarity of dreams, which give expression to repressed thoughts, or to material which is incapable of becoming conscious. In spite of this it is said that enough material remained to offend the more sensitive souls. The disfigurement or concealment of the continuing thoughts known to me could not be accomplished without leaving some trace. What I wished to repress has often against my will obtruded itself on what I have taken up, and evinced itself in the matter as an unnoticeable error. Indeed, each of the three examples given is based on the same theme: the errors are the results of repressed thoughts which occupy themselves with my deceased father.

(*ad a*) Whoever reads through the dream analysed on page 361 will find some parts unveiled; in some parts he will be able to divine through allusions that I have broken off the thoughts which would have contained an unfavourable criticism of my father. In the continuation of this line of thoughts and memories there lies an annoying tale, in which books and a business friend of my father, named *Marburg*, play a part; it is the same name the calling out of which in the southern railway-station had aroused me from sleep. I wished to suppress this Mr. *Marburg* in the analysis from myself and my readers: he avenged himself by intruding where he did not belong, and changed the name of Schiller's birthplace from *Marbach* to *Marburg*.

(*ad b*) The error *Hasdrubal* in place of *Hamilcar*, the name of the brother instead of that of the father, originated from an association which dealt with the Hannibal fantasies of my college years and my dissatisfaction with the conduct of my father towards the "enemies of our people." I could have continued and recounted how my attitude toward my father was changed by a visit to England, where I made the acquaintance of my half-brother, by a previous marriage of my father. My brother's oldest son was my age exactly. Thus the age relations were no hindrance to a fantasy which may be stated thus: how much pleasanter it would be had I been born the son of my brother instead of the son of my father! This suppressed fantasy then falsified the text of my book at the point where I broke off the analysis, by forcing me to put the name of the brother for that of the father.

(*ad c*) The influence of the memory of this same brother is responsible for my having advanced by a generation the mythological horror of the Greek deities. One of the admonitions of my brother has lingered long in my memory. "Do not forget one thing concerning your conduct in life," he said: "you belong not to the second but really to the third generation of your father." Our father had remarried at an advanced age, and was therefore an old man to his children by the second marriage. I commit the error mentioned where I discuss the piety between parents and children.

Several times friends and patients have called my attention to the fact that in reporting their dreams or alluding to them in dream analyses, I have related inaccurately the circumstances experienced by us in common. These are also historic errors. On re-examining such individual cases I have found that my recollection of the facts was unreliable only where I had purposely disfigured or concealed something in the analysis. Here again we have *an unobserved error as a substitute for an intentional concealment or repression.*

From these errors, which originate from repression, we must sharply distinguish those which are based on actual ignorance. Thus, for example, it was ignorance when on my excursion a to Wachau I believed that I had passed the resting-place of the revolutionary leader Fischof. Only the name is common to both places. *Fischof's Emmersdorf* is located in Kärnthen. But I did not know any better.

Here is another embarrassing but instructive error, an example of temporary ignorance if you like. One day a patient reminded me to give him the two books on Venice which I had promised him, as he wished to use them in planning his Easter tour. I answered that I had them ready and went into the library to fetch them, though the truth of the matter was that I had forgotten to look them up, since I did not quite approve of my patient's journey, looking upon it as an unnecessary interruption to the treatment, and as a material loss to the physician. Thereupon I made a quick survey of the library for the books.

One was *Venedig als Kunststätte*, and besides this I imagined I had an historic work of a similar order. Certainly there was *Die Mediceer (The Medicis)*; I took them and brought them in to him, then, embarrassed, I confessed my error. Of course I really knew that the Medicis had nothing: to do with Venice, but for a short time it did not appear to me at all incorrect. Now I was compelled to practise justice; as I had so frequently interpreted my patient's symptomatic actions I could save my prestige only by, being honest and admitting to him the secret motives of my averseness to his trip.

It may cause general astonishment to learn how much stronger is the impulse to tell the truth than is usually supposed. Perhaps it is a result of my occupation with psychoanalysis that I can scarcely lie any more. As often as I attempt a distortion I succumb to an error or some other faulty act, which betrays my dishonesty, as was manifest in this and in the preceding examples.

Of all faulty actions the mechanisms of the error seems to be the most superficial. That is, the occurrence of the error invariably indicates that the mental activity concerned had to struggle with some disturbing influence, although the nature of the error need not be determined but the quality of the disturbing idea, which may have remained obscure. It is not out of place to add that the same state of affairs may be assumed in many simple cases of lapses in speaking and writing. Every time we commit a lapse in speaking or writing we may conclude that through mental processes there has come a disturbance which is beyond our intention. It may be conceded, however, that lapses in speaking and writing often follow the laws of similarity and convenience, or the tendency to acceleration, without allowing the disturbing element to leave a trace of its own character in the error resulting from the lapses in speaking or writing. It is the responsiveness of the linguistic material which at first makes possible the determination of the error, but it also limits the same.

In order not to confine myself exclusively to personal errors I will relate a few examples which could just as well have been ranged under "Lapses in Speech" or under "Erroneously Carried-out Actions," but as ah these forms of faulty action have the same value they may as well be reported here.

(a) I forbade a patient to speak on the telephone to his lady-love, with whom he himself was willing to break off all relations, as each conversation only renewed the struggling against it. He was to write her his final decision, although there were some difficulties in the way of delivering the letter to her. He visited me at one o'clock to tell me that he had found a way of avoiding these difficulties, and among other things he asked me whether he might refer to me in my professional capacity.

At two o'clock while he. was engaged in composing the letter of refusal, he interrupted himself suddenly, and said to his mother, "Well, I have forgotten to ask the Professor whether I may use his name in the letter." He hurried to the telephone, got the connection, and asked the question, "May I speak to the Professor after his dinner?" In answer he got an astonished "Adolf, have you gone crazy I " The answering voice was the very voice which at my command he had listened to for the last time. He had simply "made a mistake," and in place of the physician's number had called up that of his beloved.

(b) During a summer vacation a school-teacher, a poor but excellent young man, courted the daughter of a summer resident, until the girl fell passionately in love with him, and even prevailed upon her family to countenance the matri monial alliance in spite of the difference in position and race. One day, however, the teacher wrote his brother a letter in which he said: "Pretty, the lass is not at all, but she is very amiable, and so far so good. But whether I can make up my mind to marry a Jewess I cannot yet tell." This letter got into the hands of the fiancée, who put an end to the engagement, while at the same time his brother was wondering at the protestations of love directed to him. My informer assured me that this was really an error and not a cunning trick.

I am familiar with another case, in which a woman who was dissatisfied with her old physician, and still did not openly wish to discharge him, accomplished this purpose through the interchange of letters. Here, at least, I can assert confidently that it was error and not conscious cunning that made use, of this familiar comedy-motive.

(c) Brill [L.C. p. 191] tells of a woman who, inquiring about a mutual friend, erroneously called her by her maiden name. Her attention having been directed to this error, she had to admit that she disliked her friend's husband and had never been satisfied with her marriage.

Maeder (Nouvelles contributions, etc., *Arch. de Psych.*, vi. 1908) relates a good example of how a reluctantly repressed wish can be satisfied by means of an "error." A colleague wanted to enjoy his day of leave of absence absolutely undisturbed, but he, also felt that he ought to go to Lucerne to pay a call which he did not anticipate with any pleasure. After long reflection, however, he concluded to go. For pastime on the train he, read the daily newspapers. He journeyed from Zurich to Arth Goldau, where he changed trains for Lucerne, all the time engrossed in reading. Presently the conductor informed him that he was in the wrong train — that is, he had got into the one which was returning from Goldau to Zurich, whereas his ticket was for Lucerne.

A very similar trick was played by me quite recently. I had promised my oldest brother to pay him a long-due visit at a sea-shore in England; as the time was short I felt obliged to travel by the shortest route and without interruption. I begged for a day's sojourn in Holland, but he thought that I could stop there on my return trip. Accordingly I journeyed from Munich through Cologne to Rotterdam — Hook of Holland — where I was to take the steamer at midnight to Harwich. In Cologne I had to change cars; I left my train to go into the Rotterdam express, but it was not to be found. I asked various railway employees, was sent from one platform to another, got into an exaggerated state of despair, and could easily reckon that during this fruitless search I had probably missed my connection.

After this was corroborated, I pondered whether or not I should spend the night in Cologne. This was favoured by a feeling of piety, for according to an old family tradition, my ancestors were once expelled from this city during a persecution of the Jews. But eventually I came to another decision; I took a later train to Rotterdam, where I arrived late at night and was thus compelled to spend a day in Holland. This brought me the fulfilment of a long-fostered wish — the sight of the beautiful Rembrandt paintings at The Hague and in the Royal Museum at Amsterdam. Not before the next forenoon, while collecting my impressions during the railway journey in England, did I definitely remember that only a few steps from the place where I got off at the railroad station in Cologne, indeed, on the same platform, I had seen a large sign, "Rotterdam — Hook of Holland." There stood the train in which I should have continued my journey.

If one does not wish to assume that, contrary to my brother's orders, I had really resolved to admire the Rembrandt pictures on my way to him, then the fact that despite clear directions I hurried away and looked for another train must be designated as an incomprehensible "blinding." Everything else — my well-acted perplexity, the emergence of the pious intention to spend the night in Cologne — was only a contrivance to hide my resolution until it had been fully accomplished.

One may possibly be disinclined to consider the class of errors which I have here explained as very numerous or particularly significant. But I leave it to your consideration whether there is no ground for extending the same points of view also to the more important errors of judgment, as evinced by people in life and science. Only for the most select and most balanced minds does it seem; possible to guard the perceived picture of external reality against the distortion to which it is otherwise subjected in its transit through the psychic individuality of the transit through the psychic individuality of the one perceiving it.

XI. Combined Faulty Acts

Two of the last-mentioned examples, my error which transfers the Medici to Venice and that of the young man who knew how to circumvent a command against a conversation on the telephone with his lady love, have really not been fully discussed, as after careful consideration they may be shown to represent a union of forgetting with an error. I can show the same union still more clearly in certain other examples .

(a) A friend related to me the following experience: "Some years ago I consented to be elected to the committee of a certain literary; society, as I supposed the organization might some time be of use to me in assisting me in the production of my drama. Although not much interested, I attended the meetings regularly every Friday. Some months ago I was definitely assured that one of my dramas would be presented at the theatre in F., and since that time it regularly happened that I forgot the meeting of the association. As I read their programme announcements I was ashamed of my forgetfulness. I reproached myself, feeling that it was certainly rude of me to stay away now when I no longer needed them, and determined that I would certainly not forget the next Friday. Continually I reminded myself of this resolution until the hour came and I stood before the door of the meeting-room. To my astonishment it was locked; the meeting: was already over. I had mistaken my day; it was already Saturday!["]

(b) The next example is the combination of a symptomatic action with a case of mislaying; it reached me by, remote byways, but from a reliable source.

A woman travelled to Rome with her brother-in-law, a renowned artist. The visitor was highly honoured by the German residents of Rome, and among other things received a gold medal of antique origin. The woman was grieved that her brother-in-law did not sufficiently appreciate the value of this beautiful gift. After she had returned home she discovered in unpacking that — without knowing how — she had brought the medal home with her. She immediately notified her brother-in-law of this by letter, and informed him that she would send it back to Rome the next day. The next day, however, the medal was so aptly mislaid that it could not be found and could not be sent back, and then it dawned on the woman what her "absent-mindedness" signified — namely, that she wished to keep, the medal herself.

(c) Here are some cases in which the falsified action persistently repeats itself, and at the same time also changes its mode of action:—

Due to unknown motives, Jones I left a letter[336] for several days on his desk, forgetting each time to post it. He ultimately posted it, but it was returned to him from the Dead-letter Office because he forgot to address it. After addressing and posting it a second time it was again returned to him, this time without a stamp. He was then forced to recognize the unconscious opposition to the sending of the letter.

(d) A short account by Dr. Karl Weiss (Vienna)[337] of a case of forgetting impressively describes the futile effort to accomplish something in the face of opposition. "How persistently the unconscious activity can achieve its purpose if it has cause to prevent a resolution from being executed, and how difficult it is to guard against this tendency, will be illustrated by the following incident: An acquaintance requested me to lend him: a book and bring it to him the next day. I immediately promised it, but perceived a distinct feeling of displeasure which I could not explain at the time. Later it became clear to me: this acquaintance had owed me for years a sum of money which he evidently had no intention of returning. I did not give this matter any more thought, but I recalled it the following: forenoon with the same feeling of displeasure, and at once said to myself: 'Your unconscious will see to it that you forget the book, but you don't wish to appear unobliging and will therefore do everything not to forget it.' I came home, wrapped the book in paper, and put it near me on the desk while I wrote some letters.

"A little later I went away, but after a few steps I recollected that I had left on the desk the letters which I wished to post. (By, the way, one of the letters was written to a person who urged me to undertake something disagreeable.) I returned, took the letters, and again left. While in the street-car it occurred to me that I had undertaken to purchase something for my: wife, and I was pleased at the thought that it would be only a small package. The association

---

[336] *Loc. cit.*, p. 42.
[337] Zentralb.f. Psychoanalyse, ii. 9.

'small package,' suddenly recalled 'book' — and only then I noticed that I did not have the book with me. Not only had I forgotten it when I left my home the first time, but I had overlooked it again when I got the letters near which it lay."

(e) A similar mechanism is shown in the following fully analysed observation of Otto Rank[338]:—

"A scrupulously orderly and pedantically precise man reported the following occurrence, which he considered quite remarkable: One afternoon on the street wishing to find out the time, he discovered that he had left his watch at home, an omission which to his knowledge had never occurred before. As he had an engagement elsewhere and had not enough time to return for his watch, he made use of a visit to a woman friend to borrow her watch for the evening. This was the most convenient way out of the dilemma, as he had a previous engagement to visit this lady the next day. Accordingly, he promised to return her watch at that time.

"But the following day when about to consummate this he found to his surprise that he had left the watch at home; his own watch he had with him. He then firmly, resolved to return the lady's property that same afternoon, and even followed out his resolution. But on wishing to see the time on leaving her he found to his chagrin and astonishment that he had again forgotten to take his own watch.

"The repetition of this faulty action seemed so pathologic to this order-loving man that he was quite anxious to know its psychologic motivation, and when questioned whether he experienced anything disagreeable on the critical day of the first forgetting, and in what connection it had occurred, the motive was promptly found. He related that he had conversed with his mother after luncheon, shortly before leaving the house. She told him that an irresponsible relative, who had already caused him much worry and loss of money, had pawned his (the relative's) watch, and, as it was needed in the house, the relative had asked for money to redeem it. This almost "forced" loan affected our man very painfully and brought back to his memory all the disagreeable episodes perpetrated by this relative for many years.

"His symptomatic action therefore proves to be manifoldly determined. First, it gives expression to a stream of thought which runs perhaps as follows: 'I won't allow my money to be extorted this way, and if a watch is needed I will leave my own at home.' But as he needed it for the evening to keep his appointment, this intention could only be brought about on an unconscious path in the form of a symptomatic action. Second, the forgetting expresses a sentiment something like the following: 'This everlasting sacrificing of money for this good-for-nothing is bound to ruin me altogether,

[338] Zentralb. f. Psychoanalyse, ii. 5.

so that I will have to give up everything.' Although the anger, according to the report of this man, was only momentary, the repetition of the same symptomatic action conclusively shows that in the unconscious it continued to act more intensely, and may be equivalent to the conscious expression: 'I cannot get this story out of my head.[339] That the lady's watch should later meet the same fate will not surprise us after knowing this attitude of the unconscious.'

"Yet there may be still other special motives which favour the transference on the 'innocent' lady's watch. The nearest motive is probably that he would have liked to keep it as a substitute for his own sacrificed watch, and that hence he forgot to return it the next day. He also might have liked to possess this watch as a souvenir of the lady. Moreover, the forgetting of the lady's watch gave him the excuse for calling on the admired one a second time; for he was obliged to visit her in the morning in reference to another matter, and with the forgetting of the watch he seemed to indicate that this visit for which an appointment had been made so long ago was too good for him to be used simply for the return of a watch.

"Twice forgetting his own watch and thus making possible the substitution of the lady's watch speaks for the fact that our man unconsciously endeavoured to avoid carrying both watches at the same time. He obviously thought of avoiding the appearance of superfluity which would have stood out in striking contrast to the want of the relative; but, on the other hand, he utilized this as a self-admonition against his apparent intention to marry this lady, reminding himself that he was tied to his family (mother) by indissoluble obligations.

"Finally, another reason for the forgetting of the lady's watch may be sought in the fact that the evening before he, a bachelor, was ashamed to be seen with a lady's watch by his friends, so that he only looked at it stealthily, and in order to evade the repetition of this painful situation he could not take the watch along. But as he was obliged to return it, there resulted here, too, an unconsciously performed symptomatic action which proved to be a compromise formation between conflicting emotional feelings and a dearly bought victory of the unconscious instance."

In the same discussion Rank has also paid attention to the very interesting! relation of "faulty actions and dreams," which cannot, however, be followed here without a comprehensive analysis of the dream with which the faulty action is connected. I once dreamed at great length that I had lost my pocket-book. In the morning while dressing I actually missed it; while undressing the night before the dream I had forgotten to take it out of my

---

[339] This continued action in the unconscious manifested itself once in the form of a dream which followed the faulty action, another time in the repetition of the same or in the omission of a correction.

trousers pocket and put it in its usual place, This forgetting was therefore not unknown to me; probably it was to give expression to an unconscious thought which was ready to appear in the dream content.

I do not mean to assert that such cases of combined faulty actions can teach anything new that we have not already seen in the individual cases. But this change in form of the faulty action, which nevertheless attains the same result, gives the plastic impression of a will working towards a definite end, and in a far more energetic way contradicts the idea that the faulty action represents something: fortuitous and requires no explanation. Not less remarkable is the fact that the conscious intention thoroughly fails to check the success of the faulty, action. Despite all, my friend did not pay his visit to the meeting of the literary society, and the woman found it impossible to give up the medal. That unconscious something which worked against these resolutions found another outlet after the first road was closed to it. It requires something other than the conscious counter-resolution to overcome the unknown motive ; it requires a psychic work which makes the unknown known to consciousness.

XII. Determinism — Chance — and Superstitious Beliefs

Points of View.

As the general result of the preceding separate discussions we must put down the following principle: *Certain inadequacies of our psychic capacities — whose common character will soon be more definitely determined — and certain performances which are apparently unintentional prove to be well motivated when subjected to the psychoanalytic investigation, and are determined through the consciousness of unknown motives.*

In order to belong to this class of phenomena thus explained a faulty psychic action must satisfy the following conditions:—

(*a*) It must not exceed a certain measure which is firmly established through our estimation, and is designated by the expression "within normal limits."

(*b*) It must evince the character of the momentary and temporary disturbance. The same action must have been previously performed more correctly or we must always rely on ourselves to perform it more correctly; if we are corrected by others we must immediately recognize the truth of the correction and the incorrectness of our psychic action.

(*c*) If we at all perceive a faulty action, we must not perceive in ourselves any motivation of the same, but must attempt to explain it through "inattention" or attribute it to an "accident."

Thus there remain in this group the cases of forgetting and the errors, despite better knowledge, the lapses in speaking, reading, writing, the erroneously carried-out actions, and the so-called chance actions. The explanations of these so definite psychic processes are connected with a series of observations which may in part arouse further interest.

I. By abandoning a part of our psychic capacity as unexplainable through purposive ideas we ignore the realms of determinism in our mental life. Here, as in still other spheres, determinism reaches farther than we suppose. In the year 1900 I read an essay published in the *Zeit* written by the literary historian R. M. Meyer, in which he maintains, and illustrates by examples, that it is impossible to compose nonsense intentionally and arbitrarily, For some time I have been aware that it is impossible to think of a number, or even of a name, of one's own free will. If one investigates this seeming voluntary formation, let us say, of a number of many digits uttered in unrestrained mirth, it always proves to be so strictly determined that the determination seems impossible. I will now briefly discuss an example of an "arbitrarily chosen" first name, and then exhaustively analyse an analogous example of: a "thoughtlessly uttered" number.

While preparing the history of one of my patients for publication I considered what first name I should give her in the article. There seemed to be a wide choice; of course, certain names were at once excluded by me, in the first place the real name, then the names of members of my family to which I would have objected, also some female names having an especially peculiar pronunciation. But, excluding these, there should have been no need of being puzzled about such a name. It would be thought, and I myself supposed, that a whole multitude of feminine names would be placed at my disposal. Instead of this only one sprang up, no other besides it; it was the name Dora.

I inquired as to its determination: "Who else is called Doral?" I wished to reject the next idea as incredulous; it occurred to me that the nurse of my sister's children was named Dora. But I possess so much .self-control, or practice in analysis, if you like, that I held firmly to the idea and proceeded. Then a slight incident of the previous evening soon flashed through my mind which brought the looked-for determination. On my sister's dining-room table I noticed a letter bearing the address, "Miss Rosa W." Astonished, I asked whose name this was, and was informed that the right name of the supposed Dora was really Rosa, and that on accepting the position she had to lay; aside her name, because Rosa would also refer to my sister. I said pityingly, "Poor people! They cannot even retain their own names!" I now recall that on hearing this I became quiet for a moment and began to think of all sorts of serious matters which merged into the obscure, but which I could now easily bring; into my consciousness. Thus when I sought a name for a person *who could not retain her own name* no other except "Dora" occurred to me. The exclusiveness here is based, moreover, on firmer internal associations, for in the history of my patient it was a stranger in the house, the governess, who exerted a decisive influence on the course of the treatment.

This slight incident found its unexpected: continuation many years later. While discussing in a lecture the long-since published history; of the girl called Dora it occurred to me that one of my two women pupils had the very name Dora which I was obliged to utter so often in the different associations of the case. I turned to the young student, whom I knew personally, with the apology that I had really not thought that she bore the same name, and that I was ready to substitute it in my lecture by another name.

I was now confronted with the task of rapidly choosing another name, and reflected that I must not now choose the first name of the other woman student, and so set a poor example to the class, who were already quite conversant with psychoanalysis. I was therefore well pleased when the name "Erna" occurred to me as the substitute for Dora, and Erna I used in the discourse. After the lecture I asked myself whence the name "Erna" could possibly have originated, and had to laugh as I observed that the feared possibility in the choice of the substitutive name had come to pass, in part at least. The other lady's family name was Lucerna, of which Erna was a part.

In a letter to a friend I informed him that I had finished reading the proof-sheets of *The Interpretation of Dreams*, and that I did not intend to make any further changes in it, "even if it contained *2,467* mistakes." I immediately attempted to explain to myself the number, and added this little analysis as a postscript to the letter. It will be best to quote it now as I wrote it when I caught myself in this transaction:—

"I will add hastily another contribution to the Psychopathology of Everyday Life. You will find in the letter the number 2,467 as a jocose and arbitrary estimation of the number of errors that may be found in the dream-book. I meant to write: no matter how large the number might be, and this one presented itself. But there is nothing arbitrary or undetermined in the psychic life. You will therefore rightly suppose that the unconscious hastened to determine the number which was liberated by consciousness. Just previous to this I had read in the paper that General E. M. had been retired as Inspector-General of Ordnance. You must know that I am interested in this man. While I was serving as military medical student he, then a colonel, once came into the hospital and said to the physician: 'You must make me well in eight days, as I have some work to do for which the Emperor is waiting.'

"At that time I decided to follow this man's career, and just think, to-day (1899) he is at the end of it — Inspector-General of Ordnance and already retired. I wished to figure out in what time he had covered this road, and assumed that I had seen him in the hospital in 1882. That would make 17 years. I related this to my wife, and she remarked, 'Then you, too, should be retired.' And I protested, 'The Lord forbid!' After this conversation I seated myself at the table to write to you. The previous train of thought continued, and for good reason. The figuring was incorrect; I had a definite recollection of the circumstances in my mind. I had celebrated my coming of my *24th* birthday, in the military prison (for being absent without permission). Therefore I must have seen him in 1880, which makes it 19 years ago. You then have the number 24 in 2,467! Now take the number that represents my age, 43, and add 24 years to it and you get 67! That is, to the question whether I wished to retire I had expressed the wish to work 24 years more. Obviously I am annoyed that in the interval during which I followed Colonel M. I have not accomplished much myself, and still there is a sort of triumph in the fact that he is already finished, while I still have all before me. Thus we may justly say that not even the unintentionally thrown-out number 2,467 lacks its determination from the unconscious."

Since this first example of the interpretation of an apparently arbitrary choice of a number I have repeated a similar test with the same result; but most cases are of such intimate content that they do not lend themselves to report .

It is for this reason that I shall not hesitate to add here a very interesting analysis of a "chance number" which Dr. Alfred Adler (Vienna) received from a "perfectly healthy" man.[340] A. wrote to me: "Last night I devoted myself to the *Psychopathology of Everyday Life*, and I would have read it all through had I not been hindered by a remarkable coincidence. When I read that every number that we apparently conjure up quite arbitrarily in our consciousness has a definite meaning, I decided to test it. The number 1,734 occurred to my mind. The following associations then came up: $1,734 \div 17 = 102$; $102 \div 17 = 6$. I then separated the number into 17 and 34. I am 34 years old. .. I believe that I once told you that I consider 34 the last year of youth, and for this reason I felt miserable on my last birthday. The end of my 17th year was the beginning of a very nice and interesting period of my development. I divide my life into period of 17 years. That do the divisions signify? The number 102 recalls the fact that volume 102 Of the Reclam Universal Library is Kotzebue's play *Menschenhass und Reue* (*Human Hatred and Repentance*).

"My present psychic state is 'human hatred and repentance.' No. 6 of the U. L. (I know a great many numbers by heart) is Mullner's 'Schuld' (Fault). I am constantly annoyed at the thought that it is through my own fault that I have not become what I could have been with my abilities.

---

340 Alfred Adler, "Drei Psychoanalysen von Zahlen einfällen und obsedierenden Zahlen," *Psych. Neur. Wochenschr.*, No. 28, 1905.

"I then asked myself, 'What is No. 17 of U. L.?' But I could not recall it. But as I positively knew it before, I assumed that I wished to forget this number. All reflection was in vain. I wished to continue with my reading, but I read only mechanically without understanding a word, for I was annoyed by the number 17. I extinguished the light and :continued my search. It finally came to me that number 17 must be a play by Shakespeare. But which one! I thought of Hero and Leander. Apparently a stupid attempt of my will to distract me. I finally arose and consulted the catalogue of the U. L. Number 17 was *Macbeth!* To my surprise I had to discover that I knew nothing of the play, despite the fact that it did not interest me any less than any other Shakespearean drama. I only thought of murder, Lady Macbeth, witches, 'nice is ugly,' and that I found Schiller's version of *Macbeth* very nice. Undoubtedly I also wished to forget the play. Then it occurred to me that 17 and 34 may be divided by 17 and result in 1 and 2. Numbers 1 and 2 of the U. L. is Goethe's *Faust.* Formerly I found much of Faust in me."

We must regret that the discretion of the physician did not allow us to see the significance of ideas. Adler remarked that the man did not succeed in the synthesis of his analysis. His association would hardly be worth reporting unless their continuation would bring out something that would give us the key to the understanding of the number 1,734 and the whole series of ideas.

To quote further: "To be sure this morning I had an experience which speaks much for the correctness of the Freudian conception. My wife, whom I awakened through my getting up at night, asked me what I wanted with the catalogue of the U. L. I told her the story. She found it all pettifogging but — very interesting;. *Macbeth,* which caused me so much trouble, she simply passed over. She said that nothing came to her mind when she thought of a number. I answered, 'Let us try; it.' She named the number 117· To this I immediately; replied: '17 refers to what I just told you; furthermore, I told you yesterday that if a wife is in the 82nd year and the husband is in the 35th year it must be a gross misunderstanding.' For the last few days I have been teasing my wife by maintaining that she was a little old mother of 82 years. $82 + 35 = 117$."

The man who did not know how to determine his own number at once found the solution when his wife named a number which was apparently arbitrarily chosen. As a matter of fact, the woman understood very well from which complex the number of her husband originated, and chose her own number from the same complex, which surely common it, both, as it dealt in his case with their relative ages. Now, we find it easy to interpret the number that occurred to the man. As Dr. Adler indicates, it expressed 'a repressed wish of the husband which, fully developed, would read: "For a man of 34 years as I am, only a woman of 17 would be suitable."

Lest one should think too lightly of such "playing," I will add that I was recently informed by Dr. Adler that a year after the publication of this analysis the man was divorced from his wife.[341]

Adler gives a similar explanation for the origin of obsessive numbers. Also the choice of so-called "favourite numbers" is not without relation to the life of the person concerned, and does not lack a certain psychologic interest. A gentleman who evinced a particular partiality for the numbers 17 and 19 could specify, after brief reflection, that at the age of 17 he attained the greatly longed-for academic freedom by having been admitted to the university, that at 19 he made his first long journey, and shortly thereafter made his first scientific discovery. But the fixation of this preference followed later, after two questionable affairs, when the same numbers were invested with importance in his "love-life."

Indeed, even those numbers which we use in a particular connection extremely often and with apparent arbitrariness can be traced by analysis to an unexpected meaning. Thus, one day it struck one of my patients that he was particularly fond of saying, "I have already told you this from 17 to 36 times." And he asked himself whether there was any motive for it. It soon occurred to him that he was born on the 27th day of the month, and that his younger brother was born on the 26th day of another month, and he had grounds for complaint that Fate had robbed him of so many of the benefits of life only to bestow them on his younger brother. Thus he represented this partiality of Fate by deducting 10 from the date of his birth and adding it to the date of his brother's birthday. I am the elder and yet am so "cut short."

I shall tarry a little longer at the analysis of chance numbers, for I know of no other individual observation which would so readily demonstrate the existence of highly organized thinking processes of which consciousness has no knowledge. Moreover, there is no better example of analysis in which the suggestion of the position, a frequent accusation, is so distinctly out of consideration. I shall therefore report the analysis of a chance number of one of my patients (with his consent), to which I will only add that he is the youngest of many children and that he lost his beloved father in his young years.

While in a particularly happy mood he let the number 426,718 come to his mind, and put to himself the question, "Well, what does it bring to your mind?" First came a joke he had heard: "If your catarrh of the nose is treated by a doctor it lasts 42 days, if it is not treated it lasts — 6 weeks." This corresponds to the first digit of the number (42 = 6 x 7). During the

---

[341] As an explanation of *Macbeth*, No. 17 of the U. L., I was informed by Dr. Adler that in his seventeenth year this man had joined an anarchistic society whose aim was regicide. Probably this is why he forgot the content of the play Macbeth. The same person invented at that time a secret code in which numbers substituted letters.

obstruction that followed this first solution I called his attention to the fact that the number of six digits selected by him contains all the first numbers except 3 and 5. He at once found the continuation of this solution:—

"We were altogether 7 children, I was the youngest. Number 3 in the order of the children corresponds to my sister A., and 5 to my brother L.; both of them were my enemies. As a child I used to pray to the Lord every night that He should take out of my life these two tormenting spirits. It seems to me that I have fulfilled for myself this wish: '3' and '5,' the *evil* brother and the hated sister, are omitted."

"If the number stands for your sisters and brothers, what significance is there to 18 at the end? You were altogether only 7."

"I often thought if my father had lived longer I should not have been the youngest child. If one more would have come, we should have been 8, and there would have been a younger child, toward whom I could have played the rôle of the older one."

With this the number was explained, but we still wished to find the connection between the first part of the interpretation and the part following it. This came very readily from the condition required for the last digits — if the father had lived longer. 42 = 6 x 7 signifies the ridicule directed against the doctors who could not help the father, and in this way expresses the wish for the continued existence of the father. The whole number really corresponds to the fulfilment of his two wishes in reference to his family circle — namely, that both the evil brother and sister should die and that another little child should follow him. Or, briefly expressed: *If only these two had died in place of my father!*[342]

Another analysis of numbers I take from Jones.[343] A gentleman of his acquaintance let the number 986 come to his mind, and defied him to connect it to anything of special interest in his mind. "Six years ago, on the hottest day he could remember, he had seen a joke in an evening newspaper, which stated that the thermometer had stood at 98.6° F., evidently an exaggeration of 98.6° F.[sic] We were at the time seated in front of a very hot fire, from which he had just drawn back, and he remarked, probably quite correctly, that the heat had aroused his dormant memory. However, I was curious to know why this memory had persisted with such vividness as to be so readily brought out, for with most people it surely would have been forgotten beyond recall, unless it had become associated with some other mental experience of more significance.

---

[342] For the sake of simplicity I have omitted some of the not less suitable thoughts of the patients.

[343] *Loc. cit.*, p. 36.

"He told me that on reading: the joke he had laughed uproariously, and that on many subsequent occasions he had recalled it with great relish. As the joke was obviously of an exceedingly tenuous nature, this strengthened my expectation that more lay behind. His next thought was the general reflection that the conception of heat had always greatly impressed him, that heat was the most important thing in the universe, the source of all life, and so on. This remarkable attitude of a quite prosaic young man certainly needed some explanation, so I asked him to continue his free associations. The next thought was of a factory stack which he could see from his bedroom window. He often stood of an evening watching the flame and smoke issuing out of it, and reflecting on this deplorable waste of energy. Heat, flame, the source of life, the waste of vital energy issuing from an upright, hollow tube — it was not hard to divine from such associations that the ideas of heat and fire were unconsciously linked in his mind with the idea of love, as is so frequent in symbolic thinking, and that there was a strong masturbation complex present, a conclusion that he presently confirmed."

Those who wish to get a good impression of the way the material of numbers becomes elaborated in the unconscious thinking, I refer to two papers by Jung[344] and Jones.[345]

In personal analysis of this kind two things were especially striking. First, the absolute somnambulistic certainty with which I attacked the unknown objective point, merging into a mathematical train of thought, which later suddenly extended to the looked-for number, and the rapidity with which the entire subsequent work was performed. Secondly, the fact that the numbers were always at the disposal of my unconscious mind, when as a matter of fact I am a poor mathematician and find it very difficult to consciously recall years, house numbers, and the like. Moreover, in these unconscious mental operations with figures I found a tendency to superstition, the origin of which had long remained unknown to me.

It will not surprise us to find that not only numbers but also mental occurrences of different kinds of words regularly prove on analytic investigation to be well determined.

Brill relates: "While working on the English edition of this book I was obsessed one morning with the strange word 'Cardillac.' Busily intent on my work, I refused at first to pay attention to it, but, as is usually the case, I simply could not do anything else. 'Cardillac' was constantly in my mind. Realizing that my refusal to recognize it was only a resistance, I decided to analyse it. The following associations occurred to me: *Cardillac, cardiac, carrefour, Cadillac.*

---

344 "Ein Beitrag zur Kenntnis des Zahlentraumes," *Zentralb. f. Psychoanalyse*, i. 12.
345 "Unconscious Manipulation of Numbers" (ibid., ii. 5, 1912).

"*Cardiac* recalled cardalgia — heartache — a medical friend who had recently told me confidentially that he feared that he had some cardiac affection because he had suffered some attacks of pain in the region of his heart. Knowing him so well, I at once rejected his theory, and told him that his attacks were of a neurotic character, and that his other apparent physical ailments were also only the expression of his neurosis.

"I might add that just before telling me of his heart trouble he spoke of a business matter of vital interest to him which had suddenly come to naught. Being a man of unbounded ambitions, he was very depressed because of late he had suffered many similar reverses. His neurotic conflicts, however, had become manifest a few months before this misfortune. Soon after his father's death had left a big business on his hands. As the business could be continued only under my friend's management, he was unable to decide whether to enter into commercial life or continue his chosen career. His great ambition was to become a successful medical practitioner, and although he had practised medicine successfully for many years, he was not altogether satisfied with the financial fluctuations of his professional income. On the other hand, his father's business promised him an assured, though limited, return. In brief, he was 'at a crossing and did not know which way to turn.'

"I then recalled the word *carrefour*, which is the French for 'crossing,' and it occurred to me that while working in a hospital in Paris I lived near the 'Carrefour St. Lazarre.' And now I could understand what relation all these associations had for me.

"When I resolved to leave the State Hospital I made the decision, first, because I desired to get married, and, secondly, because I wished to enter private practice. This brought up a new problem. Although my State hospital service was an absolute success, judging by promotions and so on, I felt like a great many others in the same situation, namely, that my training was ill suited for private practice. To specialize in mental work was a daring undertaking for one without money and social connections. I also felt that the best I could do for patients should they ever come my way would be to commit them to one of the hospitals, as I had little confidence in the home treatment in vogue. In spite of the enormous advances made in recent years in mental work, the specialist is almost helpless when he is confronted with the average case of insanity. This may be partially attributed to the fact that such cases are brought to him after they have fully developed the psychosis when hospital treatment is imperative. Of the great army of milder mental disturbances, the so-called border-line cases, which make up the bulk of clinic and private work and which rightfully belong to the mental specialist, I knew very little, as those patients rarely, or never, came to the State hospital, and what I did know concerning the treatment of neurasthenia and psychasthenia was not conducive to make me more hopeful of success in private practice.

"It was in this state of mind that I came to Paris, where I hoped to learn enough about the psychoneuroses to enable me to continue my specialty in private practice, and yet feel that I could do something for my patients. What I saw in Paris did not, however, help to change my state of mind. There, too, most of the work was directed to dead tissues. The mental aspects, as such, received but scant attention. I was, therefore, seriously thinking of giving up my mental work for some other specialty. As can be seen, I was confronted with a situation similar to the one of my medical friend. I, too, was at a crossing and did not know which way to turn. My suspense was soon ended. One day, I received a letter from my friend Professor Peterson, who, by the way, was responsible for my entering the State hospital service. In this letter he advised me not to give up my work, and suggested the psychiatric clinic of Zurich, where he thought I could find what I desired.

"But what does *Cadillac* mean? Cadillac is the name of a hotel and of an automobile. A few days before in a country place my medical friend and I had been trying to hire an automobile, but there was none to be had. We both expressed the wish to own an automobile — again an unrealized ambition. I also recalled that the 'Carrefour St. Lazarre' always impressed me as being one of the busiest thoroughfares in Paris. It was always congested with automobiles. Cadillac also recalled that only a few days ago on the way to my clinic I noticed a large sign over a building which announced that on a certain day 'this building was to be occupied by the Cadillac,' etc. This at first made me think of the Cadillac Hotel, but on second sight I noticed that it referred to the Cadillac motorcar. There was a sudden obstruction here for a few moments. The word Cadillac reappeared and by sound association the word *catalogue* occurred to me. This word brought back a very mortifying occurrence of recent origin, the motive of which is again blighted ambition.

"When one wishes to report any auto-analysis he must be prepared to lay bare many intimate affairs of his own life. Any one reading carefully Professor Freud's works cannot fail to become intimately acquainted with him and his family. I have often been asked by persons who claim to have read and studied Freud's works such questions as: 'How old is Freud?' 'Is Freud married?' 'How many children has he?' etc. Whenever I hear these or similar questions I know that the questioner has either lied when he made these assertions, or, to be more charitable, that he is a very careless and superficial reader. All these questions and many more are answered in Freud's works. Auto-analyses are autobiographies *par excellence*; but whereas the autobiographer may for definite reasons consciously and unconsciously hide many facts of his life, the auto-analyst not only tells the truth consciously, but perforce brings to light his whole intimate personality. It is for these reasons that one finds it very unpleasant to report his own auto-analyses. However, as we often report our patients' unconscious productions, it is but fair that we should sacrifice ourselves on the altar of publicity when occasion demands. This is my apology for having thrust some of my personal affairs on the reader, and for being obliged to continue a little longer in the same strain.

"Before digressing with the last remarks I mentioned that the word *Cadillac* brought the sound association catalogue. This association brought back another important epoch in my life with which Professor Peterson is connected. Last May I was informed by the secretary of the faculty that I was appointed chief of clinic of the department of psychiatry. I need hardly say that I was exceedingly pleased to be so honoured — in the first place because it was the realization of an ambition which I dared entertain only under special euphoric states; and, secondly, it was a compensation for the many unmerited criticisms from those who are blindly and unreasonably opposing some of my work. Soon thereafter I called on the stenographer of the faculty and spoke to her about a correction to be made in my name as it was printed in the catalogue. For some unknown reason (perhaps racial prejudice) this stenographer, a maiden lady, must have taken a dislike to me. For about three years I repeatedly requested her to have this correction made, but she had paid no attention to me. To be sure she always promised to attend to it, but the mistake remained uncorrected.

"When I saw her last May I again reminded her of this correction, and also called her attention to the fact that as I had been appointed chief of clinic I was especially anxious to have my name correctly printed in the catalogue. She apologized for her remissness and assured me that everything should be as I requested. Imagine my surprise and chagrin when on receiving the new catalogue I found that while the correction had been made in my name I was not listed as chief of clinic. When I asked her about this she was quite puzzled; she said she had no idea that I had been appointed chief of clinic. She had to consult the minutes of the faculty, written by herself, before she was convinced of it. It should be noted that as recorder to the faculty it was her duty to know all these things as soon as they transpired.[346] When she finally ascertained that I was right she was very apologetic and informed me that she would at once write to the superintendent of the clinic to inform him of my appointment, something which she should have done months before. Of course I gained nothing by her regrets and apologies. The catalogue was published and those who read it did not find my name in the desired place. I am chief of clinic in fact but not in name. Moreover, as the appointments are made only for one year, it is quite likely that my great ambition will never be actually realized.

---

[346] This is another excellent example showing how a conscious intention was powerless to counteract an unconscious resistance.

"Thus the obsessive neologism *cardillac*, which is a condensation of *cardiac*, *Cadillac*, and *catalogue*, contains some of the most important efforts of my medical experience. When I was almost at the end of this analysis I suddenly recalled a dream containing this neologism cardillac in which my wish was realized. My name appeared in its rightful place in the catalogue. The person who showed it to me in the dream was Professor Peterson. It was when I was at the first 'crossing' after I had graduated from the medical college that Professor Peterson urged me to enter the hospital service. About five years later while I was in the state of indecision which I have described, it was Professor Peterson who advised me to go to the clinic of psychiatry at Zurich where through Bleuler and Jung I first became acquainted with Professor Freud and his works, and it was also through the kind recommendation of Dr. Peterson that I was elevated to my present position."

I am indebted to Dr. Hitschman for the solution of another case in which a line of poetry repeatedly obtruded itself on the mind in a certain place without showing any trace of its origin and relation.

Related by Dr. E.: "Six years ago I travelled from Biarritz to San Sebastian. The railroad crosses over the Bidassao — a river which here forms the boundary between France and Spain. On the bridge one has a splendid view, on the one side of the broad valley and the Pyrenees and on the other of the sea. It was a beautiful, bright summer day; everything was filled with sun and light. I was on a vacation and pleased with my trip to Spain. Suddenly the following words came to me: '*But the soul is already free, floating on a sea of light.*'

"At that time I was trying to remember where these lines came from, but I could not remember; judging by the rhythm, the words must be a part of some poem, which, however, entirely escaped my memory. Later when the verse repeatedly came to my mind, I asked many people about it without receiving any information.

"Last year I crossed the same bridge on my return journey from Spain. It was a very dark night and it rained. I looked through the window to ascertain whether we had already reached the frontier station and noticed that we were on the Bidassao bridge. Immediately the above- cited verse returned to my memory and again I could not recall its origin.

"At home many months later I found Uhland's poems. I opened the volume and my glance fell upon the verse: '*But the soul is already free, floating on a sea of light,*' which were the concluding lines of the poem entitled 'The Pilgrim.' I read the poem and dimly recalled that I had known it many years ago. The scene of action is in Spain, and this seemed to me to be the only relation between the quoted verse and the place on the railroad journey described by me. I was only half satisfied with my discovery and mechanically continued to turn the pages of the book. On turning the next page I found a poem the title of which was '*Bidassao Bridge.*'

"I may add that the contents of this poem seemed even stranger to me than that of the first, and that its first verse read:

"'On the Bidassao bridge stands a saint grey with age, he blesses to the right the Spanish mountain, to the left he blesses the French land.'"

II. This understanding of the determination of apparently arbitrarily selected names, numbers, and words may perhaps contribute to the solution of another problem. As is known, many persons argue against the assumption of an absolute psychic determinism by referring to an intense feeling of conviction that there is a free will. This feeling of conviction exists, but is not incompatible with the belief in determinism. Like all normal feelings, it must be justified by something. But, so far as I can observe, it does not manifest itself in weighty and important decisions; on these occasions one has much more the feeling of a psychic compulsion and gladly falls back upon it. (Compare Luther's "Here I stand, I cannot do anything else.")

On the other hand, it is in trivial and indifferent decisions that one feels sure that he could just as easily have acted differently, that he acted of his own free will, and without any motives. From our analyses we therefore need not contest the right of the feeling of conviction that there is a free will. If we distinguish conscious from unconscious motivation we are then informed by the feeling of conviction that the conscious motivation does not extend over all our motor resolutions. *Minima non curat prætor.* What is thus left free from the one side receives its motive from the other side, from the unconscious, and the determinism in the psychic realm is thus carried out uninterruptedly.[347]

III. Although conscious thought must be altogether ignorant of the motivation of the faulty actions described above, yet it would be desirable to discover a psychologic proof of its existence; indeed, reasons obtained through a deeper knowledge of the unconscious make it probable that such proofs are to be discovered somewhere. As a matter of fact phenomena can be demonstrated in two spheres which seem to correspond to an unconscious and hence to a displaced knowledge of these motives.

---

[347] These conceptions of strict determinism in seemingly arbitrary actions have already borne rich fruit for psychology —perhaps also for the administration of justice. Bleuler and Jung have in this way made intelligible the reaction in the so-called association experiments, wherein the test person answers to a given word with one occurring to him (stimulus-word reaction), while the time elapsing between the stimulus word and answer is measured (reaction-time). Jung has shown in his *Diagnostische Assoziationsstudien*, 1906, what fine reagents for psychic occurrences we possess in this association-experiment. Three students of criminology, H. Gross, of Prague, and Wertheimer and Kiein, have developed from these experiments a technique for the diagnosis of facts (*Tatbestands-Diagnostik*) in criminal cases, the examination of which is now tested by psychologists and jurists.

(*a*) It is a striking and generally to be recognized feature in the behaviour of paranoiacs, that they attach the greatest significance to the trivial details in the behaviour of others. Details which are usually overlooked by others they interpret and utilize as the basis of far-reaching conclusions. For example, the last paranoiac seen by me concluded that there was a general understanding among people of his environment, because at his departure from the railway-station they made a certain motion with one hand. Another noticed how people walked on the street, how they brandished their walking-sticks, and the like.[348]

The category of the accidental, requiring no motivation, which the normal person lets pass as a part of his own psychic activities and faulty actions, is thus rejected by the paranoiac in the application to the psychic manifestations to others. All that he observes in others is full of meaning, all is explainable. But how does he come to look at it in this manner? Probably here as in so many other cases, he projects into the mental life of others what exists in his own unconscious activity. Many things obtrude themselves on consciousness in paranoia which in normal and neurotic persons can only be demonstrated through psychoanalysis as existing in their unconscious.[349] In a certain sense the paranoiac is here justified, he perceives something that escapes the normal person, he sees clearer than one of normal intellectual capacity, but his knowledge becomes worthless when he imputes to others the state of affairs he thus recognizes. I hope that I shall not be expected to justify every paranoic interpretation. But the point which we grant to paranoia in this conception of chance actions will facilitate for us the psychologic understanding of the conviction which the paranoiac attaches to all these interpretations. *There is certainly same truth to it*; even our errors of judgment, which are not designated as morbid, acquire their feeling of conviction in the same way. This feeling is justified for a certain part of the erroneous train of thought or for the source of its origin, and we shall later extend to it the remaining relationships.

(*b*) The phenomena of superstition furnish another indication of the unconscious motivation in chance and faulty actions. I will make myself clear through the discussion of a simple experience which gave me the starting-point to these reflections .

Having returned from vacation, my thoughts immediately turned to the patients with whom I was to occupy myself in the beginning of my year's work. My first visit was to a very old woman (see above) for whom I had twice

---

[348] Proceeding from other points of view, this interpretation of the trivial and accidental by the patient has been designated as "delusions of reference."

[349] For example, the fantasies of the hysterical regarding sexual and cruel abuse which are made conscious by analysis often correspond in every detail with the complaints of persecuted paranoiacs. It is remarkable but not altogether unexpected that we also meet the identical content as reality in the contrivances of perverts for the gratification of their desires.

daily performed the same professional services for many years. Owing to this monotony unconscious thoughts have often found expression on the way to the patient and during my occupation with her. She was over ninety years old; it was therefore pertinent to ask oneself at the beginning of each year how much longer she was likely to live.

On the day of which I speak I was hurry and took a carriage to her house. Every coachman at the cabstand near my house knew the old woman's address, as each of them had often driven me there. This day it happened that the driver did not stop in front of her house, but before one of the same number in a near-by and really similar-looking parallel street. I noticed the mistake and reproached the coachman, who apologized for it.

Is it of any significance when I am taken to a house where the old woman is not to be found? Certainly not to me; but were I *superstitious*, I should see an omen in this incident, a hint of fate that this would be the last year for the old woman. A great many omens which have been preserved by history have been founded on no better symbolism. Of course, I explain the incident as an accident without further meaning. The case would have been entirely different had I come on foot and, "absorbed in thought " or "through distraction," I had gone to the house in the parallel street instead of the correct one. I would not explain that as an accident, but as an action with unconscious intent requiring interpretation. My explanation of this "lapse in walking" would probably be that I expected that the time would soon come when I should not meet the old woman any longer.

I therefore differ from a superstitious person in the following manner:

I do not believe that an occurrence in which my mental life takes no part can teach me anything hidden concerning the future shaping of reality; but I do believe that an unintentional manifestation of my own mental activity surely contains something concealed which belongs only to my mental life — that is, I believe in outer (real) chance, but not in inner (psychic) accidents. With the superstitious person the case is reversed: he knows nothing of the motive of his chance and faulty actions; he believes in the existence of psychic contingencies; he is therefore inclined to attribute meaning to external chance, which manifests itself in actual occurrence, and to see in the accident a means of expression for something hidden outside of him. There are two differences between me and the superstitious person: first, he projects the motive to the to the outside, while I look for it in myself; second, he explains the accident by an event which I trace to a thought. What he considers hidden corresponds to the unconscious with me, and the compulsion not to let chance pass as chance, but to explain it as common to both of us. Thus I admit that this conscious ignorance and unconscious knowledge of the motivation of psychic accidentalness is one of the psychic roots of superstition. *Because* the superstitious person knows nothing of the motivation of his own accidental actions, and because the fact of this motivation strives for a place in his recognition, he is compelled to dispose of them by displacing them into the outer world. If such a connection exists it can hardly be limited to this single case. As a matter of fact, I believe that a large portion of the mythological conception of the world which reaches far into the most modern religions *is nothing but psychology projected into the outer world.* The dim perception (the endo-psychic perception, as it were) of psychic factors and relations[350] of the unconscious was taken as a model in the construction of a *transcendental reality*, which is destined to be changed again by science into *psychology of the unconscious.*

It is difficult to express it in other terms; the analogy to paranoia must here come to our aid. We venture to explain in this way the myths of paradise and the fall of man, of God, of good and evil, of immortality, and the like — that is, to transform *metaphysics* into *meta-psychology.* The gap between the paranoiac's displacement and that of superstition is narrower than appears at first sight. When human beings began to think, they were obviously compelled to explain the outer world in an anthropomorphic sense by a multitude of personalities in their own image; the accidents which they explained superstitiously were thus actions and expressions of persons. In that regard they behaved just like paranoiacs, who draw conclusions from insignificant signs which others give them, and like all normal persons who justly take the unintentional actions of their fellow-beings as a basis for 'the estimation of their characters. Only in our modern philosophical, but by no means finished, views of life does superstition seem so much out of place: in the view of life of prescientific times and nations it was justified and consistent.

The Roman who gave up an important undertaking because he sighted an ill-omened flock of birds was relatively right; his action was consistent with his principles. But if he withdrew from an undertaking because he had stumbled on his threshold (*un Romain retournerait*), he was absolutely superior even to us unbelievers. He was a better psychologist than we are striving to become. For his stumbling could demonstrate to him the existence of a doubt, an internal counter-current the force of which could weaken the power of his intention at the moment of its execution. For only by concentrating all psychic forces on the desired aim can one be assured of perfect success. How does Schiller's Tell, who hesitated so long to shoot the apple from his son's head, answer the bailiff's question why he had provided himself with a second arrow!

"With the second arrow I would have pierced you had I struck my dear child — and; truly, I should not have failed to reach you."

---

[350] Which naturally has nothing of the character of perception.

IV. Whoever has had the opportunity of studying the concealed psychic feelings of persons by means of psychoanalysis can also tell something new concerning the quality of unconscious motives, which express themselves in superstition. Nervous persons afflicted with compulsive thinking and compulsive states, who are often very intelligent, show very plainly that superstition originates from repressed hostile and cruel impulses. The greater part of superstition signifies fear of impending evil, and he who has frequently wished evil to others, but because of a good bringing-up has repressed the same into the unconscious, will be particularly apt to expect punishment for such unconscious evil in the form of a misfortune threatening him: from without.

If we concede that we have by no means exhausted the psychology of superstition in these remarks, we must, on the other hand, at least touch upon the question whether real roots of superstition should be altogether denied, whether there are really no omens, prophetic dreams, telepathic experiences, manifestations of supernatural forces, and the like. I am now far from willing to repudiate without anything further all these phenomena, concerning which we possess so many minute observations even from men of intellectual prominence, and which should certainly form a basis for further investigation. We map even hope that some of these observations will be explained by our present knowledge of the unconscious psychic processes without necessitating radical changes in our present aspect. If still other phenomena, as, for example, those maintained by the spiritualists, should be proven, we should then consider the modification of our "laws" as demanded by the new experience, without becoming confused in regard to the relation of things of this world.

In the sphere of these analyses I can only answer the questions here proposed subjectively — that is, in accordance with my personal experience. I am sorry to confess chat I belong to that class of unworthy individuals before whom the spirits cease their activities and the supernatural disappears, so that I have never been in position to experience anything personally that would stimulate belief in the miraculous. Like everybody else, I have had forebodings and experienced misfortunes; but the two evaded each other, so that nothing followed the foreboding, and the misfortune struck me unannounced. When as a young man I lived alone in a strange city I frequently heard my name suddenly pronounced by an unmistakable, dear voice, and I then made a note of the exact moment of the hallucination in order to inquire carefully of those at home what had occurred at that time. There was nothing to it. On the other hand, I later worked among my patients calmly and without foreboding while my child almost bled to death. Nor have I ever been able to recognize as unreal phenomena any of the forebodings reported to me by my patients.

The belief in prophetic dreams numbers many adherents, because it can be supported by the fact that some things really so happen in the future as they were previously foretold by the wish of the dream. But in this there is little to be wondered at, as many far-reaching deviations may be regularly demonstrated between a dream and the fulfilment which the credulity of the dreamer prefers to neglect.

A nice example, one which may be justly called prophetic was once brought to me for exhaustive analysts by an intelligent and truth-loving patient. She related that she once dreamed that she had met a former friend and family physician in front of a certain store in a certain street, and next morning when she went down town she actually met him at the place named in the dream. I may observe that the significance of this wonderful coincidence was not proven to be due to any subsequent event — that is, it could not be justified through future occurrences.

Careful examination definitely established the fact that there was no proof that the woman recalled the dream in the morning following the night of the dream — that is, before the walk and before the meeting. She could offer no objection when this state of affairs was presented in a manner that robbed this episode of everything miraculous, leaving only an interesting psychologic problem. One morning she had walked through this very street, had met her old family physician before that certain store, and on seeing him received the conviction that during the preceding night she had dreamed of this meeting at this place.

The analysis then showed with great probability how she came to this conviction, to which, in accordance with the general rule, we cannot deny a certain right to credence. A meeting at a definite place following a previous expectation really describes the fact of a rendezvous. The old family physician awakened her memory of old times, when meetings with a third person, also a friend of the physician, were of marked significance to her. Since that time she had continued her relations with this gentleman, and the day before the mentioned dream she had waited for him in vain. If I could report in greater detail the circumstances here before us, I could easily show that the illusion of the prophetic dream at the sight of the friend of former times is perchance equivalent to the following speech: "Ah, doctor, you now remind me of bygone times, when I never had to wait in vain for N. when we had arranged a meeting."

I have observed in myself a simple and easily explained example, which is probably a good model for similar occurrences of those familiar "remarkable coincidences" wherein we meet a person of whom we were just thinking. During a walk through the inner city a few days after the title of "Professor" was bestowed on me, which carries with it a great deal of prestige even in monarchical cities, my thoughts suddenly merged into a childish revenge-fantasy against a certain married couple. Some months previous they had called me to see their little daughter who suffered from' an interesting compulsive manifestation following the appearance of a dream. I took a great interest in the case, the genesis of which I believed I could surmise, but the parents were unfavourable to my treatment, and gave me to understand that they thought of applying to a foreign authority who cured by means of hypnotism. I now fancied that after the failure of this attempt, the parents begged me to resume my treatment, that they now had full confidence in me, etc. But I answered: "Now that I have become a professor, you have confidence in me. The title has made no change in my ability; if you could not use me when I was instructor you can get along without me now that I am! a professor." At this point my fantasy was interrupted by a loud "Good evening, Professor!" and as I looked up there passed me the same couple on whom I had just taken this imaginary vengeance.

The next reflection destroyed the semblance of the miraculous. I was walking towards this couple on a straight, almost deserted street; glancing up hastily at a distance of perhaps twenty steps from me, I had spied and realized their stately personalities; but this perception, following the model of a negative hallucination, was set aside by certain emotionally accentuated motives and then asserted itself in the apparently spontaneous emerging fantasy.

A similar experience is related by Brill, which also throws some light on the nature of telepathy.

"While engrossed in conversation during our customary Sunday evening dinner at one of the large New York restaurants, I suddenly stopped and irrelevantly remarked to my wife, 'I wonder how Dr. R. is doing in Pittsburg.' She looked at me much astonished and said: 'Why, that is exactly what I have been thinking for the last few seconds! Either you have transferred this thought to me or I have transferred it to you. How can you otherwise explain this strange phenomenon?' I had to admit that I could offer no solution. Our conversation throughout the dinner showed not the remotest association to Dr. R., nor, so far as our memories went, had we heard or spoken of him for some time. Being a sceptic, I refused to admit that there was anything mysterious about it, although inwardly I felt quite uncertain. To be frank, I was somewhat mystified.

"But we did not remain very long in this state of mind, for on looking toward the cloak-room we were surprised to see Dr. R. Though closer inspection showed our mistake, we were both struck by the remarkable resemblance of this stranger to Dr. R. From the position of the cloak-room we were forced to conclude that this stranger had passed our table. Absorbed in our conversation, we had not noticed him consciously, but the visual image had stirred up the association of his double, Dr. R. That we should both have experienced the same thought is also quite natural. The last word from our friend was to the effect that he had taken up private practice in Pittsburg, and, being aware of the vicissitudes that beset the beginner, it was quite natural to wonder how fortune smiled upon him.

"What promised to be a supernatural manifestation was thus easily explained on a normal basis; but had we not noticed the stranger before he left the restaurant, it would have been impossible to exclude the mysterious. I venture to say that such simple mechanisms are at the bottom of the most complicated telepathic manifestations; at least, such has been my experience in all cases accessible to investigation."

Another "solution of an apparent foreboding " was reported by Otto Rank[351]:—

"Some time ago I had experienced a remarkable variation of that peculiar coincidence wherein one meets a person who has just been occupying one's thoughts. Shortly before Christmas I went to the Austro-Hungarian Bank in order to obtain ten new silver crown-pieces destined for Christmas gifts. Absorbed in ambitious fantasies which dealt with the contrast of my meagre means to the enormous sums in the banking-house, I turned into the narrow street to the bank. In front of the door I saw an automobile and many people going in and out. I thought to myself: 'The officials will have plenty of time for my new crowns; naturally I shall be quick about it; I shall put down the paper notes to be exchanged, and say, "Please give me gold."' I realized my mistake at once — I was to have asked for silver — and awoke from my fantasies.

"I was now only a few steps front the entrance, and noticed a young man coming toward me who looked familiar, but whom I could not definitely identify on account of my short-sightedness. As he came nearer I recognized him as a classmate of my brother whose name was Gold and from whose brother, a well-known journalist, I had great expectations in the beginning of my literary career. But these expectations had not materialized, and with them had vanished the hoped-for material success with which my fantasies were occupying; themselves on my way to the bank. Thus engrossed I must have unconsciously perceived the approach of Mr. Gold, who impressed himself on my conscience while I was dreaming of material success, and thereby caused me to ask the cashier for gold instead of the inferior silver. But, on the other hand, the paradoxical fact that my unconscious was able to perceive an object long before it was recognized by the eye might in part be explained by the complex readiness (*Komplexbereitschaft*) of Bleuler. For my mind was attuned to the material, and, contrary to my better knowledge, it

---

[351] *Zenltralb. f. Psychoanalyse*, ii. 5.

guided my steps from the very beginning to buildings where gold and paper money were exchanged."

To the category of the wonderful and uncanny we may also add that strange feeling we perceive in certain moments and situations when it seems as if we had already had exactly the same experience, or had previously found ourselves in the same situation. Yet we are never successful in our efforts to recall clearly; those former experiences and situations. I know that I follow only the loose colloquial expression when I designate that which stimulates us in such moments as a "feeling." We undoubtedly deal with a judgment, and, indeed, with a judgment of cognition; but these cases, nevertheless, have a character peculiar to themselves, and besides, we must not ignore the fact that we never recall what we are seeking.

I do not know whether this phenomenon of *Déjà vu* was ever seriously offered as a proof of a former psychic existence of the individual; but it is certain that psychologists have taken an interest in it, and have attempted to solve the riddle in a multitude of speculative ways. None of the proposed tentative explanations seems right to me, because none takes account of anything but the accompanying manifestations and the favouring conditions of the phenomenon. Those psychic processes which, according to my observation, are alone responsible for the explanation of the *Déjà vu* — namely, the unconscious fantasies — are generally neglected by the psychologists even to-day.

I believe that it is wrong to designate the feeling of having experienced something before as an illusion. On the contrary, in such moments something is really touched that we have already experienced, only we cannot consciously recall the latter because it never was conscious. In short, the feeling *Déjà vu* corresponds to the memory of an unconscious fantasy. There are unconscious fantasies (or day dreams) just as there are similar conscious creations, which everyone knows from personal experience.

I realize that the object is worthy of most minute study, but I will here give the analysis of only one case of *Déjà vu* in which the feeling was characterized by particular intensity and persistence. A woman of thirty-seven years asserted that she most distinctly remembered that at the age of twelve and a half she paid her first visit to some school friends in the country, and as she entered the garden she immediately had the feeling of having been there before. This feeling was repeated as she went through the living-rooms, so that she believed she knew beforehand how big the next room was, what views one could have on looking out of it, etc. But the belief that this feeling of recognition might have its source in a previous visit to the house and garden, perhaps a visit paid in earliest childhood, was absolutely excluded and disproved by statements from her parents. The woman who related this sought no psychologic explanation, but saw in the appearance of this feeling a prophetic reference to the importance which these friends later assumed in her emotional life. On taking into consideration, however, the circumstance under which this phenomenon presented itself to her, we found the way to another conception.

When she decided upon this visit she knew that these girls had an only brother, who was seriously ill. In the course of the visit she actually saw him. She found him looking very badly, and thought to herself that he would soon die. But it happened that her own only brother had had a serious attack of diphtheria some months before, and during his illness she had lived for weeks with relatives far from her parental home. She believed that her brother was taking part in this visit to the country, imagined even that this was his first long journey since his illness; still, her memory was remarkably indistinct in regard to these points, whereas all other details, and particularly the dress which she wore that day, remained most clearly before her eyes.

To the initiated it will not be difficult to conclude from these suggestions that the expectation of her brother's death had played a great part in the girl's mind at that time, and that either it never became conscious or it was more energetically repressed after the favourable issue of the illness. Under other circumstances she would have been compelled to wear another dress — namely, mourning clothes. She found the analogous situation in her friends' home; their only: brother was in danger of an early death, an event that really came to pass a short time after. She might have consciously remembered that she lived through a similar situation a few months previous, but instead of recalling what was inhibited through repression she transferred the memory feeling to the locality, to the garden and the house, and merged it into the *fausse reconnaissance* that she had already seen everything exactly as it was.

From the fact of the repression we may conclude that the former expectation of the death of her brother was not far from evincing the character of a wish-fantasy. She would then have become the only: child. In her later neurosis she suffered in the most intense manner from the fear of losing her parents, behind which the analysis disclosed, as usual, the unconscious wish of the same content.

My own experience of *Déjà vu* I can trace in a similar manner to the emotional constellation of the moment. It may he expressed as follows: "That would be another occasion for awakening certain fantasies (unconscious and unknown) which were formed in me at one time or another as a wish to improve my situation."[352]

---

[352] Thus far this explanation of *Déjà vu* has been appreciated by only one observer. Dr. Ferenczi, to whom the third edition of this is book is indebted for so many contributions, writes to me concerning this: "I have been convinced, through myself as well as others, that the inexplicable feeling of familiarity can be referred to unconscious fantasies of which we are

V. Recently when I had occasion to recite to a colleague of a philosophical turn of mind some examples of name-forgetting, with their analyses, he hastened to reply: "That is all very well, but with me the forgetting of a name proceeds in a different manner." Evidently one cannot dismiss this question as simply as that; I do not believe that my colleague had ever thought of an analysis for the forgetting of a name, nor could he say how the process differed in him. But his remark, nevertheless, touches upon a problem which many would be inclined to place in the foreground. Does the solution given for faulty and chance actions apply in general or only in particular cases, and if only in the latter, what are the conditions under which it may also be employed in the explanation of the other phenomena?

In answer to this question my experiences leave me in the lurch. I can only urge against considering the demonstrated connections as rare, for as often as I have made the test in myself and with my patients it was always definitely demonstrated exactly as in the examples reported, or there were at least good reasons to assume this. One should not be surprise, however, when one does not succeed every time in finding the concealed meaning of the symptomatic action, as the amount of inner resistances ranging themselves against the solution must be considered a deciding factor. Also, it is not always possible to explain every individual dream of one's self of patients. To substantiate the general validity of the theory, it is enough if one can penetrate only a certain distance into the hidden associations. The dream which proves refractory when the solution is attempted on the following day can often be robbed of its secret a week or a month later, when the psychic factors combating one another have been reduced as a consequence of a real change that has meanwhile taken place. The same applies to the solution of faulty and symptomatic actions. It would therefore be wrong to affirm of all cases which resist analysis that they are caused by another psychic mechanism than that here revealed; such assumption requires more than negative proofs; moreover, the readiness to believe in a difference explanation of faulty and symptomatic actions, which probably exists universally in all normal persons, does not prove anything; it is obviously an expression of the same psychic forces which produced the secret, which therefore strives to protect and struggle against its elucidation.

On the other hand, we must not overlook the fact that the repressed thoughts and feelings are not independent in attaining expression in symptomatic and faulty actions. The technical possibility for such an adjustment of the innervations must be furnished independently of them,

---

unconsciously reminded in an actual situation. With one of my patients the process was apparently different but in reality it was quite analogous. This feeling returned to him very often, but showed itself regularly as originating in a forgotten (repressed) portion of a dream of the preceding night. Thus it appears that the *Déjà vu* can originate not only from day dreams but also from night dreams."

and this is then gladly utilized by the intention of the repressed material to come to conscious expression. In the case of linguistic faulty actions an attempt has been made by philosophers and philologists to verify through minute observations what structural and functional relations enter into the service of such intention. If in the determinations of faulty and symptomatic actions we separate the unconscious motive from its co-active physiological and psychophysical relations, the question remains open whether there are still other factors within normal limits which, like the unconscious motive, and in its place can produce faulty and symptomatic actions on the road of the relations. It is not my; task to answer this question.

VI. Since the discussion of speech blunders we have been content to demonstrate that faulty actions have a concealed motive, and through the aid of psychoanalysis we have traced our way to the knowledge of their motivation. The general nature and the peculiarities of the psychic factors brought to expression in these faulty actions we have hitherto left almost without consideration; at any rate, we have not attempted to define them more accurately or to examine into their lawfulness. Nor will we now attempt a thorough elucidation of the subject, as the first steps have already taught us that it is more feasible to enter this structure from another side. Here we can put before ourselves certain questions which I will cite in their order. (1) What is the content and the origin of the thoughts and feelings ;which show; themselves through faulty and chance actions? (2) What are the conditions which force a thought or a feeling to make use of these occurrences as a means of expression and place it in a position to do sol (3) Can constant and definite associations be demonstrated between the manner of the faulty action and the qualities brought to expression through it.

I shall begin by bringing together some material for answering the last question. In the discussion of the examples of speech blunders we found it necessary to go beyond the contents of the intended speech, and we had to seek the cause of the speech disturbance outside the intention. The latter was quite clear in a series of cases, and as known to the consciousness of the speaker. In the example that seemed most simple and transparent it was a similar sounding but different conception of the same thought, which disturbed its expression without any one being able to say why the one succumbed and the other came to the surface (Meringer and Mayers' *Contaminations*).

In a second group of cases one conception succumbed to a motive which did not, however, prove strong enough to cause complete submersion. The conception which was withheld was clearly presented to consciousness.

Only of the third group can we affirm unreservedly that the disturbing thought differed from the one intended, and it is obvious that it may establish an essential distinction. The disturbing thought is either connected with the disturbed on through a thought association (disturbance through inner contradiction), or it is substantially strange to it, and just the disturbed word is connected with the disturbing thought through a surprising outer association, which is frequently unconscious.

In the examples which I have given from my psychoanalyses it is found that the entire speech is either under the influence of thoughts which have become active simultaneously, or under absolutely unconscious thoughts which betray themselves either through the disturbance itself, or which evince an indirect influence by making it possible for the individual parts of the unconsciously intended speech to disturb one another. The retained unconscious thoughts from which the disturbances in speech emanate are of most varied origin. A general survey does not reveal any definite direction.

Comparative examinations of examples of mistakes in reading and writing lead me to the same conclusions. Isolated cases, as in speech blunders, seem to owe their origin to an unmotivated work of condensation (e.g., the *Apel*). But we should be pleased to know whether special conditions must not be fulfilled in order that such condensation, which is considered regular in the dream-work and faulty in our waking thoughts, should take place. No information concerning this can be obtained from the examples themselves. But I merely refuse from this to draw the conclusion that there are no such conditions, as, for instance, the relaxation of conscious attention; for I have learned elsewhere that automatic actions are especially characterized by correctness and reliability. I would rather emphasize the fact that here, as so frequently in biology, it is the normal relations, or those approaching the normal, that are less favourable objects for investigation than the pathological. What remains obscure in the explanation of these most simple disturbances will, according to my expectation, be made clear through the explanation of more serious disturbances.

Also mistakes in reading and writing do not lack examples in which more remote and more complicated motivation can be recognized.

There is no doubt that the disturbances of the speech functions occur more easily and make less demand on the disturbing forces than other psychic acts.

But one is on different ground when it comes to the examination of forgetting in the literal sense — *i.e.*, the forgetting of past experiences. (To distinguish this forgetting from the others we designate *sensu strictiori* the forgetting of proper names and foreign words, as in Chapters I and II, as "slips"; and the forgetting of resolutions as "omissions.") The principal conditions of the normal process in forgetting are unknown.[353] We are also

---

[353] I can perhaps give the following outline concerning the mechanism of actual forgetting. The memory material succumbs in general to two influences, condensation and disfigurement. Disfigurement is the work of the tendencies dominating the psychic life, and

811

reminded of the fact that not all is forgotten which we believe to be. Our explanation here deals only with those cases in which the forgetting arouses our astonishment, in so far as it infringes the rule that the unimportant is forgotten, while the important matter is guarded by memory. Analysis of these examples of forgetting is always an unwillingness to recall something which may evoke painful feelings. We may come to the conjecture that this motive universally strives for expression in psychic life, but is inhibited through other and contrary forces from regularly manifesting itself. The extent and significance of this dislike to recall painful impressions seems worthy of the most painstaking psychologic investigation. The question as to what special conditions render possible the universally resistant forgetting in individual cases cannot be solved through this added association.

A different factor steps into the foreground in the forgetting of resolutions; the supposed conflict resulting in the repression of the painful memory becomes tangible, and in the analysis of the examples one regularly recognizes a counter-will which opposes but does not put an end to the resolution. As in previously discussed faulty act, we here also recognize two types of the psychic process: the counter-will either turns directly against the resolution (in intentions of some consequence) or it is substantially foreign to the resolution itself and establishes its connection with it through an outer association (in almost indifferent resolutions).

The same conflict governs the phenomena of erroneously carried-out actions. The impulse which manifests itself in the disturbances of the action is frequently a counter-impulse. Still oftener it is altogether a strange impulse which only utilizes the opportunity to express itself through a disturbance in the execution of the action. The cases in which the disturbance is the result of an inner contradiction are the most significant ones, and also deal with the more important activities.

The inner conflict in the chance or symptomatic actions then merges into the background. Those motor expressions which are least thought of, or are

---

directs itself above all against the affective remnants of memory traces which maintain a more resistive attitude towards condensation. The traces which have grown indifferent merge into a process of condensation without opposition; in addition it may be observed that tendencies of disfigurement also feed on the indifferent material, because they have not been gratified where they wished to manifest themselves. As these processes of condensation and disfigurement continue for long periods during which all fresh experiences act upon the transformation of the memory content, it is our belief that it is time that makes memory uncertain and indistinct. It is quite probable that in forgetting there can really be no question of a direct function of time. From the repressed memory traces it can be verified that they suffer no changes even in the longest periods. The unconscious, at all events, knows no time limit. The most important as well as the most peculiar character of psychic fixation consists in the fact that all impressions are on the one hand retained in the same form as they were received, and also in the forms that they have assumed in their further development. This state of affairs cannot be elucidated by any comparison from any other sphere. By virtue of this theory every former state of the memory content may thus be restored, even though all original relations have long been replaced by newer ones.

entirely overlooked by consciousness, serve as the expression of numerous unconscious or restrained feelings. For the most part they represent symbolically wishes and phantoms. The first question (as to the origin of the thoughts and emotions which find expression in faulty actions) we can answer by saying that in a series of cases the origin of the disturbing thoughts can be readily traced to repressed emotions of the psychic life. Even in healthy persons egotistic, jealous and hostile feelings and impulses, burdened by the pressure of moral education, often utilize the path of faulty actions to express in some way their undeniably existing force which is not recognized by the higher psychic instances. Allowing these faulty and chance actions to continue corresponds in great part to a comfortable toleration of the unmoral. The manifold sexual currents play no insignificant part m these repressed feelings. That they appear so seldom in the thoughts revealed by the analyses of my examples is simply a matter of coincidence. As I have undertaken the analyses of numerous examples from my own psychic life, the selection was partial from the first, and aimed at the exclusion of sexual matters. At other times it seemed that the disturbing thoughts originated from the most harmless objection and consideration.

We have now reached the answer to the second question — that is, what psychologic conditions are responsible for the fact that a thought must seek expression not in its complete form but, as it were, in parasitic form, as a modification and disturbance of another. From the most striking examples of faulty actions it is quite obvious that this determinant should be sought in a relation to conscious capacity, or in the more or less firmly pronounced character of the "repressed" material. But an examination of this series of examples shows that this character consists of many indistinct elements. The tendency to overlook something because it is wearisome, or because the concerned thought does not really belong to the intended matter — these feelings seem to play the same rôle as motives for the suppression of a thought (which later depends for expression on the disturbance of another), as the moral condemnation of a rebellious emotional feeling, or as the origin of absolutely unconscious trains of thought. An insight into the general nature of the condition of faulty and chance actions cannot be gained in this way.

However, this investigation gives us one single significant fact; the more harmless the motivation of the faulty act the less obnoxious, and hence less incapable of consciousness, the thought to which it gives expression is; the easier also becomes the solution of the phenomenon after we have turned our attention toward it. The simplest cases of speech blunders are immediately noticed and instantaneously corrected. Where one deals with motivation through actually repressed feelings the solution requires a painstaking analysis, which may sometimes strike against difficulties or turn out unsuccessful.

One is therefore justified in taking the result of this last investigation as an indication of the fact that the satisfactory explanation of the psychologic determinations of faulty and chance actions is to be acquired in another way and from another source. The indulgent reader can therefore see in these discussions the demonstration of the surfaces of fracture in which this theme was quite artificially evolved from a broader connection.

VII. Just a few words to indicate the direction of this broader connection. The mechanism of the faulty and chance actions, as we have learned to know it through the application of analysis, shows in the most essential points an agreement with the mechanism of dream formation, which I have discussed in the chapter "The Dream Work" of my book on the interpretation of dreams. Here, as there, one finds the condensation and compromise formation ("*contaminations*"); in addition the situation is much the same, since unconscious thoughts find expression as modifications of other thoughts in unusual ways and through outer associations. The incongruities, absurdities, and errors in the dream content by virtue of which the dream is scarcely recognized as a psychic achievement originate in the same way — to be sure, through freer usage of the existing material — as the common error of our everyday life; *here, as there, the appearance of the incorrect function is explained through the peculiar interference of two or more correct actions.*

An important conclusion call be drawn from this combination: the peculiar mode of operation, whose most striking function we recognize in the dream content, should not be adjudged only to the sleeping state of the psychic life when we possess abundant proof of its activity during the waking state in the form of faulty actions. The same connection also forbids us assuming that these psychic processes which impress us as abnormal and strange are determined by deep-seated decay of psychic activity or by morbid state of function. *(See The Interpretation of Dreams, p. 483.)*

The correct understanding of this strange psychic work which allows the faulty actions to originate like the dream pictures will only be possible after we have discovered that the psychoneurotic symptoms, particularly the psychic formations of hysteria and compulsion neurosis, repeat in their mechanisms all the essential features of this mode of operation. The continuation of our investigation would therefore have to begin at this point.

There is still another special interest for us in considering the faulty, chance, and symptomatic actions in the light of this last analogy. If we compare them to the function of the psychoneuroses and the neurotic symptoms, two frequently recurring statements gain in sense and support— namely, that the border-line between the nervous, normal, and abnormal states is indistinct, and that we are all slightly nervous. Regardless of all medical experience, one may construe various types of such barely suggested nervousness, the *formes frustes* of the neuroses. There may, ;be cases in which only a few symptoms appear, or they may manifest themselves rarely or in mild forms; the extenuation may be transferred to the number; intensity, or to the temporal outbreak of the morbid manifestation. It may also happen that just this type, which forms the most frequent transition between health and disease, may never be discovered. The transition type, whose morbid manifestations come in the form of faulty and symptomatic actions, is characterized by the fact that the symptoms are transformed to the least important psychic activities, while everything that can lay claim to a higher psychic value remains free from disturbance. When the symptoms are disposed of in a reverse manner — that is, when they appear in the most important individual and social activities in a manner to disturb the functions of nourishment and sexual relations, professional and social life — such disposition is found in the severe cases of neuroses, and is perhaps more characteristic of the latter than the multiformity or vividness of the morbid manifestations.

But the common character of the mildest as well as the severest cases, to which the faulty and chance actions contribute, lies *in the ability to refer the phenomena to unwelcome, repressed, psychic material, which, though pushed away from consciousness, is nevertheless not robbed of all capacity to express itself.*

THE END

Printed in Great Britain
by Amazon